REVISED COMMON LECTIONARY

Daily Readings

Proposed by the

Consultation on Common Texts

Fortress Press

Minneapolis

CONTENTS

PREFACE

Consultation on Common Texts

The Consultation on Common Texts (CCT) originated in the mid-1960s as a forum for consultation on worship renewal among many of the major Christian churches in the United States and Canada. At the time of the development of *Revised Common Lectionary Daily Readings,* participants in the CCT include persons from the following churches or church agencies: American Baptist Fellowship for Liturgical Renewal, The Anglican Church of Canada, Christian Church (Disciples of Christ), Christian Reformed Church in North America, Church of the Brethren, The Episcopal Church, Evangelical Lutheran Church in America, Evangelical Lutheran Church in Canada, Free Methodist Church in Canada, International Commission on English in the Liturgy (an agency of twenty-six Roman Catholic national or international conferences of bishops), The Lutheran Church—Missouri Synod, Mennonite Church, Polish National Catholic Church of America, Presbyterian Church (U.S.A.), The Presbyterian Church in Canada, Reformed Church in America, Roman Catholic Church in the United States, Roman Catholic Church in Canada, The Unitarian Universalist Christian Fellowship, The United Church of Canada, United Church of Christ, and The United Methodist Church.

Projects and publications sponsored by the Consultation have included the following:

Revised Common Lectionary. In order to achieve even greater unity in worship, the CCT proposed a Common Lectionary as a harmonization of denominational variants in the lectionary for the Sundays and major feast days of the Christian year, based on the three-year lectionary system of the Roman Lectionary. The Common Lectionary has been revised by the Consultation on Common Texts, together with representatives of the English Language Liturgical Consultation (ELLC). This work has appeared under the title *The Revised Common Lectionary* (Nashville: Abingdon Press, 1992). The table of readings, reviewed for accuracy, appears also in the present volume.

Revised Common Lectionary Prayers. The CCT undertook this project to provide a set of ecumenical prayers specifically designed for use with the calendar of readings contained in the Revised Common Lectionary. Responding to the diverse needs of the churches for prayers in a collect form, the collection includes gathering prayers, scripture prayers, and conclusions to intercessory prayers for the Sundays of the three-year cycle and selected festival days. The prayers were published for trial use by Augsburg Fortress in 2002.

Prayers We Have in Common. This project sought to provide a contemporary and ecumenical English version of prayers for the English-speaking churches around the world. Begun by the CCT, this became part of the work of the International Consultation on English Texts (ICET). These texts have now been revised by the ELLC, ICET's successor, and published under the title *Praying Together* (Nashville: Abingdon Press, 1988). The CCT continues to work with ELLC at the international level.

A Christian Celebration of Marriage. An ecumenical liturgy for marriage was developed in response to the increasing frequency of marriage services in which more than one Christian tradition is represented. Originally published in 1985, a revised and updated version was published by Augsburg Fortress in 1995.

A Celebration of Baptism. An ecumenical liturgy for Holy Baptism was developed as a further step in the contemporary and theological convergence regarding baptism. The rite serves as an invitation to the churches to consider as official denominational rites are prepared, and it is offered for possible use in the instance of baptism when more than one Christian tradition is represented. It was published by Abingdon Press in 1988.

Earlier projects of the CCT have included *Ecumenical Services of Prayer* (1983), and *A Liturgical Psalter for the Christian Year,* prepared and edited by Massey H. Shepherd Jr. with the assistance of the CCT (1976).

INTRODUCTION

The publication of *The Revised Common Lectionary* in 1992 and its earlier edition, *The Common Lectionary* in 1983, both based on the *Ordo Lectionem Missae* of 1969, provided the ecumenical church with a three-year cycle of readings for Sundays and for many of the special liturgical days that churches hold in common. The Revised Common Lectionary has been gratefully received among churches not only in the United States and Canada, but throughout the world. Churches that have adopted it use it with the knowledge that the same cycle of scripture is being heard in other churches in common, as it were, on any given Sunday. The Revised Common Lectionary has also provided the possibility for educational and musical materials that can be shared across confessional lines, since the same readings are providing the scriptural focus for worship in the churches.

The Consultation on Common Texts (CCT), the ecumenical group that developed both of the lectionaries mentioned above, now presents this new collection of readings for the rest of the days of the week. Designed for daily use, this new lectionary recognizes that, for worshiping communities and individuals, Sunday worship is central to the Christian life. *Revised Common Lectionary Daily Readings* uses the Sunday readings of the Revised Common Lectionary as its basis, and then provides readings for the weekdays around the Sundays both to prepare for Sunday and to reflect upon it.

For whom and for what purpose has this lectionary been created?

This lectionary may well serve purposes beyond those for which it is designed. At its inception, however, it was described as a daily lectionary for use by individuals for personal devotions and meditation, and for possible corporate and liturgical use in the daily office. It was not intended as a eucharistic lectionary (for the celebration of full services of word and sacrament each day). However, it contains adequate scripture selections in the course of a week that it could be adapted for such use on occasion.

This lectionary was not designed to "teach" the Bible, but rather to illuminate the significance of the Sunday readings, to encourage a well-rounded reading of scripture over the span of the church year, and to provide a foundation for prayer. As a lectionary, it provides an ordered alternative to reading the Bible simply from start to finish. It attempts to accomplish this by the careful selection of readings with an awareness of the multiple layers of scripture and the interrelatedness of biblical stories. This allows readings to be chosen to enrich our knowledge of scripture with the same story told by other witnesses (through the use of other gospel accounts), by allusions to similar imagery in various parts of the Bible (for example, references to anointing in many times and places), or by the choice of other so-called typological selections that attempt to open up scripture in a broad way. Not every verse of the Bible is included, but the selections represent the narrative portions, the psalms, the prophets, the gospels, and the letters almost completely, with a more selective approach applied to other genres of biblical content.

At the same time, scripture begs us to not lose sight of particular stories that need to be read in their entirety. That is why *Daily Readings,* consistent with the Revised Common Lectionary, offers a pattern of semicontinuous Old Testament readings ("in-course," or *lectio continua*) during the weeks in the season after Pentecost (ordinary time). This pattern also provides a psalm related to the readings. That is to say, *Daily Readings* provides the optional use of a set of Old Testament readings selected to tell stories with narrative continuity for a period of the liturgical year, allowing these story streams to stand on their own uninterrupted.

How to use this lectionary

In general, two readings each day on Thursday, Friday, and Saturday are selected to prepare for the Sunday readings; two readings each day on Monday, Tuesday, and Wednesday are selected to reflect on the Sunday lectionary. The book is laid out on each page so that, opening to any given week, one sees Sunday in the middle, with three days preceding (the preparatory days—Thursday, Friday, and Saturday) and three days following (the reflective days—Monday, Tuesday, Wednesday). In addition, psalms are provided: one to be used during the preparatory days (the psalm for the coming Sunday) and one additional psalm for use during the reflective days.

The readings were selected to follow a usual plan or pattern:

Thursday, Friday, and Saturday (prepare)		*Monday, Tuesday, and Wednesday (reflect)*	
Psalm (repeated on each of these days)		Psalm (repeated on each of these days)	
Thursday	O.T., epistle	Monday	O.T., epistle
Friday	O.T., epistle	Tuesday	O.T., epistle
Saturday	O.T., gospel	Wednesday	O.T., gospel

The first readings to appear in this lectionary are the ones around the first Sunday of Advent, year A. They begin on the Thursday before the first Sunday of Advent, and continue through the following Wednesday. On the next page, the reader is led to preparation for the second Sunday of Advent, and so on.

Multiple options exist for using the readings provided for each day for prayer or meditation. One might, for example, want to read and pray in the morning, and use all three biblical texts—that is, the two readings assigned to the day plus the psalm. Alternately, one could be in the habit of evening devotions, or the readings might be split between morning and evening. Mealtime may be the best choice for some. There is no right or wrong way. For that matter, some people may find that their life-style does not permit them to reflect on the scripture texts daily. They might choose to read two or three days' worth of selections at a time; or, they may choose any of the week's readings for use on a particular day. A simple pattern of daily prayer, either by one's self or with others, using the daily readings may include:

the lighting of a candle or lamp
a song or hymn
the psalm
the first reading
a short time of silence and reflection
a second reading
a silence
prayer for other's needs, the world, and one's self

In addition to serving as a companion to the Sunday readings, this lectionary also provides daily readings that enrich our observances, help us prepare for the seasons, and celebrate more fully some of the commonly observed days that often are overlooked or preempted by Sunday's pericopes.

Use of the options of semicontinuous and complementary series

Two sets (or series) of readings have been provided in the weeks during the season after Pentecost. During this time in years A, B, and C, two facing pages of readings appear. The page on the left represents the semicontinuous series of Old Testament readings, with a related psalm, where biblical texts are read more or less continuously throughout this season. Some churches choose this series for Sundays. It should be noted that the readings in the semicontinuous series are not always in the order in which they appear in the Bible, but are chosen around related biblical themes or stories. They may be selected to enrich our knowledge of a biblical character, or they may provide other vignettes that help us to have a better understanding of the Sunday story. They are often selected in the same "neighborhood" of the Bible, but when dealing with broader topics, like the prophetic books, a selection might be chosen from a wider variety of biblical literature.

The page on the right (the complementary series) provides readings that are linked more closely with the other Sunday readings. Again, note that some churches choose this option, in which the gospel focus is the basis for the selection of the other Sunday readings. Understanding this can help the user, if it is desired, to stay with the series that is used in their church's Sunday worship. However, there is no right or wrong way to use the contents and patterns of readings contained in this book.

Some other ways these readings might be used

For corporate worship

A person called upon to lead a midweek gathering could read the scriptures for the day with the assurance that they would be heard in relationship to either the previous or coming Sunday and the season, thus providing continuity for the worshiping community.

For Sunday educational and leadership preparation

This lectionary can be used to enrich understandings of the Sunday readings for those who need to prepare sermons or homilies, meditations, music, and educational experiences. It may be beneficial to explore the whole week's readings, both preparatory and reflective.

For midweek services of word and sacrament

A gospel reading is not provided for each day of the week. Therefore, this lectionary is not offered as a daily eucharistic lectionary. However, it may be adapted for occasional (for example, midweek) communion services by using one of the gospel readings assigned to Saturdays and Wednesdays, perhaps pairing it with one of the other readings appointed for that week.

Some reflections by the compilers

This collection of readings is indebted to *Between Sundays: Daily Bible Readings Based on the Revised Common Lectionary* (Augsburg Fortress, 1997), compiled by Gail Ramshaw. *Between Sundays* included one reading for each weekday of the three-year cycle. When the CCT began to develop the principles upon which it would do its work, it was decided in consultation with Ramshaw that this existing work could serve as a principal foundation for an expanded set that would include two readings for each day as well as additional psalm choices. More than 2,000 readings were added.

During the multiyear process of designing and compiling this work, the committee found common hope in envisaging a daily lectionary that would broaden the exposure of Christians to scripture, in a time when some evidence pointed to lessened use of scriptures in pubic worship. It was in the process of creating the daily lectionary that the group realized its enormous potential to enrich worshipers' understandings of what is heard at Sunday worship.

The lectionary committee was also struck by the challenge of opening up more and more of the scriptures while avoiding the overuse of familiar stories. This mandate stood together with others, such as sensitivity to the roles of men and women, anti-Semitism, nationalistic references, and domestic codes of biblical cultures. Finally, the committee commends this project for use in practice, acknowledging that no project of such huge scope could possibly approach perfection or completion. The hope has been simply to provide a companion to the faithful on their daily journey of prayer and reflection.

The preparation of this document was authorized by the plenary meeting of the Consultation on Common Texts in 2000. The CCT continued throughout the project to review and advise the work. The development process began with a working group consisting of the Rev. Karen Ward, Evangelical Lutheran Church in America (ELCA), Mr. Arthur Clyde, United Church of Christ (UCC), the Rev. Dr. Horace B. Allen Jr., Presbyterian Church U.S.A. (PCUSA), and Dr. Gail Ramshaw, ELCA. The Rev. Msgr. Alan F. Detscher, Roman Catholic Church, was chair of CCT at the inception of the project.

The compilation work was completed by the Rev. Dr. Thomas E. Dipko, UCC; the Rev. Dr. Horace Allen Jr.; the Rev. Dr. Joseph P. Russell (who died in 2004), Episcopal Church; the Rev. Martin A. Seltz, ELCA; and Mr. Arthur Clyde, who chaired the working group in consultation with Dr. Fred Graham, United Church of Canada, as current Chair of the Consultation.

The Consultation on Common Texts commends this project for trial use with the hope that its use will help to perfect it. Responses and feedback to this proposal are welcome. The best way to communicate with the CCT regarding this project or any other is by visiting the Consultation's Web site at www.commontexts.org.

Advent

Christmas

Epiphany

YEAR A

First Sunday of Advent

Preparation for Sunday

THURSDAY
Daniel 9:15-19
A plea for forgiveness
James 4:1-10
A plea for God's grace and human humility

FRIDAY
Genesis 6:1-10
Humankind's wickedness, Noah's righteousness
Hebrews 11:1-7
Noah acts in faith

SATURDAY
Genesis 6:11-22
The command to build an ark: Noah's obedience
Matthew 24:1-22
The day of the Lord is coming

DAILY
Psalm 122
Gladness in God's house

First Sunday of Advent

Isaiah 2:1-5
War transformed into peace
Psalm 122
Gladness in God's house
Romans 13:11-14
Salvation is near; wake from sleep
Matthew 24:36-44
The sudden coming of salvation

Reflection on Sunday

MONDAY
Genesis 8:1-19
The flood waters subside
Romans 6:1-11
Dying and rising with Christ through baptism

TUESDAY
Genesis 9:1-17
Command to be fruitful; sign of the rainbow
Hebrews 11:32-40
The heroes of faith

WEDNESDAY
Isaiah 54:1-10
God will save the people
Matthew 24:23-35
The end is coming

DAILY
Psalm 124
We have escaped like a bird

Second Sunday of Advent

Preparation for Sunday

THURSDAY
Isaiah 4:2-6
God's promised glory for the survivors in Zion
Acts 1:12-17, 21-26
Beginnings of the apostolic ministry

FRIDAY
Isaiah 30:19-26
God's promise to be gracious to Zion
Acts 13:16-25
Paul's testimony concerning John the Baptist

SATURDAY
Isaiah 40:1-11
A voice crying in the wilderness
John 1:19-28
John the Baptist concerning his own ministry

DAILY
Psalm 72:1-7, 18-19
The righteous shall flourish

Second Sunday of Advent

Isaiah 11:1-10
A ruler brings justice and peace
Psalm 72:1-7, 18-19
The righteous shall flourish
Romans 15:4-13
Living in harmony
Matthew 3:1-12
Prepare the way of the Lord

Reflection on Sunday

MONDAY
Isaiah 24:1-16a
Judgment is coming, but glorify God
1 Thessalonians 4:1-12
Live in holiness and love one another

TUESDAY
Isaiah 41:14-20
God will not forget the poor of Israel
Romans 15:14-21
Gentiles are also called to the obedience of faith

WEDNESDAY
Genesis 15:1-18
God's covenant with Abram
Matthew 12:33-37
A good tree bears good fruit

DAILY
Psalm 21
God comes with judgment and strength

Third Sunday of Advent

Preparation for Sunday

THURSDAY
Ruth 1:6-18
Ruth's fidelity toward Naomi and her people
2 Peter 3:1-10
The promise of the Lord's coming

FRIDAY
Ruth 4:13-17
God's fidelity toward Ruth and her posterity
2 Peter 3:11-18
Prepare for the Lord's coming

SATURDAY
1 Samuel 2:1-8
Hannah sings in praise of God's fidelity
Luke 3:1-18
The proclamation of John the Baptist

DAILY
Psalm 146:5-10
God lifts up those bowed down

Third Sunday of Advent

Isaiah 35:1-10
The desert blooms
Psalm 146:5-10   *or*   Luke 1:46b-55
God lifts up those bowed down   *My spirit rejoices in God*
James 5:7-10
Patience until the Lord's coming
Matthew 11:2-11
The forerunner of Christ

Reflection on Sunday

MONDAY
Isaiah 29:17-24
The infirm will be healed
Acts 5:12-16
Many people healed by the apostles

TUESDAY
Ezekiel 47:1-12
The wilderness will flower
Jude 17-25
Prepare for the Lord's coming

WEDNESDAY
Zechariah 8:1-17
God's promise to Zion
Matthew 8:14-17, 28-34
Jesus heals

DAILY
Psalm 42
Hope in God

Fourth Sunday of Advent

Readings for Monday through Wednesday after the Fourth Sunday of Advent are provided for use if necessary. Beginning with December 22, the dated readings on the following pages may be used.

Preparation for Sunday

THURSDAY
2 Samuel 7:1-17
God will build you a house
Galatians 3:23-29
Children of God by Christ's coming

FRIDAY
2 Samuel 7:18-22
David prays for God's faithfulness toward Israel
Galatians 4:1-7
God's Son, sent in the fullness of time

SATURDAY
2 Samuel 7:23-29
David reminds God of God's promise
John 3:31-36
The one who comes from above

DAILY
Psalm 80:1-7, 17-19
Show the light of your countenance

Fourth Sunday of Advent

Isaiah 7:10-16
The sign of Immanuel
Psalm 80:1-7, 17-19
Show the light of your countenance
Romans 1:1-7
Paul's greeting to the church at Rome
Matthew 1:18-25
Our God near at hand

Reflection on Sunday

MONDAY
Genesis 17:15-22
God promises Sarah a son
Galatians 4:8-20
Paul's labor for the Galatian church

TUESDAY
Genesis 21:1-21
God saves Hagar and Ishmael
Galatians 4:21—5:1
Two women, two covenants, one freedom

WEDNESDAY
Genesis 37:2-11
The patriarch Joseph dreams
Matthew 1:1-17
Jesus' genealogy

DAILY
1 Samuel 2:1-10
Hannah's song

Days around Christmas Day

DECEMBER 22
Isaiah 33:17-22
The Lord will save us
Revelation 22:6-7, 18-20
See, I am coming soon

DECEMBER 23
2 Samuel 7:18, 23-29
Your servant will be blessed
Galatians 3:6-14
The promise of the Spirit

DECEMBER 24 (MORNING ONLY)
Isaiah 60:1-6
Arise, shine!
Luke 1:67-80
The song of Zechariah

DAILY
Luke 1:46b-55
My soul gives glory to God

Nativity of the Lord (Christmas Day)

Any of the following three propers may be used on Christmas Eve/Day.

The readings from propers II and III for Christmas may be used as alternatives for Christmas Day. If proper III is not used on Christmas Day, it should be used at some service during the Christmas cycle because of the significance of John's prologue.

Christmas, Proper I

Isaiah 9:2-7
A child is born for us
Psalm 96
Let the earth be glad
Titus 2:11-14
The grace of God has appeared
Luke 2:1-14 [15-20]
God with us

Christmas, Proper II

Isaiah 62:6-12
God comes to restore the people
Psalm 97
Light springs up for the righteous
Titus 3:4-7
Saved through water and the Spirit
Luke 2:[1-7] 8-20
The birth of the Messiah revealed to shepherds

Christmas, Proper III

Isaiah 52:7-10
Heralds announce God's salvation
Psalm 98
The victory of our God
Hebrews 1:1-4 [5-12]
God has spoken by a son
John 1:1-14
The Word became flesh

DECEMBER 26
Wisdom 4:7-15
The righteous are rewarded
Acts 7:59—8:8
Stephen is stoned to death

DECEMBER 27
Proverbs 8:22-31
Wisdom's part in creation
1 John 5:1-12
Whoever loves God loves God's child

DECEMBER 28
Isaiah 49:13-23
God comforts the suffering
Matthew 18:1-14
Become like a child

DAILY
Psalm 148
God's splendor is over earth and heaven

First Sunday after Christmas Day, December 26–31

Isaiah 63:7-9
Israel saved by God's own presence
Psalm 148
God's splendor is over earth and heaven
Hebrews 2:10-18
Christ frees humankind
Matthew 2:13-23
The slaughter of innocent children

Days of Christmas

DAILY
Psalm 20
Answer us when we call

DECEMBER 29
Jeremiah 31:15-22
Weeping in Ramah
Luke 19:41-44
Jesus weeps over Jerusalem

DECEMBER 30
Isaiah 26:1-9
Trust in God forever
2 Corinthians 4:16-18
The temporary and the eternal

DECEMBER 31
1 Kings 3:5-14
God grants a discerning mind
John 8:12-19
I am the light

**JANUARY 1—HOLY NAME OF JESUS
(MARY, MOTHER OF GOD)**
Numbers 6:22-27
The Aaronic blessing
Psalm 8
How exalted is your name
Galatians 4:4-7
We are no longer slaves
or Philippians 2:5-11
God takes on human form
Luke 2:15-21
The child is named Jesus

JANUARY 1—NEW YEAR'S DAY
Ecclesiastes 3:1-13
To everything a season
Psalm 8
How exalted is your name
Revelation 21:1-6a
New heaven and new earth
Matthew 25:31-46
Separation of the sheep and goats

JANUARY 2
Genesis 12:1-7
Abram and Sarai
Hebrews 11:1-12
Abraham's faith

The following readings are provided for use when Epiphany (January 6) is celebrated on a weekday following the Second Sunday after Christmas Day.

Second Sunday after Christmas Day, January 2–5

Jeremiah 31:7-14	*or*	Sirach 24:1-12
Joy as God's scattered flock gathers		*Wisdom lives among God's people*
Psalm 147:12-20	*or*	Wisdom 10:15-21
Praising God in Zion		*Praising the holy name*
Ephesians 1:3-14		
The will of God made known in Christ		
John 1:[1-9] 10-18		
God with us		

Days around Epiphany

Readings through January 9 are provided for use if necessary. When the Epiphany of the Lord is trans-ferred to the preceding Sunday, January 2-5, these dated readings may be used through the week that follows. When the Baptism of the Lord falls on January 11, 12, or 13, the corresponding preparation readings on the following page are used after January 9.

JANUARY 3
Genesis 28:10-22
Jacob's ladder
Hebrews 11:13-22
Abraham, Isaac, and Jacob act on faith

JANUARY 5
Joshua 1:1-9
Be strong
Hebrews 11:32—12:2
Surrounded by a cloud of witnesses

JANUARY 4
Exodus 3:1-5
The burning bush
Hebrews 11:23-31
Moses acts on faith

DAILY
Psalm 72
Prayers for the king

Epiphany of the Lord, January 6

Isaiah 60:1-6
Nations come to the light
Psalm 72:1-7, 10-14
All shall bow down
Ephesians 3:1-12
The gospel's promise for all
Matthew 2:1-12
Christ revealed to the nations

JANUARY 7
1 Kings 10:1-13
Gifts to Solomon from Sheba
Ephesians 3:14-21
Knowing the love of Christ

JANUARY 9
Micah 5:2-9
One who is to rule Israel
Luke 13:31-35
Jerusalem that kills the prophets

JANUARY 8
1 Kings 10:14-25
Solomon's splendor
Ephesians 4:7, 11-16
Gifts according to Christ

DAILY
Psalm 72
Prayers for the king

Baptism of the Lord [1]
First Sunday after the Epiphany

Preparation for Sunday

THURSDAY
1 Samuel 3:1-9
Samuel, a boy, says "Here I am"
Acts 9:1-9
Saul on the road to Damascus

FRIDAY
1 Samuel 3:10—4:1a
Samuel receives the word of God at Shiloh
Acts 9:10-19a
Ananias receives Saul into the church

SATURDAY
1 Samuel 7:3-17
Samuel guides Israel to peace
Acts 9:19b-31
Barnabas introduces Saul/Paul in Jerusalem

DAILY
Psalm 29
The voice of God upon the waters

Baptism of the Lord

Isaiah 42:1-9
The servant of God brings justice
Psalm 29
The voice of God upon the waters
Acts 10:34-43
Jesus' ministry after his baptism
Matthew 3:13-17
Christ revealed as God's servant

Reflection on Sunday

MONDAY
Genesis 35:1-15
God calls and blesses Jacob
Acts 10:44-48
Through Peter, God calls Gentiles to be baptized

TUESDAY
Jeremiah 1:4-10
God calls Jeremiah
Acts 8:4-13
Philip preaches and baptizes

WEDNESDAY
Isaiah 51:1-16
Through water God's people cross over
Matthew 12:15-21
The words of Isaiah applied to Jesus

DAILY
Psalm 89:5-37
God anoints David to be a son

Second Sunday after the Epiphany [2]

Preparation for Sunday

THURSDAY
Isaiah 22:15-25
God replaces disobedient leaders
Galatians 1:6-12
Paul's calling through a revelation of Christ

FRIDAY
Genesis 27:30-38
Isaac and Esau discover Jacob's deceit
Acts 1:1-5
The promise of the Holy Spirit

SATURDAY
1 Kings 19:19-21
Elijah calls Elisha to follow him
Luke 5:1-11
Jesus calls the first disciples

DAILY
Psalm 40:1-11
Doing the will of God

Second Sunday after the Epiphany

Isaiah 49:1-7
The servant brings light to the nations
Psalm 40:1-11
Doing the will of God
1 Corinthians 1:1-9
Paul's greeting to the church at Corinth
John 1:29-42
Christ revealed as the Lamb of God

Reflection on Sunday

MONDAY
Exodus 12:1-13, 21-28
The passover lamb
Acts 8:26-40
Philip teaches about the lamb

TUESDAY
Isaiah 53:1-12
The one like a lamb
Hebrews 10:1-4
Animal sacrifices cannot take away sins

WEDNESDAY
Isaiah 48:12-21
God saves the people through water
Matthew 9:14-17
Christ, the bridegroom, the new wine

DAILY
Psalm 40:6-17
Not sacrifice, but divine mercy

Third Sunday after the Epiphany [3]

Preparation for Sunday

THURSDAY
1 Samuel 1:1-20
The birth of Samuel
Galatians 1:11-24
The divine origin of Paul's gospel

FRIDAY
1 Samuel 9:27—10:8
Saul anointed by Samuel as king
Galatians 2:1-10
Paul's authority in the growing church

SATURDAY
1 Samuel 15:34—16:13
David anointed as king to replace King Saul
Luke 5:27-32
The call of Levi

DAILY
Psalm 27:1-6
God is light and salvation

Third Sunday after the Epiphany

Isaiah 9:1-4
Light shines for those in darkness
Psalm 27:1, 4-9
God is light and salvation
1 Corinthians 1:10-18
An appeal for unity in the gospel
Matthew 4:12-23
Christ revealed as a prophet

Reflection on Sunday

MONDAY
Judges 6:11-24
God calls Gideon to lead the people
Ephesians 5:6-14
Live as children of the light

TUESDAY
Judges 7:12-22
God leads Gideon to victory
Philippians 2:12-18
The call to shine like stars

WEDNESDAY
Genesis 49:1-2, 8-13, 21-26
Judah, Zebulun, Naphtali, and Joseph blessed
Luke 1:67-79
Christ, the light dawning

DAILY
Psalm 27:7-14
Take courage in God

Fourth Sunday after the Epiphany [4]

If this Sunday immediately precedes Ash Wednesday, the proper for Sunday and the readings for the surrounding days may be replaced, in those churches observing the Transfiguration on that Sunday, by the proper for the Last Sunday after the Epiphany and the readings for the days surrounding it.

Preparation for Sunday

THURSDAY
Deuteronomy 16:18-20
Pursue only justice
1 Peter 3:8-12
Repay evil with a blessing

FRIDAY
Deuteronomy 24:17—25:4
Do not deprive others of justice
1 Timothy 5:17-24
Good works are conspicuous

SATURDAY
Micah 3:1-4
Should you not know justice?
John 13:31-35
The new commandment

DAILY
Psalm 15
Abiding on God's holy hill

Fourth Sunday after the Epiphany

Micah 6:1-8
The offering of justice, kindness, humility
Psalm 15
Abiding on God's holy hill
1 Corinthians 1:18-31
Christ crucified, the wisdom and power of God
Matthew 5:1-12
The teaching of Christ: Beatitudes

Reflection on Sunday

MONDAY
Ruth 1:1-18
Ruth, one of the poor
Philemon 1-25
Concerning the slave Onesimus

TUESDAY
Ruth 2:1-16
Ruth, one of the hungry
James 5:1-6
A warning to the ungenerous

WEDNESDAY
Ruth 3:1-13; 4:13-22
Ruth, one of the blessed
Luke 6:17-26
The beatitudes in Luke's gospel

DAILY
Psalm 37:1-17
God will bless the righteous

Fifth Sunday after the Epiphany [5]

If this Sunday immediately precedes Ash Wednesday, the proper for Sunday and the readings for the surrounding days may be replaced, in those churches observing the Transfiguration on that Sunday, by the proper for the Last Sunday after the Epiphany and the readings for the days surrounding it.

Preparation for Sunday

THURSDAY
Deuteronomy 4:1-14
The discipline of faith
1 John 5:1-5
God's children obey God's commandments

FRIDAY
Isaiah 29:1-12
Hunger that goes unsatisfied
James 3:13-18
A gentle life born of wisdom

SATURDAY
Isaiah 29:13-16
Hearts far from God
Mark 7:1-8
The hypocrisy of lip service

DAILY
Psalm 112:1-9 [10]
Light shines in the darkness

Fifth Sunday after the Epiphany

Isaiah 58:1-9a [9b-12]
The fast that God chooses
Psalm 112:1-9 [10]
Light shines in the darkness
1 Corinthians 2:1-12 [13-16]
God's wisdom revealed through the Spirit
Matthew 5:13-20
The teaching of Christ: salt and light

Reflection on Sunday

MONDAY
2 Kings 22:3-20
Huldah urges Josiah to keep the law
Romans 11:2-10
A remnant remains faithful

TUESDAY
2 Kings 23:1-8, 21-25
King Josiah keeps the law
2 Corinthians 4:1-12
Christ, the light

WEDNESDAY
Proverbs 6:6-23
The law is a lamp
John 8:12-30
Christ the light of the world

DAILY
Psalm 119:105-112
The law is light

Sixth Sunday after the Epiphany [6]

Proper 1

If this Sunday immediately precedes Ash Wednesday, the proper for Sunday and the readings for the surrounding days may be replaced, in those churches observing the Transfiguration on that Sunday, by the proper for the Last Sunday after the Epiphany and the readings for the days surrounding it.

Preparation for Sunday

THURSDAY
Genesis 26:1-5
God blesses Isaac
James 1:12-16
God tempts no one

FRIDAY
Leviticus 26:34-46
God's covenant remembered
1 John 2:7-17
Old and new commandments

SATURDAY
Deuteronomy 30:1-9a
God's fidelity assured
Matthew 15:1-9
God's commandments and religious tradition

DAILY
Psalm 119:1-8
Happy are those who walk in the law

Sixth Sunday after the Epiphany

Deuteronomy 30:15-20   *or*   Sirach 15:15-20
Choose life   *Choose between life and death*
Psalm 119:1-8
Happy are those who walk in the law
1 Corinthians 3:1-9
God gives the growth
Matthew 5:21-37
The teaching of Christ: forgiveness

Reflection on Sunday

MONDAY
Exodus 20:1-21
The ten commandments
James 1:2-8
Facing trials

TUESDAY
Deuteronomy 23:21—24:4, 10-15
Israel's communal laws
James 2:1-13
The law, judgment, and mercy

WEDNESDAY
Proverbs 2:1-15
The way of wisdom
Matthew 19:1-12
Jesus teaches about divorce

DAILY
Psalm 119:9-16
I delight in the law

Seventh Sunday after the Epiphany [7]

Proper 2

If this Sunday immediately precedes Ash Wednesday, the proper for Sunday and the readings for the surrounding days may be replaced, in those churches observing the Transfiguration on that Sunday, by the proper for the Last Sunday after the Epiphany and the readings for the days surrounding it.

Preparation for Sunday

THURSDAY
Exodus 22:21-27
Compassion for neighbors
1 Corinthians 10:23—11:1
Do not seek your own advantage

FRIDAY
Leviticus 6:1-7
Sin against a neighbor
Galatians 5:2-6
Faith working through love

SATURDAY
Leviticus 24:10-23
An eye for an eye
Matthew 7:1-12
The golden rule

DAILY
Psalm 119:33-40
Walking in the path of the law

Seventh Sunday after the Epiphany

Leviticus 19:1-2, 9-18
Acts of mercy and justice
Psalm 119:33-40
Walking in the path of the law
1 Corinthians 3:10-11, 16-23
Allegiance to Christ, not human leaders
Matthew 5:38-48
The teaching of Christ: love

Reflection on Sunday

MONDAY
Proverbs 25:11-22
Caring for the enemy
Romans 12:9-21
Caring for the enemy

TUESDAY
Genesis 31:1-3, 17-50
Laban and Jacob reconcile
Hebrews 12:14-16
Pursue peace with everyone

WEDNESDAY
Proverbs 3:27-35
Regard for neighbors
Luke 18:18-30
The rich young ruler

DAILY
Psalm 119:57-64
Keeping the law in spite of the wicked

Eighth Sunday after the Epiphany [8]

Proper 3

If this Sunday immediately precedes Ash Wednesday, the proper for Sunday and the readings for the surrounding days may be replaced, in those churches observing the Transfiguration on that Sunday, by the proper for the Last Sunday after the Epiphany and the readings for the days surrounding it.

Preparation for Sunday

THURSDAY
Proverbs 12:22-28
Anxiety burdens the heart
Philippians 2:19-24
Timothy's worth

FRIDAY
Isaiah 26:1-6
Trust in God
Philippians 2:25-30
Paul overcomes anxiety

SATURDAY
Isaiah 31:1-9
Misplaced trust
Luke 11:14-23
A house divided falls

DAILY
Psalm 131
A child upon its mother's breast

Eighth Sunday after the Epiphany

Isaiah 49:8-16a
God's motherly compassion
Psalm 131
A child upon its mother's breast
1 Corinthians 4:1-5
Servants accountable to God
Matthew 6:24-34
The teaching of Christ: trust in God

Reflection on Sunday

MONDAY
Deuteronomy 32:1-14
God's care for the chosen people
Hebrews 10:32-39
Confidence that rewards

TUESDAY
1 Kings 17:1-16
God feeds the widow
1 Corinthians 4:6-21
The life of an apostle

WEDNESDAY
Isaiah 66:7-13
God as a nursing mother
Luke 12:22-31
Do not worry

DAILY
Psalm 104
God cares for all the earth

Ninth Sunday after the Epiphany [9]
Proper 4

The readings that follow are for churches whose calendar requires this Sunday, and who do not observe the last Sunday after the Epiphany as Transfiguration.

Preparation for Sunday

THURSDAY
Exodus 24:1-8
The blood of the covenant
Romans 2:17-29
Real circumcision a matter of the heart

FRIDAY
Deuteronomy 30:1-5
God's fidelity assured
Romans 9:6-13
God's election of Israel

SATURDAY
Amos 2:6-11
Judgment on Israel
Matthew 7:1-6
Do not judge

DAILY
Psalm 31:1-5, 19-24
I commit my spirit

Ninth Sunday after the Epiphany

Deuteronomy 11:18-21, 26-28
Keeping the words of God
Psalm 31:1-5, 19-24
I commit my spirit
Romans 1:16-17; 3:22b-28 [29-31]
Justified by God's grace as a gift
Matthew 7:21-29
The teaching of Christ: doing the works of God

Reflection on Sunday

MONDAY
Joshua 8:30-35
Joshua renews the covenant
Romans 2:1-11
The righteous judgment of God

TUESDAY
Joshua 24:1-2, 11-28
The Israelites renew the covenant
Romans 3:9-22a
All have sinned

WEDNESDAY
Job 28:12-28
The way of wisdom
Matthew 7:13-20
The narrow gate

DAILY
Psalm 52
The wicked and the righteous

Last Sunday after the Epiphany

Transfiguration Sunday

The following may be used in churches where the last Sunday after the Epiphany is observed as Transfiguration Sunday.

Preparation for Sunday

THURSDAY
Exodus 6:2-9
God promises deliverance through Moses
Hebrews 8:1-7
Christ, the mediator

FRIDAY
Exodus 19:9b-25
Israel consecrated at Sinai
Hebrews 11:23-28
The faith of Moses

SATURDAY
1 Kings 21:20-29
Elijah pronounces God's sentence
Mark 9:9-13
The coming of Elijah

DAILY
Psalm 2
The one begotten of God

Transfiguration of the Lord

Exodus 24:12-18
Moses enters the cloud of God's glory
Psalm 2   *or*   Psalm 99
The one begotten of God   *Worship upon God's holy hill*
2 Peter 1:16-21
Shining with the glory of God
Matthew 17:1-9
Christ revealed as God's beloved Son

Reflection on Sunday

MONDAY
Exodus 33:7-23
Moses asks to see God's glory
Acts 7:30-34
Moses on holy ground

TUESDAY
1 Kings 19:9-18
Elijah hears God
Romans 11:1-6
A remnant chosen by grace

DAILY
Psalm 78:17-20, 52-55
Israel led to God's holy mountain

Lent

Three Days

Easter

YEAR A

First Sunday in Lent

Ash Wednesday

Joel 2:1-2, 12-17   *or*   Isaiah 58:1-12
Return to God   *The fast that God chooses*
Psalm 51:1-17
Plea for mercy
2 Corinthians 5:20b—6:10
Now is the day of salvation
Matthew 6:1-6, 16-21
The practice of faith

Preparation for Sunday

THURSDAY
Jonah 3:1-10
Nineveh hears Jonah's preaching and repents
Romans 1:1-7
Appointed to preach the good news of Christ

FRIDAY
Jonah 4:1-11
God mercifully reproves Jonah
Romans 1:8-17
Live by faith

SATURDAY
Isaiah 58:1-12
The fast that God chooses
Matthew 18:1-7
The humble one is the greatest

DAILY
Psalm 51
Create in me a clean heart

First Sunday in Lent

Genesis 2:15-17; 3:1-7
Eating of the tree of knowledge
Psalm 32
Mercy embraces us
Romans 5:12-19
Death came, life comes
Matthew 4:1-11
The temptation of Jesus

Reflection on Sunday

MONDAY
1 Kings 19:1-8
An angel feeds Elijah in the wilderness
Hebrews 2:10-18
Christ goes before us in suffering

TUESDAY
Genesis 4:1-16
God protects Cain
Hebrews 4:14—5:10
Christ was tempted as we are

WEDNESDAY
Exodus 34:1-9, 27-28
God's revelation of mercy
Matthew 18:10-14
Not one of these little ones should be lost

DAILY
Psalm 32
Mercy embraces us

Second Sunday in Lent

Preparation for Sunday

THURSDAY
Isaiah 51:1-3
Look to Abraham and Sarah
2 Timothy 1:3-7
Faith handed down from faithful mothers

FRIDAY
Micah 7:18-20
God's faithfulness
Romans 3:21-31
Paul relates law and faith

SATURDAY
Isaiah 51:4-8
God's word means justice for all
Luke 7:1-10
Room at the table of Abraham

DAILY
Psalm 121
The Lord watches over you

Second Sunday in Lent

Genesis 12:1-4a
The blessing of God upon Abram
Psalm 121
The Lord watches over you
Romans 4:1-5, 13-17
The promise to those of Abraham's faith
John 3:1-17   *or*   Matthew 17:1-9
The mission of Christ: saving the world   *Christ revealed as God's beloved Son*

Reflection on Sunday

MONDAY
Numbers 21:4-9
Moses lifts up the serpent
Hebrews 3:1-6
Moses the servant, Christ the son

TUESDAY
Isaiah 65:17-25
God promises a new creation
Romans 4:6-13
Abraham saved through faith

WEDNESDAY
Ezekiel 36:22-32
God will renew the people
John 7:53—8:11
Jesus does not condemn the sinner

DAILY
Psalm 128
God promises life

Third Sunday in Lent

Preparation for Sunday

THURSDAY
Exodus 16:1-8
Israel complains of hunger in the wilderness
Colossians 1:15-23
Christ, the reconciliation of all things

FRIDAY
Exodus 16:9-21
God gives manna and quail
Ephesians 2:11-22
Christ, the reconciliation of Jew and Gentile

SATURDAY
Exodus 16:27-35
Manna and the sabbath
John 4:1-6
Jesus travels to Jacob's well in Samaria

DAILY
Psalm 95
The rock of our salvation

Third Sunday in Lent

Exodus 17:1-7
Water from the rock
Psalm 95
The rock of our salvation
Romans 5:1-11
Reconciled to God by Christ's death
John 4:5-42
The woman at the well

Reflection on Sunday

MONDAY
Genesis 24:1-27
Rebekah at the well
2 John 1-13
A woman reminded to abide in Christ

TUESDAY
Genesis 29:1-14
Rachel at the well
1 Corinthians 10:1-4
Drinking from Christ, the spiritual rock

WEDNESDAY
Jeremiah 2:4-13
God, the living water
John 7:14-31, 37-39
Drink of Jesus, the Messiah

DAILY
Psalm 81
We drink from the rock

Fourth Sunday in Lent

Preparation for Sunday

THURSDAY
1 Samuel 15:10-21
The prophet Samuel confronts the king
Ephesians 4:25-32
Called to honesty and forbearance

FRIDAY
1 Samuel 15:22-31
The king confesses his sinful disobedience
Ephesians 5:1-9
Now in the Lord you are light

SATURDAY
1 Samuel 15:32-34
Samuel grieves over Saul
John 1:1-9
Christ comes with light and life

DAILY
Psalm 23
My head anointed with oil

Fourth Sunday in Lent

1 Samuel 16:1-13
David is chosen and anointed
Psalm 23
My head anointed with oil
Ephesians 5:8-14
Live as children of light
John 9:1-41
The man born blind

Reflection on Sunday

MONDAY
Isaiah 59:9-19
The blindness of injustice
Acts 9:1-20
Saul is baptized, his sight restored

TUESDAY
Isaiah 42:14-21
God will heal the blind
Colossians 1:9-14
The inheritance of the saints in light

WEDNESDAY
Isaiah 60:17-22
God our light
Matthew 9:27-34
Jesus heals the blind

DAILY
Psalm 146
God opens the eyes of the blind

Fifth Sunday in Lent

Preparation for Sunday

THURSDAY
Ezekiel 1:1-3; 2:8—3:3
The word of God: lamentation and sweetness
Revelation 10:1-11
The word of God: bitter and sweet

FRIDAY
Ezekiel 33:10-16
The word of God: repent and live
Revelation 11:15-19
The word of God: thanksgiving and singing

SATURDAY
Ezekiel 36:8-15
Blessings upon Israel
Luke 24:44-53
Jesus blesses the disciples

DAILY
Psalm 130
Mercy and redemption

Fifth Sunday in Lent

Ezekiel 37:1-14
The dry bones of Israel
Psalm 130
Mercy and redemption
Romans 8:6-11
Life in the Spirit
John 11:1-45
The raising of Lazarus

Reflection on Sunday

MONDAY
1 Kings 17:17-24
Elijah raises the widow's son
Acts 20:7-12
Paul raises a young man

TUESDAY
2 Kings 4:18-37
Elisha raises a child from death
Ephesians 2:1-10
Alive in Christ

WEDNESDAY
Jeremiah 32:1-9, 36-41
Jeremiah buys a field
Matthew 22:23-33
God of the living

DAILY
Psalm 143
Save me from death

Sixth Sunday in Lent

Passion Sunday or *Palm Sunday*

Those who do not observe the procession with palms and do not wish to use the passion gospel may substitute the gospel and psalm indicated for the Liturgy of the Palms for the gospel and psalm indicated for the Liturgy of the Passion. Whenever possible, the whole passion narrative should be read.

Preparation for Sunday

THURSDAY
1 Samuel 16:11-13
Samuel anoints David
Philippians 1:1-11
Encouraged to follow Christ's righteousness

FRIDAY
Job 13:13-19
A servant keeps silence
Philippians 1:21-30
Seeing Christ in this life

SATURDAY
Lamentations 3:55-66
A cry for help
Mark 10:32-34
Going up to Jerusalem

DAILY
Psalm 31:9-16
I commend my spirit

Sixth Sunday in Lent

LITURGY OF THE PALMS
Psalm 118:1-2, 19-29
The passover praise psalm
Matthew 21:1-11
Jesus enters Jerusalem

LITURGY OF THE PASSION
Isaiah 50:4-9a
The servant submits to suffering
Psalm 31:9-16
I commend my spirit
Philippians 2:5-11
Death on a cross
Matthew 26:14—27:66 *or* Matthew 27:11-54
The passion and death of Jesus

Monday of Holy Week

Isaiah 42:1-9
The servant brings forth justice
Psalm 36:5-11
Refuge under the shadow of your wings
Hebrews 9:11-15
The blood of Christ redeems for eternal life
John 12:1-11
Mary of Bethany anoints Jesus

Tuesday of Holy Week

Isaiah 49:1-7
The servant brings salvation to earth's ends
Psalm 71:1-14
From my mother's womb you have been my strength
1 Corinthians 1:18-31
The cross of Christ reveals God's power and wisdom
John 12:20-36
Jesus speaks of his death

Wednesday of Holy Week

Isaiah 50:4-9a
The servant is vindicated by God
Psalm 70
Be pleased, O God, to deliver me
Hebrews 12:1-3
Look to Jesus, who endured the cross
John 13:21-32
Jesus foretells his betrayal

The Three Days

Holy Thursday

Exodus 12:1-4 [5-10] 11-14
The passover of the Lord
Psalm 116:1-2, 12-19
The cup of salvation
1 Corinthians 11:23-26
Proclaim the Lord's death
John 13:1-17, 31b-35
The service of Christ: footwashing and meal

Good Friday

Isaiah 52:13 — 53:12
The suffering servant
Psalm 22
Why have you forsaken me?
Hebrews 10:16-25   *or*   Hebrews 4:14-16; 5:7-9
The way to God is opened   *The merciful high priest*
John 18:1 — 19:42
The passion and death of Jesus

Holy Saturday
The following are for use at services other than the Easter Vigil.

Job 14:1-14   *or*   Lamentations 3:1-9, 19-24
Hope for a tree   *I will hope in the Lord*
Psalm 31:1-4, 15-16
Take me out of the net
1 Peter 4:1-8
The gospel proclaimed even to the dead
Matthew 27:57-66   *or*   John 19:38-42
The burial of Jesus   *The burial of Jesus*

Resurrection of the Lord, Easter Vigil

1

Genesis 1:1 — 2:4a
Creation
Psalm 136:1-9, 23-26
God's mercy endures forever

2

Genesis 7:1-5, 11-18; 8:6-18; 9:8-13
Flood
Psalm 46
The God of Jacob is our stronghold

3

Genesis 22:1-18
Testing of Abraham
Psalm 16
You will show me the path of life

4

Exodus 14:10-31; 15:20-21
Deliverance at the Red Sea
Exodus 15:1b-13, 17-18
I will sing to the Lord who has triumphed gloriously

5

Isaiah 55:1-11
Salvation freely offered to all
Isaiah 12:2-6
With joy you will draw water from the wells of salvation

6

Baruch 3:9-15, 32—4:4   *or*   Proverbs 8:1-8, 19-21; 9:4b-6
The wisdom of God   *The wisdom of God*
Psalm 19
God's statutes are just and rejoice the heart

7

Ezekiel 36:24-28
A new heart and a new spirit
Psalms 42 and 43
My soul thirsts for the living God

8

Ezekiel 37:1-14
Valley of the dry bones
Psalm 143
Revive me for your name's sake

9

Zephaniah 3:14-20
Gathering of God's people
Psalm 98
Lift up your voice, rejoice and sing

Romans 6:3-11
Dying and rising with Christ
Psalm 114
Tremble, O earth
Matthew 28:1-10
Proclaim the resurrection

Resurrection of the Lord, Easter Day

Acts 10:34-43   *or*   Jeremiah 31:1-6
God raised Jesus on the third day   *Joy at God's people restored*
Psalm 118:1-2, 14-24
On this day God has acted
Colossians 3:1-4   *or*   Acts 10:34-43
Raised with Christ   *God raised Jesus on the third day*
John 20:1-18   *or*   Matthew 28:1-10
Seeing the risen Christ   *Proclaim the resurrection*

Easter Evening

Isaiah 25:6-9
The feast of victory
Psalm 114
Tremble, O earth
1 Corinthians 5:6b-8
Set your mind on things above
Luke 24:13-49
Stay with us, Lord

Reflection on Sunday

MONDAY
Exodus 14:10-31; 15:20-21
Israel crosses over the sea
Colossians 3:5-11
The new life in Christ

TUESDAY
Exodus 15:1-18
Song at the sea
Colossians 3:12-17
The new life in Christ

WEDNESDAY
Joshua 3:1-17
Israel crosses into the promised land
Matthew 28:1-10
Proclaim the resurrection

DAILY
Psalm 118:1-2, 14-24
On this day God has acted

Second Sunday of Easter

Preparation for Sunday

THURSDAY
Song of Solomon 2:8-15
Arise, for the winter is past
Colossians 4:2-5
The new life in Christ

FRIDAY
Song of Solomon 5:9—6:3
The beloved in the garden
1 Corinthians 15:1-11
Witnesses to the risen Christ

SATURDAY
Song of Solomon 8:6-7
Love is strong as death
John 20:11-20
The witness of Mary Magdalene

DAILY
Psalm 16
Fullness of joy

Second Sunday of Easter

Acts 2:14a, 22-32
God fulfills the promise to David
Psalm 16
Fullness of joy
1 Peter 1:3-9
New birth to a living hope
John 20:19-31
Beholding the wounds of the risen Christ

Reflection on Sunday

MONDAY
Judges 6:36-40
Gideon and the fleece
1 Corinthians 15:12-20
Paul teaches the resurrection

TUESDAY
Jonah 1:1-17
Jonah saved from the sea
1 Corinthians 15:19-28
Paul teaches the resurrection

WEDNESDAY
Jonah 2:1-10
Jonah's praise for deliverance
Matthew 12:38-42
Jesus speaks of the sign of Jonah

DAILY
Psalm 114
God saves through water

Third Sunday of Easter

Preparation for Sunday

THURSDAY
Isaiah 25:1-5
Praise for deliverance
1 Peter 1:8b-12
The promised salvation comes

FRIDAY
Isaiah 26:1-4
God sets up victory like bulwarks
1 Peter 1:13-16
A holy life

SATURDAY
Isaiah 25:6-9
The feast for all peoples
Luke 14:12-14
Welcome those in need to your table

DAILY
Psalm 116:1-4, 12-19
I will call upon God

Third Sunday of Easter

Acts 2:14a, 36-41
Receiving God's promise through baptism
Psalm 116:1-4, 12-19
I will call upon God
1 Peter 1:17-23
Born anew
Luke 24:13-35
Eating with the risen Christ

Reflection on Sunday

MONDAY
Genesis 18:1-14
Abraham and Sarah eat with God
1 Peter 1:23-25
The word of God endures

TUESDAY
Proverbs 8:32—9:6
Wisdom serves a meal
1 Peter 2:1-3
Long for the pure spiritual milk

WEDNESDAY
Exodus 24:1-11
Moses and the elders eat with God
John 21:1-14
The risen Christ eats with the disciples

DAILY
Psalm 134
Praise God day and night

Fourth Sunday of Easter

Preparation for Sunday

THURSDAY
Exodus 2:15b-25
Moses the shepherd
1 Peter 2:9-12
Living as God's people

FRIDAY
Exodus 3:16-22; 4:18-20
Moses the shepherd of Israel
1 Peter 2:13-17
Living honorably in the world

SATURDAY
Ezekiel 34:1-16
God gathers the scattered flock
Luke 15:1-7
Parable of the lost sheep

DAILY
Psalm 23
God our shepherd

Fourth Sunday of Easter

Acts 2:42-47
The believers' common life
Psalm 23
God our shepherd
1 Peter 2:19-25
Follow the shepherd, even in suffering
John 10:1-10
Christ the shepherd

Reflection on Sunday

MONDAY
Ezekiel 34:17-23
God the true shepherd
1 Peter 5:1-5
Tend the flock of God

TUESDAY
Ezekiel 34:23-31
God provides perfect pasture
Hebrews 13:20-21
God's blessing through Christ the shepherd

WEDNESDAY
Jeremiah 23:1-8
God will gather the flock
Matthew 20:17-28
Jesus came to serve

DAILY
Psalm 100
We are the sheep of God's pasture

Fifth Sunday of Easter

Preparation for Sunday

THURSDAY
Genesis 12:1-3
The call of Abram
Acts 6:8-15
Stephen is arrested

FRIDAY
Exodus 3:1-12
Moses at the burning bush
Acts 7:1-16
Stephen addresses the council

SATURDAY
Jeremiah 26:20-24
A prophet of the Lord persecuted
John 8:48-59
Jesus the greater prophet

DAILY
Psalm 31:1-5, 15-16
I commend my spirit

Fifth Sunday of Easter

Acts 7:55-60
Martyrdom of Stephen
Psalm 31:1-5, 15-16
I commend my spirit
1 Peter 2:2-10
God's chosen people
John 14:1-14
Christ the way, truth, life

Reflection on Sunday

MONDAY
Exodus 13:17-22
God leads the way
Acts 7:17-40
Stephen addresses the council

TUESDAY
Proverbs 3:5-12
God, the truth and life
Acts 7:44-56
Stephen confronts the council

WEDNESDAY
Proverbs 3:13-18
God, the truth and life
John 8:31-38
Jesus, the truth of God

DAILY
Psalm 102:1-17
Prayer for deliverance

Sixth Sunday of Easter

Preparation for Sunday

THURSDAY
Genesis 6:5-22
God's command to Noah
Acts 27:1-12
Paul sails for Rome

FRIDAY
Genesis 7:1-24
The great flood
Acts 27:13-38
Paul survives shipwreck

SATURDAY
Genesis 8:13-19
The flood waters subside
John 14:27-29
Peace I leave with you

DAILY
Psalm 66:8-20
Be joyful in God, all you lands

Sixth Sunday of Easter

Acts 17:22-31
Paul's message to the Athenians
Psalm 66:8-20
Be joyful in God, all you lands
1 Peter 3:13-22
The days of Noah, a sign of baptism
John 14:15-21
Christ our advocate

Reflection on Sunday

MONDAY
Genesis 9:8-17
Sign of the covenant
Acts 27:39-44
Paul and companions come safely to land

TUESDAY
Deuteronomy 5:22-33
Moses delivers God's commandments
1 Peter 3:8-12
Seek peace and pursue it

WEDNESDAY
Deuteronomy 31:1-13
Moses promises God's presence
John 16:16-24
A little while, and you shall see

DAILY
Psalm 93
God reigns above the floods

Seventh Sunday of Easter

Ascension of the Lord, Thursday

These readings may also be used on the Seventh Sunday of Easter.

Acts 1:1-11
Jesus sends the apostles

Psalm 47   or   Psalm 93
God has gone up with a shout   *Praise to God who reigns*

Ephesians 1:15-23
Seeing the risen and ascended Christ

Luke 24:44-53
Christ present in all times and places

Preparation for Sunday

FRIDAY   **DAILY**

2 Kings 2:1-12   Psalm 93
Elijah ascends in a chariot of fire   *Praise to God who reigns*

Ephesians 2:1-7
Seated in the heavenly places with Christ

SATURDAY

2 Kings 2:13-15
The spirit rests on Elisha

John 8:21-30
Jesus speaks of going to the Father

Seventh Sunday of Easter

Acts 1:6-14
Jesus' companions at prayer

Psalm 68:1-10, 32-35
Sing to God

1 Peter 4:12-14; 5:6-11
God sustains those who suffer

John 17:1-11
Christ's prayer for his disciples

Reflection on Sunday

MONDAY
Leviticus 9:1-11, 22-24
The high priest Aaron offers sacrifice
1 Peter 4:1-6
Live by the will of God

TUESDAY
Numbers 16:41-50
The high priest Aaron makes atonement
1 Peter 4:7-11
Be good stewards of grace

WEDNESDAY
1 Kings 8:54-65
Solomon offers sacrifice
John 3:31-36
The Son and the Father

DAILY
Psalm 99
Priests and people praise God

Day of Pentecost

On the Day of Pentecost, if the Old Testament passage from Numbers is chosen for the first reading, the passage from Acts is used as the second reading.

Preparation for Sunday

THURSDAY
Exodus 19:1-9a
The covenant at Sinai
Acts 2:1-11
The giving of the Spirit

FRIDAY
Exodus 19:16-25
Moses and Aaron meet the Lord
Romans 8:14-17
Led by the Spirit of God

SATURDAY
Exodus 20:1-21
Moses brings the Ten Words to Israel
Matthew 5:1-12
Jesus brings blessings to his community

DAILY
Psalm 33:12-22
Our help and our shield

Day of Pentecost

Acts 2:1-21   *or*   Numbers 11:24-30
Filled with the Spirit   *The spirit rests on Israel's leaders*
Psalm 104:24-34, 35b
Renewing the face of the earth
1 Corinthians 12:3b-13   *or*   Acts 2:1-21
Varieties of gifts, the same Spirit   *Filled with the Spirit*
John 20:19-23   *or*   John 7:37-39
The Spirit poured out   *Jesus, the true living water*

Reflection on Sunday

MONDAY
Joel 2:18-29
The promised spirit of God
Romans 8:18-24
We have the first fruits of the Spirit

TUESDAY
Ezekiel 39:7-8, 21-29
The promised spirit of God
Romans 8:26-27
Praying in the Spirit

WEDNESDAY
Numbers 11:24-30
The spirit rests on Israel's elders
John 7:37-39
Jesus, the true living water

DAILY
Psalm 104:24-34, 35b
Renewing the face of the earth

Season

after

Pentecost

YEAR A

Trinity Sunday
First Sunday after Pentecost

Preparation for Sunday

THURSDAY
Job 38:1-11
Creation story from Job
2 Timothy 1:8-12a
Grace revealed in Christ

FRIDAY
Job 38:12-21
Creation story from Job
2 Timothy 1:12b-14
The treasure of the triune God

SATURDAY
Job 38:22-38
Creation story from Job
John 14:15-17
Father, Son, Spirit

DAILY
Psalm 8
How exalted is your name

Trinity Sunday

Genesis 1:1—2:4a
Creation of the heavens and the earth
Psalm 8
How exalted is your name
2 Corinthians 13:11-13
Paul's farewell
Matthew 28:16-20
Living in the community of the Trinity

Reflection on Sunday

MONDAY
Job 38:39—39:12
Creation story from Job
1 Corinthians 12:1-3
Faith is a gift of the Spirit

TUESDAY
Job 39:13-25
Creation story from Job
1 Corinthians 12:4-13
The Spirit in the community

WEDNESDAY
Job 39:26—40:5
Creation story from Job; Job's response
John 14:25-26
Father, Son, Spirit

DAILY
Psalm 29
Praise the glory of God

Proper 3 [8]

*Sunday between May 24 and 28 inclusive
(if after Trinity Sunday)*

Preparation for Sunday

THURSDAY
Proverbs 12:22-28
Anxiety burdens the heart
Philippians 2:19-24
Timothy's worth

FRIDAY
Isaiah 26:1-6
Trust in God
Philippians 2:25-30
Paul overcomes anxiety

SATURDAY
Isaiah 31:1-9
Misplaced trust
Luke 11:14-23
A house divided falls

DAILY
Psalm 131
A child upon its mother's breast

Sunday, May 24–28

Isaiah 49:8-16a
God's motherly compassion
Psalm 131
A child upon its mother's breast
1 Corinthians 4:1-5
Servants accountable to God
Matthew 6:24-34
The teaching of Christ: trust in God

Reflection on Sunday

MONDAY
Deuteronomy 32:1-14
God's care for the chosen people
Hebrews 10:32-39
Confidence that rewards

TUESDAY
1 Kings 17:1-16
God feeds the widow
1 Corinthians 4:6-21
The life of an apostle

WEDNESDAY
Isaiah 66:7-13
God as a nursing mother
Luke 12:22-31
Do not worry

DAILY
Psalm 104
God cares for all the earth

Proper 4 [9]

*Sunday between May 29 and June 4 inclusive
(if after Trinity Sunday)*

Preparation for Sunday

THURSDAY
Genesis 1:1—2:4a
Creation and the Sabbath
Romans 2:17-29
Real circumcision a matter of the heart

SATURDAY
Genesis 3:1-24
Expulsion from the garden
Matthew 7:1-6
Do not judge

FRIDAY
Genesis 2:4b-25
The garden of Eden
Romans 9:6-13
God's election of Israel

DAILY
Psalm 46
Our refuge and strength

Sunday, May 29–June 4

Genesis 6:9-22; 7:24; 8:14-19
The great flood
Psalm 46
Our refuge and strength
Romans 1:16-17; 3:22b-28 [29-31]
Justified by God's grace as a gift
Matthew 7:21-29
Doing the works of God

Reflection on Sunday

MONDAY
Genesis 4:1-16
Cain murders Abel
Romans 2:1-11
The righteous judgment of God

WEDNESDAY
Genesis 11:1-9
The tower of Babel
Matthew 7:13-20
The narrow gate

TUESDAY
Genesis 4:17—5:5
Beginnings of civilization
Romans 3:9-22a
All have sinned

DAILY
Psalm 69:1-3, 13-16, 30-36
Save me from the flood

Proper 4 [9]

Sunday between May 29 and June 4 inclusive
(if after Trinity Sunday)

Preparation for Sunday

THURSDAY
Exodus 24:1-8
The blood of the covenant
Romans 2:17-29
Real circumcision a matter of the heart

FRIDAY
Deuteronomy 30:1-5
God's fidelity assured
Romans 9:6-13
God's election of Israel

SATURDAY
Amos 2:6-11
Judgment on Israel
Matthew 7:1-6
Do not judge

DAILY
Psalm 31:1-5, 19-24
I commit my spirit

Sunday, May 29–June 4

Deuteronomy 11:18-21, 26-28
Keeping the words of God
Psalm 31:1-5, 19-24
I commit my spirit
Romans 1:16-17; 3:22b-28 [29-31]
Justified by God's grace as a gift
Matthew 7:21-29
Doing the works of God

Reflection on Sunday

MONDAY
Joshua 8:30-35
Joshua renews the covenant
Romans 2:1-11
The righteous judgment of God

TUESDAY
Joshua 24:1-2, 11-28
The Israelites renew the covenant
Romans 3:9-22a
All have sinned

WEDNESDAY
Job 28:12-28
The way of wisdom
Matthew 7:13-20
The narrow gate

DAILY
Psalm 52
The wicked and the righteous

Proper 5 [10]

Sunday between June 5 and 11 inclusive
(if after Trinity Sunday)

Preparation for Sunday

THURSDAY
Genesis 13:1-18
Abram and Lot separate
2 Peter 2:17-22
The world's entanglements

FRIDAY
Genesis 14:17-24
Abram blessed by Melchizedek
Acts 28:1-10
Paul in Malta heals Publius

SATURDAY
Genesis 15:1-20
Covenant with Abram and Sarai
Matthew 9:27-34
Jesus heals those who are blind or mute

DAILY
Psalm 33:1-12
Happy the people whom God has chosen

Sunday, June 5–11

Genesis 12:1-9
Journey in the promise
Psalm 33:1-12
Happy the people whom God has chosen
Romans 4:13-25
The faith of Abraham
Matthew 9:9-13, 18-26
Christ heals a woman and raises a girl

Reflection on Sunday

MONDAY
Genesis 16:1-15
The birth of Ishmael
2 Corinthians 6:14—7:2
We are the temple of God

TUESDAY
Genesis 17:1-27
The sign of the covenant
Hebrews 13:1-16
Sacrifices pleasing to God

WEDNESDAY
Genesis 18:16-33
The depravity of Sodom
Matthew 12:1-8
Mercy, not sacrifice

DAILY
Psalm 119:41-48
Salvation in God's promise

Proper 5 [10]

Sunday between June 5 and 11 inclusive
(if after Trinity Sunday)

Preparation for Sunday

THURSDAY
Lamentations 1:7-11
Jerusalem becomes unclean
2 Peter 2:17-22
The world's entanglements

FRIDAY
Lamentations 3:40-58
Let us return to God
Acts 28:1-10
Paul in Malta heals Publius

SATURDAY
Exodus 34:1-9
Moses makes new tablets
Matthew 9:27-34
Jesus heals those who are blind or mute

DAILY
Psalm 50:7-15
The salvation of God

Sunday, June 5–11

Hosea 5:15-6:6
God desires steadfast love
Psalm 50:7-15
The salvation of God
Romans 4:13-25
The faith of Abraham
Matthew 9:9-13, 18-26
Christ heals a woman and raises a girl

Reflection on Sunday

MONDAY
Leviticus 15:25-31; 22:1-9
Purity regulations
2 Corinthians 6:14—7:2
We are the temple of God

TUESDAY
Hosea 8:11-14; 10:1-2
God rejects Israel's sacrifice
Hebrews 13:1-16
Sacrifices pleasing to God

WEDNESDAY
Hosea 14:1-9
God will be merciful to Israel
Matthew 12:1-8
Mercy, not sacrifice

DAILY
Psalm 40:1-8
God's will, not sacrifice

Proper 6 [11]

*Sunday between June 12 and 18 inclusive
(if after Trinity Sunday)*

Preparation for Sunday

THURSDAY
Genesis 21:1-7
The birth of Isaac
Hebrews 3:1-6
Moses a servant, Christ a son

FRIDAY
Genesis 24:1-9
Isaac's marriage arranged
Acts 7:35-43
Israel doubts Moses, prevails upon Aaron

SATURDAY
Genesis 24:10-52
Isaac's marriage arranged
Mark 7:1-13
Moses' witness spurned by religious leaders

DAILY
Psalm 116:1-2, 12-19
Thanks for God's bounty

Sunday, June 12–18

Genesis 18:1-15 [21:1-7]
The call of Abraham and Sarah
Psalm 116:1-2, 12-19
Thanks for God's bounty
Romans 5:1-8
While we were sinners, Christ died for us
Matthew 9:35 — 10:8 [9-23]
The sending of the twelve

Reflection on Sunday

MONDAY
Genesis 23:1-19
Sarah's death and burial
1 Thessalonians 3:1-5
Timothy is sent to Thessalonica

TUESDAY
Genesis 25:7-11
The death of Abraham
2 Thessalonians 2:13 — 3:5
The life of those chosen by God

WEDNESDAY
Nehemiah 9:1-8
After exile, remembering Abraham
Luke 6:12-19
Jesus chooses the apostles

DAILY
Psalm 126
Our mouth filled with laughter

Proper 6 [11]
Sunday between June 12 and 18 inclusive
(if after Trinity Sunday)

Preparation for Sunday

THURSDAY
Exodus 4:18-23
Moses called to Egypt
Hebrews 3:1-6
Moses a servant, Christ a son

SATURDAY
Exodus 6:28—7:13
Moses and Aaron before Pharaoh
Mark 7:1-13
Moses' witness spurned by religious leaders

FRIDAY
Exodus 4:27-31
Aaron called to Moses' side
Acts 7:35-43
Israel doubts Moses, prevails upon Aaron

DAILY
Psalm 100
We are God's people

Sunday, June 12–18

Exodus 19:2-8a
The covenant with Israel at Sinai
Psalm 100
We are God's people
Romans 5:1-8
While we were sinners, Christ died for us
Matthew 9:35—10:8 [9-23]
The sending of the twelve

Reflection on Sunday

MONDAY
Joshua 1:1-11
God calls Joshua
1 Thessalonians 3:1-5
Timothy is sent to Thessalonica

WEDNESDAY
Proverbs 4:10-27
Choosing the way of wisdom
Luke 6:12-19
Jesus chooses the apostles

TUESDAY
1 Samuel 3:1-9
God calls Samuel
2 Thessalonians 2:13—3:5
The life of those chosen by God

DAILY
Psalm 105:1-11, 37-45
God saves the chosen people

Proper 7 [12]

Sunday between June 19 and 25 inclusive
(if after Trinity Sunday)

Preparation for Sunday

THURSDAY
Exodus 12:43-49
Passover directions about foreigners
Hebrews 2:5-9
Exaltation through abasement

FRIDAY
Genesis 35:1-4
Jacob returns to Bethel
Acts 5:17-26
The apostles are persecuted

SATURDAY
Ezekiel 29:3-7
Proclamation against Egypt
Luke 11:53 — 12:3
What is secret will become known

DAILY
Psalm 86:1-10
Prayer for deliverance

Sunday, June 19–25

Genesis 21:8-21
The rescue of Hagar and Ishmael
Psalm 86:1-10, 16-17
Prayer for deliverance
Romans 6:1b-11
Buried and raised with Christ in baptism
Matthew 10:24-39
The cost of discipleship

Reflection on Sunday

MONDAY
Genesis 16:1-15
The birth of Ishmael
Revelation 2:1-7
Remember from what you have fallen

TUESDAY
Genesis 25:12-18
Ishmael's descendants; his death
Revelation 2:8-11
The faithful receive the crown of life

WEDNESDAY
Jeremiah 42:18-22
Warning people not to go to Egypt
Matthew 10:5-23
Jesus speaks about persecution

DAILY
Psalm 86:11-17
Give strength to your servant

Proper 7 [12]

*Sunday between June 19 and 25 inclusive
(if after Trinity Sunday)*

Preparation for Sunday

THURSDAY
Jeremiah 18:12-17
Israel's stubborn idolatry
Hebrews 2:5-9
Exaltation through abasement

FRIDAY
Jeremiah 18:18-23
A plot against Jeremiah
Acts 5:17-26
The apostles are persecuted

SATURDAY
Jeremiah 20:1-6
Jeremiah persecuted by Pashhur
Luke 11:53—12:3
What is secret will become known

DAILY
Psalm 69:7-10 [11-15] 16-18
Draw near to me

Sunday, June 19–25

Jeremiah 20:7-13
The prophet must speak
Psalm 69:7-10 [11-15] 16-18
Draw near to me
Romans 6:1b-11
Buried and raised with Christ in baptism
Matthew 10:24-39
The cost of discipleship

Reflection on Sunday

MONDAY
Micah 7:1-7
The corruption of the people
Revelation 2:1-7
Remember from what you have fallen

TUESDAY
Jeremiah 26:1-12
Prophesy against Jerusalem
Revelation 2:8-11
The faithful receive the crown of life

WEDNESDAY
Jeremiah 38:1-13
Jeremiah imprisoned and released
Matthew 10:5-23
Jesus speaks about persecution

DAILY
Psalm 6
Prayer for deliverance

Proper 8 [13]

Sunday between June 26 and July 2 inclusive

Beware of false teachers

Preparation for Sunday

THURSDAY
Micah 7:18-20
God's faithfulness to Jacob, Abraham
Galatians 5:2-6
The nature of Christian freedom

FRIDAY
2 Chronicles 20:5-12
Abraham, "friend of God"
Galatians 5:7-12

SATURDAY
Genesis 26:23-25
God says, "I am the God of Abraham"
Luke 17:1-4
Causing little ones to stumble

DAILY
Psalm 13
Will you forget me forever?

Sunday, June 26–July 2

Genesis 22:1-14
The testing of Abraham
Psalm 13
Will you forget me forever?
Romans 6:12-23
No longer under law but under grace
Matthew 10:40-42
Welcome Christ in those Christ sends

Reflection on Sunday

MONDAY
Genesis 22:15-18
God's blessing promised again
1 Thessalonians 4:9-12
How to love one another

TUESDAY
1 Kings 18:36-39
"God of Abraham"
1 John 4:1-6
Testing the spirits

WEDNESDAY
Isaiah 51:1-3
Look to Abraham and Sarah
Matthew 11:20-24
Jesus prophesies against the cities

DAILY
Psalm 47
God's rule over the nations

Proper 8 [13]
Sunday between June 26 and July 2 inclusive

Preparation for Sunday

THURSDAY
Jeremiah 25:1-7
Israel provokes God's anger
Galatians 5:2-6
The nature of Christian freedom

FRIDAY
Jeremiah 25:8-14
Captivity of Israel foretold
Galatians 5:7-12
Beware of false teachers

SATURDAY
Jeremiah 28:1-4
Hananiah prophesies falsely
Luke 17:1-4
Causing little ones to stumble

DAILY
Psalm 89:1-4, 15-18
I sing of your love

Sunday, June 26–July 2

Jeremiah 28:5-9
Test of a true prophet
Psalm 89:1-4, 15-18
I sing of your love
Romans 6:12-23
No longer under law but under grace
Matthew 10:40-42
Welcome Christ in those Christ sends

Reflection on Sunday

MONDAY
1 Kings 21:1-16
Ahab and Jezebel rob Naboth
1 Thessalonians 4:9-12
How to love one another

TUESDAY
1 Kings 21:17-29
Elijah confronts Ahab
1 John 4:1-6
Testing the spirits

WEDNESDAY
Jeremiah 18:1-11
Jeremiah at the potter's wheel
Matthew 11:20-24
Jesus prophesies against the cities

DAILY
Psalm 119:161-168
Loving God's law

Proper 9 [14]

Sunday between July 3 and 9 inclusive

Preparation for Sunday

THURSDAY
Genesis 25:19-27
Birth and childhood of Jacob and Esau
Romans 7:1-6
Dying to the law through Christ

SATURDAY
Genesis 27:18-29
Isaac blesses Jacob
Luke 10:21-24
Jesus rejoices in the Holy Spirit

FRIDAY
Genesis 27:1-17
Rebekah and Jacob's plot
Romans 7:7-20
Sin and the law kill us

DAILY
Psalm 45:10-17
God has anointed you

Sunday, July 3–9

Genesis 24:34-38, 42-49, 58-67
Marriage of Isaac and Rebekah
Psalm 45:10-17   *or*   Song of Solomon 2:8-13
God has anointed you   *Song of love*
Romans 7:15-25a
The struggle within the self
Matthew 11:16-19, 25-30
The yoke of discipleship

Reflection on Sunday

MONDAY
Genesis 27:30-46
Esau blessed; Jacob escapes Esau
Romans 1:18-25
The guilt of humankind

WEDNESDAY
Genesis 29:31-35
Birth of Jacob and Leah's children
John 13:1-17
Jesus washes the disciples' feet

TUESDAY
Genesis 29:1-14
Jacob meets Rachel
Romans 3:1-8
The faithfulness of God

DAILY
Song of Solomon 2:8-13
Song of love

Proper 9 [14]
Sunday between July 3 and 9 inclusive

Preparation for Sunday

THURSDAY
Zechariah 1:1-6
Israel urged to repent
Romans 7:1-6
Dying to the law through Christ

FRIDAY
Zechariah 2:6-13
Exiles are the apple of God's eye
Romans 7:7-20
Sin and the law kill us

SATURDAY
Zechariah 4:1-7
By my Spirit, says God
Luke 10:21-24
Jesus rejoices in the Holy Spirit

DAILY
Psalm 145:8-14
God is full of compassion

Sunday, July 3–9

Zechariah 9:9-12
The king comes in peace
Psalm 145:8-14
God is full of compassion
Romans 7:15-25a
The struggle within the self
Matthew 11:16-19, 25-30
The yoke of discipleship

Reflection on Sunday

MONDAY
Jeremiah 27:1-11, 16-22
Jeremiah wears the evil yoke
Romans 1:18-25
The guilt of humankind

TUESDAY
Jeremiah 28:10-17
Hananiah breaks Jeremiah's yoke
Romans 3:1-8
The faithfulness of God

WEDNESDAY
Jeremiah 13:1-11
Jeremiah's loincloth
John 13:1-17
Jesus washes the disciples' feet

DAILY
Psalm 131
I rest like a weaned child on God

Proper 10 [15]

Sunday between July 10 and 16 inclusive

Preparation for Sunday

THURSDAY
Exodus 3:1-6
The God of Abraham, Isaac, Jacob
Romans 2:12-16
God judges the secret thoughts

FRIDAY
Deuteronomy 32:1-10
Jacob, personification of Israel
Romans 15:14-21
Sanctified by the Holy Spirit

SATURDAY
Isaiah 2:1-4
Jacob, collective name of Israel
John 12:44-50
I have come as light into the world

DAILY
Psalm 119:105-112
Your word is a lamp to my feet

Sunday, July 10–16

Genesis 25:19-34
Esau sells his birthright to Jacob
Psalm 119:105-112
Your word is a lamp to my feet
Romans 8:1-11
Living according to the Spirit
Matthew 13:1-9, 18-23
The parable of the sower and the seed

Reflection on Sunday

MONDAY
Micah 1:1-5
Judgment for Jacob's transgression
1 Thessalonians 4:1-8
A life pleasing to God

TUESDAY
Jeremiah 49:7-11
Edom, children of Esau, punished
Ephesians 4:17—5:2
The old life and the new

WEDNESDAY
Obadiah 15-21
Israel's triumph at Edom's expense
Matthew 13:10-17
The purpose of parable

DAILY
Psalm 142
God my refuge and portion

Proper 10 [15]

Sunday between July 10 and 16 inclusive

Preparation for Sunday

THURSDAY
Isaiah 48:1-5
What God declared long ago
Romans 2:12-16
God judges the secret thoughts

FRIDAY
Isaiah 48:6-11
You will hear new, hidden things
Romans 15:14-21
Sanctified by the Holy Spirit

SATURDAY
Isaiah 52:1-6
Sold, redeemed without money
John 12:44-50
I have come as light into the world

DAILY
Psalm 65:[1-8] 9-13
Your paths overflow with plenty

Sunday, July 10–16

Isaiah 55:10-13
The growth of the word
Psalm 65:[1-8] 9-13
Your paths overflow with plenty
Romans 8:1-11
Living according to the Spirit
Matthew 13:1-9, 18-23
The parable of the sower and the seed

Reflection on Sunday

MONDAY
Leviticus 26:3-20
A rich and a poor harvest
1 Thessalonians 4:1-8
A life pleasing to God

TUESDAY
Deuteronomy 28:1-14
The blessings of obedience
Ephesians 4:17—5:2
The old life and the new

WEDNESDAY
Proverbs 11:23-30
The fruit of righteousness
Matthew 13:10-17
The purpose of parable

DAILY
Psalm 92
The righteous as a tree

Proper 11 [16]
Sunday between July 17 and 23 inclusive

Preparation for Sunday

THURSDAY
Isaiah 44:1-5
God's blessing on Israel: "Do not fear"
Hebrews 2:1-9
Warning to pay attention

FRIDAY
Ezekiel 39:21-29
I will restore the fortunes of Jacob
Hebrews 6:13-20
The certainty of God's promises

SATURDAY
Exodus 14:9-25
God's protecting angel at the sea
Matthew 7:15-20
A tree and its fruit

DAILY
Psalm 139:1-12, 23-24
You have searched me and known me

Sunday, July 17–23

Genesis 28:10-19a
Jacob's dream of the ladder
Psalm 139:1-12, 23-24
You have searched me and known me
Romans 8:12-25
The revealing of the children of God
Matthew 13:24-30, 36-43
The parable of the weeds

Reflection on Sunday

MONDAY
Genesis 32:3-21
Jacob sends gifts to appease Esau
Revelation 14:12-20
The harvest at the end of time

TUESDAY
Genesis 33:1-17
Jacob and Esau meet
Galatians 4:21—5:1
An allegory about those saved

WEDNESDAY
Genesis 35:16-29
Benjamin is born; Rachel, Isaac die
Matthew 12:15-21
God's chosen servant

DAILY
Psalm 139:13-18
Wonderful are God's works

Proper 11 [16]
Sunday between July 17 and 23 inclusive

Preparation for Sunday

THURSDAY
Isaiah 41:21-29
The futility of idols
Hebrews 2:1-9
Warning to pay attention

SATURDAY
Isaiah 44:18-20
Idols do not know or comprehend
Matthew 7:15-20
A tree and its fruit

FRIDAY
Isaiah 44:9-17
Those who make idols are nothing
Hebrews 6:13-20
The certainty of God's promises

DAILY
Psalm 86:11-17
Teach me your ways

Sunday, July 17–23

Wisdom 12:13, 16-19   *or*   Isaiah 44:6-8
God's sovereignty   *There is no other God*
Psalm 86:11-17
Teach me your ways
Romans 8:12-25
The revealing of the children of God
Matthew 13:24-30, 36-43
The parable of the weeds

Reflection on Sunday

MONDAY
Nahum 1:1-13
The wrath and mercy of God
Revelation 14:12-20
The harvest at the end of time

WEDNESDAY
Daniel 12:1-13
The righteous will shine
Matthew 12:15-21
God's chosen servant

TUESDAY
Zephaniah 3:1-13
The wicked convert to God
Galatians 4:21—5:1
An allegory about those saved

DAILY
Psalm 75
God's judgment

Proper 12 [17]

Sunday between July 24 and 30 inclusive

Preparation for Sunday

THURSDAY
Genesis 29:1-8
Jacob meets Rachel
1 Corinthians 4:14-20
Reign of God depends not on talk but power

SATURDAY
Genesis 29:31—30:24
Children born to Jacob, Leah, Rachel
Matthew 12:38-42
Something greater than Solomon is here

FRIDAY
Genesis 29:9-14
Jacob meets Rachel's family
Acts 7:44-53
Solomon's temple cannot contain God

DAILY
Psalm 105:1-11, 45b
Give thanks to God

Sunday, July 24–30

Genesis 29:15-28
Leah and Rachel, Jacob's wives
Psalm 105:1-11, 45b   *or*   Psalm 128
Give thanks to God   *It shall be well with you*
Romans 8:26-39
Nothing can separate us from God's love
Matthew 13:31-33, 44-52
Parables of the reign of heaven

Reflection on Sunday

MONDAY
Genesis 30:25-36
Jacob and Laban argue
James 3:13-18
Two kinds of wisdom

WEDNESDAY
Genesis 46:2—47:12
Jacob settles in Goshen
Mark 4:30-34
Jesus' use of parables

TUESDAY
Genesis 30:37-43
Jacob prospers at Laban's expense
Ephesians 6:10-18
The allegory of the armor of God

DAILY
Psalm 65:8-13
Meadows clothed with flocks

Proper 12 [17]

Sunday between July 24 and 30 inclusive

Preparation for Sunday

THURSDAY
1 Kings 1:28-37
Solomon designated as king
1 Corinthians 4:14-20
Reign of God depends not on talk but power

FRIDAY
1 Kings 1:38-48
Solomon more famous than David
Acts 7:44-53
Solomon's temple cannot contain God

SATURDAY
1 Kings 2:1-4
David's instructions to Solomon
Matthew 12:38-42
Something greater than Solomon is here

DAILY
Psalm 119:129-136
Light and understanding

Sunday, July 24–30

1 Kings 3:5-12
Solomon's prayer for wisdom
Psalm 119:129-136
Light and understanding
Romans 8:26-39
Nothing can separate us from God's love
Matthew 13:31-33, 44-52
Parables of the reign of heaven

Reflection on Sunday

MONDAY
1 Kings 3:16-28
Solomon's wisdom in judgment
James 3:13-18
Two kinds of wisdom

TUESDAY
1 Kings 4:29-34
God gave Solomon wisdom
Ephesians 6:10-18
The allegory of the armor of God

WEDNESDAY
Proverbs 1:1-7, 20-33
The call of wisdom
Mark 4:30-34
Jesus' use of parables

DAILY
Psalm 119:121-128
Give me understanding

Proper 13 [18]

Sunday between July 31 and August 6 inclusive

Preparation for Sunday

THURSDAY
Isaiah 14:1-2
Compassion for Jacob
Philippians 4:10-15
Being well fed and yet hungry

FRIDAY
Isaiah 41:8-10
Jacob is God's chosen
Romans 9:6-13
True descendants of Abraham

SATURDAY
Genesis 31:1-21
Jacob flees with family and flocks
Matthew 7:7-11
Bread and stones

DAILY
Psalm 17:1-7, 15
I shall see your face

Sunday, July 31–August 6

Genesis 32:22-31
Jacob receives God's blessing
Psalm 17:1-7, 15
I shall see your face
Romans 9:1-5
The glory of God's people in Israel
Matthew 14:13-21
Jesus feeds 5000

Reflection on Sunday

MONDAY
Genesis 31:22-42
Laban overtakes Jacob
Romans 1:8-15
A harvest among the Gentiles

TUESDAY
Genesis 32:3-21
Jacob sends gifts to Esau
Acts 2:37-47
The believers breaking bread

WEDNESDAY
Isaiah 43:1-7
God's blessing prevails
Matthew 15:32-39
Jesus feeds 4000

DAILY
Psalm 17:1-7, 15
I shall see your face

Proper 13 [18]

Sunday between July 31 and August 6 inclusive

Preparation for Sunday

THURSDAY
Proverbs 10:1-5
The righteous will not go hungry
Philippians 4:10-15
Being well fed and yet hungry

FRIDAY
Isaiah 51:17-23
Drink no more from the bowl of wrath
Romans 9:6-13
True descendants of Abraham

SATURDAY
Isaiah 44:1-5
God's blessing on Israel
Matthew 7:7-11
Bread and stones

DAILY
Psalm 145:8-9, 14-21
You open wide your hand

Sunday, July 31–August 6

Isaiah 55:1-5
Eat and drink what truly satisfies
Psalm 145:8-9, 14-21
You open wide your hand
Romans 9:1-5
The glory of God's people in Israel
Matthew 14:13-21
Jesus feeds 5000

Reflection on Sunday

MONDAY
Deuteronomy 8:1-10
God will feed the people
Romans 1:8-15
A harvest among the Gentiles

TUESDAY
Deuteronomy 26:1-15
A tithe from God's harvest
Acts 2:37-47
The believers breaking bread

WEDNESDAY
Exodus 16:2-15, 31-35
God feeds the people manna
Matthew 15:32-39
Jesus feeds 4000

DAILY
Psalm 78:1-8, 17-29
God fed the people with manna

Proper 14 [19]

Sunday between August 7 and 13 inclusive

Preparation for Sunday

THURSDAY
Genesis 35:22b-29
The twelve sons of Jacob
Acts 17:10-15
The good news is shared

FRIDAY
Genesis 36:1-8
Esau's household moves
Acts 18:24-28
A new disciple preaches

SATURDAY
Genesis 37:5-11
Joseph dreams of greatness
Matthew 16:1-4
The sign of Jonah

DAILY
Psalm 105:1-6, 16-22, 45b
Remembering Joseph

Sunday, August 7–13

Genesis 37:1-4, 12-28
Joseph sold by his brothers
Psalm 105:1-6, 16-22, 45b
Remembering Joseph
Romans 10:5-15
The word of faith
Matthew 14:22-33
Jesus walking on the sea

Reflection on Sunday

MONDAY
Genesis 37:29-36
Jacob mourns Joseph's loss
2 Peter 2:4-10
God judges and rescues

TUESDAY
Genesis 39:1-23
Joseph in Potiphar's employ
Romans 9:14-29
God's wrath, God's mercy

WEDNESDAY
Genesis 40:1-23
The dreams of two prisoners
Matthew 8:23-27
Jesus stills the storm

DAILY
Psalm 28
God hears my pleadings

Proper 14 [19]

Sunday between August 7 and 13 inclusive

Preparation for Sunday

THURSDAY
1 Kings 18:1-16
God promises relief from drought
Acts 17:10-15
The good news is shared

FRIDAY
1 Kings 18:17-19, 30-40
God's flooded altar burns
Acts 18:24-28
A new disciple preaches

SATURDAY
1 Kings 18:41-46
From drought to heavy rain
Matthew 16:1-4
The sign of Jonah

DAILY
Psalm 85:8-13
I will listen to God

Sunday, August 7–13

1 Kings 19:9-18
Elijah on Mount Horeb
Psalm 85:8-13
I will listen to God
Romans 10:5-15
The word of faith
Matthew 14:22-33
Jesus walking on the sea

Reflection on Sunday

MONDAY
Genesis 7:11 — 8:5
God saves Noah from the flood
2 Peter 2:4-10
God judges and rescues

TUESDAY
Genesis 19:1-29
God saves Lot
Romans 9:14-29
God's wrath, God's mercy

WEDNESDAY
Job 36:24-33; 37:14-24
The waters of God's creation
Matthew 8:23-27
Jesus stills the storm

DAILY
Psalm 18:1-19
God saves from the waters

Proper 15 [20]

Sunday between August 14 and 20 inclusive

Preparation for Sunday

THURSDAY
Genesis 41:14-36
Joseph interprets Pharaoh's dreams
Revelation 15:1-4
All nations will worship God

FRIDAY
Genesis 41:37-57
Joseph's rise to power
Acts 14:19-28
God opens the door to Gentiles

SATURDAY
Genesis 42:1-28
Joseph's brothers come to Egypt
Matthew 14:34-36
Jesus heals the sick

DAILY
Psalm 133
How good it is to live in unity

Sunday, August 14–20

Genesis 45:1-15
Joseph reconciles with his brothers
Psalm 133
How good it is to live in unity
Romans 11:1-2a, 29-32
God's mercy to all, Jew and Gentile
Matthew 15:[10-20] 21-28
The Canaanite woman's daughter is healed

Reflection on Sunday

MONDAY
Genesis 43:1-34
Benjamin joins Joseph's brothers
Acts 15:1-21
The believing Jews accept the Gentiles

TUESDAY
Genesis 44:1-34
Judah pleads for Benjamin
Romans 11:13-29
God saves Jews and Gentiles

WEDNESDAY
Genesis 45:16-28
Pharaoh welcomes Jacob's family
Matthew 8:1-13
Jesus heals many people

DAILY
Psalm 130
With you there is forgiveness

80 YEAR A SEASON AFTER PENTECOST

Proper 15 [20]

Sunday between August 14 and 20 inclusive

Preparation for Sunday

THURSDAY
Isaiah 45:20-25
All the ends of the earth shall be saved
Revelation 15:1-4
All nations will worship God

FRIDAY
Isaiah 63:15-19
A plea for God's attention
Acts 14:19-28
God opens the door to Gentiles

SATURDAY
Isaiah 56:1-5
A covenant for all who obey
Matthew 14:34-36
Jesus heals the sick

DAILY
Psalm 67
Let all the peoples praise God

Sunday, August 14–20

Isaiah 56:1, 6-8
A house of prayer for all people
Psalm 67
Let all the peoples praise God
Romans 11:1-2a, 29-32
God's mercy to all, Jew and Gentile
Matthew 15:[10-20] 21-28
The Canaanite woman's daughter is healed

Reflection on Sunday

MONDAY
2 Kings 5:1-14
The foreigner Naaman is healed
Acts 15:1-21
The believing Jews accept the Gentiles

TUESDAY
Isaiah 43:8-13
Let all the nations gather
Romans 11:13-29
God saves Jews and Gentiles

WEDNESDAY
Isaiah 66:18-23
All nations shall come to worship
Matthew 8:1-13
Jesus heals many people

DAILY
Psalm 87
Foreigners praise God in Zion

Proper 16 [21]

Sunday between August 21 and 27 inclusive

Preparation for Sunday

THURSDAY
Genesis 49:1-33
Jacob's last words to his sons
1 Corinthians 6:1-11
When believers disagree

FRIDAY
Genesis 49:29—50:14
Jacob's death and burial
2 Corinthians 10:12-18
Let those who boast, boast in the Lord

SATURDAY
Genesis 50:15-26
Joseph's last days and death
Matthew 16:5-12
Bread as a sign of other things

DAILY
Psalm 124
We have escaped like a bird

Sunday, August 21–27

Exodus 1:8—2:10
Pharaoh's daughter takes Moses in
Psalm 124
We have escaped like a bird
Romans 12:1-8
One body in Christ, with gifts that differ
Matthew 16:13-20
The profession of Peter's faith

Reflection on Sunday

MONDAY
Exodus 1:1-7
Israel multiplies in Egypt
Romans 2:1-11
The righteous judgment of God

TUESDAY
Exodus 2:11-15a
Moses defends one of his kin
Romans 11:33-36
The riches, wisdom, and knowledge of God

WEDNESDAY
Exodus 2:15b-22
Moses flees to Midian
Matthew 26:6-13
A woman anoints Jesus

DAILY
Psalm 8
From the mouths of infants

Proper 16 [21]

Sunday between August 21 and 27 inclusive

Preparation for Sunday

THURSDAY
Ezekiel 28:11-19
Disobedience and the loss of Eden
1 Corinthians 6:1-11
When believers disagree

FRIDAY
Ezekiel 31:15-18
Israel like the cedars of Lebanon
2 Corinthians 10:12-18
Let those who boast, boast in the Lord

SATURDAY
Ezekiel 36:33-38
A desolate land becomes like Eden
Matthew 16:5-12
Bread as a sign of other things

DAILY
Psalm 138
Your love endures forever

Sunday, August 21–27

Isaiah 51:1-6
God's enduring salvation
Psalm 138
Your love endures forever
Romans 12:1-8
One body in Christ, with gifts that differ
Matthew 16:13-20
The profession of Peter's faith

Reflection on Sunday

MONDAY
1 Samuel 7:3-13
Samuel raises the Ebenezer stone
Romans 2:1-11
The righteous judgment of God

TUESDAY
Deuteronomy 32:18-20, 28-39
Praise the rock that is God
Romans 11:33-36
The riches, wisdom, and knowledge of God

WEDNESDAY
Isaiah 28:14-22
God lays a cornerstone in Zion
Matthew 26:6-13
A woman anoints Jesus

DAILY
Psalm 18:1-3, 20-32
God the rock

Proper 17 [22]

Sunday between August 28 and September 3 inclusive

Preparation for Sunday

THURSDAY
Exodus 2:23-24
God hears the cry of Israel
Ephesians 5:1-6
Do not be deceived by empty words

FRIDAY
Exodus 3:16-25
God's instructions to Moses
2 Thessalonians 2:7-12
Refusal to love the truth

SATURDAY
Exodus 4:1-9
Two signs given to Moses
Matthew 8:14-17
Jesus heals many at Peter's house

DAILY
Psalm 105:1-6, 23-26, 45b
Remembering Moses

Sunday, August 28–September 3

Exodus 3:1-15
God calls Moses
Psalm 105:1-6, 23-26, 45b
Remembering Moses
Romans 12:9-21
Live in harmony
Matthew 16:21-28
The rebuke to Peter

Reflection on Sunday

MONDAY
Exodus 4:10-31
Moses doubts, but obeys God
Revelation 3:1-6
Wake up to your faithlessness

TUESDAY
Exodus 5:1—6:13
Moses confronts Pharaoh
Revelation 3:7-13
Facing the hour of trial

WEDNESDAY
Exodus 7:14-25
First of ten plagues
Matthew 12:22-32
Jesus comes to cast out Satan

DAILY
Psalm 83:1-4, 13-18
God's power like blazing fire

Proper 17 [22]

Sunday between August 28 and September 3 inclusive

Preparation for Sunday

THURSDAY
Jeremiah 14:13-18
Denunciation of lying prophets
Ephesians 5:1-6
Do not be deceived by empty words

FRIDAY
Jeremiah 15:1-9
The consequences of sin
2 Thessalonians 2:7-12
Refusal to love the truth

SATURDAY
Jeremiah 15:10-14
Jeremiah's complaint to God
Matthew 8:14-17
Jesus heals many at Peter's house

DAILY
Psalm 26:1-8
Your love is before my eyes

Sunday, August 28–September 3

Jeremiah 15:15-21
God fortifies the prophet
Psalm 26:1-8
Your love is before my eyes
Romans 12:9-21
Live in harmony
Matthew 16:21-28
The rebuke to Peter

Reflection on Sunday

MONDAY
2 Samuel 11:2-26
David sins
Revelation 3:1-6
Wake up to your faithlessness

TUESDAY
2 Samuel 11:27b—12:15
Nathan rebukes David
Revelation 3:7-13
Facing the hour of trial

WEDNESDAY
Jeremiah 17:5-18
The vindication of the righteous
Matthew 12:22-32
Jesus comes to cast out Satan

DAILY
Psalm 17
The righteous shall see God

Proper 18 [23]

Sunday between September 4 and 10 inclusive

Preparation for Sunday

THURSDAY
Exodus 9:1-7
Another plague: Egypt's animals die
2 Corinthians 12:11-21
Sinners warned but unrepentant

FRIDAY
Exodus 10:21-29
Another plague: darkness
Romans 10:15b-21
God reaches out to erring Israel

SATURDAY
Exodus 11:1-10
Moses announces the last plague
Matthew 23:29-36
The martyrdom of the prophets

DAILY
Psalm 149
Sing praise in the congregation

Sunday, September 4–10

Exodus 12:1-14
The passover
Psalm 149
Sing praise in the congregation
Romans 13:8-14
Live honorably as in the day
Matthew 18:15-20
Reconciliation in the community of faith

Reflection on Sunday

MONDAY
Exodus 12:14-28
Instructions for the passover
1 Peter 2:11-17
Live as servants of God

TUESDAY
Exodus 12:29-42
Israel departs from Egypt
Romans 13:1-7
Obeying authority

WEDNESDAY
Exodus 13:1-10
The feast of unleavened bread
Matthew 21:18-22
Jesus teaches about praying in faith

DAILY
Psalm 121
My help is from the Lord

Proper 18 [23]

Sunday between September 4 and 10 inclusive

Preparation for Sunday

THURSDAY
Ezekiel 24:1-14
God judges unrepentant Israel
2 Corinthians 12:11-21
Sinners warned but unrepentant

FRIDAY
Ezekiel 24:15-27
God opens the prophet's mouth
Romans 10:15b-21
God reaches out to erring Israel

SATURDAY
Ezekiel 33:1-6
The prophet's vocation
Matthew 23:29-36
The martyrdom of the prophets

DAILY
Psalm 119:33-40
The path of your commandments

Sunday, September 4–10

Ezekiel 33:7-11
The prophet's responsibility
Psalm 119:33-40
The path of your commandments
Romans 13:8-14
Live honorably as in the day
Matthew 18:15-20
Reconciliation in the community of faith

Reflection on Sunday

MONDAY
Leviticus 4:27-31; 5:14-16
Atoning for sin in the community
1 Peter 2:11-17
Live as servants of God

TUESDAY
Deuteronomy 17:2-13
Punishment for sin in community
Romans 13:1-7
Obeying authority

WEDNESDAY
Leviticus 16:1-5, 20-28
The scapegoat cleanses the community
Matthew 21:18-22
Jesus teaches about praying in faith

DAILY
Psalm 119:65-72
The law humbles me

Proper 19 [24]

Sunday between September 11 and 17 inclusive

Preparation for Sunday

THURSDAY
Exodus 13:17-22
Pillar of cloud, pillar of fire
1 John 3:11-16
Love one another

FRIDAY
Exodus 14:1-18
Egypt pursues Israel
Acts 7:9-16
Joseph's family is fed in Egypt

SATURDAY
Exodus 15:19-21
The song of Miriam
Matthew 6:7-15
Forgiving one another

DAILY
Psalm 114
Tremble, O earth

Sunday, September 11–17

Exodus 14:19-31
Israel delivered at the sea
Psalm 114   *or*   Exodus 15:1b-11, 20-21
Tremble, O earth   *Song at the sea*
Romans 14:1-12
When brothers and sisters judge each other
Matthew 18:21-35
A parable of forgiveness

Reflection on Sunday

MONDAY
Joshua 3:1-17
Israel crosses the Jordan
Hebrews 11:23-29
The faith of Moses

TUESDAY
Nehemiah 9:9-15
The exodus remembered
Romans 14:13 — 15:2
Building each other up

WEDNESDAY
2 Kings 2:1-18
Prophets cross the Jordan
Mark 11:20-25
Forgiveness for those who forgive

DAILY
Psalm 77
God's way was in the sea

Proper 19 [24]

Sunday between September 11 and 17 inclusive

Preparation for Sunday

THURSDAY
Genesis 37:12-36
Joseph's brothers sin against him
1 John 3:11-16
Love one another

FRIDAY
Genesis 41:53—42:17
Joseph acts harshly against his brothers
Acts 7:9-16
Joseph's family is fed in Egypt

SATURDAY
Genesis 45:1-20
Joseph forgives his brothers
Matthew 6:7-15
Forgiving one another

DAILY
Psalm 103:[1-7] 8-13
God's compassion and mercy

Sunday, September 11–17

Genesis 50:15-21
Joseph reconciles with his brothers
Psalm 103:[1-7] 8-13
God's compassion and mercy
Romans 14:1-12
When brothers and sisters judge each other
Matthew 18:21-35
A parable of forgiveness

Reflection on Sunday

MONDAY
Genesis 48:8-22
Jacob blesses Joseph's sons
Hebrews 11:23-29
The faith of Moses

TUESDAY
Genesis 49:29—50:14
Honoring Jacob's burial wishes
Romans 14:13—15:2
Building each other up

WEDNESDAY
Genesis 50:22-26
Joseph dies
Mark 11:20-25
Forgiveness for those who forgive

DAILY
Psalm 133
How good it is to live in unity

Proper 20 [25]

Sunday between September 18 and 24 inclusive

Preparation for Sunday

THURSDAY
Exodus 15:22-27
Bitter water made sweet
2 Corinthians 13:1-4
Dissent among believers

FRIDAY
Exodus 16:1-21
Manna in the wilderness
2 Corinthians 13:5-10
Correction that builds up

SATURDAY
Exodus 16:22-30
Manna and the sabbath
Matthew 19:23-30
The last will be first

DAILY
Psalm 105:1-6, 37-45
Remembering the wilderness

Sunday, September 18–24

Exodus 16:2-15
Manna in the wilderness
Psalm 105:1-6, 37-45
Remembering the wilderness
Philippians 1:21-30
Standing firm in the gospel
Matthew 20:1-16
The parable of the vineyard workers

Reflection on Sunday

MONDAY
Exodus 16:31-35
Manna sustains for forty years
Romans 16:1-16
Diverse women and men are coworkers in Christ

TUESDAY
Numbers 11:1-9
Complaints about manna
Romans 16:17-20
A warning about troublemakers

WEDNESDAY
Numbers 11:18-23, 31-32
God sends quails
Matthew 18:1-5
True greatness

DAILY
Psalm 119:97-104
God's word sweeter than honey

Proper 20 [25]

Sunday between September 18 and 24 inclusive

Preparation for Sunday

THURSDAY
Nahum 1:1, 14—2:2
God's wrath toward Nineveh
2 Corinthians 13:1-4
Dissent among believers

FRIDAY
Nahum 2:3-13
Nineveh under siege
2 Corinthians 13:5-10
Correction that builds up

SATURDAY
Zephaniah 2:13-15
Judgment on Nineveh
Matthew 19:23-30
The last will be first

DAILY
Psalm 145:1-8
God is slow to anger

Sunday, September 18–24

Jonah 3:10—4:11
God's concern for Nineveh
Psalm 145:1-8
God is slow to anger
Philippians 1:21-30
Standing firm in the gospel
Matthew 20:1-16
The parable of the vineyard workers

Reflection on Sunday

MONDAY
Genesis 27:1-29
The younger son gets the blessing
Romans 16:1-16
Diverse women and men are coworkers in Christ

TUESDAY
Genesis 28:10-17
God blesses the runaway Jacob
Romans 16:17-20
A warning about troublemakers

WEDNESDAY
Isaiah 41:1-13
God will be with the last
Matthew 18:1-5
True greatness

DAILY
Psalm 106:1-12
God's mercy

Proper 21 [26]

Sunday between September 25 and October 1 inclusive

Preparation for Sunday

THURSDAY
Isaiah 48:17-21
God brought water from the rock
James 4:11-16
We do not know what tomorrow will bring

FRIDAY
Numbers 20:1-13
Another story of water from the rock
Acts 13:32-41
Through Jesus forgiveness is proclaimed

SATURDAY
Numbers 27:12-14
Moses' punishment for Meribah
Mark 11:27-33
Jesus' authority is questioned

DAILY
Psalm 78:1-4, 12-16
Recounting God's power

Sunday, September 25–October 1

Exodus 17:1-7
Water from the rock
Psalm 78:1-4, 12-16
Recounting God's power
Philippians 2:1-13
Christ humbled to the point of death
Matthew 21:23-32
A parable of doing God's will

Reflection on Sunday

MONDAY
Exodus 18:1-12
Moses reunited with family
Philippians 1:3-14
Paul prays for the Philippians

TUESDAY
Exodus 18:13-27
Jethro's leadership advice
Philippians 1:15-21
Christ is proclaimed regardless of the motive

WEDNESDAY
Exodus 19:9b-25
The people prepare for covenant
Matthew 9:2-8
Jesus' authority to forgive and heal

DAILY
Psalm 42
Hope in God, the rock

Proper 21 [26]

Sunday between September 25 and October 1 inclusive

Preparation for Sunday

THURSDAY
Ezekiel 12:17-28
God's judgment is timely
James 4:11-16
We do not know what tomorrow will bring

FRIDAY
Ezekiel 18:5-18
Those who repent shall live
Acts 13:32-41
Through Jesus forgiveness is proclaimed

SATURDAY
Ezekiel 18:19-24
A child does not suffer for a parent's sin
Mark 11:27-33
Jesus' authority is questioned

DAILY
Psalm 25:1-9
God's compassion and love

Sunday, September 25–October 1

Ezekiel 18:1-4, 25-32
The fairness of God's way
Psalm 25:1-9
God's compassion and love
Philippians 2:1-13
Christ humbled to the point of death
Matthew 21:23-32
A parable of doing God's will

Reflection on Sunday

MONDAY
Judges 14:1-20
Samson's riddle explained
Philippians 1:3-14
Paul prays for the Philippians

TUESDAY
Judges 16:1-22
Samson asked about his strength
Philippians 1:15-21
Christ is proclaimed regardless of the motive

WEDNESDAY
Judges 16:23-31
Samson prays to do God's will
Matthew 9:2-8
Jesus' authority to forgive and heal

DAILY
Psalm 28
Prayer to do God's will

Proper 22 [27]

Sunday between October 2 and 8 inclusive

Preparation for Sunday

THURSDAY
Exodus 23:1-9
Justice for all
Colossians 2:16-23
Hold fast to Christ, the head

FRIDAY
Exodus 23:14-19
Festivals recall the covenant
Philippians 2:14-18; 3:1-4a
Boast only in Jesus Christ

SATURDAY
Exodus 23:10-13
Sabbatical year and the Sabbath
John 7:40-52
Some accept, others reject Jesus Christ

DAILY
Psalm 19
The law rejoices the heart

Sunday, October 2–8

Exodus 20:1-4, 7-9, 12-20
The commandments at Sinai
Psalm 19
The law rejoices the heart
Philippians 3:4b-14
Nothing surpasses knowing Christ
Matthew 21:33-46
The parable of the vineyard owner's son

Reflection on Sunday

MONDAY
Deuteronomy 5:1-21
The commandments at Sinai
1 Peter 2:4-10
Christ the cornerstone

TUESDAY
Deuteronomy 5:22—6:3
Moses must proclaim the law
2 Corinthians 5:17-21
God reconciles us through Christ

WEDNESDAY
Deuteronomy 6:10-25
Keeping the commandments
John 11:45-57
Critics plan to silence Jesus

DAILY
Psalm 119:49-56
God's commandments are my songs

Proper 22 [27]

Sunday between October 2 and 8 inclusive

Preparation for Sunday

THURSDAY
Jeremiah 2:14-22
The choice vine becomes degenerate
Colossians 2:16-23
Hold fast to Christ, the head

FRIDAY
Jeremiah 2:23-37
Israel shall be shamed
Philippians 2:14-18; 3:1-4a
Boast only in Jesus Christ

SATURDAY
Jeremiah 6:1-10
Gleaning a remnant from the vine
John 7:40-52
Some accept, others reject Jesus Christ

DAILY
Psalm 80:7-15
Look down from heaven, O God

Sunday, October 2–8

Isaiah 5:1-7
The song of the vineyard
Psalm 80:7-15
Look down from heaven, O God
Philippians 3:4b-14
Nothing surpasses knowing Christ
Matthew 21:33-46
The parable of the vineyard owner's son

Reflection on Sunday

MONDAY
Ezekiel 19:10-14
A lament for Israel the vine
1 Peter 2:4-10
Christ the cornerstone

TUESDAY
Isaiah 27:1-6
God will save Israel the vine
2 Corinthians 5:17-21
God reconciles us through Christ

WEDNESDAY
Song of Solomon 8:5-14
A love song for the vineyard
John 11:45-57
Critics plan to silence Jesus

DAILY
Psalm 144
Prayer for blessing

Proper 23 [28]

Sunday between October 9 and 15 inclusive

Preparation for Sunday

THURSDAY
Exodus 24:1-8
The people pledge obedience
1 Peter 5:1-5, 12-14
Stand fast, the chief shepherd is coming

FRIDAY
Exodus 24:9-11
Feasting with God
James 4:4-10
Humble yourselves before God

SATURDAY
Exodus 24:12-18
Moses on the mountain forty days
Mark 2:18-22
No fasting when the bridegroom is present

DAILY
Psalm 106:1-6, 19-23
God's favor for the people

Sunday, October 9–15

Exodus 32:1-14
The golden calf
Psalm 106:1-6, 19-23
God's favor for the people
Philippians 4:1-9
Rejoice in the Lord always
Matthew 22:1-14
The parable of the unwelcome guest

Reflection on Sunday

MONDAY
Exodus 32:15-35
Punishment for the golden calf
Jude 17-25
Prepare for the Lord's coming

TUESDAY
Exodus 33:1-6
The people in mourning
Philippians 3:13—4:1
Hold fast to Christ

WEDNESDAY
2 Kings 17:7-20
Worshiping other gods
John 6:25-35
God will feed the believer

DAILY
Psalm 97
Light springs up for the righteous

Proper 23 [28]
Sunday between October 9 and 15 inclusive

Preparation for Sunday

THURSDAY
Isaiah 22:1-8a
A futile cry to the mountains for help
1 Peter 5:1-5, 12-14
Stand fast, the chief shepherd is coming

FRIDAY
Isaiah 22:8b-14
False joy instead of repentance
James 4:4-10
Humble yourselves before God

SATURDAY
Isaiah 24:17-23
God judges the earth from Mount Zion
Mark 2:18-22
No fasting when the bridegroom is present

DAILY
Psalm 23
You spread a table before me

Sunday, October 9–15

Isaiah 25:1-9
The feast of victory
Psalm 23
You spread a table before me
Philippians 4:1-9
Rejoice in the Lord always
Matthew 22:1-14
The parable of the unwelcome guest

Reflection on Sunday

MONDAY
Exodus 19:7-20
God meets Moses on the mountain
Jude 17-25
Prepare for the Lord's coming

TUESDAY
Amos 9:5-15
Sweet wine from the mountains
Philippians 3:13—4:1
Hold fast to Christ

WEDNESDAY
Song of Solomon 7:10—8:4
Love like rich fruit
John 6:25-35
God will feed the believer

DAILY
Psalm 34
Taste and see

Proper 24 [29]

Sunday between October 16 and 22 inclusive

Preparation for Sunday

THURSDAY
Exodus 33:7-11
The tent of meeting
3 John 9-12
Imitate what is good

FRIDAY
Exodus 31:1-11
Artisans for the tent of meeting
1 Peter 5:1-5
Exemplary leadership

SATURDAY
Exodus 39:32-43
The tabernacle completed
Matthew 14:1-12
King Herod's misuse of power

DAILY
Psalm 99
Proclaim God's greatness

Sunday, October 16–22

Exodus 33:12-23
God's glory revealed to Moses
Psalm 99
Proclaim God's greatness
1 Thessalonians 1:1-10
Thanksgiving for the church at Thessalonica
Matthew 22:15-22
A teaching about the emperor and God

Reflection on Sunday

MONDAY
Exodus 40:34-38
The cloud and the glory
Revelation 18:1-10, 19-20
The fall of Babylon

TUESDAY
Numbers 12:1-9
Aaron's and Miriam's jealousy
Revelation 18:21-24
Babylon will be found no more

WEDNESDAY
Numbers 13:1-2, 17—14:9
Scouting the land of Canaan
Matthew 17:22-27
Jesus pays the temple tax

DAILY
Psalm 63:1-8
I rejoice in the shadow of your wings

Proper 24 [29]

Sunday between October 16 and 22 inclusive

Preparation for Sunday

THURSDAY
Judges 17:1-6
Before Israel had a king
3 John 9-12
Imitate what is good

SATURDAY
Isaiah 14:3-11
The king of Babylon will fall
Matthew 14:1-12
King Herod's misuse of power

FRIDAY
Deuteronomy 17:14-20
The limitations of royal authority
1 Peter 5:1-5
Exemplary leadership

DAILY
Psalm 96:1-9 [10-13]
God's glory among the nations

Sunday, October 16–22

Isaiah 45:1-7
An earthly ruler works God's will
Psalm 96:1-9 [10-13]
God's glory among the nations
1 Thessalonians 1:1-10
Thanksgiving for the church at Thessalonica
Matthew 22:15-22
A teaching about the emperor and God

Reflection on Sunday

MONDAY
Daniel 3:1-18
Three disobey Nebuchadnezzar
Revelation 18:1-10, 19-20
The fall of Babylon

WEDNESDAY
Daniel 6:1-28
Daniel disobeys King Darius
Matthew 17:22-27
Jesus pays the temple tax

TUESDAY
Daniel 3:19-30
God saves three men in the furnace
Revelation 18:21-24
Babylon will be found no more

DAILY
Psalm 98
God reigns over the nations

Proper 25 [30]

Sunday between October 23 and 29 inclusive

Preparation for Sunday

THURSDAY
Deuteronomy 31:14-22
Moses' time to die draws near
Titus 1:5-16
Troublemakers deny God

FRIDAY
Deuteronomy 32:1-14, 18
The song of Moses
Titus 2:7-8, 11-15
A life devoted to good works

SATURDAY
Deuteronomy 32:44-47
Moses' farewell
John 5:39-47
Moses judges the disobedient

DAILY
Psalm 90:1-6, 13-17
Show your servants your works

Sunday, October 23–29

Deuteronomy 34:1-12
Death of Moses
Psalm 90:1-6, 13-17
Show your servants your works
1 Thessalonians 2:1-8
The apostle's concern
Matthew 22:34-46
Loving God and neighbor

Reflection on Sunday

MONDAY
Numbers 33:38-39
Death of Aaron
James 2:8-13
Fulfilling the royal law

TUESDAY
Exodus 34:29-35
Moses' shining face
James 2:14-26
Faith without works is dead

WEDNESDAY
Deuteronomy 26:16—27:7
The covenant ratified
Matthew 19:16-22
Keeping the commandments

DAILY
Psalm 119:41-48
I will keep God's law

Proper 25 [30]

Sunday between October 23 and 29 inclusive

Preparation for Sunday

THURSDAY
Numbers 5:5-10
Restitution for wronged neighbors
Titus 1:5-16
Troublemakers deny God

SATURDAY
Proverbs 24:23-34
Rise above retribution
John 5:39-47
Moses judges the disobedient

FRIDAY
Deuteronomy 9:25—10:5
The second set of commandments
Titus 2:7-8, 11-15
A life devoted to good works

DAILY
Psalm 1
Their delight is in the law

Sunday, October 23–29

Leviticus 19:1-2, 15-18
Acts of justice
Psalm 1
Their delight is in the law
1 Thessalonians 2:1-8
The apostle's concern
Matthew 22:34-46
Loving God and neighbor

Reflection on Sunday

MONDAY
Deuteronomy 6:1-9, 20-25
The great commandment
James 2:8-13
Fulfilling the royal law

WEDNESDAY
Proverbs 16:1-20
It is good to obey
Matthew 19:16-22
Keeping the commandments

TUESDAY
Deuteronomy 10:10-22
Moses urges the people to obey
James 2:14-26
Faith without works is dead

DAILY
Psalm 119:41-48
I will keep God's law

Proper 26 [31]

Sunday between October 30 and November 5 inclusive

Preparation for Sunday

THURSDAY
Joshua 1:1-11
God commissions Joshua
Romans 2:17-29
Real circumcision a matter of the heart

FRIDAY
Joshua 2:1-14
Rahab shelters the scouts
2 Peter 2:1-3
False prophets and their punishment

SATURDAY
Joshua 2:15-24
Rahab helps the scouts escape
Matthew 23:13-28
Woe to the scribes and Pharisees

DAILY
Psalm 107:1-7, 33-37
Thanks for a beautiful land

Sunday, October 30–November 5

Joshua 3:7-17
Crossing into the promised land
Psalm 107:1-7, 33-37
Thanks for a beautiful land
1 Thessalonians 2:9-13
The apostle's teaching
Matthew 23:1-12
Humble yourselves

Reflection on Sunday

MONDAY
Joshua 4:1-24
Another story of the crossing
1 Thessalonians 2:13-20
Words to the church

TUESDAY
Joshua 6:1-16, 20
Jericho is conquered
Acts 13:1-12
Paul and Barnabas confront a false prophet

WEDNESDAY
Joshua 10:12-14
Sun and moon stand still
Matthew 15:1-9
Lips that misrepresent the heart

DAILY
Psalm 128
It shall be well with you

Proper 26 [31]
Sunday between October 30 and November 5 inclusive

Preparation for Sunday

THURSDAY
1 Samuel 2:27-36
Hope for a better priesthood
Romans 2:17-29
Real circumcision a matter of the heart

SATURDAY
Malachi 1:6—2:9
False and true priests
Matthew 23:13-28
Woe to the scribes and pharisees

FRIDAY
Ezekiel 13:1-16
False prophets condemned
2 Peter 2:1-3
False prophets and their punishment

DAILY
Psalm 43
Send out your light and truth

Sunday, October 30–November 5

Micah 3:5-12
Judgment upon corrupt leaders
Psalm 43
Send out your light and truth
1 Thessalonians 2:9-13
The apostle's teaching
Matthew 23:1-12
Humble yourselves

Reflection on Sunday

MONDAY
Jeremiah 5:18-31
Prophets and priests who mislead
1 Thessalonians 2:13-20
Words to the church

WEDNESDAY
Proverbs 16:21-33
The wise heart and persuasive lips
Matthew 15:1-9
Lips that misrepresent the heart

TUESDAY
Lamentations 2:13-17
When prophets see false visions
Acts 13:1-12
Paul and Barnabas confront a false prophet

DAILY
Psalm 5
God blesses the righteous

Proper 27 [32]

Sunday between November 6 and 12 inclusive

Preparation for Sunday

THURSDAY
Joshua 5:10-12
Passover in the promised land
Revelation 8:6—9:12
The trumpet of God's judgment

FRIDAY
Joshua 8:30-35
Joshua renews the covenant
Revelation 9:13-21
Unrepentant humankind persists in sin

SATURDAY
Joshua 20:1-9
Joshua appoints cities of refuge
Matthew 24:1-14
Jesus foretells the end

DAILY
Psalm 78:1-7
The power of God

Sunday, November 6–12

Joshua 24:1-3a, 14-25
Joshua calls Israel to serve God
Psalm 78:1-7
The power of God
1 Thessalonians 4:13-18
The promise of the resurrection
Matthew 25:1-13
Wise and foolish bridesmaids

Reflection on Sunday

MONDAY
Joshua 24:25-33
Joshua's generation passes on
1 Corinthians 14:20-25
They will not listen to me

TUESDAY
Nehemiah 8:1-12
Ezra reads the law
1 Thessalonians 3:6-13
Stand firm in the faith

WEDNESDAY
Jeremiah 31:31-34
A new covenant
Matthew 24:29-35
My words will not pass away

DAILY
Psalm 78
God settled the tribes of Israel

Proper 27 [32]

Sunday between November 6 and 12 inclusive

Preparation for Sunday

THURSDAY

Amos 1:1 — 2:5

God judges Israel's neighbors

Revelation 8:6 — 9:12

The trumpet of God's judgment

FRIDAY

Amos 3:1-12

Israel's guilt and punishment

Revelation 9:13-21

Unrepentant humankind persists in sin

SATURDAY

Amos 4:6-13

Israel, prepare to meet your God

Matthew 24:1-14

Jesus foretells the end

DAILY

Psalm 70

You are my helper and deliverer

Sunday, November 6–12

Wisdom 6:12-16

Wisdom makes herself known

Wisdom 6:17-20

The beginning of wisdom

1 Thessalonians 4:13-18

The promise of the resurrection

Matthew 25:1-13

Wise and foolish bridesmaids

or

or

Amos 5:18-24

Let justice roll down like waters

Psalm 70

You are my helper and deliverer

Reflection on Sunday

MONDAY

Amos 8:7-14

A famine of hearing God's word

1 Corinthians 14:20-25

They will not listen to me

TUESDAY

Joel 1:1-14

Call to repentance

1 Thessalonians 3:6-13

Stand firm in the faith

WEDNESDAY

Joel 3:9-21

Promise of a glorious future

Matthew 24:29-35

My words will not pass away

DAILY

Psalm 63

God is a rich feast

Proper 28 [33]

Sunday between November 13 and 19 inclusive

Preparation for Sunday

THURSDAY
Judges 2:6-15
After Joshua's death
Revelation 16:1-7
God's judgments are true and just

FRIDAY
Judges 2:16-23
God raises up judges
Revelation 16:8-21
The judged curse God

SATURDAY
Judges 5:1-12
Song of Deborah
Matthew 12:43-45
From bad to worse

DAILY
Psalm 123
Our eyes look to God

Sunday, November 13–19

Judges 4:1-7
The judgeship of Deborah
Psalm 123
Our eyes look to God
1 Thessalonians 5:1-11
Be alert for the day of the Lord
Matthew 25:14-30
Slaves entrusted with talents

Reflection on Sunday

MONDAY
Judges 4:8-24
The judgeship of Deborah
Romans 2:1-11
The righteous judgment of God

TUESDAY
Exodus 2:1-10
Mother and sister protect Moses
1 Thessalonians 5:12-18
The Christian life

WEDNESDAY
Esther 7:1-10
Esther's victory
Matthew 24:45-51
Parable of the unfaithful slave

DAILY
Psalm 83:1-4, 9-10, 17-18
Do not be silent, O God

Proper 28 [33]

Sunday between November 13 and 19 inclusive

Preparation for Sunday

THURSDAY
Ezekiel 6:1-14
Judgment on idolatrous Israel
Revelation 16:1-7
God's judgments are true and just

FRIDAY
Ezekiel 7:1-9
The end is upon us
Revelation 16:8-21
The judged curse God

SATURDAY
Ezekiel 7:10-27
You shall know that the Lord is God
Matthew 12:43-45
From bad to worse

DAILY
Psalm 90:1-8 [9-11] 12
Number your days

Sunday, November 13–19

Zephaniah 1:7, 12-18
The day of the Lord
Psalm 90:1-8 [9-11] 12
Number your days
1 Thessalonians 5:1-11
Be alert for the day of the Lord
Matthew 25:14-30
Slaves entrusted with talents

Reflection on Sunday

MONDAY
Zechariah 1:7-17
God's judgment and mercy
Romans 2:1-11
The righteous judgment of God

TUESDAY
Zechariah 2:1-5; 5:1-4
Visions of mercy and judgment
1 Thessalonians 5:12-18
The Christian life

WEDNESDAY
Job 16:1-21
A lament about unjust punishment
Matthew 24:45-51
Parable of the unfaithful slave

DAILY
Psalm 9:1-14
God's reward for the righteous

Proper 29 [34]

Reign of Christ or *Christ the King*
Sunday between November 20 and 26 inclusive

Preparation for Sunday

THURSDAY
Genesis 48:15-22
God has been Jacob's shepherd
Revelation 14:1-11
Fear God and give God glory

FRIDAY
Isaiah 40:1-11
God will feed the people
Revelation 22:1-9
Worship God alone

SATURDAY
Ezekiel 34:25-31
A covenant of peace to come
Matthew 12:46-50
The true kindred of Jesus

DAILY
Psalm 100
We are the people of God's pasture

Sunday, November 20–26

Ezekiel 34:11-16, 20-24
God will shepherd Israel
Psalm 100
We are the people of God's pasture
Ephesians 1:15-23
The reign of Christ
Matthew 25:31-46
The separation of sheep and goats

Reflection on Sunday

MONDAY
Numbers 27:15-23
Joshua to shepherd Israel
2 Timothy 2:8-13
Those who endure with Christ reign with him

TUESDAY
Zechariah 11:4-17
Two kinds of shepherds
Revelation 19:1-9
Praise of God's judgments

WEDNESDAY
Jeremiah 31:10-14
God will shepherd the people
John 5:19-40
The judgment of the Son

DAILY
Psalm 28
Shepherd your people forever

Proper 29 [34]
Reign of Christ or *Christ the King*
Sunday between November 20 and 26 inclusive

Preparation for Sunday

THURSDAY
1 Kings 22:13-23
Israel like sheep without a shepherd
Revelation 14:1-11
Fear God and give God glory

FRIDAY
1 Chronicles 17:1-15
David, shepherd and king of Israel
Revelation 22:1-9
Worship God alone

SATURDAY
Isaiah 44:21-28
Cyrus, a shepherd for the Lord
Matthew 12:46-50
The true kindred of Jesus

DAILY
Psalm 95:1-7a
We are the people of God's pasture

Sunday, November 20–26

Ezekiel 34:11-16, 20-24
God will shepherd Israel
Psalm 95:1-7a
We are the people of God's pasture
Ephesians 1:15-23
The reign of Christ
Matthew 25:31-46
The separation of sheep and goats

Reflection on Sunday

MONDAY
Esther 2:1-18
Lowly Esther becomes queen
2 Timothy 2:8-13
Those who endure with Christ reign with him

TUESDAY
Esther 8:3-17
Queen Esther saves her people
Revelation 19:1-9
Praise of God's judgments

WEDNESDAY
Ezekiel 33:7-20
The righteous will live
John 5:19-40
The judgment of the Son

DAILY
Psalm 7
God the righteous judge

Advent

Christmas

Epiphany

Year B

First Sunday of Advent

Preparation for Sunday

THURSDAY
Zechariah 13:1-9
The coming day of God brings cleansing
Revelation 14:6-13
Hold fast to the faith

FRIDAY
Zechariah 14:1-9
God will come to rule
1 Thessalonians 4:1-18
A life pleasing God to the end

SATURDAY
Micah 2:1-13
God will gather all
Matthew 24:15-31
Be ready for that day

DAILY
Psalm 80:1-7, 17-19
We shall be saved

First Sunday of Advent

Isaiah 64:1-9
God will come with power and compassion
Psalm 80:1-7, 17-19
We shall be saved
1 Corinthians 1:3-9
Gifts of grace sustain us
Mark 13:24-37
The coming of the Son of Man

Reflection on Sunday

MONDAY
Micah 4:1-5
A promise of peace
Revelation 15:1-8
A liturgy of glory

TUESDAY
Micah 4:6-13
A promise of restoration after exile
Revelation 18:1-10
Judgment upon human pride

WEDNESDAY
Micah 5:1-5a
A promise of a shepherd
Luke 21:34-38
Be alert for that day

DAILY
Psalm 79
Prayer for deliverance

Second Sunday of Advent

Preparation for Sunday

THURSDAY
Hosea 6:1-6
Return to the God of life and love
1 Thessalonians 1:2-10
Paul thanks God for the Thessalonians

FRIDAY
Jeremiah 1:4-10
God appoints a prophet
Acts 11:19-26
The new community called "Christian"

SATURDAY
Ezekiel 36:24-28
A new heart and a new spirit
Mark 11:27-33
Jesus a prophet like John the Baptist

DAILY
Psalm 85:1-2, 8-13
Righteousness and peace

Second Sunday of Advent

Isaiah 40:1-11
God's coming to the exiles
Psalm 85:1-2, 8-13
Righteousness and peace
2 Peter 3:8-15a
Waiting for the day of God
Mark 1:1-8
John appears from the wilderness

Reflection on Sunday

MONDAY
Isaiah 26:7-15
The way of the righteous is level
Acts 2:37-42
Baptism in the name of Jesus

TUESDAY
Isaiah 4:2-6
God will wash Israel clean
Acts 11:1-18
John and Peter baptize

WEDNESDAY
Malachi 2:10—3:1
The coming messenger
Luke 1:5-17
The messenger in the temple

DAILY
Psalm 27
God's level path

Third Sunday of Advent

Preparation for Sunday

THURSDAY
Habakkuk 2:1-5
A vision concerning the end
Philippians 3:7-11
The righteousness that comes through faith

FRIDAY
Habakkuk 3:2-6
A prayer for God's glory and mercy
Philippians 3:12-16
The prize of God's call in Christ

SATURDAY
Habakkuk 3:13-19
God's devastation, God's deliverance
Matthew 21:28-32
Resistance to God in the present generation

DAILY
Psalm 126
God does great things for us

Third Sunday of Advent

Isaiah 61:1-4, 8-11
Righteousness and praise flourish like a garden
Psalm 126   or   Luke 1:46b-55
God does great things for us   *The Mighty One raises the lowly*
1 Thessalonians 5:16-24
Kept in faith until the coming of Christ
John 1:6-8, 19-28
A witness to the light

Reflection on Sunday

MONDAY
1 Kings 18:1-18
Elijah condemns King Ahab
Ephesians 6:10-17
The armor of God against the powers

TUESDAY
2 Kings 2:9-22
Elisha receives Elijah's spirit
Acts 3:17—4:4
Peter preaches about the prophets

WEDNESDAY
Malachi 3:16—4:6
Elijah and the coming one
Mark 9:9-13
Questions about Elijah

DAILY
Psalm 125
Prayer for blessing

Fourth Sunday of Advent

Readings for Monday through Wednesday after the Fourth Sunday of Advent are provided for use if necessary. Beginning with December 22, the dated readings on the following pages may be used.

Preparation for Sunday

THURSDAY
2 Samuel 6:1-11
The advent of the ark of the Lord
Hebrews 1:1-4
In the last days God speaks by a son

FRIDAY
2 Samuel 6:12-19
The ark of God enters Jerusalem
Hebrews 1:5-14
The advent of one higher than angels

SATURDAY
Judges 13:2-24
The birth of Samson
John 7:40-52
The Messiah, David, and Bethlehem

DAILY
Psalm 89:1-4, 19-26
I sing of your love

Fourth Sunday of Advent

2 Samuel 7:1-11, 16
God's promise to David
Luke 1:46b-55   *or*   Psalm 89:1-4, 19-26
The Mighty One raises the lowly   *I sing of your love*
Romans 16:25-27
The mystery revealed in Jesus Christ
Luke 1:26-38
The angel appears to Mary

Reflection on Sunday

MONDAY
1 Samuel 1:1-18
Hannah is promised a child
Hebrews 9:1-14
Christ comes as high priest

TUESDAY
1 Samuel 1:19-28
Hannah presents Samuel to God
Hebrews 8:1-13
The mediator replaces the sanctuary

WEDNESDAY
1 Samuel 2:1-10
Hannah's song
Mark 11:1-11
Jesus enters Jerusalem

DAILY
Luke 1:46b-55
The Lord lifts up the lowly

Days around Christmas Day

DECEMBER 22

Zephaniah 3:8-13
A people humble and lowly
Romans 10:5-13
The word is near you

DECEMBER 23

Zephaniah 3:14-20
God is in your midst
Romans 13:11-14
Salvation is near

DECEMBER 24 (MORNING ONLY)

Ecclesiastes 3:1-8
A time to be born
James 1:17-18
God gave us birth by the word of truth

DAILY

Psalm 96
Let the earth be glad

Nativity of the Lord (Christmas Day)

Any of the following three propers may be used on Christmas Eve/Day.

The readings from propers II and III for Christmas may be used as alternatives for Christmas Day. If proper III is not used on Christmas Day, it should be used at some service during the Christmas cycle because of the significance of John's prologue.

Christmas, Proper I

Isaiah 9:2-7
A child is born for us
Psalm 96
Let the earth be glad
Titus 2:11-14
The grace of God has appeared
Luke 2:1-14 [15-20]
God with us

Christmas, Proper II

Isaiah 62:6-12
God comes to restore the people
Psalm 97
Light springs up for the righteous
Titus 3:4-7
Saved through water and the Spirit
Luke 2:[1-7] 8-20
The birth of the messiah revealed to shepherds

Christmas, Proper III

Isaiah 52:7-10
Heralds announce God's salvation
Psalm 98
The victory of our God
Hebrews 1:1-4 [5-12]
God has spoken by a son
John 1:1-14
The Word became flesh

DECEMBER 26
Jeremiah 26:1-9, 12-15
Jeremiah threatened with death
Acts 6:8-15; 7:51-60
The plot against Stephen

DECEMBER 27
Exodus 33:18-23
Moses asks to see God's glory
1 John 1:1-9
The word of life was revealed

DECEMBER 28
Jeremiah 31:15-17
Rachel weeps for her children
Matthew 2:13-18
Death of innocent children

DAILY
Psalm 148
God's splendor is over earth and heaven

First Sunday after Christmas Day, December 26–31

Isaiah 61:10—62:3
Clothed in garments of salvation
Psalm 148
God's splendor is over earth and heaven
Galatians 4:4-7
Children and heirs of God
Luke 2:22-40
The presentation of the child

Days of Christmas

DAILY

Psalm 148

God's splendor is over earth and heaven

DECEMBER 29

Isaiah 49:5-15

God like a nursing mother

Matthew 12:46-50

Jesus' true family

DECEMBER 30

Proverbs 9:1-12

Your days will be multiplied

2 Peter 3:8-13

A thousand years as one day

DECEMBER 31

1 Kings 3:5-14

God grants a discerning mind

John 8:12-19

I am the light

JANUARY 1—HOLY NAME OF JESUS
(MARY, MOTHER OF GOD)

Numbers 6:22-27

The Aaronic blessing

Psalm 8

How exalted is your name

Galatians 4:4-7

We are no longer slaves

or Philippians 2:5-11

God takes on human form

Luke 2:15-21

The child is named Jesus

JANUARY 1—NEW YEAR'S DAY

Ecclesiastes 3:1-13

To everything a season

Psalm 8

How exalted is your name

Revelation 21:1-6a

New heaven and new earth

Matthew 25:31-46

Separation of the sheep and goats

JANUARY 2

Proverbs 1:1-7

Grow in wisdom and knowledge

James 3:13-18

The wisdom from above

The following readings are provided for use when Epiphany (January 6) is celebrated on a weekday following the Second Sunday after Christmas Day.

Second Sunday after Christmas Day, January 2–5

Jeremiah 31:7-14	*or*	Sirach 24:1-12
Joy as God's scattered flock gathers		*Wisdom lives among God's people*
Psalm 147:12-20	*or*	Wisdom 10:15-21
Praising God in Zion		*Wisdom lives among God's people*
Ephesians 1:3-14		
The will of God made known in Christ		
John 1:[1-9] 10-18		
God with us		

Days around Epiphany

Readings through January 9 are provided for use if necessary. When the Epiphany of the Lord is trans-
ferred to the preceding Sunday, January 2-5, these dated readings may be used through the week that
follows. When the Baptism of the Lord falls on January 11, 12, or 13, the corresponding preparation
readings on the following page are used after January 9.

JANUARY 3
Proverbs 1:20-33
Give heed to Wisdom, live without dread
James 4:1-10
Humble yourselves before God

JANUARY 4
Proverbs 3:1-12
Trust in God with all your heart
James 4:11-17
Our plans for our time are in God's hands

JANUARY 5
Proverbs 22:1-9
The generous are blessed
Luke 6:27-31
Do to others as you would have them do to you

DAILY
Psalm 110
Prayers for the king

Epiphany of the Lord, January 6

Isaiah 60:1-6
Nations come to the light
Psalm 72:1-7, 10-14
All shall bow down
Ephesians 3:1-12
The gospel's promise for all
Matthew 2:1-12
Christ revealed to the nations

JANUARY 7
Exodus 1:22—2:10
God saves Moses from Pharaoh
Hebrews 11:23-26
The faith of Moses

JANUARY 8
Exodus 2:11-25
Young Moses escapes from Pharaoh
Hebrews 11:27-28
The faith of Moses

JANUARY 9
Exodus 3:7-15
God speaks to Moses: I AM
John 8:39-59
Jesus' name: I AM

DAILY
Psalm 110
Prayers for the king

Baptism of the Lord [1]
First Sunday after the Epiphany

Preparation for Sunday

THURSDAY
1 Samuel 3:1-21
Samuel called by God as a prophet
Acts 9:10-19a
Saul is baptized

FRIDAY
1 Samuel 16:1-13
David anointed king by Samuel
1 Timothy 4:11-16
Gift of prophecy with laying on of hands

SATURDAY
1 Kings 2:1-4, 10-12
Solomon is designated king by David
Luke 5:1-11
Jesus calls Simon, James, and John

DAILY
Psalm 29
The voice of God upon the waters

Baptism of the Lord

Genesis 1:1-5
God creates light
Psalm 29
The voice of God upon the waters
Acts 19:1-7
Baptized in the name of Jesus
Mark 1:4-11
Jesus revealed as God's servant

Reflection on Sunday

MONDAY
Genesis 17:1-13
Circumcision a covenant sign
Romans 4:1-12
God makes righteous apart from works

TUESDAY
Exodus 30:22-38
Anointing a sign of holiness
Acts 22:2-16
Paul describes his own baptism

WEDNESDAY
Isaiah 41:14-20
God gives water in the desert
John 1:29-34
John's account of Jesus' baptism

DAILY
Psalm 69:1-5, 30-36
God will save through water

Second Sunday after the Epiphany [2]

Preparation for Sunday

THURSDAY
Judges 2:6-15
Uncertain times after Joshua's death
2 Corinthians 10:1-11
Corinthian behavior during Paul's absence

FRIDAY
Judges 2:16-23
God calls forth the judges
Acts 13:16-25
Leaders prior to Christ's coming

SATURDAY
1 Samuel 2:21-25
Eli's sons sin
Matthew 25:1-13
Wise and foolish bridesmaids

DAILY
Psalm 139:1-6, 13-18
You have searched me out

Second Sunday after the Epiphany

1 Samuel 3:1-10 [11-20]
The calling of Samuel
Psalm 139:1-6, 13-18
You have searched me out
1 Corinthians 6:12-20
Glorify God in your body
John 1:43-51
The calling of the first disciples

Reflection on Sunday

MONDAY
1 Samuel 9:27—10:8
Samuel anoints Saul king
2 Corinthians 6:14—7:1
Believers are called out

TUESDAY
1 Samuel 15:10-31
Samuel rebukes King Saul
Acts 5:1-11
Ananias and Sapphira judged

WEDNESDAY
Genesis 16:1-14
Hagar sees God and is blessed
Luke 18:15-17
Jesus blesses little children

DAILY
Psalm 86
Walking in God's way

Third Sunday after the Epiphany [3]

Preparation for Sunday

THURSDAY
Jeremiah 19:1-15
Jeremiah announces disaster
Revelation 18:11-20
Lament over a fallen city

FRIDAY
Jeremiah 20:7-13
Jeremiah denounces his persecutors
2 Peter 3:1-7
Scoffers doubt God's message

SATURDAY
Jeremiah 20:14-18
Jeremiah curses the day of his birth
Luke 10:13-16
Woe to those who reject God's messengers

DAILY
Psalm 62:5-12
In God is my safety and my honor

Third Sunday after the Epiphany

Jonah 3:1-5, 10
Repentance at Nineveh
Psalm 62:5-12
In God is my safety and my honor
1 Corinthians 7:29-31
Living in the end times
Mark 1:14-20
The calling of the disciples at the sea

Reflection on Sunday

MONDAY
Genesis 12:1-9
God calls Abram to go to Canaan
1 Corinthians 7:17-24
Live the life assigned

TUESDAY
Genesis 45:25—46:7
God calls Jacob to go to Egypt
Acts 5:33-42
The apostles are tried and flogged

WEDNESDAY
Proverbs 8:1-21
Wisdom calls the people
Mark 3:13-19a
Jesus appoints the twelve

DAILY
Psalm 46
The God of Jacob is our stronghold

Fourth Sunday after the Epiphany [4]

If this Sunday immediately precedes Ash Wednesday, the proper for Sunday and the readings for the surrounding days may be replaced, in those churches observing the Transfiguration on that Sunday, by the proper for the Last Sunday after the Epiphany and the readings for the days surrounding it.

Preparation for Sunday

THURSDAY
Deuteronomy 3:23-29
Moses sees Canaan from afar
Romans 9:6-18
God's mercy cannot be controlled

FRIDAY
Deuteronomy 12:28-32
Warnings against idolatry
Revelation 2:12-17
Idolatrous behavior is condemned

SATURDAY
Deuteronomy 13:1-5
Beware of false prophets
Matthew 8:28 — 9:1
Jesus heals the Gadarene demoniacs

DAILY
Psalm 111
The beginning of wisdom

Fourth Sunday after the Epiphany

Deuteronomy 18:15-20
The prophet speaks with God's authority
Psalm 111
The beginning of wisdom
1 Corinthians 8:1-13
Limits to liberty
Mark 1:21-28
The healing of one with an unclean spirit

Reflection on Sunday

MONDAY
Numbers 22:1-21
King Balak asks Balaam to curse Israel
Acts 21:17-26
Rules for Gentile converts

TUESDAY
Numbers 22:22-28
An angel speaks God's word to Balaam
1 Corinthians 7:32-40
Paul on marriage

WEDNESDAY
Jeremiah 29:1-14
Jeremiah speaks God's word
Mark 5:1-20
Jesus heals a man with a demon

DAILY
Psalm 35:1-10
God is our salvation

Fifth Sunday after the Epiphany [5]

If this Sunday immediately precedes Ash Wednesday, the proper for Sunday and the readings for the surrounding days may be replaced, in those churches observing the Transfiguration on that Sunday, by the proper for the Last Sunday after the Epiphany and the readings for the days surrounding it.

Preparation for Sunday

THURSDAY
Proverbs 12:10-21
The tongue of the wise brings healing
Galatians 5:2-15
The nature of Christian freedom

FRIDAY
Job 36:1-23
God's goodness is exalted
1 Corinthians 9:1-16
An apostle's life

SATURDAY
Isaiah 46:1-13
Who is equal to God?
Matthew 12:9-14
A healing on the sabbath

DAILY
Psalm 147:1-11, 20c
The Lord heals the brokenhearted

Fifth Sunday after the Epiphany

Isaiah 40:21-31
The Creator cares for the powerless
Psalm 147:1-11, 20c
The Lord heals the brokenhearted
1 Corinthians 9:16-23
A servant of the gospel
Mark 1:29-39
The healing of Peter's mother-in-law

Reflection on Sunday

MONDAY
2 Kings 4:8-17, 32-37
Elisha raises the Shunammite child
Acts 14:1-7
Resistance to the message of the apostles

TUESDAY
2 Kings 8:1-6
The Shunammite widow's land restored
Acts 15:36-41
Paul and Barnabas separate

WEDNESDAY
Job 6:1-13
Job's lament at misfortune
Mark 3:7-12
Jesus heals many people

DAILY
Psalm 102:12-28
Prayer for healing

Sixth Sunday after the Epiphany [6]

Proper 1

If this Sunday immediately precedes Ash Wednesday, the proper for Sunday and the readings for the surrounding days may be replaced, in those churches observing the Transfiguration on that Sunday, by the proper for the Last Sunday after the Epiphany and the readings for the days surrounding it.

Preparation for Sunday

THURSDAY
Leviticus 13:1-17
The law concerning leprosy
Hebrews 12:7-13
Discipline and healing

FRIDAY
Leviticus 14:1-20
The purification of persons with leprosy
Acts 19:11-20
Paul heals the sick

SATURDAY
Leviticus 14:21-32
The leprous poor also to be purified
Matthew 26:6-13
Jesus visits the home of a leprous person

DAILY
Psalm 30
You restored me to health

Sixth Sunday after the Epiphany

2 Kings 5:1-14
Naaman is healed of leprosy
Psalm 30
You restored me to health
1 Corinthians 9:24-27
Run the race
Mark 1:40-45
The healing of one with leprosy

Reflection on Sunday

MONDAY
2 Chronicles 26:1-21
Uzziah is afflicted with leprosy
Acts 3:1-10
Peter heals a crippled beggar

TUESDAY
2 Kings 7:3-10
Four men with leprosy announce good news
1 Corinthians 10:14—11:1
Do all to God's glory

WEDNESDAY
Job 30:16-31
Job's lament at his condition
John 4:46-54
Jesus heals a boy

DAILY
Psalm 6
Prayer for healing

Seventh Sunday after the Epiphany [7]

Proper 2

If this Sunday immediately precedes Ash Wednesday, the proper for Sunday and the readings for the surrounding days may be replaced, in those churches observing the Transfiguration on that Sunday, by the proper for the Last Sunday after the Epiphany and the readings for the days surrounding it.

Preparation for Sunday

THURSDAY
2 Chronicles 7:12-22
God promises Solomon healing for the nation
3 John 2-8
Well with your soul

FRIDAY
Isaiah 38:1-8
Hezekiah is healed by God
Hebrews 12:7-13
What is lame may be healed

SATURDAY
Isaiah 39:1-8
A gift for a healed king
Luke 4:38-41
The healing at Simon's house

DAILY
Psalm 41
Heal me, O God

Seventh Sunday after the Epiphany

Isaiah 43:18-25
Rivers in the desert
Psalm 41
Heal me, O God
2 Corinthians 1:18-22
Every promise of God is a "yes"
Mark 2:1-12
The healing of a paralyzed man

Reflection on Sunday

MONDAY
Isaiah 30:18-26
God promises to heal
Acts 14:8-18
Paul heals a lame man

TUESDAY
Micah 4:1-7
God gathers the afflicted into a strong nation
2 Corinthians 1:1-11
Thanksgiving after affliction

WEDNESDAY
Lamentations 5:1-22
A plea for restoration
John 5:19-29
The authority of the Son

DAILY
Psalm 38
Prayer for health and forgiveness

Eighth Sunday after the Epiphany [8]
Proper 3

If this Sunday immediately precedes Ash Wednesday, the proper for Sunday and the readings for the surrounding days may be replaced, in those churches observing the Transfiguration on that Sunday, by the proper for the Last Sunday after the Epiphany and the readings for the days surrounding it.

Preparation for Sunday

THURSDAY
Ezekiel 16:1-14
God's people like a beloved bride
Romans 3:1-8
The faithfulness of God

FRIDAY
Ezekiel 16:44-52
The disgrace of God's people
2 Peter 1:1-11
Support your faith with goodness

SATURDAY
Ezekiel 16:53-63
God's everlasting covenant
John 7:53—8:11
The woman not condemned

DAILY
Psalm 103:1-13, 22
God's compassion and mercy

Eighth Sunday after the Epiphany

Hosea 2:14-20
The covenant renewed
Psalm 103:1-13, 22
God's compassion and mercy
2 Corinthians 3:1-6
Ministers of God's new covenant
Mark 2:13-22
Eating with tax collectors and prostitutes

Reflection on Sunday

MONDAY
Hosea 3:1-5
God loves faithless Israel
2 Corinthians 1:23—2:11
About forgiveness

TUESDAY
Hosea 14:1-9
A plea for repentance
2 Corinthians 11:1-15
Christians a chaste bride to Christ

WEDNESDAY
Isaiah 62:1-5
God marries the people
John 3:22-36
Christ the bridegroom

DAILY
Psalm 45:6-17
A marriage song

Ninth Sunday after the Epiphany [9]

Proper 4

The readings that follow are for churches whose calendar requires this Sunday, and who do not observe the last Sunday after the Epiphany as Transfiguration.

Preparation for Sunday

THURSDAY
Exodus 31:12-18
The sabbath law
Acts 25:1-12
Paul is unafraid of death

FRIDAY
Leviticus 23:1-8
Sabbath, Passover, unleavened bread
Romans 8:31-39
Death cannot separate us from the love of God

SATURDAY
Leviticus 24:5-9
The bread for the tabernacle
John 7:19-24
Circumcision and healing on the sabbath

DAILY
Psalm 81:1-10
Raise a loud shout to the God of Jacob

Ninth Sunday after the Epiphany

Deuteronomy 5:12-15
Sabbath commandments
Psalm 81:1-10
Raise a loud shout to the God of Jacob
2 Corinthians 4:5-12
Treasure in clay jars
Mark 2:23—3:6
Doing the work of God on the sabbath

Reflection on Sunday

MONDAY
Exodus 16:13-26
Concerning food on the sabbath
Romans 9:19-29
God's wrath and mercy

TUESDAY
Exodus 16:27-36
Manna and the sabbath
Acts 15:1-5, 22-35
The church considers Jewish practices

WEDNESDAY
1 Samuel 21:1-6
David eats the bread of the Presence
John 5:1-18
Jesus heals on the sabbath

DAILY
Psalm 78:1-4, 52-72
God's care for the chosen people

Last Sunday after the Epiphany
Transfiguration Sunday

The following may be used in churches where the last Sunday after the Epiphany is observed as Transfiguration Sunday.

Preparation for Sunday

THURSDAY
1 Kings 11:26-40
Ahijah prophesies to Jereboam
2 Corinthians 2:12-17
God spreads the fragrance of life in Christ

SATURDAY
1 Kings 16:1-7
Jehu warns King Baasha
Luke 19:41-44
The time of God's visitation

FRIDAY
1 Kings 14:1-18
Ahijah receives Jereboam's wife
1 Timothy 1:12-20
Gratitude for mercy

DAILY
Psalm 50:1-6
God shines forth in glory

Transfiguration of the Lord

2 Kings 2:1-12
Elijah taken up to heaven
Psalm 50:1-6
God shines forth in glory
2 Corinthians 4:3-6
God's light seen in Christ
Mark 9:2-9
Christ revealed as God's beloved Son

Reflection on Sunday

MONDAY
Exodus 19:7-25
Moses meets God on the mountain
Hebrews 2:1-4
Do not neglect so great a salvation

DAILY
Psalm 110:1-4
A priest forever

TUESDAY
Job 19:23-27
Job will see God
1 Timothy 3:14-16
The mystery of our religion

Lent

Three Days

Easter

YEAR B

First Sunday in Lent

Ash Wednesday

Joel 2:1-2, 12-17   *or*   Isaiah 58:1-12
Return to God   *The fast that God chooses*
Psalm 51:1-17
Plea for mercy
2 Corinthians 5:20b—6:10
Now is the day of salvation
Matthew 6:1-6, 16-21
The practice of faith

Preparation for Sunday

THURSDAY
Daniel 9:1-14
Daniel prays for the people's forgiveness
1 John 1:3-10
The apostolic message of forgiveness

FRIDAY
Daniel 9:15-25a
An angel speaks to Daniel
2 Timothy 4:1-5
Apostolic and pastoral advice for Timothy

SATURDAY
Psalm 32
God forgives sin
Matthew 9:2-13
Jesus forgives sin and calls sinners to service

DAILY
Psalm 25:1-10
Your paths are love and faithfulness

First Sunday in Lent

Genesis 9:8-17
The rainbow, sign of God's covenant
Psalm 25:1-10
Your paths are love and faithfulness
1 Peter 3:18-22
Saved through water
Mark 1:9-15
The temptation of Jesus

Reflection on Sunday

MONDAY
Job 4:1-21
Eliphaz speaks of sin
Ephesians 2:1-10
The death of sin, the gift of grace

TUESDAY
Job 5:8-27
Seek God
1 Peter 3:8-18a
About suffering

WEDNESDAY
Proverbs 30:1-9
Plea to be safe from temptation
Matthew 4:1-11
Matthew's account of Jesus' temptation

DAILY
Psalm 77
Prayer for God to remember us

Second Sunday in Lent

Preparation for Sunday

THURSDAY
Genesis 15:1-6, 12-18
God covenants with Abraham
Romans 3:21-31
Righteousness through faith

FRIDAY
Genesis 16:1-6
Ishmael born to Abram and Hagar
Romans 4:1-12
Abraham counted righteous by God for his faith

SATURDAY
Genesis 16:7-15
An angel comforts Hagar at a spring of water
Mark 8:27-30
Peter's confession

DAILY
Psalm 22:23-31
All the earth shall turn to God

Second Sunday in Lent

Genesis 17:1-7, 15-16
God blesses Abraham and Sarah
Psalm 22:23-31
All the earth shall turn to God
Romans 4:13-25
The promise to those of Abraham's faith
Mark 8:31-38   *or*   Mark 9:2-9
The passion prediction   *Christ revealed as God's beloved Son*

Reflection on Sunday

MONDAY
Genesis 21:1-7
God gives Abraham and Sarah a son
Hebrews 1:8-12
The Son whose years will never end

TUESDAY
Genesis 22:1-19
God asks Abraham to sacrifice Isaac
Hebrews 11:1-3, 13-19
By faith Abraham obeyed God

WEDNESDAY
Jeremiah 30:12-22
God will restore Israel
John 12:36-43
The unbelief of the people

DAILY
Psalm 105:1-11, 37-45
God promises life to Abraham

Third Sunday in Lent

Preparation for Sunday

THURSDAY
Exodus 19:1-9a
Preparation for the giving of the commandments
1 Peter 2:4-10
You are God's own people

FRIDAY
Exodus 19:9b-15
Preparation for the giving of the commandments
Acts 7:30-40
God spoke to Moses at Mount Sinai

SATURDAY
Exodus 19:16-25
Preparation for the giving of the commandments
Mark 9:2-8
Moses with Elijah and Jesus on a mountain

DAILY
Psalm 19
The commandments give light to the eyes

Third Sunday in Lent

Exodus 20:1-17
The commandments given at Sinai
Psalm 19
The commandments give light to the eyes
1 Corinthians 1:18-25
Christ crucified, the wisdom of God
John 2:13-22
The cleansing of the temple

Reflection on Sunday

MONDAY
1 Kings 6:1-4, 21-22
Solomon builds the temple
1 Corinthians 3:10-23
You are God's temple

TUESDAY
2 Chronicles 29:1-11, 16-19
Hezekiah cleanses the temple
Hebrews 9:23-28
Christ as priest and once-for-all sacrifice

WEDNESDAY
Ezra 6:1-16
King Darius orders the temple rebuilt
Mark 11:15-19
Jesus cleanses the temple

DAILY
Psalm 84
How lovely is God's dwelling place

Fourth Sunday in Lent

Preparation for Sunday

THURSDAY
Genesis 9:8-17
The covenant with Noah
Ephesians 1:3-6
Blessed be God, who chose us in Christ

FRIDAY
Daniel 12:5-13
The people will be purified
Ephesians 1:7-14
We live to the praise of God's glory

SATURDAY
Numbers 20:22-29
The death of Aaron
John 3:1-13
Jesus and Nicodemus

DAILY
Psalm 107:1-3, 17-22
God delivers from distress

Fourth Sunday in Lent

Numbers 21:4-9
The lifting up of the serpent
Psalm 107:1-3, 17-22
God delivers from distress
Ephesians 2:1-10
Alive in Christ
John 3:14-21
The lifting up of the Son of Man

Reflection on Sunday

MONDAY
Exodus 15:22-27
God gives the people water
Hebrews 3:1-6
The faithfulness of Moses

TUESDAY
Numbers 20:1-13
God gives water from the rock
1 Corinthians 10:6-13
God is faithful

WEDNESDAY
Isaiah 60:15-22
God is our light
John 8:12-20
Christ the light of the world

DAILY
Psalm 107:1-16
God gives food and light

Fifth Sunday in Lent

Preparation for Sunday

THURSDAY
Isaiah 30:15-18
God's gifts of returning and rest
Hebrews 4:1-13
God promises an eternal sabbath rest

FRIDAY
Exodus 30:1-10
Aaron's responsibility for altar and atonement
Hebrews 4:14—5:4
Jesus' priesthood surpasses Aaron's

SATURDAY
Habakkuk 3:2-13
God will save the anointed
John 12:1-11
Jesus is anointed for his coming death

DAILY
Psalm 51:1-12
Create in me a clean heart

Fifth Sunday in Lent

Jeremiah 31:31-34
A new covenant written on the heart
Psalm 51:1-12   *or*   Psalm 119:9-16
Create in me a clean heart   *I treasure your promise in my heart*
Hebrews 5:5-10
Through suffering Christ saves
John 12:20-33
The grain of wheat dying in the earth

Reflection on Sunday

MONDAY
Isaiah 43:8-13
God is our savior
2 Corinthians 3:4-11
God's glory in Christ

TUESDAY
Isaiah 44:1-8
God gives life to the people
Acts 2:14-24
Peter proclaims the crucified Christ to be alive

WEDNESDAY
Haggai 2:1-9, 20-23
God promises future blessings
John 12:34-50
God gives eternal life

DAILY
Psalm 119:9-16
I treasure your promise in my heart

Sixth Sunday in Lent

Passion Sunday or *Palm Sunday*

Those who do not observe the procession with palms and do not wish to use the passion gospel may substitute the gospel and psalm indicated for the Liturgy of the Palms for the gospel and psalm indicated for the Liturgy of the Passion. Whenever possible, the whole passion narrative should be read.

Preparation for Sunday

THURSDAY
Deuteronomy 16:1-8
The feast of unleavened bread
Philippians 2:1-11
Paul's plea for Christ-like humility

SATURDAY
Jeremiah 33:10-16
In a place of desolation, God will bring gladness
Mark 10:32-34, 46-52
Jesus approaches Jerusalem

FRIDAY
Jeremiah 33:1-9
God will restore and cleanse from sin
Philippians 2:12-18
Shine like stars in the world

DAILY
Psalm 118:1-2, 19-29
Blessed is the one who comes

Sixth Sunday in Lent

LITURGY OF THE PALMS
Psalm 118:1-2, 19-29
The passover praise psalm
Mark 11:1-11   *or*   John 12:12-16
Jesus enters Jerusalem   *Jesus enters Jerusalem*

LITURGY OF THE PASSION
Isaiah 50:4-9a
The servant submits to suffering
Psalm 31:9-16
I commend my spirit
Philippians 2:5-11
Death on a cross
Mark 14:1 — 15:47 *or* Mark 15:1-39 [40-47]
The passion and death of Jesus

Monday of Holy Week

Isaiah 42:1-9
The servant brings forth justice
Psalm 36:5-11
Refuge under the shadow of your wings
Hebrews 9:11-15
The blood of Christ redeems for eternal life
John 12:1-11
Mary of Bethany anoints Jesus

Tuesday of Holy Week

Isaiah 49:1-7
The servant brings salvation to earth's ends
Psalm 71:1-14
From my mother's womb you have been my strength
1 Corinthians 1:18-31
The cross of Christ reveals God's power and wisdom
John 12:20-36
Jesus speaks of his death

Wednesday of Holy Week

Isaiah 50:4-9a
The servant is vindicated by God
Psalm 70
Be pleased, O God, to deliver me
Hebrews 12:1-3
Look to Jesus, who endured the cross
John 13:21-32
Jesus foretells his betrayal

The Three Days

Holy Thursday

Exodus 12:1-4 [5-10] 11-14
The passover of the Lord
Psalm 116:1-2, 12-19
The cup of salvation
1 Corinthians 11:23-26
Proclaim the Lord's death
John 13:1-17, 31b-35
The service of Christ: footwashing and meal

Good Friday

Isaiah 52:13 — 53:12
The suffering servant
Psalm 22
Why have you forsaken me?
Hebrews 10:16-25   or   Hebrews 4:14-16; 5:7-9
The way to God is opened   *The merciful high priest*
John 18:1 — 19:42
The passion and death of Jesus

Holy Saturday
The following are for use at services other than the Easter Vigil.

Job 14:1-14   or   Lamentations 3:1-9, 19-24
Hope for a tree   *I will hope in the Lord*
Psalm 31:1-4, 15-16
Take me out of the net
1 Peter 4:1-8
The gospel proclaimed even to the dead
Matthew 27:57-66   or   John 19:38-42
The burial of Jesus   *The burial of Jesus*

Resurrection of the Lord, Easter Vigil

1
Genesis 1:1 — 2:4a
Creation
Psalm 136:1-9, 23-26
God's mercy endures forever

2
Genesis 7:1-5, 11-18; 8:6-18; 9:8-13
Flood
Psalm 46
The God of Jacob is our stronghold

3
Genesis 22:1-18
Testing of Abraham
Psalm 16
You will show me the path of life

4
Exodus 14:10-31; 15:20-21
Deliverance at the Red Sea
Exodus 15:1b-13, 17-18
I will sing to the Lord who has triumphed gloriously

5
Isaiah 55:1-11
Salvation freely offered to all
Isaiah 12:2-6
With joy you will draw water from the wells of salvation

6
Baruch 3:9-15, 32 — 4:4   *or*   Proverbs 8:1-8, 19-21; 9:4b-6
The wisdom of God   *The wisdom of God*
Psalm 19
God's statutes are just and rejoice the heart

7

Ezekiel 36:24-28

A new heart and a new spirit

Psalms 42 and 43

My soul thirsts for the living God

8

Ezekiel 37:1-14

Valley of the dry bones

Psalm 143

Revive me for your name's sake

9

Zephaniah 3:14-20

Gathering of God's people

Psalm 98

Lift up your voice, rejoice and sing

Romans 6:3-11

Dying and rising with Christ

Psalm 114

Tremble, O earth

Mark 16:1-8

The resurrection is announced

Resurrection of the Lord, Easter Day

Acts 10:34-43   *or*   Isaiah 25:6-9
God raised Jesus on the third day   *The feast of victory*
Psalm 118:1-2, 14-24
On this day God has acted
1 Corinthians 15:1-11   *or*   Acts 10:34-43
Witnesses to the risen Christ   *God raised Jesus on the third day*
John 20:1-18   *or*   Mark 16:1-8
Seeing the risen Christ   *The resurrection is announced*

Easter Evening

Isaiah 25:6-9
The feast of victory
Psalm 114
Tremble, O earth
1 Corinthians 5:6b-8
Set your mind on things above
Luke 24:13-49
Stay with us, Lord

Reflection on Sunday

MONDAY
Genesis 1:1-19
God creates
1 Corinthians 15:35-49
The resurrected body

TUESDAY
Genesis 1:20—2:4a
God creates
1 Corinthians 15:50-58
The dead will be raised

WEDNESDAY
Song of Solomon 3:1-11
The song of the lover
Mark 16:1-8
Mark's resurrection account

DAILY
Psalm 118:1-2, 14-24
On this day God has acted

Second Sunday of Easter

Preparation for Sunday

THURSDAY
Daniel 1:1-21
Daniel in the court of Nebuchadnezzar
Acts 2:42-47
The believers' common life

FRIDAY
Daniel 2:1-23
The king searches for wisdom
Acts 4:23-31
Prayer after Peter and John's release

SATURDAY
Daniel 2:24-49
Daniel's rise to power
John 12:44-50
Believe in the one who sent me

DAILY
Psalm 133
How good it is to live in unity

Second Sunday of Easter

Acts 4:32-35
The believers' common life
Psalm 133
How good it is to live in unity
1 John 1:1—2:2
Walking in the light
John 20:19-31
Beholding the wounds of the risen Christ

Reflection on Sunday

MONDAY
Daniel 3:1-30
God saves the three men from the fire
1 John 2:3-11
A new commandment

TUESDAY
Daniel 6:1-28
God saves Daniel from the lions
1 John 2:12-17
The world is passing away

WEDNESDAY
Isaiah 26:1-15
Song of victory
Mark 12:18-27
Jesus teaches about the resurrection

DAILY
Psalm 135
Praise to God

Third Sunday of Easter

Preparation for Sunday

THURSDAY
Daniel 9:1-19
Daniel pleads for the people in prayer
1 John 2:18-25
Remain in union with God

FRIDAY
Daniel 10:2-19
Daniel's vision strengthens him
1 John 2:26-28
Have confidence in the coming one

SATURDAY
Acts 3:1-10
A man lame from birth is healed
Luke 22:24-30
Eating and drinking at Christ's table

DAILY
Psalm 4
God does wonders for the faithful

Third Sunday of Easter

Acts 3:12-19
Health and forgiveness through Jesus
Psalm 4
God does wonders for the faithful
1 John 3:1-7
The revealing of the children of God
Luke 24:36b-48
Eating with the risen Christ

Reflection on Sunday

MONDAY
Jeremiah 30:1-11a
God will save the people
1 John 3:10-16
Lay down life for one another

TUESDAY
Hosea 5:15—6:6
Salvation on the third day
2 John 1-6
Love one another

WEDNESDAY
Proverbs 9:1-6
Wisdom invites to her feast
Mark 16:9-18
Jesus appears to the disciples

DAILY
Psalm 150
Praise to God

Fourth Sunday of Easter

Preparation for Sunday

THURSDAY
Genesis 30:25-43
Jacob the shepherd
Acts 3:17-26
Peter preaches in Solomon's Portico

FRIDAY
Genesis 46:28—47:6
The shepherds of Israel sojourn in Egypt
Acts 4:1-4
Peter and John arrested

SATURDAY
Genesis 48:8-19
God has been my shepherd
Mark 6:30-34
Like sheep without a shepherd

DAILY
Psalm 23
God our shepherd

Fourth Sunday of Easter

Acts 4:5-12
Salvation in the name of Jesus
Psalm 23
God our shepherd
1 John 3:16-24
Love in truth and action
John 10:11-18
Christ the shepherd

Reflection on Sunday

MONDAY
1 Samuel 16:1-13
The shepherd David is anointed
1 Peter 5:1-5
Christ the great shepherd

TUESDAY
1 Chronicles 11:1-9
The shepherd David made king
Revelation 7:13-17
The Lamb will be the shepherd

WEDNESDAY
Micah 7:8-20
God will shepherd the people
Mark 14:26-31
Christ the shepherd

DAILY
Psalm 95
We are the sheep of God's hand

Fifth Sunday of Easter

Preparation for Sunday

THURSDAY
Amos 8:1-7
Amos' vision of the basket of fruit
Acts 8:1b-8
Philip's ministry in Samaria

FRIDAY
Amos 8:11-13
A famine of hearing the word of God
Acts 8:9-25
Philip and Simon the magician

SATURDAY
Amos 9:7-15
The mountains shall drip sweet wine
Mark 4:30-32
The kingdom like a mustard seed

DAILY
Psalm 22:25-31
All shall turn to the Lord

Fifth Sunday of Easter

Acts 8:26-40
Philip teaches and baptizes an Ethiopian
Psalm 22:25-31
All shall turn to the Lord
1 John 4:7-21
Loving one another
John 15:1-8
Christ the vine

Reflection on Sunday

MONDAY
Isaiah 5:1-7
The unfaithful vineyard
Galatians 5:16-26
The fruits of the Spirit

TUESDAY
Isaiah 32:9-20
A fruitful field
James 3:17-18
Wisdom is full of good fruits

WEDNESDAY
Isaiah 65:17-25
God's people like a tree
John 14:18-31
Keeping God's word

DAILY
Psalm 80
Israel, the vine

Sixth Sunday of Easter

Preparation for Sunday

THURSDAY
Isaiah 49:5-6
A light to the nations
Acts 10:1-34
Peter and Cornelius

FRIDAY
Isaiah 42:5-9
God declares new things
Acts 10:34-43
God shows no partiality

SATURDAY
Deuteronomy 32:44-47
Take to heart the command of God
Mark 10:42-45
Jesus came to serve

DAILY
Psalm 98
Shout with joy to God

Sixth Sunday of Easter

Acts 10:44-48
The Spirit poured out on the Gentiles
Psalm 98
Shout with joy to God
1 John 5:1-6
The victory of faith
John 15:9-17
Christ, the friend and lover

Reflection on Sunday

MONDAY
Deuteronomy 7:1-11
Keeping God's commandments
1 Timothy 6:11-12
Pursue righteousness

TUESDAY
Deuteronomy 11:1-17
The rewards of obedience
1 Timothy 6:13-16
Keep the commandments until Christ comes

WEDNESDAY
Deuteronomy 11:18-21
Teach God's words to your children
Mark 16:19-20
An account of Jesus' ascension

DAILY
Psalm 93
God reigns above the floods

Seventh Sunday of Easter

Ascension of the Lord, Thursday

These readings may also be used on the Seventh Sunday of Easter.

Acts 1:1-11
Jesus sends the apostles

Psalm 47   or   Psalm 93
God has gone up with a shout   *Praise to God who reigns*

Ephesians 1:15-23
Seeing the risen and ascended Christ

Luke 24:44-53
Christ present in all times and places

Preparation for Sunday

FRIDAY

Exodus 24:15-18
Moses on Mount Sinai for forty days

Revelation 1:9-18
A vision of the risen Christ

SATURDAY

Deuteronomy 34:1-7
Moses goes up to see the promised land

John 16:4-11
Jesus will send the Advocate

DAILY

Psalm 47
God has gone up with a shout

Seventh Sunday of Easter

Acts 1:15-17, 21-26
Matthias added to the apostles

Psalm 1
The way of the righteous

1 John 5:9-13
Life in the Son of God

John 17:6-19
Christ's prayer for his disciples

Reflection on Sunday

MONDAY
Exodus 28:29-38
Aaron prays for the people
Philippians 1:3-11
Paul prays for the church at Philippi

TUESDAY
Numbers 8:5-22
The Levites consecrated for service
Titus 1:1-9
The ministry entrusted to Titus by Paul

WEDNESDAY
Ezra 9:5-15
Ezra prays for the people
John 16:16-24
Sorrow turned to joy

DAILY
Psalm 115
God's blessings on the chosen ones

Day of Pentecost

On the Day of Pentecost, if the Old Testament passage from Ezekiel is chosen for the first reading, the passage from Acts is used as the second reading.

Preparation for Sunday

THURSDAY
Genesis 2:4b-7
God breathes life into humankind
1 Corinthians 15:42b-49
We bear Christ's image

FRIDAY
Job 37:1-13
The powerful breath of God
1 Corinthians 15:50-57
The dead will be raised

SATURDAY
Exodus 15:6-11
The breath of God rescues Israel
John 7:37-39
The living water of the Spirit

DAILY
Psalm 33:12-22
Our help and our shield

Day of Pentecost

Acts 2:1-21
Filled with the Spirit
Psalm 104:24-34, 35b
Renewing the face of the earth
Romans 8:22-27
Praying with the Spirit
John 15:26-27; 16:4b-15
Christ sends the Spirit of truth

or   Ezekiel 37:1-14
Life to dry bones

or   Acts 2:1-21
Filled with the Spirit

Reflection on Sunday

MONDAY
Joel 2:18-29
God's spirit poured out
1 Corinthians 12:4-11
Various gifts, the same Spirit

TUESDAY
Genesis 11:1-9
The fragmenting of human tongues
1 Corinthians 12:12-27
Many members, one body of Christ

WEDNESDAY
Ezekiel 37:1-14
Life to dry bones
John 20:19-23
Jesus breathes the Spirit

DAILY
Psalm 104:24-34, 35b
Renewing the face of the earth

Season

after

Pentecost

YEAR B

Trinity Sunday
First Sunday after Pentecost

Preparation for Sunday

THURSDAY
Isaiah 1:1-4, 16-20
A vision concerning God's people
Romans 8:1-8
The Spirit is life and peace

FRIDAY
Isaiah 2:1-5
A vision concerning God's people
Romans 8:9-11
The Spirit dwells in you

SATURDAY
Isaiah 5:15-24
A vision concerning God's people
John 15:18-20, 26-27
Testify in the face of persecution

DAILY
Psalm 29
Worship God in holiness

Trinity Sunday

Isaiah 6:1-8
Isaiah's vision and call
Psalm 29
Worship God in holiness
Romans 8:12-17
Living by the Spirit
John 3:1-17
Entering the reign of God

Reflection on Sunday

MONDAY
Numbers 9:15-23
God in the cloud and the fire
Revelation 4:1-8
Heaven's holy, holy, holy

TUESDAY
Exodus 25:1-22
God in the ark and its mercy seat
1 Corinthians 2:1-10
God's wisdom revealed through the Spirit

WEDNESDAY
Numbers 6:22-27
Aaronic blessing
Mark 4:21-25
Secrets come to light

DAILY
Psalm 20
The name of God

Proper 3 [8]

*Sunday between May 24 and 28 inclusive
(if after Trinity Sunday)*

Preparation for Sunday

THURSDAY
Ezekiel 16:1-14
God's people like a beloved bride
Romans 3:1-8
The faithfulness of God

FRIDAY
Ezekiel 16:44-52
The disgrace of God's people
2 Peter 1:1-11
Support your faith with goodness

SATURDAY
Ezekiel 16:53-63
God's everlasting covenant
John 7:53—8:11
The woman not condemned

DAILY
Psalm 103:1-13, 22
God's compassion and mercy

Sunday, May 24–28

Hosea 2:14-20
The covenant renewed
Psalm 103:1-13, 22
God's compassion and mercy
2 Corinthians 3:1-6
Ministers of God's new covenant
Mark 2:13-22
Eating with tax collectors and prostitutes

Reflection on Sunday

MONDAY
Hosea 3:1-5
God loves faithless Israel
2 Corinthians 1:23—2:11
About forgiveness

TUESDAY
Hosea 14:1-9
A plea for repentance
2 Corinthians 11:1-15
Christians a chaste bride to Christ

WEDNESDAY
Isaiah 62:1-5
God marries the people
John 3:22-36
Christ the bridegroom

DAILY
Psalm 45:6-17
A marriage song

Proper 4 [9]

*Sunday between May 29 and June 4 inclusive
(if after Trinity Sunday)*

Preparation for Sunday

THURSDAY
1 Samuel 1:1-18
Hannah is promised a child
Acts 25:1-12
Paul is unafraid of death

FRIDAY
1 Samuel 1:19-27
Birth and dedication of Samuel
Romans 8:31-39
Death cannot separate us from the love of God

SATURDAY
1 Samuel 2:1-10
Hannah's prayer
John 7:19-24
Circumcision and healing on the sabbath

DAILY
Psalm 139:1-6, 13-18
You have searched me out

Sunday, May 29–June 4

1 Samuel 3:1-10 [11-20]
The calling of Samuel
Psalm 139:1-6, 13-18
You have searched me out
2 Corinthians 4:5-12
Treasure in clay jars
Mark 2:23—3:6
Doing the work of God on the sabbath

Reflection on Sunday

MONDAY
1 Samuel 2:11-17
Eli's sons
Romans 9:19-29
God's wrath and mercy

TUESDAY
1 Samuel 2:18-21
Hannah visits Samuel
Acts 15:1-5, 22-35
The church considers Jewish practices

WEDNESDAY
1 Samuel 2:22-36
A prophet speaks to Eli
John 5:1-18
Jesus heals on the sabbath

DAILY
Psalm 99
Samuel called on God's name

Proper 4 [9]

Sunday between May 29 and June 4 inclusive
(if after Trinity Sunday)

Preparation for Sunday

THURSDAY
Exodus 31:12-18
The sabbath law
Acts 25:1-12
Paul is unafraid of death

FRIDAY
Leviticus 23:1-8
Sabbath, Passover, unleavened bread
Romans 8:31-39
Death cannot separate us from the love of God

SATURDAY
Leviticus 24:5-9
The bread for the tabernacle
John 7:19-24
Circumcision and healing on the sabbath

DAILY
Psalm 81:1-10
Raise a loud shout to the God of Jacob

Sunday, May 29–June 4

Deuteronomy 5:12-15
Sabbath commandments
Psalm 81:1-10
Raise a loud shout to the God of Jacob
2 Corinthians 4:5-12
Treasure in clay jars
Mark 2:23—3:6
Doing the work of God on the sabbath

Reflection on Sunday

MONDAY
Exodus 16:13-26
Concerning food on the sabbath
Romans 9:19-29
God's wrath and mercy

TUESDAY
Exodus 16:27-36
Manna and the sabbath
Acts 15:1-5, 22-35
The church considers Jewish practices

WEDNESDAY
1 Samuel 21:1-6
David eats the bread of the Presence
John 5:1-18
Jesus heals on the sabbath

DAILY
Psalm 78:1-4, 52-72
God's care for the chosen people

Proper 5 [10]
Sunday between June 5 and 11 inclusive
(if after Trinity Sunday)

Preparation for Sunday

THURSDAY
1 Samuel 4:1-22
The Philistines capture the ark
1 Peter 4:7-19
Entrusting ourselves to a faithful Creator

FRIDAY
1 Samuel 5:1-12
Trouble for the Philistines
2 Corinthians 5:1-5
What is mortal is swallowed up in life

SATURDAY
1 Samuel 6:1-18
The Philistines send back the ark
Luke 8:4-15
Hearing and living the word of God

DAILY
Psalm 138
Your love endures forever

Sunday, June 5–11

1 Samuel 8:4-11 [12-15] 16-20 [11:14-15]
Israel desires a king
Psalm 138
Your love endures forever
2 Corinthians 4:13 — 5:1
Renewed in the inner nature
Mark 3:20-35
Doing the work of God

Reflection on Sunday

MONDAY
1 Samuel 7:3-15
The people turn back to God
Revelation 20:1-6
The first resurrection

TUESDAY
1 Samuel 8:1-22
Samuel warns against kings
Revelation 20:7-15
Satan's doom

WEDNESDAY
1 Samuel 9:1-14
Saul travels to Samuel's town
Luke 11:14-28
Jesus and Beelzebul

DAILY
Psalm 108
I will sing praises among the nations

Proper 5 [10]

Sunday between June 5 and 11 inclusive
(if after Trinity Sunday)

Preparation for Sunday

THURSDAY
Isaiah 28:9-13
The people of God refuse to hear
1 Peter 4:7-19
Entrusting ourselves to a faithful Creator

FRIDAY
Deuteronomy 1:34-40
The innocent enter the good land
2 Corinthians 5:1-5
What is mortal is swallowed up in life

SATURDAY
Genesis 2:4b-14
The tree of knowledge
Luke 8:4-15
Hearing and living the word of God

DAILY
Psalm 130
With you there is forgiveness

Sunday, June 5–11

Genesis 3:8-15
God confronts Adam and Eve
Psalm 130
With you there is forgiveness
2 Corinthians 4:13—5:1
Renewed in the inner nature
Mark 3:20-35
Doing the work of God

Reflection on Sunday

MONDAY
1 Samuel 16:14-23
David calms Saul's evil spirit
Revelation 20:1-6
The first resurrection

TUESDAY
1 Kings 18:17-40
Elijah destroys the evil prophets
Revelation 20:7-15
Satan's doom

WEDNESDAY
Isaiah 26:16—27:1
God destroys Leviathan
Luke 11:14-28
Jesus and Beelzebul

DAILY
Psalm 74
God will save us from the enemy

Proper 6 [11]

*Sunday between June 12 and 18 inclusive
(if after Trinity Sunday)*

Preparation for Sunday

THURSDAY
1 Samuel 9:15-27
Saul meets Samuel
Hebrews 2:5-9
Christ tastes death for everyone

FRIDAY
1 Samuel 10:1-8
Samuel tells Saul he will be king
Hebrews 11:4-7
Without faith no one can please God

SATURDAY
1 Samuel 13:1-15a
Saul disobeys God
Mark 4:1-20
The parable of the sower

DAILY
Psalm 20
Victory for the anointed one

Sunday, June 12–18

1 Samuel 15:34—16:13
David anointed by Samuel
Psalm 20
Victory for the anointed one
2 Corinthians 5:6-10 [11-13] 14-17
In Christ, a new creation
Mark 4:26-34
The parable of the mustard seed

Reflection on Sunday

MONDAY
1 Samuel 13:23—14:23
Jonathan attacks the Philistines
Galatians 6:11-18
A new creation is everything

TUESDAY
1 Samuel 15:10-23
God rejects Saul
Revelation 21:22—22:5
Tthe tree of life

WEDNESDAY
1 Samuel 15:24-31
Samuel refuses to go with Saul
Luke 6:43-45
A tree and its fruit

DAILY
Psalm 53
God will restore Israel's fortunes

Proper 6 [11]

*Sunday between June 12 and 18 inclusive
(if after Trinity Sunday)*

Preparation for Sunday

THURSDAY
Genesis 3:14-24
Deprived of the tree of life
Hebrews 2:5-9
Christ tastes death for everyone

FRIDAY
1 Kings 10:26—11:8
Cedars more numerous than sycamores
Hebrews 11:4-7
Without faith no one can please God

SATURDAY
2 Kings 14:1-14
A thornbush confronts a cedar of Lebanon
Mark 4:1-20
The parable of the sower

DAILY
Psalm 92:1-4, 12-15
The righteous are like a cedar of Lebanon

Sunday, June 12–18

Ezekiel 17:22-24
The sign of the cedar
Psalm 92:1-4, 12-15
The righteous are like a cedar of Lebanon
2 Corinthians 5:6-10 [11-13] 14-17
In Christ, a new creation
Mark 4:26-34
The parable of the mustard seed

Reflection on Sunday

MONDAY
Ezekiel 31:1-12
Evil can be a towering cedar
Galatians 6:11-18
A new creation is everything

TUESDAY
Jeremiah 21:11-14
A fire in Judah's forest
Revelation 21:22—22:5
Tthe tree of life

WEDNESDAY
Jeremiah 22:1-9
The evil will be cut down
Luke 6:43-45
A tree and its fruit

DAILY
Psalm 52
Like an olive tree in God's house

Proper 7 [12]

Sunday between June 19 and 25 inclusive
(if after Trinity Sunday)

Preparation for Sunday

THURSDAY
1 Samuel 16:14-23
David plays the harp for Saul
Acts 20:1-16
Paul's travels

FRIDAY
1 Samuel 17:55—18:5
David becomes one of Saul's officers
Acts 21:1-16
Paul is warned about future persecution

SATURDAY
1 Samuel 18:1-4
Jonathan covenants with David
Luke 21:25-28
The roaring of the sea and the waves

DAILY
Psalm 9:9-20
Refuge in time of trouble

Sunday, June 19–25

1 Samuel 17:[1a, 4-11, 19-23] 32-49   *or*
David's victory over Goliath
Psalm 9:9-20   *or*
Refuge in time of trouble
2 Corinthians 6:1-13
Paul's defense of his ministry
Mark 4:35-41
Christ calming the sea

1 Samuel 17:57—18:5, 10-16
David becomes one of Saul's officers
Psalm 133
How good it is to live in unity

Reflection on Sunday

MONDAY
1 Samuel 18:6-30
Saul becomes David's enemy
Acts 27:13-38
Paul and the storm at sea

TUESDAY
1 Samuel 19:1-7
Saul plots David's death
Acts 27:39-44
Safe arrival on land

WEDNESDAY
1 Samuel 19:8-17
Michal helps David escape
Mark 6:45-52
Jesus walks on the water

DAILY
Psalm 119:113-128
Do not leave me to my oppressors

SEASON AFTER PENTECOST   YEAR B   162

Proper 7 [12]

*Sunday between June 19 and 25 inclusive
(if after Trinity Sunday)*

Preparation for Sunday

THURSDAY
Job 29:1-20
Job makes his defense
Acts 20:1-16
Paul's travels

FRIDAY
Job 29:21—30:15
Job laments his losses
Acts 21:1-16
Paul is warned about future persecution

SATURDAY
Job 37:1-13
Elihu extols God's power
Luke 21:25-28
The roaring of the sea and the waves

DAILY
Psalm 107:1-3, 23-32
God stilled the storm

Sunday, June 19–25

Job 38:1-11
The Creator of earth and sea
Psalm 107:1-3, 23-32
God stilled the storm
2 Corinthians 6:1-13
Paul's defense of his ministry
Mark 4:35-41
Christ calming the sea

Reflection on Sunday

MONDAY
Exodus 7:14-24
God turns the Nile into blood
Acts 27:13-38
Paul and the storm at sea

TUESDAY
Exodus 9:13-35
God sends hail
Acts 27:39-44
Safe arrival on land

WEDNESDAY
Joshua 10:1-14
God makes the sun stand still
Mark 6:45-52
Jesus walks on the water

DAILY
Psalm 65
God silences the seas

Proper 8 [13]

Sunday between June 26 and July 2 inclusive

Preparation for Sunday

THURSDAY
1 Samuel 19:18-24
Samuel helps David escape
2 Corinthians 7:2-16
Grief leads to repentance

FRIDAY
1 Samuel 20:1-25
Jonathan helps David escape
2 Corinthians 8:1-7
Encouragement to be generous

SATURDAY
1 Samuel 20:27-42
Jonathan helps David escape
Luke 4:31-37
The man with an unclean spirit

DAILY
Psalm 130
Out of the depths have I called

Sunday, June 26–July 2

2 Samuel 1:1, 17-27
Lamentation over Saul and Jonathan
Psalm 130
Out of the depths have I called
2 Corinthians 8:7-15
Excel in generosity, following Jesus
Mark 5:21-43
Christ heals a woman and Jairus' daughter

Reflection on Sunday

MONDAY
1 Samuel 23:14-18
David will be king
2 Corinthians 8:16-24
The administration of generous gifts

TUESDAY
1 Samuel 31:1-13
Saul and his sons die
2 Corinthians 9:1-5
Voluntary gifts, not extortion

WEDNESDAY
1 Chronicles 10:1-14
Jonathan's death
Mark 9:14-29
Jesus heals a child

DAILY
Psalm 18:1-6, 43-50
Steadfast love to God's anointed

Proper 8 [13]
Sunday between June 26 and July 2 inclusive

Preparation for Sunday

THURSDAY
Lamentations 1:16-22
The Lord is in the right
2 Corinthians 7:2-16
Grief leads to repentance

FRIDAY
Lamentations 2:1-12
God's warnings fulfilled
2 Corinthians 8:1-7
Encouragement to be generous

SATURDAY
Lamentations 2:18-22
Pour out your heart before God
Luke 4:31-37
The man with an unclean spirit

DAILY
Psalm 30
You have lifted me up

Sunday, June 26–July 2

Wisdom 1:13-15; 2:23-24   *or*
Humankind made for immortality
Psalm 30
You have lifted me up
2 Corinthians 8:7-15
Excel in generosity, following Jesus
Mark 5:21-43
Christ heals a woman and Jairus' daughter

Lamentations 3:22-33
Great is God's faithfulness

Reflection on Sunday

MONDAY
Leviticus 21:1-15
Dead bodies are unclean
2 Corinthians 8:16-24
The administration of generous gifts

TUESDAY
Leviticus 15:19-31
Bleeding women are unclean
2 Corinthians 9:1-5
Voluntary gifts, not extortion

WEDNESDAY
2 Kings 20:1-11
God heals Hezekiah
Mark 9:14-29
Jesus heals a child

DAILY
Psalm 88
Prayer for restoration

Proper 9 [14]
Sunday between July 3 and 9 inclusive

Preparation for Sunday

THURSDAY
2 Samuel 2:1-11
David becomes king of Judah
1 Corinthians 4:8-13
We are weak, but you are strong

FRIDAY
2 Samuel 3:1-12
Abner pledges support to David
2 Corinthians 10:7-11
Paul's bodily presence is weak

SATURDAY
2 Samuel 3:31-38
David mourns Abner's death
Matthew 8:18-22
The cost of discipleship

DAILY
Psalm 48
God our guide

Sunday, July 3–9

2 Samuel 5:1-5, 9-10
The reign of David
Psalm 48
God our guide
2 Corinthians 12:2-10
God's power made perfect in weakness
Mark 6:1-13
The Twelve sent to preach and heal

Reflection on Sunday

MONDAY
2 Samuel 5:1-10
The taking of Jerusalem
2 Corinthians 11:16-33
Paul's sufferings

TUESDAY
2 Samuel 5:11-16
Hiram recognizes David as king
James 5:7-12
Suffering and patience

WEDNESDAY
2 Samuel 5:17-25
David fights the Philistines
John 7:1-9
Unbelief of Jesus' brothers

DAILY
Psalm 21
The king trusts in the Lord

Proper 9 [14]

Sunday between July 3 and 9 inclusive

Preparation for Sunday

THURSDAY
Jeremiah 7:1-15
Do not trust deceptive words
1 Corinthians 4:8-13
We are weak, but you are strong

FRIDAY
Jeremiah 7:16-26
Walk in the way God commands
2 Corinthians 10:7-11
Paul's bodily presence is weak

SATURDAY
Jeremiah 7:27-34
Disobeying the voice of the Lord
Matthew 8:18-22
The cost of discipleship

DAILY
Psalm 123
Our eyes look to you, O God

Sunday, July 3–9

Ezekiel 2:1-5
The call of Ezekiel
Psalm 123
Our eyes look to you, O God
2 Corinthians 12:2-10
God's power made perfect in weakness
Mark 6:1-13
The Twelve sent to preach and heal

Reflection on Sunday

MONDAY
Ezekiel 2:8—3:11
Ezekiel to eat the scroll
2 Corinthians 11:16-33
Paul's sufferings

TUESDAY
Jeremiah 16:1-13
Jeremiah's celibacy and message
James 5:7-12
Suffering and patience

WEDNESDAY
Jeremiah 16:14-21
God will forgive Israel
John 7:1-9
Unbelief of Jesus' brothers

DAILY
Psalm 119:81-88
The faithful persecuted

Proper 10 [15]

Sunday between July 10 and 16 inclusive

Preparation for Sunday

THURSDAY
Exodus 25:10-22
The ark of the covenant
Colossians 2:1-5
Christ, the mystery of God

FRIDAY
Exodus 37:1-16
Building the ark
Colossians 4:2-18
Declaring the mystery of Christ

SATURDAY
Numbers 10:11-36
The ark leads the Israelites
Luke 1:57-80
The birth of John the Baptist

DAILY
Psalm 24
The King of glory shall come in

Sunday, July 10–16

2 Samuel 6:1-5, 12b-19
David dances before the ark of God
Psalm 24
The King of glory shall come in
Ephesians 1:3-14
Chosen to live in praise of God
Mark 6:14-29
The death of John the Baptist

Reflection on Sunday

MONDAY
2 Samuel 6:6-12a
The ark's power
Acts 21:27-39
Paul arrested

TUESDAY
2 Samuel 3:12-16
David claims his wife Michal
Acts 23:12-35
Plot to kill Paul

WEDNESDAY
2 Samuel 6:16-23
Michal confronts David
Luke 7:31-35
Refusing the witness of John the Baptist and Jesus

DAILY
Psalm 68:24-35
Awesome is God in the sanctuary

Proper 10 [15]

Sunday between July 10 and 16 inclusive

Preparation for Sunday

THURSDAY
Amos 2:6-16
God's condemnation of Israel
Colossians 2:1-5
Christ, the mystery of God

FRIDAY
Amos 3:1-12
Who can but prophesy?
Colossians 4:2-18
Declaring the mystery of Christ

SATURDAY
Amos 4:6-13
Prepare to meet your God
Luke 1:57-80
The birth of John the Baptist

DAILY
Psalm 85:8-13
Listen to what God is saying

Sunday, July 10–16

Amos 7:7-15
The sign of the plumb line
Psalm 85:8-13
Listen to what God is saying
Ephesians 1:3-14
Chosen to live in praise of God
Mark 6:14-29
The death of John the Baptist

Reflection on Sunday

MONDAY
Amos 5:1-9
Seek me and live
Acts 21:27-39
Paul arrested

TUESDAY
Amos 9:1-4
God searches out rebellious Israel
Acts 23:12-35
Plot to kill Paul

WEDNESDAY
Amos 9:11-15
God will restore the fortunes of Israel
Luke 7:31-35
Refusing the witness of John the Baptist and Jesus

DAILY
Psalm 142
Prayer for deliverance

Proper 11 [16]

Sunday between July 17 and 23 inclusive

Preparation for Sunday

THURSDAY
1 Chronicles 11:15-19
Water from Bethlehem's well
Colossians 1:15-23
God reconciles all things through Christ

FRIDAY
1 Chronicles 14:1-2
Hiram builds David a house
Acts 17:16-31
Assurance for all through Christ

SATURDAY
1 Chronicles 15:1-2, 16:4-13
A tent for the ark of God
Luke 18:35-43
Jesus heals a blind beggar

DAILY
Psalm 89:20-37
God's steadfast love

Sunday, July 17–23

2 Samuel 7:1-14a
God's promise to David
Psalm 89:20-37
God's steadfast love
Ephesians 2:11-22
Reconciled to God through Christ
Mark 6:30-34, 53-56
Christ healing the multitudes

Reflection on Sunday

MONDAY
2 Samuel 7:18-29
David gives thanks to God
Hebrews 13:17-25
Jesus, the great shepherd of the sheep

TUESDAY
2 Samuel 8:1-18
David's rule expands
Acts 20:17-38
The elders are shepherds

WEDNESDAY
2 Samuel 9:1-13
David adopts Jonathan's son
Luke 15:1-7
Parable of the lost sheep

DAILY
Psalm 61
Let me abide in your tent forever

Proper 11 [16]
Sunday between July 17 and 23 inclusive

Preparation for Sunday

THURSDAY
Jeremiah 10:1-16
Following scarecrows
Colossians 1:15-23
God reconciles all things through Christ

FRIDAY
Jeremiah 10:17-25
Stupid shepherds scatter the flock
Acts 17:16-31
Assurance for all through Christ

SATURDAY
Jeremiah 12:1-13
Shepherds who destroy God's vineyard
Luke 18:35-43
Jesus heals a blind beggar

DAILY
Psalm 23
The Lord is my shepherd

Sunday, July 17–23

Jeremiah 23:1-6
A righteous shepherd for Israel
Psalm 23
The Lord is my shepherd
Ephesians 2:11-22
Reconciled to God through Christ
Mark 6:30-34, 53-56
Christ healing the multitudes

Reflection on Sunday

MONDAY
Jeremiah 50:1-7
God the true pasture
Hebrews 13:17-25
Jesus, the great shepherd of the sheep

TUESDAY
Zechariah 9:14—10:2
God will save the flock
Acts 20:17-38
The elders are shepherds

WEDNESDAY
2 Samuel 5:1-12
David is to shepherd Israel
Luke 15:1-7
Parable of the lost sheep

DAILY
Psalm 100
We are God's sheep

Proper 12 [17]
Sunday between July 24 and 30 inclusive

Preparation for Sunday

THURSDAY
2 Samuel 10:1-5
The Ammonites dishonor David's envoys
Colossians 1:9-14
Growing in the knowledge of God

FRIDAY
2 Samuel 10:6-12
War with the Ammonites
Colossians 3:12-17
Let the peace of Christ rule in your hearts

SATURDAY
2 Samuel 10:13-19
Ammon defeated
John 4:31-38
Food that you do not know about

DAILY
Psalm 14
God in the company of the righteous

Sunday, July 24–30

2 Samuel 11:1-15
Bathsheba and Uriah wronged by David
Psalm 14
God in the company of the righteous
Ephesians 3:14-21
Prayer to Christ
John 6:1-21
Jesus feeds 5000

Reflection on Sunday

MONDAY
2 Samuel 11:14-21
Uriah killed in battle
Philippians 4:10-20
Christian generosity

TUESDAY
2 Samuel 11:22-27
Uriah's death reported to David
Romans 15:22-33
Gentiles share their material blessings

WEDNESDAY
2 Chronicles 9:29-31
Nathan writes a history
Mark 6:35-44
Jesus feeds 5000

DAILY
Psalm 37:12-22
The wicked plot against the righteous

Proper 12 [17]
Sunday between July 24 and 30 inclusive

Preparation for Sunday

THURSDAY
1 Kings 19:19-21
Elisha becomes Elijah's disciple
Colossians 1:9-14
Growing in the knowledge of God

FRIDAY
2 Kings 3:4-20
Elisha and the miracle of water
Colossians 3:12-17
Let the peace of Christ rule in your hearts

SATURDAY
2 Kings 4:38-41
Elisha purifies the pot of stew
John 4:31-38
Food that you do not know about

DAILY
Psalm 145:10-18
You open wide your hand

Sunday, July 24–30

2 Kings 4:42-44
Elisha feeds a hundred people
Psalm 145:10-18
You open wide your hand
Ephesians 3:14-21
Prayer to Christ
John 6:1-21
Jesus feeds 5000

Reflection on Sunday

MONDAY
Genesis 18:1-15
God eats with Abraham and Sarah
Philippians 4:10-20
Christian generosity

TUESDAY
Exodus 24:1-11
The elders eat with God
Romans 15:22-33
Gentiles share their material blessings

WEDNESDAY
Isaiah 25:6-10a
A feast on the mountain
Mark 6:35-44
Jesus feeds 5000

DAILY
Psalm 111
God gives food

Proper 13 [18]
Sunday between July 31 and August 6 inclusive

Preparation for Sunday

THURSDAY
Exodus 32:19-26a
Anger over the golden calf
1 Corinthians 11:17-22
Abuses at the Lord's Supper

FRIDAY
Joshua 23:1-16
The mighty acts of God
1 Corinthians 11:27-34
Discerning the body of Christ

SATURDAY
Judges 6:1-10
A prophet warns Israel
Matthew 16:5-12
Bread as a sign of other things

DAILY
Psalm 51:1-12
Create in me a clean heart

Sunday, July 31–August 6

2 Samuel 11:26 — 12:13a
David rebuked by Nathan
Psalm 51:1-12
Create in me a clean heart
Ephesians 4:1-16
Maintain the unity of the faith
John 6:24-35
Christ, the bread of life

Reflection on Sunday

MONDAY
2 Samuel 12:15-25
David and Bathsheba's son dies
Ephesians 4:17-24
The new life

TUESDAY
2 Samuel 13:1-19
The rape of Tamar
1 Corinthians 12:27-31
You are the body of Christ

WEDNESDAY
2 Samuel 13:20-36
Absalom's vengeance against Amnon
Mark 8:1-10
Jesus feeds 4000

DAILY
Psalm 50:16-23
God does not remain silent

Proper 13 [18]

Sunday between July 31 and August 6 inclusive

Preparation for Sunday

THURSDAY
Exodus 12:33-42
Unleavened bread for the exodus
1 Corinthians 11:17-22
Abuses at the Lord's Supper

FRIDAY
Exodus 12:43—13:2
Directions for the Passover
1 Corinthians 11:27-34
Discerning the body of Christ

SATURDAY
Exodus 13:3-10
The festival of unleavened bread
Matthew 16:5-12
Bread as a sign of other things

DAILY
Psalm 78:23-29
Manna rains down

Sunday, July 31–August 6

Exodus 16:2-4, 9-15
Manna in the wilderness
Psalm 78:23-29
Manna rains down
Ephesians 4:1-16
Maintain the unity of the faith
John 6:24-35
Christ, the bread of life

Reflection on Sunday

MONDAY
Numbers 11:16-23, 31-32
God sends quail
Ephesians 4:17-24
The new life

TUESDAY
Deuteronomy 8:1-20
You will eat your fill
1 Corinthians 12:27-31
You are the body of Christ

WEDNESDAY
Isaiah 55:1-9
Come and eat
Mark 8:1-10
Jesus feeds 4000

DAILY
Psalm 107:1-3, 33-43
God feeds the hungry

Proper 14 [19]

Sunday between August 7 and 13 inclusive

Preparation for Sunday

THURSDAY
2 Samuel 13:37—14:24
The wise woman of Tekoa
Romans 15:1-6
Living in harmony

FRIDAY
2 Samuel 14:25-33
Absalom shunned by David
Galatians 6:1-10
Bear one another's burdens

SATURDAY
2 Samuel 15:1-13
Absalom rebels against David
Matthew 7:7-11
Bread and stones

DAILY
Psalm 130
Out of the depths have I called

Sunday, August 7–13

2 Samuel 18:5-9, 15, 31-33
David laments Absalom's death
Psalm 130
Out of the depths have I called
Ephesians 4:25—5:2
Put away evil, live in love
John 6:35, 41-51
Christ, the bread of life

Reflection on Sunday

MONDAY
2 Samuel 15:13-31
David leaves Jerusalem
Ephesians 5:1-14
Fruits of the light

TUESDAY
2 Samuel 18:19-33
David learns of Absalom's death
2 Peter 3:14-18
Grow in grace and knowledge

WEDNESDAY
2 Samuel 19:1-18
Israel and Judah want David back
John 6:35-40
Doing God's will

DAILY
Psalm 57
I cry to God Most High

Proper 14 [19]

Sunday between August 7 and 13 inclusive

Preparation for Sunday

THURSDAY
1 Samuel 28:20-25
Food for Saul's journey
Romans 15:1-6
Living in harmony

FRIDAY
2 Samuel 17:15-29
Food in the wilderness
Galatians 6:1-10
Bear one another's burdens

SATURDAY
1 Kings 2:1-9
David's instructions to Solomon
Matthew 7:7-11
Bread and stones

DAILY
Psalm 34:1-8
Taste and see

Sunday, August 7–13

1 Kings 19:4-8
Elijah given bread for his journey
Psalm 34:1-8
Taste and see
Ephesians 4:25—5:2
Put away evil, live in love
John 6:35, 41-51
Christ, the bread of life

Reflection on Sunday

MONDAY
1 Kings 17:1-16
God feeds the widow of Zarephath
Ephesians 5:1-14
Fruits of the light

TUESDAY
Ruth 2:1-23
Ruth gleans in Boaz's field
2 Peter 3:14-18
Grow in grace and knowledge

WEDNESDAY
Jeremiah 31:1-6
God promises fruitful vineyards
John 6:35-40
Doing God's will

DAILY
Psalm 81
God will feed us

Proper 15 [20]

Sunday between August 14 and 20 inclusive

Preparation for Sunday

THURSDAY
1 Kings 1:1-30
Adonijah tries to become king
Acts 6:8-15
Stephen's compelling wisdom

FRIDAY
1 Kings 1:28-48
Solomon becomes king
Romans 16:17-20
Being wise in what is good

SATURDAY
1 Kings 2:1-11
David's instructions to Solomon
John 4:7-26
Christ, the living water

DAILY
Psalm 111
The beginning of wisdom

Sunday, August 14–20

1 Kings 2:10-12; 3:3-14
Solomon's prayer for wisdom
Psalm 111
The beginning of wisdom
Ephesians 5:15-20
Filled with the Spirit
John 6:51-58
Christ, the true food and drink

Reflection on Sunday

MONDAY
1 Kings 3:16-28
Solomon's wisdom displayed
Acts 6:1-7
Deacons chosen to distribute food

TUESDAY
1 Kings 7:1-12
Solomon's palace is built
Acts 7:9-16
Joseph's family is fed in Egypt

WEDNESDAY
1 Kings 8:1-21
The ark of the covenant
Mark 8:14-21
Jesus teaches about bread

DAILY
Psalm 101
I will walk with integrity of heart

Proper 15 [20]

Sunday between August 14 and 20 inclusive

Preparation for Sunday

THURSDAY
Job 11:1-20
Zophar counsels Job about wisdom
Acts 6:8-15
Stephen's compelling wisdom

FRIDAY
Job 12:1-25
Job sees wisdom and strength in God
Romans 16:17-20
Being wise in what is good

SATURDAY
Job 13:1-19
When silence is wisdom
John 4:7-26
Christ, the living water

DAILY
Psalm 34:9-14
Seeking God

Sunday, August 14–20

Proverbs 9:1-6
Invited to dine at wisdom's feast
Psalm 34:9-14
Seeking God
Ephesians 5:15-20
Filled with the Spirit
John 6:51-58
Christ, the true food and drink

Reflection on Sunday

MONDAY
Genesis 43:1-15
Joseph's brothers need food
Acts 6:1-7
Deacons chosen to distribute food

TUESDAY
Genesis 45:1-15
Joseph provides food
Acts 7:9-16
Joseph's family is fed in Egypt

WEDNESDAY
Genesis 47:13-26
Famine even in Egypt
Mark 8:14-21
Jesus teaches about bread

DAILY
Psalm 36
God saves humans and animals

Proper 16 [21]

Sunday between August 21 and 27 inclusive

Preparation for Sunday

THURSDAY
1 Kings 4:20-28
The size of Solomon's kingdom
1 Thessalonians 5:1-11
The breastplate of faith and love

SATURDAY
1 Kings 5:1-12
Hiram asked to help build the temple
Luke 11:5-13
Ask, and it will be given

FRIDAY
1 Kings 4:29-34
Solomon's wisdom recognized
Romans 13:11-14
Put on the armor of light

DAILY
Psalm 84
How dear is God's dwelling

Sunday, August 21–27

1 Kings 8:[1, 6, 10-11] 22-30, 41-43
Solomon's prayer at the temple dedication
Psalm 84
How dear is God's dwelling
Ephesians 6:10-20
Put on the armor of God
John 6:56-69
The bread of eternal life

Reflection on Sunday

MONDAY
1 Kings 5:13-18
Solomon's workers
Ephesians 5:21—6:9
A household code

WEDNESDAY
1 Kings 6:15-38
The temple interior is completed
John 15:16-25
I chose you

TUESDAY
1 Kings 6:1-14
The temple exterior is completed
Ephesians 6:21-24
Peace to the whole community

DAILY
Psalm 11
God sees all from the heavenly temple

SEASON AFTER PENTECOST   YEAR B   180

Proper 16 [21]

Sunday between August 21 and 27 inclusive

Preparation for Sunday

THURSDAY
Joshua 22:1-9
Joshua blesses eastern tribes
1 Thessalonians 5:1-11
The breastplate of faith and love

FRIDAY
Joshua 22:10-20
Concern about loyalty to God
Romans 13:11-14
Put on the armor of light

SATURDAY
Joshua 22:21-34
An altar to the one Lord
Luke 11:5-13
Ask, and it will be given

DAILY
Psalm 34:15-22
God's eyes are upon the righteous

Sunday, August 21–27

Joshua 24:1-2a, 14-18
Serve the Lord
Psalm 34:15-22
God's eyes are upon the righteous
Ephesians 6:10-20
Put on the armor of God
John 6:56-69
The bread of eternal life

Reflection on Sunday

MONDAY
Nehemiah 9:1-15
God's care of the people
Ephesians 5:21—6:9
A household code

TUESDAY
Nehemiah 9:16-31
Nehemiah confesses the people's sin
Ephesians 6:21-24
Peace to the whole community

WEDNESDAY
Isaiah 33:10-16
The righteous will eat
John 15:16-25
I chose you

DAILY
Psalm 119:97-104
God's word is sweet

Proper 17 [22]
Sunday between August 28 and September 3 inclusive

Preparation for Sunday

THURSDAY
Song of Solomon 1:1-17
Love better than wine
James 1:1-8
One who doubts is like a wave of the sea

FRIDAY
Song of Solomon 2:1-7
Love makes everything beautiful
James 1:9-16
Blessed are those who endure temptation

SATURDAY
Hosea 3:1-5
God loves faithless Israel
John 18:28-32
Ritual defilement and the Passover

DAILY
Psalm 45:1-2, 6-9
Anointed with the oil of gladness

Sunday, August 28–September 3

Song of Solomon 2:8-13
Song of two lovers
Psalm 45:1-2, 6-9
Anointed with the oil of gladness
James 1:17-27
Be doers of the word
Mark 7:1-8, 14-15, 21-23
Authentic religion

Reflection on Sunday

MONDAY
Song of Solomon 3:6-11
Groom and wedding party
1 Timothy 4:6-16
Set the believers an example

TUESDAY
Song of Solomon 5:2—6:3
A dream of love
1 Peter 2:19-25
Christ leaves an example

WEDNESDAY
Song of Solomon 8:5-7
Love cannot be quenched
Mark 7:9-23
Jesus teaches about tradition

DAILY
Psalm 144:9-15
The blessing of sons and daughters

Proper 17 [22]

Sunday between August 28 and September 3 inclusive

Preparation for Sunday

THURSDAY
Exodus 32:1-14
The Israelites make themselves a god
James 1:1-8
One who doubts is like a wave of the sea

FRIDAY
Exodus 32:15-35
Moses punishes the Israelites' evil
James 1:9-16
Blessed are those who endure temptation

SATURDAY
Exodus 34:8-28
The covenant renewed
John 18:28-32
Ritual defilement and the Passover

DAILY
Psalm 15
Dwelling in God's tabernacle

Sunday, August 28–September 3

Deuteronomy 4:1-2, 6-9
God's law: sign of a great nation
Psalm 15
Dwelling in God's tabernacle
James 1:17-27
Be doers of the word
Mark 7:1-8, 14-15, 21-23
Authentic religion

Reflection on Sunday

MONDAY
Deuteronomy 4:9-14
Teach your children
1 Timothy 4:6-16
Set the believers an example

TUESDAY
Deuteronomy 4:15-20
Do not be led astray
1 Peter 2:19-25
Christ leaves an example

WEDNESDAY
Deuteronomy 4:21-40
Moses urges faithfulness
Mark 7:9-23
Jesus teaches about tradition

DAILY
Psalm 106:1-6, 13-23, 47-48
God will remember the people

Proper 18 [23]
Sunday between September 4 and 10 inclusive

Preparation for Sunday

THURSDAY
Proverbs 1:1-19
Warnings against bad friends
Romans 2:1-11
Divine judgment applies to all

FRIDAY
Proverbs 4:10-27
The right and wrong ways
Romans 2:12-16
Gentiles obey the law instinctively

SATURDAY
Proverbs 8:1-31
In praise of wisdom
Matthew 15:21-31
Jesus heals

DAILY
Psalm 125
Trust in the Lord

Sunday, September 4–10

Proverbs 22:1-2, 8-9, 22-23
A good name
Psalm 125
Trust in the Lord
James 2:1-10 [11-13] 14-17
Faith without works is dead
Mark 7:24-37
Christ heals a little girl and a deaf man

Reflection on Sunday

MONDAY
Proverbs 8:32—9:6
Wisdom speaks
Hebrews 11:29—12:2
The heroes of faith

TUESDAY
Proverbs 11:1-31
Watch what you say and do
Hebrews 12:3-13
Trials for the sake of discipline

WEDNESDAY
Proverbs 14:1-9
Wisdom makes good sense
Matthew 17:14-21
Healing by faith

DAILY
Psalm 73:1-20
I saw the prosperity of the wicked

Proper 18 [23]

Sunday between September 4 and 10 inclusive

Preparation for Sunday

THURSDAY
Isaiah 30:27-33
God sifts the nations
Romans 2:1-11
Divine judgment applies to all

FRIDAY
Isaiah 32:1-8
The noble stand by noble things
Romans 2:12-16
Gentiles obey the law instinctively

SATURDAY
Isaiah 33:1-9
The fear of God is Zion's treasure
Matthew 15:21-31
Jesus heals

DAILY
Psalm 146
Help and hope come from God

Sunday, September 4–10

Isaiah 35:4-7a
God comes with healing
Psalm 146
Help and hope come from God
James 2:1-10 [11-13] 14-17
Faith without works is dead
Mark 7:24-37
Christ heals a little girl and a deaf man

Reflection on Sunday

MONDAY
Joshua 6:1-21
The Israelites conquer Jericho
Hebrews 11:29 — 12:2
The heroes of faith

TUESDAY
Joshua 8:1-23
The Israelites conquer Ai
Hebrews 12:3-13
Trials for the sake of discipline

WEDNESDAY
Judges 15:9-20
Samson slays the Philistines
Matthew 17:14-21
Healing by faith

DAILY
Canticle: Isaiah 38:10-20
Prayer for health

Proper 19 [24]
Sunday between September 11 and 17 inclusive

Preparation for Sunday

THURSDAY
Proverbs 15:1-17
God sees everything
Hebrews 11:17-22
Abraham, Isaac, and Jacob act on faith

FRIDAY
Proverbs 19:24-29
It is wise to be patient
James 2:17-26
Abraham and Rahab's faith

SATURDAY
Proverbs 21:1-17
God is in charge
Matthew 21:23-32
The faith of tax collectors and prostitutes

DAILY
Psalm 19
God's statutes rejoice the heart

Sunday, September 11–17

Proverbs 1:20-33
Wisdom's rebuke to the foolish
Psalm 19
God's statutes rejoice the heart
James 3:1-12
Dangers of the unbridled tongue
Mark 8:27-38
Peter's confession of faith

or

Wisdom 7:26—8:1
Ther person who lives with wisdom

Reflection on Sunday

MONDAY
Proverbs 22:1-21
Thirty wise sayings
Romans 3:9-20
The unrighteous tongue deceives

TUESDAY
Proverbs 25:1-28
More wise sayings
Colossians 3:1-11
Rid your mouth of abusive language

WEDNESDAY
Proverbs 29:1-27
Use good sense
John 7:25-36
Jesus the Messiah

DAILY
Psalm 73:21-28
You guide me with your counsel

Proper 19 [24]

Sunday between September 11 and 17 inclusive

Preparation for Sunday

THURSDAY
Joshua 2:1-14
Rahab shelters Joshua's spies
Hebrews 11:17-22
Abraham, Isaac, and Jacob act on faith

SATURDAY
Joshua 6:22-27
Rahab and her family are spared
Matthew 21:23-32
The faith of tax collectors and prostitutes

FRIDAY
Joshua 2:15-24
An oath to save Rahab and her family
James 2:17-26
Abraham and Rahab's faith

DAILY
Psalm 116:1-9
I will walk in God's presence

Sunday, September 11–17

Isaiah 50:4-9a
The servant is vindicated by God
Psalm 116:1-9
I will walk in God's presence
James 3:1-12
Dangers of the unbridled tongue
Mark 8:27-38
Peter's confession of faith

Reflection on Sunday

MONDAY
1 Kings 13:1-10
Obeying the word of God
Romans 3:9-20
The unrighteous tongue deceives

WEDNESDAY
Isaiah 10:12-20
Evil will be destroyed
John 7:25-36
Jesus the messiah

TUESDAY
1 Kings 13:11-25
Disobeying the word of God
Colossians 3:1-11
Rid your mouth of abusive language

DAILY
Psalm 119:169-176
God's law my delight

Proper 20 [25]

Sunday between September 18 and 24 inclusive

Preparation for Sunday

THURSDAY
Proverbs 30:1-10
Sayings of Agur
1 Corinthians 2:1-5
Beyond human wisdom

FRIDAY
Proverbs 30:18-33
More sayings of Agur
Romans 11:25-32
Do not claim to be wiser than you are

SATURDAY
Ecclesiastes 1:1-18
It is senseless to be wise
Matthew 23:29-39
Woe to those who kill and crucify the prophets

DAILY
Psalm 1
Delight in God's law

Sunday, September 18–24

Proverbs 31:10-31
The capable wife
Psalm 1
Delight in God's law
James 3:13 — 4:3, 7-8a
The wisdom from above
Mark 9:30-37
Prediction of the passion

Reflection on Sunday

MONDAY
Proverbs 27:1-27
Don't brag about tomorrow
James 4:8-17
Draw near to God

TUESDAY
Ecclesiastes 4:9-16
It is better to have a friend
James 5:1-6
A warning to those who trust in riches

WEDNESDAY
Ecclesiastes 5:1-20
Be careful how you worship
John 8:21-38
Being disciples of Jesus

DAILY
Psalm 128
Your wife like a fruitful vine

YEAR B

SEASON AFTER PENTECOST

Proper 20 [25]

Sunday between September 18 and 24 inclusive

Preparation for Sunday

THURSDAY

Judges 6:1-10

Israel ignores a prophet of God

1 Corinthians 2:1-5

Beyond human wisdom

FRIDAY

1 Kings 22:24-40

A prophet imprisoned

Romans 11:25-32

Do not claim to be wiser than you are

SATURDAY

2 Kings 17:5-18

Israel refuses to listen to the prophets

Matthew 23:29-39

Woe to those who kill and crucify the prophets

DAILY

Psalm 54

God is my helper

Sunday, September 18–24

Wisdom 1:16—2:1, 12-22

The righteous shall live

Psalm 54

God is my helper

James 3:13—4:3, 7-8a

The wisdom from above

Mark 9:30-37

Prediction of the passion

or   Jeremiah 11:18-20

The prophet is like a lamb

Reflection on Sunday

MONDAY

2 Kings 5:1-14

The girl servant saves her master

James 4:8-17

Draw near to God

TUESDAY

2 Kings 11:21—12:16

The boy king repairs the temple

James 5:1-6

A warning to those who trust in riches

WEDNESDAY

Jeremiah 1:4-10

God calls Jeremiah

John 8:21-38

Being disciples of Jesus

DAILY

Psalm 139:1-18

Formed in my mother's womb

Proper 21 [26]

Sunday between September 25 and October 1 inclusive

Preparation for Sunday

THURSDAY
Esther 1:1-21
Vashti disobeys Xerxes
Acts 4:13-31
The believers pray for boldness

FRIDAY
Esther 2:1-23
Esther becomes queen
Acts 12:20-25
A leader fails to give glory to God

SATURDAY
Esther 3:1-15
Haman plans to destroy the Jews
Matthew 5:13-20
You are salt and light

DAILY
Psalm 124
Escaped from the snare of the fowler

Sunday, September 25–October 1

Esther 7:1-6, 9-10; 9:20-22
Esther's intercession
Psalm 124
Escaped from the snare of the fowler
James 5:13-20
Prayer and anointing in the community
Mark 9:38-50
Warnings to those who obstruct faith

Reflection on Sunday

MONDAY
Esther 4:1-17
Mordecai seeks Esther's help
1 Peter 1:3-9
The outcome of faith is salvation

TUESDAY
Esther 5:1-14
Haman plots to kill Mordecai
1 John 2:18-25
Anointed by the Holy One

WEDNESDAY
Esther 8:1-17
A happy ending for the Jews
Matthew 18:6-9
Causing others to stumble

DAILY
Psalm 140
Deliver me from evildoers

Proper 21 [26]

Sunday between September 25 and October 1 inclusive

Preparation for Sunday

THURSDAY
Exodus 18:13-27
Moses appoints judges to keep peace
Acts 4:13-31
The believers pray for boldness

FRIDAY
Deuteronomy 1:1-18
Moses charges the judges
Acts 12:20-25
A leader fails to give glory to God

SATURDAY
Deuteronomy 27:1-10
Moses and the elders charge Israel
Matthew 5:13-20
You are salt and light

DAILY
Psalm 19:7-14
The law gives light

Sunday, September 25–October 1

Numbers 11:4-6, 10-16, 24-29
The spirit is upon seventy elders
Psalm 19:7-14
The law gives light
James 5:13-20
Prayer and anointing in the community
Mark 9:38-50
Warnings to those who obstruct faith

Reflection on Sunday

MONDAY
Zechariah 6:9-15
Far and near led to build the temple
1 Peter 1:3-9
The outcome of faith is salvation

TUESDAY
Zechariah 8:18-23
The nations seek God in Jerusalem
1 John 2:18-25
Anointed by the Holy One

WEDNESDAY
Zechariah 10:1-12
God will gather the people
Matthew 18:6-9
Causing others to stumble

DAILY
Psalm 5
Lead me in righteousness

Proper 22 [27]
Sunday between October 2 and 8 inclusive

Preparation for Sunday

THURSDAY
Job 2:11 — 3:26
Job and his friends
Galatians 3:23-29
Children of God in Christ

FRIDAY
Job 4:1-21
Eliphaz's first speech
Romans 8:1-11
Life in the Spirit

SATURDAY
Job 7:1-21
Job asks why life is so hard
Luke 16:14-18
The law endures

DAILY
Psalm 26
Your love is before my eyes

Sunday, October 2–8

Job 1:1; 2:1-10
Job's integrity in suffering
Psalm 26
Your love is before my eyes
Hebrews 1:1-4; 2:5-12
God has spoken by a Son
Mark 10:2-16
Teaching on marriage

Reflection on Sunday

MONDAY
Job 8:1-22
Bildad's first speech
1 Corinthians 7:1-9
Guidance for the married

TUESDAY
Job 11:1-20
Zophar's first speech
1 Corinthians 7:10-16
Divorce discouraged

WEDNESDAY
Job 15:1-35
Eliphaz's second speech
Matthew 5:27-36
Teachings about marriage and vow-making

DAILY
Psalm 55:1-15
It is not enemies who taunt me

Proper 22 [27]

Sunday between October 2 and 8 inclusive

Preparation for Sunday

THURSDAY
Genesis 20:1-18
Abraham pretends Sarah is his sister
Galatians 3:23-29
Children of God in Christ

FRIDAY
Genesis 21:22-34
Abraham reconciles with Abimelech
Romans 8:1-11
Life in the Spirit

SATURDAY
Genesis 23:1-20
Abraham buries Sarah
Luke 16:14-18
The law endures

DAILY
Psalm 8
You adorn us with glory and honor

Sunday, October 2–8

Genesis 2:18-24
Created for relationship
Psalm 8
You adorn us with glory and honor
Hebrews 1:1-4; 2:5-12
God has spoken by a Son
Mark 10:2-16
Teaching on marriage

Reflection on Sunday

MONDAY
Deuteronomy 22:13-30
Laws about sexual relations
1 Corinthians 7:1-9
Guidance for the married

TUESDAY
Deuteronomy 24:1-5
Laws about divorce
1 Corinthians 7:10-16
Divorce discouraged

WEDNESDAY
Jeremiah 3:6-14
God will forgive the unfaithful
Matthew 5:27-36
Teachings about marriage and vow-making

DAILY
Psalm 112
Happy are those who fear God

Proper 23 [28]
Sunday between October 9 and 15 inclusive

Preparation for Sunday

THURSDAY
Job 17:1-16
Job complains to God
Hebrews 3:7-19
Against disobedience

FRIDAY
Job 18:1-21
Bildad's second speech
Hebrews 4:1-11
The rest that God promised

SATURDAY
Job 20:1-29
Zophar's second speech
Matthew 15:1-9
Jesus teaches true commandments

DAILY
Psalm 22:1-15
Why have you forsaken me?

Sunday, October 9–15

Job 23:1-9, 16-17
The Almighty hidden from Job
Psalm 22:1-15
Why have you forsaken me?
Hebrews 4:12-16
Approach the throne of grace
Mark 10:17-31
Teaching on wealth and reward

Reflection on Sunday

MONDAY
Job 26:1-14
Who can understand God's power?
Revelation 7:9-17
The nations stand before God's throne

TUESDAY
Job 28:12—29:10
Where is wisdom found?
Revelation 8:1-5
The saints' prayers before God

WEDNESDAY
Job 32:1-22
Elihu is upset with Job's friends
Luke 16:19-31
Lazarus comforted by Abraham

DAILY
Psalm 39
Worn down by the blows of your hands

Proper 23 [28]

Sunday between October 9 and 15 inclusive

Preparation for Sunday

THURSDAY
Deuteronomy 5:1-21
The Ten Commandments
Hebrews 3:7-19
Against disobedience

FRIDAY
Deuteronomy 5:22-33
Moses meditates on God's word
Hebrews 4:1-11
The rest that God promised

SATURDAY
Amos 3:13—4:5
Judgment against oppressors
Matthew 15:1-9
Jesus teaches true commandments

DAILY
Psalm 90:12-17
Teach us to number our days

Sunday, October 9–15

Amos 5:6-7, 10-15
Turn from injustice to the poor
Psalm 90:12-17
Teach us to number our days
Hebrews 4:12-16
Approach the throne of grace
Mark 10:17-31
Teaching on wealth and reward

Reflection on Sunday

MONDAY
Obadiah 1-9
Those who ate your bread set a trap
Revelation 7:9-17
The nations stand before God's throne

TUESDAY
Obadiah 10-16
Do not gloat over another's misfortune
Revelation 8:1-5
The saints' prayers before God

WEDNESDAY
Obadiah 17-21
The dispossessed shall possess the land
Luke 16:19-31
Lazarus comforted by Abraham

DAILY
Psalm 26
Prayer for acceptance

Proper 24 [29]

Sunday between October 16 and 22 inclusive

Preparation for Sunday

THURSDAY
Job 36:1-16
God watches everything we do
Romans 15:7-13
The Gentiles glorify God

FRIDAY
Job 37:1-24
Elihu continues: I am afraid
Revelation 17:1-18
Earth's kings conquered

SATURDAY
Job 39:1-30
God confronts Job
Luke 22:24-30
The greatness of one who serves

DAILY
Psalm 104:1-9, 24, 35b
In wisdom you have made them all

Sunday, October 16–22

Job 38:1-7 [34-41]
God challenges Job
Psalm 104:1-9, 24, 35b
In wisdom you have made them all
Hebrews 5:1-10
Through suffering Christ saves
Mark 10:35-45
Warnings to ambitious disciples

Reflection on Sunday

MONDAY
Job 40:1-24
God is all-powerful
Hebrews 6:1-12
The peril of falling away

TUESDAY
Job 41:1-11
God confronts Job
Hebrews 6:13-20
The hope of God's promise

WEDNESDAY
Job 41:12-34
God's creative power
John 13:1-17
Jesus washes the disciples' feet

DAILY
Psalm 75
People will tell of your wondrous deeds

Proper 24 [29]

Sunday between October 16 and 22 inclusive

Preparation for Sunday

THURSDAY
Genesis 14:17-24
Abram is blessed by Melchizedek
Romans 15:7-13
The Gentiles glorify God

FRIDAY
Isaiah 47:1-9
Throneless nations
Revelation 17:1-18
Earth's kings conquered

SATURDAY
Isaiah 47:10-15
Futile trust in those who cannot save
Luke 22:24-30
The greatness of one who serves

DAILY
Psalm 91:9-16
The Most High, your refuge

Sunday, October 16–22

Isaiah 53:4-12
The suffering servant
Psalm 91:9-16
The Most High, your refuge
Hebrews 5:1-10
Through suffering Christ saves
Mark 10:35-45
Warnings to ambitious disciples

Reflection on Sunday

MONDAY
1 Samuel 8:1-18
Samuel warns against kings
Hebrews 6:1-12
The peril of falling away

TUESDAY
1 Samuel 10:17-25
Saul proclaimed king
Hebrews 6:13-20
The hope of God's promise

WEDNESDAY
1 Samuel 12:1-25
Israel admonished to fear God
John 13:1-17
Jesus washes the disciples' feet

DAILY
Psalm 37:23-40
God will exalt the righteous

Proper 25 [30]

Sunday between October 23 and 29 inclusive

Preparation for Sunday

THURSDAY
2 Kings 20:12-19
God's word comes to Hezekiah
Hebrews 7:1-10
The priestly order of Melchizedek

FRIDAY
Nehemiah 1:1-11
Nehemiah prays for restoration
Hebrews 7:11-22
Jesus is like Melchizedek

SATURDAY
Job 42:7-9
God corrects Job's friends
Mark 8:22-26
Jesus heals a blind man

DAILY
Psalm 34:1-8 [19-22]
Taste and see

Sunday, October 23–29

Job 42:1-6, 10-17
Job's restoration
Psalm 34:1-8 [19-22]
Taste and see
Hebrews 7:23-28
Christ, the merciful high priest
Mark 10:46-52
Christ heals blind Bartimaeus

Reflection on Sunday

MONDAY
Isaiah 59:9-19
The people confess their sins
1 Peter 2:1-10
Called to a holy priesthood

TUESDAY
Ezekiel 18:1-32
The righteous are not to blame
Acts 9:32-35
The healing of Aeneas

WEDNESDAY
Ezekiel 14:12-23
Job an example of righteousness
Matthew 20:29-34
Jesus heals two who are blind

DAILY
Psalm 28
God, my strength and shield

SEASON AFTER PENTECOST   198   YEAR B

Proper 25 [30]
Sunday between October 23 and 29 inclusive

Preparation for Sunday

THURSDAY
Jeremiah 23:9-15
False prophets of hope denounced
Hebrews 7:1-10
The priestly order of Melchizedek

FRIDAY
Jeremiah 26:12-24
Jeremiah threatened with death
Hebrews 7:11-22
Jesus is like Melchizedek

SATURDAY
Jeremiah 29:24-32
A false prophet exposed by Jeremiah
Mark 8:22-26
Jesus heals a blind man

DAILY
Psalm 126
Sowing with tears, reaping with joy

Sunday, October 23–29

Jeremiah 31:7-9
The remnant of Israel is gathered
Psalm 126
Sowing with tears, reaping with joy
Hebrews 7:23-28
Christ, the merciful high priest
Mark 10:46-52
Christ heals blind Bartimaeus

Reflection on Sunday

MONDAY
Exodus 4:1-17
Moses' power from God
1 Peter 2:1-10
Called to a holy priesthood

TUESDAY
2 Kings 6:8-23
Elisha has power over sight
Acts 9:32-35
The healing of Aeneas

WEDNESDAY
Jeremiah 33:1-11
God promises healing
Matthew 20:29-34
Jesus heals two who are blind

DAILY
Psalm 119:17-24
Open my eyes

Proper 26 [31]

Sunday between October 30 and November 5 inclusive

Preparation for Sunday

THURSDAY
Ruth 1:18-22
Ruth and Naomi
Hebrews 9:1-12
Temple sacrifices and Christ

FRIDAY
Ruth 2:1-9
Ruth meets Boaz
Romans 3:21-31
Atonement through Christ's blood

SATURDAY
Ruth 2:10-14
Boaz protects Ruth
Luke 10:25-37
Who is my neighbor?

DAILY
Psalm 146
God lifts those bowed down

Sunday, October 30–November 5

Ruth 1:1-18
Ruth remains with Naomi
Psalm 146
God lifts those bowed down
Hebrews 9:11-14
Redeemed through Christ's blood
Mark 12:28-34
Two commandments: love God and neighbor

Reflection on Sunday

MONDAY
Ruth 2:15-23
Boaz protects Ruth
Romans 12:17-21; 13:8-10
Love does no wrong to a neighbor

TUESDAY
Ruth 3:1-7
Naomi makes plans for Ruth
Acts 7:17-29
Moses becomes a resident alien

WEDNESDAY
Ruth 3:8-18
Ruth sleeps with Boaz
John 13:31-35
Commandment to love one another

DAILY
Psalm 18:20-30
You show yourself loyal

Proper 26 [31]

Sunday between October 30 and November 5 inclusive

Preparation for Sunday

THURSDAY
Exodus 22:1-15
Rules for relations with neighbors
Hebrews 9:1-12
Temple sacrifices and Christ

FRIDAY
Leviticus 19:32-37
Aliens to be treated as fellow citizens
Romans 3:21-31
Atonement through Christ's blood

SATURDAY
Numbers 9:9-14
The same statute for all
Luke 10:25-37
Who is my neighbor?

DAILY
Psalm 119:1-8
Seeking God with all our hearts

Sunday, October 30–November 5

Deuteronomy 6:1-9
Keeping the words of God
Psalm 119:1-8
Seeking God with all our hearts
Hebrews 9:11-14
Redeemed through Christ's blood
Mark 12:28-34
Two commandments: love God and neighbor

Reflection on Sunday

MONDAY
Deuteronomy 6:10-25
Keeping the commandments
Romans 12:17-21; 13:8-10
Love does no wrong to a neighbor

TUESDAY
Deuteronomy 28:58—29:1
Warnings against disobedience
Acts 7:17-29
Moses, becomes a resident alien

WEDNESDAY
Micah 6:1-8
Do justice
John 13:31-35
Commandment to love one another

DAILY
Psalm 51
A contrite heart

Proper 27 [32]

Sunday between November 6 and 12 inclusive

Preparation for Sunday

THURSDAY
Ruth 4:1-10
Boaz makes marriage plans
Romans 5:6-11
Justified by Christ's blood

FRIDAY
Ruth 4:11-17
Boaz and Ruth are married
Hebrews 9:15-24
The blood of the old covenant

SATURDAY
Ruth 4:18-22
Ruth the ancestor of King David
Mark 11:12-14, 20-24
Condemnation and blessing

DAILY
Psalm 127
Children a heritage from the Lord

Sunday, November 6–12

Ruth 3:1-5; 4:13-17
Ruth wins the favor of Boaz
Psalm 127
Children a heritage from the Lord
Hebrews 9:24-28
The sacrifice of Christ
Mark 12:38-44
A widow's generosity

Reflection on Sunday

MONDAY
Genesis 24:1-10
Isaac's marriage arranged
1 Timothy 5:1-8
Widows set their hope on God

TUESDAY
Genesis 24:11-27
Rebekah at the well
1 Timothy 5:9-16
The church assists widows

WEDNESDAY
Genesis 24:28-42
Abraham's servant finds Isaac a wife
Luke 4:16-30
Jesus praises a foreign widow

DAILY
Psalm 113
You give the barren woman a home

Proper 27 [32]

Sunday between November 6 and 12 inclusive

Preparation for Sunday

THURSDAY
Numbers 36:1-13
Women spared from poverty
Romans 5:6-11
Justified by Christ's blood

FRIDAY
Deuteronomy 15:1-11
Open your hand to the poor
Hebrews 9:15-24
The blood of the old covenant

SATURDAY
Deuteronomy 24:17-22
Laws concerning the poor
Mark 11:12-14, 20-24
Condemnation and blessing

DAILY
Psalm 146
God lifts those bowed down

Sunday, November 6–12

1 Kings 17:8-16
God feeds Elijah and the widow
Psalm 146
God lifts those bowed down
Hebrews 9:24-28
The sacrifice of Christ
Mark 12:38-44
A widow's generosity

Reflection on Sunday

MONDAY
Ruth 1:1-22
The widow's poverty
1 Timothy 5:1-8
Widows set their hope on God

TUESDAY
Ruth 3:14—4:6
The widow's next of kin receive her
1 Timothy 5:9-16
The church assists widows

WEDNESDAY
Ruth 4:7-22
The widow's life restored
Luke 4:16-30
Jesus praises a foreign widow

DAILY
Psalm 94
God will vindicate the righteous

Proper 28 [33]

Sunday between November 13 and 19 inclusive

Preparation for Sunday

THURSDAY
1 Samuel 1:21-28
Hannah gives Samuel to God
1 Timothy 6:11-21
Life that really is life

FRIDAY
1 Samuel 2:18-21
Hannah visits Samuel
Colossians 2:6-15
Christ, the head of every ruler and authority

SATURDAY
1 Samuel 3:1-18
God speaks to Samuel
Mark 12:1-12
The stone which the builders rejected

DAILY
1 Samuel 2:1-10
My heart exults

Sunday, November 13–19

1 Samuel 1:4-20
Hannah's prayers answered
1 Samuel 2:1-10
My heart exults
Hebrews 10:11-14 [15-18] 19-25
The way to God through Christ
Mark 13:1-8
The end and the coming of the Son

Reflection on Sunday

MONDAY
1 Samuel 3:19—4:2
God helps Samuel
Hebrews 10:26-31
Falling into the hands of the living God

TUESDAY
Deuteronomy 26:5-10
Thanksgiving for harvest
Hebrews 10:32-39
Call for endurance

WEDNESDAY
1 Kings 8:22-30
Solomon's prayer
Mark 13:9-23
The coming sufferings

DAILY
Psalm 3
Deliverance belongs to God

Proper 28 [33]

Sunday between November 13 and 19 inclusive

Preparation for Sunday

THURSDAY
Daniel 4:4-18
Nebuchadnezzar's dream
1 Timothy 6:11-21
Life that really is life

FRIDAY
Daniel 4:19-27
Nebuchadnezzar's dream interpreted
Colossians 2:6-15
Christ, the head of every ruler and authority

SATURDAY
Daniel 4:28-37
Nebuchadnezzar praises God
Mark 12:1-12
The stone which the builders rejected

DAILY
Psalm 16
My heart is glad

Sunday, November 13–19

Daniel 12:1-3
God will deliver the people
Psalm 16
My heart is glad
Hebrews 10:11-14 [15-18] 19-25
The way to God through Christ
Mark 13:1-8
The end and the coming of the Son

Reflection on Sunday

MONDAY
Daniel 8:1-14
A vision of destructive power
Hebrews 10:26-31
Falling into the hands of the living God

TUESDAY
Daniel 8:15-27
Signs of the end times
Hebrews 10:32-39
Call for endurance

WEDNESDAY
Zechariah 12:1—13:1
The future of Jerusalem
Mark 13:9-23
The coming sufferings

DAILY
Psalm 13
Prayer for salvation

Proper 29 [34]
Reign of Christ or *Christ the King*

Preparation for Sunday

THURSDAY
2 Kings 22:1-10
Josiah, a righteous king
Acts 7:54—8:1a
The Son at God's right hand

FRIDAY
2 Kings 22:11-20
God's judgment
1 Corinthians 15:20-28
That God may be all in all

SATURDAY
2 Kings 23:1-14
Josiah follows God's law
John 3:31-36
The one who comes from above

DAILY
Psalm 132:1-12 [13-18]
The faithful sing with joy

Sunday, November 20–26

2 Samuel 23:1-7
The just ruler like morning light
Psalm 132:1-12 [13-18]
The faithful sing with joy
Revelation 1:4b-8
Christ, the ruler of the earth
John 18:33-37
The kingdom of Christ

Reflection on Sunday

MONDAY
2 Kings 23:15-25
Josiah restores the passover
Revelation 11:1-14
The dead are filled with the breath of life

TUESDAY
1 Samuel 17:55—18:5
David becomes one of Saul's officers
Revelation 11:15-19
God's reign at the end of time

WEDNESDAY
2 Samuel 2:1-7
David becomes king of Judah
John 16:25-33
I have conquered the world

DAILY
Psalm 63
The king shall rejoice in God

Proper 29 [34]
Reign of Christ or *Christ the King*

Preparation for Sunday

THURSDAY
Ezekiel 28:1-10
A king pretends to be God
Acts 7:54—8:1a
The Son at God's right hand

FRIDAY
Ezekiel 28:20-26
Israel will be safe
1 Corinthians 15:20-28
That God may be all in all

SATURDAY
Daniel 7:1-8, 15-18
Daniel's vision of four beasts
John 3:31-36
The one who comes from above

DAILY
Psalm 93
Your throne has been established

Sunday, November 20–26

Daniel 7:9-10, 13-14
The coming one rules over all
Psalm 93
Your throne has been established
Revelation 1:4b-8
Christ, the ruler of the earth
John 18:33-37
The kingdom of Christ

Reflection on Sunday

MONDAY
Daniel 7:19-27
The holy ones receive the kingdom
Revelation 11:1-14
The dead are filled with the breath of life

TUESDAY
Ezekiel 29:1-12
Prophecy against Pharaoh
Revelation 11:15-19
God's reign at the end of time

WEDNESDAY
Ezekiel 30:20-26
I am the Lord
John 16:25-33
I have conquered the world

DAILY
Psalm 76
God is victorious

Advent

Christmas

Epiphany

Year C

First Sunday of Advent

Preparation for Sunday

THURSDAY
Nehemiah 9:6-15
Remembering the exodus
1 Thessalonians 5:1-11
Keep awake

FRIDAY
Nehemiah 9:16-25
Remembering the exodus
1 Thessalonians 5:12-22
Rejoice, pray, give thanks

SATURDAY
Nehemiah 9:26-31
Remembering deliverance from exile
Luke 21:20-24
A messianic warning

DAILY
Psalm 25:1-10
To you I lift up my soul

First Sunday of Advent

Jeremiah 33:14-16
A righteous branch springs from David
Psalm 25:1-10
To you I lift up my soul
1 Thessalonians 3:9-13
Strengthen hearts of holiness
Luke 21:25-36
Watch for the coming of the Son of Man

Reflection on Sunday

MONDAY
Numbers 17:1-11
The budding of Aaron's rod
2 Peter 3:1-18
Growing in grace

TUESDAY
2 Samuel 7:18-29
The flowering of David's line
Revelation 22:12-16
Jesus as the fulfillment of David's line

WEDNESDAY
Isaiah 1:24-31
Warning not to wither
Luke 11:29-32
The coming of the Son of Man

DAILY
Psalm 90
Prayer for life from God

Second Sunday of Advent

Preparation for Sunday

THURSDAY
Malachi 3:5-12
Return to me
Philippians 1:12-18a
Proclaiming Christ

FRIDAY
Malachi 3:13-18
Those who serve God
Philippians 1:18b-26
Paul rejoices though imprisoned

SATURDAY
Malachi 4:1-6
The sun of righteousness shall rise
Luke 9:1-6
The mission of the Twelve

DAILY
Luke 1:68-79
God's tender compassion

Second Sunday of Advent

Baruch 5:1-9
The return of scattered Israel
Luke 1:68-79
God's tender compassion
Philippians 1:3-11
A harvest of righteousness
Luke 3:1-6
Prepare the way of the Lord

or

Malachi 3:1-4
The messenger refines and purifies

Reflection on Sunday

MONDAY
Isaiah 40:1-11
The earth prepares for God
Romans 8:22-25
All creation waits

TUESDAY
Isaiah 19:18-25
All nations shall praise God
2 Peter 1:2-15
Living God's call

WEDNESDAY
Isaiah 35:3-7
God's advent will change everything
Luke 7:18-30
John the Baptist questions Jesus

DAILY
Psalm 126
Prayer for restoration

Third Sunday of Advent

Preparation for Sunday

THURSDAY
Amos 6:1-8
Punishment for self-indulgence
2 Corinthians 8:1-15
Encouragement to be generous

FRIDAY
Amos 8:4-12
Do not trample the needy
2 Corinthians 9:1-15
Generous giving bears fruit

SATURDAY
Amos 9:8-15
God will set things right
Luke 1:57-66
The birth of John the Baptist

DAILY
Isaiah 12:2-6
In your midst is the Holy One of Israel

Third Sunday of Advent

Zephaniah 3:14-20
Rejoice in God
Isaiah 12:2-6
In your midst is the Holy One of Israel
Philippians 4:4-7
Rejoice, the Lord is near
Luke 3:7-18
One more powerful is coming

Reflection on Sunday

MONDAY
Numbers 16:1-19
Korah's company rebels
Hebrews 13:7-17
Respect your leaders

TUESDAY
Numbers 16:20-35
God destroys Korah's company
Acts 28:23-31
Paul preaches in Rome

WEDNESDAY
Micah 4:8-13
God will thresh out the people
Luke 7:31-35
The Messiah and John the Baptist

DAILY
Isaiah 11:1-9
A ruler brings justice and peace

Fourth Sunday of Advent

Readings for Monday through Wednesday after the Fourth Sunday of Advent are provided for use if necessary. Beginning with December 22, the dated readings on the following pages may be used.

Preparation for Sunday

THURSDAY
Jeremiah 31:31-34
A new covenant written on the heart
Hebrews 10:10-18
New priest, new sacrifice once for all

FRIDAY
Isaiah 42:10-18
Sing to God a new song
Hebrews 10:32-39
Confidence that rewards

SATURDAY
Isaiah 66:7-11
God as a nursing mother
Luke 13:31-35
Jesus as mother hen laments over Jerusalem

DAILY
Psalm 80:1-7
Show the light of your countenance

Fourth Sunday of Advent

Micah 5:2-5a
From Bethlehem comes a ruler
Luke 1:46b-55
My soul magnifies the Lord
Hebrews 10:5-10
I have come to do your will
Luke 1:39-45 [46-55]
Blessed are you among women

or

Psalm 80:1-7
Show the light of your countenance

Reflection on Sunday

MONDAY
Genesis 25:19-28
Rebekah bears Jacob and Esau
Colossians 1:15-20
Jesus Christ, the firstborn of creation

TUESDAY
Genesis 30:1-24
Leah and Rachel bear their sons
Romans 8:18-30
The whole creation is in labor

WEDNESDAY
Isaiah 42:14-21
God is like a woman in labor
Luke 1:5-25
Elizabeth will bear a child

DAILY
Psalm 113
Praise to God, who lifts up the lowly

Days around Christmas Day

DECEMBER 22

Micah 4:1-5

A promise of peace

Ephesians 2:11-22

Christ came to bring peace

DECEMBER 23

Micah 4:6-8

Dominion shall return to Zion

2 Peter 1:16-21

Making known the coming of Christ

DECEMBER 24 (MORNING ONLY)

Micah 6:6-8

Adore God with justice, kindness, humility

Hebrews 10:5-10

I have come to do your will

DAILY

Luke 1:46b-55

My soul gives glory to God

Nativity of the Lord (Christmas Day)

Any of the following three propers may be used on Christmas Eve/Day.

The readings from propers II and III for Christmas may be used as alternatives for Christmas Day. If proper III is not used on Christmas Day, it should be used at some service during the Christmas cycle because of the significance of John's prologue.

Christmas, Proper I

Isaiah 9:2-7
A child is born for us
Psalm 96
Let the earth be glad
Titus 2:11-14
The grace of God has appeared
Luke 2:1-14 [15-20]
God with us

Christmas, Proper II

Isaiah 62:6-12
God comes to restore the people
Psalm 97
Light springs up for the righteous
Titus 3:4-7
Saved through water and the Spirit
Luke 2:[1-7] 8-20
The birth of the messiah revealed to shepherds

Christmas, Proper III

Isaiah 52:7-10
Heralds announce God's salvation
Psalm 98
The victory of our God
Hebrews 1:1-4 [5-12]
God has spoken by a son
John 1:1-14
The Word became flesh

DECEMBER 26
2 Chronicles 24:17-24
The stoning of Zechariah
Acts 6:1-7; 7:51-60
The stoning of Stephen

DECEMBER 27
Proverbs 8:32-36
Happy the one who listens to wisdom
John 21:19b-24
John's testimony

DECEMBER 28
Isaiah 54:1-13
God's steadfast love will not depart
Revelation 21:1-7
Death and mourning will be no more

DAILY
Psalm 148
God's splendor is over earth and heaven

First Sunday after Christmas Day, December 26-31

1 Samuel 2:18-20, 26
Samuel grew in favor with all
Psalm 148
God's splendor is over earth and heaven
Colossians 3:12-17
Clothe yourselves in love
Luke 2:41-52
Jesus increased in favor with all

Days of Christmas

DAILY
Psalm 147:12-20
Praise God in Zion

DECEMBER 29
1 Chronicles 28:1-10
Solomon will build the temple
1 Corinthians 3:10-17
The temple of the Spirit

DECEMBER 30
2 Chronicles 1:7-13
Solomon's prayer for wisdom
Mark 13:32-37
Keep awake

DECEMBER 31
1 Kings 3:5-14
God grants a discerning mind
John 8:12-19
I am the light

**JANUARY 1—HOLY NAME OF JESUS
(MARY, MOTHER OF GOD)**
Numbers 6:22-27
The Aaronic blessing
Psalm 8
How exalted is your name
Galatians 4:4-7
We are no longer slaves
or Philippians 2:5-11
God takes on human form
Luke 2:15-21
The child is named Jesus

JANUARY 1—NEW YEAR'S DAY
Ecclesiastes 3:1-13
To everything a season
Psalm 8
How exalted is your name
Revelation 21:1-6a
New heaven and new earth
Matthew 25:31-46
Separation of the sheep and goats

JANUARY 2
Proverbs 1:1-7
Grow in wisdom and knowledge
James 3:13-18
The wisdom from above

The following readings are provided for use when Epiphany (January 6) is celebrated on a weekday following the Second Sunday after Christmas Day.

Second Sunday after Christmas Day, January 2-5

Jeremiah 31:7-14   *or*   Sirach 24:1-12
Joy as God's scattered flock gathers   *Wisdom lives among God's people*
Psalm 147:12-20   *or*   Wisdom 10:15-21
Praising God in Zion   *Praising the holy name*
Ephesians 1:3-14
The will of God made known in Christ
John 1:[1-9] 10-18
God with us

Days around Epiphany

Readings through January 9 are provided for use if necessary. When the Epiphany of the Lord is trans-ferred to the preceding Sunday, January 2-5, these dated readings may be used through the week that follows. When the Baptism of the Lord falls on January 11, 12, or 13, the corresponding preparation readings on the following page are used after January 9.

JANUARY 3
Job 42:10-17
Job's family
Luke 8:16-21
Jesus' family

JANUARY 4
Isaiah 6:1-5
The Lord high and lofty
Acts 7:44-53
Solomon's temple cannot contain God

JANUARY 5
Jeremiah 31:7-14
Joy as God's scattered flock gathers
John 1:[1-9] 10-18
God with us

Epiphany of the Lord, January 6

Isaiah 60:1-6
Nations come to the light
Psalm 72:1-7, 10-14
All shall bow down
Ephesians 3:1-12
The gospel's promise for all
Matthew 2:1-12
Christ revealed to the nations

JANUARY 7
Daniel 2:1-19
The king searches for wisdom
Ephesians 4:17—5:1
Life lived in Christ

JANUARY 8
Daniel 2:24-49
Daniel reveals the dream's meaning
Ephesians 5:15-20
Wise living in evil days

JANUARY 9
Numbers 24:15-19
A star coming out of Jacob
Luke 1:67-79
The Savior is seen

DAILY
Psalm 72
Prayers for the king

Baptism of the Lord [1]
First Sunday after the Epiphany

Preparation for Sunday

THURSDAY
Ecclesiastes 1:1-11
There is nothing new under the sun
1 Corinthians 1:18-31
The power and wisdom of God

FRIDAY
Ecclesiastes 2:1-11
Toil for pleasure is ultimately vanity
1 Corinthians 2:1-10
The Spirit reveals the depths of God

SATURDAY
Ecclesiastes 3:1-15
All that is, is God's doing
1 Corinthians 2:11-16
God's wisdom taught by the Spirit

DAILY
Psalm 29
The voice of God upon the waters

Baptism of the Lord

Isaiah 43:1-7
Passing through the waters
Psalm 29
The voice of God upon the waters
Acts 8:14-17
Prayer for the Holy Spirit
Luke 3:15-17, 21-22
The baptism of Jesus

Reflection on Sunday

MONDAY
Judges 4:1-16
Israel's enemies drown
Ephesians 6:10-17
The Christian's spiritual armor

TUESDAY
Judges 5:12-21
The song of Deborah
1 John 5:13-21
The life of those born of God

WEDNESDAY
Numbers 27:1-11
Daughters also promised inheritance
Luke 11:33-36
Your body full of light

DAILY
Psalm 106:1-12
God saves through water

Second Sunday after the Epiphany [2]

Preparation for Sunday

THURSDAY
Jeremiah 3:1-5
Unfaithful Israel
Acts 8:18-24
God's gifts cannot be purchased

FRIDAY
Jeremiah 3:19-25
Israel is a faithless spouse
1 Corinthians 7:1-7
Guidance for the married

SATURDAY
Jeremiah 4:1-4
A call to repentance
Luke 11:14-23
Looking for signs from heaven

DAILY
Psalm 36:5-10
We feast on the abundance of God's house

Second Sunday after the Epiphany

Isaiah 62:1-5
God like the bridegroom and the bride
Psalm 36:5-10
We feast on the abundance of God's house
1 Corinthians 12:1-11
A variety of gifts but one Spirit
John 2:1-11
The wedding at Cana

Reflection on Sunday

MONDAY
Isaiah 54:1-8
God is married to Israel
Romans 12:9-21
Live in harmony with one another

TUESDAY
Song of Solomon 4:1-8
The bride's beauty extolled
1 Corinthians 1:3-17
Appeal for unity

WEDNESDAY
Song of Solomon 4:9—5:1
A love song
Luke 5:33-39
Christ the bridegroom

DAILY
Psalm 145
Praise God's faithfulness

Third Sunday after the Epiphany [3]

Preparation for Sunday

THURSDAY
Isaiah 61:1-7
The spirit of God is upon me
Romans 7:1-6
The new life of the Spirit

FRIDAY
Nehemiah 2:1-10
Nehemiah seeks the welfare of Israel
Romans 12:1-8
One body in Christ

SATURDAY
Nehemiah 5:1-13
Nehemiah deals with oppression
Luke 2:39-52
Jesus increases in wisdom

DAILY
Psalm 19
The law revives the soul

Third Sunday after the Epiphany

Nehemiah 8:1-3, 5-6, 8-10
Ezra reads the law
Psalm 19
The law revives the soul
1 Corinthians 12:12-31a
You are the body of Christ
Luke 4:14-21
Jesus reads the prophet Isaiah

Reflection on Sunday

MONDAY
Jeremiah 36:1-10
The scroll is read in the temple
1 Corinthians 14:1-12
The assembly's gifts

TUESDAY
Jeremiah 36:11-26
Jehoiakim burns the scroll
2 Corinthians 7:2-12
Grief leads to repentance

WEDNESDAY
Jeremiah 36:27-32
Jeremiah dictates a second scroll
Luke 4:38-44
Jesus heals and preaches in synagogues

DAILY
Psalm 119:89-96
The law of God gives life

Fourth Sunday after the Epiphany [4]

If this Sunday immediately precedes Ash Wednesday, the proper for Sunday and the readings for the surrounding days may be replaced, in those churches observing the Transfiguration on that Sunday, by the proper for the Last Sunday after the Epiphany and the readings for the days surrounding it.

Preparation for Sunday

THURSDAY
2 Chronicles 34:1-7
Youthful Josiah inaugurates reform
Acts 10:44-48
Gentiles receive the Holy Spirit

FRIDAY
2 Chronicles 35:20-27
Jeremiah laments the death of Josiah
Acts 19:1-10
Believers speak in tongues

SATURDAY
2 Chronicles 36:11-21
Zedekiah ignores Jeremiah and Jerusalem falls
John 1:43-51
Can anything good come out of Nazareth?

DAILY
Psalm 71:1-6
You have been my strength

Fourth Sunday after the Epiphany

Jeremiah 1:4-10
A prophet to the nations
Psalm 71:1-6
You have been my strength
1 Corinthians 13:1-13
Without love, a noisy gong
Luke 4:21-30
The prophet Jesus not accepted

Reflection on Sunday

MONDAY
1 Kings 17:8-16
The widow of Zarephath fed
1 Corinthians 2:6-16
Interpreting spiritual things

TUESDAY
2 Kings 5:1-14
Naaman the Syrian healed
1 Corinthians 14:13-25
Interpreting tongues

WEDNESDAY
Jeremiah 1:11-19
Jeremiah warns of disaster
Luke 19:41-44
Recognizing the works of God

DAILY
Psalm 56
In God I trust

Fifth Sunday after the Epiphany [5]

If this Sunday immediately precedes Ash Wednesday, the proper for Sunday and the readings for the surrounding days may be replaced, in those churches observing the Transfiguration on that Sunday, by the proper for the Last Sunday after the Epiphany and the readings for the days surrounding it.

Preparation for Sunday

THURSDAY
Numbers 20:22-29
Eleazar succeeds Aaron
Acts 9:19b-25
Saul's call is questioned

FRIDAY
Numbers 27:12-23
God's choice of Joshua
Acts 9:26-31
The apostles reluctantly welcome Saul

SATURDAY
Judges 3:7-11
God's spirit rests on Othniel
Luke 4:42-44
Jesus preaches

DAILY
Psalm 138
I will bow toward your holy temple

Fifth Sunday after the Epiphany

Isaiah 6:1-8 [9-13]
Send me
Psalm 138
I will bow toward your holy temple
1 Corinthians 15:1-11
I am the least of the apostles
Luke 5:1-11
Jesus calls the disciples to fish for people

Reflection on Sunday

MONDAY
Judges 5:1-11
Deborah the judge sings God's praise
1 Corinthians 14:26-40
Advice about worship

TUESDAY
1 Samuel 9:15—10:1b
The call of Saul
1 Timothy 3:1-9
Qualities needed by church leaders

WEDNESDAY
Isaiah 8:1-15
Resisting the call
Luke 5:27-32
The call of Levi

DAILY
Psalm 115
God blesses the chosen people

Sixth Sunday after the Epiphany [6]

Proper 1

If this Sunday immediately precedes Ash Wednesday, the proper for Sunday and the readings for the surrounding days may be replaced, in those churches observing the Transfiguration on that Sunday, by the proper for the Last Sunday after the Epiphany and the readings for the days surrounding it.

Preparation for Sunday

THURSDAY
Jeremiah 13:12-19
The threat of exile
Acts 13:26-34
God raised Jesus from the dead

FRIDAY
Jeremiah 13:20-27
Can leopards change their spots?
1 Peter 1:17—2:1
Born anew

SATURDAY
Jeremiah 17:1-4
A heritage lost
Luke 11:24-28
Blessings on those who hear the word

DAILY
Psalm 1
Trees planted by streams of water

Sixth Sunday after the Epiphany

Jeremiah 17:5-10
Those who trust the Lord are like trees
Psalm 1
Trees planted by streams of water
1 Corinthians 15:12-20
Christ has been raised
Luke 6:17-26
Blessings on the poor, woes on the rich

Reflection on Sunday

MONDAY
2 Kings 24:18—25:21
Woes come upon Jerusalem
1 Corinthians 15:20-34
The end time

TUESDAY
Ezra 1:1-11
Blessings return to Jerusalem
2 Corinthians 1:12-19
The day of the Lord Jesus

WEDNESDAY
Jeremiah 22:11-17
Woe to the unjust
Luke 11:37-52
Woe to the sinners

DAILY
Psalm 120
Woe to me

Seventh Sunday after the Epiphany [7]

Proper 2

If this Sunday immediately precedes Ash Wednesday, the proper for Sunday and the readings for the surrounding days may be replaced, in those churches observing the Transfiguration on that Sunday, by the proper for the Last Sunday after the Epiphany and the readings for the days surrounding it.

Preparation for Sunday

THURSDAY
Genesis 43:16-34
Joseph welcomes his brother Benjamin
Romans 8:1-11
You are one in the Spirit

FRIDAY
Genesis 44:1-17
Joseph detains his brother Benjamin
1 John 2:12-17
The world and its desires are passing away

SATURDAY
Genesis 44:18-34
Judah offers himself in Benjamin's place
Luke 12:57-59
Settling with your opponent

DAILY
Psalm 37:1-11, 39-40
The lowly shall possess the land

Seventh Sunday after the Epiphany

Genesis 45:3-11, 15
Joseph forgives his brothers
Psalm 37:1-11, 39-40
The lowly shall possess the land
1 Corinthians 15:35-38, 42-50
The mystery of the resurrection
Luke 6:27-38
Love your enemies

Reflection on Sunday

MONDAY
Genesis 33:1-17
Jacob and Esau reconcile
1 Corinthians 11:2-16
Advice for church life

TUESDAY
1 Samuel 24:1-22
David spares Saul's life
1 Corinthians 11:17-22, 27-33
Advice concerning the Lord's supper

WEDNESDAY
Leviticus 5:1-13
Offering for pardon
Luke 17:1-4
Forgiving seven times

DAILY
Psalm 38
Confession of sin

Eighth Sunday after the Epiphany [8]
Proper 3

If this Sunday immediately precedes Ash Wednesday, the proper for Sunday and the readings for the surrounding days may be replaced, in those churches observing the Transfiguration on that Sunday, by the proper for the Last Sunday after the Epiphany and the readings for the days surrounding it.

Preparation for Sunday

THURSDAY
Proverbs 13:1-12
A fulfilled desire is like a tree of life
Romans 5:12—6:2
Eternal life through Jesus Christ

FRIDAY
Proverbs 15:1-9
A gentle tongue is a tree of life
1 Thessalonians 4:13-18
The trumpet of resurrection

SATURDAY
Isaiah 30:8-17
Rebellion against God's word
John 16:1-4a
Remembering the words of Jesus

DAILY
Psalm 92:1-4, 12-15
The righteous flourish like a palm tree

Eighth Sunday after the Epiphany

Sirach 27:4-7
A tree's fruit discloses its cultivation
Psalm 92:1-4, 12-15
The righteous flourish like a palm tree
1 Corinthians 15:51-58
The mystery of the resurrection
Luke 6:39-49
Building on a firm foundation

or

Isaiah 55:10-13
God's word goes forth

Reflection on Sunday

MONDAY
Jeremiah 24:1-10
The good figs and the bad figs
1 Corinthians 16:1-12
Paul's travel plans

TUESDAY
Jeremiah 29:10-19
The rotten figs
1 Corinthians 16:13-24
Paul's farewell

WEDNESDAY
Proverbs 5:1-23
The bad woman or the good wife
Luke 14:34-35
Good or bad salt

DAILY
Psalm 1
The fruited tree or the chaff

Ninth Sunday after the Epiphany [9]

Proper 4

The readings that follow are for churches whose calendar requires this Sunday, and who do not observe the last Sunday after the Epiphany as Transfiguration.

Preparation for Sunday

THURSDAY
1 Kings 6:23-38
The splendor of God's temple
2 Corinthians 5:11-17
Beyond a human point of view

FRIDAY
1 Kings 8:14-21
A house for the name of the Lord
2 Corinthians 11:1-6
Beware of those who proclaim another Jesus

SATURDAY
1 Kings 8:31-40
God knows every human heart
Luke 4:31-37
Healing the man with an unclean spirit

DAILY
Psalm 96:1-9
Praise to God among the nations

Ninth Sunday after the Epiphany

1 Kings 8:22-23, 41-43
God's everlasting covenant for all
Psalm 96:1-9
Praise to God among the nations
Galatians 1:1-12
Beware of contrary gospels
Luke 7:1-10
Jesus heals the centurion's slave

Reflection on Sunday

MONDAY
Jonah 4:1-11
God's mercy on the Ninevites
Acts 8:26-40
The gospel is shared with an Ethiopian

TUESDAY
Nehemiah 1:1-11
Asking God to gather the people
Acts 3:1-10
Healing the crippled beggar

WEDNESDAY
Isaiah 56:1-8
God welcomes the outcasts
Mark 7:24-30
The Syrophoenician woman's faith

DAILY
Psalm 5
God's favor like a shield

Last Sunday after the Epiphany

Transfiguration Sunday

The following may be used in churches where the last Sunday after the Epiphany is observed as Transfiguration Sunday.

Preparation for Sunday

THURSDAY
Deuteronomy 9:1-5
God's oath to Abraham, Isaac, and Jacob
Acts 3:11-16
Abraham, Isaac, and Jacob's God glorifies Jesus

FRIDAY
Deuteronomy 9:6-14
Remember your rebellion in the wilderness
Acts 10:1-8
The vision of Cornelius

SATURDAY
Deuteronomy 9:15-24
Moses on the blazing mountain
Luke 10:21-24
Blessed are the eyes that see what you see

DAILY
Psalm 99
Worship upon God's holy hill

Transfiguration of the Lord

Exodus 34:29-35
Moses' face shone
Psalm 99
Worship upon God's holy hill
2 Corinthians 3:12—4:2
We will be transformed
Luke 9:28-36 [37-43a]
Jesus is transfigured on the mountain

Reflection on Sunday

MONDAY
Exodus 35:1-29
Offerings for the tent of meeting
Acts 10:9-23a
Peter's vision of what God makes clean

TUESDAY
Ezekiel 1:1—2:1
Ezekiel's vision of the chariot
Acts 10:23b-33
Cornelius and Peter

DAILY
Psalm 35:11-28
Do not be far from me

Lent

Three Days

Easter

First Sunday in Lent

Ash Wednesday

Joel 2:1-2, 12-17   *or*   Isaiah 58:1-12
Return to God   *The fast that God chooses*
Psalm 51:1-17
Plea for mercy
2 Corinthians 5:20b—6:10
Now is the day of salvation
Matthew 6:1-6, 16-21
The practice of faith

Preparation for Sunday

THURSDAY
Exodus 5:10-23
Israel labors in Egypt
Acts 7:30-34
Moses, called from the burning bush to the exodus

SATURDAY
Ecclesiastes 3:1-8
For everything a season
John 12:27-36
Jesus announces his passion

FRIDAY
Exodus 6:1-13
God promises deliverance
Acts 7:35-42
The people complain to Moses

DAILY
Psalm 91:1-2, 9-16
God shall keep you

First Sunday in Lent

Deuteronomy 26:1-11
Saved from Egypt
Psalm 91:1-2, 9-16
God shall keep you
Romans 10:8b-13
You will be saved
Luke 4:1-13
The temptation of Jesus

Reflection on Sunday

MONDAY
1 Chronicles 21:1-17
Satan tempts David
1 John 2:1-6
Obey God's commandments

TUESDAY
Zechariah 3:1-10
Satan tempts Joshua
2 Peter 2:4-21
Believers who fall into sin

WEDNESDAY
Job 1:1-22
Satan tempts Job
Luke 21:34—22:6
Satan enters Judas

DAILY
Psalm 17
Prayer for protection from evil ones

Second Sunday in Lent

Preparation for Sunday

THURSDAY
Genesis 13:1-7, 14-18
Abram begins his pilgrimage
Philippians 3:2-12
Paul affirms the Abrahamic tradition

FRIDAY
Genesis 14:17-24
Abram is blessed by Melchizedek
Philippians 3:17-20
Our citizenship is in heaven

SATURDAY
Psalm 118:26-29
A pilgrimage song of praise
Matthew 23:37-39
Jesus laments over Jerusalem

DAILY
Psalm 27
The Lord shall keep me safe

Second Sunday in Lent

Genesis 15:1-12, 17-18
The covenant with Abram
Psalm 27
The Lord shall keep me safe
Philippians 3:17—4:1
Our citizenship is in heaven
Luke 13:31-35   *or*   Luke 9:28-36 [37-43]
A hen gathering her brood   *Jesus is transfigured on the mountain*

Reflection on Sunday

MONDAY
Exodus 33:1-6
Abraham's descendants lament
Romans 4:1-12
The faith of Abraham

TUESDAY
Numbers 14:10b-24
Moses intercedes for the people
1 Corinthians 10:1-13
God is faithful

WEDNESDAY
2 Chronicles 20:1-22
The king prays for Jerusalem
Luke 13:22-31
The narrow door

DAILY
Psalm 105:1-15 [16-41] 42
God's covenant with Abraham

Third Sunday in Lent

Preparation for Sunday

THURSDAY
Daniel 3:19-30
Servants of God vindicated
Revelation 2:8-11
Warning to the church in Smyrna

FRIDAY
Daniel 12:1-4
God sends Michael
Revelation 3:1-6
Warning to the church in Sardis

SATURDAY
Isaiah 5:1-7
The song of the vineyard
Luke 6:43-45
A tree and its fruits

DAILY
Psalm 63:1-8
O God, eagerly I seek you

Third Sunday in Lent

Isaiah 55:1-9
Come to the water
Psalm 63:1-8
O God, eagerly I seek you
1 Corinthians 10:1-13
Israel, baptized in cloud and seas
Luke 13:1-9
The parable of the fig tree

Reflection on Sunday

MONDAY
Jeremiah 11:1-17
Judgment against the olive tree
Romans 2:1-11
Divine judgment applies to all

TUESDAY
Ezekiel 17:1-10
Allegory of the vine
Romans 2:12-16
What the law requires is written on the heart

WEDNESDAY
Numbers 13:17-27
The fruit of the promised land
Luke 13:18-21
Parables of the mustard seed, yeast

DAILY
Psalm 39
My hope is in God

Fourth Sunday in Lent

Preparation for Sunday

THURSDAY
Joshua 4:1-13
Joshua leads the people across the Jordan
2 Corinthians 4:16—5:5
Paul comforts with a promise of glory

FRIDAY
Joshua 4:14-24
God's people come through the waters dry-shod
2 Corinthians 5:6-15
Walking by faith and not by sight

SATURDAY
Exodus 32:7-14
Moses begs forgiveness
Luke 15:1-10
Parables of a lost sheep and a lost coin

DAILY
Psalm 32
Be glad, you righteous

Fourth Sunday in Lent

Joshua 5:9-12
Israel eats bread and grain
Psalm 32
Be glad, you righteous
2 Corinthians 5:16-21
The mystery and ministry of reconciliation
Luke 15:1-3, 11b-32
The parable of the forgiving father

Reflection on Sunday

MONDAY
Leviticus 23:26-41
Days for confession and celebration
Revelation 19:1-8
The marriage supper of the Lamb

TUESDAY
Leviticus 25:1-19
The jubilee celebration
Revelation 19:9-10
Blessed are those invited to the marriage supper

WEDNESDAY
2 Kings 4:1-7
The widow saved
Luke 9:10-17
Jesus feeds 5000

DAILY
Psalm 53
Restoring our fortunes

Fifth Sunday in Lent

Preparation for Sunday

THURSDAY
Isaiah 43:1-7
God will gather through fire and water
Philippians 2:19-24
Apostolic visits are promised

FRIDAY
Isaiah 43:8-15
God is Lord, Holy One, Creator, Ruler
Philippians 2:25—3:1
Paul praises a co-worker

SATURDAY
Exodus 12:21-27
Passover instituted to celebrate the exodus
John 11:45-57
Plotting against Jesus during Passover

DAILY
Psalm 126
Sowing with tears, reaping with joy

Fifth Sunday in Lent

Isaiah 43:16-21
The Lord gives water in the wilderness
Psalm 126
Sowing with tears, reaping with joy
Philippians 3:4b-14
To know Christ and his resurrection
John 12:1-8
Mary anoints Jesus for his burial

Reflection on Sunday

MONDAY
Exodus 40:1-15
Anointing the holy things
Hebrews 10:19-25
Jesus, priest for the people of God

TUESDAY
Judges 9:7-15
Anointing the bramble
1 John 2:18-28
Knowing the Son

WEDNESDAY
Habakkuk 3:2-15
God will save the anointed
Luke 18:31-34
Jesus foretells his death

DAILY
Psalm 20
Victory for God's anointed

Sixth Sunday in Lent
Passion Sunday or *Palm Sunday*

Those who do not observe the procession with palms and do not wish to use the passion gospel may substitute the gospel and psalm indicated for the Liturgy of the Palms for the gospel and psalm indicated for the Liturgy of the Passion. Whenever possible, the whole passion narrative should be read.

Preparation for Sunday

THURSDAY
Isaiah 53:10-12
The suffering one bears the sin of many
Hebrews 2:1-9
God's care for humankind

FRIDAY
Isaiah 54:9-10
God's love is steadfast
Hebrews 2:10-18
Jesus' suffering binds him to humankind

SATURDAY
Leviticus 23:1-8
Sabbath and passover
Luke 22:1-13
Jesus prepares for Passover with his disciples

DAILY
Psalm 31:9-16
I commend my spirit

Sixth Sunday in Lent

LITURGY OF THE PALMS
Psalm 118:1-2, 19-29
Blessed is the one who comes
Luke 19:28-40
Entrance into the final days

LITURGY OF THE PASSION
Isaiah 50:4-9a
The servant submits to suffering
Psalm 31:9-16
I commend my spirit
Philippians 2:5-11
Death on a cross
Luke 22:14—23:56 or Luke 23:1-49
The passion and death of Jesus

Monday of Holy Week

Isaiah 42:1-9
The servant brings forth justice
Psalm 36:5-11
Refuge under the shadow of your wings
Hebrews 9:11-15
The blood of Christ redeems for eternal life
John 12:1-11
Mary of Bethany anoints Jesus

Tuesday of Holy Week

Isaiah 49:1-7
The servant brings salvation to earth's ends
Psalm 71:1-14
From my mother's womb you have been my strength
1 Corinthians 1:18-31
The cross of Christ reveals God's power and wisdom
John 12:20-36
Jesus speaks of his death

Wednesday of Holy Week

Isaiah 50:4-9a
The servant is vindicated by God
Psalm 70
Be pleased, O God, to deliver me
Hebrews 12:1-3
Look to Jesus, who endured the cross
John 13:21-32
Jesus foretells his betrayal

The Three Days

Holy Thursday

Exodus 12:1-4 [5-10] 11-14
The passover of the Lord
Psalm 116:1-2, 12-19
The cup of salvation
1 Corinthians 11:23-26
Proclaim the Lord's death
John 13:1-17, 31b-35
The service of Christ: footwashing and meal

Good Friday

Isaiah 52:13—53:12
The suffering servant
Psalm 22
Why have you forsaken me?
Hebrews 10:16-25   *or*   Hebrews 4:14-16; 5:7-9
The way to God is opened   *The merciful high priest*
John 18:1—19:42
The passion and death of Jesus

Holy Saturday
The following are for use at services other than the Easter Vigil.

Job 14:1-14   *or*   Lamentations 3:1-9, 19-24
Hope for a tree   *I will hope in the Lord*
Psalm 31:1-4, 15-16
Take me out of the net
1 Peter 4:1-8
The gospel proclaimed even to the dead
Matthew 27:57-66   *or*   John 19:38-42
The burial of Jesus   *The burial of Jesus*

Resurrection of the Lord, Easter Vigil

1

Genesis 1:1 — 2:4a
Creation
Psalm 136:1-9, 23-26
God's mercy endures forever

2

Genesis 7:1-5, 11-18; 8:6-18; 9:8-13
Flood
Psalm 46
The God of Jacob is our stronghold

3

Genesis 22:1-18
Testing of Abraham
Psalm 16
You will show me the path of life

4

Exodus 14:10-31; 15:20-21
Deliverance at the Red Sea
Exodus 15:1b-13, 17-18
I will sing to the Lord who has triumphed gloriously

5

Isaiah 55:1-11
Salvation freely offered to all
Isaiah 12:2-6
With joy you will draw water from the wells of salvation

6

Baruch 3:9-15, 32—4:4   *or*   Proverbs 8:1-8, 19-21; 9:4b-6
The wisdom of God   *The wisdom of God*
Psalm 19
God's statutes are just and rejoice the heart

7

Ezekiel 36:24-28
A new heart and a new spirit
Psalms 42 and 43
My soul thirsts for the living God

8

Ezekiel 37:1-14
Valley of the dry bones
Psalm 143
Revive me for your name's sake

9

Zephaniah 3:14-20
Gathering of God's people
Psalm 98
Lift up your voice, rejoice and sing

Romans 6:3-11
Dying and rising with Christ
Psalm 114
Tremble, O earth
Luke 24:1-12
Women proclaim the resurrection

Resurrection of the Lord, Easter Day

Acts 10:34-43   *or*   Isaiah 65:17-25
God raised Jesus on the third day   *New heavens and a new earth*
Psalm 118:1-2, 14-24
On this day God has acted
1 Corinthians 15:19-26   *or*   Acts 10:34-43
Christ raised from the dead   *God raised Jesus on the third day*
John 20:1-18   *or*   Luke 24:1-12
Seeing the risen Christ   *Women proclaim the resurrection*

Easter Evening

Isaiah 25:6-9
The feast of victory
Psalm 114
Tremble, O earth
1 Corinthians 5:6b-8
Set your mind on things above
Luke 24:13-49
Stay with us, Lord

Reflection on Sunday

MONDAY
Joshua 10:16-27
Joshua defeats five kings
1 Corinthians 5:6b-8
Celebrating with sincerity and truth

TUESDAY
Judges 4:17-23; 5:24-31a
Jael kills Sisera
Revelation 12:1-12
The woman, the dragon, the child

WEDNESDAY
2 Samuel 6:1-15
David dances before the ark
Luke 24:1-12
Women proclaim the resurrection

DAILY
Psalm 118:1-2, 14-24
On this day God has acted

Second Sunday of Easter

Preparation for Sunday

THURSDAY
1 Samuel 17:1-23
The enemy Goliath taunts Israel
Acts 5:12-16
Signs and wonders by the apostles

FRIDAY
1 Samuel 17:19-32
David announces he will fight Goliath
Acts 5:17-26
The apostles freed from prison

SATURDAY
1 Samuel 17:32-51
David conquers Goliath
Luke 24:36-40
Beholding the wounds of the risen Christ

DAILY
Psalm 150
Let everything praise the Lord

Second Sunday of Easter

Acts 5:27-32
The God of our ancestors raised up Jesus
Psalm 118:14-29   *or*
Glad songs of victory
Revelation 1:4-8
Jesus Christ, firstborn of the dead
John 20:19-31
Beholding the wounds of the risen Christ

Psalm 150
Let everything praise the Lord

Reflection on Sunday

MONDAY
Esther 7:1-10
Esther prevails over Haman
Revelation 1:9-20
A vision of Christ

TUESDAY
Esther 8:1-17
Destruction of the Jews is averted
Revelation 2:8-11
Words to the church at Smyrna

WEDNESDAY
Esther 9:1-5, 18-23
Purim celebrates victory
Luke 12:4-12
The courage to confess Christ

DAILY
Psalm 122
Peace in Jerusalem

Third Sunday of Easter

Preparation for Sunday

THURSDAY
Isaiah 5:11-17
Appetites that lead to hunger
Revelation 3:14-22
Words to the church at Laodicea

FRIDAY
Isaiah 6:1-4
Heaven's holy, holy, holy
Revelation 4:1-11
Heaven's holy, holy, holy

SATURDAY
Genesis 18:1-8
Abraham and Sarah's hospitality to the Lord
Luke 14:12-14
Welcome those in need to your table

DAILY
Psalm 30
My wailing turns to dancing

Third Sunday of Easter

Acts 9:1-6 [7-20]
Paul's conversion, baptism, and preaching
Psalm 30
My wailing turns to dancing
Revelation 5:11-14
The song of the living creatures to the Lamb
John 21:1-19
Jesus appears to the disciples

Reflection on Sunday

MONDAY
Ezekiel 1:1-25
Ezekiel's vision of four living creatures
Acts 9:19b-31
Saul joins the apostles in Jerusalem

TUESDAY
Ezekiel 1:26—2:1
Ezekiel's vision of God's glory
Acts 26:1-18
Paul preaches before Agrippa

WEDNESDAY
Isaiah 6:1-8
Isaiah in the presence of God
Luke 5:1-11
Simon's catch of fish

DAILY
Psalm 121
God will preserve your life

Fourth Sunday of Easter

Preparation for Sunday

THURSDAY
Ezekiel 11:1-25
Ezekiel prophesies against the shepherds of Israel
Revelation 5:1-10
The throne and the elders

FRIDAY
Ezekiel 20:39-44
God will gather the scattered people
Revelation 6:1—7:4
The servants of God are sealed

SATURDAY
Ezekiel 28:25-26
God gathers the people into safety
Luke 12:29-32
Do not fear, little flock

DAILY
Psalm 23
God our shepherd

Fourth Sunday of Easter

Acts 9:36-43
Peter raises Tabitha from the dead
Psalm 23
God our shepherd
Revelation 7:9-17
A multitude sings before the Lamb
John 10:22-30
Jesus promises life to his sheep

Reflection on Sunday

MONDAY
Ezekiel 37:15-28
God will unite the flock
Revelation 15:1-4
The song of the Lamb

TUESDAY
Ezekiel 45:1-9
God promises a sanctuary
Acts 9:32-35
The healing of paralyzed Aeneas

WEDNESDAY
Jeremiah 50:17-20
Israel will be fed
John 10:31-42
The Son and the Father are one

DAILY
Psalm 100
We are God's sheep

Fifth Sunday of Easter

Preparation for Sunday

THURSDAY
Ezekiel 2:8—3:11
Eating the scroll
Revelation 10:1-11
Eating the scroll

FRIDAY
Daniel 7:13-14
An everlasting dominion is given
Revelation 11:15
God's reign at the end of time

SATURDAY
Daniel 7:27
A dominion for the holy ones of the Most High
Revelation 11:16-19
God's reign at the end of time

DAILY
Psalm 148
God's splendor is over earth and heaven

Fifth Sunday of Easter

Acts 11:1-18
God saves the Gentiles
Psalm 148
God's splendor is over earth and heaven
Revelation 21:1-6
New heaven, new earth
John 13:31-35
Love one another

Reflection on Sunday

MONDAY
1 Samuel 20:1-23, 35-42
The love of David and Jonathan
Acts 11:19-26
Christians in Antioch

TUESDAY
2 Samuel 1:4-27
David mourns Jonathan's death
Acts 11:27-30
Love embodied in care for others

WEDNESDAY
Leviticus 19:9-18
Love your neighbor
Luke 10:25-28
Love your neighbor

DAILY
Psalm 133
How good it is to live in unity

Sixth Sunday of Easter

Preparation for Sunday

THURSDAY
Proverbs 2:1-5
Knowledge of God like silver
Acts 15:36-41
Paul and Barnabas part company

FRIDAY
Proverbs 2:6-8
God gives wisdom
Acts 16:1-8
Timothy accompanies Paul

SATURDAY
Proverbs 2:9-15
Wisdom makes a home in your heart
Luke 19:1-10
Salvation makes a home with Zacchaeus

DAILY
Psalm 67
Let the nations be glad

Sixth Sunday of Easter

Acts 16:9-15
Lydia and her household are baptized
Psalm 67
Let the nations be glad
Revelation 21:10, 22—22:5
The Lamb is the light of God's city
John 14:23-29   *or*   John 5:1-9
The Father will send the Holy Spirit   *Jesus heals on the sabbath*

Reflection on Sunday

MONDAY
1 Chronicles 12:16-22
The spirit of God on Amasai
Revelation 21:5-14
Vision of the holy city

TUESDAY
2 Chronicles 15:1-15
The spirit of God on Azariah
Revelation 21:15-22
Vision of the holy city

WEDNESDAY
2 Chronicles 34:20-33
Josiah consults the prophet Huldah
Luke 2:25-38
The spirit of God on Simeon and Anna

DAILY
Psalm 93
God reigns above the floods

Seventh Sunday of Easter

Ascension of the Lord, Thursday

These readings may also be used on the Seventh Sunday of Easter.

Acts 1:1-11
Jesus sends the apostles
Psalm 47   *or*   Psalm 93
God has gone up with a shout   *Praise to God who reigns*
Ephesians 1:15-23
Seeing the risen and ascended Christ
Luke 24:44-53
Christ present in all times and places

Preparation for Sunday

FRIDAY   **DAILY**
Exodus 33:12-17   Psalm 97
Moses prays for the people   *Light dawns for the righteous*
Revelation 22:6-9
A trustworthy testimony

SATURDAY
Exodus 33:18-23
Moses asks to see God's glory
John 1:14-18
We have seen the glory of God

Seventh Sunday of Easter

Acts 16:16-34
A jailer is baptized
Psalm 97
Light dawns for the righteous
Revelation 22:12-14, 16-17, 20-21
Blessed are those who wash their robes
John 17:20-26
Christ's prayer for his disciples

Reflection on Sunday

MONDAY
Exodus 40:16-38
God's glory on the tabernacle
Acts 16:35-40
The magistrates apologize to Paul and Silas

TUESDAY
2 Chronicles 5:2-14
God's glory in the temple
Acts 26:19-29
Proclaim the light of the resurrection

WEDNESDAY
Ezekiel 3:12-21
God's glory commissions the prophet
Luke 9:18-27
God's glory and discipleship

DAILY
Psalm 29
The glory of God

Day of Pentecost

On the Day of Pentecost, if the Old Testament passage from Genesis is chosen for the first reading, the passage from Acts is used as the second reading.

Preparation for Sunday

THURSDAY
Isaiah 32:11-17
The spirit poured out to renew the earth
Galatians 5:16-25
The fruit of the Spirit

FRIDAY
Isaiah 44:1-4
The spirit poured out to renew the faithful
Galatians 6:7-10
Reaping eternal life from the Spirit

SATURDAY
2 Kings 2:1-15a
The spirit on Elijah and Elisha
Luke 1:5-17
God's Spirit to come on John the Baptist

DAILY
Psalm 104:24-34, 35b
Renewing the face of the earth

Day of Pentecost

Acts 2:1-21
Filled with the Spirit
Psalm 104:24-34, 35b
Send forth your spirit
Romans 8:14-17
The Spirit makes us children of God
John 14:8-17 [25-27]
The Spirit of truth

or

Genesis 11:1-9
God destroys the tower of Babel

or

Acts 2:1-21
Filled with the Spirit

Reflection on Sunday

MONDAY
Joel 2:18-29
God's spirit poured out
1 Corinthians 2:1-11
About the Spirit of God

TUESDAY
Ezekiel 11:14-25
God will gather the people
1 Corinthians 2:12-16
About the Spirit of God

WEDNESDAY
Numbers 24:1-14
Balaam speaks with God's spirit
Luke 1:26-38
God's Spirit comes on Mary

DAILY
Psalm 48
The God of Zion

Season
after
Pentecost

YEAR C

SEASON AFTER PENTECOST
ORDINARY TIME

Trinity Sunday
First Sunday after Pentecost

Preparation for Sunday

THURSDAY
Proverbs 3:13-18
Wisdom is a tree of life
Ephesians 1:17-19
Wisdom in the Trinity

FRIDAY
Proverbs 3:19-26
By wisdom God creates and preserves
Ephesians 4:1-6
Life in the Trinity

SATURDAY
Proverbs 4:1-9
Choose God's wisdom
Luke 2:41-52
Jesus increases in wisdom

DAILY
Psalm 8
Your majesty is praised above the heavens

Trinity Sunday

Proverbs 8:1-4, 22-31
Wisdom rejoices in the creation
Psalm 8
Your majesty is praised above the heavens
Romans 5:1-5
God's love poured into our hearts
John 16:12-15
The Spirit will guide you into the truth

Reflection on Sunday

MONDAY
Proverbs 7:1-4
Wisdom is your sister
Ephesians 4:7-16
Building up the body of Christ

TUESDAY
Proverbs 8:4-21
Wisdom's riches
Ephesians 5:15-20
Living as wise ones in the Trinity

WEDNESDAY
Daniel 1:1-21
Daniel's wisdom
Luke 1:46b-55
Mary sings of God

DAILY
Psalm 124
We have escaped like a bird

Proper 3 [8]
*Sunday between May 24 and 28 inclusive
(if after Trinity Sunday)*

Preparation for Sunday

THURSDAY
Proverbs 13:1-12
A fulfilled desire is like a tree of life
Romans 5:12—6:2
Eternal life through Jesus Christ

FRIDAY
Proverbs 15:1-9
A gentle tongue is a tree of life
1 Thessalonians 4:13-18
The trumpet of resurrection

SATURDAY
Isaiah 30:8-17
Rebellion against God's word
John 16:1-4a
Remembering the words of Jesus

DAILY
Psalm 92:1-4, 12-15
The righteous flourish like a palm tree

Sunday, May 24–28

Sirach 27:4-7
A tree's fruit discloses its cultivation
Psalm 92:1-4, 12-15
The righteous flourish like a palm tree
1 Corinthians 15:51-58
The mystery of the resurrection
Luke 6:39-49
Building on a firm foundation

or

Isaiah 55:10-13
God's word goes forth

Reflection on Sunday

MONDAY
Jeremiah 24:1-10
The good figs and the bad figs
1 Corinthians 16:1-12
Paul's travel plans

TUESDAY
Jeremiah 29:10-19
The rotten figs
1 Corinthians 16:13-24
Paul's farewell

WEDNESDAY
Proverbs 5:1-23
The bad woman or the good wife
Luke 14:34-35
Good or bad salt

DAILY
Psalm 1
The fruited tree or the chaff

Proper 4 [9]

*Sunday between May 29 and June 4 inclusive
(if after Trinity Sunday)*

Preparation for Sunday

THURSDAY
1 Kings 12:20-33
Jereboam's golden calves
2 Corinthians 5:11-17
Beyond a human point of view

FRIDAY
1 Kings 16:29-34
Ahab and Jezebel worship Baal
2 Corinthians 11:1-6
Beware of those who proclaim another Jesus

SATURDAY
1 Kings 18:1-19
Elijah confronts Ahab
Luke 4:31-37
Healing the man with an unclean spirit

DAILY
Psalm 96
Give glory to God's name

Sunday, May 29–June 4

1 Kings 18:20-21 [22-29] 30-39
Elijah and the prophets of Baal
Psalm 96
Give glory to God's name
Galatians 1:1-12
Beware of contrary gospels
Luke 7:1-10
Jesus heals the centurion's slave

Reflection on Sunday

MONDAY
Ezekiel 8:1-18
Idols in the temple, violence in the land
Acts 8:26-40
The gospel is shared with an Ethiopian

TUESDAY
Ezekiel 14:1-11
Idols in human hearts
Acts 3:1-10
Healing the crippled beggar

WEDNESDAY
Ezekiel 14:12-23
Noah, Daniel, and Job cannot save
Mark 7:24-30
The Syrophoenician woman's faith

DAILY
Psalm 135
Idols do not speak or hear

Proper 4 [9]

Sunday between May 29 and June 4 inclusive
(if after Trinity Sunday)

Preparation for Sunday

THURSDAY
1 Kings 6:23-38
The splendor of God's temple
2 Corinthians 5:11-17
Beyond a human point of view

FRIDAY
1 Kings 8:14-21
A house for the name of the Lord
2 Corinthians 11:1-6
Beware of those who proclaim another Jesus

SATURDAY
1 Kings 8:31-40
God knows every human heart
Luke 4:31-37
Healing the man with an unclean spirit

DAILY
Psalm 96:1-9
Praise to God among the nations

Sunday, May 29–June 4

1 Kings 8:22-23, 41-43
God's everlasting covenant for all
Psalm 96:1-9
Praise to God among the nations
Galatians 1:1-12
Beware of contrary gospels
Luke 7:1-10
Jesus heals the centurion's slave

Reflection on Sunday

MONDAY
Jonah 4:1-11
God's mercy on the Ninevites
Acts 8:26-40
The gospel is shared with an Ethiopian

TUESDAY
Nehemiah 1:1-11
Asking God to gather the people
Acts 3:1-10
Healing the crippled beggar

WEDNESDAY
Isaiah 56:1-8
God welcomes the outcasts
Mark 7:24-30
The Syrophoenician woman's faith

DAILY
Psalm 5
God's favor like a shield

Proper 5 [10]
Sunday between June 5 and 11 inclusive (if after Trinity Sunday)

Preparation for Sunday

THURSDAY
Exodus 29:1-9
The bread for Aaron's ordination
Acts 22:6-21
Paul, the persecutor, is healed

FRIDAY
Numbers 15:17-26
God commands a donation of bread
Acts 26:1-11
Paul pursued believers even to foreign cities

SATURDAY
Joshua 9:1-27
Shared bread saves the Gibeonites
Matthew 9:2-8
Forgiveness and healing

DAILY
Psalm 146
God lifts those bowed down

Sunday, June 5–11

1 Kings 17:8-16 [17-24]
A widow offers hospitality to Elijah
Psalm 146
God lifts those bowed down
Galatians 1:11-24
Jesus Christ is revealed
Luke 7:11-17
Jesus revives a widow's son

Reflection on Sunday

MONDAY
Job 22:1-20
Job is accused by Eliphaz
Galatians 2:1-10
Paul and the pillars of the church

TUESDAY
Job 24:9-25
Those who harm orphans and widows
Galatians 2:11-14
Paul and Peter

WEDNESDAY
Job 31:16-23
Job defends his support of the poor
Luke 8:40-56
A girl raised to life, a woman healed

DAILY
Psalm 68:1-10, 19-20
God protects the widows

Proper 5 [10]

Sunday between June 5 and 11 inclusive
(if after Trinity Sunday)

Preparation for Sunday

THURSDAY
2 Samuel 14:1-11
A woman pretends to be a widow
Acts 22:6-21
Paul, the persecutor, is healed

FRIDAY
2 Samuel 14:12-24
A plea to restore a lost son
Acts 26:1-11
Paul pursued believers even to foreign cities

SATURDAY
2 Samuel 14:25-33
David welcomes the return of Absalom
Matthew 9:2-8
Forgiveness and healing

DAILY
Psalm 30
My God, you restored me to health

Sunday, June 5–11

1 Kings 17:17-24
Elijah revives a widow's son
Psalm 30
My God, you restored me to health
Galatians 1:11-24
Jesus Christ is revealed
Luke 7:11-17
Jesus revives a widow's son

Reflection on Sunday

MONDAY
Genesis 22:1-14
God saves Isaac from death
Galatians 2:1-10
Paul and the pillars of the church

TUESDAY
Judges 11:29-40
Jephthah's daughter
Galatians 2:11-14
Paul and Peter

WEDNESDAY
Jeremiah 8:14-22
A balm in Gilead
Luke 8:40-56
A girl raised to life, a woman healed

DAILY
Psalm 68:1-10, 19-20
God protects the widows

Proper 6 [11]

*Sunday between June 12 and 18 inclusive
(if after Trinity Sunday)*

Preparation for Sunday

THURSDAY
1 Kings 20:1-22
An enemy threatens Ahab
James 4:1-7
God gives grace to the humble

FRIDAY
1 Kings 20:23-34
Ahab defeats an enemy
Romans 11:1-10
A remnant chosen by grace

SATURDAY
1 Kings 20:35-43
A prophet condemns Ahab
Luke 5:17-26
Jesus forgives sins and heals

DAILY
Psalm 5:1-8
Trust in God for deliverance

Sunday, June 12–18

1 Kings 21:1-10 [11-14] 15-21a
Ahab kills the owner of a vineyard
Psalm 5:1-8
Trust in God for deliverance
Galatians 2:15-21
Justification through grace
Luke 7:36—8:3
The woman anointing Jesus is forgiven

Reflection on Sunday

MONDAY
Genesis 31:17-35
Rachel steals Laban's gods
Galatians 3:1-9
Abraham believed God

TUESDAY
2 Samuel 19:31-43
Judah steals King David
Galatians 3:10-14
Blessing comes to the Gentiles

WEDNESDAY
Malachi 3:5-12
Do not rob God
Mark 2:1-12
Jesus forgives and heals

DAILY
Psalm 83
The crafty plot against God's people

Proper 6 [11]

Sunday between June 12 and 18 inclusive
(if after Trinity Sunday)

Preparation for Sunday

THURSDAY
2 Samuel 13:23-39
Absalom avenges Tamar's rape
James 4:1-7
God gives grace to the humble

FRIDAY
2 Samuel 15:1-12
Absalom plots against David
Romans 11:1-10
A remnant chosen by grace

SATURDAY
2 Samuel 18:28 — 19:8
David mourns Absalom
Luke 5:17-26
Jesus forgives sins and heals

DAILY
Psalm 32
You forgive the guilt of my sin

Sunday, June 12–18

2 Samuel 11:26 — 12:10, 13-15
Nathan tells the story of the lamb
Psalm 32
You forgive the guilt of my sin
Galatians 2:15-21
Justification through grace
Luke 7:36 — 8:3
The woman anointing Jesus is forgiven

Reflection on Sunday

MONDAY
2 Chronicles 29:1-19
Hezekiah renews worship of God
Galatians 3:1-9
Abraham believed God

TUESDAY
2 Chronicles 30:1-12
The people return to the Lord
Galatians 3:10-14
Blessing comes to the Gentiles

WEDNESDAY
2 Chronicles 30:13-27
The people are forgiven and healed
Mark 2:1-12
Jesus forgives and heals

DAILY
Psalm 130
Prayer for mercy

Proper 7 [12]

Sunday between June 19 and 25 inclusive
(if after Trinity Sunday)

Preparation for Sunday

THURSDAY
Genesis 24:1-21
Rebekah at the well
Romans 2:17-29
Real circumcision is a matter of the heart

SATURDAY
Proverbs 11:3-13
An intelligent person remains silent
Matthew 9:27-34
Healing the blind, casting out a demon

FRIDAY
Job 6:14-30
Teach me, and I will be silent
Galatians 3:15-22
The purpose of the law

DAILY
Psalm 42 and 43
Send out your light and truth

Sunday, June 19–25

1 Kings 19:1-4 [5-7] 8-15a
Elijah hears God in silence
Psalm 42 and 43
Send out your light and truth
Galatians 3:23-29
Clothed with Christ in baptism
Luke 8:26-39
Jesus casts out demons

Reflection on Sunday

MONDAY
2 Kings 9:1-13
The house of Ahab destroyed
1 Corinthians 1:18-31
The power and wisdom of God

WEDNESDAY
2 Kings 9:30-37
Jezebel's violent death
Luke 9:37-43a
Jesus heals a boy with a demon

TUESDAY
2 Kings 9:14-26
Injustice to Naboth avenged
Ephesians 2:11-22
One new humanity in Christ

DAILY
Psalm 59
Deliver me from my enemies

Proper 7 [12]

Sunday between June 19 and 25 inclusive
(if after Trinity Sunday)

Preparation for Sunday

THURSDAY
Isaiah 56:9-12
Israel's leaders are corrupt
Romans 2:17-29
Real circumcision is a matter of the heart

FRIDAY
Isaiah 57:1-13
The righteous perish and no one cares
Galatians 3:15-22
The purpose of the law

SATURDAY
Isaiah 59:1-8
Sin creates barriers
Matthew 9:27-34
Healing the blind, casting out a demon

DAILY
Psalm 22:19-28
I will praise you

Sunday, June 19–25

Isaiah 65:1-9
The prophet sent to a rebellious people
Psalm 22:19-28
I will praise you
Galatians 3:23-29
Clothed with Christ in baptism
Luke 8:26-39
Jesus casts out demons

Reflection on Sunday

MONDAY
Job 18:1-21
God will destroy the wicked
1 Corinthians 1:18-31
The power and wisdom of God

TUESDAY
Job 19:1-22
Job questions God's ways
Ephesians 2:11-22
One new humanity in Christ

WEDNESDAY
Ezekiel 32:1-10
Evil like a dragon will be destroyed
Luke 9:37-43a
Jesus heals a boy with a demon

DAILY
Psalm 64
Prayer for protection

Proper 8 [13]

Sunday between June 26 and July 2 inclusive

Preparation for Sunday

THURSDAY
1 Kings 22:29-40, 51-53
Ahab's chariot of death
2 Corinthians 13:5-10
Examine yourselves concerning the faith

FRIDAY
2 Kings 1:1-12
Elijah and fire from heaven
Galatians 4:8-20
Paul reproves the hearers

SATURDAY
2 Kings 1:13-18; 2:3-5
Ahaziah's apostasy; Elijah's farewell
Luke 9:21-27
Following Jesus

DAILY
Psalm 77:1-2, 11-20
You have redeemed your people

Sunday, June 26–July 2

2 Kings 2:1-2, 6-14
Elijah ascends into heaven
Psalm 77:1-2, 11-20
You have redeemed your people
Galatians 5:1, 13-25
Love is the whole of the law
Luke 9:51-62
Jesus says, Follow me

Reflection on Sunday

MONDAY
2 Kings 2:15-22
Elisha's ministry and miracles
1 John 2:7-11
Living in the light of love

TUESDAY
2 Kings 3:4-20
Pools of water without rain
Ephesians 5:6-20
The fruit of the light

WEDNESDAY
2 Kings 4:1-7
Elisha and the widow's oil
Matthew 10:16-25
Sheep in the midst of wolves

DAILY
Psalm 75
It is God who lifts up

Proper 8 [13]

Sunday between June 26 and July 2 inclusive

Preparation for Sunday

THURSDAY
Leviticus 9:22—10:11
God's fire consumes Aaron's sons
2 Corinthians 13:5-10
Examine yourselves concerning the faith

FRIDAY
2 Kings 1:1-16
God's fire consumes the king's men
Galatians 4:8-20
Paul reproves the hearers

SATURDAY
Deuteronomy 32:15-27, 39-43
God's anger like a fire
Luke 9:21-27
Following Jesus

DAILY
Psalm 16
Protect me, O God

Sunday, June 26–July 2

1 Kings 19:15-16, 19-21
Elijah says, Follow me
Psalm 16
Protect me, O God
Galatians 5:1, 13-25
Love is the whole of the law
Luke 9:51-62
Jesus says, Follow me

Reflection on Sunday

MONDAY
Genesis 24:34-41, 50-67
Rebekah follows Abraham's servant
1 John 2:7-11
Living in the light of love

TUESDAY
Jeremiah 3:15-18
Nations cease to follow their own will
Ephesians 5:6-20
The fruit of the light

WEDNESDAY
Jeremiah 23:16-22
Following stubborn hearts
Matthew 10:16-25
Sheep in the midst of wolves

DAILY
Psalm 140
Prayer for deliverance

Proper 9 [14]
Sunday between July 3 and 9 inclusive

Preparation for Sunday

THURSDAY
2 Kings 4:8-17
A barren woman longs for a child
Romans 7:14-25
I do not do the good I want

FRIDAY
2 Kings 4:18-31
Elisha and a grieving mother
2 Corinthians 8:1-7
Poverty overflows in generosity

SATURDAY
2 Kings 4:32-37
Elisha raises a beloved son
Luke 9:1-6
The mission of the twelve

DAILY
Psalm 30
My God, I cried to you for help

Sunday, July 3–9

2 Kings 5:1-14
Elisha heals Naaman's leprosy
Psalm 30
My God, I cried to you for help
Galatians 6:[1-6] 7-16
Do what is right now
Luke 10:1-11, 16-20
Jesus sends out seventy disciples

Reflection on Sunday

MONDAY
2 Kings 5:15-19a
Naaman seeks to repay Elisha
Acts 19:21-27
Demetrius opposes Paul

TUESDAY
2 Kings 5:19b-27
A servant's dishonesty brings leprosy
Acts 19:28-41
A riot follows Paul's preaching

WEDNESDAY
2 Kings 6:1-7
The miracle of the ax head
Luke 10:13-16
Woe to unrepentant cities

DAILY
Psalm 6
Be gracious and heal me

Proper 9 [14]
Sunday between July 3 and 9 inclusive

Preparation for Sunday

THURSDAY
2 Kings 21:1-15
God will wipe Jerusalem as a dish
Romans 7:14-25
I do not do the good I want

FRIDAY
Jeremiah 51:47-58
Let Jerusalem come into your mind
2 Corinthians 8:1-7
Poverty overflows in generosity

SATURDAY
Zechariah 14:10-21
Jerusalem shall abide in security
Luke 9:1-6
The mission of the twelve

DAILY
Psalm 66:1-9
God holds our souls in life

Sunday, July 3–9

Isaiah 66:10-14
Jerusalem, a nursing mother
Psalm 66:1-9
God holds our souls in life
Galatians 6:[1-6] 7-16
Do what is right now
Luke 10:1-11, 16-20
Jesus sends out seventy disciples

Reflection on Sunday

MONDAY
Jeremiah 6:10-19
Call to faithfulness
Acts 19:21-27
Demetrius opposes Paul

TUESDAY
Jeremiah 8:4-13
Call to faithfulness
Acts 19:28-41
A riot follows Paul's preaching

WEDNESDAY
Joshua 23:1-16
Joshua urges faithfulness
Luke 10:13-16
Woe to unrepentant cities

DAILY
Psalm 119:73-80
Living in faithfulness

Proper 10 [15]
Sunday between July 10 and 16 inclusive

Preparation for Sunday

THURSDAY
Amos 1:1—2:3
Judgment on Israel's neighbors
James 2:14-26
Faith produces good works

FRIDAY
Amos 2:4-11
Judgment on Judah and Israel
Acts 7:9-16
Egypt's food rescues Israel

SATURDAY
Amos 2:12—3:8
Who can but prophesy?
John 3:16-21
God's son saves the world

DAILY
Psalm 82
O God, rule the earth

Sunday, July 10–16

Amos 7:7-17
A plumb line judging the people
Psalm 82
O God, rule the earth
Colossians 1:1-14
The gospel is bearing fruit
Luke 10:25-37
The parable of the merciful Samaritan

Reflection on Sunday

MONDAY
Amos 3:9—4:5
Shameful conduct and its consequences
James 2:1-7
God has chosen the poor

TUESDAY
Amos 4:6-13
Israel, prepare to meet your God
1 John 3:11-17
Do not refuse one in need

WEDNESDAY
Amos 5:1-9
Lament for Israel's sin
Matthew 25:31-46
As you did it to one of the least of these

DAILY
Psalm 7
God is a righteous judge

Proper 10 [15]

Sunday between July 10 and 16 inclusive

Preparation for Sunday

THURSDAY
Genesis 41:14-36
Joseph plans to feed Egypt
James 2:14-26
Faith produces good works

FRIDAY
Genesis 41:37-49
God saves Egypt from starvation
Acts 7:9-16
Egypt's food rescues Israel

SATURDAY
Leviticus 19:1-4, 32-37
Mercy to the alien
John 3:16-21
God's son saves the world

DAILY
Psalm 25:1-10
Show me your ways

Sunday, July 10–16

Deuteronomy 30:9-14
God delights in your fruitfulness
Psalm 25:1-10
Show me your ways
Colossians 1:1-14
The gospel is bearing fruit
Luke 10:25-37
The parable of the merciful Samaritan

Reflection on Sunday

MONDAY
Job 24:1-8
The needy are thrust off the road
James 2:1-7
God has chosen the poor

TUESDAY
Proverbs 19:1-17
Kindness to the poor
1 John 3:11-17
Do not refuse one in need

WEDNESDAY
Ecclesiastes 9:13-18
One bungler destroys much good
Matthew 25:31-46
As you did it to one of the least of these

DAILY
Psalm 25:11-20
I take refuge in you, O God

Proper 11 [16]

Sunday between July 17 and 23 inclusive

Preparation for Sunday

THURSDAY
Amos 5:10-17
Hate evil and love good
Hebrews 5:1-6
Christ did not glorify himself

FRIDAY
Amos 5:18-27
Let justice roll down like waters
Ephesians 3:14-21
The love of Christ surpasses knowledge

SATURDAY
Amos 6:1-14
Punishment for self-indulgence
Luke 8:4-10
Jesus speaks in parables

DAILY
Psalm 52
I am like a green olive tree

Sunday, July 17–23

Amos 8:1-12
A famine of hearing God's words
Psalm 52
I am like a green olive tree
Colossians 1:15-28
A hymn to Christ
Luke 10:38-42
Choosing the better part

Reflection on Sunday

MONDAY
Amos 7:1-6
Amos pleads for forgiveness
Colossians 1:27—2:7
To know Christ

TUESDAY
Amos 8:13—9:4
No one can hide from God
1 John 2:1-6
Walking as Christ walked

WEDNESDAY
Amos 9:5-15
God will restore the fortunes of Israel
John 6:41-51
Whoever eats this bread will live forever

DAILY
Psalm 119:17-32
Put false ways far from me

Proper 11 [16]
Sunday between July 17 and 23 inclusive

Preparation for Sunday

THURSDAY
Genesis 12:10-20
Pharaoh offers hospitality to Sarai
Hebrews 5:1-6
Christ did not glorify himself

FRIDAY
Genesis 13:1-18
Abram and Lot separate peacefully
Ephesians 3:14-21
The love of Christ surpasses knowledge

SATURDAY
Genesis 14:1-16
Lot is rescued
Luke 8:4-10
Jesus speaks in parables

DAILY
Psalm 15
Leading a blameless life

Sunday, July 17–23

Genesis 18:1-10a
The hospitality of Abraham and Sarah
Psalm 15
Leading a blameless life
Colossians 1:15-28
A hymn to Christ
Luke 10:38-42
Choosing the better part

Reflection on Sunday

MONDAY
Exodus 18:1-12
Jethro's family eats before God
Colossians 1:27—2:7
To know Christ

TUESDAY
Proverbs 9:1-18
The wise and foolish women
1 John 2:1-6
Walking as Christ walked

WEDNESDAY
Deuteronomy 12:1-12
The promise to eat before God
John 6:41-51
Whoever eats this bread will live forever

DAILY
Psalm 119:97-104
God's word like honey

Proper 12 [17]

Sunday between July 24 and 30 inclusive

Preparation for Sunday

THURSDAY
Hosea 4:1-19
God condemns Israel's idolatry
Acts 1:15-20
A traitor's life ends

SATURDAY
Hosea 1:11—2:15
God's people are unfaithful
Luke 8:22-25
Jesus' disciples cry out for safety

FRIDAY
Hosea 5:1-15
Impending judgment
Acts 2:22-36
The Messiah is handed over to death

DAILY
Psalm 85
Righteousness and peace

Sunday, July 24–30

Hosea 1:2-10
Hosea's marriage
Psalm 85
Righteousness and peace
Colossians 2:6-15 [16-19]
Buried with Christ in baptism
Luke 11:1-13
Jesus teaches prayer

Reflection on Sunday

MONDAY
Hosea 2:14—3:5
God marries unfaithful Israel
Colossians 2:16—3:1
About false regulations

WEDNESDAY
Hosea 6:11—7:16
Misplaced trust
Matthew 5:43-48
Pray for those who persecute you

TUESDAY
Hosea 6:1-10
A call to repentance unheeded
Romans 9:30—10:4
Christ is the end of the law

DAILY
Psalm 44
God knows the secrets of the heart

Proper 12 [17]

Sunday between July 24 and 30 inclusive

Preparation for Sunday

THURSDAY
Esther 2:19—3:6
The Jews save a king's life
Acts 1:15-20
A traitor's life ends

FRIDAY
Esther 3:7-15
Haman's plot to kill the Jews
Acts 2:22-36
The Messiah is handed over to death

SATURDAY
Esther 4:1-17
Royal dignity for such a time as this
Luke 8:22-25
Jesus' disciples cry out for safety

DAILY
Psalm 138
Your love endures forever

Sunday, July 24–30

Genesis 18:20-32
Abraham bargains with God
Psalm 138
Your love endures forever
Colossians 2:6-15 [16-19]
Buried with Christ in baptism
Luke 11:1-13
Jesus teaches prayer

Reflection on Sunday

MONDAY
Esther 5:1-14
A banquet guest with a murderous heart
Colossians 2:16—3:1
About false regulations

TUESDAY
Esther 6:1—7:6
A royal reversal of fortunes
Romans 9:30—10:4
Christ is the end of the law

WEDNESDAY
Esther 7:7—8:17
Esther saves her people
Matthew 5:43-48
Pray for those who persecute you

DAILY
Psalm 55:16-23
Cast your burden on God

Proper 13 [18]

Sunday between July 31 and August 6 inclusive

Preparation for Sunday

THURSDAY
Hosea 8:1-14
Israel's stubborn apostasy
Romans 11:33-36
God's riches, wisdom, and knowledge

FRIDAY
Hosea 9:1-17
Punishment for Israel's sin
Ephesians 4:17-24
A new self in the likeness of God

SATURDAY
Hosea 10:1-15
Israel's sin
Mark 10:17-22
Treasure in heaven

DAILY
Psalm 107:1-9, 43
Give thanks to the Most High

Sunday, July 31–August 6

Hosea 11:1-11
Like a mother, God loves Israel
Psalm 107:1-9, 43
Give thanks to the Most High
Colossians 3:1-11
Clothed in Christ
Luke 12:13-21
Be rich toward God, your treasure

Reflection on Sunday

MONDAY
Hosea 11:12—12:14
The long history of rebellion
Colossians 3:18—4:1
A household code

TUESDAY
Hosea 13:1-16
Relentless judgment on Israel
Colossians 4:2-6
Wise conduct toward outsiders

WEDNESDAY
Hosea 14:1-9
A plea for repentance
Luke 12:22-31
Trust in God

DAILY
Psalm 60
With God we shall do valiantly

Proper 13 [18]
Sunday between July 31 and August 6 inclusive

Preparation for Sunday

THURSDAY
Proverbs 23:1-11
Resist the allure of becoming rich
Romans 11:33-36
God's riches, wisdom, and knowledge

FRIDAY
Proverbs 24:1-12
By wisdom a house is built
Ephesians 4:17-24
A new self in the likeness of God

SATURDAY
Ecclesiastes 1:1-11
Nothing new under the sun
Mark 10:17-22
Treasure in heaven

DAILY
Psalm 49:1-12
The folly of trust in riches

Sunday, July 31–August 6

Ecclesiastes 1:2, 12-14; 2:18-23
Search out wisdom
Psalm 49:1-12
The folly of trust in riches
Colossians 3:1-11
Clothed in Christ
Luke 12:13-21
Be rich toward God, your treasure

Reflection on Sunday

MONDAY
Ecclesiastes 2:1-17
The fool accumulates wealth
Colossians 3:18—4:1
A household code

TUESDAY
Ecclesiastes 3:16—4:8
Death comes to all
Colossians 4:2-6
Wise conduct toward outsiders

WEDNESDAY
Ecclesiastes 12:1-8, 13-14
Remember God
Luke 12:22-31
Trust in God

DAILY
Psalm 127
Unless the Lord builds the house

Proper 14 [19]

Sunday between August 7 and 13 inclusive

Preparation for Sunday

THURSDAY
Isaiah 9:8-17
Judgment on arrogance
Romans 9:1-9
True descendants of Abraham

FRIDAY
Isaiah 9:18—10:4
The needy deprived of their right
Acts 7:1-8
Descendants promised to Abraham

SATURDAY
Isaiah 1:2-9, 21-23
The wickedness of Judah
Matthew 6:19-24
Treasures and masters

DAILY
Psalm 50:1-8, 22-23
The salvation of God

Sunday, August 7–13

Isaiah 1:1, 10-20
Learn to do good
Psalm 50:1-8, 22-23
The salvation of God
Hebrews 11:1-3, 8-16
Abraham's faith
Luke 12:32-40
The treasure of the kingdom

Reflection on Sunday

MONDAY
Isaiah 2:1-4
A vision of peace
Hebrews 11:1-7
The ancestors' faith

TUESDAY
Isaiah 24:1-13
God lays waste the earth
Hebrews 11:17-28
The faith of Abraham's descendants

WEDNESDAY
Isaiah 24:14-23
God reigns in majesty
Luke 12:41-48
A parable of the slaves

DAILY
Psalm 11
God loves righteous deeds

Proper 14 [19]
Sunday between August 7 and 13 inclusive

Preparation for Sunday

THURSDAY
Job 21:1-16
The rich blessed with children despise God
Romans 9:1-9
True descendants of Abraham

FRIDAY
Ecclesiastes 6:1-6
Those who waste life
Acts 7:1-8
Descendants promised to Abraham

SATURDAY
Genesis 11:27-32
The ancestors of Abram and Sarai
Matthew 6:19-24
Treasures and masters

DAILY
Psalm 33:12-22
Let your loving kindness be upon us

Sunday, August 7–13

Genesis 15:1-6
God's promise of a child
Psalm 33:12-22
Let your lovingkindness be upon us
Hebrews 11:1-3, 8-16
Abraham's faith
Luke 12:32-40
The treasure of the kingdom

Reflection on Sunday

MONDAY
2 Chronicles 33:1-17
Manasseh returns to God
Hebrews 11:1-7
The ancestors' faith

TUESDAY
2 Chronicles 34:22-33
Huldah preaches the covenant
Hebrews 11:17-28
The faith of Abraham's descendants

WEDNESDAY
Jeremiah 33:14-26
God remembers the covenant
Luke 12:41-48
A parable of the slaves

DAILY
Psalm 89:1-18
God's covenant with David

Proper 15 [20]
Sunday between August 14 and 20 inclusive

Preparation for Sunday

THURSDAY
Isaiah 2:5-11
Judgment pronounced
Hebrews 10:26-31
God's judgment

FRIDAY
Isaiah 3:1-17
The people crushed
Hebrews 10:32-39
Do not abandon your confidence

SATURDAY
Isaiah 3:18—4:6
After judgment, glory
Matthew 24:15-27
The desolating sacrilege

DAILY
Psalm 80:1-2, 8-19
O God, tend this vine

Sunday, August 14–20

Isaiah 5:1-7
The vineyard destroyed
Psalm 80:1-2, 8-19
O God, tend this vine
Hebrews 11:29—12:2
The faith of the Hebrew people
Luke 12:49-56
Jesus brings fire on earth

Reflection on Sunday

MONDAY
Isaiah 5:8-23
Song of a barren vineyard
1 John 4:1-6
False prophets are in the world

TUESDAY
Isaiah 5:24-30
Foreigners invade the land
Acts 7:44-53
Our ancestors persecuted true prophets

WEDNESDAY
Isaiah 27:1-13
The keeper of the vineyard
Luke 19:45-48
Jesus cleanses the temple

DAILY
Psalm 74
Rise up, O God, plead your cause

SEASON AFTER PENTECOST 276 YEAR C

Proper 15 [20]

Sunday between August 14 and 20 inclusive

Preparation for Sunday

THURSDAY
Joshua 7:1, 10-26
Achan punished
Hebrews 10:26-31
God's judgment

FRIDAY
1 Samuel 5:1-12
The Philistines punished
Hebrews 10:32-39
Do not abandon your confidence

SATURDAY
1 Samuel 6:1-16
The Philistines atone for sacrilege
Matthew 24:15-27
The desolating sacrilege

DAILY
Psalm 82
O God, rule the earth

Sunday, August 14–20

Jeremiah 23:23-29
God's word is like fire
Psalm 82
O God, rule the earth
Hebrews 11:29—12:2
The faith of the Hebrew people
Luke 12:49-56
Jesus brings fire on earth

Reflection on Sunday

MONDAY
Jeremiah 23:30-40
False prophets
1 John 4:1-6
False prophets are in the world

TUESDAY
Jeremiah 25:15-29
The cup of God's wrath
Acts 7:44-53
Our ancestors persecuted true prophets

WEDNESDAY
Jeremiah 25:30-38
The peaceful flock is devastated
Luke 19:45-48
Jesus cleanses the temple

DAILY
Psalm 32
Prayer for forgiveness

Proper 16 [21]

Sunday between August 21 and 27 inclusive

Preparation for Sunday

THURSDAY
Jeremiah 6:1-19
Flee for safety
Hebrews 12:3-17
Call for endurance

FRIDAY
Jeremiah 6:20-30
Unacceptable offerings
Acts 17:1-9
Paul preaches Christ on the sabbath

SATURDAY
Jeremiah 1:1-3, 11-19
A vision of disaster
Luke 6:1-5
Picking grain on the sabbath

DAILY
Psalm 71:1-6
You have been my strength

Sunday, August 21–27

Jeremiah 1:4-10
Jeremiah called to be a prophet
Psalm 71:1-6
You have been my strength
Hebrews 12:18-29
Coming to the city of the living God
Luke 13:10-17
Jesus heals on the sabbath

Reflection on Sunday

MONDAY
Jeremiah 7:1-15
Jeremiah announces God's judgment
Hebrews 3:7—4:11
Sabbath rest of God's people

TUESDAY
Jeremiah 7:16-26
The people's disobedience
Revelation 3:7-13
The new Jerusalem from heaven

WEDNESDAY
Jeremiah 7:27-34
The prophet's words scorned
Luke 6:6-11
Jesus heals on the sabbath

DAILY
Psalm 10
Why do the wicked renounce God?

Proper 16 [21]

Sunday between August 21 and 27 inclusive

Preparation for Sunday

THURSDAY
Numbers 15:32-41
The severity of breaking sabbath law
Hebrews 12:3-17
Call for endurance

FRIDAY
2 Chronicles 8:12-15
Solomon honors sabbaths
Acts 17:1-9
Paul preaches Christ on the sabbath

SATURDAY
Nehemiah 13:15-22
Nehemiah enforces sabbath law
Luke 6:1-5
Picking grain on the sabbath

DAILY
Psalm 103:1-8
Crowned with mercy

Sunday, August 21–27

Isaiah 58:9b-14
Do not trample the sabbath
Psalm 103:1-8
Crowned with mercy
Hebrews 12:18-29
Coming to the city of the living God
Luke 13:10-17
Jesus heals on the sabbath

Reflection on Sunday

MONDAY
Ezekiel 20:1-17
The people profaned the sabbath
Hebrews 3:7—4:11
Sabbath rest of God's people

TUESDAY
Ezekiel 20:18-32
Israel become like the nations
Revelation 3:7-13
The new Jerusalem from heaven

WEDNESDAY
Ezekiel 20:33-44
God restores rebellious Israel
Luke 6:6-11
Jesus heals on the sabbath

DAILY
Psalm 109:21-31
Praise for healing

Proper 17 [22]

Sunday between August 28 and September 3 inclusive

Preparation for Sunday

THURSDAY
Jeremiah 11:1-17
The covenant broken
1 Peter 3:8-12
Repay abuse with a blessing

FRIDAY
Jeremiah 12:1-13
Jeremiah complains to God
1 Peter 4:7-11
Be hospitable to one another

SATURDAY
Jeremiah 2:1-3, 14-22
God pleads with Israel
Matthew 20:20-28
A request for seats of honor

DAILY
Psalm 81:1, 10-16
Honey from the rock

Sunday, August 28–September 3

Jeremiah 2:4-13
Israel forsakes the Lord
Psalm 81:1, 10-16
Honey from the rock
Hebrews 13:1-8, 15-16
God is with us
Luke 14:1, 7-14
Invite the poor to your banquet

Reflection on Sunday

MONDAY
Jeremiah 2:23-37
Israel shall be shamed
Hebrews 13:7-21
Call for faithfulness

TUESDAY
Jeremiah 3:1-14
Israel called to repentance
Titus 1:1-9
Humble and hospitable leaders

WEDNESDAY
Jeremiah 3:15-25
Shepherds chosen by God
Luke 14:15-24
God's hospitality to the humble

DAILY
Psalm 58
Like water that runs away

Proper 17 [22]
Sunday between August 28 and September 3 inclusive

Preparation for Sunday

THURSDAY
Proverbs 15:13-17
A continual feast for the poor
1 Peter 3:8-12
Repay abuse with a blessing

FRIDAY
Proverbs 18:6-12
Humility precedes honor
1 Peter 4:7-11
Be hospitable to one another

SATURDAY
Proverbs 21:1-4, 24-26
The righteous give and do not hold back
Matthew 20:20-28
A request for seats of honor

DAILY
Psalm 112
The righteous are merciful

Sunday, August 28–September 3

Sirach 10:12-18
Judgment upon the proud
Psalm 112
The righteous are merciful
Hebrews 13:1-8, 15-16
God is with us
Luke 14:1, 7-14
Invite the poor to your banquet

or

Proverbs 25:6-7
Do not put yourself forward

Reflection on Sunday

MONDAY
2 Chronicles 12:1-12
King Rehoboam humbles himself
Hebrews 13:7-21
Call for faithfulness

TUESDAY
Isaiah 2:12-17
Pride shall be brought low
Titus 1:1-9
Humble and hospitable leaders

WEDNESDAY
Isaiah 57:14-21
God blesses the humble
Luke 14:15-24
God's hospitality to the humble

DAILY
Psalm 119:65-72
God blesses the humble

Proper 18 [23]
Sunday between September 4 and 10 inclusive

Preparation for Sunday

THURSDAY
Jeremiah 15:10-21
Jeremiah complains, God reassures
Philippians 2:25-30
Welcome a faithful servant home

FRIDAY
Jeremiah 16:14—17:4
Restoration after judgment
Colossians 4:7-17
A faithful and beloved brother

SATURDAY
Jeremiah 17:14-27
God commands faithfulness
Matthew 10:34-42
The cost of discipleship

DAILY
Psalm 139:1-6, 13-18
You have searched me out

Sunday, September 4–10

Jeremiah 18:1-11
The Lord shapes Israel
Psalm 139:1-6, 13-18
You have searched me out
Philemon 1-21
Paul says, Receive Onesimus
Luke 14:25-33
Give up your possessions

Reflection on Sunday

MONDAY
Jeremiah 18:12-23
Idolatry prevails
1 Timothy 3:14—4:5
Behavior in the church

TUESDAY
Jeremiah 19:1-15
The broken earthenware jug
1 Timothy 4:6-16
Being a servant of Christ

WEDNESDAY
Jeremiah 20:1-18
A persecuted prophet laments
Luke 18:18-30
The rich ruler

DAILY
Psalm 2
Like a potter's vessel

Proper 18 [23]

Sunday between September 4 and 10 inclusive

Preparation for Sunday

THURSDAY
Genesis 39:1-23
Joseph does not sin against God
Philippians 2:25-30
Welcome a faithful servant home

FRIDAY
Deuteronomy 7:12-26
The way of obedience
Colossians 4:7-17
A faithful and beloved brother

SATURDAY
Deuteronomy 29:2-20
A renewed covenant
Matthew 10:34-42
The cost of discipleship

DAILY
Psalm 1
Delight in the law

Sunday, September 4–10

Deuteronomy 30:15-20
Walk in the way of life
Psalm 1
Delight in the law
Philemon 1-21
Paul says, Receive Onesimus
Luke 14:25-33
Give up your possessions

Reflection on Sunday

MONDAY
2 Kings 17:24-41
The Assyrians worship other gods
1 Timothy 3:14—4:5
Behavior in the church

TUESDAY
2 Kings 18:9-18
Transgressing the covenant
1 Timothy 4:6-16
Being a servant of Christ

WEDNESDAY
2 Kings 18:19-25; 19:1-7
A king repents, the nation is saved
Luke 18:18-30
The rich ruler

DAILY
Psalm 101
Choosing God's law

Proper 19 [24]
Sunday between September 11 and 17 inclusive

Preparation for Sunday

THURSDAY
Jeremiah 13:20-27
Chaff driven by desert wind
1 Timothy 1:1-11
About false teachers

FRIDAY
Jeremiah 4:1-10
God's wrath like fire
2 Peter 2:1-10a
God judges and rescues

SATURDAY
Jeremiah 4:13-21, 29-31
Judgment like a whirlwind
John 10:11-21
Jesus, the good shepherd

DAILY
Psalm 14
Who seeks after God?

Sunday, September 11–17

Jeremiah 4:11-12, 22-28
Judgment against Jerusalem
Psalm 14
Who seeks after God?
1 Timothy 1:12-17
Christ Jesus came for sinners
Luke 15:1-10
Lost sheep and lost coin

Reflection on Sunday

MONDAY
Jeremiah 5:1-17
Judgment against Jerusalem
1 Timothy 1:18-20
The danger of rejecting conscience

TUESDAY
Jeremiah 5:18-31
The people love falsehood
2 Peter 3:8-13
That all may come to repentance

WEDNESDAY
Jeremiah 14:1-10, 17-22
A plea for healing
Luke 22:31-33, 54-62
Peter denies Jesus

DAILY
Psalm 94
God disciplines the nations

Proper 19 [24]

Sunday between September 11 and 17 inclusive

Preparation for Sunday

THURSDAY
Genesis 6:1-6
Sinful humanity forgets God
1 Timothy 1:1-11
About false teachers

FRIDAY
Genesis 7:6-10; 8:1-5
God remembers faithful Noah
2 Peter 2:1-10a
God judges and rescues

SATURDAY
Genesis 8:20—9:7
A new covenant through Noah
John 10:11-21
Jesus, the good shepherd

DAILY
Psalm 51:1-10
Have mercy upon me, O God

Sunday, September 11–17

Exodus 32:7-14
Moses begs forgiveness
Psalm 51:1-10
Have mercy upon me, O God
1 Timothy 1:12-17
Christ Jesus came for sinners
Luke 15:1-10
Lost sheep and lost coin

Reflection on Sunday

MONDAY
Amos 7:1-6
God relents from punishing Israel
1 Timothy 1:18-20
The danger of rejecting conscience

TUESDAY
Jonah 3:1-10
God relents from punishing Nineveh
2 Peter 3:8-13
That all may come to repentance

WEDNESDAY
Job 40:6-14; 42:1-6
Job repents
Luke 22:31-33, 54-62
Peter denies Jesus

DAILY
Psalm 73
God is my portion

Proper 20 [25]

Sunday between September 18 and 24 inclusive

Preparation for Sunday

THURSDAY
Jeremiah 12:14—13:11
God's people like a ruined loincloth
Romans 3:1-8
The justice of God

FRIDAY
Jeremiah 8:1-13
The shameful forget how to blush
Romans 8:31-39
It is God who justifies

SATURDAY
Jeremiah 8:14-17; 9:2-11
Oppression and deceit multiply
Mark 12:41-44
A widow's offering

DAILY
Psalm 79:1-9
Deliver us and forgive our sins

Sunday, September 18–24

Jeremiah 8:18—9:1
Jeremiah laments over Judah
Psalm 79:1-9
Deliver us and forgive our sins
1 Timothy 2:1-7
One God, one mediator
Luke 16:1-13
Serving God or wealth

Reflection on Sunday

MONDAY
Jeremiah 9:12-26
A scattered people mourn
Acts 4:1-12
Salvation through Jesus Christ

TUESDAY
Jeremiah 10:1-16
Idolatry brings ruin to Israel
1 Corinthians 9:19-23
A servant of the gospel

WEDNESDAY
Jeremiah 10:17-25
Prepare for the coming exile
Luke 20:45—21:4
The rich versus the poor

DAILY
Psalm 106:40-48
God remembered the covenant

Proper 20 [25]

Sunday between September 18 and 24 inclusive

Preparation for Sunday

THURSDAY
Exodus 23:1-9
Justice for all
Romans 3:1-8
The justice of God

FRIDAY
Ezekiel 22:17-31
Israel becomes dross to God
Romans 8:31-39
It is God who justifies

SATURDAY
Isaiah 5:8-23
Calling evil good and good evil
Mark 12:41-44
A widow's offering

DAILY
Psalm 113
Our God lifts up the poor

Sunday, September 18–24

Amos 8:4-7
Those who trample the needy
Psalm 113
Our God lifts up the poor
1 Timothy 2:1-7
One God, one mediator
Luke 16:1-13
Serving God or wealth

Reflection on Sunday

MONDAY
Proverbs 14:12-31
Oppressing the poor
Acts 4:1-12
Salvation through Jesus Christ

TUESDAY
Proverbs 17:1-5
Oppressing the poor
1 Corinthians 9:19-23
A servant of the gospel

WEDNESDAY
Proverbs 21:10-16
Ears closed to the cry of the poor
Luke 20:45—21:4
The rich versus the poor

DAILY
Psalm 12
Help for the poor

Proper 21 [26]

Sunday between September 25 and October 1 inclusive

Preparation for Sunday

THURSDAY
Jeremiah 23:9-22
False prophets denounced
2 Corinthians 8:8-15
Christ became poor

FRIDAY
Jeremiah 23:23-32
God's word like a hammer
Ephesians 2:1-10
God is rich in mercy

SATURDAY
Jeremiah 24:1-10
God will bring back the exiles
Luke 9:43b-48
Welcoming little ones

DAILY
Psalm 91:1-6, 14-16
God, my refuge

Sunday, September 25–October 1

Jeremiah 32:1-3a, 6-15
Jeremiah buys a field
Psalm 91:1-6, 14-16
God, my refuge
1 Timothy 6:6-19
Pursuing God's justice
Luke 16:19-31
Poor Lazarus and the rich man

Reflection on Sunday

MONDAY
Jeremiah 32:16-35
Jeremiah's prayer, God's assurance
Revelation 3:14-22
Being rich or poor in God

TUESDAY
Jeremiah 32:36-44
I will be their God
James 5:1-6
Riches that rot

WEDNESDAY
Jeremiah 33:1-13
Healing after punishment
Matthew 19:16-22
Treasure in heaven

DAILY
Psalm 119:49-56
Your promise gives me life

Proper 21 [26]
Sunday between September 25 and October 1 inclusive

Preparation for Sunday

THURSDAY
Proverbs 22:2-16
The rich versus the poor
2 Corinthians 8:8-15
Christ became poor

FRIDAY
Proverbs 28:3-10
The rich versus the poor
Ephesians 2:1-10
God is rich in mercy

SATURDAY
Proverbs 28:11-28
Helpers of the poor lack nothing
Luke 9:43b-48
Welcoming little ones

DAILY
Psalm 146
Justice to the oppressed

Sunday, September 25–October 1

Amos 6:1a, 4-7
Warnings to the wealthy
Psalm 146
Justice to the oppressed
1 Timothy 6:6-19
Pursuing God's justice
Luke 16:19-31
Poor Lazarus and the rich man

Reflection on Sunday

MONDAY
Amos 6:8-14
Justice turned into poison
Revelation 3:14-22
Being rich or poor in God

TUESDAY
Hosea 10:9-15
Reaping injustice
James 5:1-6
Riches that rot

WEDNESDAY
Hosea 12:2-14
I have gained wealth for myself
Matthew 19:16-22
Treasure in heaven

DAILY
Psalm 62
I wait on God

Proper 22 [27]

Sunday between October 2 and 8 inclusive

Preparation for Sunday

THURSDAY
Jeremiah 52:1-11
Jerusalem besieged
Revelation 2:8-11
Be faithful until death

FRIDAY
Jeremiah 52:12-30
Burning of the temple
Revelation 2:12-29
Call to faithfulness

SATURDAY
Lamentations 1:7-15
Is it nothing to you who pass by?
Matthew 20:29-34
Mercy on persistent blind men

DAILY
Lamentations 3:19-26
Great is your faithfulness

Sunday, October 2–8

Lamentations 1:1-6
Jerusalem empty and destroyed
Lamentations 3:19-26   or
Great is your faithfulness
2 Timothy 1:1-14
Guard the treasure entrusted to you
Luke 17:5-10
Faith the size of a mustard seed

Psalm 137
Weeping by the rivers of Babylon

Reflection on Sunday

MONDAY
Lamentations 1:16-22
My eyes flow with tears
James 1:2-11
Faith produces endurance

TUESDAY
Lamentations 2:13-22
Lament over the beautiful city
1 John 5:1-5, 13-21
Faith overcomes the world

WEDNESDAY
Lamentations 5:1-22
A plea for mercy
Mark 11:12-14, 20-24
Faith that moves mountains

DAILY
Psalm 137
Weeping by the rivers of Babylon

Proper 22 [27]

Sunday between October 2 and 8 inclusive

Preparation for Sunday

THURSDAY
2 Kings 18:1-8, 28-36
King Hezekiah trusts in God
Revelation 2:8-11
Be faithful until death

SATURDAY
Isaiah 7:1-9
Standing firm in faith
Matthew 20:29-34
Mercy on persistent blind men

FRIDAY
2 Kings 19:8-20, 35-37
God saves the people
Revelation 2:12-29
Call to faithfulness

DAILY
Psalm 37:1-9
Commit your way to the Lord

Sunday, October 2–8

Habakkuk 1:1-4; 2:1-4
The wicked surround the righteous
Psalm 37:1-9
Commit your way to the Lord
2 Timothy 1:1-14
Guard the treasure entrusted to you
Luke 17:5-10
Faith the size of a mustard seed

Reflection on Sunday

MONDAY
Habakkuk 1:5-17
The wicked swallow the righteous
James 1:2-11
Faith produces endurance

WEDNESDAY
Habakkuk 2:12-20
Knowledge of the glory of God
Mark 11:12-14, 20-24
Faith that moves mountains

TUESDAY
Habakkuk 2:5-11
Those who heap up what is not theirs
1 John 5:1-5, 13-21
Faith overcomes the world

DAILY
Psalm 3
Deliverance comes from God

Proper 23 [28]

Sunday between October 9 and 15 inclusive

Preparation for Sunday

THURSDAY
Jeremiah 25:1-14
Babylonian captivity foretold
2 Timothy 1:13-18
Paul in prison

FRIDAY
Jeremiah 27:1-22
The sign of the yoke
2 Timothy 2:1-7
Share in suffering

SATURDAY
Jeremiah 28:1-17
Hananiah opposes Jeremiah
Luke 5:12-16
A leper healed

DAILY
Psalm 66:1-12
God holds our souls in life

Sunday, October 9–15

Jeremiah 29:1, 4-7
Israel plants gardens in Babylon
Psalm 66:1-12
God holds our souls in life
2 Timothy 2:8-15
We will live with Christ
Luke 17:11-19
One leper gives thanks to God

Reflection on Sunday

MONDAY
Jeremiah 29:8-23
False prophets deceive the exiles
Acts 26:24-29
Except for these chains

TUESDAY
Jeremiah 29:24-32
Jeremiah exposes a false prophet
Ephesians 6:10-20
An ambassador in chains

WEDNESDAY
Jeremiah 25:15-32
The cup of God's wrath
Matthew 10:5-15
Cure without payment

DAILY
Psalm 102:1-17
Like a lonely bird on a housetop

Proper 23 [28]

Sunday between October 9 and 15 inclusive

Preparation for Sunday

THURSDAY
Leviticus 14:33-53
Cleansing a leprous house
2 Timothy 1:13-18
Paul in prison

FRIDAY
Numbers 4:34—5:4
A census and the exclusion of lepers
2 Timothy 2:1-7
Share in suffering

SATURDAY
Numbers 12:1-15
Miriam contracts leprosy
Luke 5:12-16
A leper healed

DAILY
Psalm 111
I give thanks with my whole heart

Sunday, October 9–15

2 Kings 5:1-3, 7-15c
Naaman is cleansed
Psalm 111
I give thanks with my whole heart
2 Timothy 2:8-15
We will live with Christ
Luke 17:11-19
One leper gives thanks to God

Reflection on Sunday

MONDAY
2 Kings 5:15-19a
Naaman seeks to repay Elisha
Acts 26:24-29
Except for these chains

TUESDAY
2 Kings 5:19b-27
Greed brings leprosy to Gehazi
Ephesians 6:10-20
An ambassador in chains

WEDNESDAY
2 Kings 15:1-7
A leprous king lives in isolation
Matthew 10:5-15
Cure without payment

DAILY
Psalm 61
Prayer for a long life

Proper 24 [29]

Sunday between October 16 and 22 inclusive

Preparation for Sunday

THURSDAY
Jeremiah 26:1-15
Jeremiah threatened with death
Acts 17:22-34
God has fixed a day of judgment

FRIDAY
Jeremiah 26:16-24
Jeremiah does not deserve death
2 Timothy 2:14-26
About the Christian life

SATURDAY
Jeremiah 31:15-26
Hope for Israel's future
Mark 10:46-52
A man who would not be silenced

DAILY
Psalm 119:97-104
Your words sweeter than honey

Sunday, October 16–22

Jeremiah 31:27-34
Promise of a new covenant
Psalm 119:97-104
Your words sweeter than honey
2 Timothy 3:14—4:5
Christ the judge
Luke 18:1-8
A widow begs for justice

Reflection on Sunday

MONDAY
Jeremiah 38:14-28
King and prophet consult
1 Corinthians 6:1-11
You are washed and sanctified

TUESDAY
Jeremiah 39:1-18
Jerusalem falls
James 5:7-12
The Judge standing at the doors

WEDNESDAY
Jeremiah 50:1-7, 17-20
Judgment on Babylon
Luke 22:39-46
Jesus prays for life

DAILY
Psalm 129
My attackers have not prevailed

Proper 24 [29]

Sunday between October 16 and 22 inclusive

Preparation for Sunday

THURSDAY
Isaiah 54:11-17
God will vindicate the faithful
Acts 17:22-34
God has fixed a day of judgment

FRIDAY
Genesis 31:43—32:2
Laban and Jacob make a covenant
2 Timothy 2:14-26
About the Christian life

SATURDAY
Genesis 32:3-21
Jacob sends gifts to Esau
Mark 10:46-52
A man who would not be silenced

DAILY
Psalm 121
My help is from the Lord

Sunday, October 16–22

Genesis 32:22-31
Jacob's struggle with the angel
Psalm 121
My help is from the Lord
2 Timothy 3:14—4:5
Christ the judge
Luke 18:1-8
A widow begs for justice

Reflection on Sunday

MONDAY
1 Samuel 25:2-22
David judges against Nabal
1 Corinthians 6:1-11
You are washed and sanctified

TUESDAY
1 Samuel 25:23-35
Abigail pleads for life
James 5:7-12
The Judge standing at the doors

WEDNESDAY
1 Samuel 25:36-42
David welcomes Abigail as wife
Luke 22:39-46
Jesus prays for life

DAILY
Psalm 57
Vindication from God

Proper 25 [30]

Sunday between October 23 and 29 inclusive

Preparation for Sunday

THURSDAY
Joel 1:1-20
Lament and call to repentance
2 Timothy 3:1-9
Godlessness

FRIDAY
Joel 2:1-11
The day of the Lord
2 Timothy 3:10-15
The persecution of the godly

SATURDAY
Joel 2:12-22
Return to your God
Luke 1:46b-55
Mary's song

DAILY
Psalm 65
Your paths overflow with plenty

Sunday, October 23–29

Joel 2:23-32
The promise to restore Israel
Psalm 65
Your paths overflow
2 Timothy 4:6-8, 16-18
The good fight of faith
Luke 18:9-14
A Pharisee and tax collector pray

Reflection on Sunday

MONDAY
Joel 3:1-8
God will restore Israel and Judah
1 Peter 4:12-19
The suffering of the righteous

TUESDAY
Joel 3:9-16
The valley of Jehoshaphat
1 Peter 5:1-11
The unfading crown of glory

WEDNESDAY
Joel 3:17-20
The glorious future of Judah
Matthew 21:28-32
Faith of tax collectors and prostitutes

DAILY
Psalm 87
Glorious things are spoken of Zion

Proper 25 [30]

Sunday between October 23 and 29 inclusive

Preparation for Sunday

THURSDAY
Jeremiah 9:1-16
Israel refuses to know God
2 Timothy 3:1-9
Godlessness

FRIDAY
Jeremiah 9:17-26
Israel uncircumcised in heart
2 Timothy 3:10-15
The persecution of the godly

SATURDAY
Jeremiah 14:1-6
A drought portends destruction
Luke 1:46-55
Mary's song

DAILY
Psalm 84:1-7
Happy are they whose strength is in you

Sunday, October 23–29

Sirach 35:12-17   *or*
God is impartial in justice
Psalm 84:1-7
Happy are they whose strength is in you
2 Timothy 4:6-8, 16-18
The good fight of faith
Luke 18:9-14
A Pharisee and tax collector pray

Jeremiah 14:7-10, 19-22
Jerusalem will be defeated

Reflection on Sunday

MONDAY
1 Samuel 2:1-10
Hannah's song
1 Peter 4:12-19
The suffering of the righteous

TUESDAY
Daniel 5:1-12
A hand writing on the wall
1 Peter 5:1-11
The unfading crown of glory

WEDNESDAY
Daniel 5:13-31
Daniel urges humility
Matthew 21:28-32
Faith of tax collectors and prostitutes

DAILY
Psalm 84:8-12
A doorkeeper in God's house

Proper 26 [31]

Sunday between October 30 and November 5 inclusive

Preparation for Sunday

THURSDAY
Jeremiah 33:14-26
The righteous Branch
2 Corinthians 1:1-11
Shared suffering, unshaken hope

FRIDAY
Habakkuk 1:5-17
The wicked swallow the righteous
2 Peter 1:1-11
Participants of the divine nature

SATURDAY
Habakkuk 2:5-11
Those who heap up what is not theirs
John 8:39-47
True children of Abraham

DAILY
Psalm 119:137-144
Grant me understanding

Sunday, October 30–November 5

Habakkuk 1:1-4; 2:1-4
The righteous live by faith
Psalm 119:137-144
Grant me understanding
2 Thessalonians 1:1-4, 11-12
Faith and love amid adversity
Luke 19:1-10
Zacchaeus climbs high to see Jesus

Reflection on Sunday

MONDAY
Habakkuk 2:12-20
Knowledge of the glory of God
1 Corinthians 5:9-13
Drive out the wicked

TUESDAY
Habakkuk 3:1-16
A prophet prays
Jude 5-21
Warning against sinners

WEDNESDAY
Habakkuk 3:17-19
Trust in the midst of trouble
Luke 19:11-27
The parable of the pounds

DAILY
Psalm 142
The righteous will surround me

SEASON AFTER PENTECOST   YEAR C

Proper 26 [31]

Sunday between October 30 and November 5 inclusive

Preparation for Sunday

THURSDAY
Proverbs 15:8-11, 24-33
God welcomes the righteous
2 Corinthians 1:1-11
Shared suffering, unshaken hope

FRIDAY
Job 22:21—23:17
God hidden from Job
2 Peter 1:1-11
Participants of the divine nature

SATURDAY
Isaiah 1:1-9
Sinful Judah
John 8:39-47
True children of Abraham

DAILY
Psalm 32:1-7
Praying in time of trouble

Sunday, October 30–November 5

Isaiah 1:10-18
Learn to do good
Psalm 32:1-7
Praying in time of trouble
2 Thessalonians 1:1-4, 11-12
Faith and love amid adversity
Luke 19:1-10
Zacchaeus climbs high to see Jesus

Reflection on Sunday

MONDAY
Nehemiah 13:1-3, 23-31
Israel separates from foreigners
1 Corinthians 5:9-13
Drive out the wicked

TUESDAY
Zechariah 7:1-14
Fasting versus justice and mercy
Jude 5-21
Warning against sinners

WEDNESDAY
Amos 5:12-24
God desires justice, not offerings
Luke 19:11-27
The parable of the pounds

DAILY
Psalm 50
A sacrifice of thanksgiving

Proper 27 [32]

Sunday between November 6 and 12 inclusive

Preparation for Sunday

THURSDAY
Zechariah 1:1-17
God returns to Jerusalem
Acts 22:22—23:11
Paul confronts religious leaders

FRIDAY
Zechariah 6:9-15
Far and near led to build the temple
Acts 24:10-23
Paul testifies to the resurrection

SATURDAY
Haggai 1:1-15a
Command to rebuild the temple
Luke 20:1-8
Jesus' teaching authority

DAILY
Psalm 145:1-5, 17-21
Great is the Lord

Sunday, November 6–12

Haggai 1:15b—2:9
The promise to restore Judah
Psalm 145:1-5, 17-21
Great is the Lord
2 Thessalonians 2:1-5, 13-17
The coming of Christ Jesus
Luke 20:27-38
Jesus speaks of the resurrection

or

Psalm 98
Earth sees the victory of God

Reflection on Sunday

MONDAY
Haggai 2:10-19
A rebuke and a promise
2 Peter 1:16-21
Prophecy comes not by human will

TUESDAY
Haggai 2:20-23
God's promise to Zerubbabel
2 John 1-13
Be on your guard

WEDNESDAY
Zechariah 8:1-17
God's promise to Zion
John 5:19-29
The authority of the Son

DAILY
Psalm 98
Earth sees the victory of God

Proper 27 [32]

Sunday between November 6 and 12 inclusive

Preparation for Sunday

THURSDAY
Deuteronomy 25:5-10
Instructions for levirate marriage
Acts 22:22—23:11
Paul confronts religious leaders

FRIDAY
Genesis 38:1-26
Tamar and levirate marriage
Acts 24:10-23
Paul testifies to the resurrection

SATURDAY
Exodus 3:13-20
God appears to Moses
Luke 20:1-8
Jesus' teaching authority

DAILY
Psalm 17:1-9
Keep me as the apple of your eye

Sunday, November 6–12

Job 19:23-27a
I know that my Redeemer lives
Psalm 17:1-9
Keep me as the apple of your eye
2 Thessalonians 2:1-5, 13-17
The coming of Christ Jesus
Luke 20:27-38
Jesus speaks of the resurrection

Reflection on Sunday

MONDAY
Job 20:1-11
Mortals fly away like a dream
2 Peter 1:16-21
Prophecy comes not by human will

TUESDAY
Job 21:1, 17-34
Poor and rich lie down in the dust
2 John 1-13
Be on your guard

WEDNESDAY
Job 25:1—26:14
Even Sheol is naked before God
John 5:19-29
The authority of the Son

DAILY
Psalm 123
Our eyes look to God

Proper 28 [33]

Sunday between November 13 and 19 inclusive

Preparation for Sunday

THURSDAY
Isaiah 57:14-21
A promise of help and healing
Romans 1:18-25
The revealing of God's wrath

FRIDAY
Isaiah 59:1-15a
Sin creates barriers
2 Thessalonians 1:3-12
God's judgment

SATURDAY
Isaiah 59:15b-21
The redeemer comes to Zion
Luke 17:20-37
The judgment coming

DAILY
Isaiah 12
The Holy One in your midst

Sunday, November 13–19

Isaiah 65:17-25
A new heaven and new earth
Isaiah 12
The Holy One in your midst
2 Thessalonians 3:6-13
Do what is right
Luke 21:5-19
Suffering for Jesus' sake

Reflection on Sunday

MONDAY
Isaiah 60:17-22
Walls of salvation
Ephesians 4:25 — 5:2
Be imitators of God

TUESDAY
Isaiah 66:1-13
Rejoice in mother Jerusalem
1 Corinthians 10:23 — 11:1
Do all to the glory of God

WEDNESDAY
Isaiah 66:14-24
The reign of God
Matthew 23:37 — 24:14
The last things

DAILY
Psalm 76
God breaks the weapons of war

SEASON AFTER PENTECOST   YEAR C

Proper 28 [33]

Sunday between November 13 and 19 inclusive

Preparation for Sunday

THURSDAY

1 Samuel 28:3-19

Saul warned of God's judgment

Romans 1:18-25

The revealing of God's wrath

FRIDAY

2 Samuel 21:1-14

Violence comes on Saul's household

2 Thessalonians 1:3-12

God's judgment

SATURDAY

Ezekiel 10:1-19

God's glory leaves Jerusalem

Luke 17:20-37

The judgment coming

DAILY

Psalm 98

God judges the world

Sunday, November 13–19

Malachi 4:1-2a

A day of healing for the righteous

Psalm 98

God judges the world

2 Thessalonians 3:6-13

Do what is right

Luke 21:5-19

Suffering for Jesus' sake

Reflection on Sunday

MONDAY

Ezekiel 11:14-25

Judgment and promised restoration

Ephesians 4:25—5:2

Be imitators of God

TUESDAY

Ezekiel 39:21—40:4

Mercy on the house of Israel

1 Corinthians 10:23—11:1

Do all to the glory of God

WEDNESDAY

Ezekiel 43:1-12

Divine glory returns to the temple

Matthew 23:37—24:14

The last things

DAILY

Psalm 141

God is my refuge

Proper 29 [34]
Reign of Christ or *Christ the King*

Preparation for Sunday

THURSDAY
Jeremiah 21:1-14
Jerusalem will fall
Hebrews 9:23-28
Christ has appeared once for all

FRIDAY
Jeremiah 22:1-17
The covenant abandoned
1 Peter 1:3-9
An imperishable inheritance

SATURDAY
Jeremiah 22:18-30
The wind shepherds the shepherds
Luke 18:15-17
Receiving the kingdom of God

DAILY
Luke 1:68-79
God raises up a mighty savior

Sunday, November 20–26

Jeremiah 23:1-6
Coming of the shepherd
Luke 1:68-79
God raises up a mighty savior
Colossians 1:11-20
A hymn to Christ, firstborn of all creation
Luke 23:33-43
Jesus crucified with two thieves

Reflection on Sunday

MONDAY
Jeremiah 30:1-17
Promised restoration
Revelation 21:5-27
God reigns in the holy city

TUESDAY
Jeremiah 30:18-24
You shall be my people
Revelation 22:8-21
Surely, I am coming soon

WEDNESDAY
Jeremiah 31:1-6
Joy at God's people restored
Luke 1:1-4
That you may know the truth

DAILY
Psalm 117
God's faithfulness endures forever

Proper 29 [34]
Reign of Christ or *Christ the King*

Preparation for Sunday

THURSDAY
2 Chronicles 18:12-22
Sheep without a shepherd
Hebrews 9:23-28
Christ has appeared once for all

SATURDAY
Jeremiah 22:18-30
The wind shepherds the shepherds
Luke 18:15-17
Receiving the kingdom of God

FRIDAY
Zechariah 11:1-17
Shepherds who desert the flock
1 Peter 1:3-9
An imperishable inheritance

DAILY
Psalm 46
The God of Jacob is our stronghold

Sunday, November 20–26

Jeremiah 23:1-6
Coming of the shepherd
Psalm 46
The God of Jacob is our stronghold
Colossians 1:11-20
A hymn to Christ, firstborn of all creation
Luke 23:33-43
Jesus crucified with two thieves

Reflection on Sunday

MONDAY
Jeremiah 46:18-28
God will save Israel
Revelation 21:5-27
God reigns in the holy city

WEDNESDAY
Isaiah 60:8-16
The forsaken become majestic
Luke 1:1-4
That you may know the truth

TUESDAY
Isaiah 33:17-22
Our God rules
Revelation 22:8-21
Surely, I am coming soon

DAILY
Psalm 24
The King of glory comes

APPENDIX A

Special Days

Presentation of the Lord, February 2

Malachi 3:1-4
My messenger, a refiner and purifier
Psalm 84   *or*   Psalm 24:7-10
How dear to me is your dwelling, O God   *Lift up your heads*
Hebrews 2:14-18
Jesus shares human flesh and sufferings
Luke 2:22-40
The child is brought to the temple

Annunciation of the Lord, March 25

Isaiah 7:10-14
A young woman will bear a son
Psalm 45   *or*   Psalm 40:5-10
Your name will be remembered   *I love to do your will, O God*
Hebrews 10:4-10
The offering of Jesus' body sanctifies us
Luke 1:26-38
The angel greets Mary

Visitation of Mary to Elizabeth, May 31

1 Samuel 2:1-10
Hannah's thanksgiving
Psalm 113
God, the helper of the needy
Romans 12:9-16b
Rejoice with those who rejoice
Luke 1:39-57
Mary greets Elizabeth

Holy Cross, September 14

Numbers 21:4b-9
A bronze serpent in the wilderness
Psalm 98:1-5   *or*   Psalm 78:1-2, 34-38
God has done marvelous things   *God was their rock*
1 Corinthians 1:18-24
The cross is the power of God
John 3:13-17
The Son of Man will be lifted up

All Saints, November 1

YEAR A
Revelation 7:9-17
The multitudes of heaven worship the Lamb
Psalm 34:1-10, 22
Fear God, you saints
1 John 3:1-3
We are God's children
Matthew 5:1-12
Blessed are the poor in spirit

YEAR B
Wisdom of Solomon 3:1-9   *or*   Isaiah 25:6-9
The righteous are with God   *A feast of rich foods*
Psalm 24
They shall receive a blessing from God
Revelation 21:1-6a
A new heaven and a new earth
John 11:32-44
The raising of Lazarus

YEAR C
Daniel 7:1-3, 15-18
The holy ones of the Most High
Psalm 149
Sing praise for God's goodness
Ephesians 1:11-23
God made Christ head over all
Luke 6:20-31
Jesus speaks blessings and woes

Thanksgiving Day, October (Canada) / November (USA)

YEAR A
Deuteronomy 8:7-18
A land of streams
Psalm 65
You crown the year with your goodness
2 Corinthians 9:6-15
God provides every blessing in abundance
Luke 17:11-19
The healed leper gives thanks to Jesus

YEAR B
Joel 2:21-27
The promise to restore Jerusalem
Psalm 126
Sowing in tears, reaping with joy
1 Timothy 2:1-7
Make thanksgivings
Matthew 6:25-33
God will care for all our needs

YEAR C
Deuteronomy 26:1-11
The offering of the first fruits
Psalm 100
Enter God's gates with thanksgiving
Philippians 4:4-9
Do not worry about anything
John 6:25-35
Jesus, the bread of life

APPENDIX B

Scripture Readings in Biblical Order

Two symbols are used to indicate the two distinct patterns of Old Testament readings and psalms for the days during the season after Pentecost (Proper 4 through Proper 29). The symbol (+) indicates the pattern of semicontinuous Old Testament readings. The symbol (*) indicates the pattern of complementary readings. Entries in bold and indicated by S denote Sundays and special or festival days.

Gn 1:1-5	**Baptism/Lord [1]**	**S**	**B**
Gn 1:1-19	Easter	M	B
Gn 1:1—2:4a	**Trinity Sunday**	**S**	**A**
Gn 1:1—2:4a	Proper 4 [9]	Th	A+
Gn 1:1—2:4a	**Easter Vigil**	**S**	**ABC**
Gn 1:20—2:4a	Easter	T	B
Gn 2:4b-7	Pentecost	Th	B
Gn 2:4b-14	Proper 5 [10]	Sa	B*
Gn 2:4b-25	Proper 4 [9]	F	A+
Gn 2:15-17; 3:1-7	**Lent 1**	**S**	**A**
Gn 2:18-24	**Proper 22 [27]**	**S**	**B***
Gn 3:1-24	Proper 4 [9]	Sa	A+
Gn 3:8-15	**Proper 5 [10]**	**S**	**B***
Gn 3:14-24	Proper 6 [11]	Th	B*
Gn 4:1-16	Lent 1	T	A
Gn 4:1-16	Proper 4 [9]	M	A+
Gn 4:17—5:5	Proper 4 [9]	T	A+
Gn 6:1-6	Proper 19 [24]	Th	C*
Gn 6:1-10	Advent 1	F	A
Gn 6:5-22	Easter 6	Th	A
Gn 6:9-22; 7:24; 8:14-19	**Proper 4 [9]**	**S**	**A+**
Gn 6:11-22	Advent 1	Sa	A
Gn 7:1-5, 11-18; 8:6-18; 9:8-13	**Easter Vigil**	**S**	**ABC**
Gn 7:1-24	Easter 6	F	A
Gn 7:6-10; 8:1-5	Proper 19 [24]	F	C*
Gn 7:11—8:5	Proper 14 [19]	M	A*
Gn 8:1-19	Advent 1	M	A
Gn 8:13-19	Easter 6	Sa	A
Gn 8:20—9:7	Proper 19 [24]	Sa	C*
Gn 9:1-17	Advent 1	T	A
Gn 9:8-17	Easter 6	M	A
Gn 9:8-17	**Lent 1**	**S**	**B**
Gn 9:8-17	Lent 4	Th	B
Gn 11:1-9	Proper 4 [9]	W	A+
Gn 11:1-9	Pentecost	T	B
Gn 11:1-9	**Pentecost**	**S**	**C**
Gn 11:27-32	Proper 14 [19]	Sa	C*
Gn 12:1-3	Easter 5	Th	A
Gn 12:1-4a	**Lent 2**	**S**	**A**
Gn 12:1-7	Jan 2		A
Gn 12:1-9	**Proper 5 [10]**	**S**	**A+**
Gn 12:1-9	Epiphany 3 [3]	M	B
Gn 12:10-20	Proper 11 [16]	Th	C*
Gn 13:1-7, 14-18	Lent 2	Th	C
Gn 13:1-18	Proper 5 [10]	Th	A+
Gn 13:1-18	Proper 11 [16]	F	C*
Gn 14:1-16	Proper 11 [16]	Sa	C*
Gn 14:17-24	Proper 5 [10]	F	A+
Gn 14:17-24	Proper 24 [29]	Th	B*
Gn 14:17-24	Lent 2	F	C
Gn 15:1-6	**Proper 14 [19]**	**S**	**C***
Gn 15:1-6, 12-18	Lent 2	Th	B
Gn 15:1-12, 17-18	**Lent 2**	**S**	**C**
Gn 15:1-18	Advent 2	W	A
Gn 15:1-20	Proper 5 [10]	Sa	A+
Gn 16:1-6	Lent 2	F	B
Gn 16:1-14	Epiphany 2 [2]	W	B
Gn 16:1-15	Proper 5 [10]	M	A+
Gn 16:1-15	Proper 7 [12]	M	A+
Gn 16:7-15	Lent 2	Sa	B
Gn 17:1-7, 15-16	**Lent 2**	**S**	**B**
Gn 17:1-13	Baptism/Lord [1]	M	B
Gn 17:1-27	Proper 5 [10]	T	A+
Gn 17:15-22	Advent 4	M	A
Gn 18:1-8	Easter 3	Sa	C
Gn 18:1-10a	**Proper 11 [16]**	**S**	**C***
Gn 18:1-14	Easter 3	M	A
Gn 18:1-15	Proper 12 [17]	M	B*
Gn 18:1-15 [21:1-7]	**Proper 6 [11]**	**S**	**A+**
Gn 18:16-33	Proper 5 [10]	W	A+
Gn 18:20-32	**Proper 12 [17]**	**S**	**C***
Gn 19:1-29	Proper 14 [19]	T	A*
Gn 20:1-18	Proper 22 [27]	Th	B*
Gn 21:1-7	Lent 2	M	B
Gn 21:1-7	Proper 6 [11]	Th	A+
Gn 21:1-21	Advent 4	T	A

Reference	Occasion	Day	Year
Gn 21:8-21	**Proper 7 [12]**	**S**	**A+**
Gn 21:22-34	Proper 22 [27]	F	B*
Gn 22:1-14	**Proper 8 [13]**	**S**	**A+**
Gn 22:1-14	Proper 5 [10]	M	C*
Gn 22:1-18	**Easter Vigil**	**S**	**ABC**
Gn 22:1-19	Lent 2	T	B
Gn 22:15-18	Proper 8 [13]	M	A+
Gn 23:1-19	Proper 6 [11]	M	A+
Gn 23:1-20	Proper 22 [27]	Sa	B*
Gn 24:1-9	Proper 6 [11]	F	A+
Gn 24:1-10	Proper 27 [32]	M	B+
Gn 24:1-21	Proper 7 [12]	Th	C*
Gn 24:1-27	Lent 3	M	A
Gn 24:10-52	Proper 6 [11]	Sa	A+
Gn 24:11-27	Proper 27 [32]	T	B+
Gn 24:28-42	Proper 27 [32]	W	B+
Gn 24:34-38, 42-49, 58-67	**Proper 9 [14]**	**S**	**A+**
Gn 24:34-41, 50-67	Proper 8 [13]	M	C*
Gn 25:7-11	Proper 6 [11]	T	A+
Gn 25:12-18	Proper 7 [12]	T	A+
Gn 25:19-27	Proper 9 [14]	Th	A+
Gn 25:19-28	Advent 4	M	C
Gn 25:19-34	**Proper 10 [15]**	**S**	**A+**
Gn 26:1-5	Epiphany 6 [6]	Th	A
Gn 26:23-25	Proper 8 [13]	Sa	A+
Gn 27:1-17	Proper 9 [14]	F	A+
Gn 27:1-29	Proper 20 [25]	M	A*
Gn 27:18-29	Proper 9 [14]	Sa	A+
Gn 27:30-38	Epiphany 2 [2]	F	A
Gn 27:30-46	Proper 9 [14]	M	A+
Gn 28:10-17	Proper 20 [25]	T	A*
Gn 28:10-19a	**Proper 11 [16]**	**S**	**A+**
Gn 28:10-22		Jan 3	A
Gn 29:1-8	Proper 12 [17]	Th	A+
Gn 29:1-14	Lent 3	T	A
Gn 29:1-14	Proper 9 [14]	T	A+
Gn 29:9-14	Proper 12 [17]	F	A+
Gn 29:15-28	**Proper 12 [17]**	**S**	**A+**
Gn 29:31-35	Proper 9 [14]	W	A+
Gn 29:31—30:24	Proper 12 [17]	Sa	A+
Gn 30:1-24	Advent 4	T	C
Gn 30:25-36	Proper 12 [17]	M	A+
Gn 30:25-43	Easter 4	Th	B
Gn 30:37-43	Proper 12 [17]	T	A+
Gn 31:1-3, 17-50	Epiphany 7 [7]	T	A
Gn 31:1-21	Proper 13 [18]	Sa	A+
Gn 31:17-35	Proper 6 [11]	M	C+
Gn 31:22-42	Proper 13 [18]	M	A+
Gn 31:43—32:2	Proper 24 [29]	F	C*
Gn 32:3-21	Proper 11 [16]	M	A+
Gn 32:3-21	Proper 13 [18]	T	A+
Gn 32:3-21	Proper 24 [29]	Sa	C*
Gn 32:22-31	**Proper 13 [18]**	**S**	**A+**
Gn 32:22-31	**Proper 24 [29]**	**S**	**C***
Gn 33:1-17	Proper 11 [16]	T	A+
Gn 33:1-17	Epiphany 7 [7]	M	C
Gn 35:1-4	Proper 7 [12]	F	A+
Gn 35:1-15	Baptism/Lord [1]	M	A
Gn 35:16-29	Proper 11 [16]	W	A+
Gn 35:22b-29	Proper 14 [19]	Th	A+
Gn 36:1-8	Proper 14 [19]	F	A+
Gn 37:1-4, 12-28	**Proper 14 [19]**	**S**	**A+**
Gn 37:2-11	Advent 4	W	A
Gn 37:5-11	Proper 14 [19]	Sa	A+
Gn 37:12-36	Proper 19 [24]	Th	A*
Gn 37:29-36	Proper 14 [19]	M	A+
Gn 38:1-26	Proper 27 [32]	F	C+
Gn 39:1-23	Proper 14 [19]	T	A+
Gn 39:1-23	Proper 18 [23]	Th	C*
Gn 40:1-23	Proper 14 [19]	W	A+
Gn 41:14-36	Proper 15 [20]	Th	A+
Gn 41:14-36	Proper 10 [15]	Th	C*
Gn 41:37-49	Proper 10 [15]	F	C*
Gn 41:37-57	Proper 15 [20]	F	A+
Gn 41:53—42:17	Proper 19 [24]	F	A*
Gn 42:1-28	Proper 15 [20]	Sa	A+
Gn 43:1-34	Proper 15 [20]	M	A+
Gn 43:1-15	Proper 15 [20]	M	B*
Gn 43:16-34	Epiphany 7 [7]	Th	C
Gn 44:1-17	Epiphany 7 [7]	F	C
Gn 44:1-34	Proper 15 [20]	T	A+
Gn 44:18-34	Epiphany 7 [7]	Sa	C
Gn 45:1-15	**Proper 15 [20]**	**S**	**A+**
Gn 45:1-15	Proper 15 [20]	T	B*
Gn 45:1-20	Proper 19 [24]	Sa	A+
Gn 45:16-28	Proper 15 [20]	W	A+
Gn 45:3-11, 15	**Epiphany 7 [7]**	**S**	**C**
Gn 45:25—46:7	Epiphany 3 [3]	T	B
Gn 46:2—47:12	Proper 12 [17]	W	A+
Gn 46:28—47:6	Easter 4	F	B
Gn 47:13-26	Proper 15 [20]	W	B*
Gn 48:8-19	Easter 4	Sa	B

Reference	Occasion	Day	Year
Gn 48:8-22	Proper 19 [24]	M	A*
Gn 48:15-22	Reign of Christ [34]	Th	A+
Gn 49:1-2, 8-13, 21-26	Epiphany 3 [3]	W	A
Gn 49:1-33	Proper 16 [21]	Th	A+
Gn 49:29—50:14	Proper 16 [21]	F	A+
Gn 49:29—50:14	Proper 19 [24]	T	A*
Gn 50:15-21	**Proper 19 [24]**	**S**	**A***
Gn 50:15-26	Proper 16 [21]	Sa	A+
Gn 50:22-26	Proper 19 [24]	W	A*
Ex 1:1-7	Proper 16 [21]	M	A+
Ex 1:8—2:10	**Proper 16 [21]**	**S**	**A+**
Ex 1:22—2:10		Jan 7	B
Ex 2:1-10	Proper 28 [33]	T	A+
Ex 2:11-15a	Proper 16 [21]	T	A+
Ex 2:11-25		Jan 8	B
Ex 2:15b-22	Proper 16 [21]	W	A+
Ex 2:15b-25	Easter 4	Th	A
Ex 2:23-24	Proper 17 [22]	Th	A+
Ex 3:1-5		Jan 4	A
Ex 3:1-12	Easter 5	F	A
Ex 3:1-6	Proper 10 [15]	Th	A+
Ex 3:1-15	**Proper 17 [22]**	**S**	**A+**
Ex 3:7-15		Jan 9	B
Ex 3:13-20	Proper 27 [32]	Sa	C+
Ex 3:16-22; 4:18-20	Easter 4	F	A
Ex 3:16-25	Proper 17 [22]	F	A+
Ex 4:1-9	Proper 17 [22]	Sa	A+
Ex 4:1-17	Proper 25 [30]	M	B*
Ex 4:10-31	Proper 17 [22]	M	A+
Ex 4:18-23	Proper 6 [11]	Th	A*
Ex 4:27-31	Proper 6 [11]	F	A*
Ex 5:1—6:13	Proper 17 [22]	T	A+
Ex 5:10-23	Lent 1	Th	C
Ex 6:1-13	Lent 1	F	C
Ex 6:2-9	Epiphany Last Trfg	Th	A
Ex 6:28—7:13	Proper 6 [11]	Sa	A*
Ex 7:14-24	Proper 7 [12]	M	B*
Ex 7:14-25	Proper 17 [22]	W	A+
Ex 9:1-7	Proper 18 [23]	Th	A+
Ex 9:13-35	Proper 7 [12]	T	B*
Ex 10:21-29	Proper 18 [23]	F	A+
Ex 11:1-10	Proper 18 [23]	Sa	A+
Ex 12:1-4 [5-10] 11-14	**Holy Thursday**	**S**	**ABC**
Ex 12:1-13, 21-28	Epiphany 2 [2]	M	A
Ex 12:1-14	**Proper 18 [23]**	**S**	**A+**
Ex 12:14-28	Proper 18 [23]	M	A+
Ex 12:21-27	Lent 5	Sa	C
Ex 12:29-42	Proper 18 [23]	T	A+
Ex 12:33-42	Proper 13 [18]	Th	B*
Ex 12:43-49	Proper 7 [12]	Th	A+
Ex 12:43—13:2	Proper 13 [18]	F	B*
Ex 13:1-10	Proper 18 [23]	W	A+
Ex 13:3-10	Proper 13 [18]	Sa	B*
Ex 13:17-22	Easter 5	M	A
Ex 13:17-22	Proper 19 [24]	Th	A+
Ex 14:1-18	Proper 19 [24]	F	A+
Ex 14:9-25	Proper 11 [16]	Sa	A+
Ex 14:10-31; 15:20-21	Easter	M	A
Ex 14:10-31; 15:20-21	**Easter Vigil**	**S**	**ABC**
Ex 14:19-31	**Proper 19 [24]**	**S**	**A+**
Ex 15:1b-11, 20-21	**Proper 19 [24]**	**S**	**A+**
Ex 15:1b-13, 17-18	**Easter Vigil**	**S**	**ABC**
Ex 15:1-18	Easter	T	A
Ex 15:6-11	Pentecost	Sa	B
Ex 15:19-21	Proper 19 [24]	Sa	A+
Ex 15:22-27	Proper 20 [25]	Th	A+
Ex 15:22-27	Lent 4	M	B
Ex 16:1-8	Lent 3	Th	A
Ex 16:1-21	Proper 20 [25]	F	A+
Ex 16:2-4, 9-15	**Proper 13 [18]**	**S**	**B***
Ex 16:2-15	**Proper 20 [25]**	**S**	**A+**
Ex 16:2-15, 31-35	Proper 13 [18]	W	A*
Ex 16:9-21	Lent 3	F	A
Ex 16:13-26	Epiphany 9 [9]	M	B
Ex 16:13-26	Proper 4 [9]	M	B*
Ex 16:22-30	Proper 20 [25]	Sa	A+
Ex 16:27-35	Lent 3	Sa	A
Ex 16:27-36	Epiphany 9 [9]	T	B
Ex 16:27-36	Proper 4 [9]	T	B*
Ex 16:31-35	Proper 20 [25]	M	A+
Ex 17:1-7	**Lent 3**	**S**	**A**
Ex 17:1-7	**Proper 21 [26]**	**S**	**A+**
Ex 18:1-12	Proper 21 [26]	M	A+
Ex 18:1-12	Proper 11 [16]	M	C*
Ex 18:13-27	Proper 21 [26]	T	A+
Ex 18:13-27	Proper 21 [26]	Th	B*
Ex 19:1-9a	Pentecost	Th	A
Ex 19:1-9a	Lent 3	Th	B
Ex 19:2-8a	**Proper 6 [11]**	**S**	**A***
Ex 19:7-20	Proper 23 [28]	M	A*
Ex 19:7-25	Epiphany Last Trfg	M	B
Ex 19:9b-15	Lent 3	F	B

Scripture	Occasion	Day	Year
Ex 19:9b-25	Epiphany Last Trfg	F	A
Ex 19:9b-25	Proper 21 [26]	W	A+
Ex 19:16-25	Pentecost	F	A
Ex 19:16-25	Lent 3	Sa	B
Ex 20:1-4, 7-9, 12-20	**Proper 22 [27]**	**S**	**A+**
Ex 20:1-17	**Lent 3**	**S**	**B**
Ex 20:1-21	Epiphany 6 [6]	M	A
Ex 20:1-21	Pentecost	Sa	A
Ex 22:1-15	Proper 26 [31]	Th	B*
Ex 22:21-27	Epiphany 7 [7]	Th	A
Ex 23:1-9	Proper 22 [27]	Th	A+
Ex 23:1-9	Proper 20 [25]	Th	C*
Ex 23:10-13	Proper 22 [27]	Sa	A+
Ex 23:14-19	Proper 22 [27]	F	A+
Ex 24:1-8	Epiphany 9 [9]	Th	A
Ex 24:1-8	Proper 4 [9]	Th	A*
Ex 24:1-8	Proper 23 [28]	Th	A+
Ex 24:1-11	Easter 3	W	A
Ex 24:1-11	Proper 12 [17]	T	B*
Ex 24:9-11	Proper 23 [28]	F	A+
Ex 24:12-18	**Epiphany Last Trfg**	**S**	**A**
Ex 24:12-18	Proper 23 [28]	Sa	A+
Ex 24:15-18	Easter 7	F	B
Ex 25:1-22	Trinity Sunday	T	B
Ex 25:10-22	Proper 10 [15]	Th	B+
Ex 28:29-38	Easter 7	M	B
Ex 29:1-9	Proper 5 [10]	Th	C+
Ex 30:1-10	Lent 5	F	B
Ex 30:22-38	Baptism/Lord [1]	T	B
Ex 31:1-11	Proper 24 [29]	F	A+
Ex 31:12-18	Epiphany 9 [9]	Th	B
Ex 31:12-18	Proper 4 [9]	Th	B*
Ex 32:1-14	**Proper 23 [28]**	**S**	**A+**
Ex 32:1-14	Proper 17 [22]	Th	B*
Ex 32:7-14	Lent 4	Sa	C
Ex 32:7-14	**Proper 19 [24]**	**S**	**C***
Ex 32:15-35	Proper 23 [28]	M	A+
Ex 32:15-35	Proper 17 [22]	F	B*
Ex 32:19-26a	Proper 13 [18]	Th	B+
Ex 33:1-6	Proper 23 [28]	T	A+
Ex 33:1-6	Lent 2	M	C
Ex 33:7-11	Proper 24 [29]	Th	A+
Ex 33:7-23	Epiphany Last Trfg	M	A
Ex 33:12-17	Easter 7	F	C
Ex 33:12-23	**Proper 24 [29]**	**S**	**A+**
Ex 33:18-23		Dec 27	B
Ex 33:18-23	Easter 7	Sa	C
Ex 34:1-9	Proper 5 [10]	Sa	A*
Ex 34:1-9, 27-28	Lent 1	W	A
Ex 34:8-28	Proper 17 [22]	Sa	B*
Ex 34:29-35	Proper 25 [30]	T	A+
Ex 34:29-35	**Epiphany Last Trfg**	**S**	**C**
Ex 35:1-29	Epiphany Last Trfg	M	C
Ex 37:1-16	Proper 10 [15]	F	B+
Ex 39:32-43	Proper 24 [29]	Sa	A+
Ex 40:1-15	Lent 5	M	C
Ex 40:16-38	Easter 7	M	C
Ex 40:34-38	Proper 24 [29]	M	A+
Lv 4:27-31; 5:14-16	Proper 18 [23]	M	A*
Lv 5:1-13	Epiphany 7 [7]	W	C
Lv 6:1-7	Epiphany 7 [7]	F	A
Lv 9:1-11, 22-24	Easter 7	M	A
Lv 9:22—10:11	Proper 8 [13]	Th	C*
Lv 13:1-17	Epiphany 6 [6]	Th	B
Lv 14:1-20	Epiphany 6 [6]	F	B
Lv 14:21-32	Epiphany 6 [6]	Sa	B
Lv 14:33-53	Proper 23 [28]	Th	C*
Lv 15:19-31	Proper 8 [13]	T	B*
Lv 15:25-31; 22:1-9	Proper 5 [10]	M	A*
Lv 16:1-5, 20-28	Proper 18 [23]	W	A*
Lv 19:1-2, 9-18	**Epiphany 7 [7]**	**S**	**A**
Lv 19:1-2, 15-18	**Proper 25 [30]**	**S**	**A***
Lv 19:1-4, 32-37	Proper 10 [15]	Sa	C*
Lv 19:9-18	Easter 5	W	C
Lv 19:32-37	Proper 26 [31]	F	B*
Lv 21:1-15	Proper 8 [13]	M	B*
Lv 23:1-8	Epiphany 9 [9]	F	B
Lv 23:1-8	Proper 4 [9]	F	B*
Lv 23:1-8	Passion/Palm Sunday	Sa	C
Lv 23:26-41	Lent 4	M	C
Lv 24:5-9	Epiphany 9 [9]	Sa	B
Lv 24:5-9	Proper 4 [9]	Sa	B*
Lv 24:10-23	Epiphany 7 [7]	Sa	A
Lv 25:1-19	Lent 4	T	C
Lv 26:3-20	Proper 10 [15]	M	A*
Lv 26:34-46	Epiphany 6 [6]	F	A
Nm 4:34—5:4	Proper 23 [28]	F	C*
Nm 5:5-10	Proper 25 [30]	Th	A*
Nm 6:22-27	**Holy Name**	**S**	**ABC**
Nm 6:22-27	Trinity Sunday	W	B
Nm 8:5-22	Easter 7	T	B
Nm 9:15-23	Trinity Sunday	M	B
Nm 9:9-14	Proper 26 [31]	Sa	B*
Nm 10:11-36	Proper 10 [15]	Sa	B+
Nm 11:1-9	Proper 20 [25]	T	A+

Nm 11:4-6, 10-16, 24-29	**Proper 21 [26]**	**S**	**B***
Nm 11:16-23, 31-32	Proper 13 [18]	M	B*
Nm 11:18-23, 31-32	Proper 20 [25]	W	A+
Nm 11:24-30	**Pentecost**	**S**	**A**
Nm 11:24-30	Pentecost	W	A
Nm 12:1-9	Proper 24 [29]	T	A+
Nm 12:1-15	Proper 23 [28]	Sa	C*
Nm 13:1-2, 17—14:9	Proper 24 [29]	W	A+
Nm 13:17-27	Lent 3	W	C
Nm 14:10b-24	Lent 2	T	C
Nm 15:17-26	Proper 5 [10]	F	C+
Nm 15:32-41	Proper 16 [21]	Th	C*
Nm 16:1-19	Advent 3	M	C
Nm 16:20-35	Advent 3	T	C
Nm 16:41-50	Easter 7	T	A
Nm 17:1-11	Advent 1	M	C
Nm 20:1-13	Proper 21 [26]	F	A+
Nm 20:1-13	Lent 4	T	B
Nm 20:22-29	Lent 4	Sa	B
Nm 20:22-29	Epiphany 5 [5]	Th	C
Nm 21:4-9	Lent 2	M	A
Nm 21:4-9	**Lent 4**	**S**	**B**
Nm 21:4b-9	**Holy Cross**	**S**	**ABC**
Nm 22:1-21	Epiphany 4 [4]	M	B
Nm 22:22-28	Epiphany 4 [4]	T	B
Nm 24:1-14	Pentecost	W	C
Nm 24:15-19		Jan 9	C
Nm 27:1-11	Baptism/Lord [1]	W	C
Nm 27:12-14	Proper 21 [26]	Sa	A+
Nm 27:12-23	Epiphany 5 [5]	F	C
Nm 27:15-23	Reign of Christ [34]	M	A+
Nm 33:38-39	Proper 25 [30]	M	A+
Nm 36:1-13	Proper 27 [32]	Th	B*
Dt 1:1-18	Proper 21 [26]	F	B*
Dt 1:34-40	Proper 5 [10]	F	B*
Dt 3:23-29	Epiphany 4 [4]	Th	B
Dt 4:1-2, 6-9	**Proper 17 [22]**	**S**	**B***
Dt 4:1-14	Epiphany 5 [5]	Th	A
Dt 4:9-14	Proper 17 [22]	M	B*
Dt 4:15-20	Proper 17 [22]	T	B*
Dt 4:21-40	Proper 17 [22]	W	B*
Dt 5:1-21	Proper 22 [27]	M	A+
Dt 5:1-21	Proper 23 [28]	Th	B*
Dt 5:12-15	**Epiphany 9 [9]**	**S**	**B**
Dt 5:12-15	**Proper 4 [9]**	**S**	**B***
Dt 5:22-33	Easter 6	T	A
Dt 5:22-33	Proper 23 [28]	F	B*
Dt 5:22—6:3	Proper 22 [27]	T	A+
Dt 6:10-25	Proper 22 [27]	W	A+
Dt 6:10-25	Proper 26 [31]	M	B*
Dt 6:1-9	**Proper 26 [31]**	**S**	**B***
Dt 6:1-9, 20-25	Proper 25 [30]	M	A*
Dt 7:1-11	Easter 6	M	B
Dt 7:12-26	Proper 18 [23]	F	C*
Dt 8:1-10	Proper 13 [18]	M	A*
Dt 8:1-20	Proper 13 [18]	T	B*
Dt 8:7-18	**Thanksgiving**	**S**	**A**
Dt 9:1-5	Epiphany Last Trfg	Th	C
Dt 9:6-14	Epiphany Last Trfg	F	C
Dt 9:15-24	Epiphany Last Trfg	Sa	C
Dt 9:25—10:5	Proper 25 [30]	F	A*
Dt 10:10-22	Proper 25 [30]	T	A*
Dt 11:1-17	Easter 6	T	B
Dt 11:18-21	Easter 6	W	B
Dt 11:18-21, 26-28	**Epiphany 9 [9]**	**S**	**A**
Dt 11:18-21, 26-28	**Proper 4 [9]**	**S**	**A***
Dt 12:1-12	Proper 11 [16]	W	C*
Dt 12:28-32	Epiphany 4 [4]	F	B
Dt 13:1-5	Epiphany 4 [4]	Sa	B
Dt 15:1-11	Proper 27 [32]	F	B*
Dt 16:1-8	Passion/Palm Sun	Th	B
Dt 16:18-20	Epiphany 4 [4]	Th	A
Dt 17:2-13	Proper 18 [23]	T	A*
Dt 17:14-20	Proper 24 [29]	F	A*
Dt 18:15-20	**Epiphany 4 [4]**	**S**	**B**
Dt 22:13-30	Proper 22 [27]	M	B*
Dt 23:21—24:4, 10-15	Epiphany 6 [6]	T	A
Dt 24:1-5	Proper 22 [27]	T	B*
Dt 24:17-22	Proper 27 [32]	Sa	B*
Dt 24:17—25:4	Epiphany 4 [4]	F	A
Dt 25:5-10	Proper 27 [32]	Th	C+
Dt 26:1-11	**Lent 1**	**S**	**C**
Dt 26:1-11	**Thanksgiving**	**S**	**C**
Dt 26:1-15	Proper 13 [18]	T	A*
Dt 26:5-10	Proper 28 [33]	T	B+
Dt 26:16—27:7	Proper 25 [30]	W	A+
Dt 27:1-10	Proper 21 [26]	Sa	B*
Dt 28:1-14	Proper 10 [15]	T	A*
Dt 28:58—29:1	Proper 26 [31]	T	B*
Dt 29:2-20	Proper 18 [23]	Sa	C*
Dt 30:1-5	Epiphany 9 [9]	F	A
Dt 30:1-5	Proper 4 [9]	F	A*

Dt 30:1-9a	Epiphany 6 [6]	Sa	A
Dt 30:9-14	**Proper 10 [15]**	**S**	**C***
Dt 30:15-20	**Epiphany 6 [6]**	**S**	**A**
Dt 30:15-20	**Proper 18 [23]**	**S**	**C***
Dt 31:1-13	Easter 6	W	A
Dt 31:14-22	Proper 25 [30]	Th	A+
Dt 32:1-10	Proper 10 [15]	F	A+
Dt 32:1-14	Epiphany 8 [8]	M	A
Dt 32:1-14	Proper 3 [8]	M	A
Dt 32:1-14, 18	Proper 25 [30]	F	A+
Dt 32:15-27, 39-43	Proper 8 [13]	Sa	C*
Dt 32:18-20, 28-39	Proper 16 [21]	T	A*
Dt 32:44-47	Proper 25 [30]	Sa	A+
Dt 32:44-47	Easter 6	Sa	B
Dt 34:1-7	Easter 7	Sa	B
Dt 34:1-12	**Proper 25 [30]**	**S**	**A+**
Jos 1:1-9		Jan 5	A
Jos 1:1-11	Proper 6 [11]	M	A*
Jos 1:1-11	Proper 26 [31]	Th	A+
Jos 2:1-14	Proper 26 [31]	F	A+
Jos 2:1-14	Proper 19 [24]	Th	B*
Jos 2:15-24	Proper 26 [31]	Sa	A+
Jos 2:15-24	Proper 19 [24]	F	B*
Jos 3:1-17	Easter	W	A
Jos 3:1-17	Proper 19 [24]	M	A+
Jos 3:7-17	**Proper 26 [31]**	**S**	**A+**
Jos 4:1-13	Lent 4	Th	C
Jos 4:1-24	Proper 26 [31]	M	A+
Jos 4:14-24	Lent 4	F	C
Jos 5:9-12	**Lent 4**	**S**	**C**
Jos 5:10-12	Proper 27 [32]	Th	A+
Jos 6:1-16, 20	Proper 26 [31]	T	A+
Jos 6:1-21	Proper 18 [23]	M	B*
Jos 6:22-27	Proper 19 [24]	Sa	B*
Jos 7:1, 10-26	Proper 15 [20]	Th	C*
Jos 8:1-23	Proper 18 [23]	T	B*
Jos 8:30-35	Epiphany 9 [9]	M	A
Jos 8:30-35	Proper 4 [9]	M	A*
Jos 8:30-35	Proper 27 [32]	F	A+
Jos 9:1-27	Proper 5 [10]	Sa	C+
Jos 10:1-14	Proper 7 [12]	W	B*
Jos 10:12-14	Proper 26 [31]	W	A+
Jos 10:16-27	Easter	M	C
Jos 20:1-9	Proper 27 [32]	Sa	A+
Jos 22:10-20	Proper 16 [21]	F	B*
Jos 22:1-9	Proper 16 [21]	Th	B*
Jos 22:21-34	Proper 16 [21]	Sa	B*

Jos 23:1-16	Proper 13 [18]	F	B+
Jos 23:1-16	Proper 9 [14]	W	C*
Jos 24:1-2, 11-28	Epiphany 9 [9]	T	A
Jos 24:1-2, 11-28	Proper 4 [9]	T	A*
Jos 24:1-2a, 14-18	**Proper 16 [21]**	**S**	**B***
Jos 24:1-3a, 14-25	**Proper 27 [32]**	**S**	**A+**
Jos 24:25-33	Proper 27 [32]	M	A+
Jgs 2:6-15	Proper 28 [33]	Th	A+
Jgs 2:6-15	Epiphany 2 [2]	Th	B
Jgs 2:16-23	Proper 28 [33]	F	A+
Jgs 2:16-23	Epiphany 2 [2]	F	B
Jgs 3:7-11	Epiphany 5 [5]	Sa	C
Jgs 4:1-7	**Proper 28 [33]**	**S**	**A+**
Jgs 4:1-16	Baptism/Lord [1]	M	C
Jgs 4:8-24	Proper 28 [33]	M	A+
Jgs 4:17-23; 5:24-31a	Easter	T	C
Jgs 5:1-11	Epiphany 5 [5]	M	C
Jgs 5:1-12	Proper 28 [33]	Sa	A+
Jgs 5:12-21	Baptism/Lord [1]	T	C
Jgs 6:1-10	Proper 13 [18]	Sa	B+
Jgs 6:1-10	Proper 20 [25]	Th	B*
Jgs 6:11-24	Epiphany 3 [3]	M	A
Jgs 6:36-40	Easter 2	M	A
Jgs 7:12-22	Epiphany 3 [3]	T	A
Jgs 9:7-15	Lent 5	T	C
Jgs 11:29-40	Proper 5 [10]	T	C*
Jgs 13:2-24	Advent 4	Sa	B
Jgs 14:1-20	Proper 21 [26]	M	A*
Jgs 15:9-20	Proper 18 [23]	W	B*
Jgs 16:1-22	Proper 21 [26]	T	A*
Jgs 16:23-31	Proper 21 [26]	W	A*
Jgs 17:1-6	Proper 24 [29]	Th	A*
Ru 1:1-18	Epiphany 4 [4]	M	A
Ru 1:1-18	**Proper 26 [31]**	**S**	**B+**
Ru 1:1-22	Proper 27 [32]	M	B*
Ru 1:6-18	Advent 3	Th	A
Ru 1:18-22	Proper 26 [31]	Th	B+
Ru 2:1-9	Proper 26 [31]	F	B+
Ru 2:1-16	Epiphany 4 [4]	T	A
Ru 2:1-23	Proper 14 [19]	T	B*
Ru 2:10-14	Proper 26 [31]	Sa	B+
Ru 2:15-23	Proper 26 [31]	M	B+
Ru 3:1-5; 4:13-17	**Proper 27 [32]**	**S**	**B+**
Ru 3:1-13; 4:13-22	Epiphany 4 [4]	W	A

Ru 3:1-7	Proper 26 [31]	T	B+
Ru 3:8-18	Proper 26 [31]	W	B+
Ru 3:14—4:6	Proper 27 [32]	T	B*
Ru 4:1-10	Proper 27 [32]	Th	B+
Ru 4:7-22	Proper 27 [32]	W	B*
Ru 4:11-17	Proper 27 [32]	F	B+
Ru 4:13-17	Advent 3	F	A
Ru 4:18-22	Proper 27 [32]	Sa	B+
1 Sm 1:1-18	Advent 4	M	B
1 Sm 1:1-18	Proper 4 [9]	Th	B+
1 Sm 1:1-20	Epiphany 3 [3]	Th	A
1 Sm 1:4-20	**Proper 28 [33]**	**S**	**B+**
1 Sm 1:19-27	Proper 4 [9]	F	B+
1 Sm 1:19-28	Advent 4	T	B
1 Sm 1:21-28	Proper 28 [33]	Th	B+
1 Sm 2:1-8	Advent 3	Sa	A
1 Sm 2:1-10	Advent 4	W	B
1 Sm 2:1-10	**Visitation**	**S**	**ABC**
1 Sm 2:1-10	Proper 4 [9]	Sa	B+
1 Sm 2:1-10	Proper 28 [33]	ThFSa	B+
1 Sm 2:1-10	**Proper 28 [33]**	**S**	**B+**
1 Sm 2:1-10	Proper 25 [30]	M	C*
1 Sm 2:1-10	Advent 4	MTW	A
1 Sm 2:11-17	Proper 4 [9]	M	B+
1 Sm 2:18-20, 26	**Christmas 1**	**S**	**C**
1 Sm 2:18-21	Proper 4 [9]	T	B+
1 Sm 2:18-21	Proper 28 [33]	F	B+
1 Sm 2:21-25	Epiphany 2 [2]	Sa	B
1 Sm 2:22-36	Proper 4 [9]	W	B+
1 Sm 2:27-36	Proper 26 [31]	Th	A*
1 Sm 3:1-9	Baptism/Lord [1]	Th	A
1 Sm 3:1-9	Proper 6 [11]	T	A*
1 Sm 3:1-10 [11-20]	**Epiphany 2 [2]**	**S**	**B**
1 Sm 3:1-10 [11-20]	**Proper 4 [9]**	**S**	**B+**
1 Sm 3:1-18	Proper 28 [33]	Sa	B+
1 Sm 3:1-21	Baptism/Lord [1]	Th	B
1 Sm 3:10—4:1a	Baptism/Lord [1]	F	A
1 Sm 3:19—4:2	Proper 28 [33]	M	B+
1 Sm 4:1-22	Proper 5 [10]	Th	B+
1 Sm 5:1-12	Proper 5 [10]	F	B+
1 Sm 5:1-12	Proper 15 [20]	F	C*
1 Sm 6:1-16	Proper 15 [20]	Sa	C*
1 Sm 6:1-18	Proper 5 [10]	Sa	B+
1 Sm 7:3-13	Proper 16 [21]	M	A*
1 Sm 7:3-15	Proper 5 [10]	M	B+
1 Sm 7:3-17	Baptism/Lord [1]	Sa	A
1 Sm 8:1-18	Proper 24 [29]	M	B*
1 Sm 8:1-22	Proper 5 [10]	T	B+
1 Sm 8:4-11 [12-15] 16-20 [11:14-15]	**Proper 5 [10]**	**S**	**B+**
1 Sm 9:1-14	Proper 5 [10]	W	B+
1 Sm 9:15-27	Proper 6 [11]	Th	B+
1 Sm 9:15—10:1b	Epiphany 5 [5]	T	C
1 Sm 9:27—10:8	Epiphany 3 [3]	F	A
1 Sm 9:27—10:8	Epiphany 2 [2]	M	B
1 Sm 10:1-8	Proper 6 [11]	F	B+
1 Sm 10:17-25	Proper 24 [29]	T	B*
1 Sm 12:1-25	Proper 24 [29]	W	B*
1 Sm 13:1-15a	Proper 6 [11]	Sa	B+
1 Sm 13:23—14:23	Proper 6 [11]	M	B+
1 Sm 15:10-21	Lent 4	Th	A
1 Sm 15:10-23	Proper 6 [11]	T	B+
1 Sm 15:10-31	Epiphany 2 [2]	T	B
1 Sm 15:22-31	Lent 4	F	A
1 Sm 15:24-31	Proper 6 [11]	W	B+
1 Sm 15:32-34	Lent 4	Sa	A
1 Sm 15:34—16:13	Epiphany 3 [3]	Sa	A
1 Sm 15:34—16:13	**Proper 6 [11]**	**S**	**B+**
1 Sm 16:1-13	**Lent 4**	**S**	**A**
1 Sm 16:1-13	Baptism/Lord [1]	F	B
1 Sm 16:1-13	Easter 4	M	B
1 Sm 16:11-13	Passion/Palm Sun	Th	A
1 Sm 16:14-23	Proper 5 [10]	M	B*
1 Sm 16:14-23	Proper 7 [12]	Th	B+
1 Sm 17:[1a, 4-11, 19-23] 32-49	**Proper 7 [12]**	**S**	**B+**
1 Sm 17:1-23	Easter 2	Th	C
1 Sm 17:19-32	Easter 2	F	C
1 Sm 17:32-51	Easter 2	Sa	C
1 Sm 17:55—18:5	Proper 7 [12]	F	B+
1 Sm 17:55—18:5	Reign of Christ [34]	T	B+
1 Sm 17:57—18:5, 10-16	**Proper 7 [12]**	**S**	**B+**
1 Sm 18:1-4	Proper 7 [12]	Sa	B+
1 Sm 18:6-30	Proper 7 [12]	M	B+
1 Sm 19:1-7	Proper 7 [12]	T	B+
1 Sm 19:8-17	Proper 7 [12]	W	B+
1 Sm 19:18-24	Proper 8 [13]	Th	B+
1 Sm 20:1-23, 35-42	Easter 5	M	C
1 Sm 20:1-25	Proper 8 [13]	F	B+
1 Sm 20:27-42	Proper 8 [13]	Sa	B+
1 Sm 21:1-6	Epiphany 9 [9]	W	B

1 Sm 21:1-6	Proper 4 [9]	W	B*
1 Sm 23:14-18	Proper 8 [13]	M	B+
1 Sm 24:1-22	Epiphany 7 [7]	T	C
1 Sm 25:2-22	Proper 24 [29]	M	C*
1 Sm 25:23-35	Proper 24 [29]	T	C*
1 Sm 25:36-42	Proper 24 [29]	W	C*
1 Sm 28:3-19	Proper 28 [33]	Th	C*
1 Sm 28:20-25	Proper 14 [19]	Th	B*
1 Sm 31:1-13	Proper 8 [13]	T	B+
2 Sm 1:1, 17-27	**Proper 8 [13]**	**S**	**B+**
2 Sm 1:4-27	Easter 5	T	C
2 Sm 2:1-7	Reign of Christ [34]	W	B+
2 Sm 2:1-11	Proper 9 [14]	Th	B+
2 Sm 3:1-12	Proper 9 [14]	F	B+
2 Sm 3:12-16	Proper 10 [15]	T	B+
2 Sm 3:31-38	Proper 9 [14]	Sa	B+
2 Sm 5:1-5, 9-10	**Proper 9 [14]**	**S**	**B+**
2 Sm 5:1-10	Proper 9 [14]	M	B+
2 Sm 5:1-12	Proper 11 [16]	W	B*
2 Sm 5:11-16	Proper 9 [14]	T	B+
2 Sm 5:17-25	Proper 9 [14]	W	B+
2 Sm 6:1-5, 12b-19	**Proper 10 [15]**	**S**	**B+**
2 Sm 6:1-11	Advent 4	Th	B
2 Sm 6:1-15	Easter	W	C
2 Sm 6:6-12a	Proper 10 [15]	M	B+
2 Sm 6:12-19	Advent 4	F	B
2 Sm 6:16-23	Proper 10 [15]	W	B+
2 Sm 7:1-11, 16	**Advent 4**	**S**	**B**
2 Sm 7:1-14a	**Proper 11 [16]**	**S**	**B+**
2 Sm 7:1-17	Advent 4	Th	A
2 Sm 7:18, 23-29		Dec 23	A
2 Sm 7:18-22	Advent 4	F	A
2 Sm 7:18-29	Proper 11 [16]	M	B+
2 Sm 7:18-29	Advent 1	T	C
2 Sm 7:23-29	Advent 4	Sa	A
2 Sm 8:1-18	Proper 11 [16]	T	B+
2 Sm 9:1-13	Proper 11 [16]	W	B+
2 Sm 10:1-5	Proper 12 [17]	Th	B+
2 Sm 10:6-12	Proper 12 [17]	F	B+
2 Sm 10:13-19	Proper 12 [17]	Sa	B+
2 Sm 11:1-15	**Proper 12 [17]**	**S**	**B+**
2 Sm 11:2-26	Proper 17 [22]	M	A*
2 Sm 11:14-21	Proper 12 [17]	M	B+
2 Sm 11:22-27	Proper 12 [17]	T	B+
2 Sm 11:26—12:10, 13-15	**Proper 6 [11]**	**S**	**C***
2 Sm 11:26—12:13a	**Proper 13 [18]**	**S**	**B+**

2 Sm 11:27b—12:15	Proper 17 [22]	T	A*
2 Sm 12:15-25	Proper 13 [18]	M	B+
2 Sm 13:1-19	Proper 13 [18]	T	B+
2 Sm 13:20-36	Proper 13 [18]	W	B+
2 Sm 13:23-39	Proper 6 [11]	Th	C*
2 Sm 13:37—14:24	Proper 14 [19]	Th	B+
2 Sm 14:1-11	Proper 5 [10]	Th	C*
2 Sm 14:12-24	Proper 5 [10]	F	C*
2 Sm 14:25-33	Proper 14 [19]	F	B+
2 Sm 14:25-33	Proper 5 [10]	Sa	C*
2 Sm 15:1-12	Proper 6 [11]	F	C*
2 Sm 15:1-13	Proper 14 [19]	Sa	B+
2 Sm 15:13-31	Proper 14 [19]	M	B+
2 Sm 17:15-29	Proper 14 [19]	F	B*
2 Sm 18:5-9, 15, 31-33	**Proper 14 [19]**	**S**	**B+**
2 Sm 18:19-33	Proper 14 [19]	T	B+
2 Sm 18:28—19:8	Proper 6 [11]	Sa	C*
2 Sm 19:1-18	Proper 14 [19]	W	B+
2 Sm 19:31-43	Proper 6 [11]	T	C+
2 Sm 21:1-14	Proper 28 [33]	F	C*
2 Sm 23:1-7	**Reign of Christ [34]**	**S**	**B+**
1 Kgs 1:1-30	Proper 15 [20]	Th	B+
1 Kgs 1:28-37	Proper 12 [17]	Th	A*
1 Kgs 1:28-48	Proper 15 [20]	F	B+
1 Kgs 1:38-48	Proper 12 [17]	F	A*
1 Kgs 2:1-4	Proper 12 [17]	Sa	A*
1 Kgs 2:1-4, 10-12	Baptism/Lord [1]	Sa	B
1 Kgs 2:1-9	Proper 14 [19]	Sa	B*
1 Kgs 2:1-11	Proper 15 [20]	Sa	B+
1 Kgs 2:10-12; 3:3-14	**Proper 15 [20]**	**S**	**B+**
1 Kgs 3:5-12	**Proper 12 [17]**	**S**	**A***
1 Kgs 3:5-14		Dec 31	ABC
1 Kgs 3:16-28	Proper 12 [17]	M	A*
1 Kgs 3:16-28	Proper 15 [20]	M	B+
1 Kgs 4:20-28	Proper 16 [21]	Th	B+
1 Kgs 4:29-34	Proper 12 [17]	T	A*
1 Kgs 4:29-34	Proper 16 [21]	F	B+
1 Kgs 5:1-12	Proper 16 [21]	Sa	B+
1 Kgs 5:13-18	Proper 16 [21]	M	B+
1 Kgs 6:1-4, 21-22	Lent 3	M	B
1 Kgs 6:1-14	Proper 16 [21]	T	B+
1 Kgs 6:15-38	Proper 16 [21]	W	B+
1 Kgs 6:23-38	Epiphany 9 [9]	Th	C
1 Kgs 6:23-38	Proper 4 [9]	Th	C*

1 Kgs 7:1-12	Proper 15 [20]	T	B+
1 Kgs 8:[1, 6, 10-11] 22-30, 41-43	**Proper 16 [21]**	**S**	**B+**
1 Kgs 8:1-21	Proper 15 [20]	W	B+
1 Kgs 8:14-21	Epiphany 9 [9]	F	C
1 Kgs 8:14-21	Proper 4 [9]	F	C*
1 Kgs 8:22-23, 41-43	**Epiphany 9 [9]**	**S**	**C**
1 Kgs 8:22-23, 41-43	**Proper 4 [9]**	**S**	**C***
1 Kgs 8:22-30	Proper 28 [33]	W	B+
1 Kgs 8:31-40	Epiphany 9 [9]	Sa	C
1 Kgs 8:31-40	Proper 4 [9]	Sa	C*
1 Kgs 8:54-65	Easter 7	W	A
1 Kgs 10:1-13		Jan 7	A
1 Kgs 10:14-25		Jan 8	A
1 Kgs 10:26—11:8	Proper 6 [11]	F	B*
1 Kgs 11:26-40	Epiphany Last Trfg	Th	B
1 Kgs 12:20-33	Proper 4 [9]	Th	C+
1 Kgs 13:1-10	Proper 19 [24]	M	B*
1 Kgs 13:11-25	Proper 19 [24]	T	B*
1 Kgs 14:1-18	Epiphany Last Trfg	F	B
1 Kgs 16:1-7	Epiphany Last Trfg	Sa	B
1 Kgs 16:29-34	Proper 4 [9]	F	C+
1 Kgs 17:1-16	Epiphany 8 [8]	T	A
1 Kgs 17:1-16	Proper 3 [8]	T	A
1 Kgs 17:1-16	Proper 14 [19]	M	B*
1 Kgs 17:8-16	**Proper 27 [32]**	**S**	**B***
1 Kgs 17:8-16	Epiphany 4 [4]	M	C
1 Kgs 17:8-16 [17-24]	**Proper 5 [10]**	**S**	**C+**
1 Kgs 17:17-24	Lent 5	M	A
1 Kgs 17:17-24	**Proper 5 [10]**	**S**	**C***
1 Kgs 18:1-16	Proper 14 [19]	Th	A*
1 Kgs 18:1-18	Advent 3	M	B
1 Kgs 18:1-19	Proper 4 [9]	Sa	C+
1 Kgs 18:17-19, 30-40	Proper 14 [19]	F	A*
1 Kgs 18:17-40	Proper 5 [10]	T	B*
1 Kgs 18:20-21 [22-29] 30-39	**Proper 4 [9]**	**S**	**C+**
1 Kgs 18:36-39	Proper 8 [13]	T	A+
1 Kgs 18:41-46	Proper 14 [19]	Sa	A*
1 Kgs 19:1-4 [5-7] 8-15a	**Proper 7 [12]**	**S**	**C+**
1 Kgs 19:1-8	Lent 1	M	A
1 Kgs 19:4-8	**Proper 14 [19]**	**S**	**B***
1 Kgs 19:9-18	Epiphany Last Trfg	T	A
1 Kgs 19:9-18	**Proper 14 [19]**	**S**	**A***
1 Kgs 19:15-16, 19-21	**Proper 8 [13]**	**S**	**C***
1 Kgs 19:19-21	Epiphany 2 [2]	Sa	A
1 Kgs 19:19-21	Proper 12 [17]	Th	B*
1 Kgs 20:1-22	Proper 6 [11]	Th	C+
1 Kgs 20:23-34	Proper 6 [11]	F	C+
1 Kgs 20:35-43	Proper 6 [11]	Sa	C+
1 Kgs 21:1-10 [11-14] 15-21a	**Proper 6 [11]**	**S**	**C+**
1 Kgs 21:1-16	Proper 8 [13]	M	A*
1 Kgs 21:17-29	Proper 8 [13]	T	A*
1 Kgs 21:20-29	Epiphany Last Trfg	Sa	A
1 Kgs 22:13-23	Reign of Christ [34]	Th	A*
1 Kgs 22:24-40	Proper 20 [25]	F	B*
1 Kgs 22:29-40, 51-53	Proper 8 [13]	Th	C+
2 Kgs 1:1-12	Proper 8 [13]	F	C+
2 Kgs 1:1-16	Proper 8 [13]	F	C*
2 Kgs 1:13-18; 2:3-5	Proper 8 [13]	Sa	C+
2 Kgs 2:1-2, 6-14	**Proper 8 [13]**	**S**	**C+**
2 Kgs 2:1-12	Easter 7	F	A
2 Kgs 2:1-12	**Epiphany Last Trfg**	**S**	**B**
2 Kgs 2:1-15a	Pentecost	Sa	C
2 Kgs 2:1-18	Proper 19 [24]	W	A+
2 Kgs 2:9-22	Advent 3	T	B
2 Kgs 2:13-15	Easter 7	Sa	A
2 Kgs 2:15-22	Proper 8 [13]	M	C+
2 Kgs 3:4-20	Proper 12 [17]	F	B*
2 Kgs 3:4-20	Proper 8 [13]	T	C+
2 Kgs 4:1-7	Lent 4	W	C
2 Kgs 4:1-7	Proper 8 [13]	W	C+
2 Kgs 4:8-17	Proper 9 [14]	Th	C+
2 Kgs 4:8-17, 32-37	Epiphany 5 [5]	M	B
2 Kgs 4:18-31	Proper 9 [14]	F	C+
2 Kgs 4:18-37	Lent 5	T	A
2 Kgs 4:32-37	Proper 9 [14]	Sa	C+
2 Kgs 4:38-41	Proper 12 [17]	Sa	B*
2 Kgs 4:42-44	**Proper 12 [17]**	**S**	**B***
2 Kgs 5:1-3, 7-15c	**Proper 23 [28]**	**S**	**C***
2 Kgs 5:1-14	Proper 15 [20]	M	A*
2 Kgs 5:1-14	Proper 20 [25]	M	B*
2 Kgs 5:1-14	Epiphany 4 [4]	T	C
2 Kgs 5:1-14	**Proper 9 [14]**	**S**	**C+**
2 Kgs 5:1-14	**Epiphany 6 [6]**	**S**	**B**

2 Kgs 5:15-19a	Proper 9 [14]	M	C+
2 Kgs 5:15-19a	Proper 23 [28]	M	C+
2 Kgs 5:19b-27	Proper 9 [14]	T	C+
2 Kgs 5:19b-27	Proper 23 [28]	T	C+
2 Kgs 6:1-7	Proper 9 [14]	W	C+
2 Kgs 6:8-23	Proper 25 [30]	T	B*
2 Kgs 7:3-10	Epiphany 6 [6]	T	B
2 Kgs 8:1-6	Epiphany 5 [5]	T	B
2 Kgs 9:1-13	Proper 7 [12]	M	C+
2 Kgs 9:14-26	Proper 7 [12]	T	C+
2 Kgs 9:30-37	Proper 7 [12]	W	C+
2 Kgs 11:21—12:16	Proper 20 [25]	T	B*
2 Kgs 14:1-14	Proper 6 [11]	Sa	B*
2 Kgs 15:1-7	Proper 23 [28]	W	C*
2 Kgs 17:5-18	Proper 20 [25]	Sa	B*
2 Kgs 17:7-20	Proper 23 [28]	W	A+
2 Kgs 17:24-41	Proper 18 [23]	M	C*
2 Kgs 18:1-8, 28-36	Proper 22 [27]	Th	C*
2 Kgs 18:9-18	Proper 18 [23]	T	C*
2 Kgs 18:19-25; 19:1-7	Proper 18 [23]	W	C*
2 Kgs 19:8-20, 35-37	Proper 22 [27]	F	C*
2 Kgs 20:1-11	Proper 8 [13]	W	B*
2 Kgs 20:12-19	Proper 25 [30]	Th	B+
2 Kgs 21:1-15	Proper 9 [14]	Th	C*
2 Kgs 22:1-10	Reign of Christ [34]	Th	B+
2 Kgs 22:3-20	Epiphany 5 [5]	M	A
2 Kgs 22:11-20	Reign of Christ [34]	F	B+
2 Kgs 23:1-8, 21-25	Epiphany 5 [5]	T	A
2 Kgs 23:1-14	Reign of Christ [34]	Sa	B+
2 Kgs 23:15-25	Reign of Christ [34]	M	B+
2 Kgs 24:18—25:21	Epiphany 6 [6]	M	C
1 Chr 10:1-14	Proper 8 [13]	W	B+
1 Chr 11:1-9	Easter 4	T	B
1 Chr 11:15-19	Proper 11 [16]	Th	B+
1 Chr 12:16-22	Easter 6	M	C
1 Chr 14:1-2	Proper 11 [16]	F	B+
1 Chr 15:1-2, 16:4-13	Proper 11 [16]	Sa	B+
1 Chr 17:1-15	Reign of Christ [34]	F	A*
1 Chr 21:1-17	Lent 1	M	C
1 Chr 28:1-10		Dec 29	C
2 Chr 1:7-13		Dec 30	C

2 Chr 5:2-14	Easter 7	T	C
2 Chr 7:12-22	Epiphany 7 [7]	Th	B
2 Chr 8:12-15	Proper 16 [21]	F	C*
2 Chr 9:29-31	Proper 12 [17]	W	B+
2 Chr 12:1-12	Proper 17 [22]	M	C*
2 Chr 15:1-15	Easter 6	T	C
2 Chr 18:12-22	Reign of Christ [34]	Th	C*
2 Chr 20:1-22	Lent 2	W	C
2 Chr 20:5-12	Proper 8 [13]	F	A+
2 Chr 24:17-24		Dec 26	C
2 Chr 26:1-21	Epiphany 6 [6]	M	B
2 Chr 29:1-11, 16-19	Lent 3	T	B
2 Chr 29:1-19	Proper 6 [11]	M	C*
2 Chr 30:1-12	Proper 6 [11]	T	C*
2 Chr 30:13-27	Proper 6 [11]	W	C*
2 Chr 33:1-17	Proper 14 [19]	M	C*
2 Chr 34:1-7	Epiphany 4 [4]	Th	C
2 Chr 34:20-33	Easter 6	W	C
2 Chr 34:22-33	Proper 14 [19]	T	C*
2 Chr 35:20-27	Epiphany 4 [4]	F	C
2 Chr 36:11-21	Epiphany 4 [4]	Sa	C
Ezra 1:1-11	Epiphany 6 [6]	T	C
Ezra 6:1-16	Lent 3	W	B
Ezra 9:5-15	Easter 7	W	B
Neh 1:1-11	Proper 25 [30]	F	B+
Neh 1:1-11	Epiphany 9 [9]	T	C
Neh 1:1-11	Proper 4 [9]	T	C*
Neh 2:1-10	Epiphany 3 [3]	F	C
Neh 5:1-13	Epiphany 3 [3]	Sa	C
Neh 8:1-3, 5-6, 8-10	**Epiphany 3 [3]**	**S**	**C**
Neh 8:1-12	Proper 27 [32]	T	A+
Neh 9:1-8	Proper 6 [11]	W	A+
Neh 9:1-15	Proper 16 [21]	M	B*
Neh 9:6-15	Advent 1	Th	C
Neh 9:9-15	Proper 19 [24]	T	A+
Neh 9:16-25	Advent 1	F	C
Neh 9:16-31	Proper 16 [21]	T	B*
Neh 9:26-31	Advent 1	Sa	C
Neh 13:1-3, 23-31	Proper 26 [31]	M	C*
Neh 13:15-22	Proper 16 [21]	Sa	C*
Est 1:1-21	Proper 21 [26]	Th	B+
Est 2:1-18	Reign of Christ [34]	M	A*
Est 2:1-23	Proper 21 [26]	F	B+
Est 2:19—3:6	Proper 12 [17]	Th	C*
Est 3:1-15	Proper 21 [26]	Sa	B+

Est 3:7-15	Proper 12 [17]	F	C*
Est 4:1-17	Proper 21 [26]	M	B+
Est 4:1-17	Proper 12 [17]	Sa	C*
Est 5:1-14	Proper 21 [26]	T	B+
Est 5:1-14	Proper 12 [17]	M	C*
Est 6:1—7:6	Proper 12 [17]	T	C*
Est 7:1-6, 9-10; 9:20-22	**Proper 21 [26]**	**S**	**B+**
Est 7:1-10	Proper 28 [33]	W	A+
Est 7:1-10	Easter 2	M	C
Est 7:7—8:17	Proper 12 [17]	W	C*
Est 8:1-17	Proper 21 [26]	W	B+
Est 8:1-17	Easter 2	T	C
Est 8:3-17	Reign of Christ [34]	T	A*
Est 9:1-5, 18-23	Easter 2	W	C
Jb 1:1; 2:1-10	**Proper 22 [27]**	**S**	**B+**
Jb 1:1-22	Lent 1	W	C
Jb 2:11—3:26	Proper 22 [27]	Th	B+
Jb 4:1-21	Lent 1	M	B
Jb 4:1-21	Proper 22 [27]	F	B+
Jb 5:8-27	Lent 1	T	B
Jb 6:1-13	Epiphany 5 [5]	W	B
Jb 6:14-30	Proper 7 [12]	F	C+
Jb 7:1-21	Proper 22 [27]	Sa	B+
Jb 8:1-22	Proper 22 [27]	M	B+
Jb 11:1-20	Proper 15 [20]	Th	B*
Jb 11:1-20	Proper 22 [27]	T	B+
Jb 12:1-25	Proper 15 [20]	F	B*
Jb 13:1-19	Proper 15 [20]	Sa	B*
Jb 13:13-19	Passion/Palm Sun	F	A
Jb 14:1-14	**Holy Saturday**	**S**	**ABC**
Jb 15:1-35	Proper 22 [27]	W	B+
Jb 16:1-21	Proper 28 [33]	W	A*
Jb 17:1-16	Proper 23 [28]	Th	B+
Jb 18:1-21	Proper 23 [28]	F	B+
Jb 18:1-21	Proper 7 [12]	M	C*
Jb 19:1-22	Proper 7 [12]	T	C*
Jb 19:23-27	Epiphany Last Trfg	T	B
Jb 19:23-27a	**Proper 27 [32]**	**S**	**C***
Jb 20:1-11	Proper 27 [32]	M	C*
Jb 20:1-29	Proper 23 [28]	Sa	B+
Jb 21:1, 17-34	Proper 27 [32]	T	C*
Jb 21:1-16	Proper 14 [19]	Th	C*
Jb 22:1-20	Proper 5 [10]	M	C*
Jb 22:21—23:17	Proper 26 [31]	F	C*
Jb 23:1-9, 16-17	**Proper 23 [28]**	**S**	**B+**
Jb 24:1-8	Proper 10 [15]	M	C*
Jb 24:9-25	Proper 5 [10]	T	C+
Jb 25:1—26:14	Proper 27 [32]	W	C+

Jb 26:1-14	Proper 23 [28]	M	B+
Jb 28:12-28	Epiphany 9 [9]	W	A
Jb 28:12-28	Proper 4 [9]	W	A*
Jb 28:12—29:10	Proper 23 [28]	T	B+
Jb 29:1-20	Proper 7 [12]	Th	B*
Jb 29:21—30:15	Proper 7 [12]	F	B*
Jb 30:16-31	Epiphany 6 [6]	W	B
Jb 31:16-23	Proper 5 [10]	W	C+
Jb 32:1-22	Proper 23 [28]	W	B+
Jb 36:1-16	Proper 24 [29]	Th	B+
Jb 36:1-23	Epiphany 5 [5]	F	B
Jb 36:24-33; 37:14-24	Proper 14 [19]	W	A*
Jb 37:1-13	Pentecost	F	B
Jb 37:1-13	Proper 7 [12]	Sa	B*
Jb 37:1-24	Proper 24 [29]	F	B+
Jb 38:1-7 [34-41]	**Proper 24 [29]**	**S**	**B+**
Jb 38:1-11	Trinity Sunday	Th	A
Jb 38:1-11	**Proper 7 [12]**	**S**	**B***
Jb 38:12-21	Trinity Sunday	F	A
Jb 38:22-38	Trinity Sunday	Sa	A
Jb 38:39—39:12	Trinity Sunday	M	A
Jb 39:1-30	Proper 24 [29]	Sa	B+
Jb 39:13-25	Trinity Sunday	T	A
Jb 39:26—40:5	Trinity Sunday	W	A
Jb 40:1-24	Proper 24 [29]	M	B+
Jb 40:6-14; 42:1-6	Proper 19 [24]	W	C*
Jb 41:1-11	Proper 24 [29]	T	B+
Jb 41:12-34	Proper 24 [29]	W	B+
Jb 42:1-6, 10-17	**Proper 25 [30]**	**S**	**B+**
Jb 42:7-9	Proper 25 [30]	Sa	B+
Jb 42:10-17		Jan 3	C
Ps 1	Proper 25 [30]	ThFSa	A*
Ps 1	**Proper 25 [30]**	**S**	**A***
Ps 1	**Easter 7**	**S**	**B**
Ps 1	Proper 20 [25]	ThFSa	B+
Ps 1	**Proper 20 [25]**	**S**	**B+**
Ps 1	Epiphany 6 [6]	ThFSa	C
Ps 1	**Epiphany 6 [6]**	**S**	**C**
Ps 1	Epiphany 8 [8]	MTW	C
Ps 1	Proper 3 [8]	MTW	C
Ps 1	Proper 18 [23]	ThFSa	C*
Ps 1	**Proper 18 [23]**	**S**	**C***
Ps 2	Epiphany Last Trfg	ThFSa	A
Ps 2	**Epiphany Last Trfg**	**S**	**A**
Ps 2	Proper 18 [23]	MTW	C+
Ps 3	Proper 28 [33]	MTW	B+
Ps 3	Proper 22 [27]	MTW	C*

Ps 4	Easter 3	ThFSa	B
Ps 4	**Easter 3**	**S**	**B**
Ps 5	Proper 26 [31]	MTW	A*
Ps 5	Proper 21 [26]	MTW	B*
Ps 5	Epiphany 9 [9]	MTW	C
Ps 5	Proper 4 [9]	MTW	C*
Ps 5:1-8	Proper 6 [11]	ThFSa	C+
Ps 5:1-8	**Proper 6 [11]**	**S**	**C+**
Ps 6	Proper 7 [12]	MTW	A*
Ps 6	Epiphany 6 [6]	MTW	B
Ps 6	Proper 9 [14]	MTW	C+
Ps 7	Reign of Christ [34]	MTW	A*
Ps 7	Proper 10 [15]	MTW	C+
Ps 8	**New Year's Day**	**S**	**ABC**
Ps 8	**Holy Name**	**S**	**ABC**
Ps 8	Trinity Sunday	ThFSa	AC
Ps 8	**Trinity Sunday**	**S**	**AC**
Ps 8	Proper 16 [21]	MTW	A+
Ps 8	Proper 22 [27]	ThFSa	B*
Ps 8	**Proper 22 [27]**	**S**	**B***
Ps 9:1-14	Proper 28 [33]	MTW	A*
Ps 9:9-20	Proper 7 [12]	ThFSa	B+
Ps 9:9-20	**Proper 7 [12]**	**S**	**B+**
Ps 10	Proper 16 [21]	MTW	C+
Ps 11	Proper 16 [21]	MTW	B+
Ps 11	Proper 14 [19]	MTW	C+
Ps 12	Proper 20 [25]	MTW	C*
Ps 13	Proper 8 [13]	ThFSa	A+
Ps 13	**Proper 8 [13]**	**S**	**A+**
Ps 13	Proper 28 [33]	MTW	B*
Ps 14	Proper 12 [17]	ThFSa	B+
Ps 14	**Proper 12 [17]**	**S**	**B+**
Ps 14	Proper 19 [24]	ThFSa	C+
Ps 14	**Proper 19 [24]**	**S**	**C+**
Ps 15	Epiphany 4 [4]	ThFSa	A
Ps 15	**Epiphany 4 [4]**	**S**	**A**
Ps 15	Proper 17 [22]	ThFSa	B*
Ps 15	**Proper 17 [22]**	**S**	**B***
Ps 15	Proper 11 [16]	ThFSa	C*
Ps 15	**Proper 11 [16]**	**S**	**C***
Ps 16	**Easter Vigil**	**S**	**ABC**
Ps 16	Easter 2	ThFSa	A
Ps 16	**Easter 2**	**S**	**A**
Ps 16	Proper 28 [33]	ThFSa	B*
Ps 16	**Proper 28 [33]**	**S**	**B***
Ps 16	Proper 8 [13]	ThFSa	C*
Ps 16	**Proper 8 [13]**	**S**	**C***
Ps 17	Proper 17 [22]	MTW	A*
Ps 17	Lent 1	MTW	C
Ps 17:1-7, 15	Proper 13 [18]	ThFSa	A+
Ps 17:1-7, 15	Proper 13 [18]	MTW	A+
Ps 17:1-7, 15	**Proper 13 [18]**	**S**	**A+**
Ps 17:1-9	Proper 27 [32]	ThFSa	C+
Ps 17:1-9	**Proper 27 [32]**	**S**	**C***
Ps 18:1-3, 20-32	Proper 16 [21]	MTW	A*
Ps 18:1-6, 43-50	Proper 8 [13]	MTW	B+
Ps 18:1-19	Proper 14 [19]	MTW	A*
Ps 18:20-30	Proper 26 [31]	MTW	B+
Ps 19	**Easter Vigil**	**S**	**ABC**
Ps 19	Proper 22 [27]	ThFSa	A+
Ps 19	**Proper 22 [27]**	**S**	**A+**
Ps 19	Lent 3	ThFSa	B
Ps 19	**Lent 3**	**S**	**B**
Ps 19	Proper 19 [24]	ThFSa	B+
Ps 19	**Proper 19 [24]**	**S**	**B+**
Ps 19	Epiphany 3 [3]	ThFSa	C
Ps 19	**Epiphany 3 [3]**	**S**	**C**
Ps 19:7-14	Proper 21 [26]	ThFSa	B*
Ps 19:7-14	**Proper 21 [26]**	**S**	**B***
Ps 20		Dec 29-Jan 2	A
Ps 20	Trinity Sunday	MTW	B
Ps 20	Proper 6 [11]	ThFSa	B+
Ps 20	**Proper 6 [11]**	**S**	**B+**
Ps 20	Lent 5	MTW	C
Ps 21	Advent 2	MTW	A
Ps 21	Proper 9 [14]	MTW	B+
Ps 22	**Good Friday**	**S**	**ABC**
Ps 22:1-15	Proper 23 [28]	ThFSa	B+
Ps 22:1-15	**Proper 23 [28]**	**S**	**B+**
Ps 22:19-28	Proper 7 [12]	ThFSa	C*
Ps 22:19-28	**Proper 7 [12]**	**S**	**C***
Ps 22:23-31	Lent 2	ThFSa	B
Ps 22:23-31	**Lent 2**	**S**	**B**
Ps 22:25-31	Easter 5	ThFSa	B
Ps 22:25-31	**Easter 5**	**S**	**B**
Ps 23	Lent 4	ThFSa	A
Ps 23	**Lent 4**	**S**	**A**
Ps 23	Easter 4	ThFSa	ABC
Ps 23	**Easter 4**	**S**	**ABC**
Ps 23	Proper 23 [28]	ThFSa	A*
Ps 23	**Proper 23 [28]**	**S**	**A***
Ps 23	Proper 11 [16]	ThFSa	B*
Ps 23	**Proper 11 [16]**	**S**	**B***
Ps 24	Proper 10 [15]	ThFSa	B+
Ps 24	**Proper 10 [15]**	**S**	**B+**
Ps 24	Reign of Christ [34]	MTW	C*
Ps 24	**All Saints**	**S**	**B**
Ps 24:7-10	**Presentation**	**S**	**ABC**
Ps 25:1-9	Proper 21 [26]	ThFSa	A*

Ps 25:1-9	**Proper 21 [26]**	S	**A***
Ps 25:1-10	Lent 1	ThFSa	B
Ps 25:1-10	**Lent 1**	S	**B**
Ps 25:1-10	Advent 1	ThFSa	C
Ps 25:1-10	**Advent 1**	S	**C**
Ps 25:1-10	Proper 10 [15]	ThFSa	C*
Ps 25:1-10	**Proper 10 [15]**	S	**C***
Ps 25:11-20	Proper 10 [15]	MTW	C*
Ps 26	Proper 22 [27]	ThFSa	B+
Ps 26	**Proper 22 [27]**	S	**B+**
Ps 26	Proper 23 [28]	MTW	B*
Ps 26:1-8	Proper 17 [22]	ThFSa	A*
Ps 26:1-8	**Proper 17 [22]**	S	**A***
Ps 27	Advent 2	MTW	B
Ps 27	Lent 2	ThFSa	C
Ps 27	**Lent 2**	S	**C**
Ps 27:1-6	Epiphany 3 [3]	ThFSa	A
Ps 27:1, 4-9	**Epiphany 3 [3]**	S	**A**
Ps 27:7-14	Epiphany 3 [3]	MTW	A
Ps 28	Proper 14 [19]	MTW	A+
Ps 28	Reign of Christ [34]	MTW	A+
Ps 28	Proper 21 [26]	MTW	A*
Ps 28	Proper 25 [30]	MTW	B+
Ps 29	Baptism/Lord [1]	ThFSa	ABC
Ps 29	**Baptism/Lord [1]**	S	**ABC**
Ps 29	Trinity Sunday	MTW	A
Ps 29	Trinity Sunday	ThFSa	B
Ps 29	**Trinity Sunday**	S	**B**
Ps 29	Easter 7	MTW	C
Ps 30	Epiphany 6 [6]	ThFSa	B
Ps 30	**Epiphany 6 [6]**	S	**B**
Ps 30	Proper 8 [13]	ThFSa	B*
Ps 30	**Proper 8 [13]**	S	**B***
Ps 30	Easter 3	ThFSa	C
Ps 30	**Easter 3**	S	**C**
Ps 30	Proper 5 [10]	ThFSa	C*
Ps 30	**Proper 5 [10]**	S	**C***
Ps 30	Proper 9 [14]	ThFSa	C+
Ps 30	**Proper 9 [14]**	S	**C+**
Ps 31:1-4, 15-16	**Holy Saturday**	S	**ABC**
Ps 31:1-5, 15-16	Easter 5	ThFSa	A
Ps 31:1-5, 15-16	**Easter 5**	S	**A**
Ps 31:1-5, 19-24	Epiphany 9 [9]	ThFSa	A
Ps 31:1-5, 19-24	Proper 4 [9]	ThFSa	A*
Ps 31:1-5, 19-24	**Epiphany 9 [9]**	S	**A**
Ps 31:1-5, 19-24	**Proper 4 [9]**	S	**A***
Ps 31:9-16	Passion/Palm Sun	ThFSa	A
Ps 31:9-16	**Passion/Palm Sun**	S	**ABC**
Ps 31:9-16	Passion/Palm Sun	ThFSa	C
Ps 32	**Lent 1**	S	**A**
Ps 32	Lent 1	MTW	A
Ps 32	Lent 1	Sa	B
Ps 32	Lent 4	ThFSa	C
Ps 32	**Lent 4**	S	**C**
Ps 32	Proper 6 [11]	ThFSa	C*
Ps 32	**Proper 6 [11]**	S	**C***
Ps 32	Proper 15 [20]	MTW	C*
Ps 32:1-7	Proper 26 [31]	ThFSa	C*
Ps 32:1-7	**Proper 26 [31]**	S	**C***
Ps 33:1-12	Proper 5 [10]	ThFSa	A+
Ps 33:1-12	**Proper 5 [10]**	S	**A+**
Ps 33:12-22	Pentecost	ThFSa	A
Ps 33:12-22	Pentecost	ThFSa	B
Ps 33:12-22	Proper 14 [19]	ThFSa	C*
Ps 33:12-22	**Proper 14 [19]**	S	**C***
Ps 34	Proper 23 [28]	MTW	A*
Ps 34:1-8	Proper 14 [19]	ThFSa	B*
Ps 34:1-8	**Proper 14 [19]**	S	**B***
Ps 34:1-8 [19-22]	Proper 25 [30]	ThFSa	B+
Ps 34:1-8 [19-22]	**Proper 25 [30]**	S	**B+**
Ps 34:1-10, 22	**All Saints**	S	**A**
Ps 34:9-14	Proper 15 [20]	ThFSa	B*
Ps 34:9-14	**Proper 15 [20]**	S	**B***
Ps 34:15-22	Proper 16 [21]	ThFSa	B*
Ps 34:15-22	**Proper 16 [21]**	S	**B***
Ps 35:1-10	Epiphany 4 [4]	MTW	B
Ps 35:11-28	Epiphany Last Trfg	MT	C
Ps 36	Proper 15 [20]	MTW	B*
Ps 36:5-10	Epiphany 2 [2]	ThFSa	C
Ps 36:5-10	**Epiphany 2 [2]**	S	**C**
Ps 36:5-11	**Mon. of Holy Week**	S	**ABC**
Ps 37:1-9	Proper 22 [27]	ThFSa	C*
Ps 37:1-9	**Proper 22 [27]**	S	**C***
Ps 37:1-11, 39-40	Epiphany 7 [7]	ThFSa	C
Ps 37:1-11, 39-40	**Epiphany 7 [7]**	S	**C**
Ps 37:1-17	Epiphany 4 [4]	MTW	A
Ps 37:12-22	Proper 12 [17]	MTW	B+
Ps 37:23-40	Proper 24 [29]	MTW	B*
Ps 38	Epiphany 7 [7]	MTW	B
Ps 38	Epiphany 7 [7]	MTW	C
Ps 39	Proper 23 [28]	MTW	B+
Ps 39	Lent 3	MTW	C
Ps 40:1-8	Proper 5 [10]	MTW	A*
Ps 40:1-11	Epiphany 2 [2]	ThFSa	A
Ps 40:1-11	**Epiphany 2 [2]**	S	**A**
Ps 40:5-10	**Annunciation**	S	**ABC**
Ps 40:6-17	Epiphany 2 [2]	MTW	A
Ps 41	Epiphany 7 [7]	ThFSa	B
Ps 41	**Epiphany 7 [7]**	S	**B**
Ps 42	Proper 21 [26]	MTW	A+

Ps 42	Advent 3	MTW	A
Ps 42 and 43	**Easter Vigil**	**S**	**ABC**
Ps 42 and 43	Proper 7 [12]	ThFSa	C+
Ps 42 and 43	**Proper 7 [12]**	**S**	**C+**
Ps 43	Proper 26 [31]	ThFSa	A*
Ps 43	**Proper 26 [31]**	**S**	**A***
Ps 44	Proper 12 [17]	MTW	C+
Ps 45	**Annunciation**	**S**	**ABC**
Ps 45:1-2, 6-9	Proper 17 [22]	ThFSa	B+
Ps 45:1-2, 6-9	**Proper 17 [22]**	**S**	**B+**
Ps 45:6-17	Epiphany 8 [8]	MTW	B
Ps 45:6-17	Proper 3 [8]	MTW	B
Ps 45:10-17	Proper 9 [14]	ThFSa	A+
Ps 45:10-17	**Proper 9 [14]**	**S**	**A+**
Ps 46	**Easter Vigil**	**S**	**ABC**
Ps 46	Proper 4 [9]	ThFSa	A+
Ps 46	**Proper 4 [9]**	**S**	**A+**
Ps 46	Epiphany 3 [3]	MTW	B
Ps 46	Reign of Christ [34]	ThFSa	C*
Ps 46	**Reign of Christ [34]**	**S**	**C***
Ps 47	**Ascension**	**S**	**ABC**
Ps 47	Easter 7	FSa	B
Ps 47	Proper 8 [13]	MTW	A+
Ps 48	Proper 9 [14]	ThFSa	B+
Ps 48	**Proper 9 [14]**	**S**	**B+**
Ps 48	Pentecost	MTW	C
Ps 49:1-12	Proper 13 [18]	ThFSa	C*
Ps 49:1-12	**Proper 13 [18]**	**S**	**C***
Ps 50	Proper 26 [31]	MTW	C*
Ps 50:1-6	Epiphany Last Trfg	ThFSa	B
Ps 50:1-6	**Epiphany Last Trfg**	**S**	**B**
Ps 50:1-8, 22-23	Proper 14 [19]	ThFSa	C+
Ps 50:1-8, 22-23	**Proper 14 [19]**	**S**	**C+**
Ps 50:7-15	Proper 5 [10]	ThFSa	A*
Ps 50:7-15	**Proper 5 [10]**	**S**	**A***
Ps 50:16-23	Proper 13 [18]	MTW	B+
Ps 51	Lent 1	ThFSa	A
Ps 51	Proper 26 [31]	MTW	B*
Ps 51:1-10	Proper 19 [24]	ThFSa	C*
Ps 51:1-10	**Proper 19 [24]**	**S**	**C***
Ps 51:1-12	Lent 5	ThFSa	B
Ps 51:1-12	**Lent 5**	**S**	**B**
Ps 51:1-12	Proper 13 [18]	ThFSa	B+
Ps 51:1-12	**Proper 13 [18]**	**S**	**B+**
Ps 51:1-17	**Ash Wednesday**	**S**	**ABC**
Ps 52	Epiphany 9 [9]	MTW	A
Ps 52	Proper 4 [9]	MTW	A*
Ps 52	Proper 6 [11]	MTW	B*
Ps 52	Proper 11 [16]	ThFSa	C+
Ps 52	**Proper 11 [16]**	**S**	**C+**
Ps 53	Proper 6 [11]	MTW	B+
Ps 53	Lent 4	MTW	C
Ps 54	Proper 20 [25]	ThFSa	B*
Ps 54	**Proper 20 [25]**	**S**	**B***
Ps 55:1-15	Proper 22 [27]	MTW	B+
Ps 55:16-23	Proper 12 [17]	MTW	C*
Ps 56	Epiphany 4 [4]	MTW	C
Ps 57	Proper 14 [19]	MTW	B+
Ps 57	Proper 24 [29]	MTW	C*
Ps 58	Proper 17 [22]	MTW	C+
Ps 59	Proper 7 [12]	MTW	C+
Ps 60	Proper 13 [18]	MTW	C+
Ps 61	Proper 11 [16]	MTW	B+
Ps 61	Proper 23 [28]	MTW	C*
Ps 62	Proper 21 [26]	MTW	C*
Ps 62:5-12	Epiphany 3 [3]	ThFSa	B
Ps 62:5-12	**Epiphany 3 [3]**	**S**	**B**
Ps 63	Proper 27 [32]	MTW	A*
Ps 63	Reign of Christ [34]	MTW	B+
Ps 63:1-8	Proper 24 [29]	MTW	A+
Ps 63:1-8	Lent 3	ThFSa	C
Ps 63:1-8	**Lent 3**	**S**	**C**
Ps 64	Proper 7 [12]	MTW	C*
Ps 65	Proper 7 [12]	MTW	B*
Ps 65	Proper 25 [30]	ThFSa	C+
Ps 65	**Proper 25 [30]**	**S**	**C+**
Ps 65	**Thanksgiving**	**S**	**A**
Ps 65:8-13	Proper 12 [17]	MTW	A+
Ps 65:[1-8] 9-13	Proper 10 [15]	ThFSa	A*
Ps 65:[1-8] 9-13	**Proper 10 [15]**	**S**	**A***
Ps 66:1-9	Proper 9 [14]	ThFSa	C*
Ps 66:1-9	**Proper 9 [14]**	**S**	**C***
Ps 66:1-12	Proper 23 [28]	ThFSa	C+
Ps 66:1-12	**Proper 23 [28]**	**S**	**C+**
Ps 66:8-20	Easter 6	ThFSa	A
Ps 66:8-20	**Easter 6**	**S**	**A**
Ps 67	Proper 15 [20]	ThFSa	A*
Ps 67	**Proper 15 [20]**	**S**	**A***
Ps 67	Easter 6	ThFSa	C
Ps 67	**Easter 6**	**S**	**C**
Ps 68:1-10, 19-20	Proper 5 [10]	MTW	C+*
Ps 68:1-10, 32-35	**Easter 7**	**S**	**A**
Ps 68:24-35	Proper 10 [15]	MTW	B+
Ps 69:1-3, 13-16, 30-36	Proper 4 [9]	MTW	A+
Ps 69:1-5, 30-36	Baptism/Lord [1]	MTW	B
Ps 69:7-10 [11-15] 16-18	Proper 7 [12]	ThFSa	A*
Ps 69:7-10 [11-15] 16-18	**Proper 7 [12]**	**S**	**A***
Ps 70	**Wed. of Holy Week**	**S**	**ABC**
Ps 70	Proper 27 [32]	ThFSa	A*

Psalm	Occasion	Days	Year
Ps 70	**Proper 27 [32]**	S	**A***
Ps 71:1-6	Epiphany 4 [4]	ThFSa	C
Ps 71:1-6	**Epiphany 4 [4]**	S	**C**
Ps 71:1-6	Proper 16 [21]	ThFSa	C+
Ps 71:1-6	**Proper 16 [21]**	S	**C+**
Ps 71:1-14	**Tues. of Holy Week**	S	**ABC**
Ps 72		Jan 3-9	A
Ps 72		Jan 3-9	C
Ps 72:1-7, 10-14	**Epiphany**	S	**ABC**
Ps 72:1-7, 18-19	Advent 2	ThFSa	A
Ps 72:1-7, 18-19	**Advent 2**	S	**A**
Ps 73	Proper 19 [24]	MTW	C*
Ps 73:1-20	Proper 18 [23]	MTW	B+
Ps 73:21-28	Proper 19 [24]	MTW	B+
Ps 74	Proper 5 [10]	MTW	B*
Ps 74	Proper 15 [20]	MTW	C+
Ps 75	Proper 11 [16]	MTW	A*
Ps 75	Proper 24 [29]	MTW	B+
Ps 75	Proper 8 [13]	MTW	C+
Ps 76	Reign of Christ [34]	MTW	B*
Ps 76	Proper 28 [33]	MTW	C+
Ps 77	Proper 19 [24]	MTW	A+
Ps 77	Lent 1	MTW	B
Ps 77:1-2, 11-20	Proper 8 [13]	ThFSa	C+
Ps 77:1-2, 11-20	**Proper 8 [13]**	S	**C+**
Ps 78	Proper 27 [32]	MTW	A+
Ps 78: 1-2, 34-38	**Holy Cross**	S	**ABC**
Ps 78:1-4, 12-16	Proper 21 [26]	ThFSa	A+
Ps 78:1-4, 12-16	**Proper 21 [26]**	S	**A+**
Ps 78:1-4, 52-72	Epiphany 9 [9]	MTW	B
Ps 78:1-4, 52-72	Proper 4 [9]	MTW	B*
Ps 78:1-7	Proper 27 [32]	ThFSa	A+
Ps 78:1-7	**Proper 27 [32]**	S	**A+**
Ps 78:1-8, 17-29	Proper 13 [18]	MTW	A*
Ps 78:17-20, 52-55	Epiphany Last Trfg	MT	A
Ps 78:23-29	Proper 13 [18]	ThFSa	B*
Ps 78:23-29	**Proper 13 [18]**	S	**B***
Ps 79	Advent 1	MTW	B
Ps 79:1-9	Proper 20 [25]	ThFSa	C+
Ps 79:1-9	**Proper 20 [25]**	S	**C+**
Ps 80	Easter 5	MTW	B
Ps 80:1-2, 8-19	Proper 15 [20]	ThFSa	C+
Ps 80:1-2, 8-19	**Proper 15 [20]**	S	**C+**
Ps 80:1-7	Advent 4	ThFSa	C
Ps 80:1-7	**Advent 4**	S	**C**
Ps 80:1-7, 17-19	Advent 4	ThFSa	A
Ps 80:1-7, 17-19	**Advent 4**	S	**A**
Ps 80:1-7, 17-19	Advent 1	ThFSa	B
Ps 80:1-7, 17-19	**Advent 1**	S	**B**
Ps 80:7-15	Proper 22 [27]	ThFSa	A*
Ps 80:7-15	**Proper 22 [27]**	S	**A***
Ps 81	Lent 3	MTW	A
Ps 81	Proper 14 [19]	MTW	B*
Ps 81:1, 10-16	Proper 17 [22]	ThFSa	C+
Ps 81:1, 10-16	**Proper 17 [22]**	S	**C+**
Ps 81:1-10	Epiphany 9 [9]	ThFSa	B
Ps 81:1-10	Proper 4 [9]	ThFSa	B*
Ps 81:1-10	**Epiphany 9 [9]**	S	**B**
Ps 81:1-10	**Proper 4 [9]**	S	**B***
Ps 82	Proper 10 [15]	ThFSa	C+
Ps 82	**Proper 10 [15]**	S	**C+**
Ps 82	Proper 15 [20]	ThFSa	C*
Ps 82	**Proper 15 [20]**	S	**C***
Ps 83	Proper 6 [11]	MTW	C+
Ps 83:1-4, 13-18	Proper 17 [22]	MTW	A+
Ps 83:1-4, 9-10, 17-18	Proper 28 [33]	MTW	A+
Ps 84	Lent 3	MTW	B
Ps 84	Proper 16 [21]	ThFSa	B+
Ps 84	**Proper 16 [21]**	S	**B+**
Ps 84	**Presentation**	S	**ABC**
Ps 84:8-12	Proper 25 [30]	MTW	C*
Ps 84:1-7	Proper 25 [30]	ThFSa	C*
Ps 84:1-7	**Proper 25 [30]**	S	**C***
Ps 85	Proper 12 [17]	ThFSa	C+
Ps 85	**Proper 12 [17]**	S	**C+**
Ps 85:1-2, 8-13	Advent 2	ThFSa	B
Ps 85:1-2, 8-13	**Advent 2**	S	**B**
Ps 85:8-13	Proper 14 [19]	ThFSa	A*
Ps 85:8-13	**Proper 14 [19]**	S	**A***
Ps 85:8-13	Proper 10 [15]	ThFSa	B*
Ps 85:8-13	**Proper 10 [15]**	S	**B***
Ps 86	Epiphany 2 [2]	MTW	B
Ps 86:1-10	Proper 7 [12]	ThFSa	A+
Ps 86:1-10, 16-17	**Proper 7 [12]**	S	**A+**
Ps 86:11-17	Proper 7 [12]	MTW	A+
Ps 86:11-17	Proper 11 [16]	ThFSa	A*
Ps 86:11-17	**Proper 11 [16]**	S	**A***
Ps 87	Proper 15 [20]	MTW	A*
Ps 87	Proper 25 [30]	MTW	C+
Ps 88	Proper 8 [13]	MTW	B*
Ps 89:1-4, 15-18	Proper 8 [13]	ThFSa	A*
Ps 89:1-4, 15-18	**Proper 8 [13]**	S	**A***
Ps 89:1-4, 19-26	Advent 4	ThFSa	B
Ps 89:1-4, 19-26	**Advent 4**	S	**B**
Ps 89:1-18	Proper 14 [19]	MTW	C*
Ps 89:5-37	Baptism/Lord [1]	MTW	A
Ps 89:20-37	Proper 11 [16]	ThFSa	B+
Ps 89:20-37	**Proper 11 [16]**	S	**B+**

Psalm	Occasion	Day	Year
Ps 90	Advent 1	MTW	C
Ps 90:1-6, 13-17	Proper 25 [30]	ThFSa	A+
Ps 90:1-6, 13-17	**Proper 25 [30]**	**S**	**A+**
Ps 90:1-8 [9-11] 12	Proper 28 [33]	ThFSa	A*
Ps 90:1-8 [9-11] 12	**Proper 28 [33]**	**S**	**A***
Ps 90:12-17	Proper 23 [28]	ThFSa	B*
Ps 90:12-17	**Proper 23 [28]**	**S**	**B***
Ps 91:1-2, 9-16	Lent 1	ThFSa	C
Ps 91:1-2, 9-16	**Lent 1**	**S**	**C**
Ps 91:1-6, 14-16	Proper 21 [26]	ThFSa	C+
Ps 91:1-6, 14-16	**Proper 21 [26]**	**S**	**C+**
Ps 91:9-16	Proper 24 [29]	ThFSa	B*
Ps 91:9-16	**Proper 24 [29]**	**S**	**B***
Ps 92	Proper 10 [15]	MTW	A*
Ps 92:1-4, 12-15	Proper 6 [11]	ThFSa	B*
Ps 92:1-4, 12-15	**Proper 6 [11]**	**S**	**B***
Ps 92:1-4, 12-15	Epiphany 8 [8]	ThFSa	C
Ps 92:1-4, 12-15	**Epiphany 8 [8]**	**S**	**C**
Ps 92:1-4, 12-15	Proper 3 [8]	ThFSa	C
Ps 92:1-4, 12-15	**Proper 3 [8]**	**S**	**C**
Ps 93	Easter 6	MTW	ABC
Ps 93	**Ascension**	**S**	**ABC**
Ps 93	Easter 7	FSa	A
Ps 93	Reign of Christ [34]	ThFSa	B*
Ps 93	**Reign of Christ [34]**	**S**	**B***
Ps 94	Proper 27 [32]	MTW	B*
Ps 94	Proper 19 [24]	MTW	C+
Ps 95	Lent 3	ThFSa	A
Ps 95	**Lent 3**	**S**	**A**
Ps 95	Easter 4	MTW	B
Ps 95:1-7a	Reign of Christ [34]	ThFSa	A*
Ps 95:1-7a	**Reign of Christ [34]**	**S**	**A***
Ps 96	**Christmas Day 1**	**S**	**ABC**
Ps 96		Dec 22-24	B
Ps 96	Proper 4 [9]	ThFSa	C+
Ps 96	**Proper 4 [9]**	**S**	**C+**
Ps 96:1-9	Epiphany 9 [9]	ThFSa	C
Ps 96:1-9	Proper 4 [9]	ThFSa	C*
Ps 96:1-9	**Epiphany 9 [9]**	**S**	**C**
Ps 96:1-9	**Proper 4 [9]**	**S**	**C***
Ps 96:1-9 [10-13]	Proper 24 [29]	ThFSa	A*
Ps 96:1-9 [10-13]	**Proper 24 [29]**	**S**	**A***
Ps 97	**Christmas Day 2**	**S**	**ABC**
Ps 97	Proper 23 [28]	MTW	A+
Ps 97	Easter 7	FSa	C
Ps 97	**Easter 7**	**S**	**C**
Ps 98	**Christmas Day 3**	**S**	**ABC**
Ps 98	**Easter Vigil**	**S**	**ABC**
Ps 98	Proper 24 [29]	MTW	A*
Ps 98	Easter 6	ThFSa	B
Ps 98	**Easter 6**	**S**	**B**
Ps 98	Proper 27 [32]	MTW	C+
Ps 98	**Proper 27 [32]**	**S**	**C+**
Ps 98	Proper 28 [33]	ThFSa	C*
Ps 98	**Proper 28 [33]**	**S**	**C***
Ps 98:1-5	Holy Cross	S	ABC
Ps 99	Epiphany Last Trfg	ThFSa	C
Ps 99	**Epiphany Last Trfg**	**S**	**AC**
Ps 99	Easter 7	MTW	A
Ps 99	Proper 24 [29]	ThFSa	A+
Ps 99	**Proper 24 [29]**	**S**	**A+**
Ps 99	Proper 4 [9]	MTW	B+
Ps 100	Easter 4	MTW	A
Ps 100	Proper 6 [11]	ThFSa	A*
Ps 100	**Proper 6 [11]**	**S**	**A***
Ps 100	Reign of Christ [34]	ThFSa	A+
Ps 100	**Reign of Christ [34]**	**S**	**A+**
Ps 100	**Thanksgiving**	**S**	**C**
Ps 100	Proper 11 [16]	MTW	B*
Ps 100	Easter 4	MTW	C
Ps 101	Proper 15 [20]	MTW	B+
Ps 101	Proper 18 [23]	MTW	C*
Ps 102:1-17	Easter 5	MTW	A
Ps 102:1-17	Proper 23 [28]	MTW	C+
Ps 102:12-28	Epiphany 5 [5]	MTW	B
Ps 103:[1-7] 8-13	Proper 19 [24]	ThFSa	A*
Ps 103:[1-7] 8-13	**Proper 19 [24]**	**S**	**A***
Ps 103:1-8	Proper 16 [21]	ThFSa	C*
Ps 103:1-8	**Proper 16 [21]**	**S**	**C***
Ps 103:1-13, 22	Epiphany 8 [8]	ThFSa	B
Ps 103:1-13, 22	**Epiphany 8 [8]**	**S**	**B**
Ps 103:1-13, 22	Proper 3 [8]	ThFSa	B
Ps 103:1-13, 22	**Proper 3 [8]**	**S**	**B**
Ps 104	Epiphany 8 [8]	MTW	A
Ps 104	Proper 3 [8]	MTW	A
Ps 104:1-9, 24, 35b	Proper 24 [29]	ThFSa	B+
Ps 104:1-9, 24, 35b	**Proper 24 [29]**	**S**	**B+**
Ps 104:24-34, 35b	**Pentecost**	**S**	**ABC**
Ps 104:24-34, 35b	Pentecost	MTW	A
Ps 104:24-34, 35b	Pentecost	MTW	B
Ps 104:24-34, 35b	Pentecost	ThFSa	C
Ps 105:1-6, 16-22, 45b	Proper 14 [19]	ThFSa	A+
Ps 105:1-6, 16-22, 45b	**Proper 14 [19]**	**S**	**A+**

APPENDIXES

Psalm	Occasion	Day	Year
Ps 105:1-6, 23-26, 45b	Proper 17 [22]	ThFSa	A+
Ps 105:1-6, 23-26, 45b	**Proper 17 [22]**	S	A+
Ps 105:1-6, 37-45	Proper 20 [25]	ThFSa	A+
Ps 105:1-6, 37-45	**Proper 20 [25]**	S	A+
Ps 105:1-11, 37-45	Proper 6 [11]	MTW	A*
Ps 105:1-11, 37-45	Lent 2	MTW	B
Ps 105:1-11, 45b	Proper 12 [17]	ThFSa	A+
Ps 105:1-11, 45b	**Proper 12 [17]**	S	A+
Ps 105:1-15 [16-41] 42	Lent 2	MTW	C
Ps 106:1-6, 13-23, 47-48	Proper 17 [22]	MTW	B*
Ps 106:1-6, 19-23	Proper 23 [28]	ThFSa	A+
Ps 106:1-6, 19-23	**Proper 23 [28]**	S	A+
Ps 106:1-12	Proper 20 [25]	MTW	A*
Ps 106:1-12	Baptism/Lord [1]	MTW	C
Ps 106:40-48	Proper 20 [25]	MTW	C+
Ps 107:1-3, 17-22	Lent 4	ThFSa	B
Ps 107:1-3, 17-22	**Lent 4**	S	B
Ps 107:1-3, 23-32	Proper 7 [12]	ThFSa	B*
Ps 107:1-3, 23-32	**Proper 7 [12]**	S	B*
Ps 107:1-3, 33-43	Proper 13 [18]	MTW	B*
Ps 107:1-7, 33-37	Proper 26 [31]	ThFSa	A+
Ps 107:1-7, 33-37	**Proper 26 [31]**	S	A+
Ps 107:1-9, 43	Proper 13 [18]	ThFSa	C+
Ps 107:1-9, 43	**Proper 13 [18]**	S	C+
Ps 107:1-16	Lent 4	MTW	B
Ps 108	Proper 5 [10]	MTW	B+
Ps 109:21-31	Proper 16 [21]	MTW	C*
Ps 110		Jan 3-9	B
Ps 110:1-4	Epiphany Last Trfg	MT	B
Ps 111	Epiphany 4 [4]	ThFSa	B
Ps 111	**Epiphany 4 [4]**	S	B
Ps 111	Proper 12 [17]	MTW	B*
Ps 111	Proper 15 [20]	ThFSa	B+
Ps 111	**Proper 15 [20]**	S	B+
Ps 111	Proper 23 [28]	ThFSa	C*
Ps 111	**Proper 23 [28]**	S	C*
Ps 112	Proper 22 [27]	MTW	B*
Ps 112	Proper 17 [22]	ThFSa	C*
Ps 112	**Proper 17 [22]**	S	C*
Ps 112:1-9 [10]	Epiphany 5 [5]	ThFSa	A
Ps 112:1-9 [10]	**Epiphany 5 [5]**	S	A
Ps 113	Proper 27 [32]	MTW	B+
Ps 113	Advent 4	MTW	C
Ps 113	Proper 20 [25]	ThFSa	C*
Ps 113	**Visitation**	S	ABC
Ps 113	**Proper 20 [25]**	S	C*
Ps 114	**Easter Vigil**	S	ABC
Ps 114	**Easter Evening**	S	ABC
Ps 114	Easter 2	MTW	A
Ps 114	Proper 19 [24]	ThFSa	A+
Ps 114	**Proper 19 [24]**	S	A+
Ps 115	Easter 7	MTW	B
Ps 115	Epiphany 5 [5]	MTW	C
Ps 116:1-2, 12-19	**Holy Thursday**	S	ABC
Ps 116:1-2, 12-19	Proper 6 [11]	ThFSa	A+
Ps 116:1-2, 12-19	**Proper 6 [11]**	S	A+
Ps 116:1-4, 12-19	Easter 3	ThFSa	A
Ps 116:1-4, 12-19	**Easter 3**	S	A
Ps 116:1-9	Proper 19 [24]	ThFSa	B*
Ps 116:1-9	**Proper 19 [24]**	S	B*
Ps 117	Reign of Christ [34]	MTW	C+
Ps 118:1-2, 14-24	**Easter**	S	ABC
Ps 118:1-2, 14-24	Easter	MTW	ABC
Ps 118:1-2, 19-29	**Passion/Palm Sun**	S	ABC
Ps 118:1-2, 19-29	Passion/Palm Sun	ThFSa	B
Ps 118:14-29	**Easter 2**	S	C
Ps 118:26-29	Lent 2	Sa	C
Ps 119:1-8	Epiphany 6 [6]	ThFSa	A
Ps 119:1-8	**Epiphany 6 [6]**	S	A
Ps 119:1-8	Proper 26 [31]	ThFSa	B*
Ps 119:1-8	**Proper 26 [31]**	S	B*
Ps 119:9-16	Epiphany 6 [6]	MTW	A
Ps 119:9-16	**Lent 5**	S	B
Ps 119:9-16	Lent 5	MTW	B
Ps 119:17-24	Proper 25 [30]	MTW	B*
Ps 119:17-32	Proper 11 [16]	MTW	C+
Ps 119:33-40	Epiphany 7 [7]	ThFSa	A
Ps 119:33-40	**Epiphany 7 [7]**	S	A
Ps 119:33-40	Proper 18 [23]	ThFSa	A*
Ps 119:33-40	**Proper 18 [23]**	S	A*
Ps 119:41-48	Proper 25 [30]	MTW	A+*
Ps 119:41-48	Proper 5 [10]	MTW	A+
Ps 119:49-56	Proper 22 [27]	MTW	A+
Ps 119:49-56	Proper 21 [26]	MTW	C+
Ps 119:57-64	Epiphany 7 [7]	MTW	A
Ps 119:65-72	Proper 18 [23]	MTW	A*
Ps 119:65-72	Proper 17 [22]	MTW	C*
Ps 119:73-80	Proper 9 [14]	MTW	C*
Ps 119:81-88	Proper 9 [14]	MTW	B*
Ps 119:89-96	Epiphany 3 [3]	MTW	C
Ps 119:97-104	Proper 20 [25]	MTW	A+
Ps 119:97-104	Proper 16 [21]	MTW	B*
Ps 119:97-104	Proper 11 [16]	MTW	C*
Ps 119:97-104	Proper 24 [29]	ThFSa	C+

Ps 139:1-12, 23-24	**Proper 11 [16]**	S	A+
Ps 139:1-18	Proper 20 [25]	MTW	B*
Ps 139:13-18	Proper 11 [16]	MTW	A+
Ps 140	Proper 8 [13]	MTW	C*
Ps 140	Proper 21 [26]	MTW	B+
Ps 141	Proper 28 [33]	MTW	C*
Ps 142	Proper 10 [15]	MTW	A+
Ps 142	Proper 10 [15]	MTW	B*
Ps 142	Proper 26 [31]	MTW	C+
Ps 143	Lent 5	MTW	A
Ps 143	**Easter Vigil**	S	ABC
Ps 144	Proper 22 [27]	MTW	A*
Ps 144:9-15	Proper 17 [22]	MTW	B+
Ps 145	Epiphany 2 [2]	MTW	C
Ps 145:1-5, 17-21	Proper 27 [32]	ThFSa	C+
Ps 145:1-5, 17-21	**Proper 27 [32]**	S	C+
Ps 145:1-8	Proper 20 [25]	ThFSa	A*
Ps 145:1-8	**Proper 20 [25]**	S	A*
Ps 145:8-14	Proper 9 [14]	ThFSa	A*
Ps 145:8-14	**Proper 9 [14]**	S	A*
Ps 145:8-9, 14-21	Proper 13 [18]	ThFSa	A*
Ps 145:8-9, 14-21	**Proper 13 [18]**	S	A*
Ps 145:10-18	Proper 12 [17]	ThFSa	B*
Ps 145:10-18	**Proper 12 [17]**	S	B*
Ps 146	Proper 18 [23]	ThFSa	B*
Ps 146	**Proper 18 [23]**	S	B*
Ps 146	Proper 26 [31]	ThFSa	B+
Ps 146	**Proper 26 [31]**	S	B+
Ps 146	Proper 27 [32]	ThFSa	B*
Ps 146	**Proper 27 [32]**	S	B*
Ps 146	Proper 5 [10]	ThFSa	C+
Ps 146	**Proper 5 [10]**	S	C+
Ps 146	Proper 21 [26]	ThFSa	C*
Ps 146	**Proper 21 [26]**	S	C*
Ps 146	Lent 4	MTW	A
Ps 146:5-10	Advent 3	ThFSa	A
Ps 146:5-10	**Advent 3**	S	A
Ps 147:1-11, 20c	Epiphany 5 [5]	ThFSa	B
Ps 147:1-11, 20c	**Epiphany 5 [5]**	S	B
Ps 147:12-20		Dec 29-Jan 2	C
Ps 147:12-20	**Christmas 2**	S	ABC
Ps 148	**Christmas 1**	S	ABC
Ps 148		Dec 26-28	ABC
Ps 148		Dec 29-Jan 2	B
Ps 148	Easter 5	ThFSa	C
Ps 148	**Easter 5**	S	C

Ps 149	Proper 18 [23]	ThFSa	A+
Ps 149	**Proper 18 [23]**	S	A+
Ps 149	**All Saints**	S	C
Ps 150	Easter 3	MTW	B
Ps 150	Easter 2	ThFSa	C
Ps 150	**Easter 2**	S	C
Prv 1:1-7		Jan 2	B
Prv 1:1-7		Jan 2	C
Prv 1:1-7, 20-33	Proper 12 [17]	W	A*
Prv 1:1-19	Proper 18 [23]	Th	B+
Prv 1:20-33		Jan 3	B
Prv 1:20-33	**Proper 19 [24]**	S	B+
Prv 2:1-5	Easter 6	Th	C
Prv 2:1-15	Epiphany 6 [6]	W	A
Prv 2:6-8	Easter 6	F	C
Prv 2:9-15	Easter 6	Sa	C
Prv 3:1-12		Jan 4	B
Prv 3:5-12	Easter 5	T	A
Prv 3:13-18	Easter 5	W	A
Prv 3:13-18	Trinity Sunday	Th	C
Prv 3:19-26	Trinity Sunday	F	C
Prv 3:27-35	Epiphany 7 [7]	W	A
Prv 4:1-9	Trinity Sunday	Sa	C
Prv 4:10-27	Proper 6 [11]	W	A*
Prv 4:10-27	Proper 18 [23]	F	B+
Prv 5:1-23	Epiphany 8 [8]	W	C
Prv 5:1-23	Proper 3 [8]	W	C
Prv 6:6-23	Epiphany 5 [5]	W	A
Prv 7:1-4	Trinity Sunday	M	C
Prv 8:1-4, 22-31	**Trinity Sunday**	S	C
Prv 8:1-8, 19-21; 9:4b-6	**Easter Vigil**	S	ABC
Prv 8:1-21	Epiphany 3 [3]	W	B
Prv 8:1-31	Proper 18 [23]	Sa	B+
Prv 8:4-21	Trinity Sunday	T	C
Prv 8:22-31		Dec 27	A
Prv 8:32-36		Dec 27	C
Prv 8:32—9:6	Easter 3	T	A
Prv 8:32—9:6	Proper 18 [23]	M	B+
Prv 9:1-6	Easter 3	W	B
Prv 9:1-6	**Proper 15 [20]**	S	B*
Prv 9:1-12		Dec 30	B
Prv 9:1-18	Proper 11 [16]	T	C*
Prv 10:1-5	Proper 13 [18]	Th	A*
Prv 11:1-31	Proper 18 [23]	T	B+
Prv 11:3-13	Proper 7 [12]	Sa	C+
Prv 11:23-30	Proper 10 [15]	W	A*
Prv 12:10-21	Epiphany 5 [5]	Th	B
Prv 12:22-28	Epiphany 8 [8]	Th	A

Prv 12:22-28	Proper 3 [8]	Th	A
Prv 13:1-12	Epiphany 8 [8]	Th	C
Prv 13:1-12	Proper 3 [8]	Th	C
Prv 14:1-9	Proper 18 [23]	W	B+
Prv 14:12-31	Proper 20 [25]	M	C*
Prv 15:1-17	Proper 19 [24]	Th	B+
Prv 15:1-9	Epiphany 8 [8]	F	C
Prv 15:1-9	Proper 3 [8]	F	C
Prv 15:8-11, 24-33	Proper 26 [31]	Th	C*
Prv 15:13-17	Proper 17 [22]	Th	C*
Prv 16:1-20	Proper 25 [30]	W	A*
Prv 16:21-33	Proper 26 [31]	W	A*
Prv 17:1-5	Proper 20 [25]	T	C*
Prv 18:6-12	Proper 17 [22]	F	C*
Prv 19:1-17	Proper 10 [15]	T	C*
Prv 19:24-29	Proper 19 [24]	F	B+
Prv 21:1-17	Proper 19 [24]	Sa	B+
Prv 21:1-4, 24-26	Proper 17 [22]	Sa	C*
Prv 21:10-16	Proper 20 [25]	W	C*
Prv 22:1-2, 8-9, 22-23	**Proper 18 [23]**	**S**	**B+**
Prv 22:1-9		Jan 5	B
Prv 22:1-21	Proper 19 [24]	M	B+
Prv 22:2-16	Proper 21 [26]	Th	C*
Prv 23:1-11	Proper 13 [18]	Th	C*
Prv 24:1-12	Proper 13 [18]	F	C*
Prv 24:23-34	Proper 25 [30]	Sa	A*
Prv 25:1-28	Proper 19 [24]	T	B+
Prv 25:6-7	**Proper 17 [22]**	**S**	**C***
Prv 25:11-22	Epiphany 7 [7]	M	A
Prv 27:1-27	Proper 20 [25]	M	B+
Prv 28:3-10	Proper 21 [26]	F	C*
Prv 28:11-28	Proper 21 [26]	Sa	C*
Prv 29:1-27	Proper 19 [24]	W	B+
Prv 30:1-10	Proper 20 [25]	Th	B+
Prv 30:1-9	Lent 1	W	B
Prv 30:18-33	Proper 20 [25]	F	B+
Prv 31:10-31	**Proper 20 [25]**	**S**	**B+**
Eccl 1:1-11	Baptism/Lord [1]	Th	C
Eccl 1:1-11	Proper 13 [18]	Sa	C*
Eccl 1:1-18	Proper 20 [25]	Sa	B+
Eccl 1:2, 12-14; 2:18-23	**Proper 13 [18]**	**S**	**C***
Eccl 2:1-11	Baptism/Lord [1]	F	C
Eccl 2:1-17	Proper 13 [18]	M	C*
Eccl 3:1-8		Dec 24	B
Eccl 3:1-8	Lent 1	Sa	C
Eccl 3:1-13	**New Year's Day**	**S**	**ABC**

Eccl 3:1-15	Baptism/Lord [1]	Sa	C
Eccl 3:16—4:8	Proper 13 [18]	T	C*
Eccl 4:9-16	Proper 20 [25]	T	B+
Eccl 5:1-20	Proper 20 [25]	W	B+
Eccl 6:1-6	Proper 14 [19]	F	C*
Eccl 9:13-18	Proper 10 [15]	W	C*
Eccl 12:1-8, 13-14	Proper 13 [18]	W	C*
Song 1:1-17	Proper 17 [22]	Th	B+
Song 2:1-7	Proper 17 [22]	F	B+
Song 2:8-13	**Proper 9 [14]**	**S**	**A+**
Song 2:8-13	Proper 9 [14]	MTW	A+
Song 2:8-13	**Proper 17 [22]**	**S**	**B+**
Song 2:8-15	Easter 2	Th	A
Song 3:1-11	Easter	W	B
Song 3:6-11	Proper 17 [22]	M	B+
Song 4:1-8	Epiphany 2 [2]	T	C
Song 4:9—5:1	Epiphany 2 [2]	W	C
Song 5:2—6:3	Proper 17 [22]	T	B+
Song 5:9—6:3	Easter 2	F	A
Song 7:10—8:4	Proper 23 [28]	W	A*
Song 8:5-7	Proper 17 [22]	W	B+
Song 8:5-14	Proper 22 [27]	W	A*
Song 8:6-7	Easter 2	Sa	A
Is 1:1, 10-20	**Proper 14 [19]**	**S**	**C+**
Is 1:1-4, 16-20	Trinity Sunday	Th	B
Is 1:1-9	Proper 26 [31]	Sa	C*
Is 1:2-9, 21-23	Proper 14 [19]	Sa	C+
Is 1:10-18	**Proper 26 [31]**	**S**	**C***
Is 1:24-31	Advent 1	W	C
Is 2:1-4	Proper 10 [15]	Sa	A+
Is 2:1-4	Proper 14 [19]	M	C+
Is 2:1-5	Trinity Sunday	F	B
Is 2:1-5	**Advent 1**	**S**	**A**
Is 2:5-11	Proper 15 [20]	Th	C+
Is 2:12-17	Proper 17 [22]	T	C*
Is 3:1-17	Proper 15 [20]	F	C+
Is 3:18—4:6	Proper 15 [20]	Sa	C+
Is 4:2-6	Advent 2	Th	A
Is 4:2-6	Advent 2	T	B
Is 5:1-7	**Proper 22 [27]**	**S**	**A***
Is 5:1-7	Easter 5	M	B
Is 5:1-7	Lent 3	Sa	C
Is 5:1-7	**Proper 15 [20]**	**S**	**C+**
Is 5:8-23	Proper 15 [20]	M	C+
Is 5:8-23	Proper 20 [25]	Sa	C*
Is 5:11-17	Easter 3	Th	C
Is 5:15-24	Trinity Sunday	Sa	B
Is 5:24-30	Proper 15 [20]	T	C+

Is 6:1-4	Easter 3	F	C
Is 6:1-5		Jan 4	C
Is 6:1-8	**Trinity Sunday**	**S**	**B**
Is 6:1-8	Easter 3	W	C
Is 6:1-8 [9-13]	**Epiphany 5 [5]**	**S**	**C**
Is 7:1-9	Proper 22 [27]	Sa	C*
Is 7:10-14	**Annunciation**	**S**	**ABC**
Is 7:10-16	**Advent 4**	**S**	**A**
Is 8:1-15	Epiphany 5 [5]	W	C
Is 9:1-4	**Epiphany 3 [3]**	**S**	**A**
Is 9:2-7	**Christmas Day 1**	**S**	**ABC**
Is 9:8-17	Proper 14 [19]	Th	C+
Is 9:18—10:4	Proper 14 [19]	F	C+
Is 10:12-20	Proper 19 [24]	W	B*
Is 11:1-9	Advent 3	MTW	C
Is 11:1-10	**Advent 2**	**S**	**A**
Is 12	Proper 28 [33]	ThFSa	C+
Is 12	**Proper 28 [33]**	**S**	**C+**
Is 12:2-6	Advent 3	ThFSa	C
Is 12:2-6	**Advent 3**	**S**	**C**
Is 12:2-6	**Easter Vigil**	**S**	**ABC**
Is 14:1-2	Proper 13 [18]	Th	A+
Is 14:3-11	Proper 24 [29]	Sa	A*
Is 19:18-25	Advent 2	T	C
Is 22:1-8a	Proper 23 [28]	Th	A*
Is 22:8b-14	Proper 23 [28]	F	A*
Is 22:15-25	Epiphany 2 [2]	Th	A
Is 24:1-13	Proper 14 [19]	T	C+
Is 24:1-16a	Advent 2	M	A
Is 24:14-23	Proper 14 [19]	W	C+
Is 24:17-23	Proper 23 [28]	Sa	A*
Is 25:1-5	Easter 3	Th	A
Is 25:1-9	**Proper 23 [28]**	**S**	**A***
Is 25:6-9	**Easter**	**S**	**B**
Is 25:6-9	**Easter Evening**	**S**	**ABC**
Is 25:6-9	Easter 3	Sa	A
Is 25:6-9	**All Saints**	**S**	**B**
Is 25:6-10a	Proper 12 [17]	W	B*
Is 26:1-4	Easter 3	F	A
Is 26:1-6	Epiphany 8 [8]	F	A
Is 26:1-6	Proper 3 [8]	F	A
Is 26:1-9		Dec 30	A
Is 26:1-15	Easter 2	W	B
Is 26:7-15	Advent 2	M	B
Is 26:16—27:1	Proper 5 [10]	W	B*
Is 27:1-6	Proper 22 [27]	T	A*
Is 27:1-13	Proper 15 [20]	W	C+
Is 28:9-13	Proper 5 [10]	Th	B*
Is 28:14-22	Proper 16 [21]	W	A*
Is 29:1-12	Epiphany 5 [5]	F	A

Is 29:13-16	Epiphany 5 [5]	Sa	A
Is 29:17-24	Advent 3	M	A
Is 30:8-17	Epiphany 8 [8]	Sa	C
Is 30:8-17	Proper 3 [8]	Sa	C
Is 30:15-18	Lent 5	Th	B
Is 30:18-26	Epiphany 7 [7]	M	B
Is 30:19-26	Advent 2	F	A
Is 30:27-33	Proper 18 [23]	Th	B*
Is 31:1-9	Epiphany 8 [8]	Sa	A
Is 31:1-9	Proper 3 [8]	Sa	A
Is 32:1-8	Proper 18 [23]	F	B*
Is 32:9-20	Easter 5	T	B
Is 32:11-17	Pentecost	Th	C
Is 33:1-9	Proper 18 [23]	Sa	B*
Is 33:10-16	Proper 16 [21]	W	B*
Is 33:17-22		Dec 22	A
Is 33:17-22	Reign of Christ [34]	T	C*
Is 35:1-10	**Advent 3**	**S**	**A**
Is 35:3-7	Advent 2	W	C
Is 35:4-7a	**Proper 18 [23]**	**S**	**B***
Is 38:1-8	Epiphany 7 [7]	F	B
Is 38:10-20	Proper 18 [23]	MTW	B*
Is 39:1-8	Epiphany 7 [7]	Sa	B
Is 40:1-11	Advent 2	Sa	A
Is 40:1-11	Reign of Christ [34]	F	A+
Is 40:1-11	**Advent 2**	**S**	**B**
Is 40:1-11	Advent 2	M	C
Is 40:21-31	**Epiphany 5 [5]**	**S**	**B**
Is 41:1-13	Proper 20 [25]	W	A*
Is 41:8-10	Proper 13 [18]	F	A+
Is 41:14-20	Advent 2	T	A
Is 41:14-20	Baptism/Lord [1]	W	B
Is 41:21-29	Proper 11 [16]	Th	A*
Is 42:1-9	**Baptism/Lord [1]**	**S**	**A**
Is 42:1-9	**Mon. of Holy Week**	**S**	**ABC**
Is 42:5-9	Easter 6	F	B
Is 42:10-18	Advent 4	F	C
Is 42:14-21	Lent 4	T	A
Is 42:14-21	Advent 4	W	C
Is 43:1-7	Proper 13 [18]	W	A+
Is 43:1-7	**Baptism/Lord [1]**	**S**	**C**
Is 43:1-7	Lent 5	Th	C
Is 43:8-13	Proper 15 [20]	T	A*
Is 43:8-13	Lent 5	M	B
Is 43:8-15	Lent 5	F	C
Is 43:16-21	**Lent 5**	**S**	**C**
Is 43:18-25	**Epiphany 7 [7]**	**S**	**B**
Is 44:1-4	Pentecost	F	C
Is 44:1-5	Proper 11 [16]	Th	A+
Is 44:1-5	Proper 13 [18]	Sa	A*

Reference	Day	Day	Year
Is 44:1-8	Lent 5	T	B
Is 44:6-8	**Proper 11 [16]**	**S**	**A***
Is 44:9-17	Proper 11 [16]	F	A*
Is 44:18-20	Proper 11 [16]	Sa	A*
Is 44:21-28	Reign of Christ [34]	Sa	A*
Is 45:1-7	**Proper 24 [29]**	**S**	**A***
Is 45:20-25	Proper 15 [20]	Th	A*
Is 46:1-13	Epiphany 5 [5]	Sa	B
Is 47:1-9	Proper 24 [29]	F	B*
Is 47:10-15	Proper 24 [29]	Sa	B*
Is 48:1-5	Proper 10 [15]	Th	A*
Is 48:6-11	Proper 10 [15]	F	A*
Is 48:12-21	Epiphany 2 [2]	W	A
Is 48:17-21	Proper 21 [26]	Th	A+
Is 49:1-7	**Epiphany 2 [2]**	**S**	**A**
Is 49:1-7	**Tues. of Holy Week**	**S**	**ABC**
Is 49:5-6	Easter 6	Th	B
Is 49:5-15		Dec 29	B
Is 49:8-16a	**Epiphany 8 [8]**	**S**	**A**
Is 49:8-16a	**Proper 3 [8]**	**S**	**A**
Is 49:13-23		Dec 28	A
Is 50:4-9a	**Passion/Palm Sun**	**S**	**ABC**
Is 50:4-9a	**Wed. of Holy Week**	**S**	**ABC**
Is 50:4-9a	**Proper 19 [24]**	**S**	**B***
Is 51:1-3	Lent 2	Th	A
Is 51:1-3	Proper 8 [13]	W	A+
Is 51:1-6	**Proper 16 [21]**	**S**	**A***
Is 51:1-16	Baptism/Lord [1]	W	A
Is 51:4-8	Lent 2	Sa	A
Is 51:17-23	Proper 13 [18]	F	A*
Is 52:1-6	Proper 10 [15]	Sa	A*
Is 52:7-10	**Christmas Day 3**	**S**	**ABC**
Is 52:13—53:12	**Good Friday**	**S**	**ABC**
Is 53:1-12	Epiphany 2 [2]	T	A
Is 53:4-12	**Proper 24 [29]**	**S**	**B***
Is 53:10-12	Passion/Palm Sun	Th	C
Is 54:1-8	Epiphany 2 [2]	M	C
Is 54:1-10	Advent 1	W	A
Is 54:1-13		Dec 28	C
Is 54:9-10	Passion/Palm Sun	F	C
Is 54:11-17	Proper 24 [29]	Th	C*
Is 55:1-5	**Proper 13 [18]**	**S**	**A***
Is 55:1-9	Proper 13 [18]	W	B*
Is 55:1-9	**Lent 3**	**S**	**C**
Is 55:1-11	**Easter Vigil**	**S**	**ABC**
Is 55:10-13	**Proper 10 [15]**	**S**	**A***
Is 55:10-13	**Epiphany 8 [8]**	**S**	**C**
Is 55:10-13	**Proper 3 [8]**	**S**	**C**
Is 56:1, 6-8	**Proper 15 [20]**	**S**	**A***
Is 56:1-5	Proper 15 [20]	Sa	A*
Is 56:1-8	Epiphany 9 [9]	W	C
Is 56:1-8	Proper 4 [9]	W	C*
Is 56:9-12	Proper 7 [12]	Th	C*
Is 57:1-13	Proper 7 [12]	F	C*
Is 57:14-21	Proper 17 [22]	W	C*
Is 57:14-21	Proper 28 [33]	Th	C+
Is 58:1-12	**Ash Wednesday**	**S**	**ABC**
Is 58:1-12	Lent 1	Sa	A
Is 58:1-9a [9b-12]	**Epiphany 5 [5]**	**S**	**A**
Is 58:9b-14	**Proper 16 [21]**	**S**	**C***
Is 59:1-15a	Proper 28 [33]	F	C+
Is 59:15b-21	Proper 28 [33]	Sa	C+
Is 59:1-8	Proper 7 [12]	Sa	C*
Is 59:9-19	Lent 4	M	A+
Is 59:9-19	Proper 25 [30]	M	B+
Is 60:1-6		Dec 24	A
Is 60:1-6	**Epiphany**	**S**	**ABC**
Is 60:8-16	Reign of Christ [34]	W	C*
Is 60:15-22	Lent 4	W	B
Is 60:17-22	Lent 4	W	A
Is 60:17-22	Proper 28 [33]	M	C+
Is 61:1-4, 8-11	**Advent 3**	**S**	**B**
Is 61:1-4, 9-11	**Easter Vigil**	**S**	**ABC**
Is 61:1-7	Epiphany 3 [3]	Th	C
Is 61:10—62:3	**Christmas 1**	**S**	**B**
Is 62:1-5	Epiphany 8 [8]	W	B
Is 62:1-5	Proper 3 [8]	W	B
Is 62:1-5	**Epiphany 2 [2]**	**S**	**C**
Is 62:6-12	**Christmas Day 2**	**S**	**ABC**
Is 63:7-9	**Christmas 1**	**S**	**A**
Is 63:15-19	Proper 15 [20]	F	A*
Is 64:1-9	**Advent 1**	**S**	**B**
Is 65:1-9	**Proper 7 [12]**	**S**	**C***
Is 65:17-25	Lent 2	T	A
Is 65:17-25	Easter 5	W	B
Is 65:17-25	**Easter**	**S**	**C**
Is 65:17-25	**Proper 28 [33]**	**S**	**C+**
Is 66:1-13	Proper 28 [33]	T	C+
Is 66:7-11	Advent 4	Sa	C
Is 66:7-13	Epiphany 8 [8]	W	A
Is 66:7-13	Proper 3 [8]	W	A
Is 66:10-14	**Proper 9 [14]**	**S**	**C***
Is 66:14-24	Proper 28 [33]	W	C+
Is 66:18-23	Proper 15 [20]	W	A*
Jer 1:1-3, 11-19	Proper 16 [21]	Sa	C+
Jer 1:4-10	Baptism/Lord [1]	T	A
Jer 1:4-10	Advent 2	F	B
Jer 1:4-10	Proper 20 [25]	W	B*
Jer 1:4-10	**Epiphany 4 [4]**	**S**	**C**

Reference	Day/Proper		
Jer 1:4-10	**Proper 16 [21]**	**S**	**C+**
Jer 1:11-19	Epiphany 4 [4]	W	C
Jer 2:1-3, 14-22	Proper 17 [22]	Sa	C+
Jer 2:4-13	Lent 3	W	A
Jer 2:4-13	**Proper 17 [22]**	**S**	**C+**
Jer 2:14-22	Proper 22 [27]	Th	A*
Jer 2:23-37	Proper 22 [27]	F	A*
Jer 2:23-37	Proper 17 [22]	M	C+
Jer 3:1-5	Epiphany 2 [2]	Th	C
Jer 3:1-14	Proper 17 [22]	T	C+
Jer 3:6-14	Proper 22 [27]	W	B*
Jer 3:15-18	Proper 8 [13]	T	C*
Jer 3:15-25	Proper 17 [22]	W	C+
Jer 3:19-25	Epiphany 2 [2]	F	C
Jer 4:1-4	Epiphany 2 [2]	Sa	C
Jer 4:1-10	Proper 19 [24]	F	C+
Jer 4:11-12, 22-28	**Proper 19 [24]**	**S**	**C+**
Jer 4:13-21, 29-31	Proper 19 [24]	Sa	C+
Jer 5:1-17	Proper 19 [24]	M	C+
Jer 5:18-31	Proper 26 [31]	M	A*
Jer 5:18-31	Proper 19 [24]	T	C+
Jer 6:1-10	Proper 22 [27]	Sa	A*
Jer 6:1-19	Proper 16 [21]	Th	C+
Jer 6:10-19	Proper 9 [14]	M	C*
Jer 6:20-30	Proper 16 [21]	F	C+
Jer 7:1-15	Proper 9 [14]	Th	B*
Jer 7:1-15	Proper 16 [21]	M	C+
Jer 7:16-26	Proper 9 [14]	F	B*
Jer 7:16-26	Proper 16 [21]	T	C+
Jer 7:27-34	Proper 9 [14]	Sa	B*
Jer 7:27-34	Proper 16 [21]	W	C+
Jer 8:1-13	Proper 20 [25]	F	C+
Jer 8:4-13	Proper 9 [14]	T	C*
Jer 8:14-17; 9:2-11	Proper 20 [25]	Sa	C+
Jer 8:14-22	Proper 5 [10]	W	C*
Jer 8:18—9:1	**Proper 20 [25]**	**S**	**C+**
Jer 9:1-16	Proper 25 [30]	Th	C*
Jer 9:12-26	Proper 20 [25]	M	C+
Jer 9:17-26	Proper 25 [30]	F	C*
Jer 10:1-16	Proper 11 [16]	Th	B*
Jer 10:1-16	Proper 20 [25]	T	C+
Jer 10:17-25	Proper 11 [16]	F	B*
Jer 10:17-25	Proper 20 [25]	W	C+
Jer 11:1-17	Lent 3	M	C
Jer 11:1-17	Proper 17 [22]	Th	C+
Jer 11:18-20	**Proper 20 [25]**	**S**	**B***
Jer 12:1-13	Proper 11 [16]	Sa	B*
Jer 12:1-13	Proper 17 [22]	F	C+
Jer 12:14—13:11	Proper 20 [25]	Th	C+
Jer 13:1-11	Proper 9 [14]	W	A*
Jer 13:12-19	Epiphany 6 [6]	Th	C
Jer 13:20-27	Epiphany 6 [6]	F	C
Jer 13:20-27	Proper 19 [24]	Th	C+
Jer 14:1-6	Proper 25 [30]	Sa	C*
Jer 14:1-10, 17-22	Proper 19 [24]	W	C+
Jer 14:7-10, 19-22	**Proper 25 [30]**	**S**	**C***
Jer 14:13-18	Proper 17 [22]	Th	A*
Jer 15:1-9	Proper 17 [22]	F	A*
Jer 15:10-14	Proper 17 [22]	Sa	A*
Jer 15:10-21	Proper 18 [23]	Th	C+
Jer 15:15-21	**Proper 17 [22]**	**S**	**A***
Jer 16:1-13	Proper 9 [14]	T	B*
Jer 16:14-21	Proper 9 [14]	W	B*
Jer 16:14—17:4	Proper 18 [23]	F	C+
Jer 17:1-4	Epiphany 6 [6]	Sa	C
Jer 17:5-10	**Epiphany 6 [6]**	**S**	**C**
Jer 17:5-18	Proper 17 [22]	W	A*
Jer 17:14-27	Proper 18 [23]	Sa	C+
Jer 18:1-11	**Proper 18 [23]**	**S**	**C+**
Jer 18:1-11	Proper 8 [13]	W	A*
Jer 18:12-17	Proper 7 [12]	Th	A*
Jer 18:12-23	Proper 18 [23]	M	C+
Jer 18:18-23	Proper 7 [12]	F	A*
Jer 19:1-15	Epiphany 3 [3]	Th	B
Jer 19:1-15	Proper 18 [23]	T	C+
Jer 20:1-6	Proper 7 [12]	Sa	A*
Jer 20:1-18	Proper 18 [23]	W	C+
Jer 20:7-13	**Proper 7 [12]**	**S**	**A***
Jer 20:7-13	Epiphany 3 [3]	F	B
Jer 20:14-18	Epiphany 3 [3]	Sa	B
Jer 21:1-14	Reign of Christ [34]	Th	C+
Jer 21:11-14	Proper 6 [11]	T	B*
Jer 22:1-9	Proper 6 [11]	W	B*
Jer 22:1-17	Reign of Christ [34]	F	C+
Jer 22:11-17	Epiphany 6 [6]	W	C
Jer 22:18-30	Reign of Christ [34]	Sa	C+*
Jer 23:1-6	**Proper 11 [16]**	**S**	**B***
Jer 23:1-6	**Reign of Christ [34]**	**S**	**C+***
Jer 23:1-8	Easter 4	W	A
Jer 23:9-15	Proper 25 [30]	Th	B*
Jer 23:9-22	Proper 21 [26]	Th	C+
Jer 23:16-22	Proper 8 [13]	W	C*
Jer 23:23-29	**Proper 15 [20]**	**S**	**C***
Jer 23:23-32	Proper 21 [26]	F	C+
Jer 23:30-40	Proper 15 [20]	M	C*
Jer 24:1-10	Epiphany 8 [8]	M	C
Jer 24:1-10	Proper 3 [8]	M	C
Jer 24:1-10	Proper 21 [26]	Sa	C+
Jer 25:1-7	Proper 8 [13]	Th	A*

Jer 25:1-14	Proper 23 [28]	Th	C+		Jer 33:14-16	**Advent 1**	**S**	**C**
Jer 25:8-14	Proper 8 [13]	F	A*		Jer 33:14-26	Proper 14 [19]	W	C*
Jer 25:15-29	Proper 15 [20]	T	C*		Jer 33:14-26	Proper 26 [31]	Th	C+
Jer 25:15-32	Proper 23 [28]	W	C+		Jer 36:1-10	Epiphany 3 [3]	M	C
Jer 25:30-38	Proper 15 [20]	W	C*		Jer 36:11-26	Epiphany 3 [3]	T	C
Jer 26:1-9, 12-15		Dec 26	B		Jer 36:27-32	Epiphany 3 [3]	W	C
Jer 26:1-12	Proper 7 [12]	T	A*		Jer 38:1-13	Proper 7 [12]	W	A*
Jer 26:1-15	Proper 24 [29]	Th	C+		Jer 38:14-28	Proper 24 [29]	M	C+
Jer 26:12-24	Proper 25 [30]	F	B*		Jer 39:1-18	Proper 24 [29]	T	C+
Jer 26:16-24	Proper 24 [29]	F	C+		Jer 42:18-22	Proper 7 [12]	W	A+
Jer 26:20-24	Easter 5	Sa	A		Jer 46:18-28	Reign of Christ [34]	M	C*
Jer 27:1-11, 16-22	Proper 9 [14]	M	A*		Jer 49:7-11	Proper 10 [15]	T	A+
Jer 27:1-22	Proper 23 [28]	F	C+		Jer 50:1-7	Proper 11 [16]	M	B*
Jer 28:1-4	Proper 8 [13]	Sa	A*		Jer 50:1-7, 17-20	Proper 24 [29]	W	C+
Jer 28:1-17	Proper 23 [28]	Sa	C+		Jer 50:17-20	Easter 4	W	C
Jer 28:5-9	**Proper 8 [13]**	**S**	**A***		Jer 51:47-58	Proper 9 [14]	F	C*
Jer 28:10-17	Proper 9 [14]	T	A*		Jer 52:1-11	Proper 22 [27]	Th	C+
Jer 29:1, 4-7	**Proper 23 [28]**	**S**	**C+**		Jer 52:12-30	Proper 22 [27]	F	C+
Jer 29:1-14	Epiphany 4 [4]	W	B					
Jer 29:8-23	Proper 23 [28]	M	C+		**Lam 1:1-6**	**Proper 22 [27]**	**S**	**C+**
Jer 29:10-19	Epiphany 8 [8]	T	C		Lam 1:7-11	Proper 5 [10]	Th	A*
Jer 29:10-19	Proper 3 [8]	T	C		Lam 1:7-15	Proper 22 [27]	Sa	C+
Jer 29:24-32	Proper 25 [30]	Sa	B*		Lam 1:16-22	Proper 8 [13]	Th	B*
Jer 29:24-32	Proper 23 [28]	T	C+		Lam 1:16-22	Proper 22 [27]	M	C+
Jer 30:1-11a	Easter 3	M	B		Lam 2:1-12	Proper 8 [13]	F	B*
Jer 30:1-17	Reign of Christ [34]	M	C+		Lam 2:13-17	Proper 26 [31]	T	A*
Jer 30:12-22	Lent 2	W	B		Lam 2:13-22	Proper 22 [27]	T	C+
Jer 30:18-24	Reign of Christ [34]	T	C+		Lam 2:18-22	Proper 8 [13]	Sa	B*
Jer 31:1-6	**Easter**	**S**	**A**		**Lam 3:1-9, 19-24**	**Holy Saturday**	**S**	**ABC**
Jer 31:1-6	Proper 14 [19]	W	B*		Lam 3:19-26	Proper 22 [27]	ThFSa	C+
Jer 31:1-6	Reign of Christ [34]	W	C+		**Lam 3:19-26**	**Proper 22 [27]**	**S**	**C+**
Jer 31:7-9	**Proper 25 [30]**	**S**	**B***		**Lam 3:22-33**	**Proper 8 [13]**	**S**	**B***
Jer 31:7-14	**Christmas 2**	**S**	**ABC**		Lam 3:40-58	Proper 5 [10]	F	A*
Jer 31:7-14		Jan 5	C		Lam 3:55-66	Passion/Palm Sun	Sa	A
Jer 31:10-14	Reign of Christ [34]	W	A+		Lam 5:1-22	Epiphany 7 [7]	W	B
Jer 31:15-17		Dec 28	B		Lam 5:1-22	Proper 22 [27]	W	C+
Jer 31:15-22		Dec 29	A					
Jer 31:15-26	Proper 24 [29]	Sa	C+		Ez 1:1-3; 2:8—3:3	Lent 5	Th	A
Jer 31:27-34	**Proper 24 [29]**	**S**	**C+**		Ez 1:1-25	Easter 3	M	C
Jer 31:31-34	**Lent 5**	**S**	**B**		Ez 1:1—2:1	Epiphany Last Trfg	T	C
Jer 31:31-34	Advent 4	Th	C		Ez 1:26—2:1	Easter 3	T	C
Jer 31:31-34	Proper 27 [32]	W	A+		**Ez 2:1-5**	**Proper 9 [14]**	**S**	**B***
Jer 32:1-3a, 6-15	**Proper 21 [26]**	**S**	**C+**		Ez 2:8—3:11	Proper 9 [14]	M	B*
Jer 32:1-9, 36-41	Lent 5	W	A		Ez 2:8—3:11	Easter 5	Th	C
Jer 32:16-35	Proper 21 [26]	M	C+		Ez 3:12-21	Easter 7	W	C
Jer 32:36-44	Proper 21 [26]	T	C+		Ez 6:1-14	Proper 28 [33]	Th	A*
Jer 33:1-9	Passion/Palm Sun	F	B		Ez 7:10-27	Proper 28 [33]	Sa	A*
Jer 33:1-11	Proper 25 [30]	W	B*		Ez 7:1-9	Proper 28 [33]	F	A*
Jer 33:1-13	Proper 21 [26]	W	C+		Ez 8:1-18	Proper 4 [9]	M	C+
Jer 33:10-16	Passion/Palm Sun	Sa	B		Ez 10:1-19	Proper 28 [33]	Sa	C*

APPENDIXES

Ez 11:1-25	Easter 4	Th	C
Ez 11:14-25	Pentecost	T	C
Ez 11:14-25	Proper 28 [33]	M	C*
Ez 12:17-28	Proper 21 [26]	Th	A*
Ez 13:1-16	Proper 26 [31]	F	A*
Ez 14:1-11	Proper 4 [9]	T	C+
Ez 14:12-23	Proper 25 [30]	W	B+
Ez 14:12-23	Proper 4 [9]	W	C+
Ez 16:1-14	Epiphany 8 [8]	Th	B
Ez 16:1-14	Proper 3 [8]	Th	B
Ez 16:44-52	Epiphany 8 [8]	F	B
Ez 16:44-52	Proper 3 [8]	F	B
Ez 16:53-63	Epiphany 8 [8]	Sa	B
Ez 16:53-63	Proper 3 [8]	Sa	B
Ez 17:1-10	Lent 3	T	C
Ez 17:22-24	**Proper 6 [11]**	**S**	**B***
Ez 18:1-4, 25-32	**Proper 21 [26]**	**S**	**A***
Ez 18:1-32	Proper 25 [30]	T	B+
Ez 18:5-18	Proper 21 [26]	F	A*
Ez 18:19-24	Proper 21 [26]	Sa	A*
Ez 19:10-14	Proper 22 [27]	M	A*
Ez 20:1-17	Proper 16 [21]	M	C*
Ez 20:18-32	Proper 16 [21]	T	C*
Ez 20:33-44	Proper 16 [21]	W	C*
Ez 20:39-44	Easter 4	F	C
Ez 22:17-31	Proper 20 [25]	F	C*
Ez 24:1-14	Proper 18 [23]	Th	A*
Ez 24:15-27	Proper 18 [23]	F	A*
Ez 28:1-10	Reign of Christ [34]	Th	B*
Ez 28:11-19	Proper 16 [21]	Th	A*
Ez 28:20-26	Reign of Christ [34]	F	B*
Ez 28:25-26	Easter 4	Sa	C
Ez 29:1-12	Reign of Christ [34]	T	B*
Ez 29:3-7	Proper 7 [12]	Sa	A+
Ez 30:20-26	Reign of Christ [34]	W	B*
Ez 31:1-12	Proper 6 [11]	M	B*
Ez 31:15-18	Proper 16 [21]	F	A*
Ez 32:1-10	Proper 7 [12]	W	C*
Ez 33:1-6	Proper 18 [23]	Sa	A*
Ez 33:7-11	**Proper 18 [23]**	**S**	**A***
Ez 33:7-20	Reign of Christ [34]	W	A*
Ez 33:10-16	Lent 5	F	A
Ez 34:1-16	Easter 4	Sa	A
Ez 34:11-16, 20-24	**Reign of Christ [34]**	**S**	**A+***
Ez 34:17-23	Easter 4	M	A
Ez 34:23-31	Easter 4	T	A
Ez 34:25-31	Reign of Christ [34]	Sa	A+
Ez 36:8-15	Lent 5	Sa	A
Ez 36:22-32	Lent 2	W	A
Ez 36:24-28	Advent 2	Sa	B
Ez 36:24-28	**Easter Vigil**	**S**	**ABC**
Ez 36:33-38	Proper 16 [21]	Sa	A*
Ez 37:1-14	**Lent 5**	**S**	**A**
Ez 37:1-14	**Pentecost**	**S**	**B**
Ez 37:1-14	Pentecost	W	B
Ez 37:1-14	**Easter Vigil**	**S**	**ABC**
Ez 37:15-28	Easter 4	M	C
Ez 39:7-8, 21-29	Pentecost	T	A
Ez 39:21-29	Proper 11 [16]	F	A+
Ez 39:21—40:4	Proper 28 [33]	T	C*
Ez 43:1-12	Proper 28 [33]	W	C*
Ez 45:1-9	Easter 4	T	C
Ez 47:1-12	Advent 3	T	A
Dn 1:1-21	Easter 2	Th	B
Dn 1:1-21	Trinity Sunday	W	C
Dn 2:1-19		Jan 7	C
Dn 2:1-23	Easter 2	F	B
Dn 2:24-49	Easter 2	Sa	B
Dn 2:24-49		Jan 8	C
Dn 3:1-18	Proper 24 [29]	M	A*
Dn 3:1-30	Easter 2	M	B
Dn 3:19-30	Proper 24 [29]	T	A*
Dn 3:19-30	Lent 3	Th	C
Dn 4:4-18	Proper 28 [33]	Th	B*
Dn 4:19-27	Proper 28 [33]	F	B*
Dn 4:28-37	Proper 28 [33]	Sa	B*
Dn 5:1-12	Proper 25 [30]	T	C*
Dn 5:13-31	Proper 25 [30]	W	C*
Dn 6:1-28	Proper 24 [29]	W	A*
Dn 6:1-28	Easter 2	T	B
Dn 7:1-3, 15-18	**All Saints**	**S**	**C**
Dn 7:1-8, 15-18	Reign of Christ [34]	Sa	B*
Dn 7:9-10, 13-14	**Reign of Christ [34]**	**S**	**B***
Dn 7:13-14	Easter 5	F	C
Dn 7:19-27	Reign of Christ [34]	M	B*
Dn 7:27	Easter 5	Sa	C
Dn 8:1-14	Proper 28 [33]	M	B*
Dn 8:15-27	Proper 28 [33]	T	B*
Dn 9:1-14	Lent 1	Th	B
Dn 9:1-19	Easter 3	Th	B
Dn 9:15-19	Advent 1	Th	A
Dn 9:15-25a	Lent 1	F	B
Dn 10:2-19	Easter 3	F	B
Dn 12:1-3	**Proper 28 [33]**	**S**	**B***
Dn 12:1-4	Lent 3	F	C
Dn 12:1-13	Proper 11 [16]	W	A*
Dn 12:5-13	Lent 4	F	B

Hos 1:2-10	Proper 12 [17]	S	C+
Hos 1:11—2:15	Proper 12 [17]	Sa	C+
Hos 2:14-20	**Epiphany 8 [8]**	**S**	**B**
Hos 2:14-20	**Proper 3 [8]**	**S**	**B**
Hos 2:14—3:5	Proper 12 [17]	M	C+
Hos 3:1-5	Epiphany 8 [8]	M	B
Hos 3:1-5	Proper 3 [8]	M	B
Hos 3:1-5	Proper 17 [22]	Sa	B+
Hos 4:1-19	Proper 12 [17]	Th	C+
Hos 5:1-15	Proper 12 [17]	F	C+
Hos 5:15—6:6	**Proper 5 [10]**	**S**	**A***
Hos 5:15—6:6	Easter 3	T	B
Hos 6:1-6	Advent 2	Th	B
Hos 6:1-10	Proper 12 [17]	T	C+
Hos 6:11—7:16	Proper 12 [17]	W	C+
Hos 8:1-14	Proper 13 [18]	Th	C+
Hos 8:11-14; 10:1-2	Proper 5 [10]	T	A*
Hos 9:1-17	Proper 13 [18]	F	C+
Hos 10:1-15	Proper 13 [18]	Sa	C+
Hos 10:9-15	Proper 21 [26]	T	C*
Hos 11:1-11	**Proper 13 [18]**	**S**	**C+**
Hos 11:12—12:14	Proper 13 [18]	M	C+
Hos 12:2-14	Proper 21 [26]	W	C*
Hos 13:1-16	Proper 13 [18]	T	C+
Hos 14:1-9	Proper 5 [10]	W	A*
Hos 14:1-9	Epiphany 8 [8]	T	B
Hos 14:1-9	Proper 3 [8]	T	B
Hos 14:1-9	Proper 13 [18]	W	C+
Jl 1:1-14	Proper 27 [32]	T	A*
Jl 1:1-20	Proper 25 [30]	Th	C+
Jl 2:1-2, 12-17	**Ash Wednesday**	**S**	**ABC**
Jl 2:1-11	Proper 25 [30]	F	C+
Jl 2:12-22	Proper 25 [30]	Sa	C+
Jl 2:18-29	Pentecost	M	ABC
Jl 2:21-27	**Thanksgiving**	**S**	**B**
Jl 2:23-32	**Proper 25 [30]**	**S**	**C+**
Jl 3:1-8	Proper 25 [30]	M	C+
Jl 3:9-16	Proper 25 [30]	T	C+
Jl 3:9-21	Proper 27 [32]	W	A*
Jl 3:17-20	Proper 25 [30]	W	C+
Am 1:1—2:3	Proper 10 [15]	Th	C+
Am 1:1—2:5	Proper 27 [32]	Th	A*
Am 2:4-11	Proper 10 [15]	F	C+
Am 2:6-11	Epiphany 9 [9]	Sa	A
Am 2:6-11	Proper 4 [9]	Sa	A*
Am 2:6-16	Proper 10 [15]	Th	B*
Am 2:12—3:8	Proper 10 [15]	Sa	C+
Am 3:1-12	Proper 27 [32]	F	A*
Am 3:1-12	Proper 10 [15]	F	B*
Am 3:9—4:5	Proper 10 [15]	M	C+
Am 3:13—4:5	Proper 23 [28]	Sa	B*
Am 4:6-13	Proper 27 [32]	Sa	A*
Am 4:6-13	Proper 10 [15]	Sa	B*
Am 4:6-13	Proper 10 [15]	T	C+
Am 5:1-9	Proper 10 [15]	M	B*
Am 5:1-9	Proper 10 [15]	W	C+
Am 5:6-7, 10-15	**Proper 23 [28]**	**S**	**B***
Am 5:10-17	Proper 11 [16]	Th	C+
Am 5:12-24	Proper 26 [31]	W	C*
Am 5:18-24	**Proper 27 [32]**	**S**	**A***
Am 5:18-27	Proper 11 [16]	F	C+
Am 6:1a, 4-7	**Proper 21 [26]**	**S**	**C***
Am 6:1-8	Advent 3	Th	C
Am 6:1-14	Proper 11 [16]	Sa	C+
Am 6:8-14	Proper 21 [26]	M	C*
Am 7:1-6	Proper 11 [16]	M	C+
Am 7:1-6	Proper 19 [24]	M	C*
Am 7:7-15	**Proper 10 [15]**	**S**	**B***
Am 7:7-17	**Proper 10 [15]**	**S**	**C+**
Am 8:1-7	Easter 5	Th	B
Am 8:1-12	**Proper 11 [16]**	**S**	**C+**
Am 8:4-7	**Proper 20 [25]**	**S**	**C***
Am 8:4-12	Advent 3	F	C
Am 8:7-14	Proper 27 [32]	M	A*
Am 8:11-13	Easter 5	F	B
Am 8:13—9:4	Proper 11 [16]	T	C+
Am 9:1-4	Proper 10 [15]	T	B*
Am 9:5-15	Proper 23 [28]	T	A*
Am 9:5-15	Proper 11 [16]	W	C+
Am 9:7-15	Easter 5	Sa	B
Am 9:8-15	Advent 3	Sa	C
Am 9:11-15	Proper 10 [15]	W	B*
Ob 1-9	Proper 23 [28]	M	B*
Ob 10-16	Proper 23 [28]	T	B*
Ob 15-21	Proper 10 [15]	W	A+
Ob 17-21	Proper 23 [28]	W	B*
Jon 1:1-17	Easter 2	T	A
Jon 2:1-10	Easter 2	W	A
Jon 3:1-5, 10	**Epiphany 3 [3]**	**S**	**B**
Jon 3:1-10	Lent 1	Th	A
Jon 3:1-10	Proper 19 [24]	T	C*
Jon 3:10—4:11	**Proper 20 [25]**	**S**	**A***
Jon 4:1-11	Lent 1	F	A
Jon 4:1-11	Epiphany 9 [9]	M	C
Jon 4:1-11	Proper 4 [9]	M	C*

Mic 1:1-5	Proper 10 [15]	M	A+
Mic 2:1-13	Advent 1	Sa	B
Mic 3:1-4	Epiphany 4 [4]	Sa	A
Mic 3:5-12	**Proper 26 [31]**	**S**	**A***
Mic 4:1-5	Advent 1	M	B
Mic 4:1-5		Dec 22	C
Mic 4:1-7	Epiphany 7 [7]	T	B
Mic 4:6-8		Dec 23	C
Mic 4:6-13	Advent 1	T	B
Mic 4:8-13	Advent 3	W	C
Mic 5:1-5a	Advent 1	W	B
Mic 5:2-5a	**Advent 4**	**S**	**C**
Mic 5:2-9		Jan 9	A
Mic 6:1-8	**Epiphany 4 [4]**	**S**	**A**
Mic 6:1-8	Proper 26 [31]	W	B*
Mic 6:6-8		Dec 24	C
Mic 7:1-7	Proper 7 [12]	M	A*
Mic 7:8-20	Easter 4	W	B
Mic 7:18-20	Lent 2	F	A
Mic 7:18-20	Proper 8 [13]	Th	A+
Nah 1:1, 14—2:2	Proper 20 [25]	Th	A*
Nah 1:1-13	Proper 11 [16]	M	A*
Nah 2:3-13	Proper 20 [25]	F	A*
Hk 1:1-4; 2:1-4	**Proper 22 [27]**	**S**	**C***
Hk 1:1-4; 2:1-4	**Proper 26 [31]**	**S**	**C+**
Hk 1:5-17	Proper 22 [27]	M	C*
Hk 1:5-17	Proper 26 [31]	F	C+
Hk 2:1-5	Advent 3	Th	B
Hk 2:5-11	Proper 22 [27]	T	C*
Hk 2:5-11	Proper 26 [31]	Sa	C+
Hk 2:12-20	Proper 22 [27]	W	C*
Hk 2:12-20	Proper 26 [31]	M	C+
Hk 3:1-16	Proper 26 [31]	T	C+
Hk 3:2-6	Advent 3	F	B
Hk 3:2-13	Lent 5	Sa	B
Hk 3:2-15	Lent 5	W	C
Hk 3:13-19	Advent 3	Sa	B
Hk 3:17-19	Proper 26 [31]	W	C+
Zeph 1:7, 12-18	**Proper 28 [33]**	**S**	**A***
Zeph 2:13-15	Proper 20 [25]	Sa	A*
Zeph 3:1-13	Proper 11 [16]	T	A*
Zeph 3:8-13		Dec 22	B
Zeph 3:14-20		Dec 23	B
Zeph 3:14-20	**Easter Vigil**	**S**	**ABC**
Zeph 3:14-20	**Advent 3**	**S**	**C**
Hg 1:1-15a	Proper 27 [32]	Sa	C+

Hg 1:15b—2:9	**Proper 27 [32]**	**S**	**C+**
Hg 2:1-9, 20-23	Lent 5	W	B
Hg 2:10-19	Proper 27 [32]	M	C+
Hg 2:20-23	Proper 27 [32]	T	C+
Zech 1:1-6	Proper 9 [14]	Th	A*
Zech 1:1-17	Proper 27 [32]	Th	C+
Zech 1:7-17	Proper 28 [33]	M	A*
Zech 2:1-5; 5:1-4	Proper 28 [33]	T	A*
Zech 2:6-13	Proper 9 [14]	F	A*
Zech 3:1-10	Lent 1	T	C
Zech 4:1-7	Proper 9 [14]	Sa	A*
Zech 6:9-15	Proper 21 [26]	M	B*
Zech 6:9-15	Proper 27 [32]	F	C+
Zech 7:1-14	Proper 26 [31]	T	C*
Zech 8:1-17	Advent 3	W	A
Zech 8:1-17	Proper 27 [32]	W	C+
Zech 8:18-23	Proper 21 [26]	T	B*
Zech 9:9-12	**Proper 9 [14]**	**S**	**A***
Zech 9:14—10:2	Proper 11 [16]	T	B*
Zech 10:1-12	Proper 21 [26]	W	B*
Zech 11:1-17	Reign of Christ [34]	F	C*
Zech 11:4-17	Reign of Christ [34]	T	A+
Zech 12:1—13:1	Proper 28 [33]	W	B*
Zech 13:1-9	Advent 1	Th	B
Zech 14:1-9	Advent 1	F	B
Zech 14:10-21	Proper 9 [14]	Sa	C*
Mal 1:6—2:9	Proper 26 [31]	Sa	A*
Mal 2:10—3:1	Advent 2	W	B
Mal 3:1-4	**Advent 2**	**S**	**C**
Mal 3:1-4	**Presentation**	**S**	**ABC**
Mal 3:5-12	Advent 2	Th	C
Mal 3:5-12	Proper 6 [11]	W	C+
Mal 3:13-18	Advent 2	F	C
Mal 3:16—4:6	Advent 3	W	B
Mal 4:1-2a	**Proper 28 [33]**	**S**	**C***
Mal 4:1-6	Advent 2	Sa	C
Wis 1:13-15; 2:23-24	**Proper 8 [13]**	**S**	**B***
Wis 1:16—2:1, 12-22	**Proper 20 [25]**	**S**	**B***
Wis 3:1-9	**All Saints**	**S**	**B**
Wis 4:7-15		Dec 26	A
Wis 6:12-16	**Proper 27 [32]**	**S**	**A***
Wis 6:17-20	**Proper 27 [32]**	**S**	**A***
Wis 7:26—8:1	**Proper 19 [24]**	**S**	**B+**
Wis 10:15-21	**Christmas 2**	**S**	**ABC**
Wis 12:13, 16-19	**Proper 11 [16]**	**S**	**A***

Reference	Occasion		
Sir 10:12-18	**Proper 17 [22]**	S	C*
Sir 15:15-20	**Epiphany 6 [6]**	S	A
Sir 24:1-12	**Christmas 2**	S	ABC
Sir 27:4-7	**Epiphany 8 [8]**	S	C
Sir 27:4-7	**Proper 3 [8]**	S	C
Sir 35:12-17	**Proper 25 [30]**	S	C*
Bar 3:9-15, 32—4:4	**Easter Vigil**	S	ABC
Bar 5:1-9	**Advent 2**	S	C
Mt 1:1-17	Advent 4	W	A
Mt 1:18-25	**Advent 4**	S	A
Mt 2:1-12	**Epiphany**	S	ABC
Mt 2:13-18		Dec 28	B
Mt 2:13-23	**Christmas 1**	S	A
Mt 3:1-12	**Advent 2**	S	A
Mt 3:13-17	**Baptism/Lord [1]**	S	A
Mt 4:1-11	**Lent 1**	S	A
Mt 4:1-11	Lent 1	W	B
Mt 4:12-23	**Epiphany 3 [3]**	S	A
Mt 5:1-12	**Epiphany 4 [4]**	S	A
Mt 5:1-12	**All Saints**	S	A
Mt 5:1-12	Pentecost	Sa	A
Mt 5:13-20	**Epiphany 5 [5]**	S	A
Mt 5:13-20	Proper 21 [26]	Sa	B
Mt 5:21-37	**Epiphany 6 [6]**	S	A
Mt 5:27-36	Proper 22 [27]	W	B
Mt 5:38-48	**Epiphany 7 [7]**	S	A
Mt 5:43-48	Proper 12 [17]	W	C
Mt 6:1-6, 16-21	**Ash Wednesday**	S	ABC
Mt 6:7-15	Proper 19 [24]	Sa	A
Mt 6:19-24	Proper 14 [19]	Sa	C
Mt 6:24-34	**Epiphany 8 [8]**	S	A
Mt 6:24-34	**Proper 3 [8]**	S	A
Mt 6:25-33	**Thanksgiving**	S	B
Mt 7:1-6	Epiphany 9 [9]	Sa	A
Mt 7:1-6	Proper 4 [9]	Sa	A
Mt 7:7-11	Proper 13 [18]	Sa	A
Mt 7:1-12	Epiphany 7 [7]	Sa	A
Mt 7:7-11	Proper 14 [19]	Sa	B
Mt 7:13-20	Epiphany 9 [9]	W	A
Mt 7:13-20	Proper 4 [9]	W	A
Mt 7:15-20	Proper 11 [16]	Sa	A
Mt 7:21-29	**Epiphany 9 [9]**	S	A
Mt 7:21-29	**Proper 4 [9]**	S	A
Mt 8:1-13	Proper 15 [20]	W	A
Mt 8:14-17	Proper 17 [22]	Sa	A
Mt 8:14-17, 28-34	Advent 3	W	A
Mt 8:18-22	Proper 9 [14]	Sa	B
Mt 8:23-27	Proper 14 [19]	W	A
Mt 8:28—9:1	Epiphany 4 [4]	Sa	B
Mt 9:2-8	Proper 21 [26]	W	A
Mt 9:2-8	Proper 5 [10]	Sa	C
Mt 9:2-13	Lent 1	Sa	B
Mt 9:9-13, 18-26	**Proper 5 [10]**	S	A
Mt 9:14-17	Epiphany 2 [2]	W	A
Mt 9:27-34	Lent 4	W	A
Mt 9:27-34	Proper 5 [10]	Sa	A
Mt 9:27-34	Proper 7 [12]	Sa	C
Mt 9:35—10:8 [9-23]	**Proper 6 [11]**	S	A
Mt 10:5-15	Proper 23 [28]	W	C
Mt 10:5-23	Proper 7 [12]	W	A
Mt 10:16-25	Proper 8 [13]	W	C
Mt 10:24-39	**Proper 7 [12]**	S	A
Mt 10:34-42	Proper 18 [23]	Sa	C
Mt 10:40-42	**Proper 8 [13]**	S	A
Mt 11:2-11	**Advent 3**	S	A
Mt 11:16-19, 25-30	**Proper 9 [14]**	S	A
Mt 11:20-24	Proper 8 [13]	W	A
Mt 12:1-8	Proper 5 [10]	W	A
Mt 12:9-14	Epiphany 5 [5]	Sa	B
Mt 12:15-21	Baptism/Lord [1]	W	A
Mt 12:15-21	Proper 11 [16]	W	A
Mt 12:22-32	Proper 17 [22]	W	A
Mt 12:33-37	Advent 2	W	A
Mt 12:38-42	Easter 2	W	A
Mt 12:38-42	Proper 12 [17]	Sa	A
Mt 12:43-45	Proper 28 [33]	Sa	A
Mt 12:46-50	Reign of Christ [34]	Sa	A
Mt 12:46-50		Dec 29	B
Mt 13:1-9, 18-23	**Proper 10 [15]**	S	A
Mt 13:10-17	Proper 10 [15]	W	A
Mt 13:24-30, 36-43	**Proper 11 [16]**	S	A
Mt 13:31-33, 44-52	**Proper 12 [17]**	S	A
Mt 14:1-12	Proper 24 [29]	Sa	A
Mt 14:13-21	**Proper 13 [18]**	S	A
Mt 14:22-33	**Proper 14 [19]**	S	A
Mt 14:34-36	Proper 15 [20]	Sa	A
Mt 15:1-9	Epiphany 6 [6]	Sa	A
Mt 15:1-9	Proper 26 [31]	W	A
Mt 15:1-9	Proper 23 [28]	Sa	B
Mt 15:[10-20] 21-28	**Proper 15 [20]**	S	A
Mt 15:21-31	Proper 18 [23]	Sa	B

APPENDIXES

Reference	Occasion		
Mt 15:32-39	Proper 13 [18]	W	A
Mt 16:1-4	Proper 14 [19]	Sa	A
Mt 16:5-12	Proper 16 [21]	Sa	A
Mt 16:5-12	Proper 13 [18]	Sa	B
Mt 16:13-20	**Proper 16 [21]**	**S**	**A**
Mt 16:21-28	**Proper 17 [22]**	**S**	**A**
Mt 17:1-9	**Epiphany Last Trfg**	**S**	**A**
Mt 17:1-9	**Lent 2**	**S**	**A**
Mt 17:14-21	Proper 18 [23]	W	B
Mt 17:22-27	Proper 24 [29]	W	A
Mt 18:1-5	Proper 20 [25]	W	A
Mt 18:1-7	Lent 1	Sa	A
Mt 18:1-14		Dec 28	A
Mt 18:6-9	Proper 21 [26]	W	B
Mt 18:10-14	Lent 1	W	A
Mt 18:15-20	**Proper 18 [23]**	**S**	**A**
Mt 18:21-35	**Proper 19 [24]**	**S**	**A**
Mt 19:1-12	Epiphany 6 [6]	W	A
Mt 19:16-22	Proper 25 [30]	W	A
Mt 19:16-22	Proper 21 [26]	W	C
Mt 19:23-30	Proper 20 [25]	Sa	A
Mt 20:1-16	**Proper 20 [25]**	**S**	**A**
Mt 20:17-28	Easter 4	W	A
Mt 20:20-28	Proper 17 [22]	Sa	C
Mt 20:29-34	Proper 25 [30]	W	B
Mt 20:29-34	Proper 22 [27]	Sa	C
Mt 21:1-11	**Passion/Palm Sun**	**S**	**A**
Mt 21:18-22	Proper 18 [23]	W	A
Mt 21:23-32	**Proper 21 [26]**	**S**	**A**
Mt 21:23-32	Proper 19 [24]	Sa	B
Mt 21:28-32	Proper 25 [30]	W	C
Mt 21:28-32	Advent 3	Sa	B
Mt 21:33-46	**Proper 22 [27]**	**S**	**A**
Mt 22:1-14	**Proper 23 [28]**	**S**	**A**
Mt 22:15-22	**Proper 24 [29]**	**S**	**A**
Mt 22:23-33	Lent 5	W	A
Mt 22:34-46	**Proper 25 [30]**	**S**	**A**
Mt 23:1-12	**Proper 26 [31]**	**S**	**A**
Mt 23:13-28	Proper 26 [31]	Sa	A
Mt 23:29-36	Proper 18 [23]	Sa	A
Mt 23:29-39	Proper 20 [25]	Sa	B
Mt 23:37-39	Lent 2	Sa	C
Mt 23:37—24:14	Proper 28 [33]	W	C
Mt 24:1-14	Proper 27 [32]	Sa	A
Mt 24:1-22	Advent 1	Sa	A
Mt 24:15-27	Proper 15 [20]	Sa	C
Mt 24:15-31	Advent 1	Sa	B
Mt 24:23-35	Advent 1	W	A
Mt 24:29-35	Proper 27 [32]	W	A
Mt 24:36-44	**Advent 1**	**S**	**A**
Mt 24:45-51	Proper 28 [33]	W	A
Mt 25:1-13	**Proper 27 [32]**	**S**	**A**
Mt 25:1-13	Epiphany 2 [2]	Sa	B
Mt 25:14-30	**Proper 28 [33]**	**S**	**A**
Mt 25:31-46	**New Year's Day**	**S**	**ABC**
Mt 25:31-46	**Reign of Christ [34]**	**S**	**A**
Mt 25:31-46	Proper 10 [15]	W	C
Mt 26:6-13	Proper 16 [21]	W	A
Mt 26:6-13	Epiphany 6 [6]	Sa	B
Mt 26:14—27:66	**Passion/Palm Sun**	**S**	**A**
Mt 27:11-54	**Passion/Palm Sun**	**S**	**A**
Mt 27:57-66	**Holy Saturday**	**S**	**ABC**
Mt 28:1-10	**Easter Vigil**	**S**	**A**
Mt 28:1-10	**Easter**	**S**	**A**
Mt 28:1-10	Easter	W	A
Mt 28:16-20	**Trinity Sunday**	**S**	**A**
Mk 1:1-8	**Advent 2**	**S**	**B**
Mk 1:4-11	**Baptism/Lord [1]**	**S**	**B**
Mk 1:9-15	**Lent 1**	**S**	**B**
Mk 1:14-20	**Epiphany 3 [3]**	**S**	**B**
Mk 1:21-28	**Epiphany 4 [4]**	**S**	**B**
Mk 1:29-39	**Epiphany 5 [5]**	**S**	**B**
Mk 1:40-45	**Epiphany 6 [6]**	**S**	**B**
Mk 2:1-12	**Epiphany 7 [7]**	**S**	**B**
Mk 2:1-12	Proper 6 [11]	W	C
Mk 2:13-22	**Epiphany 8 [8]**	**S**	**B**
Mk 2:13-22	**Proper 3 [8]**	**S**	**B**
Mk 2:18-22	Proper 23 [28]	Sa	A
Mk 2:23—3:6	**Epiphany 9 [9]**	**S**	**B**
Mk 2:23—3:6	**Proper 4 [9]**	**S**	**B**
Mk 3:7-12	Epiphany 5 [5]	W	B
Mk 3:13-19a	Epiphany 3 [3]	W	B
Mk 3:20-35	**Proper 5 [10]**	**S**	**B**
Mk 4:1-20	Proper 6 [11]	Sa	B
Mk 4:21-25	Trinity Sunday	W	B
Mk 4:26-34	**Proper 6 [11]**	**S**	**B**
Mk 4:30-32	Easter 5	Sa	B
Mk 4:30-34	Proper 12 [17]	W	A
Mk 4:35-41	**Proper 7 [12]**	**S**	**B**
Mk 5:1-20	Epiphany 4 [4]	W	B
Mk 5:21-43	**Proper 8 [13]**	**S**	**B**
Mk 6:1-13	**Proper 9 [14]**	**S**	**B**
Mk 6:14-29	**Proper 10 [15]**	**S**	**B**
Mk 6:30-34	Easter 4	Sa	B
Mk 6:30-34, 53-56	**Proper 11 [16]**	**S**	**B**
Mk 6:35-44	Proper 12 [17]	W	B
Mk 6:45-52	Proper 7 [12]	W	B
Mk 7:1-8	Epiphany 5 [5]	Sa	A

Mk 7:1-8, 14-15, 21-23	**Proper 17 [22]**	**S**	**B**
Mk 7:1-13	Proper 6 [11]	Sa	A
Mk 7:9-23	Proper 17 [22]	W	B
Mk 7:24-30	Epiphany 9 [9]	W	C
Mk 7:24-30	Proper 4 [9]	W	C
Mk 7:24-37	**Proper 18 [23]**	**S**	**B**
Mk 8:1-10	Proper 13 [18]	W	B
Mk 8:14-21	Proper 15 [20]	W	B
Mk 8:22-26	Proper 25 [30]	Sa	B
Mk 8:27-30	Lent 2	Sa	B
Mk 8:27-38	**Proper 19 [24]**	**S**	**B**
Mk 8:31-38	**Lent 2**	**S**	**B**
Mk 9:2-8	Lent 3	Sa	B
Mk 9:2-9	**Epiphany Last Trfg**	**S**	**B**
Mk 9:2-9	**Lent 2**	**S**	**B**
Mk 9:9-13	Epiphany Last Trfg	Sa	A
Mk 9:9-13	Advent 3	W	B
Mk 9:14-29	Proper 8 [13]	W	B
Mk 9:30-37	**Proper 20 [25]**	**S**	**B**
Mk 9:38-50	**Proper 21 [26]**	**S**	**B**
Mk 10:2-16	**Proper 22 [27]**	**S**	**B**
Mk 10:17-22	Proper 13 [18]	Sa	C
Mk 10:17-31	**Proper 23 [28]**	**S**	**B**
Mk 10:32-34	6 Lent	Sa	A
Mk 10:32-34, 46-52	Passion/Palm Sun	Sa	B
Mk 10:35-45	**Proper 24 [29]**	**S**	**B**
Mk 10:42-45	Easter 6	Sa	B
Mk 10:46-52	**Proper 25 [30]**	**S**	**B**
Mk 10:46-52	Proper 24 [29]	Sa	C
Mk 11:1-11	Advent 4	W	B
Mk 11:1-11	**Passion/Palm Sun**	**S**	**B**
Mk 11:12-14, 20-24	Proper 27 [32]	Sa	B
Mk 11:12-14, 20-24	Proper 22 [27]	W	C
Mk 11:15-19	Lent 3	W	B
Mk 11:20-25	Proper 19 [24]	W	A
Mk 11:27-33	Proper 21 [26]	Sa	A
Mk 11:27-33	Advent 2	Sa	B
Mk 12:1-12	Proper 28 [33]	Sa	B
Mk 12:18-27	Easter 2	W	B
Mk 12:28-34	**Proper 26 [31]**	**S**	**B**
Mk 12:38-44	**Proper 27 [32]**	**S**	**B**
Mk 12:41-44	Proper 20 [25]	Sa	C
Mk 13:1-8	**Proper 28 [33]**	**S**	**B**
Mk 13:9-23	Proper 28 [33]	W	B
Mk 13:24-37	**Advent 1**	**S**	**B**
Mk 13:32-37		Dec 30	C
Mk 14:1—15:47	**Passion/Palm Sun**	**S**	**B**
Mk 14:26-31	Easter 4	W	B
Mk 15:1-39 [40-47]	**Passion/Palm Sun**	**S**	**B**
Mk 16:1-8	**Easter Vigil**	**S**	**B**
Mk 16:1-8	**Easter**	**S**	**B**
Mk 16:1-8	Easter	W	B
Mk 16:9-18	Easter 3	W	B
Mk 16:19-20	Easter 6	W	B
Lk 1:1-4	Reign of Christ [34]	W	C
Lk 1:5-17	Advent 2	W	B
Lk 1:5-17	Pentecost	Sa	C
Lk 1:5-25	Advent 4	W	C
Lk 1:26-38	**Annunciation**	**S**	**ABC**
Lk 1:26-38	**Advent 4**	**S**	**B**
Lk 1:26-38	Pentecost	W	C
Lk 1:39-45 [46-55]	**Advent 4**	**S**	**C**
Lk 1:39-57	**Visitation**	**S**	**ABC**
Lk 1:46-55	Proper 25 [30]	Sa	C
Lk 1:46b-55		Dec 22-24	A
Lk 1:46b-55		Dec 22-24	C
Lk 1:46b-55	Trinity Sunday	W	C
Lk 1:46b-55	**Advent 3**	**S**	**AB**
Lk 1:46b-55	**Advent 4**	**S**	**BC**
Lk 1:46b-55	Advent 4	MTW	B
Lk 1:57-66	Advent 3	Sa	C
Lk 1:57-80	Proper 10 [15]	Sa	B
Lk 1:67-69		Jan 9	C
Lk 1:67-79	Epiphany 3 [3]	W	A
Lk 1:67-80		Dec 24	A
Lk 1:68-79	Advent 2	ThFSa	C
Lk 1:68-79	**Advent 2**	**S**	**C**
Lk 1:68-79	Reign of Christ [34]	ThFSa	C+
Lk 1:68-79	**Reign of Christ [34]**	**S**	**C+**
Lk 2:1-14 [15-20]	**Christmas Day 1**	**S**	**ABC**
Lk 2:[1-7] 8-20	**Christmas Day 2**	**S**	**ABC**
Lk 2:15-21	**Holy Name**	**S**	**ABC**
Lk 2:22-40	**Presentation**	**S**	**ABC**
Lk 2:22-40	**Christmas 1**	**S**	**B**
Lk 2:25-38	Easter 6	W	C
Lk 2:39-52	Epiphany 3 [3]	Sa	C
Lk 2:41-52	Trinity Sunday	Sa	C
Lk 2:41-52	**Christmas 1**	**S**	**C**
Lk 3:1-6	**Advent 2**	**S**	**C**
Lk 3:1-18	Advent 3	Sa	A
Lk 3:7-18	**Advent 3**	**S**	**C**

Reference	Occasion		
Lk 3:15-17, 21-22	**Baptism/Lord [1]**	**S**	**C**
Lk 4:1-13	**Lent 1**	**S**	**C**
Lk 4:14-21	**Epiphany 3 [3]**	**S**	**C**
Lk 4:16-30	Proper 27 [32]	W	B
Lk 4:21-30	**Epiphany 4 [4]**	**S**	**C**
Lk 4:31-37	Proper 8 [13]	Sa	B
Lk 4:31-37	Epiphany 9 [9]	Sa	C
Lk 4:31-37	Proper 4 [9]	Sa	C
Lk 4:38-41	Epiphany 7 [7]	Sa	B
Lk 4:38-44	Epiphany 3 [3]	W	C
Lk 4:42-44	Epiphany 5 [5]	Sa	C
Lk 5:1-11	Epiphany 2 [2]	Sa	A
Lk 5:1-11	Baptism/Lord [1]	Sa	B
Lk 5:1-11	**Epiphany 5 [5]**	**S**	**C**
Lk 5:1-11	Easter 3	W	C
Lk 5:12-16	Proper 23 [28]	Sa	C
Lk 5:17-26	Proper 6 [11]	Sa	C
Lk 5:27-32	Epiphany 3 [3]	Sa	A
Lk 5:27-32	Epiphany 5 [5]	W	C
Lk 5:33-39	Epiphany 2 [2]	W	C
Lk 6:1-5	Proper 16 [21]	Sa	C
Lk 6:6-11	Proper 16 [21]	W	C
Lk 6:12-19	Proper 6 [11]	W	A
Lk 6:17-26	Epiphany 4 [4]	W	A
Lk 6:17-26	**Epiphany 6 [6]**	**S**	**C**
Lk 6:20-31	**All Saints**	**S**	**C**
Lk 6:27-31		Jan 5	B
Lk 6:27-38	**Epiphany 7 [7]**	**S**	**C**
Lk 6:39-49	**Epiphany 8 [8]**	**S**	**C**
Lk 6:39-49	**Proper 3 [8]**	**S**	**C**
Lk 6:43-45	Proper 6 [11]	W	B
Lk 6:43-45	Lent 3	Sa	C
Lk 7:1-10	Lent 2	Sa	A
Lk 7:1-10	**Epiphany 9 [9]**	**S**	**C**
Lk 7:1-10	**Proper 4 [9]**	**S**	**C**
Lk 7:11-17	**Proper 5 [10]**	**S**	**C**
Lk 7:18-30	Advent 2	W	C
Lk 7:31-35	Proper 10 [15]	W	B
Lk 7:31-35	Advent 3	W	C
Lk 7:36—8:3	**Proper 6 [11]**	**S**	**C**
Lk 8:4-10	Proper 11 [16]	Sa	C
Lk 8:4-15	Proper 5 [10]	Sa	B
Lk 8:16-21	Jan 3	C	
Lk 8:22-25	Proper 12 [17]	Sa	C
Lk 8:26-39	**Proper 7 [12]**	**S**	**C**
Lk 8:40-56	Proper 5 [10]	W	C
Lk 9:1-6	Advent 2	Sa	C
Lk 9:1-6	Proper 9 [14]	Sa	C
Lk 9:10-17	Lent 4	W	C
Lk 9:18-27	Easter 7	W	C
Lk 9:21-27	Proper 8 [13]	Sa	C
Lk 9:28-36	**Lent 2**	**S**	**C**
Lk 9:28-36 [37-43a]	**Epiphany Last Trfg**	**S**	**C**
Lk 9:37-43a	Proper 7 [12]	W	C
Lk 9:43b-48	Proper 21 [26]	Sa	C
Lk 9:51-62	**Proper 8 [13]**	**S**	**C**
Lk 10:1-11, 16-20	**Proper 9 [14]**	**S**	**C**
Lk 10:13-16	Epiphany 3 [3]	Sa	B
Lk 10:13-16	Proper 9 [14]	W	C
Lk 10:21-24	Proper 9 [14]	Sa	A
Lk 10:21-24	Epiphany Last Trfg	Sa	C
Lk 10:25-28	Easter 5	W	C
Lk 10:25-37	Proper 26 [31]	Sa	B
Lk 10:25-37	**Proper 10 [15]**	**S**	**C**
Lk 10:38-42	**Proper 11 [16]**	**S**	**C**
Lk 11:1-13	**Proper 12 [17]**	**S**	**C**
Lk 11:5-13	Proper 16 [21]	Sa	B
Lk 11:14-23	Epiphany 8 [8]	Sa	A
Lk 11:14-23	Proper 3 [8]	Sa	A
Lk 11:14-23	Epiphany 2 [2]	Sa	C
Lk 11:14-28	Proper 5 [10]	W	B
Lk 11:24-28	Epiphany 6 [6]	Sa	C
Lk 11:29-32	Advent 1	W	C
Lk 11:33-36	Baptism/Lord [1]	W	C
Lk 11:37-52	Epiphany 6 [6]	W	C
Lk 11:53—12:3	Proper 7 [12]	Sa	A
Lk 12:4-12	Easter 2	W	C
Lk 12:13-21	**Proper 13 [18]**	**S**	**C**
Lk 12:22-31	Epiphany 8 [8]	W	A
Lk 12:22-31	Proper 3 [8]	W	A
Lk 12:22-31	Proper 13 [18]	W	C
Lk 12:29-32	Easter 4	Sa	C
Lk 12:32-40	**Proper 14 [19]**	**S**	**C**
Lk 12:41-48	Proper 14 [19]	W	C
Lk 12:49-56	**Proper 15 [20]**	**S**	**C**
Lk 12:57-59	Epiphany 7 [7]	Sa	C
Lk 13:1-9	**Lent 3**	**S**	**C**
Lk 13:10-17	**Proper 16 [21]**	**S**	**C**
Lk 13:18-21	Lent 3	W	C
Lk 13:22-31	Lent 2	W	C
Lk 13:31-35		Jan 9	A
Lk 13:31-35	Advent 4	Sa	C
Lk 13:31-35	**Lent 2**	**S**	**C**
Lk 14:1, 7-14	**Proper 17 [22]**	**S**	**C**
Lk 14:12-14	Easter 3	Sa	A
Lk 14:12-14	Easter 3	Sa	C
Lk 14:15-24	Proper 17 [22]	W	C
Lk 14:25-33	**Proper 18 [23]**	**S**	**C**
Lk 14:34-35	Epiphany 8 [8]	W	C

Jn 6:35, 41-51	**Proper 14 [19]**	**S**	**B**
Jn 6:35-40	Proper 14 [19]	W	B
Jn 6:41-51	Proper 11 [16]	W	C
Jn 6:51-58	**Proper 15 [20]**	**S**	**B**
Jn 6:56-69	**Proper 16 [21]**	**S**	**B**
Jn 7:1-9	Proper 9 [14]	W	B
Jn 7:14-31, 37-39	Lent 3	W	A
Jn 7:19-24	Epiphany 9 [9]	Sa	B
Jn 7:19-24	Proper 4 [9]	Sa	B
Jn 7:25-36	Proper 19 [24]	W	B
Jn 7:37-39	**Pentecost**	**S**	**A**
Jn 7:37-39	Pentecost	W	A
Jn 7:37-39	Pentecost	Sa	B
Jn 7:40-52	Proper 22 [27]	Sa	A
Jn 7:40-52	Advent 4	Sa	B
Jn 7:53—8:11	Epiphany 8 [8]	Sa	B
Jn 7:53—8:11	Lent 2	W	A
Jn 7:53—8:11	Proper 3 [8]	Sa	B
Jn 8:12-19		Dec 31	ABC
Jn 8:12-20	Lent 4	W	B
Jn 8:12-30	Epiphany 5 [5]	W	A
Jn 8:21-30	Easter 7	Sa	A
Jn 8:21-38	Proper 20 [25]	W	B
Jn 8:31-38	Easter 5	W	A
Jn 8:39-47	Proper 26 [31]	Sa	C
Jn 8:39-59		Jan 9	B
Jn 8:48-59	Easter 5	Sa	A
Jn 9:1-41	**Lent 4**	**S**	**A**
Jn 10:1-10	**Easter 4**	**S**	**A**
Jn 10:11-18	**Easter 4**	**S**	**B**
Jn 10:11-21	Proper 19 [24]	Sa	C
Jn 10:22-30	**Easter 4**	**S**	**C**
Jn 10:31-42	Easter 4	W	C
Jn 11:1-45	**Lent 5**	**S**	**A**
Jn 11:32-44	**All Saints**	**S**	**B**
Jn 11:45-57	Proper 22 [27]	W	A
Jn 11:45-57	Lent 5	Sa	C
Jn 12:1-8	**Lent 5**	**S**	**C**
Jn 12:1-11	**Mon. of Holy Week**	**S**	**ABC**
Jn 12:1-11	Lent 5	Sa	B
Jn 12:12-16	**Passion/Palm Sun**	**S**	**B**
Jn 12:20-33	**Lent 5**	**S**	**B**
Jn 12:20-36	**Tues. of Holy Week**	**S**	**ABC**
Jn 12:27-36	Lent 1	Sa	C
Jn 12:34-50	Lent 5	W	B
Jn 12:36-43	Lent 2	W	B
Jn 12:44-50	Proper 10 [15]	Sa	A
Jn 12:44-50	Easter 2	Sa	B
Jn 13:1-17	Proper 9 [14]	W	A
Jn 13:1-17	Proper 24 [29]	W	B
Jn 13:1-17, 31b-35	**Holy Thursday**	**S**	**ABC**
Jn 13:21-32	**Wed. of Holy Week**	**S**	**ABC**
Jn 13:31-35	Epiphany 4 [4]	Sa	A
Jn 13:31-35	Proper 26 [31]	W	B
Jn 13:31-35	**Easter 5**	**S**	**C**
Jn 14:1-14	**Easter 5**	**S**	**A**
Jn 14:8-17 [25-27]	**Pentecost**	**S**	**C**
Jn 14:15-17	Trinity Sunday	Sa	A
Jn 14:15-21	**Easter 6**	**S**	**A**
Jn 14:18-31	Easter 5	W	B
Jn 14:23-29	**Easter 6**	**S**	**C**
Jn 14:25-26	Trinity Sunday	W	A
Jn 14:27-29	Easter 6	Sa	A
Jn 15:1-8	**Easter 5**	**S**	**B**
Jn 15:9-17	**Easter 6**	**S**	**B**
Jn 15:16-25	Proper 16 [21]	W	B
Jn 15:18-20, 26-27	Trinity Sunday	Sa	B
Jn 15:26-27; 16:4b-15	**Pentecost**	**S**	**B**
Jn 16:1-4a	Epiphany 8 [8]	Sa	C
Jn 16:1-4a	Proper 3 [8]	Sa	C
Jn 16:4-11	Easter 7	Sa	B
Jn 16:12-15	**Trinity Sunday**	**S**	**C**
Jn 16:16-24	Easter 6	W	A
Jn 16:16-24	Easter 7	W	B
Jn 16:25-33	Reign of Christ [34]	W	B
Jn 17:1-11	**Easter 7**	**S**	**A**
Jn 17:6-19	**Easter 7**	**S**	**B**
Jn 17:20-26	**Easter 7**	**S**	**C**
Jn 18:1—19:42	**Good Friday**	**S**	**ABC**
Jn 18:28-32	Proper 17 [22]	Sa	B
Jn 18:33-37	**Reign of Christ [34]**	**S**	**B**
Jn 19:38-42	**Holy Saturday**	**S**	**ABC**
Jn 20:1-18	**Easter**	**S**	**ABC**
Jn 20:11-20	Easter 2	Sa	A
Jn 20:19-23	**Pentecost**	**S**	**A**
Jn 20:19-23	Pentecost	W	B
Jn 20:19-31	**Easter 2**	**S**	**ABC**
Jn 21:1-14	Easter 3	W	A
Jn 21:1-19	**Easter 3**	**S**	**C**
Jn 21:19b-24		Dec 27	C
Acts 1:1-5	Epiphany 2 [2]	F	A
Acts 1:1-11	**Ascension**	**S**	**ABC**
Acts 1:6-14	**Easter 7**	**S**	**A**
Acts 1:12-17, 21-26	Advent 2	Th	A

Acts 1:15-17, 21-26	**Easter 7**	**S**	**B**
Acts 1:15-20	Proper 12 [17]	Th	C
Acts 2:1-11	Pentecost	Th	A
Acts 2:1-21	**Pentecost**	**S**	**ABC**
Acts 2:14a, 22-32	**Easter 2**	**S**	**A**
Acts 2:14a, 36-41	**Easter 3**	**S**	**A**
Acts 2:14-24	Lent 5	T	B
Acts 2:22-36	Proper 12 [17]	F	C
Acts 2:37-42	Advent 2	M	B
Acts 2:37-47	Proper 13 [18]	T	A
Acts 2:42-47	**Easter 4**	**S**	**A**
Acts 2:42-47	Easter 2	Th	B
Acts 3:1-10	Epiphany 6 [6]	M	B
Acts 3:1-10	Epiphany 9 [9]	T	C
Acts 3:1-10	Proper 4 [9]	T	C
Acts 3:1-10	Easter 3	Sa	B
Acts 3:11-16	Epiphany Last Trfg	Th	C
Acts 3:12-19	**Easter 3**	**S**	**B**
Acts 3:17-26	Easter 4	Th	B
Acts 3:17—4:4	Advent 3	T	B
Acts 4:1-4	Easter 4	F	B
Acts 4:1-12	Proper 20 [25]	M	C
Acts 4:5-12	**Easter 4**	**S**	**B**
Acts 4:13-31	Proper 21 [26]	Th	B
Acts 4:23-31	Easter 2	F	B
Acts 4:32-35	**Easter 2**	**S**	**B**
Acts 5:1-11	Epiphany 2 [2]	T	B
Acts 5:12-16	Advent 3	M	A
Acts 5:12-16	Easter 2	Th	C
Acts 5:17-26	Proper 7 [12]	F	A
Acts 5:17-26	Easter 2	F	C
Acts 5:27-32	**Easter 2**	**S**	**C**
Acts 5:33-42	Epiphany 3 [3]	T	B
Acts 6:1-7	Proper 15 [20]	M	B
Acts 6:1-7; 7:51-60		Dec 26	C
Acts 6:8-15	Easter 5	Th	A
Acts 6:8-15	Proper 15 [20]	Th	B
Acts 6:8-15; 7:51-60		Dec 26	B
Acts 7:1-8	Proper 14 [19]	F	C
Acts 7:1-16	Easter 5	F	A
Acts 7:9-16	Proper 19 [24]	F	A
Acts 7:9-16	Proper 15 [20]	T	B
Acts 7:9-16	Proper 10 [15]	F	C
Acts 7:17-29	Proper 26 [31]	T	B
Acts 7:17-40	Easter 5	M	A
Acts 7:30-34	Epiphany Last Trfg	M	A
Acts 7:30-34	Lent 1	Th	C
Acts 7:30-40	Lent 3	F	B
Acts 7:35-42	Lent 1	F	C
Acts 7:35-43	Proper 6 [11]	F	A
Acts 7:44-53	Proper 12 [17]	F	A
Acts 7:44-53		Jan 4	C
Acts 7:44-53	Proper 15 [20]	T	C
Acts 7:44-56	Easter 5	T	A
Acts 7:54—8:1a	Reign of Christ [34]	Th	B
Acts 7:55-60	**Easter 5**	**S**	**A**
Acts 7:59—8:8		Dec 26	A
Acts 8:1b-8	Easter 5	Th	B
Acts 8:4-13	Baptism/Lord [1]	T	A
Acts 8:9-25	Easter 5	F	B
Acts 8:14-17	**Baptism/Lord [1]**	**S**	**C**
Acts 8:18-24	Epiphany 2 [2]	Th	C
Acts 8:26-40	Epiphany 2 [2]	M	A
Acts 8:26-40	**Easter 5**	**S**	**B**
Acts 8:26-40	Epiphany 9 [9]	M	C
Acts 8:26-40	Proper 4 [9]	M	C
Acts 9:1-6 [7-20]	**Easter 3**	**S**	**C**
Acts 9:1-9	Baptism/Lord [1]	Th	A
Acts 9:1-20	Lent 4	M	A
Acts 9:10-19a	Baptism/Lord [1]	Th	B
Acts 9:10-19a	Baptism/Lord [1]	F	A
Acts 9:19b-25	Epiphany 5 [5]	Th	C
Acts 9:19b-31	Baptism/Lord [1]	Sa	A
Acts 9:19b-31	Easter 3	M	C
Acts 9:26-31	Epiphany 5 [5]	F	C
Acts 9:32-35	Proper 25 [30]	T	B
Acts 9:32-35	Easter 4	T	C
Acts 9:36-43	**Easter 4**	**S**	**C**
Acts 10:1-8	Epiphany Last Trfg	F	C
Acts 10:1-34	Easter 6	Th	B
Acts 10:9-23a	Epiphany Last Trfg	M	C
Acts 10:23b-33	Epiphany Last Trfg	T	C
Acts 10:34-43	**Baptism/Lord [1]**	**S**	**A**
Acts 10:34-43	**Easter**	**S**	**ABC**
Acts 10:34-43	Easter 6	F	B
Acts 10:44-48	Baptism/Lord [1]	M	A
Acts 10:44-48	**Easter 6**	**S**	**B**
Acts 10:44-48	Epiphany 4 [4]	Th	C
Acts 11:1-18	Advent 2	T	B
Acts 11:1-18	**Easter 5**	**S**	**C**
Acts 11:19-26	Advent 2	F	B
Acts 11:19-26	Easter 5	M	C
Acts 11:27-30	Easter 5	T	C
Acts 12:20-25	Proper 21 [26]	F	B
Acts 13:1-12	Proper 26 [31]	T	A
Acts 13:16-25	Advent 2	F	A
Acts 13:16-25	Epiphany 2 [2]	F	B

Reading	Day		
Acts 13:26-34	Epiphany 6 [6]	Th	C
Acts 13:32-41	Proper 21 [26]	F	A
Acts 14:1-7	Epiphany 5 [5]	M	B
Acts 14:8-18	Epiphany 7 [7]	M	B
Acts 14:19-28	Proper 15 [20]	F	A
Acts 15:1-5, 22-35	Epiphany 9 [9]	T	B
Acts 15:1-5, 22-35	Proper 4 [9]	T	B
Acts 15:1-21	Proper 15 [20]	M	A
Acts 15:36-41	Epiphany 5 [5]	T	B
Acts 15:36-41	Easter 6	Th	C
Acts 16:1-8	Easter 6	F	C
Acts 16:9-15	**Easter 6**	**S**	**C**
Acts 16:16-34	**Easter 7**	**S**	**C**
Acts 16:35-40	Easter 7	M	C
Acts 17:1-9	Proper 16 [21]	F	C
Acts 17:10-15	Proper 14 [19]	Th	A
Acts 17:16-31	Proper 11 [16]	F	B
Acts 17:22-31	**Easter 6**	**S**	**A**
Acts 17:22-34	Proper 24 [29]	Th	C
Acts 18:24-28	Proper 14 [19]	F	A
Acts 19:1-7	**Baptism/Lord [1]**	**S**	**B**
Acts 19:1-10	Epiphany 4 [4]	F	C
Acts 19:11-20	Epiphany 6 [6]	F	B
Acts 19:21-27	Proper 9 [14]	M	C
Acts 19:28-41	Proper 9 [14]	T	C
Acts 20:1-16	Proper 7 [12]	Th	B
Acts 20:7-12	Lent 5	M	A
Acts 20:17-38	Proper 11 [16]	T	B
Acts 21:1-16	Proper 7 [12]	F	B
Acts 21:17-26	Epiphany 4 [4]	M	B
Acts 21:27-39	Proper 10 [15]	M	B
Acts 22:2-16	Baptism/Lord [1]	T	B
Acts 22:6-21	Proper 5 [10]	Th	C
Acts 22:22—23:11	Proper 27 [32]	Th	C
Acts 23:12-35	Proper 10 [15]	T	B
Acts 24:10-23	Proper 27 [32]	F	C
Acts 25:1-12	Epiphany 9 [9]	Th	B
Acts 25:1-12	Proper 4 [9]	Th	B
Acts 26:1-11	Proper 5 [10]	F	C
Acts 26:1-18	Easter 3	T	C
Acts 26:19-29	Easter 7	T	C
Acts 26:24-29	Proper 23 [28]	M	C
Acts 27:1-12	Easter 6	Th	A
Acts 27:13-38	Easter 6	F	A
Acts 27:13-38	Proper 7 [12]	M	B
Acts 27:39-44	Easter 6	M	A
Acts 27:39-44	Proper 7 [12]	T	B
Acts 28:1-10	Proper 5 [10]	F	A
Acts 28:23-31	Advent 3	T	C
Rom 1:1-7	**Advent 4**	**S**	**A**
Rom 1:1-7	Lent 1	Th	A
Rom 1:8-15	Proper 13 [18]	M	A
Rom 1:8-17	Lent 1	F	A
Rom 1:16-17; 3:22b-28 [29-31]	**Epiphany 9 [9]**	**S**	**A**
Rom 1:16-17; 3:22b-28 [29-31]	**Proper 4 [9]**	**S**	**A**
Rom 1:18-25	Proper 9 [14]	M	A
Rom 1:18-25	Proper 28 [33]	Th	C
Rom 2:1-11	Epiphany 9 [9]	M	A
Rom 2:1-11	Proper 4 [9]	M	A
Rom 2:1-11	Proper 16 [21]	M	A
Rom 2:1-11	Proper 28 [33]	M	A
Rom 2:1-11	Proper 18 [23]	Th	B
Rom 2:1-11	Lent 3	M	C
Rom 2:12-16	Proper 10 [15]	Th	A
Rom 2:12-16	Proper 18 [23]	F	B
Rom 2:12-16	Lent 3	T	C
Rom 2:17-29	Epiphany 9 [9]	Th	A
Rom 2:17-29	Proper 4 [9]	Th	A
Rom 2:17-29	Proper 26 [31]	Th	A
Rom 2:17-29	Proper 7 [12]	Th	C
Rom 3:1-8	Epiphany 8 [8]	Th	B
Rom 3:1-8	Proper 3 [8]	Th	B
Rom 3:1-8	Proper 20 [25]	Th	C
Rom 3:1-8	Proper 9 [14]	T	A
Rom 3:9-20	Proper 19 [24]	M	B
Rom 3:9-22a	Epiphany 9 [9]	T	A
Rom 3:9-22a	Proper 4 [9]	T	A
Rom 3:21-31	Lent 2	F	A
Rom 3:21-31	Lent 2	Th	B
Rom 3:21-31	Proper 26 [31]	F	B
Rom 4:1-5, 13-17	**Lent 2**	**S**	**A**
Rom 4:1-12	Baptism/Lord [1]	M	B
Rom 4:1-12	Lent 2	F	B
Rom 4:1-12	Lent 2	M	C
Rom 4:6-13	Lent 2	T	A
Rom 4:13-25	**Proper 5 [10]**	**S**	**A**
Rom 4:13-25	**Lent 2**	**S**	**B**
Rom 5:1-5	**Trinity Sunday**	**S**	**C**
Rom 5:1-8	**Proper 6 [11]**	**S**	**A**
Rom 5:1-11	**Lent 3**	**S**	**A**
Rom 5:6-11	Proper 27 [32]	Th	B
Rom 5:12-19	**Lent 1**	**S**	**A**
Rom 5:12—6:2	Epiphany 8 [8]	Th	C
Rom 5:12—6:2	Proper 3 [8]	Th	C
Rom 6:1-11	Advent 1	M	A

Rom 6:1b-11	**Proper 7 [12]**	S	A
Rom 6:3-11	**Easter Vigil**	S	ABC
Rom 6:12-23	**Proper 8 [13]**	S	A
Rom 7:1-6	Proper 9 [14]	Th	A
Rom 7:1-6	Epiphany 3 [3]	Th	C
Rom 7:7-20	Proper 9 [14]	F	A
Rom 7:14-25	Proper 9 [14]	Th	C
Rom 7:15-25a	**Proper 9 [14]**	S	A
Rom 8:1-8	Trinity Sunday	Th	B
Rom 8:1-11	Proper 22 [27]	F	B
Rom 8:1-11	**Proper 10 [15]**	S	A
Rom 8:1-11	Epiphany 7 [7]	Th	C
Rom 8:6-11	**Lent 5**	S	A
Rom 8:9-11	Trinity Sunday	F	B
Rom 8:12-17	**Trinity Sunday**	S	B
Rom 8:12-25	**Proper 11 [16]**	S	A
Rom 8:14-17	Pentecost	F	A
Rom 8:14-17	**Pentecost**	S	C
Rom 8:18-24	Pentecost	M	A
Rom 8:18-30	Advent 4	T	C
Rom 8:22-25	Advent 2	M	C
Rom 8:22-27	**Pentecost**	S	B
Rom 8:26-27	Pentecost	T	A
Rom 8:26-39	**Proper 12 [17]**	S	A
Rom 8:31-39	Epiphany 9 [9]	F	B
Rom 8:31-39	Proper 4 [9]	F	B
Rom 8:31-39	Proper 20 [25]	F	C
Rom 9:1-5	**Proper 13 [18]**	S	A
Rom 9:1-9	Proper 14 [19]	Th	C
Rom 9:6-13	Epiphany 9 [9]	F	A
Rom 9:6-13	Proper 4 [9]	F	A
Rom 9:6-13	Proper 13 [18]	F	A
Rom 9:6-18	Epiphany 4 [4]	Th	B
Rom 9:14-29	Proper 14 [19]	T	A
Rom 9:19-29	Epiphany 9 [9]	M	B
Rom 9:19-29	Proper 4 [9]	M	B
Rom 9:30—10:4	Proper 12 [17]	T	C
Rom 10:5-13		Dec 22	B
Rom 10:5-15	**Proper 14 [19]**	S	A
Rom 10:8b-13	**Lent 1**	S	C
Rom 10:15b-21	Proper 18 [23]	F	A
Rom 11:1-2a, 29-32	**Proper 15 [20]**	S	A
Rom 11:1-6	Epiphany Last Trfg	T	A
Rom 11:1-10	Proper 6 [11]	F	C
Rom 11:2-10	Epiphany 5 [5]	M	A
Rom 11:13-29	Proper 15 [20]	T	A
Rom 11:25-32	Proper 20 [25]	F	B
Rom 11:33-36	Proper 16 [21]	T	A
Rom 11:33-36	Proper 13 [18]	Th	C
Rom 12:1-8	**Proper 16 [21]**	S	A
Rom 12:1-8	Epiphany 3 [3]	F	C
Rom 12:9-16b	**Visitation**	S	ABC
Rom 12:9-21	Epiphany 7 [7]	M	A
Rom 12:9-21	**Proper 17 [22]**	S	A
Rom 12:9-21	Epiphany 2 [2]	M	C
Rom 12:17-21; 13:8-10	Proper 26 [31]	M	B
Rom 13:1-7	Proper 18 [23]	T	A
Rom 13:8-14	**Proper 18 [23]**	S	A
Rom 13:11-14	**Advent 1**	S	A
Rom 13:11-14		Dec 23	B
Rom 13:11-14	Proper 16 [21]	F	B
Rom 14:1-12	**Proper 19 [24]**	S	A
Rom 14:13—15:2	Proper 19 [24]	T	A
Rom 15:1-6	Proper 14 [19]	Th	B
Rom 15:4-13	**Advent 2**	S	A
Rom 15:7-13	Proper 24 [29]	Th	B
Rom 15:14-21	Advent 2	T	A
Rom 15:14-21	Proper 10 [15]	F	A
Rom 15:22-33	Proper 12 [17]	T	B
Rom 16:1-16	Proper 20 [25]	M	A
Rom 16:17-20	Proper 15 [20]	F	B
Rom 16:17-20	Proper 20 [25]	T	A
Rom 16:25-27	**Advent 4**	S	B
1 Cor 1:1-9	**Epiphany 2 [2]**	S	A
1 Cor 1:3-9	**Advent 1**	S	B
1 Cor 1:3-17	Epiphany 2 [2]	T	C
1 Cor 1:10-18	**Epiphany 3 [3]**	S	A
1 Cor 1:18-24	**Holy Cross**	S	ABC
1 Cor 1:18-25	**Lent 3**	S	B
1 Cor 1:18-31	**Epiphany 4 [4]**	S	A
1 Cor 1:18-31	**Tues. of Holy Week**	S	ABC
1 Cor 1:18-31	Baptism/Lord [1]	Th	C
1 Cor 1:18-31	Proper 7 [12]	M	C
1 Cor 2:1-5	Proper 20 [25]	Th	B
1 Cor 2:1-10	Trinity Sunday	T	B
1 Cor 2:1-10	Baptism/Lord [1]	F	C
1 Cor 2:1-11	Pentecost	M	C
1 Cor 2:1-12 [13-16]	**Epiphany 5 [5]**	S	A
1 Cor 2:6-16	Epiphany 4 [4]	M	C
1 Cor 2:11-16	Baptism/Lord [1]	Sa	C
1 Cor 2:12-16	Pentecost	T	C
1 Cor 3:1-9	**Epiphany 6 [6]**	S	A
1 Cor 3:10-11, 16-23	**Epiphany 7 [7]**	S	A
1 Cor 3:10-17		Dec 29	C
1 Cor 3:10-23	Lent 3	M	B

1 Cor 4:1-5	**Epiphany 8 [8]**	**S**	**A**		1 Cor 15:1-11	Easter	S	B
1 Cor 4:1-5	**Proper 3 [8]**	**S**	**A**		**1 Cor 15:1-11**	**Epiphany 5 [5]**	**S**	**C**
1 Cor 4:6-21	Epiphany 8 [8]	T	A		1 Cor 15:12-20	Easter 2	M	A
1 Cor 4:6-21	Proper 3 [8]	T	A		**1 Cor 15:12-20**	**Epiphany 6 [6]**	**S**	**C**
1 Cor 4:8-13	Proper 9 [14]	Th	B		**1 Cor 15:19-26**	**Easter**	**S**	**C**
1 Cor 4:14-20	Proper 12 [17]	Th	A		1 Cor 15:19-28	Easter 2	T	A
1 Cor 5:6b-8	**Easter Evening**	**S**	**ABC**		1 Cor 15:20-28	Reign of Christ [34]	F	B
1 Cor 5:6b-8	Easter	M	C		1 Cor 15:20-34	Epiphany 6 [6]	M	C
1 Cor 5:9-13	Proper 26 [31]	M	C		**1 Cor 15:35-38,**	**Epiphany 7 [7]**	**S**	**C**
1 Cor 6:1-11	Proper 16 [21]	Th	A		**42-50**			
1 Cor 6:1-11	Proper 24 [29]	M	C		1 Cor 15:35-49	Easter	M	B
1 Cor 6:12-20	**Epiphany 2 [2]**	**S**	**B**		1 Cor 15:42b-49	Pentecost	Th	B
1 Cor 7:1-7	Epiphany 2 [2]	F	C		1 Cor 15:50-57	Pentecost	F	B
1 Cor 7:1-9	Proper 22 [27]	M	B		1 Cor 15:50-58	Easter	T	B
1 Cor 7:10-16	Proper 22 [27]	T	B		**1 Cor 15:51-58**	**Epiphany 8 [8]**	**S**	**C**
1 Cor 7:17-24	Epiphany 3 [3]	M	B		**1 Cor 15:51-58**	**Proper 3 [8]**	**S**	**C**
1 Cor 7:29-31	**Epiphany 3 [3]**	**S**	**B**		1 Cor 16:1-12	Epiphany 8 [8]	M	C
1 Cor 7:32-40	Epiphany 4 [4]	T	B		1 Cor 16:1-12	Proper 3 [8]	M	C
1 Cor 8:1-13	**Epiphany 4 [4]**	**S**	**B**		1 Cor 16:13-24	Epiphany 8 [8]	T	C
1 Cor 9:1-16	Epiphany 5 [5]	F	B		1 Cor 16:13-24	Proper 3 [8]	T	C
1 Cor 9:16-23	**Epiphany 5 [5]**	**S**	**B**					
1 Cor 9:19-23	Proper 20 [25]	T	C		2 Cor 1:1-11	Epiphany 7 [7]	T	B
1 Cor 9:24-27	**Epiphany 6 [6]**	**S**	**B**		2 Cor 1:1-11	Proper 26 [31]	Th	C
1 Cor 10:1-4	Lent 3	T	A		2 Cor 1:12-19	Epiphany 6 [6]	T	C
1 Cor 10:1-13	Lent 2	T	C		**2 Cor 1:18-22**	**Epiphany 7 [7]**	**S**	**B**
1 Cor 10:1-13	**Lent 3**	**S**	**C**		2 Cor 1:23—2:11	Epiphany 8 [8]	M	B
1 Cor 10:6-13	Lent 4	T	B		2 Cor 1:23—2:11	Proper 3 [8]	M	B
1 Cor 10:14—11:1	Epiphany 6 [6]	T	B		2 Cor 2:12-17	Epiphany Last Trfg	Th	B
1 Cor 10:23—11:1	Epiphany 7 [7]	Th	A		**2 Cor 3:1-6**	**Epiphany 8 [8]**	**S**	**B**
1 Cor 10:23—11:1	Proper 28 [33]	T	C		**2 Cor 3:1-6**	**Proper 3 [8]**	**S**	**B**
1 Cor 11:2-16	Epiphany 7 [7]	M	C		2 Cor 3:4-11	Lent 5	M	B
1 Cor 11:17-22	Proper 13 [18]	Th	B		**2 Cor 3:12—4:2**	**Epiphany Last Trfg**	**S**	**C**
1 Cor 11:17-22,	Epiphany 7 [7]	T	C		2 Cor 4:1-12	Epiphany 5 [5]	T	A
27-33					**2 Cor 4:3-6**	**Epiphany Last Trfg**	**S**	**B**
1 Cor 11:23-26	**Holy Thursday**	**S**	**ABC**		**2 Cor 4:5-12**	**Epiphany 9 [9]**	**S**	**B**
1 Cor 11:27-34	Proper 13 [18]	F	B		**2 Cor 4:5-12**	**Proper 4 [9]**	**S**	**B**
1 Cor 12:1-3	Trinity Sunday	M	A		**2 Cor 4:13—5:1**	**Proper 5 [10]**	**S**	**B**
1 Cor 12:1-11	**Epiphany 2 [2]**	**S**	**C**		2 Cor 4:16-18		Dec 30	A
1 Cor 12:3b-13	**Pentecost**	**S**	**A**		2 Cor 4:16—5:5	Lent 4	Th	C
1 Cor 12:4-11	Pentecost	M	B		2 Cor 5:1-5	Proper 5 [10]	F	B
1 Cor 12:4-13	Trinity Sunday	T	A		**2 Cor 5:6-10**	**Proper 6 [11]**	**S**	**B**
1 Cor 12:12-27	Pentecost	T	B		**[11-13] 14-17**			
1 Cor 12:12-31a	**Epiphany 3 [3]**	**S**	**C**		2 Cor 5:6-15	Lent 4	F	C
1 Cor 12:27-31	Proper 13 [18]	T	B		2 Cor 5:11-17	Epiphany 9 [9]	Th	C
1 Cor 13:1-13	**Epiphany 4 [4]**	**S**	**C**		2 Cor 5:11-17	Proper 4 [9]	Th	C
1 Cor 14:1-12	Epiphany 3 [3]	M	C		**2 Cor 5:16-21**	**Lent 4**	**S**	**C**
1 Cor 14:13-25	Epiphany 4 [4]	T	C		2 Cor 5:17-21	Proper 22 [27]	T	A
1 Cor 14:20-25	Proper 27 [32]	M	A		**2 Cor 5:20b—**	**Ash Wednesday**	**S**	**ABC**
1 Cor 14:26-40	Epiphany 5 [5]	M	C		**6:10**			
1 Cor 15:1-11	Easter 2	F	A		**2 Cor 6:1-13**	**Proper 7 [12]**	**S**	**B**

2 Cor 6:14—7:1	Epiphany 2 [2]	M	B
2 Cor 6:14—7:2	Proper 5 [10]	M	A
2 Cor 7:2-12	Epiphany 3 [3]	T	C
2 Cor 7:2-16	Proper 8 [13]	Th	B
2 Cor 8:1-7	Proper 8 [13]	F	B
2 Cor 8:1-7	Proper 9 [14]	F	C
2 Cor 8:1-15	Advent 3	Th	C
2 Cor 8:7-15	**Proper 8 [13]**	**S**	**B**
2 Cor 8:8-15	Proper 21 [26]	Th	C
2 Cor 8:16-24	Proper 8 [13]	M	B
2 Cor 9:1-5	Proper 8 [13]	T	B
2 Cor 9:6-15	**Thanksgiving**	**S**	**A**
2 Cor 9:1-15	Advent 3	F	C
2 Cor 10:1-11	Epiphany 2 [2]	Th	B
2 Cor 10:7-11	Proper 9 [14]	F	B
2 Cor 10:12-18	Proper 16 [21]	F	A
2 Cor 11:1-6	Epiphany 9 [9]	F	C
2 Cor 11:1-6	Proper 4 [9]	F	C
2 Cor 11:1-15	Epiphany 8 [8]	T	B
2 Cor 11:1-15	Proper 3 [8]	T	B
2 Cor 11:16-33	Proper 9 [14]	M	B
2 Cor 12:2-10	**Proper 9 [14]**	**S**	**B**
2 Cor 12:11-21	Proper 18 [23]	Th	A
2 Cor 13:1-4	Proper 20 [25]	Th	A
2 Cor 13:5-10	Proper 20 [25]	F	A
2 Cor 13:5-10	Proper 8 [13]	Th	C
2 Cor 13:11-13	**Trinity Sunday**	**S**	**A**
Gal 1:1-12	**Epiphany 9 [9]**	**S**	**C**
Gal 1:1-12	**Proper 4 [9]**	**S**	**C**
Gal 1:6-12	Epiphany 2 [2]	Th	A
Gal 1:11-24	Epiphany 3 [3]	Th	A
Gal 1:11-24	**Proper 5 [10]**	**S**	**C**
Gal 2:1-10	Epiphany 3 [3]	F	A
Gal 2:1-10	Proper 5 [10]	M	C
Gal 2:11-14	Proper 5 [10]	T	C
Gal 2:15-21	**Proper 6 [11]**	**S**	**C**
Gal 3:1-9	Proper 6 [11]	M	C
Gal 3:6-14		Dec 23	A
Gal 3:10-14	Proper 6 [11]	T	C
Gal 3:15-22	Proper 7 [12]	F	C
Gal 3:23-29	Proper 22 [27]	Th	B
Gal 3:23-29	**Proper 7 [12]**	**S**	**C**
Gal 3:23-29	Advent 4	Th	A
Gal 4:1-7	Advent 4	F	A
Gal 4:4-7	**Holy Name**	**S**	**ABC**
Gal 4:4-7	**Christmas 1**	**S**	**B**
Gal 4:8-20	Advent 4	M	A
Gal 4:8-20	Proper 8 [13]	F	C
Gal 4:21—5:1	Advent 4	T	A

Gal 4:21—5:1	Proper 11 [16]	T	A
Gal 5:1, 13-25	**Proper 8 [13]**	**S**	**C**
Gal 5:2-6	Epiphany 7 [7]	F	A
Gal 5:2-6	Proper 8 [13]	Th	A
Gal 5:2-15	Epiphany 5 [5]	Th	B
Gal 5:7-12	Proper 8 [13]	F	A
Gal 5:16-25	Pentecost	Th	C
Gal 5:16-26	Easter 5	M	B
Gal 6:[1-6] 7-16	**Proper 9 [14]**	**S**	**C**
Gal 6:1-10	Proper 14 [19]	F	B
Gal 6:7-10	Pentecost	F	C
Gal 6:11-18	Proper 6 [11]	M	B
Eph 1:3-6	Lent 4	Th	B
Eph 1:3-14	**Christmas 2**	**S**	**ABC**
Eph 1:3-14	**Proper 10 [15]**	**S**	**B**
Eph 1:7-14	Lent 4	F	B
Eph 1:11-23	**All Saints**	**S**	**C**
Eph 1:15-23	**Ascension**	**S**	**ABC**
Eph 1:15-23	**Reign of Christ [34]**	**S**	**A**
Eph 1:17-19	Trinity Sunday	Th	C
Eph 2:1-7	Easter 7	F	A
Eph 2:1-10	Lent 5	T	A
Eph 2:1-10	Lent 1	M	B
Eph 2:1-10	**Lent 4**	**S**	**B**
Eph 2:1-10	Proper 21 [26]	F	C
Eph 2:11-22	Lent 3	F	A
Eph 2:11-22	**Proper 11 [16]**	**S**	**B**
Eph 2:11-22		Dec 22	C
Eph 2:11-22	Proper 7 [12]	T	C
Eph 3:1-12	**Epiphany**	**S**	**ABC**
Eph 3:14-21		Jan 7	A
Eph 3:14-21	**Proper 12 [17]**	**S**	**B**
Eph 3:14-21	Proper 11 [16]	F	C
Eph 4:1-6	Trinity Sunday	F	C
Eph 4:1-16	**Proper 13 [18]**	**S**	**B**
Eph 4:7, 11-16		Jan 8	A
Eph 4:7-16	Trinity Sunday	M	C
Eph 4:17-24	Proper 13 [18]	M	B
Eph 4:17-24	Proper 13 [18]	F	C
Eph 4:17—5:1		Jan 7	C
Eph 4:17—5:2	Proper 10 [15]	T	A
Eph 4:25-32	Lent 4	Th	A
Eph 4:25—5:2	**Proper 14 [19]**	**S**	**B**
Eph 4:25—5:2	Proper 28 [33]	M	C
Eph 5:1-6	Proper 17 [22]	Th	A
Eph 5:1-9	Lent 4	F	A
Eph 5:1-14	Proper 14 [19]	M	B
Eph 5:6-14	Epiphany 3 [3]	M	A
Eph 5:6-20	Proper 8 [13]	T	C

Eph 5:8-14	**Lent 4**	**S**	**A**
Eph 5:15-20	**Proper 15 [20]**	**S**	**B**
Eph 5:15-20		Jan 8	C
Eph 5:15-20	Trinity Sunday	T	C
Eph 5:21—6:9	Proper 16 [21]	M	B
Eph 6:10-17	Advent 3	M	B
Eph 6:10-17	Baptism/Lord [1]	M	C
Eph 6:10-18	Proper 12 [17]	T	A
Eph 6:10-20	**Proper 16 [21]**	**S**	**B**
Eph 6:10-20	Proper 23 [28]	T	C
Eph 6:21-24	Proper 16 [21]	T	B
Phil 1:1-11	Passion/Palm Sun	Th	A
Phil 1:3-11	Easter 7	M	B
Phil 1:3-11	**Advent 2**	**S**	**C**
Phil 1:3-14	Proper 21 [26]	M	A
Phil 1:12-18a	Advent 2	Th	C
Phil 1:15-21	Proper 21 [26]	T	A
Phil 1:18b-26	Advent 2	F	C
Phil 1:21-30	Passion/Palm Sun	F	A
Phil 1:21-30	**Proper 20 [25]**	**S**	**A**
Phil 2:1-11	Passion/Palm Sun	Th	B
Phil 2:1-13	**Proper 21 [26]**	**S**	**A**
Phil 2:5-11	**Holy Name**	**S**	**ABC**
Phil 2:5-11	**Passion/Palm Sun**	**S**	**ABC**
Phil 2:12-18	Epiphany 3 [3]	T	A
Phil 2:12-18	Passion/Palm Sun	F	B
Phil 2:14-18; 3:1-4a	Proper 22 [27]	F	A
Phil 2:19-24	Epiphany 8 [8]	Th	A
Phil 2:19-24	Proper 3 [8]	Th	A
Phil 2:19-24	Lent 5	Th	C
Phil 2:25—3:1	Lent 5	F	C
Phil 2:25-30	Epiphany 8 [8]	F	A
Phil 2:25-30	Proper 3 [8]	F	A
Phil 2:25-30	Proper 18 [23]	Th	C
Phil 3:2-12	Lent 2	Th	C
Phil 3:4b-14	**Proper 22 [27]**	**S**	**A**
Phil 3:4b-14	**Lent 5**	**S**	**C**
Phil 3:7-11	Advent 3	Th	B
Phil 3:12-16	Advent 3	F	B
Phil 3:17-20	Lent 2	F	C
Phil 3:13—4:1	Proper 23 [28]	T	A
Phil 3:17—4:1	**Lent 2**	**S**	**C**
Phil 4:1-9	**Proper 23 [28]**	**S**	**A**
Phil 4:4-7	**Advent 3**	**S**	**C**
Phil 4:4-9	**Thanksgiving**	**S**	**C**
Phil 4:10-15	Proper 13 [18]	Th	A
Phil 4:10-20	Proper 12 [17]	M	B

Col 1:1-14	**Proper 10 [15]**	**S**	**C**
Col 1:9-14	Lent 4	T	A
Col 1:9-14	Proper 12 [17]	Th	B
Col 1:11-20	**Reign of Christ [34]**	**S**	**C**
Col 1:15-20	Advent 4	M	C
Col 1:15-23	Lent 3	Th	A
Col 1:15-23	Proper 11 [16]	Th	B
Col 1:15-28	**Proper 11 [16]**	**S**	**C**
Col 1:27—2:7	Proper 11 [16]	M	C
Col 2:1-5	Proper 10 [15]	Th	B
Col 2:6-15	Proper 28 [33]	F	B
Col 2:6-15 [16-19]	**Proper 12 [17]**	**S**	**C**
Col 2:16-23	Proper 22 [27]	Th	A
Col 2:16—3:1	Proper 12 [17]	M	C
Col 3:1-4	**Easter**	**S**	**A**
Col 3:1-11	Proper 19 [24]	T	B
Col 3:1-11	**Proper 13 [18]**	**S**	**C**
Col 3:5-11	Easter	M	A
Col 3:12-17	Easter	T	A
Col 3:12-17	Proper 12 [17]	F	B
Col 3:12-17	**Christmas 1**	**S**	**C**
Col 3:18—4:1	Proper 13 [18]	M	C
Col 4:2-5	Easter 2	Th	A
Col 4:2-6	Proper 13 [18]	T	C
Col 4:2-18	Proper 10 [15]	F	B
Col 4:7-17	Proper 18 [23]	F	C
1 Thes 1:1-10	**Proper 24 [29]**	**S**	**A**
1 Thes 1:2-10	Advent 2	Th	B
1 Thes 2:1-8	**Proper 25 [30]**	**S**	**A**
1 Thes 2:9-13	**Proper 26 [31]**	**S**	**A**
1 Thes 2:13-20	Proper 26 [31]	M	A
1 Thes 3:1-5	Proper 6 [11]	M	A
1 Thes 3:6-13	Proper 27 [32]	T	A
1 Thes 3:9-13	**Advent 1**	**S**	**C**
1 Thes 4:1-8	Proper 10 [15]	M	A
1 Thes 4:1-12	Advent 2	M	A
1 Thes 4:1-18	Advent 1	F	B
1 Thes 4:9-12	Proper 8 [13]	M	A
1 Thes 4:13-18	**Proper 27 [32]**	**S**	**A**
1 Thes 4:13-18	Epiphany 8 [8]	F	C
1 Thes 4:13-18	Proper 3 [8]	F	C
1 Thes 5:1-11	**Proper 28 [33]**	**S**	**A**
1 Thes 5:1-11	Proper 16 [21]	Th	B
1 Thes 5:1-11	Advent 1	Th	C
1 Thes 5:12-18	Proper 28 [33]	T	A
1 Thes 5:12-22	Advent 1	F	C
1 Thes 5:16-24	**Advent 3**	**S**	**B**
2 Thes 1:1-4,	**Proper 26 [31]**	**S**	**C**

APPENDIXES

11-12

2 Thes 1:3-12	Proper 28 [33]	F	C
2 Thes 2:1-5, 13-17	**Proper 27 [32]**	**S**	**C**
2 Thes 2:7-12	Proper 17 [22]	F	A
2 Thes 2:13—3:5	Proper 6 [11]	T	A
2 Thes 3:6-13	**Proper 28 [33]**	**S**	**C**
1 Tim 1:1-11	Proper 19 [24]	Th	C
1 Tim 1:12-17	**Proper 19 [24]**	**S**	**C**
1 Tim 1:12-20	Epiphany Last Trfg	F	B
1 Tim 1:18-20	Proper 19 [24]	M	C
1 Tim 2:1-7	**Thanksgiving**	**S**	**B**
1 Tim 2:1-7	**Proper 20 [25]**	**S**	**C**
1 Tim 3:1-9	Epiphany 5 [5]	T	C
1 Tim 3:14-16	Epiphany Last Trfg	T	B
1 Tim 3:14—4:5	Proper 18 [23]	M	C
1 Tim 4:6-16	Proper 17 [22]	M	B
1 Tim 4:6-16	Proper 18 [23]	T	C
1 Tim 4:11-16	Baptism/Lord [1]	F	B
1 Tim 5:1-8	Proper 27 [32]	M	B
1 Tim 5:9-16	Proper 27 [32]	T	B
1 Tim 5:17-24	Epiphany 4 [4]	F	A
1 Tim 6:6-19	**Proper 21 [26]**	**S**	**C**
1 Tim 6:11-12	Easter 6	M	B
1 Tim 6:11-21	Proper 28 [33]	Th	B
1 Tim 6:13-16	Easter 6	T	B
2 Tim 1:1-14	**Proper 22 [27]**	**S**	**C**
2 Tim 1:3-7	Lent 2	Th	A
2 Tim 1:8-12a	Trinity Sunday	Th	A
2 Tim 1:12b-14	Trinity Sunday	F	A
2 Tim 1:13-18	Proper 23 [28]	Th	C
2 Tim 2:1-7	Proper 23 [28]	F	C
2 Tim 2:8-13	Reign of Christ [34]	M	A
2 Tim 2:8-15	**Proper 23 [28]**	**S**	**C**
2 Tim 2:14-26	Proper 24 [29]	F	C
2 Tim 3:1-9	Proper 25 [30]	Th	C
2 Tim 3:10-15	Proper 25 [30]	F	C
2 Tim 3:14—4:5	**Proper 24 [29]**	**S**	**C**
2 Tim 4:1-5	Lent 1	F	B
2 Tim 4:6-8, 16-18	**Proper 25 [30]**	**S**	**C**
Titus 1:1-9	Easter 7	T	B
Titus 1:1-9	Proper 17 [22]	T	C
Titus 1:5-16	Proper 25 [30]	Th	A
Titus 2:7-8, 11-15	Proper 25 [30]	F	A
Titus 2:11-14	**Christmas Day 1**	**S**	**ABC**
Titus 3:4-7	**Christmas Day 2**	**S**	**ABC**

Phlm 1-21	**Proper 18 [23]**	**S**	**C**
Phlm 1-25	Epiphany 4 [4]	M	A
Heb 1:1-4	Advent 4	Th	B
Heb 1:1-4 [5-12]	**Christmas Day 3**	**S**	**ABC**
Heb 1:1-4; 2:5-12	**Proper 22 [27]**	**S**	**B**
Heb 1:5-14	Advent 4	F	B
Heb 1:8-12	Lent 2	M	B
Heb 2:1-4	Epiphany Last Trfg	M	B
Heb 2:1-9	Proper 11 [16]	Th	A
Heb 2:1-9	Passion/Palm Sun	Th	C
Heb 2:5-9	Proper 7 [12]	Th	A
Heb 2:5-9	Proper 6 [11]	Th	B
Heb 2:10-18	Lent 1	M	A
Heb 2:10-18	Passion/Palm Sun	F	C
Heb 2:10-18	**Christmas 1**	**S**	**A**
Heb 2:14-18	**Presentation**	**S**	**ABC**
Heb 3:1-6	Lent 2	M	A
Heb 3:1-6	Proper 6 [11]	Th	A
Heb 3:1-6	Lent 4	M	B
Heb 3:7-19	Proper 23 [28]	Th	B
Heb 3:7—4:11	Proper 16 [21]	M	C
Heb 4:1-11	Proper 23 [28]	F	B
Heb 4:1-13	Lent 5	Th	B
Heb 4:12-16	**Proper 23 [28]**	**S**	**B**
Heb 4:14-16; 5:7-9	**Good Friday**	**S**	**ABC**
Heb 4:14—5:10	Lent 1	T	A
Heb 4:14—5:4	Lent 5	F	B
Heb 5:1-6	Proper 11 [16]	Th	C
Heb 5:1-10	**Proper 24 [29]**	**S**	**B**
Heb 5:5-10	**Lent 5**	**S**	**B**
Heb 6:1-12	Proper 24 [29]	M	B
Heb 6:13-20	Proper 11 [16]	F	A
Heb 6:13-20	Proper 24 [29]	T	B
Heb 7:1-10	Proper 25 [30]	Th	B
Heb 7:11-22	Proper 25 [30]	F	B
Heb 7:23-28	**Proper 25 [30]**	**S**	**B**
Heb 8:1-7	Epiphany Last Trfg	Th	A
Heb 8:1-13	Advent 4	T	B
Heb 9:1-12	Proper 26 [31]	Th	B
Heb 9:1-14	Advent 4	M	B
Heb 9:11-14	**Proper 26 [31]**	**S**	**B**
Heb 9:11-15	**Mon. of Holy Week**	**S**	**ABC**
Heb 9:15-24	Proper 27 [32]	F	B
Heb 9:23-28	Lent 3	T	B
Heb 9:23-28	Reign of Christ [34]	Th	C
Heb 9:24-28	**Proper 27 [32]**	**S**	**B**
Heb 10:1-4	Epiphany 2 [2]	T	A
Heb 10:4-10	**Annunciation**	**S**	**ABC**

Heb 10:5-10	**Advent 4**	**S**	**C**
Heb 10:5-10		Dec 24	C
Heb 10:10-18	Advent 4	Th	C
Heb 10:11-14 [15-18] 19-25	**Proper 28 [33]**	**S**	**B**
Heb 10:16-25	**Good Friday**	**S**	**ABC**
Heb 10:19-25	Lent 5	M	C
Heb 10:26-31	Proper 28 [33]	M	B
Heb 10:26-31	Proper 15 [20]	Th	C
Heb 10:32-39	Epiphany 8 [8]	M	A
Heb 10:32-39	Proper 3 [8]	M	A
Heb 10:32-39	Proper 28 [33]	T	B
Heb 10:32-39	Advent 4	F	C
Heb 10:32-39	Proper 15 [20]	F	C
Heb 11:1-3, 13-19	Lent 2	T	B
Heb 11:1-3, 8-16	**Proper 14 [19]**	**S**	**C**
Heb 11:1-7	Advent 1	F	A
Heb 11:1-7	Proper 14 [19]	M	C
Heb 11:1-12		Jan 2	A
Heb 11:4-7	Proper 6 [11]	F	B
Heb 11:13-22		Jan 3	A
Heb 11:17-22	Proper 19 [24]	Th	B
Heb 11:17-28	Proper 14 [19]	T	C
Heb 11:23-26		Jan 7	B
Heb 11:23-28	Epiphany Last Trfg	F	A
Heb 11:23-29	Proper 19 [24]	M	A
Heb 11:23-31		Jan 4	A
Heb 11:27-28		Jan 8	B
Heb 11:29—12:2	Proper 18 [23]	M	B
Heb 11:29—12:2	**Proper 15 [20]**	**S**	**C**
Heb 11:32-40	Advent 1	T	A
Heb 11:32—12:2		Jan 5	A
Heb 12:1-3	**Wed. of Holy Week**	**S**	**ABC**
Heb 12:3-13	Proper 18 [23]	T	B
Heb 12:3-17	Proper 16 [21]	Th	C
Heb 12:7-13	Epiphany 6 [6]	Th	B
Heb 12:7-13	Epiphany 7 [7]	F	B
Heb 12:14-16	Epiphany 7 [7]	T	A
Heb 12:18-29	**Proper 16 [21]**	**S**	**C**
Heb 13:1-8, 15-16	**Proper 17 [22]**	**S**	**C**
Heb 13:1-16	Proper 5 [10]	T	A
Heb 13:7-17	Advent 3	M	C
Heb 13:7-21	Proper 17 [22]	M	C
Heb 13:17-25	Proper 11 [16]	M	B
Heb 13:20-21	Easter 4	T	A
Jam 1:1-8	Proper 17 [22]	Th	B
Jam 1:2-8	Epiphany 6 [6]	M	A
Jam 1:2-11	Proper 22 [27]	M	C

Jam 1:9-16	Proper 17 [22]	F	B
Jam 1:12-16	Epiphany 6 [6]	Th	A
Jam 1:17-18		Dec 24	B
Jam 1:17-27	**Proper 17 [22]**	**S**	**B**
Jam 2:1-7	Proper 10 [15]	M	C
Jam 2:1-10 [11-13] 14-17	**Proper 18 [23]**	**S**	**B**
Jam 2:1-13	Epiphany 6 [6]	T	A
Jam 2:14-26	Proper 25 [30]	T	A
Jam 2:14-26	Proper 10 [15]	Th	C
Jam 2:17-26	Proper 19 [24]	F	B
Jam 2:8-13	Proper 25 [30]	M	A
Jam 3:1-12	**Proper 19 [24]**	**S**	**B**
Jam 3:13-18	Epiphany 5 [5]	F	A
Jam 3:13-18	Proper 12 [17]	M	A
Jam 3:13-18		Jan 2	B
Jam 3:13-18		Jan 2	C
Jam 3:13—4:3, 7-8a	**Proper 20 [25]**	**S**	**B**
Jam 3:17-18	Easter 5	T	B
Jam 4:1-7	Proper 6 [11]	Th	C
Jam 4:1-10	Advent 1	Th	A
Jam 4:1-10		Jan 3	B
Jam 4:4-10	Proper 23 [28]	F	A
Jam 4:8-17	Proper 20 [25]	M	B
Jam 4:11-16	Proper 21 [26]	Th	A
Jam 4:11-17		Jan 4	B
Jam 5:1-6	Epiphany 4 [4]	T	A
Jam 5:1-6	Proper 20 [25]	T	B
Jam 5:1-6	Proper 21 [26]	T	C
Jam 5:7-10	**Advent 3**	**S**	**A**
Jam 5:7-12	Proper 9 [14]	T	B
Jam 5:7-12	Proper 24 [29]	T	C
Jam 5:13-20	**Proper 21 [26]**	**S**	**B**
1 Pet 1:3-9	**Easter 2**	**S**	**A**
1 Pet 1:3-9	Proper 21 [26]	M	B
1 Pet 1:3-9	Reign of Christ [34]	F	C
1 Pet 1:8b-12	Easter 3	Th	A
1 Pet 1:13-16	Easter 3	F	A
1 Pet 1:17-23	**Easter 3**	**S**	**A**
1 Pet 1:17—2:1	Epiphany 6 [6]	F	C
1 Pet 1:23-25	Easter 3	M	A
1 Pet 2:1-3	Easter 3	T	A
1 Pet 2:1-10	Proper 25 [30]	M	B
1 Pet 2:2-10	**Easter 5**	**S**	**A**
1 Pet 2:4-10	Proper 22 [27]	M	A
1 Pet 2:4-10	Lent 3	Th	B
1 Pet 2:9-12	Easter 4	Th	A
1 Pet 2:11-17	Proper 18 [23]	M	A

Reference	Occasion	Day	Year
1 Pet 2:13-17	Easter 4	F	A
1 Pet 2:19-25	**Easter 4**	**S**	**A**
1 Pet 2:19-25	Proper 17 [22]	T	B
1 Pet 3:8-12	Epiphany 4 [4]	Th	A
1 Pet 3:8-12	Easter 6	T	A
1 Pet 3:8-12	Proper 17 [22]	Th	C
1 Pet 3:8-18a	Lent 1	T	B
1 Pet 3:13-22	**Easter 6**	**S**	**A**
1 Pet 3:18-22	**Lent 1**	**S**	**B**
1 Pet 4:1-6	Easter 7	M	A
1 Pet 4:1-8	**Holy Saturday**	**S**	**ABC**
1 Pet 4:7-11	Easter 7	T	A
1 Pet 4:7-11	Proper 17 [22]	F	C
1 Pet 4:7-19	Proper 5 [10]	Th	B
1 Pet 4:12-14; 5:6-11	**Easter 7**	**S**	**A**
1 Pet 4:12-19	Proper 25 [30]	M	C
1 Pet 5:1-5	Easter 4	M	A
1 Pet 5:1-5	Proper 24 [29]	F	A
1 Pet 5:1-5	Easter 4	M	B
1 Pet 5:1-5, 12-14	Proper 23 [28]	Th	A
1 Pet 5:1-11	Proper 25 [30]	T	C
2 Pet 1:1-11	Epiphany 8 [8]	F	B
2 Pet 1:1-11	Proper 3 [8]	F	B
2 Pet 1:1-11	Proper 26 [31]	F	C
2 Pet 1:16-21	**Epiphany Last Trfg**	**S**	**A**
2 Pet 1:16-21		Dec 23	C
2 Pet 1:16-21	Proper 27 [32]	M	C
2 Pet 1:2-15	Advent 2	T	C
2 Pet 2:1-3	Proper 26 [31]	F	A
2 Pet 2:1-10a	Proper 19 [24]	F	C
2 Pet 2:4-10	Proper 14 [19]	M	A
2 Pet 2:4-21	Lent 1	T	C
2 Pet 2:17-22	Proper 5 [10]	Th	A
2 Pet 3:1-7	Epiphany 3 [3]	F	B
2 Pet 3:1-10	Advent 3	Th	A
2 Pet 3:1-18	Advent 1	M	C
2 Pet 3:8-13		Dec 30	B
2 Pet 3:8-13	Proper 19 [24]	T	C
2 Pet 3:8-15a	**Advent 2**	**S**	**B**
2 Pet 3:11-18	Advent 3	F	A
2 Pet 3:14-18	Proper 14 [19]	T	B
1 Jn 1:1-9		Dec 27	B
1 Jn 1:1—2:2	**Easter 2**	**S**	**B**
1 Jn 1:3-10	Lent 1	Th	B
1 Jn 2:1-6	Lent 1	M	C
1 Jn 2:1-6	Proper 11 [16]	T	C
1 Jn 2:3-11	Easter 2	M	B

Reference	Occasion	Day	Year
1 Jn 2:7-11	Proper 8 [13]	M	C
1 Jn 2:7-17	Epiphany 6 [6]	F	A
1 Jn 2:12-17	Easter 2	T	B
1 Jn 2:12-17	Epiphany 7 [7]	F	C
1 Jn 2:18-25	Easter 3	Th	B
1 Jn 2:18-25	Proper 21 [26]	T	B
1 Jn 2:18-28	Lent 5	T	C
1 Jn 2:26-28	Easter 3	F	B
1 Jn 3:1-3	**All Saints**	**S**	**A**
1 Jn 3:1-7	**Easter 3**	**S**	**B**
1 Jn 3:10-16	Easter 3	M	B
1 Jn 3:11-16	Proper 19 [24]	Th	A
1 Jn 3:11-17	Proper 10 [15]	T	C
1 Jn 3:16-24	**Easter 4**	**S**	**B**
1 Jn 4:1-6	Proper 8 [13]	T	A
1 Jn 4:1-6	Proper 15 [20]	M	C
1 Jn 4:7-21	**Easter 5**	**S**	**B**
1 Jn 5:1-5	Epiphany 5 [5]	Th	A
1 Jn 5:1-5, 13-21	Proper 22 [27]	T	C
1 Jn 5:1-6	**Easter 6**	**S**	**B**
1 Jn 5:1-12		Dec 27	A
1 Jn 5:9-13	**Easter 7**	**S**	**B**
1 Jn 5:13-21	Baptism/Lord [1]	T	C
2 Jn 1-6	Easter 3	T	B
2 Jn 1-13	Lent 3	M	A
2 Jn 1-13	Proper 27 [32]	T	C
3 Jn 2-8	Epiphany 7 [7]	Th	B
3 Jn 9-12	Proper 24 [29]	Th	A
Jude 5-21	Proper 26 [31]	T	C
Jude 17-25	Advent 3	T	A
Jude 17-25	Proper 23 [28]	M	A
Rev 1:4-8	**Easter 2**	**S**	**C**
Rev 1:4b-8	**Reign of Christ [34]**	**S**	**B**
Rev 1:9-18	Easter 7	F	B
Rev 1:9-20	Easter 2	M	C
Rev 2:1-7	Proper 7 [12]	M	A
Rev 2:8-11	Proper 7 [12]	T	A
Rev 2:8-11	Lent 3	Th	C
Rev 2:8-11	Easter 2	T	C
Rev 2:8-11	Proper 22 [27]	Th	C
Rev 2:12-17	Epiphany 4 [4]	F	B
Rev 2:12-29	Proper 22 [27]	F	C
Rev 3:1-6	Proper 17 [22]	M	A
Rev 3:1-6	Lent 3	F	C
Rev 3:7-13	Proper 17 [22]	T	A
Rev 3:7-13	Proper 16 [21]	T	C

Rev 3:14-22	Easter 3	Th	C
Rev 3:14-22	Proper 21 [26]	M	C
Rev 4:1-8	Trinity Sunday	M	B
Rev 4:1-11	Easter 3	F	C
Rev 5:1-10	Easter 4	Th	C
Rev 5:11-14	**Easter 3**	**S**	**C**
Rev 6:1—7:4	Easter 4	F	C
Rev 7:9-17	Proper 23 [28]	M	B
Rev 7:9-17	**All Saints**	**S**	**A**
Rev 7:9-17	**Easter 4**	**S**	**C**
Rev 7:13-17	Easter 4	T	B
Rev 8:1-5	Proper 23 [28]	T	B
Rev 8:6—9:12	Proper 27 [32]	Th	A
Rev 9:13-21	Proper 27 [32]	F	A
Rev 10:1-11	Lent 5	Th	A
Rev 10:1-11	Easter 5	Th	C
Rev 11:1-14	Reign of Christ [34]	M	B
Rev 11:15	Easter 5	F	C
Rev 11:15-19	Lent 5	F	A
Rev 11:15-19	Reign of Christ [34]	T	B
Rev 11:16-19	Easter 5	Sa	C
Rev 12:1-12	Easter	T	C
Rev 14:1-11	Reign of Christ [34]	Th	A
Rev 14:6-13	Advent 1	Th	B
Rev 14:12-20	Proper 11 [16]	M	A
Rev 15:1-4	Proper 15 [20]	Th	A
Rev 15:1-4	Easter 4	M	C
Rev 15:1-8	Advent 1	M	B
Rev 16:1-7	Proper 28 [33]	Th	A

Rev 16:8-21	Proper 28 [33]	F	A
Rev 17:1-18	Proper 24 [29]	F	B
Rev 18:1-10	Advent 1	T	B
Rev 18:1-10, 19-20	Proper 24 [29]	M	A
Rev 18:11-20	Epiphany 3 [3]	Th	B
Rev 18:21-24	Proper 24 [29]	T	A
Rev 19:1-8	Lent 4	M	C
Rev 19:1-9	Reign of Christ [34]	T	A
Rev 19:9-10	Lent 4	T	C
Rev 20:1-6	Proper 5 [10]	M	B
Rev 20:7-15	Proper 5 [10]	T	B
Rev 21:1-6a	**New Year's Day**	**S**	**ABC**
Rev 21:1-6a	**All Saints**	**S**	**B**
Rev 21:1-6	**Easter 5**	**S**	**C**
Rev 21:1-7		Dec 28	C
Rev 21:5-14	Easter 6	M	C
Rev 21:5-27	Reign of Christ [34]	M	C
Rev 21:10, 22—22:5	**Easter 6**	**S**	**C**
Rev 21:15-22	Easter 6	T	C
Rev 21:22—22:5	Proper 6 [11]	T	B
Rev 22:1-9	Reign of Christ [34]	F	A
Rev 22:6-7, 18-20		Dec 22	A
Rev 22:6-9	Easter 7	F	C
Rev 22:8-21	Reign of Christ [34]	T	C
Rev 22:12-14, 16-17, 20-21	**Easter 7**	**S**	**C**
Rev 22:12-16	Advent 1	T	C

A History of Civilization

A History of

Crane Brinton

John B. Christopher

University of Rochester

Robert Lee Wolff

Archibald Cary Coolidge Professor of History, Harvard University

Civilization

Prehistory to 1300

Fourth Edition

Prentice-Hall, Inc., Englewood Cliffs, New Jersey

A History of Civilization

Prehistory to 1300, Fourth Edition

Brinton, Christopher, and Wolff

Design by Mark A. Binn

Maps by Vincent Kotschar

PRENTICE-HALL INTERNATIONAL, INC., *London*
PRENTICE-HALL OF AUSTRALIA, PTY. LTD., *Sydney*
PRENTICE-HALL OF CANADA, LTD., *Toronto*
PRENTICE-HALL OF INDIA PRIVATE LTD., *New Delhi*
PRENTICE-HALL OF JAPAN, INC., *Tokyo*

Current printing:

1   2   3   4   5   6   7   8   9   10

0-13-389502-5

Preface

In preparing this fourth edition of *A History of Civilization* we have tried to incorporate the new discoveries that continue to add to our knowledge of the past, especially the remote past. Where new theories or approaches to a major subject have seemed to warrant change, we have made the change. We have recorded and sought to interpret the events of the years since 1967, when the third edition was published. Perhaps naturally, we regard this latest edition as a better book than its predecessors.

In particular, there is now a wholly new chapter on the ancient Near East, and there are wholly rewritten chapters on the Greeks and the Romans. The medieval chapters have also undergone substantial revision, especially in those sections that deal with letters and with art. Throughout the rest of the work, especially of course in Chapters 30 and 31, which deal with the quarter century since the end of World War II, we have recast and reinterpreted our materials. Extensive revisions have brought abreast of recent scholarship the chapters on the Reformation, the seventeenth century, and the economic and intellectual revolutions of the nineteenth century. We think the new illustrations are perhaps more successfully married to the text than ever before, and there are more of them in full color than there have been in earlier editions. Finally, our book is now available in three paperback volumes, with the chronological breaks coming at 1300 and 1815, as well as in two hardbound volumes dividing at 1715; the innovation, we hope, offers more flexibility for courses such as those scheduled on a quarter or trimester basis.

Our senior co-author, Crane Brinton, died on September 7, 1968, and we have had to try to carry on without him. His extraordinary gift for hitting off what he called the style—or essence—of a period, a nation, even a whole civilization, we shall always admire, and we have greatly missed. But the reader of this edition will find, we hope, that much of the substance and all of the spirit of his contributions to the earlier editions have been maintained.

We should like here to thank Elizabeth Genovese for her taste and resourcefulness in obtaining illustrative materials; Mark A. Binn and Helen Maertens of the Project Planning Department at Prentice-Hall, who have applied their skills and energies most generously and effectively; and Cecil Yarbrough, Project Planning editor, whose ingenuity, efficiency, wisdom, and tact have made the preparation of these volumes a pleasure.

A Note on the Reading Suggestions

A list of reading suggestions is appended to each chapter of this book. Almost all historical bibliographies nowadays begin with the statement that they are highly selective and do not, of course, aspire to be exhaustive. This apology is hardly necessary, for the fact is that in most fields of history we have outrun the possibility of bringing together in one list all the books and articles in all languages on a given topic. There are for the wide fields of this book, and in English alone, thousands of volumes and hundreds of thousands of articles in periodicals. The brief lists following each chapter are simply suggestions to the reader who wishes to explore a given topic further.

Each list attempts to give important and readable books, with special attention to paperbacks (noted in the list with an asterisk), which are often the editions most available in a college community. A useful guide is *Paperbound Books in Print,* a monthly review of new paperbacks, with encyclopedic cumulative issues published three or four times a year. In addition, good readings in original sources, the contemporary documents and writings of an age, are sometimes listed, though the reader can supplement these listings from the text itself and from the footnotes. In addition, there are many good collections of sources for European history, notably the *Introduction to Contemporary Civilization in the West* (3rd ed., 1960), prepared by faculty members at Columbia University; this begins with the Middle Ages and gives much longer selections from the sources than such compilations usually do. Other good collections are to be found in the Portable Readers (published by Viking). There are also many sourcebooks and pamphlets on central or controversial problems in European history. A good example is K. M. Setton and H. R. Winkler, eds., *Great Problems in European Civilization* (Prentice-Hall, 2nd ed., 1966). Another is the series of pamphlets edited by R. W. Greenlaw under the general title "Problems in European Civilization" (D. C. Heath).

Our lists also include historical novels and, occasionally, dramas. Professional historians are likely to be somewhat severe in their standards for a historical novel. They naturally want its history to be sound, and at bottom they are likely to be somewhat prejudiced against the form. The historical novels listed here are all readable and all reasonably good as history. But note that historical novels, like historical films, though accurate on such material matters as authentic settings and appropriate costumes, often fail to capture the immaterial aspects—the psychology, the spirit—of the age they are written about. Many such novels motivate their characters, especially in love, as if they were modern Europeans and Americans. Exceptions to this rule are noted in the lists.

It is easy to assemble more material on a given topic than is furnished by our reading lists. American libraries, large and small, have catalogs with subject and title listings, as well as a section of reference books with encyclopedias and bibliographies. Many libraries have open shelves where, once a single title is discovered, many others may be found in the immediate area. Perhaps the first printed list of books to be consulted is *A Guide to Historical Literature* (Macmillan, 1931) and its sequel, *The American Historical Association's Guide to Historical Literature* (Macmillan, 1961). For more recent books one can turn, for American history, to the *Harvard Guide to American History* (Belknap, 1954), edited by O. Handlin and others. And for the history of Europe and other areas there are many good bibliographies; see, for example, those in "The Rise of Modern Europe" series edited by W. L. Langer (Torchbooks); in the multivolumed *Oxford History of England;* and in R. R. Palmer and J. Colton, *A History of the Modern World* (Knopf, 1970). For historical fiction, one may consult two older specialized guides: E. A. Baker, *A Guide to Historical Fiction* (Macmillan, 1914) and J. Nield, *A Guide to the Best Historical Novels and Tales* (Elkins, Mathews, and Marrot, 1929). The more recent *Fiction Catalogue* (Wilson, 1951), while covering much besides historical fiction, does furnish keys to books that cover particular countries and particular historical eras.

What is much more difficult than assembling titles is securing an evaluation of individual books. For older books the *Guide to Historical Literature,* already mentioned, gives the most useful references to critical reviews of the titles it discusses. *The Book Review Digest* gives capsule reviews and references to longer ones. For current books the weekly book section of *The New York Times* and *The Times Literary Supplement* (published in London) usually provide informative reviews of historical works soon after they are published. Later—sometimes as much as three years later—full scholarly appraisals are published in the *American Historical Review,* its British equivalent, the *English Historical Review,* and in more specialized reviews, such as the *Journal of Modern History, Speculum* (for medieval studies), *The Middle East Journal,* and many others. An American scholarly journal, *History and Theory,* covers a field of great interest to historians today. By reading a few reviews of a book one can usually get a fair indication of its scope and quality. In our reading suggestions we have tried, within a very brief compass, to give comparable indications.

Contents

Maps

A History of Civilization

What Good Is History?

A little less than two centuries ago, just about the time of the American Revolution, a learned Englishman, Edward Gibbon, had completed a new volume of his famous work, *The Decline and Fall of the Roman Empire*, and called upon a royal duke, a brother of King George III, to give him a copy. The duke, taking the present, said "Another damned thick book. Always scribble, scribble, scribble. Eh, Mr. Gibbon?"

If you stop to think about it, there was really very little that Gibbon could say in reply. He might have pointed out that the earlier volume had been a best seller, and was on the dressing tables of most of the fashionable ladies of the duke's acquaintance. But that would probably not have changed the duke's opinion very much. The duke was bored by history, and that was that. There have always been people like the duke and there always will be. Nor have they always been merely stupid, as one must admit that the duke was. Henry Ford Sr., inventive genius whose cheap cars changed the whole way of life of twentieth-century America, once remarked feelingly "History is bunk," and there is no reason to think that he did not mean it or that he ever changed

his views. And Henry Ford in his own way was brilliant. An even more brilliant man, a deeply original thinker in the field of psychology, in 1970 an active scholar and colleague of one of the authors of this history book you are reading, once said with deep feeling "I hate history." It is true that he said it at a cocktail party, but he surely meant it. Once his listener had overcome the shock of hearing so extravagant a statement from such a source, the remark even became understandable.

Like the duke and Henry Ford, the psychologist was made uncomfortable by history. How many complications we could avoid if we did not know anything about the past: what our forefathers in America and our ancestors in other countries and men and women in civilizations other than our own had done in their lives. If we could ignore everything that had happened yesterday or the day before or last year or ten or a hundred or a thousand years ago, we could face our own problems cleanly, without trying to hark back and solve them by remembering and acting upon some precedent. Or could we? We could avoid the clutter of past thinkers' unreliable, fumbling, inappropriate efforts to work things out, and so avoid a war, clean up a mess, end injustice (if any) by the sheer fresh simple use of our own brilliant intuition. Or could we? If indeed we could, why should we bother about the past? Yet if it were merely boring (as the duke said) or bunk (as Henry Ford said) we really could ignore it, and it would not only not be necessary to study it, or a good idea to reflect upon it: it would be forgotten and better forgotten. Yet it is not forgotten, it is remembered; it somehow will not go away, and people do keep on trying to guide themselves by its lessons.

By introducing a necessary complication into human calculations, the past, or our memory of it, prevents the solution of human problems by simple, straightforward, direct means: it gets in the way of neatness, and somehow fogs things up, irritating our friend the psychologist. Remembrance of the past, of what happened to us the last time we crossed the street against the traffic light, of what happened to our father in the Korean War, or what happened to *his* father in the stock market crash of 1929 cannot help but affect us every day, as we go for a walk, think about Vietnam, or contemplate investing in a speculative stock. Whether we get useful or nonuseful signals from our memories of the past, good or bad advice, is another question. One traffic crossing is not the same as another; two wars are not the same; maybe the fact that grandpa was burned by speculating in 1929 should not stop us from trying the same kind of thing today, because times have changed, haven't they? Or haven't they? That is the thing that continues to puzzle us. And if times have changed, how ought the change to affect our decisions?

When one begins to contemplate this as a problem, one can sympathize with the psychologist, if not share his views. We simply cannot escape the past, at least in the sense of our own immediate memories and the memories of those whom we have known. But of course this is a long way from the study of the past. If we cannot prevent ourselves from acting at least partly in accordance with our knowledge of past experience—our own and that of others—we can at least not bother to find out about more remote things, things that happened in more distant times and places to people we never heard of. We do not *need* to study history. And many today echo in their own way the voices of the duke, of Henry Ford, and of the psychologist. Usually they say that history is not "relevant." Are they right? Is it "relevant?" What good is it?

A team of doctors in the Panama Canal Zone at the beginning of the present century found ways to defeat the deadly disease of yellow fever. Of course they had studied biology, chemistry, and medicine. History would hardly have helped them much, except possibly in giving them knowledge of the failures of previous scientists or of the dreadful toll past yellow fever epidemics had taken. Other scourges like polio have more recently yielded to similar researches. Who can question the "relevance" of studies that lead to results like these? We would cheerfully agree that history is simply not "relevant" in the same way. No matter how hard we study the past history of racial discrimination, for instance, and no matter how much we know about the evils it has wrought, our knowledge will not lead directly to its elimination from the hearts of other men, although indeed such knowledge may help us conquer it in ourselves. So even here, "relevance" by no means disappears.

It is often said, of course—so often that practically everybody who reads this will expect us to be saying it at just this moment—that we can solve the problems of the present—or even the future—by using the lessons of the past. True, a person who has recovered from being run over after crossing the street against a red light will quite probably wait for the light the next time. This past experience has solved a present problem. But as soon as the problem becomes more than an individual one, involving, say, national policy, the statement about the lessons of the past needs to be modified at once. The United States fought in World War I in 1917 and 1918. Should we therefore have been able to avoid fighting in World War II, which in fact we found ourselves doing between 1941 and 1945? The answer can only be that the lessons of history are never so clear. Everything changes, so that the range of problems the second time is very different from the range of problems the first time. It is not like a single person facing the same red light twice. The

intersection has changed, the lights are different colors, and the rules are not the same. In 1941 we faced the Japanese as enemies; they had been on our side in World War I. In 1941 we faced a Germany under Hitler quite different from the Germany of the Kaiser of World War I. Our mere act of participation in the First World War could not teach us how to avoid the Second.

On a more complex level, of course, perhaps we could have learned some lessons that we did not learn. Instead of participating in international organizations to keep the peace after World War I—the League of Nations—the United States stayed out of the League, which never managed to become an effective agency against war. People often say that had the United States joined the League, it would have been able to prevent World War II. But this is far from clear. After World War II, we did join the United Nations, successor to the League. But the United Nations has not proved any more effective with us than the League proved without us: wars continue to be fought, and the United States itself has been involved in two major ones, in Korea and in Vietnam, since World War II ended. While it is true that World War III has so far indeed been avoided, that is probably more due to the general belief that the existence of nuclear weapons means that mankind might well be exterminated in such a war than to any other factor. And that belief is hardly a lesson from history.

If complex problems never present themselves twice in the same or even in recognizably similar form, if—to borrow a frequent image from the military world—our generals always prepare for the last war instead of the next war, then does the study of history in fact offer mankind any help in solving its problems? The answer is, surely, yes: but only in a very limited way. It does offer a rich collection of clinical reports on human behavior in various situations—individual and collective, political, economic, military, social, cultural—that informs us in detail on the way the human race has at times conducted its own affairs, and that surely suggests ways of handling even distantly similar problems in the present. President Truman's secretary of state, the former chief of staff General George Marshall, once remarked that nobody could "think with full wisdom and deep conviction" about the problems of the 1950's who had not reflected upon the fall of Athens in the fifth century B.C. He was thinking of the extraordinary history of the Peloponnesian War between Athens and Sparta written just after the war was over by Thucydides the Athenian, a participant in the struggle. There were no nuclear weapons, no telecommunications, not even any guns and gunpowder, in the fifth century B.C.; the logistics of the war were altogether primitive, yet one of the most distinguished leaders of American military and political affairs twenty-three hundred years later found Thucydides indispensable to his thinking about the problems of the United States.

History, then, can, though only roughly, only approximately, show the range—or the spectrum—of human behavior, with some indication of its extremes and averages. It can, though again by no means perfectly, show how and within what limits human behavior changes. This last is especially important for the social scientist, for the economist, the sociologist, the applied anthropologist. For if these experts studied only the people and institutions existing today, they would have but imperfect notions of the real capacities of human beings. They would be like biologists with no knowledge of the contributions of historical geology and paleontology to their understanding of organic evolution. History, then, provides materials that even the inspiring leader of men into new ways and new worlds—the prophet, the reformer, or the columnist—will do well to master before he tries to lead us into those new ways.

For it can tell us something about what human material can stand and what it cannot stand, just as the many contributory sciences and technologies involved can tell the engineer what stresses his metals can stand. The historian, incidentally, knows that human beings can stand a lot—much more than any metal. History can give an awareness of the depth of time and space that should check the optimism and the overconfidence of the reformer. Millions of man-hours, for example, are wasted in the process of teaching children to read English, with its absurd spelling and its over-refined punctuation. Yet the slightest background of history will show that human societies usually resist changes like the reform of spelling, or accept them only in times of revolution, as when the metric system was introduced during the French Revolution; or under dictatorship, as when the Turkish alphabet was changed from Arabic to Roman by the twentieth-century dictator Atatürk.

You may still wish to reform our spelling, even though you know these historic difficulties; but if you have learned from history, you will never look at the problem of getting English-speaking peoples to change their spelling as if it were a problem like that of designing a superhighway. You will, or should, however, learn through the study of history something about the differences between *designing* such a highway, an engineer's job, and getting the highway built, a much more complicated job for government experts, economists, businessmen, contractors, workers of many kinds of training, politicians local, state, and national, conservationists and other pressure groups, and ultimately a problem for us as taxpayers and voters.

So, if you are willing to accept a "relevance"

more difficult to see at first than the immediate applicability of science, and more remote than direct action, you will have to admit that history is "relevant." It may not actually build the highway or clear the slum, but it can give enormous help to those who wish to do so. And failure to take it into account may bring about failure in the sphere of action. We are not, you notice, making grandiose claims for history. Nor do we think we can convince those among you who already hate it, like the professor of psychology, although maybe we have a chance with those of you who so far agree only with Henry Ford or with Gibbon's duke. There is, however, one undeniable fact that will help us, and we hope will help you: many people actively *enjoy* history.

Whether it is historical gossip they prefer (how many lovers did Catherine the Great of Russia actually take during a given year and how much political influence did their activity in the imperial bedroom in fact give them?), or the details of historical investigation (how does it happen that the actual treasures found in a buried Viking ship correspond to those described in an Anglo-Saxon poetic account of a ship-burial?), or more complex questions of cause and effect (how influential have the writings of revolutionary intellectuals been upon the course of actual revolutions?), or the relationships between politics and economics (how far does the rise and decline of Spanish power in modern times depend upon the supply of gold from the New World colonies?), or cultural problems (why was it classical Greek and Roman art and literature that men revived in the earliest period of modern times, instead of turning to some other culture or to some altogether new experiment?), those who enjoy history will read almost greedily to discover what they want to know. And having discovered it, they may want to know how we know what they have learned, and turn to far more detailed and scholarly accounts than we have been able to provide here, or even to those sources closest in time to the persons and questions concerned, and presumably the best informed. So we know in advance that some of you already like history, for whatever reason, and we know too that others of you will soon be hooked. Unashamedly we admit it: the study of history can be enormous fun. Otherwise why should we have scribbled away and produced another damned thick book?

The historical record is most imperfect, and even the labors of generations of scholars have not filled it out. Notably, historians until quite recently have usually been more interested in the pomp and drama of the lives of the great than in the conditions of life for the masses. Battles and treaties have studded their pages. They have studied with care political and religious behavior, it is true, and within the last few generations they have studied economic behavior. Until recently they have paid less attention to social behavior and to folkways. Since the historians of one generation make the historical record that is handed down to later historians, our record is very faulty and cannot always be improved. No one can ever conduct a sort of retrospective Gallup Poll, for instance, to find out just what millions of fifteenth-century Frenchmen thought about Joan of Arc. Yet our ignorance must not be exaggerated either. As you can learn from any manual of historiography—that is, the history of the writing of history—historians have in the last few hundred years built up a technique and a body of verifiable facts that have made history not an exact science, but a useful body of knowledge.

History is no longer merely "past politics"—and past wars; it is "past everything." Geographically, it is no longer just the history of Europe and North America; it is the history of the whole world.

No sensible person will deny that these newer interpretations have greatly enriched and deepened the study of history. On the other hand, this new history is much more complex, difficult, and unwieldly than was the old. When you add China, India, the Aztecs, and a lot more in space, and add the centuries back to ancestral subhumans in time, and add all the innumerable activities of all men to the dramatic activities of a few in politics and war, you create an unmanageable mass of detail, and the result is sometimes a longer and more arid catalog of details than the lists of kings, queens, presidents, consuls, generals, popes, and cardinals that used to fill the older histories. After all, a list of poets, or even of inventors, is not in itself very illuminating; and even a hasty epithet or two—"ethereal" Shelley, "sweet-voiced" Keats, "ingenious and laborious" Edison—adds very little.

The present book is in part—though only in part—a reaction against the attempt to cover all the past

everywhere on earth. We hope to retain the best of the old and add the best of the new. As for space, we shall concentrate on the history of one part of the world, the Europe sometimes scornfully called a "small peninsula of Asia." We shall trace the expansion of that Europe as Europeans explored, settled, colonized, and traded in all parts of the globe. But we shall be concerned with non-European peoples only as they and their histories impinged on the development of European cultures. We are not motivated by any self-worship, certainly not by any contempt for Asians or Africans, but rather by a desire to get our own record straight. We are not against the study of "world history," but we do hold that it is unwise to begin with world history; we think it wiser to know one's own civilization well before one tries to understand all others. As for time, after a very brief look at the ages-long prehistoric past of Western man and the beginnings of his history in the Near East, we shall be mostly concerned with the last two thousand years or so.

Obviously, this is not all a good American citizen of the second half of the twentieth century needs to know about the past of *Homo sapiens*. But it is an essential part of what he needs to know, probably the part he *most* needs to know if he is to face the problems of human relations on this planet.

In discussing the past of our own civilization, we shall try manfully to see our forebears in their religious and cultural lives, and engaging in all their manifold social and economic activities. But "what really happened" still primarily means to us, as we think it must to all who are writing an introductory work, politics: politics in the sense of past government, past domestic policy, past foreign policy, and therefore—as always—past wars and past peace. So it will be around the political lives, political expediencies, political inventions, and political behavior of men from the first civilizations to the present that we hope to organize this work.

Prehistory to 1300

I

Man's First
Civilizations

I Before Writing

History and Prehistory

Within the lifetime of men now in their forties
and fifties, archaeology, with the new tools supplied by other sciences, has revolutionized what
human beings know about the remoter past of
our earth and the people who live on it. Discoveries continue at a rapid pace. In the 1930's,
'40's, and '50's, no writer could have put on
paper many of the major statements in this chapter. In the 1980's and '90's, perhaps even sooner,
our successors will know enough to dispute or
modify or at least greatly add to what we here
set forth.

It may at first seem strange that our concepts
of the distant past are changing much faster than
our concepts of the periods much closer to us in
time and much better known. But when we
consider the ways in which we know about the

*Above: Portrait head of Queen Nefertiti
(fourteenth century B.C.), wife and sister of
the Egyptian pharaoh Ikhnaton.
Above right: Details of pillars in the temple at Karnak,
Egypt. Right: Ruins of the Palace of Minos
at Knossos, Crete, ca. 1600 B.C.*

6

past we can quickly see that—far from strange—this is entirely natural. If we want to know about something—almost anything—that happened, let us say, during the American Revolution, we have the letters of George Washington and his contemporaries, the written records of the British government that tried to suppress the American colonists' rebellion, the proceedings of the Continental Congress, the Declaration of Independence, and literally thousands of other *written sources*—diaries, memoirs, documents, newspapers, propaganda leaflets—that bring us instantly into the minds of the men of that time and enable us to work out for ourselves what probably happened. And if we cannot go directly to these written sources for history, we have hundreds of books written since the events of the Revolution by the historians who have been interested in it and who have set down their view of what happened, for us to accept or challenge, but at least to consider. New sources may be discovered and fresh light thrown on some event we thought we understood: we may find out that Paul Revere's teacher at school had been reading radical pamphlets (something that previous students had not known) and that this helped prepare Paul as a youth for his famous ride. But the new sources probably would not force us to reject or even to reconsider everything we had learned before they were discovered.

Most of the sources we would read about the American Revolution would be written in English. But if we wanted to find out about the part played by Lafayette and Rochambeau we would soon find ourselves compelled to read documents in French; if we asked ourselves why a Pole, Taddeusz Kościuzsko, joined the American side, we might have to learn Polish—and Russian and German—in order to find out. If we were interested in the ideas of Thomas Jefferson, we would have to study several of his favorite classical authors—who wrote in Greek or Latin—and, though we would find translations available, we might feel it important to read them as Jefferson did, in the original. But whatever the problems of learning languages, or of trying to decide which of two contradictory accounts of the same event to follow, or of interpreting what we might find (this is what George III *said;* but what did he *really* think?), we would always be dealing with abundant written sources in languages that modern men know how to read.

For events 2,000 years or more before the American Revolution, or less well known, or taking place in Europe or Asia, we would still usually have written sources, in Persian or Sanskrit, Greek or Latin or Chinese, sometimes fragmentary instead of full, sometimes so biased as to be unreliable, but written. Where possible we would supplement these with all kinds of other evidence: the coins that rulers struck with pictures or inscriptions on them that might tell us things we could not find out any other way; the statues or paintings or poems or songs of the age that might reflect the attitudes of the artists and their society more surely than a document; in-

Tools of early man: (left) Paleolithic; (right) Neolithic.

deed, anything that we could find from the period and the place to supplement our written sources.

But suppose our written sources were written in a language we could not read? Or suppose we had no written sources at all? As we move backward in time through human history these problems confront us more and more urgently. The discovery of texts written in both a known and a previously unknown language has over the last couple of centuries enabled scholars to read the language of the Egyptians, and those of the peoples of the ancient Mesopotamian river valleys in the Near East, although uncertainties often remain. Brilliant use of the techniques of cryptography in the 1950's cracked one of the two scripts commonly used in ancient Crete and on the Greek mainland. But the earlier Cretan script remains to be deciphered. Nobody has yet cracked Etruscan, the language—written in Greek letters—of the people that ruled in Italy before the Romans.

And of course there were long, long, *long* centuries and millennia before man had learned to write at all. Only his bones and the bones of his animals and some of the things he made remain to tell us about him: they are our only sources. The recent development of the carbon-14 technique, whereby radioactive carbon is used to enable us to date ancient objects within a couple of centuries, has proved to be a great help in straightening out chronology. Nothing seems surer, however, than that scholars will find many more new objects and new ways of dating them and so will enable our successors to write with more certainty than we about our earliest ancestors.

The Old Stone Age

In the seventeenth century, an Anglican archbishop named James Ussher carefully worked out from data given in the Bible the date of the creation of the world by God. It proved to be precisely 4004 B.C.; so if you added the 1,600-odd years since the birth of Christ, you came up with a figure of considerably less than 6,000 years for the age of our earth. We smile now at the generations that accepted Ussher's views—though everybody did so until the nineteenth century—because all of *us* know that the earth is billions of years old; that organic life may go back several billion years; that remains of an animal recognizable as an ancestor of modern man have been recently found in Africa and dated as perhaps two million years old. This creature and his fellows were perhaps the ancestors of both apes and men; he was much older than the remains scientists had previously found and dated. After him, it seems to have taken a mere 1,300,000 years before the first of the true men that scientists have found made his appearance, six or seven hundred thousand years ago. A true man has a larger skull, with more brains in it, than an ape, and a true man *makes tools*.

Yet even though we can identify our remote ancestors so many hundreds of thousands of years before Ussher thought the world was made, we know so little about what was happening during all those hundreds of millennia before Ussher's creation date of 4004 B.C. that for the historian—as distinguished from the anthropologist—almost all of that time belongs to "prehistory." We can be certain that during those long, long centuries the advance of the human animal was enormously slow. The first real tools, found in Kenya and dated by radiocarbon at about 600,000 B.C., were stones used to chip other stones into useful instruments. And it was by stone weapons and tools that early man lived for hundreds of thousands of years: lived in a stone age, as the terms that scholars use to describe his life make abundantly clear.

From roughly the beginning to roughly 8000 B.C.—varying by a few thousand years or so according to the region one is describing—man lived in the Old Stone Age—Paleolithic. By about 8000 B.C. in some places—much later in others—he passed into a New Stone Age, Neolithic, marked by certain great changes that we shall consider in a moment. By about 3000 B.C. we are at the beginning of the Bronze Age, and of even greater transitions to new forms of human life and society. And still later came the Iron Age. Wrong though Archbishop Ussher is about the age of the earth, he is none the less ironically almost right about what a historian can say about the period before 4004 B.C.

Paleolithic man left remains scattered widely in Europe and Asia, and took refuge in Africa from the glaciers that periodically moved south over the northern continents and made life impossible there. Wherever he went, he hunted to eat, and fought and killed his enemies. His skull formation took on different developments in different portions of the world at different times: hence the anthropologist's *Australopithecus* (southern apelike creature), *Pithecanthropus erectus* (the ape-man that stands erect), and many others. Toward the end of the Paleolithic period we find Neanderthal man, named from the valley of the Neander in Germany, who was in fact far less apelike than the frequent modern "restorations" of his features have usually shown him. A recent excavation of a Neanderthal burial has shown that the corpse was buried on a heaping bouquet of flowers, a more delicate attention than one might have expected. Paleolithic man learned how to cook his food, how to take shelter from the cold in caves where there were caves, and eventually how to specialize his tools: he made bone needles with which to sew animal hides into clothes with animal sinews; he made hatchets, spears, arrowheads, awls.

One day in 1940, when two boys in southwest France went hunting rabbits, their pet dog suddenly disappeared down a hole and did not come

Bull from the cave at Lascaux, ca. 12,000 B.C.

back. Following the dog, they literally fell into an underground grotto, hidden for thousands of years. The light of their torches revealed an extraordinary series of paintings on its limestone walls and roofs, of animals portrayed in brilliant colors with astonishing realism and artistry: deer, bison, horses, and others. These were the achievement of Cro-Magnon man, toward the end of the Paleolithic period, perhaps about 12,000 B.C. Lascaux, where they were found, became one of the great tourist centers of Europe. By 1960, despite all the precautions of the authorities, the breath of so many thousands of visitors gazing in awe and wonder began to damage the pictures, which had been sealed away from moisture for so many millennia; so the cave has had to be closed to the public. At Altamira, in northern Spain, similar contemporary cave-pictures, not quite so splendid, had long been known, but had suffered somewhat from early souvenir hunters. Long exposed to air and changing temperatures, they are happily immune to moisture, and now remain the most easily visible monument of the great skills of Paleolithic man.

We can only guess but not know for certain why the Paleolithic artist painted the pictures: did he think that by putting animals—in all their realism—on his walls, he could improve his chances in the hunting field? Would their pictures give him power over them, and so ensure his supply of food? Were the different animals also totems of different families or clans? These are probably good guesses. In the paintings so far discovered, no human beings appear—at least none drawn or painted with the same loving attention to form and detail: an occasional little stick-figure is probably a person. Yet the artists of Altamira or Lascaux could have produced human portraits of surpassing beauty had they thought of it or wished to do so. Perhaps that would have been "bad magic" instead of the "good magic" that came from painting animals. Paleolithic man did occasionally produce small female statuettes: crude, often armless, usually grossly overemphasizing the breasts, buttocks, and sexual organs, found widely scattered (and sardonically called "Venuses" by modern archaeologists). Were these fertility symbols? or love charms? Quite probably.

Sometimes on the walls of the caves we find paintings of human hands, often with a finger or fingers missing. Were these hands simple testimony of appreciation for one of man's most extraordinary physical gifts: the hand with its apposable thumb (not found in apes), which alone made tool-making possible? or were they efforts to ward off evil spirits by upholding the palm or making a ritual gesture? or were they prayers by hunters and warriors that they should not suffer mutilation of their fingers or that they might retain their strength despite some mutilation they had already suffered? Perhaps. We can say for sure only that by the end of the Old Stone Age man was still perhaps a savage, but he was also an artist.

The New Stone Age

When man first built houses, learned how to bake clay pots, and domesticated animals, he was on his way out of the Old Stone Age. Various terms (e.g., Mesolithic) are used for this period of transition from Paleolithic to Neolithic, which lasted longer in some regions than in others. By common consent, however, the transition is over when men settle down to live in their houses and grow their own food; once this is accomplished man has entered the New Stone Age (Neolithic). Three recent excavations, all in the Near East, have pushed back our previous earliest Neolithic dates; and with the boundaries between periods thus in flux and the terms intended only to be useful and not to confuse, it is probably better here not to try to fix any firm boundaries between late Paleolithic and early Neolithic.

At Jericho in Palestine during the 1950's, archaeologists excavated a town of about 7800 B.C. (radiocarbon dating) that extended over about eight acres and included perhaps 3,000 inhabitants. These people lived in round houses with conical roofs—the oldest permanent houses known—and they had a large, columned building in which were found many mud-modeled figurines of animals and modeled statues of a man, woman, and male child; it was almost surely a temple of some kind. All this dates from a time when people did not yet know how to make pots, which appear only at a later stage. Next oldest, and most recent of the new finds, is Çatalhüyük in southern Turkey, discovered only in 1961, and dating to 6500 B.C. The people who lived there had a wide variety of pottery, grew their own grain, kept sheep, and wove their wool into

textiles. A woman sculptured in relief in the posture of giving birth to a child, a bull's head, boars' heads with women's breasts running in rows along the lower jaws, and many small statuettes were all found together in what we can be sure was their shrine. The bull and a double axe painted on a wall seem to look forward to main features of the better-known religion of ancient Crete, as we shall see.

Far to the east, in modern Iraq (ancient Mesopotamia) near the Iranian border, lay Jarmo, to be dated about 4500 B.C., a third Neolithic settlement. A thousand years later than Jarmo, about 3550 B.C., and far to the south, at Uruk on the banks of the Euphrates River, men were using the plow to scratch the soil before sowing their seeds, and were already keeping the accounts of

The Venus of Willendorf, a Neolithic statuette found in Austria.

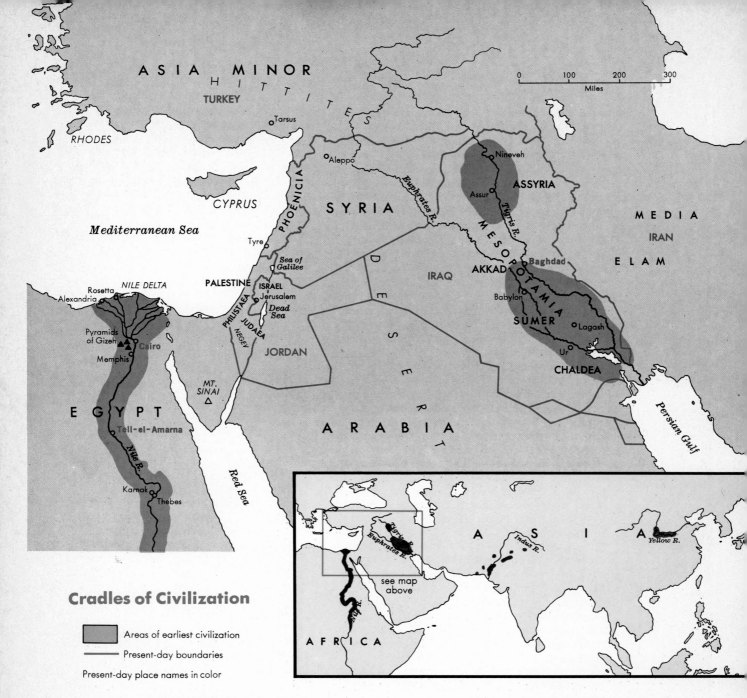

Cradles of Civilization

▨ Areas of earliest civilization

— Present-day boundaries

Present-day place names in color

their temple in simple picture-writing. This was the great leap forward that took man out of pre-history and into history. Similar advances are found in Egypt too, at roughly the same time. But archaeology seems to show that Mesopotamia took the lead, and indeed that it was from Mesopotamia that major cultural contributions—especially the all-important art of writing—penetrated into Egypt and gave the Egyptians a great push into history.

The Neolithic people of Mesopotamia and of Egypt were not necessarily any more intelligent than those elsewhere. Indeed, Neolithic remains have been found also in many places in the Mediterranean region, and even far to the north. But in those places climate was far less favorable, and even when Neolithic man managed to triumph over his environment—as in the lake settlements of Switzerland, where he built frame houses on piles over the water—the triumph came later (in this case about 2500 B.C.). In Australia and New Guinea and in South America there are people today who still live in the Neolithic Age. It was the inhabitants of the more favored regions who got to the great discoveries first. It was they who learned copper-smelting and the other arts of metallurgy, and who thus led the human race out of the Stone Age—after 597,000 years or so—and into the Bronze Age. And it was they who first lived in cities. Writing, metallurgy, and urban life: these are the marks of civilization. Soon after these phenomena appeared in the Tigris-Euphrates valleys and along the Nile, they appeared also in the valley of the Indus, and along certain Chinese rivers. But it is not to India or China but to Mesopotamia and Egypt that we can trace our own civilization, and it is to these that we must now turn.

II   The Valley Peoples

Mesopotamia

SUMERIANS   North of the Persian Gulf, in the fertile lower valleys of the Tigris and Euphrates and in the land between them ("Mesopotamia": the land between the rivers, today southern Iraq), the Sumerians were already well established by the year 3000 B.C., living and writing in cities. We have known about the Sumerians for only a hundred years. Archaeologists working at Nineveh in northern Mesopotamia in 1869 found many Babylonian inscribed clay tablets, which they could read because the inscriptions were written in a known Semitic language (Akkadian). But some of the tablets also had writing in another language that was not Semitic, and was previously unknown. Some of these inscriptions made reference to the "king of Sumer and Akkad," and so a scholar suggested that the new language be called Sumerian. But it was not until the 1890's that archaeologists digging far to the south of Nineveh found many thousands of tablets inscribed in Sumerian only. Since then, excavations have multiplied; the material has poured in; by working from known Akkadian to previously unknown Sumerian, scholars have pretty well learned how to read the language.

We now know that it was the Sumerians who invented writing on clay, using at first a kind of picture-writing, and over the thousand years between 3000 and 2000 B.C. developing a phonetic alphabet. With a reed pen they impressed into the wet clay tablet little wedge-shaped marks, producing a script that we call cuneiform from the Latin *cuneus,* meaning a wedge. The first thousand years of Sumerian history we know from tens of thousands of these tablets that are mostly economic or administrative in their content. It is not until the second thousand years (after 2000 B.C.) that we get purely literary materials, but 5,000 tablets from that period do provide us with them, some short, some very long, many of them not yet transcribed or translated.

In the earliest days, the Sumerians governed themselves through a council of elders, who derived their authority in turn from a general assembly of all the adult free men. This assembly, which decided on such questions as making war and peace, sometimes would grant supreme authority to an individual leader for a limited time. The arrangement—which seems astonishingly "modern" and "democratic" to us—apparently did not last long, and was replaced by one-man rule in each city. But the human ruler acted only as the representative on earth of the god of the city. In this capacity he built temples to the god to keep him appeased, and especially to obtain his divine protection against the floods that often swept torrentially down the river valleys in the springtime with disastrous results for the people in their way. The lives and religion and literature of the peoples of Mesopotamia were pervaded by terror of floods: it is virtually certain that the story of the flood in Genesis echoes the ancient tradition of the Sumerians. The Sumerians devised an elaborate system of canals not only for irrigation but to control the force of the floods, and each city required the blessing of its god on its labors.

Indeed, it took the toil of many centuries for the Sumerians to transform the bleak marshes of the river valleys into fertile and productive farmland, dotted with prosperous cities, each with its own political bureaucracy and its religious institutions; and, as with all human societies, each passing through occasional oppressions, upheavals, and political overturns many of which are recorded by surviving inscriptions. Cities warred with one another, and about 2350 B.C. we find the first inscription recording the ambition of one city ruler to rule the entire region, to be the first universal monarch in history. Moreover, the Sumerians had to fight against infiltrating Semites from the Arabian deserts to the west, and from the hills to the north. In taking the lead against invaders, Gudea, ruler of the city of Lagash, united the Sumerians about 2050 B.C. Soon after he died, Ur replaced Lagash as the capital city, and for a century its rulers played the role of universal monarch. That they called themselves "kings of Sumer and Akkad" shows the fusion between the non-Semitic Sumerians and the Semitic Akkadians from the north that had already begun to take place. Much of what we know about the Sumerians comes from the recent systematic excavation of Ur. About 1950 B.C. the Semitic desert invaders destroyed Ur too, and with it Sumerian power.

In addition to their city-gods, the Sumerians worshiped a god of the heavens, a god of the region between heaven and earth (the air, hence storms and winds), and a god of earth. Another trinity included gods of the sun and moon, and a goddess of the morning star, who was also associated with fertility. With this female deity was associated a young male god who died and was reborn as a symbol of the seasons.

Here, in the first religion recorded in sources that we can read and therefore interpret surely, we find elements common to all subsequent efforts of men to deal with the supernatural. It was Enki, God of Earth, for instance, who poured the water into the two great fertilizing rivers, Tigris and Euphrates, and stocked them with fish; who created grain, filled the land with cattle, built houses and canals, and set sub-gods over each enterprise.

The Sumerian gods were portrayed in human form, and lived recognizably human lives, with rivalries among themselves. Sumerians also believed in a multitude of demons, mostly bad. Because the temples of the city-god and other gods actually owned most of the land, most of the population worked as serfs of the temple. But the produce of the land was distributed as pay to them. Life was highly diversified: blacksmiths, carpenters, and merchants now appear alongside the hunters, farmers, and shepherds of the older days. Fathers exercised many rights over their children. The society was monogamous, and women held a high position. Punish-

ments seem mild relative to those later found in the Babylonian society that grew out of the Sumerian; in Sumer, they consisted mostly of fines.

In many epic poems, the Sumerians celebrated the brave exploits of Gilgamesh, a mighty hero. He undertakes perilous journeys, fights and overcomes dreadful monsters, and performs great feats of strength. But even Gilgamesh, strong though he was, had to die; and a mournful tone, which scholars recognize as typical of the society, pervades Sumerian literature: hymns, lamentations, prayers, fables, and even schoolboy compositions.

Yet a Sumerian proverb sagely says,

Praise a young man, and he will do whatever you want;
Throw a crust to a dog, and he will wag his tail before you.

Obviously these were people who observed each other keenly; they are very recognizably of the same human breed as ourselves. In their literature they often dealt with the seeming injustice of this life, where even righteous men who lead good lives must suffer. We can recognize the type of the future Old Testament Job, and the moral is the same: glorify God, await the end of life, which will set you free from earthly suffering.

Sumerian art was entirely religious, official in intent, and impersonal in style. It changed very little for a millennium and more. The Sumerians built their temples of baked brick. In the shrine was an altar against a wall; other rooms and an outer courtyard were later added. The most striking feature of the temple was that the whole structure was set upon a terrace, a first stage toward the multiplication of terraces, each above and smaller than the last, with the sanctuary at the top, reached by stairs from terrace to terrace. This was the *ziggurat*, the typical Mesopotamian temple, whose construction itself reflects perhaps the rigidly hierarchical Sumerian social order. It was a great ziggurat that suggested the tower of Babel to the author of Genesis. Sumerian tombs were simple chambers, but were often filled with objects intended for use in the afterlife, which Sumerians envisioned as mournful and dreary, to be spent in darkness and dust. Their statuary consisted of clothed human figures, solemn and stiff, with large, staring eyes: gods were shown as larger than kings, and ordinary human beings as smaller. On monumental slabs (steles), on plaques, and especially on seals the Sumerians showed themselves skillful at carving in relief.

AKKADIANS: BABYLONIANS AND ASSYRIANS
Now that scholars have learned so much about the Sumerians, they have realized the enormous debt to Sumer owed by the people who succeeded them as rulers of Mesopotamia: the Semitic Akkadian-speakers, to whom belonged first the Babylonians and then their successors, the Assyrians, both originally descended from the nomads of the Arabian desert. Power first passed to the Semites with Sargon the Great of Babylon (2350 B.C.), and returned to them after an interlude, about 2000 B.C., with the invasions of the Amorites from the west.

Since 1935 excavations at Mari in the middle Euphrates valley have turned up a palace with more than 260 rooms containing many thousands of tablets throwing much new light on the Amorite kingdom. Mari was one of its main centers, and the documents we have, mostly from the period between 1750 and 1700 B.C., consist of the royal archives, and include the official letters to the king from his own local officials scattered through his territories and from other rulers of local city-states and principalities many of which were previously unknown to scholars. Among the correspondents was an

Amorite prince named Hammurabi, who just before 1700 B.C. made his own Babylonian kingdom supreme in Mesopotamia. His descendants were able to maintain their power down to 1530.

Hammurabi's famous code of law, engraved on an eight-foot pillar, though in part modeled on its Sumerian predecessors, exhibits a much harsher spirit in its punishments. Yet, as its author, the king boasted not of his warlike deeds but of the peace and prosperity he had brought. The code reveals a strongly stratified society: a patrician who put out the eye of a patrician would have his own eye put out; but a patrician who put out the eye of a plebeian had only to pay a fine. Yet perhaps it is most important to note that even the plebeian had rights that, to a degree at least, protected him against violence from his betters. Polygamy and divorce have now made their appearance. The code, in fact, is just about what we would expect: it owes its literary form to Sumerian models, and like them describes individual crimes and punishments instead of theorizing about principles, but it reflects the needs of a society with a different social structure.

New nomads, the Kassites from the east (Iran), shattered Babylonian power about 1530; and gradually supremacy in Mesopotamia passed to the far more warlike Semitic Assyrians, whose power had been rising in Nineveh for several centuries. About 1100 their ruler Tiglath-pileser I reached both the Black Sea and the Mediter-

Panel from Nimrud showing Shalmaneser III, king of Assyria, receiving homage from Jehu, king of Israel; 841 B.C.

ranean on a conquering expedition north and west, after which he boasted that he had become "lord of the world." Assyrian militarism was harsh, and the conquerors regularly transported into captivity entire populations of defeated cities. By the eighth century the Assyrian state was a kind of dual monarchy: Tiglath-pileser III, their ruler, also took the title of ruler of Babylonia, thus consciously accepting the Babylonian tradition. During the 670's B.C. the Assyrian king Esarhaddon invaded and conquered Egypt. Then in turn the mighty Assyrian Empire fell to a new power, the Medes (Iranians related to the Persians), who took Nineveh (612 B.C.) with Babylonian help.

For less than a century thereafter (612–538 B.C.) Babylonia experienced a rapid, brilliant revival, during which King Nebuchadnezzar overthrew Jerusalem and took the Hebrews into captivity, and at the end of which the Hebrew prophet Daniel showed King Belshazzar the moving finger on the wall of the banquet-chamber that told him his kingdom was to be given to the Medes and the Persians. Daniel was right, of course, and Cyrus the Great of Persia took Babylon in 538 B.C., ending the history of the Mesopotamian empires after two and a half millennia at least.

In addition to their cuneiform writing, the Babylonians and Assyrians took much of their religion from the Sumerians. The cosmic gods remained the same, but the local gods of course were different, and under Hammurabi one of them, Marduk, was exalted over all other gods and kept that supremacy thereafter. The religious texts left behind outnumber those of the Sumerians and give us a more detailed picture of Babylonian-Assyrian belief: demons became more numerous and more powerful, and a special class of priests was needed to fight them. Magic practices multiplied; soothsayers consulted the livers of animals in order to predict the future. All external happenings—an encounter with an animal, a sprained wrist, the position and color of the stars at a vital moment—had implications for one's own future that must be discovered. Starting with observation of the stars for such magical purposes, the Babylonians developed substantial knowledge of their movements, and the mathematics to go with it. They even managed to predict eclipses. They could add, subtract, multiply, divide, and extract roots. They could solve equations, and measure both plane areas and solid volumes. But their astronomy and their mathematics remained in the service of astrology and divination.

Like the Sumerians, the Babylonians were a worried and a gloomy people, who feared death and regarded the afterlife as grim and dusty, in the bowels of the earth. Even this depressing fate could be attained only if the living took care to bury the dead and to hold them in memory. Otherwise one had only restlessness and perhaps a career as a demon to look forward to. In Babylonian literature, we find Marduk the center of an epic of the creation; we encounter Gilgamesh again, in a more coherent epic than that of the Sumerians, in which he declines a goddess's offer to make him a god because he knows he is sure to die.

Similarly in art the inspiration remains unchanging, but some variations appear: unlike the Sumerians, the Babylonians in some regions had access to stone, and so now incorporated columns in their buildings; and especially the Assyrians showed greater interest, as one would expect, in scenes of combat. In Assyria too one finds the orthostat, a statue inserted into a wall, and so appearing in high relief; typical Assyrian versions appear as bulls, lions, and fantastic winged beasts. Jewels, gold, and ivory-carving now reached new and extraordinarily beautiful heights, as shown especially in the finds at Nimrud.

Egypt

CHARACTER OF THE SOCIETY   What the Tigris and the Euphrates rivers did for the land between them—Mesopotamia—the Nile River, rising in the hills of Ethiopia and flowing a thousand miles north through Egypt into the Mediterranean, did for the strip of land along its banks on both sides, beyond which, east and west, stretched the dry and inhospitable sands of desert. Nobody can be certain how many millennia had passed in which the people along the Nile had slowly learned to take advantage of the annual summer flood by tilling their fields to receive the silt-laden river waters, and by regulating its flow, but about 3000 B.C., approximately the same time when the Sumerian civilization emerged in Mesopotamia, the Egyptians had reached a comparable stage in their devel-

opment. Much better known to us than Mesopotamia—most of us, even as small children,
already knew about the pyramids, the sphinx,
and King Tut's tomb—Egypt was the other ancient valley civilization that made major contributions to our own.

No sweeping generalizations about peoples
and societies are ever wholly acceptable; yet,
speaking roughly, scholars who have studied the
sources for both Egypt and Mesopotamia and
who have compared the two often note that the
Egyptians are generally more cheerful and confident than the gloomy and apprehensive Sumerians, Babylonians, and Assyrians; more tolerant
and urbane and less harsh and obdurate; more
speculative and imaginative and less practical
and literal-minded; and—despite the long cen-

turies of apparent sameness—more dynamic and
less static in their attitudes and achievements.
Life after death the Egyptians regarded as a
happy continuation of life on earth with all its
fleshly pleasures, not as a dismal eternal sojourn
in the dust. When we think of Mesopotamian art
we think of temples made of brick and of public
monuments; when we think of Egyptian art we
think of tombs made of stone and of private
monuments. The Mesopotamians have left few
statues, the Egyptians many. The Mesopotamian
rulers—both the early city-lords and the later
kings who aspired to universal monarchy—were
agents of the gods on earth; the Egyptian rulers
from the beginning were themselves regarded as
gods. So, despite the many similarities between
the two societies, and the mutual influences

The temple at Idfu, third century B.C., best preserved of the Egyptian temples.

which we now know to have passed from each to the other—though chiefly in the direction of Egypt from Mesopotamia—each had its own distinct characteristics.

Because Egyptian territory consisted of the long strip along the banks of the Nile, it always was hard to unify. At the very beginning—3000 B.C.—we can distinguish two rival kingdoms—Lower Egypt: the Nile Delta (so called because it is shaped like the Greek letter of that name)—the wedge-shaped triangle nearest the Mediterranean where the river splits into several streams and flows into the sea; and Upper Egypt: the land along the course of the river for 800 miles between the Delta and the First Cataract. Periodically the two regions were unified in one kingdom, but the ruler, who called himself "king of Upper and Lower Egypt," by his very title recognized that his realms consisted of two somewhat disparate entities, one looking toward the Mediterranean and outward to the other civilizations growing up around its edges, and the other more isolated by its deserts and more self-regarding. The first unifier, perhaps mythical, was a certain Menes, whose reign (about 2850 B.C.) scholars take as the start of the first standard division of Egyptian history, the Old Kingdom (2850–2200).

OLD, MIDDLE, AND NEW KINGDOMS   When the king is god, his subjects need only listen to his commands to feel sure they are doing the divine will. As each Egyptian king died, his great sepulchral monument in the form of a pyramid told his subjects that he had gone to join his predecessors in the community of gods. The largest of the pyramids took several generations to build, and involved the continual labor of thousands of men, a token that the society accepted and took pride in the divinity of its rulers. A highly centralized bureaucracy carried out the commands of the king. A stratified society worked for him. His forces advanced at times westward into the Libyan desert, and at other times—drawn by the pull that we find exerted on every ruler of Egypt from Menes to President Nasser—east and north into Palestine. The Old Kingdom was first disturbed and eventually shattered by a growing tendency among district governors to pass their offices on to their sons, who in turn tended to strike out on their own or at least to regard their territories as hereditary fiefs and thus to weaken the central authority.

At the same time we know the priests of the Sun had also made good their claims to special privileges that helped diminish royal power. After an interim period of disorder lasting perhaps two centuries (2200–2000 B.C.), a new dynasty (eleventh of the thirty in Egyptian history) restored unity in what is known as the Middle Kingdom (2100–1800 B.C.), distinguished for its rulers' land-reclamation policies and its victories abroad.

Growing internal weakness combined with a foreign invasion and conquest put an end to the Middle Kingdom about 1800 B.C. The conquerors were called Hyksos, and were Asian nomads of uncertain origin, who imported the war chariot and perhaps the bow. The Egyptians hated their rule, which lasted something over a century, and eventually rallied behind a new dynasty (the seventeenth) to drive out the invaders. By 1600 B.C. the task was accomplished and the New Kingdom (1600–1100 B.C.) well launched. The five centuries of the New Kingdom saw extraordinary advances: in foreign affairs, the Egyptians engaged in a struggle for Syria and Palestine not only with the great powers of Mesopotamia but with the mountain and desert peoples who lived between the two great valley civilizations. The Egyptian ruler (now called pharaoh) Thutmose I reached the Euphrates on the east, and marched far south into Nubia (what we today call the Sudan). Thutmose III (1501–1447 B.C.) fought seventeen campaigns in the East, and even crossed the Euphrates and beat his Mesopotamian enemies on their own soil. The walls of the great temple of Karnak preserve his own carved account of his military achievements and the enormous tribute paid him by his conquered enemies. It is his obelisk, popularly known as Cleopatra's Needle, that stands in Central Park in New York. The Egyptians established their own network of local governors throughout the conquered territories, but ruled mildly, and did not, as the Assyrians were soon to do, deport whole masses of the population into captivity.

It was the pharaoh Amenhotep IV (1375–1358 B.C.) who caused a major internal upheaval in the successful New Kingdom by challenging the priests of the sun-god Amen, who had become a powerful privileged class. Amenhotep urged the substitution for Amen of the sun-disk, Aten, and, even more dramatic, commanded that Aten alone be worshiped and that all the

The pharaoh Ikhnaton. This statue from Karnak is a remarkable example of seemingly modern distortion in ancient art

multitude of other gods, whom we shall shortly discuss, be abandoned. Amenhotep changed his name to Ikhnaton, "Pleasing to Aten," in honor of his only god. Some have seen in this famous episode a real effort to impose monotheism on Egypt; others doubt that one can be certain. To mark the new policy, Ikhnaton and his beautiful wife Nefertiti, whose statue is widely reproduced, ruled from a new capital in Amarna. Amarna gives its name to the Amarna Age (ca. 1417–ca. 1358 B.C.). Nearby—beginning in the 1880's—were found the famous Tell-el-Amarna letters, a collection of about four hundred tablets including the diplomatic correspondence of Ikhnaton and his father with the rulers of western Asia, in many languages, an invaluable source for scholars.

Ikhnaton's effort to overthrow the entrenched priesthood led to internal dissension and the loss of external strength. His son-in-law, Tutankhamen (1361–1352 B.C.), was eventually sent to rule in Thebes, city of the priests of Amen, with whom he compromised: this was "King Tut," the discovery of whose tomb with all its magnificent contents was the archaeological sensation of the 1920's. With Ikhnaton's death, the

Giant statues of Ramses II at the rock temple formerly at Abu Simbel, now rconstructed atop the escarpment to avoid the waters of the Aswan High Dam.

new religious experiment collapsed, and the pharaohs strove to make up for the interval of weakness by restoring their foreign conquests.

About 1300 B.C. we find Ramses II reaching a treaty with a people from Asia Minor, the Hittites. This treaty, of which we have texts both in Egyptian and Hittite, called for a truce in the struggle for Syria and provided for a dynastic marriage between the pharaoh and a Hittite princess. The interlude was short, however, and soon after 1200 B.C. the New Kingdom in its turn fell to a general invasion of the eastern Mediterranean shores by mixed bands of Sea Peoples, probably including ancestors of the later Greeks and Sicilians, and others.

Now Egypt entered into a period of decline, marked by renewed internal struggles for power between the secular authorities and the priests, and among local and central rulers. Then came the Assyrian conquest of the seventh century, the Persian conquest of 525 B.C., the conquest by Alexander the Great of Macedonia in 331 B.C., and the conquest by Rome in 30 B.C.

RELIGION Religion was the most powerful force animating Egyptian society, and it was so complicated a religion that modern authorities are hard put to describe it. One of the greatest writes that if one asked an ancient Egyptian "whether the sky was supported by posts or held up by a god, the Egyptian would answer: 'Yes, it is supported by posts or held up by a god—or it rests on walls, or it is a cow, or it is a goddess whose arms and feet touch the earth.' " * So the Egyptian was ready to accept multiple and overlapping divinities, and to add new ones whenever it seemed appropriate: if a new area was incorporated into the Egyptian state, its local gods would be added to those already worshiped.

From the beginning, Egyptian cults included animals, totems perhaps: sheep, bulls, gazelles, and cats, still to be found carefully buried in their own cemeteries. As time passed, the figures of Egyptian gods became human, but often retained an animal's head, sometimes an animal's body. Osiris, the Egyptian god best known to most of us, began as a local Nile Delta deity. He taught mankind agriculture; Isis was his wife, and Set (animal-headed) his brother and rival. Set killed Osiris; Isis persuaded the gods to bring

* J. A. Wilson, in *The Intellectual Adventure of Ancient Man*, ed. Henri Frankfort (Chicago, 1946), p. 44.

him back to life, but thereafter he ruled below (obviously a parallel to the fertility and vegetation-cycle beliefs we have already encountered in Mesopotamia and will encounter in Greece). Naturally enough, Osiris was identified with the life-giving, fertilizing Nile, and Isis with the receptive earth of Egypt.

Horus the sun defeated the evil Set after a long struggle. But Horus was only one kind of sun-god: there was also Re, later joined with Amen, and still later Aten, as we saw. The moon-god was the ibis-headed Thoth. In the great temple-cities like Heliopolis, priests worked out and wrote down hierarchies of divinities. Out in the village, all the forces of nature were deified and worshiped: one local god was part crocodile, part hippopotamus, and part lion, a touching and economical revelation of what simple farmers along the riverbanks had to worry about. However numerous the deities, Egyptian religion itself was unified; unlike a Sumerian temple, however, which was the political center of its city, and for which the population toiled, the Egyptian temple had a more limited religious function.

The Egyptians were preoccupied with life after death. They believed that after death each human being would appear before Osiris and recount all the bad things he had *not* done on earth: "I have not done evil to men. I have not ill-treated animals. I have not blasphemed the gods," and so on, a negative confession, to justify his admission into the kingdom of the blessed. Osiris would then have the man's heart weighed, to test the truth of his self-defense; and he would be admitted or else delivered over to judges for punishment.

Egyptians believed not only in body and soul, but in *ka,* the indestructible vital principle of each human being, which left the body at death but could and did return at times. That is why the Egyptians preserved the body in their elaborate art of mummification: so that the *ka* in its return would find it not decomposed; and that is why they filled the tombs of the dead with all the objects that the *ka* might need or find delightful on its returns to the body. Otherwise it might come back and haunt the living.

CIVILIZATION We know Egyptian civilization so intimately because of the great number of inscriptions, that give us the historical materials, and of papyri (fragments of the ancient material the Egyptians wrote on, made of the pith of a water-plant), that give us the literary materials. Yet what we have represents a smaller percentage of what once existed and of what may yet be found than does our collection of Mesopotamian literature on its carefully copied myriads of clay tablets. The Egyptian language first yielded its secrets only in the 1820's, when the French scholar Champollion first saw on a late obelisk that several Greek personal names were repeated in the Egyptian hieroglyphic (literally, "sacred writing"). With these as a start, Champollion turned to a famous trilingual inscription, the Rosetta Stone, found in the Nile Delta in 1799, that bears the same text in Greek, in hieroglyphic, and in another script used in Egypt after hieroglyphics had gone out of fashion. The Rosetta Stone was soon deciphered, and the lessons learned have been applied to all the texts discovered before and since. Visitors to the British Museum can still see the extraordinary slab that made it possible for men of the nineteenth and twentieth centuries A.D. to understand ancient Egypt.

The famous Egyptian *Book of the Dead* brings together stories of the gods and hymns and prayers, and teaches us much of what we know of Egyptian religion. The Egyptian literature we have includes no epic story of a hero comparable to Gilgamesh, a mortal who cannot quite attain immortality, no doubt because the Egyptians confidently did expect to attain it, whether heroic or not. But it does include love-songs, banquet-songs, and what we would call fiction, both historical and fantastic. "If I kiss her," says an Egyptian lover, "and her lips are open, I am happy even without beer," * a sentiment that seems irreproachably up-to-date even at the distance of three millennia. "Enjoy thyself as much as thou canst," says a banquet-song, "For a man cannot take his property with him," † though actually nobody ever tried harder than the Egyptians to do so. The historical romance of Sinuhe tells the story of an Egyptian noble who was forced by intrigue into exile in Asia, was elected chief of a tribe there, won a magnificent single combat against a local champion, and, at the end, full of longing for Egypt, was happily re-

called by the pharaoh and richly dressed, honored, and given a pyramid of his own for his future sepulcher. In another story we hear of the young man who resisted a lady's advances only to find that she was accusing him of having made advances to her: a predicament similar to that of Joseph in Egypt itself as reported by the Old Testament, and to many similar tales in the folklore of other peoples.

We have all seen pictures of Egyptian pyramids and temples, gigantic sculptured pharaohs and divinities, and the rich and ostentatious gold and jewels of a splendid sepulcher like King Tut's. The use of stone in building, the skillful use of great spaces, the skillful portraiture of individuals rather than types, the obelisks and sphinxes, the absence of perspective: these are familiar characteristics of Egyptian art. But less well known are the many scenes of ordinary country or family life that characterize Egyptian painting and that show a characteristic enjoyment and even a sense of humor distinctly not found in Mesopotamia. On the wall of an Egyptian tomb a young man and his wife sit happily

From the tomb of Ramose in Thebes: the brother and sister-in-law of the deceased, ca. 1375 B.C.

* A. Erman, *Literature of the Ancient Egyptians*, trans. A. M. Blackman (London: Dutton, 1927), p. 244.

† J. H. Breasted, *The Dawn of Conscience* (New York, 1933), pp. 163–164.

playing checkers or listening to music or watching the dancing girls. A thief steals a cow while the herdsman's eyes are elsewhere; a crocodile waits for a baby hippopotamus to be born so that at last he may have his lunch. The people who lived along the Nile all those millennia ago speak to us clearly, and we listen with fascination and recognition.

III   Peoples Outside the Valleys

For well over a thousand years after their first flourishing (3000 B.C.), the peoples of the valley civilizations had held the stage virtually alone. But the Hyksos invasion of Egypt (ca. 1800), the Kassite invasion of Mesopotamia, and the Hittite attacks on both have already warned us that the men of the mountains and deserts outside the valleys had begun to compete fiercely with the more settled valley societies. The outsiders too had centuries of history behind them, still not well known to scholars, but by 1500 B.C. the Kassites in southern Mesopotamia, the Hurrians with their state of Mitanni in northern Mesopotamia, and the Hittites in Anatolia (Asian Turkey) had all emerged as rivals both to Babylon and to Egypt.

All of them had strong Indo-European ethnic elements: that is, elements of a strain that will become predominant in Iran, and later in the Mediterranean and the West. All of them were ruled by kings, but their kings were neither the Mesopotamian agents of god on earth nor the Egyptian deified monarchs: rather they ruled as the most powerful among a noble class that controlled the instruments of conquest—horses and chariots—and shared the fruits of conquest, dividing new land among themselves. We begin now to find records, not only of war between these newly emerging peoples and the settled valley societies, but also of their diplomatic exchanges and their peace settlements.

For communication everybody used Akkadian, a Semitic tongue often foreign to both parties in a negotiation. The Egyptians, for example, corresponded in it with the peoples who ruled Syria, who did not speak it either. As with the language and the cuneiform letters in which it was written, so with the culture generally: the outside peoples were deeply influenced by Mesopotamian religion and literature and art. Though the outsiders dealt severe blows to the valley societies and sometimes seemed temporarily to have overthrown them, the valley societies—Mesopotamian and Egypt—did not in fact succumb during the centuries from 1500 to 1200 B.C., when the threat was greatest.

The Hittites

Until the twentieth century A.D., we knew the Hittites only from a few mentions in other sources—Uriah, whom King David so reprehensibly arranged to have killed in battle in order to keep his wife Bathsheba, was a Hittite, for instance. But the discovery of the Hittite capital, Hattushash, now called Bogazköy, in the high plateau of Anatolia revealed not only monumental inscriptions but also several thousand tablets, largely cuneiform in script and written not only in the Indo-European Hittite language but in many others as well. These finds enable us to date at ca. 1700 B.C. the emergence of a strong Hittite kingdom, with its Indo-European ruler and aristocracy in control over the native Anatolian population; to note its great conquests between 1700 and ca. 1590, its resumption of successful expansion toward Babylon about 1530, its internal crises and recovery about 1500 with the first of the hereditary monarchs, and its height under Suppiluliumas (1380-1346), contemporary of Ikhnaton, who took advantage of Egyptian weakness to assert his own strength.

Surely it was no coincidence that Suppiluliumas began after his intimate contact with the Egypt of Ikhnaton to insist that he be addressed as "my Sun" and to use the solar disk as a symbol. Henceforth Hittite sovereigns were deified, but only after death: it is from about this time that the written sources we have begin to speak of a king as "becoming a god" at death. The onslaught of the Sea Peoples that destroyed the Egyptian New Kingdom about 1200 also put an end to the centralized Hittite state, although various smaller "neo-Hittite" petty principalities continued to exist in Asia Minor in the face of Assyrian expansion down to the late eighth century B.C.

To Hittite religion the native Anatolians, the Indo-European Hittite upper crust, the Mesopotamians, and the Egyptians all made contributions: foreign gods were made welcome and domesticated. Once part of Hittite religion, no matter where they had originally come from, they received homage in forms derived from Mesopotamia. But there were differences here to: women played a more prominent role in Hittite religion and society than they did either in Mesopotamia or in Egypt. And alone among the peoples of the ancient Near East, the Hittites cremated their kings.

This has reminded scholars that in Homer's *Iliad* the Trojans cremated their dead prince Hector, and that Troy itself stood on the edge of Anatolia and so would have been close to areas of predominant Hittite influence. When to this is added the fact that Hittite sources apparently refer to the Achaeans (the name that Homer gives his Greeks) and to Troy, many have been tempted to see a close historical connection between the Hittites and the tale told by Homer.

That portion of Hittite literature which is preserved is full of Mesopotamian echoes, but it is distinguished by its sober official histories, which—alone up to that time among the literary works of the ancient Near East—sought to determine and record the motives of the rulers for their actions. The treaty, too, as a special literary and diplomatic instrument, was apparently a Hittite invention. Hittite architecture expressed itself in fortresses on peaks, which became the nuclei of cities. Otherwise, the buildings show Mesopotamian influence, as does the sculpture; but the Hittites produced no monumental human statues.

Hurrians, Canaanites, Philistines, Phoenicians

Far less well known than the Hittites and still posing many unsolved problems are the Hurrians, whose state, called Mitanni, was established about 1500 B.C. in northern Mesopotamia and lasted only about a century and a third. No local archaeological finds comparable to Bogazköy for the Hittites have yet turned up; and what we know about the Hurrians comes from Egyptian, Hittite, Amorite, and western Palestine documents. Like the Hittites, the Hurrians had an Indo-European ruling class, and worshiped some Indo-European deities. Their great importance was to act as intermediaries between the great civilization of Mesopotamia and the less advanced peoples to the north and west, especially the Hittites.

Besides the mountains of Anatolia and northern Mesopotamia, the deserts of Syria (the Old Testament land of Canaan) gave rise to a number of Semitic peoples who from time to time invaded the valley societies. Indeed, the Akkadians themselves, both Babylonians and Assyrians, and the Amorites as well had first emerged into history along this path. But there remained behind, of course, other Semitic peoples who never penetrated into the valleys, and who created societies of their own along the Syrian coast of the Mediterranean and in its hinterland.

At Ugarit on the coast—in the northern portion called Phoenicia—archaeologists in 1929 found the royal palace of a Canaanite state that flourished between 1400 and 1200 B.C., complete with tablets in a northwest Semitic tongue—Ugaritic—containing several poems highly important for our knowledge of the religion and culture of the people, and also the archives of official correspondence, including a treaty with the Hittites, written in Akkadian and showing that the Canaanites were under Hittite domination. Though extremely important because of its far-flung relationships with contemporary states, and as a forerunner of the Phoenicians, Ugarit was only one of many Canaanite city-states, and it went down in the general chaos of 1200 B.C. caused by the Sea Peoples' invasion. Among these invading Sea Peoples, we know, were the Indo-European Philistines, who settled to the south of the Canaanites and gave their name to Palestine.

The Canaanites apparently matched their extreme political localism with extreme religious localism, and they seem often not to have taken much trouble to sort out their gods: several gods presided over any given department of life, and gods were sometimes male and sometimes female, as if nobody was quite sure or cared very much. If this seems primitive, the impression is reinforced by the Canaanite practices of human sacrifice and of religious prostitution. The supreme Canaanite god was El, whose name simply means "god" and who is little known. Baal, on the other hand, whose name means "lord," was a storm-god—like the Sumerian god of the air, the region between heaven and earth. Baal and his wife Astarte, like Osiris and Isis in Egypt and parallel figures in Mesopotamia, symbolized the seasons and cyclical fertility.

In the period after 1300 the Phoenicians, still another Semitic people, flourished along the coast south of Ugarit, and carried on a brisk trade with the western Mediterranean, founding Carthage as a colony about 800 B.C. The Phoenicians (whose very name comes from the word for the Tyrian purple dye made from shellfish found along the coast of their capital, Tyre) thus brought their Semitic tongue (Punic) more than halfway to the Straits of Gilbraltar, through which in fact their ships had often sailed. Many Phoenician names, as we shall see, appear among the names the Greeks gave to their gods; and the Phoenician alphabet, a real advanced alphabet, not, like cuneiform, a collection of signs that stood for whole syllables, and perhaps inspired by Ugaritic, became the immediate ancestor of the Greek alphabet.

Land of Canaan, Baal, Philistines: these names have been familiar to us all since childhood. For we have now come into the place and time of the Old Testament, and are prepared to understand some of the regional and cultural background of the Hebrews, who in turn were to pass on so much to the peoples of Europe and America.

The Hebrews

HISTORY AND THE OLD TESTAMENT With the Hebrews we have reached our first people whose history is recorded in a series of books providing a consecutive story over many centuries. This is of course the Old Testament, which includes much besides the historical accounts in Genesis, Exodus, Joshua, Judges, Samuel, and Kings: genealogy and ritual law (Numbers, Leviticus, and Deuteronomy), tales (Ruth and Job), proverbs (Proverbs, Ecclesiastes), prophetic utterances (Isaiah, Jeremiah, and the rest), and lyric poems (The Psalms, The Song of Solomon). Because for many centuries these books were held by Jew and Christian alike to express the literal and sacred truth, it was not

until relatively recently that scholars began to apply to them the same tests of authenticity that they apply to ordinary works of history. Nineteenth-century scholars found much material in the Old Testament that they took to be legendary and mythical, and they often questioned its historical accuracy. But most such doubts have tended to be dispelled in our own time, as hard archaeological evidence has piled up in support of the general narrative that the Old Testament gives us. It is true that the Old Testament was not written down as the events happened, that many of its earliest portions were compiled long after the event, that the writings were not arranged in their present form until the second century B.C., and that many folklore elements can be easily identified. But the weight of the evidence tends to confirm the biblical story.

Even the biblical account of the mist-shrouded beginnings of the Hebrews now seems authentic: they may well have migrated from Ur "of the Chaldees" sometime after 1950 B.C., when that Sumerian center in southern Mesopotamia was destroyed, northwest to the prosperous center of Haran. Abraham then may well have migrated westward into Canaan, as Genesis says. The accounts in Genesis of the origins of the universe and the racial origins of the Hebrews, and the stories of Eden, the Flood, and the Tower of Babel all fit into the supposition of a northern Mesopotamian—and no other—place of residence for the Hebrews before about 1500 B.C., when the westward migration took place. Probably a racial mixture including some non-Semitic elements (Hurrian?) from the beginning, the Hebrews may well be the same as a people called Khapiru who appear beginning about 1900 B.C. in the cuneiform tablets and in both Hittite and Egyptian sources as raiders, wanderers, and captives. Historians also are convinced that some of the Hebrews at least did live for several centuries in the Nile Delta during the Hyksos period, before Moses (whose name is Egyptian) became their leader and led them about 1300 B.C. to within sight of the Promised Land. Even the miraculous crossing of the Red Sea in Exodus is not incompatible with the shallow waters, the reedy growth, and the winds of the region.

Outsiders battering their way back into Canaan against the entrenched resistance of those who already lived there, the Hebrew confederation of tribes was held together by the new religion that Moses gave them—the Ten Commandments, the Ark of the Covenant, the many observances that God prescribed. Gradually by ruthless conquest they added to their holdings (Joshua took Jericho about 1230 B.C.), and after the period of the Judges—when many minor leaders directed Hebrew affairs, and battles were fought against Canaanites and Philistines—the loose confederation became a monarchy in about 1020 B.C., when the phophet Samuel chose Saul to be the first king. Saul's son-in-law, rival, and successor, David, so well known to us by the virtually contemporary account (1000–960 B.C.)

in the Book of Samuel, united the kingdom and strengthened it. His luxury-loving son Solomon brought the Palestinian kingdom of the Jews to new heights of prosperity, but even then it was small in size and resources compared to Sumer, Babylon, Assyria, or Egypt.

But Solomon (960–922 B.C.) lacked the character of David, and in 933 B.C. the kingdom split in two: the northern kingdom of Israel (933–722 B.C.), stronger but lacking the great center of Jerusalem, and the southern kingdom of Judah (933–586 B.C.), which held Jerusalem but had little real strength. The Assyrians destroyed

Mosaic map of Palestine, the oldest existing map of the country, in Madaba, Jordan.

Israel in 722 B.C., and the Babylonians—then, as we have seen, experiencing a brief revival—destroyed Judah in 586 and took the Jews into captivity. When the Persians under Cyrus the Great in turn conquered Babylonia and freed the Jews to return to Palestine after 538, the Jews no longer had a state, but a religious community only. From then on they were held together by religion alone, and depended politically on one empire or another: in succession, the Persian, the Macedonian, the Roman.

RELIGION   Indeed, had it not been for their extraordinary religion, the Hebrews would seem to us just another people of the ancient Near East, less numerous than most, less talented artistically than any. But of course we would probably not know much about them had it not been for their religion, which gave them and us the books of the Old Testament and an enduring tradition. Many of the most fundamental ideas of Hebrew religion go back to the days when the Hebrews were still nomads, before they had adopted a settled life. Thus God's commandments to Moses on Mount Sinai that "Thou shalt have no other gods before me," "Thou shalt not make unto thee a graven image," and "Thou shalt not take the name of the Lord thy God in vain"—which long preceded the settlement in Palestine—determined three fundamental and permanent aspects of Judaism which were new among Near Eastern religions.

The religion of the Hebrews was monotheistic, recognizing only a single god. Despite the experiment of Ikhnaton in Egypt and a few Babylonian texts that try to associate all divine power with the chief god, Marduk, alone, the Jews were the first to insist that their god was the only god, and a universal god. Second, the Jews were forbidden to represent him in sculpture or painting—which was an enormous contrast with all other religions of the ancient world. More than that: they were forbidden to make *any* images of living beings, flesh, fish, or fowl, no doubt because their leaders feared that if they did make such images, they would end by worshiping them; and so from these earliest days their art was confined to nonrepresentational subjects. When they deviated from this law, as they sometimes did, it was usually because of the influence upon them of neighbors whose traditions did not forbid animal or human representations in art. Third, the religion of the Hebrews

from the beginning would regard the *name* of God—Yahveh or Jehovah, meaning "he causes to be," or "the creator"—as literally not to be spoken, a reverence quite different from any we have found in other ancient Near Eastern religions. From the nomadic period of Hebrew life also come the feast of the Passover, with its offering of a spring lamb and of unleavened bread, celebrating the escape from Egypt; the keeping of the sabbath on the seventh day; the annual day of expiation (Yom Kippur); and other holy days still honored by the Jews in our own times.

The Old Testament swarms with episodes in which the Hebrews proved unable to keep the first commandment, broke away from the worship of the single God, tried to propitiate other gods, and were punished. Yet however often they disobeyed, the first commandment remained the central feature of their religion. With monotheism from the first went morality, as shown in the remaining commandments forbidding murder, adultery, stealing, false witness, and covetousness of one's neighbor's property. Jehovah himself, both merciful and righteous, creator of all things, was human in form, but was not visible to the human eye. Unlike the gods of all the other peoples, he did not lead a human life; he had no family; he dwelt, not in a palace like a human palace only more splendid, but in heaven. When he wished to speak to the leader of his people, he descended onto a mountain top (Mount Sinai) or into a burning bush or into the space left for him by his own direction between the wings of the cherubim to be set atop the sacred box in which the Ten Commandments on their two tablets of stone were to be kept.

This was the Ark of the Covenant, built by artisans to the special orders of God as relayed by Moses. The Covenant was the special pact between God himself and his chosen people, all the tribes of the Hebrews, in tribal confederation, held together by their regard for this most sacred of objects. Kept at first in a very special tent, a portable tabernacle, the ark moved with the Hebrews, first to Shiloh, where the Philistines captured it about 1050 B.C., and then into the temple built for it by Solomon in Jerusalem, a royal chapel, whose decorations included many that violated the commandment about graven images. Solomon's temple was built by a Canaanite architect using Phoenician models, showing the increasing influence of non-Israelite peoples on the cult.

There were prophets (men called by God) among the Jews from the beginning; but they naturally multiplied during the division of the people into the two kingdoms of Israel and Judah. They summoned the people to return to the original purity of the faith and to avoid the paganism that seemed to be threatening if Canaanite influences continued. In ecstasy perhaps brought on by dances, they solemnly warned of fearful punishment to come if the people did not heed them. After the punishment, however, the prophets (notably Isaiah) promised that Israel would rise again, and that a descendant of David would appear as the Messiah to usher in a new golden age. The disaster came, of course, with the Babylonian captivity; and now that the prophecies of evil had been fulfilled, the prophet Ezekiel had a vision of new life being breathed into the dead bones of Israel, and urged the preparation for its restoration. (It was in exile, in the sixth century B.C., that the sacred writings were selected and arranged in a form not unlike the Old Testament we know.) The captivity once over, the priests became the dominant figures in the restored community, with its rebuilt temple but without a state of its own. They strove deliberately to return to what they believed to be the practices of their remote ancestors.

As one would expect, there was much about Hebrew society that recalls what we have already observed about the remaining peoples of the ancient Near East. The father exercised supreme authority within the family; polygamy and divorce were permitted; and, as among the Hittites, a widow married her dead husband's brother. The Hebrews had slaves, but a Hebrew slave could be made to serve no more than six years. A man who had injured his slave was required to set him free. Otherwise the law of an eye for an eye, a tooth for a tooth, held sway. Yet the general prescriptions, such as the Commandments, and even some of the specific regulations—not to wrong strangers, not to exact usurious interest for a loan, to help one's enemies as well as one's friends—strike an ethical note deeper than any that we have found in the earlier Mesopotamian Near East, and presage the Christian principles that would—within another half-millennium—emerge from this Hebrew society.

IV   Crete and Mycenae

Minoans Before Mycenae

Among the notable finds in Ugarit was an ivory relief of a bare-breasted goddess, holding wheat ears in each hand and seated between two goats standing on their hind legs. She is like nothing from Mesopotamia or Egypt, but she greatly resembles the goddesses frequently found on the large Mediterranean island of Crete, on the westernmost fringe of the Near East, where there developed beginning about 2600 B.C. the last of the Bronze Age civilizations we shall consider. Like the others, it had been preceded by untold numbers of centuries of gradual Stone Age advance. Bronze Age Cretan civilization is often called Minoan, after Minos, the legendary founder of the local dynasty, whose monarchs were all called Minos after him.

Sir Arthur Evans, the British archaeologist whose brilliant work on Crete in the first half of our own century enabled modern scholars to appreciate Minoan society at its true worth, divided the culture into three main periods, Early (from ca. 2600 to about 2000 B.C.), Middle (from ca. 2000 to about 1600 B.C.), and Late Minoan (from ca. 1600 to about 1100 B.C.); and each of these three is regularly further subdivided three times to enable easy discussion of the objects found. For all such dating pottery is the key. Different styles found at different levels permit scholars to work out a chronological framework. In Crete such dating is of surpassing importance, partly because we have not yet learned how to read the earliest writing, some of it in hieroglyphics and some of it in a script known as Linear A. The number of Linear A tablets is relatively small compared with the tens of thousands of Mesopotamian writings at our disposal; and no inscription has yet been found written in both Linear A and a known language: Crete has no Rosetta Stone. Since they cannot read the writ-

The Toreador Fresco from Crete, ca. 1500 B.C.

ing, scholars who try to reconstruct Cretan society in its early phases have nothing to go on except the objects uncovered by the archaeologist. Of these the greatest are the palace of Minos at Knossos (modern Heraklion), found and partly reconstructed by Evans, and other palaces and tombs in other parts of the island.

The Cretans were—we think—not Indo-Europeans but descendants of Anatolian immigrants to the island. Pottery and seals found on Crete show that the Cretans were in touch both with Egypt and with Mesopotamia. In fact, this was a busy maritime people, whose ships not only plied the Mediterranean but presumably managed to defend the island against invaders, since none of the palaces was fortified. Expanding at the expense of other islanders, the Cretans had garrisons and even colonies abroad, a small scale empire exacting tribute from other powers.

The Palace of Minos is a Middle Minoan triumph, resting on earlier foundations, characterized by many rooms, a great staircase, strikingly beautiful wall-frescoes (recovered from the ruins in fragments), massive columns, many six-foot-tall stone storage jars for olive oil or wine, and an elaborate plumbing system with pipes, running water, and ventilation. So complex was the palace that Evans himself believed—probably rightly—that he had discovered the very building which had inspired the ancient Greek legend of the Labyrinth, the palace on Crete with a system of rooms and corridors so mazelike that nobody could find his way without a guide or a thread to unwind behind him as he went, so that he might later retrace his steps.

Minoan craftsmen produced delicate pottery hardly thicker than an eggshell, decorated with birds, flowers, and marine animals; ivory or pottery statuettes of the bare-breasted goddess, who sometimes holds a snake in each hand; and many paintings of bulls, some showing young athletes —girls and boys—leaping over a bull's back, in what was clearly something like a ritual game. Athenian legend (no doubt a memory of tribute of grain once sent to Crete) said that long ago the Athenians had been forced to send each year young men and maidens to be sacrificed by the Cretans to their half-man, half-bull monster called the Minotaur (a Minos-bull, supposedly the fruit of a union between the Cretan queen Pasiphaë and a bull). This reminiscence too, and the fact that many pairs of bullhorns have been found in Knossos and elsewhere, illustrate the importance of the animal in the Cretan religion, in which a double axe, found in many sizes, from full-sized models in bronze to tiny miniatures in gold, also played a role. The word *labyrinth* itself means "place of the double axe."

Society at Knossos, at least from the Middle Minoan period on, was elegant. Sophisticated court ladies wearing embroidered dresses and gold or silver necklaces enjoyed dances or strolled about viewing the fountains, the carefully laid-out flower beds, and the rock gardens. But Crete had its troubles too, though conjecture must help us in any effort to say just what they were. Was it natural catastrophes (earthquakes, tidal waves, and fires) that destroyed the palace of Minos a little after 1600 B.C., and again about 1500, and a third time about 1400? Or did invading Hyksos, on their way out of Egypt after their occupation, do the damage of 1600? Did mainland Greeks, crossing from the north, cause the destruction of 1500? Nobody can be quite sure about the earlier destructions, which were repaired; but the last disaster of 1400 may well be attributable to actions of mainland Greeks.

Mycenaeans and Minoans

In Greece too, Bronze Age civilization had taken root. Greece was a largely barren land, mountainous, and divided into small valleys and plains, separated from each other, but none of them far from the sea. From the earliest times the inhabitants took advantage of the rugged coasts and islands, with their many shelters and good harbors, to sail from place to place, seldom if ever losing sight of land, profiting by the exchange of olive oil and wine for grain and metal and slaves. About 2000 B.C. the village Bronze Age culture of the inhabitants—who were not Indo-Europeans but, like the Cretans, presumably a mixture of Stone Age indigenous peoples and Anatolians who had invaded about 3000 B.C. —was interrupted by the invasion from the north of the first true Greeks: Indo-Europeans, who first destroyed and then settled, no doubt intermarrying with the previous inhabitants. This society had one of its chief centers at Mycenae in the Peloponnesus, suitably situated to control land trade and not far from the sea.

The Mycenaeans were led by warrior chieftains, but they also engaged in commerce with Crete. Minoan objects have been found in the famous royal tombs at Mycenae that perhaps span the century from 1600 to 1500 B.C. In fact, so profound was the Minoan influence at work upon the arts of the mainland that scholars speak now of the Minoanization of mainland Greece. The most celebrated objects are the great gold

masks of the warrior princes buried in the tombs and the daggers inlaid with various metals that show hunting scenes of astonishing realism and beauty. When the great German archaeologist Heinrich Schliemann found these in the 1870's he was looking for the tomb of the Homeric hero Agamemnon, and thought that he had found it. But, as we shall see, Agamemnon actually lived about three hundred years later. Egypt and Anatolia too shared in the Mycenaean trade, but the chief influences in mainland Greece were Minoan.

Interchange, we now believe, went both ways. Mycenaean Greeks visited Crete as traders or even as tourists; perhaps they observed the absence of physical fortifications that left Knossos vulnerable. Then (it is conjectured) they moved in and seized power, perhaps about 1480, presumably having first built their own fleet. No longer did they need to send to Knossos whatever tribute is remembered in the Minotaur legend. Indeed, they now controlled the very center of the civilization that had already taught them so much. Certain military innovations now took place in Crete: chariots were introduced and arrows stored for large bodies of troops, but the invaders built no fortifications, presumably because they expected no new invasion. In the palace at Minos the Greeks installed a throne-room of the type they were accustomed to build

The Harvester Vase, ca. 1600 B.C., from the villa of Hagia Triada in southern Crete.

in their own mainland palaces. But, most important, the Minoans showed them how useful it was to keep records; and since Linear A, devised for a non-Indo-European language from Anatolia, would not do, the scribes presumably invented a new script—Linear B—in which to write the language of the conquerors: Greek. On the other hand, Linear B may have been developed gradually out of Linear A.

It is the very existence of this new script, and the conclusive proof worked out only in 1952 by Michael Ventris that in fact it *is* early Greek, that has made possible the foregoing tentative reconstruction of events that are still somewhat uncertain. Of course Evans had found the Linear B tablets in great numbers in his Cretan excavations; but no such tablets were known *from mainland Greece* until 1939, when an American scholar, Carl Blegen, discovered the first of what proved to be a large collection of them in Pylos, where he was excavating a Mycenaean palace, and since then many more have turned up elsewhere in Greece, including some in Mycenae itself. Acting on the assumption that it was probably Greek (since he now knew that Greeks were keeping records in it on the mainland), Ventris used the techniques of cryptography to demonstrate that the signs in the language each represented a syllable (not a single letter), and then cracked the code. The thousands of Linear B tablets have by no means all been read even now, and by no means all readings are certain; but Greek it is. It is too bad in some ways that the tablets are mostly prosaic inventory-lists of materials stored in the palaces or of persons in the royal services.

But the disappearance in Crete of Linear A, and the substitution for it about 1460 B.C. of the new Linear B (Greek), points clearly to a Mycenaean occupation of the island that preceded the last great violent destruction of about 1400 B.C. and lasted almost a century. We cannot be sure to what degree the new Greek rulers of Knossos were independent of direct authority from the mainland: they may have been subordinate Mycenaean princes. The great palace of Knossos and a number of other major Cretan centers were burned down about 1400, apparently after looting. We do not know who did it. Perhaps the Cretans rose against their Greek masters and burned down their own cities; though it has been plausibly suggested that such an act would have invited fierce reprisals and

continued occupation after reconstruction. There was no reconstruction. Instead there was permanent disruption. So perhaps it was the Mycenaeans themselves who—in revenge against Cretan rebelliousness which may have made the island ungovernable—decided to cut their losses and destroy the Cretan centers and sail away. Or perhaps it was a volcanic upheaval of the seabed. The recent rediscovery (1967) and present active excavation of a Minoan city on the volcanic island of Santorin (Thera) to the north of Crete may furnish us with new evidence and enable us to decide the question one way or another. We do know that after the disaster of 1400 B.C. Crete lost its Mediterranean importance, which passed definitely to the aggressive mainland peoples.

Mycenae, 1400-1100 B.C.

We still know relatively little about Mycenaean politics and society. We can tell from excavated gold treasures that Mycenae itself was wealthy, which is not surprising, considering that it had conquered Crete. But the Myce-

Gold votive ax found in a cave near Knossos.

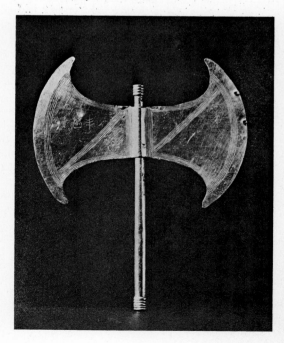

naeans seem not to have been overseas empire-builders even in the sense that the Cretans had been; their occupation of Crete may well have been undertaken by an invading captain who retained power for himself in Crete, however much of its revenue he sent back home. The Achaeans (Greeks) of whom the Hittite sources speak may well not have been the Greeks of Mycenae at all but Greeks of Rhodes, another island principality. And there were other settlements in the Peloponnesus itself—Pylos, Tiryns (the latter very close to Mycenae)—which seem to have been extensive too, and, perhaps, under local rulers equally powerful but bound in alliance to the Mycenaeans: a kind of loose confederacy among equals seems to fit best with the evidence. Each of the cities was walled. The walls of Mycenae survive, with their famous Lion Gate showing the two great sculptured beasts who lean forward to face each other, separated by a slender column, over the huge lintel above the gateway.

Tombs from the period before 1400 B.C. are of two sharply distinct types: those carefully built to take the bodies of kings and important noblemen, and simple burial places for the rest of the population. Tombs from the period between 1400 and 1200 show a rise in the general wealth: more chamber-tombs have been found with more gifts to the dead. At Mycenae itself, and at Tiryns, Pylos, Athens, and Thebes there arose now great palaces as community centers, with workshops, storage areas, guardrooms, and lesser dwelling-houses attached. Others certainly existed, and more will be found. Good roads with bridges and culverts connected the main towns, and good water-supply systems characterized them. Artisans attached to the palace built and repaired chariots, made jars to hold the wine and oil, tanned leather, wrought bronze in the forge, made bricks, and sewed garments; workmen stored goods for preservation and for sale and exchange. A Mycenaean palace was a businesslike (and noisy) place. The Linear B tablets preserve records of special royal furniture most elaborately inlaid in ivory, glass, and gold: like the Egyptian pharaohs, the Mycenaean rulers obviously valued things most when they took a lot of time and effort to make. Smaller than the great palaces on Crete, those of the Mycenaeans on the mainland nonetheless testify to the vibrant life of an advanced society. One of the richest hoards, containing treasures in gold

and jewels and bronze made over a period of five centuries, was found in a private house in Tiryns: it was obviously the stolen booty of a Mycenaean grave-robber, with a fine taste in antiques, who like all men before and since could not take his possessions with him.

Mycenaean religion remains a puzzle. Unlike Crete, where shrines and evidence of worship are everywhere, the Greek mainland furnishes no separate shrines at all, although there are some fragments of an altar in the great room or the courtyard of the palaces, and some portable altars have also been found. The reason is that the Greeks, unlike the Cretans, made burnt and blood offerings to their gods. Gems found in the Mycenaean royal tombs clearly show Cretan deities and religious scenes; so the Cretan goddess was also revered on the mainland. The Linear B tablets from Pylos kept records of offerings made to certain gods—Poseidon, the god of the sea, Ares, the god of war, Artemis, the moon-goddess, and even Zeus and Hera, to later Greeks the ruler of the gods and his consort. But there are other gods who did not survive the Dark Age and who never reappear in classical Greece.

The most famous Mycenaean exploit of the three centuries 1400–1100 was of course the Trojan War, now dated about 1240 B.C., known to every Greek of the classical period from the poems of Homer written down four to five centuries after the event, and known in some measure to all civilized westerners ever since. This was a great expedition led by the king of Mycenae, Agamemnon, in command of a fleet and an army contributed by the other towns and islands of Mycenaean Greece, against Troy, a rich city on the northwest coast of Asia Minor (Anatolia) not far from the mouth of the Dardanelles, the straits that lead from the Aegean into the Sea of Marmora. The Trojans were Indo-Europeans like the Greeks but not so advanced: they did not write or paint their own pottery; they seem to have had few contacts with their neighbors in the Aegean, the Cretans, or their neighbors in Anatolia, the Hittites. They had a powerfully fortified city, and they traded with mainland Greece (many Mycenaean objects have been found in the ruins of Troy), though what they gave in exchange is not certain: perhaps horses, grain, purple dye, silver, and textiles.

Scholars now dismiss as romance the famous

tale of the rape by the Trojan prince Paris of Helen, wife of Menelaus, Mycenaean prince of Sparta, and the war of revenge that followed; and we must believe instead that the Mycenaean expedition was undertaken for plunder of the Trojan citadel. Romantic too—or at least unproven—are the traditions that the siege lasted ten years and that great numbers of ships and men were involved. Agamemnon's force won, and burned Troy. Excavation carried on first by Schliemann and later by other scholars shows that the Troy destroyed by Agamemnon's famous expedition was probably a patched-up reconstruction of a richer Troy that may well have suffered destruction in an earlier Greek attack about 1300.

Soon after the siege of Troy there began the upheaval in the Mediterranean world to which we have already several times referred, the great raiding expeditions of the Sea Peoples that eventually—among other things—shattered the Egyptian New Kingdom and the Hittite state and left the Philistines washed up on the shores of Palestine. Egyptian and Hittite sources show that there were perhaps Greeks among the Sea Peoples, but we cannot tell where these "Achaeans" (or "Argives") and "Danaans" came from. In this period of raiding and migration the general violence did not spare Mycenaean Greece, which began about 1200 to suffer a great wave of destruction.

The great palaces were burned, some perhaps

The Lion Gate at Mycenae.

by fellow Mycenaean Greeks, others perhaps by fragments of other Sea People little better than pirates who landed and conducted hit-and-run raids, and still others perhaps by a new wave of Greek invaders from the north, adding to the general confusion now by entering the Mycenaean society as conquerors. These last were the Dorians, whom scholars can later identify by their special dialect of Greek in inscriptions but who at the beginning were illiterate. It took them a century to obtain mastery in Greece. To them scholars used to attribute most of the destruction that ushered in the Dark Age that began about 1100, but probably much of the destruction preceded their invasion and made it easier.

The Dark Age; Homer

With the destruction of the Mycenaean cities there set in at least three centuries that are called the Dark Age: dark in that we have little conclusive evidence from them to give us a picture of the life, and dark also in that the interlude surely marked a great series of steps backward in Greek civilization. Literacy vanished, for example. It is sometimes argued that Linear B was too clumsy a script ever to have been useful for anything much beyond keeping business records and that in any case only a very small proportion of Mycenaean Greeks (perhaps five percent) could ever have been able to read and write in it; so that its disappearance now was a positive benefit, for when literacy returned it would be in the new Greek alphabet taken from the Phoenicians. Even this argument would, however, concede the end of progress and the reversion to more primitive conditions, characteristic of the Dorian domination. The political units of the Mycenaean world, already small, gave way to still smaller communities.

There were, we know, migrations of Greeks from Greece itself to the Aegean coasts of Asia Minor: to the central region (later called Ionia) that emerges into daylight again about 800 B.C.; and other Greeks, speaking other dialects into the regions to the north (Aeolic) and south (Doric) of Ionia. In the hinterland behind these regions lived the Anatolian peoples in their own kingdoms: Lydia, Caria, Phrygia. Other Greeks on the mainland were lucky enough to miss the

full impact of the Dorian invasion, notably the Athenians, whose later leadership of Greece, once the Dark Age cleared, may perhaps be attributable to a head start gained in this way.

The end of the Dark Age is closely tied in with the writing down of the Homeric poems, the *Iliad* and the *Odyssey*. Did the same person commit both to writing? Was it Homer? Did the *Iliad* precede the *Odyssey*? No certain answer can be given to these questions, but it seems highly likely that at some time between 850 and 750 B.C. (some say even later) both were recorded permanently, and we may as well call the man who did it Homer. Together the two great epics represent only a fraction of the epic material that existed in the Dark Age; there were many other tales of the great deeds of heroes. Minstrels who accompanied themselves on stringed instruments sang the separate songs to audiences around the banquet tables in a princely palace, or to a gathering of villagers in a public square, or to soldiers around a campfire. The songs that together make up the much longer epics that have come down to us were no doubt among the most popular, and the minstrel who put them down was selecting from his repertory the stories that had best stood the test of performance.

The *Iliad* tells the story of a single incident that took place during the siege of Troy: the wrath of the Greek hero Achilles, who stopped fighting and sulked in his tent because the commander Agamemnon had taken from him a Trojan girl captive. Agamemnon had allowed himself to be persuaded to restore to her family his own captive girl, and so made up for his loss by taking Achilles' prize away. While Achilles refused to fight, the great combat continued, and eventually, when Hector the Trojan prince had killed Achilles' best friend and comrade-in-arms, Patroclus, Achilles returned to the battle and in turn slew Hector, whose body at the very end he returned to Hector's sorrowing father, old King Priam. The *Odyssey* tells of the ten-year wanderings of another Greek hero, Odysseus, after the siege of Troy was over; of the extraordinary places and peoples he visited on his way back to his home on the island of Ithaca, where his faithful wife Penelope awaited him despite the attention of many suitors, and whence their son Telemachus had set out in order to find his father.

Put in this summary form, the two stories

perhaps seem blunt and commonplace. But a deep humanity pervades both. Despite the continual bloody fighting in the *Iliad*, the modern reader—like all before him—is moved by the terror of Hector's baby son, Astyanax, when he sees his father with his fierce plumed war-helmet on, until Hector takes it off and shows the child who it really is; feels the truth of the passage when the old men of Troy admit that Helen—beautiful as a goddess—was well worth all the fuss; shares the grief and dignity of Priam as he begs Achilles to return Hector's body for decent burial; and appreciates Achilles' courteous generosity to an enemy when he reluctantly agrees. The romantic *Odyssey*, with its lotus-eaters, sirens, men turned to swine by enchantment, and fierce one-eyed giant, provides similar moments of high human drama in the actual homecoming of Odysseus in disguise, and the responses of his favorite dog and his old nurse, or in the sorrow of the beautiful island princess Nausicaa, first seen playing ball on the beach

The gold Mycenaean death mask known as the Mask of Agamemnon.

with her maidens, when she finds that Odysseus will not stay and be her lover.

In both poems, the gods—now the standard collection of Greek divinities: Zeus, Hera, Apollo, Artemis, Aphrodite, and the rest—play an intimate part in the affairs of the mortals, intervening in the fighting to give victory to their favorites, supplying Achilles with an extraordinary shield on which are displayed many scenes in cunning metalwork, saving Odysseus from the perils of his voyage. The gods and goddesses on Olympus are only a little more outsize than the heroes; they live thoroughly human lives, quarreling over the affairs of the mortals and giving way to fits of bad temper. The epics take the reader into the world of a heroic age, like the later and lesser epics that reflected other heroic ages: such as *Beowulf* or *The Song of Roland.*

We hear at every turn and in great detail about the armor, ships, houses, domestic arrangements, and social behavior of the personages. It has always been a great temptation for scholars to reconstruct Mycenaean society from Homer. But Homer was writing five hundred years after the Trojan War. How far back did even a powerful oral tradition reach? In describing Odysseus' bed was he describing a real Bronze Age Mycenaean bed or the kind of bed that a prince would have slept in in his own day or a little before? Sometimes archaeology helps us here; more often it either does not help or adds to the confusion, as when the word that Homer uses for Nestor's drinking cup (*depas*) is found scratched on a Mycenaean storage jar far too big for anyone to drink from. Was Homer sometimes consciously trying to show his readers a world five hundred years earlier than theirs, and

if so to what extent and in what passages? How safe are we in using him as a historical source?

To these largely unanswerable questions scholars give varying answers; but most in recent years have preferred to use Homer sparingly if at all. Yet there is the long interpolated catalog of the ships in the *Iliad* that lists the contingents supplied to the Greek armies by the various Greek settlements and names their commanders. Many authorities think it is a genuine Bronze Age document that provides hard, usable evidence with regard to the diverse political organization of Mycenaean society: partly by city, partly by the captain the people follow, partly by tribe. So too the description of Odysseus' household as including more than fifty slaves is taken as an indication of the prevalence of slavery in Mycenaean times, and conclusions are reached from episodes in Homer with regard to the inheritance of royal power and the existence of assemblies of elders. Other scholars would reject such conclusions as dangerous. But whether we use Homer as history or not, the Greeks themselves from his time on certainly did so, and formed their own conception of their ancestral past from the *Iliad* and the *Odyssey*. Together with the Old Testament, some of which was being committed to writing at about the same time, these two poems form the greatest literary and cultural and spiritual legacy of ancient man.

Indeed, certain modern scholars would maintain that both Homeric and Hebrew civilization grew directly from a common eastern Mediterranean background, and they point to many parallels in action and attitude. In many respects archaeological evidence serves to suggest that this viewpoint probably deserves a wider acceptance than it has yet won.

Reading Suggestions on Man's First Civilizations

PREHISTORY   W. F. Albright, *From the Stone Age to Christianity*, 2nd ed. (*Anchor). A superb up-to-date survey of a field in which modern scholarship has made remarkable advances.

G. Gamow, *Biography of the Earth* (*Mentor). A very good introduction to the earth sciences, and an indispensable background for human history.

J. Pfeiffer, *From Galaxies to Man: A Story of the Beginnings of Things* (Macmillan, 1959). A good popular account of the most recent evolutionary concepts.

L. B. S. Leakey, *Adam's Ancestors: The Evolution of Man and His Culture* (Harper, 1960; *Torchbooks).

A. L. Kroeber, *Anthropology* (Harcourt, 1948). A masterly review of the subject in its general ramifications, with much material that is really philosophy of history.

C. Ceram, *Gods, Graves, and Scholars* (Knopf, 1951). A bestseller, deservingly so, for it makes clear to the reader what archaeology is all about.

H. L. Shapiro, ed., *Man, Culture, and Society* (Oxford Univ. Press, 1956). A good collaboration; a scholarly work, advanced but not difficult.

V. Gordon Childe, *What Happened in History* (*Penguin). Prehistory and ancient history down to the Greeks. A rapid but suggestive survey by an ethnologist and archaeologist, "rationalist" in point of view.

Jacquetta Hawkes and Sir Leonard Wooley, *History of Mankind,* Vol. I (Harper, 1963). The first volume of UNESCO's collaborative work. The first part, by Miss Hawkes, has been much praised.

L. Pareti, *The Ancient World* (Harper, 1965). The second volume of the UNESCO series. Critics find this book, the result of many collaborators, generally unsatisfactory. Apparently there can be an excess of collaboration, at least in writing history.

Ralph Linton, *The Tree of Culture* (Knopf, 1955; *Vintage). An admirable recent survey of cultural anthropology.

R. Coulborn, *The Origin of Civilized Societies* (Princeton Univ. Press, 1959). A scholarly, readable, and stimulating study.

P. L. Ralph, *The Story of Our Civilization: Ten Thousand Years of Western Man* (*Everyman). A thoughtful survey in 300 pages.

NEAR EASTERN HISTORY: GENERAL ACCOUNTS

H. B. Parkes, *Gods and Men: The Origins of Western Men* (Knopf, 1959). A perceptive survey, "rationalist" at bottom, but respectful, even warm, toward the early religions of the West. Fine brief reading lists.

S. Moscati, *The Face of the Ancient Orient: A Panorama of Near Eastern Civilization in Pre-Classical Times* (Quadrangle Books, 1960). A good introductory survey.

G. Bibby, *Four Thousand Years Ago* (Knopf, 1962). A most readable account of the crucial second millennium B.C. (2000–1000 B.C.).

H. Frankfort, *The Birth of Civilization in the Near East* (Indiana Univ. Press, 1951; *Anchor). A brief and stimulating essay by an expert in the field.

H. Frankfort and others, *Before Philosophy* (*Penguin). Admirable essays in the intellectual history of the ancient Near East.

Christopher Dawson, *The Age of the Gods* (Sheed and Ward, 1934). An admirable introduction to these earliest Western civilizations.

V. M. Scramuzza and P. L. MacKendrick, *The Ancient World* (Holt, 1958). A good, up-to-date, standard textbook.

NEAR EASTERN HISTORY: ACCOUNTS BY AREA AND PEOPLE

Egypt: The distinguished Egyptologist J. H. Breasted wrote several books on aspects of ancient Egyptian history. One of his last works was *The Dawn of Conscience* (Scribner's, 1933); a study of Egyptian religious and ethical beliefs.

J. A. Wilson, *The Burden of Egypt* (Univ. of Chicago Press, 1951). The best single-volume study of Egyptian culture.

H. Kees, *Ancient Egypt: A Cultural Topography* (Univ. of Chicago Press, 1961). Very detailed and not very readable, but full of concrete details and illustrations.

A. Mekhitarian, *Egyptian Painting* (Skira, 1954). Expensively and superbly illustrated.

Mesopotamia: S. N. Kramer, *History Begins at Sumer* (*Anchor). Incorporates the latest research in this rapidly growing field; see also Kramer's more scholarly *The Sumerians* (Univ. of Chicago Press, 1963).

J. Laessoe, *People of Ancient Assyria* (Barnes and Noble, 1963). Attempts to show the Assyrians as more than mere militarists.

C. W. Ceram, *The Secret of the Hittites*, trans. R. C. Winston (Knopf, 1956). A most readable popular account of this people as resurrected by modern archaeology.

R. N. Frye, *The Heritage of Persia* (World, 1963). Authoritative general survey by a specialist.

The Jews: The best introduction of all, of course, is the Old Testament itself, the national epic of the early Jews. Other helpful accounts are:

H. M. Orlinsky, *Ancient Israel* (Cornell Univ. Press, 1954). A good introductory manual.

L. Finkelstein, ed., *The Jews: Their History, Culture, and Religion,* 3rd ed., 2 vols. (Harper, 1960). Comprehensive; popular in the best sense.

M. L. Margolis and H. Marx, *A History of the Jewish People* (*Meridian). The 1960 edition of the well-known general history.

Cyrus H. Gordon, *Introduction to Old Testament Times* (Ventnor, 1953). See note on Gordon's writings under next heading.

CRETE AND EARLY GREECE

L. R. Palmer, *Mycenaeans and Minoans* (Knopf, 1962). Controversial reassessment in the light of the Linear B tablets. J. Chadwick, *The Decipherment of Linear B* (*Vintage). By Ventris' collaborator.

C. W. Blegen, *Troy and the Trojans* (Praeger, 1963), and Lord William Taylor, *Mycenaeans* (Praeger, 1964). Clear scholarly introductions.

Emily Vermeule, *Greece in the Bronze Age* (Univ. of Chicago Press, 1964). Thorough survey of Mycenaean Greece.

Cyrus H. Gordon, *Before the Bible* (Collins, 1962) and *Ugarit and Minoan Crete* (Norton, 1966). Two books that draw highly daring parallels between ancient Near Eastern and Homeric Civilization.

2

The Greeks

I   The Greeks
Before the Persian Wars

In the first chapter, seeking to chronicle and understand man's experience from about 3000 B.C. to about 850 B.C.—or in some instances a few centuries later—we have concentrated primarily on the ancient Near East: Mesopotamia, Egypt, the peoples outside the valleys, and the Hebrews; and we have examined as well the Minoan–Mycenaean civilization that grew up on Crete and on the mainland of Greece, peripheral to the Near East but closely connected with it. Sometime about 850, though one would not wish to insist too firmly on any precise date, the focus for chroniclers and interpreters like us shifts away from the Near East to a people that has hitherto been peripheral: the Greeks. Of course, the Near East after 850 continues to engage our attention: indeed we have already noted the military adventures of the Assyrians in the eighth and seventh centuries and the Babylonian cap-

Above: Geometric vase with prothesis (lying-in-state of the dead), eighth century B.C.
Above right: Three goddesses, from the east pediment of the Parthenon (ca. 437–431 B.C.), now in the British Museum. Right: The Propylaea (entrance gate) and the Temple of Athena Nike on the Acropolis, Athens (437–424 B.C.).

tivity of the Hebrews and their release from it by the Persians in the sixth. The Persians we shall soon encounter again. But for fresh ideas, for new contributions to our own heritage, for new attitudes toward the outside world and toward man himself it is the Greeks who move to the center of the stage between the ninth and the third centuries B.C.

What the Greeks Were Like

The Greeks were different from the other peoples we have come to know. For one thing, they were more curious: it is still proverbial that a Greek always wants to know some new thing, and that he will ask questions tirelessly of anybody who knows something he does not yet know himself. Where does the stranger come from? how big is his family? how much money does he have? what does it cost to live in his country? The questions may range from such relatively superficial personal matters—the answers to which will only temporarily assuage the questioner's itch for all knowledge—to the most fundamental problems, abstract or practical: how do we really know what we *think* we know? what is the universe made of? what causes men to suffer fevers? what are the various possible ways for men to live together and govern themselves? and the myriad other questions to which there may be no real answers but only a multitude of approximations, any one of which will please some Greeks and none of which will please them all; so the argument can continue and the fun rage unchecked.

Then too, the Greeks were less otherworldly than the other peoples. The Mesopotamians and Egyptians—though with differing attitudes—both concentrated their attention upon the life to come; the Greeks were far more interested in life on earth. They did not deny that death was inevitable, and they suffered the fears and anxieties common to the human lot; but they had no feeling of hopelessness with regard to earthly life, and found it delightful to engage in tackling its manifold problems. The Hebrews submitted to the will of an all-powerful single god, who directed not only the footsteps of the entire people but the lives of each of its individual members; the Greeks had no such divinity and no such law, and so man himself, human reason,

and human answers to human problems took a central place in their hearts and minds. Gods of course they had, and proper service to the gods they felt it seemly to render; indeed they would often, even usually, attribute human action to the influence of a god; but one gets the feeling that for them this was often only a manner of speaking. They say "Ares strengthened the hero's arm for the deadly spear-thrust" when they seem to mean little more than "the hero summoned up all the resources of his muscular right arm, and let the enemy have it with a spear."

We often hear that the Greeks invented democracy: literally, government by the people. Indeed they did, but they also invented oligarchy: government by the few; and aristocracy: the rule of the best, or noblest or richest; and they also produced many refinements on rule by one man, which they called a tyranny even when it was mild and just and popular. Moreover, although they invented democracy, they had terrible difficulties in making it work. Fierce political infighting between rival groups and rival politicians usually characterized their political life. Rather than absorb a political loss at home, a Greek politician would often intrigue with a foreign enemy.

Modern students have often taken their picture of Greek politics in general from the superb speech that Pericles, the most celebrated of the leaders of Athens, made in 430 B.C. over the Athenian soldiers killed in the first year of a great war against Sparta, as reported in the history of the war by the historian Thucydides. Praising Athenian democracy, Pericles said that at Athens the law guaranteed equal justice to all, that talent and not wealth was the Athenian qualification for public service, that Athenians expected of everybody a lively interest and participation in public affairs. In fact, his picture corresponded more to an ideal world than to the real Athenian world, where the courts were often markedly prejudiced, where wealth remained an important qualification for office, and where individual political ambition burned as hotly and was often pursued as ruthlessly and unscrupulously as anywhere on earth. In the tough world of Athenian politics one can without much effort see strong parallels to human behavior in other more modern democracies. The Greeks invented democracy but seldom practiced it; when they did, it usually fell far short of their own ideals as expressed by Pericles.

We know their politics in great detail—more fully than those of any people we have yet considered.

Then too, the Greeks had far more humor than any of the other peoples, who, as we have seen—except for an occasional bit of playfulness the Egyptians reveal in their art—were by and large a solemn lot. The Greeks enjoyed laughter, whether playful and gentle or raucous and cruel. Moderns who enjoy the American musical comedy *Of Thee I Sing*, which satirizes our powerless vice-presidency and our tendency to be sentimental over politics, or who admire the Gilbert and Sullivan operettas that poke fun at the civilian head of Queen Victoria's Nav-vee or lampoon the aesthetic movement of which Oscar Wilde was the symbol, will find comparable topical satire in a light and witty mood in the comedies of Aristophanes. But Aristophanes is also capable of violence and vulgarity. Touches of Charlie Chaplin and of the Marx

Detail of a bronze statue of a charioteer, from the shrine of Apollo at Delphi, ca. 470 B.C.

Brothers make him instantly understandable and delightful. Brilliant, funny, energetic, inventive, opinionated, arrogant, and immensely quarrelsome, the Greeks are the first people of the ancient world whom we can feel we actually know.

Revival After the Dark Age

For the Greeks the Dark Age began to dissipate about 850 B.C., with the renewal of contact between the mainland and the Near East: Phoenicia, whose trade continued brisk, lay close to the Greek island of Cyprus, where Mycenaean culture had continued after the Dorians had ruined it on the mainland. Objects from Phoenicia now appear in mainland Greece; and the earliest traces of the Phoenician alphabet as adapted to the writing of Greek are now dated about 825 B.C. New letters were added for peculiarly Greek sounds. The general disorders of the Dark Age were coming to an end, and orderly life began to resume. New styles of pottery also testify to the renewal of communications. Greece proper now received the Homeric poems, first written down in the Ionian Greek settlements of Asia Minor, and bringing back to the mainland the sense of its glorious and heroic past.

In Greece itself, the poet Hesiod, writing in the language of Homer and in the same meter, in his *Works and Days* (ca. 800 B.C.) set down the proper rules of life for the small farmer, and admonished his own brother, who had tried to take more than his fair share of the family estate. Hesiod also wrote a genealogy of the gods (*Theogony*), giving the traditional view of the way the universe had come into being: the gods were the children of earth and heaven, and had themselves created mankind. Preaching justice, human and divine, Hesiod's verse reflected the religious ideas of the Greeks in an early phase, perhaps partly under the influence of the oracle at Delphi, a mountain shrine of the sun-god Apollo in central Greece where a divinely inspired prophetess gave advice to all comers. The invading Dorians had become particular sponsors of the shrine at Delphi. To this earliest period of the revival also belongs the foundation of a famous Greek institution, the Olympic games, held every four years beginning with 776

B.C. at Olympia, shrine of Zeus in the western Peloponnesus. The records of the Olympic victors were preserved in the temple, and together with lists of kings and magistrates formed a source for the first Greek historians.

The Polis: Sparta

The chief social and political form to emerge in reviving Greece was the *polis,* or city-state, which had begun in the Greek settlements of Asia Minor, and consisted of the municipality itself and the territory immediately surrounding it: small in size and in population, often centering on a fortress built on a hill—the high city or Acropolis. It was in the Dorian centers—first Crete, and then especially Sparta on the mainland—that such city-states first emerged. The one at Sparta is of course responsible for the overtones that the word "Spartan" still has in our ordinary language today.

Here, in what the philosopher Aristotle later called "an association of several villages which achieves almost complete self-sufficiency," only the upper five to ten percent of the population were citizens; descendants of the Dorian conquerors, they were the rulers, hereditary landowners, and soldiers. The overwhelming majority of the people belonged to the *helot* class, farm laborers bound to the soil, servants of the ruling group. In between was a free class called *perioikoi* ("dwellers around"), descendants of the pre-Dorian residents of neighboring areas, who lived in the villages under Spartan control and had personal freedom but no right to participate in politics or to intermarry with the Spartans. The ruling Spartans lived in constant fear of revolution; they kept their secret agents planted among the helots to report subversive talk, and indeed barely managed to put down a helot uprising in the late seventh century.

The constitution, which the Spartans attributed to a divinely inspired lawgiver, Lycurgus, dating perhaps from about 825 B.C., provided that there should be two kings, descendants of two rival Dorian families. Real political power came to reside in five *ephors* (overseers) elected annually by an assembly of all Spartan citizens over 30, excluding women, helots, and perioikoi. There was, besides, a kind of council of thirty elders representing the more powerful families.

War dominated Spartan thinking. The males lived under military discipline from the age of seven, when a boy was taken from his parents, and taught reading and music and running and fighting. Weak-looking babies were abandoned to die. So that there might be healthy children, girls too were given strenuous training. Adult males lived in the barracks until they were 30, though they might marry at 20, but they dined in the mess-hall until they were 60. It was a harsh, bleak life, "Spartan" in its merits and in its defects.

The army was excellent and the citizens were patriotic and able to bear misfortune. The need to keep hostile neighbors under control led the Spartans also to introduce clumsy iron bars as money in order to make ordinary commercial pursuits as unattractive and difficult as possible.

Their earliest poets wrote fine, sensitive lyrics, but soon this art vanished, and war-songs first, and then no poetry at all, replaced it. The Spartans were not artists, but fighters. A barracks-state, Sparta reminds twentieth-century students of the fascist states of the 1920's and '30's.

Colonization

Together with the establishment of city-states there took place a large-scale movement of Greek colonial expansion. The city-states of Asia Minor and of Greece proper sent out naval expeditions of their citizens to plant new settlements in non-Greek areas where there was no power strong enough to prevent it: around the edge of the Black Sea, along the African shore of the Mediterranean in what we now call Libya, in Sicily, and along the Italian coasts (which the Romans later called *Magna Graecia,* "Great Greece"), and as far west as the coasts of France and Spain. Each new colony became a new city-state, independent of its mother-city but bound to it by sentimental and economic ties and by similar political and religious practices. It was no doubt overpopulation and internal strife in the settled cities together with the wish for trade and adventure that advanced the colonizing movement. Trebizond in Asia Minor, Panticapaeum in the Crimea, Byzantium (later to be Constantinople and still later Istanbul) at the Black Sea Straits, Syracuse in Sicily, Naples in southern Italy, Marseilles in southern France, and Cadiz beyond the Straits of Gibraltar on the Atlantic southern coast of Spain are among the famous cities that started their lives as Greek colonies.

Such foundations, and many others, combined with the decline of Egypt and the Assyrian conquests in western Asia, set off a whole new period of Mediterranean trade focusing on Greece. First one of the Greek cities and then another would assume prominence in the busy traffic: the Dorian-founded settlements on Crete, Rhodes, Corinth (with its strategic position at the isthmus that attaches the Peloponnesus to northern Greece), Megara: all became powerful and prosperous, as to a lesser extent did many other cities. By the mid-seventh century, coins, invented in the Anatolian kingdom of Lydia, had begun to be struck on the island of Aegina in Greece, where silver was the only precious metal available, and soon this convenient system spread westward. The coins of Aegina had turtles on them, those of Corinth foals, those of Athens from the sixth century onward the owl of Athena, goddess of the city.

The owl, sacred to Athena, appeared on Athenian coins from the sixth century onward. This silver coin is from the fifth century.

Athens

DRACO AND SOLON   Athens—which had never undergone a Dorian occupation—did not become a polis as soon as Sparta and Corinth, but lingered as an old-fashioned aristocratic tribal state,

dominating the large surrounding hinterland of Attica. It was divided territorially into plains, hills, and coastal land, and politically into four tribes, each of which had three brotherhoods (*phratries*) or territorial subdivisions (*trittyes*). Within each phratry a further distinction was drawn between those who owned and worked their farms (the *clans*)—which were the earliest category—and those who belonged to a guild of artisans or merchants. The clans included numerous related families or households of varying degrees of nobility. Land descended in the clan and might not be alienated. With it went a deep attachment to the local religious shrines, whose priests were clansmen. Later in creation, the guildsmen were citizens but not aristocrats, and presumably could sell or transfer their property. Each mature male was admitted into a phratry either as a clansman or as a guild-member.

Three *archons* (leaders or principal persons)—one of whom managed religious affairs, one military affairs (the *polemarch*), and one civil affairs—were joined in the seventh century by a board of six recording archons, making nine in all. Each was elected for a year, at the end of which all nine automatically became members of the Council of the Areopagus (the hill of Ares, god of war, in Athens), the chief judicial and policy-making body. Although a general assembly of all the people directly elected the archons and so the future members of the Areopagus Council, only clansmen—people of birth and wealth, not guildsmen—could be elected.

Already ancient in the seventh century B.C., these political arrangements were challenged in 632 by a young noble's plot to seize power, which led to a scandal when his followers were massacred though they had taken sanctuary at the altar of Athena. The noble family held responsible for the sacrilege was banished, and in 621 a specially appointed official, Draco, published the first Athenian law-code, famous for its severe penalties: hence our term a "Draconian" measure. Harshest of all were the laws on debt: a bankrupt clansman could never sell off or mortgage his land, but was compelled to mortgage the produce of it to the debtor. Thus he would oblige himself and his heirs to work it indefinitely for somebody else, and in effect would lose his own freedom. Bankrupt guildsmen actually became the property of their creditors, as slaves. The growing inequity of this system led to civil strife.

In the 590's the reformer Solon freed both clansmen and guildsmen actually suffering these penalties for debt, cancelled current debts, and abolished the harsh system. He repealed almost all Draco's laws, and published a new code. He tried to improve the general prosperity by emphasizing the need to abandon complete economic dependence on agriculture and to foster a lively new commerce. He even offered citizenship to citizens of other poleis who would come to work in Athens. He opened the most important offices of state to rich guildsmen as well as rich clansmen: money, not birth, now counted chiefly.

He is also said to have founded a new body, the Council of Four Hundred, consisting of one hundred members from each of the four tribes, all named by Solon himself, to act as a kind of inner circle of the general assembly of the people, preparing the materials for discussion and making recommendations for action: the general assembly now could not act without such a recommendation; but it could vote against it, and it still elected the archons. And Solon also made it a kind of court, by selecting a panel of assembly-members by lot to review the work of the magistrates.

Introducing these democratic innovations but keeping both the older aristocratic election only of the rich to magistracies and the oligarchic power of the few in the Council of the Areopagus, Solon's reforms were really a radical set of compromises. In one of his own poems he says of his actions: "I stood holding my stout shield over both parties [the poor and the rich]; I did not allow either party to prevail unjustly." By justice Solon meant more than legal justice; he meant what we would call social justice. Though some of his fellow Athenians jeered at him for not taking advantage of his extraordinary powers to line his own pockets, he answered (again in a poem) that "money flits from man to man, but honor abides forever." Urging the Athenians to abide by his laws for a hundred years, he withdrew from the scene for a decade.

PEISISTRATUS AND CLEISTHENES Civil strife at once began again. Athenians seem to have lined up in accordance with both region and class: the plains-people being mostly aristocrats

Late sixth-century bronze figure of a banqueter, probably from the Peloponnesus.

who felt Solon had gone too far, the hill-people mostly poor farmers who felt he had not gone far enough, and the coast-people mostly artisans who thought he was about right. In 561 B.C. their quarrels gave Athens into the hands of a "tyrant," as the Greeks called a dictator, however benevolent: Peisistratus, a noble, who had made himself leader of the hill-people. In and out of office for some years, Peisistratus once managed to get back into power by dressing up a beautiful girl as Athena to show the citizens that the goddess herself wanted him admitted to her sanctuary on the Acropolis. His final return in 546 he owed to vast sums of money that he had made from the silver mines on his estates in the north, and to mercenary troops from Argos whom he hired with his wealth. Peisistratus and his sons dominated Athens until 510 B.C.

Though Solon's constitutional measures had not prevailed, his economic policy made Athens rich, as Athenian pottery became the best and most sought-after in Greece. Peisistratus—who collected ten percent of all revenues for his personal fortune—pushed commercial success still further, partly by shrewd alliances with other poleis. At home, his was the only party. He exiled those aristocrats who refused to support him; he would often keep the son of a noble family as a hostage to ensure the family's loyalty. Having come to power as leader of the poor, he made them loans, embarked on a lavish program of public works to be sure there were jobs for all, subsidized the arts, and increased the magnificence of state religious celebrations. His sons, who succeeded him on his death in 528 B.C., followed his policies; but of course the noble families whom their father had displaced continued opposition, often from exile. When Hipparchus, one of the sons, was assassinated for personal reasons in 514 B.C., executions multiplied, government grew more tyrannical, and the exiled nobles came back in 510 B.C. By 508 Cleisthenes, one of the exiles, who appealed for the support of the guildsmen—already so much favored by Peisistratus—succeeded in his turn in coming to power by promises of constitutional reform.

These promises he fulfilled by striking at the influence of the clans in elections, and giving the guildsmen equal weight. Using as the basic new political unit an old territorial division called a *deme,* a small area something like a ward in a modern city, Cleisthenes ordered all citizens registered as voters within their demes, irrespective of their origins, thus giving the guildsmen equal franchise with the clansmen. Whoever was a member of a given deme in the year 508–507 B.C. remained so permanently, and so did his descendants even if they moved away.

Cleisthenes also rezoned Attica into three new regions that did not coincide with the former coast, hill, and plain. He regrouped the demes into trittyes which, unlike the twelve older trittyes, were in general not arranged compactly and next to each other, but chosen from all three territorial subgroupings. Finally, by drawing lots he put every three trittyes together into a political "tribe." Instead of the four old racial (or genuinely tribal) tribes, there were ten of these new political tribes whose membership cut across the old family and regional and class lines. Each of these new, nontribal, artificial tribes had members from each of the three new territorial divisions, and the former influence of the noble families had been effectively cut down. Cleisthenes had invented a fundamental tool of democracy: the gerrymander.

Each deme annually elected a number of its members (proportionate to its population) as its representatives, and from them the new ten tribes selected by lot fifty each to be members of the new Council of Five Hundred, replacing Solon's Council of Four Hundred. Solon had given Athenians equality before the law; Cleisthenes gave them equality at the ballot box. The four old racial or tribal tribes, the old brotherhoods, the clans, continued to play a major part in religious and social life, but their political role was over.

Of course, the system was clumsy. The archons continued to administer, except that now (501) the whole Assembly of the People elected ten generals a year to serve as operational commanders under the polemarch. The Council of the Areopagus (ex-archons) retained its powers and its aristocratic complexion. Archons and generals continued to be aristocrats, and though they were often able, experienced, and patriotic, they struggled with each other for power and prestige, and tended to become the chiefs of rival factions. These rivalries would lead individuals to take different positions at different times in their careers. Cleisthenes himself had fluctuated between supporting and opposing the family of Peisistratus, had worked with and against both Spartans and Persians, and had at one time appealed to the nobles, at another to the people. These switches in loyalty were normal in Athenian politics but naturally increased its instability.

The ten groups of fifty tribal members of which the Council of Five Hundred was made up each governed in continual session for a tenth of the year (roughly 36 days), and the chairman of the committee of fifty that was sitting at any given time was selected afresh by lot every day. During each continual 36-day session the committee members (*prytaneis*) lived in a special state building and were fed at public expense. They could summon the remaining 450 councillors to a full session whenever they wished. No citizen between the ages of 30 and 60 could be a member of the council more than twice or chairman of a day's session more than once. Thus, with swiftly changing large groups of citizens receiving responsibilities for short times, almost any citizen could hope to enjoy the experience at some time during his life. Fortified by their new constitution—giving all citizens a stake in the community—the Athenians were prepared for their famous historic confrontation with the Persian Empire.

II   Persia and the Greeks, to 478 B.C.

The Persian Empire

We have already encountered the Medes, an Indo-European people of the Near East, who in 612 B.C. cooperated with the briefly recovering Babylonians to destroy Nineveh and bring down the hated empire of the brutal Assyrians. We have also seen the Medes' southern relatives, the Persians, destroy Babylon (538) and allow the captive Hebrews to return to Jerusalem. It was Cyrus, the Persian ruler (557–529 B.C.) of the southern province, the captor of Babylon and liberator of the Jews, who attacked his northern kinsmen the Medes and took their capital (Ecbatana, south of the Caspian Sea), and so began a meteoric rise toward universal empire, the greatest to come out of the ancient Near East.

Uniting his territory with that of the Medes and bypassing Babylon, Cyrus moved westward into Anatolia, absorbed the Lydian kingdom of the rich king Croesus, and then attacked and conquered the Greek cities of Ionia along the Aegean coast. Next he moved east all the way to the borders of India, conquering and annexing as he went, but imposing no such tyranny as the Assyrian. Instead of deporting whole populations, Cyrus allowed them to worship as they pleased, honored their gods and their customs, and allowed them to keep on governing themselves in their own way under his representatives. The fall of Babylon led to the Persian conquest of Syria. Cyrus' son Cambyses (529–522 B.C.) invaded and conquered Egypt, and died on his way home to put down a revolution, which his brother-in-law and successor Darius (521–486 B.C.) succeeded in quelling.

It was Darius who subdivided the empire into twenty provinces (satrapies), each with its political governor, its military governor, and its tax-collector, but otherwise running its own affairs. Royal agents crossed and crisscrossed the vast area from the Aegean to the Indus, collecting intelligence for the king. Darius took from the Lydians the practice of coining money and introduced it into all his dominions. The highway system was a marvel, a great network whose largest thread was the royal road that ran more than 1,600 miles from Susa, Darius' capital, to Sardis, the chief city of Lydia. It is likely that Darius himself introduced Zoroastrianism, the religion of Zarathustra, who had died only a generation earlier. In any case, Darius himself accepted the religion, and paid honors to its great god Ahuramazda without repudiating other gods.

Zoroastrianism began as a monotheistic faith, proclaiming the one god Ahuramazda, whose chief quality was his wisdom. He is the only intellectual deity we have so far encountered, and the other divinities around him were not gods and goddesses but abstract qualities such as Justice and Integrity, which he had created. It was the existence of evil in the universe that led Zarathustra to imagine that life was a constant struggle between a good spirit and an evil spirit, *both* subordinate to Ahuramazda. A wise man will ponder and then choose the good way; a foolish man will choose the evil way; and the supreme spirit will reward the wise and punish the foolish.

Ancient Greece

Athenian Empire, 450 B.C.

■ Battle sites

THRACE

Black Sea

Bosporus

Byzantium

Propontis
(Sea of Marmora)

MACEDONIA

Amphipolis

Aegospotami

CHALCIDICE

Hellespont

Troy

EPIRUS

MT. OLYMPUS

Dodona

THESSALY

LESBOS

LYDIA

PHRYGIA

Arginusae Is.

CHIOS

Sardis

Thermopylae

Ionian Sea

ITHACA

Delphi

Thebes

EUBOEA

Athens

Aegean Sea

SAMOS

Mycale

Miletus

Corinth

Mycenae

Argos

DELOS

Halicarnassus

Olympia

PELOPONNESUS

see inset below

COS

PERSIAN EMPIRE

Pylos

Sparta

LACONIA

MELOS

Cretan Sea

RHODES

**THERA
(SANTORIN)**

0   50   100
Miles

Knossos

CRETE

Mediterranean Sea

MT. PARNASSUS

Delphi

Chaeronea

PHOCIS

EUBOEA

BOEOTIA

Thebes

Leuctra

Delium

Gulf of Corinth

Plataea

ATTICA

Marathon

Megara

Eleusis

Corinth

Salamis

Athens

Piraeus

PHOCIS

*Saronic
Gulf*

MT. LAURION

Mycenae

Mantinea

Argos

Epidaurus

Tiryns

AEGINA

0   25
Miles

Greek Colonial World

Areas of Greek settlement

0   500
Miles

ALPS

CRIMEA

Panticapaeum

Black Sea

PYRENEES

Massilia

ITALY

ILLYRIA

Trebizond

IBERIA

CORSICA

SARDINIA

Byzantium

ASIA MINOR

Paestum

Croton

Megara

Phocaea

IONIA

Cadiz

Segesta

"MAGNA
GRAECIA"

Corinth

Athens

SYRIA

Str. of Gibraltar

Syracuse

SICILY

GREECE

RHODES

PHOENICIA

CYPRUS

Carthage

Agrigento

CRETE

Mediterranean Sea

Cyrene

LIBYA

EGYPT

AFRICA

Intellectual and abstract, lacking ritual and priesthood, early Zoroastrianism was perhaps too impersonal and rarefied for a popular faith, and was modified after its founder's death. By identifying Ahuramazda with the good spirit, the next generations in effect demoted the supreme god, who was now no longer the ruler over the evil spirit (Ahriman) but only a contender with him. From a monotheism the religion became dualistic (giving comparable power to good and evil) and also revived elements of earlier polytheism, as old deities and ceremonies reappeared and a powerful priesthood asserted itself. At the moment of Darius' reign, however, the religion was still in its earliest phase.

The Ionian Cities; the Threat to Greece; Marathon

Though tolerant with regard to religion and local custom, as we have seen, the new Persian rulers would not allow their subjects political freedom, which was precisely what the now captive Ionian Greek cities most valued. Their prosperity also declined, as the Persians drew toward Asia the wealth of the trade routes that had formerly enriched the Aegean towns. By 513, the Persians had crossed the Bosporus on a pontoon bridge, sailed up the Danube, and moved north across modern Romania into the Ukraine in a campaign against the nomadic people called Scythians. Though indecisive, the new advance into Europe alarmed the Greeks, who were now receiving overtures for an alliance from the Scythians: it looked as if Darius would move south against European Greece from his new base in the northern Balkans.

Some of the Greek poleis—Sparta and her allies—were hostile to the Persians; but there were others that had pro-Persian rulers. One of Peisistratus' sons, Hippias, had taken refuge with the Persians, who were backing his return to Athens, but about 505 B.C. the Athenians refused to accept him, and soon afterwards decided to give help to the captive Ionian cities in their resistance to Persian rule. The Ionians then rebelled; with Athenian help they burned down Sardis, the former Lydian capital and now headquarters for the Persians in Asia Minor (499 B.C.). Encouraged, many other Greek cities joined the rebellion.

But the Persians struck back, and by 495 B.C. had defeated the ships of the Greek cities in the Aegean; they burned the most important Ionian city—Miletus—massacred many of its men, and deported its women and children. By 493 B.C. the Ionian revolt was over, and in the next two years the Persians extended their authority along the northern coasts of Greece proper, directly threatening Athens. It was probably Hippias who advised the Persian commanders whom he was accompanying to land at Marathon, in a region once loyal to his father Peisistratus, only about 25 miles north of Athens. There a far smaller Athenian force decisively led by Miltiades defeated the Persians and put an end for ten years to the Persian threat to Greece. Because the Spartans had been celebrating a religious festival during which military operations were taboo, they had been unable to participate in the fighting; only the much smaller polis of Plataea had sent 1,000 troops to join the 10,000 Athenians. The credit for driving off the Persians therefore went primarily to Athens. Darius now planned a much greater invasion, but first an Egyptian uprising and then his death (486) delayed it. His successor Xerxes (486–465), having subdued the Egyptians in 485, resumed the elaborate preparations.

The 480's

By the time Xerxes was ready to try again, the Athenians had removed their hero Miltiades from an active role in their affairs. Like other Athenian leaders he had had the usual varied career: at one time pro-Peisistratus, at another anti-, at one time pro-Persian, at another the hero of Marathon. A leader of the nobles, he was eventually brought down by a rival faction.

It was probably now (488 B.C.) that some leader first invented the famous practice known as ostracism. The word comes from *ostrakon*, a fragment of a clay pot on which the individual citizens scribbled the name of any politician they wished to exile from the city for a period of ten years. Apparently a majority of a meeting of 6,000 citizens (i.e., 3,001 votes) was needed to ostracize. The 480's—the decade of preparation for Xerxes' expected attacks—was the decade of ostracism par excellence: many hundreds of the original clay potsherds still exist with the names of prominent politicians written on them, a sort of negative ballot. We know that by and large the citizens ostracized the leaders of the Peisistratid party and many other politicians. By 480 they had been eliminated, and Themistocles had emerged as the popular choice to lead the resistance to the new Persian invasion.

The 480's also saw a reform in the method of choosing the nine archons, who after 487 were no longer elected by the people but selected by lot from a preliminary list, drawn up by the demes, of five hundred candidates, who still had to be among the richer citizens. Each deme could put down on the list a number of its own men in proportion to its population. This reform further reduced the influence of the aristocratic clans. Moreover, it gradually reduced the influence of the Council of the Areopagus (made up of ex-archons), since more and more its members became men chosen in the new way. Because the generals were still elected, the old political rivalry for the archonship now shifted to the office of general, and factional struggle continued.

New supplies of silver were discovered in the nick of time, and Themistocles persuaded the Athenians to use the money to build a new fleet instead of passing it out among the citizens, a decision that probably determined the outcome of the Persians' new effort, and that incidentally suited the poor, who built the ships and rowed them and whose fortunes were associated with the navy. As the leading military power of Greece, with many allies including Athens, Sparta took over the leadership of the anti-Persian Greek poleis, which together formed an anti-Persian league with a congress of delegates from the individual cities and a unified command. Knowing that its forces would be greatly outnumbered (perhaps 110,000 against 500,000 Persians), the league did not try to defend the northern cities, where the Persian cavalry could operate freely, but instead abandoned them.

Xerxes Invades

The events of the year 480 B.C. are deservedly celebrated: Xerxes' huge army, its supply-lines greatly overextended and its speed slowed down by its very numbers, crossed into Europe and swung south into Greece, while a fleet, possibly of 3,000 ships of various sizes, sailed along the coast. At the pass of Thermopylae in central Greece a Greek traitor showed the Persians how to outflank the defenders, but a small army of Spartans—only 300 strong—defended the pass to the last man, taking a terrible toll of the Persian infantry. A storm, a battle, and a second storm cut the Persian fleet in half. The Delphic oracle had mysteriously prophesied that Athens would be destroyed but had advised the Athenians to put their trust in their "wooden walls." Themistocles succeeded in persuading the Athenians that the message meant they should abandon the city and rely upon their fleet—their wooden ships—for their defense.

Athens was accordingly evacuated, except for the defenders of the Acropolis, who were killed. Xerxes' men plundered the city. But the fleet in the narrow waters of the harbor of Salamis off Athens awaited the Persian attack, despite fierce debate and disagreement among the Greeks. Themistocles eventually sent a misleading message to the Persians pretending that he would betray the Greeks, and so persuaded them that it was safe to attack. The Greek fleet—helped by deserters from the Persians who revealed Xerxes' battle-plans—won a smashing victory, which Xerxes himself watched from a great throne set up on shore. Xerxes had to withdraw from Greece, for autumn was setting in. In the next year (479) at Plataea the united Greek forces numbering more than 100,000 men defeated the Persian troops once again, after Attica had again been invaded and devastated. This time they massacred the enemy.

The maintenance of Greek unity was most impressive: in spite of the thousands of personal and municipal rivalries among the Greeks, all members of the league had kept the oath "I shall fight to the death, I shall put freedom before life, I shall not desert colonel or captain alive or dead, I shall carry out the general's commands, and I shall bury my comrades-in-arms where they fall and leave none unburied." A wildly individualistic people had shown that they could put the general interest ahead of all else. Soon afterwards at Mycale (478 B.C.) the Greeks scored another victory on land and sea. The Persians, as it turned out, had been stopped forever, although peace was not formally made until 448, and at many times during those three decades the threat of renewed invasion hung over the heads of the Greeks.

III   The Athenian Empire, 478-404 B.C.

Postwar Reorganization

When the Athenians began to rebuild and refortify Athens, the Spartans asked them to stop, maintaining that the new walls might be useful to the Persians if they ever again invaded Greece; but Themistocles, as ambassador to Sparta, trickily played for time until the walls had already been built. The episode once again shows Themistocles as able and somewhat unscrupulous; it serves as a symbol of Athens' unwillingness to let Sparta, as the strongest military power, take the lead in planning for the future defense against Persia. It was indeed Athens, from 478 on the strongest naval power, that organized the new Greek alliance, designed to liberate the Ionian cities still subject to Persia and to maintain the defenses. Athens contributed most of the ships, but the other cities were assessed contributions in both ships and money. The treasury of the alliance was on the island of Delos; therefore the alliance is sometimes called the Delian League. It scored a major victory over the Persians in Asia Minor about 467 B.C.

Domestic Athenian politics continued savage: Themistocles was ostracized about 472; while in exile, he was charged with corruption; he fled to the Persians, was given rich revenues, and died in the service of Xerxes' son and successor. Immensely able, Themistocles somehow seemed not quite trustworthy. He accurately foresaw both the successes and the great danger that lay ahead for Athens: the long-range threat from Sparta. Like Miltiades, he lost the confidence of the Athenians after he had done them invaluable service.

In 462 a new reform further democratized Athenian government: the Areopagus Council was shorn of its powers and left a mere figurehead, while the Council of Five Hundred and the Assembly were the beneficiaries. Though put through largely by Ephialtes, the reform was partly inspired by a brilliant young aristocratic politician named Pericles (a grandson of Cleisthenes). By about 457 the patriotic and incorruptible Pericles had become the leading Athe-

nian politician, responsible for the many military and naval operations conducted simultaneously against the Persians (chiefly in Egypt: an expensive failure), the Spartans, and certain members of the Athenian alliance itself who resented the dictatorial ways of Athens.

At home Pericles pushed democracy, inaugurating a system of state pay, first for the jurymen (drawn from a panel 6,000 strong, 600 from each tribe) and later for those rendering other services to the state. State service was thus transformed from an activity that the poor could not afford to one that they welcomed. In order to limit the number of those eligible for such payment, Pericles also now limited Athenian citizenship to those both of whose parents were Athenian. The money to pay all these people could come only from the allies.

From Alliance to Empire

In fact, Pericles was in the process of turning the Athenian alliance into an empire, with the subject members providing the money for Athens, which in turn would defend them all, and would be able to challenge Sparta. In 454 the treasury of the alliance was moved from Delos to Athens, and became in effect a major Athenian resource. Since 470, no ally had been allowed to secede. During a truce with the Spartans (451–446 B.C.), the Athenians, operating in the Aegean, increased the number of their allies (about 170 cities at the peak), and in 448 made a peace with Persia that liberated the Ionian cities and bound the Persians not to come within three days' journey of the coast.

Athenian settlements were founded on the territories of some allied states, and Athenian coinage was standard. Resentment against Athens was naturally widespread among the allies. But in 446–445 a new thirty years' treaty with Sparta provided that neither side would commit aggression against the other. Both had lost the good will of the other Greek poleis: Athens was now ruling an empire by force and

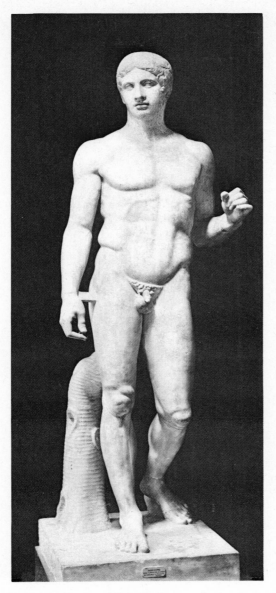

Roman marble copy of Polyclitus' statue of a spearbearer (The Doryphorus). The original was sculpted ca. 450–440 B.C., at about the time that Phidias was at work on the Acropolis.

dominate the affairs of state, but he was elected general democratically every year. He had at his disposal the large surpluses in the imperial treasury, which mounted in these years of peace, and which with Athens' other revenues were much more than enough to pay the 10,000 rowers of the warships, the 700 officials, the 500 councillors, the 6,000 jurors, and many others. Pericles embarked upon a great program of public works, of which the two most famous buildings were the temple of Athena Parthenos (the virgin), the celebrated Parthenon, and the Propylaea (monumental gateway), both on the Acropolis. After one had mounted the steps that led up to the Propylaea, and passed through it, there at the top of the hill was the giant bronze statue of Athena sculptured by Phidias, a personal friend of Pericles, and behind it and to the right was the entrance portico of the magnificent new temple. Inside was another statue of Athena, this one in gold and ivory, also by Phidias.

There were plenty of jobs available in the building program, and slaves as well as freemen participated and were well paid. There was money and opportunity for everybody: for the 30,000 resident aliens (metics), who had to pay a special tax, and were not allowed to own land or participate in politics, but contributed to the city's and their own good fortune in a variety of ways, chiefly commercial; for the 200,000 slaves, whose lot was easier than it was elsewhere, and who were often set free; and most of all for the 168,000 Athenian citizens (4,000 upper class, 100,000 middle class, and 64,000 lower class).*

The Peloponnesian War

THE FIRST FIFTEEN YEARS, 431–416 B.C.   The splendid civilization of Athens in the fifth century depended upon the continued exercise of complete control over the subject poleis in the empire. A growing number of incidents in which the Athenians ruthlessly asserted their power alarmed the Spartans: if they did not fight soon, they feared, they might not be able to win. They tried to force the Athenians to make concessions, but Pericles, with the support of the Assembly, said only that Athens would consent to have all disputed questions arbitrated.

*All such statistics are mere approximations. No exact figures can be given.

its services against the Persians seemed less magnanimous; Sparta had suffered defeats and its reputation was dimmed.

The thirty years' truce, as it turned out, lasted only for fifteen (446–431). It was a prosperous period, during which Pericles continued to

In 431 began the ruinous Peloponnesian War (431–404 B.C.). The Spartans invaded Attica in order to force a military decision. Pericles countered by withdrawing the entire population within the city walls, which had been extended to include the suburbs and to give access to the sea. He intended to avoid pitched battles with the superior Spartan troops on land, and to match his defensive policy on land by an offensive policy at sea, launching seaborne raids against enemy territory and inviting naval battles.

These tactics worked well in the first year of the war; but in 430 a terrible plague broke out in Athens, where the whole population of Attica was cooped up with no sanitation. In 429 Pericles himself died of it, leaving Athens without the trusted leader who could make even unpopular policies acceptable. The plague raged until the end of 426, and cost Athens about a third of its population, including its best troops. It did not deter the Athenians from continuing the war, with general though costly success at sea and even, contrary to Pericles' policies, on land.

By 424, Athens could probably have ended the war on favorable terms, and the upper and the middle classes that had suffered most from it were eager to do so: it was their lands in Attica which the Spartans ravaged, and their members who made up most of the land-forces that did the heavy fighting. But the lower classes, identified with the fleet, which was still in fine condition, wanted to continue the war in the hope of greater gains; and since they now dominated the city's politics, the war continued.

Not until 421 could the peace party conclude the Peace of Nicias (so called after its leader), which provided that each side restore captured places and prisoners, and remain at peace with the other for fifty years. This was soon supplemented by an actual Spartan-Athenian alliance, also concluded for fifty years, but intended chiefly to give each power a chance to put its own alliance in order while secure from an attack by the other. The war had been marked by numerous acts of brutality on both sides: brutality not only by our modern standards (which offer little cause for boasting in any case) but by Greek standards: prisoners were slaughtered and enslaved, and agreements broken in a way that contemporaries felt to be blameworthy.

ALCIBIADES AND FAILURE   The peace lasted five years, 421–416 B.C., which saw the gradual rise to eminence in Athenian politics of Pericles' nephew, Alcibiades, a brilliant, ambitious, dissolute, and unstable youth, who succeeded the demagogic Cleon as leader of the lower-class war party against the restrained and unglamorous Nicias. Athenian efforts to support Argos against Sparta only ended in the defeat of Argos and Athens and the strengthening of Spartan prestige. By killing all the adult males of the island of Melos and enslaving the women and children as a punishment for Melos' insistence on staying neutral in the war (415), Athens underlined its own ruthlessness. By deciding, against Nicias' prudent counsel, to send off a large naval expedition to Sicily to attack the great Greek city of Syracuse, the Athenian assembly once again followed Alcibiades' lead—he said there would be great glory in it, and that all Sicily and then Greece would become subject to Athens.

Ten-drachma silver coin from Syracuse, 479 B.C.

Yet the project bore no real relationship to Athenian interests: it was irrelevant to the politics of mainland Greece, and the Athenians had little sound military intelligence about Sicily. Just before the expedition sailed, a scandal broke out in Athens: the statues of Hermes that stood before the doors of temples and houses were mutilated in the night (the sexual organ was broken off), and Alcibiades—who was known to have committed similar sacrilege before when in a wild and dissipated mood—was suspected. But he went off to Sicily, as co-commander with his opponent, the unwilling Nicias, of the greatest naval expedition ever sent out by a Greek polis. Before the fleet reached Syracuse, Alcibiades was recalled to stand trial for the mutilation of the Hermae; but he escaped to Sparta.

The siege of Syracuse was long drawn out (414–413), enormously expensive in ships, money, and men (200 ships, more than 40,000 seamen, at least 10,000 troops), and a total failure: Nicias and other leaders were captured and killed. While it was going on, Sparta, now advised by Alcibiades (who also seduced the wife of the Spartan king, Agis), renewed the war at home, and sent troops to help the Syracusans. The Spartans also stirred up the Ionian cities to revolt against Athens. The Persian satraps in Asia Minor, hoping to regain sea-coast towns lost so long before, joined with the Spartans. Alcibiades, who had worn out his welcome in Sparta, now joined the Persians.

Ironically enough the balance of power between the two great Greek poleis that in 490 and 480–479 had so gloriously expelled the Persians from Greece was now, in 412, held by the very same Persians. Alcibiades tried to blackmail the Athenians by telling them that if they would install an oligarchic government, he would return and exercise his influence with the Persians on their behalf; while the Spartans promised the Persians that in exchange for paying for their fleet, they would permit the cities of Ionia to fall into Persian hands once more.

Civil strife accompanied by assassinations of those who opposed a change in the constitution created a turbulent atmosphere in Athens. A group of conspirators first prevailed on the Assembly to appoint a team to draft a new oligarchic constitution, and then persuaded a rump session to accept the recommendation that the existing officials be dismissed. A group consisting of five presidents appointed a hundred associates, who in turn co-opted three hundred more, and this now became the new Council of State, which ousted the former Council of Five Hundred by an armed but bloodless coup d'état. The new Four Hundred could summon at will a new Five Thousand, ostensibly to replace the traditional assembly of all the citizens. The democratic forces still controlled the fleet.

The leading oligarchs would now have liked to proceed at once to peace with Sparta, and probably intended that the Five Thousand should never be summoned. From exile, Alcibiades, however, did not back their aims, but indicated his preference for the summoning of the Five Thousand. After a naval defeat, the citizens actually deposed the oligarchic Four Hundred and elected the Five Thousand—all upper class— which governed the city from 411 to 410 B.C. when, after some Athenian successes at sea, democracy was restored.

Alcibiades continued to command Athenian naval forces at sea without returning home until 407, when he came to Athens and was absolved for the mutilation of the Hermae; but the Spartan fleet defeated him in 406, and he went into retirement on his estates along the Dardanelles, where he was murdered three years later by Spartan and Persian agents. His career vividly illustrates the vulnerability of the Athenian democracy to a plausible, charming, talented scoundrel. Another weakness—the temptation to yield to impluse—was displayed soon afterwards, when the Athenians had defeated the Spartan fleet (at Arginusae) but had suffered heavy casualties, and the Council was intimidated by the mourning families of the drowned soldiers into ordering the collective executions of six generals, on the charge of not rescuing the troops in the water. The Council paid no attention to the fact that one of the generals had himself been swimming for safety at the time. The people later regretted their act, but the generals were dead.

In the final naval action of the war, the Spartans captured most of the Athenian fleet empty on a beach in the Dardanelles while the sailors were hunting food on shore (Aegospotami, 405), and the Spartan infantry rounded up thousands of Athenian prisoners, of whom 3,000 were executed as direct reprisal for recent Athenian atrocities. Starving, blockaded by land and sea, its alliance in ruins because the allies had defected or joined the Spartans, Athens had no choice but to surrender. Some of the Spartan allies wanted to punish the Athenians as the Athenians had punished the Melians, but the Spartans refused. The Athenians were forced to demolish their long walls, abandon their empire, surrender their fleet, and undertake to follow the Spartan lead in foreign policy. But they were not massacred.

IV   The Fourth Century B.C. and the Hellenistic Age

Spartan Hegemony

As the victors, the Spartans found themselves dominant in a Greece where polis hated polis and, within each polis, faction hated faction. From Ionia, which the Spartans had sold back to Persia as the price of victory, the Persians loomed once more as a threat to the whole Greek world. By mid-century the new state of Macedonia in the north menaced the Greeks. Perhaps wiser or more vigorous leaders would have been able to create some sort of federation among the individual poleis that could have withstood the Persians and the Macedonians, and, still later, the Romans. But since this did not happen, it seems more likely that the polis as an institution was no longer the appropriate way for the Greek world to be organized. Perhaps it was too small, too provincial, too old-fashioned to keep the peace and give men room for economic advancement and intellectual growth.

Sparta proved as unable as Athens to manage Greece. The Spartan government, suitable for a state that had no purpose but war, was largely in the hands of the elders, too conservative to meet new challenges. Gold and silver had found their way into the simple agricultural economy whose founders had preferred to use bars of iron as exchange. Many Spartans for the first time found themselves disfranchised for debt, and so relegated to the status of inferiors. They joined the helots and perioikoi as part of a discontented majority, at precisely the moment when Sparta needed more equals—full, enfranchised fighting citizens. Away from home the Spartans could neither relinquish the cities of the former Athenian Empire in which they had installed governments of their own oligarchic type, nor occupy them satisfactorily.

At Athens, for example, an oligarchy of thirty (the thirty tyrants) instituted a reign of terror (instigated by the extremist Critias) not only against democrats associated with past regimes but also against moderate oligarchs. In 403 an invading force of exiled democrats killed Critias, and touched off a brief civil war. At Athens they restored democracy, but the thirty tyrants and their sympathizers were set up as a Spartan puppet state nearby at Eleusis. Nobody was allowed to move between the two separate Athenian states. In 401 the Athenians treacherously killed the generals of the Eleusis armies, and the two states were reunited. It was the government of this insecurely re-established Athens that tried and condemned the philosopher Socrates in 399 B.C.

The Spartans could not pose as the leaders of Greece and simultaneously keep their bargain with the Persians to sell Ionia back to them; yet if they went back on this bargain, the Persians would start a new war. So in 401 B.C., when the younger brother of Artaxerxes II, king of Persia —Cyrus the Younger, governor of Asia Minor— rebelled against Artaxerxes and asked for Spartan aid, Sparta gave it to him. Cyrus was soon killed in a battle deep in Mesopotamia, and his Greek troops were left high and dry in the heart of Persia. Their disciplined march north to the shores of the Black Sea and the Greek city of Trebizond on its shore forms the substance of a book called the *Anabasis* ("The March Back") by the Athenian Xenophon, one of their officers. The episode left the Spartans at war with Persia.

The Spartans did not unite their land and sea commands, but gave the Persians time to build a fleet, which they put under an Athenian admiral, Conon. The Persians also bribed Thebes, Corinth, Argos, and Athens to stir up so much trouble against Sparta that Spartan troops had to be recalled from Persia to fight a new war in Greece proper. It lasted eight years (to 386); saw the self-assertion of Thebes; seemed to produce the threat of a renewed Athenian Empire; and ended in stalemate, as the Persians and Spartans finally got together and imposed a peace ("The King's Peace," 380 B.C.) by which the Persians resumed control of all Greek states in Asia, and the rest were autonomous.

Thebes Rises to Hegemony

Raising money from their allies, hiring mercenaries to intimidate all resistance, the Spartans systematically disciplined and punished the cities that dared resist, installing an oligarchy at Thebes (382) and in lesser places, breaking their promise to respect the autonomy of all Greek cities. A group of Theban democratic exiles conspired to overthrow the pro-Spartan regime there (379 B.C.), and when the Spartans tried to punish them, a new war broke out, in which Athens participated after 377 as the leading power in a new anti-Spartan league, joined by many Greek cities.

By 371, the Spartans were ready for peace, a guarantee of independence to all Greek states, and disarmament. But the wording of the treaty gave Persia and Athens the leading roles as guarantors, and deliberately limited the Thebans to signing for Thebes only, not for their own league of allies (the Boeotian League). So Epaminondas, the chief Theban delegate, refused to sign, and soon afterward roundly defeated the Spartans at the battle of Leuctra. Cities subject to Sparta began to oust their oligarchic governments and install democracies. Epaminondas followed up his successes by two invasions of the Peloponnesus (369, 368), which destroyed Spartan power in its own homeland. Ugly and tyrannical, Spartan power vanished from Greece unmourned. It was no credit to Athens that in the final stages she helped Sparta out of fear of Thebes.

As head of the Boeotian League, Thebes under Epaminondas not only had a democratic government of its own, but treated its allies rather as equals than as subjects, and so commanded a true federation rather than an empire like the first Athenian Alliance or the Spartan Alliance. Other local leagues of cities followed the Boeotian example and were affiliated with Thebes. Warfare continued despite the effort of the Persians to dictate a general peace (367), as the Athenians reverted to their former imperialist practices and installed colonies of Athenian settlers on the soil of conquered cities. The Thebans fought in the Peloponnesus, in the north, against Athens at sea, and finally in the Peloponnesus again, where an alliance of Sparta and Athens and several other poleis met them in battle at Mantinea (362).

Epaminondas was killed at a moment when his forces were winning, but they stopped fighting when they heard of his death, and their enemies got away. All hope that Thebes could put an end to the interminable fighting among Greeks died with Epaminondas, a leader of extraordinary military talent and political generosity, who preferred leadership to domination, but whose own people, the Boeotians, largely deserved their reputation elsewhere in Greece as country bumpkins, uncultivated and crude, with a strong streak of ruthlessness which even Epaminondas could not always control.

Though a new league of city-states was now formed (362) to end war and to enable the Greeks as a whole to determine their foreign policy, Athens continued to act as the rival of Thebes and to play the traditional political game of alliance-building within the league. Though ineffective, the league was an important effort to create something like a United States of Greece. Without its restraints, Thebes found itself broken in war against the city of Phocis, whose general had seized the shrine of Delphi and used the accumulated funds there to create a large army of mercenaries (354). For its part Athens strove to reconstruct its old Aegean empire, but in 357 found that many of its most important outposts had rebelled (the "Social War": i.e., war of the allies, 357–355), and was forced to grant them freedom in 355. Athens was exhausted and broke and weak.

Ironically enough, the inability of the Greek cities to give up fighting was almost surely due in part to general prosperity. Whereas during the fifth century only Athens and Sparta had been able to afford large armies and navies, during the fourth many other cities grew rich enough to support such forces. Brisk Mediterranean commerce brought wealth to the distant Greek settlements from the Crimea to Spain; it was not only goods that flowed but also slaves and mercenary troops: it is estimated that shortly after mid-century the Persians alone had 50,000 Greek troops fighting in their armies.

Many of the devices of modern capitalism to make international trade easier now first made their appearance: banking and credit, insurance, trade-treaties, and special privileges. Private wealth grew apace, and was widely distributed. Slaves grew in number; we know of several

Alexander the Great depicted on a four-drachma silver coin of about 300 B.C. with the horns of Amen.

people who owned more than a thousand of them; by 338 B.C. there may have been as many as 150,000 in Attica, working in the mines and at other occupations. All this prosperity meant that states quickly recovered from defeats in war and could quickly afford to try again. Patriotism became more and more a matter of cutting up the melon of profits. At the same time, the poor grew poorer; unwilling to declass themselves by engaging in the manual labor that was now the work of slaves, they became vagrants or mercenary soldiers.

Macedon

North of Thessaly, and extending inland into areas that are today part of Yugoslavia and Albania, lay the kingdom of Macedon, with a considerable coastline along the Aegean. The Macedonians were a mixture of peoples, including some of Greek origin; they were organized into tribes, worshiped some of the Greek gods, and spoke a native language which the Greeks could not understand, although it included many words of Greek origin. Their hereditary kings—who were also elected by the people—claimed Greek descent; indeed they believed they were descendants of the hero Herakles, son of Zeus himself.

The king spoke Greek as well as the native language, had title to all land, and ruled absolutely so long as he was not charged with treason (when the people might depose him). He was advised by councillors who were selected from among the nobles of each tribe and felt themselves to be his social equals. Although the Greeks had planted some poleis along the Macedonian shore, and although Greek cultural influence and Greek trade had penetrated deeply into Macedon by the fourth century, Macedon did not copy Greek political institutions, but kept its own, much more nearly like those of Mycenaean Greece in the days of Agamemnon. Traditionally the Macedonians relied on cavalry in war, but in the fourth century they added foot-soldiers in order to fight their neighbors from the west and north, the Illyrians (probable ancestors of the Albanians of today). Both Athens and Sparta interfered and intrigued in internal Macedonian affairs.

THE ACHIEVEMENT OF PHILIP   In 359, a prince of the ruling house, Philip, became regent for his infant nephew, the king. Having lived for three years as a hostage in Thebes, where he knew Epaminondas, Philip was well versed in Greek affairs. He applied Theban military principles to his army (emphasizing infantry tactics), led it in person, defeated the Illyrians and various rivals for power within Macedon, was elected king in his own right, and broke the power of Athens in the territory neighboring his own to the east (359–354 B.C.). He exploited the rich gold and silver mines in his kingdom, and struck

his own coinage. He scored successes in Thessaly and in Thrace, where he threatened Athenian possessions along the shore of the Dardanelles (354–351).

Athenian politicians viewed Philip's advance with mixed feelings. Some favored him, others opposed. It was not until he had won still more territory and begun to use a fleet successfully that the famous Athenian orator Demosthenes began to warn against the threat from Macedon. But Philip had annexed the peninsula of Chalcidice and detached the big island of Euboea, close to Attica itself, from its Athenian loyalties.

At that point he suggested peace and an alliance with Athens, which was reached with the approval even of Demosthenes (346), though Philip meanwhile had secured control over the Delphic oracle. He was moving south and consolidating his power as he came. By 342, the Athenians had acquired new allies in the Peloponnesus. In retaliation Philip moved into Thrace (modern Bulgaria) to cut off the Athenian grain supplies coming from the Black Sea, and to avert a new Persian–Athenian alliance. Once again Demosthenes pressed for war, and Athens took military action in Euboea (341, 340). Philip declared his intention of punishing her now for unneutral acts. By late 339 he was deep in Greece once again, only two days distant from Attica. Acting under the gun, Demosthenes now arranged an eleventh-hour alliance with Thebes, which however proved unavailing. Protesting at intervals his wishes for peace, Philip totally defeated the Athenian–Theban alliance at Chaeronea in Boeotia (338 B.C.). He occupied Thebes, which had surrendered, but spared Athens a military occupation on condition that the Athenian Alliance be dissolved and an alliance with Macedon adopted. He showed leniency, and proved that in fact he had never intended to destroy Athens, as Demosthenes had maintained.

Philip's victories aroused in many the hope of a unified Greece. In the Peloponnesus all the poleis except Sparta honored him. At Corinth in 337 B.C., all the poleis (again with the exception of Sparta) met and organized a league that called itself The Greeks, all members of which bound themselves to stop fighting and intervening in each other's affairs. This was a far more closely knit body than the abortive league of 362. It immediately allied itself with Macedon, and then joined with Philip in a declaration of war on Persia to revenge the sacrilege of Xerxes' inva-

58

sion of 143 years earlier. Philip was to command the expedition. By 336 B.C. the advance forces of the army were already liberating the Ionian cities from Persia. But Philip, aged only 46, was now assassinated at his daughter's wedding by a Macedonian noble who was acting for personal rather than political motives.

Philip's accomplishments greatly impressed his contemporaries, who realized that no such powerful consolidated state as his Macedon had ever existed west of Asia. Instead of allowing the resources of Macedon to be dissipated in flashy conquests, he organized the people he conquered, both in the Balkan area from the Adriatic to the Black Sea and in Greece. He kept morale high in the army, and had the various contingents from the various regions competing to see who would do the best job. He differentiated his troops into more specialized units for diverse tasks in war, and he took personal command of the unit that had the roughest assignment. He could appreciate the strengths of his Greek opponents, and when he had defeated them he utilized their skills and made sure of their loyalty by decent treatment. By his final effort to unify them against their traditional Persian enemy, he associated himself with the ancient patriotic cause that so many of them had so often betrayed but that obviously still had great appeal to them. Though he felt himself to be part of Greek civilization, he reminds many students of the Greece of an earlier age than his own, and is often regarded as a kind of Homeric hero in the flesh almost a thousand years after the siege of Troy.

THE ACHIEVEMENT OF ALEXANDER Philip's son Alexander the Great belongs to legend as much as to history. Alexander loved war, politics, athletics, alcohol, poetry, medicine, and science. He was only twenty when he came to the throne. Within a dozen years he led his armies on a series of triumphal marches that won for Macedon the largest empire yet created in the ancient world. He began by crushing a Greek revolt led by Thebes (335 B.C.), whose entire population he sold into slavery (he did not massacre the males, as the Spartans and Athenians often did). Next he crossed the Aegean into Asia Minor to continue the war of the Greek League against Persia, and recapture the Ionian cities. He defeated the Persians at the river Granicus (334 B.C.), and took over Ionia, where he established democracies in the poleis. In ter-

ritories belonging to the Persians he took title to all land, thus replacing the Persian king, whom he defeated again at Issus (333 B.C.), and so opened up Syria. He reduced Tyre by siege, and refused King Darius' offer of a Persian princess and all territory west of the Euphrates.

Egypt was next, and it fell easily. Here he founded the great port of Alexandria in the Nile Delta (332), a Greek city from the beginning. But he paid his respects to the Egyptian divinities, and allowed himself to be treated as a god, according to the Egyptian way. Then he marched east and defeated the Persians again in Mesopotamia (Gaugamela, near Nineveh, 331 B.C.). The Persian Empire was smashed. Alexander sacrificed to Marduk in Babylon, and ordered his temple restored; the Persians had destroyed it. Vast mopping-up operations continued in Persia proper (330–327), as Alexander's armies seized the chief cities and all the Persian royal treasure—perhaps half a billion dollars in cash. But he treated the Persian royal family with great courtesy, and acted toward his new subjects just as a king of Persia would have done. The Persian nobles came to acknowledge him as king by the grace of Ahuramazda. In fact, Alexander *was* king of Persia, and so called himself, just as he was pharaoh of Egypt, king of Babylon, king of Macedon, and commander (*hegemon*) of the Greek League.

Far out in central Asia, Alexander fell in love with and married the daughter of a local chieftain, who joined forces with the conqueror (327 B.C.). This marriage enhanced the new loyalty of the Persians to him, but it helped to strain the loyalty of his own Macedonian noble companions, who also disliked Alexander's own occasional adoption of Persian dress and Persian custom for the benefit of his new subjects, despite the fact that he did not change his own attitude toward or traditional relationships with the Macedonians. In fact, he continued to regard himself as a Greek and as the descendant of Zeus. He had paid his respects to the shade of his ancestor Achilles at Troy before he began his Eastern campaigns, and his favorite reading was the *Iliad*. But Alexander was forced to put to death his own most faithful commander, Parmenio, whose son had plotted against the king: Macedonian law required that all male relatives of a plotter be killed. And in 328 B.C. at Samarkand (now Soviet Uzbekistan), Alexander in a drunken fury killed one of his own

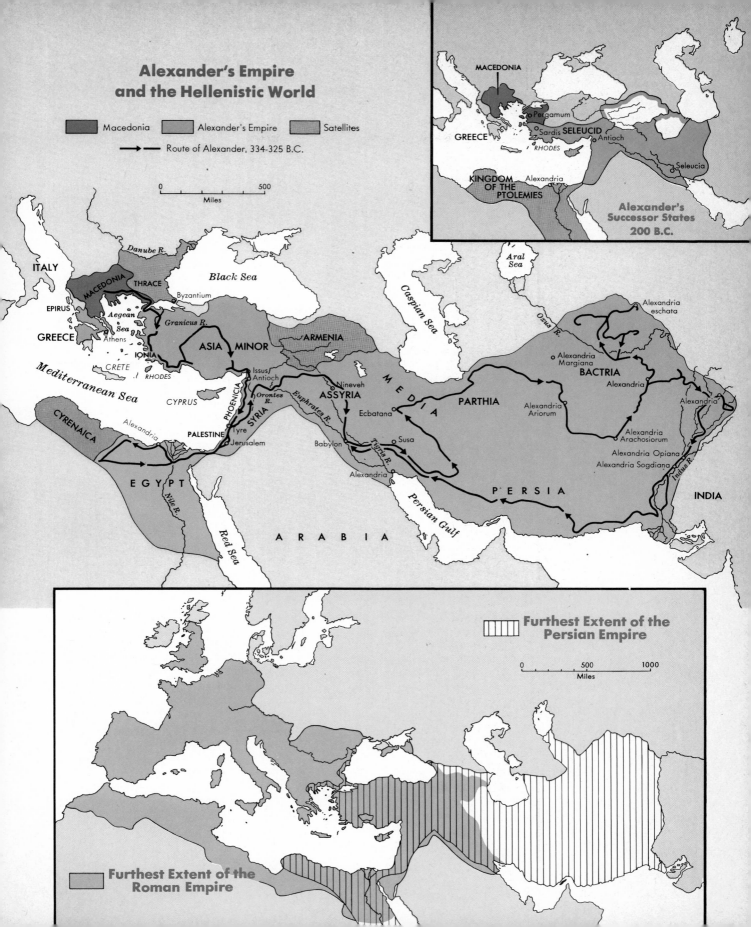

Alexander's Empire and the Hellenistic World

Macedonia   Alexander's Empire   Satellites

→ Route of Alexander, 334–325 B.C.

0   500
Miles

Alexander's Successor States 200 B.C.

MACEDONIA

GREECE

Pergamum
Sardis   SELEUCID
RHODES
Antioch

KINGDOM OF THE PTOLEMIES

Alexandria

Seleucia

ITALY

Danube R.

Black Sea

MACEDONIA   THRACE
Byzantium

EPIRUS

Aegean Sea
GREECE   Athens
Granicus R.
IONIA
CRETE   RHODES

Mediterranean Sea

CYRENAICA

Alexandria

PHOENICIA
Issus/Antioch
Orontes R.
SYRIA
PALESTINE   Tyre
Jerusalem

E G Y P T

Nile R.

Red Sea

A R A B I A

ASIA MINOR

ARMENIA

Caspian Sea

Aral Sea

Ozus R.

Euphrates R.
ASSYRIA   Nineveh
M E D I A
Ecbatana
Tigris R.
Babylon   Susa
Alexandria

PARTHIA

Alexandria Ariorum

Alexandria eschata

Alexandria Margiana   BACTRIA
Alexandria

Alexandria Arachosiorum
Alexandria Opiana
Alexandria Sogdiana

Indus R.

Alexandria

INDIA

P E R S I A

Persian Gulf

Furthest Extent of the Persian Empire

0   500   1000
Miles

Furthest Extent of the Roman Empire

senior companions for having taunted him with his Persian ways.

The tensions of the conquest did not diminish its efficiency: new levies of troops came out from Europe and were raised in Asia; new roads, new money, and new towns sprang up, each named after Alexander. Believing that India was the last region in Asia, that it was small, and that after India one would come upon Ocean, via which one could perhaps return to Europe by sea, Alexander next set out to conquer India (327 B.C.) from a base in what is now Afghanistan. He soon found himself doing battle with the hill tribes and with princes of Kashmir and Punjab (now Pakistan). At first the Indian war elephants terrified Alexander's cavalry and his men, but soon the Macedonians learned how to defeat them, and won many victories. Alexander moved on east; but India · was not small, as he had thought, and his troops eventually mutinied. Alexander had to give in, and call off any further advance (326 B.C.). He led his troops on riverboats down the Indus southward toward the Indian Ocean, fighting all the way, and sacrificing a gold cup to Poseidon when he reached the ocean shore. Several new Alexandrias were founded, including the town that is now Karachi (Pakistan), before Alexander led his forces westward again across the southern Persian deserts back to Susa (324).

Here he punished those who had become unruly or corrupt during his long absence, and dramatically pursued his plan to combine the best features of the Macedonian and the Persian nobilities by staging a mass marriage between 80 Macedonian officers and 80 Persian noblewomen. He himself took a new Persian wife, and blessed the unions of 10,000 Macedonian troops with Persian women. Macedonian troops who wished to return home were sent off well rewarded, and those who wished to stay were combined with newly trained Persian recruits. A great double naval expedition from the mouths of the Tigris–Euphrates eastward along the shore of the Persian Gulf to India, and westward around Arabia (never yet circumnavigated) to Egypt, was in preparation at Babylon, where Alexander had great dockyards built. From the Greeks, who had enjoyed a longer period of internal peace than any for over a century, Alexander asked for divine honors: not to be a new god, as has sometimes been thought, but to be

recognized as a general benefactor. In 323 B.C., at Babylon, he caught a fever and died, aged 33.

Imagination can hardly conceive of what Alexander might have accomplished had he lived: he might well have made Greece the center of his empire, and would surely have been able to conquer the two states in the western Mediterranean already looming on the horizon as powers there: Carthage and Rome. He respected all races and religions, and believed in decent politics and a booming economy. Each of the Alexandrias he settled with Greeks and planned as a center for the diffusion of Greek culture. A superb general, a clever governor of subject peoples, a pious believer in the Greek gods, a passionate man who sometimes acted impulsively and bitterly regretted it later, Alexander astonished his contemporaries, and it is little wonder that he became to later generations the hero of a great cycle of romances that circulated in every country, in every language, and among every people, down virtually into our own day.

Heirs of Alexander

As soon as the news of Alexander's death was known, his faithful generals began a fierce scramble for portions of his empire. They combined against each other in various shifting alliances, and arranged many intermarriages and murders, in a period of kaleidoscopic political and military change. By about 300 B.C. three dynasties had emerged as supreme, each in a different portion of the empire: the Ptolemies in Egypt, the Seleucids in Asia, and the Antigonids in Macedon and Greece. In addition, there were various lesser kingdoms, chiefly in Asia Minor. Fighting continued almost without interruption until the rising power of Rome began to challenge them and to destroy and then absorb them one by one.

In Egypt the Ptolemies followed the ancient pattern of government, turning themselves into successors of the pharaohs. They became gods, they sometimes married their sisters, they exploited the agricultural wealth of the country to the limit. They claimed title to all land, some of which was farmed by peasants directly for their benefit, and some let out to temples or to military settlers or officials. The Ptolemies' own land gave them all its produce except what was needed to feed the farm workers. Land let to others paid the Ptolemies a percentage of the wheat. Oil, flax, and papyrus were royal monopolies. No tree in Egypt could be cut down without royal permission. The Ptolemies governed largely through their Greek officials, who poured into Egypt for several generations after Alexander's death. Even the armies of the first three Ptolemies were made up wholly of Greeks. It was not until 217 B.C. that Egyptian troops participated in the wars of the dynasty, which were directed chiefly against the Seleucids of Asia for the possession of Syria, and against the Antigonids for islands of the Aegean and the Anatolian coasts.

Alexandria, the capital, had two great harbors, broad streets, luxurious palaces, a famous

Building in the caravan town of Petra, in present-day Jordan, carved directly into the red rock hills.

library with 700,000 rolls of papyrus, and a museum where scholars, freed from all duties by state subsidies, conducted their researches as they chose ("fat fowls in a coop," a skeptical poet called them). The towering lighthouse 400 feet high was regarded as one of the wonders of the world, and had an elevator that took the attendant from street level to the lamp at the top. This was the biggest city of the ancient world until Rome eventually outstripped it; there were perhaps a million inhabitants of Alexandria in the first century B.C., some of them living in multistoried apartment houses. Alexandria was far too big to be a polis; but its Greek population had its own political organization, as did the Jews and the Egyptians. At Alexandria stood also the Ptolemies' big barn, where all the royal grain was stored after it had come down the Nile.

The Egyptian population lived under its own law, and was judged in its own courts. Those who were discontent with the system that exploited them so thoroughly—and there were many—had no escape except to take sanctuary in a temple; and the government always tried to reduce the number of temples that had the right to provide sanctuary. For a long time the Greek population, with its own language, law-courts, culture, and ways of life, did not mingle with the Egyptians, but remained a large collection of foreigners who were getting rich as fast as they could. By the early second century Greek immigration had tapered off. Greek–Egyptian intermarriages had begun, and the army was more Egyptian and less effective. Rome began to intervene; disorganization set in; and by 118 B.C. Ptolemy VII had to issue a series of decrees calling for reform that show how far the system had begun to disintegrate.

Seleucus I was also one of Alexander's generals, who began as governor of Babylon and eventually won control over all of Alexander's Asian lands except northern and western Asia Minor and the Indian regions in the East, which had to be given up by 303 B.C. Seleucid territorial holdings fluctuated a good deal, however. We know much more about the Ptolemaic kingdom than about the Seleucid because many papyri have survived in the dry climate of Egypt that preserve details of economic and social life; no such source exists for Asia. The Seleucids' Ionian territories centered on the former Lydian capital of Sardis, their Syrian territories on the

Dionysus sailing. Attic kylix (drinking cup) painted by Exekias ca. 540 B.C.

new city of Antioch-on-Orontes in northern Syria, and their Mesopotamian territories on the new city of Seleucia not far from Babylon. As the heirs of the ancient Near Eastern empires, the Seleucids used the former Assyrian and Persian administrative forms, and revived Babylonian religion and Babylonian literature, still written in cuneiform. Some scholars believe that by deliberately sponsoring a Babylonian religious revival the Seleucids were seeking a counterweight to Zoroastrianism, the Persian faith. It does appear that the Seleucids failed to achieve what

Alexander had so well begun: the securing of Persian cooperation in managing the huge Asian territories.

The Seleucids could not count on deification, like the Ptolemies, nor could they create in Asia anything like the extremely centralized Ptolemaic system of exploitation. In Asia, unlike Egypt, there was too vast an area to be governed, there were too many varied traditions of authority, too many local governors to be considered. The Seleucids instead did something the Ptolemies did not do: they founded Greek cities, and sponsored their development. To do this they gave up large areas that were their own royal land, and they also transferred the land of powerful individual landowners to the cities. In such cases the lot of the peasant improved, as he ceased to be private property and gained his freedom. The Greek cities were military colonies, with money and land given by the king, and settlement, housing, financial, and other questions delegated to a military governor. The settlers received land, and were required to serve in the army in exchange.

Like Alexander the Seleucid rulers named the cities for themselves; there were many Antiochs named for the Antiochus who had been Seleucus I's father and whose name continued to be given to many of the monarchs of the dynasty; there were also Seleucias, Laodiceas named after Seleucus' mother, and Apameas named after his wife. Some of the earlier Alexandrias now had their names changed to Antioch. The multiple founding of Greek cities all over Asia was a bold attempt to solve the problem of military security, and it failed partly because there were not enough Greeks available to populate the cities and man the armies, partly because the Seleucids did not command the loyalty of the Persian population.

As for Macedon and Greece, the family that won out there were the descendants of Alexander's governor of the western Anatolian province of Phrygia, the Antigonids. It was not until 276 B.C., almost half a century after Alexander's death, that the son of the first Antigonus, known as Antigonus Gonatas, was accepted as king of Macedon; and his success there came because he was such an able general that he had defeated the marauding Gauls. These were Celts (Indo-Europeans) from distant western Europe who were now migrating eastward along the Danube, and bursting southward from the wilder and unsettled portion of the Continent on raids into Italy, Greece, and eventually Asia Minor, where they were given a kingdom of their own called Galatia. Having protected Greece from the Gauls (277 B.C.), Antigonus proved a successful ruler in Macedon.

Though the Greek cities were now grouped together into two leagues, the Aetolian and the Achaean, larger in membership and more representative in their joint rule than the Athenian and Spartan alliances of earlier times, they fought against each other and against the Antigonid kings of Macedon with the usual Greek vigor; so that by the 220's, the Greeks were largely independent of Macedon. In these times Athens had become famous largely as a university town, and usually stayed out of the perpetual brawls of the other cities. But Sparta, true to its traditions, tried to take over the Achaean League, and would have succeeded had not the Macedonians been brought back into Greece in 222, to defeat the Spartans finally. By the 220's, however, Rome had begun her interventions in the Greek world, and these were quickly to lead to conquest.

V   The Civilization of Greece

The Gods

The Olympian gods are already old acquaintances, whom we first learned to know in Homer. The citizens of a polis naturally had special devotion for the divinity who had founded it: Athens for Athena, Sparta for Zeus, but they worshiped the other gods as well. Everybody worshiped the goddess of the hearth, Hestia, the protectress of each individual person's own home and fireside. Births and deaths in a family, solemn political actions in the state, were accompanied by religious rites. Poleis in large numbers grouped together in special devotion to regional shrines: the temple of Apollo at Delphi and of Zeus at Olympia we know; Zeus had another shrine at Dodona. The Olympic games were followed by others held in honor of Apollo at Delphi, of Poseidon the sea-god on the Isthmus of Corinth. At the games religious solemnities accompanied the sports: racing, jumping, throwing the discus, wrestling. The winners were crowned with laurel, as were those who won drinking contests or beauty contests or contests for the best poem or musical composition, including hymns to the god which lovingly and realistically retold the myths that surrounded his birth and life, almost as if he were a human hero.

Two Greek cults of particular importance began outside the ordinary worship of the Olympian gods: that of Demeter at Eleusis near Athens, and that of Dionysus. Demeter (the name means literally "earth-mother") was the goddess of fertility and of the harvests: her daughter (by Zeus), Persephone, was snatched away by the god of the underworld, and had to spend a third of the year with him: the months of barrenness, late autumn and winter. Every spring she returned, and the fields became fertile again. Like the Mesopotamians from Sumer on and like the Egyptians, the Greeks too invented a story to account for the miracle of rebirth every spring. At Eleusis Demeter was worshiped in ceremonies which all initiates swore to keep secret. We know few of the details, but certainly there was a kind of ritual drama in which the initiates acted out the sorrow of the goddess searching for her lost daughter; there was a ritual meal, with communion in bread and water; and there was a sacred purifying bath in the salt waters of the nearby sea. Probably the participants expected that they would enjoy some sort of afterlife.

Dionysus, the god of wine, was not Greek in origin, but a northern foreigner, who also stood for fertility in its more openly sexual aspects: his celebrants originally carried phalluses in his procession, and were themselves often dressed as goats. In its original form the cult inspired its followers with wild frenzy in which they tore up and ate the flesh of living animals, and so acted out the devouring of the god himself. The cult was tamer in Greece, where songs were early written for the god.

Tragedy

From these songs there developed at Athens the art of tragedy: the word means "goat-song," and shows the close connection with the god Dionysus. At first largely sung by a chorus and formally religious in tone, the tragedies began to deal with more personal human problems, and individual actors' roles became more and more important. The first competition to choose the best tragedy was sponsored by Peisistratus in 534 B.C., and annual contests were held thereafter. Many hundreds of tragedies were written; comparatively few have survived in full—prob-

ably the best—and we have fragments of others. The later Greek philosopher Aristotle believed that it was the purpose of tragedy to arouse pity and terror in the spectators; to purge or purify them by causing them to reflect on the fearful punishments that highly placed men and women brought upon themselves by their own sins, the worst of which was hubris, arrogance.

The first, and some would still say the greatest, of the three chief tragedians whose works survive was Aeschylus (ca. 525–456 B.C.), of whose seventy-odd tragedies we have seven. The earliest in time was *The Persians* (472 B.C.), in which Aeschylus explained the defeat of the Persians as the result of Xerxes' efforts to upset the international order established by the gods, and of the arrogance by which he offended Zeus. The audience could ponder recent history (it was only seven years since the Persians had been defeated) and consider the moral reasons for their own victories: such a play would tend to sober up any fireeater who thought one Greek could lick ten Persians.

In *Prometheus Bound,* Aeschylus dealt with the punishment meted out by Zeus to Prometheus the Titan, who had stolen fire as a gift to mankind and who now lay chained to a rock while a vulture pecked at his liver. Zeus himself behaved tyrannically—he was new to the job of being king of the gods when Prometheus committed his offense—and only gradually learned to temper his wrath with mercy. Just as Xerxes had offended against the proper order of things by trying to impose Persian rule on Greece, so Prometheus had, even out of good will, offended by trying to get mankind the great gift of fire too soon. In the trilogy *The Oresteia,* all three plays of which survive, Aeschylus dealt with the ghastly tragedies in the family of Agamemnon, who sacrificed his daughter Iphigenia to get a favorable wind to go to Troy, was murdered by his unfaithful wife Clytemnestra on his return, and was avenged by his son Orestes, who killed his mother on orders of Apollo. Orestes suffered torments by the Furies, and was acquitted by a court presided over by Athena; but only Zeus succeeded in transforming the Furies into more kindly creatures. Crime and punishment, remorse and release, a benevolent god over all: these Aeschylus portrayed in lofty, moving verse.

Sophocles, the second of the three greatest tragedians (496–406 B.C.), wrote many tragedies, of which only ten survive. He believed deeply in

Athenian institutions and in the religion of his fellow Greeks, and took an active part in the public life of Periclean Athens. In his *Antigone*, the niece of Creon, tyrant of Thebes, defied her uncle's harsh decision that the body of her brother, killed while leading a rebellion, must be exposed to be devoured by beasts of prey. Proclaiming that divine law required decent burial, she disobeyed Creon, and caused the proper ceremonial earth to be sprinkled on the body. She knew she would die for her defiance, but she acted in obedience to her conscience and resisted the dictator. The *Antigone* has carried its message of the sanctity of the individual conscience down the centuries, proclaiming the eternal superiority of what is right and decent to any mere dictator's brutal whim.

Living to be ninety, Sophocles saw the ruin brought by the Peloponnesian War, and his last tragedy, *Oedipus at Colonus*, produced after his death, dealt with the old age of the famous Theban king who in ignorance had killed his father and married his mother, and had torn out his own eyes in horror when he discovered what he had done. A blind beggar, outcast, Oedipus now knew that he could not have avoided the pollution of his unwitting crimes, and that his self mutilation too was justified. Tempered by years of suffering, he sought sanctuary to die, and received it from Theseus, king of Athens: Oedipus' tomb would forever protect the Athenians against Thebes. Reflecting upon the terrible story of Oedipus and on the trials of all human life, Sophocles' chorus sang that for mankind the best thing is never to be born, and the next best to die as soon as possible after birth: the passions of youth, the blows dealt one in middle life, and the anguish of old age are not worth it.

Nineteen plays remain of the many written by the third and last of the Attic tragedians, Euripides (ca. 485–406 B.C.), who focused rather more upon human psychology, with far less emphasis on divine majesty. More realistic in their introduction of children, slaves, and other characters upon the scene, his plays were also more romantic in their exploration of the far

The theater at Epidaurus, ca. 330 B.C.

reaches of the human mind. The *Hippolytus* showed the uncontrollable sexual passion of a decent woman—Phaedra—for her ascetic stepson Hippolytus, who rejected it as he would all passion. She was ashamed of her lust but, as in the case of Potiphar's wife and Joseph, accused Hippolytus of having attacked her; he was executed, she committed suicide. The *Medea* showed a woman so far gone in agony brought about by rejection of her love that she killed her children in a fit of madness. The *Alcestis* showed a husband so selfish that he gladly accepted the offer of his devoted wife to die for him so that she might prolong his life; and then suffered agonies of remorse at his folly, when he had lost her.

The Trojan Women presented the sufferings of the women of Troy at the hands of the Greeks. It was staged in the same year as the Athenian atrocity at Melos, and must have caused the audience many uncomfortable moments of self-questioning. *The Bacchae* explored the excesses of religious ecstasy: in a frenzy a queen tore her own son to bits, thinking he was a lion. Was Euripides saying that men under the impulse of strong emotion were beasts, or that the old religion had too much that was savage in it, or only that the young king had defied the god and his hubris had brought him a fate that he well deserved?

Comedy

Comedy, like tragedy, also began at the festivals of Dionysus. Aristophanes (ca. 450–ca. 385 B.C.) has left eleven complete plays and parts of a twelfth. Besides making his audience laugh, he hoped to teach them a lesson through laughter. A thoroughgoing conservative, Aristophanes was suspicious of all innovation. In *The Frogs*, for instance, he brought onto the stage actors playing the parts of the two tragedians Aeschylus (then dead) and Euripides (still alive). The god Dionysus himself solemnly weighed verses from their plays on a giant pair of scales. Every time, the rather solemn, didactic, and old-fashioned Aeschylus outweighed the innovating, skeptical, febrile, modern Euripides: a tragedian's duty, Aristophanes thought, was to teach.

In *The Clouds* Aristophanes ridiculed the philosopher Socrates, whom he showed in his "think-shop" dangling from the ceiling in a basket so that he could voyage in air and contemplate the sun. Aristophanes meant to call attention to the dangers offered to Athenian youth by the so-called Sophists. His identification of Socrates with them was somewhat unfair; but, like the others, Socrates taught young men to question the existing order, and he was therefore fair game.

Aristophanes opposed the Peloponnesian War not because he was a pacifist, but because he thought it unnecessary. In his *Lysistrata* the women denied themselves to their husbands until the men made peace, and in other plays Aristophanes denounced the Athenian politicians, including Pericles himself, for going to war. In *The Birds* the leading characters set off to found a Birdville (Cloud-cuckoo-land) to get away from war. In one of his later plays, of which we have only two, the women took over the state and proposed to share all the men among them, putting prostitutes out of business; in the other, Poverty and Wealth appeared in person and argued their cases.

These later plays provided a transition to the New Comedy of the fourth century, gentler and more domestic. We have several New Comedies by Menander, including one published for the first time only in the late 1950's. The drama was of course only one form that Greek poetic genius took. From the earliest days, the Greeks were the masters of lyric poetry as well (we have quoted one or two of Solon's own poems above): among the most celebrated are poems of love by the poetess Sappho, of war by Spartan poets in the very early days, and of triumph in the games by Pindar.

History

A large proportion of what we know about the Greeks before and during the Persian Wars we owe to the industry and intelligence of Herodotus (ca. 484–420 B.C.), who began to write his history as an account of the origins and course of the struggle between Greeks and Persians, and expanded it into an inquiry into the peoples of the whole world known to the Greeks. Born in Halicarnassus on the Ionian coast of Asia

Minor, Herodotus was a great traveler, who visited Egypt, Italy, Mesopotamia, and the lands around the Black Sea, collecting information and listening to whatever stories people would tell him about their own past and about their present customs. He recorded what he learned, much of it of course tinged with myth, and he loved a good story; but he was both experienced and sensible, and he often put his reader on his guard against a story that he himself did not believe but set down in order to fill out the record.

Some have tended to scoff a little, especially at Herodotus' tales of a past that was remote even when he was doing his research; but, like those who have rashly questioned some of the history of the Old Testament, these doubters have often been silenced by recent archaeological finds. Herodotus, for instance, said that the founder of Thebes, the semimythical Cadmus, was a Phoenician who had brought Phoenician letters with him from Phoenicia to Greece, where he founded Thebes about 1350 B.C., or about 900 years before Herodotus' own day. Herodotus added that Cadmus' dynasty was ousted about 1200 B.C. This was often disbelieved. But in A.D. 1964 archaeologists at Thebes found in the palace of Cadmus a large collection of fine cuneiform seals, one of which was datable to 1367–1346 B.C. These instantly demonstrated the high probability of Herodotus' account of Cadmus' origin, date of arrival, and bringing of letters. Even the date of the ouster was verified, since the seals were in a layer of material that had been burned about 1200 B.C. and had survived because they were already baked clay. Herodotus wrote so well and so beguilingly that we would read him with delight even if he were not so reliable. Nor was he a mere collector and organizer of material. Though he wandered far, he never lost sight of his main theme: the conflict between East and West, which he interpreted as a conflict between despotism and freedom.

Always coupled with Herodotus we find the equally intelligent but very different historian Thucydides (ca. 460–ca. 400 B.C.), who wrote the account of the origins and course of the Peloponnesian War. The difference between the two arose partly from their subject matter: Herodotus was dealing largely with events that had happened before his own time, and he had to accept traditions, and often hearsay accounts.

Thucydides was dealing largely with events in which he himself had been a participant: he was an unsuccessful general on the Athenian side in the war, and had been punished for his defeat; but he remained impersonal, scientific, and serious, collecting and weighing his information with the greatest care. Though he followed Herodotus' custom of putting into the mouths of his leading characters words—sometimes long speeches—which represented what they might have said rather than what they actually said, in his introduction he warned his readers what he was doing: the actual words were not available, but the arguments on both sides of any issue could be revived and written up in the form of speeches. Pericles' funeral oration of 430 B.C. with its praise of Athenian democracy is perhaps the most famous; but Thucydides also put into the mouths of the Melians, about to suffer the terrible slaughter and enslavement at Athenian hands, the moving arguments appropriate to those who were about to be massacred.

As deep a student of human psychology as any of the tragedians, Thucydides found in men and nations the cause of war; he knew as much about war and human behavior as anybody since has been able to learn. He wrote as a loser, but not as a mere loser in a sporting event, where time, and perhaps a return match, will assuage the hurt: Thucydides had seen his own Athens, so admirable in its best qualities, brought down by the Spartan militarists. He hoped that human intelligence would in the future realize how risky war was and what damage it did to the highest human values, but he knew that human nature would always respond to certain challenges by force, and that the lessons of the past were hard to learn. He wrote in pain and in iron detachment. His narrative of the great military events, such as the siege of Syracuse, Alcibiades' ill-conceived project, moves with great speed and well-concealed artistry. The much less talented and more pedestrian Xenophon, author of the *Anabasis,* wrote—in the *Hellenica*—a continuation of Thucydides' work down to the year 362 B.C. And the still less talented Arrian, writing very late but basing his work largely on the now lost account by Ptolemy I himself, has left us an account of Alexander's campaigns.

But for the century or so that followed the death of Alexander we have no historical work comparable with the histories of Herodotus,

Fifth-century bronze statue, probably Zeus or Poseidon, now in the National Museum, Athens.

Thucydides, Xenophon, or Arrian. Therefore, we know the period less intimately than any since the Dark Age. It is only with the decade of the 220's that we once again encounter a narrative history, and then its author and his purpose themselves symbolize the change that has taken place. He was Polybius, a Greek who wrote in Greek but who had spent much time in Rome, where he had become an admirer and agent of the Romans, and the subject of his book was the rise to power of Rome. That he began his account with the year 221 B.C. clearly suggests that by that date the focus of world affairs had begun to shift from Greece to Rome.

Science and Philosophy

Possessed of inquiring, speculative minds, the Greeks showed a deep interest in science. Stimulated by their acquaintance with Egyptian science, the Ionians and later the European Greeks, though they lacked instruments to check and refine their results, correctly attributed to natural rather than supernatural causes a good many phenomena. They knew that the Nile flooded because annual spring freshets took place at its source in Ethiopia. They decided that the straits between Sicily and Italy and Africa and Spain had been caused by earthquakes. They understood what caused eclipses, and knew that the moon shone by light reflected from the sun. Hippocrates of Cos (ca. 460–377) founded a school of medicine, from which there survive the Hippocratic oath, with its high concept of medical ethics, and detailed clinical accounts of the symptoms and progress of diseases so accurate that modern doctors have been able to identify cases of diphtheria, epilepsy, and typhoid fever.

The mathematician Pythagoras (ca. 580–500) seems to have begun as a musician interested in the mathematical differences among lyre-strings needed to produce various notes. The theorem that in a right-angled triangle the square of the hypotenuse is equal to the sum of the squares of the other two sides we owe to the followers of Pythagoras. They made the concept of numbers into a guide to the problems of life, elevating mathematics almost to a religious cult, perhaps the earliest effort to explain the universe in abstract mathematical language. Pythagoras is said to have been the first to use the word *cosmos* —harmonious and beautiful order—for the universe. Earlier Greeks had found the key to the universe in some single primal substance: water, fire, or air; and Democritus (460–370) decided that all matter consisted of atoms.

The Hellenistic astronomer Aristarchus, in the mid-third century, concluded that the earth revolves around the sun, a concept not generally accepted till almost 2,000 years later, while his younger contemporary, Eratosthenes, believed that the earth was round, and estimated its circumference quite accurately. Euclid, the great geometrical systematizer, had his own school at Alexandria in the third century B.C., and his pupil Archimedes won a lasting reputation in both theoretical and applied physics, devising machines for removing water from mines and irrigation ditches ("Archimedes' screw," a hand-cranked device, is still in use in Egypt), and demonstrating the power of pulleys and levers by singlehandedly drawing ashore a heavily laden ship. Hence his celebrated boast: "Give me a lever long enough and a place to stand on, and I will move the world."

The Greek scholars of the fifth and fourth centuries B.C. were not specialists like those in a modern university. The same man would study and write books on physics, mathematics, astronomy, music, logic, and rhetoric. Rhetoric became an increasingly important subject, as the Greeks reflected on their own language and developed high standards of self-expression and style. The subject really began with political oratory, as politicans wished to make more and more effective speeches—particularly essential in wartime, when the population was excited anyhow, and each leader strove to be more eloquent than the last. These multipurpose scholars who taught people how to talk and write and think on all subjects were called Sophists: wisdom-men. Sophists generally tended to be highly skeptical of accepted standards of behavior and morality, questioning the traditional ways of doing things.

How could anybody really be sure of anything?, they would ask, and some would answer that we cannot know anything we cannot experience through one or more of our five senses. How could you be sure that the gods existed if you could not see, hear, smell, taste, or touch them? Perhaps you could not know, perhaps they did not exist after all. If there were no gods and therefore no divine laws, how should we behave? Should we trust laws made by other men like us? And what sort of men were making laws and in whose interest? Maybe all existing laws were simply a trick invented by powerful people— members of the establishment—to protect their position. Maybe the general belief in the gods was simply a "put-on," invented by clever people to whose interest it was to have the general public docile. Not all Sophists went this far, of course; but in Athens during the Peloponnesian

War, many young people, already troubled by the war or by the sufferings of the plague, were ready to listen to suggestions that the state should not make such severe demands upon them. Such young people would have burned their draft cards if they had had any, and their troubled parents, god-fearing and law-abiding, greatly feared the Sophists as the corrupters of the youth.

It is only against this background that we can understand the career and the eventual fate of Socrates (469–399 B.C.), whose method was that of the Sophists—to question everything, all the current assumptions about religion, politics, and behavior—but who retained unwavering to the end his own deep inner loyalties to Athens and to God. Socrates wrote no books, and held no professorial chair; but we know him well from contemporary reports, chiefly those of his pupil, Plato. Socrates was a stonemason who spent his life talking and arguing in the Assembly, in public places, and in the homes of his friends in Athens. He thought of himself as a gadfly, challenging everything anybody said to him, and urging people not to take their preconceptions and prejudices as truths. Only a never-ending debate, a process of question and answer—the celebrated "Socratic method"—could lead human beings to truth. Reasoning led Socrates to conclude that man was more than an animal, that he had a mind, and, above all, that he had a true self, a kind of soul or spirit. Man's proper business on earth was to fulfill this true soul and cultivate the virtues that were proper to it—temperance, justice, courage, nobility, truth. Socrates himself listened to the voice of God that spoke within him.

We have already seen Socrates in his basket in mid-air in Aristophanes' *Clouds*. Of course he irritated and alarmed those who were worried about the youth of the day, and who thought of him as just another Sophist and one of the most vocal and dangerous. So when he was about 70 years old he was brought to trial on charges of disrespect to the gods and corrupting the youth of Athens. He argued that he had followed the prescribed religious observances and that he wanted only to make men better citizens; and he defended his gadfly tactics as necessary to stir a sluggish state into life. But a court of 501 jurors voted the death penalty by a narrow margin. Socrates could have gotten off by suggesting that

he be punished in some other way. Instead he ironically asked for a tiny fine, and forced the court to choose between that and death. It condemned him again. Socrates drank the poison cup of hemlock, and waited for death serenely optimistic: he was "of good cheer about his soul." Many contemporaries and most men since have recognized that he was the victim of hysteria following a dreadful war.

Thereafter, it was Plato (ca. 429–347 B.C.) who carried on his work. Plato founded a school in Athens, the Academy, and wrote a large number of celebrated dialogues: earnest intellectual conversations, in which Socrates and others discuss problems of man and the human spirit. Much influenced by the Pythagoreans, Plato retained a deep reverence for mathematics, but he found cosmic reality in Ideas rather than in numbers. As man has a "true self" (soul) within and superior to his body, so the world we experience with our bodily senses has within and superior to itself a "true world," an invisible universe or cosmos. In the celebrated dialogue *The Republic,* Plato has Socrates compare the relationship between the world of the senses and the world of Ideas with that between the shadows of persons and objects as they would be cast by firelight on the wall of a cave, and the same real persons and objects as they would appear when seen in the direct light of day. So man sees the objects—chairs, tables, trees—of the world as real, whereas they are only reflections of the true realities—the universals—the Idea of the perfect chair, table, or tree. So man's virtues are reflections of ideal virtues, of which the highest is the Idea of the Good. Man can and should strive to know the ultimate Ideas, especially the Idea of the Good.

This theory of Ideas has proved to be one of the great wellsprings of Western thought and has formed the starting point for much later philosophical discussion. Moreover, in teaching that the Idea of the Good was the supreme excellence and the final goal of life, Plato was advancing a kind of monotheism and laying a foundation on which pagan and Christian theologians both would build.

Politically, Athenian democracy did much to disillusion Plato: he had seen its courts condemn his master Socrates. On his travels he had formed a high opinion of the tyrants ruling the cities of Magna Graecia. So when Plato came to sketch the ideal state in *The Republic,* his system resembled that of the Spartans. He recommended that power be entrusted to the Guardians, a small intellectual elite, specially bred and trained to understand Ideas, governing under the wisest man of all, the Philosopher-King. The masses would simply do their jobs as workers or soldiers, and obey their superiors.

Plato's most celebrated pupil was Aristotle (ca. 384–322 B.C.), called the "master of those who know." Son of a physician at the court of Philip of Macedon, and tutor to Alexander the Great, Aristotle was interested in everything. He wrote on biology, logic, literary criticism, political theory, ethics. His work survives largely in the form of notes on his lectures taken by his students; despite their lack of polish, these writings have had a prodigious later influence. He wrote 158 studies of the constitutions of Greek cities. Only the study of Athens survives.

Aristotle concerned himself chiefly with things as they are. The first to use scientific methods, he classified living things into groups much as modern biologists do, and extended the system to other fields—government, for example. He maintained that governments were of three forms: by one man, by a few men, or by many men; and that they were good and bad types of each, respectively monarchy and tyranny, aristocracy and oligarchy, polity and democracy (mob rule). Everywhere—in his *Logic, Poetics, Politics*—he laid the foundation for later inquiry. Though he believed that men should strive and aspire, he did not push them on to Socrates' goal of self-knowledge or to Plato's lofty ascent to the Idea of the Good. He urged instead the cultivation of the golden mean, the avoidance of excess on either side: courage, not foolhardiness or cowardice; temperance, not overindulgence or abstinence; liberality in giving, not prodigality or meanness.

Later, in the period after Alexander, two new schools of philosophy developed, the Epicurean and the Stoic. Epicurus (341–270 B.C.) counseled temperance and common sense, carrying further the principle of the golden mean. Though he defined pleasure as the key to happiness, he ranked spiritual joys above those of the body, which he recommended should be satisfied in moderation. The Stoics, founded by Zeno, got their name from the columned porch (Stoa) in Athens where he first taught. They preferred to repress the physical desires altogether. Since only the inward man counted, the Stoics preached total disregard for social, physical, or economic differences among men. They became the champions of slaves and other social outcasts, anticipating to some degree one of the moral teachings of Christianity.

The Arts

The incalculably rich legacy left by the Greeks in literature was well matched by their achievements in the plastic arts. In architecture, their characteristic public building was a rectangle, with roof supported by fluted columns. Over the centuries, the Greeks developed three principal types or orders of columns, still used today in "classical" buildings: the Doric column, terminating in a simple, unadorned square flat capital; the Ionic, slenderer and with simple curlicues (volutes) at the four corners of the capital; and the Corinthian, where acanthus leaves rise at the base of the volutes. Fluting gives an impression of greater height than the simple cylindrical Egyptian columns.

No matter what the order of the columns, a Greek temple strikes the beholder as dignified and simple. On the Acropolis of Athens, the Parthenon, greatest of all Doric temples, rose between 447 and 432 B.C. as the crowning achievement of Pericles' rebuilding program. By means of subtle devices—slightly inclining the columns inward so that they look more stable, giving each column a slight bulge in the center of the shaft so that it does not look concave—the building gives the illusion of perfection. In the triangular gable-ends that crowned its front and back colonnades (the pediments) and on the marble slabs between the beam ends above the columns (the metopes) stood a splendid series of sculptured battle-scenes, most of whose remains are now in the British Museum (the Elgin Marbles). Originally, the Parthenon and its statues were brightly painted. The building survived almost undamaged until 1697, when a Venetian shell exploded a Turkish powder magazine inside.

The achievement of Phidias and the other sculptors of the Periclean Age had gradually developed from the "archaic" statues created a century or more earlier, usually of young men

72

rather rigidly posed, with their arms hanging at their sides and a curiously uniform serene smile on their lips. Probably influenced by Egyptian models, these statues have great charm for moderns, who sometimes find the realism of the finished classical work rather tiresome. Phidias' great gold and ivory statues of Athena and the Olympian Zeus long ago fell to looters. So did most of the Greeks' sculpture in bronze; but every so often a great bronze statue is fished out of the sea or (as happened in 1959) is found under the pavement of a street being excavated for a sewer.

Though Greek painting as such has almost disappeared, we know from written texts that

The Laocoön Group. First-century B.C. marble in the Vatican Museum.

public buildings were adorned with paintings of Greek victories and portraits of political and military leaders. Moreover, the thousands of pottery vases, plates, cups, and bowls that have been discovered preserve on their surfaces—in black on red or in red on black—paintings of extraordinary beauty and of great variety. They show mythological scenes, illustrations to the *Iliad* and *Odyssey,* and the daily round of human activity: an athlete, a fisherman, a shoemaker, a miner, even a drunk vomiting while a sympathetic girl holds his head.

In the Hellenistic age sculpture became more emotional and theatrical: compare the Laocoön group, with its writhing serpents crushing their victims, to a statue of the Periclean period. The Venus de Milo and the Winged Victory of Samothrace are two of the most successful Hellenistic works of art; but there are a good many imitative and exaggerated efforts which are regarded as comparative failures. In literature, too, beginning with Menander's New Comedy, vigor and originality ebbed, while sophistication and a certain self-consciousness took over.

Such a summary account of the splendors of Greek civilization runs the risk of creating the impression that the Greeks were supermen living in a paradise of physical and cultural triumphs. In fact, of course, few Greeks could understand or follow the ideas of a Plato or an Aristotle, or could afford to spend a great deal of time at the games, at the theater, or arguing with Socrates. Most Greeks worked hard, and their standard of living would seem extremely low today. In all of Athens at its height we know of only one establishment that employed over a hundred workmen. Even wealthy Athenians resided in small, plain houses of stucco or sun-dried brick: nobody until the Hellenistic period lived pretentiously. Athens was a huddle of mean little streets; there was little or no drainage; lighting was by inadequate, ill-smelling oil lamps. Inside a smithy or a pottery, it was so hot that the smith or potter often worked naked, as we know from vase-paintings. But relaxation was at hand: a musician might play in the smithy; and the climate made outdoor living agreeable much of the year.

On the one hand, the Greeks discovered or invented democracy, drama, philosophy. But on the other, they clung to their old-fashioned religious rituals and could not make themselves give up civil war between their city-states. The freedom-loving Athenians executed Socrates. Though they formulated the wisdom of "Know Thyself" and the golden mean, created a beautifully balanced and proportioned architecture, and organized an education that trained the whole man, intellectual and physical, they too often exhibited hubris, the unbridled arrogance that they felt to be the most dangerous of mortal vices. And, as it did in the tragedies of the stage, so in their own lives, their hubris brought nemesis upon them. Their achievements, however, have lived after them, inspiring most of the values that Western man holds dearest.

Reading Suggestions on the Greeks

GENERAL ACCOUNTS

N. G. L. Hammond, *A History of Greece to 322 B.C.,* 2nd ed. (Oxford Univ. Press, 1967). A good up-to-date survey.

M. I. Finley, *The Ancient Greeks* (*Compass). Compact, up-to-date, and perceptive introduction to Greek life and thought.

H. D. F. Kitto, *The Greeks* (*Penguin). Useful, though opinionated, introduction.

G. E. Robinson, *Hellas: A Short History of Greece* (*Beacon). Good survey by a scholar who has written extensively on Greek history.

M. I. Rostovtzeff, *Greece* (*Galaxy). A famous older account by a distinguished Russian scholar; now somewhat out of date.

J. B. Bury, *A History of Greece to the Death of Alexander the Great,* 3rd ed. rev. (Macmillan, 1951). Another celebrated older account, stressing war and politics.

Will Durant, *The Life of Greece* (Simon and Schuster, 1939). A clear and careful presentation designed for the general public.

A. Bonnard, *Greek Civilization,* 3 vols. (Macmillan, 1957–1961). Stimulating chapters on many aspects of Greece by a European scholar.

R. M. Cook, *The Greeks till Alexander* (Thames & Hudson, 1961). Well-illustrated survey stressing material accomplishments.

SPECIAL STUDIES:
THE POLIS

G. Glotz, *The Greek City and Its Institutions* (Knopf, 1929). Celebrated study by a French scholar; now somewhat out of date.

A. Andrewes, *The Greek Tyrants* (*Torchbooks). Very informative comparative survey of emerging Greek constitutions.

Victor Ehrenberg, *The Greek State* (*Norton). A solid scholarly introduction.

A. H. M. Jones, *Athenian Democracy* (Praeger, 1957). An up-to-date interpretation.

A. E. Zimmern, *The Greek Commonwealth* (*Oxford Univ. Press). A celebrated older account, highly sympathetic in tone.

A. R. Burn, *Pericles and Athens* (*Collier). Popular introduction to the Athenian Golden Age.

H. Michell, *Sparta* (Cambridge Univ. Press. 1964). A comprehensive survey, rather more favorable in tone than most treatments of the subject.

Kathleen Freeman, *Greek City-States* (*Norton). Excellent overview, focusing on interesting examples usually neglected in the concern for Athens and Sparta.

A. G. Woodhead, *The Greeks in the West* (Praeger, 1962), and J. M. Cook, *The Greeks in Ionia and the East* (Praeger, 1963). Volumes in the series "Ancient Peoples and Places," highlighting the geographical outposts of the Greek world, likewise often neglected.

W. S. Ferguson, *Greek Imperialism* (Houghton, 1913). Brilliant lectures on the topic.

SPECIAL STUDIES:
GREEK CIVILIZATION

W. Jaeger, *Paideia*, 3 vols. (Oxford Univ. Press, 1939–1944; Vol. 1 also in paper-back). An advanced study of Greek civilization and ideals.

C. M. Bowra, *The Greek Experience* (*Mentor). With stress on interpretation rather than fact; by a literary scholar.

Edith Hamilton, *The Greek Way to Western Civilization* (*Mentor). Enthusiastic popular treatment by a great admirer of the Greeks.

G. Lowes Dickinson, *The Greek View of Life* (*Collier). Greek culture appraised from an old-fashioned point of view.

M. Hadas, *A History of Greek Literature* (*Columbia Univ. Press). Helpful survey.

Edith Hamilton, *Mythology* (*Mentor). Brief introduction, centered on Greek myths.

W. K. C. Guthrie, *The Greek and Their Gods* (*Beacon). Detailed but stimulating study of the origins and nature of Greek religion.

M. P. Nilsson, *Greek Folk Religion* (*Torchbooks). Informative lectures on popular beliefs and practices.

F. M. Cornford, *Before and After Socrates* (*Cambrige Univ. Press). First-rate short introduction to Greek science and philosophy.

E. Bréhier, *The Hellenic Age* (*Phoenix). The first volume of a detailed history of philosophy by a French scholar.

H. I. Marrou, *A History of Education in Antiquity* (*Mentor). A useful account, also treating the Romans and early Christians.

J. B. Bury, *The Greek Historians* (*Dover). Appraisal by a celebrated English historian.

Rhys Carpenter, *The Esthetic Basis of Greek Art* (*Midland). Analysis by an expert.

SPECIAL STUDIES:
THE HELLENISTIC
WORLD

W. W. Tarn, *Alexander the Great* (*Beacon). A sympathetic (and not always convincing) study by the foremost expert on the subject.

A. R. Burn, *Alexander the Great and the Hellenistic World* (*Collier). Brief popular account.

P. Bamm, *Alexander the Great* (Thames & Hudson, 1970). Beautiful pictures of the remains and scenery of Alexander's world; text disappointing.

W. W. Tarn, *Hellenistic Civilization* (*Meridian). Comprehensive survey of civilization under Alexander's successors.

M. Rostovtzeff, *The Social and Economic History of the Hellenistic World* (Clarendon, 1941). Detailed study by a great historian.

M. Hadas, *Hellenistic Culture* (Columbia Univ. Press, 1959). Good evaluation.

E. Bréhier, *The Hellenistic and Roman Age* (*Phoenix). Another volume of the French scholar's history of philosophy.

SOURCES

Note: The following list includes only the most famous works, many of which are available in many other translations and editions.

W. H. Auden, ed., *The Portable Greek Reader* (*Viking). Excellent short anthology.

A. J. Toynbee, ed, *Greek Civilization and Character* and *Greek Historical Thought* (*Mentor). Two volumes of excerpts from Greek writers affording a kaleidoscopic view of Greek attitudes.

Homer, *The Iliad*. Two of many translations: That of R. Lattimore (*Phoenix) is a good poetic translation; W. H. D. Rouse's (*Mentor) is in modern English prose.

W. J. Oats and E. O'Neill, Jr., eds., *The Complete Greek Drama* (Random House, 1938). A selection of dramas by the same editors may be found in *Seven Famous Greek Plays* (*Modern Library).

The Dialogues of Plato, trans. B. Jowett, (Clarendon, 1953). New edition of a famous (and controversial) old translation.

The Works of Aristotle, ed. W. D. Ross, (Clarendon, 1908–1931). Selections by the same editor are also available (*Scribner's).

Thucydides, *History of the Peloponnesian War*, trans. B. Jowett, (*Bantam).

Herodotus, *The Histories,* trans. A. de Selincourt (*Penguin).

Xenophon, *Anabasis: The March Up Country*, trans., W. H. D. Rouse (*Ann Arbor).

HISTORICAL FICTION   Mary Renault, *The King Must Die* and *The Last of the Wine* (*Pocket Books). Two of the several novels with Hellenic backgrounds written by an accomplished practicioner of historical fiction. The first is set in Mycenaean Greece and Minoan Crete, the second in Athens during the Peloponnesian War.

3

The Romans

I   Pre-Roman Italy

The earliest beginnings of what would become an empire more splendid and stable than any we have yet encountered are obscure indeed. Centuries later, when they had become a mighty people, the proud Romans—anxious to document their own mysterious past—collected every available myth, and cherished a story that in part we recognize as a tissue of invention. It told how Aeneas, a Trojan prince, but the son of the goddess Venus, had fled from burning Troy, led his fugitive followers to Italy, and founded a state on the banks of the Tiber. The poet Vergil (70–19 B.C.) immortalized the myth—already well known among the Romans—in his epic *Aeneid*, written in the imperial days of the first Roman emperor, the divine Augustus. After Aeneas, said the legend-makers, came a royal dynasty at Alba Longa, and eventually the famous nurslings of the she-wolf, Remus and his brother Romulus (traditionally 753–716 B.C.), who built Rome

Above: The tetrarchy of Diocletian, co-rulers of the Roman Empire, a sculpture now in St. Mark's, Venice. Above right: Hercules and Telephus, a first-century B.C. wall painting from Herculaneum. Right: Early fifth-century bronze wolf ("the Capitoline wolf") with Renaissance figures of Romulus and Remus.

itself and slew Remus for mockingly jumping over the low earthen city wall. These and other legends the later historian Livy (59 B.C.–A.D. 17), only a few years younger than Vergil, wove together to give his contemporaries the kind of remote past in which they could take pride.

Yet archaeology, as we know, has often shown how rash it is to belittle legend. If myths are not true in every detail, they may yet reflect in a general way some actual historic event. Thus the advent of a mythical prince from the East (Aeneas) can be made to symbolize the undoubted flow into Italy of men from the eastern Mediterranean and Greece, and the later pervasive influence of Greek civilization upon the Romans: when he wrote the *Aeneid* Vergil himself was both consciously and unconsciously borrowing from Homer. And the modern archaeologist has found at Alba Longa pottery and other artifacts similar to the earliest finds at Rome, suggesting that Livy's date for the mythical Romulus may be reasonably accurate.

In Italy, the plains were more extensive and more fertile than in Greece, and the mountains less of a barrier to land communication. South of the site of Rome stretched the plain of Latium, which lent itself well to intensive farming, especially after drainage and irrigation ditches had been dug. The surrounding hills provided good timber- and pastureland. Only fifteen miles from the sea, overlooking the Tiber, Rome could share in the trade of the peninsula; its seven hills could be easily fortified and defended. And its inhabitants were to prove themselves great builders, generals, administrators, and lawgivers.

To the south, as we know, by the year 600 B.C. Greek colonies dotted the shores of Italy and Sicily: this was Magna Graecia. To the north, the dominant power was held by the Etruscans, a mysterious people, perhaps from Asia Minor, who had invaded the peninsula and conquered the region north of Latium by 700 B.C. Thereafter they extended their power southward, surrounding Rome, which they seized soon after 600. Although we have rich Etruscan remains—pottery, weapons, sculpture, painting, mostly found in tombs—nobody has yet altogether deciphered the language: the Etruscans wrote in Greek letters, but their tongue is not Indo-European. No key like the Rosetta Stone

Detail of an Etruscan mosaic from the "Tomb of the Bulls," Corneto, Italy.

has turned up, and so far no expert like Ventris has turned up either. But most of the 10,000 existing inscriptions are very short: even if one could read them, one might not learn very much.

The Etruscans were expert farmers and miners, they built huge stone walls around their settlements, and they practiced divination, foretelling the future from observing flocks of birds in flight or from examining the entrails of an animal slain as a sacrifice. Their tomb-decoration seems to show that, like the Egyptians, they believed the afterlife was similar to this one, and that they accorded their women a more nearly equal status with men than was usual in ancient society. They also enjoyed gladiatorial combat as a spectacle, a taste which the Romans borrowed from them.

When the Etruscans moved into Latium and took over Rome, the people they conquered were apparently Latin tribesmen, descendants of the prehistoric inhabitants of the peninsula, and Rome itself must have been little more than a collection of hovels, probably no more significant in appearance than many of its neighboring villages. Under its Etruscan kings, Rome prospered during the sixth century. The Etruscans built new stone structures and drained and paved what became the Forum. But the native population resented foreign rule, and joined with other Latin tribes in a large-scale rebellion. The traditional date for the expulsion from Rome of the last Etruscan king, Tarquin the Proud, is 509 B.C. What he left behind was an independent Latin city-state, still including some Etruscan notables, much smaller than Athens or Sparta, sharing Latium with other city-states. Yet in less than 250 years Rome would dominate the entire Italian peninsula.

II   The Roman Republic

Politics and Society

How did the Romans manage to do it? Surely their own special form of government gave them strength. Once they had ousted Tarquin, the dominant aristocratic forces at Rome set up a republic. Only the well-established land-owning families, the patricians (Latin *pater*, "father")—perhaps not more than ten percent of the population—held full citizenship. The remaining ninety percent were plebeians (Latin *plebs*, "the multitude"), who included those engaged in trade or labor, the smallest farmers, and all those who were debtors as the result of the economic upheaval after the expulsion of the Etruscans. The plebeians had no right to hold office; they could amass as much money as they pleased, however, and wealthy plebeians would eventually lead the campaign to gain political emancipation for their class. Fifth-century Rome, then, was not unlike sixth-century Athens before the reforms of Cleisthenes.

The patrician class supplied the two consuls, the executive chiefs of state who governed jointly for a term of a year, enjoying full imperium, supreme political power, each of them exercising it alone in alternate months. Each had the right of veto over the other; so that both had to sup-port a measure before it could be put through. Ordinarily they were commanders of the army, but in wartime this power was often wielded, for a period not longer than six months, by an elected *dictator*. (Despite the modern meaning of the term, in the Roman republic it meant a commander who had obtained his authority constitutionally and had to give it up when his term was over.) The consuls usually followed the policies decided on by the Senate, a body consisting of about 300 members, mostly patricians and all ex-officials like the members of the Athenian Council of the Areopagus. The Senate was so important that it stood first in the famous Roman political device: S.P.Q.R.—*Senatus Populusque Romanorum* (The Senate and the People of the Romans). The reigning consuls were themselves senators, and appointed new senators. The entire Roman people in arms, patrician and plebeian alike, constituted another deliberative body, the Centuriate Assembly (so called from the century, the smallest unit—100 men—in the army). Its powers at first glance seem very great: it elected the consuls and other officials, and could approve or reject all laws submitted to it by the consuls and the Senate. But when one realizes that it could neither initiate proposed legislation nor discuss the matters submitted to it, and further learns that older and richer men predominated in it, one sees that it actually was less powerful than the Senate.

Before a man could be chosen consul, he had to pass through an apprenticeship in other posts. The job that led directly to the consulate was that of praetor (*prae-itor,* "the one who goes in front"). Elected by the Centuriate Assembly for a term of a year, the praetor served as a judge; he often had an army command, and later a provincial governorship. In the beginning there was only one praetor; but the number later rose to eight. Men seeking election as praetor or consul wore a special robe whitened with chalk, the *toga candida,* whence our word "candidate." From among the ex-consuls, the Assembly elected also two censors, for an eighteen-month term. They took the census that determined which of the population was financially qualified for army service. They also secured the right to pass on the moral qualifications of men nominated for the Senate, and they barred those whom they thought corrupt or too luxury-loving—whence the connotation of our words "censor" and "censorship."

This regime was well designed to carry on the chief business of the Roman state: war. The Roman army at first had as its basic unit the phalanx, about 8,000 foot soldiers, armed with helmet and shield, lance and sword, who took the field in massed array. But experience led to the substitution of the far more maneuverable legion, consisting of 3,600 men divided into 60- or 120-man bodies called maniples, armed with the additional weapon of the iron-tipped javelin which they hurled at the enemy from a distance. Discipline was harsh; punishment for offenses was summary and brutal; but the officers also understood the importance of generous recognition and reward of bravery as an incentive.

The plebeians naturally resented their exclusion from political authority. As early as the 490's, they threatened to withdraw from Rome and to found nearby a new city-state of their own, and when this tactic won them a concession, they continued to use it with great effect on and off during the next two hundred years. First (494) they got the right to have officials of their own, the tribunes of the people, to protect them from unduly harsh application of the laws. By 457 there were ten of these. The plebeians also (471) gained their own assembly, the Tribal Assembly (so named because of the subdivision of the population into tribes), which chose the

tribunes and had the right, like the Centuriate Assembly, to pass on new laws. They complained that, because the laws had never been written down, the patrician judges could manipulate them for their own purposes. After a lengthy political struggle the laws were engraved on wooden tablets in 451 B.C. and publicly exhibited. These were the Twelve Tables, beginning the epochal history of Roman law.

In the early days of the republic, plebeian debtors lost their farms and were forced into slavery. Property therefore accumulated in the hands of the patrician landowners. The plebeians obtained legislation limiting the size of the estate that any one man might accumulate, abolishing the penalty of slavery for debt, and opening newly acquired lands to settlement by landless farmers. The farmer–debtor problem, though eased, remained to plague the Romans to the end. During the fifth and fourth centuries, the plebeians won the right to hold all the offices of the state, even that of consul (366 B.C.). They also forced the abrogation of the laws that forbade their intermarriage with patricians. The fusion of wealthy plebeians and patricians formed a new class, the *nobiles,* who were to dominate the later republic as the patricians had the earlier.

The Conquest of Italy

In a long series of wars the Romans made good their supremacy over the other Latin towns, the Etruscan cities, and the half-civilized tribes of the central Apennines (the mountain backbone of the peninsula). Early in the third century B.C. they conquered the Greek cities of southern Italy. Meanwhile, in the north, the Celtic Gauls had crossed the Alps and settled in the Lombard plain; their expansion was halted at the little river Rubicon, which formed the northern frontier of Roman dominion.

The expansion of Rome in Italy demonstrated imaginative statesmanship as well as military superiority. In conquered areas, the Romans sometimes planted a colony of their own land-hungry plebeians. Usually they did not try to force the resident population into absolute subjection, but accepted them as allies, and respected their institutions. The cities of Magna Graecia continued to enjoy home rule. In some of the conquered cities the Romans offered members of the upper classes full Roman citizenship, but more often they gave Italians the status of part-citizens, without the right to participate in the Roman assemblies.

The Punic Wars

The conquest of Magna Graecia made Rome a near neighbor of the Carthaginian state. Carthage—modern Tunis—was originally a Phoenician colony, but had long since liberated itself from its motherland, and expanded along the African and Spanish shores of the Mediterranean and into the Balearic islands, Sardinia, and the western parts of Sicily. Ruled by a commercial oligarchy, Carthage held a virtual monopoly of western Mediterranean trade. When the Carthaginians began to seize the Greek cities in eastern Sicily also, the Sicilian Greeks appealed to Rome. So the Romans no doubt welcomed the opportunity to launch the First Punic (from the Latin word for "Phoenician") War, 264–241 B.C.

The Romans won by building their first major fleet in a genuine "crash program" and defeating the Carthaginians at sea. They forced Carthage to give up all claim to eastern Sicily and to cede western Sicily as well, thus obtaining their first territory outside the Italian mainland. In 237 they added Sardinia and Corsica. In 227 Sicily became a province of Rome, and Sardinia-Corsica another, each with its Roman governor. Thereafter the provincial governors were ex-consuls (and called proconsuls).

Trying to make up for their losses by expanding their holdings in Spain, rich in minerals and manpower, the Carthaginians sent their general Hannibal to lead their campaigns there. In 218, when the Second Punic War (218–201 B.C.) broke out, Hannibal led his forces across southern Gaul and then over the Alps into Italy, losing in the snow many of the elephants he used as pack-animals. In northern Italy he recruited many Gauls, and won a string of victories as he marched southward. The Roman general Fabius Cunctator, the Delayer, tried to exhaust the Carthaginians by his famous "Fabian" tactics: refraining from all-out battle while attacking Carthagian supply-trains and patrols and trying to wear them out. When the Romans reversed these tactics and impatiently tried to hit the Carthaginians at Cannae (216 B.C.), they suffered a shattering defeat.

It was several years before a new general, Scipio, emerged to defeat the Carthaginians, first in Spain and then in Africa itself (Zama, 202 B.C.), receiving the title "Africanus" as a reward for his successes. The Romans forced the Carthaginians to surrender southern and eastern Spain, which they made into two new Roman provinces. From this base Rome continued to fight the native Spaniards in central and northern Spain for about two centuries more. Carthage also had to pay a large sum of money, and promise to follow Rome's lead in foreign policy. Hannibal fled to the court of the Seleucid king Antiochus III.

Although Carthaginian power had been broken, the speedy recovery of the city's prosperity alarmed a war party at Rome, which agitated for its complete destruction. Cato the censor and senator would end each of his speeches with the word *Delenda est Carthago* ("Carthage must be destroyed"). In the Third Punic War (149–146 B.C.) the Romans leveled the city, sprinkled salt on the earth, and took over all its remaining territory, which became the Roman province of Africa (modern Tunisia).

The Conquest of Greece

While the Punic Wars were still going on, Rome had become embroiled in the Balkans and in Greece, sending fleets to put down the Illyrian pirates who were operating in the Adriatic from bases in what is now Albania. By 219, the Greeks, who had been suffering as much as anybody from the Illyrian raids, were so grateful to Rome for intervening that they admitted Romans to the Eleusinian mysteries and the Isthmian Games. But Philip V (221–178 B.C.), Antigonid king of Macedon, viewed with great suspicion Roman operations on his side of the Adriatic, and tried to help Hannibal during the Second Punic War. A Roman fleet prevented Philip from crossing to Italy, and many of the Greek cities, opponents of Philip but not yet of Rome, came to Rome's aid in the fighting that ensued. The First Macedonian War ended in 205 B.C. with the Romans and Philip agreeing to the existence between them of buffer states on the eastern shore of the Adriatic.

But in 202 several powers—Athens, Ptolemy V of Egypt, his ally Attalus, ruler of the powerful independent kingdom of Pergamum in Asia Minor, and Rhodes, head of a new naval league—appealed to Rome to intervene again against Philip, who had been interfering in the buffer states and arousing Roman suspicion. In the Second Macedonian War (200-197 B.C.) Rome defeated Philip's armies on their own soil (Cynoscephalae, 197) and forced him to withdraw from Greece altogether and to become an ally of Rome. At the Isthmian Games of 196, a solemn Roman proclamation declared the Greeks to be free. Two years later, after more fighting (chiefly against Sparta), the Roman armies left Greece and a largely disillusioned population.

Antiochus III (223-187 B.C.), Seleucid king in Asia, profited by the defeat of Macedon to take over the Greek cities on the Aegean coast of Asia Minor and to cross into Europe and campaign there. Worried at his advance, the Romans, who had their hands full with wars in Spain, kept on negotiating with him. But Antiochus, who had with him the refugee Hannibal, preferred to fight, hoping vainly for Greek support. At Thermopylae in 191 B.C. the Romans defeated him, and then invaded Asia, forcing Antiochus in 188 to surrender all the Seleucid holdings in Asia Minor. Hannibal got away, but poisoned himself in 183 as he was about to be surrendered to Rome. Rome had become the predominant power in the Greek world.

For the next forty years, the Romans found themselves obliged to arbitrate the constantly recurring quarrels among the Greek states. Rebellions forced repeated armed intervention. Philip V's son and successor, Perseus (179-168 B.C.), seemed to threaten to unite Greece against the Romans, and in the Third Macedonian War (171-168 B.C.) he was captured and his forces were routed at the decisive battle of Pydna (168 B.C.). The Romans came off with great booty. They imposed a ruthless settlement, breaking Macedon up into four republics and exiling from Greece many who had sympathized with Perseus. Twenty years later, after intervening against a leader called Andriscus, who pretended he was a son of Perseus, the Romans annexed Macedon (148 B.C.), their first province east of the Adriatic; and two years after that they defeated a desperate uprising of the Achaean League, and marked their victory by a particularly brutal sack of Corinth. All the men were killed, the women and children were sold as slaves, and the city was leveled to the ground. It was the same year as the total destruction of Carthage.

The Romans henceforth governed Greece from Macedon, but did not yet annex it as a province. Internal fighting in Greece came to an end; there was a religious and economic revival. Rome's prestige was now so great that in 133 the king of Pergamum, whose family had been helpful allies of the Romans—and much hated elsewhere for that reason—bequeathed his flourishing Asia Minor state to Rome in his will. It became the new province of Asia. The first Roman advances into southern Gaul followed in the next two decades.

Economic Strain: the Gracchi

As Roman territory increased, signs of trouble multiplied. The republic allowed a few overseas cities to retain some self-government, but usually organized its new territories as provinces under governors appointed by the Senate. Some of the governors proved oppressive and lined their own pockets, but as long as they collected taxes they had a free hand. In Italy, pressure mounted from Rome's allies, who demanded full citizenship and a share in the new wealth flowing into the capital. With the gradual exhaustion of Italian soil, grain had to be imported from Africa; former Italian grainfields were transformed into mixed farms or large cattle-ranches run by slaves, whom only big landowners could afford. More and more small farmers lost their land and became penniless and resentful refugees in the city of Rome.

The proprietors of latifundia (big estates) and certain merchants and contractors who had built roads for the state or furnished supplies to the army combined to form a new class of very rich men called equites (knights—the name had originally been used for those who could afford to equip themselves for service in the cavalry, the most expensive branch of the army, but no longer had any military significance). Sometimes they managed to join the Senate—that small group of about 300 men who actually governed Rome, and who had been steadily growing more powerful because they had managed the Punic

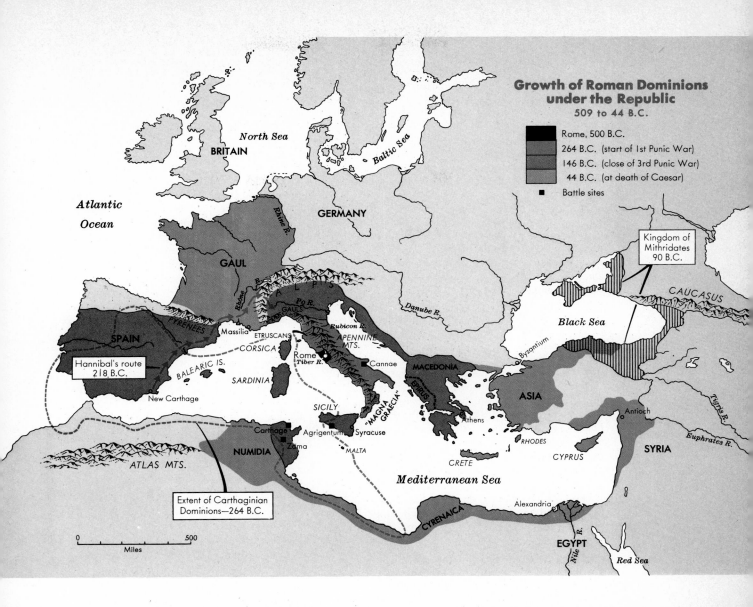

**Growth of Roman Dominions
under the Republic**
509 to 44 B.C.

- Rome, 500 B.C.
- 264 B.C. (start of 1st Punic War)
- 146 B.C. (close of 3rd Punic War)
- 44 B.C. (at death of Caesar)
- Battle sites

Kingdom of Mithridates 90 B.C.

North Sea

BRITAIN

Baltic Sea

Atlantic Ocean

GERMANY

GAUL

Rhone R.

ALPS

CAUCASUS

Danube R.

Black Sea

Hannibal's route 218 B.C.

SPAIN

PYRENEES

Massilia

ETRUSCANS

Po R.

GAULS

Rubicon R.

APENNINE MTS.

Byzantium

ASIA

Tigris R.

Euphrates R.

Antioch

SYRIA

CORSICA

Rome

Tiber R.

Cannae

MACEDONIA

EPIRUS

BALEARIC IS.

SARDINIA

"MAGNA GRAECIA"

Athens

RHODES

CYPRUS

New Carthage

SICILY

Carthage

Agrigentum

Syracuse

Zama

MALTA

CRETE

ATLAS MTS.

NUMIDIA

Mediterranean Sea

Extent of Carthaginian Dominions—264 B.C.

CYRENAICA

Alexandria

EGYPT

Nile R.

Red Sea

0 — 500 Miles

Wars so successfully—but it was almost impossible to crash the magic inner circle of the Senate that actually made policy and dominated Roman affairs. A group of about twenty families of *nobiles* (descendants of consuls) monopolized the highest offices, and so blocked for most others the path to noble status. By making combinations among themselves, by handing out patronage to their loyal henchmen, by controlling senatorial elections, by representing themselves as the repository of all the old Roman virtues of simplicity and hard work and true patriotism, this tight little oligarchy ran things in its own way. Naturally its exclusiveness produced severe tensions.

Among the senators themselves, those who were content with things as they were called themselves optimates, while those who found themselves unable to get things done their way sometimes tried to get support from the people at large in the Tribal Assembly, and so got from their opponents the name populares. The increase in wealth led to increased bribery at election-time, and to more lavish spectacles staged for the entertainment of the public. There were many thousands of foreign slaves now, ranging from pampered Greek intellectuals, much in demand as tutors in the household, to brutally abused farm- or mine-laborers, who sometimes organized revolts—70,000 in Sicily in 135 B.C., for example. Even military discipline was less reliable. The machinery that had successfully guided a small city-state was proving inadequate to deal with the problems of empire, of social strain, of economic distress, and of growing corruption.

Two brothers named Gracchus, grandsons of Scipio, hero of the Punic War, and themselves nobles, emerged during the late 130's and the 120's as the particular champions of the dispossessed. Tiberius Gracchus, who served as tribune of the people in 133 B.C., and Gaius, who held the post from 123 to 121, sought to increase the role of the tribunes and the Tribal Assembly at the expense of the Senate. The wild beasts, said Tiberius, have their dens, but the Roman soldiers have not a clod of earth to call their own. The brothers wanted to limit the size of estates that could be owned by one family; to resettle landless farmers either on state-owned lands in Italy that had been leased to capitalist farmers or in a new colony founded at Carthage; and to give the city poor of Rome relief by allowing them to buy grain from the state at cost. Politically, they wanted to give certain privileged financial and judicial posts to the equites, to extend Roman citizenship to all Latins, and to raise other Italians to Latin status, which would have appeased much bitter anti-Roman feeling among the republic's own Italian allies.

The efforts of the Gracchi largely failed. Of their economic program only the proposal to sell the Roman people cheap grain remained on the books after their overthrow. In the succeeding centuries the state had to lower the price until the poor were getting their bread free. This in itself reveals the relative failure of the resettlement program: had enough dispossessed farmers actually received new allotments, the number in the city needing cheap bread would presumably have fallen off sharply. The agrarian capitalists, after being forced by the Gracchi to give up much of the land they rented from the state, were soon expanding their holdings once more. The latifundia had come to stay. Moreover, on the political side, the Senate resented the extension of rights and privileges to the equites, and balked at granting Roman citizenship to non-Roman Italians.

Meantime, politics turned unconstitutional and violent. Tiberius Gracchus ousted a tribune of the people who was blocking his program; both brothers defied precedent and ran for re-election as tribunes. The senators themselves resorted to murder to stop the Gracchi, killing Tiberius and three hundred of his supporters in 133; in 121 Gaius killed himself to avoid a similar fate, amidst a massacre of his followers ordered by the consul. Were the Gracchi high-minded "New Dealers" blocked by the vested interests of the senators, or unstable radicals whose high-handed methods only added to the discord? Probably both; at any rate the deadlock between impatient Gracchan reformism and stodgy senatorial conservatism revealed the inadequacy of the Roman government.

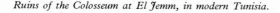

Ruins of the Colosseum at El Jemm, in modern Tunisia.

III Twilight and End of the Republic

After the Gracchan interlude, political leadership passed to generals who cared less for principle than for power. In the provinces the misrule of the governors provoked uprisings. A victorious general would celebrate in Rome with a great "triumph," a parade of his successful troops and of their prisoners and booty that would dazzle the public. And the troops, properly rewarded by their commanders, became loyal to them rather than to the state. The way to get ahead in Roman politics was to make a record as a successful general.

Marius and Sulla

The first of the generals to reach power was Marius, a "new man" who had married into the highest Roman aristocracy. Marius had won victories against the Numidians in North Africa—in what is now eastern Algeria (111–105 B.C.)—and against a group of Germanic peoples called the Cimbri and Teutones, who with some Celtic allies had caused Rome a great deal of alarm before he beat them at what is now Aix-en-Provence in southern France (102 B.C.). Violating the custom that a consul had to wait ten years before serving a second term, Marius had himself elected six times between 107 and 100 B.C. He began a major reorganization of the army by abolishing the last remains of a property qualification. Professional soldiers now gradually replaced the former citizen-soldiers, who in the past had gone back to their normal peacetime occupations once the fighting was over. The danger for the state in this change was soon made manifest: such troops would count on their commanders to look after them in times of peace, especially since there was no system of state pensions. The way would soon lie open for rival commanders to compete against one another for dictatorial powers.

Marius strove to inculcate in the individual soldier a feeling of special loyalty to his legion, and increased mobility by requiring the men to carry their own equipment as far as possible.

"Marius' mules" his men were soon called. Once peace had come (100 B.C.) Marius got his troops the land allotments they craved, but he proved incapable of understanding—much less solving— the persistent political and social problems of the republic. He retired in 99 B.C. amidst disorders caused largely by his political allies.

Smoldering during the 90's B.C., the old issue of Roman citizenship for the Italian cities burst into flames once more at the end of the decade, when the Senate stubbornly refused to see that the question had become crucial. The Italians felt passionately that their assistance to the Roman state should be rewarded by official recognition of their equality. When they could not gain this end by persuasion, they rebelled in a full-scale war for independence (called the Social War from socius, "ally," 91–88 B.C.), striking their own coins, one of which showed the Roman she-wolf being gored by the bull, the symbol of Italy, the new state they hoped to found. It took major Roman military operations to put down this bitter revolution, and success came in the end only because the Romans gave in on the main issue. During the fighting itself the state began to pass a series of laws gradually opening Roman citizenship to all Italians south of the river Po, a process not truly completed until 84 B.C. Among the leading generals who had fought the rebels was Sulla, who became consul in 88 B.C.

In that year Mithridates VI, the ambitious king of Pontus, on the south shore of the Black Sea, seized the Roman province of Asia and provoked the massacre of 80,000 Romans in a single night. Mithridates, a partly Hellenized oriental despot who had recently conquered rich new lands on the northern coast of the Black Sea and in the Crimea, soon became involved in anti-Roman activities in Greece as well. The Senate gave Sulla—who had already held Eastern commands—charge of the new expedition to punish him. But Marius now emerged from retirement and demanded the job for himself. Civil strife broke out between the rival generals.

Sulla's troops took Rome, and Marius fled to Africa; then Sulla went off to fight Mithridates, and Marius came back and seized Rome. Elected consul for 86 B.C., Marius died at the age of seventy. It took Sulla until 84 to defeat Mithridates, who had to evacuate all Roman territory and pay an indemnity. Sulla imposed a ruthless settlement on the cities that had been disloyal to Rome. His forces sacked Athens for sympathizing with Mithridates, and plundered Zeus's treasury at Olympia and Apollo's at Delphi.

When he got back from Asia in 83, Sulla had to fight a bloody war against his Roman political opponents in Italy. For two years thousands were killed in battle or massacred after defeat, and during 81 Sulla conducted savage mopping-up operations in the provinces and butchered his surviving enemies in Rome and those Italian cities that had opposed him. By the time it was over, even the Senate was reduced to about 150 members. Sulla raised the number to something between 500 and 600, drawing heavily on his own supporters and adding also 300 members of the equites, perhaps in the hope of blunting the ancient rivalry between the two groups. He strove to restore to this reconstituted Senate its ancient position as the chief force in political life. In a great mass of new legislation Sulla tried to keep young men out of office by setting minimum ages for office-holding; he stringently curtailed the powers of the tribunes and the Tribal Assembly, and he reformed the law courts. He prolonged his own tenure as dictator beyond the traditional fixed limit of six months. He did retire in 79 B.C., and died a year later, aged sixty.

Pompey and Caesar

Within ten years, Pompey, a ruthless and arrogant young veteran of Sulla's campaigns, won victories first in Italy against an over-ambitious consul, then in Spain against a Roman governor who was building an independent power there, and then at home once more against a slave rebellion led by Spartacus (73–71 B.C.). In 70 B.C. Pompey became consul before he had reached the minimum legal age, and with his colleague Crassus, a millionaire who had in fact played a larger part than Pompey in subduing the revolt of Spartacus, forced the Senate to undo much of the work of Sulla, especially by restoring their old power to the tribunes and the Tribal Assembly. Next, Pompey became grand admiral of Roman naval forces against the troublesome pirates of the Mediterranean. After promptly defeating them (67 B.C.), he took command of a new war against Mithridates, who had attacked Rome again in order to prevent the Romans from picking up a neighboring kingdom (Bithynia) in Asia Minor that had been left them in the will of the king.

It was initially the tribunes of the people, newly restored to influence in large part through Pompey's own pressure, who now—against bitter senatorial opposition—forced through the measures that gave Pompey unprecedented special powers and huge resources in men, money, and supplies in his two successive commands, and so helped further to destroy the machinery that Sulla had constructed in the hope of maintaining senatorial supremacy. But after Pompey had beaten the pirates, even moderate men (like the great lawyer and aspiring politician Cicero) and future opponents of Pompey (like the talented Julius Caesar) supported the renewal and extension of the powers.

In the East, Pompey defeated Mithridates, and drove him into his Crimean fortress of Panticapaeum, where he committed suicide (63 B.C.). Pompey also defeated Mithridates' son-in-law Tigranes, king of Armenia, and then moved into Syria. Here the last effective Seleucid had died as early as 129 B.C., and Pompey now turned Syria too into a Roman province, and captured Jerusalem itself (64 B.C.), rudely entering the shrine of the Temple but not disturbing the Ark. The western fringe of Asia was now effectively Roman, governed either directly by Rome, or by local kings who acknowledged themselves to be Roman clients and thus followers of Rome in all aspects of their foreign policy. Following the policies of Alexander and the Hellenistic kings, Pompey also deliberately rebuilt many of the former Greek city-states in western Asia, thus not only binding the loyalties of the local populations to him, and through him to Rome, but also almost doubling the annual Roman revenue in tribute.

While Pompey was in the East, his former co-consul, the rich and ambitious Crassus, by intrigue tried to build up his own power for what he foresaw as a certain showdown with the popular military hero. Egypt seemed to offer opportunities, when the alleged will of one of the Ptolemies—which may even have been genuine—left the kingdom to Rome; but Crassus' efforts to get the Senate to approve annexation were blocked by Cicero and the optimates, acting in Pompey's interests.

Then, in 63, there came to light the famous conspiracy of Catiline, a frustrated and impoverished noble who had been trying vainly for some time to win political office and who now gathered a disreputable band of malcontents around him in the hope of pulling off a successful coup in Rome. Cicero, now consul and personal target of the revolutionaries, exposed the plot in the Senate: his speeches there against Catiline have given much instruction and some pain to generations of schoolboys. Supported by Cato the younger, great-grandson of the enemy of Carthage, Cicero called for the death penalty for the conspirators. The Senate approved, despite the efforts of Julius Caesar to substitute life imprisonment (efforts which helped give rise to the probably unfounded suspicion that Caesar and Crassus might have been involved in the conspiracy). But the Senate was not a court of law, and had no power to impose death sentences. So when Cicero proceeded to have five ringleaders executed, he was acting illegally, if

patriotically. Soon afterward Catiline himself was killed in battle against Roman troops.

Cicero now made overtures to Pompey suggesting that they cooperate in establishing a general harmonious concord among all Romans of good will (he had been heartened by the support that he had received against Catiline from patriotic Romans of all shades of political opinion). But Cicero lacked the family background and personal following necessary to reach the top; he was a lawyer and not a general; and Pompey may well have resented the fact that it had been Cicero and not he who had saved the republic from Catiline. In any case, Pompey was not responsive. He returned to Italy (62 B.C.), and retired into private life, dismissing his armies and making no attempt to seize power.

However, he soon found himself balked by the Senate in his efforts to have his Eastern settlement ratified, and to have land provided in the usual way for his veteran troops. Rebuffed also in certain (quite reasonable) proposals of their own, Crassus and Caesar joined with Pompey in a loose three-man political alliance ("triumvirate") to assist one another. Cicero

Outfall into the Tiber of the Cloaca Maxima, draining the Forum at Rome.

refused to come in with them, but together they got everything they wanted. In 59 B.C. Caesar became consul, and Pompey married his daughter. With Caesar's backing, Pompey's former troops received large grants of land, much of it near Naples, where the peasantry had to be dispossessed. Pompey's Eastern settlement was duly confirmed. Caesar himself received—in two installments—both provinces of Gaul to govern. On leaving Rome, he secured the election as tribune of a certain Clodius. Only a few years earlier, Clodius had created a scandal by disguising himself as a woman and attending a religious ceremony supposedly reserved exclusively for females. He had been tried for sacrilege and acquitted by bribery, despite Cicero's objections. The religious festival was taking place in Caesar's own house, and it was generally believed that Clodius and Caesar's wife were having an affair: it was then that Caesar had divorced her because "Caesar's wife must be above suspicion."

Clodius put through certain new laws making bread distributions to the citizens altogether free—thus speeding demoralization and enhancing his own popularity—and authorizing the formation of political clubs, which in fact were soon to become little private armies. Clodius,

Shops and private houses along a street in the ruins of Pompeii.

who had been waiting for a chance to get back at Cicero ever since Cicero had objected to his acquittal, now got Cicero sent into exile because of his execution without trial of the Catilinarian conspirators. Clodius even began to harass Pompey himself, who soon formed his own private gang of supporters and struck back at Clodius by getting Cicero recalled from exile. By 56 B.C. strains were appearing in the triumvirate, as Pompey and Crassus became rivals for a mission to Egypt, and Pompey began to think that Crassus was behind the attacks of Clodius' gang upon him.

But the triumvirs got together at a conference, and it was agreed that Caesar would continue his work in Gaul, while Crassus would become governor of Syria and Pompey of Spain. Clodius was to be curbed. Cicero himself recanted and supported the triumvirs. Crassus went off to Syria, but in 53 B.C. was killed in a terrible Roman defeat in Mesopotamia (Carrhae) by the forces of the Parthians, the dynasty that had risen in Persia to replace the Seleucids. Even before that, Pompey's wife, Caesar's daughter, died, and the bonds between the two men were loosened. The former chief of Pompey's private gang now murdered Clodius, and in 52 Pompey became sole consul, retaining his Spanish command as well, but staying in Rome as the most powerful politician there. The triumvirate had come to an end, and Pompey was anxiously watching the activities of Caesar, who had spent most of the 50's campaigning.

In Gaul lived Celtic tribes, mostly farmers and cattle-raisers. There was some mining, and a good deal of trade along the rivers, but there were only a few small cities. The tribes were often at odds with each other. Here Caesar had conquered for Rome the large area corresponding to most of modern France and Belgium. He had even twice crossed the English Channel to punish the Celtic Britons for helping their fellow Celts in Gaul, though he did not attempt to conquer Britain permanently. Caesar was a magnificent general, distinguished especially by the speed with which he moved and the decision with which he acted. After once submitting, the Gallic tribes often showed a tendency to revolt again, and a lesser genius than Caesar would have allowed himself to become discouraged at watching his work come unstuck.

Moreover the Germanic tribes east of the Rhine frequently intervened in Gaul and made the problem even more difficult. Against the Germans Caesar showed extreme ruthlessness. He impressed upon them the lesson that they must stay on their own side of the Rhine by massacring two whole German tribes in Gaul, and then rapidly building a bridge across the Rhine, invading and devastating the territory on the east bank, returning to Gaul, and destroying the bridge after he had crossed it. Even after the Gallic tribes had learned to unite against him in the great revolt of Vercingtorix (52 B.C.) Caesar overcame them decisively. Caesar's transformation of Gaul into Roman territory meant that—like Italy and Spain—the future France would have a civilization firmly based on Rome and a language based on Latin. In order to give his achievements maximum publicity in Rome, Caesar now wrote his *Gallic Wars* (much easier Latin to read than Cicero).

Caesar's Victory, Death, and Achievements

Warily watching Caesar's growing triumphs, the optimates at Rome, who disapproved of Pompey but feared Caesar's popularis background and tendencies even more,* succeeded in persuading Pompey to accept the command of all troops in Italy. Pompey and Caesar were now facing each other for a showdown that neither of them seems really to have wanted. Caesar himself blamed the optimates for blocking his efforts to run for the consulship without having first given up his command. At any rate, when in 49 Caesar defied the Senate and led his loyal troops south across the Rubicon River boundary, he was entering Roman territory proper illegally under arms, and had opened a civil war.

Within two months Caesar was master of Italy, and Pompey with his troops had fled to Greece. Cicero later joined him. Caesar, who had no ships and so could not cross to Greece, left two of his supporters—Mark Antony and Lepidus—in charge of Italy and Rome itself, and went off to campaign against Pompey's supporters in Spain, a task that took him only three

---

*Caesar often reminded the Roman people that his aunt had been Marius' wife, which made him an impeccable popularis, while on the other hand he was also descended directly from Aeneas and so from the gods.

months despite great odds against him. Both in Italy and Spain he treated his defeated opponents with mercy, not repeating the bloodbaths of Sulla. Having been appointed dictator, he got himself elected consul at Rome, resigned the dictatorship after only eleven days, and put through a law to the advantage of debtors. In 48 B.C. he defeated Pompey's forces at Pharsalus, in Greece. Pompey escaped with some followers to Egypt, but was murdered there by troops of Ptolemy XII, the ten-year-old ruler eager to win Caesar's support against his eighteen-year-old sister, wife, and rival, Cleopatra.

Caesar's own famous trip to Egypt and love affair with Cleopatra came immediately afterwards, accompanied by successful warfare against her brother, who was killed and succeeded by a still younger brother, Ptolemy XIII, though real power remained in Cleopatra's hands. Caesar's celebrated trip up the Nile with Cleopatra quite possibly never actually happened. But he certainly defeated pro-Pompey forces in Asia Minor, returned to Rome to deal with the disorders that creditors and their supporters had caused in protest against the new law on debtors, and generously greeted Cicero (back in Rome again after Pompey's defeat). He cleaned up the dangerous situation in North Africa (47–46 B.C.), which was held by Pompey's followers, including Cato (who now committed suicide); and he set up Cleopatra and their infant son Caesarion in his own house. Despite the unpopularity of this action, he also had her made officially a Friend of the Roman People, which seems fair enough.

A final victory over the large armies that Pompey's sons had been massing in Spain, and Caesar was back in Rome for another triumph in 45 B.C. Less than a year later—the Ides of March, 44 B.C.—he lay stabbed to death on the floor of the Senate at the foot of Pompey's statue. His dictatorship had been twice renewed, the third time for life; he had been consul five times, sometimes alone; he had the title "Liberator"; his enemies had been forgiven.

He did not have much time for the program of social reform that Cicero urged him to undertake, and that he himself wished to put through. But he did help the debtors and suppress the political clubs that had led to the private armies. He sharply cut down the bread dole, with the intention of settling more than half of its former recipients in new colonies, which were also founded for his own troops in Africa, Spain, and Greece. He began an active program of using new city charters for the Italian towns. He admitted to Roman citizenship a Gallic legion, and several cities in the provinces. He issued the first gold coins, reformed the calendar to bring it into line with the solar year (the Julian calendar, which, as slightly modified by Pope Gregory XIII in the eighteenth century, is still in use), and set fixed taxes for many areas, enabling the inhabitants to know from year to year what would be expected of them. He added new buildings to Rome; he planned new highways, systems of Tiber flood-control, and even a canal through the Isthmus of Corinth in Greece. Politically he created many new senators (the number rose to 900), and controlled the elections to the other public offices. The threads of power were all in his hands.

His opponents said he wanted to become king, and to be worshiped as a god. About monarchy they may have been right. Several times before his death Caesar was offered crowns or refused crowns: was he testing public sentiment? In any case he denied any wish for a crown. Was that mere window-dressing? Quite likely he had not yet made up his mind what kind of form or title to give his own autocracy. About divinity his opponents were probably wrong: like other Roman generals, Caesar had been given divine honors in the East, but like other Romans he probably saw no need for a divine cult of himself in Rome during his lifetime. Whatever his real views may have been, he had indeed ridden roughshod over the Roman constitution; he acted personally in an overbearing way. Patriots among his own supporters—who had nothing to gain by his death—certainly joined the conspiracy against him, feeling that killing a tyrant would be a patriotic act. The celebrated Brutus, who had been a partisan of Pompey but had been pardoned by Caesar, was the half-nephew and son-in-law of Cato the Younger, that self-appointed symbol of the old republican virtues. Others among the conspirators were no doubt merely disloyal or jealous. The leader was Cassius.

Yet the rank and file of Romans seem to have regarded Caesar as a great benefactor, the restorer of law and order. The conspirators found the public hostile, and were forced to accept a compromise with Caesar's supporters, worked out by Cicero: the murderers would not be punished, but Caesar would be solemnly buried and his will would be respected. The will was in the hands of Caesar's aide, the ambitious and unscrupulous consul Mark Antony; it left a bequest of money to each individual Roman citizen. This generous legacy, combined with Antony's fiery praise of Caesar at the funeral, aroused the mob to fury against the conspirators, who fled from Rome, leaving Antony in control.

Antony and Octavian: The End of the Republic

But much to Antony's distress Caesar in his will had adopted as his son and left three-quarters of his huge fortune to Octavian, his grand-nephew, still only nineteen years old, who now came to Rome to claim his inheritance, which Antony refused to turn over. Claiming the providences of Gaul for his own, Antony had to fight to get them. As Demosthenes had once warned the Athenians against Philip, Cicero now repeatedly warned the Romans that Antony wanted to be dictator and urged that Octavian should be used against him for the benefit of the republic.

But once Antony had been defeated by the forces of Octavian and the two consuls, the Senate turned with relief to various prominent members of the conspiracy against Caesar, and to Pompey's son, Sextus Pompeius. Octavian refused to cooperate with these people, marched on Rome, and got himself elected consul; Caesar's murderers were soon outlawed. Joined by Lepidus, another former important aide to Caesar, Antony won his fight in Gaul. With characteristic shrewdness, Octavian now reached an agreement with Lepidus and Antony: together, the three formed the second triumvirate, official this time, and assumed for five years the right to make laws and appoint officials. Antony took two Gallic provinces, Lepidus the rest of Gaul and Spain, Octavian Africa, Sicily, and Sardinia. Caesar's outlawed murderers, Brutus and Cassius, had large and threatening armies in Macedonia and Asia Minor; Sextus Pompeius had a fleet.

To raise money, the triumvirs now reverted to the ruthlessness of Sulla, executing two thousand rich equities and three hundred senators and confiscating their estates. Among the victims was Cicero, murdered at Antony's order, and his severed head and hands savagely exhibited in public. In 42 B.C. Octavian and Antony moved east and at Philippi twice defeated Caesar's murderers: both Cassius and Brutus committed suicide. Octavian now took over all of the Western provinces except Gaul, and prepared to deal with Sextus Pompeius, while Antony went east to re-establish Roman rule. This time Lepidus' claims were temporarily ignored pending a clarification of his behavior: he was thought to have been in treasonable contact with Sextus Pompeius, but soon afterwards he was given Africa. Thus the inevitable rivalry had begun within the second triumvirate.

It continued, as members of Antony's family seized Rome briefly and forced Octavian to fight them. Only after a renewal of the old agreement in 40 B.C. was Antony allowed officially to return to Italy, where he married Octavian's sister, Octavia, thereby postponing a civil war. In 37 B.C. the triumvirate was renewed for a second five-year term. But it was not until 36 that Octavian was able to dispose of Sextus Pompeius, who with his ships had set himself up as ruler of Sicily and had several times defeated Octavian. Sextus Pompeius fled to the East, where Antony had him executed. Lepidus tried to seize Sicily on his own account, but failed, and Octavian dropped him from the triumvirate, sparing his life. There were now only two triumvirs left. Octavian controlled the entire West, which he made even more secure by a successful campaign against the tribesmen and pirates of Illyricum—part of modern Yugoslavia (35–33 B.C.). Octavian, whose late adoptive father Julius Caesar had long since been recognized as a god, now began to call himself Imperator Caesar. He began to beautify Rome with new buildings, and to receive general credit for the better conditions that his rule had brought to Italy.

In the East, meanwhile, Antony, who probably at first was interested chiefly in her money, had summoned Cleopatra from Egypt (where she had returned after Caesar's death), and had killed Ptolemy XIII, the second of her younger brothers and husbands to die. They began their famous love affair in Asia Minor, and continued it in Egypt. She bore him twins, and he went through some form of marriage to her, although still married to Octavia. Invaders in Macedonia were troublesome to Antony, but the attacks in Syria and Asia Minor of the Parthians (one of whose commanders was a Roman officer and

former supporter of Cassius) were worse, and Antony suffered a great defeat in what is now northwest Persia, which he partly redeemed by a victory in Armenia (34 B.C.). The triumph and accompanying ceremonies he and Cleopatra put on for themselves in Alexandria afterwards sounded clear warnings to Octavian.

Caesar's ostensible son by Cleopatra, Caesarion or Ptolemy Caesar, they proclaimed to be the true heir of Julius, and King of Kings (Octavian of course was not mentioned), while Cleopatra herself was Queen of Kings. She was already ruling portions of Asia Minor and the island of Cyprus, and her twins by Antony, Alexander Helios (the Sun) and Cleopatra Selene (the Moon), each were now assigned provinces, as was the newborn baby Ptolemy Philadelphus. Though Antony remained only triumvir, it was natural for Octavian to exploit to the full for propaganda purposes in Italy all these most un-Roman oriental arrangements. When the triumvirate expired in 33 B.C., it was not renewed; and Octavian, who no longer needed the title, dropped it. It was, however, the only claim to authority that Antony had, and he continued to use it.

The quarrel soon emerged fully into the open. Both consuls of 32 B.C. and 300 senators were partisans of Antony, and went to Egypt to join him; he formally divorced Octavia. By reading Antony's will to the remaining senators, Octavian persuaded them that its provisions with regard to Cleopatra and her children implied that Antony intended to abandon Rome, and make Alexandria the imperial capital. As the Italian and other western population rallied behind him, Octavian deprived Antony of his office, declared war on Cleopatra, and crossed to Greece to fight them both. At Actium, off the western coast of northern Greece (31 B.C.), Octavian's ships won a critical naval battle; in the next year Octavian himself occupied Alexandria. Antony and Cleopatra committed suicide, and Caesarion was executed, but Cleopatra's other children were spared, and Octavia brought them up. Rome thus acquired Egypt, the last of the great Hellenistic states to disappear. But Egypt did not become a Roman province. It became the personal property of the Roman emperor, administered for him by his agents. And Octavian had become sole and undisputed master of the entire Roman heritage. The republic had come to an end.

IV   The Empire

Rome and the Provinces at the End of the Republic

There was no sharp break with republican governmental practices, no abolition of the republic or proclamation of an empire. Octavian was too intelligent, too shrewd, too conscious that he was heir to a long tradition, to startle or alienate the people of Rome. But while seeking to preserve traditional forms, he was none the less determined to get on with the business of remaking the government along the lines suggested by Julius Caesar, so that Rome would have the authority and the machinery to manage the huge territories it had acquired. The almost perpetual internal strife characteristic of the last sixty years of the republic had left the population eager for a ruler who could guarantee order, and less sensitive about traditional Roman freedoms than earlier generations.

Each of the political generals in turn had had to settle his veterans—perhaps half a million in all—on new allotments in Italy, a process that had helped make the peninsula itself more homogeneous, and that had assured the continued existence of small farms alongside the large estates of the rich, characterized by absentee owners and slave labor. Prosperous and populous (perhaps fourteen million people, of whom about a third were slaves), Italy continued to be largely agricultural, though much building activity was carried on in Rome and the other towns, with tools produced by local industry. Roman businessmen enthusiastically exploited the provinces, to which many of them flocked to make money in trade, especially the luxury trade.

As wealth increased, so did the demand for jewels, works of art, and exotic foods, and though admirers of traditional Roman simplicity and self-denial deplored the changes, it would be wrong to think that new-rich showy ways triumphed everywhere, or that the old families alone could enjoy material comfort. Cicero himself, for example, despite his energy, ambition, and high character, could never achieve real power in Rome, but he did become consul, and

he made a great deal of money in his legal practice: he had eight country houses that we know of besides his house in Rome. The Roman jet set did indeed pay less attention to the domestic virtues than their ancestors had paid, and the growing divorce rate and loose morality shocked the conservatives; but many of the upper classes used their wealth to foster literature and art, and lived quiet, happy family lives.

The equites were distinguished from the nobles only by their origins, not by their economic or social position. Nobles and equites alike had their circles of clients in the professions or trades, and there were in addition independent small shopkeepers and merchants. Living in squalid apartment houses, six or seven stories tall, the Roman lower classes, assured at least of free grain for bread, presumably also made money by selling their votes to the highest bidder at election time, and may have got by with doing little if any work. They did insist on, and obtain, increasingly elaborate and violent public spectacles at more and more frequent intervals. Rome itself probably had about a million inhabitants.

In the provinces, Roman practice varied with existing conditions. In the West—Spain or Gaul, for example—the Romans had to deal with the Celtic tribes. In the ancient Mediterranean lands—largely Greek—to the east, they built on the existing traditional system of city-states. The basic charter issued to each such province at the time of its annexation would exempt certain cities permanently from taxation, allow them to continue to be governed by their local laws, release them from the obligation to give free housing and food to Roman soldiers stationed there, and even exempt their citizens from the draft. Taxes were usually not high, and included a fixed tax, a tenth of agricultural produce, and customs tolls. By way of appeasing the equites, Gaius Gracchus in 123 B.C. had given them the right to bid for the privilege of collecting the taxes in Asia, which was a profitable business. The provincial governor, an ex-consul or ex-praetor at Rome, usually served between three and five years, and enjoyed unlimited power, although Roman citizens living under his rule could appeal against any of his actions that they considered illegal. He was responsible for justice and for defense, and his accounts were scrutinized carefully before he could go home. Some Roman governors were corrupt and made fortunes; but we would not even know about them if they had not later been tried and punished for their offenses.

The provincials under Roman rule usually found themselves at peace with each other, an inestimable benefit in Greece, for example, with its traditions of perpetual strife between city-states. Nor did the Romans interfere with local ways of life. The frequent unpopularity of their rule we can attribute in part to the privileged position of the Roman residents, and in part to the natural dislike of human beings to be gov-

A contemporary marble bust of Augustus as a youth.

erned by foreigners. And of course when challenged by rebellion or "treachery" in a province, Roman punishment was usually speedy and severe.

Octavian Becomes Augustus

Facing these realities, and aware that he could neither dilute his authority nor fully exercise it, Octavian moved gradually in the years after Actium. He gradually demobilized his huge armies, founding some new settlements in Italy and abroad for 100,000 ex-soldiers. Enormously rich already, he now had personally available to him all the revenues of Egypt in addition, and he paid for the soldiers' pensions out of his own pocket. Now that his enemies had been destroyed, he issued an amnesty. Consul every year, imperator, governor in his own right of Spain, Gaul, and Syria, princeps—that is, first—among the senators, in 27 B.C. he received further honors from the Senate, including most notably the new title of Augustus, the revered one, by which he was thereafter known to history, and by which we refer to him hereafter.

The continued personal control over three provinces assured him of more troops personally loyal to himself than any other provincial governor or combination of governors would be able to command. The title "princeps," which he always said was his own favorite, was not a new one, and so it had a reassuring republican ring: Augustus said he was the "restorer" of the republic. As the first citizen and the one to whom reverence was due, he enjoyed by common consent more prestige, more authority, than anybody else. Men could feel that they were still living, or rather living again, in the Roman Republic, while not failing to see that its affairs were in the hands of its single most important citizen.

In 23 B.C., after four years in the provinces, Augustus modified his position further by resigning the consulship, which he had continued to hold annually, and accepting from the Senate three new grants: of tribunician powers which enhanced his supremacy in Rome, of "greater" powers in provincial affairs than those of any other provincial governor, and of the right to introduce the first measure at any meeting of the Senate, which he could summon. To the tribunician powers he gave full publicity, thus reminding the public of Rome that he was *their* magistrate. The other powers he had in reserve if he should want to exercise them, and so he did not need to give them publicity. These measures of 23 B.C. stabilized Augustus' rule, which was to last another thirty-seven years, until A.D. 14. He spent nine of these years away from Rome.

The Senate of course continued to share in the processes of government. Augustus reduced its numbers in 29 B.C. from 1000 to 800 members and again in 18 B.C. to 600 members. He gave it a small inner steering committee, on which he himself sat. He also enabled men not of senatorial birth who were distinguished for their military service, their wealth, or their character to serve as members; and in fact he could and did appoint anybody he thought suitable. He used the equites in administrative posts, thereby diminishing their grievances at being left out, and added new recruits to this class too by judicious selection. The sons of senators were equites until their twenty-fifth birthdays. What Augustus did was to create a civil service that opened careers to talent and that rewarded service with regular salaries and recognition by advancement.

Both the Senate and Augustus could issue laws; both the Senate and Augustus sitting as judges could try certain capital cases involving important people; it was the Senate that authorized Augustus to draw from the treasury the money that he would need, but he was so rich that in fact he often spent his own money for public purposes, and went through most of his huge personal fortune in this way. Recognizing that future veterans should not have to be dependent on the private fortunes of their future commanders, he founded with his own money a special veterans' pensions department, and assured its further support by assigning to it the revenues from two new taxes, a sales tax of one-hundredth and an estate tax of one-twentieth. Both the Senate and Augustus could mint coinage, but after 12 B.C. only Augustus' new mint at Lugdunum (the modern Lyon) in Gaul struck gold and silver coins, the Senate's mint at Rome issuing copper and bronze. Similarly with the provinces: Augustus governed some and the Senate others. Theirs was a fruitful cooperation in running the empire; but his was in each case the guiding hand. And the people of Rome—the ancient and traditional partner of the Senate—had for practical purposes no function except to approve.

Augustus himself took the lead in introducing new social reforms: adultery became for the first time a crime against the state; those who failed to marry and have children found themselves limited in the amounts of money they could legally inherit; married men had certain advantages in running for political office; all except members of the senatorial class might now legally marry former slaves. These measures to strengthen the family probably had the desired effect of increasing the population. It became somewhat more difficult, however, to set slaves free, and for freedmen to obtain Roman citizenship, measures probably designed to keep intermarriage between ex-slaves (foreigners) and Romans down in number.

Among the many public buildings restored by Augustus were dilapidated temples of the gods. He also built—often at his own expense—many new ones, and other grand public buildings such as baths and theatres, boasting justly that he had found Rome a city of brick and left it a city of marble. Less spectacular perhaps, but probably even more important, he founded the city's first regular fire department and police force; and instituted new measures to maintain and improve the highway system throughout Italy, to make travel fast and safe, and to bind together the outlying cities and veterans' colonies with the capital.

The far-flung imperial frontiers needed of course to be defended; but the generals who defended them must be kept from using their forces against the central government of Augustus himself. Once the armies had been reduced in size, each legion (there were 28 after 13 B.C. and 25 after 9 B.C.) was made into a permanent unit 5,620 men strong, of which 5,500 were infantry. Made up of Roman citizens who volunteered, they served for 26 years, receiving a bonus at the end of their service equivalent to about 14 years' salary. Auxiliary forces amounting to an equal number of troops were stationed with each legion. These were noncitizens, who received citizenship after 30 years' service. Thus provincials shared with Romans the responsibility for their own defense, and won a substantial reward. This army, totaling about 300,000 men, was stationed in permanent garrison-camps along the frontiers in the provinces, where the troops worked in peacetime on public projects such as aqueducts or canals.

To the provinces they would bring Roman ways, and their camps would naturally become the centers of something like cities, as tradesmen would come to supply their needs. Less important but by no means neglected, the navy too was reorganized by Augustus to keep down pirates, to move troops by sea, and to man a far-flung system of naval bases. As an innovation, Augustus created the Praetorian Guard: about 9,000 specially privileged and highly paid troops, of whom about a third were regularly stationed in Rome. Usually they did not go on campaign unless Augustus himself or some member of his family was personally engaged.

Augustus' Campaigns

In the East, Augustus annexed some new territories in Asia Minor, and, most important, was able by a show of strength in Armenia to reach a satisfactory diplomatic settlement with the Parthians, avoiding what would surely have been an expensive and perhaps a dangerous war for Rome. Judea during this time was ruled by Herod, a client king of Jewish faith, whom Antony had installed in 37 B.C. The kingdom prospered, but the Orthodox Jews resented Herod's aping of the Hellenistic kings, his subservience to the Romans, and his cruelty in putting down his domestic enemies. After his death in 4 B.C., the Romans took over Judea proper from his incompetent son, Archelaus, and ruled through a Roman procurator, who remained outside Jerusalem. This was a concession to the Jews, whom the Romans also allowed to worship freely, not to serve in the Roman armies, and to use coinage without any graven image (i.e., the portrait of Augustus).

North Africa and Spain saw the usual fighting against tribesmen, and by 19 B.C. most of the Iberian peninsula had been permanently subdued. In Gaul, an occasional rising still occurred, but Roman administration extended throughout the land, and Lugdunum (Lyon) emerged not only as the site of the imperial mint but also as the road and river communications-center of the entire area. (A huge new altar of Rome and Augustus was erected there in 12 B.C. by the sixty-four Gallic tribes.) Immediately

north of the Alps, Augustus campaigned successfully in areas that are now Switzerland and Austria, and then undertook a series of campaigns eastward along the Danube, extending Roman power into present-day Hungary, Yugoslavia, and Bulgaria, all the way to the Black Sea (13 B.C.–A.D. 9).

It was in the year A.D. 9, however, that Roman arms suffered a disaster in Germany, when, as the climax of more than twenty years of raiding and campaigning east of the Rhine and up to the Elbe, three legions were attacked and wiped out by the German leader Arminius, who had been in the Roman auxiliary forces and had obtained Roman citizenship and the rank of *eques*. Old and disinclined for more fighting, Augustus did not try to avenge the defeat, and the Rhine frontier proved to be the final limit of Roman penetration into north-central Europe. The enormously important result, as we shall see, was that the Germans never became Romanized.

Administered by the professionals in the new civil service, the provinces—whether senatorial or imperial—were now probably better governed than under the republic. A system of regular censuses enabled the central government to assess provincial taxes fairly. Improved communications made it easier to punish swiftly and effectively those offenses that did occur, and the provincial councils—primarily designed to further the local cult of the emperor—also served as a natural source of complaints against his officials. In the urbanized areas the cities, and in Gaul the tribes, still served as the underlying basis for provincial government, and administered the affairs of the larger number of provincials according to their own traditional customs. Local civic pride could flourish under Roman domination. From Augustus' first acceptance of that title in 27 B.C., the celebrated *Pax Romana*—the Roman Peace—lasted more than 200 years, until A.D. 180. It was an enormous boon.

Augustus himself had since 42 B.C. officially been the "son" of the deified Julius Caesar, and his name after 29 B.C. appeared in hymns to the gods; his "genius" (*numen*) had an altar of its own from the year before his death (A.D. 13). None of this was equivalent to open direct worship of Augustus in Rome itself or in Italy. But in the Eastern provinces he was deified in accordance with ancient tradition, and we have already seen him furthering the importation of his cult—in association with that of deified Rome —into tribal Gaul. Whatever his faults of character, it is impossible to deny that he should be remembered as he wished to be remembered, as one who had maintained the Roman state firmly in its position, and had laid the lasting foundations of its future constitution.

The Successors of Augustus, to A.D. 96

Family tragedies among the heirs of Augustus (his son-in-law and loyal and efficient supporter Agrippa died, as did both of Agrippa's sons, Augustus' grandsons) compelled him to select as his heir his stepson, Tiberius, son of his wife Livia by her first husband. Although he was an experienced and successful general and diplomat, Tiberius had become resentful when Augustus had forced him to divorce his wife and marry Augustus' daughter and Agrippa's widow, and the resentment had increased when he became the heir only because his stepsons, the preferred candidates, were dead. Fifty-five years old, and personally of a gloomy disposition, he did, however, accept tribunician and proconsular powers like those of Augustus himself, and a few weeks after Augustus' death became princeps at the invitation of the Senate. He reigned twenty years, until A.D. 37.

Down to A.D. 23 he followed the example of Augustus, cooperating with the Senate and refusing the consulship except for three special years. But thereafter Sejanus, prefect (commander) of the Praetorian Guard, now specially housed in Rome, conspired to win the succession for himself. As Tiberius' son and heir Drusus had died, Sejanus played upon Tiberius' jealousy of his niece-in-law and her sons, now the nearest in line for power. In 26 Tiberius retired to Capri, giving Sejanus the opportunity to mature his plot; but in 31 Tiberius became convinced that Sejanus was a traitor, and denounced him to the Senate, which ordered him killed. When Tiberius came to believe that Sejanus had himself killed Drusus and seduced Drusus' wife, his disillusionment was complete: he stayed for the rest of his life on Capri, although he continued to govern effectively.

Tiberius has suffered from a bad press: in fact there is no real evidence that on Capri he gave himself up to vice (in any case he was now in his seventies), nor was the number of trials and executions for treason extraordinarily high (as sometimes asserted) in view of the extensive conspiracy of Sejanus. Personally not extravagant, Tiberius reduced taxes, took measures to enable debtors to borrow interest-free, and left a full treasury. But his distaste for public games and his absence from Rome made him unpopular, and his reign was felt to have been a failure. His heir was his great-nephew Gaius (reigned A.D. 37–41), always called Caligula from the little military boots he had worn in his childhood.

After only a few months, Caligula emerged from an illness, perhaps insane and certainly brutish. He took the consulship himself in three of his four years, and in the other year ousted the two consuls by force, though the story that he planned to bestow the office upon his favorite horse is not provable. Challenging the Senate's partnership, he had many prominent persons accused of treason and executed, confiscating their property to spend on his own lavish amusements. Committing incest with his sister, he also founded a temple to himself in the oriental way. Inevitably there were conspiracies against him, which culminated in his assassination A.D. 41. In the provinces he had been almost as eccentric: at different times he seemed on the point of invading both Germany and Britain, and preparations were far advanced; but in the end he did nothing. In Egypt the jealousy and hatred of the Greeks for the Jews of Alexandria led them to demand that the Jews be forced to install statues of the emperor in the synagogues; and Caligula made matters worse by ordering his statue set up in the rebuilt temple in Jerusalem. At the moment of his death Judea was on the verge of an uprising.

Caligula was succeeded by his uncle Claudius (41–54), the youngest of Tiberius' nephews. Found hiding behind the palace curtains by a member of the Praetorian Guard, Claudius was uncertain whether he was to be killed or placed in power. But the Guard preferred to maintain the family line, especially after Claudius promised its members a rich present. The Senate had to concur. Physically weak and fifty years old, Claudius had all his life been harshly treated by his cruel relatives; but he was a man learned in Roman history, and a practicing scholar in both Greek and Latin, with a knowledge even of Etruscan, and a deep appreciation both of the republican past and of the work of Julius Caesar

Mosaic at Ostia, the seaport of ancient Rome.

and Augustus. He had bad luck with his wives, and contemporaries often scorned him; but he proved a good judge of men and an able administrator until the later years of his reign. He tried to restore the Augustan cooperation with the Senate, but like Augustus did not hesitate to add to its members and to require attendance at its meetings. In the navy, in the management of Rome's seaport of Ostia, in the treasury, and elsewhere he substituted his own administrators for those of the Senate, whom he found inefficient. He also executed perhaps as many as thirty-five senators and three hundred equites.

Claudius greatly enlarged the role of his own personal bureaucrats, mostly freedmen in origin. Beginning with Augustus, each emperor had employed such a staff as a matter of course, but Claudius was the first to divide its work departmentally, with a freedman at the head of each department, not unlike a cabinet in more modern governments. This private imperial civil service rose parallel to that formed by senators and equites, and now began a steady growth:

for the first time there appeared a bureau-chief of the imperial correspondence, one for finances (with subchiefs for the emperor's private funds), another in charge of petitions, and others. Dependent for their advancement and their fortunes entirely on the emperor personally, these men often became very rich. Since it was their efficiency that determined their advancement, they were usually efficient, and of course bitterly hated. Claudius took a personal interest in the administration of justice, sped up the workings of the courts, and sometimes—probably too often—acted as judge himself in trials held secretly in his own apartments. Drainage-projects and harbor-works, encouragement of commerce by the first insurance policies against storm-losses at sea: these were some of the distinguishing aspects of his reign at home.

Abroad, Claudius extended Roman territory, thus disregarding the principles of Augustus, who had decided after A.D. 9 that the empire should be kept within its boundaries. Mauretania (the Morocco of today) was conquered and became two new provinces (A.D. 44). Thrace and Lycia were added about the same time. In 43, ninety-eight years after Julius Caesar's first invasion, Claudius invaded Britain, where rival Gallic tribes had been competing and the demand for Roman goods had been rising. A tribal ruler of Surrey and Sussex had been expelled, and had fled to Rome and appealed to Claudius for help. Probably in part because he felt the need of military victory to enhance his position with the armies and people, Claudius in person led the invasion and conquered southeast England, which became the province of Britain. The Roman advance continued after he had returned to Rome, and the Celtic rulers of Lincoln became allies, while hostilities extended into Wales.

By establishing Roman colonies at Cologne on the Rhine and Trier (Treves) on the Moselle, Claudius also improved the defenses of Gaul against the Germans. Everywhere in Roman territory he was generous with grants of Roman citizenship, thus winning the devotion of the provincials. Since all citizens could run for office and thus become senators, some Gauls now tried to do so, and Claudius forced the Senate unwillingly to remember that in the past Rome had always gained by the extension of Roman rights to non-Romans.

By far the most competent ruler since Augustus, Claudius was ruined by the wretched character of his family. His third wife, Messalina, in 48 publicly "married" her lover, probably as part of a conspiracy, and had to be executed. His fourth wife, Agrippina, was also his niece, and already twice a widow and the mother of a favorite son, Nero, whom Claudius was persuaded to adopt. In her campaign to clear the way for Nero's succession, Agrippina poisoned or otherwise disposed of many, allegedly culminating with Claudius himself, to whom she gave poisoned mushrooms in 54. Nero (reigned 54-68) succeeded at the age of sixteen, and began by giving a large gift to the Praetorian Guard and promising to abandon Claudius' unpopular practices of holding secret trials and of advancing former freedmen.

The ambitious Agrippina clearly hoped to wield the real power herself, but Nero in 59 had her murdered. This crime was the darkest act of his first five years as emperor, during which his tutor, the playwright Seneca, and the commander of the Praetorian Guard actually managed the affairs of state jointly. But where a ruler is essentially absolute, his personality becomes of extreme importance, and Nero was profligate and so proud of his own artistic talents as to verge on insanity. He wanted to transform the Roman public spectacles into something more like the Greek Olympic games. He sang, played the harp, acted, and drove a chariot in person at such spectacles. Among others he murdered his wife, Claudius' daughter Octavia, and married his mistress, Poppaea, whom he later kicked to death in a fit of temper. He did not start the great fire that burned down much of Rome in 64, nor did he fiddle while it burned; indeed, he personally took part in the efforts to put it out, and did what he could for those who had lost their homes. But the dispossessed did blame him, and to find a scapegoat he accused the sect of the Christians—now for the first time attracting attention at Rome—whose secret meetings had led to charges of immorality against them. Nero persecuted them to take the attention away from himself.

Maladministration in Britain led to the revolt (61) of the famous Boadicea (Boudicca), and severe Roman losses before it was suppressed. The chief threat in the provinces arose in Palestine. Here the various Jewish sects detested each other and the Christians, while all except the upper class disliked Roman rule, which had swung back and forth between extremes of tolerance (Augustus) and intolerance (Caligula). Roman officials usually had too few troops and too little skill to keep order in an increasingly tense situation. Gangs of bandits—some with professed social aims—and groups of Jewish zealots added to the trouble, which culminated in the massacre of a Roman garrison (66) after the Jewish high priest had refused to sacrifice to Jehovah for the special benefit of the Roman emperor.

The Roman general Vespasian had begun to reconquer Palestine, when Nero found himself faced with a rising of Roman troops in Gaul and Spain, where the governor, Galba, was disloyal to him. Hesitating too long to call on the Praetorian Guard, Nero lost his hold over them. One of their prefects came out for Galba, who was proclaimed emperor by the Senate, and Nero committed suicide (68).

Up to this moment, each new emperor—duly named by the Senate—had been a member, though sometimes a distant one, of the family

Bust of the emperor Vespasian.

paign through to its violent conclusion with the sack of Jerusalem (70) and the final destruction of the rebuilt temple.

Vespasian (69–79), a man not of senatorial origins, proved as competent an emperor as he was a general. He founded a second dynasty, the Flavian, the throne passing successively to his two sons, Titus (79–81) and Domitian (81–96). Vespasian added new blood to the Senate by appointing non-Romans, especially Spaniards, re-establishing finances on a sound basis, put down a major Gallic revolt, continued to advance in Britain, and succeeded in overcoming the opposition to a dynastic succession. He and his successors helped prevent a recurrence of military uprisings by using some troops to build public works, stationing others in dangerous areas of the frontier, and keeping the numbers concentrated in any one place too few to encourage an ambitious commander to revolt. It was during the brief reign of Titus that the famous eruption of Vesuvius wiped out the population of the prosperous provincial town of Pompeii, leaving behind an unequaled body of evidence for the future about the daily life of the period. The brutal Domitian alienated the Senate by forcing it to go along with his own tyrannical condemnation of individual senators whom he suspected. Though he raised the pay of the army, and conducted successful operations along the Rhine and Danube, a palace conspiracy brought him down in 96, ending the Flavian rule, and reopening the possibility of new strife for the throne.

of Julius Caesar and Augustus. Tiberius, Caligula, Claudius, and Nero are called the Julio-Claudian emperors. But now the line had run out, and the Senate and people of Rome learned that emperors could be found in other families and chosen in other ways. The year 68–69 saw the rapid election of four successive emperors, each supported by rival armies, the first three dying by violence in their turn. So Galba, the commander of the legions in Spain, gave way to Otho, his own lieutenant and the candidate of the Praetorian Guard, who lost out to Vitellius, the commander of the army on the German frontier, who was defeated by Vespasian, the general who had already begun to subdue Palestine, where his son Titus was carrying the cam-

From Nerva to Marcus Aurelius (96–180)

The Senate, so subservient to an emperor in his lifetime, had, when an emperor died, the power of appointing his successor, much as the College of Cardinals in our own day acquires and exercises real authority only during the interlude between the death of one pope and its election of a new one. In 96 the Senate chose a mild sixty-five-year-old lawyer named Nerva—childless and therefore certain not to found a dynasty—who promptly freed Domitian's prisoners and ceased persecuting Jews and Christians. He founded a new charity that gave loans to Italian farmers to provide food for orphans.

100

Relief of a Roman battle on the Column of Trajan, Rome.

Indeed he was so mild that a consul is supposed to have grumbled that Domitian had been bad because he let nobody do anything, but Nerva was worse because he let anybody do everything. Nerva did have to permit the Praetorian Guard to punish the murderers of Domitian. But this weakness in the face of military pressure he counteracted by the extraordinary judgment he showed in adopting as his son, and so nominating as his successor, the great general Trajan, who succeeded him peacefully at his death in 98. The adoption proved to be only the first of a series of four successive fortunate adoptions that gave the empire its most prosperous and peaceful years, 98–177.

Called by the Senate "the best of emperors," Trajan (98–117), of Spanish origin, "restored to Rome not only the security of life but its dignity also," as the writer Pliny said of him. Except for executing the Praetorians who had made difficulties for Nerva, Trajan's domestic rule was serene and uneventful. Abroad he extended Roman territories in a series of glittering but expensive campaigns: across the Danube into Dacia—part of the Romania of today—which became a new Roman province in 106, and across the Euphrates against the Parthians into Mesopotamia, a war that ended in failure in 115 and was followed by a massive revolt of the Jews that was still unsettled when Trajan died, just after having adopted his nephew Hadrian (117–138).

Experienced as a military commander, as a provincial governor (Pannonia, Syria), and as a politician (consul at the age of thirty-three), Hadrian was a highly cultivated man. He had the troops and the firm resolution needed to put down the Jewish revolt and to frustrate his possible rivals for power. He realized that the Roman lines of communication became too long and hard to protect whenever Roman troops moved east and south of the Syrian desert; so he abandoned Trajan's Parthian war and eventually made formal peace with the Parthians. Moderate and generally conciliatory toward the Senate, he gained public popularity by canceling all private debts to the government, furthering charities, and sponsoring great spectacles in the circus. He further opened the ranks of the civil service to talented aspirants; he made the expensive official Roman postal service a central government department instead of requiring local contributions to its cost. His immediate advisers (*consilium*) included some distinguished lawyers, who helped him adjust taxes and control prices in bad years, and improve the legal position of slaves and soldiers. By bringing into a uniform code the past decisions of the praetors, Hadrian's lawyers enabled all citizens to know when they could bring a case, and assured them of uniform procedures. Born in Spain and widely traveled throughout the empire, Hadrian had no great personal fondness for Italy or for Rome. He believed that the provinces of the empire should be equal under Roman imperial benevolence, with himself as true "father of the fatherland" (*pater patriae*), a title awarded occasionally under the republic (Cicero) but usually accepted by the emperors from the Senate without much consideration as to its precise meaning.

Hadrian applied the principle by recruiting the armies for provincial defense within each province itself, maintaining the Guard as a special privileged corps of men of Italian blood. Most dramatic, he spent many years away from home, residing in turn in Britain (where he built across the entire island the famous defensive system of forts and walls and ditches still known as Hadrian's Wall, as a flexible means of containing invasions from the north), in Provence (southern France), in Spain, in Morocco, in Asia Minor, in Greece, in Tunisia and Libya, in Greece again, in Syria and Palestine (where he replanned and changed the name of Jerusalem, forbade circumcision, and eventually had to put down another Jewish revolt), in Egypt. Everywhere he inspected troops and defenses and built new buildings; everywhere but Palestine he made himself known to and usually admired by the population. Back in Rome after a decade, he began the construction of what is still known as Hadrian's Villa, at Tivoli near Rome, something like a World's Fair exposition-ground with whole areas reminiscent of his favorite Greece and Egypt.

Ruins of Hadrian's Wall in Northumberland.

Before he died in 138, Hadrian adopted as son and successor Antoninus, a man of fine character and great wealth, whose grandfathers had each been consul twice, and who was given the name Pius in recognition of his filial devotion. As part of the plan, Antoninus Pius (138–161) immediately adopted as his son and prospective heir his nephew, the young and cultivated Marcus Aurelius (161–180). The forty-two years of their combined reigns won glowing praise at the time from certain articulate Romans as an era of peace and prosperity. Later students of Roman history have also singled them out as unique; the eighteenth-century English scholar Edward Gibbon remarked that there had never been another time "in which the happiness of a great people was the only object of government." Gibbon was echoing Antoninus Pius' contemporary, the Greek orator Aelius Aristides, who wrote that the Persian rulers killed and exiled people and broke their oaths, and even the ancient Greek city-states who had resisted the Persians had failed in governing Greece; but within the Roman Empire

Neither sea nor land is any bar to citizenship, and Asia is treated exactly the same as Europe. In your empire, every avenue of advancement is open to everyone. No one who deserves office or responsibility remains an alien. A civil world-community has been set up as a free republic, under a single ruler, the best ruler and teacher . . . of order. From Rome, the centre, there emanates throughout the world a security that rests on a power compared with which the walls of Babylon were mere child's play and women's work. All depends on the legions, who assure the perpetual peace, because Mars, whom you have never slighted, dances his ceaseless dance upon the banks of the outer rivers [Rhine, Danube, Euphrates] and thus averts the shedding of blood.*

Certainly if we use as a measure of general happiness the absence of civil strife, the continued building of great public buildings, and the ability of the comfortable to lead their comfortable lives undisturbed, the period deserves Aelius Aristides' warm words. On the other side, it is sometimes argued that Egypt, for example, the private financial province of the Roman emperors, was cruelly exploited; but in fact this

* Adapted and abbreviated from the edition of J. H. Oliver, "The Ruling Power," *Transactions of the American Philosophical Society*, XLIII (1953), part 4.

had always been true under native Egyptian rule and under the Ptolemies, and continued to be true under Egypt's successive rulers down virtually to the present day. One might add that for the less privileged in Rome itself and in Italy, at least, the Antonine monarchy showed much consideration and averted the worst blows of poverty. Yet it was certainly those already fortunate who benefited most from the good fortunes of these reigns.

Moreover, while Hadrian had ensured security by his energetic travels and his regular personal scrutiny of the far-flung armies, Antoninus Pius was more lethargic, and never left Italy. So the dance of Mars upon the banks of the outer rivers was less vigorous than Aelius Aristides had boasted. As a result, Marcus Aurelius, a cultivated Stoic philosopher, who derived no enjoyment from his might as emperor and whose own melancholy *Meditations* serve as a corrective to Aelius Aristides, found himself obliged to campaign actively beyond the Danube in Dacia, and against the Parthians in the East. Even his victories carried with them the warnings of future dangers: he allowed certain barbarians to settle within the imperial frontiers and to be enrolled in the Roman armies, thus jeopardizing the traditional defensive system, and his troops brought back to Rome from their triumph over the Parthians a dreadful plague.

The Downward Slide: Commodus to Diocletian (180–284)

With the succession of Commodus (180–192), the flesh-and-blood son of Marcus Aurelius, the line of fortunate adoptions came to an end, and with it the happy period that had begun with Nerva almost a century before. Cruel, capricious, extravagant, and without talent, except perhaps as a gladiator, Commodus revived the bad days of Nero or Domitian, and was swayed by one or another favorite until he was murdered by his own closest advisers. Within a year, the Praetorian Guard installed and murdered two emperors, the second of whom had obtained the office by outbidding his rival. He was replaced by the commander of the troops in Pannonia (Hungary), Septimius Severus, a native Punic-speaking North African (193–211), who marched his armies into Rome; disbanded the Praetorian

Guard and created a new one from amongst his own troops; and put down two successive rivals in the first civil strife Rome had experienced in more than a century. After a successful campaign against the Parthians, Septimius added Mesopotamia to the empire as a province. Dependent upon the armies, he showered favors upon them: better food, better pay, better conditions—recognition of marriages between native women and Roman legionaries, permission for married legionaries to live off the base. He also favored the equites as against the senators. The prefects of the Praetorian Guard began to play a very important part in the economic and judicial sphere; there were now usually two, one of whom was a professional lawyer. The legal treatment of the poor—the reservoir of potential soldiers—improved.

Septimius died while on campaign in Britain (211) and was succeeded by his two sons, Geta and Caracalla, who ruled jointly for a year until Caracalla had Geta killed in the very lap of their mother, the intellectual Syrian Julia Domna. The brutality of the act is a good index to the character of Caracalla (211–217), who embarked on a purge that may have cost the lives of 20,000 victims, and who enjoyed driving a chariot and slaughtering wild beasts in the arena. Adopting the cult of Alexander the Great, Caracalla in his disordered imagination hoped to rival Alexander's achievements. He spent much of his reign

Fourth-century Sassanian cameo showing the defeat and capture of Valerian by King Shapur I, A.D. 260.

campaigning, and tried to live like the common soldier. Hearing that the Alexandrians were calling him the Emperor Oedipus, in allusion to the rumors of improper relations between him and his mother, he entered the city on an ostensible state visit and had the inhabitants massacred indiscriminately.

Apart from his atrocities and from a treacherous and brutal victory over the Parthians, Caracalla is remembered for his edict of 212 extending Roman citizenship to all freeborn inhabitants of the empire. Though in some ways a liberal measure, and the climax of earlier extensions of citizenship, Caracalla's edict was also intended as a money-raising device: as Roman citizens, the newly enfranchised subjects would have to pay inheritance taxes that they would otherwise not have owed. Naturally enough, Caracalla was assassinated. So were his sixteen immediate successors.

It is an unedifying parade: the Moorish Macrinus (217–218) with his single earring and military incompetence, was followed by the fourteen-year-old immensely rich homosexual Syrian priest of the sun-god, Elagabalus (218–222), great-nephew of Julia Domna fobbed off on the Romans as a son of Caracalla. Alexander Severus (222–235), a cousin of Elagabalus, soberer and more virtuous, tried to revive cooperation with the Senate, and to restore the traditional virtues to Roman life, but he too was only fourteen on his accession and was dominated by his greedy and parsimonious mother; the Senate was now impotent, and the army resented Alexander's neglecting to appease it by the now traditional bribes. Though his campaign against the new Sassanian dynasty that had replaced the Parthians in Persia was a success (231–233), his military zeal was half-hearted, and in Germany on another campaign he fell victim to another military conspiracy. During the next half-century (235–284), there were twenty-six emperors, of whom twenty-five were murdered: most of them were chosen by their troops, held power briefly, and were in turn supplanted by another ambitious military commander.

Attracted by Roman weakness and pushed from behind by other people on the move, the barbarians crossed the frontiers at many points. One Roman emperor (Decius, 252) was killed in battle by them. Another (Valerian, 260) was captured by the Sassanians, and died or was killed in captivity. Plagues raged; whole provinces temporarily escaped the central authority; population fell off; order disappeared. The tide turned in the reign of Aurelian (270–275), the "restorer of the world," and definitively with the accession of Diocletian (284–305).

The New Empire: Diocletian and Constantine

But to turn the tide demanded a thoroughgoing series of reforms, internal as well as external. Diocletian and his successors, especially Constantine (306–337), accomplished them, though we often do not know exactly when each new measure was adopted. The term "new empire" is often applied to the result, but what appeared to be new was often a return to something that had been tried before; it was rather the combination of such experiments that was new.

Under Diocletian there evolved gradually—each step resulting from local emergencies in one part or another of the empire—a system which when complete was called the tetrarchy, or rule by four men. Diocletian as Augustus first appointed a talented officer as Caesar, an action often taken previously, and then was forced by circumstances to promote him to Augustus, or co-emperor, though it was understood that Diocletian was the senior Augustus. Soon each Augustus had in turn appointed a Caesar of his own, whom he also adopted as his son. Such adoption too, we know, was an old practice. It was understood that the two emperors would eventually abdicate, each to be succeeded by his own Caesar, who upon becoming Augustus would appoint a new Caesar as his son and eventual successor. The scheme was obviously designed to assure a peaceful succession and to end the curse of military seizures of the throne. The empire, though in practice ruled by four men—a tetrarchy—still in theory remained a single unit.

This was particularly important, because accompanying the gradual establishment of the tetrarchy there was a territorial shift in administration, as each of the four new rulers took primary responsibility for his own large area. Diocletian made his headquarters at Nicomedia, on the eastern shore of the Sea of Marmara, in western Asia Minor, and from there governed Asia Minor, Syria, and Egypt, plus Thrace in Europe, the whole becoming the prefecture of the East. His Caesar had his headquarters at Sirmium in what is now Yugoslavia, and governed from there the Balkans including Greece, which became the prefecture of Illyricum. Diocletian's co-Augustus, the junior emperor Maximian, had his headquarters at Milan, and from there governed Italy and North Africa, together with parts of what is now Austria, which became the prefecture of Italy. And *his* Caesar had his headquarters at Trier (Treves) on the Moselle River in western Germany, and governed Gaul, Spain, and Britain, which became the prefecture of Gaul. Diocletian remained supreme over the others.

What is of course most obviously striking is that not even the prefecture of Italy was governed from the imperial capital of Rome. The new imperial territorial reorganization exposed as a hollow sham the ancient pretense that the emperor shared power with the Senate. Diocletian simply walked out on Rome, leaving the citizens with their free bread and circuses. It is of great importance too that he chose the East as the site of his own headquarters. Diocletian indeed now adopted the full trappings of oriental monarchy: he wore silk robes of blue and gold to symbolize the sky and the sun; he sprinkled his hair with gold dust to create the nimbus when the light shown down upon him. His clothes glittered with jewels; he wore ruby and emerald bracelets, necklaces, and rings; his fingernails were gilded; and his boots—which were to become *the* new symbol of imperial power—were of purple leather. He entered his throne-room carrying a golden scepter topped with a golden ball—the earth—on which was seated a Roman gold eagle with a sapphire in its beak—the heavens. Servants followed sprinkling the air with perfume, and fan-bearers spread the scent abroad. Every person in the room sank to the floor until Diocletian was seated on his throne, after which the privileged might kiss the hem of his garment.

The first Augustus would have been revolted. Occasionally Rome had seen similar displays, notably under the perverted Elagabalus, himself the priest of a Syrian sun-god, but even in its degenerate days Rome always hated such display, and Elagabalus was murdered. Diocletian's pomp had nothing to do with effeminacy or

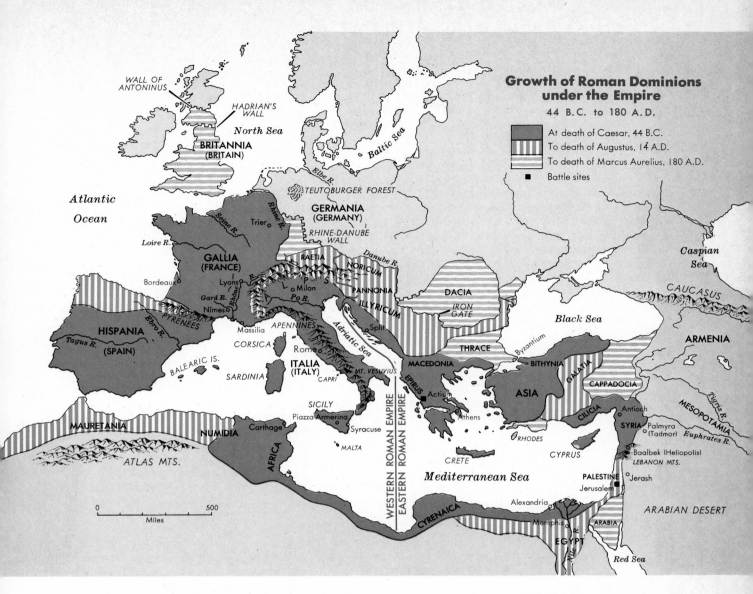

Growth of Roman Dominions under the Empire
44 B.C. to 180 A.D.

- At death of Caesar, 44 B.C.
- To death of Augustus, 14 A.D.
- To death of Marcus Aurelius, 180 A.D.
- ■ Battle sites

perverted tastes: he was a rough Balkan soldier. Rather he was making a deliberate attempt to elevate the prestige of the emperor—the divine and deified emperor—so high that his divinity would not be shaken by the ambitions of his rivals. It was no accident that Diocletian chose the additional surname Jovius, thus associating himself with Jupiter (Jove), the ruler of the gods.

No mere mechanical reorganization and geographical regrouping of forces could have prevented the recurrence of military uprisings. Diocletian now firmly separated the military from the civil power, so that the generals and colonels in command of local garrisons throughout the empire had no local political authority. The new civil officials whom he appointed had no military authority. Moreover, Diocletian subdivided the old provinces, so that the number of provinces rose to over one hundred, each of course vastly smaller than a province had formerly been; and these in turn were regrouped into twelve so-called dioceses, which made up the four great prefectures. The bureaucracy grew enormously: the various financial departments, the secret service, the post, and foreign relations each had its own structure, and the top officials became a kind of advisory body, almost a Cabinet. While an individual Roman senator might find a place in such a system, it was independent of the Senate as such, and as a body the Senate continued only as a group of privileged magnates. Diocletian also adapted military tactics to a new age, introducing heavy-armed cavalry for the first time, and inventing a flexible system of frontier defenses that made it possible for troops to move rapidly to a point where danger threatened.

Diocletian and Constantine also took steps to deal with the economic misery and social unrest that had accompanied the political and military disorders of the later third century. By using as a unit of land-measurement for tax purposes the amount of land that could be cultivated by a single farm laborer, and by trying to force the farm laborer to stay put, work his land, and pay his taxes, the new empire greatly stimulated the growth of the class of rural resident called the colonus, who was attached to the soil. He was not a slave, and could not be sold apart from the land he cultivated, but when it was sold he went with it. Other men in other walks of life also were bound to their various jobs, and sons to their fathers' jobs after them. Sons of bakers had to become bakers, sons of goldsmiths goldsmiths. In his efforts to stabilize the economic situation, Diocletian also tried to fix prices, but was thwarted by black-marketing and riots.

At the lowest territorial administrative level, the civitas (each city and portions of the surrounding countryside), the city senators (curiales) had to make up out of their own pockets any difference between the tax payments assessed for the civitas and the amount actually collected. From being an honor, the position of curialis became a burden, and curiales too had to be compelled to stay in their posts, to do their duty, and to pass their jobs on to their eldest sons. Society in the new empire became more rigidly stratified than ever before in Roman history. The combination of this increased social stratification with oriental despotism, a huge bureaucracy, and a continuing dependence on the military made ordinary life extremely bleak: corruption, violence, inequity, individual despair were frequent.

The Roman Empire survived in both Eastern and Western portions (though the days of the Western empire proved numbered), but its citizens were probably unhappier than they had ever been. Writing a few decades later, the historian Ammianus Marcellinus said:

Rich men could buy acquittals, and poor men were condemned; the depravity of judges and lawyers sold the interests of the poor to military

commanders and influential persons. The Emperor considered nothing but how he might amass money. Ruinous titles, privileges, and exemptions ate up the fortunes of poor and rich. Every class and profession was exposed to annoyance and the insatiable greed of the imperial tax-collectors. People were eager for any change at all.

Diocletian retired in 305 and left his half of the empire to his Caesar; and he forced his fellow Augustus, Maximian, to do the same. Each of the new Augusti in turn named a Caesar; but the system now broke down, as the four top officials began to struggle against each other for supreme power. By 324, Constantine, who had begun as the son of the Western Caesar, boss of Gaul, emerged as sole Augustus, and the empire was reunited. Though the tetrarchy did not survive, the other reforms of Diocletian and his immediate successors certainly helped to stave off collapse. But, of course, they did not prevent it.

Few subjects have been more debated than the reasons for the decline of the Roman Empire. The celebrated eighteenth-century historian Edward Gibbon blamed Christianity, charging that it destroyed the civic spirit of the Roman by turning his attention to the afterlife and away from his duties to the state. Michael Rostovtzeff, a learned Russian scholar writing in the 1920's and 1930's, attributed the decline in part to the constant pressure of the underprivileged masses to share in the wealth of their rulers, of which there was not enough to go around anyhow. Gibbon and Rostovtzeff each reflected his own time and experience, Gibbon the anticlerical rationalism of the eighteenth century, Rostovtzeff the bitter lesson of the Bolshevik Revolution in his native Russia. Others have emphasized the influx of Greeks and Orientals into Roman society, and intimated that the original "pure" Roman racial virtues were thus diluted, a view shared by few reliable historians. Still others have talked of climatic change, but with little evidence.

Economically, losses in population caused by plagues and civil war crippled agriculture, already hampered by backward methods. The growing concentration of land in large estates and the absorption of free farmers into the status of coloni diluted Roman prosperity, already suffering from feeble purchasing power and inflation. Psychologically, the masses became alienated from their rulers: the substitution of the mercenary for the old citizen-soldier testified to the decline of the old Roman patriotism. Yet even with all these factors, it would be hard to imagine Roman decline without the terrific pressure of outside forces: the third and fourth centuries were the time when the barbarian world began to move, and it was the barbarian threat that eventually brought about the collapse of the Roman structure in the West while permitting its survival in the East in a modified form.

V   The Civilization of Rome

Greek Influences

In the years following the end of World War II, when American military power emerged as the decisive force in European affairs, many Europeans unkindly compared the Americans to the Romans and themselves to the Greeks. The Americans, they felt, were uncultivated boors without much of a civilization of their own, but with a great deal of impressive military hardware, trying to tell newly weakened peoples with old and proud military and political traditions how to run their affairs, and at the same time goggling admiringly at the surviving monuments of European culture.

It is of course true that American civilization is newer, and that if Americans wish to see ancient temples, medieval castles, and cathedrals, they must go to Europe to do so. But the parallel breaks down in many places. America did not attack and conquer Europe or attempt to govern it. Rome did these things to Greece. America was founded by Europeans, and inherited its civilization from them; so that Homer, Dante, and Shakespeare are as much a part of our tradition as of theirs. Rome was not founded by Greeks. And if many Americans regarded Europe as a museum for their entertainment and instruction, was it not because they recognized themselves as part of the same tradition rather than because they had found something new and different?

However faulty the modern part of the parallel may be, the ancient generalization still holds true: Greece, though conquered, took her conqueror captive. Indeed, Greek influence from Magna Graecia affected the Romans long before they conquered Greece itself. In the arts, the Romans found virtually their entire inspiration in Greek models. In literature the Greeks supplied the forms, and often much of the spirit, but the best Roman literary achievements could not be mistaken for Greek works: they have a Roman spirit and quality. In science and engineering the Romans had greater natural talent and originality than the Greeks, as they did in law and the arts of government.

The Greece the Romans gradually conquered was not the Greece of Homer or Pericles; so that the Romans, for example, did not imitate the Greek tragedians of the fifth century B.C.: there was no Roman Aeschylus, Sophocles, or Euripides. This was the Greece of the decades after the death of Alexander, of the New Comedy of Menander, not the Old Comedy of Aristophanes, when literature—much of it produced in Alexandria—was more artificial, more purely charming and graceful, often trivial, less grand, less concerned with the central themes of human existence. The surviving Alexandrian epic, Apollonius Rhodius' *Argonautica,* which tells of the adventures of the mythical hero Jason on his way to find the golden fleece, was a scholar's careful (and not very successful) effort to be Homeric long after the heroic age was over. When the Romans first began to imitate the Greeks, the greatest Greek works, though deeply respected, were no longer being written: it was a lesser age.

Religion

Before the first contacts with the Greeks, of course, the Romans, in their central Italian provincial agricultural city-state, had already evolved their own religion, the worship of the household spirits, the lares and penates, that governed their everyday affairs, along with those spiritual beings that inhabited the local woods and springs and fields. Like the Greek Hestia, the Roman Vesta presided over the individual hearth, and had in her service the specially trained Vestal Virgins. From the Etruscans the Romans took the belief, which they never abandoned, in divination: they too foretold the future through observing the flight of birds (the auspices) and examining the entrails of animals (the auguries). From Greece there came the entire Olympic collection of gods and goddesses, some of them merging their identities in existing divinities, and most of them changing their names. Zeus became Jupiter, Hera Juno, Poseidon Neptune, and so on, though Apollo remained Apollo. But the Romans had nothing like the Greek Olympic games or the festivals of Dionysus that had led to the writing of Athenian tragedy and comedy.

Julius Caesar, as we know—and after him most of the emperors beginning with Augustus— was deified after death, and Augustus consented to be worshiped jointly with Rome at the great altar in Gaul. But in the imperial cult as in other religious observances, except for certain notable festivals each year, the individual Roman took little part. The official priests performed most rites, headed by their chief priest, the pontifex maximus, a title and role taken over by the emperors themselves. The state religion early lost its appeal for the Romans, and, since there was no reason why they could not worship as many other gods as they chose in addition, after rendering due veneration to the ordinary deities, including the emperor, Rome early imported cults from other places, chiefly the East, which competed for popularity. Since Christianity eventually joined and won the competition, we postpone discussion of its competitors until the next chapter, where we can more easily examine the reason for its victory.

Literature

Quintus Ennius (239-169 B.C.), who was born and brought up in Magna Graecia, naturally turned to Homer for inspiration when he put into epic form his patriotic account (the *Annales*) of Roman successes down to his own time. Although only fragments (in all between six and seven hundred lines) are preserved, we have enough to appreciate Ennius' thoroughly Roman admiration for the military virtues, and to understand his lasting influence on later Roman writers. Just as Ennius used Homeric verse

to celebrate Roman toughness and resilience, Plautus (254-184 B.C.) and Terence (195-159 B.C.) found their inspiration in the Greek New Comedy of Menander. Plautus was the more raucous and knockabout: it was he who wrote the play about the two sets of twins, masters and servants who are always being taken for each other, that Shakespeare eventually imitated in *A Comedy of Errors*. And other characters from Plautus—the rich but stupid young gentleman with an immensely clever and resourceful valet, the money-grubbing miser—recur throughout the course of western European—and Russian— literary history. Gentler and milder in every sense, Terence stuck closer to the Greek originals, but was not a success in his own day. After Plautus and Terence, various Roman authors tried to write comedies with a native Italian inspiration, but none of their work survives. In addition to these sophisticated works, the Romans enjoyed crude farces of the kind that had always been staged in the villages.

During the late republic appeared two of Rome's greatest poets, Lucretius (94-55 B.C.) and Catullus (84-54 B.C.), alike only in their mastery of their chosen verse forms and the genuineness of their emotions. Lucretius—a serious disciple of the Greek philosopher Epicurus—wrote a long poem *On the Nature of Things* (*De Rerum Natura*) putting into moving poetry his master's beliefs that there is no human survival after death, and that the gods—far from governing the affairs of men—do not intervene at all. The universe is made of atoms, whose motions and behavior are governed by fixed laws, right out to the edges, the "flaming walls of the universe," except that men control their own actions. Catullus, looking to certain Alexandrian poets of the emotions, wrote passionate love-lyrics recording his feelings for his mistress Clodia (sister of the tribune Clodius), to whom he gives the name of Lesbia. Sometimes playful and charming, as in the poems addressed to Lesbia's pet sparrow or celebrating the first days of returning spring, sometimes bitter and obscene (Lesbia was unfaithful and made Catullus miserable), these brief poems, in a meter new to Rome, seem to some readers the highest achievement of Roman literature. Catullus also wrote a long, sustained, and extraordinarily gripping poem about the exaltation and self-mutilation of the devotees of Cybele, the great mother-goddess of Asia Minor, and her consort

Attis, whose cult was becoming popular at Rome.

In Cicero (106–43 B.C.), whom we have already so often encountered in his role as a lawyer and politician, the late republic produced its greatest writer of prose. His oratorical skill of course furthered his career as a successful lawyer and politician; his speeches in the courtroom or in the Senate were carefully prepared and effective pleas. He deliberately won his listeners with an occasional quick injection of a witty or ironical phrase into an otherwise somber and stately passage. He carefully studied not only what he wanted to say but how he could choose the most effective—sometimes the most unexpected—words in which to say it, and how he could combine them into a rhythmical and pleasing pattern, so that the sound and the sense would combine to make his point irresistibly. As the recognized supreme master of the art, he also wrote treatises on oratory. We also have almost a thousand letters that Cicero wrote to his friends and acquaintances, and some of their answers to him. The correspondence includes not only exchanges of letters with the most important Roman public figures of the period but also many intimate letters to Cicero's best friend, Atticus, that reveal his personal joys and sorrows.

Philosophically, Cicero in large measure agreed with the views of the Stoics as modified by Greek teachers who had adapted the originally abstract and remote concepts of Stoicism to Roman taste, by allowing for the exercise in ordinary life of the Stoic virtues, and admitting that one can have some virtues without possession of all knowledge. Cicero, himself not an original thinker, deliberately helped popularize these ideas in his philosophic essays—on Old Age, on Friendship, on the Nature of the Gods, and on other political and social subjects. Into the Latin language he introduced for the first time terms capable of conveying the meaning of the Greek concepts he was discussing. His fellow Romans first learned from him about the concept of a "natural law," for example, that existed independent of all human legislative actions, or a "law of nations" that should regulate the relationships of different peoples toward each other. The influence of these Ciceronian works radiated far into future human history: the early Christian Church Fathers went to school to Cicero, as did the humanists of the Italian Renaissance, and the men who made the eighteenth-century revolutions in America and in France and who wrote the Declaration of Independence and the Constitution of the United States.

It was the writers of the Age of Augustus who gave Rome its literary Golden Age. And, as in the other enterprises of his era, Augustus himself took an active part in recruiting and subsidizing talent, even genius, to proclaim the glories of the new era, his new era. Vergil (70–19 B.C.) in his *Georgics* and *Eclogues* followed the models of Greek pastoral poetry, and praised the pleasures and satisfactions of rural life. Written before Augustus reached political supremacy, these poems helped Augustus advance his later program of propaganda to get men back to the farm. He persuaded Vergil to write the *Aeneid*, the great epic of Rome's beginnings, in which the poet could "predict" the future glories that Augustus' rule would bring. Though designed in part to please Augustus, these passages none the less reveal Vergil's own sincere and intense patriotism. Vergil often reflects upon the sacrifices that necessarily accompany a rise to greatness, on sorrow, and on death.

His fellow poet Horace (65–8 B.C.) had more humor, and expressed a greater variety of feelings in a greater number of meters. In short poems on more limited subjects he too praised the joys of rural life, and the virtues of moderation, but also in more solemn terms celebrated the Roman qualities of quiet toughness, the simple life, the traditional religious attitudes. Ovid (43 B.C.–A.D. 17) gave worldly advice—often cynical—on the art of love; and elsewhere told the stories of the mythical transformations reported in Greek myths, as various divinities became birds or animals or plants. Ovid died in exile because of his involvement in a scandal affecting the granddaughter of Augustus.

To match in prose Vergil's epic of Rome's early days and to stress again the virtues that had made Rome great, the historian Livy (59 B.C.–A.D. 17) set out to write a prose history of the city from the moment of its founding. Only 35 of the 142 books into which he divided his work have come down to us complete, but we have summaries of the missing portions—most of the second and all of the first century B.C. Livy could use as his sources the compilations of many Roman writers now lost; but for the earliest periods he had to fall back on legend. He knew the difference between reliable and unreliable accounts, but often had only the latter available, and so used them. Vividly written, his work was indeed very long, and soon was put into *Reader's Digest* form for the unambitious. The future emperor Claudius had Livy as his tutor, and it would probably be safe to attribute Claudius' own success as emperor to the training he received from the historian.

The insistence on the great Roman virtues reflected an uneasy sense of their decline. In the period after Augustus, as the government became more arbitrary and autocratic, and writers began to fear the consequences of expressing themselves too freely, disillusionment set in. Moreover, the general admiration for the achievements of the Augustan writers, especially Vergil, became so intense that poets were often content to try to imitate the authors of the Golden Age, and to suppress their own originality. The greatest of all the Roman historians, Tacitus (ca. 55-117 A.D.), himself a master of prose style, was convinced that Romans had degenerated. In his *Germania* he wrote an essay ostensibly in praise of the rugged and still primitive way of life of the German barbarians, but in fact an acid commentary on the qualities the Romans had once had and had now lost. Similar disillusionment pervades his works of history, originally covering the period from Tiberius to Domitian, but not entirely preserved. Brilliant and prejudiced, allowing his personal opinions to color his accounts (sometimes in ways we cannot surely check), he was the greatest of the writers of the period between Tiberius and Hadrian, known as the Silver Age.

Silver Age poets included notably Seneca, Nero's tutor, by birth a Spaniard, a Stoic philosopher, and author of nine tragedies imitating Greek originals but far more bombastic and sensational. Seneca perhaps also wrote an extant satire on Claudius—a man easy to poke fun at especially after he was dead, but morally worth several Senecas and any number of Neros. Seneca's nephew, Lucan, wrote an epic poem (*The Pharsalia*) about the struggle between Caesar and Pompey. In successive generations, Persius (34-62 A.D.) and Juvenal (50-130) satirized contemporary society, and, as satirists often do, overstated the case: Juvenal enjoyed painting the vulgarities and wretchedness, the cruelties and greed of Rome in the harshest colors. His crass characters the Romans would have met frequently not only on the streets but in the pages of a famous obscene novel, the *Satyricon,* attributed to one of Nero's court officials, Petronius, which has an unforgettable episode of a wild banquet given by a newly rich ex-slave.

Law

The legal code published on the Twelve Tables in the fifth century B.C. reflected the needs of a small city-state, not those of a huge empire. As Rome became a world capital, thousands of foreigners flocked to live there to pursue their businesses, and of course they often got into disagreements with each other or with a Roman. But Roman law developed the flexibility to adjust to changing conditions: the enactments of the Senate and Assemblies, the decrees of each new emperor, and the decisions of the judges who were often called in as advisers—all of these contributed to a great body of legal materials.

It was the praetors, the chief legal officers, who heard both sides in every case, and determined the facts before turning over the matter to the judex, a referee, for decision. The judices had to develop a body of rules for deciding cases that were not covered by existing law. As they dealt with many different breeds of foreigners, they worked out a body of legal custom common to all of them, the law of the peoples (*jus gentium*), that would be acceptable to all comers. As each new praetor took office for a year, he would announce the laws by which he intended to be bound, usually following his predecessors, and adding to the body of law as necessary. Romans too gradually acquired the benefits of the law of the peoples.

The expert advisers (jurisconsults) to both praetor and judex felt an almost religious concern for equity: it was the spirit rather than the letter of the law that counted. This humane view found support in the philosophical writings of the Stoics, who believed as we saw that above all manmade law stood a higher "natural" law, divinely inspired, and applying to all men everywhere. In practice, of course, judges were often ill trained, the emperors brutal or arbitrary; Roman law could be used to exalt the authority of the state over the individual. Yet the law recognized the rights of the citizen, afforded legal redress even to slaves, and gave wide scope to local legal practices. Its superiority made it victor over other legal systems; the law of much of western Europe today goes back to its provisions.

Engineering and Medicine

The Romans devised a formula for making concrete from sand, lime, silica, stone, and water. They combined this concrete with large stones in building roads and bridges so well designed and so long-lasting that even today a few are still in use. The network of roads spread throughout the empire, making travel overland swift and easy. The Romans went to great trouble and

The Pont du Gard, Roman aqueduct at Nimes, first century A.D.

expense to provide their cities with pure and abundant water. A dozen aqueducts served Rome itself, and from Constantinople to Segovia aqueducts form the most spectacular Roman ruins. The concern for water reflected a real interest in bathing and in hygiene: the Romans had the highest sanitary standards known in Europe until the nineteenth century.

Roman surgeons made a variety of ingenious instruments for special operations, including the Caesarean operation—supposed (probably wrongly) to have been first performed at the birth of Julius Caesar—to deliver babies unable to be born normally. The Romans invented the first hospitals, military and civilian. Much superstition survived in Roman medicine, and it was the Greeks, notably Galen (A.D. 131–201), who continued to make the chief theoretical contributions, compiling medical encyclopedias and diffusing learning. What Galen did for medicine, his contemporary Ptolemy of Alexandria did for ancient geography; both remained the chief authorities on their subjects down to the sixteenth century. Some learned Romans followed the Alexandrian Eratosthenes in believing that the earth was round. Pliny the Elder in the first century A.D. made observations of ships approaching the shore to support this view: it was the tip of the mast that appeared first to an observer on shore and the hull last, a proof, Pliny felt, that the surface of the earth was curved.

Architecture, Sculpture, and Painting

Roman architecture borrowed the Greek column, usually Corinthian, but made wide use also of the round arch, originated by the Etruscans, and from this developed the barrel vault, a continuous series of arches like the roof of a tunnel which could be used to roof over large areas. The Romans introduced the dome, and a splendid one surmounts the Pantheon at Rome, built to honor the divine ancestors of Augustus. Roman structures emphasized bigness: the Colosseum seated 45,000 spectators; the Baths of the emperor Caracalla accommodated thousands of bathers at a time (its ruins are still used for grand opera); Diocletian's palace at Split in modern Yugoslavia contains most

The interior of the Pantheon, in a painting by Giovanni Panini (1691-1765).

and the mosaic floors of public and private buildings, where a favorite subject was a hunting scene in the landscape of the Nile, with crocodiles and hippopotamuses among the papyrus plants. The recently discovered imperial villa at Piazza Armerina in Sicily has a superb series of these floors, including a scene of bathing girls in bikinis tossing a beach ball from hand to hand.

A Final Appraisal

Tacitus was certainly right in thinking that Rome had lost some of its traditional virtues with its conquest of huge territories, its accumulation of wealth, and its assumption of imperial responsibilities. Nevertheless, the first two centuries of the empire mark the most stable and prosperous era that had yet occurred in human history. No doubt, the profits of flourishing commercial life were unevenly distributed, and there were glaring contrasts between riches and poverty. But many of the harshest aspects of ancient society elsewhere were softened at Rome: slaves could obtain their freedom more easily; women had more rights and commanded more respect (we have much evidence of harmonious family life, though there were more divorces perhaps than at any time until our own day); physical comforts were abundant for those who could afford them.

In Rome itself, however, great areas were slums: six- and seven-story wooden tenements that burned down repeatedly and were rebuilt despite building codes and fire departments. Worst of all was the chronic urban unemployment: at the height of the Pax Romana, perhaps half the population of the capital was on the bread dole. The inhabitants also were given free circuses in the form of chariot races and gladiatorial combats, and the poor squandered their pennies on betting. Bloodshed exerted a morbid fascination: criminals were crucified and even burned alive on the stage as part of spectacles to entertain the populace, and in the last century of Roman life these shows had become so popular that they had superseded the circus, despite the protests of the occasional horrified citizens, pagan or Christian.

Though the structure of the Roman state would disappear in the West by the end of the fifth century A.D., Roman influence has given a

of the modern city inside its walls. All over the Middle East and North Africa, as well as western Europe, one finds amphitheaters, temples, villas, and other monumental remains of the Roman domination.

Roman statues, though derived from Greek and Hellenistic models, often had a realism all their own, as in the cases of imperial portrait busts. In a sculptured frieze running spirally up a monumental column the victories of the emperor Trajan are vividly recorded. Of Roman painting we have chiefly the pretty—sometimes obscene—wall decorations of the villas at Pompeii (the resort town near Naples that was literally buried A.D. 79 by the sudden eruption of Vesuvius that covered it in a rain of hot ash), permanent shape to western Europe. Italian, French, Spanish, Portuguese are all languages derived from Latin, and our own English tongue is a hybrid with almost as many Latin as Germanic words. Roman legal concepts provided the foundations of respectability for many a squalid barbarian society. Rome itself, finally, would become the capital of Christianity and its administrative organization a model for the structure of the Church.

Gladiators: detail of a mosaic pavement ca. A.D. 300 now in the Borghese Gallery, Rome.

Reading Suggestions on the Romans

GENERAL ACCOUNTS

M. Rostovtzev, *Rome* (*Galaxy). Excellent survey by a famous Russian scholar.

A. E. R. Boak, *A History of Rome to 565 A.D.*, 5th ed. (Macmillan, 1965). A standard textbook.

C. E. Robinson, *Apollo History of Rome* (*Apollo). A clear introductory account.

T. Mommsen, *The History of Rome* (*Meridian). A detailed study by a great German scholar of the nineteenth century; still worth reading, though its interpretations are sometimes out of date.

M. Grant, *The World of Rome* (World, 1960). General introduction to imperial Rome; handsomely illustrated.

R. H. Barrow, *The Romans* (*Penguin). Sound popular introduction.

Tenney Frank, *A History of Rome* (Holt, 1923). Useful, though opinionated, survey by an American scholar.

THE ETRUSCAN BACKGROUND
AND THE ROMAN REPUBLIC

O. W. von Vacano, *The Etruscans in the Ancient World* (Edward Arnold, 1960). Scholarly study carefully based on archaeological evidence.

D. H. Lawrence, *Etruscan Places* (*Viking). Charming popular introduction by the famous novelist, now often outdated in information.

R. Bloch, *The Etruscans* (Praeger, 1958). General introduction, generously illustrated, in the series, "Ancient Peoples and Places." The same author's *The Origins of Rome* (Praeger, 1960), another volume in the series, takes the story of Rome to the early fifth century B.C.

A. Alföldi, *Early Rome and the Latins* (Univ. of Michigan Press, 1963). Detailed and erudite study of relations of Rome with the other Latin towns and with the Etruscans.

H. H. Scullard, *Roman Politics, 220–150 B.C.* (Clarendon, 1951). Detailed study of the era when Rome began to dominate the Mediterranean world. Scullard's *From the Gracchi to Nero* (*Barnes & Noble) is an up-to-date, clear, and balanced history of the later republic and early empire.

R. E. Smith, *The Failure of the Roman Republic* (Cambridge Univ. Press, 1955). A provocative essay critical of the Gracchi.

THE ROMAN EMPIRE

L. Homo, *Roman Political Institutions* (Knopf, 1930). Scholarly survey, now somewhat outdated.

E. Badian, *Roman Imperialism in the Late Republic* (Blackwell, 1968). A brief and original series of lectures substantially revising previous scholarship.

Anthony Birley, *Marcus Aurelius* (Little, Brown, 1966). Useful and well-written up-to-date study.

George C. Brauer, Jr., *The Young Emperors* (Crowell, 1967). The only recent monograph on the subject.

Stuart Perowne, *Hadrian* (Norton, 1960). Lively modern treatment.

H. J. Haskell, *The New Deal in Old Rome* (Knopf, 1939). The reforms of the Gracchi seen in the light of the American New Deal of the 1930's; by a newspaper editor and amateur historian.

R. Syme, *The Roman Revolution* (*Oxford Univ. Press). Detailed study of the transformation of the Roman state and society under Caesar and Augustus.

H. T. Rowell, *Rome in the Augustan Age* (Univ. of Oklahoma Press, 1962). Sympathetic appraisal of Augustus and his work.

T. W. Africa, *Rome of the Caesars* (Wiley, 1965). The era of the Pax Romana interpreted through biographical sketches of some of its leading figures.

M. P. Charlesworth, *The Roman Empire* (Oxford Univ. Press, 1951). Informative general sketch.

S. Dill, *Roman Society from Nero to Marcus Aurelius* (*Meridian). A classic of social history.

J. Carcopino, *Daily Life in Ancient Rome* (*Yale Univ. Press). A lively introduction.

ROMAN CIVILIZATION

C. Bailey, ed., *The Legacy of Rome* (Oxford, 1923). Informative essays on a variety of topics.

W. C. Greene, *The Achievement of Rome* (Harvard Univ. Press, 1933). Useful cultural survey.

Edith Hamilton, *The Roman Way* (*Norton). Sympathetic appraisal, based chiefly on Latin literature.

Tenney Frank, *Life and Literature in the Roman Republic* (*Univ. of California Press). Helpful survey.

H. Mattingly, *Roman Imperial Civilization* (*Anchor). Instructive study based largely on coins.

M. Clarke, *The Roman Mind* (Cohen & West, 1956). Studies in the history of thought from Cicero to Marcus Aurelius.

H. J. Rose, *Religion in Greece and Rome* (*Torchbooks). Detailed handbook.

E. Bréhier, *The Hellenistic and Roman Age* (*Phoenix). The second volume in a history of philosophy by an able French scholar.

M. Wheeler, *Roman Art and Architecture* (*Penguin). Clear, well-illustrated introduction.

ROMAN DECLINE   M. Rostovtzeff, *The Social and Economic History of the Roman Empire*, 2nd ed. (Clarendon, 1957). Detailed, scholarly study, magnificently illustrated, with interesting speculations on the reasons for Rome's decline.

R. M. Haywood, *The Myth of Rome's Fall* (*Apollo). Scholarly study of the centuries of decline, directed to the general reader.

Edward Gibbon, *A History of the Decline and Fall of the Roman Empire* (*many editions, usually abridged). The earliest chapters of this famous old work relate to the third and fourth centuries.

G. Milner, *The Problem of Decadence* (Williams & Norgate, 1931). Comprehensive, if inconclusive, bird's-eye view of conflicting interpretations of the reasons behind Roman decline.

SOURCES   N. Lewis and M. Reinhold, *Roman Civilization,* 2 vols. (*Torchbooks). A highly useful compilation, with enlightening editorial comments.

B. Davenport, ed., *Portable Roman Reader* (*Viking). Helpful anthology.

Vergil *The Aeneid,* trans. R. Humphries (*Scribner's). A good modern translation.

Tacitus, *On Britain and Germany,* trans. H. Mattingly (*Penguin).

Tacitus, *The Annals of Imperial Rome,* trans. M. Grant (*Penguin).

Plutarch, *Makers of Rome,* trans. I. Scott-Kilvert (*Penguin). Biographies by a cultivated Greco-Roman gentleman, who lived about A.D. 100.

Marcus Aurelius, *Meditations* (*several editions).

HISTORICAL FICTION   E. L. White, *Andivius Hedulio* (Dutton, 1933). A novel about the adventures of a
AND DRAMA   Roman nobleman in the days of the empire.

W. E. Bryher, *The Coin of Carthage* (*Harvest) and *The Roman Wall* (*Vintage). By a first-rate historical novelist; the one is set against the Second Punic War, and the other against the Alpine frontier in the era of decline.

G. B. Shaw, *Caesar and Cleopatra* (*Penguin). Caesar characterized as a wise and talkative dictator.

Stimulating and imaginative, if not always historical, portraits of famous Romans are drawn by Shakespeare in *Julius Caesar, Antony and Cleopatra* (with a devastating characterization of the ambitious young Augustus), and *Coriolanus* (which takes a very disenchanted view of the Roman Republic, especially the Tribunes of the People).

4

Christianity

I   Religion in the Later Roman World

Greek scientific theory and Roman technical skills had brought the ancient world to the threshold of an industrial age. A century before Christ, Hero of Alexandria had even discovered the engineering usefulness of steam pressure in a boiler, and conceived a model of a fire engine, including the piston. It would have been only a short step to the building of steam devices. Why did more than 1700 years pass before man took that step?

The answer must lie in the attitudes of the ruling groups in Roman times. Science formed no part of their education, and scattered statements show that they scorned what we would call research. They feared new inventions that might put still more people out of work: the emperor Tiberius once executed a man who had invented a process for making unbreakable glass. Although the earlier advance of science in the

Above: "The Good Shepherd": fourth-century marble statue now in the Lateran Museum, Rome. Right: Wall of the nave of S. Apollinare Nuovo, a fifth-century church in Ravenna, Italy.

Greek and Hellenistic world had given rise to small groups of rationalists who believed in improving their lives by using their reasoning powers, even these minorities seem virtually to have disappeared. Everywhere in Rome the student can observe a mounting pessimism and a lack of faith in man's ability to work out his own future.

The old gods seemed powerless to intervene; life appeared to be a matter of luck. And so, beginning as early as the third century B.C. and gathering increasing momentum later on, the cult of the goddess Fortune became immensely popular in the Mediterranean world: chance governed everything; today's prosperity might vanish tomorrow; the best thing to do was to enjoy luck while it lasted. Closely related was the belief in Fate: what happened was inevitable, because it had been fated from the beginning; when you were born, the moment of your death was already fixed. Some, like Cicero, protested that men could contribute to their own fate and so take advantage of fortune; Vergil attributed both fate and fortune to the will of the divine providence; but most Romans, like Tacitus, seem to have felt helpless to change their own fates or to influence events.

Astrology

To escape this feeling, most Romans came to believe that the movements of the heavenly bodies influenced the fortunes and the fate of men and governed the decisions they made. Thus the science of astronomy became lost in the false speculation of astrology. If you could do nothing to change your destiny, you could at least try to find out what it might be by consulting an expert astrologer. He would study the seven planets (Saturn, Jupiter, Mars, the Sun, Venus, Mercury, the Moon), each of which had its own will, character, sex, plants, numbers, and animals, and each of which was lord of a sphere. Seven transparent but impenetrable concentric spheres, with Earth at the center, cut man off from heaven. Each planet had its own day: hence the seven-day week. Seven itself became a mystic number: there were seven ages of man, seven wonders of the world. Then too there were the twelve Houses of the Sun, constellations of stars through which the sun passed on his path around

the earth: these were the signs of the zodiac.*

From the position of the heavenly bodies and the signs of the zodiac at the moment of your conception or birth, astrologers would draw up a horoscope foretelling your fate. The Roman emperors, like most of their subjects, profoundly believed in astrology. And of course some people have continued to believe, even to our own day. Especially valuable for the art of prophecy were unnatural events: the appearance of a comet, the birth of a monster. Similarly, men believed in all sorts of magic, and tried by its power to force the heavenly bodies to grant their wishes.

New Cults: Cybele, Isis, Mithra

The state religion of the Olympian gods and of the deified emperor still commanded the loyalty of many Romans, who regarded the proper observance of its rites as the equivalent of patriotism. But the old faith no longer allayed the fears of the millions of people believing in blind fate and inevitable fortune. More and more men sought for a religion that would hold out the hope for an afterlife better than the grim life here on earth. So, along with astrology and magic, a large number of mystery religions began to appear in Rome.

All the new faiths taught that a human being could save his soul by uniting it with the soul of a saviour, who in many cases had himself experienced death and resurrection. Union with the saviour was accomplished by a long initiation, marked by purifications, ritual banquets, and other ceremonies. As the candidate cast aside human unworthiness, the god would enter him, and so after death he would be saved. The initiate sought a mystical guarantee that he would not perish but would survive hereafter. It was perfectly possible to join as many of these cults as one liked and yet at the same time continue to practice the state religion.

The Greeks had had such cults in the rites of Demeter at Eleusis and in the mysteries of Dionysus. The rites of Dionysus, now called Bacchus, became popular at Rome, celebrating as they did the animal side of human nature and the

* Not until the sixteenth century did man discover that the earth was not at the center of our universe, and that it revolved around the sun.

abandonment of all restraint. On hundreds of Roman sarcophagi can be seen the Bacchic procession, celebrating the joys of drink and sex. But the cult of Bacchus was too materialistic to satisfy all Romans.

One of its major competitors was the cult of the great mother-goddess Cybele, transplanted from Asia Minor. Her young husband, Attis, died and was reborn annually (like Demeter's daughter, Persephone). Attis was thus a symbol of renewed fertility. The rites of Cybele included fasting, frenzied processions, and the self-flagellation and even self-mutilation of the priests. The first temple to Cybele at Rome dated from 204 B.C., but the zenith of the cult came in the second century A.D. and later. By that time the rites in-

cluded the slaughter of a bull above a pit into which the initiate had descended in order to be bathed by the blood. The cult, as we have seen, was the subject of a long dramatic poem by the poet Catullus.

Even more popular—especially among women —was the cult of the Egyptian Isis, whose consort, Osiris, also died and was reborn each year. All feminine elements, both lascivious and chaste, were concentrated in an elaborate ritual of worship for Isis, the loving mother-goddess, who promised her adherents personal immortality.

From Persia via Asia Minor came the cult of the god Mithra, allied to the supreme powers of good and light and so connected with the Sun.

Taurobolium (sacrifice of a bull in Mithraism): a Roman relief.

120

The male initiates passed in succession through seven grades of initiation (corresponding to the seven planets and named after animals), qualifying for each by severe tests. Baptism and communion were also part of the ritual. Unconquered, physically tough, and self-denying, Mithra became a model for the Roman soldier, to whom he held out the hope of salvation. Mithraism had no priests and welcomed the gods of other cults; it tended to absorb the other sun-worshiping cults, including that of Apollo, into one new cult, often heartily supported by the emperor. From London to Alexandria and from the Rhine to the Euphrates, temples of Mithra, with altars and statues, have been found.

Mysticism for the Intellectuals

In addition to these well-defined cults, most of which appealed to the masses rather than to the highly educated, there were certain notable new trends in mystical thinking that were popular among the intellectuals. Halfway between religion and philosophy lay the writings of the so-called thrice-great Hermes (Hermes Trismegistus) and his school, who prescribed abstinence, concentration, and study as a preparation for a flash of ecstasy and a spiritual rebirth. The Epicureans tried to banish pain, fear, and desire by repose and reflection, and the Stoics still calmly looked forward to an absorption after death in the impersonal fiery breath of the divinity. Stronger still was the current called

Neoplatonic, since its adherents claimed to be disciples of Plato. They taught that each human soul makes a pilgrimage toward an eventual union with the divine incorporeal essence, the One, the True, the Good, the last great abstraction. By contemplation the mystic can gradually free himself from material ties and achieve ecstatic vision. Neoplatonism soon became contaminated with far less lofty and rarefied rites, like those of the cults. Incantations against demons helped the seeker on his way, and mumbo-jumbo sometimes replaced philosophy. For the Neoplatonist the divine reason, the *logos*, joined with the divine soul and the ultimate divinity itself as a sort of Trinity.

Christianity

But no single one of the mystery religions or philosophic movements appealed to men and women of all classes at Rome. Mithraism, which perhaps had the most adherents, especially in the army, excluded women and lacked love and tenderness. Neoplatonism had no appeal for the masses. In the Roman world, we have already noted the presence of Christians, especially under Nero, who made them the scapegoat for the great fire of 64. Indeed, Christianity competed with the cults in the Roman world for more than three centuries after the death of its founder, with no assurance that it would triumph. Sharing some things in common with them, it also possessed qualities they lacked.

II Jesus; The First Christians

The Historical Jesus

About the accuracy of the biblical story of Jesus, his mission, his crucifixion and resurrection, there has been much debate ever since the beginnings of modern scholarly biblical criticism in the nineteenth century. Some of the more extreme of those who pursued this "higher criticism," such as the German philosopher Bruno Bauer, denied that Jesus had ever existed; for Bauer, Jesus was a myth. For the most part, however, these critics confined themselves to questioning the objectivity and accuracy of our historical sources for the life of Jesus.

Jesus was born in Palestine sometime between the years we call 8 and 4 B.C., and was crucified probably A.D. 29, 30, or 33. There are no sources absolutely contemporary with his life, but Paul's Epistles to the Corinthians were written about A.D. 55, the Acts of the Apostles about 60–62, and the Gospels in the years that followed: Mark about 65, Matthew and Luke about 80–85, and John about 100. Late in the second or early in the third century these texts were revised in Alexandria. We have no canonical Christian text written down before this revision. Before the year 60 a collection of the sayings of Jesus himself existed, written in Aramaic, the Semitic language that he spoke; this is lost. In addition, many other texts existed that were not regarded as canonical. Among them we may note the so-called Gospel of Thomas, of which fragments were found in Egypt in 1945 and 1946, consisting of 114 sayings attributed to Jesus, and dating from the early second century. Thus, because we have no precise, contemporary accounts, the exact details of the preachings of Jesus during his own lifetime cannot always be determined.

Most scholars would now agree that the first generation or so of "higher" critics of the Bible in the nineteenth century went too far in concluding that, because the life of Jesus is not *documented* in the sense, say, that the life of any great modern man is documented, the gospel account is fiction. The extremists who deny the historicity of Jesus have had few followers, even among the scholars who are outside Christian belief. Indeed it seems safe to say that our sources give us a faithful reflection of the life of Jesus.

Jesus was born in a Palestine that was a satellite kingdom of the new world-state of the Roman Empire. Like much of the rest of the civilized world, the people of Palestine had been groping for firm religious beliefs. The mingling of men in this world of conquests and trade had been accompanied by an unsettling mingling of gods and creeds. Even the Jews were not wholly outside this melting pot of religious beliefs and emotions. Many members of their upper classes had been influenced by Greek philosophy, and the Jewish royal family of Herod the Great, king of Judea from 37 to 4 B.C., had been thoroughly Hellenized. Jesus was himself a Jew, and his followers inherited with his own teaching the uncompromising monotheism of the Old Testament, the Jewish tradition of regular education of the faithful, the belief that they formed a chosen people, the acceptance of authority, and the constant indoctrination of the faithful with a code of behavior. The Gospels of Matthew and Luke in particular refer to Jesus as the Teacher of Righteousness.

New light on these specifically Palestinian traditions in Christianity may be provided by the Dead Sea Scrolls, which were discovered in caves in Palestine beginning in 1947. The scrolls, dating from 200 to 70 B.C., contain fragments of

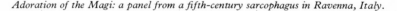

Adoration of the Magi: a panel from a fifth-century sarcophagus in Ravenna, Italy.

the teachings of a heretical Jewish sect, the Essenes, who lived in an isolated community and shared their property; their buildings were destroyed by the Romans A.D. 68. The Dead Sea Scrolls make repeated reference to a Teacher of Righteousness, a Suffering Just One, in whom some see a forerunner of Christ. Although after the Teacher's death, probably a violent one, his followers did not claim that he had been the Messiah awaited by the Jews, there is one passage in which the Teacher spoke of himself as producing a man-child who would have all his own powers. The New Testament makes no reference at all to the Essenes, and Jesus may have had no contact with them or with their tradition, yet the scrolls reveal a reforming movement within Judaism that apparently had much in common with later Christianity.

In Jesus' own time, the Jewish faithful were torn between two sects, the Sadducees and the Pharisees. From a religious point of view the priestly Sadducees were conservative and recognized only the law of the Old Testament. The Pharisees, who were more progressive, recognized the authority of oral tradition and religious speculation as supplementing the law. From these sources they developed ideas about resurrection from the dead, reward after death for the good and punishment for the wicked, and belief in a Messiah. All these beliefs are given later development in Christianity. It is significant that the Christian New Testament attacks the Pharisees more sharply than the Sadducees. Though such comparisons are always imperfect, we may point out that radicals often, if not usually, find liberals more objectionable than conservatives.

Jesus preached in the towns and villages and gathered small groups of followers. His doctrines brought him the enmity of influential Jewish groups, and possibly also that of the Roman resident administrators. It might have seemed to the people in power that he was preaching social revolution. In the eyes of conventional Jews, he was pretty clearly a dangerous rebel.

The Teachings of Jesus

The general nature of Jesus' message is clear enough. Although he appealed to the poor, the unlearned, and the weak, he was no simple social revolutionary, no revivalist, no ascetic. He preached the enjoyment of the good things of this world, an enjoyment freed from rivalry, ostentation, and vulgarity. He was kind but stern: good intentions are not enough; "he that heareth, and doeth not, is like a man that without a foundation built a house upon the earth . . ." (Luke 6:49). Above all he preached gentleness and love: humility, charity, honesty, toleration ("Judge not, that ye be not judged"—Matt. 7:1); but he warned that "wide is the gate, and broad is the way, that leadeth to destruction" (Matt. 7:13). Though he preached that men should turn the other cheek, he also said at another time that he came not to bring peace, but a sword. Plain people understood him, and took comfort from his words.

From Jesus' preaching there emerged theological conclusions of great importance: he spoke of his Father in heaven, referred to himself as the Son of Man, and taught that God the Father had sent him to redeem mankind from sin. Those who hearkened and led decent lives on earth would gain eternal bliss in heaven; those who turned a deaf ear and continued in their evil courses would be eternally damned in hell. The Gospels add that Christ (the word means "the anointed one") had died on the cross as the supreme act of redemption, that he had risen from the dead on the third day, and that he would soon return, during the lifetime of some of his hearers, to end this world in a final Day of Judgment. So the earliest Christians expected the Second Coming of Christ momentarily, and thought little of their earthly lives. Soon the literal expectation of Christ was transformed into a more mystical expectation of "the Comforter."

Christ was miraculously born of a virgin mother. He was baptized by John the Baptist in the waters of the Jordan, and his followers too were baptized by their priests. He himself had given bread and wine to his followers, and told them that it was his body and his blood. The virgin mother, the purifying bath, and the mysterious sacrificial meal of communion recall elements that were present in the various mystery cults, as of course does the promise of eternal life. But the Christians held in contempt the excesses of the cult of Cybele, for example, and regarded the Mithraic baptism and sacred communion as fiendish parodies of their own practices. Moreover, Jesus' sacrifice of his life for mankind and the intimacy with God promised during the future eternal life gave Christianity an immediacy and an appeal that no mystery religion could duplicate. Christ's message of love—for man, woman, and child, for the weak and lowly—supplied the tenderness that was lacking in the world of every day.

The First Christians

After the crucifixion of Jesus, a little group of his followers held together in Jerusalem. These first Christians were Jews who followed, as indeed Jesus himself followed, the Jewish law. They might well have remained no more than a humble Jewish sect or splinter group. But Christian belief had drawing powers that were bound to exceed the limits of the Jewish communities. Christ had told his followers, "There be some standing here, which shall not taste of death, till they see the Son of man coming in his kingdom" (Matt. 16:28). Add to this doctrine of the Second Coming the immediacy of the emotional tie which Christianity brought between the individual believer and Christ, and among individuals in the Christian brotherhood, and you have indeed an evangel, the "glad tidings" that made Christians out of Jews, Greeks, Romans, all the varied folk of the Roman Empire.

The full social and psychological consequences of this widespread belief we cannot really know. Some of the first Christians were so convinced of the closeness of the Day of Judgment that they gave up everything that touched the world of the senses and common sense and turned wholly to prayer, self-denial, and ecstasy. But clearly this belief was useful in making converts to Christianity and, given the organizing gifts of the apostles and their successors, it was also useful in maintaining the loyalty and enthusiasm of converts. Quite as clearly, this belief in an immediate Second Coming began to prove an embarrassment after the first generation or so, and had to be spiritualized into a theological doctrine of salvation.

It has never been easy for the individual Christian to know whether or not he is a true Christian. But membership in the kind of organized society we call a church has always been for most Christians an indispensable accompanying condition of salvation. In the early and struggling years of Christianity, this condition was reasonably easy to fulfill. For in spite of doctrinal and disciplinary problems, problems complicated by the appeal of the Gospel to troubled and excitable souls, the early Christians were united to an extraordinary degree in the primitive Church.

Saint Paul

They owed that union in part to the tireless activities of the early organizers, of whom the most remarkable was Saul of Tarsus, a converted Jew who had never seen Christ. Saint Paul, as he is known in Christianity, after having helped to persecute the first little band of Christians in Jerusalem, himself experienced on a journey to Damascus a deep emotional conversion. Paul and his helpers have left behind them records in the Acts and the Pauline and other Epistles of the New Testament. From these we can learn how the new faith was incorporated into an organized church, and we can come to know Paul as a person much more thoroughly and reliably than we know most personalities of the ancient world.

Paul is called the Apostle to the Gentiles, and he seems to have led the way in taking the one step that had to be taken before Christianity could become a universal religion. The first Christians, as we have seen, were religious Jews who thought of themselves as followers of Yahweh and his law. This law included among other things an elaborate set of ritual ways that a Jew mastered only slowly as he grew up among his people. It was a stumbling block in the way of adult Greeks and other Gentiles who might find the preachings of Jesus attractive. Even though Jesus himself had been what we call liberal in his interpretation of the law, he had, according to the Gospels, made some strong statements, notably: "Think not that I am come to destroy the law, or the prophets: I am not come to destroy, but to fulfill. For verily I say unto you, Till heaven and earth pass, one jot or one tittle shall in no wise pass from the law, till all be fulfilled" (Matt. 5:17–18).

The Jewish ritual requirement of male circumcision is a simple example of the hindrances that stood in the way of conversion to Christianity as long as it remained a Jewish sect. For an adult in those days, without antiseptics and without anesthesia, circumcision was a dangerous and dreaded operation. But Paul had a remedy: he announced that the Greek or Syrian convert to Christianity need not undergo circumcision. Similarly, he proclaimed that the convert need not abstain from pork or follow the detailed prescriptions of the law. Paul said all this many times and in many ways: "For by one Spirit are we all baptized into one body, whether we be Jews or Gentiles, whether we be bond or free" (1 Cor. 12:13). And most simply: "For the letter killeth, but the spirit giveth life" (2 Cor. 3:6). The Christian was to be saved, not by the letter of the Jewish law, but by the spirit of the Jewish faith in a righteous God.

In a way that was surely never common in early history—one finds no such union in an Ikhnaton or a Plato—Paul united in his own person the mystic who would transcend the world and the flesh, the gifted spiritual adviser of ordinary men and women troubled in their everyday lives, and the able administrator of a growing Church. In all Paul's writings there are passages which show him to have been ascetic in his morality and firmly convinced that Christian truth is not a matter of habit or reasoning, but of transcending faith:

Howbeit we speak wisdom among them that are perfect: yet not the wisdom of this world, nor of the princes of this world, that come to nought: But we speak the wisdom of God in a mystery, even the hidden wisdom, which God ordained before the world unto our glory; Which none of the princes of this world knew: for had they known it, they would not have crucified the Lord of glory. [1 Cor. 2:6–8.]

Yet Paul was no oriental mystic who wholly denied the reality or goodness of this world; he never preached denial of this world in mystic ecstasy. Indeed he expresses clearly that characteristic Christian tension between this world and the next, between the real and the ideal, which has ever since firmly marked Western society. This tension—better, this *awareness*—he expressed as the mystic union of Christ and Christian: "Always bearing about in the body the dying of the Lord Jesus, that the life also of Jesus might be made manifest in our body" (2 Cor. 4:10), a magnificent passage much used in funeral services. Christians are not merely animals, or merely men: They are children of God who are destined, if they are true Christians, to eternal bliss. But on this earth they must live in the constant imperfection of the flesh, not wholly transcending it, always aware that they are at once mortal and immortal.

A large part of the Pauline Epistles deals with matters of church discipline. Here we see Paul charged with the curing of souls, keeping a firm but not despotic hand over scattered and struggling Christian congregations in Corinth, in Rome, and in many parts of the empire. We see him trying to tame the excesses to which the emotionally liberating new doctrines so readily gave rise. We find him urging the newly emancipated not to interpret Christian love as sexual promiscuity, not to take their new wisdom as an opportunity for wild ranting ("speaking with tongues"), not, in short, to indulge in excesses, but to accept the discipline of the Church, to lead quiet, faithful, but firmly Christian lives.

The Early Spread of Christianity

Paul, of course, was not one of the twelve apostles, actual companions of Christ, who, according to tradition, separated after the crucifixion to preach the faith in the four corners of the earth. But he has been accepted as their equal in his apostolate. Of the twelve, Peter, after

Christian in a Roman toga: mural from a Roman catacomb.

working in the East, went to Rome, of which he was the first bishop, and so the first pope, and was there martyred under Nero—tradition said on the very same day as Paul, who had also come to Rome. Thus the Church of Rome had both Peter and Paul as its founders. In the imperial capital, the first Christians were a despised sect, suspected of all sorts of horrid crimes, such as incest and infanticide as well as ritual murder. But by the year 100, the new faith had long since found a foothold outside the Jewish communities of its origin, had penetrated the Eastern regions of the empire, and had even established a foothold in the West. It was still a small, obscure, persecuted sect, and only a visionary could have predicted its eventual triumph. If the blood of the martyrs is the seed of the Church, Paul was its most skillful cultivator, nursing the new plants. They were already so hardy that not even the bitter winds of persecution could kill them.

III   Christianity in the Pagan World

The Reasons for Persecution

What to Christians is known as persecution was to the authorities of Rome simply their duty as defenders of public order against men and women who seemed to them traitors or irresponsible madmen. The Christians ran afoul of the Roman civil law not so much for their positive beliefs and practices, but rather for their refusal to accept the divinity of the emperor, and to sacrifice to him as a god. The emperor was not *their* god, and they were ready to suffer the punishment of death for not worshiping him. To cultivated Greeks and Romans of these first centuries Christians seemed wild and indecent enthusiasts, and to the masses they were disturbers, cranks, revolutionaries. But the empire was not very concerned with the details of the morals and faiths of its hundreds of component city-states, tribes, and nations. Scores of gods and goddesses, innumerable spirits and demons, filled the minds of the millions under Roman rule, and the rulers, themselves usually Stoics with a philosophic, though scornful, toleration of mass superstitions, were willing to tolerate them all as part of the nature of things.

There was, however, a practical limit to this religious freedom, which after all was based on no ideal of religious liberty, and certainly not on any concept of separation of Church and State. To hold this motley collection of peoples in a common allegiance, to give them something like the equivalent of a modern national flag and pledge of allegiance, the emperor was deified. Simple rites of sacrifice to him were added to local religions and local rites. After all, one more god gave no trouble to those who believed in the Greco-Roman pantheon or in Isis or Cybele or in any other conventional polytheism; one more pinch of incense on one more altar was simple enough. Those who did not believe in the customary local gods—and such disbelief was widespread in the Roman Empire—had no trouble in doing what was expected of them, for they did not take with undue seriousness any religion, new or old.

The Christians, however, could not sacrifice to the emperor any more than the Jews of old could sacrifice to Baal. Indeed, they felt that, insofar as the emperor pretended to be a god, he was in fact a devil. The more cautious administrators of the growing Christian Church were anxious to live down their reputation for disorderliness, and by no means sought to antagonize the civil authorities. These leaders may have been responsible for the familiar "Render therefore unto Caesar the things which are Caesar's; and unto God the things that are God's" (Matt. 22:21), which historians believe is clearly a later addition to the text of the New Testament. But sacrifice was a thing of God's. The true Christian, then, could not bring himself to make what to an outsider or a skeptic was merely a decent gesture, like raising one's hat today when the flag goes by in a parade. Moreover, if he was a very ardent Christian, he might feel that the very act of sacrifice to Caesar was a wicked thing, even when performed by non-Christians, and he might show these feelings in public.

The Persecutions

But the imperial authorities did not consistently seek to stamp out the Christian religion. The persecutions were sporadic. They came in some half-dozen major waves over three centuries, and they were subject to great local variations. The first persecution, as we know, came in 64 under the emperor Nero, and Tacitus called it a deliberate attempt by Nero to find a scapegoat for the fire:

Therefore, to scotch the rumour [that he himself had set the fire] Nero substituted as culprits, and punished with the utmost refinements of cruelty, a class of men, loathed for their vices, whom the crowd styled Christians. Christus, the founder of the name, had undergone the death penalty in the reign of Tiberius, . . . and the pernicious superstition was checked for a moment, only to break out once more, not merely in Judaea, the home of the disease, but in the capital itself, where all things horrible or shameful in the world collect and find a vogue. First, then, the confessed members of the sect were arrested; next, on their disclosures, vast numbers were convicted, not so much on the count of arson as for hatred of the human race.*

There was no doubt in Tacitus' mind that the Christians were criminals, but a faint doubt did creep into the mind of an able and conscien-

* *The Annals,* trans. John Jackson (Cambridge, Mass., 1937), XV, xliv.

Catacomb of the church of S. Sebastiano, Rome.

tious member of the imperial ruling class, Pliny the Younger. Pliny wrote to his emperor, Trajan (98–117), from Bithynia in Asia Minor that he was puzzled about the Christians. Should he punish a Christian just because he admitted to being a Christian, or must he have evidence of the horrid crimes that Christians were alleged to commit? Should he trust an unknown informer who had furnished him with a list of alleged Christians? Many, he wrote, had actually recanted and worshiped Trajan's image. But, he went on:

> They affirmed, however, the whole of their guilt, or their error, was, that they were in the habit of meeting on a certain fixed day before it was light, when they sang in alternate verses a hymn to Christ, as to a god, and bound themselves by a solemn oath, not to any wicked deeds, but never to commit any fraud, theft or adultery, never to falsify their word, nor deny a trust when they should be called upon to deliver it up; after which it was their custom to separate, and then reassemble to partake of food—but food of an ordinary and innocent kind. . . . I judged it so much the more necessary to extract the real truth, with the assistance of torture, from two female slaves, who were styled *deaconesses:* but I could discover nothing more than depraved and excessive superstition.*

Trajan, in accordance with his own judicious and moderate character, replied:

> No search should be made for these people; when they are denounced and found guilty, they must be punished; with the restriction, however, that when the party denies himself to be a Christian, and shall give proof that he is not (that is, by adoring our Gods) he shall be pardoned on the ground of repentance, even though he may have formerly incurred suspicion. Informations without the accuser's name subscribed must not be admitted in evidence against anyone, as it is introducing a very dangerous precedent, and by no means agreeable to the spirit of the age.†

One sees that the men who directed that measures be taken against the Christians were often not themselves men of passionate religious convictions. At moments of crisis they sought to get

rid of people like Christians, but they did not have the fanaticism of the true persecutor. They could not fight fire with fire of their own.

Persecution, then, was not steady but sporadic. Christian willingness to undergo martyrdom rather than worship the gods was regarded by most pagan Romans, including the Stoic emperor Marcus Aurelius, as a kind of exhibitionism. Marcus Aurelius persecuted the Christians both in Asia Minor and in Gaul. In the third century, as the Roman world seemed to be coming apart at the seams, persecutions became more frequent and more severe; Diocletian was especially harsh. The persecutions claimed many martyrs. But by going underground—in the city of Rome, *literally* underground to worship in the catacombs—by glorifying the memory of the martyrs, by persistent proselytizing, by taking advantage of the kind of good will or at least neutrality evident in Trajan's letter, the Church grew stronger and its members more numerous throughout these centuries. After a final major persecution in the early fourth century, official toleration was achieved in 311 in an edict signed on his deathbed by the persecuting emperor Galerius. The emperor Constantine (306–337) confirmed the policy of toleration in an agreement with his rival Licinius about 313.

The Conversion of Constantine

In 312 Constantine himself had a religious experience akin to Paul's on the Damascus road: just before going into battle, it is said, the emperor saw in the heavens the sign of a cross against the sun and the words "conquer in this." He put the sign on the battle-standards of his army, won the battle, and attributed the victory to the god of the Christians. Though the story has often been challenged, there is little evidence for the counterargument that Constantine acted because he simply foresaw the eventual triumph of Christianity. He continued to appease the sun-god as well as the god of the Christians, but he regarded himself a Christian. At the time of his death in 337, the Church was on its way to becoming the official state religion of the Roman Empire.

One last major official attempt was made at a formal restoration—or, rather, reconstruction—

---

* Pliny, *Letters,* trans. W. Melmoth (London, 1915), X, xcvi.

† Ibid., X, xcvii.

128

of the old polytheism of the empire. The emperor Julian the Apostate (361–363), pagan and philosopher much influenced by the Neoplatonists, was persuaded that the "Galileans," as he called the Christians, were adherents of an inferior oriental superstition. But Julian's substitute for Christianity was a hopeless hodgepodge of Neoplatonic and oriental religious ideas and practices.

At his death only two years after he had assumed the imperial crown, Christianity quickly regained and extended a position that had never been greatly threatened by Julian's activities. The emperor Theodosius I (379–395) made Christianity the official religion of the empire and began to persecute the pagans. Paganism continued in the countryside and among the upper classes and the intellectuals for another century or so, but in the cities it was no longer an organized force.

The Christian Triumph as a Historical Problem

Why did Christianity triumph? It was at the beginning a despised sect of simple enthusiasts in a rich, well-organized, sophisticated society. Yet it took over the society. In general, we may postulate the need for a religion of love in the savage world of Rome; and in particular we have noted some of the advantages that Jesus' teachings gave Christianity over the mystery cults. The cult of Isis lacked a missionary priesthood, that of Mithra any priesthood at all. Isis was chiefly for women, Mithra altogether for men. Apuleius, a second-century Latin novelist, in the eighth book of his *Golden Ass*, describes a troupe of emasculated priests of Isis carrying about their "omnipotent and omnipresent Syrian goddess" and behaving like a rowdy circus troupe. Apuleius himself appears fond of magic and new cults, and ends his story with a long account of his own initiation into the cult of Isis, a rite full of flubdubbery.

So the evangel was really "good news," with its promise of personal immortality, its admonition to behave with kindness and with love to one's fellow human beings, its lofty moral code. The Church provided a consoling and beautiful and dramatic ritual, and the opportunity to become a part of the exciting, dangerous, and thoroughly masculine task of spreading the gospel.

The would-be convert could find in it ideas and rites closely related to those of Egyptians, Greeks, and Jews. It was at Ephesus, the shrine of the peculiar virgin mother-goddess known as Diana of the Ephesians, that the quarrelsome Christian theologians of the fifth century would proclaim the Virgin Mary the mother of God.

From its cradle in Jerusalem, Christianity never penetrated far into the lands of Zoroastrian, Hindu, and other Eastern faiths, nor far into Africa. Instead it spread north and west into Europe, essentially *within* the Roman Empire. It needed the political and cultural structure of the empire to work within. And, of course, only a few centuries later a fiery and militant new monotheism, Islam, arose and overwhelmed some of the Eastern outposts of Christianity.

Christianity succeeded not only because it set itself against the earthly compromises and indecencies of pagan cults, the dryness and sterility of later pagan philosophy, but also because it contained so much of paganism, because, in short, it was by no means wholly new. This point is often referred to as the *syncretistic* nature of Christianity—that is, the new religion's capacity for borrowing and absorbing the doctrines and practices of older beliefs. Christian notions of immortality and resurrection are related to Egyptian, Greek, and Hebrew notions; Greek and Roman philosophies, especially mystical Neoplatonism, contributed a great deal to developed Christianity. Even more important perhaps is the extent to which Christianity allowed the old uses, the old rites and habits, the unintellectual "practical" side of religion, to survive, and the extent to which it mastered and tamed pagan habits. So, when the crowds of Ephesus in the fifth century hailed the victory of the theologians who were defending the Virgin's motherhood, one might almost hear an echo, "Great is Diana of the Ephesians." Christmas is the birth of Jesus, but also the turning northward at last of the European winter sun, the promise of its returning warmth; and Easter is an echo of thousands of prehistoric years of celebrations of the actual coming of spring, the resurrection of life in nature.

Yet all these many reasons pale into abstraction before the fact that Christianity prevailed because it won its way into the hearts of living men and women. Christianity brought to the confused millions of a world that was almost as self-conscious and worried as our own a feeling of belonging, of understanding, of loving and of being loved. Here is one of the many Christian inscriptions that have survived from early tombs:

I, Petronia, wife of a deacon, of modest countenance, here lay down my bones and place them in their resting place. Cease from weeping, my husband and sweet children, and believe that it is not right to mourn one that lives in God.*

Christianity, although it achieved the status of legal religion in the Roman Empire early in the fourth century, enjoyed no full and undisputed triumph. After the persecutions and the competition with pagan beliefs, long, serious struggles sprang up within Christianity itself over the forms and nature of its own beliefs and rituals. We may now follow the story of Christianity until the end of the historical period that our fathers called Antiquity. For clarity of analysis, we shall treat separately the evolution of the two great elements in Christianity, ideas and spirit on one side, political and social organization on the other. But we must always remember that in real life the two elements were inseparable, each always conditioning and altering the other, a process of mutual *reinforcement*.

IV   The Organization of Christianity

Just what was the organization of the early Christian churches, and especially of the primitive churches of the first generation or two after the death of Christ? There has been the same kind of debate over this question as over the problems of the historicity of Jesus and the sources of the New Testament. Since the late Middle Ages, men have sought to find in the primitive Church a pattern, an authority, a confirmation of their own conceptions of what church government ought to be. They have found, in part at least because they wanted to find their own kind of government, that the early Christian Church was episcopalian (ruled by bishops) or presbyterian (ruled by elders) or congregational (ruled by the members of the church) or even that the primitive Church had no government but was simply a spontaneous gathering of the faithful. The historian will conclude that there were in fact in the early Church elements of all these, even of the last.

Commentators on early Christian organization often differ on important details, such as the question of the role of Peter and Paul in the early Church at Rome. But almost all agree on two very broad generalizations. First, the primitive churches frequently had excited and excitable members who had somehow to be tamed, disciplined, and perhaps rejected if any kind of mundane order was to be maintained in the Church. Second, in all the primitive churches gradually grew up a distinction between lay and clerical members.

The organizers of early Christianity had, in addition to the troubles that always face the worldly organizers of an otherworldly faith, the grave difficulty of achieving this organization in the midst of a great bureaucratic empire that was committed in principle to the suppression of Christianity. The wild enthusiast—in the phrase of Paul, the "speaker with tongues"—was usually an unreliable member of an organized underground.

Yet Christianity did triumph, and its organization was already taking shape by the end of the second century. In the first churches, the little groups organized by the first missionaries, there were men called variously prophets, teachers, and the like. The names suggest that these men worked basically on the feelings of their co-religionists, that perhaps many of them were mystical believers rather than worldly organizers. But almost as early we also find that these groups have elders, overseers, and presidents. And *these* names suggest in fact what we call government—Church government, to be sure, and not political government, but essentially a source of law and authority.

The Early Church

More and more, the overseer (Greek *episkopos*) appeared in authority over a compact administrative area, his see. This was the bishop,

* H. P. V. Nunn, *Christian Inscriptions* (London, 1920), No. 41.

who became the key figure in church administration. Each see claimed to have been founded by one of the original apostles; and its bishop thus held office through "apostolic succession." Since it had been Christ himself who had chosen the apostles, every bishop, in effect, became a direct spiritual heir of Christ. Groups of bishoprics or episcopal sees often were gathered together into larger units, owing obedience to an archbishop, a head-overseer (*archiepiskopos*). Just as the bishop often had his headquarters in a Roman civitas, or city-state unit, and exercised authority over the churches in the countryside roundabout, so the archbishop governed the civitates from a mother-city, a metropolis, usually the capital of a Roman province, and his see was called a province.

At the top of the hierarchy stood the bishop of the imperial capital, Rome itself, the father of them all, *papa* or pope, who claimed supreme authority. The prestige of Rome contributed powerfully to his claim. So did the association of Peter and Paul with Rome. Christ had said to Peter, "Thou art Peter and upon this rock I will build my church," a celebrated Greek pun, since the word for Peter is *Petros* and that for rock *petra*. Because Peter had been martyred in Rome, the bishops of that city could claim that Christ himself had picked Rome as the rock upon which to build: a claim that was embodied in their "Petrine theory." The bishops of the great cities of the eastern Mediterranean, Alexandria and Antioch, however, claimed to exercise a paternal rule equal in authority to that of the pope. They called themselves patriarch (fatherly governor). Still later, after Constantine had moved the imperial capital from Rome to Constantinople (A.D. 330), its bishop, also a patriarch, would oppose papal claims to supremacy.

With the departure of imperial government from Rome, the popes gradually made themselves more and more responsible for the government of the great city. And as the barbarians began to pour in and Rome itself came under attack, the pope became the symbol of the old Roman regularities and certainties, a rock indeed. A succession of outstanding men became Bishop of Rome, notably Leo the Great (reigned 440–461), a theologian, a splendid administrator, and a brave man, who saved the city from the Hun, Attila. By the time of the break-up of the Roman Empire, in the fifth century, nobody in the West would have disputed the claim of papal supremacy; the papacy had emerged as the firmest institution in a new and terrible world.

The government of the Church thus exhibited important characteristics. First, it had arisen gradually, in response to need. Second, the Church strengthened its organization by utilizing the existing political machinery of the Roman Empire, placing its major officials in centers which were already administrative capitals. Third, the bishops and archbishops, meeting in councils, determined which religious ideas or practices would be accepted and which rejected, which writings were truly Christian and which false. In this way the Church selected from other writings the twenty-seven canonical books of the New Testament, written in Greek, and the Old Testament writings as preserved in a Greek translation from the Hebrew. In the Greek church today, these versions are still in use; in the Roman church, the Latin version called the Vulgate, made by St. Jerome in the fourth century, is used. Many of the writings that the Church rejected have survived. Though not canonical, they have much interest for the modern historian and theologian.

Each individual bishop presided over several churches. Each church was under the care of a priest (Greek *presbyteros*, "elder"), who had been qualified by special training and by the ceremony of ordination. The area served by each church and its priest came to be known as the parish. In the early Church the office of deacon, often held by a man who had other occupations besides the service of the Church, had much importance. In some of the early churches, the congregation itself elected its officers, and the church was governed by boards of elders (presbyteries); but the system of appointment from above prevailed over that of election, although the congregation was often consulted. Before long, then, the distinction between those who were merely faithful worshipers (the laity) and those who conducted the worship and administered the affairs of the church (the clergy) became well defined. Despite frequent rumbles of protest during the two thousand years of Christianity, and despite differences of degree in the Christian churches, some distinction between laity and clergy is maintained in all, even the Society of Friends (Quakers), who have no formally separate body of clerics.

By the seventh century the broad lines of church government in both the East and the

Spread of Christianity, to 11th Century

NORWAY
SWEDEN
DENMARK
SCOTLAND
IONA
IRELAND
ENGLAND
York
Oxford
Lindisfarne
Whitby
Salisbury
Canterbury
Winchester
Louvain
Cologne
Berlin
GERMANY
Trier
Mainz
Paris
Toul
Sens
Clairvaux
Tours
Citeaux
Basel
Constance
Cluny
FRANCE
Milan
Po R.
Padua
Bologna
Ferrara
Florence
Assisi
ITALY
Rome
Monte Cassino
CORSICA
SARDINIA
BALEARIC IS.
SICILY
Santiago de Compostela
SPAIN
Hippo
RUSSIA
Kiev
BYZANTINE
EMPIRE
Constantinople
Chalcedon
Nicaea
Thessalonica
Ephesus
Corinth
Athens
Tarsus
Antioch
RHODES
CRETE
CYPRUS
Damascus
Nazareth
Jerusalem
SYRIA
Alexandria
EGYPT

Atlantic Ocean
Mediterranean Sea
Black Sea
Baltic Sea

Rivers: *Elbe R.*, *Oder R.*, *Vistula R.*, *Niemen R.*, *Duna R.*, *Oka R.*, *Volga R.*, *Dnieper R.*, *Don R.*, *Danube R.*, *Rhone R.*, *Seine R.*, *Loire R.*, *Ebro R.*, *Tagus R.*

Dates (boxed): 995, 1155, 1202, 829, 560, 440, 1125, 1124, 1230, 690, 787, 597, 10th C., 988, 722, 590, 966, 496, 739, 880, 517, 7th C., 863, 950, 10th C., 863, 550

0 ___ 500 Miles

Spread of Christianity, to 11th Century

▨	to 600 A.D.
▨	600-800 A.D.
▨	800-1100 A.D.

*In some cases part of the population remained pagan for some time thereafter; in other cases Arian Christianity was already established before the date indicated.

Dates indicate conversion to Christianity*

The Holy Land

0 10 20 30 40
Miles

Tyre
Dan
L. Huleh
Acre
Safad
Haifa
Sea of Galilee
MT. CARMEL
Nazareth
Caesarea
Bethshean
Jordan R.
Mediterranean Sea
Nablus
Jaffa
Lydda
Ramallah
Ramle
Jericho
Jerusalem
Bethlehem
Hebron
Dead Sea
Gaza
Beersheba

West had been laid out. The organization was hierarchical—that is, there was a regular series of relations of subordinate to superior from priest to pope or patriarch, somewhat, though by no means exactly, as military lines of command run from second lieutenant to general. But this hierarchy was not without principle of mutual consultation. At almost every level, for bishoprics, for archbishoprics, and for the Church as a whole, there were councils made up of officials who met and debated problems and made decisions. Church government, then, was no simple relation of silent underling to commanding superior. Indeed, in these early centuries the critical decisions were made by assemblies rather than by individuals. Once the papacy had become firmly established, however, the popes maintained the position—when they could—that the pope was superior even to a general council, and was not bound by its decisions.

From the conversion of Constantine, the first Christian emperor, the election of bishops became a matter of particular concern to the state. In order to retain the initiative, the officials of the church worked to put the election of each new bishop into the hands of the clergy of the cathedral (episcopal church) of his see. Practice remained uneven, however. Sometimes the citizens simply gave assent to an accomplished fact by approving elections. At other times the people had real power, as when Roman mobs under the sway of rival political leaders controlled the choices to the papal throne. Since bishops often exercised actual governing power and had their own law courts, lay rulers often insisted on approving or even selecting them. The problem of the degree to which laymen could participate in the choice of the bishops remained acute down into the eleventh century, as the popes strove to have the ultimate say.

In a sense, however, this very struggle was one of the major sources of our present democratic institutions. The point becomes clear when we look at the very different history of Church and State in the East. In the East, the emperor at Constantinople was in fact head of both Church and State. No organized clerical body could tell him where to stop. Although religious disputes regularly broke out in the Eastern empire, there emerged from them no clearcut moral or legal code to set limits to the emperor's *rights*. The Russian church inherited this Eastern tradition. In the West, however, pope and emperor waged a fruitful, if sometimes bitter and cruel, struggle. From this struggle there gradually emerged in practice acceptance of a situation in which no absolute authority, at once political *and* religious, was combined in a single person or institution. This acceptance, though very far from being what we now call separation of Church and State, is nevertheless one of the roots of what we now call civil rights of the individual and of smaller groups within the political state.

Within three or four centuries, then, the Catholic church had come a long way from the humble group of dissident Jews who gathered to mourn the death, and to rejoice at the resurrection, of Jesus Christ. Hostile critics of all sorts, both within and outside Christianity, have maintained that by engaging itself in the affairs of this world, by acquiring property, by taking over legal and administrative tasks, and by accepting rich and powerful men as members of the Christian communion, the Church betrayed its founder. They quote such words of Jesus as "How hardly shall they that have riches enter into the kingdom of God" (Luke 18:24) or "except ye . . . become as little children, ye shall not enter into the kingdom of heaven" (Matt. 18:3). Yet Christianity has always held as a central mission its duty not to shun or deny or denigrate this world and this life but to work in the world; not indeed to accept the world as it is, but to accept it as a challenge, that is, to compromise with it in order to improve it. Once the expectation of the immediate Second Coming had passed, the Church in a sense compromised with this world of living men and women. But this compromise must seem to most of us in the Western tradition a strength rather than a weakness.

Monasticism

Deacons, priests, bishops, archbishops, all serve the laity of this world, and are called *secular* clergy (Latin *saeculum*, "world"). Early in the history of the Church, however, another kind of devotee to Christianity appeared in Syria and Egypt—the monk, a man who felt that he must deny the urges of his own flesh and become an ascetic. Monks would leave civilization behind and go into the desert to live in solitude, meditation, and prayer, subsisting on the minimum of food and drink. By the third century, there were a good many of these hermits, who enjoyed reputations for extreme holiness and often competed with each other in torturing themselves or in self-denial; some lived in trees or in holes in the ground, others on the tops of columns, to which they would haul up the food that pious devotees would supply.

To keep the extremists from using the cloak of holiness to cover un-Christian self-assertion, certain leaders, such as St. Anthony, early collected groups of monks around themselves and formed communities, living by a rule. The Greek St. Basil (329–379) wrote the most famous of these rules, which became standard in the Greek church and still regulates Greek monasticism today. Basil prescribed celibacy and poverty but combated the dangers of extreme asceticism by requiring that the monks work in the fields or elsewhere to make their communities as self-supporting as possible. Because, after Basil, monks lived by a rule, they are known as the regular clergy (Latin *regula,* "rule"), as contrasted with the secular clergy. In Greek monasticism, the monks not only worshiped but also ate and worked together. Although they were dedicated to a life outside this wicked world, they were also to do works of charity, such as setting up orphanages and hospitals near the monastery grounds.

Similarly, in the West the problem was met by the rule of St. Benedict, who founded the great abbey at Monte Cassino in southern Italy in the 520's. His Latin rule, like Basil's Greek rule, prescribed hard work for all and urged the monks to try to be tolerant of each other's interests and infirmities. In the West particularly, the monks broke new ground around their monasteries, acted as pioneers in opening up the wilderness, performed missionary service among the still unconverted heathen tribes, and did much charitable and medical work among the poor and the sick. In both East and West, scholarship early became one of the recognized occupations for monks, and the monastic scribe, who copied the works of the ancients and built up the library of his foundation, helped preserve the literature of the past.

Benedict's own rule is one of the most important documents of Christianity. Its spirit is evident in a short extract that sets forth the Benedictine cure for that form of pride which had arisen in the very first days of monasticism, the desire to outshine one's fellows in *something:*

As there is an evil and bitter emulation which separates from God and leads to hell, so there is a good spirit of emulation which frees from vices and leads to God and life everlasting. Let monks therefore practise this emulation with most fervent love; that is to say, let them in honour prevent one another, let them bear most patiently with each other's infirmities, whether of body or of manner. Let them contend with one another in their obedience. Let no one follow what he thinks most profitable to himself, but rather what is best for another. Let them show brotherly charity with a chaste Love.*

We shall learn more about what sent men and women into the monastic movement when, in the final section of this chapter, we examine the Christian way of life. The New Testament sounds an ascetic note that is firm and clear, especially in some of the writings of Paul. First in emphasis among the renunciations of the monk and the nun is sexual intercourse; Christianity has from the beginning found sexuality one of those phases of human nature that need most control. But the monastic movement also meant renunciation or at least disciplining of other pleasures of the flesh, and indeed of all pleasures in the ordinary sense. For many people, the monastic life has satisfied a strong need for security, communion, renunciation, and spiritual orderliness. This need has perhaps been more common in troubled times like those of the late Roman Empire, but during the last two thousand years it has never been absent from our society. To maintain monastic standards required a constant struggle, and we shall repeatedly encounter—and learn to expect—periodic monastic reform movements designed to correct abuses and to return monasticism to its original ideals.

Although monasticism contributed great services to the Christian commonwealth, it also posed grave problems to those who had charge of the affairs of the Church. No body of men, even though they are deeply consecrated men, fails to develop some sense of what Benedict called emulation. Both secular clergy and regular clergy have sometimes been tempted into emulation that has not had holiness as its goal. The secular clergy have felt that they were the true soldiers of the Lord in this harsh world, and that the regular clergy were dodging their responsibilities.

---

* *The Rule of St. Benedict,* ed. Cardinal Gasquet (London, 1936), Ch. LXXII. "Prevent" in this passage has an archaic sense: "anticipate in action."

134

The regular, on the other hand, have felt that they were leading purer, more ascetic lives, nearer what Jesus had preached. The tension and rivalry between secular and regular clergy complicated the organization of the Church. The monasteries, and the abbots who headed them, needed to be integrated into that organization; in a sacramental religion such as Christianity, the bishop *had* to be brought into monastic life. Abbots, however, were often at odds with bishops and archbishops. They resented the attempts of the secular clergy to see that the high standards of monastic discipline were maintained.

In the long run, these difficulties were largely overcome. Later in the Middle Ages the monastic orders achieved a more centralized organiza-

tion that made their own self-policing more effective. Meanwhile, though most of the monks lived in and for their monasteries, their officials, particularly the abbots, were integrated into the general government of the Church. These officials took part in the councils or synods that were of such great importance in the formation of Church doctrine and discipline; sometimes they rose to papal office. As centers of learning, the monasteries played a great part in building not only the structure of Christian theology but also the church or canon law that entered so essentially into medieval law and institutions, and thus into our own. In sum, the regular and secular clergy in the West were both recognized parts of a great whole.

V   The Ideas of Christianity

The Christian clergy could hardly have attained their great power had they not been essential intermediaries between this visible world of actuality and an invisible other world that to the true Christian is as real as this one. In Christianity certain important ideas about the other world are embodied in ritual acts called *sacraments*. These sacraments, administered by the clergy, are central to Christianity, the chief of the many bridges that Christianity has sought to throw between this world and the other world, between the imperfect and the perfect, the "real" and the "ideal."

The Eucharist and Salvation

The central mystery of Christianity is the sacrament of the Eucharist. It is a mystery made available to simple men and women, as a part of ordinary living, by the services of the Church. The sacrament stems from Jesus' last supper with his disciples, where he

. . . took bread, and blessed it, and brake it, and gave it to the disciples, and said, Take, eat; this is my body. And he took the cup, and gave thanks, and gave it to them, saying, Drink ye all of it; For this is my blood of the new testament, which is shed for many for the remission of sins [Matt. 26:26–28].

By the third century, the Eucharist had become the miraculous ceremony that made the Christian believer feel emotionally his link with God, that made him feel the wonder of salvation. If the sacrament of *baptism* figuratively washed away the stain of original sin, and made the individual a Christian, then the sacrament of the *Eucharist* enabled him to remain in the Christian communion—subject always to good behavior—and sustained him in its faith and fellowship. There were to be many grave theological disputes over the doctrine of the Eucharist, notably at the time of the Protestant revolt. But it has remained central to the drama of the Christian faith even when, as for some Protestants, it is but a commemoration of the Lord's Supper.

Around this symbolic act of the Mass, or Eucharist, theological explanations were woven. For the common man, these explanations could be very simple; for theologians, they could be very complex. The reader must not expect from our account the kind of universally agreed-upon statements he would get in an elementary geometry, for example. We may start with the basic doctrine of original sin, according to which Adam was given the chance for a perfect life on earth but disobeyed God, was driven from Eden, and was exposed to death and suffering here on earth. All Adam's descendants shared this fate. But the Jews, in spite of individual and group backslidings, kept alive their faith in God; and after generations of suffering God took mercy and sent to earth his only begotten son, Jesus. By his sufferings on the cross, Jesus *atoned* for human sins, made redemption to God the Father, and made it possible in the future for those who believed in him to avoid the ultimate consequences of Adam's sin. He made it possible for good Christians to be saved, to enjoy in the other world after death the immortal happiness which they could anticipate, so to speak, in this one, but which they could not completely enjoy here because this earth is no longer the Garden of Eden. It should be noted, however, that among the very first Christians the belief in the immediate Second Coming of Christ amounted to a belief that this world of Adam's sons was about to end and that some would be transported to an eternal Eden, others to an eternal hell worse than this world.

Even so elementary an outline of the doctrine of salvation bristles with the kind of difficulties Christians have been arguing about for centuries. What was the relation between God the Father and his only begotten son? In this context, what does the term "begotten" actually mean? What was Adam's original sin? How did a man go about the task of attaining salvation; was it enough to belong to the Church, or must he have some inward sign? This latter question raises what has been for two thousand years perhaps the central point of debate in Christianity, the problem of faith or good works.

If you hold strongly that salvation is purely inward and emotional, that is the outflowing of the individual soul through God's grace to its source in God, then outward acts, such as the sacraments, become superfluous—or worse, a possible refuge for hypocrites. If you hold strongly that God expects his true children to act on this earth in accordance with patterns he has laid down and given to his Church to administer, you may hold that doing prescribed things (i.e., "good works") is what really counts here on earth, since this is the only way a man can be known by his fellows. The first extreme could logically make the organized Church quite unnecessary, and could lead to the "priesthood of the individual believer." The second extreme could make outward conformity the sole test of salvation, and could lead to the complete control of daily life by an all-powerful clergy. Neither extreme position has ever in fact been taken, except in words and on paper. In daily Christian living there is actually no conflict between faith

and works. *To the Christian, one is impossible without the other.*

The Seven Sacraments

As time passed, the sacraments, the core of the system of good works, grew in number to seven. They were: (1) baptism, by which the infant was washed of the stain of original sin and brought into mystical union with Christ; (2) confirmation, by which, on attaining an age at which he could understand Christian doctrine, the child was formally brought into the discipline of the Church; (3) the Eucharist, the central act of the Christian drama; (4) penance, whereby the confessed and repentant sinner, granted absolution by the priest, had the guilt of his sin and *eternal* punishment remitted, subject to a *temporal* punishment assigned as penance; this temporal punishment might or might not be sufficient to satisfy God's justice, and hence a given penance itself could not guarantee the penitent's salvation; (5) extreme unction, "the last rites of the Church," a ceremony performed by the priest at the dying moments of the Christian to prepare him for the life to come; (6) ordination, the ceremony by which a candidate was made a priest; and (7) matrimony. Baptism and the Eucharist (the latter is often called the Lord's Supper or Communion) have remained as sacraments in almost all the Protestant groups. Of the other sacraments, the one that has been most heavily attacked and most vigorously rejected by Protestants generally is that of penance.

Heresy

The early centuries of Christianity saw a series of struggles to define the accepted doctrines of the religion—orthodoxy—and to protect them against the challenge of rival doctrinal ideas —heresy. The first heresies appear almost as soon as the first clergy. In fact, the issue between those who wished to admit Gentiles who were outside the law and those who wished to confine the gospel to the Jews foreshadowed the kind of issue that was to confront Christianity in the first few centuries, when heresy followed on heresy. The points at issue sometimes seem unreal and un-

Virgin and saints, from the chapel of a Coptic monastery in Egypt.

important, even ludicrous to us today. But it is a grave error of understanding and of historical perspective for us to regard these religious debates as trivial or childish, on the assumption that we ourselves have outgrown such things. One must remember that men believed that their future salvation depended upon the proper definition and defense of religious belief and practice. In addition, bitter political, economic, and national issues often underlay disputes that took a theological form.

These theological disputes of the first few Christian centuries concerned men's understanding of God's universe and of God's means of providing salvation for sinful man. Behind them lay real differences of personality and of national and class interests. The very existence of these heresies is a sign of the vitality of youthful Christianity, of the wholeheartedness and energy with which men and women threw themselves into the new movement. To regard divisions and struggles over ideas and ideals as a weakness in a social movement is a superficial judgment. Western history indicates that such divisions, if not carried too far, are rather signs of strength and growth. The overcoming of these divisions was a part of the process by which the Church acquired the unity and the resiliency, the store of political skills, with which it was able to organize Europe after the barbarian invasions, and to salvage much of the culture of the Greco-Roman world.

Gnostics and Manichaeans

Men have always had difficulty in understanding and explaining how evil can exist (as it obviously does) in a physical world created by a good God. The Gnostics (from the Greek word for "knowledge") affirmed that only the world of the spirit is real (and good); the physical world is evil, or an evil illusion. Thus they could not accept the Old Testament, whose God created this world; they regarded him as a fiend or decided that this world had been created by Satan. Nor could they accept Jesus' human life and work and martyrdom in this world, an essential part of Christian belief. They could not accept baptism because to them water was matter, or venerate a crucifix which to them was just two pieces of wood. The sharp distinction that the Gnostics drew between the evil present world and the good world of the spirit is often called *dualist*. Clearly heretical, the Gnostics focused on Christ's miracle-working and on other sorts of magic. Among them there arose a sharp distinction between an elite, whose members led especially pure lives, and the ordinary flock, less able to bear self-denial or the mysteries of the faith, who usually worked hard to support the elite.

Closely related to Gnosticism were the ideas of Mani, a third-century Mesopotamian prophet, who also echoed the dualistic views of the Persians and preached that the God of light and goodness and his emanations were in constant conflict with the god of darkness, evil, and matter and his emanations. These Manichaean views became immensely popular, especially along the North African shores of the Mediterranean during the third and fourth centuries. The Christians combated them, and throughout the Middle Ages tended to label all doctrinal opposition as Manichaean. Yet the dualist ideas persisted, more or less underground, and cropped up every few decades for a thousand years.

Donatists and Arians; The Council of Nicaea

Within Christianity itself, heresy sometimes involved very practical problems. The emperor Constantine faced the so-called Donatist movement in North Africa. The movement arose because, during the Roman persecutions of the Christians, a number of priests had lacked the courage to court martyrdom, and had instead handed over to the Roman authorities the sacred books. After the persecutions had come to an

end, these "handers-over" (*traditores*) had resumed their role as priests. Donatus, bishop of Carthage, and his followers maintained that the sacraments administered by such a *traditor* were invalid. While one can understand Donatus' wish to punish weakling or collaborationist priests, one can also see that, once a believer suspected the validity of the sacraments as received from one priest, he might suspect it as received from any other. Amidst much bitterness and violence Constantine finally ruled that once a priest had been properly ordained, the sacraments administered at his hands had validity even if the priest had himself acted badly.

Heresy also arose over essentially philosophical issues. Such was Arianism, named after Arius, a priest of Alexandria who early in the fourth century put forth the view that if God the Father had begotten God the Son (through God the Holy Ghost), then God the Son, as begotten, could not be exactly of the *same* essence (*homoousios* in Greek) as God the Father, but must be somehow inferior to, or dependent upon, or at least later in time than his begetter, of a *similar* essence (*homoiousios* in Greek) but not the same. It is difficult to refute this position on the basis of logical argument alone. Far from a quarrel over one letter (*homoousios* or *homoiousios*), Arius' view threatened to belittle the divinity of Christ as God the Son and to separate Christ from the Trinity. Arius' bitter opponent, Athanasius, bishop of Alexandria, fought him passionately, disdaining logic and emphasizing mystery. Athanasius and his follower maintained that Christians simply had to take it as a matter of faith that Father and Son are identical in essence and that the Son is equal to, independent of, and contemporaneous with the Father; even though the Father begat the Son, it is heresy to say that there was ever a time when the Son did not exist. In the Greek East especially, this abstract philosophical argument was fought out not only among churchmen and thinkers but in the barbershops and among the longshoremen. A visitor to Constantinople at that time complained: "I ask how much I have to pay; they talk of the born and the unborn. I want to know the price of bread; they answer 'the father is greater than the son.' I ask if my bath is ready; they say 'the son has been made out of nothing.' " The fact that most people did not understand what they were talking about did not prevent their rioting against their opponents.

After trying hard to stay out of the quarrel and urging the bishops to stop discussing it, Constantine realized that it would have to be settled. He himself summoned in 325 the first council of the whole Church, a council called ecumenical (from the Greek *oikoumene*, "the inhabited world"), at Nicaea, across the straits from Constantinople. A large majority of the bishops decided in favor of the Athanasian view, which was then embodied in the famous Nicene Creed, issued with all the force of an imperial decree by Constantine himself:

We believe in one God, the Father all-sovereign,
    maker of all things, both visible and invisible:
And in one Lord Jesus Christ,
    the Son of God,
begotten of the Father, and only-begotten,
that is from the essence [*ousia*] of the Father.
        God from God
        Light from light,
        True God from true God,
begotten not made,
being of one essence [*omoousion*] with the Father;
by whom all things were made,
    both things in heaven and things on earth;
who for us men and for our salvation came down from heaven and
    was made flesh, was made man
        suffered and rose again on the third day,
        ascended into heaven,
        cometh to judge quick and dead:
And in the Holy Spirit.
But those who say
    that there was once when he was not
    and before he was begotten he was not
    and he was made of things that were not
Or maintain that the Son of God is of a different
    essence or substance
    or created or subject to moral change or alteration—
Them doth the Catholic and Apostolic Church
    anathematize [condemn to damnation].

The emperor had presided over the council, and against his will found himself assuming the role of head of the church, giving legal sanction to a purely doctrinal decision and so playing the role both of Caesar and of Pope. This "Caesaropapism," in fact, became the tradition of Empire and Church in the East.

But the decree of Nicaea did not dispose of Arianism. Arians disobeyed; Constantine himself wavered; and his immediate successors on the imperial throne were Arians. Between 325 and 381, there were thirteen more councils that dis-

cussed the problem, deciding first one way, then another. One pagan historian sardonically commented that one could no longer travel on the roads because they were so cluttered up with throngs of bishops riding off to one council or another. Traces of Arianism remained in the empire for several centuries after Nicaea, and, because the missionary Ulfilas preached the Arian form of Christianity to the barbarian Goths beyond the frontiers of the empire, the heresy was spread among many Germanic peoples.

The Two Natures of Christ

Long before Arianism disappeared, a new and related controversy had shaken the Eastern portion of the empire to its foundations. Exactly what was the relationship of Christ the God and Christ the man? He was both man and God, but just exactly how was this possible? And was the Virgin Mary—a human woman—perhaps the mother only of his human aspect, or, if not, how could a human being be the mother of God? One extreme position was that of the dyophysites (two-nature-ites), who separated the human nature of Christ from the divine and so refused to regard the human virgin as the *mother of God*. The dyophysite view later became (unfairly) linked with the name of Nestorius, bishop of Constantinople in the early fifth century, and its followers were called Nestorians. They took refuge in Asia—Persia and beyond, all the way to China. The other extreme view was that of the monophysites (one-nature-ites), who argued that Christ's human and divine natures were totally merged; but they carried their thesis so far that they almost forgot Christ's human attributes and tended to make him a god only. Again the dispute flared up in physical violence in the East; again the decision hung in the balance; again the emperor (Marcian, reigned 450–457) called an ecumenical council, this one at Chalcedon, near Constantinople, in 451. Supported by Pope Leo the Great, the council condemned monophysitism and, like the Council of Nicaea, took a mystical rather than a rational decision: the true believer must believe in the two natures of Christ, human and divine, coexisting yet not distinct from each other; the Virgin is properly called the mother of God.

But like the decision at Nicaea, the decision at Chalcedon did not completely or definitively dispose of the opposition. Monophysites were concentrated in the provinces of Egypt and Syria and apparently expressed in their religious beliefs the resentment of the ancient Mediterranean cities of Alexandria and Antioch against the new domination by the upstart Constantinople. So, perhaps partly because it was identified with what we would call nationalism, monophysitism did not die out, and the emperors strove to deal with it by one compromise or another. But, since there were no monophysites in the West, the Roman church regarded the issue as closed; every time an emperor at Constantinople tried to appease his Egyptian and Syrian monophysite subjects, he would be condemned by the pope for heresy. The problem remained unsolved.

The disaffection of the monophysite provinces of Syria and Egypt was to facilitate their conquest in the seventh century by the new religion of Islam. To this day there are still monophysite Christians in Egypt and Syria, and Nestorian remnants in further Asia. The continuing quarrel illustrates the lasting political impact that theological disagreement sometimes provided.

Other Heresies

In the Roman West, as contrasted with the Greek East, the serious heresies were less philosophical and more practical. Pelagianism, for example, took its name from Pelagius, a British monk who argued that human beings held in their hands the control of their moral fate. They were not tainted by original sin; they did not need divine grace to obtain personal salvation. In short, Pelagius believed in complete freedom of will. But complete freedom of will is again a tipping of the complex balance that is orthodox Christianity. The idea tends to exalt human pride and human independence, and to lessen the majesty and suprarational power of God. Pelagianism is simply too hopeful, without the note of tragedy, to be genuinely Christian. Yet in one form or another it has tended to crop up constantly in the history of Western culture. The last major appearance was perhaps in the optimistic Enlightenment of the eighteenth century.

VI   Thought and Letters in the First Christian Centuries

Though a good deal of dislike and mutual misunderstanding had always characterized the attitudes of Greeks and Romans toward each other, Roman admiration for Greek literature and art had given its stamp to the works of Roman writers and artists. The triumph of Christianity tended to contribute, as we have seen, new sources of misunderstanding and tension to the relationships between Easterners and Westerners. The political division imposed by Diocletian and repeated by many of his successors expressed the undoubted geographic distinction between Eastern and Western provinces. As the barbarian inroads began increasingly in the fourth and fifth centuries to disrupt communications and threaten all the established institutions in the West, the opportunities for Westerners to know Greek and embrace the great classical tradition were fewer. In the Eastern provinces few except soldiers and professional administrators had ever spoken or read Latin, though it remained the official language of legislation at Constantinople down through the fifth century.

Despite the growing division, however, the literature and art of the late Roman and early Christian world may be treated as a single whole.

Julian and the Cappadocians

In this period letters declined and almost disappeared in the pagan West, while in the East only a few passionate devotees of the old gods and opponents of Christianity still made their voices heard. Notable among these were the teachers of the nephew of Constantine, the young Julian, who became emperor in 361. In a brief reign of two years, Julian, embued with classical philosophy in its more mystical (Neoplatonic) forms, tried to restore the old beliefs, reviving the sacrifices in the temples, forbidding Christians to teach, threatening new persecutions, even trying to construct a kind of hierarchy to give to the pagan faiths the efficiency of the Christian Church. Julian himself was the

St. Jerome in His Study: a panel by Jacopo di Paolo da Bologna (1384–1426).

author of satirical and moralistic essays and orations. His program was doomed to failure, but it has always interested poets and novelists as well as scholars.

Christian letters began to take the center of the stage. In the East, many of the best writers devoted much energy to polemical writings on the burning doctrinal questions and disputes of the day. In both East and West the best minds among Christians faced the problem of how to treat the classical heritage. A few thinkers, mostly in the West and especially at first, advised against the reading of anything but Scripture, for fear of pagan error. They later came to acknowledge that one had to read the great pagans of the past in order to be able to refute pagan philosophical ideas. Still, there was always the danger that in the pleasure of reading a delightful classical author one might forget that the prime concern was to expose his errors and refute his argu-

ments. The Greek Christians worried far less about this problem, and in the fourth century the three great Cappadocian fathers (so called from the province of Asia Minor where they were born)—Basil, author of the monastic rule; his brother, Gregory of Nyssa; and their friend, Gregory of Nazianzos—all had an excellent classical education and used the techniques of the pagan philosophers in discussing religious ideas.

Jerome, Ambrose, and Augustine

Jerome, who studied with Gregory of Nazianzos, produced the Latin Bible, the Vulgate, as the climax of a life of devoted scholarship that had made him the master of Hebrew and Greek as well as Latin. Ambrose (ca. 340–397), a Roman civil servant who became bishop of Milan, wrote many theological works and commentaries, christianizing much that he found in the classics, particularly in Cicero; he transformed Cicero's Stoic concept of duty to the state into a Christian concept of duty to God. Ambrose put his own preaching into practice when he publicly humiliated the emperor Theodosius I (reigned 379–395) and forced him to do penance for savagely punishing some rioters. The act symbolizes the Western church's insistence that, in matters of morals and of faith, the Church would be supreme, an attitude that ran exactly counter to the practice already growing up in the East.

Augustine (354–430), the greatest of the Western church fathers and a native of North Africa, himself had been a Stoic, a Manichaean, and a Neoplatonist before he studied under Ambrose and was converted to Christianity. He then became bishop of the North African city of Hippo, and engaged in energetic controversy with heretics. He was the author of the *Confessions,* a vivid, mystical autobiography, and *The City of God,* which he wrote to refute the pagan argument that Christianity, by undermining the old Roman virtues and offending the gods, had led to the decline and the misfortunes of Rome. He easily showed that pagan empires innocent of Christianity had often fallen in the past, and he then moved far beyond the specific controversy to outline a complete Christian philosophy of history.

Augustine also established the characteristic Western Christian attitude toward the grave and unavoidable problem of the freedom of the will. Here again we encounter what to the unbeliever, or merely to the simplifier, is a contradiction, an effort to have one's cake and eat it. Augustine held that God is all-knowing, all-good, all-powerful; nothing could be that he had not known and intended; our actions are *determined,* better, predetermined, by God. Pelagius, who preached that men have full freedom of will, and can will independently of God's will, was to Augustine a dangerous heretic. And yet Augustine had to preserve human moral responsibility; the Christian must be able to choose between doing right and doing wrong. The Christian may not say that when he does wrong it is because God planned for him to do wrong, and thus *made* him do wrong. God has put us on this earth for his glory and our eventual salvation; without the testing of our moral strength—without our being able to feel that *in a sense* we have "freedom of the will"—we should be poor creatures indeed, mere animals. But we are not gods ourselves, not free as God is free; we may not—as a twentieth-century anthropoligist was to put it—believe that "man makes himself."*

Augustine maintained that God's plan for humanity involved a continuing struggle between the community of those who will be saved, God's community or city, *civitas Dei,* and the community of those who reject God, the earthly community, *civitas terrena.* Ultimately, of course, the triumph of the city of God is assured; its members will be saved, while those of the earthly city will be damned. Since human history is all a preparation for the Last Judgment, the individual should turn his will toward God, and with the help of divine grace may so order his earthly life by decency, tolerance, trust, and discipline that he may deserve and receive heavenly citizenship hereafter. The help of the divine grace, Augustine taught, was necessary to fortify human wills (even those that had already chosen God) because original sin (inherited from Adam) had turned man away from God, and God's grace must help him to return. At times Augustine's argument led him to minimize the value of good works, or even of the sacraments, for the achieving of salvation: he came near to a belief in predestination: the belief that God has chosen in advance an elect company of men for salvation. The later church fathers did not follow Augustine, but insisted that both good works and grace were essential to salvation.

So to the Christian, although the heavenly city is the goal, his conduct and attitudes in the earthly city have the utmost importance. He must curb his pride and ambition, control his natural appetites, and avoid yielding too exclusively to the pull of family ties. This does not mean the annihilation of self in extreme asceticism, but rather the combination of control of self with love and kindness for others: all others, high and low. The Christian must love even the sinner, though not the sin. Nor may he, out of softness, attribute sin to environment or temporary influences; sin is *there,* and will be permanent in the earthly city. Nor may a Christian trust too fully the experiences of his senses alone, and try to explain all phenomena by reason and by naturalistic arguments. He must have faith, "the substance of things hoped for, the evidence of things unseen." He must not try to put himself in the place of God, who alone can "understand" the universe. Instead he must believe in God, for then he can feel that the universe is not the puzzling or hostile place it seems to men who do nothing but reason. Yet he must also strive to improve the world around him and the other human beings who live in it, in order to make the earthly city as nearly as possible resemble the city of God.

The Christian Way of Life

By the fourth and fifth centuries, it had become clear that East and West were interpreting much of the message of the Gospels in different ways. It is true that some fiction of unity continued to be maintained, and also that throughout the first Christian millennium Rome and Constantinople seem disputants within a common heritage. But the facts of the separation are clear enough to us now. In this chapter we are concerned above all with the spirit of *Western* Christianity.

Western Christianity has sought to promote on this earth a life in which are mingled (though not confused) the practical and the ideal, the commonplace and the heroic, sensual pleasure and ascetic self-denial. Like any other great effort of the human spirit, Christianity has never been in actuality quite what it is in ideal. It has,

* The title of a book (London, 1936) by V. Gordon Childe.

however, consistently maintained the relation between the ideal and the actual *as in fact a relation,* a coming together, not a flying apart. On the one hand, Christianity was often tempted, in an excess of idealism, to deny the reality or at any rate the importance of the actual, the sense world of our human experiences. On the other hand, in the duty of living it was often tempted to betray or simply to neglect its ideals. But it has on the whole maintained a fruitful tension between this world and the next. It has never quite, never totally, like some oriental cults, sought to deny or escape from the sense world, or to suppress that world by some continued magic or mystery. Nor has it ever quite, like crude hedonism or certain kinds of philosophical materialism, been willing to accept the sense world at whatever face value common sense or uncorrected human reason might give that world.

One of the clearest notes of Christianity is simply a distrust of the flesh, a rejection of the idea that the natural human appetites and instincts are adequate to serve as a sole guide to human conduct. This distrust inspires one of the major doctrines of Christianity, that of original sin, which is *not* a belief that man is naturally wicked, but rather a belief that without divine aid he must lapse into the wickedness which is a heritage from Adam. This profound distrust of the natural man of flesh and blood runs all through Christianity and takes many forms. Our Freudian time is tempted to believe that the early Christians were obsessed with sex, that the original sin of Adam and Eve was sexual intercourse, that the appetite in natural man most distrusted by Christianity is sexual appetite. Orthodoxy does not accept such a confined definition of original sin; for Christianity, pride is the great sin. Yet it is not unfair to say that most Christian thought distrusts the whole unaided natural man —his appetites for food, drink, gaming, fighting, and vainglory, as well as for sexual indulgence. Catholic Christianity has always provided a place for the rare individual who wishes to subdue the flesh by fleeing this world. Protestant Christianity has been less successful with such people, who under Protestantism have more generally had to turn their ascetic drive toward reforming the conduct of others on earth.

In practice, the traditional Christian way of life has not been wholly different from older ways, such as that of the Greeks of the great culture. We noted that for the Greek of the great age overeating and undereating, gluttony and ascetic abstinence, were *both evils,* and that the sensible man sought the golden mean by eating moderately but well. So too, in fact, with the good conventional Christian. Gluttony was for him worse than abstemiousness, because, being more common, it was therefore more dangerous. There remains in the background of Christian feeling on this subject something that is reflected in the popular saying "It is better to eat to live than to live to eat." But the view that Christianity is a gloomy faith, that the Christian may never under any conditions enjoy food, drink, and lovemaking on this earth is false. The note of asceticism is in Christianity, and if you listen for it with either a friendly or a hostile ear, you can always hear it. But there are many other notes, sounding simultaneously in chords of great complexity.

The Individual and Society

One of these other notes is that of unselfishness, unselfconsciousness. From one point of view, Christianity is an individualistic faith, concerned with the salvation of individual souls. The Christian at his highest moments is alone with God, responsible to God alone. State, vocation, family are all distractions of this world, yet in daily living Christianity accepts and emphasizes social and family responsibility. In the true Christian life all men are one, and subsidiary groups are a distraction—or, worse, a manifestation of selfishness. The important thing is for the individual to avoid all kinds of personal triumphs over others, all competitive successes, all the things that set off and sharpen his ego. Christianity as a great world religion, especially in its Catholic form, has never carried this annihilation of the individual ego to an extreme. Men who have competed very successfully with their fellows in this world have been professing Christians; even Napoleon was a professed Christian. Nevertheless, the ideal of unselfishness is there. Christianity tries to tame the more extravagant flights of the competitive human spirit, tries to subdue self-assertiveness, truculence, boasting, pride, and other manifestations of the "natural" man. It distrusts them quite as much as—indeed, properly, more than—it distrusts man's simpler appetites for food, drink, and sex, all the pleasures of the flesh.

A third note of Christianity is simply the

other side of unselfconsciousness. The Christian should not only subdue his own ego; he should open his heart in loving-kindness to all his fellow men. Modern rationalists have often been so shocked by the fact that some Christians burned, imprisoned, or otherwise silenced fellow men who disagreed with them on theological matters that they have refused to hear this note of love and charity in Christianity. But it is there, and without it Christianity is incomplete. The note is not quite the one we today recognize as sentimental humanitarianism, not quite the note of pity the crusading reformer feels for criminals, defectives, failures, and all other underdogs. The Christian is expected to love the "upperdog" as well as the underdog, a duty many humanitarian reformers seem not to acknowledge.

Christian loving-kindness, for all its affinities with gentler emotions, is also based on resignation in face of a universe that is not to be shaped wholly by man's will. For the Christian regards sin as a fact. He may not deny the existence of sin, nor hold that, left to himself, treated permissively, the sinner will somehow cease to sin. He must forgive the truly repentant sinner, he must pity the sinner, he must indeed love the sinner. But he may not love the sinner for his sin. Above all, he may not regard sin as an illusion, nor as the result of poor physical and social environment alone, nor as the result of temporary and wholly human or physical influences. For the orthodox Christian loving-kindness can therefore never be optimistic about the perfectibility of man, nor can it ever be pure humanitarianism.

Reason and Faith

A fourth note of Christianity is its distrust of certain kinds of thinking. Christianity is by no means opposed to all thought. We have already seen that its theology is an intellectual structure of great subtlety and complexity; we shall see that at its medieval climax Christianity held reason in the highest esteem. But Christianity has always distrusted the kind of thinking we nowadays usually call rationalism; it has always been afraid that the human mind will *think away the supernatural,* the transcendental, the miraculous. Thus, though it is unfair to Christianity to say that it has always opposed full intellectual freedom, or to say that modern science has de-

veloped only in spite of Christian antagonism, there remains a grain of truth in these extreme statements. At the very least, the Christian must at some point begin to believe what his sense experience, his instruments, and his science give him no direct evidence for. Indeed, pure rationalism must remain for the Christian the indecent self-assertion of the rationalist, a sin perhaps worse than the self-assertion displayed by the sensualist or the show-off, a sin nearer the heart of pride. The natural man can think as well as lust. Only the spiritual man can have faith, "the substance of things hoped for, the evidence of things not seen."

Throughout the ages, Christianity has firmly maintained its belief that this world as presented to the mind by the conventional five senses is not representative of the whole universe. The universe is for the Christian ultimately a problem, an intellectual as well as a moral and emotional problem. There is a God for whom nothing is a problem, a God who "understands" the universe. Men cannot possibly put themselves in God's place, and they cannot understand the universe by ordinary intellectual activity such as logic, science, or common sense. But through the intercession of God they can by a different sort of activity acquire a kind of certainty quite different from worldly knowledge, which latter is no more than the product of intellectual activity working on sense perception.

The kind of activity by which men arrive at this certainty we call *faith.* It is not thinking, not feeling, not anything the psychologist or physiologist in his laboratory can get at, any more than the chemist in his laboratory can get at the miracle of the Eucharist. Through faith, men cannot know the universe as they know, for instance, that oaks grow from acorns. Through faith they *can* be certain that God does exist, that the universe is not the puzzling, even hostile place it seems to a man thinking and worrying, and that the universe is indeed made for man and the drama of his salvation.

But—and this is the last note we shall dwell on—Christianity also attaches a very great importance, a very great degree of reality, to this world of the senses. This world is the testing ground for entrance into the next world. The faith of the Christian, which we have above sought to separate sharply from other human activities, does teach him that these other activities are indispensable to his salvation, that they must be well conducted here on earth. But more than this, the good Christian wants other men to be good; he wants to make this imperfect world as nearly as possible like that perfect world his faith tells him about.

This emphasis on bettering mankind is called melioristic. Christianity is in many ways a pessimistic faith, with no concrete notions of *its own* about progress on this earth, indeed with quite definite notions about this earth as frequently a vale of tears. And yet Christianity has been intensely melioristic in practice. It has been a reforming religion, anxious to make this world a better place for human beings, more peaceful, more prosperous, more friendly, more decent. It has believed in improvement, if not in formal progress of the kind first clearly formulated in the eighteenth century.

Finally, Christianity has in its central tradi-tion never really been straitjacketed by formulas or dogmas that confined its appeal to one sort of person. It has been universal in its appeal. It has made room for mystics, for ascetics, for intellectuals, for soldiers, for rulers and administrators, for orators and salesmen, for artists and seers, and above all for ordinary men and women. In all these it has sought to tame the "natural" man (as Christianity must call him) of self-assertive pride, has sought to make him a Christian living a Christian life. Unlike the Greek polytheistic cults which sought only to keep the gentlemanly few at the gentlemanly level, Christianity has sought to ennoble us all. Its standards of conduct are high—quite as high as, and indeed not so very different from, the best of Greek ideals. It seeks to extend these standards not just to an aristocracy, but to all mankind.

Reading Suggestions on Christianity

GENERAL ACCOUNTS

L. M. O. Duchesne, *Early History of the Christian Church*, 3 vols. (Longmans, 1912–1924). A lengthy standard account; very readable.

K. Latourette, *History of Christianity* (Harper, 1953). A short survey; both well-balanced and sympathetic.

C. Guignebert, *Christianity Past and Present* (Macmillan, 1927). One of the best surveys, written by a French scholar who, though not sympathetic to Christianity, is fair-minded.

C. Dawson, *Religion and the Rise of Western Culture* (*Image). Excellent survey to the thirteenth century.

A. C. McGiffert, *A History of Christian Thought*, Vol. I (Scribner's, 1932). A good brief account from a Protestant position.

H. B. Parkes, *Gods and Men: The Origins of Western Culture* (Knopf, 1959). A clear and sympathetic account with a fine reading list.

R. M. Pope, *The Church and Its Culture* (Bethany, 1965). A brief sympathetic account, with a full, up-to-date bibliography.

SPECIAL STUDIES

F. Cumont, *The Oriental Religions in Roman Paganism* (Open Court, 1911; *Dover). A classical introduction to the general religious climate in which Christianity took root.

John Ferguson, *The Religions of the Roman Empire* (Cornell Univ. Press, 1970). Up to date and comprehensive.

A. Toynbee, ed., *The Crucible of Christianity* (World, 1969). Learned essays by leading scholars, including the editor, on Judaism, Hellenism, and the historical background of Christianity. Splendidly illustrated.

E. Renan, *Life of Jesus* (Modern Library). This famous book, written a century ago, was one of the first attempts to deal with Jesus as a historical figure. Its scholarship is now outdated, but it is interesting for its skeptical point of view.

M. Burrows, *The Dead Sea Scrolls* (Viking, 1955). Of the many books on the subject this is perhaps the most useful for the student of general history.

E. Wilson *Scrolls from the Dead Sea* (Oxford Univ. Press, 1955). Both readable and thought-provoking.

A. Schweitzer, *The Quest of the Historical Jesus,* new ed. (Macmillan, 1948). Somewhat detailed and specialized, but an excellent introduction to the fascinating question of the historicity of Jesus.

B. H. Streeter, *The Four Gospels* (Macmillan, 1930). A good middle-of-the-road study by a Protestant cleric.

S. J. Case, *The Social Origins of Christianity* (Univ. of Chicago Press, 1923). Fully lives up to its title; emphasizes interrelations of environment and ideas.

E. R. Goodenough, *The Church in the Roman Empire* (Holt, 1931). A brief, balanced account directed to the beginning student.

R. Bultman, *Primitive Christianity in Its Contemporary Setting,* trans. R. H. Fuller (*Meridian). An up-to-date scholarly treatment.

Walter Nigg, *Warriors of God* (Knopf, 1959) and *The Heretics* (Knopf, 1962). Readable and sound accounts of monasticism and heresies from Simon Magus and the Gnostics to Leo Tolstoy.

A. D. Nock, *St. Paul* (Oxford Univ. Press, 1955). A classic treatment, originally published in 1938.

W. H. C. Frend, *Martyrdom and Persecution in the Early Church* (Basil Blackwell, 1965). A scholarly yet readable account with a full bibliography.

SOURCES

The New Testament is, of course, the best source reading. The inquisitive reader may wish to compare several versions: The Authorized version (many editions) is substantially the King James version; the Revised Standard version (Nelson, 1952) has created some unfavorable comment both from literary reviewers and from fundamentalist Protestants; a recent American edition of the Douay (Roman Catholic) version was published in 1950 (Catholic Book Publishing Company); finally, there is an American Protestant version by Smith and Goodspeed (Univ. of Chicago Press, 1939).

Next to the New Testament may be ranked the writings of St. Augustine—his spiritual autobiography, *The Confessions,* trans. J. F. Sheed, (Sheed and Ward, 1947), and the more difficult *City of God,* trans. G. E. McCracken, 6 vols., (Harvard Univ. Press, Loeb Classical Library).

H. S. Bettenson, ed., *Documents of the Christian Church,* 2nd ed. (Oxford Univ. Press, 1963). An excellent collection, accompanied by enlightening summaries and editorial comments; useful not only for the early period but also for the whole history of Christianity.

P. R. Coleman-Norton, ed., *Roman State and Christian Church,* 3 vols. (S.P.C.K., 1966). Translations of the key legal documents down to 535.

5

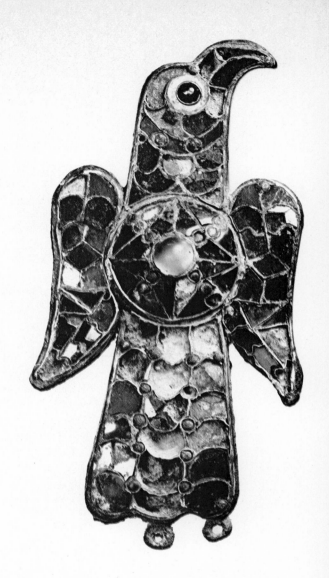

The West

Early Middle Ages

I The Breakdown of Roman Civilization

The period from the collapse of the Roman Empire in the West down to about A.D. 1000 provides an outstanding example of the breakdown of a whole civilization. Historians used to call these early medieval centuries from 500 to 1000 the Dark Ages. This term still properly suggests a gloomy barbarian interruption between a bright classical flowering and a later bright recovery or rebirth (renaissance). But today historians prefer the more neutral term "early Middle Ages"—for they have come to believe that "dark" is a misleading exaggeration. For if much of Roman civilization was lost in these years, much, including above all Christianity, was retained and developed, and many new ways of life and even new techniques were adopted and discovered. Feudal society—springing from both Roman and barbarian origins—created new kinds of human

Above: An eagle fibula (clasp) from Spain, second half of the sixth century.
Above right: Cross section of the underground mausoleum of Abbot Mellebaude at Poitiers, seventh century.
Right: Part of a seventh-century purse cover, with gold, garnets, and enamel, from the ship-burial found at Sutton Hoo, England.

146

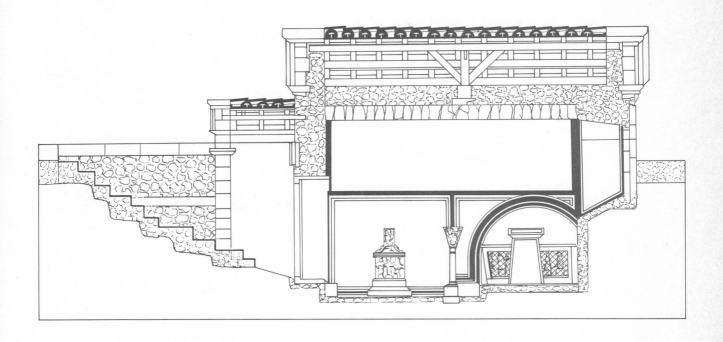

relationships, while new inventions such as deeper plowing and better drainage, the horse-collar (a great improvement on the old yoke), and the seaworthy Norse ships (which could face the hazards of Atlantic navigation in a way the old Mediterranean vessels never could) marked an advance and not a retreat. Yet, by the standards of classical civilization, the early Middle Ages in many ways represented a catastrophic decline, a dark and barbarous age indeed.

Viewed in the long perspective of world history, the barbarian conquest of the Roman Empire is no more than another instance of a mature, no doubt in some respects decadent, civilization falling to simpler peoples of primitive background. As we know, even the centuries of the *Pax Romana* had been filled with Roman combat against the barbarians on the far side of the Rhine–Danube line. Tacitus had lectured his fellow Romans on the instructive contrast between their own soft degeneracy and what he regarded as the simple toughness and harshness of the Germans. His account of the Germans, partisan though it may be, is the fullest report we have on their simple tribal life before their first major breakthrough to the Roman side of the frontier, which did not take place until the fourth century. In spite of Tacitus' fears, it was apparently not so much Roman decline that opened the way to the Germans as sheer pressure on the Germans from other tribes that drove them in panic to try to cross the Roman borders, by force if necessary.

Indo-European in language, like the Greeks, the Romans, and the Celts, the Germans seem to have dwelled originally along the shores of the Baltic, both on the Continent and in Scandinavia. Very early in ancient times they migrated southward. When the Romans first began to write about them, they were already divided into tribes, but had no overall political unity. One group of Germanic tribes, the Goths, had settled in what we now call Romania, on the north side of the Danube boundary, and in the adjacent plains of what is now southern Russia, the Ukraine. In the fourth century, conditions in central Asia about which we still know almost nothing precipitated a fierce Asian people known as the Huns into the territory of the Goths. Living on horseback for days, traveling swiftly, and reveling in cruelty, the Huns started a panic among the Goths and other Germanic tribes. The shock waves, beginning in the last half of the fourth century, continued throughout the fifth and into the sixth. They shattered the Roman structure in the West and left its fragments in barbarian hands. The Eastern territories suffered much less, and the imperial tradition continued uninterrupted in Constantinople.

In addition to barbarian military raids, penetrations, and conquests, there were slower and more peaceful infiltrations lasting over long periods. German laborers settled and worked on the large Roman estates, especially in Gaul. Moreover, before, during, and after the invasions, individual barbarians joined the Roman side, often rising to high positions and defending the old empire against their fellow barbarians. The Romanized barbarian became as familiar a figure as the barbarized Roman.

Thanks to many surviving chronicles and histories, almost all written in Latin by monks, we know a great deal about the routes of the invading bands, about their chiefs, and about the politics of the separate states they set up. But these historical accounts are inferior to the best Greek and Roman historical writings in depth and composition and in psychological insight and accuracy. The modern student of social problems would like to know many things about the German wanderings which the sources do not tell him. Then too, partly because these narratives were written by clerics, whose ideals and property suffered so much from the invaders, they almost certainly exaggerate the cruelty and destructiveness of the invasions.

We do not know how numerous the invaders were in proportion to the invaded population; we do not know to what degree the barbarians replaced peoples who were there before them; we do not know whether the total population of western Europe was greater or less under the barbarians than under the late Roman Empire. Modern research has generally tended to diminish the numerical importance of the German invaders. It seems clear that there were more Germans in proportion to non-Germans in Britain and Belgium, with the proportion of Germans steadily diminishing from north to south. Biologically, racially, the Western world was just a bit more mixed after the invasions than before.

But may not this small German admixture have been qualitatively important? Proud patriots, especially in Germany and Britain during the nineteenth and early twentieth centuries, used to argue that this "new blood" brought a youthful energy that ultimately made possible medieval and modern civilization. But nowadays we are properly more than skeptical about all such improbable and unscientific racial claims.

How complete was the breakdown of Roman civilization in the West? The loss can be seen most clearly at the level of large-scale political and economic organization. These early medieval centuries, with the brief but important interlude of Charlemagne's revived empire, just before and after the year 800, were marked by a failure in human ability to organize and administer as an effective state and society any large territorial group. Only the Roman Catholic church was consistently able to transcend the relatively narrow limits of the medieval duchy, county, or other small unit that was coming into existence, and to maintain an effective organization to which millions of human beings adhered. And even the Church was subject to grave lapses of discipline and control. Its local clergy were caught up in the web of local lay rule, and weakness and disorder appeared in its very heart at Rome. It struggled everywhere to preserve its unity and strength.

Roads, postal systems, even sea transport declined from the Roman efficiency that had allowed both men and things an almost modern freedom and ease, if not speed, of travel and communication. Thousands of little districts came to depend on themselves for almost everything they used, and thus became relatively autarkic (self-sufficient). And these same little districts took to fighting among themselves. Some invading Germanic tribes did exercise a rough control over sizable areas, but these areas were much smaller than the old empire had been, and the control was ordinarily uncertain and unsophisticated, when compared to that made possible by the complex Roman governmental machinery.

With this loss of ability to run anything big, there went a loss of discipline, a loss of morale, a loss of the older, orderly ways. Save for rare exceptions, mostly in the Church, the almost instinctive network of habits of command and obedience that keep a great, complex community together was rudely cut. Long centuries later, it had to be gradually and painfully restored.

The traditional classical artistic skills—in sculpture, painting, architecture—tended to weaken, though they by no means disappeared and though new inspiration was not lacking. Sculptors no longer carved the human body realistically, though it is possible that they stopped because they did not want to do so, not because they did not know how. Their art may have rejected "realism." Still, it is hard to look at the art that has survived from the earliest part of the early Middle Ages without seeing signs that basic skills have been lost. Even though we may admire the vigor and power of an early medieval statue, for example, and prefer it to the smooth—even slick—perfection of a Roman one, we are forced to admit that the medieval artist is crude by comparison, as indeed our own tastes may be.

Similarly, the early Middle Ages lost command over the classical tools of scholarship and science. Spoken Latin gradually broke down into local languages—"vernaculars"—French, Italian, and Spanish in the making. Even where it survived as a learned tongue, written as well as spoken, Latin was debased and simplified. The general level of cultivated literature and philosophy was primitive. Most writers in Latin—and there were not many—were clumsy and inept imitators of the already enshrined "classics" like Cicero and Vergil.

But much of ancient civilization did survive the early Middle Ages. Men could weave, farm, use horses, and make pottery, swords, and spears quite as well in the year 1000 as in the year 100; in some ways and in some places, they could do these things better in 1000 than in 100. Among churchmen there survived, in libraries, and to some degree in the education of the cleric, an admiration for and some varying familiarity with the classics. The barbarian chiefs so admired the Rome they were destroying that they retained an almost superstitious reverence for its laws and institutions even if they understood them only faintly and in part. As we shall see, the most striking political event of the early Middle Ages is the actual revival in the West, under Germanic kings, of the title and the claims of the Roman Empire.

Visigoths, Vandals, Anglo-Saxons

When the fourth-century Hunnic push against them began, one tribe of Goths, the Visigoths, or West Goths, petitioned to be allowed to cross

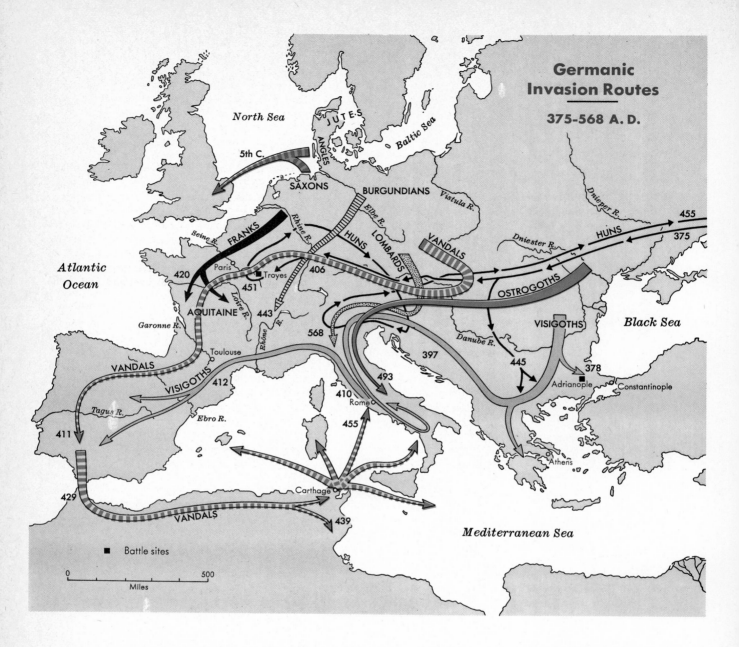

Germanic Invasion Routes

375-568 A.D.

North Sea

JUTES

ANGLES

5th C.

SAXONS

BURGUNDIANS

Baltic Sea

Vistula R.

Dnieper R.

455

375

HUNS

FRANKS

Rhine R.

HUNS

Elbe R.

LOMBARDS

VANDALS

Atlantic Ocean

420

Paris

Troyes

451

406

Dniester R.

Seine R.

OSTROGOTHS

Black Sea

AQUITAINE

443

Loire R.

Rhône R.

568

VISIGOTHS

Garonne R.

Toulouse

Danube R.

445

Adrianople

378

Constantinople

VANDALS

VISIGOTHS

412

397

493

Tagus R.

Ebro R.

410

Rome

455

411

429

Carthage

439

VANDALS

Athens

Mediterranean Sea

■ Battle sites

0   500
Miles

the Danube and settle in Roman territory, on the south bank, in present-day Bulgaria. The Roman border guards took cruel advantage of their fear and hunger; and soon there were many desperate Goths milling about only a few miles from Constantinople. In the year 378, at Adrianople, the mounted Goths defeated the Roman legions of the Eastern emperor Valens, who was killed in battle. More and more Goths now freely entered the empire. Unable to take Constantinople or other fortified towns, they proceeded south into the Balkans, under their chieftain, Alaric, ravaged Greece, including Athens, and then

marched north again around the head of the Adriatic and south into Italy. In 410, Alaric and his Goths sacked Rome itself, an event that made a staggering impression on the inhabitants of the empire. Pagan and Christian blamed each other for the disaster, and, as we know, it inspired Augustine's *City of God*. Alaric died soon afterwards, and his successors led the Visigoths north across the Alps into Gaul, and then south again across the Pyrenees into Spain.

Here, in the westernmost reaches of the continental Roman Empire, the Visigoths, after their long wanderings, founded a Spanish kingdom that would last until the Muslim invasions of the seventh century. In southern Gaul they had a large area (Aquitaine) given them by the Western Roman emperor Honorius (ruled 395–423), into whose family their king married; but this area they would lose in less than a century to a rival German tribe, the Franks. Since the Visigoths were Arians, they had some difficulty in ruling the orthodox Christians among their subjects.

Almost simultaneously with the Visigothic migration, another Germanic people, the Vandals, still resident in Germany, crossed the Rhine westward into Gaul and moved southward into southern Spain, where they settled in 411. Next, the Roman governor of North Africa made the mistake of inviting them across the Straits to help him in a struggle against his Roman masters. The Vandals came in 429, but soon seized North Africa for themselves. They moved eastward across modern Morocco and Algeria and established their capital at Carthage (Tunis). Here they built a fleet and raided the shores of Sicily and Italy, finally sacking Rome (455) in a raid that has made "vandalism" synonymous to this day with destruction of property. Like the Visigoths, the Vandals were Arian, and they, too, often persecuted the orthodox. They held on in North Africa until the 530's, when, as we shall see, the Eastern emperor Justinian put an end to their state.

Under pressure on the Continent, the Romans early in the fifth century began to withdraw their legions from Britain. As they left, Germanic tribes from across the North Sea in what we would now call north Germany and Denmark began to filter into Britain. These Angles, Saxons, and Jutes, coming from an area that had undergone little Roman influence, were still heathen. In England they gradually established their authority over the Celtic Britons, many of whom survived as a subject class. The barbarians soon founded seven Anglo-Saxon kingdoms, of which Northumbria, Mercia, and Wessex successively became the most important. Scotland and Wales remained Celtic, as of course did Ireland, which was in large measure converted to Christianity in the fifth century by Catholic missionaries from Gaul, led by Saint Patrick.

Ireland escaped the first great wave of barbarian invasions, and its Celtic church promoted learning, poetry, and the illumination of manuscripts such as the famous *Book of Kells*, one of the wonders of the era. By the end of the sixth century Catholic Christianity was moving into England from two directions at once: Celtic Ireland and Rome. This "Celtic Christianity" developed several practices that differed from those of the Roman church, notably in the method of determining the date of Easter. In Britain disputes over these questions were eventually settled (Whitby, 664). In time, Irish monasticism became so strong that many Irish monks and scholars moved out of Ireland as missionaries to convert the heathen on the continent too. Saint Columban, for example, born in Leinster, headed missions from the Low Countries up to the Rhine to Switzerland and even into Italy in the seventh century.

Huns, Ostrogoths

Not only the Germanic peoples but the Asian Huns themselves participated in the onslaught on Roman territories. Emerging into Europe from the East early in the fifth century, the Huns soon conquered what we would call Romania, Hungary, and parts of Yogoslavia, Poland, and Czechoslovakia. Under their domination lived a large collection of German tribes. The Hunnic rulers extracted tribute-money from the Roman emperors at Constantinople. Under their ruler, Attila, this savage horde pressed westward, crossed the Rhine, and met with defeat in Gaul in 451 at the hands of a Roman general in a battle usually called Châlons. Pope Leo the Great persuaded Attila to withdraw from Italy without attacking Rome.

Like many nomad empires, that of the Huns in central Europe fell apart after the death of the conquering founder (452). A plague decimated their ranks, and many withdrew into Asia once more. But other related Asian peoples, nomads and pagans like the Huns, and like them Mongol in appearance, entered Europe before the age of the barbarian invasions was over: Avars in the sixth century, Bulgars in the sixth and seventh, and Magyars or Hungarians in the ninth. The Magyars eventually set up a lasting state in the Danubian plain, and their europeanized descendants still inhabit modern Hungary. As the first Asian invaders, the Huns had not only touched off the invasions of the terrified Germanic tribes but had directly helped to smash Roman influence in central Europe.

Among the German tribes liberated by the

collapse of the Hunnic Empire, the first to make a major impact were the Ostrogoths (East Goths). They moved into the general disorder left in Italy after the last of the Western emperors, Romulus Augustulus (the little Augustus), had been dethroned by his barbarian protector Odovacar in 476, the date often used by historians to mark the "end" of the Roman Empire in the West. Actually, like his immediate predecessors, Romulus Augustulus had been an ineffectual tool of the nearest barbarian general who could command loyal troops. Roman imperial power, however, continued uninterruptedly in the East. In fact, it had been the Eastern emperor Zeno in Constantinople who had hired the Ostrogoths to intervene in Italy on his behalf against Odovacar.

The leader of the Ostrogoths, Theodoric, had been educated in Constantinople, and admired both Greek civilization and the Roman Empire as an institution. For most of his long rule in Italy (489–526) he was content to serve as nominal subordinate to Emperor Zeno and his successors in the East, as a kind of governor of Italy. Theodoric was also king of his own Gothic people, and established his capital at Ravenna. Like many other christianized German tribes, the Ostrogoths were Arian. In the eyes of the popes and of the Italians, they were therefore heretics as well as German foreigners. Although Theodoric hoped to impose upon his Germanic subjects the civilization of the Roman Empire, he did not have enough time to bring about any real assimilation. Moreover, toward the end of his reign, Theodoric, who had made dynastic marriages with the Vandal and other Germanic ruling houses, became suspicious of the empire and planned to go to war against Constantinople, but died before he could do so.

Many other barbarian peoples participated in the break-up of Roman territory and power in the West during the fifth and sixth centuries, but failed to found any lasting state. They remain mere tribal names: Sciri, Suevi, Alamanni—the German forests seem to have had an inexhaustible supply of them. There were two other German tribes, however, whose achievements we still remember: the Burgundians, who moved into the valleys of the Rhone and Saône rivers in Gaul in the 440's and gave their name to a succession of "Burgundies," varying in territory and government, and the Franks—most important of all—from whom modern France itself derives its name.

II   The Franks; the Building of an Empire

Destined to found the most lasting political entity of any of the Germanic tribes, the Franks appeared first as dwellers along the lower Rhine. They engaged in no long migrations, but simply expanded gradually west and south from their native territory until eventually they were to create an empire that would include most of western Europe except for the Iberian peninsula and the British Isles. Clovis (reigned 481–511), descendant of the house of Merwig or Merovech, called Merovingian, was the founder of Frankish power. Moving into Gaul, he defeated successively a Roman army (486), the Alamanni (496), and the Visigoths of Aquitaine (at the battle of Vouillé, 507). Large areas of modern France, northwest Germany, and the Low Countries were now Frankish.

The most important factor in Clovis' success, aside from his skill as a general, was his conversion to Christianity, not as an Arian heretic but as an orthodox Catholic. This gave him the instant support of the clergy of Gaul, especially of the powerful bishops of Aquitaine, who welcomed the Franks as a relief from the Arian Visigoths. Probably the greatest liability of the Franks was their habit of dividing up the kingdom between the king's sons in every generation. This meant not only a constant parceling out of territory into petty kingdoms and lordships but constant secret intrigues and bloody rivalries among brothers and cousins and other relatives who strove to reunite the lands. Indeed, Merovingian history forms one of the most sordid and savage chapters in the whole record of Western society.

Here is a sample of what went on, as reported by the sixth-century historian Gregory of Tours. A grandson of Clovis, King Chilperic, married Fredegund, who was not of noble birth. Fredegund determined to make herself queen in fact as well as in name. She stopped at nothing to achieve her ambitions and to eliminate her rivals. When her sons perished in an epidemic, she sent Chlodovech, Chilperic's son by an earlier marriage, to the same place "that he too might die the same death." Chlodovech survived, but only until his stepmother had him stabbed to death. Next, Fredegund tried to dispose of her sister-in-law, Brunhild, by sending "a cleric of her household to ensnare and slay that queen." Brunhild, however, discovered the would-be assassin and sent him back to Fredegund, who

"punished him by having his hands and feet cut off." Finally Fredegund turned against her own daughter, Rigunth:

Sometimes they even came to blows and buffets. One day her mother said to her: "Why doest thou set thyself against me, O my daughter? Here are possessions of thy father which I have under my control; take them and do with them as seemeth good to thee." She then went into her treasure-room, and opened a chest full of necklets and precious ornaments, for a long time taking out one thing after another, and handing

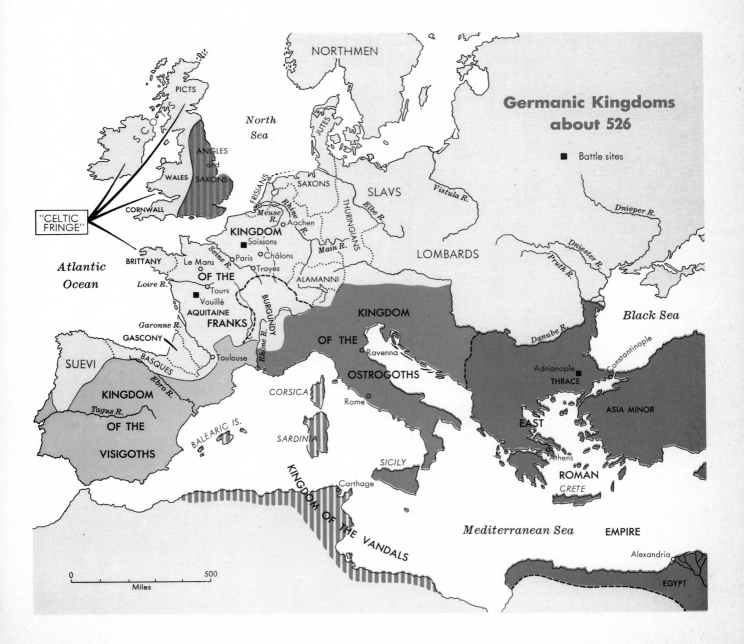

them to her daughter, who stood by. At last she said: "I am weary; put thou in thy hand, and take out what thou mayst find." Rigunth put her arm into the chest to take out more things, when her mother seized the lid and forced it down upon her neck. She bore upon it with all her strength, until the edge of the chest beneath pressed the girl's throat so hard that her eyes seemed about to start from her head. . . . The attendants outside . . . broke into the small chamber, and brought out the girl, whom they thus delivered from imminent death.*

By the end of the seventh century, the Merovingian kings themselves became so degenerate that they are known as *rois fainéants* (do-nothing kings). They delegated real power to their chief officials, the "mayors of the palace," a title showing the close connection between the household service of the monarch and the actual government. By the eighth century one particular family had made this office hereditary from father to son—the Carolingians (from *Carolus,* Latin for Charles). One of the mayors, Charles (ruled 714–741), called Martel, "the hammer," organized the Frankish nobles into a dependable cavalry and in 732 near Tours defeated a roving band of Muslims that had been raiding northward from Spain. There was no real danger that the Muslims would conquer Frankish territory, yet since Tours was the farthest north in Europe that the Muslims ever came, the battle is a landmark in Western history. Charles Martel's son, Pepin the Short (ruled 741–768), assumed the title of king of the Franks and consolidated the kingdom once again. Pepin's adventurous policy with regard to Italy initiated a whole new chapter in Western history.

Italy from Theodoric to Pepin

Soon after the death of Theodoric, the great Eastern emperor Justinian (ruled 527–565—see below, Chapter 6) launched from Constantinople an ambitious effort to reconquer the major areas of the West that had been lost to the barbarians. The imperial forces tackled the Vandals of North Africa first, and then, before consolidating their successes, invaded Italy from Carthage, via Sicily. For almost twenty years (535–554) in-

*Gregory of Tours, *History of the Franks,* ed. O. M. Dalton (Oxford, 1927), Book IX, 34.

creasingly savage and destructive warfare ravaged the peninsula, as Justinian's troops fought the Ostrogoths. The towns and countryside of Italy were left depopulated, and the survivors reduced to misery. So Justinian's proclamation of an imperial restoration (554) was hollow indeed. In the same year imperial forces took back a portion of southern Spain from the Visigoths.

But only three years after Justinian's death, a new Germanic tribe, the Arian Lombards, entered Italy (568) from the north. They easily conquered the north Italian plain that still bears their name (Lombardy), and established a kingdom with its capital at Pavia. Further to the south, they set up two duchies (Benevento and Spoleto). Italy lay once again in fragments. Still under imperial domination were Ravenna and the territory surrounding it, the island settlement of Venice, Rome, Naples, and the toe and heel of the peninsula, as well as Sicily. The emperor at Constantinople appointed a governor called the exarch, who had his headquarters at Ravenna and was particularly charged with organizing the defense of Italy.

But Constantinople was far away; dangers threatened the emperors from the East, and they often could not afford to pay much attention to Italy's needs or send money and troops to help the exarchs fight the Lombards. In this situation the Church emerged more and more as the protector of the Catholic population, the bishops often receiving privileges from the Arian Lombard conquerors that conferred upon them virtual governing rights in the towns. Among the bishops, the pope of course took the lead, and, among the popes, the most remarkable in every way was Gregory I, the Great (reigned 590–604).

Child of a rich and aristocratic Roman family, Gregory abandoned worldly things and became a monk and founder of monasteries. His administrative talents were extraordinary: he served as papal ambassador to the Roman imperial court at Constantinople before becoming pope in 590. Besides his religious duties, he had to take virtually full responsibility for maintaining the fortifications of Rome, for feeding its population, for managing the great financial resources of the Church and its lands in Italy, for conducting diplomatic negotiations with exarchate and Lombards, and even for directing military operations. It was he who sent the mission to Britain (596) that began the papal contribution to the conversion of the Anglo-Saxons. Gregory had an exalted conception of papal power, and stoutly defended its supremacy over the Church in his letters to the emperor and to the patriarch at Constantinople.

During the seventh and early eighth centuries, the alienation between the empire in the East and the papacy was greatly increased by religious disagreements and a related political and economic dispute (see below, Chapter 6). And simultaneously, the Lombards gradually consolidated and expanded their power, taking Ravenna in 751 and putting an end to the exarchate. Menaced by the Lombards and unable to count on help from Constantinople, Pope Stephen II in 753 paid a visit to King Pepin of the Franks.

Pepin was unsure of his position, being only a descendant of a line of Mayors of the Palace for the Merovingians. So, in exchange for papal approval of his new title of king, he attacked the Lombards and forced them to abandon Ravenna and other recent conquests. Then he gave a portion of these lands to the pope, as the celebrated Donation of Pepin. Of course the lands did not belong to Pepin but to the emperor at Constantinople, but this did not prevent Pepin's disposing of them. Together with Rome itself and the lands immediately around it, the Donation of Pepin formed the territory over which the pope ruled as temporal sovereign down to the nineteenth century. These were the Papal States, and Vatican City is their present-day remnant. Pepin's son, Charles the Great (Charlemagne), completed the destruction of the Lombard kingdom in 774 and assumed the Iron Crown of Lombardy.

From the papal point of view, the new alliance with the Franks marked the end of dependence upon the empire and the beginning of the papacy as a territorial power. The Franks, too busy to take over these Italian lands themselves and no doubt also aware of the pious responsibilities that they had acquired when they became the protectors of the Church, did not try to dictate to the popes. Soon after Pepin's donation, the clerks of the papal chancery forged "proof" that Pepin had only been confirming a gift of lands to the Church made long ago by the emperor Constantine. The forgery (the so-called Donation of Constantine) stated, in addition, that Constantine had directly declared that:

inasmuch as our imperial power is earthly, we have decreed that it shall venerate and honor his most holy Roman Church and that the sacred see of blessed Peter shall be gloriously exalted above our empire and earthly throne. We attribute to him the power and glorious dignity and strength and honor of the Empire, and we ordain and decree that he shall have rule as well over the four principal sees, Antioch, Alexandria, Constantinople, and Jerusalem, as also over all the churches of God in all the world. And the pontiff who for the time being presides over that most holy Roman Church shall be the highest and chief of all priests in the whole world, and according to his decision shall all matters be settled which shall be taken in hand for the service of God or the confirmation of the faith of Christians.*

For about seven hundred years, until the Italian Renaissance scholar Lorenzo Valla proved it a forgery, men believed this extraordinary document to be genuine.

Charlemagne and the Revival of Empire

Pepin's son Charlemagne (Charles the Great, reigned 771–814)—so Einhard, his contemporary biographer, tells us—was a vigorous, lusty, intelligent man who loved hunting, women, and war. All his life he wore Frankish costume and thought of himself as a Frankish chieftain. Although he could read, and kept pen and ink under his pillow, he could never teach himself how to write. He spoke Latin, however, and understood some Greek. A great conqueror, Charlemagne turned his armies east and crossed the Rhine. In campaigns lasting more than 30 years, he conquered the heathen Saxons, living south of Denmark, and converted them at sword's point to Christianity. Monks and priests followed his armies.

Charlemagne thus made the first successful invasion of Germany. This spawning-ground of the barbarians who had shattered Roman society in the West then began the long, slow process of assimilation to Western civilization. In addition to the lands of the Saxons, Charlemagne added to his domain the western areas of

---

*Documents of the Christian Church, ed. Henry Bettenson (New York, 1947), p. 140.

A thirteenth-century fresco depicting the Donation of Constantine.

modern Czechoslovakia (Bohemia), much of Austria, and portions of Hungary and Yugoslavia; the eastern boundaries of his realm reached the Elbe River in the north, and the Danube, where it turns sharply south below Vienna. Along these wild eastern frontiers he established provinces (marks or marches). His advance into eastern Europe brought him victories also over the Asian Avars, successors to the Huns along the lower Danube. Far to the west, Charlemagne challenged Muslim power in Spain and set up a Spanish march in what is today Catalonia. An unimportant defeat of his rear guard at the pass of Roncesvalles in the Pyrenees Mountains in 778 formed the theme of the

heroic epic *The Song of Roland* (*Chanson de Roland*), which in its surviving form was composed several centuries later.

By the end of the eighth century, Charlemagne had reunited under Frankish rule all of the western Roman provinces except for Britain, most of Spain, Southern Italy, Sicily, and North Africa, and had added to his domains central and eastern European areas which the Romans had never possessed. On Christmas Day, 800, the pope himself, Leo III, crowned Charlemagne emperor in Rome. So mighty was the tradition of Roman Empire and so great its hold on the minds of men that, more than three centuries after the disappearance of Romulus Augustulus, last of the Western emperors, the chief bishop of the Christian church, seeking to honor and recognize his mighty Frankish patron, automatically crowned him "Roman" emperor. Even before the coronation, a poet in Charlemagne's own circle had hailed him as "Augustus." Indeed, Einhard modeled his biography of his imperial master so closely upon Suetonius' famous biography of Augustus that one has to be careful in its use.

It is quite possible that Charlemagne himself was surprised and not altogether pleased by the coronation; he probably relished his title, but he almost surely disliked the role played by the pope and the implication that the pope had the right to choose and crown emperors. The Roman emperors at Constantinople were horrified at the insolence of the barbarian Charlemagne in assuming the sacred title.

Within his territories Charlemagne was, by virtue of his consecration, a sacred ruler, with spiritual rights and duties as well as temporal ones. His lofty concept of his office and his personal power enabled him to influence the Church —even in matters of doctrine—more like Constantine or other Eastern emperors than any other Western monarch. He himself named Louis the Pious, by then his only living son, his successor in 813; the pope had no part in the ceremonies.

Charlemagne's government was very simple. Had not all but one of his sons died before him he would have divided the kingdom in the standard Frankish way. His personal household staff were also the government officials: the chamberlain, the count of the stable (constable), and so on. On major decisions the emperor conferred with great nobles of state and church, but he told them what he (and they) were going to do rather than asking them for advice and permission. Since the Franks, like other Germans, believed that law *existed* and could not be made by men, even Charlemagne could not in theory legislate. But he did issue instructions to his subjects, divided into subheadings or chapters and therefore called *capitularies,* which usually dealt with special administrative problems. It was a highly personal rule. Einhard says about it:

> When he had taken the imperial title he noticed many defects in the legal systems of his people; for the Franks have two legal systems, differing in many points very widely from one another, and he therefore determined to add what was lacking, to reconcile the differences, and to amend anything that was wrong or wrongly expressed. He completed nothing of all his designs beyond adding a few capitularies, and those unfinished. But he gave orders that the laws and rules of all nations comprised within his domains which were not already written out should be collected and committed to writing.

> He also wrote out the barbarous and ancient songs, in which the acts of the kings and their wars were sung, and committed them to memory. He also began a grammar of his native language.*

In a restored eighth-century mosaic from St. John Lateran Saint Peter is shown conferring symbols of spiritual authority and temporal power on Pope Leo III and Charlemagne.

* *Early Lives of Charlemagne,* ed. A. J. Grant (London, 1922), pp. 44-45.

Since Einhard also tells us that Charlemagne himself could not write, we know that this passage must mean that Charlemagne did not do this writing himself but ordered it to be done.

Charlemagne's territories included about 300 counties, each governed by a count. The counties that lay in former Roman territory corresponded to the lands of a former Roman *civitas*. The count had to maintain order, render justice, and recruit and command soldiers. Alongside the count, the bishop of the diocese and the various local magnates might have considerable powers of their own on their own lands. Only a powerful king could keep the local authorities from arrogating too much power to themselves. Charlemagne required his counts to appoint teams of judges, called *scabini*, whose appointment he would then ratify, and who would actually take over much of the counts' role in rendering justice. He also sent out from his own central administrative staff pairs of royal emissaries (the *missi dominici*, literally "the lord's messengers"), usually a layman and a cleric, to investigate local conditions and correct abuses. As representatives of the emperor, they could overrule the count.

The Carolingian Empire depended too much upon Charlemagne personally; he had assembled more territory than could any longer be effectively governed, in view of the degeneration of administrative machinery and of communications since Roman days. Under his less talented successors, the old Frankish habit of dividing up lands and authority among the heirs to the throne reasserted itself. Quarrels over the allotment of territory raged among brothers and cousins. The title of emperor descended to a single heir in each generation, but as early as the middle of the ninth century it had become an empty honor.

Thus Charlemagne's achievement was short-lived if brilliant. Historians have taken differing views of it; some have emphasized its brevity and denied its lasting influence. Others have stressed its brilliance, and declared that the mere resurrection of the Roman imperial title in the West helped determine the future direction of European political action: the next time a new revival began, men instinctively launched it by resuscitating the Roman Empire once again. But these historians add that, as events turned out, this title lured later generations of German rulers over the Alps into Italy in search of an illusory honor, prevented them from forging Germany into a national unity, and so kept Italy and Ger-

Detail of a fourteenth-century reliquary bust of Charlemagne.

many tied together in an utterly unnatural relationship that helps explain why neither became a nation until the nineteenth century.

Some would insist that Charlemagne's revival of the imperial title kept alive, even though in a tenuous and almost unreal form, at least the ideal of a unified Christian Western society, not merely a collection of parochial states devoted to the cutthroat competition of war and so-called peace. Others maintain that, thanks to Charlemagne's act, a lay power with universal or at least pan-Western temporal aspirations was able through the medieval centuries to oppose the temporal claims of a spiritual power, the papacy; and, of course, a spiritual power well anchored in Italy could oppose the temporal power. The existence of these two claimants to supreme power, the pope and the emperor, saved the West from the extremes of lay domination of religion on the one hand and religious domination of the state on the other. This rivalry and tension—they argue—helped promote such

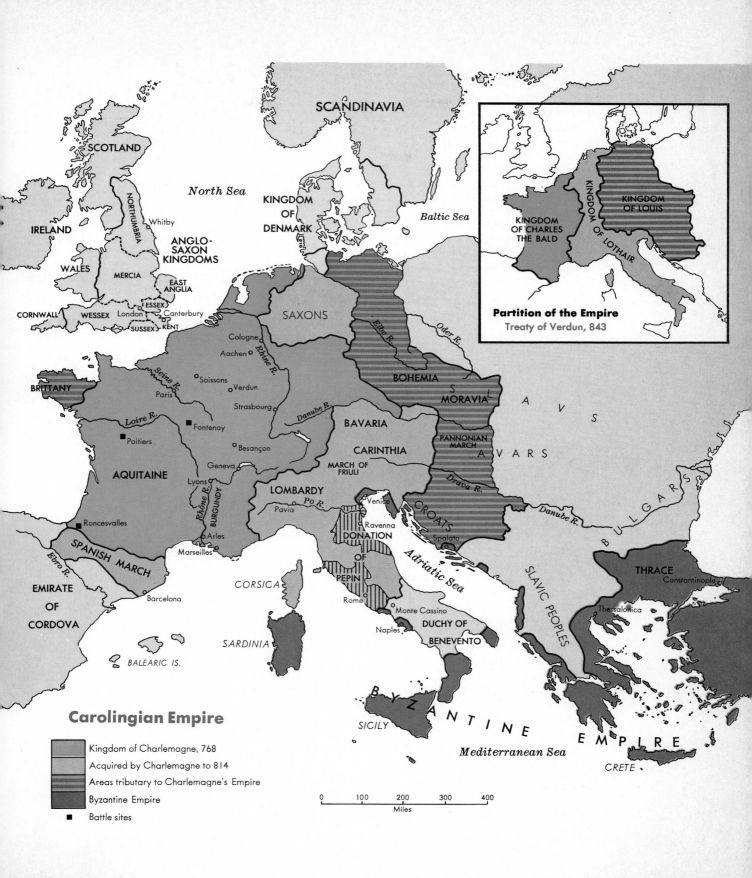

SCANDINAVIA

SCOTLAND

IRELAND

North Sea

KINGDOM OF DENMARK

Baltic Sea

NORTHUMBRIA
Whitby

ANGLO-SAXON KINGDOMS

WALES

MERCIA

EAST ANGLIA

CORNWALL   WESSEX   London   ESSEX   Canterbury
SUSSEX   KENT

SAXONS

Cologne
Aachen

Rhine R.

Elbe R.

Oder R.

BOHEMIA

MORAVIA

A   V   S

Seine R.
Soissons
Paris
Verdun
Strasbourg

Danube R.

BAVARIA

CARINTHIA

PANNONIAN MARCH

A V A R S

BRITTANY

Loire R.
Fontenoy
Poitiers
Besançon
Geneva

MARCH OF FRIULI

Drava R.

AQUITAINE

Lyons

Rhône R.   BURGUNDY

LOMBARDY

Pavia   Po R.

Venice

Ravenna

CROATS

Spalato

Danube R.

BULGARS

DONATION OF PEPIN

Adriatic Sea

Arles
Marseilles

Roncesvalles

SPANISH MARCH

Ebro R.

Rome

Monte Cassino

SLAVIC PEOPLES

THRACE

Constantinople

EMIRATE OF CORDOVA

Barcelona

CORSICA

SARDINIA

BALEARIC IS.

Naples

DUCHY OF BENEVENTO

Thessalonica

B   Y   Z   A   N   T   I   N   E   E   M   P   I   R   E

SICILY

Mediterranean Sea

CRETE

Carolingian Empire

- Kingdom of Charlemagne, 768
- Acquired by Charlemagne to 814
- Areas tributary to Charlemagne's Empire
- Byzantine Empire
- ■ Battle sites

0   100   200   300   400
Miles

Partition of the Empire
Treaty of Verdun, 843

KINGDOM OF CHARLES THE BALD

KINGDOM OF LOTHAIR

KINGDOM OF LOUIS

typically Western institutions and attitudes as individual rights, the rule of law, and the dignity of man.

All of this lies in the realm of political theory and speculation and of course none of it can be "proved." Nevertheless, it is clear that the revival of the old Roman imperial idea is one of the great threads that run through all subsequent European history. With Charlemagne the "Roman" empire became in fact largely a German one, but there always remained about the very name "empire" some suggestion of a common political order within which war was somehow "unnatural," not right. In this sense, the medieval empire, reinforced by the concept of Christendom, is a link—admittedly verbal, idealistic, even "ideological" rather than legal or institutional—between the One World of Rome and the One World of twentieth-century aspiration. And apart from political theorizing, all students of the intellectual and artistic revival in the time of Charlemagne and his successors would agree that the period provided a dazzling flash of light after centuries that had indeed been relatively dark.

In the struggle among Charlemagne's grandsons, one episode deserves special notice: the Strasbourg Oaths of 842. Two of the grandsons, Charles the Bald, who held the Western regions, and Louis the German, who held the Eastern regions, swore an alliance against their brother, the emperor Lothair, whose lands lay between theirs. Each swore in the language of the other's troops: Louis in a Latin-like language on its way to becoming French, which scholars call Romance, and Charles in Germanic. Of course this does not mean that there was a France or a Germany in 842: only that the western and eastern Frankish lands spoke divergent tongues. But the symbolism is a striking sign of things to come in European history. Charles and Louis could hardly have chosen a more appropriate place than Strasbourg—chief city of Alsace, in the heart of the middle zone, long a bone of contention between modern France and Germany—to swear their bilingual oath. In the ninth century, however, there were as yet no national states in Europe. Indeed, instead of coalescing into large national units, the Frankish dominions were even then in the process of breaking up into much smaller ones. As the power of the central Frankish state was frittered away in family squabbles, smaller entities, duchies or counties, emerged as virtually autonomous units of government, many with names we still recognize as belonging to provinces of modern France or Germany: Champagne, Britany, Saxony, Bavaria.

III After Charlemagne: The Northmen

Charlemagne's conquests in Germany had for the first time brought into the area of Western civilization the breeding-ground of many of the barbarians. Still outside lay Scandinavia, from whose shores there began in the ninth century a new wave of invasions that hit Britain and the western parts of the Frankish lands with savage force. The Northmen conducted their raids from small ships that could easily sail up the Thames, the Seine, or the Loire. Their appetite for booty grew with their successes, and soon they organized fleets of several hundred ships, ventured farther abroad, and often wintered along a conquered coast. They ranged as far south as Spain, penetrated into the Mediterranean through the Straits of Gibraltar, and raided Italy. To the west they proceeded far beyond Ireland, and reached Iceland and Greenland. Later on, some almost certainly landed in Newfoundland, Labrador, or even New England, although some scholars still question the validity of the evidence we have for this.

The longing for booty may not by itself account for the Norse expansions. Polygamy was common among the upper classes of the pagan Scandinavians (the lower ones could not afford it), and it is probable that the younger sons of these Viking chiefs either had to leave home or stop living in the style to which they had grown accustomed. This possible cause for the Norse expansion is suggested by the fact that even after the Vikings had conquered their first European base of settlement, the younger sons continued to go abroad to plunder and to settle.

The Norsemen's first captured base was the region along the lower Seine River, which is still called Normandy after them. In 911, the Frankish king was forced to grant the Norse leader

An early tenth-century Irish sculptured cross, "the Muiredach Cross."

Dnieper, consolidated the first Russian state (see below, Chapter 6).

While the Normans were raiding and developing Normandy, other Scandinavians were almost paralleling their achievements in the British Isles. In Ireland the Northmen were soon firmly established, especially in the ports of Dublin and Waterford, and in the Shannon River port of Limerick. But in the interior, the Celtic chieftains held on. In 1014, under the leadership of Brian of Munster, these chieftains won the battle of Clontarf against the Northmen and their native allies. Finally, the Northmen were absorbed into the texture of Irish society. But the two centuries of struggle had provided a fatal interruption in the brilliant development of Irish civilization, and thereafter tribal warfare was to reign unchecked until the English invasion of the twelfth century.

The Anglo-Saxon Kingdoms and the Danes

In England, too, the savage Danish attacks on the northern and eastern shores soon led to settlement. The chief organizer of defense against the Danes was the Anglo-Saxon kingdom of Wessex under Alfred the Great (ruled 871–899). Although Alfred finally defeated the Danes, he was not strong enough to expel them, and had to concede the whole northeast of England to them, a region thereafter called the Danelaw.

Far more advanced at this stage than the Danes, Alfred's kingdom was governed through the royal household and clerical staff. The king's great council, the *witenagemot*, made up of important landholders, churchmen, and officials, advised him when he asked for advice, acted as a court of justice, and elected and deposed kings. The king could count on revenue from his own estates, and also from a special tax imposed for defense against the Danes, called the Danegeld. He also received two-thirds of all the fines imposed by local courts. His army was still the old Germanic host (*fyrd*), in which every landholder was obliged to serve, but he also had additional household troops. Anglo-Saxon institutions in the tenth century were not very different from those of the Franks before Charlemagne or those of any settled Germanic tribe.

Soon after the turn of the eleventh century, new waves of Danes scored important successes

Rolf (or Rollo) a permanent right of settlement. The Normans became an efficient and powerful ruling class—in fact, the best administrators of the new "feudal" age. From Normandy soon after the year 1000 younger sons would go off to found a flourishing state in the southern Italian and Sicilian territories that still belonged to the Eastern Roman Empire. And from Normandy in 1066, as we shall see, Duke William and his followers would conquer England.

Kinsmen of these Norsemen who had settled in Normandy also did great deeds. In the 860's the first wave of Viking invaders crossed the Baltic Sea to the territory that is now Russia, and penetrated deep inland to the south along the river valleys. They conquered the indigenous Slavic tribes, and, at Kiev on the middle under the command of Canute (Knut), the king of Denmark. In 1017 Canute was chosen king of England by the Anglo-Saxon witenagemot. Able ruler of a kind of northern empire (he was also king of Norway), Canute allied himself with the Roman church, and brought Scandinavia into the Christian community. His early death (1035) without competent heirs led to the break-up of his holdings, and England reverted to a king of the house of Alfred (Edward the Confessor). The work of Canute in England, though it did not last, belongs with that of the Scandinavians in Normandy, in southern Italy, and in Russia as an example of the political and administrative ability so widely demonstrated by the Scandinavians once they had settled down.

Carolingian Decline: The Saxon Empire

By the end of the ninth century, the power of the Carolingians in their German territories had almost disappeared in the face of domestic challenge by ambitious local magnates and foreign threats from Norsemen, Slavs, and the Asian Magyars, who poured into the Hungarian plain in the mid-890's. Their predecessors, the Huns and Avars, had vanished, but the Magyars would stay, and form the nucleus of a Hungarian state.

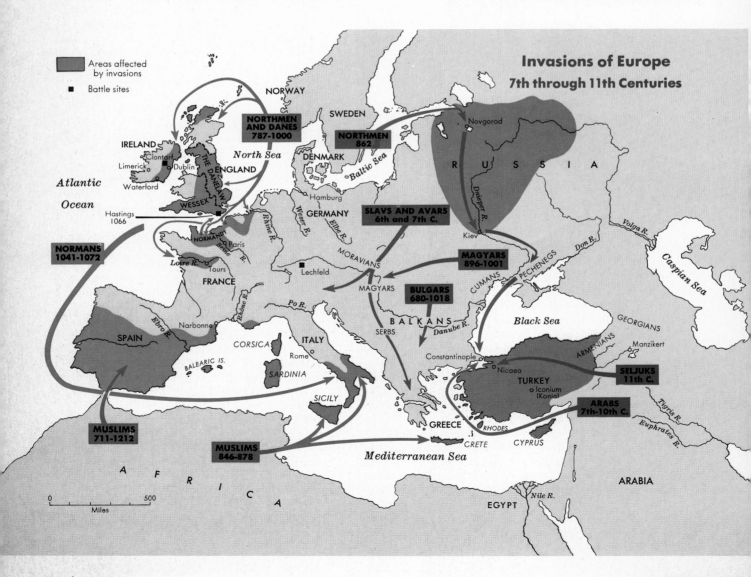

Invasions of Europe
7th through 11th Centuries

The Hungarian language thus remains today the only non-Indo-European tongue in Europe except for Finnish and Basque.

When the last nominal Carolingian ruler, Louis the Child, died in 911, the German magnates elected the duke of Franconia as King Conrad I (reigned 911–918). The most important units in Germany were now the duchies—Franconia, Saxony, Swabia, and Bavaria—each under its autonomous ruler. Conrad I failed to control either the other dukes or the Magyars, and finally nominated his strongest enemy, Henry, duke of Saxony, to succeed him. Henry's son, Otto I (936–973), both checked the rival dukes and, at the Battle of Lechfeld, 955, defeated the Magyars.

Master of his German territories, the Saxon Otto next sought to revive Charlemagne's title of Roman emperor, which had passed from one shadowy Carolingian prince to another until it lapsed in 924. Deep in decline after the reign of the great pope Nicholas I (858–867), the papacy had fallen into the hands of rival Roman noble families, corrupt and ineffectual. Without strong central administration and under attack from Muslims and Magyars, Italy had become anarchic. Yet Rome, even at its lowest depths in the mid-tenth century, continued to act as an irresistible magnet for those seeking supreme power. Like Charlemagne almost two hundred years before him, Otto went to Italy. He had himself crowned emperor by the degenerate Pope John XII (962), and then had John deposed for murder and installed his own candidate on the papal throne. He forced the Roman aristocracy to promise that imperial consent would hereafter be necessary to papal elections, and he renewed the Donation of Pepin and the subsequent grants of the Carolingians to the papacy. Though the papacy for the next hundred years was hardly more than an instrument manipulated by Otto's German successors, Otto's action eventually ensured the continuity of the papacy as an independent institution; it also tightly linked the political fortunes of Germany and Italy for centuries to come.

In the western Carolingian lands, which we may now call France, partitioning, strife, and feebleness led to the fragmentation of both territory and power among ambitious landowners. As early as 887 one faction of these magnates chose a non-Carolingian, Odo, count of Paris, as king, and civil war between him and the Carolingian claimant added to the chaos. For the next century the families of the two rivals alternated in power. Finally, in 987 the magnates elected as king a descendant of the early count of Paris, Hugh Capet. Though several of the nobles who chose Hugh were actually more powerful than he, he founded the dynasty that would last almost to our own time. (When Louis XVI went to the guillotine in 1793, his executioners called him "Citizen Capet.")

Europe about 1000

About the year 1000, then, England was a centralized monarchy; France was nominally ruled by an elected king who was feebler than his great supporters; Germany was divided into duchies, one of which—Saxon—had asserted its supremacy and claimed the old imperial title; and Italy still remained anarchic, but a revived papacy had begun to emerge. Out of the debris of the Roman Empire, buffeted by two successive waves of barbarian invasions and held together only by their common Christian faith, these major fragments had begun to take on, even as early as this, certain features that we can still recognize today. Elsewhere, the Scandinavian kingdoms had imposed order on the turbulent peoples who had made the Viking expansion, and the little Christian kingdoms in the north of Spain were only beginning their struggle with the Muslim tide that had engulfed the peninsula (see below, Chapter 6).

In the East, the empire, with its direct descent from Rome and its Greco-oriental character, still stood firm at Constantinople after many shocks. It had started its work of christianizing those Slavic peoples nearest to it—the Bulgarians, the Russians, the Serbs. The western Slavs—Czechs, Poles, Croats, and others—and the Magyars, lying between the Germans and the influences radiating from Constantinople, had received the attention of Roman missionaries. By the year 1000 there was already visible a fateful line of demarcation between the Western Catholic world and Eastern Orthodox world, with its different alphabet and its different outlook.

IV Feudal Europe

If the old Roman ways of governing largely collapsed, as they did, during the centuries that we have called the early Middle Ages, what replaced them? It is all very well to speak of relative "anarchy" before and after the interval provided by Charlemagne, but what was "anarchy" like, and how were human relations governed? Did everybody just slaughter everybody else indiscriminately? What were the rules that enabled life to go on, however harshly?

In fact, of course, there were mutual arrangements between men that allowed people to work and fight, and to survive if they could. In these arrangements, about which we still know much less than we might like to know, we can discern elements surviving from Roman times, innovations introduced by the barbarians, and changes linked with conversion to Christianity. The settled inhabitants of western Europe and the invaders underwent a long period of slow mutual adjustment, as new and old ways of regulating human affairs competed and often combined with each other.

Feudalism: The Rulers

To these widely varied social and political combinations scholars give the name *feudalism*. Feudal institutions were the arrangements—personal, territorial, and governmental—between persons that made survival possible under the conditions that obtained in western Europe during the Dark Ages. The arrangements were made between important people who were concerned with maintaining order; feudal institutions involved the governors—the upper classes, both laymen and clerics—not the masses of the population. Because central authority was no longer able to maintain itself locally, local authority had to be improvised to replace it. But because the processes and their results were anything but systematic, we do not here use or recommend the outmoded term "feudal system."

One of the most influential arrangements between persons among the barbarians was the war-band (or *Gefolge*) of all the early Germans, the *comitatus*, as Tacitus called it in Latin. In the war-band, the leader commanded the loyalty of his followers, who had put themselves under his direction for fighting and winning of booty. It was one of the most important institutions of the Scandinavian invaders of future Russia, where it acquired the Slavic name of *druzhina*. Among the Anglo-Saxons, the word for its chieftain was *hlaford*, the direct origin of our word "lord." Chief and followers consulted before a raid or before making peace; those who disagreed might go and serve another chief; booty was divided.

In the Roman provinces, too, local landowners had often built their own private armies, while in Rome itself the magnates had long maintained their groups of *clients*, to whom they acted as *patron* and gave legal protection. When a humble man wanted to enter the client relationship, he asked for the *patrocinium* of the great man and secured it by performing the act of *commendation*, recommending or entrusting himself to the patron. He remained free, but obtained food and clothing in exchange for his services, whatever they might be. If the man was of the upper classes, he was called *fidelis*, a faithful man. By the Carolingian period, the term *vassus*, originally denoting a man of menial status, had come to mean a man who rendered military service to his patron, or lord. To be a vassus or vassal meant no disgrace; it was the new name for the status gained by the act of commendation. So a combination of old Germanic and old Roman practices contributed to new relationships described in new terms.

A Roman patron sometimes had retained the title to a piece of property but granted a client the temporary use of it, together with the profits to be derived from it so long as he held it, often for life. The Romans used the term *precarium* for this kind of tenure, and the Carolingian rulers commonly adopted the old practice—sometimes using the old Roman term, sometimes the newer *beneficium*, benefice, to describe the land temporarily held by the vassal in exchange for service. By the year 1000 the act of becoming a vassal usually meant that a man got a benefice; indeed he might refuse faithful service or loyalty unless he was satisfied with the land he received. The feeble later Carolingians and their rivals outbid each other in giving benefices to their supporters in order to obtain armed support and service. This was one of the practices that depleted the royal estates.

In the later Carolingian period, the benefice came to be called *feudum,* a fief, the term that has given us the words "feudal" and "feudalism." When the benefice became a fief, it also became hereditary. Though title to the fief remained with the lord who granted it, the fief itself passed, on the death of a vassal, to the vassal's heir, who inherited with it the obligations to serve the lord and his heirs.

The man who received a fief often got with it certain rights to govern the farmers who lived and worked on the lands that made it up. This practice too had its precedents: in late Roman times, the emperors had often granted an *immunity* to their own estates, an understanding that the people who lived on these lands would not be visited by imperial tax-collectors or other law-enforcing officials. Because the immunity exempted the inhabitants from onerous duties, it was hoped that the farmers would enjoy their privileged status, and therefore stay put and supply the emperor with needed produce. The Frankish kings adopted this practice, sometimes extending it to lands of the Church and even to those of private proprietors. By the tenth century an immunity meant that the king undertook to keep his officials off the privileged lands, and that the holder of the lands would himself perform such governmental functions as collecting taxes, establishing police arrangements, and setting up a court of justice, of which he might keep the profits coming from fines or assessments.

From late Roman times, too, came the local offices of duke and count. Originally military commanders, they took over increasing civil authority as the power of the central government relaxed. In Frankish times they might be very powerful rulers, kings in all but name. In the disorders of the Carolingian decline, these offices gradually became hereditary; at the same time, the dukes and counts were the vassals of the Carolingians. So the title and office, the duties of the vassal, and the fief (or territory of the office) all became hereditary.

Vassals and Lords

Feudalism and feudal practice did not extend uniformly over all of Europe. Northern France and the Low Countries were the most thoroughly feudalized areas, Germany perhaps the least. Everywhere some pieces of land never became fiefs, but remained the fully owned private property of the owners; these were called *allods*. Feudal practices varied from place to place, and they developed and altered with the passage of time. But certain general conceptions were held pretty much everywhere.

One of the most significant was that of a feudal contract: the lord—or *suzerain,* as he was often called—owed something to the vassal just as the vassal owed something to the lord. When they entered upon their relationship the vassal rendered formal homage to his lord; that is, he became the lord's "man." He also promised him aid and counsel. *Aid* meant that he would appear when summoned, fully armed, and participate as a knight in the lord's wars (subject perhaps to limits on the number of days' service owed in any one year). *Counsel* meant that he would join with his fellow vassals—his *peers,* or social equals—to form the lord's court of justice that alone could pass judgment on any one of them. He might also be required at his own expense to entertain his lord for a visit of specific length, and to give him money payments on special occasions—the marriage of the lord's eldest daughter, the knighting of his eldest son, or—later on—his departure on a crusade. The vassal also swore *fealty* (fidelity) to his lord. The lord was understood to owe, in his turn, protection and justice to his vassal.

If the vassal broke this contract, the lord would have to get the approval of the court made up of the vassal's peers before he could proceed to a punishment such as depriving the vassal of his fief (*forfeiture*). If the lord broke the contract, the vassal was expected to withdraw his homage and fealty in a public act of defiance before proceeding to open rebellion. Sometimes the contract was written, sometimes it was oral. Sometimes the ceremony included a formal *investiture* by the lord: he would give his kneeling vassal a symbol of the fief that was being transferred to him, a twig or a bit of earth. When lord or vassal died, the contract had to be renewed with his successor. The son of a vassal, upon succeeding to his father's fief, often had to pay *relief,* a special, and often heavy, cash payment like a modern inheritance tax. If the vassal died without heirs, the fief would *escheat,* or revert to the lord, who could bestow it on another vassal or not as he saw fit. If the vassal's heir was still a minor, the lord exercised the right of *wardship* or guardianship until he came of age; this meant that the lord received the revenues from the fief, and if he was unscrupulous he could milk it dry.

Within a feudal kingdom, the king theoretically occupied the top position in an imaginary pyramid of society. Immediately below him would be his vassals, men who held fiefs directly from the king, called *tenants-in-chief.* But they in turn would be feudal lords: that is, they would have given out various parts of their own property as fiefs to their own vassals. These men, the king's vassals' vassals, would be the king's *rear vassals,* and so at the next lower level of the theoretical pyramid. But they too would often have vassals, and so on, for many more levels—a process called *subinfeudation.* But this was only theory.

Practice was more complicated still. A tenant-in-chief might hold only a very small fief from the king and not be a very important person at all, while a vassal's vassal's vassal might be rich and powerful. The dukes of Normandy, who were vassals to the king of France, were for some centuries much stronger than their overlord. An individual might receive fiefs from more than one lord, and so be vassal, owing homage and fealty, to both. What was he to do if one of his lords quarreled with another and went to war? Which of his lords would have a prior right to count on his military help? This kind of thing happened very often: one Bavarian count had twenty different fiefs held of twenty different lords. Gradually, there arose a new concept, that of a *liege* lord, the one to whom a vassal owed service ahead of any other. But in practice the difficulties often persisted. Even though feudal law became more and more subtle and complex, this was an era when armed might counted for more than legality.

Manorialism

All the complicated arrangements we have been discussing directly involved only the governing persons who fought on horseback as mounted knights and whose fiefs consisted of landed property known as manors or estates. Even if we include their dependents, the total would hardly reach ten percent of the population of Europe. Most of the other ninety percent of the people worked the land. In late Roman times, the large estate, owned by a magnate and worked by tenant farmers, had been called a *latifundium.* The tenant farmers, or *coloni,* were often descendants of small landowners who had turned over their holdings to the magnate in exchange for a guarantee of protection and a percentage of the crop. While the coloni were personally free, not slaves, they could not leave the ground they cultivated, nor could their children.

If the coloni lived in groups of houses close together, the latifundium could be described as a *villa.* Though conditions varied widely, we shall not be far wrong if we think of the late Roman latifundium becoming the medieval manor, the late Roman villa becoming the medieval village, and the late Roman coloni becoming the medieval serfs. As we shall see, the early German village community also contributed to the new social structure. While the Roman landed estate had often produced its food for sale at a profit in the town and city, the long centuries of disorder beginning with the Germanic invasions led to a decline of commerce, of cities, and of agriculture for profit. The medieval manor usually produced only what was needed to feed its own population.

The oldest method of cultivation was the two-field system, alternating crops and fallow so that fertility could be recovered. Later, especially in grain-producing areas, a three-field system was devised—one field for spring planting, one for autumn planting, and the third lying fallow. Elsewhere—in the mountains, in wine-growing areas, in the "Celtic fringes" of Brittany and Wales, and in the new areas of pioneer settlement in Eastern lands, there were many variant agricultural techniques and social arrangements. Here, as so often, there was no simple "typical" medieval way.

On the manor, oxen had originally pulled the plow, but the invention of the horse-collar (so that the horse would not strangle on the old-fashioned strap around his neck) and the use of horseshoes (which allowed the horse to plow stony soil that hurt the oxen's feet) helped make it possible to substitute horses for oxen. So did the increasing use of tandem harnessing, en-

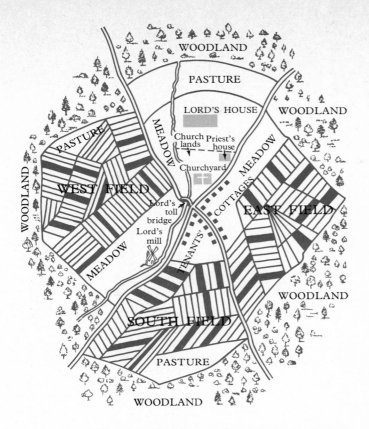

Plan of a medieval manor; the solid strips are the lord's demesne.

abling the horses to work in single file instead of side by side. A heavy-wheeled plow made its appearance in advanced areas.

The pattern of agricultural settlement, then, varied from region to region. But so far as a "typical" manor existed, each of its peasant families had holdings, usually in the form of scattered long strips, in the big open fields. In theory this gave each family a bit of the good arable land, a bit of the less good land, a bit of woodland, and so on. The strips might be separated from each other by narrow, unplowed *balks,* but there were no fences, walls, or hedges. The lord of the manor had his own strips, his *demesne* (perhaps a quarter to a third of the land), reserved for the production of the food that he and his household needed. It was understood that the peasants had to work this demesne land for the lord, often three days a week throughout the year, except perhaps in harvest time, when the lord could command their services until his crops were safely in the barns. Of course, the size of the lord's household varied, depending on how important a person he was in his feudal

relations with the king and other magnates. The more important he was, the more armed men he had to feed, and the more dependents and servants they all had, the more numerous and bigger would be his fiefs, and the more peasants he would need to work the manors that made up the fiefs.

When a serf died, his son made the lord a payment (*heriot*) in order to inherit his father's right to cultivate the family strips. In exchange for permission to pasture their beasts in the lord's meadows, the serfs might perform other duties. They often had to dig ditches or maintain the roads. They paid to have their grain ground at the lord's mill and their bread baked in his oven. They could not marry or allow their daughters to marry outside the manor without the lord's permission and usually the payment of a fine (*merchet*). They were bound to the soil, a hereditary caste of farm laborers, serfs. But they were not slaves; the lord could not sell them; they and their children descended with the land to the lord's heirs. On such a manor the peasants would live in a cluster of houses. A big manor might have several such villages, with perhaps isolated farmsteads in addition. On the other hand, a single village might lie partly in one manor and partly in another belonging to a different lord.

Undoubtedly the bulk of the man-hours of labor on the manor went directly into farming, and the bulk of the farming was grain-farming. But everywhere some of the manor's inhabitants would be craftsmen, such as blacksmiths or tanners. They too would cultivate their own plots of land. Each manor would have at least one church of its own, with its priest. If the lord was a great lord, he might have several priests, including his own chaplain for the household and a village priest for the local church.

The organization of the countryside by manors was earliest developed in eastern France and in parts of Italy and Germany. Even at its height, it did not include some parts of these and other European countries. But in the large areas where manorialism did prevail, the old Roman landlord's economic power over his tenants had fused with the traditional Germanic village chief's political power, and, by the eleventh century, with the governing rights that the lord received with his fief. The deep respect for custom probably tended to prevent the lord's extorting from his peasants more work or more food than they traditionally owed him. But they had no rights, and nowhere to appeal in cases where the lord was oppressive. Custom prevailed in the lord's court of justice, when he or his steward sat in judgment on the serf-tenants, enforcing the traditional rules of the village community. Custom regulated the bargaining agreements reached among the peasants for the use in common of plows and plowteams. Custom no doubt retarded inventiveness and stifled initiative, but it was the only thing that gave a serf the sense that he was protected against exactions and cruelties.

As for true slavery, where human beings are bought and sold like chattels, it hardly existed in early medieval Western Europe. If the serf was tied to the land, the land, in effect, was also tied to the serf. The serf could not be dispossessed unless he failed to live up to his obligations. Thus he could claim certain rights, even if they were only customary rights—his share of the complex manorial farming operations, his use of the strips which he *felt* to be his own. Moreover, as a Christian, the serf had a soul and could not be treated as a mere animal. Christianity never fitted well with a slave society, and throughout the Middle Ages the Church sought to make the serf's customary rights into real rights.

By no means all the peasants on every manor were serfs, however. Some of them were freemen, called *franklins* in England, who virtually owned the land they worked. And between the freemen and the serfs there were probably always landless laborers who were not tied to the land as serfs, and peasants with dues so light that they were almost freemen.

The manor was nearly, but not wholly, autarkic. The picture of a self-sufficient manor suggests a little community in which nothing is used that comes from the outside, in which long hours of labor are required simply to feed and clothe the community. Yet we know that nobles and their retinues fought lustily all through these years, and that they fought in armor, used swords, and built stone castles. Surely not every one of the thousands of manors could have produced steel and iron, or the salt, spices, building stones, lumber, furs, wines, and other commodities that never vanished altogether from Western life. Some of these wares were luxuries, and others were durable goods that were needed only occasionally. But they were in demand, and they were produced and sold. The manor then was only *comparatively* self-sufficient and unspecialized. It had surpluses and deficiencies which gave it the motives and the means for trade with outsiders. It provided something above a bare minimum of livelihood for at least a minority of its residents. Even in the early Middle Ages Western society was not reduced to a hand-to-mouth existence.

V   The Civilization of the Early Middle Ages in the West

A General View

In letters and in the arts, the early medieval centuries saw a severe, perhaps catastrophic, decline in the skills that had characterized the men of the Roman Empire, even in its latest periods. Judged by comparison with the achievements of Greek, Hellenistic, or Roman civilizations, or by those of the contemporary eastern Mediterranean world, Byzantine and Muslim, those of western Europe in these centuries may sometimes seem feeble or primitive, sometimes even pathetic. But this is only what one would expect in a world where the masters usually did not have the taste or the judgment to patronize writers or artists, and where life was often too turbulent to give men much leisure for the exercise of creative skills. Roads and postal systems—so effective in Roman days—now deteriorated; sea transport was far more uncertain; and cities, generally in human history the homes of culture and the commerce that makes the culture possible and available, often subsided into mere shells of their former splendor: mere forts in the countryside, where they had once been vibrant centers of communication, both physical and human. Technical skills were lost, and so was the command over what had become the whole western European language of intellectual and literary men: Latin. Nobody spoke good Latin any more, and few could write it. The slowly developing vernacular languages: the Romance-French, or the German, were used only infrequently, and usually hesitantly, for literary purposes.

All this is true, and yet a large question remains. Can one fairly use classical standards to judge the writing and the art of a postclassical age, evolving in many new directions? Most scholars would now be reluctant to do so, which is of course why we have avoided, though mentioning, the term "dark" in connection with these centuries. In fact, so much is known in our times about the original barbarian contributions to the culture of this period that it can probably now be evaluted with less prejudice than ever before. Not only did many barbarians love and admire the Roman world that their fellow barbarians were engaged in destroying, and therefore painstakingly keep alive, however crudely, the Roman literary and artistic tradition, but the widely traveled invading tribesmen brought with them art forms of their own, poetry, sculpture, and painting that only recently have begun to receive from scholars the appreciation that is their due.

Everywhere in the West, then, the story in general is the same, although it varies greatly in detail: the men of these centuries were moving gradually away from their Roman past, though still cherishing and often trying with varying degrees of success to imitate Roman models; and at the same time they were also creating new and original artifacts that reflected their own barbarian past. While the Christian faith that the invaders took from the dwellers in the Roman Empire gave them a more permanent and firmer link with Rome itself and with its traditions than they would otherwise have had, they could neither absorb the Roman heritage entire nor wholly abandon their own traditions and practices. In the cultural realm, then, as in the realm of institutions, what we shall find is an amalgam, a new combination of old elements. If we meet no Homer, no Virgil, no Phidias in the pages that follow, it may not necessarily mean that the men we shall encounter—many of them anonymous—are less worthy of our study or deserve our contempt. It means instead that they lived in different times, under different pressures, and expressed their artistic and intellectual drives in new and different ways. Far less well known than the civilizations of the ancient world, this early medieval western European civilization merits far more attention than it usually gets.

Latin Literature: Italy

It was naturally in Italy that the fight against the loss of the classical heritage was waged most vigorously and most successfully. Under the rule of the Ostrogothic king Theodoric (489–526), a great admirer of the Greek and Latin cultural tradition, two distinguished intellectuals combated the general decline: Boethius and Cassidorus.

Boethius (ca. 480–524), unlike most of his contemporaries, knew both Greek and Latin. Learned and versatile, he advised Theodoric on many points. He gave detailed directions to the king's brother-in-law, ruler of the Burgundians, for the making of a water-clock. He was a recognized authority on music, and in person he picked the best available harpist to play at the court of Clovis, the king of the Franks. He thwarted an effort of Theodoric's military paymaster to cheat the troops, by showing that the paymaster had "sweated" the silver from the coins. He held the posts of consul (now of course honorary, but still carrying enormous prestige) and of Master of the Offices, something very much like a prime minister and by no means honorary only.

Boethius planned a Latin translation of all the voluminous works of Plato and Aristotle, and in those small portions of the work that he completed he took care to make his translation as literal as possible. He also made the first efforts to use Aristotle's logical methods in dealing with Christian theology, writing works of his own on the art of argument. These were to serve as the inspiration, not to men of his own time, most of whom had little interest or ability in philosophical discourse, but to scholars and thinkers who lived six hundred and more years after his death, when philosophical disputation on theological questions became the fashion and the chief sign of an intellectual revival (see Chapter 8). Had Boethius survived to complete or even carry very far his plans for rendering the greatest Greek philosophers into Latin, western Europe perhaps would not have been denied these materials for another half millennium, and intellectual development in the West might have been speeded up. But only two years after making him Master of the Offices, Theodoric imprisoned Boethius on a charge of treasonable plotting against him.

After a year in jail, Boethius was executed at the age of forty-four, perhaps because he was sharply opposed to Arianism, the form of Christianity to which Theodoric and the Ostrogoths adhered.

In the later years of his life, Boethius wrote not only a treatise on music, but several influential works on theology, against the Arian and monophysite heretical views. In jail, he wrote his most famous work, *The Consolation of Philosophy,* a dialogue between himself in his cell and the female personification of Philosophy, who appears to him. Partly in verse, partly in prose, and wholly in excellent Latin, the *Consolation* is a moving and noble work, in which the prisoner seeks—and is helped by Philosophy to find—answers not only to the injustice he feels he is suffering, but also to the larger questions of human life and death on earth, and the relationships between man and God. Full of reminiscences of classical authors (Boethius was extremely well read in the classics, and probably had few if any books to refer to in prison) and so sometimes criticized for its lack of originality, the book dwells on the commonness of suffering, on the fickleness of fortune, which often punishes unjustly an innocent man, and on the transitoriness and relative worthlessness of worldly triumphs in any case. Everything we gain here on earth, even fame, will vanish away. Largely owing to this book, however, Boethius' own fame survived far more securely than that of any other mere successful Master of the Offices: *The Consolation of Philosophy* became one of the most popular books (and schoolbooks) of all later medieval centuries.

Cassiodorus (ca. 490–580) managed to stay in Theodoric's good graces, and long survived him. During the life of the Ostrogothic king, Cassidorus, like Boethius, became consul and Master of the Offices. He collected his royal master's official correspondence. But his great ambition was to found a new Christian university in Rome, where the sadly neglected classical subjects could be taught and where a real revival of learning and scholarship might take place. Perhaps it was too late for this in any case, but the terrible disorders that accompanied Justinian's reconquest of Italy from the Goths between 535 and 554 made fulfillment of the idea altogether impossible. Thwarted, Cassiodorus founded instead a monastery near Squillace, his birthplace on the Adriatic shore of the heel of Italy. Here among the brethren of his community—who lived, of course, according to the Rule of St. Benedict (see above, Chapter 4)—Cassiodorus tried to keep learning alive in its Christian form. The monks copied by hand not only the Bible but the best pagan Latin authors—Cicero, Virgil, and the rest—and those who had no taste for this bookish work cultivated the gardens and wheatfields and took care of the fishponds, which became especially famous, in order to feed the community. Cassiodorus himself wrote books: on spelling, to help the monastic scribes with their task: on the Psalms, to provide the biblical text with a classical commentary; and on the Soul, following in the footsteps of Cicero and his Greek masters. Some of his monks translated Greek works into Latin.

Far more typical of the period, however, were the views of Pope Gregory the Great (ca. 540–604, pope 590–604), whom we have already encountered as the talented administrator who kept the Church alive and kept Italy from falling into total chaos in the strife between Lombards and exarchate. Practical in every way, Gregory was ready to abandon the classical past if he could bring more order into the barbarian and Christian present. "The same lips," he wrote one of his bishops, "cannot sound the praises of Jupiter and the praises of Christ," and firmly enjoined him to stop holding conferences where ancient literature was read. In Gregory's own writings, the same practical tendency appears: his so-called *Dialogues* deal in four volumes with the lives and miracles of the Italian church fathers, providing edifying anecdotes in order to attract Christian readers away from pagan authors and toward the proper contemplation of their own future salvation. His commentary on the Book of Job interprets the Old Testament story in New Testament terms: Job becomes a type of Christ in his suffering, and the aim of the book is to make its readers behave better in this world.

But perhaps the most important of Gregory's writings is the great body of his surviving correspondence, more than a thousand letters dating from the fourteen-year period of his papacy. Sent to literally all corners of the Christian world, and dealing with every sort of problem in the management of the Church and its relations to the secular rulers, from the Byzantine emperor and the exarch down, these letters reflect Gregory's humanity, commanding habits, enormous sense of the importance of his office, and even, at times, unexpected humor. To a bishop in far-off Asia Minor, who had been trying unsuccessfully to convert a refugee Persian prince to Christianity, Gregory wrote that it was too bad the bishop had not yet succeeded in his pious aim, but that what really mattered was the effort, and the bishop would surely reap his heavenly reward just for trying. To lend point to this, he quoted a proverb apparently popular at the time: "Black the Ethiopian goes into the bath, and black he emerges, but the bathman gets his fee just the same." No other pope of the early Middle Ages has left us so large a number of letters, nor is there anything remotely resembling these documents as a vivid historical source: they provide a sustained flash of light for the scholar in a period very little known to us both before and after they were written.

Latin Literature: Gaul and Spain

As one moves away from Italy, the center of the Roman world, the survival and cultivation of Latin letters naturally grows even feebler. In Gaul, a highly romanized province, there did remain even into the period of the invasions a cultivated group of upper-class landowners and churchmen who still found it natural to communicate with each other in Latin, in the old-fashioned way, and with much of the old-fashioned style. There were good poets among them, but perhaps the most distinguished writer of all was chiefly a prose stylist, Sidonius Appolinaris (ca. 431–ca. 475).

Born of a family long prominent in imperial affairs, and educated at the school of Lyon (still a major Roman provincial center), Sidonius eventually became bishop of Auvergne in south-central France during the invasions of Visigoths and Burgundians, while Huns and Franks were active nearby. Yet in 147 letters, written with a conscious eye to future preservation and publication, Sidonius—essentially an aristocrat in his habits and tastes—writes almost as if nothing very alarming were happening in the outside world and as if he and his fellow nobles, well born and well educated, still had the say about what would happen in the future. True, he refers to the Germanic invaders, but with gentlemanly distaste, as underbred and coarse, not with the apprehension that they were bringing with them the doom of Sidonius and all his friends. He sneers at one of his fellow nobles who had forgotten himself so far as to learn the language of the barbarian German invaders.

Decorous parties on country estates, beautifully situated, with luxurious baths, tastefully decorated, sparkling drawing-room discussion full of epigram, careful cultivation of ornamental gardens as well as of vineyard and olive-grove, lavish picnics spread by devoted servants, due attention to setting a new mosaic floor, reading in the estate's library, and discussion of Virgil or Terence, games of tennis and dice: these are the occupations that chiefly concerned Sidonius and his wide circle of friends, all as proud of their noble Roman origins as he was himself. But he was a good Christian, made financial sacrifices for his flock, and showed vigor in combating the Arianism and barbarism of the Germans. His letters provide a corrective to the over-simple view of the barbarian inroads as producing a chaotic social upheaval.

By the time of the Frankish triumph in the next generation, the Gallo-Roman culture that Sidonius so proudly stood for had virtually died. There was now very little literary activity. We have some moving Latin hymns by a writer called Fortunatus, and of course we have the prose document already cited, the history of Gregory, bishop of Tours. As we know, it chronicles in a Latin that would have shocked Sidonius, much less Cicero, the unedifying behavior of the Merovingian rulers. But there is a vigorous if primitive quality about Gregory, a mixture of credulity, native goodness, and calm acceptance of atrocities that gives the reader deep insight into the Merovingian age. In Spain, too, further from Rome than Gaul but still a romanized province, there was a good deal of writing in Latin, at least down into the seventh century, which saw the *Etymologies* of Isidore (ca. 570–636), archbishop of Seville, a sort of encyclopedia. It reflects Isidore's own learning, extraordinary for its time, and his superstition and ignorance, which were far more typical. With all the defects that make a modern reader smile or shudder, Isidore's book became a standard reference work for several centuries after he wrote it.

Latin Literature: Britain, and the Continent Once More

The seventh century, then, saw the virtual end of literary activity in the classical vein on the Continent, and marks the low point of intellectual effort there as of political stability. For a different spirit, destined eventually to restore Roman culture to the Continent, we must turn to Britain, during Roman times a peripheral province, hardly participating in Roman civilization, and producing no Latin authors before the barbarian invasions. Christianity came to Britain, as we have seen, in two waves: one from Ireland, where it was of Gallic origin, and the other from Rome, at the very end of the sixth century and the beginning of the seventh in the mission sent by Gregory the Great, headed by a Greek from Asia Minor. And it was Christianity that produced in England, not a revival, but the very first original writing in Latin. The combined influence of the Celtic and the Roman tradition brought such fruitful results that by the end of the eighth century it was men from Britain who stimulated a revival on the Continent—sponsored by Charlemagne himself, who provided the necessary interest and patronage.

Of a large number of cultivated men, the greatest was Bede (ca. 672–735). Abbot of his own monastery, he could read Greek, knew the Latin writings of the church fathers intimately, and himself wrote a famous *Ecclesiastical History of the English People,* covering the story of the spread of Christianity in England from the arrival in 597 of the missions sent by Gregory the Great down to 732, almost to the moment of Bede's own death. Written in a Latin of astonishing vigor and purity, it tells us almost everything we know of the progress of the new religion among the pagan Anglo-Saxons, about the Church's relationship with the Anglo-Saxon kings, and about the foundation of the many monastic houses, where book-loving monks found a shelter for themselves and the books they loved. Bede's own even-tempered personality shines through the work, which sometimes rises to true poetic greatness.

For example, Bede tells how, in 627, when the still pagan king Edwin of Northumbria had received a letter from the pope, and a Latin missionary was at his court urging him to accept Christianity, he naturally called his witenagemot to consult them on the matter. One of Edwin's counselors then said:

Man's life here on earth, O King, seems to me—so far as its uncertainties go—just the same as if, when you were sitting at dinner in the wintertime with your companions in arms and their servants, and a great fire had been kindled in the middle of the hall, and the hall was warm with its heat, but outside all about there raged the storms of winter rain and snow, a sparrow might come to the house, and fly through it swiftly, entering at one window and flying out at another. For the time while the bird is inside the house, it feels no chill from the winter blast, but after this tiny spell of fair weather has passed, that lasts only for a moment, the sparrow quickly passes again from winter to winter, and so is lost to your view. In the same way, this life of men comes into being for a brief moment, but what follows it and what went before it we certainly do not know. So if this new teaching [i.e. Christianity] has brought us anything surer to cling to, I think it should be followed.*

Soon after, Edwin was converted. And the metaphor about human life on earth remains a moving and effective one more than thirteen centuries later.

It was churchmen from this cultural world of Britain that thrived while the Continent stagnated who helped make possible the great flowering of Latin letters that took place under Charlemagne. Alcuin of York (ca. 735–ca. 804), who had studied under a pupil of Bede, came to Charlemagne's court in 782, and helped to transform the palace school there into a serious and practical educational institution, where men studied the seven liberal arts, as generally understood by the medieval layman and cleric alike: grammar, rhetoric, and dialectic (the art of argument), and arithmetic, geometry, astronomy, and music. Alcuin wrote much himself, prose and verse, and took the lead in reviving biblical scholarship and in teaching such practical subjects as legible handwriting to the scribes who now began to copy manuscripts in monasteries. The survival of much of Latin literature we owe to the efforts of these Carolingian scribes.

Other literary men in great numbers worked in Charlemagne's time. Einhard imitated Suetonius in his biography of Charlemagne, but he also turned his hand to various other arts, including bronze-foundry and metalwork in general, taking the nickname of Bezaleel (the artisan in Exodus to whom the making of the Ark of the Covenant was entrusted) to show his craftsmanship. The splendid bronze grill around

*Bede, *Historia Ecclesiastica Gentis Anglorum,* Book II, chap. xiii (London and New York: Loeb Classical Library, 1930), I, 283 ff. Translation ours. In the distant Soviet Union there survives a manuscript of Bede's history contemporary with the author, with some notes written in a handwriting that scholars believe is that of Bede himself.

the gallery in Charlemagne's palace church at Aachen, still to be seen there (though now a part of the much later city hall), is thought to be Einhard's own work, or at least executed under his direction.

Another prolific writer was Theodulf, bishop of Orléans born in southern Gaul near the Spanish border, where classical civilization had never died out. He is now recognized as the author of the anonymous *Libri Carolini,* (*Books of Charles,* i.e., Charlemagne), an imposing theological treatise dealing with the problem of whether it was idolatrous to venerate holy images—a problem then severely agitating the Byzantine Empire (see Chapter 6), with which Charlemagne had diplomatic relations. Theodulf, who traveled widely, (he was one of Charlemagne's *missi dominici*) wrote verse accounts of his voyages and of the works of art he saw on his way. He had at least two of the most splendid surviving Bibles of the entire Middle Ages copied for him, written in gold letters on vellum entirely stained purple. On his estate of Germigny-des-Près along the Loire River, he also built for himself a private chapel than can still be seen, altered in many ways but containing the only surviving mosaic picture of the period in the West, a picture of the Hebrew Ark of the Covenant described in Exodus: it is no coincidence that Theodulf's chapel is the only church in Christendom dedicated to no saint, not even to Christ, but to God the Father himself.

The foundations laid by men such as these and others like them permitted their successors in the next two generations, after Charlemagne's empire had disintegrated, to write history, poetry, saints' lives, works on theology and ethics, and vast numbers of personal letters in Latin. In new monastic centers such as St. Gall in Switzerland, and across the Rhine in newly christianized Germany, the literary work made possible by the British immigrants who had been responsible for the "Carolingian Renaissance" went on, and the continuity of Western civilization had been assured.

Vernacular Literature: *Beowulf*

As we have seen, the distance of Britain from Rome and its failure to become completely latinized during antiquity paradoxically allowed it to profit greatly from the double wave of Latin

A page from Alcuin's edition of the Vulgate.

Christian missionaries—Celtic and papal—and so provide the needed stimulus for the Carolingian Latin literary revival. But by the same token, the thinness of the Latin veneer probably encouraged the Angles and Saxons and Jutes to produce a literature in their own language (we call it Anglo-Saxon or Old English) while the continental former Roman provinces were too inhibited by the overpowering prestige of Latin, and perhaps also delayed by far less stable political conditions than prevailed in Britain. At any rate, there were a good many writers in England who did not hesitate to write in their own language. Sometimes they were translators: Boethius' *Consolation of Philosophy* was rendered into Old English, and King Alfred the Great himself translated Bede's *Ecclesiastical History.* Sometimes they were original writers, setting down a group of proverbs, or the life of a saint, or a chronicle, or—in verse—an account of one battle or another.

But by far the most remarkable Old English literary survival is *Beowulf,* a poem of almost 3,200 lines, preserved in only a single manuscript in the British Museum, written down about the year 1000. Hundreds of scholars have written thousands of pages about this poem: almost every statement about it might be questioned by some authority, and what we say here is no exception. A fire damaged the unique manuscript in 1731; it was rebound in the 1860's in such a way that more words disappeared; after the fire but before the rebinding, two copyists, one an Icelander, had made transcripts of it in the 1780's: all this has naturally tended to keep hot the fires of scholarly controversy.

It is clear that the poem was composed well before the date of our present manuscript, perhaps as early as about 680 (it includes historical characters from the 500's), perhaps as late as 800 or even later. Until 1939, some scholars thought it had been composed in Northumbria, some in Mercia; but in that year a spectacular archaeological discovery at Sutton Hoo in Essex (East Anglia) turned up the ship-tomb of an East Anglian king dating from the late seventh or early eighth century and containing a harp, jewels, and armor like those described in *Beowulf*, which also includes a description of a ship-funeral. So now some scholars think the poem may be of East Anglian origin. Some scholars argue fiercely that the poem was written by a single author, others that it is a composite; some that it is a pagan poem with Christian interpolations, others that it breathes a wholly Christian spirit. Some think it has two parts, some six, some three. These arguments and others are likely to go merrily on without resolution. The poem has been described as "a museum for the antiquarian, a sourcebook for the historian, a treatise for the student of Christian thought, and a gymnasium for the philologist." It is, however, also unmistakably a poem.

Beowulf begins in Denmark, where it tells of the founding of the Danish royal line, and the building of the great hall called Heorot by King Hrothgar. Heorot is repeatedly raided by a savage monster, Grendel, who seizes and eats the Danish warriors as they lie asleep after dinner, until from over the sea in southern Sweden comes a hero, Beowulf, a Geat in the service of the Geatish king, Hygelac. Beowulf has come to rescue the Danes from the curse of Grendel; he lies in wait for the monster, and in single combat so severely grips his hand that Grendel has to flee, leaving his entire arm, ripped out at the socket, in the hands of Beowulf. The wound is fatal, of course. But Grendel's mother, in some ways more terrifying than her son, tries to avenge him, and Beowulf has to do combat with her at the bottom of a wild and lonely lake; he kills her too, and the Danes celebrate in delight. Then Beowulf returns home to the land of the Geats, and reports to his master, Hygelac, who receives him warmly. Eventually Beowulf himself becomes king of the Geats, and at the very end of a long life has a last victorious combat with a dragon who has stolen a hoard of treasure and is ravaging the country. The treasure is recovered, but Beowulf dies in the fight, and his funeral ceremonies end the poem.

Such a narrative of fighting and treasure would have surely provided rich entertainment to warriors gathered in a hall, perhaps like that of Edwin in the excerpt from Bede we have quoted above. *Beowulf* exalts the ideal of heroic behavior, but, again like Edwin's counselor, is deeply concerned with the transitoriness of human life: the climax of all Beowulf's heroism, and the end of the poem, is the hero's death and funeral. The monsters may be thought of as mere mythical creatures, but they have been assimilated by the poet into the framework of Christianity: he tells us that Grendel and his mother are descendents of Cain. But it is an almost incidental Christianity: the name of Christ is not mentioned nor is there reference to the Incarnation, the Crucifixion, or the Resurrection. The Christianity of the poem seems to have been superficially grafted on to a pagan stem. The fierceness of combat itself, the immense sensitivity of heroes to slights, real or imagined, and the heroic response to courteous treatment for a traveler or a man who saved one's life: these are familiar from other poems of heroic ages, like the *Iliad* and the *Odyssey*.

Here is a recent translation into modern English of several short passages from the poem:

Beowulf's trip to Denmark:

Foaming at the prow and most like a sea-bird
The boat sped over the waves, urged on by the wind;
until next day, at the expected time
so far had the carved prow come
that the travellers sighted land,
shining cliffs, steep hills,
broad headland. So did they cross the sea;
their journey was at an end. [ll. 217–224.]

Hrothgar's queen, Wealhtheow, thanks Beowulf for killing Grendel:

To him she carried the cup, and asked in gracious words
if he would care to drink; and to him she presented
twisted gold with courtly ceremonial—
two armlets, a corslet and many rings,

and the most handsome collar in the world.
I have never heard that any hero had a jewel
to equal that.... [ll. 1190–1196.]

       Applause echoed in the hall.
Wealhtheow spoke these words before the company:
"May you, Beowulf, beloved youth, enjoy
with all good fortune this necklace and corslet,
treasures of the people; may you always prosper;
win renown through courage, and be kind in your
    counsel
to these boys [her sons]; for that, I will reward you
    further.
You have ensured that men will always sing
your praises, even to the ends of the world,
as far as oceans still surround cliffs,
home of the winds. May you thrive, O prince,
all your life. I hope you will amass
a shining hoard of treasure. O happy Beowulf,
be gracious in dealing with my sons.
Here, each warrior is true to the others,
gentle of mind, loyal to his lord;
the thanes are as one, the people all alert,
the warriors have drunk well. They will do as I
    ask."
       Then Wealhtheow retired to her seat
beside her lord. That was the best of banquets. . . .
[ll. 1215–1234.]

Beowulf goes to Grendel's mother's lake:

Then the man of noble lineage left Heorot far
    behind,
followed narrow tracks, string-thin paths
over steep, rocky slopes—remote parts
with beetling crags and many lakes
where water-demons lived. He went ahead
with a handful of scouts to explore the place;
all at once he came upon a dismal wood,
mountains trees standing on the edge
of a grey precipice, the lake lay beneath,
blood-stained and turbulent. . . . [ll. 1407–1416.]*

    Although we shall find a spirit somehow simi-
lar to *Beowulf* in the later Old French *Song of
Roland*, there is no contemporary vernacular
poem truly comparable to it in any language.

The Arts

    In the arts, as in literature, the story is one
of a very gradual transition away from Roman

---

* Reprinted by permission of Farrar, Straus & Giroux,
Inc., and Macmillan & Co. Ltd. from Kevin Crossley-Hol-
land's translation of *Beowulf*. Translation © 1968 by Kevin
Crossley-Holland; introductory matter © 1968 by Bruce
Mitchell.

forms, thoroughly standardized and understood
in all the continental provinces, and adapted to
Christian needs and uses for at least two centuries before the barbarians arrived, toward
newer achievements introduced as the barbarians
themselves became more cultivated. The early
great churches of such important imperial cities
as Milan (San Lorenzo) or Trier were still the
large rectangular basilicas taken over from the
secular architecture of the Romans, but for certain smaller Christian structures, especially bap-
tisteries, then built detached from the main
church, innovations were tried: some were
square, with corner niches and a drum (Fréjus,
in southern France), others were polygonal
(Albenga, in northern Italy), and rich mosaic
decoration was characteristic. As soon as a barbarian tribe was firmly established in its new
territory, its kings as a matter of prestige built
churches, often small, it is true, but generally
imitative of the Roman models. Most of these
have disappeared, but we know from contemporary written accounts and from archaeological research that they often had domes, and tin
or gilded bronze roof tiles that shone in the sun.
In Merovingian times, marble quarries were
worked, especially in southwest France, and fine
stone capitals and slabs were even exported.
    From the Visigothic occupation in Spain
there survive several churches, such as the
seventh-century San Pedro de la Nave near the
Portuguese frontier, whose architecture is late
Roman but whose sculpture is clearly unclassical and in a new mood: in a capital showing
the sacrifice of Isaac, the hand of God emerges
from the heavens representing the voice of the
Lord telling Abraham to hold his upraised hand
and spare his son.
    For a still-existing Merovingian building one
must examine the seventh-century Baptistery of
St. John at Poitiers, later remodeled to some
extent, but still clearly showing its debt to later
Roman buildings, even though the sculptural
decoration and the ornamentation in terra-cotta
are now far cruder. At Poitiers too is the underground mausoleum of a seventh-century abbot,
Mellebaude (p. 147), modeled on the Gallo-
Roman tomb-chambers in which such a noble
as Sidonius, for example, or indeed any of his
ancestors for centuries before him, might have
been buried. In very good Latin on the wall are
painted inscriptions, well lettered, one of which
says "Everything goes from bad to worse, and

Exterior of San Pedro de la Nave from the southwest.

the end of time is near," a quite un-Roman senti-ment that reflects the pessimism of men who felt the degeneration of the times they lived in. Even more representative of a new era is a sculptured representation in the tomb-chamber itself: the two thieves crucified with Christ, each bound to a cross of his own that no Roman sculptor could have carved, so primitive are the figures, so star-ing the eyes, so crude the execution. Here, as for example in certain sculptured slabs of the same period found in excavations at St. Denis, just outside Paris (a most ancient and celebrated church in which French kings were later buried), one sees unmistakably the barbarian hand work-ing in a tradition that is all its own.

Also still almost miraculously preserved at Poitiers by the nuns at the Abbey of the Holy Cross is a small carved wooden bookstand owned by a Merovingian queen, Radegund, at the end of the sixth century. In the center of the carved reading surface is a lamb, representing Christ, and in each corner is the symbol of one of the four apostles, an eagle's head for John and a man's for Matthew, a bull's for Luke and a lion's for Mark. At the top, between two doves, is the Greek monogram for Christ, while at bottom, between two doves, is a cross in a circle. Along the sides two crosses in still another form balance each other. The whole is simple and harmonious, and thoroughly Mediterranean in inspiration, but in execution perhaps more primitive, show-

ing possibly the limitations of a barbarian wood-carver, and suggesting—if one is impression-able—both the piety and the ingenuousness of a Christian barbarian queen.

Two sculptured tombs in the crypt (under-ground chapel) of Jouarre, east of Paris, further illustrate the complexity of the era. The tomb of Agilbert, of the late seventh century, with its extraordinarily vivid and poignant representa-tion of men and woman praying at the Last Judgment, their arms upraised, is so unlike all other sculpture of the period in its intensity that it has been conjectured that the artist was an Egyptian Christian, one of those known to have fled from the Arab Muslim conquest (see Chap-ter 6). By contrast, the tomb of Theodechilde, of the first half of the eighth century, with its splendid carved shells and beautifully lettered Latin inscription, is in the fullest Roman tradi-tion. Jouarre had close connections with Britain, and its sculptures have been compared with those of the early sculptured crosses of Ireland (p. 161) and northern England, where it is possible also that Egyptian influences had penetrated.

Not only Egypt but the Byzantine Empire too made its contribution to the art of the West during these centuries. There were of course the great monuments built in Rome and Ravenna itself by Greeks or artists trained in the Greek school, dating back to the sixth century, all well known. But this was imperial territory down to

751. More striking are the frescoes in the tiny church in a remote village in northern Italy, Castelseprio, where the bishops of Milan had a summer residence. Totally unknown until 1944, these were revealed when some soldiers scraped the plaster off the wall. Although there is still much debate among scholars as to the date when they were painted, it seems probable that they belong to the eighth or early ninth century, and they reflect a classical revival that had been taking place at Byzantium itself since the seventh century. Compared with the figures of the tomb of Mellebaude, these frescoes reveal an extraordinary sophistication.

To find clear-cut examples of the kind of art the barbarians brought with them, it is easiest to turn to the "minor arts" of goldsmithing and jewelry. As the Huns drove before them into Europe the Germans who had settled along the shores of the Black Sea, the Germans brought with them objects made there by local craftsmen working in an Iranian or other Eastern tradition, and characterized by brilliant color and the use of gems (often from as far away as India) or colored glass for ornamentation. Once inside the borders of the Roman Empire, the tribes-men, notably the Ostrogoths, naturally retained their taste for this sort of thing, and presumably artists they had brought with them as well as their own craftsmen continued the tradition. Many of these marvelous (and altogether unclassical) objects have been found in barbarian graves in central Europe, and also in Gaul, Spain, and Italy. An eagle-shaped clasp from Spain (p. 146) is a fine example of a not uncommon type of ornament of this school.

To understand the influences exerted by the Byzantine outpost of the exarchate at Ravenna, we must make a point often overlooked: between 642 and 752 virtually all the popes were themselves Greek or Syrian by origin. These Eastern popes surely sponsored further imports from the East and fostered a continued popularity of Eastern objects. The magnificent jeweled gold bookcovers made probably in Rome for the Bible that Pope Gregory the Great himself gave to the Lombard queen Theodelinde provide a convincing example. Four large jewels in the corner of each cover are actually classical portrait-gems, often now taken out of some treasured collection to embellish this sort of artwork of a quite different tradition.

The sacrifice of Isaac: capital at San Pedro de la Nave. The hand of God, representing the voice of the Lord, emerges from the heavens at the critical moment to stop Abraham from killing his son.

The sculptured figures in Mellebaude's tomb: the two thieves who were crucified with Christ, bound to their crosses.

From later in the seventh century comes the jeweled gold crown of the Visigothic king Recceswinth (see color plates), one of a large collection of Visigothic royal crowns, of which several can be seen in the Cluny Museum in Paris. Similar jeweled objects—a purse (p. 147), a harp, and weapons—were found in the great Sutton Hoo ship-burial in Essex, England, in 1939, to which we have referred in connection with *Beowulf*. To those astonished archaeologists and students of Old English poetry who first looked at the Sutton Hoo find, it must have seemed as if they were seeing illustrated in real life the lines of the poem that tell how

*. . . then they laid their dear lord,
the giver of rings, deep within the ship
by the mast in majesty; many treasures
and adornments from far and wide were gathered
   there.
I have never heard of a ship equipped
more handsomely with weapons and war-gear,
swords and corselets; on his breast
lay countless treasures that were to travel far
with him. . . .* *

And the presence in the royal funeral-ship at Sutton Hoo of a massive round silver plate made at Byzantium in the period 491–518, and of two silver spoons with Greek inscriptions, helped to emphasize the continuous contacts between the barbarians and the East.

It was indeed the influences from the East greatly stimulated by the influx of barbarians that led to the gradual abandonment of the realistic representation of men and beasts in art. Imported Byzantine silver, ivories, and textiles, as well as the Byzantine monuments like those of Ravenna, on Italian soil, surely helped speed the change in styles. Though the story of Eastern influences and its expression by Western artists is a complicated one, it is strikingly exemplified by an extraordinary row of six stucco

* Reprinted by permission of Farrar, Straus & Giroux, Inc., and Macmillan & Co., Ltd. from Kevin Crossley-Holland's translation of *Beowulf*. Translation © 1968 by Kevin Crossley-Holland; introductory matter © 1968 by Bruce Mitchell.

The carved wooden reading desk of the saintly Merovingian queen Radegund.

The baptistery of St. John, Poitiers, from the northeast.

statues of saints that decorates the front of a small church (Santa Maria in Valle) at Cividale in northern Italy. These saints were carved by sculptors whose skills would have permitted them to do anything they chose. The stiff ceremonial garments obviously cover genuine human bodies; and though hieratic positions are preferred for the figures, the detail is deliberately realistic. Scholars now date these remarkable statues to about the year 800 and ascribe them to Byzantine artists working in Italy.

In strong contrast is the almost abstract effect

of a relief of the Adoration of the Magi on the altar of Duke Ratchis, in the same small town of Cividale, ascribed to native Lombard craftsmen and to a period a little more than half a century earlier. Here we are almost back to the primitive quality of the two thieves in Abbot Mellebaude's tomb at Poitiers. But we have come the full distance and more when we consider a seventh-century German tomb-slab (stele) now at Bonn. On one side the warrior stands sword in hand, about to be bitten by the serpent of death; on the other, Christ stands over his tomb with a halo (but also with a spear!).

Although in a few cases, such as the paintings at Castelseprio and the stucco saints at Cividale, we have found monuments reflecting powerful classicizing influences, we must wait until the Carolingian period for a full revival. Surviving monuments in Italy gave the artists some of their inspiration, and Charlemagne's desire and ability to attract the best craftsmen from anywhere in Europe enabled them to put it into effect. Paintings and mosaics in Roman churches —Santa Maria Antiqua and Santa Maria Maggiore in particular, dating to the fifth and sixth centuries, illustrated for the men of the eighth and ninth centuries, as they do today, what could be made of Christian subjects treated in the classical style.

Wall paintings and mosaics are fixed monuments, and only a traveler can visit them if they are widely separated from each other; but books are transportable, and it was largely through book illustration—the famous illumination of manuscripts—that inspirations from one region

Details from two sculptured tombs in the crypt of Jouarre: (left) the tomb of Agilbert;
(right) the tomb of Theodechilde.

From Cividale: (above) three holy women; (below) the sculptured Adoration of the Magi.

and one school intermingled in other regions with influences from other schools. So north Italian books in which all these classical and Byzantine influences had been brought to bear traveled across the Alps, into Gaul, and into Britain with Gregory the Great's missionaries: there actually survive two illustrations from a Bible that came along on the expedition, which together with other books and objects, now lost or unidentifiable, brought the Mediterranean traditions into England, already exposed to them indirectly by the Celtic missionaries from Ireland. And in due course the same influences penetrated into Germany by the same route, where artists under the Ottonian Emperors would pick them up.

Illustrative of this north Italian school of painting, so influential in transmitting its influences northward, is a drawing from a manuscript of a book of church law (early ninth century) at Vercelli. Constantine the Great is shown on his throne at the Council of Nicaea with the bishops who signed its decrees, while below the throne, books propounding the Arian heresy are being burned.

To the "Carolingian Renaissance," notably marked by manuscript illustration, the specifically barbarian contribution came not in the form of figure-drawing, either of persons or of animals, but in the decorative geometric patterning that often characterized barbarian craftsmanship in the metal objects we have discussed. It appears as well in the contemporary written descriptions of other objects (Beowulf was given by a Dane a sword whose "iron blade was engraved with deadly twig-like patterning"—ll. 1458-1459)—which we are specifically told was an heirloom); and it reappears in book illustration with the breathtaking patterns to be seen in the great Celtic manuscripts: the Books of Durrow, Echternach (brought from Britain to Germany), Lindisfarne, and Kells, executed in the seventh and eighth centuries (see color plates). A page with interlace border from the earliest of these, the Book of Durrow, shows St. Matthew in a cloak of complex checkerboard design; both border and cloak are of barbarian inspiration. The Celtic missionaries who went from Ireland to the Continent and founded the monastery at Bobbio in Italy took these talents with them, and there learned what the indigenous craftsmen had to teach them. By the time we reach the celebrated Book of Kells the

A tomb stele now at Bonn: on one side a warrior, on the other Christ.

earlier stiffness of the human figure is gone, and the geometric patterns have enriched themselves and proliferated; in some cases the birds and fish that were used by continental artists for ornamentation also appear. Coptic influences from Egypt, and even Iranian ones can also be seen in some of the manuscript illuminations produced just before the time of Charlemagne, notably at the French monastery of Corbie.

Charlemagne himself made five trips to Italy, which have been called "the stages by which Frankish culture climbed to the level of Caro-

lingian culture," deepening and carrying further the connection begun by Pepin. Lombards from northern Italy joined the Anglo-Saxons like Alcuin at a court that had no permanent residence during the long years of continual campaigning, but that settled in 794 at Aachen, where the new royal (soon imperial) residence was built at forced-draft speed. From Rome and Ravenna there poured in exciting works of art, many of which have of course disappeared, like the equestrian statue of Theodoric, itself an imitation of that of Marcus Aurelius. We have

One of the jeweled gold bookcovers for the Bible that Gregory the Great gave to the Lombard queen Theodelinde.

Book illustration: Constantine at Nicaea, from a canon-law book at Vercelli.

preserved a model in bronze of a similar statue of Charlemagne himself. In the chapel at Aachen, Charlemagne's marble throne is still in place.

To Aachen came Romans, Lombards, Greeks from southern Italy and probably from Byzantium itself, Syrians, Anglo-Saxons, Irishmen, Spaniards from the Visigothic parts of Spain, Jews, Arabs, and every sort of inhabitant of Gaul and Germany. Architects and artisans—including, perhaps, some Greeks—were striving to

create a kind of synthesis between the imperial palace in Constantinople and the papal residence in the Palace of St. John Lateran in Rome. Charlemagne especially enjoyed receiving foreign travelers, who came from everywhere, many of them, especially officials, bringing rich gifts—relics, books, textiles, jewels. In 796 arrived the treasure captured from the Avars, who had been pillaging for two centuries. It filled sixteen ox-carts. The most sensational present was sent in 802 by the caliph at Bagdad, Harun al Rashid (see Chapters 6 and 9): the famous white elephant, Abu'l Abbas, who became a general favorite at Aachen, and whose bones remained a wonder for many centuries after he died. Harun also sent Charlemagne a marvelous clock of gilded bronze, with twelve mounted mechanical knights who on the stroke of noon emerged from twelve little doors that shut behind them. Silken tents, perfumes, oriental robes abounded. The exotic atmosphere of the court remained a vivid memory for many centuries after the glory had departed. Charlemagne had a good many beautiful daughters, whom the gentle aging Alcuin nicknamed "the crowned doves that flit about the chambers of the palace," and against whom he warned his students.

In a New Testament made expressly for Charlemagne in the early 780's and richly illustrated, the dedication verses read "Charles, the pious king of the Franks with Hildegard his glorious wife ordered me to write down this work," and the simple words conceal only momentarily the appearance of a new factor in early medieval art, the presence and determination of a powerful royal patron that provided a wholly new stimulus to artists. A portrait of Christ from this early manuscript reflects the influence of paintings recently done at Rome. It is only one of literally hundreds of miniature paintings from surviving Carolingian books, among which scholars distinguish between those painted at court and those produced in provincial centers. Similarly the art of the worker in precious metals and jewels flourished with new vigor, and that of the bronze-founder—having virtually perished—was revived at Aachen, where the still-existing grillwork around the gallery of Charlemagne's palace-chapel illustrates the development of a variety of styles, and where great bronze doors, several with ornamental lion's-head handles, testify to classicizing influence at work. And these and all the other currents can be seen in ivory carvings of the period.

With the Carolingian artistic explosion and its continuation in modified form by the Ottonians, after a lapse during the decline of the early tenth century, we have returned to monuments far better known to students than those of the earlier so-called "darker" ages, upon which we have therefore concentrated our attention, in an effort to restore the balance in a summary account.

Reading Suggestions on the West in the Early Middle Ages

GENERAL ACCOUNTS

T. Hodgkin, *Italy and Her Invaders,* 8 vols. (Clarendon, 1885–1899). A detailed treatment of these centuries in Italy, a monumental work of nineteenth-century scholarship, by no means superseded.

J. B. Bury, *The Invasion of Europe by the Barbarians* (Macmillan, 1928). A helpful shorter account.

E. A. Thompson, *The Early Germans* (Oxford Univ. Press, 1965). A brief up-to-date general study.

F. Lot, *The End of the Ancient World and the Beginnings of the Middle Ages* (Knopf, 1931). A balanced survey by a French historian.

The Cambridge Medieval History, Vol. II (Macmillan, 1913). One of the few scholarly surveys of the whole period in a single volume.

C. Dawson, *The Making of Europe* (Macmillan, 1933; *Meridian). A scholarly Catholic account.

SPECIAL STUDIES

J. M. Wallace-Hadrill, *The Barbarian West: The Early Middle Ages, A.D. 400–1000* (*Torchbooks). Up-to-date brief account.

J. H. Clapham and E. Power, eds., *The Cambridge Economic History,* Vol. I (Cambridge Univ. Press, 1941). A scholarly study of agrarian life in the Middle Ages.

A. Dopsch, *The Economic and Social Foundations of European Civilization* (Harcourt, 1937). An important work revising earlier notions of the breakdown that occurred after the "fall" of Rome.

S. Dill, *Roman Society in Gaul in the Merovingian Age* (Macmillan, 1926), and *Roman Society in the Last Century of the Western Empire,* 2nd ed. (Macmillan, 1899; *Meridian). Useful social and cultural accounts.

Carl Stephenson, *Medieval Feudalism* (*Great Seal Books). The best simple introductory manual.

M. Bloch, *Feudal Society,* English trans., 2 vols. (Univ. of Chicago Press, 1961–1964). The masterpiece of a great French scholar.

A. C. Flick, *The Rise of the Medieval Church and Its Influence on the Civilization of Western Europe from the First to the Thirteenth Century* (Putnam's, 1909). A good survey.

L. J. Daly, *Benedictine Monasticism: Its Formation and Development Through the Twelfth Century* (Sheed and Ward, 1965). A valuable general account of a major monastic order.

H. Pirenne, *Mohammed and Charlemagne* (Norton, 1939). Defense of the highly controversial thesis that the Arab conquest of the Mediterranean harmed western Europe more than the German invasions had done.

R. Winston, *Charlemagne: From the Hammer to the Cross* (Bobbs-Merrill, 1952). The best biography available in English.

H. Fichtenau, *The Carolingian Empire: The Age of Charlemagne* (*Torchbooks). A competent study.

C. H. Haskins, *The Normans in European History* (Houghton, 1915). A very readable and sympathetic introduction.

G. Duby and R. Mandrou, *A History of French Civilization,* trans. from the French (Random House, 1964). Though this admirable book is useful for all French history right up to the present, its first few pages provide a particularly good bird's-eye view of France at the end of the early Middle Ages.

F. M. Stenton, *Anglo-Saxon England,* 2nd ed. (Clarendon, 1950). A standard account.

P. H. Blair, *Roman Britain and Early England, 55 B.C.–871 A.D.* (Nelson, 1963). Supplements Stenton and is equally scholarly.

D. Whitelock, *The Beginnings of English Society* (*Penguin). A briefer introduction to Anglo-Saxon England.

E. K. Rand, *Founders of the Middle Ages* (Harvard University Press, 1928). Excellent essays on early medieval men of letters.

M. L. W. Laistner, *Thought and Letters in Western Europe, A.D. 500 to 900* (Methuen, 1931). A good scholarly study.

R. W. Chambers, *Beowulf: An Introduction to the Study of the Poem,* suppl. C. L. Wrenn, 3d ed. (Cambridge Univ. Press, 1959). A full compendium of the scholarship on the poem.

Gwyn Jones, *The Norse Atlantic Saga* (Oxford Univ. Press, 1964) and *A History of the Vikings* (Oxford Univ. Press, 1968). The two latest and best studies.

J. Hubert, J. Porcher, and W. F. Volbach, *Europe of the Invasions* (Braziller, 1969). Excellent picture book with short texts.

SOURCES   Gregory of Tours, *History of the Franks* ed. O. M. Dalton (Clarendon, 1927). The account of a sixth-century historian.

A. J. Grant, ed., *Early Lives of Charlemagne* (Chatto & Windus, 1922).

Sidonius, *Poems and Letters,* trans. W. B. Anderson (Harvard Univ. Press, 1936). The observations of a fifth-century Roman aristocrat.

Venerable Bede (Beda Venerabilis), *Ecclesiastical History of the English Nation* (Dutton, 1954). An adequate translation.

Beowulf, trans. Kevin Crossley-Holland (Farrar, 1968). A good recent translation.

HISTORICAL FICTION   H. Muntz, *The Golden Warrior* (Scribner's, 1949). A well-written, historically sound novel of the Norman conquest of England.

W. Bryher, *The Roman Wall* (Pantheon, 1954). A short novel of life on the frontier of the Roman Empire during the decline.

W. Bryher, *The Fourteenth of October* (Pantheon, 1952). Another good novel about the Norman conquest of England.

6

Eastern Christendom and Islam

To the Late Eleventh Century

I Byzantium: The State

At the far southeastern corner of Europe, on a little tongue of land still defended by a long line of massive walls and towers, there stands a splendid city. Istanbul it is called now, a Turkish corruption of three Greek words meaning "to the city." After 330, when the Roman emperor Constantine the Great, abandoning Rome, decided to make it his capital, it was often called Constantinople, the city of Constantine, but it also retained its ancient name: Byzantium. For more than eleven hundred years thereafter it remained the capital of the Roman Empire, falling to the Ottoman Turks in 1453.

The waters that surround it on three sides are those of the Sea of Marmora, the Bosporus, and the city's own sheltered harbor, the Golden Horn. A few miles north, up the narrow swift-flowing Bosporus, lies the entrance into the Black Sea. To the southwest of the city, the Sea

Above: Sixth-century ivory figure of the archangel Michael, probably made at Constantinople.
Above right: The creation of the world: mosaic scenes from Genesis in St. Mark's, Venice.
Right: Pages from a fourteenth-century Arabic manuscript of the Koran: Sura II, verses 254–259.

186

of Marmora narrows into the Dardanelles, the long passage into the Aegean, an island-studded inlet of the Mediterranean. The Dardanelles, the Sea of Marmora, and the Bosporus not only connect the Black Sea with the Mediterranean but separate Europe from Asia. Together, these are the "Straits," perhaps the most important strategic waterway in European diplomatic and military history. The city dominates the Straits. In the fifth century before Christ, a shrewd Persian general was told that the earliest Greek settlers had built a town across the Straits in Asia, some seventeen years before anyone had colonized the European site of Istanbul. "Then," said he, "they must have been laboring under blindness. Otherwise, when so excellent a site was open to them, they would never have chosen one so greatly inferior."*

To the Slavs, both of Russia and of the Balkans, who owe to it their religion and their culture, Byzantium has always been Tsargrad, city of the emperor. This was the center of a civilization in many ways similar to that of western medieval Europe, yet in others startlingly different.

The Emperor

Byzantium called itself New Rome. Its emperors ruled in direct succession from Augustus. Its population, predominantly Greek in race and language, called itself not Hellene (the name of the ancient Greeks for themselves) but Rhomaean, Roman. Despite the importance of the Roman tradition, many non-Roman elements—Christian, Greek, Armenian—became increasingly important in Byzantine society. A Roman of the time of Augustus, to say nothing of the republic, would have found himself ill at ease and out of place in, say, eleventh-century Byzantium. After Constantine himself had become a Christian, the emperor was of course no longer God. But he was ordained of God, and his power remained divine. As there could be but one God in heaven, so there could be but one emperor on earth. The pagan tradition of the god-emperor was modified, not abandoned.

In theory, the will of God manifested itself in the unanimous consent of the people, the senate

* Herodotus, *History,* trans. G. Rawlinson (New York, 1862), IV, 144.

(established at Constantinople in the Roman pattern by Constantine himself), and the army to the choice of each new emperor. In practice, the reigning emperor usually chose his own heir, often his own son, by co-opting him during his own lifetime, as he had done at Rome. When an emperor selected somebody not his son, public opinion required that he should adopt him formally. Byzantine dynasties sometimes lasted several centuries. But politicians and the mob often intervened. They imprisoned and exiled emperors, murdered them, blinded or mutilated them (which made them ineligible to rule again), and enthroned their own candidates.

Each new emperor was raised aloft on a shield as a sign of army approval, so becoming imperator, commander in chief. By the mid-fifth century, he was also formally crowned by the highest dignitary of the Church, the patriarch of Constantinople. He would swear to defend the Christian faith, and in addition to the crown received a purple robe and a pair of high purple boots. In the seventh century, the emperor began to call himself *basileus*, King of Kings, in token of his military victory over the Persians. Later still, he added the term *autokrator*. Empresses bore corresponding feminine titles and in general played an important role. Their images often appeared on the imperial coinage. Three times in Byzantine history women ruled alone, without a male emperor.

The emperor was an absolute ruler. Though now only the servant of the Christian God, he was still hedged about by the old divinity. God bestowed his position upon him, and lent victory to his arms. Since the state was founded on the favor of heaven, there could be no need for change. Although the individual autocrat might be overthrown by the conspiracy of a rival, autocracy as such was never challenged. And of course these divinely awarded powers entailed immense earthly responsibilities: "Imperial power," says an eighth-century text, "is a legal authority established for the good of all subjects. When it strikes a blow, it is not through hatred; if it grants a reward, it is not through favoritism; but like the referee in a fight, it awards to each man the recompense he deserves." "And if," added a ninth-century patriarch more daring than most, "the Emperor, inspired by the devil, gives a command contrary to the divine law, no-one should obey him. Every subject can rebel against any administrative act which runs counter to the law, and even against the Emperor if he allows himself to be governed by his passions." Thus the Byzantines believed that revolution was the only recourse against imperial tyranny.

An elaborate and rigid code of etiquette governed every movement the emperor made every day of the year. So complex were the rules of his life that entire treatises were written to describe them. His subjects remained silent in his presence. He spoke and gave his commands through simple, brief, and established formulas. When he gave gifts, his subjects hid their hands beneath their cloaks, a Persian ritual gesture implying that the touch of a mere human hand would soil his. Those admitted to audience approached him with their arms held fast by officials, and ceremoniously fell on their faces in obeisance when they reached the throne. On public occasions the emperor was acclaimed in song, to the sound of silver trumpets.

The Law

As the direct agent of God, the emperor was responsible for the preservation of the tradition of the Roman law. He alone could modify the laws already in effect or proclaim new ones. From time to time the emperor ordered the periodic redrafting and recompiling of the statute books. Thus he had ready to his hand an immensely powerful instrument for preserving and enhancing his power.

Justinian (reigned 527–565) between 528 and 533 ordered his lawyers to dispose of obsolete, repetitious, and conflicting enactments, and thus to codify existing law. His *Code* included all legislation since Hadrian (117–138). The authoritative opinions of legal experts were codified in

Sixth-century mosaic in the Church of San Vitale, Ravenna, showing the emperor Justinian and attendants.

the *Digests,* an even bulkier work. The *Institutes,* a handbook for students, served as an introduction to both compilations. All these were set down in the Latin in which they had been issued, but Justinian's own laws, the *Novels,* or newly passed enactments, appeared in Greek.

Not until the eighth century did a new collection appear—the *Ekloga* (wholly in Greek)—which modified Justinian's work in accordance with Christian attitudes toward family relationships and with the decreasingly Roman and increasingly Greek and oriental character of the empire. The *Ekloga* softened the death penalty provided for many offenses by earlier law, and substituted punishments less severe, though still often entailing cruel mutilations. Under Leo VI (886–912), a new collection, called the *Basilics,* made its appearance. Leo's own new laws show the emperor rejecting much that dated from an earlier period when the absolutism of the emperor had not been so fully developed.

In the Byzantine Empire, justice could be rendered only in the emperor's name. He was the supreme judge, and the rendering of justice was perhaps his most important function. Subordinate officials handed down decisions only by virtue of the power he had delegated to them, and could in theory always be overruled on appeal to him. The emperors themselves often rendered judgment in person in quite ordinary cases brought to them by their subjects. Heraclius (610–641) punished an officer who had stolen the land of a poor widow and had beaten her son to death. Theophilus (829–842) appeared every week on horseback at a given church, and handed down judgments so fair and equitable and unbiased that they have passed into legend:

One day when the emperor appeared, a poor woman threw herself at his feet in tears, complaining that all light and air had been shut off from her house by a huge and sumptuous new palace which a high official of the police was building next door. Moreover, this official was the brother of the Empress. But the Emperor paid no heed to this. He ordered an instant inquiry, and when he found that the woman had told the truth, he had the guilty man stripped and beaten in the open street, commanded the palace to be torn down, and gave the land on which it stood to the woman. Another time, a woman boldly seized the bridle of the horse which the Emperor was riding, and told him that the horse was hers. As soon as Theophilus got back to the palace, he had her brought in, and she testified that the general of the province where she lived had taken the horse away from her husband by force, and had given it to the Emperor as a present to curry favor with him. Then he had sent the rightful owner of the horse into combat with the infantry, where he had been killed. When the general was haled before the Emperor and was confronted by the woman, he finally admitted his guilt. He was dismissed from his post, and part of his property confiscated and given to the plaintiff.*

The emperors of the later ninth century took greater care in the systematic appointment of judges and created a kind of legal-aid bureau to enable the poor of the provinces to make appeals to the capital. Judges were obliged to render written decisions and to sign them all. New courts were set up and new officials were created. Later, even in the provinces, side by side with the martial law administered by the local commanding general, we find instances when even soldiers were tried in civil courts for civil offenses.

The "sacred palace," the emperor's residence, was the center of the state, and the officials of the palace were the most important functionaries of the state: administrative, civil, and military. All officials had a title that gave them a post in the palace, as well as a rank among the nobility. At Byzantium, many of the greatest and most influential officials were eunuchs, an oriental feature of the state that astonished Westerners and made them uneasy. There was never a prime minister, but in practice an imperial favorite often controlled policy.

War

As defenders of the faith, the Byzantine emperors fought one enemy after another for eleven hundred years. Sometimes the invaders were moving north and west from Asia: Persians in the seventh century, Arabs from the seventh century on, and Turks beginning in the eleventh century.

The Byzantine Empire was often shaken by these blows: the provinces of Syria and Egypt were lost forever in the seventh century as a result of the impact of Persians and Arabs. And western Europe was not entirely spared the effects of these invasions. The Arab expansion

*C. Diehl, "La Légende de Théophile," *Seminarium Kondakovianum,* IV (1931), 35. Our translation.

brought waves of Muslims into Sicily and southern Italy, and across the Straits of Gibralter into Spain, whence a small force even challenged the Franks at Tours in 732. But Charles Martel's victory at Tours was a far less significant achievement in checking the Muslim tide at high-water mark than the victory of the Byzantine emperor Leo III the Isaurian, who had repelled a major Arab attack on Constantinople itself in 717, fifteen years before. Had it not been for Byzantium, we might all be Muslims.*

Byzantium thus served as a buffer that absorbed the heaviest shock of Eastern invasions, and cushioned the West against them. The Byzantine state was also engaged on all its frontiers in almost constant warfare against a variety of other enemies. Sometimes they were Asians, who had drifted into Europe from what is now Russia. In this category belong the Huns of the fifth century, the Avars of the sixth and seventh, the Bulgars of the seventh and succeeding centuries, the Magyars of the ninth and later centuries, and the Pechenegs and Cumans of the eleventh, twelfth, and thirteenth centuries. All these peoples were initially Turkic or Finnish or Mongolic nomads, living in felt tents, drinking fermented mare's milk and eating cheese, and quite at home for days at a time on the backs of their swift horses.

Sometimes the enemies were native Europeans, like the Slavs, who first appeared in the sixth century and filtered gradually south into the empire thereafter in a steady human flow that covered the entire Balkan Peninsula, even Greece, with Slavic settlement. In the northeastern part of the Balkan Peninsula just south of the Danube, the Slavs were conquered by the Hunnic tribe of the Bulgars, but they slowly absorbed their conquerors. By the tenth century the Bulgarians had no recognizable Asiatic traces left, but were thoroughly Slavic. These Bulgars, and much later the Slavic Serbs to the west of them, fought long and exhausting wars against Byzantium. So did the Russians, another Slavic people, whose Scandinavian upper crust was gradually absorbed by a slavic lower class. They first assaulted Byzantium from the water in 860, having floated in canoes down the river Dnieper and sailed across the Black Sea; and they several times repeated the attack. Beginning in the eleventh century, the enemies were western

* Which does not mean we would be any worse, only that we would be different.

Europeans: Normans from the southern Italian state in Italy and Sicily, Crusaders from France and Germany and Italy, freebooting commercial adventurers from the new Italian cities seeking to extract economic concessions by force or to increase the value of the concessions they already held.

For more than seven hundred years after Constantine, until the late eleventh century, when Turks and Normans alike inflicted serious defeats, the Byzantines were able to hold their own. Though hostile forces sometimes swarmed to the very foot of the land walls or threatened to launch a maritime invasion from across the Straits, Constantinople itself remained inviolable and secure until 1204. In that year it was taken for the first time by a mixed force of Venetian traders eager for profit, and French, Italian, and German Crusaders, who should have been fighting the Muslims in Palestine.

Only a state with phenomenally good armies and navies could have compiled so successful a military record. From all periods of Byzantine history there survive treatises on the art of war, discussing new ways of fighting, new weapons. The Byzantines were adaptable, learning and applying lessons from their successive enemies. Often commanded by the emperor in person, carefully recruited and thoroughly trained, well armed and equipped, entertained by bands playing martial music, served by medical and ambulance corps, a signal corps with flashing mirrors, and intelligence agencies far more competent than those maintained by their rivals, the Byzantine armies, though occasionally defeated, by and large maintained their superiority.

The same is almost as true of the Byzantine navies. The appearance of a Muslim fleet in the eastern Mediterranean in the seventh century forced a naval reorganization by the Byzantines, who by the tenth century had recaptured their former control of these waters. In the eleventh century, like all other Byzantine institutions, the navy suffered a decline from which it never recovered. Gradually, the developing Italian merchant cities replaced Byzantium as the great Mediterranean naval power. This was one of the main causes of the empire's downfall. At its height, however, the Byzantine fleet played a major role in imperial defense. It was equipped with one of the real secret weapons of the Middle Ages: Greek fire, a chemical compound squirted from tubes or siphons in the shape of lions' heads

A thirteenth-century manuscript illumination illustrating the use of Greek fire.

of gilded bronze mounted on the prows of the Byzantine ships, which would set enemy vessels aflame, and strike terror into the hearts of their sailors.

Diplomacy

The Byzantines fought only when they had to, preferring to negotiate whenever possible. Diplomacy too they brought to a high level: we have the records and reports of a good many Byzantine embassies, and can appreciate the subtlety of the instructions given the envoys. First Persia, and then to some extent the Muslim caliphate, were the only states whose rulers the Byzantine emperors regarded as equals. All others were barbarians, and when they claimed an imperial title, as in the case of the Franks or the later German emperors, the claim was usually passed over in scornful silence or openly disputed.

Yet, although the theory of empire proclaimed that the Byzantine Empire was universal, in their constant effort to protect their frontiers the Byzantine emperors dealt realistically with those "barbarian" peoples whom they could not con-

quer. They negotiated treaties securing to themselves military assistance, and graciously allowing the vassal peoples to bask in the reflected light of imperial prestige and to enjoy the luxuries that Byzantine money could buy. A kind of "offiice of barbarian affairs" kept imperial officials supplied with intelligence reports on the internal conditions of each barbarian people so that a "pro-Byzantine" party might be created among them and any internal stresses and quarrels might be turned to the advantage of the Byzantines.

As in Roman times, when the emperor sent arms for the chieftain of a foreign tribe, the act was the equivalent of adoption. The Christian Byzantine emperor could make the paternal relationship even stronger by sponsoring the barbarian ruler at his eventual baptism. The son of such a chief might be invited to be educated at Byzantium and thus introduced to all the glories of Byzantine civilization. Titles in the hierarchy of the palace, with their rich and valuable insignia, were bestowed on barbarian rulers; and on occasion a royal crown might even be granted. Marriage was also a most useful instrument. Barbarian leaders were delighted to marry Byzantine girls of noble family; and when it was a question of a particularly desirable alliance, the emperor himself might marry a barbarian princess or arrange to give a princess of the imperial house to a foreigner.

A solemn formal reception at the imperial court usually dazzled a foreign ruler or envoy, even a sophisticated Western bishop like Liudprand, ambassador of Berengar, king of Italy, who has left us this account from the year 948:

Before the emperor's seat stood a tree made of bronze gilded over, whose branches were filled with birds, also made of gilded bronze, which uttered different cries, each according to its varying species. The throne itself was so marvellously fashioned that at one moment it seemed a low structure and at another it rose high into the air. It was of immense size and was guarded by lions, made either of bronze or of wood covered over with gold, who beat the ground with their tails and gave a dreadful roar with open mouth and quivering tongue. Leaning upon the shoulders of two eunuchs I was brought into the emperor's presence. At my approach the lions began to roar and the birds to cry out, each according to its kind. . . . After I had three times made obeisance to the emperor with my face upon the ground, I lifted my head and behold! the man whom just before I had seen sitting on a mod-

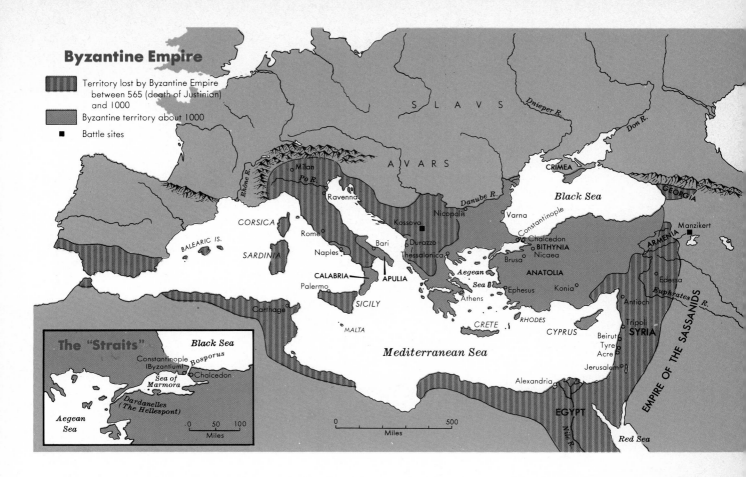

Byzantine Empire

- Territory lost by Byzantine Empire between 565 (death of Justinian) and 1000
- Byzantine territory about 1000
- ■ Battle sites

SLAVS

Dnieper R.

Don R.

AVARS

CRIMEA

Black Sea

GEORGIA

Manzikert

Milan

Rhône R.

Po R.

Ravenna

Danube R.

Nicopolis

Varna

Constantinople

Chalcedon

BITHYNIA

Nicaea

ARMENIA

CORSICA

Rome

Kossovo

Durazzo

Thessalonica

Brusa

ANATOLIA

Edessa

Euphrates R.

BALEARIC IS.

Bari

SARDINIA

Naples

CALABRIA

APULIA

Aegean

Sea

Ephesus

Konia

Antioch

EMPIRE OF THE SASSANIDS

Palermo

Athens

SICILY

Carthage

MALTA

CRETE

RHODES

CYPRUS

Tripoli

Beirut

Tyre

Acre

SYRIA

Mediterranean Sea

Jerusalem

Alexandria

EGYPT

Nile R.

Red Sea

Miles | 0 ——— 500

The "Straits"

Black Sea

Constantinople (Byzantium)

Bosporus

Chalcedon

Sea of Marmora

Dardanelles (The Hellespont)

Aegean Sea

0   50   100
Miles

---

erately elevated seat had now changed his raiment and was sitting on the level of the ceiling. How it was done I cannot imagine, unless perhaps he was lifted up by some sort of device as we use for raising the timbers of a wine-press. On that occasion he did not address me personally, since even if he had wished to do so the wide distance between us would have rendered conversation unseemly, but by the intermediary of a secretary he enquired after Berengar's doings, and asked after his health. I made a fitting reply and then, at a nod from the interpreter, left his presence and retired to my lodging.*

The Economy

Good armies and navies and shrewd diplomacy always cost money and depend directly upon the economic strength of the state that creates and uses them. Byzantium was enormously rich. It was a great center of trade, to

Antapodosis, VI, v, in *Works of Liudprand of Cremona*, trans. F. A. Wright (London, 1930), pp. 207–208.

which came vessels from every quarter of the compass. From the countries around the shore of the Black Sea came furs and hides, grain, salt, wine, and slaves from the Caucasus. From India, Ceylon, Syria, and Arabia came spices, precious stones, and silk; from Africa, slaves and ivory; from the West, especially Italy, merchants eager to buy the products sold in Constantinople, often the products of the imperial industries.

The Byzantine emperors themselves were able for many centuries to maintain a monopoly of the manufacture and sale of silk textiles, purple dye, and gold embroidery, which were not then merely luxuries, but absolute necessities for the dignitaries of church and state in the West as in the East. For long a closely guarded secret of the Persians, silk manufacture came to Byzantium in the middle of the sixth century, when— so the story goes—two monks explained to the emperor that the mysterious cloth was the product of silkworms. Later, bribed by the promise of a great reward, they actually brought back silkworms' eggs hidden in a hollow cane. They taught the emperor that the worms must be fed mulberry leaves; great plantations of mulberries were established, especially in Syria; and a mighty enterprise was under way.

The power that was derived from the control over the manufacture and sale of silk has rightly been compared with modern controls over strategic materials like coal, oil, and iron. But it was not only the imperial treasury that profited: the rich were able to embellish their persons and their homes; many middle-class merchants and craftsmen found a livelihood in the industry; and the flow of revenue into the imperial treasuries made it possible for the emperors to tax the lower classes less than would otherwise have been necessary for national defense and other official expenses. An elaborate system of control over manufacture (which was in the hands of carefully regulated imperial guilds) and over sales (which were permitted only in official salesrooms) safely secured the monopoly down to the eleventh century.

Besides controlling silk, the emperor forbade the export of gold, a measure obviously designed to prevent the depletion of reserves. The nomisma, as the Byzantine gold coin was called, was standard all over the Mediterranean and even in the East. Until the late eleventh century it was almost never debased, and even then only under the impact of crisis brought about by civil strife and foreign invasion, and only gradually. But for eight hundred years this money was stable.

All visitors noticed and envied the wealth of Byzantium, especially those from the West, whose own largely rural society and meager way of life contrasted so strikingly with the urban glitter and sophistication of the imperial capital. Westerners admired the splendid silken garments embroidered with gold, the palaces and churches aglow with mosaics and richly carved columns of semiprecious stones imported at great expense from distant lands, the jewelry and gold and ivory worn by the wealthy citizens and displayed in their houses. Beneath the splendor and the show lay the hard economic realities that preserved the state for centuries: a thriving commerce and industry and a substantial revenue.

Throughout Byzantine history, the sources of state income remained pretty much the same. Money came in from state property in land— farms, cattle ranches, gold and silver mines, marble quarries—as distinct from the money that came in from the emperor's personal estates. Booty seized in war or fortunes confiscated from rich men in disgrace provided cash. And of course there was also revenue from taxation: on land and persons, sales and profits, imports and exports, and inheritances.

From Diocletian (284–305) the Byzantines inherited the concept that land and labor were taxable together. The territory of the empire was considered to be divided into units called yokes, each of which was defined as the amount of land that could feed a single laboring farmer. In order to be taxable as a unit of land, each yoke had to have its farmer to work it; in order to be taxable as a person, each farmer had to have a yoke to work. In a period of labor shortage, the government thus had to find a person to cultivate every yoke; otherwise there would have been no revenue.

It was this concept that led to the binding of many peasants to the soil and to their slow degeneration into serfs. Large private landowners naturally flourished under such a system, since it was easier for the state to lease them large tracts of land and leave it to them to find the supply of labor. Moreover, inferior land or abandoned or run-down farms were compulsorily assigned to nearby landowners, who were responsible for the taxes on this property as on their more productive acres. Only if a landowner had a substantial acreage of rich and productive farm land could he be expected to pay such taxes on the more marginal farms. So this aspect of the system also contributed to the growth of large private estates. Yet, though the large estate may have predominated in the early period, the small private freeholder seems never to have disappeared. In later centuries, as we shall see, the balance between the two types of holding would several times swing one way or the other.

The Capital and the Factions

As the capital, Constantinople had its own special administration, under a prefect of the city, or *eparch*. He was mayor, chief of police, and judge rolled into one, responsible for public order, inspecting the markets, fixing fair prices for food, and supervising the lawyers, notaries, money-changers, and bankers, as well as merchants. The city artisans and tradesmen were organized into guilds or corporations, each with its own governor, under the authority of the prefect. The eparch upheld standards of quality in food supplies and in manufactured goods and punished misrepresentations of quality by overenthusiastic or dishonest salesmen. By the eleventh century, the eparch was often left in charge in the emperor's absence.

Byzantium inherited from Rome rival parties of chariot-racers, each with its own stables and equipment and colors, the Blues and the Greens. We can best understand these circus factions if we imagine that in, let us say, present-day Chicago, the White Sox and the Cubs were not only the city's passionately loved baseball teams who played each other exclusively, and about whose rivalry the entire community was wildly concerned, but also represented opposing factions on all the political, religious, economic, and social issues of the day, and in addition had certain military duties in defense of the city in time of war.

The Blues and Greens were influential during the early centuries of the empire; the emperor himself always joined one group or the other. He fixed the days on which races were to be held at the Hippodrome, a vast stadium near the cathedral church of Santa Sophia that was attached to the sacred palace. On the appointed days, the turbulent populace would throng the stands and root frantically for the charioteers of their party.

Blues and Greens seem to have come from different quarters of the city, and from different social classes. The Blues were by and large the party of the aristocracy, the Greens of the lower classes; the Blues were the party of strict Christian orthodoxy, the Greens were frequently the party of questionable orthodoxy, since new heresies naturally took root among the poor. Those emperors who were strictly orthodox themselves enrolled as Blues; those who leaned toward heterodoxy and felt the need for mob support enrolled as Greens. This division existed in the great provincial cities, too, but at Constantinople it took on special virulence. The factional strife manifested itself sometimes in the Hippodrome, when the faction opposed to the emperor would riot against him; sometimes in the streets of the city, when roving bands belonging to one faction would invade the quarter of the other and burn down houses.

The most celebrated riot in all Byzantine history was the Nika revolt of 532 (so called because of the cry of the rioters, meaning "victory"). On this occasion the Blues and Greens temporarily united in the Hippodrome to try to force Justinian to be merciful to two condemned criminals, one Green and one Blue, who had escaped execution by accident. When the emperor, who had been a Blue, but who now tried to assume an impartially severe attitude toward both parties, failed to assent to their joint request, they revolted simultaneously and burned most of the public buildings of the city. The seriousness of the riot was greatly increased by the presence in the city of a large number of poor peasants from the country, who had fled their farms as a result of heavy taxation, and who joined the factions in what became a revolution.

Justinian might well have lost his throne had it not been for the coolness and bravery of his celebrated Empress Theodora:

My opinion is that now, above all other times, is a bad time to flee, even if this should bring safety. Once a man has seen light, he must surely die; but for a man who has been an emperor to

The empress Theodora: detail of a mosaic in the Church of San Vitale at Ravenna.

become a refugee is not to be borne. May I never be separated from the purple [the symbol of imperial rank] and may I no longer live on that day when those who meet me shall not call me mistress. Now if you wish to save yourself, O Emperor, this is not hard. For we have much money; there is the sea, here are the boats. But think whether after you have been saved you may not come to feel that you would have preferred to die. As for me, I like a certain old proverb that says: royalty is a good shroud.*

The emperor took heart, and the revolt was put down. It was the destruction of the old cathedral during this riot that made necessary the construction of the new Santa Sophia.

The Nika affair was exceptional in its severity and in the combination of the rival factions. But every reign from the end of the fourth century to the middle of the seventh was marked by outbursts of disorder between the two parties. All this time, both the Blues and Greens also had military and municipal duties, helping with the construction of the walls, and bearing a heavy share of the responsibility for defense. This made for instability, since it was never certain that mutual hatred would yield in the face of common danger. In the seventh and eighth centuries the emperors in some unknown fashion finally succeeded in clipping the wings of the factions. They took over the management of the public entertainments in the Hippodrome and left only an unimportant role to the leaders of the Blues and Greens, who were restricted to acclaiming the emperor on public occasions.

II Byzantium: Religion and Civilization

Religion at Byzantium

All aspects of Byzantine life were deeply permeated by Christianity. Religion pervaded social life: from birth until death, at every important moment in the life of every person, the Church played an important role, governing marriage and family relations, filling leisure time, helping determine any critical decision. Religion pervaded intellectual life: the most serious intellectual problems of the age were those of theology, and they were attacked with zest by brains second to none in power and subtlety. Religion pervaded aesthetic life: the arts were largely, though by no means entirely, devoted to the representation of ecclesiastical subjects, and serving the Church offered one of the best opportunities to exercise a creative talent. Religion pervaded economic life: business was carried on under the auspices of the Church, and a substantial part of the citizens' income went to support the Church.

Religion also pervaded political life. What we would call the domestic issues, about which the people got excited, were political issues centering on theological problems. What was the true relationship of the members of the Trinity to one another? What was the true relationship of the human to the divine nature of Christ? Was it proper to worship the holy images? It was not only in monasteries and universities that such problems were argued, but also in the streets. Either faction would riot in the Hippodrome if the Emperor opposed its views on such questions. The right answer meant salvation and future immortality, whereas the wrong answer meant damnation and eternal punishment.

What we would call the issues of foreign policy too were pervaded by religion: when the emperor went forth to war, he went as the champion of the faith. Most often, the enemies were not Christians, or were heretics or schismatics. The emperor went into battle against them with a sacred picture borne before him, an icon (image) of the Virgin, perhaps one of those which legend said had been painted by Saint Luke, or not even made by human hands at all, but miraculously sent from heaven itself. In a sense, all Byzantine wars were crusades.

Contrast with the West

Yet much of this was true also in the medieval West. The real contrast we see most clearly when

* Procopius, *History of the Wars*, I, xxiv, 35–38. Our translation.

we compare the relationship between Church and State in the West with that in the East. The very abandonment of Rome had permitted the local bishops to create the papal monarchy and challenge kings and emperors. In Constantinople, however, the emperor remained in residence. No papacy could develop. Constantine himself summoned the Council of Nicaea in 325; he paid the salaries of the bishops, presided over their deliberations, and as emperor gave to their decrees the force of imperial law. When he legislated as head of the Christian church in matters of Christian dogma, he was doing what no layman in the West could do; he still had some of the attributes of the Roman pontifex. In the East the emperor regularly deposed patriarchs and punished clerics. He took the initiative in church reforms. The faith was a principle of civil law; the emperor often helped prepare canon law. Constantine's successors were often theologians themselves and enjoyed argument and speculation on theological questions. Sometimes they even legislated on matters of faith without consulting churchmen. In short, the Church was a kind of department of state, and the emperor was the effective head of it as he was of the other departments. One of his titles was "equal to the Apostles."

The state of affairs in which a single authority plays the role of both emperor and pope is known as Caesaropapism, and the term is often applied to the behavior of the Byzantine emperors. Sometimes, it is true, a patriarch of Constantinople challenged an emperor successfully. Moreover, absolute though they were, none of the emperors could afford to impose new dogma without church support, or could risk offending the religious susceptibilities of the people. Some scholars therefore prefer not to use the term "Caesaropapism," but the exceptions seem to us less important than the rule.

The Theological Controversies

As we know, Constantine had not wanted to intervene in the theological quarrel over Arianism, but he did so because the very structure of the empire was threatened. The Council of Nicaea failed to impose a settlement, and the quarrel continued for another three-quarters of a century. Then, after a pause of only fifty years, there began the new and even more desperately fought battles over the relationship between the human and divine natures in Christ. This controversy was concentrated in the eastern Mediterranean world, where most Egyptian, Syrian, Ethiopian, and Armenian Christians were monophysites, as they are to this day—that is, they believed that the human and divine natures in Christ are one, a view that tends to make the believer forget Christ's humanity. And they resisted vigorously attempts to force them to compromise.

The antagonism grew partly out of the jealousy felt by the older Mediterranean capitals of Antioch and Alexandria for the imperial city of Constantinople, an upstart from their point of view, which churchmen and laymen alike blamed for the decline in their commerce. Antioch and Alexandria had been patriarchates, like Rome, from early days, whereas Byzantium had been only an obscure bishopric until it became the capital, under Constantine, and had become a patriarchate only after 381. It was only the presence of the emperor that won so great a rank for his city.

As the Council of Nicaea of 325 offered a solution to the Arian controversy that remained unacceptable, so the Council of Chalcedon of 451 offered a solution to the monophysite controversy that remained unacceptable. This internal dissension over theology and prestige in the empire helped to soften the imperial defenses against the Muslims, whose success in Syria and Egypt is partly due to the failure of these provinces to develop a sense of solidarity with Byzantium. During the entire controversy, the emperors, especially Zeno (474–491), Justinian (527–565), and Heraclius (610–641), strove repeatedly to arrange compromises that would permit a settlement; but all efforts failed.

In the course of the two great theological controversies, which lasted with intervals from the fourth to the late seventh centuries and which culminated in the loss of the Eastern provinces of the empire, almost every possible intellectual subtlety had been introduced into the discussion. From the point of view of intellectual advance, of philosophical development, theology had reached a dead end. From here on, Byzantine Christianity was increasingly preoccupied with ritual.

Monasticism and the Sacraments

The Byzantines assumed, to a far greater extent than the western Europeans, that the individual had very little chance of salvation. In the East, more than the West, monasticism became *the* Christian life, since to become a monk was to take a direct route to salvation. Worldly men, including many emperors, became monks on their deathbeds to increase their chances of going to heaven. At Byzantium, monks enjoyed enormous popular prestige and often influenced political decisions; monks provided the highest ranks of the Church hierarchy; rich and powerful laymen, from the emperor down, founded new monasteries as an act of piety. Often immune from taxation, monasteries acquired vast lands and much treasure. Some emperors tried to check monastic growth, but the monks remained powerful and continued to influence policies because of their hold over the popular imagination.

For the ordinary Christian, the sacraments of the Church provided the way to salvation. In the East every religious act took on a sacramental quality. Every image, every relic of a saint, was felt to preserve the essence of the holy person in itself. In the same way God was felt to be actually present in the sanctuary; He could be reached through—and only through—the proper performance of the ritual. In the East the emphasis fell on mystery, magic, ritual, a personal approach to the heavenly Saviour, more than on the ethical teachings of Christianity. Once a believer had accepted the proper performance of a magical action as the right way to reach God, he could not contemplate any change in it: if the old way was wrong, one's parents and grandparents were all damned.

Quarrels and Schism with the West

A slight difference in the wording of the liturgy, it is sometimes argued, caused the schism, or split, between the Eastern and Western churches in 1054. The Greek creed states that the Holy Ghost "proceeds" from the Father, the Latin adds the word *filioque*, meaning "and from the son." But this and other differences might never have received much notice, and would surely not have led to schism, had it not been for the political questions at issue and for the increasing divergences between the two civilizations.

More than three hundred years earlier, in the eighth century, a new religious controversy had raged in the Byzantine Empire over the use of sculptured and painted sacred images and the nature and amount of reverence that a Christian might properly pay them. Something very like idolatry was widespread in the East, and twice for long periods (726–787 and 813–842) the emperors adopted the strict Old Testament rule that all images must be banned (iconoclasm, image-breaking). The impulse apparently came from the puritanism of the army, country boys from Anatolia and Armenia who were able to install their officers on the imperial throne. The popes, who believed that images were educational and might be venerated, were shocked, and condemned iconoclasm. In the end, the emperors restored the images, but as early as the 730's an iconoclastic emperor had punished the pope by removing from papal jurisdiction southern Italy, with its rich church revenues, and Illyricum (the Balkan provinces), and placing them under the patriarch of Constantinople. Even more decisive than iconoclasm was the pope's belief that Byzantium could not or would not defend Italy and the papacy against Lombards and Muslims, and his decision to turn to Pepin and Charlemagne.

Again, in the 860's, competition between papal and Byzantine missionaries to convert the Bulgarians had led to a political quarrel. It was only then that the Greeks "discovered" the Roman "error" in adding *filioque* to the creed. Though the disagreement of the late ninth century was eventually settled, the underlying mistrust persisted. It was increased by the deep corruption into which the papacy fell during the tenth century. The Byzantines became accustomed to going their own way without reference to the bishops of Rome. When the papacy was eventually reformed in the eleventh century, the Byzantines did not understand that they were no longer dealing with the slack and immoral popes they had grown used to.

Under these circumstances, they were unprepared for a revival of the old papal determination to recover jurisdiction over southern Italy, still a part of the Byzantine Empire and still therefore under the patriarch of Constantinople. As the Norman adventurers, newly arrived in southern Italy in the eleventh century, began to make conquests in this Byzantine territory, they turned over to the jurisdiction of the popes the churches and church revenues in the lands and cities they conquered. Naturally, the ambitious and vigorous popes welcomed the return of souls and revenues that they had never given up claim to. Naturally, the Byzantine patriarch was unhappy over his losses. A violent and powerful man, he dug up the old *filioque* controversy again as a pretext for pushing his more solid grievances, and in answer to his complaints the pope sent to Byzantium one of his most energetic and unbending cardinals named Humbert. The interview ended in mutual excommunication. Cardinal Humbert shook the dust of Constantinople from his feet and sailed for home. Despite numerous efforts at reconciliation since 1054, these mutual excommunications were lifted only in 1965.

Antagonism between East and West

Besides the political issues that contributed to the split between the churches, we must record the growing mutual dislike between Eastern and Western Christians. To the visiting Westerner, no doubt in part jealous of the Byzantine standard of living, the Greeks seemed soft, effeminate, and treacherous. To the Byzantine, the Westerner seemed savage, fickle, and dangerous, a barbarian like all other barbarians. Nowhere is the Western attitude shown any better than by Bishop Liudprand, who had been so impressed by the emperor's throne when he visited Constantinople in the year 948. On a second official visit, this time for the Western emperor Otto I in 969, he describes his reception by the emperor Nicephorus Phocas:

On the fourth of June we arrived at Constantinople, and after a miserable reception . . . we were given the most miserable and disgusting quarters. The palace where we were confined was certainly large and open, but it neither kept out the cold nor afforded shelter from heat. Armed soldiers were set to guard us and prevent my people from going out and any others from coming in. . . . To add to our troubles the Greek

wine we found undrinkable because of the mixture in it of pitch, resin, and plaster. The house itself had no water, and we could not even buy any to quench our thirst. . . . On the sixth of June . . . I was brought before the Emperor's brother Leo . . . and there we tired ourselves with a fierce argument over your [Otto's] imperial title. He called you not emperor, which is Basileus in his tongue, but insultingly Rex, which is King. . . . On the seventh of June . . . I was brought before Nicephorus himself. . . . He is a monstrosity of a man, a dwarf, fat-headed and with tiny mole's eyes; disfigured by a short, broad thick beard half going gray; disgraced by a neck scarcely an inch long; piglike by reason of the big close bristles on his head; in color an Ethiopian, and, as the poet says, "you would not like to meet him in the dark."*

As might have been expected, Liudprand, the defender of the West, and Nicephorus, the Byzantine, whose unattractiveness his guest certainly exaggerated in order to curry favor with his German imperial master, had a vigorous set-to on questions of prestige. Finally, when Liudprand was about to go home, he left behind him scrawled upon the wall of his uncomfortable quarters a long anti-Greek poem, which begins:

Trust not the Greeks; they live but to betray;
Nor heed their promises, whate'er they say.
If lies will serve them, any oath they swear,
And when it's time to break it feel no fear.†

On the other side, the Byzantine reaction to Westerners is illustrated by a document written by the princess Anna Comnena more than a century later, the famous *Alexiad,* a history of her father, Emperor Alexius I Comnenus (1081–1118). Here is what she says about the Norman crusader Bohemond:

Now, Bohemond took after his father in all things, in audacity, bodily strength, bravery, and untamable temper. . . . These two, father and son, might rightly be termed "the caterpillar and the locust"; for whatever escaped Robert, that his son Bohemond took to him and devoured. . . .
For by nature the man was a rogue and ready for any eventualities; in roguery and cunning he was far superior to all the Latins [Westerners]. . . . But in spite of his surpassing them all in superabundant activity in mischief, yet fickleness

* *Works of Liudprand of Cremona,* trans. F. A. Wright, (London, 1930), pp. 235–236.
† Ibid., p. 270.

like some natural appendage attended him too. . . .

He was such a man, to speak briefly, as no one in the Empire had seen before, . . . for he was a wonderful spectacle. . . . He was so tall that he surpassed the tallest man by a cubit [about eighteen inches]; he was slender of waist and flank, broad of shoulder, and fullchested; his whole body was muscular. . . . His body as a whole was very white; his face was mingled white and ruddy-color. His hair was a shade of yellow, and did not fall upon his shoulders like that of other barbarians; the man avoided this foolish practice, and his hair was cut even to his ears. I cannot say whether his beard was red or some other color; his face had been closely shaved and seemed as smooth as chalk. . . . A certain charm hung about the man but was partly marred by a sense of the terrible. There seemed to be something untamed and inexorable about his whole appearance, . . . and his laugh was like the roaring of other men. . . . His mind was manysided, versatile, and provident. His speech was carefully worded and his answers guarded.*

The mutual dislike between Byzantines and Westerners was to grow steadily more intense in the period after the late eleventh century, until it reached a climax in the tragedy of 1204, as we shall see.

Byzantine Civilization

Until less than a century ago, the study of Byzantine history was under a cloud. German classical scholars felt that it was somehow not decent to investigate the history of a people who could not write good classical Greek. The French usually referred to Byzantium as the *bas-empire,* literally the low or degenerate empire, whose achievements they scornfully contrasted with the glorious literary and artistic performance of Greece and Rome. From Gibbon on, the English were equally indifferent or scornful. The Victorian scholar Lecky wrote:

Of that Byzantine Empire the universal verdict of history is that it constitutes, without a single exception, the most thoroughly base and despicable form that civilization has yet assumed. . . . There has been no other enduring civilization

so absolutely destitute of all the forms and elements of greatness. . . . The history of the empire is a monotonous story of the intrigues of priests, eunuchs, and women, of poisonings, of conspiracies, of uniform ingratitude, of perpetual fratricides*

Lecky was writing a history of European morals; and one must cheerfully admit that a Victorian moralist would find much to shudder at in the private lives of the individual Byzantine emperors. Yet this is almost irrelevant to the historian's estimate of Byzantine civilization.

That achievement was varied, distinguished, and of major importance to the West. Byzantine literature does indeed suffer by comparison with the classics; but the appropriate society with which to compare medieval Byzantium is not classical antiquity but the contemporary Europe of the Middle Ages. Medieval western European civilization and medieval Byzantine civilization are both Christian and both the direct heirs of Rome and Greece. The Byzantines created art as admirable in its way as anything produced in the West; they maintained learning on a level much more advanced than did the West; the West itself owes a substantial cultural debt to Byzantium.

Byzantium as Preserver of the Classics

In the West, long centuries passed during which the knowledge of Greek had disappeared and nobody had access to the great works of philosophy, science, and literature written in Greek by the ancients. During all this time the Byzantines preserved these masterpieces, copied and recopied them, by hand of course, and gave them constant study.

Again, in contrast to the West, study was not confined to monasteries, although the monks played a major role. It was also pursued in secular libraries and schools. The teacher occupied an important position in Byzantine society; books circulated widely among prominent men in public life; many of the emperors were scholars and lovers of literature. In the early days of the empire, the greatest university was still at Athens,

---

* Translation partly ours, partly from E. A. S. Dawes' translation of the *Alexiad* (London, 1928), pp. 37-38, 266, 347.

* W. H. Lecky, *History of European Morals from Augustus to Charlemagne* (New York, 1869), II, 13-14.

but because of its strong pagan tradition the pious Christian emperor Justinian closed the university there in the sixth century. The imperial university at Constantinople, which probably dates from Constantine himself, supplied a steady stream of learned and cultivated men to the bureaucracy, the church, and the courts. The emphasis in its curriculum was on secular subjects: philosophy, astronomy, geometry, rhetoric, music, grammar, law, medicine, and arithmetic. The School of the Patriarch, the Archbishop of Constantinople, also in the capital, provided instruction in theology and other sacred subjects.

Had it not been for Byzantium, it seems certain that Plato and Aristotle, Homer and Sophocles, would have been lost. We cannot even imagine what such a loss would have meant to Western civilization, how seriously it would have retarded us in science and speculation, in morals and ethics, how crippled we should have been in our efforts to deal with the fundamental problems of human relationships, what a poor and meager cultural inheritance we should have had. That these living works of the dead past have been preserved to us we owe to Byzantium.

Original Writing

Too often, however, people have thought of the Byzantine cultural achievements as limited to preservation and transmission. The Byzantines were themselves creative. We have, for instance, an epic poem, from the tenth or eleventh century, describing the heroic activity of a frontier warrior who had lived some two to three centuries earlier, Basil Digenes Akritas (Basil, of the two races, the frontiersman). Half Greek, half Arab, he fights wild beasts and brigands, preserves order on the border between Byzantine and Muslim territory, seizes a fair bride and forces her family to consent to the marriage, defeats a magnificent Amazon (female) warrior, and even tells the emperor how to behave. Though the creator of this hero was no Homer, he is fully comparable with the Western authors who sang of Roland, of the Cid, and of the Scottish borderers. Like Basil, all these heroes were men of the frontiers, Daniel Boones of the Middle Ages, pursuing adventure and righting wrongs among the medieval equivalents of the Red Indians.

In prose, we find an almost unbroken line of those who over the long centuries wrote the history of the empire. Writing in a popular style, the chroniclers took their story back to the Creation or continued the work of a predecessor who had done so. The true historians wrote for intellectuals, and limited themselves to the story of their own times, perhaps with an introduction describing a period immediately before their own about which they had some first-hand information. We must be careful to weigh what they tell us, because they were often violently partisan in the quarrels of their day and may sometimes be found blackening the innocent or whitewashing the guilty for their own purposes. But if we proceed cautiously, the great series of Byzantine historians opens up for us a world as yet little known. There is no comparable body of literature to tell us about men and events in the medieval West, which all too often can be discovered only from the bare bones of legal documents or from a tantalizingly dry and brief mention in some book of annals.

As we might expect, theological writing forms a substantial part of the prose literature. In the early period the Byzantine theologians hotly debated the great controversies that rent the empire about the true relationship between God the Father and God the Son, or between the divine and human natures of Christ. In a society like the Byzantine, such works had the importance that may be ascribed, for example, to those of Freud or Marx in our own day. Too difficult for most people to read or understand, they none the less had enormous influence over the lives of everybody: the leaders of the society were directly or indirectly affected by their answers to the problems of human social and economic life in general, or of the life of the human individual in particular and of his prospects of eternal salvation or damnation. The early theologians also drew up appropriate rules for monks, balancing the need for denying the desires of the flesh by providing reasonable opportunities for work, an arrangement which worked in the East to prevent many of the difficulties that arose in Western monasticism. Finally, under the influence of the Neoplatonic philosophers, the theologians developed a mystic strain, in which they urged contemplation and purification as stages toward illumination and the final mystic union with God.

For the ordinary man, the mysteries of his faith were enhanced by the beauties of the church service, where magnificent hymns were sung, often composed by men whom we would consider to be major poets. Saints' lives, usually written for a popular audience, took the place of the novel in our society. They told a personal story, often including adventure, anxiety, deprivation, violence, and agony of various sorts, and they set forth the final triumph of virtue and piety. The eyes of the reader were elevated to consider his heavenly reward, since the hero of the story was often martyred here on earth. Exciting and edifying, these tales were not only immensely popular in their day, but help the scholar of our own. They often supply valuable bits of information about daily life, especially among the humbler classes, and about the attitudes of the people, for which we sometimes have no other source.

Here is an episode from the life of Theodore of Sykeon, a seventh-century saint who wrought miracles in Asia Minor:

. . . The holy Theodore sent his archdeacon to the capital, Constantinople, to buy a chalice and a paten of silver. . . . The archdeacon went and bought from a silversmith a pure and well-finished vessel, so far as concerned the quality of the silver and the workmanship, and he brought it back to the monastery. . . . When the saint looked at them, he . . . condemned them as being useless and defiled. But the archdeacon who looked at the appearance and not at what was hidden, pointed out the perfect and well-wrought workmanship and the quality proved by the five-fold stamp upon it, and thought by these facts to convince the Saint. But the Saint said "I know, yes, I know, son, that so far as eyes can see, it appears a beautiful specimen of craftsmanship and the worth of the silver is evident from the stamps on it, but it is another, an invisible cause which defiles it. I fancy the defilement comes from some impure use. But if you doubt it, pronounce the verse for our prayers and be convinced." Then whilst the archdeacon chanted the verse of Invocation, the Saint bent his head in prayer, and after he had filled the chalice, the chalice and the paten turned black. . . . Then the archdeacon returned to Constantinople and gave them back to the dealer in silver and told him the reason. The dealer made inquiries of . . . his manager and his silversmith who fashioned the vessels, and found out that they came from the chamberpot of a prostitute. . . . He gave him other and very beautiful vessels, and these the archdeacon carried to the Saint, and reported to him and to the monks the cause of defilement in the earlier vessels, and they all gave thanks unto God.*

From this passage we learn quite incidentally a good bit about the organization of the silver business in Byzantium: a merchant is shown employing a manager and an artisan, and we find that a fivefold hallmark was the Byzantine equivalent of our "sterling" stamped on an object. Also, we discover that then as now ladies of easy virtue sometimes became quite prosperous.

Unique among these saints' lives is one extraordinary document of the tenth century: a highly polished tale of an Indian king, who shuts away his only son Ioasaph in a remote palace to protect him from the knowledge of the world and especially to prevent his being converted to Christianity. But the prince cannot be protected; he sees a sick man, a blind man, and a dead man; and when he is in despair at life's cruelties a wise monk in disguise, named Barlaam, succeeds in reaching him by pretending to have a precious jewel that he wishes to show. The jewel is the jewel of the Christian faith, and the rest of the long story is an account of the wise monk Barlaam's conversion of Prince Ioasaph. In the course of the conversion, Barlaam tells Ioasaph ten moral tales illustrating the Christian life. One of these is known to us as the casket-story of Shakespeare's *Merchant of Venice;* another is the tale of Everyman, which later became common in all Western literatures; others of Barlaam's stories were used by hundreds of other Western authors and preachers of all nationalities.

Yet what is most fascinating about this piece of Byzantine literature is that it originally comes from India: the life of Ioasaph is a Christianized version of the life of Buddha, the great Indian religious leader of the sixth century B.C. His life story passed through Persia via the Arabs to the Caucasus kingdom of Georgia before it was turned into Greek legend and transmitted to the West. And the stories that Barlaam tells to convert Ioasaph are also Indian in origin and are either Buddhist birth-stories (recitals of the Buddha's experiences in earlier incarnations used as comment upon what was going on around him), or Hindu moral-comic tales. Indeed the very name "Ioasaph" was once "Bodasaph," and so is the same as the Indian word "Bodhisattva," which means a person destined to attain Buddha-

*N. H. Baynes and E. A. S. Dawes, *Three Byzantine Saints* (Oxford, 1948), 117–118.

Interior of Santa Sophia, with Turkish medallions.

Façade of St. Mark's, Venice.

hood. Prince Ioasaph has been canonized a saint of both the Orthodox and the Roman Catholic churches, and it is thus an odd but true fact that through this legend Buddha himself became and has remained a Christian saint.

The Arts

When we turn to the field of the plastic arts, we can see the Byzantine achievement with our own eyes. In Constantinople the Church of Santa Sophia, built in the sixth century, was designed to be "a church the like of which has never been seen since Adam nor ever will be." The dome, "a work at once marvelous and terrifying," says a contemporary, "seems rather to hang by a golden chain from heaven than to be supported by solid masonry"; and Justinian (527–565), the emperor who built it, was able to exclaim "I have outdone thee, O Solomon!" "On entering the church to pray," says Justinian's historian,

Procopius, "one feels at once that it is the work not of man's effort or industry, but in truth the work of the divine power; and the spirit, mounting to heaven, realizes that here God is very near, and that He delights in this dwelling that He has chosen for Himself." The Turks themselves, who seized the city in 1453, ever since have paid Santa Sophia the sincerest compliment of imitation; the great mosques that throng present-day Istanbul are all more or less directly copied after the great church of the Byzantines.

Before Santa Sophia could be built, the other cities of the empire, particularly Alexandria, Antioch, and Ephesus, had produced the necessary architectural synthesis: a fusion of the Hellenistic or Roman basilica with a dome taken from Persia. This is just one striking example of the way in which Greek and oriental elements were to be blended in the new society. In decoration, the use of brilliantly colored marbles, enamel, silken and other fabrics, gold, silver, and jewels, and the paintings and glowing mosaics on the walls and ceilings, reflect the sumptuousness of the Orient.

The tourist of today wishing to see a Byzantine church of Justinian's time need not go all the way to Istanbul. On the Adriatic coast of Italy, south of Venice, at Ravenna, there are three wonderful smaller churches of the sixth century with superb mosaics still well preserved, including portraits of Justinian himself and of his Empress Theodora. And at Venice itself, first the client, then the equal, and finally the conqueror of Byzantium, St. Mark's is a true Byzantine church of the later period, whose richness and magnificence epitomize perhaps better than any surviving church in Istanbul itself the splendor of later Byzantine architecture.

Along with the major arts of architecture, painting, and mosaics went the so-called minor arts, whose level the Byzantines raised so high that the term "minor" seems almost absurd. The silks, the ivories, the work of the goldsmiths and silversmiths, the enamel and jeweled bookcovers, the elaborate containers made especially to hold the sacred relics of a saint, the great

Hungarian sacred Crown of Saint Stephen, the superb miniatures of the illuminated manuscripts in half a hundred European libraries—all testify to the endless variety and fertility of Byzantine inspiration.

Even in those parts of western Europe where Byzantine political authority had disappeared, the influence of this Byzantine artistic flowering is often apparent. Sometimes we are dealing with actual creations by Byzantine artists produced in the West or ordered from Constantinople by a connoisseur. These are found in Sicily and southern Italy, in Venice, and in Rome itself. Sometimes the native artists work in the Byzantine manner, as in Spain, in Sicily, and in the great Romanesque domed churches of southern France. Often the new native product is not purely Byzantine, but rather a fusion of Byzantine with local elements, a new art diverse in its genius, but one of whose strands is clearly native to Constantinople.

III   The Fortunes of Empire, 330-1081

When we are dealing with a period of more than eleven hundred years of history, as in the case of Byzantium from its dedication by Constantine in 330 to its capture by the Turks in 1453, it is useful to subdivide it. The late eleventh century provides the major break in Byzantine history: by then the decline in imperial strength can be plainly seen. So in this chapter we shall bring the story down only as far as 1081. In each of the shorter periods that can for convenience be distinguished between 330 and 1081, we shall not only single out for emphasis the major trends of foreign and domestic policies but we shall also trace the more gradual course of changes to be found in government, society, and economic life.

The Main Periods of Byzantine History, 330-1081

The first period runs from Constantine's dedication of his capital in 330 to the accession of the emperor Leo III in 717. Despite their efforts, the Roman emperors at Constantinople

could not reconquer the West and thus reconstitute the Roman Empire of Augustus. Indeed, theological controversy, reflecting internal political strain, and combined with Persian and Arab aggression, cost the empire Syria and Egypt. The internal structure was modified in accordance with the new situation.

From 717 to 867, the threat of Arab conquest was safely contained, the Bulgarians were converted, the major religious and political struggle over church images was fought and decided, and the big landowners began to emerge as a threat to the financial and military system.

From 867 to 1025, the Byzantine Empire was at its height; the emperors went over to the counterattack against the Arabs and regained much territory and prestige; the grim Bulgarian struggle was fought to a bloody conclusion; the Russians were converted; and the emperors made every effort to check the growth of the great landowning aristocracy.

The years 1025-1081 represented a period of decline, slow at first, but accelerated as the period drew to a close: external military disaster accompanied, and was related to, the triumph of the landowners.

Silver plate showing the emperor Theodosius, with his sons Honorius and Arcadius on either side, bestowing the insignia of office on a local official. Found in the mid-nineteenth century in western Spain by two peasants, who, before they could be stopped, split it in order to divide the profits.

330-717

In the period from 330 to 717, the emperors immediately following Constantine were Arians. Theodosius the Great (379-395), the first truly orthodox emperor after Constantine, proclaimed Orthodox Nicene Christianity (381) to be the sole permitted state religion. All those who did not accept the Nicene Creed were to be driven from the cities of the empire. Theodosius' enactment is a landmark along the road to the creation of the Orthodox Eastern empire, and demonstrates once more the close relation of theology to politics and to imperial initiative in matters of faith. Although the empire east and west was united under Theodosius, his sons Arcadius (395-408) and Honorius divided it, with Arcadius ruling at Constantinople. It was never again fully united in fact, although in theory it had never been divided.

Over the whole period until the accession of

Justinian in 527, the eastern portion of the empire was able to use the German barbarians as troops in its own armies, and at the same time usually managed to deflect the new blows of further invaders so that they fell chiefly upon the West. Though the Huns and the Persians presented a challenge, the cities of the East continued prosperous, and government operated undisturbed. Only the monophysite controversy warned of the internal weakness that was threatening stability. The subtleties of theological argument only partly concealed the real issue: Would Alexandria successfully challenge Constantinople for leadership in the ecclesiastical world of the eastern Mediterranean?

With Justinian (527-565) we encounter an emperor so controversial that even his own historian, Procopius, in addition to several works praising him to the skies, wrote a *Secret History,* never published in his own day, and discovered only much later. The *Secret History* denounces Justinian in the most unrestrained way and tells some shocking stories about his past and that of his famous Empress Theodora, who in her youth had been an entertainer in the Hippodrome. On the basis of the full record we can safely conclude that Justinian was not greater than Cyrus the Great or Themistocles, as Procopius says when praising him. But we do not have to believe either that he was a demon who walked around the palace at night without his head, as Procopius tells us in the *Secret History.*

By strenuous military efforts, Justinian's armies reconquered North Africa from the Vandals, Italy from the Ostrogoths, and southern Spain from the Visigoths, a last desperate effort to reunite all of Rome's Mediterranean lands and recreate a territorial unity that was by now in fact unmanageable. Both the long drawn-out campaigns and a vast new system of fortifications proved extremely costly. The focus of imperial attention on the West permitted the Persian danger on the Eastern frontier to grow to the point where Justinian's immediate successors could not check it, while in Europe Slavs and Avars were able to dent the Danube line and filter into the Balkans.

Justinian began a process of administrative reorganization that his successors would finish. In the provinces of the Roman Empire, Constantine had seen to it that civil and military authority were never united in the hands of the same official. This was an obvious precaution against repeated revolts by ambitious generals like those that had characterized the third century. But now, Justinian's conquests in the West imposed so severe a strain on the system, and unrest in Egypt and elsewhere was so alarming, that the emperor occasionally entrusted both civil and military power to a single officer. After Justinian's death the militray emergency caused in Italy by the invasion of the Lombards and in North Africa by the savage native Berbers forced the authorities to create in both places large military districts. Here the military commanders, called exarchs, also served as civil governors, and their areas of command were called exarchates. The exarchs of Italy and Africa, with their headquarters respectively at Ravenna and Carthage, became virtual vice-emperors.

The empire did not have to pay the full bill for Justinian's policies until the early years of the seventh century. Under the reign of Phocas (602–610), internal bankruptcy and external attacks from the Persians seemed to threaten total destruction. It was Heraclius (610–641), the son of the exarch of Africa, who sailed in the nick of time from Carthage to Constantinople and seized the throne. He spent the first years of his reign in military preparations, absorbing heavy losses as the Persians took Antioch, Damascus, and Jerusalem, bearing off the True Cross in triumph. Soon afterwards they entered Alexandria, and Egypt too was gone. After 622 Heraclius began his great counteroffensive. At one moment in 626 the Persians threatened Constantinople from the Asian side of the Straits, while the Slavs and Avars were besieging it in Europe; but the Byzantines beat off the double threat. Heraclius defeated the Persians on their own territory, recaptured all the lost provinces, and returned the True Cross to Jerusalem in 629.

But only a few years later, the new movement of Islam, which we shall examine shortly, exploded out of Arabia and took away once more the very provinces that Heraclius had recaptured from the Persians. In both the Persian and the Muslim victories over Byzantium the disaffection of the monophysite Syrians and Egyptians played a major part. From Egypt the Muslims pushed on westward and took Carthage in 698, putting an end to the North African exarchate. Muslim ships began to operate from Cyprus and Rhodes. In northern Italy the Lombard kingdom had increased its power, while two separate Lombard duchies, one at Spoleto in central Italy,

the other at Benevento farther south, threatened the imperial possessions. Heraclius' work and that of Justinian were seemingly undone.

The Reorganization of the Seventh and Eighth Centuries

But despite the desperate crisis, the emperors, beginning with Heraclius, completely overhauled the administrative machinery of the state. They now gradually extended to their remaining territories in Asia Minor and the Balkans the system of government previously introduced into the two exarchates. The loss of Syria and Egypt required the transformation of Asia Minor into a reservoir of military manpower and an orderly stronghold of defense. The perpetual raids of Slavs, Avars, and Bulgars into the Balkan provinces made the emergency the more acute, and increased still more the dependence on Asia Minor. So now the emperors divided Asia Minor and the Balkans into what we would call army corps areas, with the local military commanders also exercising civil authority.

These new military districts were called *themes,* from a word meaning a permanent garrison. In each theme the troops were recruited from the native population; in return for their services, the sturdy, independent yeoman farmers were granted land, but they were not allowed to dispose of it or to evade their duties as soldiers. Their sons inherited the property along with the obligation to fight. The commanding generals of a theme, though in theory responsible to the emperor, often revolted, and in the seventh and eighth centuries many of them seized the throne. Gradually, the imperial government strove to combat this danger, inevitable when broad military and civil powers were united in the same hands, by dividing up the large original themes into smaller ones. From seven big themes at the end of the seventh century, the number mounted to about thirty small ones by the year 900. From the start, one of the themes was naval. In addition to the troops supplied by the commanders of the themes, the emperors had at their disposal other forces, both land and sea, quartered in the capital itself.

The emperors also asserted more and more their direct supervisory authority over the civil service departments. As the reorganization proceeded, the old title of a formerly influential job was sometimes bestowed as a purely honorary reminder of past duties, much as the English title of duke, for example, no longer means that the bearer is a true dux, or army commander. In this way a hierarchy of honorary titles came to exist side by side with the hierarchy of real jobs. Military and civil officials, eunuchs, clerics, and even foreign ambassadors to the Byzantine court all had their places both in the galaxy of honorary titles and in the hierarchy of real positions. Special treatises were needed to remind court officers of the proper precedence at banquets and other festivities.

The new system also embodied a change in concepts of taxation. New immigration and settlement had apparently put an end to the labor shortage of earlier centuries. It was now possible to separate the land tax from the tax on persons. The latter was transformed into a hearth tax, which fell on every peasant household without exception. For purposes of the land tax, each peasant village was considered a single unit. Imperial tax-assessors regularly visited each village, calculated its total tax, and assessed the individual inhabitants the portion of the tax that each would owe. The community as a whole was held responsible for the total tax, and often the neighbor of a poor peasant or of one who had abandoned his farm would have to pay the extra amount to make up the total. This obligation was onerous, and when the tax could not be collected the state itself sometimes had to take over the property and resell or re-lease it.

garian menace reached a new peak of severity.

During the period when iconoclastic emperors held the throne (726–787 and 813–842) the movement took on in its later phases a violent anti-monastic aspect, since the monks at Byzantium were the great defenders of the images. During this phase of the struggle we find some of the monks actually challenging the right of the emperors to legislate in matters of religion. But the images were twice restored by imperial decree (each time by an empress) as they had twice been banned by imperial decree. The position of the emperor in church affairs remained supreme despite these murmurs against his authority, and the restoration of the images was a concession to the weight of public opinion. As a result of the struggle, the Byzantines drew more careful distinctions between superstitious adoration paid to images and proper reverence. When the controversy closed, it was tacitly understood that no more religious statues would be sculptured in the round.

Although the new system of military small-holdings and the growth of a free peasantry retarded the development of large estates during the eighth and ninth centuries, we have clear evidence that once again large landlords were beginning to accumulate big properties. One cause may have been the ruin of the small farmers in Asia Minor as a result of the dreadful disorders that accompanied a great rebellion led by a certain Thomas the Slav. After threatening to subvert the throne, this rebellion was put down in 823.

717–867

867–1081

In 717, Leo III won a splendid victory over the Arabs, who were besieging the capital itself. Thereafter the struggle against the Muslims gradually became stabilized along a fixed frontier in Asia Minor. But the Muslim capture of Crete and Sicily opened the way for repeated pirate raids against the shores of imperial lands in Greece and southern Italy. In northern Italy, the Lombards extinguished the exarchate of Ravenna in 751, and Byzantine rule was interrupted by the alliance between the Franks and the papacy. The Byzantine *dux* of Venetia moved his headquarters to the famous island of the Rialto, and thus became the forerunner of the *doges* of Venice. And in the Balkans, the Bul-

Although intrigue and the violent overthrow of sovereigns remained a feature of Byzantine politics, the people developed a deep loyalty to the new ruling house that was established in 867 by the Armenian Basil I (867–886) and called the Macedonian dynasty. Even usurpers now took pains to legitimatize themselves by marrying into the imperial house. As political disintegration began to weaken the Muslim world, the Byzantines went over to the counteroffensive in the tenth century. Their fleets and armies recaptured Crete (961) and soon afterward Antioch and much of northern Syria, after three centuries of Arab domination.

A new Muslim dynasty in Egypt, which took

over in Palestine also, stopped the Byzantine advance short of Jerusalem. But much like the later Crusaders from the West, the Byzantine emperors hoped to liberate Christ's city from the infidel. While pushing back the Muslims, the Byzantines allied themselves with the Armenians, penetrated the state of Armenia, and at the end of the period annexed it. This was almost surely an error in judgment: what had been a valuable buffer against the Turks of Central Asia, who were beginning to raid into eastern Asia Minor, now lay open to attack. Firmly re-established in southern Italy in the face of the Muslim threat from Sicily, the Byzantines dominated the neighboring Lombard duchies until after the advent of the Normans in the early eleventh century. These adventurers displayed their usual savagery in local warfare and their usual ability in carving out estates for themselves and gaining a foothold in the peninsula. With the critically important fight against the Bulgarians we shall deal below.

Under the early emperors of the Macedonian dynasty the large landowners continued to flourish. Whole dynasties of nobles came to exist on their great estates. They were "the powerful," who were constantly acquiring more land at the expense of "the poor." The more they got, the more they wanted. They bought up the holdings of "the poor" and made the peasantry once more dependent upon them. The growing power of "the powerful" threatened the state in two important ways: not only was it losing its best taxpayers, the free peasants, but also its best soldiers, the military settlers.

During the tenth and eleventh centuries, there developed a great struggle between the emperors and "the powerful," parallel in some ways to the struggle between the monarchy and the feudal nobility in France, but destined to end differently. For while in France over the centuries the nobility was curbed and a strong centralized monarchy was established, in the East, where absolutism as such was never questioned, "the powerful" thwarted all imperial attempts to check the growth of their economic and military power, and eventually seized the throne itself. Repeated laws striving to put an end to the acquisition of land by "the powerful" could not be enforced; in times of bad harvest especially, the small free proprietor was forced to sell out to his rich neighbor.

The great emperor Basil II (976–1025) made the most sustained efforts to reverse this process.

A law of Basil has been preserved, with marginal notes and comments of his own, which vividly illustrates the problem and his attitude toward it. It tells how Basil, in the course of his travels in the empire, had received thousands of complaints about "the powerful" who were buying up or seizing lands belonging to "the poor." He names names:

The patrician Constantine Maleinos and his son the magistros Eustathius have for a hundred years, or perhaps even a hundred and twenty, been in undisputed possession of lands unjustly acquired. It is the same way in the Phocas family, who, from father to son, for more than a century, have also succeeded in holding on to lands wrongly obtained. In more recent times certain newly rich men have done the same. For example Philokales, a simple peasant who lived for a long while in poverty by the work of his hands and paid the same taxes as the other peasants his brothers, now has obtained various offices of the palace, because he had made a fortune . . . and acquired vast estates. He has not gone unpunished. When we arrived in the region where his property is located, and heard the complaints of those whom he had dispossessed we commanded that all the buildings he had built be razed and that the lands ravished from the poor be returned to them. Now this man is living again on the small piece of property which he owned at the start of his career and has once more become what he was by birth, a simple peasant. Our imperial will is that the same should happen to all those of our subjects, whether of noble birth or not, who have in this way seized the land of the poor. It is for this reason that we proclaim what follows: Every estate which was established before the time of our maternal grandfather Romanos I [919–944] shall remain in the hands of its proprietor, provided that he can prove by authentic documents that his title goes back before that time. All estates acquired since, and contrary to my grandfather's laws, shall be considered to be illegally owned. . . . The peasants, the original owners, who were long since expelled by the owners of the large estates, have the right to reclaim the immediate and complete restitution of their property without being required to repay the sales price, or to pay for any improvements which may have been installed by the proprietors who are about to be dispossessed.*

Shortly afterward, the emperor, returning from a campaign in the Caucasus, visited the enormous estates in Asia Minor belonging to that

* G. L. Schlumberger, *L'Epopée Byzantine* (Paris, 1896–1905), II, 122. Our translation.

very Eustathius Maleinos whom he had denounced in his law. Maleinos was able not only to entertain the emperor himself in sumptuous style, but also to feed the entire army. On the pretext of wishing to repay his hospitality, Basil took this great potentate back to Constantinople with him, where he kept him, like a bird in a cage, until he died. Thereupon all his estates were seized by the crown. As a final blow to "the powerful," Basil II ordained that they would have to pay all the tax arrears of the delinquent peasants, thus relieving the village communities of the heavy burden that was so difficult for them to bear, and placing it on the shoulders of the rich.

But a few years after Basil died, this law was repealed under the influence of "the powerful," and thenceforth they did indeed prove "more merciless than famine or plague." As the landlords got more and more of the free military peasants as tenants on their estates, their own military role grew more and more important, and they became virtual commanders of private armies. After Basil, only the civil servants acted

as a counterweight to the landowners. In an effort to reduce their power, the civil servants tried to cut down the expenses of the army, in which the landlords were now playing the leading role.

Strife between these two parties weakened the imperial defenses. The Normans drove the Byzantines from the Italian peninsula by taking the great southern port of Bari in 1071. In the same year, after three decades of raids across the eastern frontier of Asia Minor, the Seljuk Turks defeated the imperial armies at Manzikert in Armenia, and captured the emperor Romanos IV. Asia Minor itself, mainstay of the empire, now lay open to the Turks, who pushed their way to the Straits and established their capital in Nicæa. Meanwhile other Turkic tribes, Pechenegs and Magyars, raided southward into the Balkans almost at will. In 1081, there came to the throne one of the "powerful" magnates of Asia Minor, Alexius I Comnenus. The story of the ways in which he and his successors built still another military and social system and staved off collapse for more than a century properly belongs to a later chapter.

IV   Byzantium and the Slavs

Of all the achievements of the Byzantines, none is so remarkable as their impact on the Slavic world. Here we are dealing with the transfer of a civilization, substantially unmodified, from a more advanced to a less advanced group of peoples. Much as old Rome civilized and eventually christianized large groups of "barbarians" in western Europe, so Constantinople, the new Rome, civilized and christianized the Slavs. Many of the problems that beset the West today in its dealings with the Soviet Union arise from the fact that the Soviet Union is first and foremost Russia, a country in the Orthodox and not in the Western Christian tradition, a country that still shows the effects of having experienced its conversion from Byzantium.

Conversion of the Bulgarians

The first of the Slavic peoples to fall under Byzantine influence were the Bulgarians, who

were the product of a fusion between a Slavic population and a smaller group of Asiatic Bulgar invaders. From the time these barbarians crossed the Danube in the late seventh century, they engaged in intermittent warfare against the Byzantine Empire. In 811, the ruler of the Bulgarians, Krum, defeated the imperial forces, and the emperor Nicephorus I (802–811) was killed, the first emperor to fall in battle since the death of Valens at Adrianople in 378. Krum took the skull of Nicephorus, had it hollowed out and lined with silver, and used it as a drinking cup—behavior that vividly shows the level of Bulgarian civilization at the time. Bulgarian religion was primitive: the sun and moon and stars were worshiped and propitiated with sacrifices of horses and dogs. The overwhelming masses of the people were peasants living in huts.

Yet the rulers of this people had created a powerful state, which by the middle of the ninth century had reached the stage all barbarian tribes eventually reached—preparedness for conversion to Christianity, for the reception of the religion that alone could accompany a position of prestige in the medieval world. Already Greek artisans were imported into Bulgaria to build the palaces of the native rulers. Since there was no Bulgarian alphabet, Greek letters had to be used in the royal inscriptions. But the Bulgarian rulers hesitated to accept missionaries from Byzantium, since this would surely mean the extension of Byzantine political power.

At the same time, a Slavic people called the Moravians, who lived far to the west in what is now Czechoslovakia, had also established a state of their own and had reached a stage similar to that reached by the Bulgarians. Their rulers felt themselves ready for Christianity. But, just as the Bulgarians associated the religion with their powerful neighbors, the Byzantines, and feared Byzantine imperial political encroachment, so the Moravians associated it with their powerful neighbors the Germans, and feared both German and papal encroachment. In 862, the king of the Moravians began the process that was to culminate in the conversion of the Slavs. He sent to Byzantium, in order to avoid German or papal influence, and asked that a Greek missionary be sent to teach the Moravian people Christianity in their own Slavic language.

The Byzantine emperor Michael III sent to Moravia two missionaries, Cyril (or Constantine) and his brother Methodius, called the Apostles to the Slavs. They knew the Slavic tongue and had invented two alphabets in which it could be written. The simpler and more useful is the alphabet still employed by the Russians, the Bulgarians, and the Serbs, and still called Cyrillic after its inventor. Almost at once, as a countermove, Boris, ruler of the Bulgarians, asked for Christianity from the Germans. But these efforts on the part of the two Slavic rulers to avoid accepting conversion at the hands of their powerful neighbors and to obtain it instead from a less threatening distant court were doomed to failure. In spite of the efforts of Cyril and Methodius among the Moravians, German pressure and eventual papal reluctance to give final sanction to the conduct of church services outside the Latin tongue proved too strong. After some years, it was the German clergy and the Roman form of Christianity that triumphed in Moravia.

Similarly, despite Boris' negotiations with the Germans and a long correspondence with the popes, during which the Roman pontiff on one occasion gave him advice about wearing trousers

(permissible) and eating all his meals by himself (permissible but rude), the nearby power of Byzantium was too strong, and Roman Christianity had to yield. At first, the Byzantines forced their faith on Boris by the sword. Boris yielded, but the flood of Greek priests that followed, and the Byzantine attempts to prescribe the proper duties of the Christian prince, annoyed him and he turned to Rome. His flirtation with the papacy, however, ended in disillusionment when it became clear that Rome would not allow him to have an independent church of his own. He moved back to the Byzantine church, and this time the Byzantines did not repeat their mistakes. They permitted the Bulgarians virtual ecclesiastical autonomy. Only in the fold of the Eastern church could Boris unify his country and consolidate his own autocratic power. The Byzantine patriarch, unlike the pope, made no temporal claims. In Bulgaria, then, from the late ninth century on, the language of the church was the native Slavonic tongue preached by followers of Cyril and Methodius.

Of course, the conversion of Bulgaria did not mean that an era of perpetual good relations was now established between Byzantium and the new converts. The ambitions of the Bulgarian rulers were too great for that. Under Simeon (893–927), second son of Boris, himself educated in Constantinople and called "half-Greek" by his contemporaries, there began a bitter hundred-years' war, during which the Bulgarians tried to make themselves emperors by conquering Constantinople itself. Toward the end of the tenth century, the rivalry became more intense than ever under a Bulgarian ruler named Samuel. In 1014, Basil II (976–1025) whom we have already seen curbing his own great landowners, captured fourteen or fifteen thousand Bulgarian prisoners and savagely blinded ninety-nine out of every hundred. The hundredth man was allowed to keep the sight of one eye, so that he could lead his miserable fellows home. At the ghastly sight of his blinded warriors, Samuel fell dead of shock. Basil II took the appropriate name of "Bulgar-slayer." Shortly afterward, Byzantine domination over Bulgaria became complete, and the country was ruled as a conquered province. But its inhabitants were never deprived of their own church, whose archbishop had just as much jurisdiction as he had had in the days of Bulgarian independence.

The great expenditures of money and man-

Fourteenth-century Slavonic manuscript depicting Basil II's defeat of the Bulgarians (top). Basil blinded the prisoners and sent them back to King Samuel, who died of shock at the sight (bottom).

power incidental to the long pursuit of the Bulgarian war played their part in weakening Byzantium for the military disasters that were to come at Manzikert and at Bari in 1071. But Boris' decision to accept Christianity from Constantinople, and the subsequent Byzantine military conquest of his country, helped to determine where the line between East and West would be drawn for all future history. The Bulgarians are an Orthodox people to this day, and their architecture, their literature, and their art throughout the Middle Ages directly reflected the overpowering influence of Byzantium. In much the same way, more than three hundred years later, the western neighbors of the Bulgarians, the Serbs, also took their faith from the Greek East after a flirtation with the Latin West. And the Serbs acted for the same reason: the attractions of Byzantium.

The Early Russian State

To the north and east of the Balkan Bulgarians lie the great plains between the Baltic and the Black seas, the plains of European Russia. Here movement is easiest by water, along the valleys of the rivers that flow north into the Baltic or south into the Black or Caspian seas. Beginning in the eighth century, the Scandinavians, whom we have already encountered in their invasions of England and of western Europe, expanded into Russia also. First taking control of the Baltic shore, they then began to move south along the rivers to the Sea of Azov and the northern Caucasus. Their name, in the period of expansion, was Rus, which has survived in the modern term "Russia." Gradually they overcame many of the Slavic, Lithuanian, Finnish, and Magyar peoples who were then living on the steppe. The details of this process are very little known. The story told in the Old Russian *Primary Chronicle*, compiled during the eleventh century, is suggestive of what may have happened among the inhabitants of Russia sometime in the 850's:

There was no law among them, but tribe rose against tribe. Discord thus ensued among them, and they began to war one against another. They said to themselves "Let us seek a prince who may rule over us and judge us according to the law." They accordingly went overseas to the Varangian [i.e., Scandinavian] Russes . . . and said to the people of Rus, "Our whole land is great and rich, but there is no order in it. Come to rule and reign over us."*

This is the story of the "calling of the princes." The *Chronicle* goes on to tell how Rurik (who has now been successfully identified with a Danish warrior known from other sources) accepted the invitation and settled in the town of Novgorod, already an important trading center.

*Samuel H. Cross, *The Russian Primary Chronicle*, in *Harvard Studies and Notes in Philology and Literature*, XII (1930), 145.

From Novgorod, within a few years, Scandinavian princes moved south along the Dnieper River. On the middle course of the Dnieper they seized the settlement called Kiev, still today the major city of the Ukraine, and made it the center of a state at first very loosely controlled and devoted especially to trade. And in 860, for the first time, a fleet of two hundred of their warships appeared off Constantinople, where they at first caused panic but were eventually repulsed. During the next two centuries there were three further attacks of varying seriousness, as well as other wars, which the Byzantines won.

But the normal state of affairs was not war between Byzantium and Russia. The texts of the trade treaties concluded between the two reflect close economic ties. We find the Byzantines promising to feed the visiting Russian traders and to furnish them baths and supplies for the homeward voyage. The Russians agreed to live in a special quarter outside the city during their stay in Constantinople and to be registered by imperial officials. One treaty reads "They shall not enter the city save through one gate, unarmed and fifty at a time, escorted by soldiers of the emperor." But at the same time that the Byzantines were anxious to protect the lives and property of their citizens from the wild barbarians, they were eager to obtain the merchandise that the Russians brought them.

Conversion of the Russians

Most important, however, was the continuing religious influence that Byzantium exercised upon the Russians. No doubt numerous individual Russians were converted from their primitive polytheistic faith simply as a result of their impressions during a visit to Byzantium. In the trade treaty of 945, we find that some of the Russian envoys are already Christians and are already swearing by the Holy Cross to observe the provisions of the treaty. In the 950's, Olga, the ruling princess of Kiev, visited the emperor at Constantinople:

Olga came before him, and when he saw that she was very fair of countenance and wise as well, the Emperor wondered at her intellect. He conversed with her, and remarked that she was worthy to reign with him in his city. When Olga heard these words, she replied that she was still a

Early Russia about 1100

pagan, and that if he desired to baptize her, he should perform this function himself: otherwise she was unwilling to accept baptism. The Emperor, with the assistance of the Patriarch, accordingly baptized her. . . . After her baptism, the Emperor summoned Olga and made known to her that he wished her to become his wife. But she replied, "How can you marry me, after baptizing me yourself and calling me your daughter? For among Christians that is unlawful, as you must know." Then the Emperor said, "Olga, you have outwitted me."*

The Russians were converted as a people during the late 980's in the reign of Vladimir. He felt the inadequacy of the old faith, about which we do not know very much except that the Russians worshiped forest and water spirits and a god of thunder. According to the partly legendary story in the *Chronicle*, Vladimir was visited by representatives of the different faiths, who told him about their beliefs. He discarded the faith of Mohammed, because circumcision and absti-

*Ibid., pp. 168–169.

Thirteenth-century manuscript illumination depicting Russian envoys to Byzantium.

Shortly afterward, Vladimir was baptized and married a Byzantine princess. Returning to Kiev, he threw down all the idols in the city, and in one day forcibly baptized the entire population in the waters of the Dnieper.

Despite its legendary features, the whole story reflects the various cultural influences to which the Kievan state was in truth exposed. It had Muslim, Jewish,* and Roman Catholic Christian neighbors; but the most powerful and influential neighbor was the Orthodox and Greek Byzantium, and doubtless the marriage alliance with the Byzantine princess and the resulting gain in prestige played a part in Vladimir's decision. To secure the conversion of the Russians to the Byzantine form of Christianity was also important for the Byzantines, who needed to protect their possessions along the Black Sea and their capital itself against Russian attack.

nence from pork and wine were disagreeable to him. "Drinking," said he, "is the joy of the Russes. We cannot exist without that pleasure." Judaism he rejected because the God of the Jews had not been strong enough to enable them to stay in their native Jerusalem. Roman Christianity he rejected because it required a certain amount of fasting, as of course did the Christianity of the Greeks. But the cautious Vladimir did not accept this fourth possibility, Orthodox Christianity, until he had sent a commission to visit the countries where all the faiths were practiced, and to report back to him.

The envoys reported, "When we journeyed among the Moslems, we beheld how they worship in . . . a mosque, . . . and there is no happiness among them but only sorrow and a dreadful stench. Their religion is not good. Then we went among the Germans [Roman Catholics], and saw them performing many ceremonies in their temples; but beheld no glory there. Then we went on to Greece [Byzantium], and the Greeks led us to the edifices where they worship their God, and we knew not whether we were in heaven or on earth. For on earth there is no such splendor or such beauty, and we are at a loss how to describe it. We only know that God dwells there among men, and their service is fairer than the ceremonies of other nations. For we cannot forget that beauty.*

*Ibid., p. 199.

Effects of Conversion

Conversion meant great changes in the Russians way of life. The church became an important social force in Kievan society, and the clergy formed an entirely new and highly influential social class. In spite of the fact that the Byzantines always asserted theoretical sovereignty over the Russian church, and in spite of the fact that the archbishops of Kiev in the early period were mostly Greeks, and appointed from Byzantium, the Russian church quite early asserted its practical independence. The church in Russia from the first became an important landowner, and, as in the Byzantine Empire, monasteries multiplied. The clergy came to have legal jurisdiction over all Christians in cases involving morals, family affairs, and religious matters. A new and more advanced concept that crimes should be punished by the state replaced the old primitive feeling the punishment was a matter of personal revenge. For the first time, formal education was established. The Cyrillic alphabet was adopted, and literature in Russian began to appear, almost all of it ecclesiastical. Byzantine art forms were imported and imitated; the great Church of St. Sophia at Kiev is in its way as magnificent as its namesake in Constantinople. The old pagan faith persisted in

* The Turkic tribe of the Khazars, settled along the lower Don River, had been converted to Judaism.

the countryside; enormous rural areas remained backward, and culture was largely confined to the few cities and to the monasteries. In the main, however, the conversion of the Russians had a civilizing effect.

Yet the short-run gain may well have been outweighed by a long-run loss. The very use of the native language in the liturgy, which was so great an advantage to the Byzantines when, as missionaries, they sought to spread their faith without insisting on the use of their language, meant that the culture of Russia remained poor by contrast with that of the West. In the West, every priest and every monk had to learn Latin. As soon as he did so, he had the key to the treasures of Latin classical literature and the works of the Latin church fathers, who had themselves been formed in the schools of pagan rhetoric, philosophy, and literature. The educated man in the West, usually a cleric, had access to Vergil, to Ovid, to Cicero, and to a large number of lesser authors, some of whom may not have been in the least suitable for clerical reading, but all of whom gave the reader a sense of style, a familiarity with ancient taste and thought, and sometimes solid instruction. He had Jerome, who had gone to school to Cicero, and Augustine, whose *City of God* was the classic expression of Christian philosophy, written in magnificent Latin prose. The educated man in the West had a whole library of commentaries on the classical authors designed to reconcile them with Christian doctrine, and to make it legitimate to study them, to teach them, and to copy them for posterity. Not every priest and monk in the West could qualify as a professor of classics, but for those who had the leisure, the talent, the inclination, and the luck to find themselves in a monastery with a good library, the opportunity for learning and cultivation was open.

The fact that the Byzantines did not insist on the use of Greek in the liturgy meant that the Russian clergy did not automatically learn Greek, as French or English or German or Spanish priests had to learn Latin. And of course the Latin heritage was not available to the Russians either. A very few Russians did learn Greek, but by and large the great Greek classical heritage of philosophy and literature was closed to the Russians. Byzantine sermons, saints' lives, some chronicles and history, and certain other pieces of Byzantine literature, including both the epic of Basil Digenes Akritas and the tale of

Barlaam and Ioasaph, were indeed translated and circulated in Slavonic. But these, as we have seen, were hardly substitutes for Plato and Aristotle, Homer and the dramatists. The conversion to Christianity from Byzantium thus had the effect of stunting the intellectual and literary progress of Russia. It is clear, of course, that the Kievan Russians of the tenth century were not ready for Plato and Aristotle, but when a time in their development came when they would have been ready, they were cut off from access to the treasurehouse.

Indeed, in the nineteenth century a very influential group of Russian thinkers argued that conversion from Byzantium had led Russia into hopeless stagnation and wretched intellectual sterility, because it had cut Russia off from Rome, the fountainhead of the vigorous intellectual and spiritual life of the West, without providing a substitute. Their opponents argued just as vigorously that it was precisely the Orthodox faith accepted from Byzantium that gave modern Russia her high degree of spirituality, her willingness to bend to the will of God, and indeed all the virtues which they found in the Russian character and the Russian system. This difference of opinion persists, but it may be said without much fear of contradiction that modern Russia has shown a considerable cultural lag in comparison with Western countries, that this cultural lag is partly attributable in the first place to the fact that Christianity was accepted from Byzantium, and that the very privilege of using Slavonic in the church services prevented the growth in Russia of a class of men educated in the wisdom of the ancient world.

It would be a grave mistake, however, to attribute the cultural lag solely to these factors. It was perhaps in even greater measure due to the effect on Russian development of the Tatar invasions and domination of the thirteenth and fourteenth centuries, as we shall see.

Kievan Russia

Kievan Russia itself, in spite of whatever drawbacks conversion from Byzantium may have had, developed a society not very unlike that in contemporary western medieval Europe. From being a mere Scandinavian warband sworn to assist the prince in battle and entitled to divide

Early Russian architecture: the Church of the Savior on the Nereditsa, Novgorod.

the booty with him, the prince's entourage had now become that upper ruling group of councillors appropriate to a settled state. The Kievan law codes reflect the social conditions of the time and place: arson and stealing horses were the worst crimes, more heavily punished than murder or mutilation. The penalty was the same for stealing a beaver out of another man's trap, for trespassing on his land, for knocking out his tooth, or for killing his slave. This was a society that put its emphasis on the value of property.

There has been some dispute among scholars over whether agriculture was more or less important than commerce in Kievan Russia. Although it is clear that farming played a large role, the emphasis should certainly be put upon trade. In this trade, with Byzantium in particular, the Russians sold mostly furs, honey, and wax, not products of agriculture at all, but of hunting and bee-keeping. Since the Byzantines paid in cash, Kiev had much more of a money economy than did western Europe. Viewed from the economic and social point of view, Kievan Russia was in some ways more advanced than backward manorial western Europe, where markets, fairs, and industries were only beginning to spring up in Flanders, along the Baltic shore, and in northern Italy.

During the period before the Tatar invasions, which began in the early 1200's, this Kievan state began to have close diplomatic and political re-lations with the West. Dynastic marriages were arranged between the ruling house of Kiev and the royal families of Sweden and France, and alliances were reached with the Holy Roman Empire of Germany. Merchants from the West appeared in Russia, especially at Novgorod in the north, and at Kiev itself. It is then conceivable that whatever handicap was imposed by Byzantine Christianity might have been overcome, had Kiev been allowed to maintain its free lines of communications with the West. Its advance might have come through developing further this vigorous and valuable exchange. But as things turned out, Russia was denied this opportunity.

The Kievan state had internal political weaknesses, especially the failure to make any rules for the succession to the throne, and the practice (similar to that of the Franks) of dividing up the land among the prince's sons as if it were the private property of the prince. The fragmentation of the Kievan state into mutually hostile provinces weakened it in the face of outside dangers. Beginning in the eleventh century the Turkish tribe of Polovtsy or Cumans appeared on the southern steppes of Russia just as the Huns had swept into Europe earlier. The Russian princes warring against one another made a tragic error by hiring bands of Polovtsy. Thus when the Mongol Tatars appeared in the early thirteenth century, Kievan Russia had been softened for the blow. The sole surviving heroic poem of the Kievan period, the *Song of the Expedition of Igor,* reproves the Russian princes:

Voices have grown mute, revelry has waned. . . . Lower your banners, sheath your damaged swords, for ye have already strayed far from the glory of your grandsire. For with your own treasons ye began to bring the infidels upon the Russian land. . . . For through civil strife came violence from the land of the Polovtsians.*

Never entirely centralized politically, the Kievan state none the less strove for unity. It be-

*La Geste du Prince Igor, ed. H. Grégoire, R. Jakobson, and M. Szeftel (New York, 1948), p. 171, trans. S. H. Cross. The *Igor Tale* was preserved in a single manuscript only, which perished in the burning of Moscow during Napoleon's invasion of Russia in 1812. Scholars have long debated its authenticity, and recently the theory that it may be a brilliant eighteenth-century forgery has once more gained some currency. But we believe these arguments are far from conclusive, and prefer to accept the poem as a genuine—and remarkably beautiful—Kievan work.

queathed the ideal of unity to the future Russian state that was to emerge after more than two centuries of Mongol domination. The common heritage of a literary language and of a single Christian faith laid the basis for a future unified state.

It was this later state, the state of Moscow, that was to take from the Byzantines not only their form of religion, already deeply entrenched in the Russia of Kiev, but also their political theory of autocracy, and much of their political practice.

V   Islam before the Crusades

Islam (the Arabic word means "submission") is the most recently founded of the world's great religions. Its adherents (Muslims, "those who submit") today inhabit the entire North African coast of the Mediterranean, part of Yugoslavia and Albania, Egypt, Turkey, the entire Near and Middle East, Pakistan, parts of India, the Malay Peninsula, Indonesia, and the Philippine Islands, to say nothing of Russian Central Asia and portions of China. From the point of view of Western civilization, relationships with the Muslim world have been of crucial importance since Mohammed founded Islam in the early seventh century. In an incredibly short time Islamic society joined the Latin and Greek Christian societies as the third major civilization west of India.

Mohammed

What we know of Mohammed is derived from Muslim authors who lived some time after his death; it is not easy to decide what is true and what is fictional in their accounts. The Arabia into which he was born about the year 570 was inhabited largely by nomadic tribes, each under its own chief. These nomads lived on the meat and milk of their animals, and on dates from the palm trees. They raided each other's flocks of camels and sheep, and often feuded among themselves. The religion of the Arabs was pagan, centering around sacred stones and trees. Their chief center was Mecca, fifty miles inland from the coast of the Red Sea, where there was a sacred building called the Kaaba, or cube, in which the Arab worshipers did reverence to a large number of idols, especially to a small black stone fallen from heaven, perhaps a meteorite. To this place the pagan Arabs seem to have made a pilgrimage of some sort.

In the sixth century, Mecca was inhabited by a tribe called the Kuraish, a trading people who lived by caravan commerce with Syria. Mohammed was born into one of the poorer clans of the Kuraish. Early orphaned, he was brought up by relatives and as a young man entered the service of a wealthy widow much older than himself, whom he later married, after successfully performing several trading missions for her. Now prosperous, Mohammed was free to devote himself to his divine mission. We do not know how he became convinced that he was the bearer of a new revelation. He certainly could read no language except Arabic, and there were no religious books written in Arabic. His ideas and information on the beliefs of other religions must therefore have been derived from observations on his caravan journeys and from conversations with members of Christian and Jewish communities. In any case, he seems to have spent much time in fasting and in vigils, perhaps suggested by Christian practice. He surely suffered from nervousness and hysteria, and seems to have had paroxysms during which he suffered high fevers. He became convinced that God was revealing the truth to him and had singled him out to be his messenger. The revelations came to him gradually over the rest of his life, often when some crisis arose. He probably wrote them down himself, in a rhythmic, sometimes rhyming Arabic prose, and included entertaining stories from the Old Testament of the Hebrews, and from popular and current Arabian folklore, such as the legends that had come to surround the memory of Alexander the Great.

The whole body of Muslim revelation was not put together until some little time after Mohammed's death. This is the Koran, or "book." The chapters were not arranged in order by subject matter, but put together mechanically by length, with the longest first. This makes the Koran difficult to follow. Moreover, it is written in a

Sixteenth-century Persian miniature showing Mohammed, his face veiled, ascending to Paradise.

Mohammed was a firm monotheist. His God is the God of the Jews and Christians, yet Mohammed did not deny that his pagan fellow Arabs had knowledge of God. He declared only that it was idolatry to worship more than one god, and he believed the trinity of the Christians to be three gods and therefore idolatry. A major innovation for the Arabs was Mohammed's idea of an afterlife, which was to be experienced in the flesh. The delights of paradise for Mohammed are fleshly indeed, and the punishments of hell are torture.

The requirements of Islam are not severe. Five times a day in prayer, facing toward Mecca, the Muslim must bear witness that there is no God but God and that Mohammed is his prophet. During the sacred month of Ramadan— perhaps suggested by Lent—he may not eat or drink between sunrise and sunset. He must give alms to the poor. And, if he can, he should at least once in his lifetime make a pilgrimage to the sacred city of Mecca. This was, and is, all, except for regulation of certain aspects of daily life—for example, the prohibition against strong drink, and other rules about food and its preparation, mostly taken from Jewish practice. The rest is social legislation: polygamy is sanctioned, but four wives are the most a man, save for the Prophet himself, may have. Divorce was easy for the husband, who need only repeat a prescribed formula. The condition of women and of slaves was markedly improved by the new laws.

At first, Mohammed preached this faith only to members of his family; then he preached to the people of Mecca, who repudiated him scornfully. In 622, some pilgrims from a city called Yathrib, two hundred miles north of Mecca, invited Mohammed to come to their city to settle a local feud. He accepted the invitation. This move from Mecca is the famous Hegira, from which the Islamic calendar has ever since been dated. The year 622 is the Muslim year 1. And Yathrib, to which he went, had its name changed to al-Medina, *the* city. Medina became the center of the new faith, which grow and prospered. The Jews of Medina, however, on whom Mohammed had been counting to become converted, did not do so, and aroused his hostility. He came to be more and more dependent upon the Arabs of the desert, the nomads, and became less and less universal in his appeal. God told him to fight against those who had not been converted. The holy war, or *jihad*, is a concept very like the Christian cru-

peculiar style, full of allusions to things and persons who are not called by their right names. Readers are often puzzled by the Koran, and a large body of Muslim writings explaining it has grown up over the centuries. Mohammed regarded his revelation as the confirmation of Hebrew and Christian scriptures. Islam is a religion designed for all men, the perfection of both Judaism and Christianity, the final revelation of God's truth.

sade: those who die in battle against the infidel die in a holy cause. In 630 Mohammed returned to Mecca as a conqueror, cleansed the Kaaba of all the idols except the black stone, and incorporated it into his religion. Two years later, in 632, he died. Perhaps a third of Arabia had by then become Muslim, but it seems clear that many Arabs had not yet even heard of the new faith. Yet only one century later, Charles Martel was having to battle Mohammed's co-religionists in far-off France; the great Byzantine Empire was locked in a struggle with them for its very existence; and Islam had reached India.

Expansion of Islam

Scholars used to believe that this startling expansion was due to the religious zeal of the con-verts to the new faith. Now, students of early Islam often argue that overpopulation of the Arabian peninsula set off the explosion of the Arabs into so huge an area. In fact, Arabs had been quietly emigrating from Arabia for some time, to settle in Iraq, Palestine, and Syria. Now they had the new faith to serve as a symbol of their new unity, and the first stages of their advance took them into lands already infiltrated by fellow Arabs. So the movement quickly gathered momentum: Islam might be its battle-cry, but its motives seem to have been the age-old ones of conquest for living-space and booty. Toward Christians and Jews the conquering Muslims generally were tolerant, regarding both as fellow monotheists and "peoples of the Book."

Syria and Persia were conquered almost simultaneously by two armies. The Syrian province, disaffected from Byzantium by mono-physitism, fell easily. And the Persians, because

The Great Mosque at Mecca, with the Kaaba in the foreground.

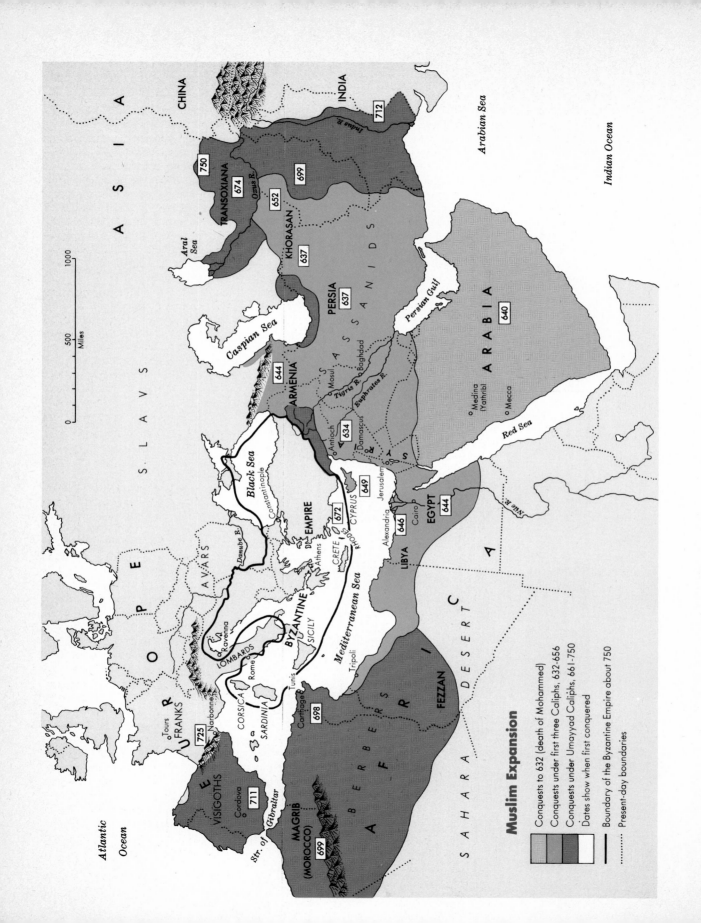

Atlantic
Ocean

Arabian Sea

Indian Ocean

A S I A

CHINA

INDIA

712

750

TRANSOXIANA

674

Oxus R.

699

Aral
Sea

652

KHORASAN

637

PERSIA

637

S A S S A N I D S

ARABIA

640

1000

500

0

Miles

Caspian Sea

644

ARMENIA

Baghdad

Mosul R.

Tigris R.

Euphrates R.

Persian Gulf

Medina
(Yathrib)

Mecca

Antioch

634

Damascus

Red Sea

Nile R.

S L A V S

Black Sea

Constantinople

BYZANTINE

EMPIRE

649

Jerusalem

572

CYPRUS

RHODES

CRETE

Athens

Alexandria

Cairo

EGYPT

644

646

LIBYA

E U R O P E

Danube R.

AVARS

LOMBARDS

Ravenna

Rome

SICILY

BYZANTINE

Tripoli

Mediterranean Sea

A F R I C A

FEZZAN

B E R B E R S

S A H A R A   D E S E R T

FRANKS

Tours

725

Narbonne

CORSICA

SARDINIA

Carthage

Tunis

698

VISIGOTHS

Cordova

711

Str. of Gibraltar

MAGRIB
(MOROCCO)

699

Muslim Expansion

Conquests to 632 (death of Mohammed)

Conquests under first three Caliphs, 632–656

Conquests under Umayyad Caliphs, 661–750

Dates show when first conquered

Boundary of the Byzantine Empire about 750

Present-day boundaries

of their weakness after recent defeats at the hands of Heraclius, failed to put up the resistance that might have been expected. By 639 Jerusalem had been captured; in 641 the native Persian dynasty was ended. During 639–40 the Arabs added Egypt, the major Byzantine naval base, which was also monophysite in religion and ripe for conquest. Launching ships, they now seized the islands of Cyprus and Rhodes, and began attacking southern Italy and Sicily. Moving west across North Africa, they took Carthage in 698 and conquered the native Berber tribes, who had resisted Romans, Vandals, and Byzantines. In 711 with a mixed force of Berbers and Arabs, under the command of a certain Tarik, they launched the invasion of Spain across the Straits of Gibraltar. The very name "Gibraltar" is a corruption of Arabic words meaning "Rock of Tarik." By 725, the first Arabs had crossed the Pyrenees, to meet Charles Martel at Tours seven years later. Meanwhile, they had been spreading east from Persia throughout what is today Russian Turkestan, and in 724 they had reached the Indus and the western frontiers of China. Simultaneously, they moved south from Egypt and North Africa into the little-known and un-civilized desert regions of Central Africa. These conquests of the first century of Islam were virtually final. Only the Mediterranean islands and Spain were ever permanently reconquered by Christians.

Disunity in Islam

The unity of these enormous conquests was of course more apparent than real. The Arabs had overrun a vast collection of diverse peoples with diverse customs. Moreover, the Arabs themselves were experiencing internal dissensions that made impossible the establishment of a unified state to govern the whole of the conquered territory. After Mohammed's death, there was disagreement over the succession. Finally, Mohammed's eldest companion, Abu Bekr, was chosen *khalifa* (caliph, the representative of Mohammed). Abu Bekr died in 634, and the next two caliphs were also chosen from outside Mohammed's family, to the distress of many Muslims. Moreover, many Arabs resented the caliphs' assertion of authority over them and longed for their old freedom as nomads. In 656,

the third caliph was murdered. By then, those who favored choosing only a member of Mohammed's own family had grouped themselves around Ali, son-in-law of the prophet. This party also opposed all reliance on commentaries, or supplemental works explaining the Koran. Fundamentalists with regard to the Koran, they were known as Shiites (the sectarians). Opposed to them were the Sunnites (traditionalists), who favored the election to the caliphate of any eligible person and approved of supplementing the Koran with commentaries called "traditions."

In 656 Ali was chosen caliph. Civil war broke out, and Ali was murdered in 661. His opponent, Muawiyah, of the Umayyad family, leader of the Sunnites, had already proclaimed himself caliph in Damascus in 660. Thus began the Umayyad caliphate (660–750). On the whole, it was a period of prosperity, good government, brisk trade, and cultural achievement along Byzantine lines, of which the famous "Dome of the Rock" mosque in Jerusalem is the outstanding example. The civil service was manned by Greeks, and Greek artists worked for the caliph; the Christian population, except for the payment of a poll tax, were on the whole unmolested and better off than they had been before.

Shiite opposition to the Umayyads, however, remained strong. There was almost no difference between the two groups with regard to religious observances and law. But the Shiites felt it their duty to curse the first three caliphs, who had ruled before their hero, Ali, while the Sunnites deeply revered these three caliphs. The Shiites were far more intolerant of the unbeliever, conspired in secret against the government, and were given to self-pity and to wild emotional outbursts of grief for Ali's son Husein, who was killed in 680. Southern Iraq was then the center of Shiite strength, although in modern times Persia has become the center.

From these Eastern regions came the leadership of the plot which in 750 was responsible for the overthrow and murder of the last of the Umayyad caliphs at Damascus, together with ninety members of his family. The leader of the conspirators was Abu-'l Abbas, not a Shiite himself, but the great-grandson of a cousin of Mohammed. The caliphate was shortly afterward moved east to Baghdad, capital of present-day Iraq, and was thereafter known as the Abbasid caliphate. The days when Islam was primarily an Arab movement under Byzantine influence were over. At Baghdad, the caliphate took on more and more of the color of the Persian Empire, in whose former territory it was situated. But even now, its Christian subjects were on the whole well treated.

Meanwhile, the rest of the Muslim world fell away from its dependence upon the Abbasids. One of the few Umayyads to escape death in 750 made his way to Spain, and built himself a state centered around the city of Cordova. Rich and strong, his descendants declared themselves caliphs in 929. Separate Muslim states appeared in Morocco, in Tunis, and in Egypt, where still another dynasty, this time Shiite, built Cairo in the tenth century and began to call themselves caliphs. Rival dynasties also appeared in Persia itself, in Syria, and in the other Eastern provinces. At Baghdad, though the state took much of its chraacter and culture from its Persian past, the power fell gradually into the hands of Turkish troops. And it was the Seljuk Turks who emerged supreme from the confused struggle for power when they took Baghdad in 1055. Although the caliphate at Baghdad lasted down to 1258, when the Mongols finally ended it, the caliphs were mere puppets in Turkish hands.

Islamic Civilization

More interesting perhaps than the shifts in political and military fortunes of Islamic rulers is the extraordinary development of Islamic civilization. The Arab conquerors were moving into provinces that had an ancient tradition of culture, regions which, until the Arabs appeared, had been parts of the East Roman or Persian empires. The Arabs brought their new religion and their language to the peoples whom they conquered. The religion often stimulated new artistic and literary development, and, through its requirement of pilgrimage, brought about mobility among the Muslims and encouraged the exchange of ideas with fellow Muslims from the other end of the Muslim world. The language had to be learned by everybody who wished to read the Koran, since it was the rule that the Book might not be translated. Since Arabic is an extraordinarily flexible and powerful instrument, it became the standard literary language of the whole Islamic world. Indeed, the

Muslims were highly conscious of its merits. They felt that incessant study of it was necessary for comprehension, and they gave the highest position among the arts to the composing of poetry, rating it even ahead of science. But aside from religion and language, the chief contribution to Muslim culture came from the civilizations of Persia and of the Greco-Roman world. Islamic government learned much from the Persian tradition; Islamic philosophy learned much from the classical tradition; and Islamic literature learned much from both.

Like both Roman and Greek Christianity, Islam was convinced of its superiority to all other religions and ways of life. Like Byzantium, Islam aspired to dominate the civilized world, which it thought of as divided between those lands already part of Islam, and those lands still to be conquered. Like the Byzantine emperor, the caliph was an absolute autocrat, a vicar of God, chosen by a mixture of election and hereditary principle, who could not be mutilated and still keep the throne. The caliph, of course, could not add to or change the religious law, although we have seen the emperor pronounce on dogma. Both courts went in for show and ceremony.

Christians and Muslims, however strong their mutual hatred, felt themselves to be worshipers in two religions that were on the same level of intellectual advancement and parallel in many respects: in their attitude toward creation, human history, the last judgment, and the instability of everything mortal. When at peace with the Muslims, the Byzantines thought of them as the successors of the Persians, and as such the only other civilized nation. As a concession to the Muslim attitude toward women, diplomatic protocol prescribed that ambassadors from the caliph were not to be asked the customary question about the health of the ladies of the caliph's household. And the caliph's ambassadors had the highest places at the imperial table. Each court had the highest respect for the other's attainments in science.

Science

The reign of Mamun (813–833) is often said to mark the high point in the civilization of the caliphate. In Baghdad he built observatories, founded a university, and ordered the great works of Greek and Indian scientists and philosophers translated into Arabic. We hear of a young Byzantine geometry student who was taken prisoner by the Muslims and brought to Baghdad as a slave:

One day his master's conversation turned on the Caliph, and he mentioned Mamun's interest in geometry. "I should like," said the Greek youth, "to hear him and his masters discourse on that subject." . . . Mamun . . . eagerly summoned him to the palace. He was confronted with the Moslem geometers. They described squares and triangles; they displayed a most accurate acquaintance with the nomenclature of Euclid; but they showed no comprehension of geometrical reasoning. At their request he gave them a demonstration, and they inquired in amazement how many savants of such a quality Constantinople possessed. "Many disciples like myself," was the reply, "but not masters." "Is your master still alive?" they asked. "Yes, but he lives in poverty and obscurity." Then Mamun wrote a letter to the master, Leo, inviting him to come to Bagdad, offering him rich rewards. . . . The youth was dispatched as ambassador to Leo. Leo discreetly showed the Caliph's letter to an imperial official, who brought the matter to the Emperor's attention. By this means Leo was discovered and his value appreciated. The Emperor gave him a salary and established him as a public teacher. . . . Mamun is said to have communicated with Leo again, submitting to him a number of geometrical and astronomical problems. The solutions he received made him more anxious than ever to welcome the mathematician at his court, and he wrote to the Emperor begging him to send Leo to Bagdad for a short time, as an act of friendship, and offering in return eternal peace and 2,000 pounds of gold [about a million dollars]. But the Emperor, treating science as if it were a secret to be guarded like the manfacture of Greek fire, and deeming it bad policy to enlighten barbarians, declined.*

Although the charge that the Muslim mathematicians did not understand geometrical reasoning is surely an absurd invention, the story none the less reflects a real situation—the immense eagerness of the Muslims to acquire Greek learning, which seems to have served as a stimulus to the Byzantines to appreciate their own neglected men of science. In any case, the last portion of the story, showing how jealously guarded were not only the secret weapons of the Byzantines but also what we would call today their basic research in mathematics, has a modern ring indeed. Aristotle and the other philosophers and scientists of the ancient world were in any case available to the Arabs, whether in the original Greek or in Syriac or Persian translations. Under Harun al-Rashid (785–809), the caliph of *Arabian Nights* fame, who walked about the streets of Baghdad in disguise looking for amusement and adventure, schools of translators were set up and manuscripts were ordered from Constantinople and elsewhere. Even more was done by Mamun.

One of the chief fields of interest was medicine, which the Muslims developed beyond the standard works of the Greek masters. They wrote texbooks, for instance, on diseases of the eye, on smallpox, and on measles, which remained the best authorities on those subjects until the eighteenth century. Al-Razi, a Persian of the tenth century, wrote a famous twenty-volume compendium of all medical knowledge, and Avicenna (980–1037) was perhaps even more famous for his systematization of all known medical science. In physics, Al-Kindi wrote more than two hundred and fifty works, on such diverse fields as music, optics, and the tides.

Muslim scientists adopted the Indian numerals, the very ones that we use today and call "Arabic." The new numerals included the zero, a concept unknown to the Romans, without which it is hard to see how higher mathematical research could be carried on. The Muslims began on analytical geometry and founded plane and spherical trigonometry. They progressed much further than their predecessors in algebra; and "algebra" is itself an Arabic word like "alcohol," "cipher," "alchemy," "zenith,'" "nadir," and others that testify to early Muslim scientific achievement.

Philosophy, Literature, and the Arts

On the philosophical side, the Muslims eagerly studied Plato, Aristotle, and the Neoplatonists. Like the Byzantines and the western Europeans, the Muslims used what they learned to enable them to solve their own theological

*Slightly adapted from J. B. Bury, *A History of the Eastern Roman Empire* (London, 1912), pp. 437-438.

problems. These did not involve such questions as the relationships of the members of the Trinity to each other or the human and divine natures in Christ, but focused on the nature and the power of God and his relationship to the universe. Efforts to reconcile philosophy and religion occupied the great Spanish Muslim Averroës (1126–1198), whose commentaries on Aristotle translated from Arabic into Latin were available to the Christian West before the original Greek text of Aristotle himself. Thus it was that the Muslims came to share with the Byzantines the role of preserver and modifier of the classical works of philosophy and science. And eventually, in the twelfth century and later, when the West was ready and eager for the intellectual banquet of ancient learning, it was the Muslims in Sicily and in Spain, as well as the Greeks, who could set it before them.

Indeed, the process began even earlier in Spain, where the physical splendor and intellectual eminence of Cordova caused its fame to spread abroad. Cordova was only dimly known to non-Spaniards, but they were deeply aware of its superiority to their own cities. In Spain itself, a Spanish Christian in 854 complained that his fellow Christians were irresistibly attracted by Muslim culture:

My fellow-Christians delight in the poems and romances of the Arabs; they study the works of Moslem theologians and philosophers, not in order to refute them, but to acquire a correct and elegant Arabic style. Where today can a layman be found, who reads the Latin Commentaries on the Holy Scripture? Who is there that studies the Gospels, the Prophets, the Apostles? Alas! the young Christians who are most conspicuous for their talents have no knowledge of any literature or language save the Arabic; they read and study Arabian books with avidity, they amass whole libraries of them at immense cost, and they everywhere sing the praises of Arabian lore.*

These Arabic poems of which the Spaniard speaks went back in part to the pre-Islamic classical Arab tradition, and portrayed life in the desert, with its camels and horses, its warfare and hunting, its feasts and drinking-bouts. Love is a favorite subject, but it was bad form to mention a lady's real name unless she was a slave girl.

Composition was governed by a strict code of convention. It was customary, for example, for the poet to praise himself, but not possible for him freely to portray human character. Still, much understanding of fundamental human experience shines through. Here is a portion of a poetic treatise on the calamities of love, which describes the kinds of "avoidance" a lover encounters:

The first kind is the avoidance required by circumstances because of a watcher being present, and this is sweeter than union itself. Then there is the avoidance that springs from coquetry, and this is more delicious than many kinds of union. Because of this it happens only when the lovers have complete confidence in each other. Then comes avoidance brought about by some guilty act of the lover. In this there is some severity, but the joy of forgiveness balances it. In the approval of the beloved after anger there is a delight of heart which no other delight can equal. Then comes the avoidance caused by boredom. To get tired of somebody is one of the inborn characteristics of man. He who is guilty of it does not deserve that his friends should be true to him. Then comes the avoidance brought about when a lover sees his beloved treat him harshly and show affection for somebody else, so that he sees death and swallows bitter draughts of grief, and breaks off while his heart is cut to pieces. Then comes the avoidance due to hatred; and here all writing becomes confused, and all cunning is exhausted, and trouble becomes great. This makes people lose their heads.*

Arabic love poetry, especially as developed in Spain, deeply influenced the lyricists across the Pyrenees in Provence, in the south of France. "Earthly love" became an important element of medieval literature. The troubadours' songs spread to Germany, where the minnesinger adopted the convention. Some of the greatest masterpieces of Western love poetry thus find their ancestry in the songs of the Muslims of Spain.

Besides poetry there is a great deal of interesting autobiography and excellent history in Arabic, but no drama. The fiction is of a limited sort only—sad misfortunes of a pair of lovers, exciting incidents of urban life in the

* G. E. von Grunebaum, *Medieval Islam* (Chicago, 1946), pp. 57–58.

* Ibid., pp. 269–270. Slightly adapted and abridged.

capital, with the caliph and the vizier participating, or the adventures of a rogue. These stories were collected in the celebrated *Arabian Nights* between 900 and 1500. Stories of Indian and Jewish origin are included, as well as some that derive from the Greek classics and from works of the Hellenistic period. Even when the plots are not so derived, much of the detail, especially geographical detail, is. Thus Sinbad the Sailor's famous roc with its enormous egg comes from the Greek romance of Alexander, and the *Odyssey* supplies the source of the adventure with the blinded giant.

In the arts, the Muslims developed their own adaptation of Byzantine churches in their mosques, which needed a front courtyard with a fountain, since Muslims must wash before entering. Because there were neither priests nor elaborate ritual, all that was necessary inside was a quiet and dignified place to pray and rest, with a small niche in the wall showing the direction of Mecca, and a pulpit from which the Koran might be read aloud. Since the faithful had to be summoned by the muezzin's call to prayer, slender towers or minarets were built next to the mosque. Beautiful and elaborate geometric patterns, in wood, stone, mosaic, and porcelain tile, characterize the interior decoration. Arabic script itself lends itself well to use in decoration; and the names of the first four caliphs and passages from the Koran are regularly found. The great mosques of Damascus and Cairo, Jerusalem and Cordova are perhaps the greatest surviving specimens, but there are thousands of others all over the Muslim world. The Gothic architecture of the West owes a still not fully explored and largely unacknowledged debt to the pointed arches and ribbed vaults, the stone tracery (often called arabesque) and the other striking features of these buildings. In the architecture of the Norman period in Sicily we can see direct traces of Muslim influence, as of course we can in Spain, whose entire civilization has been permanently shaped by the Muslims.

Finally, in music, we must point to a substantial Muslim contribution that is seldom recognized. The Morris dance, for instance, is simply a "Moorish dance." "Lute," "tambourine," "guitar," and "fanfare" are all words of Arabic origin. From the Muslims of Spain across the Pyrenees into France and thence to the whole western European world came not only the poetry of courtly love but the instruments which the singer played while he sang of his beloved. Through Sicily and through Spain came Greco-Roman and Muslim science, philosophy, and art. When we consider the contributions of the Byzantines and the Muslims to the culture of our Western society, we are altogether justified in saying that much light came from the East.

Reading Suggestions on Eastern Christendom and Islam

GENERAL ACCOUNTS — G. Ostrogorsky, *History of the Byzantine State*, trans. J. Hussey (Rutgers Univ. Press, 1957). A brilliant historical synthesis, with rich bibliography.

A. A. Vasiliev, *History of the Byzantine Empire, 324-1453,* 2 vols. (*Univ. of Wisconsin Press). A good comprehensive work.

J. Hussey, *The Byzantine World* (Hutchinson's University Library, 1957). Useful shorter sketch.

The Cambridge Medieval History. Vol. IV: *The Byzantine Empire*. Part I: *Byzantium and Its Neighbours*, ed. J. M. Hussey (Cambridge Univ. Press, 1966). Collaborative work with contributions by many excellent scholars. Full bibliographies.

V. O. Kluchevsky, *A History of Russia,* 5 vols. (Dent, 1911-1931). The greatest single work on Russian history, its usefulness impaired by a poor translation.

Michael Florinsky, *Russia: A History and an Interpretation,* Vol I (Macmillan, 1953). A good textbook, solid and accurate.

H. A. R. Gibb, *Mohammedanism: An Historical Survey* (*Galaxy). An excellent essay by the greatest Western contemporary authority on the subject.

Bernard Lewis, *The Arabs in History,* 3rd ed. (*Torchbooks). A reliable short treatment.

P. K. Hitti, *History of the Arabs from the Earliest Times to the Present,* 8th ed. (*St. Martin's). A detailed treatment, useful for reference.

G. E. von Grunebaum, *Medieval Islam,* 2nd ed (*Phoenix). A learned essay on Islamic culture, in part controversial.

F. Rahman, *Islam* (Weidenfeld & Nicholson, 1966). Sound comprehensive introduction by a Muslim scholar.

W. Montgomery Watt, *Muhammad: Prophet and Statesman* (*Oxford). Clear and informative study.

SPECIAL STUDIES A. H. M. Jones, *Constantine and the Conversion of Europe* (Macmillan, 1948). A sensible and helpful introduction.

C. Diehl, *Byzantine Portraits* (Knopf, 1927). A collection of excellent essays on important Byzantine personalities.

J. B. Bury, *A History of the Later Roman Empire, 395–802,* 1st ed. 2 vols (Macmillan, 1889). The first edition of a work later revised only down to 565. The second edition (*Dover) is the best work on the period 395–565.

J. B. Bury, *A History of the Eastern Roman Empire, 802–867* (Macmillan, 1912). Distinguished scholarly treatment.

R. J. H. Jenkins, *Byzantium: The Imperial Centuries, A.D. 610–1071* (Random House, 1967). Reliable narrative.

G. Every, *The Byzantine Patriarchate, 451–1204* (S.P.C.K., 1947). A good summary.

J. M. Hussey, *Church and Learning in the Byzantine Empire, 867–1185* (Oxford Univ. Press, 1937). Good introduction to the subject.

G. Ostrogorsky, "Agrarian Conditions in the Byzantine Empire in the Middle Ages," and R. S. Lopez, "The Trade of Mediaeval Europe: The South," in *The Cambridge Economic History,* Vols. I and II, respectively. Brief modern discussions of these topics.

S. Runciman, *History of the First Bulgarian Empire* (Bell, 1930). Lively and reliable.

A. Grabar, *Byzantine Painting* (Skira, 1953). Superb reproductions of mosaics and frescoes.

David Talbot Rice, *The Art of Byzantium* (Thomas & Hudson, London: 1959). A beautiful picture-book.

G. Vernadsky, *Kievan Russia* (Yale Univ. Press, 1948). Vol. II of the Yale History of Russia, authoritative and complete.

G. P. Fedotov, *The Russian Religious Mind,* 2 vols. (Harvard Univ. Press, 1946 and 1966). A study of the Kievan period of Russian history from a most unusual point of view.

W. Muir, *The Caliphate,* rev. ed. (Grant, 1915); and G. Le Strange, *Baghdad during the Abbasid Caliphate* (Oxford Univ. Press, 1924). Standard works on these subjects.

SOURCES *Procopius,* trans. H. B. Dewing, 7 vols. (Loeb Classical Library, 1914-1940). The writings of a major historian who lived through the events he recounts. His work includes histories of Justinian's wars and of his activities as a builder, and also a scurrilous secret denunciation of Justinian.

Constantine Porphyrogenitus, *De Administrando Imperio,* ed. G. Moravcsik, trans. R. J. H. Jenkins (Budapest, 1949). A letter of advice written by an emperor to his son and heir, telling much about the various "barbarian" peoples on the imperial frontiers.

Michael Psellus, *Chronographia,* trans. E. R. A. Sewter (Yale Univ. Press, 1953). A contemporary account of eleventh-century history.

Digenes Akrites, trans. J. Mavrogordato (Clarendon, 1956). The first English translation of the Byzantine frontier epic, with a good introduction.

St. John Damascene, *Barlaam and Ioasaph,* trans. G. R. Woodward and H. Mattingly (Macmillan, 1914, Loeb Classical Library). The transformed life of Buddha discussed in the text above. The attribution to St. John of Damascus is no longer regarded as correct.

The Russian Primary Chronicle, Laurentian Text, ed. S. H. Cross and O. P. Sherbowitz-Wetzor, (Mediaeval Academy, 1953). Our oldest source for early Russian history.

A. J. Arberry, *The Koran Interpreted* (*Macmillan).

HISTORICAL FICTION

W. S. Davis, *The Beauty of the Purple* (Macmillan, 1924). The career of Leo the Isaurian in eighth-century Byzantium.

F. Harrison, *Theophano* (Harper, 1904). Byzantium toward the end of the tenth century.

7

Monarchy
in the Medieval West

To the Early Fourteenth Century

I Introduction

Most of us think of a Frenchman as intelligent and volatile, individualistic, disliking authority and regimentation, cynical about sweeping statements of principle, passionately patriotic, but hating his political opponents because they do not share his assumptions about the framework within which the country's destinies are to be worked out. He has become inured to unstable government. We probably think of an Englishman as sensible and calm, feeling the need to act on principle, devoted to political freedom, law-abiding, and willing to work in harness with even his bitterest political enemy, since all agree on the basic assumptions about the country. He is accustomed to a political stability that is unparalleled elsewhere, and takes it entirely for granted. We probably think of a German as talented and hardworking, eager both to exercise authority over others and to have it exercised

Above: Emperor Henry IV kneeling at Canossa, requesting the abbot Hugh of Cluny and the countess Matilda of Tuscany to intercede with Pope Gregory VII.
Above right: The fortress towers of San Gimignano, in Tuscany. Right: A scene from the Bayeux Tapestry, depicting the Norman fleet under William the Conqueror crossing the English Channel.

MARE TRANSIVIT

over him, convinced of his own superiority to men of other nations, disciplined but sometimes gulled by demagogues with glittering promises, and given to aggression against others. We probably think of an Italian as volatile, artistically brilliant and sensitive, but indifferent to or cynical about politics, and willing to accept great social and economic contrasts: the poor and illiterate forever poor and illiterate and the rich and powerful forever rich and powerful.

Such stereotypes are altogether unscientific. But they would not even be recognizable if a great many people, on much or little evidence, had not reached these conclusions. If asked to explain historically why we think these people are the way we think they are, most of us would say of France: "France has been attacked three times by Germany since 1870, and has been weakened and disillusioned. Besides, since the Revolution of 1789 the French have never been able to agree on whether they shall have a democratic republic or not." Many would say of England: "In the eighteenth century the English were able to get such a head start in the Industrial Revolution that in the nineteenth century London became the economic capital of the world; economic power and a widespread empire have meant political stability." Many would say of Germany: "The Germans were not unified into one nation until the late nineteenth century, and when they were unified they accepted the ideas of Prussian military discipline and absolute government. The defeat in World War I, the punitive Treaty of Versailles, and the depression were the things that made them fall for Hitler."

Many would say of Italians: "Italy's political unity too was delayed until recent times, and has often been more apparent than real. Italians' primary loyalties often go to one or another of their great cities. The Roman heritage and the Mediterranean tradition that social differences are a matter of God's choosing have played an important part."

Now all these explanations are roughly true, but do they really explain anything? *Why* have a large number of Frenchmen never fully reconciled themselves to democracy? *Why* did the English get a head start in industrialization and colonial expansion? *Why* was German and Italian unity retarded? The trouble with all our answers is that they come out of the recent past, the period since the eighteenth century. They are good as far as they go, but they do not go far enough. We could answer our second set of questions accurately but inadequately with answers out of the sixteenth and seventeenth centuries, but a new set of unanswered questions would instantly present itself that could be answered only from a still earlier period. Until we get back to the time when there were no Frenchmen, Englishmen, Germans, or Italians in our modern sense, and then begin from the beginning and try to watch them develop along differing lines, we are not likely to come up with a set of satisfactory historical explanations for our stereotypes. This chapter begins in the tenth century, at a time when the national differentiation between the peoples of western Europe was still in its earliest stages. If our answers are to be found anywhere, this seems the place to look.

II   The Development of France: Hugh Capet to Philip the Fair

The Capetians

When Hugh Capet came to the throne of France in 987, there was little to distinguish him from the last feeble Carolingians. Yet he was different, if only because he was the first of a male line that was to continue uninterrupted for almost 350 years. Like the Byzantine emperors, but with better luck, the Capetians procured the election and coronation of the king's eldest son during his father's lifetime, and then took him into the government. When the father died, the son would already be king. After two centuries, when Philip II Augustus (ruled 1180–1223) decided for reasons of his own not to follow this practice, the hereditary principle had become so well established that the succession was no longer questioned.

For a hundred years before the accession of Hugh Capet, his ancestors had been rivals of the Carolinginans for the throne. As king of France,

Hugh was recognized by all the feudal lords as their suzerain, but they were actually more powerful than he and could if necessary defy him with impunity. Thus he might not be able to collect the aid (military service), the counsel, and the feudal dues which his vassals in theory owed him. He was also, of course, lord of his own domain, the Île de France. This was a compact strip of land including Paris and the land immediately adjacent, and extending south to Orléans on the Loire. The Île de France was far smaller than the domain of any of the great feudal lords: the dukes of Normandy or Burgundy or Aquitaine, the counts of Flanders, Anjou, Champagne, Brittany, or Toulouse. It may indeed have been for this very reason that Hugh was chosen to be king: he seemed less likely to be a threat than any of the better-endowed lords. Yet the Capetian domain was compact, not scattered, and central, not peripheral; it was easy to govern and was advantageously located. Hugh and his immediate successors concentrated on it.

In addition to their position as the suzerain of suzerains and as feudal lords of their own domain, the Capetians enjoyed the sanctity of kingship that came with coronation and unction (anointing) with the holy oil, which tradition said a dove had brought down from heaven for Clovis at his baptism. In the eyes of his people, this ecclesiastical ceremony brought the king very close to God. He could work miracles, it was soon believed. In this way the king was raised above all other feudal lords, however powerful: he had no suzerain. Furthermore the Church was his partner: he defended it, according to his coronation oath, and it assisted him. In the great sees near Paris, the king could nominate successors to vacant bishoprics and archbishoprics, and he could collect the income of bishoprics during vacancies. All through the West, as we shall see, these great powers of the lay lords, and especially of kings, in church affairs aroused the opposition of the papacy during the eleventh century. In France, the pope was eventually able to force the king to abandon lay investiture—the actual presentation of ring and staff (symbols of his office) to a new bishop. But the king retained his right of intervention in episcopal elections, and the bishops still took oaths of fealty to the king and accepted their worldly goods at his hands. This partnership with the Church greatly strengthened the early Capetian kings.

The history of the Capetians, during their first two centuries of rule in France, is on the surface far less eventful than the contemporary history of several of their great vassals, such as the dukes of Normandy, who were conquering England, and whose vassals were establishing a great state in Sicily, or the dukes of Burgundy, whose relatives were taking over the throne in Portugal. The Capetian kings stayed at home, made good their authority within their own domain, and, piece by piece, added a little neighboring territory to it. They put down the brigands who made a mockery of their authority on the roads. By the time of Louis VII (ruled 1137–1180), faraway vassals in the south of France and elsewhere, recognizing royal prestige and authority, were appealing to the king more and more often to settle local disputes. The king's duty to maintain peace throughout the realm had become more than a theoretical right.

Within the royal domain itself, the Capetians increased their control over the *curia regis,* the king's court, which consisted of an enlargement of the royal household. The great offices had at first tended to become hereditary, thus concentrating power in the hands of a few families. Under Louis VI (ruled 1108–1137) a single individual held the key household offices of chancellor and seneschal (steward) as well as five important posts in the Church. Louis VI, however, ousted this man and his relatives from their posts, and made appointments of his own choosing. These new men were lesser nobles, lower churchmen, and members of the middle classes that were now emerging in the towns. Since they owed their careers to the Crown alone, they were loyal and trustworthy royal servants. Most important among them was Suger, the abbot of St. Denis, a man of humble origin who efficiently served both Louis VI and Louis VII for decades.

Besides ensuring the loyalty and efficiency of the central administration, the Capetians replaced hereditary local officials. They introduced royal appointees known as *prévôts* (provosts) to administer justice and taxation in the lands of the royal domain. Furthermore, Louis VI granted royal charters to rural colonists and to new towns, because he recognized that the colonization of waste lands and the growth of new towns would be advantageous to the monarchy. In these ways, the French kings began their long and significant alliance with the middle classes.

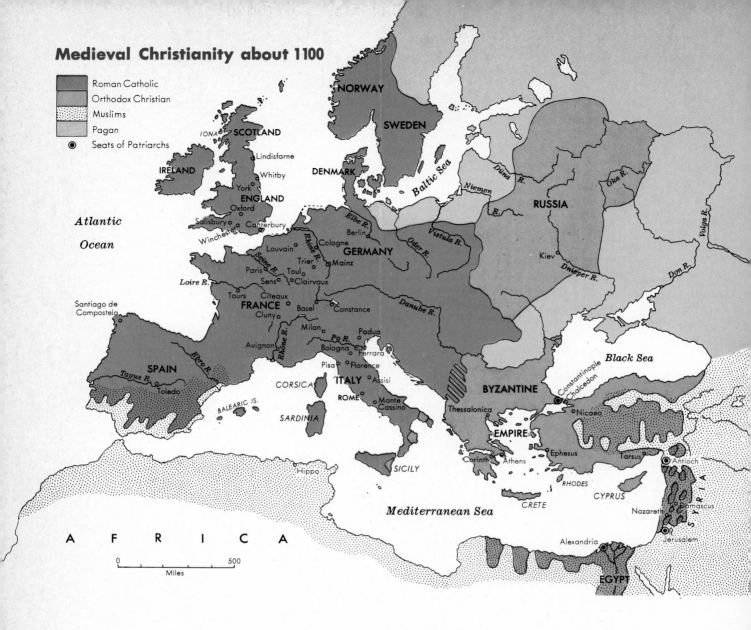

Medieval Christianity about 1100

- Roman Catholic
- Orthodox Christian
- Muslims
- Pagan
- ⊙ Seats of Patriarchs

Atlantic

Ocean

NORWAY

SWEDEN

Baltic Sea

SCOTLAND

IONA

Lindisfarne

Whitby

IRELAND

York

DENMARK

Niemen R.

Dvina R.

Oka R.

RUSSIA

Volga R.

England

Oxford

Berlin

Elbe R.

Oder R.

Vistula R.

Salisbury

Canterbury

Winchester

Louvain

Cologne

GERMANY

Kiev

Dnieper R.

Don R.

Paris

Rhine R.

Seine R.

Trier

Mainz

Toulo

Tours

Sens

Clairvaux

Loire R.

Cîteaux

FRANCE

Basel

Constance

Danube R.

Santiago de Compostela

Cluny

Milan

Padua

Po R.

Avignon

Rhône R.

Bologna

Ferrara

Black Sea

Ebro R.

Pisa

Florence

Constantinople

Chalcedon

SPAIN

Tagus R.

Toledo

CORSICA

ITALY

Assisi

BYZANTINE

Nicaea

Thessalonica

Tarsus

Antioch

BALEARIC IS.

ROME

Monte Cassino

EMPIRE

SARDINIA

Ephesus

SYRIA

Corinth

Athens

Damascus

Hippo

SICILY

RHODES

CYPRUS

Nazareth

CRETE

Mediterranean Sea

Alexandria

Jerusalem

A F R I C A

EGYPT

0   500

Miles

The Contest with Normans and Angevins

The most important single factor in the development of Capetian France, however, was the relationship of the kings with their most powerful vassals, the dukes of Normandy. By the mid-eleventh century, the dukes had centralized the administration of their own duchy, compelling their vassals to render military service, forbidding them to coin their own money, and curbing their rights of justice. The viscounts, agents of the ducal regime, exercised local control. After Duke William conquered England in 1066 and became its king, he and his successors were still vassals of the Capetians for Normandy. But they became so much more powerful than their overlords that they did not hesitate to conduct regular warfare against them. Norman power grew even greater during the early twelfth century, when an English queen married another great vassal of the French king, the count of Anjou. In the person of their son, King Henry II (ruled 1154–

1190), England was united with the French fiefs of Normandy, Anjou, Maine, and Touraine in what is sometimes called the Angevin Empire.

But this was not all. King Louis VII of France had married Eleanor, the charming heiress of Aquitaine, a great duchy in the southwest of France. When he got the marriage annulled (1152) for lack of a male heir, Eleanor lost no time in marrying the Angevin Henry II and adding Aquitaine to his already substantial French holdings. When Henry became king of England in 1154, he was also lord of more than half of France. He added Brittany and still other French territories to his realm. This Angevin threat was the greatest danger faced by the Capetian monarchs, and it was their most signal achievement that they overcame it.

The first round in the victorious struggle was the achievement of Philip II, Philip Augustus (ruled 1180–1223), who quadrupled the size of the French royal domain. Shrewd, calculating, bald, one-eyed, and fierce-tempered, Philip first supported Henry II's rebellious sons against him. Then, after Henry's death, Philip plotted with Henry's younger son, John, against John's older brother, Richard the Lionhearted—Philip's former companion on the Third Crusade (see Chapter 9) and now (1191–1194) a captive in Austria. Philip even married a Danish princess with the idea of using the Danish fleet against England and making himself heir to the Danish claims to the English throne. When John succeeded Richard in 1199, however, Philip Augustus strongly supported a rival claimant to the English throne—John's nephew, the young Arthur of Brittany.

Through legal use of his position as feudal suzerain, Philip managed to ruin John. In 1200 John foolishly married a girl who was engaged to somebody else. Her father, vassal of the king of France, complained in proper feudal style to Philip, his suzerain and John's. Since John would not come to answer the complaint, Philip declared his fiefs forfeit and planned to conquer them with young Arthur's supporters. When John murdered Arthur (1203), he played right into Philip's hands, lost his supporters on the Continent, and in 1204 had to surrender Normandy, Brittany, Anjou, Maine, and Touraine to Philip Augustus. Only Aquitaine was now left to the English, who had been expelled from France north of the Loire. In 1214, at the famous battle of Bouvines in Flanders, Philip Augustus defeated an army of Germans and English under the emperor Otto IV, John's ally. Unable to win back their former French possessions, the English confirmed this territorial settlement by treaty in 1259. England's remaining possessions in France were to be the cause of much future fighting. But John's great losses were added to the French royal domain. The French kings now had possession of the efficiently run duchy of Normandy, which they could use as a model for the rest of France.

The Albigensian Crusade and the Winning of the South

Next the Capetians moved south to the rich and smiling land of Languedoc and Toulouse, the true Mediterranean south. Its people drew much of their culture from Muslim Spain and spoke a dialect different from that of the north of France. And many of them belonged to the

The tomb figure of Eleanor of Aquitaine in the abbey church of Fontevrault.

heretical church of the *Cathari* (Greek for "pure ones"), with its center at the town of Albi.

The Albigensians, as the Cathari were called, believed that the history of the universe was one long struggle between the forces of light (good) and the forces of darkness (evil). The evil forces (Satan) created man and the earth, but Adam had some measure of goodness. Jesus was not born of woman, nor was he crucified, because he was wholly good, wholly of light. Jehovah of the Old Testament was the God of evil. The Albigensians had an elite of their own ("the perfect") who devoted themselves to pure living. Some of them forbade the veneration of the cross; others forbade infant baptism, the celebration of the Mass, or the holding of private property. Many of them denied the validity of one or more of the sacraments. Some even said the Catholic church itself was Satan's. The Albigensians were strongest among the lower classes, but they often had the support of nobles who adopted their views in order to combat the Church politically.

This heresy, which reminds one of the Gnostics' dualist views, had originated in the third century A.D. in Mesopotamia in the teachings of the Manichaeans, whose doctrines appeared in the Byzantine Empire, spread thence to the Balkans, to northern Italy, and finally to France. The Church proclaimed a crusade against these heretics in 1208, after the count of Toulouse had connived at the murder of a papal legate.

Philip Augustus did not at first participate in the expeditions of his nobles, who rushed south to plunder and kill in the name of the Catholic church. By the year of his death (1223), however, after the war had gone on intermittently for fourteen years, the territorial issue had become confounded with the religious one. Northern French nobles were staking out their claims to the lands of southern French nobles who embraced the heresy; so Philip finally sponsored an expedition led by his son, Louis VIII (ruled 1223–1226). Assisted by a special clerical court called the Inquisition, which was first set up to extirpate this heresy, Louis VIII and his son Louis IX (ruled 1226–1270) carried on the campaign, which by the 1240's had driven the heresy underground. Languedoc itself was almost entirely taken over by the Crown, and it was arranged that the lands of Toulouse would come by marriage to the brother of the king of France when the last count died. This happened in 1249.

Royal Administration

Administrative advance kept pace with territorial gain. Indeed, it is doubtful if Philip Augustus and his successors could have added to the royal domain if they had not overcome many of the disruptive elements of feudalism and if they had not asserted their authority effectively in financial, military, and judicial matters. Philip Augustus systematically collected detailed information on precisely what was owing to him from the different royal fiefs. He increased the number of his own vassals, and he reached over the heads of his vassals to *their* vassals, in an attempt to make the latter directly dependent on him.

He exacted stringent guarantees—such as a promise that if a vassal did not perform his duties within a month, he would surrender his person as a prisoner until the situation was resolved. Moreover, if a vassal did not live up to this agreement, the Church would lay an interdict upon his lands. This dreadful punishment meant that everyone resident on the lands was denied access to most of the sacraments and comforts of religion. The people naturally feared an interdict above all else, since they could not marry, or have their babies baptized, or have their sins forgiven before they died.

Philip and his officials were alert to increase the royal power by purchasing new estates, by interfering as much as possible in the inheritance of fiefs upon the death of their holders, and by providing suitable husbands of their own choosing for the great heiresses. Since the men of those days led violent lives, a lady would sometimes outlast three or four husbands, inheriting from each, and thus each time becoming a more desirable prize, and offering the king a chance to marry her off with profit to himself.

The local officials of the Crown, the *prévôts*, had regularly been rewarded by grants of land, which, together with the office, tended to become hereditary. The Crown lost both income and power as well as popularity when a local *prévôt* made exactions on his own behalf. Early in his reign, Philip Augustus held an investigation and heard the complaints to which the system had given rise. He appointed a new sort

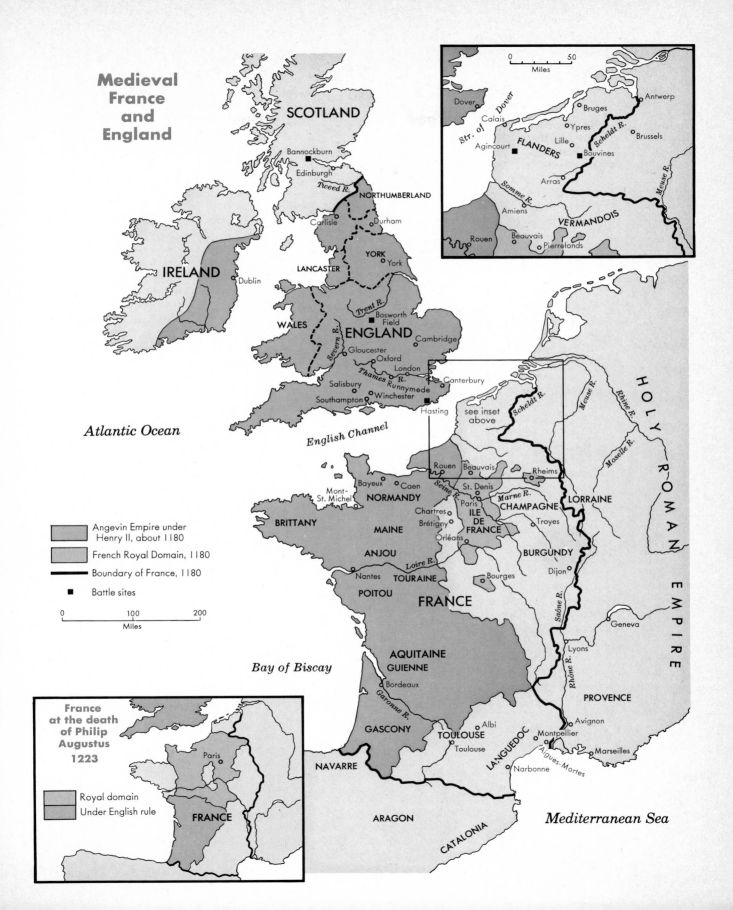

Medieval France and England

SCOTLAND

Bannockburn

Edinburgh

Tweed R.

NORTHUMBERLAND

Carlisle
Durham

IRELAND

Dublin

LANCASTER

YORK
York

Trent R.

Bosworth
Field

WALES

ENGLAND

Cambridge

Severn R.

Gloucester
Oxford

Thames R.
London

Salisbury
Runnymede
Canterbury

Southampton
Winchester

Hasting

Atlantic Ocean

English Channel

see inset
above

Rouen
Beauvais

Rheims

Bayeux
Caen

Mont-
St. Michel

NORMANDY

Seine R.

St. Denis

Chartres
Brétigny

Paris

Marne R.

CHAMPAGNE

LORRAINE

BRITTANY

MAINE

ILE
DE
FRANCE

Troyes

Meuse R.

Moselle R.

H O L Y   R O M A N   E M P I R E

ANJOU

Loire R.

Orléans

BURGUNDY

Nantes

TOURAINE

Bourges

Dijon

POITOU

FRANCE

Saône R.

Geneva

Bay of Biscay

AQUITAINE

GUIENNE

Bordeaux

Lyons

Rhône R.

PROVENCE

Garonne R.

GASCONY

TOULOUSE

Albi

Toulouse

LANGUEDOC

Avignon

Montpellier

Marseilles

Aigues-
Mortes

NAVARRE

Narbonne

ARAGON

CATALONIA

Mediterranean Sea

Angevin Empire under
Henry II, about 1180

French Royal Domain, 1180

Boundary of France, 1180

■ Battle sites

0   100   200
Miles

Inset (top right)

0   50
Miles

Dover

*Str. of
Dover*

Calais

Bruges

Antwerp

Ypres

Agincourt

FLANDERS

Lille

Scheldt R.

Brussels

Bouvines

Arras

Somme R.

Amiens

VERMANDOIS

Rouen

Beauvais

Pierrefonds

Meuse R.

Inset (bottom left)

**France
at the death
of Philip
Augustus
1223**

Paris

Royal domain

Under English rule

FRANCE

of official, not resident in the countryside, but tied to the court, who would travel about, enforcing the king's will in his domain, rendering royal justice on his behalf, and collecting moneys due to him. This official received no fiefs to tie him to a given region; his office was not hereditary. He was a civil servant appointed by the king, who paid him a salary and could remove him at will. In the north, where this system was introduced, he was called a *bailli* (bailiff), and his territory a *baillage* (bailiwick). In the south, to which the new system was extended, he was called a *sénéschal* (not to be confused with the old officer of the household), and his district a *sénéchaussée*.

Like any administrative system, this one had its drawbacks: a *bailli* or *sénéschal* far from Paris might become just as independent and unjust as the old *prévôt* had been, without the king's being aware of it. Louis IX (ruled 1226–1270) had to limit the power of these officials in two ways. He made it easy for complaints against them to be brought to his personal attention. And he appointed a new kind of official to take care of the caretakers. These were the *enquêteurs* or investigators, royal officials not unlike Charlemagne's *missi*. The *enquêteurs* had supervisory authority over the *baillis* and seneschals, and traveled about the country inspecting their work. This whole complex of new civil servants introduced in the late twelfth and thirteenth centuries meant that the king was in a position to interfere with almost all local and private transactions, to exact his just due, and to supply royal justice at a price.

Naturally the king's court (*curia regis*) was so swamped with new business that the old haphazard feudal way of attending to it could no longer be followed. To depend, like Hugh Capet, on officers of the household, would have been a little like the United States government of today trying to get along with no filing system except an old chest of drawers belonging to George Washington. The administration of France in the thirteenth century was nowhere near as complicated as that of the United States in the twentieth, and there was plenty of time for gradual experiment and development.

What happened was something like this. The king's household differentiated itself into departments, most of which had little to do with government. Rather, they attended to the needs of the king and the curia regis. This court consisted not only of retainers but of clerics and others who served as advisers on day-to-day problems. When a major policy question affecting the realm was up for decision, or when a major legal case needed to be tried, the king was entitled to summon his vassals (both lay and clerical) for counsel, and those he summoned were obliged to come. They then joined the rest of the curia regis in a kind of enlarged royal entourage.

When the curia regis sat in judgment on a case, it came to be known as the *parlement*, a high judicial tribunal. Naturally, as law grew more complex, trained lawyers had to handle more and more of the judicial business. At first, they explained the law to the vassals sitting in judgment, and then, as time passed, they formed a court of justice and arrived at decisions themselves in the name of the king. By the fourteenth century, this court of justice was called the *Parlement de Paris,* because Paris was its headquarters.

When the curia regis sat in special session on financial matters, auditing the reports of income and expenditure, it acted as a kind of government accounting department. By the fourteenth century, this was called the *chambre des comptes,* or chamber of accounts. Naturally enough, it engaged more and more professional full-time employees, clerks and auditors and the like.

Cash flowed to the Crown from the lands of the royal domain, from customs dues and special tolls, from fees for government services, and from money paid in by vassals in order to avoid rendering such outmoded feudal services as entertaining the king and his court. But, in spite of this variety of revenue, the king of France could not levy regular direct taxes on his subjects. During the twelfth century the regular collection of feudal aids accustomed the nobles to paying money to the Crown. Then a special levy was imposed on those who stayed home from the crusade of 1145. In 1188, Philip Augustus collected one-tenth of the movable property and one-tenth of a year's income from all who failed to join in a crusade. These extraordinary imposts, however, never failed to arouse a storm of protest.

Saint Louis

New advances in royal power came with Louis IX (ruled 1226–1270), in many ways the greatest of all medieval kings. Deeply pious, almost monastic in his personal life, Louis carried his own high standards over into his role as king. He wore simple clothes, gave alms to beggars, washed the feet of lepers, built hospitals, and created in Paris the Sainte Chapelle (Holy Chapel), a small church that is a real jewel-box of glowing stained glass, to hold Christ's Crown of Thorns. The Church made him a saint in 1297, less than thirty years after his death.

One of his knights, the Sieur de Joinville, tells this characteristic story about Saint Louis in his memoirs:

Of his mouth he was so sober, that on no day of my life did I ever hear him order special meats, as many rich men are wont to do; but he ate patiently whatever his cooks had made ready. . . . In his words he was temperate; for on no day of my life did I ever hear him speak evil of any one; nor did I ever hear him name the Devil—which name is very commonly spoken throughout the kingdom, whereby God, as I believe, is not well pleased.

He put water into his wine by measure, according as he saw that the strength of the wine would suffer it. . . . He asked me why I put no water into my wine; and I said this was by order of the physicians, who told me I had a large head and a cold stomach, so that I could not get drunk. And he answered that they deceived me; . . . if I drank pure wine in my old age, I should get drunk every night, and that it was too foul a thing for a brave man to get drunk.*

Saint Louis was a dutiful husband and an energetic king. During the early years of his reign, when he was still a youth, his very able mother, Blanche of Castile, acted as regent on his behalf and kept the great lords from successful revolt. Louis was grateful to her, yet he resented her attempts to dominate his relations with his wife, Queen Margaret. Joinville recalls:

The unkindness that the Queen Blanche showed to the Queen Margaret was such that she would not suffer, in so far as she could help it, that her son should be in his wife's company, except at night when he went to sleep with her. The palace where the king and his queen liked most to dwell was at Pontoise, because there the king's chamber was above and the queen's chamber below; and they had so arranged matters between them that they held their converse in a turning staircase that went from the one chamber to the other; and they had further arranged that when the ushers saw the Queen Blanche coming to her son's chamber, they struck the door with their rods, and the king would come running into his own chamber so that his mother might find him there.*

Saint Louis did not let his own devotion to the Church stop him from defending royal prerogatives against every attempt of his own bishops or of the papacy to infringe upon them. For example, when the popes tried to enforce the theory that "all churches belong to the pope," and to assess the churches of France for money and men for papal military campaigns, the king declared that church property in France was "for the requirements of himself and his realm," and was not to be despoiled by Rome (1247). Yet when he himself became deeply interested in the crusading movement (see Chapter 9), he found himself in need of papal support to enable him to tax the French clergy. Indeed, the clergy then complained to the pope concerning the king's exactions.

In the towns, too, those old allies of the Capetian dynasty, there were difficulties during Louis's reign. These difficulties arose in large measure out of internal conflicts between the small upper class of rich merchants, who kept city government a kind of oligarchy, and the lower class of tradesmen and artisans, who felt oppressed and excluded from their own government. When the Crown intervened, it was out of concern not so much for the poor and humble as for the maintenance of order and the continued flow of funds to the royal coffers. Louis began to send royal officials into the towns, and in 1262 issued a decree requiring that the towns present their accounts annually.

This decree itself is a further instance of the king's assertion of royal prerogative. It was a new sort of enactment, the *ordonnance,* or royal command issued for all of France without the previous assent of all the vassals. Royal power and prestige had now progressed to the point where Louis did not feel the need to obtain all his vassals' consent every time he wished to govern their behavior. Ordonnances signed by some vassals governed all. Examples of Louis' ordonnances are his prohibition of private warfare and his law providing that royal money was valid everywhere in France. Both show his advanced

*Joinville's Chronicle of the Crusade of Saint Louis, in Memoirs of the Crusades, Everyman ed. (New York, 1933), pp. 139–140.

* Ibid., p. 288.

Carcassonne, a restored medieval walled town in southern France.

views as well as his determination to strengthen the power of the monarchy.

Royal justice had now become a widely desired commodity, and appeals flowed in to the parlement from the lower feudal courts. The royal court of justice alone came to be recognized as competent to try cases of treason and of breaking the king's peace, and the extension of royal justice to the towns was secured by bringing in to the parlement's deliberations representatives of the middle classes: the king's bourgeois. So fair and reasonable was the king's justice felt to be that his subjects often applied to him personally for it. He made himself available to them by sitting under an oak tree in the forest of Vincennes, near Paris and listening to the case of anybody, high or low, who wished to tell him his story. He maintained no royal protocol on these occasions, and there were no intermediaries. His justice was prized not only in France but also abroad. He settled quarrels in Flanders, Navarre, Burgundy, Lorraine, and elsewhere. He reached a reasonable territorial settlement with England

in 1259, and in 1264 was asked to judge a dispute between King Henry III of England and the English barons.

Remarkable though he was, Louis was simply a remarkable man of the thirteenth century. In his devotion to the crusading enterprise, for instance, he was embracing wholeheartedly the highest ideals of the period. But he never seemed to realize that crusades were now no longer very practicable (see Chapter 9 for details). Moreover, it cost France dear to have the king delayed abroad for years and to have him languish in captivity from which he was redeemed only at great expense. Yet, for all his human failings, Saint Louis typifies the medieval ideal that the divine law of God's revelation was mirrored in our human law. As God ordered the universe, so human law established the proper relationships of men to one another in society. In human society, the king had his special role, and Saint Louis, in his conception and enactment of that role, reached heights that had not been attained by other monarchs.

The System Hardens: Philip the Fair

After the death of St. Louis, the French kingship experienced the general change that was coming over the entire world of the Middle Ages during the late thirteenth and fourteenth centuries. Old conventions and forms persisted, but they seemed to be hardening, to be losing the possibility of fresh and vigorous new expression. In the political history of France, these tendencies begin with the reign of Saint Louis's grandson, Philip IV (1285–1314). Called "the Fair" because he was handsome, Philip offered a striking contrast to Louis in personality and in character. Ruthlessly, he pushed the royal power and consolidated the royal hold; the towns, the nobles, and the Church all suffered invasions of their rights from his ubiquitous agents. Against the excesses of Philip the Fair, the medieval checks against tyranny, which had been successful against many other aggressive kings, failed to operate. His humiliation of the papacy alone helped as much as any other event of the Middle Ages to bring an end to the Christian commonwealth to which Saint Louis had been so devoted. The multiplying *gens du roi*, "the king's men," used propaganda, lies, and trickery to undermine all authority except that of the king.

This undermining was a steady war that went on in a series of small engagements in local courts of justice, with the king's lawyers pushing his rights. One of the devices used was *prevention:* a rule that if a case was started in a court, it had to be finished there, no matter what court was properly competent to try it. If the king's agents managed to bring a case into the royal court, it had to be completed there, even if the royal court was not the proper place for it. Another device was *défaute de droit:* a rule that if justice were refused in a lower court, the plaintiff had a right to appeal to his suzerain's court. The king's agents would urge plaintiffs to claim on any and all occasions that they had been denied justice in their lord's court, and to bring the case to the royal court. Still another device was *faux jugement:* a rule that if a man lost a suit he would be entitled to an appeal by challenging the judge, calling him "wicked and false." On the appeal, the judge would be the defendant in the next higher court. By using this device at the high level of the great lords' courts, the king's men would bring appeals into the royal courts. The system of royal justice was gradually swallowing up the system of feudal justice.

And, as the new cases flowed in, the parlement became ever more specialized and professionalized. The *chambre des requêtes* (chamber of petitions) now handled all requests that the royal court intervene. The *chambre des enquêtes* (chamber of investigations) would establish the facts in new cases. In the *chambre des plaids* (chamber of pleas) the lawyers actually argued the cases, and judgments were handed down. Members of the parlement now traveled to the remotest regions of France, bringing royal justice to all parts of the king's own domain, and more and more taking over the machinery of justice in the great lordships.

At the same period, the most intimate advisers of the king in the curia regis, whom he regularly consulted, became differentiated as the "narrow" or "secret" council, while the larger groups of advisers, consisting of the remaining lords and high clerics, was called the "full council." In 1302, for the first time, representatives of the towns attended a meeting of this large council. At the moment when townsmen first participate, we are making a transition to a new kind of assembly, the Estates General (though the term would not be used in France for some time). An estate is a social class. Traditionally, the clergy is the first estate, the nobility the second, and the townsmen the third. When all three estates are present, an assembly is an Estates General. Though the clerics and nobles acted as individuals, the townsmen came as chosen delegates from the corporations of their municipalities, and so acted as representatives.

Philip the Fair's Struggle for Money

War with England kept Philip pressed for cash during much of his reign. He summoned the estates to explain his need for money and to obtain their approval for his proceeding to raise it. He usually asked for funds in a general way, but did not fix the amount, since the groups whom he was asking to contribute always had the right to bargain. Since the medieval man felt that no action was proper unless it had always been customary, whenever the king wanted to do anything new he had to try to make it somehow seem like something old. A protest that such and such attempt to get money was an *exactio inaudita* (an unheard-of exaction) often was enough to frustrate the king's efforts. Philip tried all the known ways of getting money. One of the most effective was to demand military service of a man, and then permit him to buy himself off by paying a specific amount assessed on his property. When protests arose, the king usually had to swallow them and retreat to more orthodox methods. Requests for revenue that had hitherto been irregular were made regular. Forced loans, debasement of the coinage, additional customs dues, and royal levies on commercial transactions also added to the royal income.

Need for money explains the two most celebrated incidents of Philip's reign, his quarrel with the papacy and his suppression of the Knights Templars. Philip claimed the right to tax the clergy for defense. In 1296, the vigorous pope Boniface VIII (1294–1303) forbade kings and princes to tax the clergy for their countries without papal consent. Philip clapped an embargo on exports from France of precious metals, jewelry, and currency. The order threatened the elaborate financial system of the papacy so severely that under pressure from his distressed bankers, the pope retreated, saying in 1297 that in an emergency the king of France could go ahead and tax the clergy without papal consent, and that the king would decide when an emergency had arisen.

But a new quarrel arose in 1300 over the trial in Philip's courts of a French bishop accused of treason. Although at the urging of his clergy Philip did send the case to Rome, the pope was so angry that he made the mistake of giving Philip a public dressing-down in a bull entitled *Ausculta fili* ("Listen, son"), in which he declared that when a ruler was wicked the pope might take a hand in the temporal affairs of that realm. Philip replied in scornful and sarcastic language, calling the pope "your fatuousness." When Boniface pushed his claims still further in a still more famous bull, which declared that it was necessary to salvation for every human creature to be subject to the pope, and when

he threatened to excommunicate the king, Philip issued a whole series of extreme charges against Boniface and sent a gang of thugs to kidnap him. They burst into the papal presence at the Italian town of Anagni (September 7, 1303), and threatened him brutally, but did not dare put through their plan to seize him. None the less, Boniface, who was over eighty, died not long after this humiliation. Philip then obtained the election of a French pope, who never went to Rome at all. Thus began the "Babylonian captivity" of the papacy at Avignon (1305–1378).

Philip used the docile papacy of Avignon in his attacks on the Knights Templars, a crusading order that had become a rich banking house. He owed them money, and to avoid paying it brought them to trial on a series of charges of vicious behavior. With papal cooperation he used as evidence against them confessions extorted by the Inquisition. In 1312 the order was abolished. Philip did not pay them what he owed, and took over their funds, while a rival order was allowed to annex the Templars' lands. Philip also proceeded against others with money, arresting the Jews, stripping them of their property, and expelling them from France in 1306. In 1311 he expelled the agents of Italian bankers. All debts owing the Jews and Italians were simply collected by royal agents, and the Crown kept the money.

Protest in France

Just before Philip died in 1314, the towns joined with the lords in forming a series of local leagues that put on a taxpayers' strike in protest against the king's having raised money for a war in Flanders and then having made peace instead of fighting. Louis X (ruled 1314–1316) calmed the unrest by revoking the aid, returning some of the money, and making scapegoats of the more unpopular bureaucrats. He also issued a series of charters to several of the great vassals, confirming their liberties. The episode resembled in many ways the protest that had arisen in England a century earlier and had culminated there in one great charter—Magna Carta—as we shall see.

But taxation was still thought of as inseparably connected with military service, and military service was an unquestioned feudal right of the king. So the king was still free to declare a military emergency, to summon his vassals to fight, and then to commute the service for money, just as Philip the Fair had done. For this reason the charters of Louis X did not put an effective halt to the advance of royal power, and there was no committee of barons (as there had been in England) to make sure that the king lived up to his promises. Because the French barons did not defend their corporate interests, the French monarch could continue to enjoy a position unique among the kings of western Europe.

III   The Development of England, 1066-1307

The Norman Conquest

The England that threatened the security of France had first become a major power as a result of the Norman conquest of 1066. In that year, William the Conqueror and his invading Normans defeated the Anglo-Saxon forces at

William the Conqueror as depicted in a thirteenth-century manuscript illumination.

Hastings on the south coast of England. The expedition of 1066, motivated in part by William's personal claim to the English crown, marked an important stage in the process of Norman expansion which spanned the tenth and eleventh centuries and reached from the British Isles to the south of Italy.

Fat, intelligent, and violent, the Conqueror, as King William I of England (1066–1087), had the advantage of a conquered country to work in. As we know, Anglo-Saxon England had already developed its own institutions—its thirty-four shires and their sheriffs, its system of hundred and shire courts, its royal tax of the Danegeld, and its national militia of the *fyrd*. William could use or modify these institutions as he saw fit.

By 1071 the whole land was conquered, and William personally owned it all. He kept about a sixth as royal domain, gave about half as fiefs to his great Norman barons, and returned to the church the quarter that it had held before. Although many of his barons subinfeudated their lands, their vassals owed military service only to William, and swore primary allegiance to him (Salisbury Oath, 1086), giving him an advantage that no French king would ever enjoy. The bishops and abbots held of him, and owed him feudal services. He alone claimed all castles, and none could be built without a license from him. He forbade private war and allowed only royal coinage. He continued to levy the Danegeld, to impose judicial fines, and to summon the *fyrd* as well as the feudal array. He kept the Anglo-Saxon system of courts, and bound the sheriffs closely to the Crown by giving them wide local authority at the expense of bishop and earl.

The Conqueror thus maintained old English custom and law, but superimposed the Norman feudal structure, with its mounted knights and castles. The sheriffs provided continuity. The Norman curia regis superseded the Anglo-Saxon witenagemot; it met regularly three times a year, but could be summoned at any time. It gave counsel and tried the cases of the great vassals. Its members could be asked to perform special tasks in the shires. In 1086 William ordered a careful survey of all landed property in England. The record of the survey is the famous Domesday Book, which included for every piece of land a full statement of ownership, past and present, and a listing of all resources, so that the royal administration might ascertain whether and where more revenue could be obtained. Tenants, plows, forest land, fish ponds, all were listed in Domesday Book. Contemporary accounts reveal the thoroughness of William's inquiry and the resentment it caused:

So very narrowly did he have it investigated, that there was no single hide nor a yard of land, nor indeed (it is a shame to relate but it seemed no shame to him to do) one ox nor one cow nor one pig was there left out, and not put down on his record: and all these records were brought to him afterward. . . .

Other investigators followed the first; and men were sent into provinces which they did not know, and where they themselves were unknown, in order that they might be given the opportunity of checking the first survey and, if necessary, of denouncing its authors as guilty to the king. And the land was vexed with much violence arising from the collection of the royal taxes.*

No such monument was ever compiled for any other country in the Middle Ages.

William, with the assistance of the able Italian Lanfranc, whom he made Archbishop of Canterbury, established continental practices in the English church. But he refused the pope's demand that feudal homage be done to him as overlord of England. Rightly maintaining that none of his predecessors on the English throne had ever acknowledged papal suzerainty, he agreed only to pay the accustomed dues to the Church of Rome. The English church recognized no new pope without the king's approval, and accepted no papal commands without his assent. When William died in 1087, the English monarchy was stronger than the French was to be for more than two hundred years.

* *Anglo-Saxon Chronicle* and a note by the Bishop of Hereford, *English Historical Documents, 1042–1189,* ed. D. C. Douglas and G. W. Greenaway (New York, 1953), II, 161, 851.

Scene from the Bayeux Tapestry: William's Normans defeat Harold's Anglo-Saxons at Hastings.

Henry I and Henry II: Administration and Law

William's immediate successors extended the system. More and more they made their administrators depend upon the king alone by paying them fixed salaries, since payments in land (fiefs) often led the recipient to try to make his office hereditary, and since clerical administrators might feel the rival pull of papal authority. Household and curia regis grew in size, and special functions began to develop. Within the curia regis, the king's immediate advisers became a "small council." The full body met less often. The royal *chancery* or secretariat also grew, since the king was duke of Normandy, and had much business on the Continent.

Henry I (ruled 1100–1135) allowed his vassals to make payments (*scutage,* "shield money") to buy themselves off from military service. He also exempted the boroughs from Danegeld but collected still heavier payments from them. To handle the increased income, the first specialized treasury department came into existence, the *exchequer,* so called because the long table on which the clerks rendered to the officers of the curia regis their semiannual audit of the royal accounts was covered with a cloth divided into checkerboard squares representing pounds, shillings, and pence.

Because Henry's only legitimate son died before his father, the succession was disputed between Henry's daughter Matilda, wife of Geoffrey of Anjou, and Henry's nephew Stephen. A period of civil war (1135–1154) between their partisans produced virtual anarchy in England, and showed what could happen when the strong royal hand disappeared from the helm. Yet when the Angevin Henry II (ruled 1154–1189), son of Matilda and Geoffrey, succeeded to the throne, he found the foundations of a powerful monarchy still intact. We have already encountered him as the lord of half of France.

Stormy and energetic, Henry II systematically cut at the roots of the anarchy: he had more than 1,100 unlicensed castles destroyed. From the contemporary *Dialogue Concerning the Exchequer,* written by his treasurer, we learn how the money rolled in: from scutage plus special fees for the privilege of paying it, from fines, from aids, from tallage paid by the boroughs, and from a new tax collected from the knights who did not go on crusades. Even more important than this re-establishment and strengthening of the financial institutions was Henry's contribution to the law of England, built on that of Henry I.

In our own day, when the making of new laws is something we take for granted, it requires a real effort of the imagination to think of a period in which new law could not, in theory, be made at all. Law was what had always existed, and it was the job of the lawyers and government officials to discover what this was and proclaim it. Henry I and Henry II therefore did not fill whole statute books with new enactments: they could never have dreamed of such a thing. Instead, Henry I claimed that he was ruling in accordance with the law of the Saxon King Edward the Confessor, and the law-books issued in his period contain a mixture of Anglo-Saxon and other materials, including, for example, fixed schedules of money payments imposed as penalties for crime. It was not by issuing laws that Henry I and Henry II transformed the legal practices of England. By developing old instruments in new combinations they created the new common law, law common to all of England because it was administered by the royal courts. Though the hundred and shire courts continued to exist, their jurisdiction had been diluted by that of the competing baronial courts, lay and ecclesiastical. Moreover, only the king could give Englishmen better ways of settling their quarrels among themselves than the old trial by ordeal or trial by battle. The chief instruments were writs, juries, and itinerant justices.

If, for example, somebody seized a subject's property, by the middle of Henry II's reign the victim could buy quite reasonably a royal writ: an order from the king directing a royal official to give the plaintiff a hearing. The official would assemble a group of twelve neighbors who knew the facts in the case; they took an oath, and were therefore called a jury (from *juré,* "man on oath"); and then they told the truth as they knew it about whether dispossession had taken place, answering yes or no, and thus giving a verdict (from *veredictum,* "a thing spoken truly"). These early juries were *not* trial juries in the modern sense but men who were presumed to be in the best position to know the facts already. By similar machinery of writ and jury, inheritances unjustly detained could be recovered, and a man unjustly held as a serf could win his freedom. Thus, though the use of a jury, or sworn inquest, dated back to the ninth-century Carolingians, and had come to England with the Conqueror, its application to civil cases between individuals was a new procedure, and so was the flexibility permitted by a variety of writs. No matter who won, the royal exchequer profited, since the loser had to pay a fine. Also, judgments rendered by royal judges in effect became new law without any legislation in the modern sense.

Building on the practice begun by Henry I, Henry II also regularly sent itinerant justices out to the shires. On their travels they were instructed in each shire to receive reports from the local officials, and to try all cases pending in the shire court. Moreover, the sheriffs had to bring before the justices from each hundred and township a group of sworn men to report under oath all crimes that had occurred since the last visit of the justices, and to indicate whom they considered to be the probable criminal in each case. This is another use of the jury, the jury of presentment, since it presented the names of suspect criminals. It is the ancestor of the modern grand jury ("grand" simply in the sense of large), consisting of greater numbers of men than the twelve that took part in the petty juries. Again the treasury profited, as the itinerant justices imposed heavy fines. Again blatant innovation was avoided; again refinements and combinations of existing instruments produced new legal conditions. Of course, we are still in the Middle Ages. The usual means of proof in a criminal trial was still under Henry II the ordeal by cold water: If the accused, with hands and feet tied, floated in a pool blessed by the Church, he was guilty: if he sank, he was innocent.

An Italian depiction of the martyrdom of Thomas à Becket: fresco from SS Giovanni e Paolo, Spoleto.

Henry II and Becket

Where Henry II failed was in an effort to limit the competing system of canon law. Confident that he would have a pliant assistant, he appointed his friend and chancellor, Thomas à Becket, to be archbishop of Canterbury. But once he had become archbishop, Becket proved inflexibly determined not to yield any of the Church's rights, but rather to add to them whenever he could. The great quarrel between the two broke out over the question of "criminous clerks"—that is, clerics convicted of crime. In publishing a collection of earlier customs relating to the Church (Constitutions of Clarendon, 1164), Henry included one provision that clerics charged with crimes should be indicted in the royal court before being tried by the bishop's court, and then if convicted returned to the royal authorities for punishment. Becket refused to agree to this part of the document and appealed to the pope for support.

Although the issue was compromised after a dispute that lasted six years, Henry, in one of his fits of temper, asked whether nobody would rid him of Becket. Four of his knights responded by murdering Becket in his own cathedral at Canterbury. Henry swore to the pope that he was innocent of complicity in the murder, but he had to undergo a humiliating penance and, more important, he had to yield on the issue. The Church in England won the sole right to punish its clergy—"benefit of clergy," the principle was called. Moreover, Henry had to accept the right of litigants in church courts to appeal to Rome direct, without royal intervention or license of any sort. This meant that the papacy had the ultimate say in an important area of English life. It was a severe defeat for Henry's program of extending royal justice. Yet the other clauses in the Constitutions of Clarendon were not challenged, and the king continued to prevent the pope from taxing the English clergy directly. For his part, Becket was made a saint only two years after his death, and pilgrimages to his miraculous tomb at Canterbury became a standard part of English life.

Henry's reign was also notable for the reorganization of the old Anglo-Saxon *fyrd* by the Assize of Arms, 1181, which made each free man responsible, according to his income, to maintain suitable arms for the defense of the realm. Forests, floods, the ingredients and prices of bread and beer, and of course the warfare with France all occupied Henry's attention. Unfortunately, he could not control his own sons, who rebelled against him and made his last years miserable by attacking his possessions on the Continent. When he died, he is said to have turned his face to the wall and said, "Shame, shame on a conquered king!"

Richard I and John

Henry II's son, Richard the Lionhearted (ruled 1189–1199), spent less than six months of his ten-year reign in England. But the country did not revert to the anarchy that had been characteristic of the reigns of Stephen and Matilda. Henry II had done his work too well for that. The bureaucracy functioned without the presence of the king. Indeed, it functioned all too well for the liking of the population. For Richard needed more money than had ever been needed before to pay for his crusade, for his ransom from captivity, and for his wars against Philip Augustus of France. Heavy taxes were levied on income and on personal property; certain kinds of possessions, including silver plate, were sim-

A fourteenth-century manuscript illumination showing King John hunting deer.

ply confiscated; a large number of charters was sold to cities. Thus it was that Richard's brother, John (ruled 1199–1216), who was clever but unreliable, greedy, and tyrannical, succeeded to a throne whose resources had been squandered. John had the great misfortune to face three adversaries who proved too strong for him: Philip Augustus, who expelled the English from France north of the Loire; Innocent III, the greatest of medieval popes; and the outraged English baronage.

In 1206 the election to the archbishopric of Canterbury was disputed between two candidates, one of whom was favored by John. The pope refused to accept either, and in 1207 procured the election of a third, Stephen Langton. John exiled the members of the cathedral chapter of Canterbury and confiscated the property of the see. Innocent responded by putting all England under an interdict (1208) and by excommunicating John (1209). He threatened to depose John, and thought of replacing him with a Capetian; he corresponded with Philip Augustus, who prepared to invade England. Fearing with good reason that his own vassals would not stay loyal in the face of such an invasion, John gave in (1213). Not only did he accept Langton as archbishop of Canterbury and promise to restore Church property and to reinstate banished priests, but he also recognized England and Ireland as fiefs of the papacy, and did homage to the pope for them. In addition, he agreed to pay an annual tribute to Rome. All this of course represented a startling papal victory. From now on, Innocent sided with John in his quarrel with a large faction of the English barons—a quarrel that became acute after the French had won the Battle of Bouvines (1214). "Since I have been reconciled to God, and have submitted to the Roman Church," John exclaimed when the news of Bouvines was brought to him, "nothing has gone well with me."

John and the Barons: Magna Carta

The quarrel with perhaps a third of the English barons arose from John's ruthlessness in raising money for a campaign in France, and from his habit of punishing vassals without trial. At the moment of absolution by the pope in 1213, John had sworn to Stephen Langton that he would "restore the good laws of his predecessors." But he violated his oath. After Bouvines, the barons hostile to John renounced their homage to him and drew up a list of demands, most of which they forced him to accept on June 15, 1215, at Runnymede, one of the most celebrated occasions in all human history. The document that he agreed to send out under the royal seal to all the shires of England had sixty-three chapters, in the legal form of a feudal grant or conveyance, known as Magna Carta, the Great Charter.

In Magna Carta one finds a feudal document, a list of specific concessions drawn up in the interest of a group of great barons at odds with their feudal lord, the king. The king promises reform in his exactions of scutage, aids, reliefs, and in certain other feudal practices. He makes certain concessions to the peasantry and the tradesmen (uniform weights and measures, town liberties) and to the Church (free elections to bishoprics and maintenance of liberties).

Why do English and American historians and politicians often call this medieval special-interest document the foundation-stone of our present liberties? Largely because in later centuries some of its provisions could be and have been given new and expanded meanings. For instance, the provision "No scutage or aid, save the customary feudal ones, shall be levied *except by the common consent of the realm*" in 1215 meant only that John would have to consult his great council (barons and bishops) before levying extraordinary feudal aids. Yet this could later be expanded into the doctrine that all taxation must be by consent, that taxation without representation was tyranny, which would have astonished everybody at Runnymede. Similarly, the provision that "No freeman shall be arrested or imprisoned, or dispossessed or outlawed or banished or in any way molested; nor will we set forth against him, nor send against him, unless by the lawful judgment of his peers and by the law of the land" in 1215 meant only that the barons did not want to be tried by anybody not their social equal, and that they wished to curb the aggressions of royal justice. Yet it was capable of later expansion into the doctrine of due process of law, that everybody was entitled to a trial ("by his peers").

Although medieval kings of England reissued the charter with modifications some forty times, it was to be ignored under the Tudor monarchy in the sixteenth century, and Englishmen did not appeal to it until the revolt against the Stuarts in the seventeenth century. By then, the Middle Ages had long since been over, and the rebels against Stuart absolutism could read into the medieval clauses of Magna Carta many of the same modern meanings that we, just as inaccurately, see in them at first glance. Thus Magna Carta's lasting importance lies partly in what later interpreters were able to read into its original clauses. It also lies perhaps even more, however, in two general principles underlying the whole document: that the king was subject to the law and that he might, if necessary, be forced to observe it. This is why this document, more than seven centuries old, dealing with a now obsolete social system, still carries vitally important implications for us in the twentieth century.

As soon as John had accepted the charter, he instantly tried to break his promises; the pope declared the charter null and void; and Langton and the barons opposed to John now took the pope's former place as supporters of a French monarchy for England. Philip Augustus' son actually landed in England and occupied London briefly; but John died in 1216 and was succeeded by his nine-year-old son, Henry III (ruled 1216–1272), to whose side the barons rallied. The barons then expelled the French from England. It was not until 1258 that the king found himself again actually at open war with a faction of his own barons. Yet, during the interval, there were warnings of future trouble.

Henry III and the Barons

In Henry's reissue of Magna Carta (1216 and 1217), the clause requiring the great council to approve unusual taxation was omitted. In 1232, Henry appointed a French favorite to the highest post in his administration, replacing a loyal Englishman who had become identified with the barons' revolt. Frenchmen in high places in the state were now added to the host of Italians appointed by the pope to high places in the English church. Since both the French and the Italian appointees were avaricious, many English nobles felt a deep resentment toward these foreigners. Henry's marriage to a French princess (1236) fanned the flames. The great council flatly refused to give Henry money for a campaign in France, and its members discussed plans for limiting the royal power. In 1254 Henry received from the pope the crown of Sicily for his second son, and in 1257 he permitted his brother to seek election as Holy Roman Emperor. Both were highly expensive undertakings, since Sicily had to be conquered and the empire had to be bought. Things came to a head in 1258, a year of bad harvest, when Henry asked for one-third of the revenues of England as an extra grant for the pope.

Now the barons openly rebelled. They came armed to the session of the great council and secured the appointment of a committee of twenty-four of their number, which then issued a document known as the Provisions of Oxford. This document created a council of fifteen without whose advice the king could do nothing. The committee put its own men in the high offices of state. It also replaced the full great council with a baronial body of twelve. This provision clearly contained the seeds of a baronial tyranny per-

haps worse than the king's own. The foreigners were expelled. But the barons were ridden by dissension among themselves; the pope declared the Provisions null and void, and Henry III resumed his personal rule. Civil war broke out in 1263 between the king and the baronial party headed by Simon de Montfort. When in the next year Louis IX was called in to arbitrate, he ruled in favor of the king and against the barons. Simon de Montfort, however, would not accept the decision, took arms again, captured the king in 1264, and set up a regime of his own based on the restoration of the Provisions of Oxford. This regime lasted fifteen months. In 1265, Simon de Montfort called an assembly of his supporters, which, as we shall see, was a step in the evolution of Parliament. But in this same year, the heir to the throne, the lord Edward, defeated and killed Simon de Montfort, and restored his father, Henry III, to the throne. For the last seven years of Henry's reign (1265–1272), as well as for the next thirty-five years of his own rule (1272–1307), Edward I was the real ruler of England.

The Origins of Parliament

The revolts of the thirteenth century had given the barons experience in the practical work of government, and many of their reforms had been accepted by the royal governments that followed. Still more important, during the course of the struggle the local communities of England had emerged as significant elements in the operations of the central administration. Indeed, it is to these years of Henry III that historians turn for the earliest signs of the greatest contribution of the English Middle ages to mankind: the development of Parliament.

The word *parliament* is French and simply means a "talking" or "parley," a conference of any kind. The French historian Villehardouin refers to a discussion between the French and Venetian leaders in the fourth crusade (1204) as a *parlement*. Joinville, the biographer of St. Louis, refers to his hero's secret conversations with his wife on the palace staircase as *parlements*. And we have already encountered the word as applied in France to that part of the *curia regis* which acted as a court of justice. In England, during the thirteenth century, the word is found more and more often in reference to the assemblies summoned by the king, especially those that were to hear petitions for legal redress. In short, a parliament in England in the thirteenth century is much like the parlement in France: a session of the king's large council acting as a court of justice.

The Anglo-Saxon witenagemot had been an assembly of the great churchmen and laymen of the kingdom who advised the king on taxation and on matters of policy, and who could also act as a supreme court in important cases. In these respects the great council of the Norman and Angevin kings was not much different from the witenagemot. Feudal law simply reinforced the king's right to secure from his chief vassals both aid (that is, military service) and counsel (that is, advice on law and custom and a share in judicial decisions). The Norman kings made attendance at sessions of the great council compulsory; it was the king's privilege, not his duty, to receive counsel, and it was the vassal's duty, not his privilege, to offer it.

But by requiring the barons to help govern England, the kings entirely unconsciously, and indeed contrary to their own intentions, actually strengthened the assembly of the vassals, the great council. The feeling gradually grew up that the king *must* consult the council; this feeling is reflected in the scutage and aid provision of Magna Carta. Yet the kings generally consulted only the small council of their permanent advisers; the great council met only occasionally and when summoned by the king. The barons who sat on the great council thus developed a sense of being excluded from the work of government in which they felt entitled to participate. It was this baronial discontent, perhaps as much as the issues we have already considered, that led to the troubles under Henry III. When the barons took over the government in 1258, they determined that the great council should meet three times a year, and they called it a parliament. When Henry III regained power, he continued to summon the feudal magnates to the great council, to parliament.

Knights of the Shire and Burgesses

The increasing prosperity of England in the thirteenth century had enriched many members of the landed gentry who were not necessarily the king's direct vassals, and might occupy a position fairly far down in the feudal pyramid. The inhabitants of the towns had also increased in number and importance with the growth of trade. Representatives of these newly important classes in country and town now began to attend parliament at the king's summons. They were the knights of the shire, two from each shire, and the burgesses of the towns. Accustomed since Anglo-Saxon times to the compulsory participation in their local hundred and shire courts, the knights of the shire were landholders with local standing, and they were often rich men. By the time of Richard the Lionhearted, some were occasionally selected to bring court records to the judges. For other purposes (bringing in accounts or documents to show title) townsmen, too, had been chosen by the towns at royal command to appear before royal justices either on circuit in the shires or in London. In 1213, 1226, and 1227, knights of the shire had been summoned by the king to discuss current problems; in 1254 they were summoned for the first time to a meeting of the great council. Meanwhile, burgesses or townsmen were also being summoned by the king to appear before his justices either on circuit in the shires or in London; they brought accounts or legal documents.

Although controversy on the subject still rages, recent research has made it seem probable that the chief reason for the king's summons to the shire and town representatives was his need for money. By the thirteenth century the sources of royal income, both ordinary and extraordinary, were not enough to pay the king's ever-mounting bills. Thus he was obliged, according to feudal custom, to ask for "gracious aids" from his vassals. These aids were in the form of percentages of personal property, and the vassals had to assent to their collection. So large and so numerous were the aids that the king's immediate vassals naturally collected what they could from *their* vassals to help make up the sums. Since these subvassals would contribute such a goodly part of the aids, they, too, came to feel that they should assent to the levies. The first occasion when we can be sure that the king summoned subvassals for this purpose was the meeting of the great council in 1254, to which he called the knights of the shire. It should be emphasized that this was not exactly a great innovation; the knights of the shire, as we have seen, were already accustomed to bringing information to the king and speaking on behalf of their shires.

The towns also came to feel that they should be consulted on taxes, since in practice they were often able to negotiate with the royal authorities for a reduction in the levy imposed on them. Burgesses of the towns were included for the first time in Simon de Montfort's "parliament" of 1265. Knights of the shire likewise attended this meeting, because Simon apparently wanted to muster the widest possible support for his program, and believed that an assembly of the direct vassals would not be representative enough. But only known supporters of Simon were invited to attend the parliament.

Scholars no longer believe, as they once did, that de Montfort had a twentieth-century democrat's devotion to representative institutions, or even that he regarded the assembly he was summoning as establishing a precedent for the future. Yet it did prove to be such a precedent, and the simultaneous presence of shire and town representatives made it the first true ancestor of the modern House of Commons. Not all subsequent parliaments had representatives from shire and town, and not all assemblies attended by knights and burgesses were parliaments. Knights and burgesses had no "right" to come to parliament; no doubt, they often felt it a nuisance and an expense to come, and not a privilege. But gradually they came to attend parliament regularly.

Edward I

Edward I, who became an extraordinary legislator, also tried but failed to unite all Britain into a single kingdom. In 1283 he put down a revolt of the Welsh, executed the brother of the last native prince, and proclaimed his own infant son prince of Wales. Ever since, this title has been reserved for the eldest son of the English monarch. In the 1290's a disputed succession to the throne of Scotland, and the formation of a Franco-Scottish alliance, brought Edward to Scotland as invader. Although he declared himself king of Scotland in 1296, and carried off the Stone of Scone, the symbol of Scottish kingship, to Westminster Abbey, William Wallace's rebellion (1297-1305) required a second conquest

of Scotland and led to the capture and execution of Wallace. Edward incorporated Scotland with England. However, the celebrated Robert Bruce now rebelled, and Edward I died while on an expedition against him (1307). Edward II (ruled 1307-1327) lost Scotland to Bruce at the Battle of Bannockburn (1314). So it was not until 1603 that England and Scotland were joined under the same king (James I), and he was a Scot who became king of England.

By the late thirteenth century the earlier medieval belief that law is custom, and that it cannot be made, was disappearing. In Edward I England found a law-giver who enacted a great series of systematizing statutes. Indeed, Edward is sometimes called, a bit misleadingly, "the English Justinian." Edward's statutes were framed by the experts of the small council, who elaborated and expanded the machinery of government, and under whose rule parliament's function was more judicial than legislative or consultative. Each of the statutes was really a large bundle of different enactments. Taken together, they reflect a declining feudalism, and show us an England in which the suzerain-vassal relationship was becoming more and more a mere landlord-tenant relationship, and in which the old duties of fighting were becoming less important than the financial aspects of the matter. The Second Statute of Westminster (1285), for example, was designed to assure the great landowner that an estate granted to a tenant could not be disposed of except by direct inheritance; this is what we would call entail. Similarly, the Statute of Mortmain (1279) prevented transfer of land to the Church without the consent of the suzerain. The Church placed a "dead hand" (*mortmain*) on land and could hold on forever to any land it received; lay landlords, therefore, found it highly unprofitable to see portions of their holdings transferred to clerical hands.

In addition to these statutes, which redounded to the interest of the landlord, Edward I in another statute commanded the barons to show by what authority (*quo warranto*) they held any privilege, such as the right to have their own court of justice. Some privileges (franchises) he revoked, but his chief aim was to assert the principle that all such franchises came from the king, and that what he had given he could take away. Under Edward the business of royal justice increased steadily, and specialized courts began to appear, all of them the offspring of the central

The Court of King's Bench in the fifteenth century.

permanent the king's share in export duties on wool and leather, the burden of which fell mostly on foreigners, and in customs dues on foreign merchandise, which soon became the most important single source of royal income, eloquent testimony to the flourishing commerce of the period. At the behest of parliament, Edward expelled the Jews from England in 1290; they were not allowed to come back until the mid-seventeenth century. After their expulsion, the Italians assumed the role of moneylenders.

Edward required all freemen to be responsible for military service and to equip themselves appropriately. The less well-off served as footsoldiers. But those with a certain minimum amount of property were compelled to become knights (distraint of knighthood) and serve on horseback, in part for financial reasons: Once they had achieved knight's status the king could collect feudal dues from them. Edward's vigorous extension of royal power aroused the same sort of opposition that had plagued John and undone Henry III. In 1297 both the clergy (under the influence of Pope Boniface VIII) and the barons refused to grant the aid that Edward wanted; they were able to make him confirm Magna Carta and promise not to levy any further taxes without first obtaining consent.

Edward I's parliament of 1295 is traditionally called the Model Parliament, because it included all classes of the kingdom, not only barons, higher clergy, knights of the shire, and burgesses, but also representatives of the lower clergy. In the royal summons of 1295 we find a celebrated clause: "What touches all should be approved by all." This echoes a famous provision of Roman law, and pays at least lip service to the principle that consent to taxation was necessary. Again, in 1297, Edward declared that the "good will and assent of the archbishops, bishops, and other prelates, earls, barons, knights, burgesses, and other freemen of our realm" were *essential* to a royal levy of a tax. This principle was frequently reasserted in later years, and parliament sometimes made its confirmation a condition for the grant of money. The regular presence of the knights and burgesses had gradually made them more and more nearly indispensable to the king's business. Unlike the French monarchs, the English had encountered a corporate baronial opposition, which by forcing consultation upon the king had begun to create brand-new institutions.

curia regis. The Court of Common Pleas, which handled cases that arose between subjects, had begun to take shape earlier, but now crystallized into a recognizable, separate body. The new Court of King's Bench handled criminal and Crown cases, and the special Court of Exchequer dealt with disputes pertaining to royal finance.

Edward I also regularized and improved existing financial and military practices. He made

IV   Germany and Italy, Empire and Papacy, 911-1273

Dukes and King

In Germany, strong monarchy won a secure footing earlier than it had in either England or France. As the Carolingian Empire gradually disintegrated in the late ninth and early tenth centuries, five duchies arose in the East Frankish lands of Germany. They were Franconia, Saxony, Thuringia, Swabia, and Bavaria. These duchies were military units organized by the local Carolingian administrators, who took the title of duke (army commander). At first, these military leaders were loyal to the Carolingian monarchy, and, after the Carolingian dynasty had become extinct, they chose one of their own

number, Conrad, duke of Franconia, as their king in 911. The dukes felt that this was the best way to protect their lands against the threat of the Magyar invaders (see Chapter 5). Conrad, however, could not claim the deference that his Carolingian predecessors had enjoyed. His efforts to exact it, coupled with his failure as a military leader, led the dukes for the first time to assert themselves as rivals to the Crown and to build up their duchies into petty kingdoms. Each duke made himself hereditary ruler and took control over the Church in his own duchy. Each tried to arouse the loyalty of his people and to dominate the local administrators of the king, the counts.

These decentralizing processes had only be-

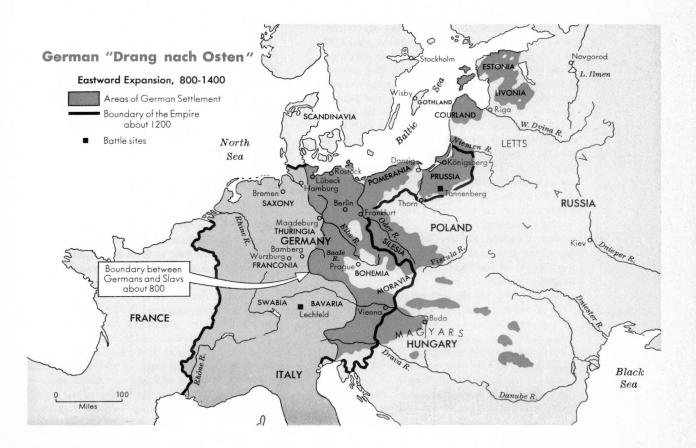

German "Drang nach Osten"

Eastward Expansion, 800-1400

Areas of German Settlement

Boundary of the Empire
about 1200

■ Battle sites

gun when Conrad died, having named as his successor the duke of Saxony, who became King Henry I (919–936). A struggle with the duchies ensued, in which Henry and his descendants—notably Otto I (936–973) and Otto III (983–1002)—were able to reassert the power of the monarchy. They successfully combated the ducal tendency to dominate the counts and to control the Church; they made the counts serve under the Crown, and regained the right to appoint bishops. In 939, moreover, the Crown obtained the duchy of Franconia; thenceforth the German kings, no matter what duchy they came from, would also have Franconia as the royal domain. Parts of Saxony, too, became Crown land.

Saxon Administration

The Saxon dynasty established by Henry I relied on the Church to perform much of the work of governing Germany. Henry welcomed the alliance between Church and monarchy, partly because bishops, unlike counts, could not pass on their offices to their sons, and partly because bishops were better educated than laymen. And the Church welcomed the alliance because a strong central government was its best guarantee of stability. In the tenth century the papacy itself recognized the rights of the German kings to appoint their own bishops. The later Saxon monarchs received church and abbey lands into their special protection, exempting them from the authority of the counts, and bringing them directly under the Crown. The bishops were given the right to administer justice within their own domain, and in fact were invested with the powers of counts. In 1007, for instance, the bishops of the great sees of Bamberg and Würzburg were given all the rights that had formerly belonged to counts.

In addition to efficient administration, the Church supplied the German king with much of his revenue, and tenants of church lands furnished three-quarters of his army. The Church also shared largely in the German expansion to the east—the celebrated *Drang nach Osten*—in the defeat of the Magyars (955), in the push into Slavic lands along the Elbe and Saale rivers, and in the advance into Silesia. New German bishoprics were set up, with Magdeburg as center, and subject sees were established east of the Elbe. The Church, in consequence, was now able to impose Christianity upon the vanquished Slavs.

The Empire

When King Otto I took the title of emperor in the year 962, he created for his successors a set of problems that far transcended the local problems of Germany, and that profoundly affected Germany itself. The old concept of the Roman Empire as the only possible true secular power had continued unchanged in the Eastern empire of Byzantium.

In the Carolingian West, however, this idea had become much diluted, and "emperor" had come to mean a ruler who controlled two or more kingdoms, but who did not necessarily claim supremacy over the whole inhabited world. The kingdoms that the Western emperor was likely to control were Germany, Burgundy, and Italy. Burgundy had grown up under ambitious rulers in the region between the eastern and western Frankish lands. Italy, on the other hand, was weak, divided, and open to invasion.

Thus the king of Germany had something to gain if he could secure the title of emperor even in its diluted new meaning. And, if he did not make himself emperor, he faced a real danger that somebody else would. That somebody might easily be the duke of Swabia or of Bavaria, in which case the struggle of the Saxon kings to control the dukes would have proved unavailing. When viewed in this light, Otto I's fateful trip to Italy and his assumption of the imperial title appear not as a mere urge for conquest but as a move in self-defense. Moreover, it was the natural step for the heir to the Carolingians to take.

Otto I's grandson, the brilliant young Otto III (983–1002), used a seal with the words *Renewal of the Roman Empire*. In Rome itself he strove to restore a Roman imperial palace, Roman titles, and Roman glory, possibly acting under the influence of his Byzantine mother, and surely hoping to win the support of the Roman aristocracy. He also tried to make imperial power real in Italy by putting German officials on Church lands to keep these lands out of the hands of the Italian nobility, and by appointing German bishops to Italian sees in an effort to build up the sort of government he had at home. Since Otto III did not ignore Germany but paid careful attention to relations between Germany and the Slavs, German contemporaries seem to have felt that his intervention in Italy was proper and legitimate. He was not trying to dominate the entire West, but rather to establish himself as emperor in the new dilute sense, and to consolidate the rule of the Saxon dynasty in Italy, Burgundy, and Germany.

German culture and German trade benefited from the Italian connection. By the early eleventh century, the right of the German king to be king of Italy and emperor was taken for granted; even if a new king had not yet been crowned emperor by the pope, he called himself "king of the Romans, still to be promoted to emperor." Italy benefited, now that her long period of anarchy had finally come to an end. The emperors raised the level of the papacy from the degradation it had reached in the tenth century. But, as the emperors sponsored reforming movements within the Church, they set in motion forces that would make the papacy a world power and bring about their own eventual ruin.

Salian Administration

The hereditary principle had by now been established in the German monarchy; regional barriers within Germany were gradually disappearing; and a sense of German national unity was asserting itself, evidenced by the general use of the term *teutonici* (Teutons or Germans). When the Saxon dynasty died out in 1024, the widow of the last Saxon designated Conrad II (1024–1039) of the Salian dynasty. The new dynasty, which came from Franconia, produced some first-rate administrators. Conrad II modified the Saxon policy of entrusting the duchies and the great episcopal sees to members of the imperial family. He ruled instead through the counts, and permitted their office to become hereditary, something that the greater nobles had opposed. Conrad thus experimented with a political alliance between the Crown and the lesser nobles (the counts) against the pretensions of the great dukes.

Yet this sort of alliance, which had been effective elsewhere in Europe, could not succeed in Germany. The counts, who did not usually feel oppressed by the dukes, were not ready to ally themselves with the king against them; if anything, the counts felt more oppressed by the king and were more likely to ally themselves with the dukes against the Crown. For Conrad II to permit the office of count to become hereditary was to establish a dangerous precedent. Conrad's successors therefore abandoned the alliance with the counts.

But they did accept and develop another of Conrad's administrative innovations: the training of members of the lower classes to serve as administrators: the *ministeriales*. The Church had long used such men to run its great estates, and now the kings used them to run the lands of the Crown. Though they often received lands as a reward, their lands were usually not hereditary, and so did not become fiefs. Thus the *ministeriales* depended directly on the Crown, had a status that could not be described as feudal, and remained a class peculiar to Germany. Often they had highly successful careers. The ministerialis who was comptroller-general of the imperial estates under Henry III (1039–1056) ended his career as a bishop. Under Henry IV (1056–1106) the great nobles began to complain that the king listened only to low-born fellows.

Henry III chose Goslar in the Harz mountains as the first permanent royal residence, and the German royal court gave up its previous practice of moving from place to place. Henry IV ordered a survey of Crown lands in 1064–1065 to discover how much revenue he could count on. The survey did not extend to other people's land, and so was by no means as comprehensive as the English Domesday Book. But by the 1070's the German monarchy was almost as effectively administered as Norman England, and far more so than France would be until Philip Augustus, more than 100 years later.

Moreover, Germany, unlike France, was not a fully feudalized country. In France, the Carolingian counts had become feudal lords, each in his own county, whereas in Germany the dukes had no such feudal position. Free men in Germany did not have to choose between becoming vassals of the dukes and ceasing to exist; both large and small estates continued to be owned outright by free men. Although the social distinction between the rich and poor was great, both were more often free of feudal ties than anywhere else in western Europe. Technically, as we have seen, land that was still free was called an *allod* (from *allodium,* the opposite of *feudum,* a fief) and allods were far more numerous in Germany than elsewhere.

Though the class of free landholders had no feudal ties, it had no royal ties either. So, when the attack came on the increasing centralization of the eleventh-century German monarchy, it came from these free landowners, a class that had no exact counterpart in France or England. They had strengthened their position by becoming the guardians or "advocates" (German: *Vogt*) of monasteries, a process that was aided for a time by the Crown itself. In 973 there were in Germany 108 abbeys, probably all attached to the Crown; in 1075, there were more than 700, and almost all the new ones were attached to members of the landowner class. A new monastic foundation in Germany was not only a sign of the founder's piety. Monks opened up and colonized new lands, and the resulting revenues went to the founder of the house, who as "advocate" also had jurisdiction over the tenants. (The English term for this practice is *advowson;* the German, *Vogtei.*)

To keep these valuable monasteries out of royal hands, the German nobles often made them the legal property of the pope, who was far away and could not interfere as readily as the king could. Thus, side by side with what may be termed the "royal" church and its bishops, there grew up in Germany a "noble" church based largely on monastic foundations.

Opposition to the royal church, to the ministeriales, and to the trend toward monarchical centralization all led the German nobility to revolt. In 1073, the nobles rose in Saxony against the emperor Henry IV; in 1075, Henry crushed the uprising. But only a few weeks later there began the open struggle with the papacy that gave the nobles new occasion to rebel. This was the Investiture Controversy, destined to last half a century and to end in the ruin of the German monarchy.

The Investiture Controversy

TO 1077   The origins of this struggle go back to the year 1046, when the emperor Henry III had first intervened in Rome, at a moment when three rival popes were simultaneously in office while rival mobs of their supporters rioted in the streets. Henry deposed all three and named a German, who soon died, and was replaced by a second German, who also lived only a short time. In 1049, Henry named a third German, his own uncle, Bishop Bruno of Toul, who became pope as Leo IX. Leo fought abuses bravely and was committed to the Cluniac program of monastic reform (see Chapter 8). But Leo and especially his younger assistant, Hildebrand, also favored the extension of reform beyond the monasteries. The whole church hierarchy, they insisted, must be purged of secular influences, and over it all the pope must reign supreme. Ironically enough, the emperor Henry III had put into power reformers whose chief target would be his own imperial system of government in Germany.

In 1073 Hildebrand himself became pope as Gregory VII. He was determined to push ecclesiastical reform by ensuring the canonical (regular) election of all bishops and abbots. This would mean sweeping away the system of royal selection and appointment, and the subsequent ceremony of lay investiture—that is, the conferring of the prelate's insignia of office (for bishops a ring and a staff)—by a layman, the emperor. Yet the German royal administration largely depended on this royal appointment of prelates, which involved not only lay investiture but the sale of church offices and many other corrupt practices.

Gregory VII now girded himself for the attack. And, though personally humble and saintly, he was a statesman of such vigor, shrewdness, intellect, and passion that modern historians agree with his contemporaries in judging him, with Gregory the Great and Innocent III, as one of the Church's greatest and most effective popes. He believed that, as the wielder of supreme spiritual authority, the pope had jurisdiction over temporal things as well, and that temporal princes who defied his command were followers of Antichrist. These were quite new ideas.

In the great struggle with the emperor, the pope seemed to enjoy many advantages. The papacy had recently (1059) put the election of new popes into the hands of the newly founded College of Cardinals, thus depriving the emperors of their former role. Moreover, in its attacks on lay investiture and on the imperial administrative and ecclesiastical system in Germany, the papacy was assured of the support of the German nobles, who had helped spread the

Cluniac order in Germany. Also, the pope was now allied, after a long period of hostility, with the new Norman rulers of southern Italy.

Gregory VII took the offensive in 1075 by forbidding lay investiture. In 1076, Henry IV and his bishops responded by declaring Gregory's election as pope null and void. Gregory then excommunicated Henry and declared him deposed, and deprived the bishops loyal to the emperor of their offices. Urged on by papal legates, Henry's noble opponents in Germany joined forces with the pope, and made Henry promise to clear himself of the excommunication within four months, on pain of the loss of his crown, and meanwhile to accept the papal sentence and to withdraw from public life. Henry's opponents also invited the pope to Germany.

To prevent this unwelcome visit, Henry himself secretly went to Italy in 1077, and appeared before the castle of Canossa, where Gregory was temporarily staying on his way north. Henry declared himself a penitent, and Gregory kept him waiting outside the castle for three days, barefoot and in sackcloth. When he was finally admitted he did penance, and Gregory absolved

Illumination from a twelfth-century chronicle. Top: Henry IV and his antipope expelling Gregory VII from Rome. Bottom: Gregory's death.

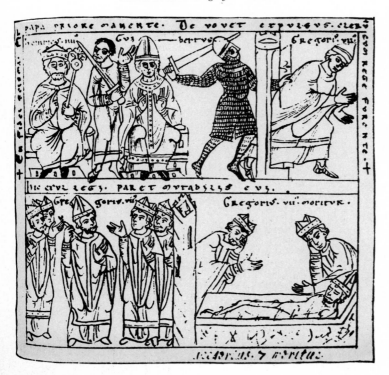

him. The drama and symbolism of this famous episode have often led historians to marvel at the power of the pope. But it struck contemporaries the other way: by allowing himself to be publicly humiliated, Henry had actually forced Gregory's hand. The pope had had to absolve him, and once absolved, Henry could no longer be deposed.

1077 TO 1122   Before Henry returned home, his German opponents, in their resentment at his stealing a march on them, had elected a new ruler, an "antiking," Rudolf of Swabia. This development resulted in a fearfully destructive civil war in Germany. By refraining for three years (until 1080) from making a decision between the rival kings, Gregory VII did what he could to prolong the civil war. When he did decide, it was in favor of Rudolf and against Henry, whom he solemnly deposed and excommunicated once more. But the pope's efforts failed. Rudolf was killed in battle, and a new antiking commanded even less support. The German clergy again declared the pope deposed, and Henry marched to Italy in 1081, took Rome in 1084, installed an antipope, and had himself crowned emperor by this antipope. Gregory summoned his Norman vassals and allies, but they did not arrive until after Henry had returned to Germany. Gregory died in defeat in 1085. By 1091, the last vestige of the revolt against Henry in Germany had been stamped out.

It must be realized that to many pious men of the Middle Ages Gregory's new claim that he could make and unmake kings seemed a dreadful thing. Implicit in it, they thought, lay future civil strife: the pope was destroying monarchy, something that had been established by God at the beginning of time. Thus the imperial theorists in the struggle were the conservatives, and the papal theorists were the revolutionaries.

Gregory VII's successors were reformers like him. They renewed his excommunication of Henry IV, supported civil war in Germany, and virtually put an end to imperial power in Italy. In 1106, Henry IV died and was succeeded by his son, Henry V (1106–1125). Just as Henry IV had tried to make his peace with the Church at Canossa in 1077 in the hope of defeating the princes, so now his son, Henry V, made his peace with the princes in the hope of defeating the Church. In doing so, he changed the character of the German monarchy. The nobles kept most of the gains they had won in the revolt of 1077. Consequently, feudal warfare continued in Germany, the ravaged royal lands could not be reassembled and put in order, and Henry V was unable to carry out the "Domesday Book" type of survey that he had planned (he was married to the daughter of Henry I of England). No final settlement was reached with the Church until the princes forced the issue and dictated imperial policy.

In the ecclesiastical settlement of 1122, the famous Concordat of Worms, Henry V renounced the practice of investing bishops with the clerical symbols of ring and staff. The pope permitted imperial investiture with the *regalia* (wordly goods pertaining to the bishop's office). The investiture was to take place before the bishop was consecrated, thus assuring the emperor of a previous oath of fealty from the bishop. Moreover, clerical elections in Germany were to be carried out in the presence of the emperor (or his representatives), thus giving him an opportunity to exercise a strong influence over the decisions. In Italy and Burgundy, the emperor retained less power; consecration was to take place *before* the regalia were conferred, and the emperor could not attend clerical elections. The Concordat of Worms was a compromise that in effect ended the Investiture Struggle, despite its failure to settle many other issues.

AFTERMATH   As a result of this struggle, Germany had become feudalized. During the years between 1076 and 1106 the princes and other nobles acted on the pretext that there was no king, since the pope had deposed him. They extended their powers, increasing the number of their dependents and administering their land without reference to the monarchy. Feudal castles multiplied and became centers of administrative districts; free peasants fell into serfdom; the absence of central authority drove lesser nobles to become dependent on greater nobles—in short, the familiar feudalizing process that had gone on in ninth- and tenth-century France now was operating in eleventh- and early twelfth-century Germany.

The princes had many assets in addition to their great allodial holdings. They employed ministeriales of their own, had a variety of vassals bound to them by feudal ties, and increased their power by combining and pyramiding their

monastic "advocacies." The royal government did not extend outside the royal domains. The aristocracy were the "lords of the land" and their lands were their own. The foundations of the future German territorial principalities and of what is known as German *particularism* had been laid.

In Italy, the Investiture Controversy had seen the further rise of the Norman kingdom of the south, controlling the island of Sicily, and the toe and heel of the Italian boot to a point well north of Naples. The struggle had also been responsible for the growth of communes in the cities of the north. The communes had begun as sworn associations of lesser nobles, who banded together to resist the power of the local bishops. In Lombardy, the communes were favored by Gregory VII.

They took advantage of his support to usurp the powers of municipal government. In Tuscany, where the ruling house was pro-papal, the communes allied themselves with the emperor, who granted them their liberties by charter. Thus, in Germany, the Crown faced a newly entrenched aristocracy; in Italy, it faced a new society of powerful urban communes.

The German nobles now controlled the election of the emperor. In 1138 they chose Conrad of Hohenstaufen, a Swabian prince, who became Emperor Conrad III (1138–1152). In so doing, they passed over another claimant, Henry the Proud, duke of Bavaria and Saxony and marquis of Tuscany in Italy, a member of the powerful Welf family. Because of their ancestral estate, the Hohenstaufens were often known as Waiblings; in Italian, *Waibling* became *Ghibelline* and *Welf* became *Guelf*. Thus in the first half of the twelfth century, the Guelf-Ghibelline, or Welf-Hohenstaufen, feud—one of the most famous, lasting, and portentous in history—got under way. Henry the Proud, the Welf leader, refused homage to Conrad III; Conrad, in turn, deprived Henry of Saxony and Bavaria. Once more feudal warfare raged in Germany.

Frederick Barbarossa

In 1152, there came to the throne of this sadly divided Germany Frederick I Hohenstaufen (1152–1190), called Barbarossa ("redbeard"), who reorganized and rebuilt the monarchy. Us-

Frederick Barbarossa portrayed as a crusader, from a Bavarian manuscript of 1188.

Italy with its greater wealth, and on Burgundy, both of which were near his native Swabia.

Frederick married the heiress to Burgundy in 1156, and took possession of this great province, which had slipped out of imperial control during the Investiture Controversy. He made Switzerland the strategic center of his policy, since it was adjacent to Burgundy and Swabia and since it controlled the Alpine passes into Italy. For the first time, Germany, northern Italy (Lombardy), and Burgundy were firmly united. Frederick tried to build in Swabia the sort of compact, well-run royal domain that the Capetians enjoyed in the Île de France. But the new royal power could be based only on feudal suzerainty over cooperative great vassals in Germany, and on an alliance with the northern Italian communes—a pattern not unlike the one that Philip Augustus would work out in France.

Frederick Barbarossa made six trips to Italy. He intervened first at Rome, where, in 1143, a commune had risen up in protest against papal rule. The leader of the commune, Arnold of Brescia, strongly favored the Church's return to apostolic poverty and simplicity. Barbarossa won papal good will by offering the pope assistance not only against Arnold but also against the Normans and against a Byzantine threat to southern Italy. He was crowned emperor in Rome in 1155, after a famous argument over whether he would hold the pope's bridle and stirrup as well as kiss his foot (Frederick lost). At the pope's request, the emperor hanged and burned Arnold, whose death he is later said to have regretted. The pope, however, soon reached an accommodation with the Normans and quarreled with Frederick once more (1157).

ing the Roman law as the source for his arguments, Frederick defended the power of the empire against the Church, declaring that he was the lawful heir of the lands and titles that Charlemagne had won by conquest, and not merely king by God's grace. Frederick could not rely upon the great churchmen as administrators, as his predecessors had; the Investiture Controversy had made that impossible. Since his own landed possessions in Germany were not great enough to give him a basis for a full restoration of royal power, he focused his attention on

The Struggle with the Italian Towns

Frederick returned to Italy in 1158 for the special purpose of subduing the leading north Italian commune, Milan. At Roncaglia (1158) he held a conference (diet) that was designed to define his regalia—that is, the rights of the emperor in the Italian towns. During the past three hundred years, these old imperial rights had been passed from the Frankish counts to the bishops, and had then been seized from the bishops by the communes. At stake were such matters as appointing dukes and counts, coining money, collecting a special tax to support the imperial army, and collecting custom dues and other taxes. Although Frederick did not necessarily intend to resume exercising the regalia, he wanted it recognized that they really belonged to him, and that he alone could grant them to others. He was also prepared to appoint imperial officials "with the consent of the people" in those towns he did not trust; elsewhere he left the choice of officials to the communes themselves.

But the pope opposed this consolidation of imperial power, and so did the Lombard League of communes, headed by Milan. Frederick was forced into war against the Lombard League and the papacy. Although he defeated the pope and occupied Rome in 1168, a devastating plague forced him to retreat. Then he was utterly defeated by the Lombard League at Legnano in 1176. In 1177, at Venice, Frederick reached an agreement with the pope, and in 1183 he made the Peace of Constance with the Lombard towns.

The towns kept the regalia within their own walls; but outside the walls they retained only those rights which they had already purchased, or might in the future buy, from the emperor. After free election by those towns which possessed the right, communal officials were to take an oath of fealty to the emperor. Frederick retained the special tax to support the imperial army and recognized the Lombard League as a legitimate organization. The league paid a large sum of money in return for this peace. Although Frederick had made concessions of self-government to the communes, he had succeeded in establishing his claims as feudal suzerain.

The Peace of Constance enabled the emperor to assert himself strongly in central Italy, where he established a direct imperial government rather than a feudal government, as he had in the north. Finally, in 1186, Frederick married his son, Henry, to the heiress of Norman Sicily. This was to prove one of the most important dynastic marriages of the Middle Ages. The papal territories, now in the hands of a weak pope, were gravely threatened by this union between the heir to Germany and northern Italy and the heiress to southern Italy. When a strong pope again came to the throne, it was clear that he would have to fight against this strangulation of his temporal power.

Barbarossa's German Policies

In line with his policy of consolidating his strength to the south, Frederick Barbarossa made certain concessions to the German princes. His great Welf rival, Henry the Lion (son of Henry the Proud), for example, obtained the right to invest the bishops of several important sees. Moreover, Henry was the leader of a great wave of German eastward expansion into the Slavic lands across the Elbe, where he ruled independently of his imperial overlord. He married the daughter of Henry II of England, received envoys from the Byzantine emperor, and conducted an almost independent foreign policy. By the 1160's Frederick was gradually beginning to counter this Welf threat by building up his own estates in Swabia and elsewhere. Then when Frederick ran into trouble in Italy and needed reinforcements, Henry tried to bargain with the emperor and in general showed that he was not a loyal vassal. Frederick, in turn, determined to assert his authority as suzerain and punish Henry.

This he did by the same means that Philip Augustus would use against King John. Frederick received complaints against Henry from his vassals, summoned Henry into the royal court to answer these complaints, and, when Henry refused, declared him contumacious and deprived him of his property (1180). The great territorial possessions of the Welf family were now broken up and divided among other smaller princes. The very act of parceling them out instead of adding them to the royal domain shows how feudalized Germany had become. Frederick could not hold onto these lands as Philip Augustus would hold onto Normandy because he simply did not control his vassals as effectively as the French king did.

In the same year (1180), Frederick's immediate vassals were recognized as princes of the empire. This step gave formal recognition to the new feudal order in Germany by creating a new class that was jealous of its prerogatives. Other seeds of future crisis had been sown by Frederick's reliance on the resources of Italy, where resentment against German rule was strong, and especially by his tight organization of central

Italy and his alliance with the south Italian Normans, both of which threatened the popes.

In 1190, Frederick was drowned in a river in Asia Minor while away on the Third Crusade. His great achievements, and the fact that he had died in a far-off land, gave rise to the legend that he was still alive, but asleep in a mountain cave, with his great red beard flowing over the table on which his arm rested. Some day "the old emperor" would come back, bringing glory and union to Germany. So Frederick joined King Arthur and Charlemagne's mighty peer, Holger the Dane, as heroes whom their people could not bear to lose.

Consequences of Henry VI's Sicilian Marriage

Barbarossa's son, Henry VI (1190–1197), changed the hitherto limited concept of the imperial role in the West. When Henry married Constance, the heiress of Sicily, he acquired by marriage an extraordinary kingdom. This kingdom had been built up in less than two centuries by the descendants of a small band of Norman adventurers, who in the early eleventh century had taken Apulia and Calabria (the heel and the toe of Italy) from the Byzantine Greeks. By 1091, the Normans had seized Sicily from the Muslims. Their great Roger II, who had been crowned king of Sicily in 1130, was an ally of the papacy. Ruling over a mixed population of Catholics, Orthodox Greeks, and Muslims, the small Norman upper class tolerated all faiths, and patronized and assimilated the Byzantine and Muslim cultures. Characteristically, they issued official documents in Arabic and Greek as well as in Latin.

The Norman kings of Sicily demonstrated the usual Norman gift for government. Ruling as absolute monarchs, and living the luxurious lives of oriental potentates at their splendid capital of Palermo, they traded with the entire Mediterranean world. Their administration was professional, not feudal. The members of the curia regis were not hereditary vassals, but appointees of the king. Royal officials called justiciars gave justice to the provinces, and royal chamberlains supervised local financial administration. The army combined Arab professional-

ism with feudal Norman practice. It was this heritage to which Henry VI succeeded.

But Richard the Lionhearted of England united with the German Welfs and the papacy to back a rival to Henry for control over the Norman Sicilian kingdom. Henry dissolved the alliance through skillful use of his capture of Richard (1192) as a diplomatic weapon. He held Richard for ransom and applied pressure on Richard's German allies. He then forced Richard to become his vassal and used the ransom money to finance a campaign in Sicily. Sicily was won by 1194, and Henry refused to do homage to the pope for it. Now Henry planned to acquire the Byzantine Empire, against which the Normans had waged intermittent warfare since the early eleventh century. He had secured the homage of the kings of Cyprus and Armenia, and he was building up a fleet to invade the eastern Mediterranean, when he died suddenly in 1197.

It was Henry VI's union of Germany, not only with Sicily, but also with the traditional Norman ambitions in the Mediterranean, that widened the hitherto limited Western concept of empire—and that was to have such grave consequences for the structure that Frederick Barbarossa had reared so painfully. Henry's Sicilian policy required him to make further concessions to the German princes. He made still more during his efforts to get them to recognize the hereditary right of his son, Frederick II, to succeed him, a problem that would not even have arisen in England or France, where hereditary royal succession was established. In this attempt, Henry offered the princes the same hereditary rights in their own fiefs that he asked of them.

The minority of Henry VI's infant son, Frederick II, saw a renewed civil war (1197–1215) in which the great pope Innocent III (1198–1216) determined to destroy the German-Sicilian combination, which had caught the papal lands in central Italy in an imperial pincers. Innocent III backed a Welf, educated in England, Otto of Brunswick, son of Henry the Lion, against the brother of Henry VI, Philip of Swabia, who initially had the support of the German princes and became king in 1198. The pope revived the claim of Gregory VII that no emperor could rule without papal confirmation, while Philip argued that an emperor duly elected by the princes was emperor whether the pope approved or not. To assure himself of papal support, Otto promised to give up all the rights with regard to investiture that the emperors had managed to salvage for themselves from the Investiture Controversy. Richard the Lionhearted and then King John of England backed their Welf nephew, Otto, and Philip Augustus of France naturally opposed the English–Welf coalition by backing Philip of Swabia.

When Philip Augustus defeated John in Normandy in 1204, he strengthened the cause of Philip of Swabia. By 1208, even Innocent III was preparing to accept Philip of Swabia, when Philip was assassinated. Now the German princes elected Otto, but, once he had been crowned by the pope in 1209, Otto began to act like a Hohenstaufen instead of a protégé of the papacy. He undertook to conquer Sicily, the very thing Innocent III wanted most to prevent. So in 1210 the pope excommunicated his former protégé and turned to the young Frederick Hohenstaufen, son of Henry VI. Supported by the pope and given money by Philip Augustus of France, Frederick reorganized the Hohenstaufen party in Germany and was crowned king in 1212. When Otto was defeated at Bouvines by Philip Augustus in 1214, Frederick's position became more secure.

Frederick II

But to establish his authority with the German princes and with the pope, Frederick II (1212–1250) had to make still more concessions. He had to give up control of the German church, exactly as Otto had done, and he promised not to reunite Germany and Sicily. In 1215 Innocent III seemed to have won a resounding victory. Yet the possibilities for a reconstruction of the German monarchy lay open to a ruler who would devote himself to reestablishing his position in Germany. Frederick II, however, chose to give his attention to Sicily. It was in that civilized society where his mother, Constance, had grown up, that he felt at home. He disliked Germany and spent only nine years there.

Frederick II is perhaps the most interesting monarch of medieval history. Brilliantly intelligent and highly cultivated, he spoke Arabic and Greek as well as half a dozen other languages, took a deep interest in scientific experiment, collected wild animals and women, and wrote poetry in the Italian vernacular. He patronized the arts, wrote a book on the sport of falconry, and was a superb politician. He was cynical, hard-boiled, a sound dilpomat, an administrator with capacity and vision, and a statesman in the imperial mold, with his father's vision of a Mediterranean empire.

It was Germany's misfortune, however, that the base for his operations had to be his beloved Sicily. The Germans felt more and more that they had no stake in his empire. It was Frederick's own misfortune that he encountered, after the death of Innocent III, three successive popes—Honorius III (1216–1227), Gregory IX (1227–1241), and Innocent IV (1243–1254)—who were not only consistently determined to prevent him from achieving his aims but entirely competent to fight him on even terms. It is little wonder that Frederick could never extend to Germany the centralized administration he built in southern Italy, and that German particularism, already blossoming, came into full flower. Frederick's reign condemned Germany to six hundred years of disunity.

In 1220, Frederick obtained for his son, Henry, election as king of Germany and a promise that Henry would be the next emperor. To do this he granted great privileges to the bishops and abbots. These ecclesiastical princes were already elected without imperial interference. Now Frederick abandoned his right to set up mints and customs stations in their territories, together with royal rights of justice. He promised to exclude from imperial cities any serfs who might run away from church lands to try their fortunes in the towns, and he agreed to build no new towns or fortresses on church lands. Thus he made the mistake that the French and English kings had avoided from the first: He acted against the towns, failing to see that they were his natural allies. In 1231 the secular princes exacted from Frederick a privilege parallel to that which he had already granted to the great church magnates. As regarded royal justice, mints, runaway serfs, and the rest, the lay lords now enjoyed the same sort of rights as the clerical. Both the secular and the ecclesiastical princes had become virtually independent potentates. The German crown had surrendered its hard-won rights.

In startling contrast is Frederick's administrative work in Sicily. Here, like William the Conqueror in England, Frederick assumed royal title to all property. In the Constitutions of Melfi, of 1231, he imposed his own completely centralized monarchical form of government upon his Italian subjects. Some of this centralization was a reassertion of the policies and programs of Frederick's Sicilian ancestor, Roger II. Much of the rest came from Roman law, with its extraordinarily lofty conception of the emperor's position. Feudal custom was wiped out, and trial by battle was forbidden as antiquated and absurd. At Naples Frederick founded a university, which became a state training school in which officials could be grounded in the Roman law. Frederick's army and navy were organized on a paid rather than a feudal basis. Finances were regularized and modernized, and an imperial bureaucracy collected tariffs on incoming and outgoing merchandise. State monopolies like those at Byzantium (see Chapter 6) controlled certain key industries, such as silk. Frederick became rich and powerful—the nearest approach to a modern national monarch that the West produced in the Middle Ages.

Frederick II and the Papacy

Yet the keynote of Frederick II's reign was his tremendous and ultimately unsuccessful conflict with the papacy, beginning in the 1220's. During the emperor's absence from Italy on a crusade, the pope's newly hired mercenary armies attacked his southern Italian lands. When Frederick returned, he was able to make peace temporarily. But he soon created further trouble. After he had defeated the Lombard towns in 1237 for refusing to keep the Peace of Constance, he announced a new plan to extend imperial administration to all Italy, including Rome. So in 1239 the pope excommunicated him, and war was resumed. Violent propaganda

Emperor Frederick II, in the ship on the left, watching his soldiers assaulting church-men on their way to the council summoned by Gregory IX.

North Sea

Danzig PRUSSIA

Lübeck
Hamburg
Bremen *Weser* Elbe R. POMERANIA
FRIESLAND
SAXONY BRANDENBURG *Vistula R.*
HARZ MTS. Magdeburg
Meuse R. Goslar POLAND
Cologne KINGDOM Oder R. SILESIA
LOWER Aachen THURINGIA Elbe R.
LORRAINE *Rhine R.* *Saale R.*
Frankfurt *Main R.* Prague
Trier Mainz Würzburg Bamberg BOHEMIA MORAVIA
Worms Wurzburg OF
UPPER PALATINATE FRANCONIA Ratisbon
LORRAINE *Danube R.* Augsburg AUSTRIA
Strasbourg GERMANY Vienna
FRANCE SWABIA BAVARIA
Constance STYRIA
A L P S CARINTHIA
Saône R. TYROL CARNIOLA HUNGARY
KINGDOM OF BURGUNDY Brescia *Adige R.* Trieste *Drava R.*
(KINGDOM OF ARLES) Legnano ■ Milan Venice *Danube R.*
LOMBARDY Pavia *Po R.*
Rhône R. Roncaglia Ferrara Danube
Alessandria Ravenna R.
Genoa Canossa Bologna ROMAGNA Zara SERBIA
Avignon KINGDOM Florence Ancona
Arles OF ITALY Pisa Assisi *Adriatic Sea*
Siena
TUSCANY Ragusa

CORSICA PAPAL Tagliacozzo ■
(to Pisa) Rome Anagni Bari
STATES
Melfi APULIA
Naples Taranto
SARDINIA Amalfi Salerno
(to Pisa and Genoa)
KINGDOM CALABRIA
OF THE
TWO SICILIES
(Hohenstaufen, 1194)

Medieval Germany and Italy

at death of Frederick II, 1250

Palermo

SICILY

Syracuse

0   100   200
Miles
■ Battle sites

—— Boundary of the Holy Roman Empire
▦ Kingdom of the Two Sicilies
▤ Papal States
▨ Claimed by Papacy
■ Venetian possessions

Mediterranean Sea

pamphlets were published and circulated by both sides. The pope called Frederick a heretic who was trying to found a new religion. Frederick called the pope a hypocrite, and urged all monarchs in Europe to unite against the pretensions of the Church. Hemmed in at Rome by the encroaching imperial system, the pope summoned a church council, presumably to depose Frederick. But Frederick's fleet captured the entire council of more than one hundred high churchmen. Just as Frederick was about to enter Rome itself, Pope Gregory IX died (1241); Frederick tried to install a new pope favorable to himself, but failed. The new pope, Innocent IV, fled from Italy, summoned a council to Lyons (1244), and deposed Frederick. There followed five more years of struggle. Frederick died in 1250, before the conflict had been settled.

After Frederick's death, the papacy pursued his descendants with fury. His son, Conrad IV, died in 1254, leaving a young son who was called Conradino, "little Conrad." In 1255, Frederick's illegitimate son, the gifted and capable Manfred, gained control of Sicily, which the popes had been trying to give to the second son of Henry III of England. But in 1266 a long-maturing papal plan succeeded. Saint Louis's brother, the ruthless and able Charles of Anjou, was brought into Italy as the papal candidate for the southern territories. He defeated and killed Manfred, and established himself as king in the south. When Conradino, aged fifteen, led an army south

from Germany to combat the cruel and tyrannical regime of Charles, he was defeated and captured at the Battle of Tagliacozzo in 1268, and soon afterward was executed at Naples. Angevin rule continued in Naples until 1435, although the Aragonese took Sicily in 1282.

By 1268 the breed of the Hohenstaufen was extinct. The Holy Roman Empire, begun by Frederick Barbarossa, and given an Italian rather than a German base by Henry VI and Frederick II, had been destroyed by the papacy. Yet within forty years of Charles of Anjou's entry into Italy as the instrument of papal vengeance, Charles' grandnephew, Philip the Fair, was to puncture the inflated temporal claims of the papacy and take it off to Avignon.

In Germany the imperial throne remained vacant from 1254 to 1272. The princes consolidated their power during this interregnum by taking advantage of the large grants made by rival candidates to the throne, all foreigners, in the hope of receiving their support. But the princes were pleased for a time not to have an emperor; their usurpation of rights that had formerly belonged to the monarchy was now well on its way to completion. Meanwhile, the old links with Italy were virtually broken, and the earlier form of the imperial idea vanished. The allodial nobility, the Investiture Controversy, and the preoccupation with Italy had ensured that the princes would emerge as the real rulers of Germany.

V   Conclusion

Our examination of four Western peoples through these centuries of their medieval development suggests a preliminary set of explanations for the stereotypes of national character with which we began this chapter. Already, at the beginning of the fourteenth century, we can see, in the contrasting institutional development of France, England, and Germany, the emergence of national units somehow recognizable as the ancestors of the nations we know.

In France, the Capetian kings, beginning as relatively powerless and insignificant local lords, have extended the sway of their royal administration into the lands of their great vassals, and created the institutions of a powerful centralized

monarchy. The question of the English claims to large areas on the Continent remains to be settled in the grim struggle of the Hundred Years' War (see Chapter 10). In England, on the other hand, the Norman conquerors have proved able to make the most of existing Anglo-Saxon institutions, and to superimpose effective feudal monarchy, while they and their Angevin successors have developed the common law, bringing not only money and power to the monarch but security to the subject.

Whereas in France the vassals are unaware of the danger to their position until it is too late, and are too divided among themselves to unite in opposition to the monarch's aggressions, in

England the vassals early recognize the need for presenting a united corporate opposition if they are to preserve their rights. And out of their opposition there have emerged the guarantees that limit the king: promises given in the first instance on behalf of the great vassals, but later subject to much broader interpretation. By the early fourteenth century, out of the king's need to obtain assent for taxation and out of the custom of consultation between king and subject, there is beginning to emerge Parliament, "incomparably the greatest gift of the English people to the civilization of the world."

In Germany, the monarchy, which effectively asserts itself in the earlier period, is fatally weakened by the prevalence of an allodial rather than a feudal nobility, which cooperates with the papacy in an assault upon the German administrative system. After the Investiture Controversy, once the country has been feudalized, the monarchy fails to realize, as both the French and the English have done, the advantages of an alliance with the towns. It is further weakened by Henry VI's marriage to Constance, the heiress of the Sicilian kingdom, the shift of the center of gravity to Sicily, and the virtual abandonment of power in Germany to the great princes.

In Italy, the disunity of the earlier medieval period is enhanced and perpetuated. The papal territories—dating from the time of Pepin—in the central region of the peninsula effectively separate the northern lands, where the German rulers seek their base and where the town communes grow, from the Norman kingdom in the south. When north and south threaten to combine against the center, the popes find ways to prevent it. Even the mere concept of unity has less meaning in Italy than in Germany, and centralization here is never achieved even temporarily as it is everywhere else.

Reading Suggestions on Monarchy in the Medieval West

GENERAL ACCOUNTS: FRANCE

A. Tilley, *Mediaeval France* (Cambridge Univ. Press, 1922). Political-historical essays.

SPECIAL STUDIES: FRANCE

A. Luchaire, *Social France at the Time of Philip Augustus* (Peter Smith, 1929). A well-written account, perhaps overemphasizing the seamy side of life.

A. R. Kelly, *Eleanor of Aquitaine and the Four Kings* (Harvard Univ. Press, 1950; *Vintage). A learned and lively treatment, the best in English.

R. Fawtier, *The Capetian Kings of France* (*Papermac). Most up-to-date account.

J. Evans, *Life in Mediaeval France* (Oxford Univ. Press, 1925). Good picture of French society.

GENERAL ACCOUNTS: ENGLAND

A. L. Poole, *From Domesday Book to Magna Carta, 1087–1216* (Clarendon, 1951), and F. M. Powicke, *The Thirteenth Century, 1216–1307* (Clarendon, 1953). Good accounts.

D. M. Stenton, *English Society in the Early Middle Ages,* and A. R. Myers, *England in the Late Middle Ages* (*Penguin). Useful introductory volumes at the popular level.

H. M. Cam, *England before Elizabeth* (Hutchinson's University Library, 1950), and F. M. Powicke, *Mediaeval England, 1066–1485* (Home University Library, 1948). Excellent.

SPECIAL STUDIES: ENGLAND

G. O. Sayles, *Th Medieval Foundations of England* (*Perpetua). Excellent basic study. With H. G. Richardson, Sayles is co-author of *The Governance of Medieval England from the Conquest to Magna Carta* (Edinburgh, 1963), a brilliant and provocative analysis.

B. Wilkinson, *The Constitutional History of England, 1216–1399* (Longmans, 1948–1952). Uses the latest scholarly investigations of a much-debated subject.

David Charles Douglas, *William the Conqueror and the Norman Impact upon England* (Univ. of California Press, 1964), and Frank Barlow, *William I and the Norman Conquest* (English University Presses, 1965). Respectively, scholarly and popular.

F. M. Powicke, *King Henry III and The Lord Edward* (Clarendon, 1947). Scholarly.

G. L. Haskins, *Growth of English Representative Government* (*Perpetua). A clear account of a most difficult and vital subject.

George C. Homans, *English Villagers of the Thirteenth Century* (Russell & Russell, 1960). Interesting study of social organization and behavior.

GENERAL ACCOUNTS: GERMANY AND ITALY

G. Barraclough, *The Origins of Modern Germany* (Blackwell, 1949). The best general treatment of medieval Germany in English.

J. Bryce, *The Holy Roman Empire,* rev. ed. (Macmillan, frequently reprinted). A brilliant undergraduate essay, whose conclusions have been modified by recent investigation.

SPECIAL STUDIES: GERMANY AND ITALY

G. Barraclough, *Mediaeval Germany, 911–1250,* 2 vols. (Blackwell, 1938). A series of scholarly essays by German historians, conveniently translated and commented upon.

J. W. Thompson, *Feudal Germany* (Univ. of Chicago Press, 1928). The only work in English on this subject.

E. Kantorowicz, *Frederick the Second, 1194–1250* (R. R. Smith, 1931). Scholarly and imaginative treatment; some scholars deplore the imagination, but not the scholarship.

SOURCES

D. C. Douglas and G. W. Greenaway, eds., *English Historical Documents, 1042–1189* (Oxford Univ. Press, 1953). Volume II of a monumental series still in publication.

The Chronicle of Jocelin of Brakelund, H. E. Butler, trans. (Nelson, 1949). Medieval monastery life.

HISTORICAL FICTION

W. E. Bryher, *The Fourteenth of October* (Pantheon, 1952), and H. Muntz, *The Golden Warrior* (Scribner's, 1949). Good novels about the Norman conquest of England.

Z. Oldenbourg, *The World Is Not Enough* (Pantheon, 1948). A highly successful effort to recapture in fiction the life, violence and all, of twelfth-century France.

8

Medieval Society and Civilization in the West

I   The Society and Its Economy

The Turning Point of the Eleventh Century

The eleventh century proved to be a major turning point in the social and economic life of the West, although nobody alive at the time could have been fully conscious of what was happening. As the raids of the Northmen tapered off, most of western Europe found itself secure against outside attack. By the end of the century, western Europe was able to take the offensive and invade the lands of Islam in the crusades, as we shall see. During the eleventh century, the population grew rapidly. Although scholars cannot really account for this, it may have reflected the greater security of the individual and his increased expectancy of life. By modern standards, of course, human beings were still exposed every day to dangers that seem to us fantastic: from

Above: Two standing Old Testament figures, from the north porch of Chartres Cathedral, ca. 1215–1225. Above right: The nave of Pisa Cathedral, an Italian church of the Romanesque period. Right: Ground plan of the Cathedral of Speyer in western Germany, begun ca. 1030.

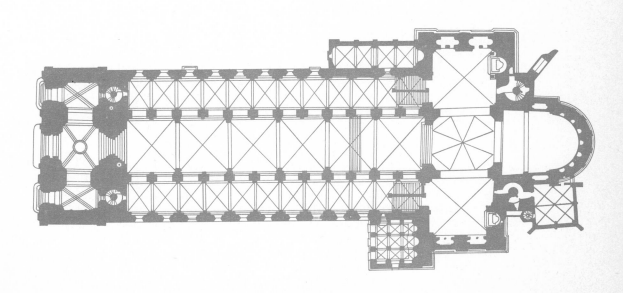

diseases that nobody could cure, from under-nourishment and famine that nobody could assuage, and often from violence that nobody could combat or police.

The larger population needed more food and more land. Pioneers felled trees, drained swamps, opened up new areas for farming. When forests or marsh lay within a manor, a lord would often offer special inducements to his serfs to get them to undertake the extra heavy labor of clearing and farming it. Sometimes a group of peasants would move into a new region that had lain empty before, and would clear it and farm it by introducing the usual strip system. If such un-inhabited land belonged to a lord, he might invite peasants to colonize it, and offer them freedom from serfdom and the chance to pay a money rent instead of the usual services. This would bring profit to the lord and great advantages to the emancipated serfs.

New technology helped to improve the farmer's life. Farmers adopted some devices that had been known earlier, such as the heavy wheeled plow, with horses to draw it. Wind-mills made their first appearance on the European landscape, especially in flat areas like the Low Countries, where there was no falling water to run a watermill. Slowly the anonymous inventors of the Middle Ages perfected systems of gears that would turn the millstones faster and produce more meal in less time.

Trade and Town

During the eleventh century also, and as part of the same general development, trade began slowly to revive. Medieval farmers were helpless in the face of a bad harvest year, and plenty or scarcity varied widely from region to region. It was the natural thing to bring surpluses into areas of famine and sell them at high prices to the hungry. The first new commercial centers arose in places such as Venice and the Low Countries, where the local farms could not feed the increasing population. Even in the earlier Middle Ages such trade had never disappeared altogether, but now the incentives to increase its scale were pressing.

When the proprietor of a manor found that year after year he could make large sums by selling a certain crop, he began to plant more and more of that crop, and to use the money gained by its sale to buy the things he was no longer raising. Once he had more money than he needed for necessities, he began to think of how to spend it on something extra, a luxury. Such a demand quickly creates its supply: what was once a luxury comes to seem a necessity. Thus, for example, the people of Flanders, living in an area that was poor for growing grain but good for raising sheep, sold their raw wool, developed a woolen-manufacturing industry, and imported the food they needed.

The recovery of commerce and the beginnings of industries stimulated the growth of towns. Old Roman towns like London and Marseilles revived. New towns grew around a castle (*bourg* in France, *burgh* in England, *burg* in Germany), especially if it was strategically located for trade as well as for defense. And so the resident *bourgeois, burgesses,* or *burghers* enter the language as castle-dwellers, but soon become recognizable as residents of towns, engaged in commerce. Protected by the lord of the castle, or sometimes by the abbot of a local monastery, the townsmen built walls and pursued their trade. They would band together into guilds to protect themselves from brigands on the roads, and to bargain with the lord of the next castle, who might be showing unpleasant signs of confiscating their goods or charging indecently high tolls whenever they crossed his land. Grouped in a guild, merchants could often win concessions: if the lord they were bargaining with seemed unreasonable, they might threaten to take a route across the lands of some less rapacious lord and pay a more moderate toll.

Mutual advantage soon led proprietors, including kings as well as lesser lords, to grant privileges to the townsmen by issuing a charter. Although the contents of such documents vary, most of them guaranteed free status to the townsmen; even an escaped serf within the town would acquire freedom if he could avoid capture for a year. The charter might also grant the townsmen the right to hold a perpetual market, to transfer property within the town walls, and to have their lawsuits tried in a town court by town custom, which slowly developed into a whole new kind of law, the *law merchant.*

Industry followed commerce into the town. The merchant, with his experience of distant markets, learned how to buy raw material, to have workmen do the manufacturing wherever it was cheapest, and to sell the finished products wherever he could get the best price. The workmen also soon began to organize themselves into craft guilds, which provided medical care and burial for the members, and often fixed minimum wages, the standards of quality of the product, and even the prices to be asked.

Enterprise was neither free nor private. It was highly regulated, not only as an effort to reduce outside competition, but also as a reflection of the ideas of the age. Men believed that a "just price" for a pair of shoes included the cost of the leather and the thread, the amount needed to sustain the shoemaker at his usual standard of life while he made the shoes, and a small addition to pay the seller for his time and trouble. To "make money," in the modern sense of charging all that the traffic will bear, was in theory to cheat the customer. No doubt many medieval customers were in fact cheated in this sense, but the ethics of the time condemned the action. Finance capitalism—the use of money to make money, the investment of funds at interest—was condemned as usury.

Town and Countryside

In their turn, the towns greatly affected the overwhelming mass of the population who remained in the countryside, who now had a place to sell their surplus and so an incentive to produce it. Some peasants saved enough cash to buy their freedom; some fled to the town in the hope of acquiring freedom, or at least in the hope that

their children might acquire it. The very word "cash" suggests a most important development, the flourishing of a money economy instead of the economy of barter. Barter still continued, but as the magnates came to want more and more manufactured or imported or luxury items, they wanted cash rather than services: a serf's labors would produce more grain, but not the money to buy a piece of armor. So the lord would let the peasant pay him cash, and would forgive (commute) the serf's obligation to work on his land. More demand for money led to more money in circulation, and to a slowly inflationary rise in wages and prices.

With the increase in demand for goods, large-scale fairs became a regular feature of medieval life. Some of them brought together merchants and products from a relatively narrow region, but others attracted men and goods from all over the European world. In Champagne, in northeastern France, for example, there were several great annual fairs each year. The count of Champagne not only collected a fee from the towns for the privilege of holding the fair but also got the revenues from a special court set up to try cases that arose there. As large-scale transactions became more frequent, it became less practical for merchants to carry around large amounts of cash, and during the thirteenth century merchants came to use a written promise to pay instead. Acceptance of these bills of exchange, a kind of primitive bank-check, often made it unnecessary to transport money at all, since a Parisian creditor of a London merchant could call upon a Parisian debtor of the same merchant to pay the amount owed.

II   The Medieval Church

Medieval Christianity

It is easy to write—and read—the commonplace that the Christian faith as embodied in the Church was supreme in the medieval West. But we moderns, no matter how good Christians we may be, need to exercise our imaginations to understand just what that statement means. For the medieval man, God made the weather, as he made everything else. God could and did interfere with the regular processes of nature. A

lightning bolt was not an electrical discharge that could be simulated in the laboratory; it was not even quite what we mean by a "natural phenomenon"; it was an instrument in the hand of God, an instrument with which he could strike down a sinner. For the masses, God with his thunderbolt differed little from Jupiter or Thor with his. Although the educated minority no longer held this crude view, even it thought of God as somehow working directly on natural forces.

In medieval times Christianity occupied a

place very different from the place it holds in our culture. The separation of church and state is for most of us today an accepted fact. And though we hardly permit a man to belong to no state, we do permit him to belong to no church. Moreover, we readily accept the existence of many mutually exclusive churches, the so-called denominations. In the medieval West there was but one church, and noble, peasant, and townsman, in England or on the Continent, belonged to it. Only the Jews were apart, and though they commonly could worship freely and pursue careers in finance, they often suffered disabilities, such as having to live in a separate quarter (ghetto). Further, popular passion occasionally unleashed persecution or even massacre, as during the first days of the Crusades, and sometimes a monarch—Edward I, Philip the Fair—expelled them from the land. Heretics like the Albigensians who repudiated some specific practices or beliefs of the Church were religious outlaws, not allowed to exist peacefully in society; usually they had to worship secretly. And in the end they were exterminated.

For the medieval man, religious and political governance were both necessary instruments of the divine scheme for maintaining human society; they were, in medieval terms, the "two swords" of God. They were wielded by different sets of God's human agents, and they were *both* necessary.

The question of which sword was in fact the greater sword on this earth was a major source of dispute in medieval times. This was the issue in the Investiture Controversy, in the conflict between Henry II and Becket, and in the conflict between Philip the Fair and Boniface VIII (see Chapter 7). Innocent III in 1198 was certain of the answer:

The creator of the universe set up two great luminaries in the firmament of heaven, the greater light to rule the day, the lesser light to rule the night. In the same way for the firmament of the universal Church, which is spoken of as heaven, he appointed two great dignities; the greater to bear rule over souls (these being, as it were, days), the lesser to bear rule over bodies (these being, as it were, nights). These dignities are the pontifical authority and the royal power.*

* *Documents of the Christian Church,* ed. Henry Bettenson (New York, 1947), pp. 157-158.

No pope of Carolingian times could possibly have made such a statement. The medieval church, like medieval society as a whole, had in the intervening centuries taken its opportunity to develop its own organization into a wealthy, centralized, and powerful authority. Its theorists and pamphleteers, such as those of Gregory VII (Hildebrand) in the eleventh century, had laid the groundwork for Innocent's extravagant claim, against which the secular monarchs struggled with varying success.

The Reform Movement

CLUNY By the time Innocent III could seriously talk as he did, much had happened to the corrupt Church of the tenth century. As we know, it was the monks of Cluny in France who, with their program for reforming the purchase and sale of church offices (simony), concubinage, lay investiture, and other abuses, gave the initial great impulse to reform.

Founded in 910, this great monastery saw its monks strive to restore the primitive simplicity and strict asceticism of Benedict's original rule. From Cluny reforming monks went out to found "daughter" monasteries, all inspired by the same ideal. Eventually the "mother" abbey attentively and strictly ruled over more than 300 of these widely scattered centers of reforming zeal. Together they acted as a kind of organized pressure group, a catalyst or leaven for the whole process of clerical housecleaning.

We have seen how eventually men trained in the Cluniac spirit reached the papal throne itself as nominees of the emperor Henry III. They established the principle of clerical celibacy, which preserved Catholic priests from the natural tendency of fathers to provide property for their offspring. The reformers checked, though of course they did not completely abolish, simony. Gregory VII (Hildebrand), as we know, expanded the ideas of reform into a generalized effort to root out secular influences from the entire Church, which would then move forward under militant papal leadership. The Lateran Synod of 1059 issued the decree establishing the College of Cardinals, a group of certain key clerics ("cardinal" from *cardo,* a hinge), who were to elect each new pope. The system remains in force today.

The Cluniac movement was also the first of several great waves of reforming zeal that swept the Church at intervals until the sixteenth century without disrupting its organizational unity. The power of the medieval Church lay *both* in its other-worldly ideals *and* in its this-worldly skill in human government. Nothing is clearer evidence of this power than the Church's success in controlling these potentially revolutionary outbursts of desire to reform humanity, to have men and women everywhere and always behave like Christians.

Like almost all the great revivals of the Christian spirit, the Cluniac movement bore the stamp of Puritanism. Puritanism often relies on authoritarian rule, for it seems that the only way to get large groups of men to keep on denying the flesh for a long period of time is to police them. Perhaps the most striking thing about the Cluniac order is not its revival of the strict Benedictine rule but its enforcement of that rule through a centralized authority. The Abbot of Cluny was the theocratic ruler of the whole order. The daughter houses enjoyed no real home rule; instead, they were held in firm obedience to the mother house.

What happened to the Cluniac order set a pattern for later reforming orders. The ideal was poverty and humility; the result was riches and pride. By the twelfth century the Cluniac houses were becoming prodigiously wealthy, and their rule had relaxed. Perhaps this lapse was hastened by the very centralization of power in the mother house and its abbot. Since everything depended on the personality of the ruler, a succession of weak or selfish abbots could do more harm than it would in an order that granted more home rule to the individual houses.

ST. BERNARD AND THE CISTERCIANS The same pattern was repeated by the Cistercians, a new offshoot of the Benedictines, founded at the very end of the eleventh century in a dismal, uncultivated waste at Cîteaux (Cistercium) in Burgundy, a site far from the distractions and temptations of worldly life. They set to work with the diligence of the first Benedictines, for whom hard work on the land was a prime need, and they eventually transformed the spot into a garden. The order's greatest leader was Bernard of Clairvaux (1091–1153), who in 1115 led a small band of Cistercians to Clairvaux, a nearby spot as unpromising as Cîteaux itself. From Clairvaux the unworldly Bernard influenced the affairs of the world to a degree almost beyond our modern understanding.

St. Bernard not only upbraided clergyman for their laxity in observing ecclesiastical rules but also helped to organize a crusade to the Holy Land, advised the kings of France, and chastened even the greatest feudal nobles. For example, the duke of Aquitaine, the father of the famous Eleanor, had expelled bishops from their sees. Bernard, after trying unsuccessfully to win the duke over in a conference, celebrated the Mass in his presence. Bearing aloft the sacred Host in the midst of the congregation, Bernard challenged the duke to pit his will against God's. The Duke had armies, Bernard had none; but the duke collapsed—literally, for he could not stand —and the bishops were restored.

The Cistercians, apparently warned by the overcentralization of the Cluniac system, gave their daughter houses genuine self-rule. As a result, their houses clung together far more successfully. Yet the Cistercians, too, failed to hold to the ideals of their founder. By the thirteenth century, the great Cistercian monasteries—Fountains Abbey in English Yorkshire, for instance, whose ruins are still magnificent—were great and wealthy centers of agricultural and craft production. The expensive arts of architecture and sculpture—scorned initially by Bernard himself as devilish devices that took men's attention from worship—were lavished on their buildings. These Cistercian monasteries had become great corporations, thoroughly tied into the increasingly complex web of economic life.

FRANCISCANS AND DOMINICANS The next wave of reform sought not so much to purify monasticism from within as to bring Christian charity to the new urban masses, often neglected by the Church, and often hostile to its rich and worldly clergy.

Unlike the Cluniacs and Cistercians, the friars of the new orders founded by Saint Francis (1182–1226) and Saint Dominic (1170–1221) did not intend to live apart from the world. Gentle, charming, and ascetic, Saint Francis, son of a merchant family, had undergone religious conversion in his youth. He prescribed for his followers total poverty: they were to have no monastic house, but were rather to go and preach, and were to rely on charity for their food and shelter:

272

The brethren shall nothing appropriate to them, neither in housing nor in lands, nor in rent nor in any manner of thing, but like pilgrims and strangers in this world, in poverty and meekness, serving Almighty God. They shall faithfully, boldly and surely and meekly go for alms. . . .

And those that be unlearned shall not busy themselves to be lettered and learned; but they should attend and take heed above all things, and desire to have the spirit of our Lord and his holy operation to pray always to almighty God with a pure spirit and a clean heart.*

Francis called his order Friars Minor ("little brothers"), and their dependence on alms led to the term "mendicant"—begging—friars. In 1210, Innocent III approved Francis' foundation, but even before Francis died (1226) the papacy against his wishes permitted a revised rule, which allowed the friars land and buildings. So worldly concerns began to preoccupy some of the friars, to the dismay of the rest. Though Francis had repudiated book-learning and books, later Franciscans often studied in the universities and became distinguished scholars.

Saint Dominic, a Spaniard, well born like Saint Francis, founded his own mendicant order in 1215. From the beginning, study was a cardinal duty of his followers, who were to educate the laity of the world by preaching to them. The Dominicans were given the name Order of Preachers. Their monastic houses or priories (for they, too, soon began to acquire property) were governed by monks elected by the members, and the officials of each priory in turn elected the superior officials of the order.

The reforming movements of the eleventh, twelfth, and thirteenth centuries within the Church helped to keep piety constantly renewed, dispelled the threat of mass disaffection, and played a major role in the intellectual as well as the social life of the age. Dominicans and Franciscans served as the staff of the permanent papal tribunal of the Inquisition formed in 1233 to find, interrogate, judge, and punish suspected heretics and to deliver those who persisted in their heresy to the secular authorities to be burned at the stake.

LOLLARDS AND HUSSITES In the fourteenth and fifteenth centuries, as manorial self-suf-

*Adapted from *Monumenta Fransiscana*, ed. R. Howlett (London 1882), II, 69–70, 73.

ficiency continued to decline and more and more people were thrown into a money economy with its dangers of unemployment and job displacement, social problems became increasingly severe. The ravages of the Black Death, an epidemic which struck with particular force in the mid-fourteenth century, further disrupted the medieval order. Under these conditions, the Church was obliged to contend with newer and more intransigent reform movements that might be thought of as aiming at social revolution. The English priest John Wycliffe (ca. 1320–1384) and his Lollard followers mixed together religious, social, and economic aims; they were for the "people" and against those in power, the establishment. The term "Lollard" means "babbler," and it is a good example of the common practice in all societies (which are normally conservative or, at any rate, not radical) of fastening a bad name on rebels. The Lollards had a part in stirring up the English Peasants' Revolt, one of the leaders of which was the priest John Ball. Its slogan has a "socialist" touch you will not find in St. Francis:

*When Adam delved and Eve span
Who was then the gentleman?*

In the fifteenth century, a somewhat similar movement in Bohemia, the western province of modern Czechoslovakia, took its name from another religious leader, John Hus (1369–1415). The Hussite movement was a compound of religious and social aims, with a strong component of what we should now call Czech nationalism. Hus wanted to end many clerical abuses, notably the domination of the Church in Slavic Bohemia by German prelates. Neither Wycliffe nor Hus, however, quite broke up the unity of the church.

The Challenge of the New Dynastic States

The challenge to the unity of western Christendom was not confined to such social movements as those of Wycliffe and Hus. Another challenge came from the newly developing dynastic states, forerunners of the nation-states of modern times. When Boniface VIII came out second best in his encounter with Philip the Fair

Fresco depicting the return of Pope Gregory XI to Rome from Avignon in 1377, ending the Babylonian Captivity.

(see Chapter 7), the drive toward a Gallican, i.e., French national, church was greatly strengthened. Gallicanism did not aim to separate the Church in France (Gallia) from the Catholic communion, but it did aim to make it a thoroughly *French* church that would be more under the royal than papal control.

In Italy, the intervention of Philip the Fair had unleashed hostility against foreigners, and the city of Rome grew too disorderly for Boniface's successor, Benedict XI (1303-1304), who withdrew to Perugia. When Benedict's successor, the Frenchman Bertrand de Got, was elected pope as Clement V (1305-1314), the cardinals hoped that he could somehow compromise with King Philip of France and restore papal prestige. Clement, on the contrary, turned out to be what we should now call pro-French. He set up the papal capital at Avignon, in what is now southern France, where from 1305 to 1377 the seat of the papacy remained. Here in Avignon, the popes were subject to the will of the kings of France, a development that was a tremendous comedown for the holder of the See of Peter. This period was later known as the Babylonian Captivity, a term coined by the Italian poet Petrarch in allusion to the captivity of the ancient Jews at Babylon.

Pope Gregory XI returned to Rome in 1377, ending the Babylonian Captivity. On his death in 1378 the College of Cardinals elected Urban VI. But a part of the College declared the election invalid and chose a rival pope, Clement VII, who ruled from Avignon. From 1378 to 1417, a period known as the Great Schism, there were two popes—one at Rome, the other at Avignon. The states of Europe gave their allegiance either to Rome or to Avignon, depending on their international alliances and emnities. France was of course pro-Avignon; England, the enemy of France—this was in the midst of the Hundred Years' War—was pro-Rome; and Scotland, the enemy of England and the ally of France, was pro-Avignon.

The Conciliar Movement

Against the scandal of the Great Schism the Church rallied in the Conciliar Movement, a series of general councils beginning at Pisa, 1409, and continuing at Constance, 1414-1417, and at Basel, 1431-1449. The Council of Pisa failed so dismally that it actually chose a *third* claimant to the papal throne, John XXIII, who cast such discredit on that name that no pope chose it again until 1958.* The Council of Constance at least solved the problem of the schism. With the election of Martin V in 1417, the unity of Western Christendom was restored. But the schism had been an obvious symptom of more deep-seated troubles. Among these troubles were national rivalries; the decline and corruption of the monasteries; worldliness in the secular clergy, and especially in the upper clergy; the failure of the Church to keep in touch with the masses, who had been unsettled by the economic and social changes that were making the modern world—all the troubles, in short, that were to come to a head in the Protestant Reformation of the next century.

Against these difficulties, the Conciliar Movement made little headway. Hus, in spite of an imperial guarantee of his safety, was tried at Constance for doctrinal heresy and was condemned to death in 1415. But the Hussite heresy was merely driven underground. The general councils attempted to supplant papal absolutism with a kind of constitutional government within

* The John XXIII of 1410 is not counted as a legitimate pope, but an "antipope."

the Church; the councils of the whole Church were to be called regularly, and would constitute a parliament. The pope would be a constitutional monarch. Could such councils with full powers have forestalled the Reformation by reforming the Church from within? The question is unanswerable, for they were never given the chance. They did produce a considerable amount of writing on political philosophy which anticipated modern discussion of constitutional government. But papal supremacy simply did not give way to constitutional government.

Our brief survey of the reform movements from the Cluniac to the Conciliar must not give the impression that medieval Christianity was weak and unstable. On the contrary, the very success of the medieval Church in absorbing rebels is proof of its strength and stability. For these movements were not suppressed by force, but softened, tamed, and absorbed into the unity of the Church. From them the Church gained more than it lost; it gained in renewal of piety, in closer contact with the masses, in wealth, and in learning.

III   Medieval Thought

Education

It was the Church that alone directed and conducted education in medieval Europe. Unless destined for the priesthood, young men of the upper classes had little formal schooling, though the family chaplain often taught them to read and write. Their training was in war and hunting, and sometimes in the problems of managing their property. But the monastic schools educated future monks and priests, and the Cluniac reform, with its increased demand for piety, stimulated study and the copying of manuscripts. Medieval men still reckoned that there were seven liberal arts, divided into the trivium (grammar, rhetoric, dialectic) and the quadrivium (arithmetic, geometry, astronomy, and music), the first three including much of what we might call humanities today, the last four corresponding to the sciences. Only a few monastic schools in the eleventh century were prepared to offer instruction in all seven, and in general monks thought of their work as the preservation rather than as the advancement of knowledge.

The cathedral schools, on the other hand, whose teachers were often less timid about studying pagan writings from the great classical past, fostered a more inquiring spirit. In France during the eleventh century at the cathedral schools of Paris, Chartres, Reims, and other towns, distinguished teachers now were often succeeded by men whom they had trained themselves, and distinguished pupils went on to join or found other schools. Scholarship no longer depended on the occasional advent of a single first-class mind. In Italy, where the connection with cathedrals was not so close, the medical school at Salerno had a tradition stretching back into the early Middle Ages; at Bologna law became the specialty, beginning as a branch of rhetoric and so within the trivium. Students were attracted to Bologna from other regions of Italy and even from northern Europe, and in the early twelfth century, as education became fashionable for young men ambitious for advancement in the Church or in the royal service, the numbers of students grew rapidly.

Universities

The student body at Bologna organized itself into two associations: students from the near side of the Alps and students from the far side, and the two incorporated as the whole body, the *universitas,* or university. As a corporate body, they could protect themselves against being overcharged for food and lodging by threatening to leave town; they had no property, and could readily have moved. If the students did not like a professor, they simply stayed away from his lectures, and he starved or moved on, for he was dependent on tuition fees for his living. Soon the *universitas,* that is to say the students, fixed the price of room and board in town, and fined professors for absence or for lecturing too long. The professors organized too, and admitted to their number only those who had passed an examination, and so won a *license* to teach, remote ancestor of all our academic degrees.

Scenes of student life in the Middle Ages, from "Statutenbuch des Collegium Sapentiae."

In Paris and elsewhere in the north, the cathedral schools were the immediate forerunners of the universities, and it was the teachers, not the students, who organized first, as a guild of those who taught the seven liberal arts and who got their licenses from the cathedral authorities. By the thirteenth century pious citizens had founded in Paris the first residence halls for poor students, who might eat and sleep free in these "colleges." The practice crossed the Channel to Oxford and Cambridge. As in later times, the authorities of these medieval universities stoutly defended against encroachment by the secular powers. Students were not very different then:

Well-beloved father, I have not a penny, nor can I get any save through you, for all things at the University are so dear: nor can I study in my Code or my Digest, for they are all tattered. Moreover, I owe ten crowns in dues to the Provost, and can find no man to lend them to me; I send you word of greetings and money.*

* Quoted in G. G. Coulton, *Life in the Middle Ages* (Cambridge Univ. Press, 1929), III, 113.

The friction of "town and gown" also dates from medieval times. The students played, drank, sang, hazed freshmen, organized hoaxes and practical jokes, and staged riots. University authorities did not like this sort of thing, and passed many ordinances, usually in vain, against student sports and brawls. Student life in the Middle Ages was hard; it was little softened by what we call "activities." Here is a ducal ordinance of 1476 for the University of Louvain in the Low Countries:

The tutors shall see that the scholars rise in the morning at five o'clock, and that then before lectures each one reads by himself the laws which are to be read at the regular lecture, together with the glosses. . . . But after the regular lecture, having if they wish, quickly heard mass, the scholars shall come to their rooms and revise the lectures that have been given, by rehearsing and impressing on their memory whatever they have brought away from the lectures either orally or in writing.*

* H. Rashdall, *The Universities of Europe in the Middle Ages*, rev. ed. (Oxford, 1936), II, 341.

Much of the curriculum did involve memory work, rote learning. But remember that in these days before printing, ready reference works were scarce. Moreover, though again the formal rules of scholarly debate were fixed, there was, nonetheless, lively discussion available for those who worked to sharpen their minds, not just to load their memories.

The Question of Universals

Much of the learning taught and studied in the Middle Ages seems strange to us today, and it requires imagination to understand how exciting intellectual exercise was to men discovering it for the first time. At the turn of the eleventh century, Gerbert of Aurillac, who spent the last four years of his life as Pope Sylvester II (999–1003), stood out as the most learned man of his day; the smattering of mathematics and science that he had been able to pick up caused his contemporaries to suspect him of witchcraft. His interest lying in logic, he turned to the work of Boethius (see Chapter 5). For the first time, across the gulf of centuries, a probing mind moved into the portions of Aristotle that Boethius had translated, and discovered in logic a means to approach the writings of the ancients and of the church fathers in a systematic way. By the end of the century, churchmen could debate whether it was proper to use human reason in considering a particular theological question (for example, was Christ present in the sacramental wafer and wine?), and in all efforts to explain away inconsistencies in the Bible and the Fathers in general. Even those who attacked the use of reason used it themselves in making new definitions that enabled them to argue that bread and wine could indeed, in a certain way, become flesh and blood.

Once the new method became available, the men of the late eleventh and early twelfth centuries employed it largely in a celebrated controversy over the philosophical problem of "universals." A universal is a whole category of things; when we say "dog" or "table" or "man," we may mean not any specific individual dog or table or man, but the idea of all dogs, tables, or men: dogdom, tabledom, mankind. The question that exercised the medieval thinkers was whether universal categories have an existence: *is* there such a thing as dogdom, tabledom, or mankind?

If you said no, you were a *nominalist;* that is, you thought dogdom, tabledom, mankind were merely *nomina, names* that men give to a general category from their experience of individual members of it. We experience dogs, tables, men, and so we infer the existence of dogdom, tabledom, mankind because the individual members of the category have certain points of resemblance; but the category, the universal, has no existence in itself. If you said yes, you were a *realist;* that is, you thought that the general categories did exist. Many realists took this view a large step further, and said that the individual dog, table, or man was far less real than the generalizing category or universal, or even that the individual dog, table, or man was a mere reflection of one aspect of the category, and existed by virtue of belonging to the category; a man exists only because he partakes of the nature of mankind, a dog because he partakes of the nature of dogdom.

If one transfers the problem to politics, and thinks of the state and the individual, one can see at once how great its practical importance may be. A pure nominalist would say that the state is just a name, and exists only by virtue of the fact that the individuals who make it up are real; he would argue that the state must then serve its subjects, since after all it is only the sum of their individualities. A pure realist would say that the state is the only real thing, that the individual subjects exist only so far as they partake of its general character, and that the state by virtue of its existence properly dominates the individual. In religion, an extreme nominalist, arguing that what one can perceive through one's senses is alone real, might even have trouble believing in the existence of God. An extreme realist would tend to ignore or even to deny the existence of the physical world and its problems. Moderate realists have to start with faith, to believe so that they may know, as the English saint Anselm put it.

Peter Abelard (1079–1142), a popular lecturer in the University of Paris, tried to compromise the question. He argued that universals were not merely names, as the nominalists held, nor did they have a real existence, as the realists held. They were, he said, *concepts* in men's minds, and as such had a real existence of a special kind in the mind, which had created them out of its experience of particulars: mankind from men, dogdom from dogs, and so on. Abelard's compromise between nominalism and realism is called conceptualism.

Abelard insisted on the importance of understanding for true faith; he put reason first, and thus understood in order that he might believe, instead of the other way around. His most famous work, *Sic et Non* (*Yes and No*), lists over 150 theological statements and cites authorities both defending and attacking the truth of each. When Scripture and the Fathers were inconsistent, he seems to argue, how could a man make up his mind what to believe unless he used his head? A rationalist and lover of argument, Abelard was none the less a deeply pious believer. The mystical Saint Bernard, however, suspicious of reason, believed him heretical, and had his views condemned and denounced repeatedly.

Thomas Aquinas

By the time of Abelard's death in the mid-twelfth century, the Greek scientific writings of antiquity—lost all these centuries to the West—were on their way to recovery, often through translations from Arabic into Latin. In civil law, the great code of the Emperor Justinian became the text commonly used in the law schools. In canon law, the scholar Gratian published at Bologna about 1140 what became the standard collection of decrees, and reconciled by commentary apparently contradictory judgments.

In the second half of the century came the recovery of Aristotle's lost treatises on logic, which dealt with such subjects as how to build a syllogism, how to prove a point, or how to refute false conclusions. Using these instruments, medieval thinkers were for the first time in a position to systematize and summarize their entire philosophical position. Yet the recovery of Aristotle posed certain new problems. For example, the Muslim philosopher Averroës, whose comments accompanied the text of Aristotle's *Metaphysics*, stressed Aristotle's own view that the physical world was eternal; since the soul of man —a nonphysical thing—was essentially common to all humanity, no individual human soul could be saved by itself. Obviously this ran counter to fundamental Christian teaching. Some scholars tried to say that both views could be true, Aristotle's in philosophy and the Christian in theology; but this led directly into heresy. Others tried

to forbid the study and reading of Aristotle, but without success. It was the Dominican Albertus Magnus (1193–1280), a German, and his pupil Thomas Aquinas (1225–1274), an Italian, who—in massive multivolume works produced over a lifetime—succeeded in reconciling the apparent differences between Aristotle's teachings and those of the Christian tradition. They were the greatest of the Schoolmen, exponents of the philosophy historians call Scholasticism.

Aquinas' best-known writings were the *Summa Theologica* and the *Summa contra Gentiles*. He discussed God, man, and the universe, arranging his material in systematic, topical order in the form of an inquiry into and discussion of each open question. First, he cited the evidence on each side, then he gave his own answer, and finally he demonstrated the falsity of the other position. Though Aquinas always cited authority, he also never failed to provide his own logical analysis. For him, reason was a most valuable instrument, but only when it recognized its own limitations. When reason unaided could not comprehend an apparent contradiction with faith, it must yield to faith, since reason by itself could not understand the entire universe. Certain fundamentals must be accepted as unprovable axioms of faith, although, once they had been accepted, reason could show that they were probable.

If a man put a series of arguments together and came out with a conclusion contrary to what orthodox Christians believed, he was simply guilty of faulty logic, and the use of correct logic could readily show where he erred. Indeed, Aquinas delighted in the game of inventing arguments against accepted beliefs, matching them with a set of even more ingenious arguments, and then reconciling the two with an intellectual skill suggesting the trained athlete's ability in timing and coordination.

Here is an example of the mind and method of Aquinas. It is a relatively unimportant part of the *Summa Theologica*, but it is fairly easy to follow, and it brings out clearly how close to common sense Aquinas can be. He is discussing the specific conditions of "man's first state," the state of innocence before the Fall. He comes to the question of what children were like in the state of innocence. Were they born with such perfect strength of body that they had full use of their limbs at birth, or were they like human children nowadays, helpless? In the Garden of

Eden, one might think that any form of helplessness would detract from perfection, and that God might well have made the human infant strong and perfect, or might even have had men and women born adult. Aquinas did not think so; even his Eden was as "natural" as he could make it:

By faith alone do we hold truths which are above nature, and what we believe rests on authority. Wherefore, in making any assertion, we must be guided by the nature of things, except in those things which are above nature, and are made known to us by Divine authority. Now it is clear that it is as natural as it is befitting to the principles of human nature that children should not have sufficient strength for the use of their limbs immediately after birth. Because in proportion to other animals man has naturally a larger brain. Wherefore it is natural, on account of the considerable humidity of the brain in children, that the sinews which are instruments of movement, should not be apt for moving the limbs. On the other hand, no Catholic doubts it possible for a child to have, by Divine power the use of its limbs immediately after birth.

Now we have it on the authority of Scripture that *God made man right* (Eccles. vii. 30), which rightness, as Augustine says, consists in the perfect subjection of the body to the soul. As, therefore, in the primitive state it was impossible to find in the human limbs anything repugnant to man's well-ordered will, so was it impossible for those limbs to fail in executing the will's commands. Now the human will is well ordered when it tends to acts which are befitting to man. But the same acts are not befitting to man at every season of life. We must, therefore, conclude that children would not have had sufficient strength for the use of their limbs for the purpose of performing every kind of act; but only for the acts befitting the state of infancy, such as suckling, and the like.*

This apparently trivial passage contains much that is typical of Thomism, as the philosophy of Aquinas is termed. It reveals the clear supremacy that is granted to "truths which are above nature," which we hold by faith and receive through divine authority; the belief that God usually prefers to let nature run its course according to its laws; the belief that there is a "fitness" in human action conforming to these laws of nature; and, finally, the appeal to authority,

* The Summa Theologica of St. Thomas Aquinas, 2nd ed. London, 1922), Vol. IV, pt. I, Quest. XCIX.

in this case the Old Testament and Augustine. Notice also that Aquinas never even brings up the kind of question anticlerical rationalists were later to ask, such as just how were children procreated before the Fall? Or were there any children, anybody but Adam and Eve, in Eden before the Fall?

Political Thought

In dealing with problems of human relations, medieval thinkers again used a vocabulary that is different from ours. Yet they come fairly close in many ways to modern democratic thinking. Except for extreme realism, medieval thought was emphatically not totalitarian. To the medieval thinker the perfection of the kingdom of heaven could not possibly exist on earth, where compromise and imperfection are inescapable.

Full equality could not exist on earth. Medieval political thought accepts as its starting point an order of rank in human society. The twelfth-century *Policraticus (Statesman's Book)* of the English Scholastic philosopher John of Salisbury (ca. 1115–1180) provides a complete statement of this social theory. The prince (or king) is the head of the body of the commonwealth; the senate (legislature) is the heart; the judges and governors of provinces are the eyes, ears, and tongue; the officials and soldiers are the hands; the financial officers are the stomach and intestines; and the peasants "correspond to the feet, which always cleave to the soil." This "organic" theory of society, is a great favorite with those who oppose change. For obviously the foot does not try to become the brain, nor is the hand jealous of the eye; the whole body is at its best when each part does what nature meant it to do. The peasant, the blacksmith, the merchant, the lawyer, the priest, and the king himself all have been assigned a part of God's work on earth.

Medieval thought thus distinguished among vocations, but it also insisted on the dignity and worth of all vocations, even the humblest. It accepted the Christian doctrine of the equality of all souls before God and held that no man can be a mere instrument of another man. Even the humblest person on this earth could in the next world hope to enjoy a bliss as full and eternal as any king's. Furthermore, medieval political theory was by no means opposed to all change on earth. One might assume that it would have opposed any and all resistance to existing authority. Certainly the medieval thinkers were not democratic in the sense of believing that the people have a right to, or can, "make" their own institutions. But they did not hold that, since God has arranged authority as it now is in this world, we should preserve existing conditions, come what may. If existing conditions were bad, it was likely to be a sign that originally good conditions had been perverted. The thing to do was to try to restore the original good conditions, God's own plan.

A relatively rigid and authoritarian society needs a sovereign authority whose decisions are final. In ancient Sparta, for instance, there was no appeal from the decisions of the rulers, and in eastern Europe the Byzantine emperor, and his Russian successor, the czar, were perhaps such final authority. At the very highest level, the popes and emperors each claimed supremacy. Able and lucky emperors, like Otto the Great and Frederick Barbarossa, came close to exercising such authority; Pope Innocent III almost attained it in the thirteenth century. Both the imperial and the papal sides enlisted medieval thinkers. Dante spent a great deal of energy on a long political pamphlet, *De Monarchia* (*Concerning Monarchy*), in which he urged the world rule of the emperor as a solution for the evils of war. Thomas Aquinas concluded that the pope had "an indirect rather than a direct authority in temporal matters"—another example of his bent toward moderation.

In the strife of propaganda—for such it was—the imperialists insulted the papalists and the papalists insulted the imperialists. Each side, however, had to find backing for its claims to authority. Marsiglio of Padua (ca. 1290-1343), the author of *Defensor Pacis* (*Defender of the Peace*), an imperialist pamphlet, found the only true source of authority in a commonwealth to be the *universitas civium*, the whole body of the citizens. Marsiglio probably did not mean to be as modern as this may seem. He still used medieval terms, and the constitutionalism, the notions of popular sovereignty, that have been attributed to him are a long way from our notion of counting votes with "one man, one vote" to determine political decisions. But Marsiglio did in all earnestness mean what a great many other medieval thinkers meant: No man's place in the order of rank, even if he is at the top of it, is such that

those of lower rank must always and unquestioningly accept what he commands. If worst came to worst, medieval political thinkers were often willing to approve tyrannicide, a doctrine by no means in good odor in our time.

Finally, the feudal relation itself, which held the nobility together as lords and vassals, is an admirable example of medieval insistence that the order of rank is not one of mere might. The feudal relation was a contract that was binding on *both* parties. And the elaborate code of chivalry developed by this feudal class insisted on the personal dignity and standing of each initiate.

The Law of Nature

Let us take one final illustration of medieval ways of thought. As we saw in Chapter 7, to the medieval mind, even to that of the lawyer, the law was not made but found. Law for common, everyday purposes was what we should call custom. On the manor, for instance, the customary arrangements for use of the field were found by consulting the men of the manor and learning what had been done time out of mind. Medieval thought also recognized something beyond custom, something beyond law in the sense of what people were used to doing. This was the *law of nature*, or natural law.

To the medieval thinker the law of nature was something like God's word translated into terms that made it usable by ordinary men on earth. It was the ethical ideal, the "ought to be," that was discernible by men of good will who were thinking rightly. This was not natural law as most modern scientists would interpret the term, for the scientist finds traditional moral distinctions vague and subjective, always open to dispute and misunderstanding. A thermometer, as well as common sense, can tell us when water becomes ice. But what instrument, what human faculty, can tell us in a similarly precise way when a man is acting in accordance with the law of nature, and when he is not so acting?

The medieval thinker would answer that the thermometer, even common sense, can decide only limited question of material fact. But, by using our full human faculties as God intended, we can answer with even more certainty the questions of right and wrong. To do so, we need the whole resources of the human community. We need the word of God as revealed in the Christian church, the wisdom handed down to us by our ancestors, the skills and learning each of us has acquired in his calling, and the common sense of the community. Of course, due weight must always be given to those who are specially qualified by their position. Medieval opinion would insist that even though a commonsense test, or a thermometer, can give the correct answer, men will not necessarily take the right action. No instrument (that is, no scientific knowledge) can protect men from sin. Protection from sin is afforded only by being a full member of the Christian church. Such a member will know right from wrong, natural from unnatural, by the fact of his membership.

The Medieval and the Modern Outlooks Contrasted

We have looked at two concrete instances of medieval attitudes—the notion of an organic stratified society in which each man plays the part God sent him to play, and the concept of a natural law to be understood by reason that regulates as well as explains human relations on earth. Behind all these ideas is the medieval idea of this earthly world as *static*. The Middle Ages thought that change was accidental and random, not what we call progress. No medieval person believed, or could believe, in progress in anything like our modern sense. Some changes, of course, did occur in the Middle Ages. Workmen improved their tools and indulged in that very modern form of change known as invention. Some merchants made money, often by methods that were not too different from those of today. In the last few medieval centuries, corruption, competition, and rapid social change were so visible that even the theorist saw them. Wycliffe and many another rebel were fully aware of living in a changing society. Yet they thought that their society had *lapsed* from what God and natural law intended, not that it was progressing to new ideals.

The medieval intellectual, then, assumed that the universe was at bottom static; the modern intellectual assumes that it is at bottom dynamic. The one assumed that laws for right human action had been, so to speak, designed for all time

by God in heaven, and that those laws were clear to the good Christian. The other assumes that laws for right human action are in fact worked out in the very process of living, that no one can be sure of them in advance, and that new ones are constantly being created. The medieval man, puzzled, tended to resolve his problem by an appeal to authority, the best or the natural authority in which he had been trained to put his faith. He turned to Aristotle and Aquinas if he was a Schoolman, to the customary law of the land if he was a lawyer, to his father's farming practices if he was a farmer. And—this is very important— he usually believed that no perfectly satisfactory solution of his problems would be available until he went to heaven. The modern man, puzzled, tends at least to consult several different authorities and to compare them before he makes up his own mind. He may also try some experiments on his own. He usually feels that if he goes about it in the right way, he can in fact solve his difficulty. The right way for the medieval man already existed, and had at most to be *found;* the right way for the modern man may have to be *invented, created.*

Mysticism

Although Scholasticism set faith above reason, nevertheless it held that the instrument of thought is a divine gift, and that it must be used and sharpened here on earth. This exaltation of reason would be unacceptable to a mystic at any time in the world's history. And medieval mysticism was also a strong current. Thus in 1140 Saint Bernard secured the condemnation of the disputatious philosopher Abelard for false teaching. Bernard was the mystic of action, a man in some ways like Saint Paul, a great organizer and a commanding personality.

Saint Francis was a very different kind of mystic. But for him, too, formal Scholastic thought was futile and harmful. Christ was no philosopher. Christ's way was the way of submission, of subduing the mind as well as the flesh. How Francis felt about learning is clear from the following:

My brothers who are led by the curiosity of knowledge will find their hands empty in the day of tribulation. I would wish them rather to be strengthened by virtues, that when the time of tribulation comes they may have the Lord with them in their straits—for such a time will come when they will throw their good-for-nothing books into holes and corners.*

The quality of Francis' piety comes out in this fragment of a work which is almost certainly by his own hand, the *Canticle of the Brother Sun:*

Most High, omnipotent, good Lord, thine is the praise, the glory, the honour and every benediction;
Praised be thou, my Lord, with all thy creatures, especially milord Brother Sun that dawns and lightens us;
Be praised, my Lord, for Sister Moon and the stars that thou has made bright and precious and beautiful.
Be praised, my Lord, for Brother Wind, and for the air and cloud and the clear sky and for all weathers through which thou givest sustenance to thy creatures.
Be praised, my Lord, for Sister Water, that is very useful and humble and precious and chaste.
Be praised, my Lord, for Brother Fire, through whom thou dost illumine the night, and comely is he and glad and bold and strong.
Be praised, my Lord, for Sister, Our Mother Earth, that doth cherish and keep us, and produces various fruits with coloured flowers and the grass.†

Aquinas' Franciscan contemporary Bonaventura (John of Fidanza, 1221–1274) preached to his students in Paris that the human mind, as an organ of Adam's sinful and unredeemed descendants, could understand only things of the physical world. Only by divine illumination could men hope to gain cognition of the divine or supernatural. Prayer, not study, love and longing for God, not reason—this was the answer of Bonaventura, as it always is for mystics. Yet Bonaventura was an accomplished philosopher, quite able to deal on even terms with his rationalist opponents. In his *Voyage of the Mind to God* he echoes Augustine and the earlier Platonists: the grace of God helps the mind achieve the degree of love it needs to undergo the ultimate mystical experience of union with the divine.

Finally, here is a characteristic bit from Meister Eckhart (1260–1327), a German mystical preacher:

* Quoted in H. O. Taylor, *The Mediaeval Mind* (New York, 1930), I, 444–445.
† Ibid., 455–456.

It is God's nature to be without a nature. To think of his goodness, or wisdom, or power is to hide the essence of him, *to obscure it with thoughts about him. Even one single thought or consideration will cover it up.* . . . When God finds this order in a soul, he begets his Son, and the soul bursts into light with all its energy, and from that energy, that light, there leaps a flame. That is love; and the soul, with all its energy, has penetrated to the divine order.*

Science

Historians of science today recognize that the Middle Ages saw considerable achievement in natural science. They have indeed revised downward the reputation of the Oxford Franciscan Roger Bacon (ca. 1214–1294?) as a lone, heroic devotee of "true" experimental methods; but they have revised upward such reputations as those of Adelard of Bath (twelfth century), who was a pioneer in the study of Arab science, and Robert Grosseteste (ca. 1170–1253), who clearly did employ experimental methods. No doubt much theological and philosophical thinking of the Middle Ages was concerned with forms of human experience that natural science is not concerned with; but in many ways even modern Western science goes back at least to the thirteenth century.

First, especially in the late Middle Ages, real progress took place in the arts and crafts that underlie modern science—in agriculture, in mining and metallurgy, and in the industrial arts generally. Accurate clockwork, optical instruments, and the compass all emerged from the later Middle Ages. Even such sports as falconry, and such dubious subjects as astrology and alchemy, helped lay the foundations of modern science. The breeding and training of falcons taught close observation of the birds' behavior; astrology involved close observation of the heavens, and complicated calculations; alchemy, though it was far short of modern chemistry, nevertheless brought the beginnings of the identification and a rough classification of elements and compounds. Second, mathematics, a deductive study quite in keeping with medieval intellectual properties, was pursued throughout the period; thanks in part to Arab influences, it had

* *Meister Eckhart*, trans. R. B. Blakney (New York, 1941), p. 243. Italics ours.

been fashioned into a tool ready for the use of early modern scientists. Through the Arabs, medieval Europeans learned Arabic numerals and the symbol for zero, which originated apparently in India—a small thing, but one without which the modern world could hardly get along. If you doubt this, try doing long division with Roman numerals—dividing, say, MCXXVI by LXI. The process is difficult and time-consuming.

Finally, and of major importance, the intellectual discipline of Scholasticism, antagonistic as it often was to experimental science, formed a trained scholarly community that was accus-tomed to a rigorous intellectual discipline. Natural science uses deduction as well as induction, and early modern science inherited from the deductive Scholasticism of the Middle Ages the meticulous care, patience, and logical rigor without which all the inductive piling up of facts would be of little use to scientists. There was no direct "psychological" transfer of skills from the medieval philosophers to the early modern scientists; the transfer was the inheritance of an intellectual tradition of close, almost "unnatural" attentiveness and hard mental work that cannot grow up overnight in any society.

IV   Literature and the Arts

In literature and the arts, as in the social and economic life of medieval men, the eleventh century provides a convenient turning-point for the student. Latin, as we have abundantly seen, continued to be the language of the Church and of learned communication everywhere in western Europe. In fact, men wrote it far better and more fluently than they did in the earlier Middle Ages, when, with the exception of the Carolingian period, literacy was in some measure kept alive by the half-literate. All the churchmen we have been discussing in this chapter—John of Salisbury, Abelard, Bernard, Aquinas, and the rest—wrote Latin even when corresponding informally with their friends. Schoolboys, often destined for the Church or they might not have been schoolboys at all, began their academic lives by learning it. It was also the language of the law and of politics: all documents, such as a title deed to a piece of property, a royal enactment, a treaty of peace, or a letter from one monarch to another or between laymen and clerics, were still written in Latin as a matter of course. Sermons were written and delivered in Latin, hymns were composed and sung in Latin, and much verse was still written in Latin, even extremely colloquial or satirical verse, such as the famous student songs of the twelfth century, still preserved in a single manuscript found in a German monastery.

These songs, all anonymous, are called Goliardic because the authors—mostly, we imagine, wild young renegade clerics wandering about Europe from one lecturer to another—claimed to be in the service of a certain Golias, a kind of satanic figure perhaps deriving originally from the Old Testament giant, Goliath, whom David slew with a stone from his sling. Their verses mocked the form and the values of the serious religious poetry of the time, and goodhumoredly, though very roughly, satirized the clergy and the Church and even the Bible. No doubt the Goliardic verses in praise of wine, women, and song shocked the virtuous, as they were intended to do. Here is the way in which the Confession of Golias, so called, defined the highest good:

My intention is to die
In the tavern drinking;
Wine must be on hand, for I
Want it when I'm sinking.

Angels when they come shall cry
At my frailties winking:
"Spare this drunkard, God, he's high,
*Absolutely stinking."**

But if Latin persisted and was widely used for all literary purposes, the period after the eleventh century marks the gradual triumph of the vernacular languages all over Europe for the literature of entertainment, of belles lettres. Whereas *Beowulf*, coming from a Britain never thoroughly Latinized, was our only important literary vernacular poem during the early Middle Ages, now such poems began to appear in ever greater

* From *The Goliard Poets* by George F. Whicher. Copyright 1949 by George F. Whicher. Reprinted by permission of New Directions Publishing Corporation.

numbers on the Continent as well. A particularly celebrated one is *The Song of Roland,* in Old French, whose earliest surviving manuscript was probably written down a little after the year 1100. It breathes a spirit as heroic as that of *Beowulf,* but it was molded in an environment vastly different from the Scandinavian and Germanic forests and lakes where Grendel and his mother lived.

The poem deals with a historic episode, then already far in the past: the defeat of Charlemagne's rear guard by the Muslims in the year 778, in a mountain pass at Roncevaux in the Pyrenees. Even though our earliest written version dates from after 1100, we know that earlier versions of the story were sung well before that date: for example, as William the Conqueror's men were about to go into battle at Hastings in 1066, a minstrel sang to them about Charlemagne and Roland and Oliver and the vassals of the great king who died at Roncevaux. We also accept, as some scholars do not, the argument that many of the otherwise incomprehensible names of tribes and persons appearing in one episode of the poem can readily be understood in terms of tribes and persons and place names actually connected with the Normans of southern Italy in their invasion of the Balkan lands of the Byzantine Empire across the Adriatic Sea in 1081–1082.

In the *Song of Roland,* human beings have replaced monsters as the enemy; the landscape has brightened; a more intense Christian piety softens some of the worst violence: Roland sees to it that his comrades slain by the infidel receive a Christian blessing. It is human treachery—by the villainous Ganelon—that brings down tragedy on the heroic forces of Charlemagne, leaving the noble Oliver dead, and Roland and the king grief-stricken. The highest virtue in the poem is loyalty to one's lord: a quality that was the first necessity in a feudal society which only the knight's loyalty to his suzerain saved from anarchy. And, as the knight was always defined as a mounted man, a man on a horse, so the unwritten but generally accepted code that during these centuries came to govern his behavior in more and more elaborate detail as time went on was called *chivalry,* from the word that means a horse: chivalric actions are those knightly deeds to be expected from a mounted man.

In the *Song of Roland* at the very end of its 4,000 lines, after the traitor Ganelon has been torn limb from limb by horses, Charlemagne is immediately summoned by a new emergency:

St. Gabriel came to him with a message from God: "Charles, summon the armies of the empire! By force shalt thou enter the land of Bire and bring succour to king Vivien in his city of Imphe, which the heathen have besieged. The Christians are crying out and calling for thee." The emperor had no wish to go. "God," he said, "how full of toil is my life!" And the tears flowed from his eyes and he tore at his white beard.

The final note, then, is of an old man (for the poet had forgotten that Charlemagne in 778 was not yet old and was not yet even emperor) tormented by the great weight of earthly responsibilities, and tired and human after all, rather than heroic or superhuman. And in Roland's deep loyalty to his lord, Charlemagne, we find something new: a love for "sweet France," a patriotic note of love for country struck at just about the earliest moment that we can speak of Europeans as having a country.

Many other songs were sung about Charlemagne's captains, and stories told about them; and other such "cycles" of stories also evolved at the same period around other great heroes. King Arthur of Britain, far more legendary than Charlemagne, was of course one of the most famous, and the exploits of his knights were celebrated not only among Arthur's fellow Celts in Wales, Ireland, and Britanny but in France as well, by such poets as Marie de France and Chrétien de Troyes. From France they passed in the thirteenth century into Germany, where Wolfram von Eschenbach wrote a splendid long poem about King Arthur's knight Sir Percival, and gave new impetus to an old tradition that would not culminate perhaps until Wagner's opera of the nineteenth century. If Wagner found inspiration in the Arthurian cycle, so did Tennyson, Edwin Arlington Robinson, and a host of other moderns, always ready to retell a well-known story in a way that would speak afresh to the psychological attitudes of new generations.

Similarly, the men of the thirteenth century rediscovered the story of the Trojan war, itself an event already almost 3,000 years in the past. It was of course not yet Homer, himself still unknown in the Latin West, but two rather humdrum summary accounts in Latin supposedly by one Dares the Phrygian and Dictys the Cretan (imaginary figures, both of them) that supplied the impetus to the revival of interest in Troy. And current or recent events, like the Crusades, led to dozens of other poetic narratives of adventure: a *Song of Antioch* (Old French), for example, dealing with the adventures of the Crusaders near that historic Eastern city. To read any large number of these medieval vernacular poems is to encounter again and again the same attitudes toward noble action, and the same chivalric virtues of loyalty and good faith and courage that were celebrated in the *Roland.* Collectively these poems, chiefly a northern French phenomenon, are called the *Chansons de Geste:* songs of deeds, or songs of action.

In southern France, things were gentler. No doubt the sunny climate, the greater leisure, and the proximity to the cultivated Muslims of Spain all played a part. Here lyric poetry flourished, with love as its favorite theme. But love in southern France soon had a curious code of its own: *courtoisie,* or courtly love. The singer's lady was never a properly attainable sweetheart, unmarried and perhaps ready to be won. She was always the wife of another; she was worshiped from afar; and the singer celebrated in ecstasy even the slightest kindness she might offer him. Her merest word was a command, and her devoted knight undertook without question even the most arduous mission she might propose to him, without hope of a reward. But a lady who failed to reward him, at least to some degree, was not playing by the rules of this elaborate and artificial game. The twelfth-century troubadours who sang in the southern French language (called Provençal after the large region of Provence, and quite a different dialect from that spoken in the north) were often half-humorous as they expressed their hopeless longings for the unattainable lady.

Aquitaine, the southwestern portion of France, was long a center for this form of lyric poetry. Duke William IX in the early twelfth century was himself a troubadour, and his granddaughter, Eleanor—the wife successively of Louis VII of France and then of Henry II of England—held "courts of love." Here, in sessions patterned mockingly on those of feudal courts of justice, the lovesick troubadors sang their songs and had their cases judged, and petitions from ladies and gentlemen crossed in love received mock-serious attention. So the southern French modified the general feudal attitude toward women as mere breeders of new genera-

tions of fighters, and made life more agreeable and far more sophisticated for all who heard the songs of courtly love.

The influence of the troubadours penetrated into Germany, where courtly love was soon called *Minne,* and its celebrants the minnesingers. Needless to say, few medieval nobles behaved according to the code, and yet portions of the conceptions fostered among the troubadours did become part of the developing notions of chivalry. In such a thirteenth-century figure as Saint Louis, we find as nearly as truly chivalrous figure as can have ever existed. His faithful biographer, Joinville, from whom we have already quoted passages illustrating Louis's character, was himself the personification of a loyal vassal, as he accompanied his royal master on his ill-fated Crusades. And Joinville's work is one of the two most important vernacular French prose documents of the thirteenth century, the other being the only slightly earlier account by Villehardouin of the Fourth Crusade and the capture of Constantinople. When historians began to write for their audiences in the language of every day rather than in Latin, the triumph of the vernacular was at hand.

In Italy, the original home of the Latin language, vernacular was somewhat slower to develop. But here too, at the sophisticated and cosmopolitan court of the emperor Frederick II (1215–1250) in Palermo, some of Frederick's chief advisers began to write love poetry in what they themselves called the "sweet new style" (*dolce stil nuovo*), and soon the fashion of writing at least that form of literature in the vernacular spread northward. But it was not until somewhat later, with Dante Alighieri (1265–1321) of Florence, that the vernacular Italian tongue scored its definitive triumph. It is significant to note that Dante himself, among his other books, felt impelled to write—in Latin—a stirring defense of vernacular Italian: *De Vulgari Eloquentia (Concerning the Speech of Every Day).* And for his own greatest work, *The Divine Comedy,* he himself chose Italian.

Among the writers in the Western tradition, Dante belongs with Homer, Vergil, and Shakespeare as a supreme master; so that it would be absurd to try to "appreciate" him here. Moreover, as a towering intellectual figure he heralds the new age of rebirth at least as loudly as he sounds the familiar medieval note; and we shall be discussing him again when we consider the

Renaissance. It would distort our picture, however, not to examine here *The Divine Comedy* as a medieval book, a very long book, perhaps the most celebrated and in some ways the most typical of all medieval books.

Lost in a dark wood, in his thirty-fifth year ("halfway along the road of our human life"), Dante encounters the Roman poet Vergil, who consents to act as his guide through two of the three great regions of the afterlife of man: Hell and Purgatory. Descending through the nine successive circles of Hell, where the eternally damned must remain forever, the two meet and converse with individual souls in torment, some of them historic persons like Judas or Brutus, others recently deceased Florentines of Dante's own acquaintance, about whose sins he knew at first hand. In Purgatory, less sinful human beings are working out their punishment before they can be saved. The souls of the great pagan figures, born too early to have become Christians, are neither in Hell nor in Purgatory but in Limbo, a place on the edge of Hell, where Vergil himself must spend eternity. Here he introduces Dante to the shades not only of such ancients as Homer, Plato, and Socrates, but of characters in ancient myth and poetry such as Hector, Odysseus, and Aeneas. Even the Muslim scholar Averroës and the Muslim hero Saladin are in Limbo, not in Hell.

When the poet comes to the gates of Paradise, Vergil cannot continue to escort him; so the guide to the final region of the afterlife is Beatrice, a Florentine girl with whom Dante himself had fallen desperately in love as a youth but whom he had worshiped only at a distance. Here Dante was consciously transforming one of the central experiences of his own life into literature in accordance with the traditions of the code of courtly love. In Paradise, of course, are the Christian worthies and the saints,—Benedict, Bernard, Aquinas, and others—and at the climax of the poem, a vision of God himself.

This voyage through the afterlife is designed to show in new pictorial vividness an ancient concept: that man's actions in this life determine his fate in the next. From the lost souls in Hell, who have brought themselves to their hopeless position ("Abandon Hope, All Ye Who Enter Here" reads the inscription over the gates of Hell), through those who despite their sufferings in Purgatory confidently expect to be saved and will indeed be saved, to those whose pure life on earth has won them eternal bliss, Dante shows the entire range of human behavior and its eternal consequences. It is a majestic summary of medieval Christian moral and ethical ideas, and has often been compared in its completeness and its masterful subordination of detail to general vision with the philosophical work of Aquinas. The *Divine Comedy* is a poetic and moving *summa*.

In the generation after Dante's death, the Italian authors Petrarch and Boccaccio became the chief intellectual and literary figures of Europe. We will consider them among the forerunners of the Italian Renaissance. Here, however, we must stop to pay tribute to a poet perhaps greater than they, one who knew Petrarch personally and had read many of Boccaccio's works, but who is none the less in many ways a medieval figure: Geoffrey Chaucer (1340–1400). In England, where the vernacular had always been strong, the Old English of the pre-Conquest period had by Chaucer's time evolved into a new form of the language usually called Middle English, quite recognizable to most of us today as an archaic version of the language we ourselves speak (although we may sometimes be perplexed by its forms). Chaucer is the supreme poet of Middle English, and surely the most brilliant English literary voice before Shakespeare. Not a scholar but an experienced man of affairs, who made several trips to the Continent on business for the king of England, and who eventually became Controller of Customs and Clerk of the King's Works, Chaucer left behind many literary works, including several allegorical poems, some of which seem to satirize contemporary politics, and a long and moving verse narrative love story full of passion and beauty, *Troilus and Criseyde,* deriving its characters from the Trojan War stories now so fashionable in western Europe.

But of course Chaucer's most celebrated work is the *Canterbury Tales,* and the student sometimes comes to feel that if nothing else had survived of medieval literature, we should still be able to learn most of what we know about it from the *Tales* alone. The *Tales* are told by a group of pilgrims on their way to the tomb of Thomas à Becket, the archbishop of Canterbury murdered under Henry II and now a saint. The pilgrims come from all walks of English life except the high nobility, and include a knight, a squire, a prioress, a clerk, a monk, a friar, a sailor, a miller, and others. In a brilliant prologue, Chaucer, who was himself one of the group, characterizes his fellow pilgrims, each of whom emerges as a living person. On the way from London, each tells at least one story, fully consonant with his personality and experience.

The knight tells a romantic story of chivalric love: two cousins, Palamon and Arcite, both fall in love with a maiden whom they have barely glimpsed from the window of their prison cell. Deadly rivals thereafter, they continue to cherish their mutual strife, in prison and out, without the lady's ever being aware of them. When she learns, she does very little about it, and in the end one kills the other, and wins her as his own. It is indeed a strange story to us: the lady's passivity, the two knights' lovesickness unfed by any encouragement; but it is a true story of courtly love, and befits the experienced warrior who tells it. The miller tells a raw story of a young wife's deception of her elderly husband with a young lover, a barnyard anecdote, in effect, but full of liveliness and good humor. The prioress tells a saint's legend, the squire an (unfinished) story full of semiscientific marvels, and so on. Chaucer does not hesitate to satirize his churchmen: as we shall see, the fourteenth century was a period of much discontent with the English church, and the poet was striking a note that was sure to be popular. The sophistication, delicacy, power, passion, and humor that Chaucer commands put him in the same class with Dante, and with no other medieval writer in any country.

V The Arts

As in literature, so in the arts, the centuries beginning with the eleventh saw notable changes in Europe and in Britain. Evolving from the Ottonian styles of the earlier period, the Romanesque style dominated the eleventh and most of the twelfth centuries. The Gothic style, following it and developing from it, began in the twelfth century and continued to prevail down to the fifteenth. The transition between Romanesque and Gothic is complex; and art historians have recently begun to see the years between about 1180 and about 1220, especially in northern France, as a fairly distinct period which they have labeled transitional.*

But the whole matter of terminology is difficult here: the term "Romanesque" is sometimes rather loosely used for buildings as early as the Carolingian and Ottonian periods, but many prefer to use "pre-Romanesque" and "proto-Romanesque" for these, both terms suggesting, quite properly, that we are on our way to something that we have not yet quite reached. Beginning in Lombardy, where the first schools of craftsmen were formed, and from which the builders traveled wherever they were needed and summoned, their skills and styles traveled across southern France to northern Spain: in both regions Catalan craftsmen practiced the art. One of the very earliest Romanesque churches, high up in the French Pyrenees, is St. Martin du Canigou, built in the first quarter of the eleventh century. Like many of these new buildings, it is a monastic church, far larger than most of the churches of the earlier period, and its interior provides examples of two important adaptations

The monastery of St. Martin du Canigou high in the French Pyrenees, an early Romanesque building.

* The concept was probably brought closer to general acceptance by an extraordinary exhibition of art called "The Year 1200," held in New York in 1970 to celebrate the hundredth anniversary of the Metropolitan Museum of Art, which concentrated upon the glories and problems of these years.

of earlier Roman architectural devices: the barrel or tunnel vault, or continuous round-arch roofing, now used for far larger spaces than before; and the groin vault, at first used in crypts only, and then later moved above ground to the main church. To the groin vault ribbing was sometimes added for strengthening. At St. Martin, the tower and cloister and body of the church are in harmonious balance, and all are adapted to the precipitous slope on which the church was built.

Most Romanesque churches had as their fundamental ground plan a Latin cross, with a long staff and shorter cross-arms; the shrine of the church, where stood the altar with the relics of the saint, was at the east end, and usually its walls formed a curved arc: this was the apse. Within this portion of the church also the choir sang. The arms of the cross extended north and south, usually from a point immediately west of the apse; these were the transepts. And the long portion of the cross, extending westward to the west front, was the nave, usually with an aisle at each side. Towers might be built over the crossing of nave and transepts, and at either side of the west front. Some churches had none or only one, some as many as six, if additional ones were built at the ends of the transepts. Around the interior of the apse—sometimes called simply "the choir" —there often opened a series of chapels, usually reflected in the exterior design by smaller arcs emerging from the apse wall, like bulges, little apses, or absidioles, as they are called. Of course, the ground plans varied greatly in detail from church to church, according to the wealth and taste of the community and the length of time that construction took, since as fashions changed, innovations could and would be incorporated in any church that remained a long time in the building.

Among the great Romanesque churches were those built at Mainz, Worms, and Speyer in western Germany by the Holy Roman emperors of the Salian line, of which we reproduce the ground plan of Speyer, mostly of the eleventh century, with later additions (page 267), and a view of the exterior of Worms as it is today. Surely one of the best ways to gain an impression of a great Romanesque monastery church, with its surrounding buildings (now so destroyed and rebuilt that no spectator can tell what they once looked like), is to examine the painstaking reconstructions made by a brilliant student of past

The Cathedral of Worms, western Germany, begun in the eleventh century.

architecture, Professor K. J. Conant. Here is Conant's drawing of his model of the entire complex of Cluny as it was in 1157. And to be compared with the church at Cluny is a reconstruction of the noble pilgrimage church of St. James (Santiago) at Compostela in far northwestern Spain.

To Compostela from all over western Europe but especially from France there flooded in these years throngs of pilgrims to worship at the shrine of the saint. And along the routes, to accommodate the pilgrims, hospices were built, and monasteries and churches flourished. It has long been realized that Romanesque architecture spread along these routes as well, and "pilgrimage churches," great Romanesque buildings at which the pilgrims would stop to worship along their way, were built in many key centers. The interior

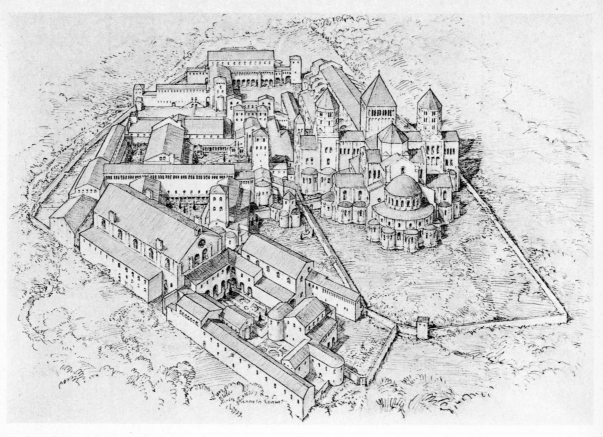

Drawing of a model of the monastery of Cluny as constructed by Professor Conant.

Santiago de Compostela, the goal of western European pilgrims: a drawing of a restoration to its medieval state.

The Medieval West

Admirers of the Middle Ages often claim that the medieval craftsman worked in anonymity, content to carve or paint for the glory of God and the joy of creating beauty, and not for fame or money. Perhaps so, though the reason we do not know the names of many medieval architects and sculptors is simply that the records have been lost. Yet art and artists seem to have been closely tied to the community in the Middle Ages. The greatest of medieval arts, architecture, clearly shows this community stamp. In a medieval town the cathedral, parish churches, town hall, guild halls, and other *public* buildings dominate.

All the fine arts contributed to these great community buildings; indeed, they had hardly any other major outlet. Painting was subordinated to architecture. While the medieval church had no place for the canvas designed to be hung for exhibition, mosaics, wall painting, and above all stained glass contributed to the total design.

Sculpture, too, was subordinated to the building. Statues and carvings were fitted into the design of the great churches, in niches on the fronts and porches, or on altars and shrines in the interior. Medieval sculpture is never simply realistic in the way of the portrait bust, nor independently grand in the way of equestrian statue. It is always part of the "stone Bible."

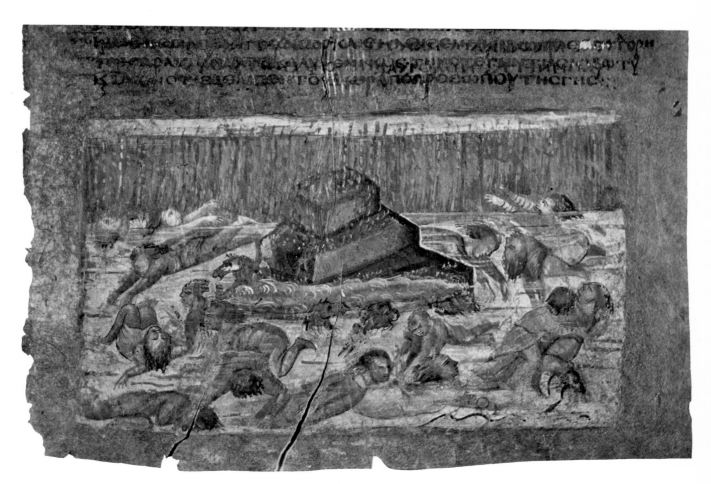

The Flood: an illumination from the sixth-century manuscript known as the Vienna Genesis.

Saint Matthew: folio 21v of the late seventh-century Book of Durrow.
Trinity College Library, Dublin; The Green Studio.

Saint John: folio 291v from the late eighth-century Book of Kells.

Trinity College Library, Dublin; The Green Studio.

Detail of the Bayeux Tapestry, ca. 1073–1083.

European Art Color, Peter Adelberg, N.Y.C.

Opposite: The seventh-century jeweled gold crown of the Visigothic king Recceswinth.

Museo Arqueologico Nacional, Madrid.

*The Angel of the Four Winds: a ceiling panel in the Church of St. Martin,
Zillis, Switzerland, ca. 1350.*

European Art Color, Peter Adelberg, N.Y.C.

Twelfth-century bas-relief of the baptism of Christ, Müstair, Switzerland.

European Art Color, Peter Adelberg, N.Y.C.

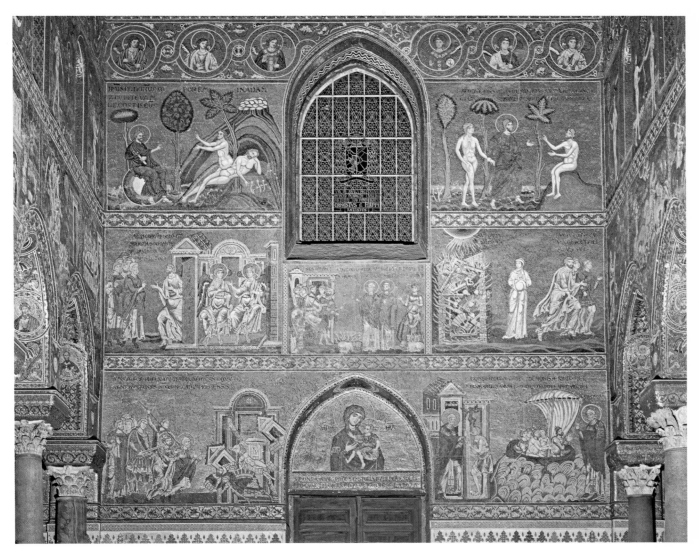

Mosaic scenes from Genesis: The west wall of the nave of the Cathedral of Monreale, Sicily, showing Byzantine and Muslim influence.

Opposite: The Presentation in the Temple: fresco in the twelfth-century church of Nohant-Vic, France.

The Last Judgment: a page from the psalter made for Ingeborg, Danish wife of King Philip Augustus of France (reigned 1180-1223).

Giraudon, Paris.

*Jonah and the whale: a champlevé enamel plaque from Nicholas of Verdun's
Klosterneuburg altarpiece, 1181.*

European Art Color, Peter Adelberg, N.Y.C.

*Stained glass window from Chartres Cathedral, depicting the erection of the
church of Pamplona by Charlemagne.*

European Art Color, Peter Adelberg, N.Y.C.

Head of Christ, by Claus Sluter, Archaeological Museum, Dijon, France.

European Art Color, Peter Adelberg, N.Y.C.

Donors: the left wing of a triptych (the Campin Altarpiece) by Robert Campin.

The Metropolitan Museum of Art, the Cloisters Collection, purchase.

Opposite: .The Adoration of the Magi, by Hieronymus Bosch.

The Metropolitan Museum of Art, Kennedy Fund, 1912.

Landscape detail from the center panel of an altarpiece, The Nativity, from the workshop of Rogier van der Weyden.

The Metropolitan Museum of Art, the Cloisters Collection, purchase, 1949.

of Ste. Foi at Conques in south-central France, with its groin vaulting in the nave, is typical.

Variations on the typical Romanesque church can be seen, for example, in southwestern France, where a group of churches, unlike those anywhere else, have domed roofs, sometimes with the domes placed in a row above the nave, and, at St. Front of Perigueux, placed in a Greek (equal-armed) cross pattern, with a central dome, surrounded by four side domes, like St. Mark's at Venice, itself an imitation of the (lost) Church of the Holy Apostles in Byzantium. It has long been argued, and cogently, that Greek influence was somehow at work in this corner of France. The effect upon the worshiper standing under a roof made up of a series of domes is entirely different from that produced by the ordinary Romanesque barrel of groin vaulting, a point well illustrated by the interior of the Cathedral of Angoulême. That Romanesque was a truly international style despite its many variations may be seen in further examples, the interiors of two widely separated cathedrals: that of Pisa, in Italy (page 267), and that of Durham, in northern England.

A little before the year 1100, there began an extraordinary revival of European sculpture. While the tradition had never been lost, as we know from looking at monuments as late as the early medieval Irish and English crosses, and at the extraordinary figures at Cividale, the finest surviving examples of the art of sculpture before the Romanesque revival were the smaller examples in ivory and in metalwork that we have also noted. But now, quite suddenly, with joy and exuberance, the stones of the Romanesque churches we have been discussing came literally to life. The older classical columns usually had Corinthian capitals with their acanthus leaves. But now capitals began to blossom out with rosettes, palm-leaf ornament, and grapevines, and amidst the foliage there suddenly proliferated a whole race of marvelous beasts. Some were carved as if they were illustrations to the popular bestiaries (collections of anecdotes about real and mythical animals, usually with a Christian allegorical explanation of the animals' incredible characteristics); some were taken from real life, and some from the teeming imagination of the sculptors. At such places as Chauvigny, in western France, lions and pelicans, horses and elephants, griffins and dragons, and mermaids and other weird monsters, savage harpies attacking each other, all now edified the beholder, or, as

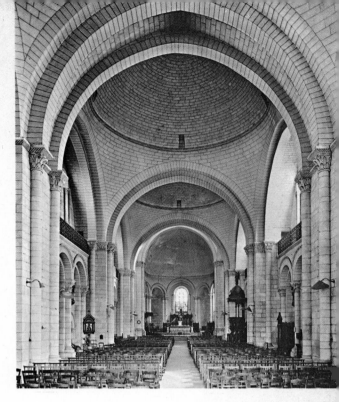

Angoulême: The nave of a church whose roof is a series of domes.

Durham: nave of the Cathedral. Romanesque (or Norman, as it is always called in England).

The Magi all tucked up for their dreams: from Autun.

Saint Bernard stoutly maintained, distracted him from his real business in church: the capitals at his church of Clermont and at Cîteaux were severely plain.

Of course, scenes from the Bible also appeared on the capitals, and elsewhere in the churches, but now often interpreted with a freedom from the traditional ways of showing such subjects, and with a due consideration for the space available to the artist within the small compass of the top of a column. On some capitals, the three magi (wise men from the East) sleep happily under the same blanket with their crowns on. Judas hangs himself, while terrifying winged demons pull actually and symbolically at each end of the rope. And from the capitals, of course, the sculpture spread to the available large flat and vertical surfaces available to the artist in a Romanesque church: for example, to the arched space over the outside of the front portal, the tympanum, as it is called.

Here Christ himself could be shown enthroned, often with the Virgin and the saints at his side, and surrounding and beneath them a depiction of the Last Judgment, the souls of the damned being eternally rejected at the moment of the Second Coming of the Lord, while those of the blessed rise from the tomb to enjoy their eternal salvation. At Vézelay and Autun in Burgundy, at Conques and Beaulieu and many other Romanesque churches of the pilgrimage routes, such large-scale representations of this complicated composition gave the sculptor scope for his versatility at filling space and portraying what is after all the sublimest moment in the Christian's conception of his universe.

On the doorposts, and in the repeated hollow indented narrow arches around the portals (called *voussures*), sculptured ornament also took over. At Moissac and Souillac in southern France, a frantic series of grotesque beasts, each gripping and eating the next, climbs and struggles its way up an entire vertical column or door-post. Human and animal heads look out side by side from the voussures surrounding the tympanum. In one region of southwest France, specially noted for its breeding of horses, it is horses' heads alone that ornament the church portals and façades. In the cloister of San Domingo de Silos in northern Spain, or in Chichester Cathedral in southern England, one still can see large plaques sculptured with splendid representations of biblical scenes. Romanesque sculpture is almost always in relief rather than in the full round.

In the nature of things, far less survives of Romanesque painting than of Romanesque sculpture. In the first place, when anti-Christian vandals in later periods of revolution set about the business of defacing earlier Christian monuments, they naturally found it somewhat easier to destroy paintings by scraping them off the walls or tearing out illuminations from books than to shatter stone monuments completely. In the second place, a painting on a plaster wall, for example, deteriorates faster with the passage of time than does a piece of sculpture, especially one that is indoors. However, enough survives, often in out-of-the-way places, to show that painting too experienced a revival no less significant than sculpture. In León in northern Spain, in many churches of Catalonia, and in a few places in England, France, and Italy, wall paintings can still be seen from this early period.

Probably the most complete series still visible is in the abbey church of St.-Savin-sur-Gartempe, not far from Poitiers in western France, and only a few moments' drive from the grotesque capitals at Chauvigny. At St.-Savin, the walls and ceiling of the apse and the entire long

The west tympanum at Autun.

Chartres: the west portals.

barrel vaulting of the ceiling of the nave were covered with an elaborate series of paintings, the nave with scenes from the Old Testament: Creation, the murder of Abel, Noah's Ark, the stories of Abraham and Joseph, and the Tower of Babel; and the apse with scenes from the New, including the deposition from the Cross and the Resurrection. One may also consider as a special kind of Romanesque painting the unique and famous Bayeux tapestry (actually an embroidery) commemorating the Norman Conquest of England and made soon afterwards.

Such elaborate "programs" of painting as that at St.-Savin are more familiar to us from the monuments of Italy, where the painting often took the ancient form of mosaic, used by the Romans but perfected for Christian art and for wall decoration by the Byzantines. Just as in the earlier period Eastern influence produced the great mosaics in Ravenna, we find in the Romanesque period especially rich mosaic paintings in the churches of Norman Sicily, always open to Eastern influences, and still inhabited by and visited by many Greeks. In Palermo alone, the chapel of the royal palace of the Norman kings (Cappella Palatina), the church of the Martorana, and the magnificent nearby Cathedral of Monreale all display these Byzantine-influenced mosaic paintings against the usual gold ground, and present a rich variety of scenes. Not far away at Cefalù is still another large church with mosaic decoration. The earliest surviving mosaics at St. Mark's in Venice—also intimately linked with Byzantium, as we know—date shortly after the beginning of the thirteenth century.

We turn now briefly to the changes that came over the Romanesque beginning in the late twelfth century. In architecture, the arches, from being round, now gradually rose to points at the peak, and similarly the roofs, once barrel-vaulted (or barrel-vaulted with groins and ribs), now also rose more and more sharply, as the smooth flow of the arc was sharply broken, and two loftier curves now met instead at a point. The continuous Romanesque barrel vault pressed down upon its supporting walls with even stress, and the walls had to be made very strong, with few openings, and often with buttresses—stone supports built at right angles to the main wall to take part of the outward push. But the chief feature of the newer medieval architecture always known as "Gothic" was precisely this pointed arch, a new device by which the builder could carry his buildings to soaring heights. The vaulted ceiling now rested upon a series of masonry ribs, in groups of four, two rising from each side of the wall, and each group supported by a massive pillar. Four pillars therefore could now be made to take the place of a whole section of solid Romanesque wall, and the spaces between the pillars could be freed for windows. From the beginning, therefore, Gothic churches were far lighter inside than Romanesque churches.

Outside too, a new effect of increased lightness and soaring height was achieved by moving the vertical buttress of the Romanesque period away from the walls of the church, and by bridging the gap between buttress and church wall with an arched support that looked as if it were actually flying between the now distant vertical and the lofty masonry wall, part of whose outward thrust it was designed to take. These "flying buttresses" also freed the builder to soar upward. Into the new window spaces made possible by the new architectural devices the craftsmen of the thirteenth century and later fitted a new form of painting: the window in multicolored (stained) glass, glittering with gemlike color in ruby, sapphire, and emerald, and showing biblical episodes or episodes from the life of the saint whose church they illuminated.

Gothic architecture flourished for at least two

Amiens: The nave.

King's College Chapel, Cambridge.

centuries everywhere in Europe. Its first and perhaps greatest moments came in northern France, with the building—all between the 1190's and about 1240—of the cathedrals of Chartres, Reims, Amiens, Notre Dame of Paris, and other celebrated churches. Sometimes the ambition of a designer extended beyond his control of engineering: the architect of Beauvais, who managed to build the loftiest apse and transepts of any Gothic church, found that he could not get his nave to stand up; so it fell, and what remains still looks like an exercise in defiance of the law of gravity.

Open and vast, but solidly built, soaring upward according to well-worked-out and usually well-understood mathematical architectural proportional formulas, the Gothic cathedral terminates in aerial towers. Though its great windows let in the light, the stained glass keeps the interior dim and awe-inspiring. In England, York and Canterbury, Salisbury and Wells, Ely and Winchester among a good many other cathedrals still stand as the best of island Gothic, fully comparable with the best on the Continent. With the passage of time in the fourteenth and fifteenth centuries ornamentation grew richer, decoration became more intricate, literally flame-like, or "flamboyant," and Gothic architecture on the Continent moved toward its decline. The later tower at Chartres illustrates this overripe

look; in England, however, the later richer Gothic has given us such marvels as King's College Chapel in Cambridge and the Henry VII Chapel at Westminster Abbey in London.

Of sculpture in the years between 1180 and 1220 it has been recently said that ". . . for practically the first time since ancient Greek and Roman times, draperies curl and caress the bodies underneath; limbs themselves are proudly and successfully shown as organic entities; strength becomes a thing of muscles rather than size alone; physiques are neither camouflaged nor ignored, but studied and presented to our eyes in an almost overpowering beauty. Faces become truly alive, eyes shine with an inner light, gestures seem to develop an entirely new expressive poetry of their own. Drama is supreme."* Refusing to call this style either Romanesque or Gothic, and discarding even the name "transitional," but preferring simply the slightly awkward term "Style 1200," recent scholars point to the work in metals of Nicholas of Verdun and of sculptors working in the valley of the Meuse, where France, Belgium, Holland, and Germany are close together, as marking the beginning of the new school; but more generally northern

---

* Thomas P. F. Hoving, in his Foreword to *The Year 1200: A Centennial Exhibition at the Metropolitan Museum of Art* (New York: The Metropolitan Museum of Art, 1970), I, vii.

"Style 1200": Two of Nicholas of Verdun's enameled plaques made for the Klosterneu-burg altarpiece—Christ enthroned, and the mouth of Hell. In the former, note the folds of the draperies and the genuine bodies beneath.

France, western Germany, and England all saw its activity.

Gradually during this period, sculpture in the round became more and more common, beginning with figures that were carved fully in the round from the mid-sections of columns, engaged in the façade or the portal of a church only at the top and at the base. The lifelike representation of drapery, the firm balance of the figures on their feet, are principal characteristics of these new statues, chiefly occurring in northern France (see page 266). Similar influences are shown elsewhere in metalwork and in manuscript illumination, rather than in monumental sculpture, and it is agreed that the influences from outside that help make the development possible must be sought in Byzantine art, then itself undergoing a kind of classical renaissance, and available to Western eyes through renewed and intensified contacts between East and West by pilgrims, travelers, and warriors during the period of the Crusades. What we have here is an artistic revival more splendid and more complicated even than had hitherto been suspected.

"Style 1200": Silver-gilt figure of St. Simon sculpted by Nicholas of Verdun for the Shrine of the Three Kings, Cologne.

Chartres: the façade.

An aerial view of Beauvais Cathedral.

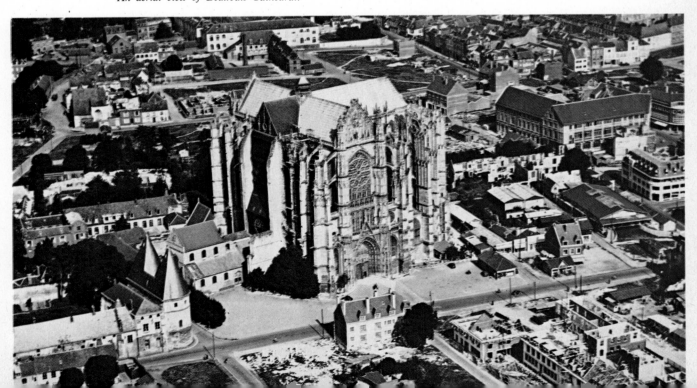

Reading Suggestions on Medieval Society and Civilization in the West

GENERAL ACCOUNTS

H. O. Taylor, *The Mediaeval Mind,* new ed. (Harvard Univ. Press, 1949). Sympathetic and objective in its treatment of the Middle Ages, but in some respects outdated.

H. Adams, *Mont-St. Michel and Chartres* (*Anchor). By a distinguished American of a generation back, very much disturbed by the machine age and attracted to the Middle Ages. An unreliable but highly stimulating introduction to the beauties of medieval architecture and literature.

G. C. Coulton, *Medieval Panorama* (Macmillan, 1938; *Meridian). This and other writings of Coulton are full of interesting details, but are basically "anticlerical" and unsympathetic toward much of medieval culture.

M. De Wulf, *Philosophy and Civilization in the Middle Ages* (Princeton Univ. Press, 1922; *Dover). Popular lectures by a great medieval scholar.

D. Knowles, *The Evolution of Medieval Thought* (*Vintage). Stresses the continuity between classical and Scholastic thought.

F. B. Artz, *The Mind of the Middle Ages, A.D. 200–1500,* 2nd ed. (Knopf, 1954). A very useful survey.

C. S. Lewis, *The Discarded Image: An Introduction to Medieval and Renaissance Literature* (Cambridge Univ. Press, 1964). An essentially revisionist commentary.

David Knowles, *The Evolution of Medieval Thought* (Helicon Press, 1962). Emphasizes continuity between classical and Scholastic thought.

A. L. Poole, ed., *Medieval England,* 2 vols. (Oxford Univ. Press, 1958). Two nicely illustrated volumes, essentially a medley of essays by specialists, on such aspects of culture as landscape, communications, architecture, heraldry, education, recreation and other matters; uneven, but with much not elsewhere available to the general reader.

S. H. Thomson and others, *Perspectives in Medieval History* (Univ. of Chicago Press, 1963). Five American medievalists sew up their generation's view of the subject.

SPECIAL STUDIES

J. H. Clapham and E. Power, eds., *The Cambridge Economic History,* Vol. I, and M. Postan and E. E. Rich, eds., Vol. II (Cambridge Univ. Press, 1944, 1952). A definitive survey of many aspects of the material basis of medieval civilization in the West.

P. Boissonade, *Life and Work in Medieval Europe* (Knopf, 1927). A good introduction to the social and economic life of villages, manors, countryside, and towns in the Middle Ages.

J. W. Baldwin, "The Medieval Theories of the Just Price," *Transactions* of the American Philosophical Society (July 1959). A study of characteristic twelfth-and-thirteenth-century theories of what prices were legitimate.

W. Ullman, *Principles of Government and Politics in the Middle Ages* (Barnes and Noble, 1961). Ambitious synthesis, not acceptable to all specialists.

L. White, Jr., *Medieval Technology and Social Change* (Oxford Univ. Press, 1962). Scholarly, readable, suggestive.

H. Pirenne, *Medieval Cities* (Princeton Univ. Press, 1925; *Anchor). An excellent, readable short essay.

S. Painter, *French Chivalry* (Johns Hopkins Univ. Press, 1940; *Cornell Univ. Press). A very good survey of the ideals and behavior of feudal society.

H. Rashdall, *The Universities of Europe in the Middle Ages,* new ed., 3 vols. (Clarendon, 1936). The classic account; full and readable.

C. H. Haskins, *The Renaissance of the Twelfth Century* (*Meridian). An important work, stressing "modern" elements in medieval civilization.

C. H. Haskins, *The Rise of Universities* (Peter Smith, 1940; *Cornell Univ. Press). A delightful series of short essays.

L. Thorndike, *A History of Magic and Experimental Science,* 8 vols. (Macmillan, 1923–1956), and A. C. Crombie, *Augustine to Galileo: The History of Science, A.D. 400–1650* (Harvard Univ. Press, 1953). A detailed and a briefer account, both good.

S. Baldwin, *The Organization of Medieval Christianity* (Holt, 1929). An introductory study.

A. C. McGiffert, *History of Christian Thought,* Vol. II (Scribner's, 1933). A good survey.

C. Dawson, *Religion and the Rise of Western Culture* (Sheed and Ward, 1950; *Image). An admirably sympathetic but also realistic survey in terms of cultural history.

E. Gilson, *The Spirit of Medieval Philosophy* (Scribner's, 1936), and *Reason and Revelation in the Middle Ages* (*Scribner's). By a distinguished French Catholic scholar, author of many other important works sympathetic to the Middle Ages.

M. D. Chenu, *Toward Understanding St. Thomas* (Regnery, 1964). Standard work translated from the French.

H. Daniel Rops, *Bernard of Clairvaux,* translated from the French (Hawthorne, 1964). An excellent account of a very medieval figure.

P. Sabatier, *Life of St. Francis of Assisi* (Scribner's, 1912). A well-balanced biography of a personality hard to evaluate objectively.

C. S. Lewis, *The Discarded Image: An Introduction to Medieval and Rennaissance Literature* (Cambridge Univ. Press, 1964). A subtle commentary, revising traditional interpretations.

H. Waddell, *The Wandering Scholars* (Constable, 1927; *Anchor). A good study.

Kenneth J. Conant, *Carolingian and Romanesque Architecture, 800 to 1200.* Standard work.

The Year 1200: A Background Survey, ed. Florens Deuchler, 2 vols. (The Cloisters Studies in Medieval Art, 1970). Provocative text and splendid illustrations.

HISTORICAL
FICTION

There are many historical novels about the Middle Ages, a few of them quite good (see the suggestions for Chapters 5 and 7). But the best literary introduction to the many-sided human beings of the Middle Ages is provided by Chaucer's *Canterbury Tales.* E. Power's *Medieval People* (*Anchor) is an admirable set of brief biographical sketches of a half-dozen individuals from various walks of medieval life. Zoe Oldenbourg's *The Cornerstone* (Pantheon, 1955) is a remarkably frank "realistic" novel about an early thirteenth-century French noble family. Helen Waddell's *Peter Abelard* (*Compass) is a novel about the famous love affair with Heloise. An interesting narrative poem is C. Whitman's *Peter Abelard* (Harvard Univ. Press, 1965).

9

The East

Late Middle Ages

I   The Main Threads

In the past few chapters we have been considering separately three great societies—Roman Christendom, Greek Christendom, and Islam. In the third quarter of the eleventh century, the relations between them entered upon a long period of crisis that was fundamentally important for the future of all three. Our first task in this chapter is to deal with the late medieval interaction of these three societies, particularly in the movement called the Crusades. Next, we shall consider the decline and final collapse of the Byzantine Empire. And, finally, we shall trace the fortunes down to the end of the seventeenth century of the two states that, in different senses, were its successors: the Ottoman Empire, and Muscovite Russia. In this introductory section we shall examine the main pattern of all these developments before discussing them in detail in subsequent sections.

Above: A contemporary stone head of Frederick II. Above right: A Russian prince and his bodyguard. Right: Mosque of the emperor Suleiman the Magnificent, Istanbul, sixteenth century.

300

By the eleventh century, each of the three societies had well-established relationships with the other two. Byzantium had conducted diplomatic negotiations with many Western monarchs; the papacy had maintained regular official contact with the Byzantines even after the official break in 1054; and southern Italy had been a Byzantine outpost. The Byzantines had been involved in more or less continuous war and diplomacy with the caliphate and the local Muslim dynasties in Syria. Islam had touched Roman Christendom in Spain and Sicily, and Western pilgrims had thronged, as we shall see, to the shrines of Christendom in Muslim Palestine. But after 1071, when the Normans took Bari and drove the Byzantines from Italy, and the Seljuk Turks won at Manzikert and battered their way into the central Byzantine stronghold of Asia Minor, the tempo of the relationship steadily quickened. For the next six centuries, the fate of each society became ever more closely bound up with the fate of the other two.

The Norman assault on the Byzantines now moved eastward from Italy across the Adriatic to the Balkan shores of the empire itself. In order to ward it off, the Byzantine emperors, pressed as they were simultaneously by the Seljuks, in 1082 made an alliance with the booming port of Venice—once their vassal, now their equal. In exchange for naval assistance, they gave the Venetians commercial concessions in the empire. Permitted to import and export at special tariff rates, and given a quarter in Constantinople itself, with warehouses, churches, and dwelling places, the Venetians and later the Genoese joined the sailors of Amalfi and Pisa in taking over the carrying-trade of the eastern Mediterranean.

The Crusades

Meanwhile, the papacy, stimulated by Byzantine appeals for military assistance against the Seljuks, proclaimed a holy war against Islam. This concept had already become familiar in the Byzantine wars against the Muslims and in the Catholic attempts to reconquer Spain and Sicily. In 1095 Pope Urban II launched the great military movement of the Crusade. The recovery of the Holy Sepulcher was the ultimate aim, and the Crusaders fought with the cross as their symbol. They were granted special privileges as soldiers of the Lord. From then on for a period of almost two hundred years, expedition after expedition was hurled against the Muslims, most often in Syria and Palestine, but also in Egypt, North Africa, and even Portugal. The armies were sometimes commanded by kings and emperors, sometimes by lesser nobles. Sometimes they came by sea, sometimes by land, sometimes by a combined land-and-sea route. Sometimes they scored successes, great or small; more often they met with partial or total failure. Reinforcements from the West flowed to the East in an almost continuous stream. Therefore, the practice of calling certain specific expeditions the Second, Third, or Fourth Crusade, and so on up to the Eighth, is really not very accurate, though it is often useful.

As a result of the First Crusade, the Westerners established in Muslim territory in Syria four independent states of their own, usually called the Latin or Frankish states (to the Muslims all Westerners were "Franks"). These states were ruled by Europeans of various origins, jealous of each other and often at odds. After the First Crusade, many of the later expeditions were directed toward meeting some emergency that had arisen in the Latin states. Here in the East, a new society sprang up, in which Western feudal practice could combine with Muslim local practice. Yet by 1187 the Muslims, overcoming their disunity, had swept away all but a remnant of the Western outposts. After a century of epilogue, the process was complete by 1291.

Thereafter, although the crusading ideal continued to be preached in the West, no major expedition was ever again launched to reconquer the Holy Land, which remained in Muslim hands. In the fourteenth and fifteenth centuries some of the Western expeditions against the Ottoman Turks took on various aspects of a crusade, but they were never the genuine article.

The Downfall of Byzantium

Most of the important crusading expeditions passed through Byzantium. From the first, the emperors were embarrassed by the presence of the often uncontrollable "barbarian" armies in their territory. Naturally, they tried to move the Westerners as quickly as possible on to Muslim soil and into the combat against the infidel for which they had come. But the Westerners tended to regard these precautions as perfidy, and distrusted the Greeks. The vast material wealth of Constantinople appealed greatly to the greedy eyes of the western European military commanders. There were profound religious and social differences between the Greeks and Latins, and the Byzantines hated the Italian merchants resident among them, as well as the Western armies pouring through the capital. Tension mounted throughout the twelfth century. Internal disorder increased, signalized by a great increase in Byzantine feudal decentralization.

Finally, in 1204, the Fourth Crusade, which had set out from Venice by sea to fight in the Holy Land, was diverted for political reasons to Constantinople, and took the city by storm. This was the first time the Byzantine capital had been taken, and it marks a landmark in the history of the relations between Eastern and Western Christians. The Westerners set up a "Latin Empire" in Constantinople, gained a foothold in Asia Minor, and founded feudal principalities throughout Greece and in the islands of the Aegean. Meanwhile, the Byzantines, driven from their capital, founded two Greek states in Asia Minor, Trebizond and Nicaea, and one in Europe, Epirus. All three eventually called themselves empires.

In 1261 the Latins, deprived of help from home, without roots, hated by the Greeks, were driven from Constantinople by the Greek emperor of Nicaea, and the Byzantine Empire was restored. But from then on for the next two centuries, the empire was merely a shadow of its former self. Though expelled as rulers from the capital, the Westerners remained in Greece and on the islands. Venetians and Genoese retained and strengthened their privileged positions in Constantinople. In the Balkans, the Serbians rose to a position of power, and menaced Byzantium itself. It proved entirely impossible to restore the Byzantine military or economic system. Although its pretensions to being the only civilized state in the world and its theoretical aspirations to world empire were never abandoned, Byzantium was now only a Balkan state. And, toward the end of the thirteenth century the Byzantine emperors became aware of how great a danger was presented by a new Turkish people, the Osmanlis, or Ottoman Turks. Muslims like the rest, the Ottoman Turks in only a few generations had been able to consolidate their power in northwestern Asia Minor, opposite Constantinople.

The Ottoman Turks

Themselves a product of a fusion between Greek natives and Turkish invaders, the Osmanlis crossed the Straits into Europe in the mid-fourteenth century, were invited to assist the parties in the ever-growing internal Byzantine strife, and gradually became a European power. They occupied most of the former Byzantine territory, except for the capital itself. A variety of efforts to reunite the Eastern and Western churches and to obtain assistance from the Roman Catholic West for the Byzantines, who were beleaguered by their Muslim enemy, all met with failure. In 1453 the Osmanlis besieged and captured the city of Constantine, and the empire that proudly traced its origins to Augustus finally came to an end.

Yet the end, though definite enough, was in some ways more of an appearance than a reality. The Ottoman Turks by 1453 had become a partly European people, and, though their system had many features that may be considered purely Turkish, they too, like so many of the earlier enemies of the empire, were overwhelmed by their sense of its prestige. With Constantinople as their capital, the Ottoman sultans ruled like Byzantine emperors. Though Muslim, they permitted their Christian subjects to worship in their own way. Although the Christians suffered certain disabilities, the religious life of the Orthodox continued to be governed by the patriarch of Constantinople, a Greek as always. Byzantine ways persisted throughout the Balkan region. In a real sense, the Ottoman Empire, despite its own peculiar institutions, was a successor state to Byzantium, and many of its inhabitants were descendants of the Byzantines.

Extraordinarily successful as a military power, the Turks, during the first two centuries of their domination at Constantinople, repeatedly threatened Europe. Twice they advanced as far as

Vienna, and they fought naval wars all over the Mediterranean. Although a new general crusade against them was never launched successfully, many crusades were preached. The West did develop strong defenders, especially the Hapsburg rulers of the Holy Roman Empire, now centered at Vienna, who in the end were able to resist the Ottoman onslaught. And meanwhile, after the end of the sixteenth century, the Ottoman system itself was in full internal decay. The astonishing thing is that it was able to forestall total disruption. By the end of the seventeenth century, European rulers were already beginning to discuss how they should divide the Turkish lands when the empire fell apart. But contrary to all calculations, the Ottoman Empire, perhaps largely because its existence was valuable to some of the European powers, continued to exist down to the end of World War I in our own twentieth century.

Post-Kievan Russia

Although the Ottoman Empire represented a kind of successor state to Byzantium, it was still a Muslim state. There was, however, another state, which, though it occupied no Byzantine territory and never included within its borders more than a handful of Byzantine subjects, was also in its way a successor state to Byzantium, and which regarded itself as the new leader of the Orthodox world. This was Russia, whose story we left at the time of the decline of Kiev, when it was torn by internal dissension and was as well a prey to invasion by the Mongol Tatars.

In the thirteenth, fourteenth, and early fifteenth centuries, the extreme western portions of the Kievan state fell under Polish and Lithuanian influence. At the same time, the city of Novgorod in the north continued to develop its trade with the West, chiefly Germany, and its municipal institutions. But the most striking feature of Russian development was the Tatar domination of the entire northeastern and eastern regions. The Tatars exercised their domination from afar, and, except for devastating raids, did not occupy the country, though they did levy a large annual tribute upon the Russians. Not until the fifteenth century were the princes of Moscow, who for a variety of reasons had emerged as the leading power in the region, able to throw off this obligation, and even after this, the Tatars continued to maintain important settlements on Russian soil. The most important effect that the Tatar domination had on the future development of Russia was the cutting off of so vast an area from the West, and the consequent deepening of the cultural lag that we have already observed as one of the consequences of Kievan Russia's having been converted to Christianity from Byzantium.

Moreover, the princes of Moscow, in establishing themselves as supreme over the Russian lands, received from the Orthodox church, which was backing them in their endeavor, a full-fledged ideology: that Moscow was the successor of Byzantium, which had fallen to the Turks, and thus of Rome, which had fallen to the schismatic Roman Catholics. Moscow was thus the third and final Rome, and the rulers of Moscow were the direct heirs of the Byzantine emperors. The importance of this concept for future Russian historical development is sometimes disputed by scholars. But we shall try to show how deeply affected by it the Russian princes actually were, and how greatly it contributed over the centuries to their absolutist rule in practice.

II The Crusades

The Idea of a Holy War

In 964, when the Byzantine emperor Nicephorus Phocas (ruled 963–969) was about to go to war against the Arabs, he wrote a long letter to the caliph, full of insults, threats, and boasts of his previous victories:

We have conquered your impregnable fortresses . . . left piles of corpses with blood still pouring from them . . . rendered your peasants and their wives helpless in the very midst of their flocks. Lofty buildings have been destroyed. . . . When the owl hoots there now, echo answers. . . . People of Baghdad, flee at once, and bad luck to you, for your weakened empire will not last. . . . I shall march with all speed toward Mecca, bringing in my train a throng of soldiers black as night. I shall seize that city, and stay there a time at my ease, so that I may establish there a throne for the best of beings: Christ.*

In 975 Nicephorus' assassin and successor, John Tsimisces (ruled 969–976), wrote a letter to his ally, the king of Armenia, telling of his campaigns of that year against the Muslims in Syria. He had taken Damascus, he wrote, and Nazareth:

People came from Ramleh and Jerusalem, to beseech our majesty for grace. They asked of us a leader, and declared themselves to be our subjects. We gave them what they asked for. It was our wish to free the holy tomb of Christ from the insults of the Muslims. . . . If those accursed Africans [i.e., Egyptian Muslims] who now live in Caesarea on the seacoast had not taken refuge in the castles along the shore, we should have marched into the holy city of Jerusalem and should have been able to pray in those holy places.†

These two tenth-century Byzantine documents breathe the spirit of the later Western movement known as the Crusades: a holy war against the Muslims for the possession of the Holy Places. Although the Byzantines never were able to fulfill their ambition, they had the will and the intention.

Similarly, in the West, the idea of a holy war was not new in 1095. In Spain, the fighting of Christian against Muslim had been virtually continuous since the Muslim conquest in the eighth century. The small Christian states of the north pushed southward when they could, and retreated again when they had to. Just after the year 1000, the great Cordovan Caliphate weakened, and the Spanish Christian princes of the north won the support of the powerful French abbey at Cluny. Under prodding from Cluny, French nobles joined the Spaniards in warring on the Muslims. And soon the pope offered an indulgence to all who would fight for the Cross in Spain. In 1085 the Christians took the great City of Toledo, but a new wave of Muslim Berbers from North Africa set them back for a time.

* G. L. Schlumberger, *Nicéphore Phocas* (Paris, 1923), pp. 348 ff. Our translation.
† G. L. Schlumberger, *L'Epopée Byzantine* (Paris, 1896), I, 287–288. Our translation.

The Christian movement continued during the remainder of the eleventh century, and on into the twelfth. It recovered a large area of central Spain, and it was itself a crusade: a holy war against the infidel supported by the papacy. So too were the wars of the Normans in southern Italy against the Muslims of Sicily.

Pilgrimages

From the third century on, Christians had visited the scenes of Christ's life. At Jerusalem, Constantine's mother, Saint Helena, discovered the true cross and other relics of the Passion. Her son built the Church of the Holy Sepulcher. Before the Muslim conquest in the seventh century, pilgrims came from Byzantium and the West, often seeking sacred relics for their churches at home. For a while after the Muslim conquest, pilgrimages were very dangerous, and could be undertaken only by the hardiest pilgrims. Saint Willibald, an Englishman who made the journey between 722 and 729, encountered freezing cold and hunger in Asia Minor, captivity and imprisonment as a spy by Muslims in northern Syria, sickness on three different occasions, blindness at Gaza, a savage lion in the olive groves of Esdraelon, severe Muslim customs officers at Tyre (Willibald was smuggling at the time), and a volcanic eruption on an Italian island on the way home.

During the reign of Charlemagne, conditions improved for Western pilgrims, largely because of the excellent relations between Charlemagne and the famous caliph Harun al-Rashid (see Chapter 6). The caliph made him a present of the actual recess in which Christ was buried. Charlemagne was allowed to endow a hostel in Jerusalem for the use of pilgrims. He gave a splendid library to the Latin church of St. Mary, and sent money and bought land to support Christian foundations. So deep was Charlemagne's interest that there sprang up a legend that he had somehow acquired from Harun a "protectorate" over the Holy Land, and another that he had actually made a pilgrimage to the East in person. Neither of these stories is true, but they reflect the importance of the pilgrimage in Charlemagne's period.

In the tenth century, the belief grew that pilgrimage would procure God's pardon for sins.

St. James (Santiago) of Compostella in Spain, and of course Rome itself, became favorite places of pilgrimage, but no place could compare in importance with the shrines of Palestine. Large organized groups began to replace the individual journey. Great lords with suites of followers came, as well as humble clerics from all over Europe. We know of more than one hundred Western pilgrimages during the eleventh century. On one occasion, contemporaries report 7,000 German pilgrims, all traveling together.

The Late-Eleventh-Century Crisis

Stable conditions in both Muslim and Byzantine dominions were essential for the easy and safe continuance of pilgrimages. But in the early eleventh century the half-mad Egyptian ruler of Palestine, Hakim, himself a Muslim heretic, abandoned the tolerant practices of his predecessors, and began to persecute Christians and make travel to the Holy Places unsafe. Moreover, with the death of the last ruler of the Macedonian house in 1057, there began at Byzantium an open struggle between the party of the court civil servants and the military party of the great Asia Minor landowners. Simultaneously came Pecheneg invasions of the Balkans, Norman attacks on Byzantine southern Italy, and the rise in Asia of the Seljuk Turks. By 1050 the Seljuks had created a state centering on Persia. In 1055 they entered Baghdad on the invitation of the Abbasid caliph himself, and became the champions of Sunnite Islam against the Shiite rulers of Egypt. In the 1050's, Seljuk forces appeared in Armenia and Asia Minor; they raided deep into Anatolia, almost to the Aegean. Their advance culminated in the catastrophic Byzantine defeat of Manzikert in 1071, followed by the occupation of most of Asia Minor, and the establishment of a new sultanate with its capital at Nicaea. The Seljuks conquered not only much of Asia Minor but also Syria and Palestine. Jerusalem fell in the very year of Manzikert and Bari, 1071, and became part of a new Seljuk state of Syria.

Amid disorder and palace intrigue, with the empire reduced in territory and the capital in danger, there came to the Byzantine throne in 1081 Alexius I Comnenus, a general and a great

landowner, who was to found a dynasty that staved off disaster for over a century. Between 1081 and 1085, he held off the Norman attack on the Dalmatian coast by means of his alliance with Venice. He was at home in the slippery field of intrigue, playing one local Turkish potentate off against another, and slowly reestablishing a Byzantine foothold in Asia Minor. Civil wars among the Turks and the multiplication of brigands on the highways in Anatolia and Syria made pilgrimage in the two decades after Manzikert a dangerous pursuit indeed, despite the relatively decent conditions in Palestine itself.

The schism between Eastern and Western churches provided the papacy with an additional incentive for intervention in the East. The vigorous reforming popes of the later eleventh century felt that the disunity of Christendom was intolerable, the rending of a seamless garment. In 1073 Pope Gregory VII (Hildebrand) sent an ambassador to Constantinople, who reported that the emperor was anxious for a reconciliation, and emphasized the dreadful conditions brought about for travelers by the Turkish conquests in Asia Minor. Gregory VII planned to extend the holy war from Spain to Asia by sending the Byzantines an army of Western knights. Even more striking, he intended to lead them himself, and thus put himself in a position to bring about a reunion of the churches. It was only the quarrel with the German emperor (see Chapter 7) that prevented the pope from carrying out this plan. But here, more than twenty years before the opening of the First Crusade, all the elements are combined: a holy war, to be fought in alliance with the Greeks against the Muslims in Asia, under the direct sponsorship of the papacy.

The First Crusade

Pope Urban II (1088–1099) carried on the tradition of Gregory VII. To his Council at Piacenza in 1095 came envoys from Alexius, who asked for military help against the Turks. Turkish power was declining, and now would be a good time to strike. The Byzantine envoys also seem to have stressed the sufferings of the Christians in the East. Eight months later, at the Council of Clermont, Urban preached to a throng of the faithful. He emphasized the appeal received from the Eastern Christians, brothers in difficulty, and painted in dark colors the hardships that now faced pilgrims to Jerusalem. He summoned his listeners to form themselves; rich and poor alike, into an army, which God would assist. Killing each other at home should give way to fighting a holy war. Poverty at home would yield to the riches of the East (a theme especially important in view of the misery in which so many Europeans lived). If a man were killed doing this work of God, he would automatically be absolved of his sins and assured of salvation. The audience greeted this moving oration with cries of "God wills it." Throngs of volunteers took a solemn oath, and sewed crosses of cloth onto their clothes. Recruitment was under way. The First Crusade had been launched.

On the popular level, a certain Peter the Hermit, an unkempt, barefoot old man, who lived on fish and wine and was a moving orator, proved the most effective preacher of the crusade. Through France and Germany he recruited an undisciplined mob of ignorant peasants, including women and children, many of them serfs living wretched lives, suffering near-starvation as a result of crop failure. Often they believed that Peter was leading them straight to heaven, the New Jerusalem, flowing with milk and honey, which they confused with the Jerusalem on earth. People less well fitted for the tasks of the holy war can hardly be imagined.

In two installments, the rabble poured up the Rhine, across Hungary, where 4,000 Hungarians were killed in a riot over the sale of a pair of shoes, and into Byzantine territory at Belgrade. The Byzantines, who had hoped for the loan of a few hundred well-trained knights, were appalled at the prospect of the enormous armies of human locusts about to descend on them from the West. They proceeded to arrange military escorts and to take all precautions against trouble. Despite their best efforts, the undisciplined Crusaders burned houses and stole everything that was not chained down, including the lead from the roofs of churches.

Once in Constantinople, they were graciously received by Alexius Comnenus, who none the less felt it necessary to ship them across the Straits as quickly as possible. In Asia Minor they quarreled among themselves, murdered the Christian inhabitants, scored no success against the Turks, and were eventually massacred. The trouble brought upon the Byzantines by this first mob of Crusaders was a symbol of future difficulties.

Meanwhile, at the upper levels of Western society, no kings had enlisted in the Crusade, but a considerable number of great lords had been recruited, including a brother of the king of France, the duke of Normandy, and the count of Flanders. The most celebrated, however, were Godfrey of Bouillon (duke of Lower Lorraine), and his brother Baldwin, Count Raymond of Toulouse, Count Stephen of Blois, and Bohemond, a Norman prince from southern Italy. Better equipped and better disciplined, the armies led by these lords now began to converge on Constantinople by different routes, arriving at intervals. Still, there was plenty of trouble for the people on the routes. "My lips are tight," wrote the distressed Byzantine archbishop of Bulgaria, through whose see so many of the Crusaders passed. "The passage of the Franks, on their invasion, or whatever you want to call it, has upset and gripped us all. . . . As we have grown accustomed to their insults, we bear trouble more easily than we used to. Time can teach a person to get used to anything." *

The emperor Alexius was in a very difficult position. He was ready to have the Western commanders carve out principalities for themselves from the Turkish-occupied territory which they hoped to conquer. But he wanted to assure himself that lands properly Byzantine would be returned to his control, and that whatever new states might be created would be dominated by him. He knew of the Western custom of vassalage, and the importance attached to an oath taken to an overlord. So he decided to require each great Western lord to take an oath of liege homage to him on arrival. To obtain these oaths, Alexius had to resort to bribery with splendid gifts, and to all sorts of pressure, including in some cases the withholding of food supplies from the unruly crusading armies.

The armies were all ferried across the Straits. There was no supreme command, but the armies acted as a unit, following the orders of the leaders assembled in council. In June of 1097 at Nicaea, the Seljuk capital, the Turks surrendered at the

---

* J. P. Migne, *Patrologia Graeca*, CCXXVI, 324–325. Our translation.

last minute to Byzantine forces rather than suffer an assault from the Crusader armies. This the Crusaders bitterly resented, since they had not been informed of the negotiations for surrender, and had been looking forward to plundering the town. Crossing Asia Minor, the Crusaders defeated the Turks in a battle at Dorylaeum, captured the Seljuk sultan's tent and treasure, and opened the road to further advance. Godfrey's brother Baldwin, leaving the main army, marched to Edessa, a splendid ancient imperial city near the Euphrates, strategically situated for the defense of Syria from attacks coming from the East. Here, after negotiations with the local Armenian rulers, he became count of Edessa, lord of the first Crusader state to be established (1098).

Meanwhile, the main body of the army was besieging the great fortress city of Antioch, which finally was conquered by treachery after more than seven months. Antioch became the center of the second Crusader state, under the Norman Bohemond. The other Crusaders then took Jerusalem itself by assault in July 1099, followed by a slaughter of Muslims and Jews, men, women, and children.

The Crusader States

The Lorrainer Godfrey of Bouillon was chosen, not king, for he would not consent to wear a royal crown in the city where Christ had worn the crown of thorns, but "defender of the Holy Sepulcher." The third Crusader state had been founded. When Godfrey died, not long afterward, his brother Baldwin of Edessa became first king of Jerusalem in 1100.

Venetian, Genoese, and Pisan fleets now assisted in the gradual conquest of the coastal cities, ensuring sea communications with the West and the vital flow of supplies and reinforcements. In 1109 the son of Raymond of Toulouse founded the fourth and last of the Crusader states, centering around the seaport of Tripoli. The king of Jerusalem was the theoretical overlord of the other three states, but was often unable to enforce his authority. The Byzantine emperors never relinquished the rights that had been secured to them by the oath that the Crusaders had made to Alexius, and were, especially in the case of Antioch, occasionally able to assert those rights successfully.

An illumination from a fourteenth-century manuscript shows Godfrey of Bouillon before Jerusalem in 1099. At the left is Peter the Hermit.

The holdings of the Westerners lay within a long narrow coastal strip, extending from the Euphrates River to the borders of Egypt, more than five hundred miles long and seldom as much as fifty miles wide. From the Muslim cities of Aleppo, Hamah, Emesa (Homs), and Damascus, just inland from the strip, and from Fgypt to the southwest, danger constantly threatened. The Westerners failed to take obvious measures for the common defense. The great lords built superb castles at strategic places but often fought with one another, sometimes in alliance with neighboring Muslims.

The Assizes of Jerusalem—not written down until the thirteenth century, when the Muslim reconquest was nearly complete—record the governmental practice of the Crusader states. The great officers of the realm were the officers of the king's household: seneschal, constable, marshal, and the like. The high court of the barons not only adjudicated disputes but acted as council of state for the king's business. The lords had rights of justice on their own fiefs. Police and civil cases were under the direction of the viscounts, royal officers in the towns, and there were special commercial and maritime courts. The Italian commercial cities, as colonial powers, had quarters of their own in the coastal cities, with privileged status. Revenues were raised by carefully collected customs dues, by

monopolies on tanning and similar industries, by
a poll tax on Muslims and Jews, and by a land
tax on the native population. Yet in the early
days especially, money was scarce, and the kings
raided Muslim caravans or married rich wives
in an effort to bolster their shaky finances. Ecclesiastical organization was complex—the two
Latin patriarchs of Jerusalem and Antioch each
had a hierarchy of Roman Catholic archbishoprics and bishoprics subject to them, but Greek,
Syrian, and Armenian churches continued to exist, each with its own clergy, in addition to the
Muslim and Jewish faiths.

The Military Orders

Early in their colonial occupation the Westerners founded the "military orders" of knighthood. The first of these were the Templars,

started about 1119 by a Burgundian knight who
sympathized with the hardships of the Christian
pilgrims, and who banded together with several
others in a group designed to afford protection to
the helpless on their way to pray at the holy
places. The knights took the vows of poverty,
chastity, and obedience, and were given headquarters near the Temple of Solomon—hence the
name Templars. Saint Bernard himself inspired
their rule, based on the rules for his own Cistercians, and confirmed by the pope in 1128. A second order, founded shortly after, was attached to
the ancient Hospital of Saint John of Jerusalem,
and was therefore called the Hospitalers. Made
up of knights, chaplains, and serving brothers,
under the command of a master, with subordinate provincial commanders both in the East and
at home in the West, the two orders put into the
field the most effective fighting forces in the Holy
Land. Each eventually obtained a special uniform, the Templars wearing red crosses on

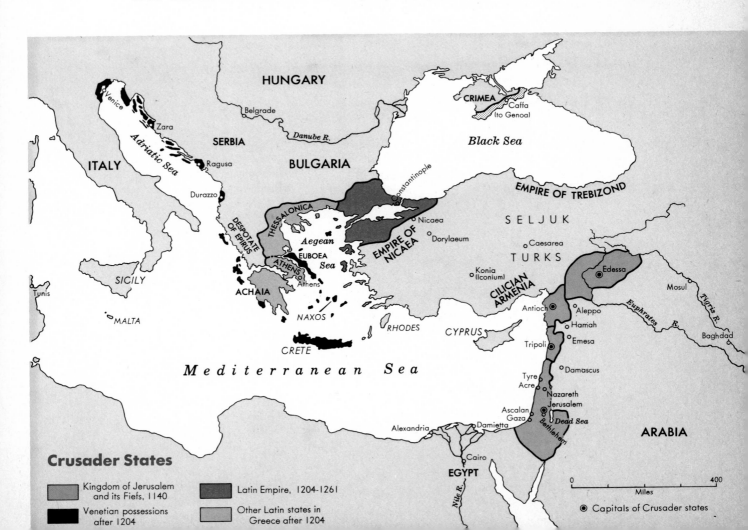

Crusader States

Kingdom of Jerusalem and its Fiefs, 1140
Venetian possessions after 1204
Latin Empire, 1204-1261
Other Latin states in Greece after 1204
● Capitals of Crusader states

white, the Hospitalers white crosses on black. Later, a third, purely German group became the order of the Teutonic Knights, and wore black crosses on white.

After their establishment, the orders grew rapidly in wealth; they had fortresses and churches of their own in the Holy Land, and villages of which they obtained the produce. Moreover, Western monarchs endowed them richly with lands in Europe. Their original purposes were soon dimmed or lost sight of, and they became another element in the complicated political, military, and ecclesiastical tangle in the Crusader states. They often allied themselves with Muslims when they thought such an alliance would be useful in pursuing their own quarrels with the nobility of the Holy Land, with its clergy, with new arrivals, with the Italian cities, and with one another. The orders so far forgot the original vows of poverty that they engaged in banking and large-scale financial operations. In the early fourteenth century, the Templars were destroyed by Philip IV of France for political reasons of his own (see Chapter 7). The Teutonic Knights, most of whose fighting was done not in the Holy Land but against the pagans of the eastern Baltic shore, were disbanded only in 1525, and transmitted some of their lands and much of their outlook toward the world to the modern state of Prussia. The Hospitalers moved first to Cyprus, and then to Rhodes in the early fourteenth century. They were driven to Malta by the Turks in 1522 and continued there until Napoleon's seizure of the island in 1798.

The Muslim Reconquest

Tormented as the Crusader states were by the political disunity that was so characteristic of feudal society at its height, it is a wonder that they lasted so long. It was not the castles or the military orders that kept them in being so much as it was the disunion of their Muslim enemies. When the Muslims did achieve unity under a single powerful leader, the Christians suffered grave losses. Thus, beginning in the late 1120's, Zangi, governor of Mosul on the Tigris (the town that gives its name to our muslin cloth), succeeded in unifying the local Muslim rulers of the region. In 1144 he took Edessa, first of the Crusader cities to fall. It was never to be recaptured. Two years later, Zangi was assassinated, but the Muslim reconquest had begun.

As an answer to the loss of Edessa, Saint Bernard himself preached the so-called Second Crusade in Europe. He aroused enormous enthusiasm, and for the first time Western monarchs—King Louis VII of France and King Conrad III of Germany—came to the East. But the Second Crusade proved a shattering failure. As the German and French armies passed through Constantinople, relations with the Byzantines were worse than ever. It is quite likely that the emperor, Manuel Comnenus (1143–1180), whose capital the Crusaders seriously considered attacking, mixed chalk with the flour that he sold them before he managed to get them across the Straits, and altogether possible that he was in touch with the Turks.

The Western armies were almost wiped out in Asia Minor. When the remnants reached the Holy Land, they found themselves in hopeless conflict with the local lords, who feared that the newcomers would take over the kingdom, and who sabotaged what might otherwise have been a successful siege of the key Muslim city—Damascus. The Crusaders' failure to take Damascus in 1149 brought its own punishment—in 1154 Zangi's son, Nureddin, took it, and Muslim Syria was united against the Latins. Saint Bernard had boasted of his success in recruiting the Crusade: "Because of my preaching, towns and castles are empty of inhabitants. Seven women can scarcely find one man." He now lamented:

We have fallen on evil days, in which the Lord, provoked by our sins, has judged the world, with justice, indeed, but not with his wonted mercy. . . . The sons of the Church have been overthrown in the desert, slain with the sword, or destroyed by famine. . . . The judgments of the Lord are righteous, but this one is an abyss so deep that I must call him blessed who is not scandalized therein.*

The next act of the Muslim reconquest was carried out in Egypt by a general of Nureddin's, who was sent in to assist one of the quarreling factions in Cairo. This general became vizier of Egypt and died in 1169, leaving his office to his nephew, the great Saladin, celebrated in both

* Quoted in T. A. Archer and C. L. Kingsford, *The Crusades* (New York, 1895), p. 220.

Krak des Chevaliers, a Crusader fortress built by the Hospitalers and taken by Saladin in 1188.

history and legend, who became the greatest single Muslim leader of the Crusade period. A vigorous and successful general, often moved by impulse, Saladin was also a chivalrous knight, whose humanity often prevailed over his natural enmity for the Christians.

Saladin brought the Muslim cities of Syria and Mesopotamia under his control and distributed them to faithful members of his own family. By 1183 his brother ruled Egypt, his sons ruled Damascus and Aleppo, and close relatives ruled all the other important centers. Internal decay in the kingdom of Jerusalem and a squabble over the throne gave Saladin his chance, and a violation of a truce by an unruly Crusader lord gave him his excuse. In 1187 Jerusalem fell, and soon there was nothing of the kingdom left to the Christians except the port of Tyre.

The Later Crusades

These were the events that elicited the Third Crusade (1189–1192). The Holy Roman Emperor, Frederick Barbarossa, led a German force through Byzantium, and aroused the usual fears with the usual foundation. But Frederick was drowned in a river in Asia Minor (1190) before reaching the Holy Land. Some of his troops, however, continued to Palestine. There they were joined by Philip Augustus of France and Richard the Lionhearted of England, deadly rivals in the West. Each was at least as interested in thwarting the other as he was in furthering what was supposed to be the common cause. The main operation of the Third Crusade was a long siege of the seaport of Acre, which lasted a year and a half, and which was finally successful in 1191. Jerusalem itself could not be recaptured, but Saladin signed a treaty with Richard allowing Christians to visit the city freely. A small strip of seacoast with Acre as center remained in the hands of the Crusaders as a pitiful remnant of the kingdom of Jerusalem. The cities of Tripoli and Antioch, their surrounding territories greatly shrunken, were also preserved.

Saladin died in 1193. His dominions were divided among his relatives, and the Christians obtained a respite. But from the end of the twelfth century on, the story of the Crusades and of the Crusader states in Syria is a mere epilogue to what has gone before. Reinforcements from the West now dwindled away to a very small trickle.

Innocent III's great effort at a Fourth Crusade was, as we shall see, diverted from the Holy Land against Byzantium, where the foundation of the Latin Empire and of a new series of states on Greek soil partly distracted the attention of Western knights. They could now choose to crusade against the schismatic Greeks instead of the infidel Muslims. The failures in the East were partly balanced by the successes in Spain, where, by the end of the thirteenth century, the Christians had restricted the Muslims to the kingdom of Granada in the southeastern corner of the peninsula. Far to the northeast, the pagan Lithuanians and Slavs received the attention of the Teutonic Knights in the Baltic region.

The zeal that had driven men toward the Holy Land was diluted, perhaps most of all, by the struggle between the papacy and its European opponents: first, the Albigensian heretics of southern France between 1208 and 1240, and second, the emperor Frederick II between 1220 and 1250 (see Chapter 7). In these affairs the popes were offering those who would fight against a purely European and nominally Christian enemy the same indulgence as they offered those who fought the infidel. All these factors no doubt brought disillusionment, especially when combined with the spectacle of repeated military failure and internal Christian dissension in the Holy Land itself.

The high point of tragic futility was the famous Children's Crusade of 1212, when throngs of French and German children went down to the Mediterranean in the expectation that its waters would divide before them and open a path to the Holy Land, along which they could march to a bloodless victory. When this failed to happen, several thousand pushed on to Marseilles and other seaports, and many were sold into slavery.

The more serious military efforts can be quickly reviewed. In the Fifth Crusade the Christians attempted the conquest of Egypt, on the sound theory that this was the center of Muslim strength. Although they took the fortress of Damietta on the Nile late in 1219, the Crusaders could not continue to Cairo, and had to surrender Damietta in 1221. Emperor Frederick II led the Sixth Crusade. The papacy excommunicated him once for failing to go on the Crusade, and a second time for going on it. No fighting was involved, partly because the Syrian Christians

would not support a ruler at odds with the pope, partly because Frederick was too sophisticated to fight when he could get what he wanted by diplomacy. Speaking Arabic and long familiar with the Muslims from his experience in Sicily, he was able to secure more for the Christians by negotiation than any military commander since the First Crusade had secured by war. In 1229 he signed a treaty with Saladin's nephew, which actually restored Jerusalem to the Latins again, except for the site of the Temple, where stood the great mosque of the Dome of the Rock. Bethlehem and Nazareth were also handed over and a ten-year truce was agreed upon.

But the gains were mourned by the Muslims and not welcomed by the Christians, who put Jerusalem under an interdict when Frederick visited it to crown himself king. The Egyptian ruler now took into his service several thousand Turks from central Asia, who had been displaced from their homes by the terrible invasions of Genghis Khan and his Mongols, then raging through western Asia and eastern Europe. These Turks took Jerusalem in 1244 and shortly thereafter thoroughly defeated the Latins in a great battle at Gaza. Jerusalem remained in Muslim hands until 1917. The Mongols themselves appeared in the neighborhood of Antioch and forced the ruler of the principality to pay tribute.

Now Saint Louis, king of France, launched the first of his two crusades, sometimes called the Seventh. Aimed at Egypt, the expedition captured Damietta once again in 1249, but Louis himself was taken prisoner in the next year and had to pay a very heavy ransom. His years in the East (1248–1254) had little practical result.

In 1250, the household troops of the Egyptian sultan, called Mamluks or slaves, took power into their own hands in Egypt. Soon after, the Mongols, fresh from their victories in Asia, where they had finally extinguished the Abbasid Caliphate in Baghdad (1258), invaded Syria itself and were defeated in an important battle in 1260 by the Mamluk general Baibars, who immediately proceeded to make himself sultan. Baibars, who had none of Saladin's chivalry, had much of his ability, and proceeded by degrees to reduce the number of strongholds remaining to the Crusaders, taking Antioch in 1268. He delayed his advance in fear of a new crusade (the Eighth) of Saint Louis in 1270, but resumed it when the king landed in Tunis and died there. The

Muslims took Tripoli in 1289 and finally Acre in 1291, massacring 60,000 Christians. The century-long epilogue to the first hundred years of crusading fervor was now over, and the Christian settlements were wiped out. They were not deeply mourned even in the lands of western Europe, from which so much blood and treasure had flowed for their establishment and defense.

The Meeting of East and West

In the minds of the men who came out to the new Crusader states, the wish to make a pilgrimage and to win the indulgence that came with the war against the infidel mingled from the first with the wish for gain and the love of adventure. Although many came only with the idea of returning home again, many others migrated with the intention of remaining. Although the population fluctuated, a new world neither Eastern nor Western but compounded of both was growing up in the narrow strip of Crusader territory. As one Crusader put it:

God has poured the West into the East; we who were Westerns are now Easterns. He who was a Roman or a Frank is now a Galilean or Palestinian. He who was from Rheims or Chartres is now a Tyrian or an Antiochene. We have all forgotten our native soil; it has grown strange unto us.*

Or if we look at it from the Muslim point of view, we find a Syrian warrior and cultivated gentleman of the twelfth century telling some revealing stories (remember as you read what follows that Mecca is *southeast* of Jerusalem):

Everyone who is a fresh immigrant from the Frankish lands is ruder in character than those who have become acclimatized and have held long association with Muslims. . . . Whenever I visited Jerusalem, I always entered the Aqsa Mosque . . . which was occupied by the Templars who were my friends. The Templars would evacuate the little adjoining mosque so that I might pray in it. One day I entered this mosque, repeated the first formula "Allah is great," and stood up in the act of praying upon which one

of the Franks rushed on me, got hold of me, and turned my face eastward saying "This is the way thou shouldst pray!" A group of Templars hastened to him, seized him, and repelled him from me. I resumed my prayer. The same man, while the others were otherwise busy, rushed once more on me and turned my face eastward, saying "This is the way thou shouldst pray!" The Templars again came in to him and expelled him. They apologized to me, saying "This is a stranger who has only recently arrived from the land of the Franks and he has never before seen anyone praying except eastward." Thereupon I said to myself, "I have had enough prayer."*

Yet, after a while, the "Franks" learn civilization:

Among the Franks are those who have become acclimatized and have associated long with Muslims. These are much better than the recent comers from the Frankish lands. But they constitute the exception, and cannot be treated as a rule. . . . We came to the home of a knight who belonged to the old category of knights who came with the early expeditions of the Franks. He had been by that time . . . exempted from service, and possessed in Antioch an estate, on the income of which he lived. The knight presented an excellent table, with food extraordinarily clean and delicious. Seeing me abstaining from food, he said, "Eat, be of good cheer! I never eat Frankish dishes, but I have Egyptian women cooks and never eat except their cooking. Besides pork never enters my home."†

Here in Usamah we find reflected the essential spirit of tolerance that moved both Christians and Muslims once they had begun to mix. Each side respected the valor of the other. The Latins were never numerous enough to cultivate the soil of Syria, and needed the labor of the Christian and Muslim peasants.

The natives were also most useful in commerce. As time passed, some Westerners married Easterners, and a race of halfbreeds came into existence. Even those who did not intermarry often had their houses, palaces, or churches built by native craftsmen. They wore oriental clothes, let their beards grow, and ate squatting on carpets, Eastern-style. Whenever

---

* Fulcher of Chartres, quoted ibid., p. 170.

* *Memoirs of Usamah Ibn-Munqibh,* trans. P. K. Hitti, (Princeton, 1930), pp. 163-164.
† Ibid., pp. 169-170.

they could get away with it, they liked to watch the Muslim dancing girls. They hired Muslim physicians, joined Muslims in tournaments and hunts, shared certain shrines, and debated the theology of each other's religions. The prince of Antioch struck a coin showing himself wearing a Muslim turban, and another with a Greek inscription describing him as the "grand Emir." The Venetians in the kingdom of Jerusalem struck coins bearing Arabic passages from the Koran. We have a respectful Arabic account of the main Christian customs house at Acre, where Arabic-speaking and Arabic-writing Christian officials sat on a carpeted platform behind gold-trimmed ebony desks, examining the merchandise arriving by caravan.

Impact of the Crusades on the West

These easternized Westerners were suspect to their fellow countrymen who were freshly arrived from the West for a pilgrimage only. Yet the temporary visitors, by the mere fact of their numbers and their return to their homes in western Europe, probably had a greater effect on European society than those who stayed in the East. The number of those who went to the East and returned home was large. From Marseilles alone, the ships of the Hospitalers and the Templars carried six thousand pilgrims a year, so many that the shipowners of the port sued the knightly orders for unfair competition. The result was what has been called a "small folk-migration," and "an active and peaceful binding together of Western Europe and Western Asia." Arabic words in Western languages testify to the concepts and products borrowed by the Westerners: in commerce, *bazaar, tariff,* the French *douane,* and the Italian *dogana* (a customs house, from the Arabic *diwan,* the sofa on which the officials sat); in foods, sugar, saffron, rice, lemons, apricots, shallots and scallions (both words derive from the name of the city of Ascalon), melons, and pistachios; in manufactured goods, cotton, muslin, damask (from Damascus), and many others.

All the new products proved a stimulus to the markets and fairs, and to the growing commercial life of the West. Venice and Genoa, the ports from which much of the produce of the East was funneled into Europe, prospered exceedingly. So did the cities of Flanders, whose own manufacture of woolen goods was stimulated by the availability of Eastern luxuries for trade. Letters of credit and bills of exchange became a necessity in an ever more complex commercial and financial system, stimulated by the vast numbers of men traveling and making financial arrangements for a journey and a long absence from home. Italian banking houses sprang up with offices in the Holy Land. The orders of knighthood—especially the Templars—played their own role in the money trade.

Thus the Crusades contributed to the introduction of new products, first luxuries and then necessities, and they helped create the conditions that called for the beginnings of modern methods of finance. In the long run, too, they probably stimulated the movement of population from the country to the towns, which in turn permitted the smaller rural population to live better on their lands, and perhaps to improve their methods of agriculture. Yet these changes, though surely speeded by the Crusades, were under way before they began, as a result in part of contact with Islam in Spain and Sicily.

About the political and religious impact of the crusading experience upon Western society, it is impossible to do more than speculate. Some historians believe that the Crusades helped to weaken and impoverish the feudal nobility, and that therefore the monarchies benefited. It is certain that kings were able to tax directly for the first time as a result of the need to raise money for the expeditions to the Holy Land. The papacy was no doubt strengthened in its climb to leadership over all Western Christendom by the initiative it took in sponsoring so vast an international movement and by the degree of control it exercised over its course; yet this short-run gain may have been outweighed by a long-run loss. The religious motive, never present unmixed even at the beginning, was more and more diluted by more worldly considerations. The spectacle of churchmen behaving like any layman in their human frailty, the misuse of the crusading indulgences for purely European papal purposes, and the cumulative effect of failure and incompetence piled upon failure and incompetence surely contributed to a disillusionment with the papal concept of the Crusades. Moreover, the mere discovery that all Muslims were not savage beasts, that profit lay in trade with them, and that living together was possible must have broadened the outlook of those who made the discovery and must have led them to question authoritative statements to the contrary even when these statements emanated from Rome.

On the whole, the influence of the Crusades upon western European art and architecture seems to have been relatively slight. It was greater in the writing of history and personal memoirs, especially in the vernacular language. In the thirteenth century, Villehardouin wrote his account of the Fourth Crusade, against Constantinople, and Joinville wrote his moving and vivid life of Saint Louis, including an account of the Seventh Crusade. The stuff of poetry was greatly enriched by the crusading experience, and whole families of *chansons de geste* owe to it their theme, their scenery, and their appeal. Still more important was the great increase in geo-graphical interest and knowledge; our first reliable maps and the beginnings of European journeys to the Far East date from the crusading period.

The fourteenth- and fifteenth-century Europeans who fought against the Ottoman Turks, who explored the West African coasts and rounded the Cape of Good Hope, emerging into the Indian Ocean and fighting Muslims there, who eventually crossed the broad Atlantic with the mistaken idea that they would find at the other side that old hypothetical ally against the Turks, the lord of the Mongols (see Chapter 14), were the direct descendants of the Crusaders of the earlier period. It is perhaps as a medieval colonization movement, inspired, like all else in the Middle Ages, largely by the Church, that the Crusades are best considered. The Westerners called the Crusader states in Syria *Outremer*, the "land beyond the sea." They were as truly overseas colonists as the followers of Columbus.

III The Fortunes of Empire, 1081-1453

Western Influences at Byzantium

During its last 372 years, the fate of the Byzantine Empire became increasingly dependent upon the actions of western Europeans. The establishment of the Italian merchants and their increasing economic power robbed the emperors of their independence on the sea. The floods of Crusaders rendered the Byzantines first uneasy, then insecure. Popular hatred mounted on both sides, until, the end of the twelfth century, it broke out in a series of violent acts, of which the Latin sack of Constantinople itself in 1204 was the climax. During the years between 1204 and 1261, while the Byzantine government was in exile from its own capital, its chief aim was to drive out the hated Latin usurper. But even after the Byzantine leaders had succeeded in 1261, they found themselves still unable to shake off the tentacles of the West. The economic and military dominance of Westerners was such that twice (1274 and 1439) the Byzantine emperors actually concluded a formal "union" with the Church of Rome, only to have it repudiated by the forces of Greek public opinion.

The Western attitude is revealed in the crisp words of the great fourteenth-century Italian poet Petrarch, who wrote:

I do not know whether it is worse to have lost Jerusalem or to possess Byzantium. In the former Christ is not recognized, in the latter he is neglected while being worshiped. The Turks are enemies but the schismatic Greeks are worse than enemies. The Turks openly attack our Empire [the Empire of the West]; the Greeks say that the Roman Church is their mother, to whom they are devoted sons; but they do not receive the commands of the Roman pontiff. The Turks hate us less because they fear us less. The Greeks both hate and fear us deep in their bellies.*

The corresponding attitude of the Greeks is shown by the famous remark of a fifteenth-century Greek churchman: that he would rather see the turban of the Turk in Constantinople than the red hat of a cardinal. Those who shared this attitude got their wish in 1453. Not even the

---

* H. A. Gibbons, *Foundation of the Ottoman Empire* (New York, 1916), p. 133. Our translation.

Ottoman Turks themselves had so great a responsibility for the downfall of Eastern Christian society as did the Western Christians. Fraternal hatred spelled disaster.

Byzantine Feudalism

This great drama of the last centuries was played out to the accompaniment of internal decay. "The powerful," in the person of Alexius Comnenus, had captured the throne itself in 1081. Thereafter the accumulation of lands and tenants—who could serve as soldiers in the landlords' private armies—seems to have gone unchecked. With the weakening of the central government and the emergence of the local magnates, a form of feudalism became the characteristic way of life on Byzantine soil. As early as the middle of the eleventh century we find the emperor granting land to be administered by a magnate in exchange for military service. Such a grant was called *pronoia*. Although it was not hereditary, and although no pronoia was held except from the emperor directly, these differences do not obscure the fundamental similarity between the pronoia and the Western fief. Military service now depended on the holders of pronoias.

In the cities, imperial police officials or local garrison commanders often formed petty dynasties of their own, acting as virtually independent potentates. Many individual Western knights entered imperial service. We find the Byzantines familiar with Western feudal concepts as early as the oath exacted by Alexius from the Crusaders; and Alexius' successors acted as feudal suzerain of the Latin principality of Antioch. Manuel Comnenus (1143–1180) had a fondness for the externals of Western life, and especially enjoyed tournaments. But the prominence of individual Westerners and the fashionable popularity of some Western customs are only surface symptoms of the feudalizing tendencies hard at work within Byzantine society.

Along with political feudalism went economic ruin and social misery, which mounted steadily as the twelfth century wore on. Periodic reassessment of the taxes gave the assessors unlimited opportunity for graft. They demanded food and lodging, presents and bribes. They would agree to turn in a fixed sum to the treasury and would then pocket the difference between this and what they could squeeze out of the taxpayer. They would seize cattle on the pretext that they were needed for work on state projects, and then sell them back to the owners and keep the money for themselves. Irregular taxes for purposes of defense gave further chances to oppress the population. With the decline of the navy, piracy became a major problem of state. The indented coasts of the Greek mainland and the numerous islands became nests of sea-raiders, preying not only on merchant shipping but upon the population on shore. Bands of wandering monks, at odds with the secular clergy, swarmed everywhere. They had no visible means of support and simply acted as brigands.

The archbishop of Athens at the end of the twelfth century tells us that a large part of the population of the countryside had actually decamped, ruined by taxes and unable to bear the exactions any longer. Those free peasants who remained were selling their land to great landowners and were becoming serfs. The end of the free peasantry, as the archbishop said, meant economic ruin to the state.

Toward the end of the twelfth century, the processes we have been describing accelerated and rapidly reached a climax. In 1171 Manuel Comnenus made a desperate effort to rid the capital of Venetian merchants by suddenly arresting all he could lay his hands on in one day. More than ten thousand were imprisoned. But the economic hold of Venice was too strong, and the emperor was soon forced to restore its privileges, though its rulers naturally remained angry with the Byzantines. In 1182, a passionate wave of anti-Latin feeling led to a savage massacre by the Constantinople mob of tens of thousands of Westerners who were resident in the capital. In 1185 the Normans of Sicily, pursuing their century-old wars against the empire, avenged the Latins by sacking Thessalonica, second city of the Byzantines. The last of the Comnenian dynasty, Andronicus I (ruled 1183–1185), was torn to pieces by the frantic citizens of Constantinople as the Norman forces approached the city walls. The weak dynasty of the Angeloi succeeded.

Four years later, in 1189–90, the crusading forces of the Western emperor Frederick Barbarossa nearly opened hostilities against the Greeks. Frederick's son, Henry VI, married a

Norman Sicilian princess and inherited both her ancestors' feud with the Byzantines and his own father's frustrated wish to seize Constantinople. Henry prepared a great fleet designed for a major attack on Byzantium, but he died in 1197 just as it was about ready to sail. Against this background of smoldering hatred, always on the point of bursting into the flames of open warfare, we can best understand the "diversion" of the Fourth Crusade.

The Fourth Crusade

In 1195 Alexius III Angelus deposed, blinded, and imprisoned his elder brother, Emperor Isaac Angelus (ruled 1185–1195). Just three years later, there came to the papal throne the great Innocent III, who soon called for a new crusade. No monarchs were to go on this expedition, but Count Baldwin of Flanders, and numbers of other powerful lords, took the cross. They decided to proceed to the Holy Land by sea and applied to the Venetians for transportation and food. The Venetians agreed to furnish these at a high price, more than the Crusaders could pay, and also to contribute fifty armed warships, on condition that they would share equally in all future conquests. It is quite likely that the shrewd old doge (duke) of Venice, the eighty-year-old, blind Enrico Dandolo, intended from the first to use the Crusaders' indebtedness to him as an excuse to employ their military might for his own purposes. Indeed, he agreed to forgive the debt temporarily if the Crusaders would help him reconquer Zara, a town on the Dalmatian side of the Adriatic, down the coast from Venice, which had revolted against Venetian domination and had gone over to the king of Hungary. So the Crusade began with the sack and destruction of a Roman Catholic town in 1202. Angrily, the pope excommunicated the Crusaders. But worse was to follow.

The son of the blinded Isaac Angelus, known as the young Alexius, had escaped to the West and was trying hard to recruit assistance to overthrow his uncle, the usurper Alexius III, and to restore Isaac. The brother of the late Henry VI, Philip of Swabia, candidate for the Western imperial throne, had married a daughter of Isaac, and welcomed his brother-in-law, the young

Alexius, with sympathy not unmixed with the family's traditional ambitions. Philip had many followers among the Crusaders. At this moment, after the siege of Zara, the young Alexius offered to pay off the rest of the Crusaders' debt to Venice and to assist their efforts in the Holy Land if they would go first to Constantinople and restore his father. This suited the ambitions of both the Venetians and the sympathizers of Philip of Swabia. Although many of the knights disapproved of the "diversion" and some left the Crusade to go on their own to Palestine, most went along with the decision.

Thus it was that in the spring of 1203 the Venetian fleet with the Crusaders aboard made its appearance in the Sea of Marmora:

Now you may know that those who had never before seen it gazed much at Constantinople; for they could not believe that there could be in all the world so mighty a city, when they saw those high walls and those mighty towers, with which it was girt all round, and those rich palaces and lofty churches, of which there were so many that no man could believe it unless he had seen it with his own eyes, and the length and breadth of the city, which of all others was the sovereign. And know well that there was no man so bold that his flesh did not creep, and this was no wonder; for never was so great an undertaking entered upon by human beings since the world was made.*

In July 1203 the Crusaders took the city by assault. Isaac was set free and his son, the young Alexius, was crowned as Alexius IV. Alexius III fled with as much treasure as he could carry. During the next few months, the Crusaders stayed in the neighborhood of the capital, waiting for Alexius IV to pay off his obligation to them. A great fire broke out, for which the Greek population blamed the Latins. A popular revolution put on the throne a new anti-Latin emperor, who strangled Alexius IV. In March 1204 the Crusaders drew up a solemn treaty with their Venetian allies, agreeing to seize the city a second time, to divide up all the booty, to elect a Latin emperor, who was to have a quarter of the empire, and to divide the other three-quarters

---

* G. de Villehardouin, *La Conquête de Constantinople*, ed. E. Faral (Paris, 1938), I, 131. Our translation.

evenly between the Venetians and the non-Venetians. If the emperor proved to be a Venetian, the non-Venetians were to name a Latin patriarch, and vice versa.

Then came the second siege, the second capture, and the dreadful sack of Byzantium. Here is the account of a Greek historian:

How shall I begin to tell of the deeds done by these wicked men? They trampled the images underfoot instead of adoring them. They threw the relics of the martyrs into filth. They spilt the body and blood of Christ on the ground, and threw it about. . . . They broke into bits the sacred altar of Santa Sophia, and distributed it among the soldiers. When the sacred vessels and the silver and gold ornaments were to be carried off, they brought up mules and saddle horses inside the church itself and up to the sanctuary. When some of these slipped on the marble pavement and fell, they stabbed them where they lay and polluted the sacred pavement with blood and filth. A harlot sat in the Patriarch's seat, singing an obscene song and dancing frequently. They drew their daggers against anyone who opposed them at all. In the alleys and streets, in the temple, one could hear the weeping and lamentations, the groans of men and the shrieks of women, wounds, rape, captivity, separation of families. Nobles wandered about in shame, the aged in tears, the rich in poverty.*

The pope himself fulminated against the outrages committed by the Crusaders. What was destroyed in the libraries of the capital we shall never know. Besides the relics, some of the most notable works of art were sent to the West, among them the famous gilded bronze horses from the Hippodrome, still to be seen over the door of St. Mark's in Venice.

The Latin Empire

After the sack, the Latins set about governing their conquest. They elected Baldwin of Flanders as first Latin emperor, and the title continued in his family during the fifty-seven years of Latin occupation. The Venetians chose the first Latin patriarch and kept a monopoly on that rich office. The territories of the empire were divided on

paper, since most of them had not yet been conquered. The Venetians secured for themselves the long sea route from Venice by claiming the best coastal towns and strategic islands. A strange hybrid state was created, in which the emperor's council consisted half of his own barons and half of members of the Venetian merchant colony under the leadership of their governor. Though in theory the Latin emperors were the successors of Constantine and Justinian, and wore the sacred purple boots, in practice they never commanded the loyalty of the Greek population and could never make important decisions without the counsel of their barons.

They were not only surrounded by hostile Greeks but had as neighbor the new Bulgarian Empire, whose ruler promptly went to war against them, took Baldwin prisoner, and had him murdered in prison. Across the Straits, Greek refugees from Constantinople, under Theodore Lascaris, set up a state in Nicaea. The Latins could not concentrate upon the enemies in Asia because of the threat from Europe. Outnumbered, incompetent as diplomats, slow to learn new military tactics, miserably poor after the treasures of Byzantium had been siphoned away, the Westerners could not maintain their Latin Empire, especially after its main sponsors ceased to be able to assist it. When the popes became deeply involved in their quarrel with the Western emperor Frederick II, the Latin Empire was doomed. It was the Greeks of Nicaea who eventually recaptured their capital in 1261 and reestablished the Byzantine Empire.

Meanwhile, however, the Latins had fanned out from Constantinople, and also had made landings in continental Greece. Greece was divided into a whole series of feudal principalities. There were now French dukes of Athens, worshiping in the Parthenon, which had been an Orthodox church of the Virgin and now became a Roman Catholic shrine dedicated to her. The Peloponnesus, the southern peninsula of Greece, became the principality of Achaia, with twelve great feudal baronies and many minor lordships. Thessalonica became the capital of a new kingdom, which, however, fell to the Greeks in 1224. In the islands of the Aegean a Venetian adventurer established the "duchy of the Archipelago" (from the words meaning "Aegean Sea"), and other barons, mostly Italian, founded themselves tiny lordships among the islands. The Venetians held Crete

* Nicetas Choniates, *Historia*, ed. I. Bekker (Bonn, 1835), pp. 757 ff. Condensed; our translation.

Two of the gilded bronze horses taken by the Venetians from the Hippodrome at Byzantium and installed at St. Mark's Cathedral, Venice.

and the long island of Euboea off the coast of Attica.

In the new world of Latin Greece, chivalry, castles, tournaments, all the externals of Western feudal society, were so faithfully copied that in the 1220's Pope Honorius III called it "as it were, New France." Templars, Hospitalers, and Teutonic Knights had lands there. The laws were codified in the Assizes of Romania, like the Assizes of Jerusalem a valuable sourcebook of feudal custom. As in the Latin states of Syria, intermarriage took place between Latins and Greeks, but the native population never really became reconciled to alien domination. As in Syria, the traces of Latin rule are seen most clearly only in the remains of the great castles and not in any lasting impression upon the native society. The feudal states of Greece lasted for varying periods, but most of them were wiped out during the long process of Turkish conquest in the fifteenth century, and none existed after the sixteenth.

Byzantium after 1261

When the Greeks of Nicaea, under Michael VIII Palaeologus (1258–1282), recaptured their capital, they found it depopulated and badly damaged, and the old territory of the empire mostly in Latin hands. It was impossible for Michael and his successors to reconquer more than occasional fragments of continental Greece

317

or the islands, to push the frontier in Asia Minor east of the Seljuk capital of Konia, or to deal effectively with the challenge of the Serbians in the Balkans. Michael VIII's diplomacy was distinguished for its subtlety even by Byzantine standards. He staved off the threat posed to his empire by Charles of Anjou, younger brother of Saint Louis, to whom the popes had given the south Italian kingdom of the Normans and Hohenstaufens. Just as a new and powerful force appeared headed for Byzantium from Sicily, Michael helped precipitate the revolt of 1282, known as "the Sicilian Vespers." The French were massacred by the population, Charles of Anjou's plans had to be abandoned, and the way was open for the conquest of Sicily by the Aragonese from Spain.

So incompetent and frivolous were most of the successors of Michael VIII that they contributed materially to the decline of their own beleaguered empire. Wars among rival claimants for the throne tore the empire apart internally at the very moment when the preservation of unity in the face of external enemies seemed of the utmost necessity. The social unrest that we noticed as characteristic of the period before the Latin conquest reappeared in even sharper form, as Thessalonica, second city of the empire, was torn by civil strife. For a few years in the 1340's, Thessalonica was run as a kind of independent republic by a lower-class party known as the zealots. New theological controversy, which, as usual, barely concealed political disagreements, rent the clergy, already tormented by the choice between uniting with Rome or perishing. The currency, debased for the first time under the Comnenoi, was now allowed to drift.

At one moment in the 1350's the leader of the Serbian state, the lawgiver king Stephen Dushan, proclaimed himself emperor of the Serbians and Greeks (much as the Bulgarian prince Simeon had done in the tenth century). In 1355 Dushan was about to seize Constantinople and make it the capital of a new Greco-

The Anastasis: fresco in the Church of the Chora, Istanbul (fourteenth century). Note the locks, bolts, and hinges of the smashed gates of Hell, as Christ raises Adam and Eve from the dead.

Slavic state when he suddenly died. The Genoese and the Venetians, usually at war with each other, interfered at every turn in the internal affairs of the empire.

The Advance of the Ottoman Turks

It was the Ottoman Turks, however, who gave the empire the final blow. These Turks were the ablest and luckiest of the groups to whom the Seljuk Empire in Asia Minor was now passing as it disintegrated. We find them in the last quarter of the thirteenth century settled on the borders of the province of Bithynia, across the Straits from Constantinople. This region had been the center of Greek resistance to the Latins during the Latin Empire and the base of the movement for the reconquest of the capital. Economic and political unrest led the discontented population of this region to turn to the Ottomans in preference to the harsh and ineffetual officials of the Byzantine government. As a whole, the Turks were not fanatical Muslims, and they had no racial distaste for the Greek population, from whom, in fact, they were anxious to learn.

The Ottoman conquest of Bithynia was a kind of gradual penetration, beginning with cattle raids and continuing with the acquisition of land. The farmers willingly paid tribute to the Turks, and as time went on many of them were converted to Islam in order to avoid the payment. They learned Turkish, and taught the nomadic Turkish conquerors some of the arts of a settled agricultural life; the Turks, in turn, adopted Byzantine practices in government. One interesting institution that probably speeded the process of assimilation of the two peoples was the Ottoman corporations of the Akhis, a curious combination of craft guild, monastic order, and social service agency. Highly tolerant, the Akhis were organized according to the craft or trade of their members. They were intensely pious Muslims who were determined to fight tyrannical government. In the towns of Anatolia they built hostels for travelers, where they gave religious dances and read the Koran. They presented Islam at its most attractive and thus aided the Christians to become converted. Within a generation or two it is likely that the original Ottoman Turks had become very highly mixed with the native Greeks of Anatolia.

Even before this process had got very far the Turks had begun to conquer the cities of Bithynia, and to engage in open warfare with the Byzantines. The Turks built a fleet and began raiding in the Sea of Marmora and the Aegean. It was not long before they were invited into Europe by one of the rival claimants to the Byzantine throne, who in 1354 allowed them to establish themselves in the Gallipoli peninsula. Soon they were occupying much of the neighboring province of Thrace. In 1363 they moved their capital to the city of Adrianople, on the European side of the Straits. Constantinople was now surrounded by Turkish territory, and could be reached from the west only by sea. In order to survive at all, many of the later emperors had to reach humiliating arrangements with the Turkish rulers—in some cases becoming their vassals.

The Byzantine Empire survived down to 1453. But its survival was no longer in its own hands. The Turks chose to conquer much of the Balkan region first, putting an end to the independent Bulgarian and Serbian states in the 1370's and 1380's. The final defeat of the Serbs at the battle of Kossovo on June 28, 1389, has long been celebrated by the defeated Serbs themselves in poetry and song. June 28, Saint Vitus' day, is their national holiday, and the day on which the archduke Franz Ferdinand was assassinated by the Serb nationalists in 1914. A European "crusade" against the Turks was wiped out at Nicopolis on the Danube in 1396.

But Turkish conquests were delayed for half a century when a new wave of Mongols under Timur (celebrated in our literature as Tamerlane) emerged from central Asia in 1402 and defeated the Ottoman armies at Ankara in the Anatolian plateau, the present-day capital of Turkey. Like most Mongol efforts, this proved a temporary one, and the Ottoman armies and state recovered. In the 1420's and 1430's, the Turks moved into Greece; and the West, now thoroughly alarmed at the spread of Turkish power in Europe, tried to bolster the Byzantine defenses by proposing a union of the Eastern and Western churches in 1439 and by dispatching another "crusade" to Bulgaria in 1444. Both efforts proved futile.

With the accession of Mohammed II to the Ottoman throne in 1451, the doom of Constantinople was sealed. His skillful Hungarian engineer cast for him an enormous cannon that fired great stone balls. It took two months to drag the cannon from Adrianople to the walls of Constantinople. New Turkish castles on the Bosporus were able to prevent ships from delivering supplies to the city. In 1453 strong forces of troops and artillery were drawn up in siege array, and at one moment the Turks dragged a fleet of small boats uphill on runners and slid them down the other side into the Golden Horn itself. As final defeat grew more and more inevitable, the Greeks and Latins inside the city took communion together inside Santa Sophia for the last time, and the last emperor, Constantine XI, died bravely defending the walls against the Turkish onslaught.

On May 29, 1453, with the walls breached and the emperor dead, the Turks poured into the city. Mohammed II, the Conqueror, gave thanks to Allah in Santa Sophia itself and ground the altar of the sanctuary beneath his feet. Thenceforth it was to be a mosque. When he passed through the deserted rooms of the imperial palace, he is said to have quoted a Persian verse on the transitoriness of human power: "The spider has become the chamberlain in the palace of Afrasiab, and has woven her curtain before the door; the owl is now the trumpeter upon the battlements thereof." Shortly thereafter, he installed a new Greek patriarch, and proclaimed himself protector of the Christian church. On the whole, during the centuries that followed, the Orthodox church accepted the sultans as successors to the Byzantine emperors.

IV   The Ottoman Successor-State, 1453-1699

Part of the Ottomans' inheritance no doubt came from their far-distant past in central Asia, when, like other Turks, they had almost surely come under the direct or indirect influence of China, and had lived like other nomads of the steppe. Their fondness and capacity for war and their rigid adherence to custom may go back to this early period, as did their native Turkish language. From the Persians and the Byzantines, who themselves had been influenced by Persia, the Turks seem to have derived their exaltation of the ruler, their tolerance of religious groups outside the state religion, and their practice of encouraging such groups to form independent communities inside their state. Persian was always the literary language and the source of Turkish literature, both in form and in content. From Islam, the Turks took the sacred law and their approach to legal problems, the Arabic alphabet in which they wrote their Turkish tongue, and the Arabic vocabulary of religious, philosophical, and other abstract terms. All the wellsprings of their inheritance—Asiatic, Persian-Byzantine, and Muslim—tended to make them an exceptionally conservative people.

The Ottoman System

Fortunate in finding their neighbors weak as they themselves grew in strength, and fortunate in their geographic position as near neighbors to the Byzantines, the Ottomans allowed the peoples that they conquered to pass through a stage of vassalage rather than insisting upon immediate annexation by force. Until the sixteenth century they showed tolerance to their infidel subjects, permitting Christians and Jews to serve the state, and allowing the patriarch of Constantinople and the Grand Rabbi to act as leaders of their own religious communities, or *millets*. The religious leader not only represented his flock in its dealings with the Ottoman state but also had civil authority over them in civil, judicial, and financial matters that affected them alone. Non-Muslims paid a head-tax and lived in peace. The patriarch of Constantinople exercised far more power than he ever had under the Byzantines.

From 1280 to 1566 ten successive able sultans ruled the Ottomans. They received early training in administration, and were expected on their accession to kill off all their brothers—on one occasion there were nineteen victims—in order to forestall civil strife. In theory, the sultan possessed the entire wealth of his dominions, and his object was to exploit it to the full. To do so he maintained an elaborate system of administrators whose lives and property belonged absolutely to him, all of whom were slaves (*kullar*), and at the same time members of the ruling class (Ottomans). To belong to the ruling class a man had to be loyal to the sultan, a Muslim, and a true

Sultan Mohammed II (ruled 1451–1481): a painting by Gentile Bellini.

Ottoman: that is, he had to master the "Ottoman way" of speaking and behaving. All those who lacked one or more of these attributes were not members of the ruling class, but subjects (*raya*, literally "cattle"). A raya could become an Ottoman by acquiring the three necessary attributes. Beyond the activities of collecting, spending, and increasing the imperial revenues, and defending and adding to the imperial possessions, the Ottomans had no duties, and rayas could, in their own millets, take care of everything else.

The Ottoman ruling class included four subdivisions, the "men of the emperor," the "men of the sword," the "men of the pen," and the "sages." The first—the imperial class—comprised an inner service, embracing the sultan himself and his wives, sons, servants, private purse, and palace attendants, including the entire harem;

and an outer service, including the grand viziers and the other highest officers of the state, those who directed all the other branches of the service. In the early days of the Ottoman Empire, the Turkish princely families from Anatolia virtually monopolized both the inner and the outer services of this imperial class. But as early as the fourteenth century, and even more markedly in the fifteenth, the sultans learned to balance their influence by recruiting new talent from among the newly acquired Christian subjects. Some entered the system as prisoners of war; some the sultan bought or received as presents. But most he obtained through the regular levying of the *devshirme*, or tribute of children.

Every four years until sometime in the seventeenth century, specially trained officers, each with a quota of places to fill, visited the Balkan and Anatolian villages and selected and took away the strongest and ablest-appearing unmarried Slavic or Albanian or Greek youths, between the ages of ten and twenty, especially those between fourteen and eighteen. Though many Christian families naturally hated and feared the practice, some may even have welcomed it, since it held out to the luckiest and most intelligent unlimited opportunities for advancement. The recruits had to accept Islam, and though we know of a few cases of resistance or escape, most seem to have become good Muslims, or at least indifferent to religious matters. All then received a systematic education, perhaps a tenth of the group every year going on to higher studies, and the very cream of the crop attending the sultan's own palace school as pages in his household. Here they studied languages, Muslim and Turkish law, ethics, and theology, as well as horsemanship and military science. Each year the state increased their allowance and reviewed their progress. If a man who had not at first been selected for one of the higher schools proved unexpectedly able, he would be transferred to one.

All left school at the age of twenty-five, and the top men received posts in the imperial class. One sixteenth-century Slav graduated from the page corps as a gatekeeper, advanced to chief taster to the sultan, moved to the cavalry and became a general, then equerry, then commander of the picked infantry corps, governor of Egypt, and finally passed through the three grades of vizier, finishing his career as grand vizier, the very top officer of the state. So the devshirme recruits, all originally Christian, competed with the older Turkish aristocratic families for the honor of staffing the imperial class. A grand vizier presided over the council of state, and if the sultan trusted him might exercise great influence. If not, the sultan would depose or kill him: as a slave, the vizier was completely subject to the sultan's whim.

The "men of the sword" included all those connected with the Ottoman armies. In addition to the usual irregular troops and the garrison forces, these were the cavalrymen, or *spahis,* who predominated in the early centuries of Ottoman history. They received fiefs of land, (*timars,* or in the case of big fiefs, *ziamets*) in exchange for service and could administer these fiefs as they wished, collecting taxes from their tenants and keeping order and justice among them. The infantrymen, at first far less important, received fixed salaries from the treasury. But with the introduction of gunpowder and the development of artillery and rifles, the Ottomans founded a special new corps to use these weapons, the *yeni cheri* (new troops, janissaries). Most of the janissaries came from the devshirme recruits who were not selected for training for the imperial class. The janissaries lived in special barracks in the capital and enjoyed special privileges. A source of strength, they also posed a constant potential danger to the state.

At the height of Turkish military successes, the Sultans could put into the field formidable armies, sometimes amounting to more than a quarter of a million men on the march. They were absolutely fearless in battle and were the terror of all opponents. An ambassador from the Hapsburgs who spent eight years in Constantinople between 1554 and 1562 compares their endurance favorably with that of European troops. The Turks, he says:

. . . take out a few spoonfuls of flour and put them into water, adding some butter, and seasoning the mess with salt and spices; these ingredients are boiled and a large bowl of gruel is thus obtained. Of this they eat once or twice a day. . . . It is the patience, self-denial, and thrift of the Turkish soldier that enable him to face the most trying circumstances and come safely out of the dangers that surround him. What a contrast to our men! Christian soldiers on a campaign refuse to put up with their ordinary food and call for thrushes, and other such like dainty dishes. . . .

It makes me shudder to think what the result of a struggle between such different systems can be. . . .*

The "men of the pen" performed the other duties of government, striving to see that all land was tilled and all trade carried on as profitably as possible so that the sultan might obtain his share in taxes. Once the money came in, these officials spent it on the necessary expenses of state, including all salaries for troops and other employees. To keep an official honest and zealous, the Ottoman system often rewarded him by giving him in lieu of salary a portion of the sultan's property to exploit for himself, a kind of fief, from which he might make as much money as he could by administering it. Sometimes he had to turn in a portion of his proceeds as revenue to the sultan, and more rarely he received a salary and had to turn in all the proceeds. In the countryside every farm and village, in town every business and trade, in the government every job thus became a kind of fief. As the Ottoman system declined in the seventeenth and eighteenth centuries, the transformation of these fiefs in land or money into private possessions without obligations signalized the loss by the sultan's administration of its former power to extract wealth from all its resources.

The "sages" (*ulema*) included all those connected with religion: the judges who applied Muslim law in the courts, the teachers in the schools, and the scholars of the Koran and the holy law (*Shariya*), the *muftis.*

The muftis, or jurists, answered questions that arose in the course of lawsuits and that were submitted to them by the judges. It was their function to apply the sacred law of Islam, and they usually gave short replies, without explanation. These replies settled the case. The grand mufti in Istanbul, whom the sultan himself consulted, was known as the *Sheikh-ul-Islam,* the ancient or elder of Islam, and outranked everybody but the grand vizier. Since he could speak the final word on the sacred law, he may even be said to have exercised a kind of check on the absolute power of the sultan himself. He alone could proclaim the beginning of war, or denounce a sultan for transgression of the sacred

* O. G. Busbecq, *Turkish Letters,* trans. C. T. Forster and F. H. B. Daniell (London, 1881), I, 220–221.

law, and summon his subjects to depose him. The opinions of the muftis were collected as a body of interpretative law, lying between the changeless, age-old sacred law of Islam and the current enactments of the sultans. The general acceptance by all Muslims of the supremacy of the sacred law and the reluctance of the muftis to accept change were two of the factors that accounted for the failure of the Ottoman system to develop with the times. There are no "reformations" in Turkish history until the twentieth century.

The effectiveness of this entire structure depended upon the character of the sultan himself. After the mid-sixteenth century, all were brought up in the stifling seclusion of the harem, with its constant quarrels and intrigues between rival concubines, and its often debilitating pleasures. After the first ten generations, the sultans mostly were weaklings, drunkards, debauchees, and men of little experience or political understanding. Harem intrigue played a great role in the state. But in its earlier centuries the Ottoman system flourished and its territories grew.

Ottoman Expansion to 1566

By the end of the 1460's most of the Balkan Peninsula had been consolidated under Turkish rule, except for the tiny Slavic mountain region of Montenegro, which maintained a precarious independent existence. Thus the core of the new Ottoman state was Asia Minor and the Balkans, the same core around which the Byzantine Empire had been built. From this core before the death of Mohammed II in 1481, the Turks expanded across the Danube into modern Romania, seized the Genoese outposts in the Crimea, and made this southern Russian region a vassal state under its Tatar rulers. They also fought against the Venetians and even landed forces in Italy. The limits of their expansion were marked by the great Hungarian fortress of Belgrade, key to a further advance into central Europe, and the island fortress of Rhodes in the Mediterranean, stronghold of the Hospitalers and key to a further naval advance westward.

Sultan Selim I (1512–1520) nearly doubled the territories of the empire, but almost exclusively in Asia, at the expense of the Persians, and

in Africa, where Egypt was annexed in 1517 and the rule of the Mamluks ended. From them the sultan inherited the duty of protecting Mecca and Medina. He also assumed the title of caliph, with the sacred insignia of office. It is doubtful whether this alone greatly enhanced his prestige, since the title had for centuries been much abused. At one moment in his reign, Selim contemplated a general massacre of all his Christian subjects. Only the refusal of the Sheikh-ul-Islam to grant his consent saved the Christians. This episode vividly illustrates the precariousness of Christian life under the Turks. It also demonstrates that the character of the Ottoman state was substantially altered by the acquisition of so much territory. It was now no longer necessary to appease the Christians by generous treatment, because the overwhelming majority of the population was Muslim. Moreover, most of the newly acquired Muslims were Arabs, more fanatical than the Ottoman Turks had hitherto been.

Suleiman the Magnificent (1520–1566), contemporary of the Western emperor Charles V and of Francis I of France and Henry VIII of England, resumed the advance into Europe. Indeed, the Ottoman Empire now became deeply involved in western European affairs. It participated in the dynastic wars between the imperial house of Hapsburg and the French Valois, and affected the course of the Protestant Reformation in Germany by the threat of military invasion from the southeast. The newly consolidated national monarchies of the West had begun to outclass the old European enemies of the Turks, the Venetians and the Hungarians. Charles V had inherited Spain and now had to face the naval attacks of the Ottoman fleets. His younger brother, Ferdinand, as ruler of the Austrian and later the Hungarian territories, bore the brunt of the Turkish attacks on land. Cheering the Turks on were the French. Even though their king was the eldest son of the Church, their wars against the Hapsburgs came first.

In 1521 Suleiman took Belgrade, and in 1522 Rhodes, thus removing the two chief obstacles to westward advance. In 1526, at Mohács in Hungary, he defeated the Christian armies, and the Turks entered Buda, the Hungarian capital on the middle Danube. In September 1529 Suleiman besieged Vienna itself, posing a threat to Christendom greater than any since Leo III and Charles Martel had defeated the advance guard of the Arabs in the early eighth century. But the Turkish lines of communication were greatly overextended; Suleiman had to abandon the siege after two weeks. Finally, in 1533, Ferdinand recognized Suleiman as overlord of Hungary. In the years that followed, Suleiman made good his claim to actual control over the south-central portion of Hungary, and added other lands north and east of the Danube. In North Africa he acquired Algeria, which remained an Ottoman vassal state in the western Mediterranean until the nineteenth century. In Asia he defeated the Persians, annexed modern Iraq, including Baghdad itself, and secured an outlet on the Persian Gulf. He even fought naval wars against the Portuguese in the Persian Gulf and the Indian Ocean.

The emperor Charles V shown victorious over Suleiman in a sixteenth-century painting ascribed to Cornelis Cornelisz.

In 1536 a formal treaty was concluded between France and the Ottoman Empire, the first of the famous "capitulations." It permitted the French to buy and sell throughout the Turkish dominions on the same basis as any Turk. They could have resident consuls with civil and criminal jurisdiction over Frenchmen in Turkey. In Turkish territory, Frenchmen were to enjoy complete religious liberty, and were also granted a protectorate over the Holy Places, the old aim of the Crusades. This was a great advance in prestige for the Roman Catholic church. The Orthodox church never accepted this settlement, and the same old dispute helped touch off the Crimean War in the nineteenth century. These "capitulations" gave the French a better position in the Ottoman Empire than that of any other European power and thus contributed to the wealth and prestige of France. They also brought the Turks into the diplomatic world of western Europe. And they are particularly interesting as parallels to the earlier Byzantine trade treaties with Venice and Genoa, who had received virtually the same privileges beginning at the end of the eleventh century. In this respect, as in so many others, the Ottoman sultans were behaving as the successors of the Byzantine emperors.

Ottoman Decline, 1566-1699

After Suleiman, the Ottoman system, already manifesting signs of weakness, deteriorated despite occasional periods of Turkish success. The Ottoman capture of Cyprus in 1571 led to the formation of a Western league against the Turk, headed by the pope, an enterprise as near to a crusade as the sixteenth century could produce. In 1571 the league won the great naval battle of Lepanto, off the Greek coast. It destroyed the Ottoman fleet, but failed to follow up the victory, permitting the Turks to recover.

By the end of the century, the sale of government offices had become a regular practice, and the repeated rebellions of janissaries were jeopardizing the sultan's position. In 1606, a peace was signed that put an end to one of the perennial wars with the Hapsburgs. Previously, all treaties with Western states had been cast in the form of a truce granted as a divine favor from the sultan to a lesser potentate, and had been accompanied by a provision that the other party would

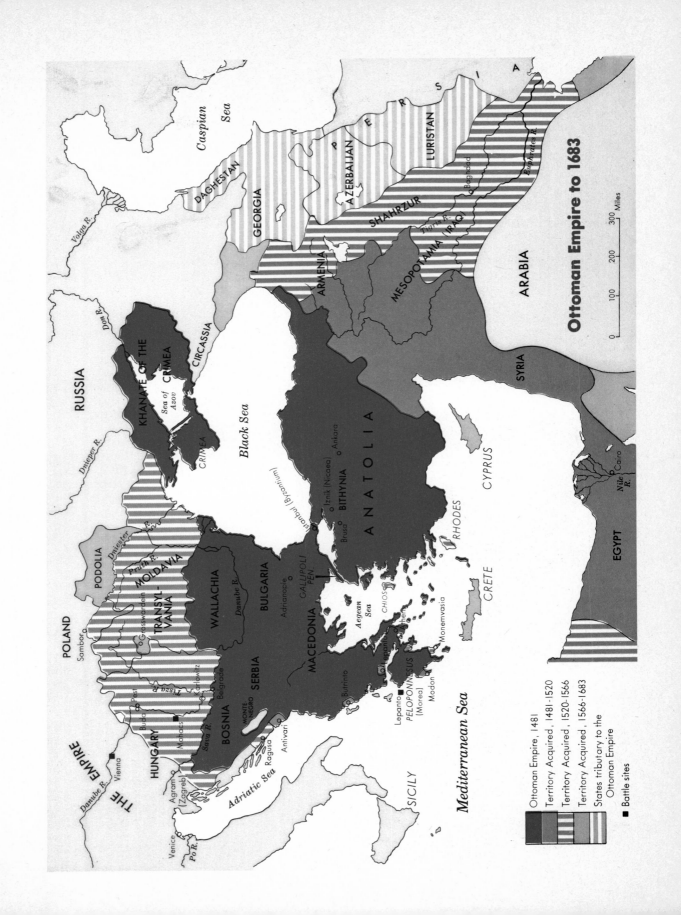

Ottoman Empire to 1683

0   100   200   300   Miles

RUSSIA

Caspian Sea

DAGHESTAN

GEORGIA

P E R S I A

AZERBAIJAN

LURISTAN

Euphrates R.

Baghdad

SHAHRZUR

Tigris R.

ARMENIA

MESOPOTAMIA (IRAQ)

CIRCASSIA

ARABIA

Volga R.

Don R.

Dnieper R.

KHANATE OF THE CRIMEA

Sea of Azov

CRIMEA

Black Sea

ANATOLIA

Ankara

Iznik (Nicaea)

BITHYNIA

Brusa

Istanbul (Byzantium)

SYRIA

CYPRUS

Cairo

Nile R.

EGYPT

POLAND

Dniester R.

PODOLIA

Prut R.

MOLDAVIA

TRANSYL-VANIA

Grosswardein

Sombor

Tisza R.

Karlowitz

Belgrade

WALLACHIA

Danube R.

BULGARIA

Adrianople

GALLIPOLI PEN.

Aegean Sea

CHIOS

RHODES

CRETE

Monemvasia

Athens

Lepanto

PELOPONNESUS (Morea)

Modon

Butrinto

Mediterranean Sea

SICILY

THE EMPIRE

HUNGARY

Vienna

Danube R.

Buda

Pest

Mohacs

SERBIA

Sava R.

BOSNIA

MONTE NEGRO

Ragusa

Antivari

Adriatic Sea

Agram (Zagreb)

Venice

Po R.

MACEDONIA

Legend:
- Ottoman Empire, 1481
- Territory Acquired, 1481-1520
- Territory Acquired, 1520-1566
- Territory Acquired, 1566-1683
- States tributary to the Ottoman Empire
- ■ Battle sites

pay tribute as part of the settlement. This time the Turks had to negotiate as equals. They gave the Hapsburg emperor his proper title, and were unable to demand tribute.

Indeed, had it not been for the convulsion of the Thirty Years' War, which preoccupied the states of western Europe (see Chapter 13), the Ottoman Empire might have suffered even more severely in the first half of the seventeenth century than it did. As it was, internal anarchy rent the state; troops rioted, and several sultans were deposed within a few years; the Persians recaptured Baghdad; and rebellion raged in the provinces. In 1622, the British ambassador wrote to his government:

The Empire has become, like an old body, crazed through many vices. All the territory of the Sultan is dispeopled for want of justice, or rather by reason of violent oppression: so much so that in his best parts of Greece and Anatolia a man may ride three, four, and sometimes six days, and not find a village to feed him and his horse. The revenue is so lessened that there is not wherewithal to pay the soldiers and maintain the court.*

Here we are already encountering what nineteenth-century statesmen two hundred years later were still calling the "sick man of Europe."

Yet a firm sultan, Murad IV (1623-1640), temporarily restored order through the most brutal means. Despite a temporary retrogression after his death, what looked like a real revival began with the accession to power of a distinguished family of viziers, the Köprülü. The first Köprülü ruthlessly executed 36,000 people in a five-year period (1656-1661), hanged the Greek patriarch for predicting in a private letter that Christianity would defeat Islam, rebuilt the army and navy, and suppressed revolt. Between 1661 and 1676 the second Köprülü led the Ottoman navies to a triumph in Crete, which they took from Venice. The Turks temporarily won large areas of the Ukraine from the Russians and Poles, only to lose them again in 1681. In 1683 the Turks again penetrated the heart of Europe, and for the last time Vienna was besieged, with all Europe anxiously awaiting the outcome. For the second time in two centuries, the Turkish

wave was broken, and now Europe began a great counter-offensive against the Turks. Although the Köprülü had galvanized the warlike Ottoman armies into a last successful effort, they did not touch and could not touch the real evils of the Ottoman system.

The End of an Era

Now the Hapsburgs drove the Turks out of Hungary, and the Venetians seized the Greek Peloponnesus. The Turks needed peace. In 1699, after an international congress at Karlovitz on the Danube, most of the gains of the European counteroffensive were recognized, including those of the Austrians, Poles, Venetians, and Russians. The Russians had appeared for the first time since the Tatar invasion on the shores of the Sea of Azov, which opens into the Black Sea. The extensive territorial losses suffered by the Turks, the strengthening of the Hapsburgs to the east, and the appearance of Russia as an important enemy of the Turks all mark this settlement as a landmark. From now on the western European powers could stop worrying about the Ottoman menace, which had preoccupied them ever since the fourteenth century, and which had replaced the Crusades as a great cause for which Christendom could occasionally be united. From now on, the importance of Turkey is no longer its military potential, but its diplomatic position as a power in decline over whose possible disintegration and division the states of Europe might squabble and negotiate. With Karlovitz, what we call the "Eastern question" may be said to have begun.

With this shift from the military offensive, which had been their only policy since their arrival in Bithynia in the thirteenth century, to a new enforced policy of defensive diplomacy, the Ottoman Turks were forced to go outside their slave-family for administrators. Nobody trained in the old way had the proper equipment to act in the new. Thus it was that during the eighteenth century the Turks were forced, against their will, to rely more and more upon Christian Greeks to fill certain high offices of state. Born negotiators, with centuries of experience in commerce, and perhaps retaining the talents of their Byzantine ancestors, the Greeks now appear as the chief Ottoman diplomats. It is striking that

* Quoted by E. S. Creasey, *History of the Ottoman Turks* (London, 1854), I, 392-393.

the Turkish representative at Karlovitz should have been a Greek named Mavrogordato, from the island of Chios, who is said to have settled the disturbing question of protocol and precedence at the peace conference by inventing a round chamber with a door for each delegate, in the middle of which stood a round table. Each delegate could enter by his own door at the same moment, and sit in his own place at the round table with no question of higher and lower stations. This was a typically Greek idea, which no Turk could have had, and it may serve as a convenient symbol for the opening of a new era in administration and diplomacy.

V   Russia from the Thirteenth to the End of the Seventeenth Century

With the collapse of Kievan Russia about the year 1200, Russian development entered upon a confused and difficult period of about two hundred and fifty years. During this time, even the shrewdest contemporary observer would have been hard pressed to predict the future course of Russian history, or even the likely center for a future Russian state. There were at least four main centers of Russian national life, exposed to different enemies, undergoing different internal stresses, and shaping themselves in different ways.

The Western Lands

The southwestern portion of Russian territory, including the old capital at Kiev, became a virtually independent principality during the thirteenth century. It was distinguished by a particularly unruly nobility, which hampered all efforts of the princes to achieve consolidation in the face of the constant pressure from their Polish and Lithuanian neighbors. A parallel development occurred in the northwest portion, centering around the cities of Polotsk and Smolensk. No Russian prince after the end of the thirteenth century was able to maintain himself in the face of these pressures.

By the early fourteenth century, the grand duke of Lithuania, with his capital at Vilna, ruled nominally over most of the western Russian lands. The Lithuanians, still mostly pagan, gradually took over the language and manners of their more advanced Russian vassals. But in 1386, a celebrated dynastic marriage united Lithuania to Poland instead of to Russia. As a result, the Polish Roman Catholic church and the Po-

lish nobility now came to the fore. Had it not been for the antagonism between Orthodox Russians and Catholic Poles, and for the conflicting interests of the nobles of different religions and languages, the original Lithuanian-Russian combination might just possibly have proved to be the center around which Russia could reunite. Yet even before the addition of the largely unassimilable Polish element, this region had become so feudal in character that its potential ability to unify Russia is extremely doubtful. Even under the grand duke of Lithuania, most of the lands nominally affiliated with his duchy were ruled without interference by local nobles bound to him only by an oath of fealty and by their obligations to render military service. A parliament of nobles also limited the political authority of the grand duke. As in the West, the economic basis of the society in the western Russian lands was manorial. We find restrictions on the movement of the peasant farmer here long before we find them elsewhere in Russia.

The North

The northern regions of Russia, between the Baltic shore and Lake Ilmen, stretching far away to the north and northeast all the way to the Arctic Ocean and nearly to the borders of Siberia, were distinguished in this period by the growth of the town commonwealth of Novgorod (Newtown). This city, spread out along the banks of the Volkhov River where it flows out of Lake Ilmen, came to rule over the vast, empty, infertile northern regions, which were explored by armed merchants and pioneers in search of furs and other products of the forests and tundra.

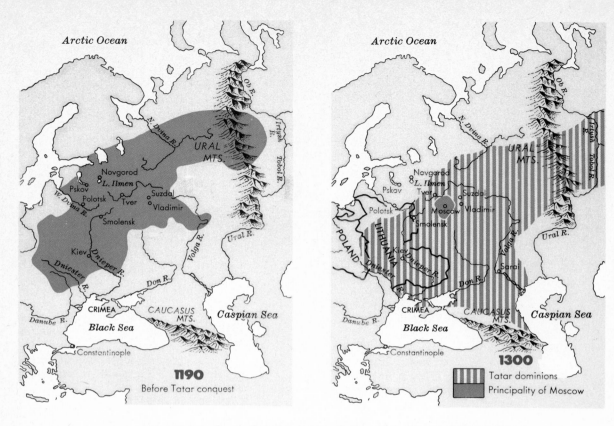

Arctic Ocean

URAL MTS.

N. Dvina R.

Ob R.

Irtysh R.

Tobol R.

Novgorod

L. Ilmen

Pskov

Polotsk

W. Dvina R.

Tver

Suzdal

Vladimir

Smolensk

Kiev

Dnieper R.

Dniester R.

Danube R.

Don R.

Volga R.

Ural R.

CRIMEA

Black Sea

CAUCASUS MTS.

Caspian Sea

Constantinople

1190
Before Tatar conquest

Arctic Ocean

URAL MTS.

N. Dvina R.

Ob R.

Irtysh R.

Tobol R.

Novgorod

L. Ilmen

Pskov

Tver

Moscow

Suzdal

Vladimir

POLAND

LITHUANIA

Polotsk

Smolensk

Kiev

Dnieper R.

Dniester R.

Danube R.

Don R.

Volga R.

Ural R.

Sarai

CRIMEA

Black Sea

CAUCASUS MTS.

Caspian Sea

Constantinople

1300

Tatar dominions

Principality of Moscow

Medieval and Early Modern Russia, 1190-1689

Arctic Ocean

URAL MTS.

N. Dvina R.

Ob R.

Irtysh R.

Tobol R.

Novgorod

L. Ilmen

Pskov

Kazan

Polotsk

LITHUANIA

Moscow

Smolensk

Kulikovo

POLAND

Kiev

Dnieper R.

Dniester R.

Volga R.

Don R.

Ural R.

Astrakhan

Danube R.

CRIMEA

Black Sea

CAUCASUS MTS.

Caspian Sea

Constantinople

1505
At death of Ivan III

Arctic Ocean

URAL MTS.

N. Dvina R.

Ob R.

Irtysh R.

Tobol R.

Novgorod

L. Ilmen

Pskov

W. Dvina R.

Kazan

Moscow

LITHUANIA

POLAND

Kiev

Dnieper R.

Dniester R.

COSSACKS

Don R.

Volga R.

Ural R.

Astrakhan

Danube R.

CRIMEA

Black Sea

CAUCASUS MTS.

Caspian Sea

1689
At accession of Peter the Great

In Novgorod even before the collapse of Kiev there grew up a tradition of municipal independence. The town council, or *veche* (pronounced *vyé-che*), became very strong. The lifeblood of the city was its trade with the West: Russian furs, wax, honey, tar, and tallow were exchanged for German cloth and metalwork. The Germans had their own quarter in Novgorod, which they maintained for several centuries despite constant friction with the Russians. The town.grew rich and strong. One might have expected this city to serve as the agent to reunify Russia, although its territory was exposed to and suffered attack by the Teutonic Knights and the Swedes.

But internally Novgorod had an extremely rigid class system. The representatives of the richer merchants came to control the veche. A few powerful families concentrated the city's wealth in their hands and disputed with each other for political power. Economic discrepancies between rich and poor grew very wide. A man who could not pay his debts would be made a slave, and slaves frequently revolted and became brigands. Because the surrounding countryside had little good soil, the city depended upon the region to the southeast, around Moscow, for its grain. Yet its rulers did not have the sense to realize that Moscow possessed this weapon against them. When in the fifteenth century the Polish-Lithuanian state and the state of Moscow were competing, the class struggle inside Novgorod was reflected in the allegiances of the population. The upper classes favored the Poles and Lithuanians, the lower favored Moscow. In 1478 the ruler of Moscow conquered the city, took away the bell, the symbol of its independence, and wiped out the upper classes. Novgorod may be compared with Venice and with other commercial patrician oligarchies in

The thirteenth-century Kremlin at Pskov.

the West. But its inability to solve its own internal problems deprived it of its chance to unify Russia.

The Northeast:
Moscow and the Tatars

Thus both Western feudalism and Western urban commercial development had their counterparts on Russian soil during the period after the collapse of Kiev. But it was the principality of Moscow, northeast of Kiev, east of Smolensk, and southeast of Novgorod, that succeeded where the other regions failed. Here neither feudality nor commercial oligarchy triumphed. This was the region where the prince was strong.

At the end of the Kievan period, the region of Moscow was still a frontier area, newly settled. Agriculturally poorer than the fertile southwest, it was richer than the north, could provide food enough for its people, and had flourishing forest industries. The cities remained small, and the pioneers turned neither to the nobility nor to the veche, since neither existed to any notable extent. Instead, they turned to the prince. This was also the region most exposed to the Tatar conquests of the thirteenth century.

By the early years of the thirteenth century, the celebrated Genghis Khan had succeeded in consolidating under his command a large number of those Mongolian nomads of central Asia who before, as Huns, Avars, and Polovtsy, had repeatedly erupted into Europe. Having conquered northern China and Asia from Manchuria to the Caspian Sea, Genghis Khan led his savage Tatars across the Caucasus and into the steppes of southern Russia, defeating Russians and Polovtsy together in 1223, but then retreating to Asia, where he died in 1227. His nephew Baty brought the Tatar hordes back again in the 1230's, sacked Moscow in 1237 and Kiev in 1240, and moved on into the western Russian regions and into Poland, Hungary, and Bohemia. Everywhere the Tatars went, devastation and slaughter marked their path.

Their success seems to have been due to their excellent military organization: unified command, general staff, clever intelligence service, and deceptive battle tactics. Though Baty defeated the Poles and the Germans in 1241, political affairs in Asia drew him eastward again,

and the Tatars never again appeared so far to the west. Baty retreated across Europe, and at Sarai, near the great bend of the Volga, close to modern Volgograd (formerly Stalingrad), he founded the capital of a new state. This was the Golden Horde, which accepted the overlordship of the far-off central government of the Mongols, in Peking.

Other Mongol leaders were responsible for ending the Abbasid Caliphate in 1258 and were defeated by the Mamluks in 1260. The enmity between Mongols and Muslims led the popes, Saint Louis, and other leaders of western Europe to hope that they could bring the Mongol rulers into an alliance directed against the Muslims, and so crush the opponents of Christianity between Eastern and Western enemies. The existence of various Christian sects in distant Asia lent strength to the hope that the khan himself could be converted. Considerable diplomatic correspondence was exchanged, and several embassies were sent to Mongolia and China during the thirteenth and fourteenth centuries with this end in view. But nothing ever came of all this, except a great increase in geographical knowledge derived from the extraordinarily interesting accounts of the European ambassadors, who were usually Franciscans or Dominicans. Their reports of their journeys into Asia and of their varied receptions at the court of the Mongol rulers rival any travel books ever written.

The most lasting effect on Europe of the Tatar invasions is found in Russia. Here the Tatars' main purpose was the efficient collection of tribute. Although they laid waste the territory while they were in the process of conquering it, after the conquest had been achieved they shifted to a policy of exploitation. They took a survey of available resources and assessed tribute at the limit of what the traffic would bear. It was not to their interest to disturb economic life, so long as their authority was recognized. They did draft Russian recruits for their armies, but after a while they made the local Russian princes responsible for the deliveries of men and money, and stayed out of Russian territory except occasionally to take censuses, survey property, and punish the recalcitrant. They had to confirm their tributary Russian princes, each of whom traveled to Sarai on his election to do homage. Some of them had to go all the way to China. Although no part of Russia was exempt from Tatar attacks during the period of conquest, thereafter the expensive burden of tribute and the humiliating sense of subservience fell most heavily upon the region of Moscow.

Toward the end of the fourteenth century, as the Mongol Empire itself grew feebler, the Russians became emboldened. The first Russian victories over the Tatars, scored by a prince of Moscow in 1378 and 1380, were fiercely avenged. Yet they served to show that the Tatars could be attacked and defeated. The Golden Horde did not disintegrate until the early fifteenth century, and even then the Tatars did not disappear from Russian life. Three separate khanates, or Tatar states, were formed from the debris of the Golden Horde: one at Kazan on the middle Volga, where it blocked the course of the river for another century and a half to Russian trade; one at Astrakhan at the mouth of the Volga on the Caspian; and one in the Crimea, where it later became a vassal of the Ottoman sultan.

Tatar Impact
on Russian Civilization

Historians have long debated the effect upon Russia of the "Tatar yoke"; one school has recently argued that the experience was somehow beneficial, because it eventually enabled the centralizing influence of the prince of Moscow, successor of the Tatar khan, to prevail. They add that trade with Asia helped Russia. They minimize the devastation wrought by the Tatar forces, and emphasize the fact that except for an occasional punitive expedition the Russian people never saw a Tatar after the conquest itself was over.

Yet it seems sure that the Tatar conquest also had a very serious negative effect on Russia. As the great nineteenth-century Russian poet Pushkin remarked, the Tatars brought to the Russians "neither algebra nor Aristotle." By this he meant to contrast the cultural impact of the Tatars on Russia with that of the Muslims on, let us say, Spain. Rule by an alien power is sometimes tolerable if the aliens are the bearers of a higher culture. But the Tatars, despite their military efficiency, were bearers of a lower culture than the Russians of the Kievan period had already achieved.

As we have seen (Chapter 6), there was no inherent reason why Russia in the late twelfth century should not have developed as a European state with highly individual characteristics of its own. After two centuries of Tatar domination, however, it had not advanced; rather, it had gone backward. Contemporaries felt that the Tatar yoke was a calamity, and historians have yet to demonstrate convincingly that it was anything else. When the Tatar power was finally shattered in the fifteenth century, Russian civilization was far behind that of the West. To the retarding effect of Byzantine Christianity there had been added the tremendous handicap of two centuries of cultural stagnation.

The Development
of the Muscovite State

During these two centuries, the princes of Moscow asserted themselves and assumed leadership. Moscow had a favorable geographical position, near the great watershed from which the Russian rivers, always the great routes for trade, flow north into the Baltic or south into the Black Sea. Thus, when the Tatar grip relaxed, and trade could begin again, Moscow was advantageously located. Moreover, Moscow was blessed with a line of remarkably able princes, not so much warriors as grasping, shrewd administrators, anxious to increase their holdings and to consolidate their own authority within the steadily expanding borders of their principality. They married into powerful families, acquired land by purchase and by foreclosing mortgages, and inherited it by will. They established the principle of seniority, so that their domain was not divided among their sons in each generation, and the tragedy of Kiev was not repeated.

Then too, they developed useful relations with their Tatar overlords. It was the princes of Moscow whom the Tatars chose to collect the tribute from other neighboring princes, and to deliver it at Sarai. Thus the princes were able to point to their success in excluding the Tatar agents from Russia, and to attract settlers to their lands. They were enabled to keep a close watch on the Tatars, so that when the moment of Tatar weakness came, it was they who could take advantage of it and marshal armies against them. They scored the first victories over the Tatars, and could truthfully claim to be the agents of liberation and the champions of Russia.

Finally, and very possibly most important, the princes of Moscow secured the support of the Russian church. In the early fourteenth century, the metropolitan archbishop transferred his see to Moscow, and made it the ecclesiastical capital of Russia. When the effective line of Muscovite princes faltered temporarily, it was the metropolitan who administered the principality loyally and effectively until the royal house recovered. Thus the Russian church deliberately bet on Moscow, and consciously decided to throw in its lot with the Muscovite house rather than with any other. The metropolitan who first moved to Moscow is said by his biographer to have advised the prince as follows:

If you build a church of the Virgin in Moscow, my son, and bury me in this city, so will you yourself become famous above the other princes, and also your sons and grandchildren from generation to generation. And this city will become celebrated above all the other Russian cities, and bishops will live here, and they will turn the city's forces against your enemies, and will praise God here.*

The Autocracy

By the middle of the fifteenth century, Moscow was a self-conscious Russian national state that was able to undertake successful wars against both the Polish-Lithuanian state and the Tatars. Ivan III (ruled 1462–1505) put himself forward as the heir to the princes of Kiev, and declared that he intended to regain the ancient Russian lands that had been lost to foreign Poles and Tatars—a national appeal, although a purely dynastic one. Many nobles living in the Western lands came over to him with their estates and renounced their loyalties to the Lithuanian-Polish state. In 1492, the Prince of Lithuania was forced to recognize Ivan III as sovereign of "all the Russias." This new national appeal was fortified by a religious appeal as well, for in addition to being sovereign Ivan was also the champion of Orthodoxy against the Catholic Poles and the Muslim Tatars. His wars took on the character

of a purely Russian crusade. But he felt himself to be much more than a mere Russian prince.

In 1472 Ivan had married the niece of the last Byzantine emperor, Constantine XI, who had been killed fighting against the Turks on the battlements of Constantinople in 1453. Ivan adopted the Byzantine title of autocrat, used the Byzantine double eagle as his seal, and began to behave like a Byzantine emperor. He sometimes used the title czar (caesar). He no longer consulted his nobles, but reached decisions in solitude. Italian architects built him an enormous palace, the Kremlin, a building set apart, like the one at Byzantium. When the Holy Roman emperor in the 1480's decided to make an alliance with Ivan III and to arrange for a dynastic marriage, Ivan responded:

By God's grace we have been lords in our land since the beginning of time, since the days of our earliest ancestors. God has elevated us to the same position which they held, and we beg him to grant it to us and our children. We have never desired and do not now desire confirmation of this from any other source.*

Here is the claim to unlimited power derived directly from God that the Byzantine emperor had been accustomed to make.

When a rebellious noble fled Russia under the reign of Czar Ivan IV, the Terrible (1534–1584), he wrote the czar from abroad, denouncing him for failing to consult his nobles on important questions, as had been the custom in the days of Kievan Russia. Ivan replied that he was free to bestow favors on his slaves or inflict punishment on them as he chose. The czar thought of Russian nobles as his slaves. He scorned Queen Elizabeth of England for living among merchants, whom she permitted to influence her. In short, from the late fifteenth century on, we find the czars calling themselves autocrats and acting like autocrats.

Part of the explanation for the immensely rapid growth of an autocratic theory and practice lies in the fact that Russia lived in a constant state of war or preparation for war. A national emergency prolonged over centuries naturally led to a kind of national dictatorship. Perhaps

---

* E. Golubinsky, *Istoriya Russkoi Tserkvi*, 2nd ed. (Moscow, 1901–11), II, 1, p. 144. Our translation.

* F. Adelung, *Kritisch-literarische Übersicht der Reisenden in Russland* (St. Petersburg and Leipzig, 1846), I, 153. Our translation.

more significant is the fact that in Moscow's lands feudalism had not, as it had in the West, developed a united class of selfconscious nobles who would fight for the rising monarchy for their privileges. Instead of uniting against the pretensions of the monarch, the Muscovite nobility produced various factions, with which the monarch could deal individually. Moreover, the absolutism of the Tatar khans probably helped furnish a model.

But most important of all was the ideology supplied by the Church and taken over largely from Byzantium. In the West, the Church itself was a part of feudal society, and jealous of its prerogatives. In Russia, as we have seen, it became the ally of the monarchy and something like a department of state. Russian churchmen were entirely familiar with Rome's claim to world empire, and to Constantinople's centuries-long position as "new Rome." They knew many written Byzantine claims to world domination, and they were conscious of many historical legends that could be useful to them. With the fall of Constantinople (Czargrad) to the Turks, they elaborated a famous theory that Moscow was the successor to the two former world capitals:

The Church of Old Rome fell because of its heresy; the gates of the Second Rome, Constantinople, have been hewn down by the axes of the infidel Turks; but the Church of Moscow, the Church of the New Rome, shines brighter than the Sun in the whole Universe. . . . Two Romes have fallen, but the Third stands fast; a fourth there cannot be.*

Russian churchmen spread the story that Rurik, the first political organizer of Russia, was descended from the brother of Augustus. They claimed that the Russian czars had inherited certain insignia and regalia not only from the Byzantines but even from the Babylonians. All the czars down to the last, in 1894, were crowned with a cap and clothed with a jacket that were actually of Byzantine manufacture, though of uncertain history. Thus the Church supplied the state with justification for its behavior. Imperial absolutism became one of the chief political features of modern Russia.

* Quoted by A. J. Toynbee, *Civilization on Trial* (New York, 1948), p. 171.

Nobles and Serfs

Between the accession of Ivan III in 1462 and the accession of Peter the Great in 1689, the autocracy succeeded in overcoming the opposition of the old nobility. This was done in part by virtually creating a new class of military-service gentry who owed everything to the czar. Their estates (*pomestie*), at first granted only for life in exchange for service, like the Byzantine pronoia, eventually became hereditary, like the western European fief. The estates of the old nobility (*vochina*), which had always been hereditary but for which they had owed no service, became service-estates, and thus like fiefs too. By the end of the period, the two types of noble and the two types of estate had by a gradual process become almost identical. The hereditary nobles often owed service. The military-service nobles often had hereditary land. Under Peter the Great (1689–1725) this process was to be completed and state service was to become universal. A central bureau in Moscow kept a census of the "service" men and of their obligations in time of war.

This tremendously important social process was accompanied by another, which is really the other side of the coin—the growth of serfdom. In a fashion familiar to us from our study of the West and of Byzantium, economic factors and political unrest in Russia had forced more and more peasants to seek out large landowners for dependence. The peasants would accept contracts that required rent in produce and service on the landlord's own land, and that involved the receipt of a money loan which had to be repaid over a period of years with interest or in the form of extra services. By the early seventeenth century it had become customary that the peasant could not leave his plot until he had paid off his debt. Since the debt was often too big for him to repay, he could in practice never leave.

The process was enormously speeded up when the czars gave estates to the new military-service gentry. An estate was not much good unless there was farm labor to work it. In periods of bitter agrarian and political crisis such as the sixteenth and seventeenth centuries, it became advisable for the government to help the service gentry to keep their farmers where they were. And, since the peasants paid most of the taxes, it was easier for the government to collect its own revenues if it kept the peasants where they were. Gradually it was made harder and harder for a tenant to leave his landlord, until by 1649 the avenues of escape were closed, and the serf was fixed to the soil. The landlord administered justice, and had police rights on the estate. He collected the serfs' taxes. He himself could sell, exchange, or give away his serfs. And the serf status became hereditary; children of serfs were enrolled on the estate's census books as serfs like their fathers.

The Russian serfs were not emancipated until 1861. Together with the absolute autocracy, the institution of serfdom is the most characteristic feature of Russian society. It affected every Russian, whether landowner, serf, or neither, for all the centuries it existed. In a very real sense, the consequences of Russian serfdom are still with us today, posing a serious problem not only for the rulers of the Soviet Union but for all the world that has to deal with them. Russian serfdom became a fixed custom far later in time than did western European serfdom. In fact, it was most widely extended during the eighteenth century, at a moment when the serfs in western Europe had long been on their way to complete liberation. This is another illustration of the fact that Russia went through many of the same processes as the West, but with greater intensity and at a later time.

The Reign of Ivan the Terrible

Most of the disorders that characterize Russian history in the sixteenth and seventeenth centuries have their origin in the long reign (1534–1584) of Ivan IV, the Terrible. Pathologically unbalanced, Ivan succeeded to the throne as a small child. He experienced helplessly the indignities inflicted on him by the various rival groups of nobles who were maneuvering and intriguing for power. Devoted to the rites of the Church, and fancying himself as a theologian, Ivan was none the less horribly cruel. He had perhaps as many as seven wives; he murdered his own son in a fit of lunatic rage. Soviet historians have tried to turn him into a hero by explaining that his wrath was directed against the selfish nobles who were conspiring to take over Russia. But, though the nobles were selfish enough, the danger of their intrigues was surely hugely exaggerated by the czar.

When Ivan finally was strong enough, in 1547, to assume the crown and throw off the tutelage of the boyars, he embarked upon a period (1547–1560) usually regarded as one of sound government and institutional reform. He regulated the rapacity of the imperial administrators in the provinces, who had oppressed the population. He also convoked the first *zemski sobor* (land assembly), a consultative body consisting of nobles, clerics, and representatives from the towns, to assist with the imperial business, particularly with important questions of war and peace. Though comparable in its social composition to the various assemblies of the medieval western European world, the zemski sobor under Ivan seems to have met only once, and can in no sense be regarded as a parliamentary body.

A contemporary portrait of Ivan the Terrible.

When Ivan fell ill in 1553, the nobles refused to take an oath of allegiance to his son. This action apparently reawakened all his savagery, and upon his recovery he created a fantastic new institution: the *oprichnina,* or "separate realm," to belong to him personally, while the rest of Russia continued to be administered as before. The men whom Ivan now appointed to run the oprichnina (called oprichniks), grimly dressed in black and riding black horses, bore on their saddlebows a dog's head (for vigilance) and a broom (symbolizing a clean sweep). They were the forerunners of the grim secret police forces that have long characterized Russian society. They waged a fierce, relentless war on the nobles, confiscating their estates, exiling them, killing them off. The czar, as was said, had divided his realm in two, and had set one part of it warring on the other. And in the diary of one oprichnik we find this revealing entry: "Today I did no harm to anyone: I was resting." The oprichniks took over the old estates of the men whom they were destroying. By the time of Ivan's death, many of the oprichniks themselves had been murdered at his orders, and Russian administration had degenerated to a state approximating chaos. Yet Ivan was able to extend Russian authority far to the east against the Kazan and Astrakhan Tatars, thus for the first time opening the whole Volga waterway to Russian commerce, and facilitating expansion further east, into Siberia.

The Time of Troubles

Though the territory was wide and the imperial rule absolute, ignorance, illiteracy, and inefficiency weakened the structure of Russian society. The few foreign observers who knew the Russia of Ivan could foresee chaos ahead. And the czar himself had his own dire forebodings: "The body is exhausted, the spirit is ailing, the spiritual and physical wounds multiply, and there is no doctor to cure me,"* he wrote in his last will. Though the old nobility had been dealt a series of blows, the new gentry has as yet no sense of corporate entity and therefore was not firmly in control of the machinery. Ivan's son

*Quoted by M. T. Florinsky, *Russia: A History and an Interpretation* (New York, 1953), I, 208.

and heir, Fëdor (1584–1598), was an imbecile, and with his death in 1598 the Moscow dynasty, descended from the rulers of the former Kievan state, died out. The cliques of rival nobles intrigued for power. Fëdor's brother-in-law, Boris Godunov, emerged as the dominant figure in the state.

Though Boris Godunov was probably a man of talent, he could not overcome his handicaps: Ivan's legacy of disorder, the intrigues of the nobility, and the famine and plague that began in 1601. Bands of brigands roamed the countryside, and when in 1603 a pretender arose under the protection of the king of Poland and declared that he was a son of Ivan the Terrible—who had in fact died long before—he was able to capture the support of many of the discontented. Russia was launched on the decade known as the Time of Troubles (1603–1613).

After Boris Godunov's death (1605), the pretender ruled briefly as czar. But within a year he was murdered, and was succeeded by a certain Shuiski, a representative of the ancient aristocracy. But new pretenders arose; the mobs of peasants and brigands were rallied once again; civil war continued, as Poles and Swedes intervened. Shuiski fell in 1610, and was succeeded by no one czar but by a small group of nobles who planned that the heir to the Polish throne would become czar of Russia.

Polish forces took over in Moscow, and it soon appeared that the king of Poland intended not to turn over the power to his son but to reign in Russia himself. It was this specter of a foreign and Catholic domination that aroused the national sentiments of the Russians. In answer to a summons from the patriarch, there assembled a kind of national militia, drawn largely from the prosperous free farmers of the middle Volga region, organized by a butcher named Kuzma Minin, and led by a nobleman named Dmitri Pozharski. These two are the national heroes of the Time of Troubles. Under their command the militia won the support of other rebellious elements and drove the Poles from Moscow in 1613.

The Role of the Zemski Sobor

A zemski sobor now elected Czar Michael Romanov. From the election of Michael in 1613 to the Russian Revolution of 1917, the Romanov dynasty held the throne. Michael succeeded with no limitations placed upon his power by the zemski sobor or by any other body; he was that curious anomaly, an elected autocrat. For the first ten years of the reign of Michael Romanov, the zemski sobor stayed in continual session. Since it had picked the new czar in the midst of crisis, it had indeed performed a constitutional function. It even included some representatives of the free peasantry. It assisted the uncertain new dynasty to get under way by endorsing the policies of the czar and his advisers, and thus lending them the semblance of popular support. One might have supposed that this would be the beginning of a new kind of partnership, and that, as had sometimes happened in the West, representatives of the various social classes would gain more and more political self-confidence and power, and might even transform the zemski sobor from a consultative to some sort of legislative assembly, a parliament.

But this was not to be. After 1623, the zemski sobor was summoned only to help declare war or make peace, to approve new taxation, and to sanction important new legislation. It endorsed the accession of Michael's son Alexis (ruled 1645–1676), and in 1649 confirmed the issuance of a new law code, summarizing and putting in order past statutes. After 1653 Alexis did not summon it again, nor did his son and successor, Fëdor (ruled 1676–1682). Its last meetings were in 1682.

No law abolished the zemski sobor. None had created it. The dynasty was entrentched and no longer needed it. Czardom, autocratic czardom, was taken for granted. No czar needed consult with any of his subjects unless he felt the need to do so. No subject had the right to insist on being consulted, though all subjects had the duty to give advice when asked for it. As the Romanovs became entrenched, they no longer felt the need to consult anybody's wishes except their own and those of their court favorites.

Individually, the early Romanovs were neither distinguished nor talented. The central government consisted of a number of bureaus or ministries or departments (*prikazy*), often with ill-defined or overlapping areas of competence. Provincial governors continued to milk the long-suffering population, and local efforts at self-government were in practice limited to the choice of officials obliged to collect and hand over taxes to the central authorities. Opposition

to the system there certainly was, but it came not from articulate or literate citizens offering criticism or suggestions for improvement. It came from below, from the oppressed and hungry peasantry. And it expressed itself in the only form of action the serf knew: large-scale or small-scale revolt, the burning of the manor house, the slaughter of the landlord or the tax-collector, the ill-directed march about in the vast flat countryside. Such affairs were a matter of yearly occurrence, the largest and most famous being that of Stenka Razin (1676), the "Russian Robin Hood." Such Russian uprisings were almost never directed against the czar but against the landlords and officials, of whose misdeeds the czar was supposed not to know. Often indeed the peasant leaders would arouse their followers *in the name* of the czar. Sometimes, as during the Time of Troubles, the leaders pretended to be czars in order to obtain more followers.

The Role of the Church

The Church remained the partner of the autocracy. The czar controlled the election of the metropolitan of Moscow, and after 1589 he controlled the election of the newly proclaimed patriarch of Moscow, a rank to which the Metropolitan was elevated. In the seventeenth century there were two striking instances when a patriarch actually shared power with the czar. In 1619 the father of Czar Michael Romanov, Filaret, who had become a monk, became patriarch and was granted the additional title of "great sovereign." He assisted his son in all the affairs of state. In the next generation Czar Alexis (ruled 1645–1676) appointed a cleric named Nikon to the patriarchal throne and gave him the same title and duties. Nikon proved so arrogant that he aroused protests from clergy as well as laity. He also seriously put forth the theory that the authority of the patriarch in spiritual affairs exceeded that of the czar, and that, since the spiritual realm was superior to the temporal, the patriarch was actually superior to the czar. This was a claim parallel to the one that was regularly made in the West by the more powerful popes but that was almost never advanced in Byzantium or in Russia. In 1666 a Church council deposed Nikon, who died a mere monk. These two experiments with two-man government (dyarchy, it was called, in contrast with monarchy) were never repeated, and they are interesting because they are the exceptions that prove the rule in Russia: the Church depends upon the state. Peter the Great was to abolish the patriarchate largely because he did not wish Nikon's claims ever to be repeated.

As in the Byzantine Empire, so in Russia, monasteries became immensely rich. By 1500 it is estimated that they owned more than a third of the land available for cultivation. Opposition to monastic worldliness arose within the Church itself, and one might have supposed that the government would have supported this movement. But those who favored monastic poverty also wished to enforce the noninterference of the state in monastic affairs. To preserve their right to control the monasteries in other respects, the government of the czar was obliged to oppose this reforming movement with respect to monastic property.

The Church, almost alone, inspired the literature and art of the Muscovite period. History was written by monks, in the form of chronicles.

St. Basil Cathedral, Moscow, built 1554–1560.

Travel literature took the form of accounts of pilgrimages to the Holy Land, although we have one secular travel book, a report by a Novgorod merchant who went to India on business. A handbook of etiquette and domestic economy, called *Household Management,* advises how to run a home and how to behave in company, revealing a conservative, well-ordered, solid, and smug society. Theological tracts attack the Catholics, and also the Protestants, whose doctrines were known in the western regions. This literature is limited, and it was still dominated by the Church several centuries after the West had made the break. Almost all of it was written in Old Church Slavonic, the language of the liturgy and not the language of everyday speech. Though stately and impressive, Old Church Slavonic was not an appropriate vehicle for new ideas. There was no secular learning, no science, no flowering of vernacular literature, no lively debates on the philosophical level in the field of theology. In painting, the icon, inherited from Byzantium, did flourish mightily, and various local schools produced works of great beauty and character. The greatest are reminiscent of some of the "Italian primitives," which also were painted under the influence of Byzantium.

The Expansion of Russia

The sixteenth and seventeenth centuries saw the tremendous physical expansion of the Russian domain. Russian pioneers, in search of furs to sell and new land to settle, led the way, and the government followed. Frontiersmen in Russia were known as Cossacks (*kazakh* is a Tatar word meaning "free adventurer"). It is a common error to suppose that they were somehow racially different from the mass of Russians. They were not; they were simply Russians living on the frontiers, organizing themselves for self-defense against the Tatars as our American pioneers did against the Indians. The Cossack communities gradually grew more settled, and two Cossack republics, one on the Dnieper, the other on the Don, were set up. These republics lived in a kind of primitive democracy relatively independent of Moscow; they fought Tatars and Turks quite at their own free will. As time passed, more Cossack groups formed in the Volga, in the Urals, and elsewhere.

The expansion movement took the Russians eastward into the Urals and on across Siberia—one of the most dramatic chapters in the expansion of Europe. Far more slowly, because of Tatar, Turkish, and Polish opposition, the Russians also moved southeast toward the Caucasus and south toward the Black Sea. Repeated wars were fought with Poland over the old west-Russian territory of the Ukraine. Sometimes the Cossacks favored the Poles, and sometimes the Russians. But by 1682 the Poles were weakening, and were soon to yield. On the European frontiers it was the Swedes, still blocking the Baltic exit, against whom Russia's future wars would be fought. The struggle with the Tatars of the Crimea, whose lands extended far north of the peninsula, was also a constant feature. The Ottoman Turks, overlords of the Tatars, held the key fort of Azov, controlled the Black Sea, participated in the wars over the Ukraine, and now for the first time became perennial enemies of the czars.

Russia and the West

A final development of these two centuries was to prove of the utmost importance for the future Russia. This was the slow and gradual penetration of foreigners and foreign ideas, a process warmly welcomed by some Russians, deeply deplored by others, and viewed in a rather mingled light by still others, who prized the technical and mechanical learning they could derive from the West but feared Western influence on Russian society and manners. This ambivalent attitude toward Westerners and Western ideas became characteristic of later Russians: they loved what the West could give, but they often feared and even hated the giver.

The first foreigners to come were the Italians, who helped build the Kremlin at the end of the fifteenth century. But they were not encouraged to teach Russians their knowledge, and failed to influence even the court of Ivan III in any significant way. The English, who arrived in the mid-sixteenth century as traders to the White Sea, were welcomed by Ivan the Terrible, who had tried to attract German and other artisans, but who had been blocked by Swedish control of the Baltic shore. He gave the English valuable privileges and encouraged them to trade their woolen cloth for Russian timber and rope, pitch,

and other naval supplies. These helped build the great Elizabethan fleets that sailed the seas and defeated the Spanish Armada. The English were the first foreigners to penetrate Russia in any numbers and the first to teach Russians Western industrial techniques. They got along well with the Russians and supplied a large number of officers to the czar's armies, mostly Scotsmen. Toward the middle of the seventeenth century, the Dutch were able to displace the English as the most important foreign group engaged in commerce and manufacturing. The Dutch had their own glass, paper, and textile plants in Russia.

After the accession of Michael Romanov in 1613, the foreign quarter of Moscow, always called "the German suburb," grew rapidly. Foreign technicians of all sorts—textile weavers, bronze founders, clockmakers—received enormous salaries from the state. Foreign merchants sold their goods, much to the distaste of the native Russians, who begged the czars to prevent the foreigners from stealing the bread out of their mouths. Foreign physicians and druggists became fashionable, though always suspected by the superstitious common people of being wizards. By the end of the seventeenth century, Western influence is apparent in the life of the court. The first play in Russia was performed in 1672, and although it was a solemn biblical drama about Esther, it was at least a play. A few nobles began to buy books and form libraries, to learn Latin and French and German. People were eating salad and taking snuff, and shyly beginning to try their skills at some of the social arts, such as conversation. A few Russians went abroad to travel, and, of these few, all who could refused to go back.

The people, meanwhile, distrusted and hated the foreigners, looted their houses when they dared, and jeered at them in the street. As one intelligent writer of the seventeenth century put it:

Acceptance of foreigners is a plague. They live by the sweat and tears of the Russians. The foreigners are like bear-keepers who put rings in our noses and lead us around. They are Gods, we fools, they dwell with us as lords. Our Kings are their servants.

The most dramatic outbreak of anti-foreign feeling took place, as might have been expected, in the field of religion. Highly educated clerics from the western lands (the Ukraine) and Greek scholars recommended to Patriarch Nikon that the Holy Books be revised and corrected in certain places where the texts were not sound. Resentment against this reform took the form of a great schism in the Russian church itself. Given the deep Russian regard for the externals, the rite, the magic, rather than for the substance of the faith, we must not be surprised at the horror that was aroused when the Russians were told that for centuries they had been spelling the name of Jesus incorrectly and had been crossing themselves with the wrong number of fingers. As at Byzantium, the religious protest reflected a deep-seated hatred of change, particularly change proposed by foreigners. Declaring that the end of the world was at hand (since Moscow, the Third Rome, had now itself become heretical),

about 20,000 of the schismatics shut themselves up in their huts and burned themselves alive. When the world did not end, those schismatics who survived, always known as the Old Believers, settled down and became sober, solid Russian citizens, many of them merchants and well-to-do peasants. Some later governments persecuted them; most did not. But, whatever the policies of the state might be toward them, the Russian church itself was weakened as a result of the schism.

Peter the Great is usually thought of as the initiator of westernization for Russia. But before he had ever come to the throne, Russian society had been profoundly split at its heart, the Church, by the influx of foreigners and foreign ways during the sixteenth and seventeenth centuries.

VI   Conclusion

In this complex chapter we have handled as a unit events whose relationship is not often recognized by historians. Yet it has seemed to us that their true significance is comprehensible only if some of the more conventional dividing lines are disregarded. We have seen how, beginning in the last quarter of the eleventh century, the medieval West undertook a prolonged onslaught against the Muslim and Orthodox East. The crusades against Islam, the Norman and Hohenstaufen attacks on Byzantium, the ambitions of the Italian cities, the Western distaste for the schism between the churches—all came together in the attack on Constantinople in 1204 and in the collapse of the Byzantine Empire, already deeply penetrated by the West. Yet the Crusader states founded on Syrian and Greek soil proved ephemeral. In Syria the Muslims had put an end to them by the close of the thirteenth century. In the Byzantine world, though

the empire was reestablished in 1261, the future lay with the Osmanli Turks, whose long slow rise to supremacy forms the central theme of the later Middle Ages in the southeast. Dominating the old Byzantine and Islamic worlds down to the end of the seventeenth century, the Ottoman empire was the successor-state to both. Meanwhile, Orthodox Russia—forced by the Tatar invasion to remain medieval long after the western European world had emerged into a new period—took its character from Moscow, the Third Rome, and in its way proved itself also the heir of the Byzantine heritage. In dealing with the East, we perceive the fundamental continuities only by disregarding the conventional periods that are useful for the West: long after the West had emerged from the Middle Ages—in fact, down to the end of the seventeenth century—the Ottoman Empire and Russia are still medieval.

Reading Suggestions on the East in the Late Middle Ages

(See also the listings for Chapter 6.)

GENERAL ACCOUNTS

A History of the Crusades. Vol. I: *The First Hundred Years,* ed. Marshall W. Baldwin; Vol. II: *The Later Crusades, 1189–1311,* ed. Robert Lee Wolff and H. W. Hazard (Univ. of Pennsylvania Press, 1955, 1962; (2nd ed. Kenneth M. Setton, general ed., Univ. of Wisconsin Press, 1969). Collaborative work with authoritative contributions by many scholars; good bibliographies.

S. Runciman, *A History of the Crusades,* 3 vols. (Cambridge Univ. Press, 1951–1954). The fullest treatment of the subject by a single scholar.

E. S. Creasy, *History of the Ottoman Turks,* 2 vols. (1854–1856), new ed., intro. Zeine Zeine (Beirut Khayats, 1961). Despite its age, still the only good general account in English based on a ten-volume German work.

SPECIAL STUDIES

J. L. LaMonte, *Feudal Monarchy in the Latin Kingdom of Jerusalem* (Mediaeval Academy, 1932). A study of the institutions of the Crusader States in the Levant.

W. Miller, *The Latins in the Levant: A History of Frankish Greece* (1204–1566) (John Murray, 1908), and *Essay on the Latin Orient* (Cambridge Univ. Press, 1921). Two good studies of the "Latins" in Greece.

C. M. Brand, *Byzantium Confronts the West, 1180–1204* (Harvard Univ. Press, 1968). Scholarly study of the diplomacy of an important period.

J. W. Barker, *Manuel II Palaeologus, 1391–1425* (Rutgers Univ. Press, 1969). Good monograph on a late Byzantine emperor.

A. S. Atiya, *The Crusade in the Later Middle Ages* (Methuen, 1938). A study of the propaganda and the expeditions that marked the decline of the crusading movement.

E. Pears, *The Destruction of the Greek Empire and the Story of the Capture of Constantinople by the Turks* (Longmans, 1903). A solid work not superseded by more recent studies.

H. A. Gibbons, *The Foundation of the Ottoman Empire* (Century, 1916). An older work whose conclusions are again finding favor.

P. Wittek, *The Rise of the Ottoman Empire* (Royal Asiatic Society, 1938). A suggestive essay on the elements that helped to advance the Ottoman state.

H. A. R. Gibb and Harold Bowen, *Islamic Society and the West,* Vol. I, Parts 1 and 2 (Oxford Univ. Press, 1950, 1956). The most authoritative survey of Ottoman institutions.

B. Lewis, *The Arabs in History* (*Torchbooks). Crisp and suggestive survey.

B. Miller, *Beyond the Sublime Porte* (Yale Univ. Press, 1931), and *The Palace School of Mohammed the Conqueror* (Harvard Univ. Press, 1941). Studies of the Ottoman imperial palace and the Ottoman educational system, respectively.

A. H. Lybyer, *The Government of the Ottoman Empire in the Time of Suleiman the Magnificent* (Harvard Univ. Press, 1913). A pioneering work on Ottoman institutions, now out of date in many details.

Dorothy M. Vaughan, *Europe and the Turk: A Pattern of Alliances, 1350–1700* (Liverpool Univ. Press, 1954). Role of the Ottoman Empire in European diplomacy.

G. Vernadsky, *The Mongols and Russia* (Yale Univ. Press, 1953). Volume III of the Yale History of Russia; authoritative and complete.

J. L. I. Fennell, *Ivan the Great of Moscow* (Macmillan, 1961). Valuable monograph.

SOURCES

Anna Comnena, *The Alexiad,* trans. E. A. S. Dawes (Kegan Paul Trench, Trübner, 1928). The life and reign of Emperor Alexius Comnenus (1081–1118), by his daughter.

Fulcher of Chartres, *Chronicle of the First Crusade,* trans. M. E. McGinty (Univ. of Pennsylvania Press, 1941).

An Arab-Syrian Gentleman and Warrior in the Period of the Crusades: Memoirs of Usamah ibn-Munqidh, trans. P. K. Hitti (Columbia Univ. Press, 1929).

William, Archbishop of Tyre, *A History of Deeds Done Beyond the Sea,* trans. E. A. Babcock and A. C. Krey, 2 vols. (Columbia Univ. Press, 1943). The greatest of the contemporary accounts of the Crusaders' Levant.

Memoirs of the Crusades, including Villehardouin's chronicle of the Fourth Crusade and Joinville's of the crusade of St. Louis, trans. F. T. Marzials (*Dutton). Eyewitness accounts by prominent participants.

Robert of Clari, *The Conquest of Constantinople,* trans. E. H. McNeal (Columbia Univ. Press, 1936). Eyewitness account by a humble participant in the events of 1204.

P. W. Topping, *Feudal Institutions as Revealed in the Assizes of Romania, The Law Code of Frankish Greece* (Univ. of Pennsylvania Press, 1949).

Kritovulos, *History of Mehmed the Conqueror,* trans. C. T. Riggs (Princeton Univ. Press, 1954). A Greek life of Mohammed the Conqueror.

The Life and Letters of Ogier Ghiselin de Busbecq, ed. C. T. Forster and F. H. Blackburne Daniell, 2 vols. (C. K. Paul, 1881). Perceptive and amusing reports of a Hapsburg ambassador to Suleiman the Magnificent.

The Correspondence between Prince A. M. Kurbsky and Tsar Ivan IV of Russia, 1564–1579, ed. and trans. J. L. I. Fennell (Cambridge Univ. Press, 1955), and *Kurbsky's History of Ivan IV,* ed. and trans. J. L. I. Fennell (Cambridge Univ. Press, 1965). Hitherto regarded as fundamental sources for the political theories of the czar and his noble opponents. The most recent scholarship casts grave doubt on their authenticity.

IO

The West

Late Middle Ages

I Introduction

In eastern Europe, as the last chapter showed, medieval institutions continued to flourish long after the Turks captured Byzantium in 1453, the date often cited as the turning-point from medieval to modern. And, indeed, in Russia the Middle Ages ended only recently, with the emancipation of the serfs in 1861. In western Europe, by contrast, the Middle Ages really did come to an end about five centuries ago. No one year or one event can be singled out; rather, a series of crucial developments took place over the span of half a century in the later 1400's and early 1500's —the consolidation of royal authority in the national monarchies of France, England, and Spain; the discovery of America; the virtual disappearance of serfdom in the West; and Martin Luther's revolt. This chapter surveys the political, economic, and social forces that destroyed traditional feudal and manorial society. Succeed-

Above: A silver groat, ca. 1500, with a likeness of King Henry VII. Above right: Florence in 1490. Right: Leonardo's drawing of a condottiere. Far right: Verrocchio's monument to the condottiere Bartolommeo Colleoni.

342

ing chapters will examine the famous twin movements of the Renaissance and the Reformation that disrupted the Christian cultural synthesis and the religious unity of the Middle Ages.

During the fourteenth and fifteenth centuries old forms and attitudes persisted in Western politics but, in a manner characteristic of an era of decline, became more rigid and less flexible, more sterile and less creative. Political leaders sometimes acted as though they were living centuries earlier: the Holy Roman emperor Henry VII in the early 1300's sought to straighten out the affairs of Italy in the old Ghibelline tradition, even though he had few of the resources that had been at the command of Frederick Barbarossa. The nobles of France and England, exploiting the confusion of the Hundred Years' War, built again the private armies and the great castles of the feudal heyday and attempted to transfer power back from the monarch to themselves. Their movement has been called "bastard feudalism," for service in these new feudal armies hinged upon money, not upon the traditional feudal elements of personal loyalty and mutual respect and guarantees.

Manifestations like these have been interpreted as symptoms of senility, a hardening of the arteries of the body politic, and so in some senses they were. But they may also be viewed as expedients or experiments in the adjustment of old institutions to new demands. The nobles who practiced bastard feudalism were not only taking selfish advantage of a prolonged war but also putting soldiers in the field at a time when neither the French or English monarchies could sustain a military effort decade after decade. The importance of the monetary factor—the soldier hired for money, the ex-serf paying rent in money, the banker earning his livelihood handling money—was characteristic of the transition from medieval to modern.

By the close of the fifteenth century it was evident that the future lay not with neofeudal lords but with "new" monarchs, who had little interest in reviving faded glories and were very much committed to what the twentieth century knows as power politics. While politics and power had always gone hand in hand, what distinguished the "new" monarchs from their predecessors was the candor and the professionalism of their operations. They made no bones about the pursuit of power, naked and unadorned with medieval trappings; and they were served by better instruments of government, better soldiers, diplomats and bureaucrats. Outstanding representatives of the new professionalism were Louis XI of France, Henry VII of England, and Ferdinand and Isabella of Spain, all of them monarchs of developing national states. On a local or regional scale, the princes of the particular German states and the despots of the Italian city-states often qualified.

Meanwhile, the economy and society of western Europe were experiencing even more strain and upheaval. In the countryside by the early fourteenth century the older patterns of manorialism, serfdom and payment in kind, coexisted with the newer patterns of free peasants, producing for the cash market and paying rents and taxes in cash as well. The old customs displayed some of the rigidity of the age. Former serfs often found that a lord could still oblige them to use his bake oven or flour mill or wine press and pay a stiff fee for the privilege. They also found that in times of trouble they could no longer turn to a lord for protection. The uncertainties and perplexities of a world no longer wholly medieval nor yet wholly modern underlay the numerous outbreaks of agrarian violence like the French Jacquerie or the English Peasants' Revolt. Comparable crises convulsed urban life—civil war in the woolen-manufacturing towns of Flanders, chronic strife between the wealthy and the poorer classes in Florence. Here the rigid old institution was the guild, which was losing much of its old fraternal spirit; the unsettling new element was the aggressive entrepreneur.

Two particular social traumas sapped the morale and resilience of fourteenth-century Europe. The first was the great famine of 1315–1317, caused apparently by a protracted spell of bad weather just at the time when the long medieval process of clearing forests and draining marshes for new farmland was coming to a halt. Europe was unable to produce enough grain to provide its population with sufficient bread, at that time the mainstay of the diet. The result was widespread starvation. It is known that about 10 percent of the inhabitants of the Flemish town of Ypres died in a six-month period. The second and greater trauma was the Black Death of 1347–1350, which is estimated to have killed between a third and half of the European population. This ghastly epidemic was apparently the first appearance in Europe of bubonic plague, introduced by ships coming from the Near East. A major social consequence of the plague was a severe shortage of labor, which depressed the economy for several decades and emboldened the peasants and workers who did survive to press for greater rights, usually with only temporary success.

II   The Emerging National Monarchies

Outbreak of the Hundred Years' War

At the death of Philip the Fair in 1314, the Capetian monarchy of France appeared well on the way to establishing a new-model state manned by efficient and loyal bureaucrats. Philip Augustus, Louis IX, and Philip the Fair had all consolidated the royal power at the expense of their feudal vassals, including the kings of England. Soon, however, France became embroiled in an almost interminable contest with England that crippled the monarchy for a century. This was the celebrated Hundred Years' War.

The nominal cause of the war was a dispute over the succession to the French throne. For more than three hundred years, ever since Hugh Capet had been succeeded by his son, son had followed father as king of France. This remarkable streak of good fortune came to an end with the three sons of Philip the Fair. Each of them ruled in turn between 1314 and 1328, but none of them fathered a son who survived infancy. Consequently, the crown passed to Philip of Valois, Philip VI (1328–1350), a nephew of Philip the Fair and the first cousin of his sons; the Valois dynasty thereby succeeded the Capetian dynasty. In order to make the succession legal, the lawyers had to dispose of a dangerous claim to the throne—that of the king of England, Edward III (1327–1377), whose mother Isabella had been a daughter of Philip the Fair. As nephew of the last Capetian kings, did not Edward have a better right to succeed than their first cousin, Philip of Valois? To settle the question, French lawyers went all the way back to a Frankish law of the sixth century which said that a woman could not inherit land. Although this so-called Salic law had not applied in France for centuries, the lawyers now interpreted it to mean that a woman could not transmit the inheritance to the kingdom. The legal quibble was to serve Edward III as pretext for beginning the Hundred Years' War.

Edward's claim to the French throne was not, of course, the only reason for the outbreak of war. England's continued possession of the rich land of Aquitaine, with its lucrative vineyards and its prosperous wine-shipping port of Bordeaux, was an anomaly in an increasingly unified France. As suzerains over Aquitaine, the kings of France encroached upon the feudal rights of the kings of England. They encouraged the local knights to appeal to them over the head of the English king, and then cited him before their own court. The English, for their part, wished not only to keep what they had, but to regain Normandy and the other territories they had lost to Philip Augustus.

The most pressing issue arose farther north, in Flanders. This small but wealthy area, which today lies on both sides of the frontier between Belgium and France, was ruled in medieval times by the count of Flanders, a vassal of the king of France. The thriving Flemish cloth manufacturers bought most of their wool from England and sold much of their finished cloth there; the English crown collected taxes both on the exported wool and on the imported woolens. Inside Flanders, the artisans and tradesmen of the towns were in almost constant conflict with the rich commercial ruling class. The rich sought the backing of their lord, the count of Flanders, and he in turn sought that of his overlord; the workers got the help of the English, who feared the disruption of their lucrative trade. Warlike incidents multiplied during the early fourteenth century. In 1302, the Flemish town militias defeated Philip the Fair. In 1326, the count of Flanders arrested and jailed all Englishmen on his lands; the king of England forbade the export of raw wool, or the import of finished goods, and caused a crisis in Flanders that brought the French armies back in 1328, this time to win a victory. King Edward III, however, allied him-

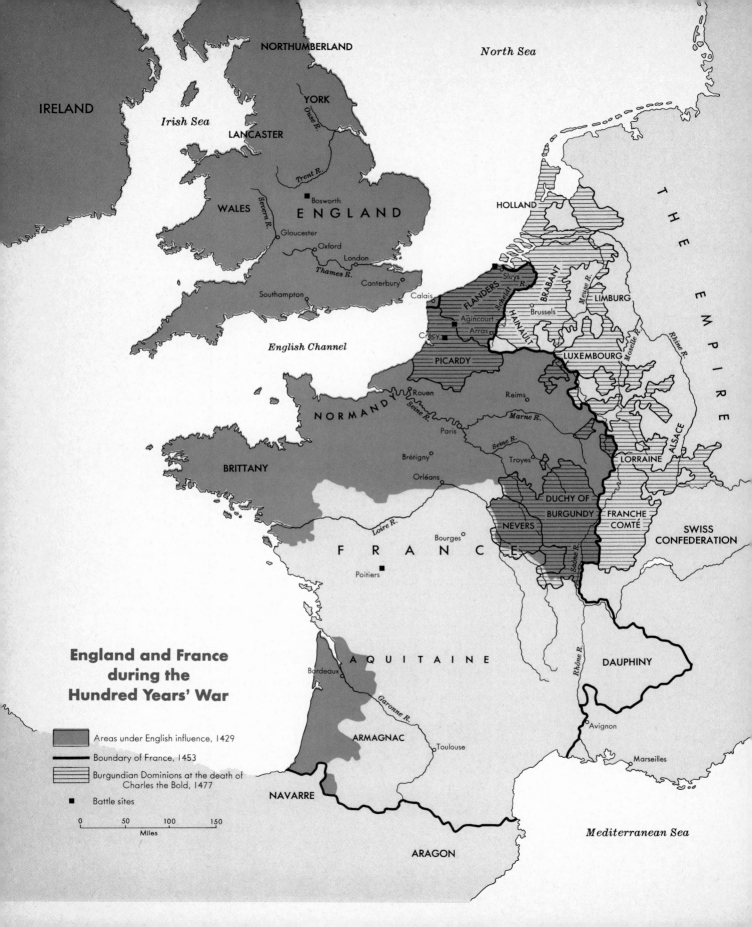

NORTHUMBERLAND

North Sea

IRELAND

Irish Sea

YORK

LANCASTER

■ Bosworth

WALES

E N G L A N D

HOLLAND

Severn R.

○ Gloucester

○ Oxford
London ○

Thames R.

Canterbury ○

Southampton ○

Calais

■ Sluys

FLANDERS

BRABANT

Scheldt R.

LIMBURG

Brussels ○

HAINAULT

Meuse R.

■ Agincourt

Arras ○

LUXEMBOURG

English Channel

■ Crécy

PICARDY

Moselle R.

N O R M A N D Y

○ Rouen

Seine R.

Reims ○

Marne R.

ALSACE

○ Paris

Seine R.

LORRAINE

Rhine R.

BRITTANY

Brétigny ○

Troyes ○

Orléans ○

DUCHY OF

BURGUNDY

FRANCHE

COMTÉ

SWISS
CONFEDERATION

NEVERS

Loire R.

Bourges ○

F R A N C E

Saône R.

Poitiers ■

**England and France
during the
Hundred Years' War**

A Q U I T A I N E

Rhône R.

DAUPHINY

Bordeaux ○

Garonne R.

Avignon ○

	Areas under English influence, 1429
	Boundary of France, 1453
	Burgundian Dominions at the death of Charles the Bold, 1477
■	Battle sites

ARMAGNAC

Toulouse ○

Marseilles ○

0   50   100   150
Miles

NAVARRE

Mediterranean Sea

ARAGON

T
H
E

E
M
P
I
R
E

self with a Flemish merchant, Jacob van Artevelde, who expelled both the ruling Flemish oligarchy and the French, and organized his own government of Flanders. It was in response to pressure from these Flemish allies that Edward III put forth his claim as king of France and precipitated war in 1337.

The war was synonymous with the history of France for a troubled century. The Valois kings, with the notable exception of Charles V, the Wise (1364–1380), were far less effective rulers than the Capetians had been. The English won all the greatest battles and gained by treaty huge amounts of French territory. France was racked by the Black Death and swept by social crisis and civil war. Yet the English were overextended, and in the end the French drove them out and completed the unification of their country under a strong national monarchy. Necessity obliged the Valois kings to develop a standing army, finance it from a system of direct taxation, and enlist the support of the middle classes, on whose assistance, indeed, the whole accomplishment depended.

The first major operation of the war was an English naval victory at Sluys (1340), which gave the English command of the Channel for many years. When their Flemish ally, Van Artevelde, was killed in 1345, the English invaded northern France to obtain a foothold on the Continent. In 1346 came the first of the great English victories, at Crécy. Despite inferior numbers, the English profited by the incompetent generalship of the French and by their own successful—and very unfeudal—experiments in relying upon large numbers of infantrymen, armed with the longbow. From higher ground English archers poured arrows down on a confused crowd of mounted French knights and of mercenaries armed with the crossbow, a weapon rather like a giant slingshot and more cumbersome than the longbow. Next the English took Calais, which gave them a port in France. When open warfare was resumed after the Black Death, the English again compensated for inferior numbers by superior tactics. At Poitiers (1356), in western France, the English not only defeated the French again but also captured the French king John, (1350–1364) and carried him off to England, where he settled down to a carefree life in luxurious captivity. In France his son, the future king Charles the Wise, served as regent, but

France's feudal armies had been shattered and the machinery of government had been sadly weakened.

The Estates General and Charles the Wise

In these years the French monarchy faced not only a triumphant foreign enemy but also increasingly hostile criticism at home, focused in the central representative assembly, the Estates General. When summoned in 1355 to consent to a tax, the Estates General insisted on fixing its form—a general levy on sales and a special levy on salt—and demanded also that their representatives rather than those of the Crown act as collectors. Moreover, the Estates for the first time scheduled future meetings "to discuss the state of the realm." After the defeat at Poitiers, they demanded that the regent, Charles, dismiss and punish the royal advisers and substitute for them twenty-eight delegates chosen from the Estates. When Charles hesitated to accept the demands of the Estates, their leader Etienne Marcel, a bourgeois merchant of Paris, led a general strike and revolution in the capital, the first of many in French history, and forced Charles to consent. In his *grande ordonnance* of 1357, he accepted the Estates' demands for a complete administrative housecleaning.

But this was as far as the success of the Estates went. Marcel made two cardinal mistakes. He allied himself with a rival claimant to the throne, and he assisted a violent peasant revolt, the Jacquerie (so called from the popular name for a peasant, Jacques Bonhomme—James Goodfellow). Already harrowed by the Black Death, the peasants endured fresh suffering as a result of the war—from bands of soldiers living off the land, and from demands for more taxes and also for money to pay the ransom of nobles taken prisoner along with King John. In desperation they rose up in 1358, without a specific program and without effective leadership, murdering nobles and burning chateaux. The royal forces, in disarray though they were, put down and massacred the peasants (the death toll has been estimated at 20,000). The outcome of the Jacquerie showed that, put to the test, the country failed to support the more radical Parisians—

this, too, was to be a familiar pattern in later French history. In the final flare-up, Marcel was killed, and Charles won his struggle.

Although the Estates had in effect run France for two years during 1356 and 1357, they had imposed no principle of constitutional limitation upon the king; they had not made themselves permanent or necessary to the conduct of government. After all, with the country in chronic danger of invasion, even rebellious Frenchmen wished to meet the emergency by strengthening rather than weakening their monarchy. They were willing to criticize its methods but not to limit them. Moreover, the opponents of the Crown—clergy, nobles, townsmen—came from all three estates and mistrusted one another because of conflicting class interests; even members of a single estate were divided by the differing interests of the provinces from which they came. Some of the southern French lands had their own regional estates and were not represented in the Estates General of the 1350's. Class and local antagonisms gave the Crown an advantage which Charles the Wise was not slow to take. As early as 1358 the reasons why the Estates General would never become in France what Parliament was in England are clear.

In 1360 the Hundred Years' War entered another pause with the Treaty of Calais. Edward III renounced his claim to the French crown, but only in exchange for all southwestern France (Aquitaine plus Poitou) and lands bordering the Channel near Calais. The king of England was to annex these lands outright, not simply hold them as the vassal of the king of France. An enormous ransom was agreed upon for the captive French king John. But John broke his parole, and relations deteriorated once more. When the war was resumed in 1369, the French made impressive gains under Charles the Wise and his capable middle-class advisers. By his death in 1380, they had ejected the English from all but a string of seaports, including Bordeaux and Calais. For the first time since the beginning of the war, the French fleet was able to sail freely in the Channel and raid the English coasts. At home, Charles regularized the salt tax and kept the upper hand over the Estates General as well, securing their agreement that other existing taxes were to be made permanent.

Burgundians and Armagnacs

But, instead of initiating a period of reconstruction and recuperation, the successes of Charles the Wise were only the prelude to a period of still worse suffering. Charles VI (1380–1422) went insane and never ruled effectively. A struggle broke out between one of the king's uncles, the duke of Burgundy, and the king's brother, the duke of Orléans, for control of France. The whole conflict illustrated the danger of a king's giving provinces (called *appanages*) to any of his sons other than the heir to the throne himself. Such a son might himself be loyal, but within a generation or two his heirs would be remote enough from the royal family to feel themselves rivals. It was essentially this pattern that had ruined the Carolingians. In 1361, King John revived the practice and opened the door to bastard feudalism by assigning the important duchy of Burgundy as the appanage of his youngest son, Philip. He thus revived the old political entity of Burgundy in a new form that was to threaten France herself.

The rivalry between Burgundy and Orléans led to the murder of the duke of Orléans in 1407 by assassins hired by the Burgundians. The Orléanists, now led by the father-in-law of the new duke, Count Bernard of Armagnac, were known thereafter as the Armagnacs. They commanded the loyalty of much of southern and southwestern France, while the Burgundians controlled the north and east. The Armagnacs were strongest among the great nobles, and were professedly anti-English; the Burgundians, whose duke had inherited Flanders and had thus become immensely rich, were pro-English, and had the support of the upper bourgeoisie in the towns.

Under these circumstances, the English reopened the war in alliance with the Burgundians. Their king, Henry V, won the celebrated battle of Agincourt (1415), where the heavily armored French knights were mired in the mud. Thus Henry temporarily undid the work of Philip Augustus and Charles the Wise by reconquering Normandy. The Burgundians took over in Paris, massacring partisans of the Armagnacs, whose party fled in disorder to set up their own rival regime south of the Loire, headed nominally by the dauphin, the heir to the throne. When the English took the Norman capital, Rouen (1419), the alarmed Burgundians tried to patch up a truce with the Armagnacs. But the duke of Burgundy was assassinated to avenge the murder of the duke of Orléans a dozen years earlier. Next, Charles VI cast off his own son, the dauphin, as illegitimate (the title of dauphin and the right to hold the province of Dauphiné, in southeastern France, were reserved for the eldest son of the king). By the Treaty of Troyes (1420), he adopted Henry V of England as heir and as his regent during his lifetime. Henry married Charles VI's daughter, and was allowed to retain as his own all the conquests north of the Loire until he should inherit all of France on the death of Charles VI.

This fantastic settlement, which threatened to put an end to French national sovereignty altogether, was supported by the Burgundians, the Estates General, and the University of Paris. Had Henry V lived, it is barely possible that the entire future would have been changed. But French national consciousness was now aroused; the dauphin ruled at Bourges as King Charles VII (1422–1461) with Armagnac support. England, too, was torn with faction and could not or would not supply enough troops to hold down conquered northern France. In any case, Henry V and Charles VI both died during 1422, and the regent for the infant English king Henry VI prepared to move south against Charles VII.

Joan of Arc and Charles VII

At this juncture, the miracle of Joan of Arc saved France. The wretched, demoralized forces of Charles VII were galvanized into action by the visionary peasant girl from Lorraine who reflected the deep patriotism of the French, and who touched a responsive chord at a moment when all seemed lost. The story is well known: how saints and angels told Joan that she must bring the pitiful Charles VII to be crowned at Reims, traditional coronation place for the kings of France; how she was armed and given a small detachment that drove the English out of Orléans; how the king was crowned, Joan taken prisoner by the Burgundians, sold to the English,

Charles VII of France presiding over the Court of Parlement, 1458: a painting attributed to Jean Fouquet.

turned over to the French Inquisition, and burned at Rouen (1431). The papacy itself undid the verdict against her in 1456 and made her a saint in 1919.

Against heavy odds the French monarchy managed to sustain the impetus provided by the martyred Joan. In 1435, at Arras, Charles VII and Burgundy concluded a separate peace which made it impossible for the English to win the war. Charles now recovered Paris (1436), but for ten years the countryside was ravaged and pillaged by bands of soldiers organized into private companies. They were known as "flayers" (*écorcheurs*), a term indicating vividly their mode of treating the peasantry. Moreover, leagues of nobles, supported by the new dauphin, the future Louis XI, revolted in 1440. Fortunately for the Crown, the Estates General in 1439 granted the king the permanent right to enjoy two essential nonfeudal resources—to keep a standing army, and to levy the *taille* (from a French word meaning "cut"), a tax paid directly by individuals and collected by royal agents.

With these instruments ready to his hand, with additional financial aid from the great merchant prince Jacques Coeur, and with assistance from professional military experts, Charles VII embarked on reforms which at last ended the medieval system that had for so long shown itself inadequate. Twenty companies of specialized cavalry were organized, 1,200 to a company, under commanders of the king's personal choice. These companies, which supplanted the contingents of écorcheurs, were assigned to garrison the towns. Professionals supervised the introduction of artillery, which became the best in Europe. The new French force drove the English out of Normandy and Aquitaine (1449–1451) so that Calais alone in France remained in English hands when the Hundred Years' War finally ended in 1453. The standing army, based on direct taxation that had been granted by the Estates as a royal right, had enabled France to overcome the English threat.

Meantime, Charles had scored against another institution, the Church, that might have weakened the Crown. In 1438, he regulated church–state relations by the Pragmatic Sanction of Bourges ("pragmatic sanction" is simply a name for a solemn royal pronouncement). This document laid down the policy known as Gallicanism, claiming for the Gallican, or French, church a virtually autonomous position within the Church Universal. It greatly limited papal control over ecclesiastical appointments and revenues in France and asserted the superiority of church councils over popes.

The Burgundian Threat and King Louis XI

Against one set of enemies, however, Charles VII was not successful—his rebellious vassals, many of them beneficiaries of bastard feudalism, who still controlled large areas of the kingdom (nearly half of the total), that were not part of the royal domain. The most powerful of these vassals was the duke of Burgundy, Philip the Good (1419–1467), whose authority reached far beyond the duchy of Burgundy in eastern France and the adjoining Franche-Comté (Free County of Burgundy—still technically part of the Holy

Roman Empire) and extended to Flanders and other major portions of the Low Countries. This sprawling Burgundian realm almost deserved to be called an emerging national state. But it was a divided state. The two main territorial blocs in eastern France and the Low Countries were separated by the non-Burgundian lands of Alsace and Lorraine. And it was a personal state, for Duke Philip had assembled it as much by good luck as by good management, inheriting some lands and acquiring others by conquest or negotiation. Yet it was also a menacing state, which might have interposed itself permanently as a middle kingdom between France and Germany. Philip behaved as though he were a monarch of the first magnitude. He used the wealth of the Flemish and Dutch towns to support the most lavish court in Europe, and his resources at least equaled those of his feudal suzerains, the king of France and the Holy Roman emperor. He also had defied Charles VII by allying with England in the Hundred Years' War.

The decisive trial of strength between France and Burgundy took place under the successors of Charles VII and Philip the Good. The new French king was Louis XI (1461–1483), who as dauphin had repeatedly intrigued against his father but who now pursued energetically the policies that Charles had initiated. At his accession Louis was already a crafty and practiced politician, who despised the pageantry of kingship, liked a simple tavern meal better than elaborate royal fare, and preferred secret diplomacy to open war, soon earning the nickname "the Universal Spider." One of his aides, the statesman and historian Philippe de Comines (1447–1511), drew a notable portrait of him:

Amongst all those I have ever known, the most skillful at extricating himself out of a disagreeable predicament in time of adversity was King Louis XI . . . , the most humble person in terms of speech and manner and the prince who worked more than any other to gain to his cause any man who could serve him or who could be in a position to harm him. And he was not discouraged if a man he was trying to win over at first refused to cooperate, but he continued his persuasion by promising him many things and actually giving him money and dignities which he knew the other coveted. . . .

He was naturally a friend to those of middle rank and an enemy of all the powerful lords who could do without him. No man ever gave ear to people to such an extent or inquired about so many matters as he did, or wished to make the acquaintance of so many persons. For indeed he knew everyone in a position of authority and of worthy character who lived in England, Spain, Portugal, Italy, in the territories of the Duke of Burgundy, and in Britanny, as well as he knew his own subjects. These methods and manners which he had . . . saved the crown for him, in view of the enemies he had acquired for himself at the time of his accession to the throne.

But above all his great liberality served him well. For although he was a wise leader in time of adversity, as soon as he believed himself to be secure . . . , he began to antagonize people by means of petty actions. . . . he spoke slightingly of people in their presence as well as in their absence, except in the case of those he feared; and they were numerous because he was by nature rather apprehensive. When as a result of his words some harm came upon him or if he suspected that it might, he wanted to make amends and would make the following speech to the person he had offended: "I well realize that my tongue has brought me great disadvantage, but it has also occasionally brought me much pleasure. It is reasonable, however, that I should make reparation for my blunder." And he never said these kind words without granting the person whom he thus addressed a favor, and no small one at that.*

Louis returned to the strong monarchical tradition of Philip Augustus and Philip the Fair. He forced his protesting subjects to pay higher taxes but granted favors to the men of the middle class and gave them responsible posts in his administration. He propitiated the pope by withdrawing the Pragmatic Sanction of 1438 but in practice continued most of its restrictions on papal control over the Gallican church. He enlarged the army bequeathed him by his father yet conserved its use for the direst emergencies only.

Where Louis XI was cautious, Charles the Bold was audacious to the point of folly. His temperament and policies were nicely assessed by Comines, who had served Charles before he shifted his allegiance to Louis:

I have not seen any reason why he should have incurred the wrath of God, unless it was

because he considered all the graces and honors which he had received in this world to have been the result of his own judgment and valor, instead of attributing them to God, as he should have. For indeed he was endowed with many good qualities and virtues. No prince ever surpassed him in eagerness to act as patron to great men. . . . No lord ever granted audience more freely to his servants and his subjects. . . . He was very ostentatious in his dress and in everything else—a little too much. He was very courteous to ambassadors and foreigners; they were well received and lavishly entertained. . . . He desired great glory, and it was that more than anything else which made him engage in these wars. He would have liked to resemble those princes of antiquity who remained so famous after their death. And he was as daring as any man who ruled in his time.*

Charles determined to build a true middle kingdom by bridging the territorial gap between Burgundy and the Low Countries and seizing Lorraine and Alsace. But, since Alsace was a confused patchwork of feudal jurisdictions overlapping northern Switzerland, his designs threatened the largely independent Swiss confederation. Subsidized by Louis XI, the Swiss defeated Charles three times in 1476 and 1477; in the last of the battles Charles was slain.

Since Charles left no son, his lands were partitioned. The Duchy of Burgundy passed permanently, and the Franche-Comté temporarily, to France. The Low Countries went to Mary, the daughter of Charles; she married Maximilian of Hapsburg, who later became Holy Roman emperor. Their son was to marry the daughter of Ferdinand and Isabella of Spain, and their grandson, the emperor Charles V, was to rule Germany, the Low Countries, Spain, and the fast-growing Spanish empire overseas, and to threaten the kingdom of France with hostile encirclement.

Louis XI, though he did not keep all the Burgundian inheritance out of the hands of potential enemies, did shatter the prospect of a middle kingdom. More than that, he broke the strength of the Armagnac faction as well, recovered most of the territory held as appanages, and doubled the size of the royal domain. At his death, French bastard feudalism was virtually eliminated. The only major region still largely independent of

*S. Kinser, ed., and I. Cazeaux, trans., *The Memoirs of Philippe de Commynes* (University of South Carolina, 1969), I, 130–131.

* Ibid., I, 325.

the Crown was the duchy of Brittany, and this was brought under royal control during the reign of his son. The France of Louis XI was not yet a full-fledged national monarchy, but by his consolidation of territory and by his competent central administration, Louis laid the indispensable foundations for the forging of the French people into a proud, cohesive, confident nation in subsequent centuries.

England: Edward II and Edward III

England, too, was emerging as a national monarchy. Here too, social and political dissension had accompanied the Hundred Years' War, and bastard feudalism flourished until Edward IV and Henry VII reasserted the royal power in the later fifteenth century, much as their contemporary, Louis XI, did in France. But, however close the links and parallels between the two countries, there was also an all-important difference. Whereas in France the Estates General was becoming the docile servant of the monarchy, the English Parliament was slowly setting the precedents and acquiring the powers that would one day make it the master of the Crown.

In England, after the death of the strong and successful Edward I in 1307, the political tide turned abruptly against the monarchy. His athletic son, Edward II (1307–1327), was a weak and inept ruler, dominated by his favorites and by his French queen, Isabella. In 1314 he lost the battle of Bannockburn to the Scots, and with it the short-lived English hegemony over Scotland. Meantime, Edward II faced baronial opposition much like that which had harassed his grandfather, Henry III. In the Ordinances of 1311, the barons virtually reenacted the Provisions of Oxford of 1258. This time they set up as the real rulers of England twenty-one "lords ordainers," who had to consent to royal appointments, to declarations of war, and to the departure of the king from England. Like the barons of Henry III, however, the barons of Edward II were as selfish as the king's bureaucrats had been, and Parliament repealed the ordinances in 1322. In the end, noble malcontents gathered around Edward's queen, Isabella, who led a revolt against her husband. Imprisoned, then murdered, Edward II was succeeded on the throne by his fifteen-year-old son, Edward III, a knightly and vigorous figure.

The reign of Edward III (1327–1377) was marked not only by the stunning English victories in the early campaigns of the Hundred Years' War but also by the great economic crisis following the Black Death. The plague created a terrible shortage of manpower; crops rotted in the fields for lack of harvesters, and good land dropped out of cultivation. The agricultural laborers of England, aware of their suddenly increased bargaining power, and of the enhanced wealth gained by their masters from the French war, demanded better working conditions, or left home and flocked to the towns. In 1351, Parliament passed the Statute of Laborers, an attempt to fix wages and prices as they had been before the plague. It also included regulations forbidding workmen to give up their jobs, and requiring the unemployed to accept work at the old rates. The law was not a success, and the labor shortage hastened the end of serfdom and paved the way for the disorders that took place under Edward's successor. The cause of the peasants was defended most effectively in a striking item of medieval literature, the verse satire of Edward's reign called *The Vision of Piers Plowman,* which denounced the corruption of officials and especially of the clergy.

The attempts to enforce the Statute of Laborers were made by the justices of the peace, a notable English institution first appearing under Edward III. The justices were all royal appointees, selected in each shire from the gentry, who were substantial landholders and accustomed to exercising leadership in local matters. Since they received no pay, they accepted office from a sense of duty or from a fondness for prestige. As the old shire and hundred courts disappeared, the justices of the peace became the chief local judges and, almost down to our own day, were also virtually the rulers of rural England.

The reign of Edward III also witnessed the growth of English national feeling, fostered by the long war with France. The fact that the popes now resided at Avignon and were thought to be under the thumb of the French made the papacy a particular target of nationalist suspicion. In 1351, Parliament passed the Statute of Provisors restricting the provision (that is, the appointment) of aliens to church offices in England. Two years later, Parliament checked the appeal of legal cases to the papal curia by the Statute of Praemunire (the Latin term refers to the prosecution of a legal case). Another example of nationalistic legislation came in 1362, when Parliament declared English the official language of the courts. Norman French, the old language of the ruling classes, continued to be used for some legal documents. As the years passed, English was taught in the schools, and in 1399 it was used to open Parliament. This increased use of the English language expressed the developing sense of national identity and in turn doubtless quickened national feeling.

Nationalism, the dislike of the papacy, and the widespread social and economic discontent were all reflected in England's first real heresy, which appeared at the close of Edward III's reign. This was the doctrine preached by John Wycliffe, an Oxford scholar who died in 1384. Advocating a church without property, in the spirit of the early Christians, Wycliffe called for the direct access of the individual to God, and for the abolition or weakening of many of the functions of the priest. He denied, for example, that in the Mass the bread was miraculously transsubstantiated into the body of Christ. He and his followers were also responsible for the preparation and circulation of an English translation of the Bible. Wycliffe's views were indeed heretical, for the Church had long insisted that the priest was the indispensable intermediary between man and God, and that the Bible should remain in its Latin version, the Vulgate, and should not be translated into the vernacular.

The Evolution of Parliament

The most significant constitutional development of Edward III's long reign was the evolution of Parliament, both in organization and in function. The division of Parliament into two houses was beginning to appear in the fourteenth century, although the terms "House of Commons" and "House of Lords" were not actually used until the fifteenth and sixteenth centuries, respectively. Edward I's Model Parliament of 1295 had assembled not only barons, the higher clergy, knights of the shire, and burgesses but also representatives of the lower clergy. It did not prove to be an exact model for later parliaments, since the lower clergy soon dropped out,

preferring to limit their attendance to the assembly of the English church known as Convocation. But all the other groups present in 1295 continued to appear. The higher clergy, the lords spiritual, also attended Convocation, but as vassals of the king they had to come to Parliament too. As time wore on, this group coalesced with the earls and barons, the lords temporal, to form the nascent House of Lords. The knights of the shire and the burgesses coalesced to form the nascent House of Commons.

The gradual coalescence of knights and burgesses was an event of capital significance—an event that laid the social foundation of the future greatness of the House of Commons. It brought together two elements, the one representing the gentry, the lower level of the second estate, and the other representing the third estate, which always remained separate in the assemblies of the continental monarchies. Little is known about the precise reasons for this momentous development. We do know that in the fourteenth century the knights of the shire were far from feeling a sense of social unity with the burgesses; instead they felt closer to the great lords, with whom they had many ties of blood and common interests in the countryside. But we also know that some of the smaller boroughs were represented by knights from the countryside nearby. At any rate, the king regarded both knights and burgesses as separate from the great lords, and during the reign of Edward III the two groups regularly deliberated together. By the end of the fourteenth century, the important office of Speaker of the House was developing, as the Commons chose one of their members to report to the king on their deliberations. The parliamentary coalition of knights and burgesses evidently came into existence well before their sense of social closeness.

Meantime, the political foundations of the future greatness of the House of Commons were also being laid. In the fourteenth century the chief business of Parliament was judicial. From time to time, the knights and burgesses employed the judicial device of presenting petitions to the king; whatever was approved in the petitions was then embodied in statutes. This was the faint beginning of parliamentary legislative power. Under Edward III, furthermore, the growth of parliamentary power was stimulated by Edward's constant requests to Parliament for new grants of money to cover the heavy expenses of the Hundred Years' War. More and more, Parliament took control of the pursestrings, while Edward, who had little interest in domestic affairs other than finances, let the royal powers be whittled away imperceptibly. Significantly, the responses to the major economic and nationalistic grievances of the mid-fourteenth century took a parliamentary form—the Statutes of Laborers, Provisors, and Praemunire.

Richard II
and Bastard Feudalism

When Edward III died, his ten-year-old grandson succeeded as Richard II (1377–1399). Richard's reign was marked by mounting factionalism on the part of royal relatives and their noble followers and by an outbreak of social discontent on the part of the peasants. Both conflicts strongly resembled their French counterparts, the strife between Burgundy and Armagnac, and the Jacquerie of 1358.

The social disorders arose out of protests against the imposition of poll (head) taxes, which fell equally upon all subjects. In 1380, the poorer classes bitterly resented paying their shilling a head for each person over fifteen, whereas the well-to-do scarcely noticed it. Riots provoked by attempts to collect the tax led to the Peasants' Revolt of 1381. The peasants burned manor records to destroy evidence of their obligations; they also murdered the archbishop of Canterbury. When they marched on London, the fifteen-year-old king interviewed them and promised to meet their demands, which included the ending of serfdom and the seizing of clerical wealth, and thus showed Wycliffe's widespread influence among the lower classes. Richard II saved his own life by offering to lead the peasants himself, but he failed to keep his promises. The rebels experienced severe reprisals, and king and Parliament would have restored serfdom had it been economically possible. Wycliffe, discredited by the excesses of the peasants, retired to private life.

Under Richard II and his successors, though there were interludes of peaceful, constitutional rule, factional strife assumed critical dimensions as a result of the new bastard feudalism. During the fourteenth century, the baronage, which still dominated the scene, had become a smaller, richer class of great magnates. The relationship of the great lords to their vassals grew to be based more and more on cash, and less and less on military service and protection. These lords recruited the armed following they still owed to the king, not by bringing into his increasingly professional army their tenants duly equipped as knights, but by hiring little private armies to go to war for them. Soldiers in these armies, while often members of the country gentry, were bound not by the old feudal ties but by "written indenture and a retaining fee." The custom was known as "livery and maintenance," since the lord provided uniforms for his retainers, who, in turn, "maintained" the lord's cause, especially in legal disputes. Though forbidden by statute in 1390, this practice continued to flourish. The danger from private armies became greater during each interlude of peace in the war with France, as mercenaries used to plundering for a livelihood in a foreign country were suddenly turned loose in England.

The trouble had begun during the last years of Edward III, when effective control of the government passed from the aging king to one of his younger sons, John of Gaunt, duke of Lancaster, and his corrupt entourage. John of Gaunt could mobilize a private army of 1,500 men, and his faction persisted after the accession of Richard II; and new factions also appeared, centered on two of the young king's uncles, the dukes of York and Gloucester. In 1387, Gloucester defeated Richard II's supporters in battle. Then, in a packed Parliament (1388), which was called either the "wonderful" Parliament or the "merciless" Parliament, depending on one's factional ties, Gloucester had royal ministers condemned for treason. The baronage seemed now to control the Crown. It commanded superior armies, it put its own people into royal administrative commissions, and it packed Parliament. Richard II took no steps against Gloucester until 1397, when he arrested him and moved against his confederates. The king packed Parliament in his own favor and had it pass extraordinary new antitreason laws, many of which were retroactive. He grew tremendously extravagant and imposed heavy fiscal exactions on his subjects.

Richard's confiscation of the estates of his first cousin, Henry of Bolingbroke, son of the late John of Gaunt, precipitated a revolution. Its success rested not so much on the popularity of the exiled Bolingbroke as on the great alarm

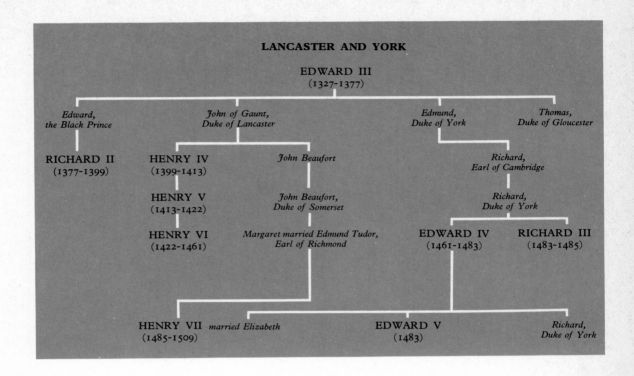

LANCASTER AND YORK

EDWARD III
(1327-1377)

Edward,
the Black Prince

John of Gaunt,
Duke of Lancaster

Edmund,
Duke of York

Thomas,
Duke of Gloucester

RICHARD II
(1377-1399)

HENRY IV
(1399-1413)

John Beaufort

Richard,
Earl of Cambridge

HENRY V
(1413-1422)

John Beaufort,
Duke of Somerset

Richard,
Duke of York

HENRY VI
(1422-1461)

Margaret married Edmund Tudor,
Earl of Richmond

EDWARD IV
(1461-1483)

RICHARD III
(1483-1485)

HENRY VII married Elizabeth
(1485-1509)

EDWARD V
(1483)

Richard,
Duke of York

created by Richard's doctrine that the king could control the lives and property of his subjects. Henry's conspiracy against Richard and his landing in England, therefore, gained wide support. Richard was defeated, was forced to abdicate in 1399, and was later murdered; Bolingbroke now became Henry IV (1399-1413), first monarch of the House of Lancaster.

Lancaster and York

To recover from the upheavals of Richard II's reign and to check the growth of bastard feudalism, England badly needed a long period of stable royal rule. But this the Lancastrian dynasty in the long run was unable to provide. Henry IV owed his position in part to confirmation by Parliament, and Parliament in turn, mindful of its experience with Richard II, was very sensitive about allowing any assertion of the royal authority. As a result, Henry and Parliament did not get on smoothly. Moreover, Henry faced not only hostile factions but also a whole series of revolts—by dispossessed sup-

porters of Richard, by the Welsh aristocracy, and by the great family of the Percies in Northumberland, on the Scottish border. And, as if this were not enough, the last years of his reign were troubled by his own poor health and by the hostility of his son, the "Prince Hal" made famous by Shakespeare.

The son came to the throne as King Henry V (1413-1422), renewed the Hundred Years' War, and scored spectacular victories. At home, he embarked on a course of royal assertiveness, tempered by his need to secure parliamentary support in financing his military campaigns in France. He also persecuted vigorously the followers of Wycliffe in an attempt to suppress the social and religious discontent evidenced in the Peasants' Revolt. The untimely death of Henry V in 1422 ended the brief period of Lancastrian success, for it brought to the throne Henry VI (1422-1461), an infant nine months old at his accession who proved mentally unstable as he grew up.

The reign of this third Lancastrian king was a disaster for England. Her forces went down to defeat in the last campaigns of the Hundred Years' War, and, while the feebleness of Henry

VI did strengthen the hand of Parliament, it strengthened still more the power of bastard feudalism. As corrupt noble factions competed for control of government, a serious quarrel broke out between Henry VI's queen, Margaret of Anjou, and her English allies on the one side, and, on the other, Richard, duke of York, a great-grandson of Edward III and heir to the throne until the birth of Henry's son in 1453. These quarrels led directly to the Wars of the Roses (1455–1485), named for the red rose, the badge of the House of Lancaster, and the white rose, the badge of the House of York.

In thirty years of sporadic fighting, Parliament became the tool of rival factions, and the kingdom itself changed hands repeatedly. In 1460 Richard of York was killed, and the ambitious Earl of Warwick, the "kingmaker," took over the leadership of the Yorkist cause. In the next year Warwick forced the abdication of Henry VI and placed on the throne the son of Richard of York, Edward IV (1461–1483). The king and the kingmaker soon fell out, and in 1470–1471 Warwick staged an abortive revolution that restored the throne briefly to the hapless Henry VI. Edward IV quickly regained control, and Henry VI and Warwick were killed. With Edward securely established, firm royal government returned to England, seemingly on a permanent basis.

Again, however, the prospect of stability faded, for Edward IV died in 1483 at the threshold of middle age. The crown passed momentarily to his twelve-year-old son, Edward V, who was under the domination of his mother and her ambitious relatives; he was soon pushed aside by his guardian and uncle, brother of the older Edward, Richard III (1483–1485), last of the Yorkist kings. Able, courageous, and ruthless, Richard III may not have been quite the villainous figure indelibly imprinted on history by Shakespeare's play. There is still controversy over whether he was responsible for the death of the "little princes of the Tower"—Edward V and his younger brother. In any case, factional strife flared up again as Richard's opponents found a champion in the Lancastrian leader, Henry Tudor, who had the backing of the French. In 1485, on Bosworth Field, Richard III was slain, and the Wars of the Roses at last came to an end. The battle gave England a new monarch, Henry VII, and a new dynasty, the Tudors.

Henry VII

Henry VII (1485–1509) was descended from a bastard branch of the Lancastrian family (his great-grandfather was the illegitimate son of John of Gaunt). His right to be king, however, derived not from this tenuous hereditary claim but from his victory at Bosworth and subsequent acceptance by Parliament. The new monarch had excellent qualifications for the job of tidying up after the dissipations of civil war. Shrewd, able, working very closely with his councillors, waging foreign policy by diplomacy and not by war, Henry VII had a good deal in common with Louis XI of France; they were both professionals. Unlike Louis, however, Henry was devout and he was generous, maintaining a lavish court and endowing at Westminster Abbey the magnificent chapel which bears his name and, with its spectacular fan-vaulting, is such a fine example of the very late and very elaborate Gothic style.

Henry formally healed the breach between the houses of the rival roses by marrying the Yorkist heiress Elizabeth, daughter of Edward IV. Some of the magnates attempted to continue the old factional strife by supporting Perkin Warbeck, an imposter who claimed to be Elizabeth's brother, the younger of the "little princes of the Tower." Henry dealt very firmly with this rebellion and with other uprisings. He deprived the nobles of their private armies by forbidding livery and maintenance, and also banned the nobles' old habit of interfering in the royal courts to intimidate the litigants.

Measures like these had been tried by Henry's predecessors but had ultimately failed for lack of enforcement. Henry, however, enforced his measures most vigorously. In 1487 a parliamentary statute charged a special committee of the King's Council with the task of seeing that the apparatus of the law should not be used to back up factional interests, juridical abuses, or other measures of resistance to what Henry wanted. The new committee became the administrative court known as the Star Chamber, from the star-painted ceiling of the room in which it met. While its operations were sometimes high-handed and arbitrary, it had no direct connection with the later court of the same name, under the seventeenth-century Stuart kings, which made "star chamber proceedings" synonymous with abuse of judicial authority. In fact Henry VII abandoned the experiment with the Star Chamber after a few years and relied on the ordinary courts, particularly those of the justices of the peace, to do the work of the "Big Policeman."

While Henry depended heavily on the country gentry and other traditional mainstays of monarchical government, he also welcomed new men, from the prosperous urban merchant class, or from the ranks of churchmen who had worked their way up and owed their careers to him, like the able lawyer Morton, who became archbishop of Canterbury. Henry rewarded many of his advisers with lands confiscated from his opponents at the end of the Wars of the Roses. The king and his councillors more than doubled the revenues of the central government, partly by using such high-handed methods as "Morton's Fork," attributed (though probably wrongly) to Archbishop Morton. When prelates were summoned to make special payments to the king, those who dressed magnificently in order to plead exemption on the grounds of the cost of high ecclesiastical office were told that their rich apparel argued their ability to make a large payment. The other tine of the fork caught those who dressed shabbily to feign poverty, for their frugality argued that they, too, could afford a large contribution. Such practices enabled Henry to avoid a clash with Parliament, because he seldom had to raise taxes requiring parliamentary sanction. The king's obvious efficiency and his avoidance of costly wars, won him support in the increasingly significant business community. Since foreign vessels still carried the bulk of England's trade, Henry dared not revoke the special privileges of foreign merchants. But he used the threat of revocation to gain trading privileges for English merchants abroad, especially in Italy.

Henry VII reestablished prosperity, law, and order in an England weary of rebellion and civil war. His policies set the stage for the more dramatic reigns of his illustrious successors, Henry VIII and Elizabeth I. He restored the prestige of the monarchy, made it the rallying point of English nationalism, and fixed the pattern for the Tudor policy toward Parliament, a policy often given the misleading label of "Tudor absolutism." Henry VII and his successors were indeed strong monarchs, but they were not absolute in the sense that they attempted to trample over Parliament or to ignore it. Henry, as we have just seen, asked Parliament for money as infrequently as possible; during the last dozen years of his reign he had to summon only one Parliament, which met for a few weeks in 1504. Even so, when it refused to give him all the monies he wanted, he yielded gracefully and avoided a confrontation. Henry VII was well aware that precedents for limiting a monarch's authority lay at hand ready for use against an arbitrary ruler. As a foreign visitor noted, "if the king should propose to change any old established rule, it would seem to every Englishman as if his life were taken from him."*

Spain

The accomplishments of Henry VII and Louis XI, impressive though they were, were overshadowed by those of their great Spanish contemporaries, Ferdinand and Isabella. Henry and Louis ruled kingdoms which, however racked by internal dissensions, had long been well-defined states with established central institutions. Ferdinand and Isabella inherited a Spain that had never really been united; they had to build the structure of central government from the very foundations.

The decisive event in the early medieval history of the Iberian peninsula was the Muslim conquest, starting in the year 711. The whole peninsula, with the exception of the extreme north, came under Muslim control. In the eighth and ninth centuries, Christian communities free of Muslim domination survived only in the Carolingian march of Catalonia and in the tiny states of Galicia, the Asturias, León, and Navarre. From the ninth century through the fifteenth, the Christian states of the north pressed southward until the Muslim remnant at Granada fell in 1492. This slow expansion by Catholic Spaniards has often been likened to a crusade more than five hundred years long. It was indeed

*Quoted by R. L. Storey in *The Reign of Henry VII* (London, 1968), p. 121.

a crusade, and the proud, militant, intolerant spirit of the crusader left a permanent mark upon the Spanish "style." The reconquest of Spain, like the great Crusades to the Holy Land, was a disjointed movement, undertaken in fits and starts by rival states that sometimes put more energy into combating each other than into fighting the Muslim.

Three Christian kingdoms dominated the Iberian peninsula in the middle of the fifteenth century. Castile, the largest and most populous, occupying the center of the peninsula, had originated as a frontier province of León and had assumed the leadership of the reconquest. The capture of Toledo in central Spain (1085) and the great victory over the Muslims at Las Navas de Tolosa (1212) were landmarks in its expansion southward. The power of the Castilian kings, however, did not grow in proportion to their territory. The powerful organization of sheep-ranchers, the *Mesta,* controlled vast stretches of Castilian territory and constituted a virtual state within the state. Both the nobility and the towns, which played a semi-independent part in the reconquest, maintained many rights against the royal authority. Both were represented, together with the clergy, in the Cortes, the medieval Castilian counterpart of the English Parliament and the French Estates General, which had become largely powerless by the fifteenth century.

To the west of Castile, along the Atlantic coast, lay the second Christian kingdom, Portugal. Once a Castilian province, Portugal had won independence in the twelfth century. Though still retaining close links with Castile, the Portuguese were nurturing their own particular national interests, especially in exploration and commerce overseas.

The third kingdom, located in northeastern Spain, was Aragon, which was as much a Mediterranean power as a Spanish one. Its kings controlled the Balearic Islands, ruled lands along the Mediterranean on the French side of the Pyrenees, and had an important stake in southern Italy. In the breakup of the Hohenstaufen Empire Aragon took the island of Sicily (1282). King Alfonso the Magnanimous (1416–1458) added the mainland territories of Naples (1435); at Alfonso's death his inheritance was divided: Sicily and Aragon went to his brother, John (1458–1479), and Naples to his illegitimate son,

Ferrante. In Aragon, as in Castile, the oldest established political institutions were those limiting the Crown—the nobility, the towns, and the Cortes, much more powerful here than in Castile. Two of the territories belonging to the Crown of Aragon on the Spanish mainland had Cortes of their own and so many other autonomous privileges that they were in effect separate states. These were Valencia, dominated by the city of the same name on the Mediterranean, and, farther north, Catalonia, centered on the prosperous port of Barcelona.

Ferdinand and Isabella

In 1469, Ferdinand, later king of Aragon (1479–1516), married Isabella, later queen of Castile (1474–1504), and thus made the dynastic alliance that eventually consummated the political unification of Spain. The obstacles confronting them were immense. Not only was the royal power weak in both states; the inhabitants of Castile and Aragon did not always speak the same language, a difference still evident today in the distinction between the Castilian Spanish spoken in Madrid and the Catalan of Barcelona, whose closest linguistic relative is the Provençal once spoken in the south of France. Aragon looked toward the Mediterranean, Castile toward the Atlantic so that the union of Castile with Portugal might have been more natural.

Even today, Spanish nationalism is diluted by strong regional feelings, especially in Catalonia; Ferdinand and Isabella, however, made an impressive beginning on the very long task of forging a single Spanish nation. Though very different in personality, they made a good political partnership. He was a wary realist of the stamp of Louis XI and an ardent promoter of Aragon's interests in Italy, where he regained Naples. Though given the honorific title of "The Catholic" by the pope, he was skeptical and tolerant in religion and an unfaithful spouse in marriage. Isabella, on the other hand, was devout to the point of fanaticism, adored the pomp and circumstance of the throne, and in politics was wholly absorbed in the consolidation of her authority in Castile. She vested much of the executive authority in a potent new instrument of absolutism staffed by royal appointees, the

Council of Castile. She allied herself with the middle class of the towns against the nobles and drew military support more from town militias than from feudal levies. Her sovereignty was jeopardized by the existence of three large military brotherhoods controlled by the Castilian nobility and founded in the twelfth century to advance the reconquest. Isabella imposed royal authority on all three brotherhoods by the simple device of insisting that Ferdinand be made the head of each. Toward the Mesta Isabella was more indulgent, since payments made by the sheep interests were the mainstay of royal revenue until the wealth of the New World began to pour in.

Ferdinand and Isabella relied heavily on the Church in advancing the royal power. The Queen was pious, but she was also determined to bring the Church under royal discipline and prescribed a much-needed purge of ecclesiastical corruption. The purified Spanish church was later to assume leadership of the Catholic Reformation. The Spanish monarchs also obtained from the papacy the right to make appointments to high offices in the Spanish church and to dispose of parts of its revenue. Like the Gallican church, the Spanish church was half-independent of Rome; far more than the Gallican church, it was the prop of royal absolutism.

An individual and an institution cemented the alliance of church and state in Spain. The individual was Cardinal Jiménez (1436–1517), the archbishop of Toledo, and Isabella's chief minister. Jiménez executed her policies of purify-

ing the Church, curbing the aristocracy, and making an alliance with the towns. The institution was the Inquisition, brought into Spain in 1478. The Spanish Inquisition was from the first a royal rather than a papal instrument; it sought to promote Spanish nationalism by enforcing universal Catholicism, to create loyal subjects of the Crown by obliging men to be obedient children of the Church.

The chief targets of the new policy were the two important Spanish religious minorities—the Muslims and the Jews. Both groups had long enjoyed toleration; both owned some of the most productive farms and businesses in Spain; and the Jews, because of their economic capacity and political reliability, were favorite agents of the Crown until Isabella's alliance with the Christian townsmen. In the fourteenth century, however, fear and envy of Jewish success had promoted anti-Semitic outbreaks which led many Jews to become converts to Christianity. It was in order to check backsliding among these New Christians that the Inquisition was established. The persecution was so menacing, with its tortures and burnings at the stake, that more than 100,000 New Christians fled the country. In 1492 unconverted Jews were confronted with the alternatives of immediate baptism or immediate exile with the loss of their property; about 150,000 Jews went into exile. Ten years later it was the turn of the Muslims, who received no choice except baptism. Catholicism thereby won many nominal new adherents who continued to conform only because they dreaded what the In-

Christian Reconquest of Spain

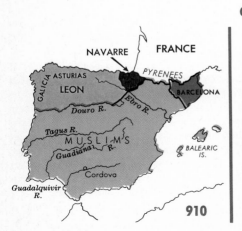

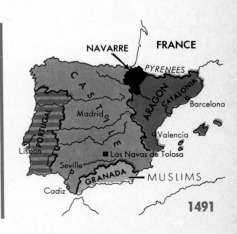

quisition had in store for those who wavered in their new faith. Isabella and Jiménez had secured religious uniformity but had alienated some of the most productive groups in Spanish society.

The year 1492, accordingly, may be viewed as the most crucial date in the whole of Spanish history. It began, on January 2, with the triumphal entry of Ferdinand and Isabella into the Alhambra of Granada, marking the conquest of the last fragment of independent Muslim Spain.

Later in the year, the way was opened for fresh conquests on a scale undreamt when Columbus sailed from a Castilian Atlantic port on the first of his momentous voyages to the New World. But in the same year persecution on a grand scale was confirmed as national policy. The new Spanish monarchy already bore the stamp of the intolerant nationalism that was to be at once its strength and its weakness in generations to come.

III Particularism in Germany and Italy

The Interregnum and Its Results

In contrast to the new monarchies of western Europe, Germany had monarchs but no national monarchy, as power shifted steadily from the emperor to the princes of the particular states. Once, indeed, for a span of almost two decades there was no emperor at all—the Interregnum (1254–1273) following the death of the last Hohenstaufen emperor, Conrad IV, the son of Frederick II. During the Interregnum, the princes brought closer to completion their usurpation of rights that had formerly belonged to the monarchy. They also enhanced their power by taking advantage of the large grants made by rival foreign candidates for the imperial throne in the hope of receiving princely support. Meanwhile, the old links between Germany and Italy were sundered, and the earlier idea of an emperor who ruled lands outside Germany vanished.

The imperial title, however, did not vanish. It went to Rudolf of Hapsburg (1273–1291), first emperor to be chosen after the Interregnum. Scion of a family of lesser German nobility, whose estates lay mostly in Switzerland, Rudolf cared nothing for imperial pretensions. What he wanted was to establish a hereditary monarchy for his family in Germany and to make this monarchy as rich and as powerful as possible. He added Austria to the family holdings, and his descendants ruled at Vienna until 1918. Since Hapsburg interests were focused on the southeastern part of the empire, Rudolf was willing to make concessions to the French in the western

imperial territories in order to get their support for the new Hapsburg monarchy.

After 1270, consequently, the French moved into imperial territories that had once belonged to the old Carolingian middle kingdom. They thereby secured lands east of the Rhone and a foothold in Lorraine. The German princes, however, especially the great archbishops of the Rhine Valley, opposed the Hapsburg policy of propitiating the French. Thus, during the century following the Interregnum, two parties developed in Germany. There was a Hapsburg party, anti-imperial (in the sense of being indifferent to the territorial integrity of the empire), in favor of a strong hereditary monarchy, eastern-based, and therefore pro-French. And there was an opposition party, pro-imperial, against a strong hereditary monarchy, western-based, and therefore anti-French. Since both parties on occasion elected emperors, the imperial office was no longer monopolized for long periods by one family but was held at various times by the houses of Nassau, Luxemburg, Bohemia, and Hapsburg, and by the Wittelsbach family of Bavaria.

This division on the imperial question frustrated the development of German national unity. German political life, like that of contemporary France and England, showed some of the sterility and the exaggerated concern for empty forms that characterized the later Middle Ages. Thus the emperor Henry VII (1308–1313) intervened in Italy just as if he could still perform the impossible and unite that divided country, and just as if the imperial dreams of the Hohenstaufens could be made realities without the resources and the loyalties which the Hohenstau-

fens had commanded. Similarly, in a long
conflict between the papacy and the emperor
Louis of Bavaria (1314–1347), the "captive"
popes at Avignon asserted pretensions to omni-
potence which even Gregory VII and Innocent
III had not been able to make good.

The Golden Bull

Rudolf of Hapsburg had pursued territorial
aims in order to strengthen the monarchy. But
in time, as the imperial crown passed from
family to family, matters were reversed. The
princes wanted the crown because it would help
them add to their own possessions. As each
German emperor strove to achieve family territorial aims, the position of the monarchy became
simply that of another territorial princedom.
The pursuit of such aims engaged all the princes,
whether their houses happened to be in temporary control of the imperial throne or not.
Thus, toward the middle of the fourteenth century, the principle of elective monarchy finally
triumphed and the princes as a class secured a
great victory.

Their victory was embodied in the Golden
Bull of 1356, issued by the emperor Charles IV.
It reaffirmed what the German princes had
themselves declared in 1338 during Louis of Bavaria's conflict with the papacy: that the imperial
dignity was of God, that the German electoral
princes chose the emperor, and that the choice
of the majority of the electors needed no confirmation by the pope. In 1356, it was expressly
stated that a candidate receiving the majority of
electoral votes had been unanimously elected
emperor. Furthermore, the position of the electors was now regularized. They were to number
the three Rhenish ecclesiastical princes—the
archbishops of Mainz, Trier, and Cologne—and
four secular princes—the count palatine of the
Rhine, the duke of Saxony, the margrave of
Brandenburg, and the king of Bohemia. The
rights of the four lay electors were to pass to
their eldest sons and their territories could never
be divided. Each of the seven electors was to be
all but sovereign in his own territory, with full
rights of coinage and of holding courts from
which there was no appeal. It is little wonder
that the Golden Bull has been termed "the
Magna Carta of the German princes."

*Illustrations from the fourteenth-century "Mirror of
Saxony" ("Der Sachsenspiegel"). Top: The pope (center)
receives the key from Saint Peter; the emperor is at the
left. Center: The pope and emperor embrace, symbolizing
the coordination of spiritual and temporal power. Bottom:
The pope consecrates the emperor; six electors look on at
the left.*

Princes, Cities, and Estates

During the fourteenth century, the German
princes inside their own principalities had been
facing the threat of a new political fragmentation. This came especially from their own administrative officials, the ministeriales, who were
originally from the lower classes but who had
turned their lands and powers into feudal rights,
had assumed knighthood, and had virtually

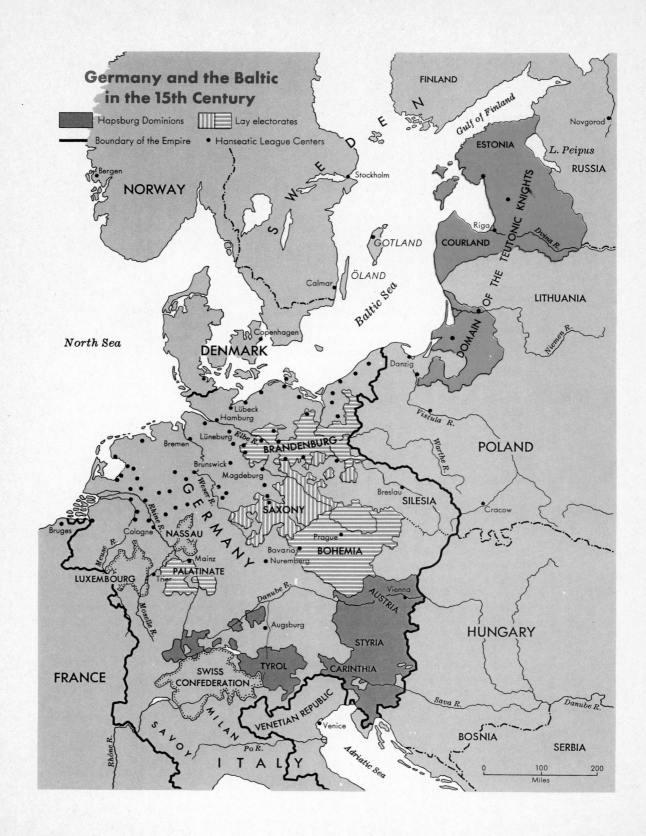

Germany and the Baltic in the 15th Century

Hapsburg Dominions
Lay electorates
Boundary of the Empire
Hanseatic League Centers

FINLAND

NORWAY

Bergen

SWEDEN

Stockholm

GOTLAND

ÖLAND

Calmar

Baltic Sea

Gulf of Finland

Novgorod

ESTONIA

L. Peipus

RUSSIA

Riga

COURLAND

DOMAIN OF THE TEUTONIC KNIGHTS

Dvina R.

LITHUANIA

Niemen R.

North Sea

DENMARK

Copenhagen

Danzig

Vistula R.

POLAND

Lübeck
Hamburg
Lüneburg
Bremen
Brunswick
Magdeburg

Elbe R.
Weser R.

BRANDENBURG

Warthe R.

SAXONY

Breslau

SILESIA

Cracow

GERMANY

Rhine R.

Bruges

Cologne

NASSAU

Meuse R.

LUXEMBOURG

Moselle R.

Trier

Mainz

PALATINATE

BOHEMIA

Prague

Bavaria

Nuremberg

Danube R.

Augsburg

Vienna

AUSTRIA

STYRIA

HUNGARY

FRANCE

SWISS
CONFEDERATION

TYROL

CARINTHIA

Sava R.

Danube R.

SAVOY

Rhône R.

MILAN

Po R.

VENETIAN REPUBLIC

Venice

Adriatic Sea

BOSNIA

SERBIA

ITALY

0   100   200
Miles

merged with the old nobility. It appeared as if a permanent state of feudal anarchy might prevail within the German states. To levy taxes, the princes had to obtain the consent of the nobles and knights along with that of the other estates, the clergy and the towns. The estates often won privileges from the princes in exchange for money. As late as 1392 in Brunswick, for example, the estates forced the duke to give them far-reaching concessions, which amounted to establishing them as rival rulers of the duchy. This period of increasing power of the estates also saw the rise of the famous Hanse of North German commercial towns and the increasing prominence of sovereign "free cities" all over Germany. But the rise of the estates meant also a rise in public disorder as urban–rural antagonism increased, robber barons infested the roads, and wars between rival leagues became common.

By about 1400, the power of the estates had reached its height; then it slowly yielded to other forces that had begun to operate after the enactment of the Golden Bull. The princes who were not electors gradually adopted for their own principalities the rules of primogeniture and indivisibility which the Golden Bull had prescribed for the electoral principalities. The princes were assisted in their assertion of authority by the spread of Roman law. As the Roman law had helped the emperors in ages past, it now helped the prince to make good his claims to absolute control of public rights and offices. Gradually, in half a hundred petty states, orderly finance, indivisible princely domains, and taxation granted by the estates became typical.

By the end of the fifteenth century, then, the German princes had achieved on a local or regional scale the kind of stability and constitutional balance which the king of France had first achieved in his kingdom two centuries earlier. As in England, the estates sometimes aired their grievances at meetings and obtained redress. Instead of mutual hostility between them and the princes, there was now cooperation. This was the pattern that was to typify German political life for the centuries ahead.

The Empire and Nationalism

With a host of sovereign princes firmly established in their particular states and with a long roster of "free cities" enjoying virtual political independence, the empire itself had become almost meaningless. In the two centuries following the Interregnum, it had lost control not only over the western lands taken by France but also over other frontier areas, notably Switzerland. In 1291, three forest cantons in the heart of the country had made a successful bid for effective selfrule. By the early sixteenth century, the number of confederated cantons had quadrupled, and the Swiss, backed by France, had checked both Burgundian and German attempts to subjugate them. The Swiss Confederation, though nominally still subject to the empire, was in fact an independent entity, with boundaries beginning to resemble those of present-day Switzerland. Another national state was emerging, but one distinguished by the absence of a strong central authority. The Swiss federal government was extremely weak, and the individual cantons enjoyed many prerogatives of the kind that Americans of today would call "states' rights."

As territorial losses and other visible signs of the empire's weakness multiplied, the Germans themselves began to undergo a national awakening. The emperor would have been the natural rallying point of emerging national feeling, if that office had not already become an instrument to advance the interests of particular dynasties. In 1438, the emperorship, though still elective, passed permanently to the house of Hapsburg. Forty-five years later a most attractive scion of that house, Maximilian I (1493–1519), became emperor. He was a gentleman and a scholar, and an athlete and warrior as well, and he had acquired great riches by marrying Mary of Burgundy, the daughter of Charles the Bold and the heiress of the Low Countries. Under his weak predecessors, the Hapsburg position in central Europe had deteriorated. Maximilian reestablished firm Hapsburg power in Austria and its dependencies. He also arranged for his children and grandchildren marriages that promised to add vast new territories to the family possessions and that would make his grandson, Charles V, the ruler of half of Europe. On the other hand, Maximilian's projects for reforming the empire came to little, not only because of the vested interests of German particularism but also because of Maximilian's own dynastic concerns. German nationalism was still awaiting a leader.

Despots and Condottieri in Italy

Italians, too, were experiencing the growth of national awareness and lacked any central authority to give it effective political expression. With the disintegration of the Hohenstaufen Empire in the thirteenth century the last shadows of the emperor's control over Italian affairs vanished, and Italy, too, witnessed the advance of particularism and the emergence of powerful local rulers. In Germany the fifteenth century was the Age of the Princes; in Italy it was the Age of the Despots, power politicians par excellence, brilliant and ruthless and cultivated rulers who did much to set the style of the Renaissance.

Despots had not always ruled in Italy. As we saw in Chapter 7, the struggle between popes and emperors had promoted the growth of independent communes or city-states, particularly in northern Italy. In the twelfth and thirteenth centuries, the communes were oligarchic republics, dominated by the nobility and by the newly rich businessmen. The ruling oligarchies, however, were torn by the strife between the pro-papal Guelfs and the pro-imperial Ghibellines. Meantime, something close to class warfare arose between the wealthy, on the one hand, and the small businessmen and wage earners on the other. In town after town, from the thirteenth century on, social and political dissensions grew so bitter that arbitrary one-man government seemed to be the only remedy. Sometimes a despot seized power; sometimes he was invited in from outside by the contending factions. Often he was a *condottiere,* a captain of the mercenaries whom the states hired under contract to fight their wars (*condotta* is Italian for "contract," whence *condottiere,* "contractor," *condottieri* in the plural). One of the first great condottieri was an Englishman, Sir John Hawkwood, who went to Italy during the lull in the Hundred Years' War following the Treaty of Brétigny in 1361. In the fifteenth century the most celebrated condottieri were native sons, scions of local noble dynasties like the Gonzaga of Mantua, the Malatesta of Rimini, and the Montefeltro of Urbino or ambitious plebeians who viewed the military profession as an avenue to riches and power. Typical of these careerists

were Francesco Sforza, who became duke of Milan, and two men whose exploits are now largely forgotten but whose professional toughness lives on in famous equestrian sculptures—Erasmo Gattamelata, in the statue by Donatello in Padua, and Bartolommeo Colleoni, in that by Verocchio in Venice.

By the fifteenth century, the fortunes of war and politics had worked significant changes in the map of Italy. Especially in the northern half of the peninsula, many city-states that had been important a century or two before were sinking into political obscurity, subjugated or at least eclipsed by their stronger neighbors, though often still participating vigorously in economic or cultural life. Genoa, Pisa, Siena, and Lucca are cases in point. Half a dozen states now dominated Italian politics—the Two Sicilies in the south, the States of the Church in the center, and in the north the duchy of Milan and the republics of Florence and Venice.

Sicily, Naples, and Rome

The Two Sicilies comprised the island of Sicily and the mainland territory of Naples, confusingly named the Kingdom of Sicily. Both territories had long been subject to foreign domination, Byzantine and Arab, Norman and Hohenstaufen. In 1268, Charles of Anjou, the brother of Louis IX of France, conquered them from the grandson of the emperor Frederick II. Insular Sicily revolted against Angevin rule in the bloody uprising known as the Sicilian Vespers (1282) and passed to the control of Aragon, and eventually to the Spain of Ferdinand and Isabella. Naples remained Angevin until 1435, when it was taken by Alfonso the Magnanimous of Aragon. In 1458, it became an independent state again, ruled by Alfonso's illegitimate son Ferrante (Ferdinand, 1458–1494), a particularly ruthless despot. Under Angevin and Aragonese rule, the Two Sicilies never fully recovered the vigor, the prosperity, and the cultural leadership they had enjoyed in their great medieval days. But their eclipse was by no means total; Alfonso the Magnanimous was a generous patron of art and learning, and Naples played at least a econdary role in the Renaissance.

Like the Two Sicilies, the States of the Church suffered a material decline. They vir-

SWITZERLAND

TYROL

Drava R.

FRANCE

DUCHY
OF
MILAN
•Milano

DUCHY
OF
SAVOY
•Pavia
Turin

L. Como

Verona

•Padua

Trieste

Venice

Sava R.

Rhône R.

MANTUA

Po R.

Genoa

FERRARA

Ravenna

Bologna• ROMAGNA
•Zara

OTTOMAN

Avignon
(to the
Papacy)

REPUBLIC
OF
GENOA

Arno R.
Pisa

Florence
TUSCANY

Spalato

EMPIRE

REP. OF
FLORENCE

Siena

Urbino
•Assisi

STATES

Adriatic Sea

CORSICA
(to Genoa)

of the

CHURCH

Rome•
Tiber R.

KINGDOM

Bari

Garigliano R.

Naples

APULIA

Taranto

SARDINIA
(to Aragon)

of the

TWO

CALABRIA

SICILIES

IONIAN IS.
(to Venice)

Renaissance Italy
about 1494

Palermo

Messina

SICILY

Mediterranean Sea

Syracuse

0   100   200
Miles

CRETE   RHODES   CYPRUS

Danube R.

VENETIAN REPUBLIC

tually disintegrated as a political unit during the
fourteenth century and the first half of the
fifteenth, when the popes sustained the successive blows of the Babylonian Captivity, the Great
Schism, and the struggle with the Councils. The
city of Rome relapsed into the hands of rival
princely families; the outlying territories fell to
local feudal lords or despots.

After 1450, the popes once more concentrated
their attention on central Italy. Beginning with
Nicholas V (1447-1455), and continuing with
Pius II (1458-1464) and Sixtus IV (1471-1484),
the papacy was held by a series of ambitious
men, often highly cultivated, and often very
secular as well, openly acknowledging their
children and lavishing favors on them and on
other relatives. They restored Rome to its old
importance as a center of art and learning, and
they began the reconquest of the papal domin-

ions. The Borgia pope, Alexander VI (1492-
1503), greatly aided by his aggressive and unscrupulous son, Cesare, made notable progress
in subjugating the lords of central Italy and in
breaking the power of the Roman princely
families. Cesare Borgia employed almost any
means—treachery, violence, assassination by poisoning—to gain his ends. The next pope, Julius
II (1503-1513), a nephew of Sixtus IV, was a
statesman and general who commanded his
troops in person and who consolidated further
the temporal authority of the papacy. Soon,
however, the political ambitions of these ecclesiastical condottieri collapsed under the double
blow of the wounds inflicted on the Church by
the Reformation and the damage sustained by
Italy as the battleground in a prolonged war between the Hapsburgs and the Valois kings of
France.

365

Milan

In the late Middle Ages, both the States of the Church and the Two Sicilies were overshadowed by the three great north Italian states. Of these, the Duchy of Milan occupied a site of great strategic and economic value in the midst of the fertile Lombard plain, within sight of the Alps. Milan was the center of the breadbasket of Italy and the terminus of trade routes through the Alpine passes from northern Europe. It was also a textile and metallurgical center, famous for its velvets and brocades, its weapons and armor.

Milan had began to play a major political role in the twelfth century, when it headed the Lombard League in a successful contest with Frederick Barbarossa. At that time its territories reached from Lake Como in the Alps south to Pavia on the Po River. Later, the Milanese extended their dominions south of the Po and threatened to annex both Florence and Genoa. Twelfth-century Milan was a republic, run by the nobility in conjunction with a *Parlamento*, or great council, in which all citizens of modest means could participate. This mixture of aristocracy and democracy, however, proved unworkable, the more so since it was complicated by outbreaks of Guelf and Ghibelline factionalism. In 1277, authority was seized by the noble Visconti family, henchmen of the powerful archbishops of Milan, who soon secured recognition from the emperor as dukes of Milan. Their highhanded methods, together with the great prosperity of the city and its agrarian hinterland, gave them an income higher than that of many kings. The age of despotism, begun by the Visconti, continued when their direct line died out in 1447. Attempts to revive the old republican government were quickly countered by the son-in-law of the last Visconti duke, Francesco Sforza, an energetic condottiere who usurped the ducal office in 1450. He maintained the Visconti tradition of arbitrary rule but made it more tolerable by his soldierly efficiency and by his generous support of public works. He founded a great hospital in the city, completed its elaborate Gothic cathedral, and extended irrigation canals throughout the duchy.

The most famous of the Sforza dukes was a younger son of Francesco, Ludovico Il Moro, 1451-1508 (Lewis "the Moor"—the nickname has been traced both to "Maurus," his middle name, and to his dark, "Moorish" appearance). Like his father, Il Moro was a usurper; he seized the government in 1479 from his weak and sickly nephew. He assembled a retinue of outstanding artists and intellectuals, headed by the renowned Leonardo da Vinci, and made the court of Milan perhaps the most brilliant in Europe. Il Moro had the reputation of being the craftiest diplomat of the age. All his craftiness, however, did not suffice to defend him against the armies of France and Spain, which invaded Italy in the 1490's. Driven from his throne in 1500, Il Moro died in a French prison eight years later. The Duchy of Milan came under direct Spanish rule in 1535 and remained under the control of Spain for almost two hundred years. The Sforzas were true condottieri, soldiers of fortune who gained power—and lost it—almost overnight.

Florence

Not condottieri but bankers, merchants, and industrial entrepreneurs governed the Republic of Florence, on the banks of the Arno in Tuscany, midway between Milan and Rome. Class conflicts largely determined the course of politics in this pioneering center of industry and finance. By the thirteenth century, the struggle between Guelfs and Ghibellines had become a contest for power between two noble factions, one (the Guelf) ready to open its ranks to newly rich commoners, the other (the Ghibelline) reluctant to do so. In the late 1200's, Guelf capitalists prevailed over the Ghibelline aristocrats and proceeded to revise the constitution of the republic so that a virtual monopoly of key government offices rested with the seven major guilds, which were controlled by the great woolen masters, bankers, and exporters. They denied any effective political voice, to the craftsmen and shopkeepers of the fourteen lesser guilds as well as to Ghibellines, many nobles, and common laborers. But feuds within Guelf ranks soon caused a new exodus of political exiles, among them the poet Dante, whose attempts to heal the divisions among his fellow Guelfs resulted in his permanent banishment (1302) and his adoption of the lost Ghibelline cause of imperial rule for divided Italy.

Throughout the fourteenth century and into the fifteenth, political factionalism and social and economic tensions continued to torment Florence, though they did not prevent the remarkable cultural burgeoning of the city, as we shall see in the next chapter. The politically unprivileged—almost everyone outside the dominant Guelf oligarchy—sought to make the republic more democratic; they failed in the long run because of the oligarchy's resilience and also because the reformers themselves were torn by the hostility between the lesser guilds and the poor day laborers, often termed *Ciompi,* which literally meant "wool carders." In the 1340's disastrous bank failures weakened the major guilds enough to permit the fourteen lesser guilds to gain supremacy. Unrest persisted, however, reaching a climax with the revolution of the Ciompi in 1378. Wool carders, weavers, and dyers all gained the right to form their own guilds and to have a minor say in politics. Continued turbulence permitted the wealthy to get the upper hand over both the Ciompi and the lesser guilds and to reestablish oligarchic rule. Their prestige rose when they defended Florence successfully against the threat of annexation by the aggressive Visconti of Milan. Finally, in the early 1400's, a new rash of bankruptcies and a series of military reverses weakened the hold of the oligarchs. In 1434, some of its leaders were forced into exile, and power passed to a political champion of the poor, Cosimo de' Medici.

For the next sixty years (1434–1494) Florence was run by the Medici, who had large woolen and banking interests and were perhaps the wealthiest family in the whole of Italy. Their application of the graduated income tax bore heavily on the rich, and particularly on their political enemies, and the resources of the Medici bank were also employed to weaken their opponents and assist their friends. The Medici were despots, but despots rather like some tyrants of ancient Greece, who did a good deal to improve the position of the lower classes. They operated quietly behind the façade of republican institutions, Cosimo, for example, seldom holding any public office and keeping himself in the background. It was an old Floren-

tine custom that the municipal officials should be chosen every two months in a sort of political lottery by the random selection of names from leather purses containing the names of all eligible citizens. It was also an old custom that the guilds rigged the lottery so that only the names of their adherents were ever selected, and all Cosimo had to do was abide by the traditional fraud. The turnover of personnel every two months hardly promoted political stability, however, and Cosimo's grandson made a new Council of Seventy, with permanent membership, the real center of administration.

The grandson of Cosimo was Lorenzo, the most famous of the Medici, ruler of Florence from 1469 to 1492 and known as *Il Magnifico* for want of a formal title. An equally celebrated Florentine, Machiavelli, drew an admiring portrait of Lorenzo the Magnificent:

It was throughout his aim to make the city prosperous, the people united, and the nobles honored. He loved exceedingly all who excelled in the arts, and he showered favors on the learned. . . . Lorenzo delighted in architecture, music, and poetry. . . . To give the youth of Florence an opportunity of studying letters he founded a college at Pisa, to which he had appointed the most excellent professors that Italy could produce. . . . His character, prudence, and good fortune were such that he was known and esteemed, not only by the princes of Italy, but by many others in distant lands. . . . In his conversation he was ready and eloquent, in his resolutions wise, in action swift and courageous. There was nothing in his conduct, although inclined to excessive gallantry, which in any way impaired his many virtues; it is possible he found more pleasure in the company of droll and witty men than became a man of his position; and he would often be found playing among his children as if he were still a child. To see him at one time in his grave moments and at another in his gay was to see in him two personalities, joined as it were with invisible bonds. . . . There had never died in Florence—nor yet in Italy—one for whom his country mourned so much, or who left behind him so wide a reputation for wisdom.*

Lorenzo possessed in abundance many of the qualities most admired in his time. In addition

---

* Machiavelli, *Florentine History,* trans. W. K. Marriott (New York, 1909), pp. 359–360.

Terra-cotta bust of Lorenzo de' Medici by Verrocchio.

to those noted by Machiavelli, he was tolerant, and he was devoted to sports and rural pleasures; he had great charm and a most decided way with women; and he lavished money on the beautification of the city of Florence. Yet neither his appearance (he had a deformed nose) nor his policies were perfect. Lorenzo's neglect of military matters, his financial carelessness, and the failure of the Medici bank left Florence ill prepared for the wars that engulfed Italy at the turn of the century from the fifteenth to the sixteenth.

Like the story of Milan after Il Moro, the story of Florence after Lorenzo is one of rapid political decline. Following the death of Lorenzo in 1492, the Florentines made two short-lived attempts to drive the Medici from power and to reestablish a genuine republic. In 1512 and again in 1530 the Medici returned. In 1569, they converted the Florentine republic, which had now lost any claim to grandeur, into the Grand Duchy of Tuscany, with themselves as hereditary grand dukes.

Venice

The third great north Italian state, Venice, enjoyed a political stability that contrasted sharply with the turbulence of Florence and Milan. By the fifteenth century, the Republic of St. Mark, as it was called, was in fact an empire. Its territories included the lower valley of the Po River (annexed to secure its defenses and its food supply), the Dalmatian shore of the Adriatic Sea, and part of the Greek islands and mainland. The empire reflected the Ventians' leadership in the Fourth Crusade and their dominance over the Eastern trade, which was unchallenged after they outdistanced the rival Genoese in the fourteenth century. The government likewise reflected the paramountcy of the republic's commercial interests, since, unlike Florence or Milan, Venice had no traditional landed nobility.

The Venetian constitution assumed its definitive form in the early fourteenth century. Earlier, the chief executive had been the doge or duke, first appointed by the Byzantine emperor, then an elected official; the legislature had been a general assembly of all the citizens, somewhat resembling the Parlamento of Milan. The

Venetian merchants, however, feared that a powerful doge might establish a hereditary monarchy, and they found the assembly unwieldly and unbusinesslike. Accordingly, they relegated the doge to an ornamental role like that of a constitutional monarch today. Conveyed in a gorgeously outfitted barge and attended by a host of citizens and foreign visitors, the doge annually cast a huge "wedding ring" into the Adriatic. He thus "married" the sea and paid yearly tribute to the source of Venetian wealth. At the same time, the merchants made the old assembly into the Great Council, a closed corporation whose membership of 240 men was limited to the families listed in a special Golden Book. The Great Council, in turn, elected the doge and the members of the smaller councils, which really ran the government. Foremost among these was the Council of Ten, a powerful secret agency charged with maintaining the security of the republic.

The Venetian elite was a much tighter and more closed group than that of fourteenth-century Florence, where successful and aggressive newcomers could gain membership in one of the seven greater guilds. The Venetian system vested a permanent monopoly of political power in the old merchant families listed in the Golden Book, about 2 percent of the total population. One can appreciate why the label of "Venetian oligarchy" has often been pinned on any government that seeks to perpetuate the privileges and profits of the few. The oligarchs of Venice, however, while denying the many a voice in politics and sternly repressing all opposition, did institute many projects for the general welfare, from neighborhood fountains on up to the great naval arsenal. They treated the subject cities of the empire with fairness and generosity, and they were pioneers—at least in the Western world—in the development of a corps of diplomats to serve the far-reaching concerns of a great commercial power. Though they were unable to prevent the eventual decline of the city, they did pursue their business aims with single-minded efficiency for several hundred prosperous years. Venice was unique among Italian states for its political calm and order. There were no upheavals, no sudden seizures or losses of power by rival factions or ambitious despots. Seldom in history have political means been so perfectly adapted to economic ends.

Reception of a Venetian ambassador in Cairo: painting of the school of Gentile Bellini.

The "School of Europe"

The Italian states of the fifteenth century have been called the "school of Europe," instructing the other European states in the new realistic ways of power politics. Despots like Il Moro, Cesare Borgia, Lorenzo the Magnificent, and the oligarchs of Venice might well have given lessons in statecraft to Henry VII of England or Louis XI of France. They were the most hard-boiled rulers in a hard-boiled age. In international affairs, the experiments with diplomatic missions made by Venice, by the Visconti of Milan, and by the Gonzaga family in the small north Italian state of Mantua were soon copied by the national monarchies farther north and west. Italian reliance on condottieri foreshadowed the general use of mercenaries and the abandonment of the old feudal levies. The rival Italian states, though their mutual competition

often led to open conflict, yet learned to coexist in a precarious balance of power. This balance served as a model or precedent for the European monarchies in later centuries.

This very example, however, also reveals that Italy was the "school of Europe" in a negative sense, for she also furnished a compelling object lesson in how not to behave politically. By the close of the fifteenth century, it was evident that the balance established among the Italian states was too precarious to preserve their independence. Beginning with the French invasion of 1494, Italy became a happy hunting ground for the new national and dynastic imperialists of France, Spain, and the Hapsburg realm and ended as a Spanish preserve, as a later chapter will show in more detail. The national monarchy was the wave of the future, at least of a successful political future; the city-state was not, even when it was run by an efficient despot, or even when, like Venice, it ruled an empire. The Italians of the Renaissance, like the Greeks of antiquity whom they so frequently resembled,

Anonymous portrait of Cesare Borgia.

were victimized by stronger neighbors and were penalized for their failure to form "one Italy."

Machiavelli

These lessons from the "school of Europe" were first drawn by Niccolò Machiavelli (1469–1527). A diplomat who served the restored Florentine republic in the early 1500's, Machiavelli was exiled when the Medici returned in 1512. Soon after, he wrote *The Prince* and dedicated it to the Medici ruler in the vain hope of regaining political favor. While this famous little essay often makes rather tame reading today, it still contains the statements that have given the word "Machiavellian" its sinister reputation. *The Prince* makes a low estimate of human nature:

For it may be said of men in general that they are ungrateful, voluble, dissemblers, anxious to avoid danger, and covetous of gain; as long as you benefit them, they are entirely yours; they offer you their blood, their goods, their life, and their children, . . . when necessity is remote; but when it approaches, they revolt.*

One might term this a secular adaptation of original sin, a transfer of Christian pessimism about mankind from the realm of religion to that of social and political psychology. The politics of *The Prince* follow directly from its estimate of human nature:

A prudent ruler ought not to keep faith when by so doing it would be against his interest, and when the reasons which made him bind himself no longer exist. If men were all good, the precept would not be a good one; but as they are bad, and would not observe their faith with you, so you are not bound to keep faith with them. . . .†

Accordingly, Machiavelli praises the vigorous and unscrupulous absolutism of Francesco Sforza, of Lorenzo the Magnificent, and, above all, of Cesare Borgia. After surveying the bad faith and deception practiced by Cesare Borgia to tighten his hold on the States of the Church, Machiavelli concludes:

I find nothing to blame, on the contrary, I feel bound . . . to hold him up as an example to be imitated by all who by fortune and with the arms of others have risen to power.‡

The Prince was, first and last, a tract for the times, a drastic prescription against the severe political maladies afflicting Italy in the early 1500's. But what precisely was Machiavelli's diagnosis of Italy's ills, and what precisely were his recommended prescription? Scholars do not entirely agree. A majority of them believe that *The Prince* is to be taken literally and that Italy's desperate plight in the face of foreign invasion— "without a head, without order, beaten, despoiled, lacerated, and overrun," as Machiavelli wrote in the emotional final chapter—required a desperate remedy. A minority, however, argue that Machiavelli's intention was satirical and that he was really warning his compatriots against relying on excessive despotism, even at the moment of national emergency.

* *The Prince*, Chap. 17. This and succeeding quotations from Machiavelli are from the Modern Library edition of *The Prince and The Discourses.*
† Ibid., Chap. 18.
‡ Ibid., Chap. 7.

The minority view gains some plausibility when *The Prince* is compared with Machiavelli's longer work, *The Discourses on the First Ten Books of Titus Livius* (the Roman historian Livy). In *The Discourses* he addresses not the immediate Italian crisis but the universal problem of building a lasting government, and argues that the state requires something more than a single prince endowed with power, more power, and yet more power. In a chapter entitled "The People Are Wiser and More Constant than Princes," Machiavelli writes:

I say that the people are more prudent and stable, and have better judgment than a prince. . . . We also see that in the election of their magistrates they make far better choice than princes; and no people will ever be persuaded to elect a man of infamous character and corrupt habits to any post of dignity, to which a prince is easily influenced in a thousand different ways. . . . We furthermore see the cities where the people are masters make the greatest progress in the least possible time, and much greater than such as have always been governed by princes; as was the case with Rome after the expulsion of the kings, and with Athens, after they rid themselves of Pisistratus; and this can be attributed to no other cause than that the governments of the people are better than those of princes.*

In *The Discourses*, Machiavelli thus presents both an estimate of human nature and a political program seemingly in conflict with the statements of *The Prince*. But the conflict is perhaps more apparent than real. *The Discourses* concerned people, like the Athenians and Romans of old, who had great civic virtues and were capable of self-government. *The Prince* concerned people, Machiavelli's Italians, who in his judgment had lost their civic virtues and therefore required the strongest kind of government from above. It seems as though the majority of

scholars may be correct in their interpretation of *The Prince* after all.

Machiavelli blamed the Church for the Italians' loss of civic spirit. *The Discourses* attacked the papacy in particular for preventing Italian unity because of its temporal interests, and then questioned the values of Christianity itself:

Reflecting now as to whence it came that in ancient times the people were more devoted to liberty than in the present, I believe that it resulted from this, that men were stronger in those days, which I believe to be attributable to the difference of education, founded upon the difference of their religion and ours. For, as our religion teaches us the truth and the true way of life, it causes us to attach less value to the honors and possessions of this world; whilst the Pagans, esteeming those things as the highest good, were more energetic and ferocious in their actions. . . . The Pagan religion deified only men who had achieved great glory, such as commanders of armies and chiefs of republics, whilst ours glorifies more the humble and contemplative men than the men of action. Our religion, moreover, places the supreme happiness in humility, lowliness, and a contempt for worldly objects, whilst the other, on the contrary, places the supreme good in grandeur of soul, strength of body, and all such other qualities as render men formidable. . . .*

Machiavelli evidently believed that the purpose of government was not to prepare men for the City of God but to make upstanding citizens of this world, ready to fight, work, and die for their earthly country.

In defending nationalism, Machiavelli was exalting the doctrine that was to contribute so much to shaping the modern world. In defending secularism and power politics, Machiavelli preached what others had already practiced. Henry VII, Louis XI, Ferdinand of Aragon, and the Italian despots, in their different ways, were all good Machiavellians.

IV   Business and Businessmen

The businesslike politics of most fifteenth-century heads of state accorded well with the economic temper of the age. It was the age not

only of the condottiere and despot but also of the businessman—the aggressive merchant and banker, the capitalist who, by definition, did not

* *The Discourses*, Book I, Chap. 58.

* *The Discourses*, Book II, Chap. 2.

spend all he made but risked his savings by investing them in new enterprises. It was the age when the more developed areas of Europe which are sometimes loosely termed the West—that is, the areas to the west of the Adriatic Sea and the Elbe River—were taking new steps along the road from the subsistence economy of the early Middle Ages to a money economy with its greater emphasis on the exchange of goods.

It was a long and uneven road from an economy based on home-grown produce paid for in kind to one relying heavily on imports paid for in money. By the fifteenth century the West had long been importing salt, from the land deposits in Germany or the sea-salt pans of the Atlantic coast, in order to preserve food. To make food tasty if it had begun to spoil, the West had long sought the spices of the East; and to wash it down western Europeans had already developed a taste for the wines of the Rhine, of Burgundy, and of Bordeaux (in one year in the fourteenth century the wine exports of Bordeaux, in Aquitaine, totaled 25,000,000 gallons). Since drafty medieval buildings made warm clothing essential, the furs of eastern Europe, the wool of England and Spain, and the woolen cloth of Flanders and Italy all commanded good markets. At the close of the Middle Ages, supplies of palatable food and comfortable clothing were steadily increasing. Salt fish, for example, was cheap and easily kept from spoiling. In the fourteenth century, a great boom occurred in the herring fisheries along the narrow Baltic waters between Denmark and Sweden. According to the exaggerated report of one traveler, the Baltic fisheries employed 300,000 people in catching fish, salting them down, and making the barrels to pack them in.

Trade did not expand at a uniform rate. Overall, it slumped in the fourteenth century because of the serious economic depression which, as we noted at the start of this chapter, began in the early 1300's and was prolonged by the Black Death and by the Hundred Years' War. Recovery came in the fifteenth century, and by the later 1400's the trade of the West could for the first time be compared in volume and variety with that of Rome in the days of the empire, of Byzantium at its tenth-century peak, and of Norman and Hohenstaufen Sicily. Meantime, Western merchants developed more elaborate commercial procedures and organizations, of which the Hanseatic towns of the Baltic and the trading cities of Italy provide the most telling illustrations.

The Hanse

The great Hanse (the German word means "league" or "confederation") of north German trading towns flourished in the fourteenth and fifteenth centuries. Among its leaders were Lübeck, Hamburg, Bremen, and Danzig; its membership included at one time or another almost a hundred towns. Because the Holy Roman Empire was so weak, and also because many of the Hanseatic towns began as autonomous frontier outposts east of the Elbe in the course of the *Drang nach Osten,* the Hanse long exerted extensive political and military influence in addition to economic power.

The Hanse was not the first important confederation of commercial towns in Europe, nor was it the first to throw off control by a higher political authority. Alliances of communes in Lombardy and in Flanders had blocked the ambitions, respectively, of Hohenstaufen emperors and French kings. The Hanse, however, operated on a grander scale. Its ships carried Baltic fish, timber, grain, furs, metals, and amber to western European markets and brought back cloth, wine, spices, and luxuries. For a time, Hanseatic vessels controlled the lucrative business of transporting wool from England to Flanders. Hanseatic merchants, traveling overland with carts and pack trains, took their Baltic wares to Italy. The Hanse maintained especially large depots at Venice, at Bruges, at Russian Novgorod, and at London, where its headquarters was known as the Steelyard. At the Norwegian port of Bergen, the Hanseatic contingent was said to number 3,000 individuals. These establishments enjoyed so many special rights, and they were so largely ruled by their own German officials and their own German laws, that they were Hanseatic colonies on foreign soil.

The Hanse had all the appurtenances of political independence. Its policies were determined by meetings of representatives from the member towns, held usually in the guild hall at Lübeck. It had its own flag, its own diplomats, and its own legal code, the Law of Lübeck. It made treaties, declared war, and sometimes used the weapon of undeclared war. When English

374

merchants attempted to get a foothold at Bergen, the Hanseatic colony there destroyed the intruders' property and then ejected them by force. In 1406, to teach a forceful lesson to English vessels poaching on Hanseatic fishing waters off Norway, Hanseatic captains seized ninety-six English seamen, bound them hand and foot, and threw them overboard.

The Hanseatic complex almost added up to an independent power of the first magnitude—almost, but not quite. It was weakened by the mounting conservatism and rigidity of its mer-

chants and by the rivalries between competing member towns and rival merchant families. Trading was carried on not by a few established firms but by a multitude of individuals who entered temporary partnerships for a single venture. It has been estimated that about two hundred and fifty independent merchants engaged in the transport of English wool to Flanders. Only a minority of the towns belonging to the Hanse usually sent representatives to the deliberations in Lübeck, and scarcely any of the members could be counted on for men and

A panoramic view of the city of Venice in 1500: a woodcut by Jacobo de Barbari. The Doge's palace is in the right foreground, with the Cathedral of Saint Mark's behind it.

arms in an emergency. For all these reasons, the fortunes of the Hanse declined rapidly after 1500. The shifting of trade routes from the Baltic to the Atlantic also sapped the prosperity of the Hanseatic towns to the advantage of Holland and England. The loosely organized Hanse was no match for the stronger monarchical governments that were growing up along the rim of its old Baltic preserve in Sweden, in Russia, and even, with the consolidation of princely power, in Germany itself.

Venice

The truly big business of the last medieval centuries was to be found not along the Baltic but in the cities of the Mediterranean, many of which were already thriving veterans of trade, toughened and enriched by the Crusades. In Italy, besides Venice with its empire strung along the sea route from the northern Adriatic to Byzantium, there were Genoa, Lucca, Pisa, Florence, Milan, and a dozen others; in southern France there were Narbonne, Montpellier, and Marseilles; and in Spain there was Barcelona. Venice may serve as an example. The trade that brought wealth to Venetian merchants was the East-West traffic—spices, silks, cotton, sugar, dyestuffs and the alum needed to set them, from the East; wool and cloth essentially from the West. The area of Venetian business was enormous, stretching from Flanders and England in the West to the heart of Asia. In the thirteenth century, the Venetian Marco Polo reached China after a great journey overland.

The main carrier of Venetian trade was the galley. By 1300, the designers of the arsenal, the government-operated shipyard, had improved the traditional long, narrow, oar-propelled galley of the Mediterranean into a swifter and more capacious merchant vessel, relying mainly on sails and employing oarsmen chiefly for getting in and out of port. In the fifteenth century, these merchant galleys had space for 250 tons of cargo. Although this figure is unimpressive in our day, when the capacity of freighters is computed in thousands and tens of thousands of tons, spices and luxuries were small in bulk and large in value. Records from the early fifteenth century show approximately forty-five galleys sailing annually, among them four to Flanders, four to Beirut on the Lebanon coast, three to the Black Sea, three to Alexandria, two to southern France, and two or three transporting pilgrims to Jaffa in the Holy Land. The Flanders galleys touched both at Sluys, the harbor of Bruges, and at the English ports of London and Southampton. First sent out in 1317, and making an annual voyage thereafter, the Flanders fleet was a very important European economic institution. It provided the first regular all-water service between Italy and northwestern Europe and made shipments cheaper and more secure than they had been on the older overland route.

The state supervised the activities of these galleys from the cradle to the grave. Since the average life of galleys was ten years, government experts tested their seaworthiness periodically, and the arsenal made needed replacements. The government provided for the defense of the galleys and their cargoes by requiring that at least twenty of the crew be bowmen. The captains of the Flanders galleys were directed to protect the health of the crew by enlisting a physician and a surgeon, and to maintain the prestige of the city with two fifers and two trumpeters. For the Flanders fleet the government also determined the time of sailing (the spring), the number of galleys (usually four to six), and the policies of the captains (avoid "affrays and mischiefs" in English ports, even if the crew have to be denied shore leave, and, above all, get to Bruges before the Genoese do). Officials back home were furious when, as occasionally happened, the Genoese did get to Bruges first and skimmed the cream off the Flemish market. To smooth the way for Venetian merchants, the republic maintained an ambassador in England.

Industry

The expansion of trade stimulated the industries that furnished the textiles, metals, ships, and other requirements of the merchants. By 1300, the towns of Flanders and Italy had developed the weaving of woolen cloth into a big business, with a large production, large numbers of workmen, and large profits for a relatively few entrepreneurs. In the early fourteenth century, it is estimated, 200 masters controlled the wool guild of Florence, which produced nearly 100,000 pieces of cloth annually and employed

30,000 men. By and large, only the 200 had the capital—the saved-up funds—to finance the importation of fine raw wool from England and see it through all the processes that ended with the finished cloth. The older medieval concept that all artisans engaged in making a single product should belong to a single guild was giving way to the modern division between capital and labor, and in the case of labor between the highly skilled and the less skilled. A compelling instance is the strife in Florence among the seven great guilds, the fourteen lesser guilds, and the Ciompi.

Despite the growth of capitalism, Europe had not yet experienced a true industrial revolution. In 1500, according to an informed estimate, industry employed less than 5 percent of the European population. Manufacturing continued to be what the Latin roots of the word suggest that it was—making by hand—though many hand tools were ingenious and efficient. Power-driven machines did not exist, except for an occasional experimental device operated by water or by draft animals. The modern aspects of late medieval industry, confined largely to a few advanced crafts, were the increase in output, the

Jean Fouquet's "Descent of the Holy Ghost" has fifteenth-century Paris as its background.

trend toward mass production of standardized articles, and the complementary trend toward the specialization of the labor force.

In Lübeck, Hanseatic capitalists promoted the mass output of rosaries by supplying materials and wages to beadmakers and by promoting a standard product. In the Hapsburg lands of central Europe, the silver mines anticipated modern practice by dividing their labor force into three parts, each working an eight-hour daily shift. In Florence, twenty or more different specialized crafts participated in woolen production—washing, combing, carding, spinning, weaving, dyeing, and so forth. But the actual work was subcontracted, in effect, to small domestic shops according to the "put-out system": instead of the worker's going to a mill or a factory, the work went to the worker in his home.

Probably the largest industrial establishment in Europe was the Venetian arsenal, which normally employed a thousand men, and many more in time of emergency. These workmen, called *Arsenalotti*, formed a kind of pyramid of skills. At the bottom were the stevedores, helpers, and other unskilled laborers; then came the sawyers, who cut the timbers for the galleys, and the caulkers, who made the wooden hulls seaworthy; then the pulleymakers and mastmakers; and finally, at the top, the highly skilled carpenters, who did the all-important work of shaping the lines of the hull. Supervisors, like modern foremen, disciplined the arsenalotti, checking on their presence at their posts during the working day; anyone who reported late, after the arsenal bell had ceased tolling its summons to work, forfeited a day's pay. By the sixteenth century, the process of adding a superstructure to the hull and outfitting the vessel was so efficiently arranged that the arsenalotti could complete and equip a hundred galleys for a campaign against the Turks in the space of two months.

Banking

The expansion of industry and trade promoted the rise of banking. New enterprises required new money, which in turn was supplied by merchants anxious to invest the excess capital they had accumulated. The risks of lending were great; kings in particular, we shall see,

were likely to repudiate their debts. But the potential profits were also very large. Florentine bankers were known to charge 266 percent annual interest on an especially risky loan, and in 1420 the Florentine government vainly tried to put a ceiling of 20 percent on interest rates. The high rate of interest also reflected the demand for money. Kings, popes, and lesser rulers needed it for war and administration; businessmen needed it to finance trading voyages.

Bankers were moneychangers as well as moneylenders. Only an expert could establish the relative value of the hundreds upon hundreds of coins in circulation, varying wildly in reliability and precious metallic content and minted by every kind of governmental unit from the big monarchy down to the small city and the tiny feudal principality. Bankers also facilitated the transfer of money over long distances. Suppose an English exporter, A, sold wool to an Italian importer, Z; it would be slow and risky for Z to pay A by sending actual coins on the perilous trip between the two countries. Now suppose that two other businessmen enter into the transaction—Y, an Italian woolen manufacturer who has shipped cloth to B, an English importer. Obviously it is safer and often far swifter if Z pays Y in Italy what he really owes to A in England, and if B pays A what he really owes to Y. This sort of transaction was facilitated through the commercial device of bills of exchange, which bankers bought and sold.

The great European bankers were Italians, the "Lombard" bankers, though many of them came not from Lombardy but from Florence, Siena, and other towns in Tuscany. By the late 1200's, Italian bankers had become the fiscal agents of the pope, charged with the transfer of papal revenues from distant countries to Rome. Florence was the Wall Street of the early fourteenth century, literally the "Evil Street," for the great import-export houses were grouped into the *Arte di Calimala* (The Guild of the Evil Street), named after a thoroughfare once notorious for riffraff. The beautiful florins minted by the city were the first gold coins made outside Byzantium to gain international currency because of their reliability. The great Florentine banking families of the Bardi and the Peruzzi financed imports of English wool and the export of finished cloth; they also advanced large sums to the kings of England and France. Then, when the expenses of the Hundred Years' War led

Edward III of England to default on his debts to the Bardi and the Peruzzi, both firms failed in the 1340's. The repercussions, felt for more than a generation, included new attempts to democratize the Florentine government and the revolt of the Ciompi in 1378. Florentine banking rallied in the fifteenth century under the dynamic Cosimo de' Medici, whose activities involved companies for woolen and silk manufacture as well as the Medici bank and branch firms in Venice, Milan, Rome, Avignon, Geneva, Bruges, and London. The inefficiency of branch managers together with the extravagance of Lorenzo the Magnificent caused the failure of the bank before the century was out.

Meanwhile, money and banking were thriving elsewhere. The golden ducats of Venice joined the florins of Florence in international popularity, and the Bank of St. George, founded at Genoa in 1407, eventually took over much of the Mediterranean business done by Spanish Jews before the persecution of the late 1400's. In Catalonia, Barcelona established an important municipal bank in 1401. In London, the celebrated merchant and moneylender Sir Richard (Dick) Whittington served as lord mayor for three terms around 1400, while France had its Jacques Coeur and Germany its Fugger family.

Jacques Coeur and the Fuggers

A citizen of Bourges in central France, the son of an ordinary craftsman, Jacques Coeur (1395–1456) used private wealth to secure public office, and public office to augment his private wealth. And he employed both for the greater glory of France and of the Church. Coeur made a fortune by trading with the Muslim Near East and by running a ship service for pilgrims to the Holy Land. King Charles VII of France sent him on diplomatic missions, made him the chief royal fiscal agent, and placed him in charge of the royal mint; Coeur, indeed, financed the final campaigns of the Hundred Years' War. Aided by the royal favor, Coeur acquired a string of textile workshops and mines, bought landed estates from impoverished nobles, lent money to half the dignitaries of France, and obtained noble husbands and high church offices for his own middle-class relatives. At Bourges, he met the cost of embellishing the cathedral and built himself a private palace, one of the showplaces of France.

Coeur demonstrated dramatically the wealth and the power that a mere bourgeois could attain. Yet it was all too good to last, for too many highly placed people owed him too much money. To avoid repayment, Charles VII had him disgraced on the trumped-up charge of poisoning the favorite royal mistress. A refugee from France, Coeur was starting to recoup his losses when he died while leading a papal expedition against the Turks.

In the little Bavarian cities of Augsburg and Nuremberg, a series of great banking families flourished, of whom the most famous were the Fuggers of Augsburg. The founder of the family's prosperity was a linen weaver and trader in the late fourteenth century. His sons and grandsons imported textiles and luxuries from Venice and began buying up silver and lead mines, which were experiencing a prolonged boom. In the late 1400's, they became bankers to the Hapsburgs and, after the failure of the Medici bank, to the papacy as well. With the Fuggers, as with Jacques Coeur, wealth bred more wealth, power, and eventual ruin. Through Hapsburg favor they secured silver, iron, and copper mines in Hungary and the Tyrol. At the peak of their prosperity in the 1540's, the family fortune is estimated to have reached a figure worth over a quarter of a billion of our present-day dollars. Thereafter it dwindled as the flood of gold and silver from America ended the central European mining boom, and as the Fuggers themselves made extensive loans to the Hapsburg Philip II of Spain who went through repeated bankruptcies. In 1607, the family firm went bankrupt.

Two quotations will convey something of the personality of these German bankers. First, there is the prideful note of rugged individualism in the epitaph that Jacob Fugger, a grandson of the founder, composed for his own tomb in the early sixteenth century:

To the best, greatest God! Jacob Fugger of Augsburg, the ornament of his class and people, imperial councillor under Maximilian I and Charles V, who was behind no one in the attainment of extraordinary wealth, in generosity, purity of morals, and greatness of soul, is, as he

The house of Jacques Coeur in Bourges, France (fifteenth century).

was not comparable with anyone in his lifetime, even after death not to be counted among the mortals.*

But the haughty Fuggers were not just "robber barons," and so there is this note of philanthropy in the inscription at the entrance to the Fuggerei, a charming garden village that they built for the poor of Augsburg:

Ulrich, George, and Jacob Fugger of Augsburg, blood brothers, being firmly convinced that they were born for the good of the city, and that for their great prosperity they have to thank chiefly an all-powerful and benevolent God, have out of piety, and as an example of special generosity founded, given, and dedicated 106 dwellings, both buildings and furnishings, to those of their fellow citizens who live righteously, but are beset by poverty.*

Town and Countryside

Augsburg, with its special housing development for low-income families, begins to sound like a modern city. Yet we must not exaggerate,

*Quoted by Miriam Beard, *A History of the Business Man* (New York, 1938), pp. 239-240.

*J. Strieder, *Jacob Fugger the Rich* (New York, 1931), p. 176.

for the total population of Augsburg at the zenith of Fugger power probably never exceeded 20,000. In fact, none of the centers of international economic life five or six hundred years ago was really a big city at all. One set of estimates for the fourteenth century puts the population of Venice, Florence, and Paris in the vicinity of 100,000 each; that of Genoa, Milan, Barcelona, and London at about 50,000; and that of the biggest Hanseatic and Flemish towns between 20,000 and 40,000. At the close of the Middle Ages, most Europeans still lived in the countryside.

The urban minority, however, was beginning to bring important changes to the life of the rural majority. In those days, farms usually came right up to the city walls. Ties between town and countryside were especially close in areas where towns were numerous—Lombardy, Tuscany, Flanders, the Rhine Valley, and northern Germany. Merchants often invested their wealth in farm properties, nobles who acquired interests in towns usually retained their country estates, and peasants often moved to town as workmen or became part-time artisans on the farm itself under the put-out system. Rural laborers made prayer beads for the capitalists of Lübeck and spun woolen yarn for the guild masters of Florence. Town governments sometimes improved adjacent farmland on the pattern established by the medieval communes of Milan and Siena, which had drained marshes nearby to increase the area under cultivation.

Moreover, the growth of trade and the increased use of money were transforming the agrarian institutions of western Europe. Many manors now specialized in a single commodity like grain or wool, olives or grapes, and so had to purchase the necessities that they themselves no longer produced. The lords of these one-crop manors, depending increasingly on a monetary income, thus became capitalists, albeit on a modest scale. The more enterprising among them wanted to sweep away what seemed to be inefficient medieval survivals. They demanded that their peasants pay their rent in money rather than in commodities or in work on the demesne land. The sheep-raising capitalists of sixteenth-century England were to secure the right of enclosure, of fencing off for their own flocks common lands where the peasants had traditionally pastured their own livestock. In Spain, the great guild of sheep-raisers, the Mesta, secured comparable exclusive rights to vast tracts of pasture.

Businessmen, too, attacked medieval economic customs. They wanted property in a form that they might readily buy and sell, free from the restrictions of feudal tenure. And they wanted laborers whom they could hire and fire, free from the restrictions of serfdom. All these forces, together with the labor shortage and peasant unrest created by the Black Death, precipitated the end of serfdom. Serfs had virtually disappeared in Italy, with its robust urban life, by 1300; two centuries later they had vanished in most areas of western Europe.

Thus, at the heart of economic and social relationships, the cash nexus of the capitalist was beginning to replace the medieval complex of caste and service. These new developments blurred the old lines between classes. The ordinary individual very probably made a gain in real income by becoming a wage-earning worker or rent-paying tenant farmer instead of a serf. Yet he also lost something—the security, the inherited job, the right to certain lands—which he had possessed in the days of manorialism. Despair and discontent came to the surface in rebellions like the Jacquerie and the English rising of 1381 and continued as undercurrents in the more prosperous Europe of the fifteenth century. In towns and cities, too, pressures mounted, as the guilds became more exclusive and the separation between the wealthy master and the ordinary workman widened. Sometimes the tensions were kept under control, as in Venice, but sometimes they exploded, as in the Flemish towns on the eve of the Hundred Years' War and in the revolt of the Florentine Ciompi.

The New Importance of the Bourgeoisie

Perhaps the most important political result of the economic changes we have been surveying was the enlarged role of the business class, the celebrated bourgeoisie. Sometimes the bourgeois themselves ruled, as did the Medici in Florence and the merchants in Venice and the Hanse. Sometimes the bourgeois provided monarchs with the money or the professional skills, or both, to further dynastic and national interests. Archbishop Morton helped Henry VII bring law and order back to England; Fugger money supported the Hapsburgs; Jacques Coeur was, at least for a time, indispensable to Charles VII of France. Coeur's ultimate disgrace underscored the fact that, while the holders of political power were beholden to the wielders of economic power, the reverse was also true.

The economic leaders made their impact not only on politics but also on the whole style of the age. The medieval outlook on man was undergoing a significant change: witness the extreme of worldly pride asserted in the epitaph of Jacob Fugger. No medieval man, except perhaps such a very rare specimen as the emperor Frederick II, would have been so presumptuous, so self-centered, so lacking in humility. The bourgeois were beginning to invade the Church's near-monopoly of the support of culture. The Fuggers, the Medici, Jacques Coeur, and the well-to-do in general were undertaking the pa-

tronage of art and learning, and financing the building of public monuments. The palace or the library of the rich man challenged the monastery or the Church-dominated university as a center of scholarship. In the late 1400's, as the next chapter will show, the intellectual life of Florence revolved around the Platonic Academy, subsidized by Lorenzo the Magnificent.

More and more, there was little to distinguish the rich and cultivated prelate from the rich and cultivated layman. The popes of the later 1400's and early 1500's—Sixtus IV, Alexander VI, Julius II—like their contemporaries in the business world were great admirers and amassers of material wealth and great connoisseurs of art. But, while they participated to the hilt in the great outburst of cultural energy we know as the Renaissance, the Church, the very keystone of medieval civilization, cracked, split, and threatened to crumble.

Reading Suggestions on the West in the Late Middle Ages

GENERAL ACCOUNTS

D. Hay, *Europe in the Fourteenth and Fifteenth Centuries* (Holt, 1966). Excellent survey of social, political, and economic developments, with useful bibliographical footnotes.

W. K. Ferguson, *Europe in Transition, 1300-1520* (Houghton, 1963). Another useful survey.

E. P. Cheyney, *The Dawn of a New Era, 1250-1453,* and M. Gilmore, *The World of Humanism, 1453-1517* (*Torchbooks). Good introductory accounts, with very full bibliographies, in the important series "The Rise of Modern Europe," edited by W. L. Langer.

Cambridge Medieval History, Vols. VII and VIII (Cambridge Univ. Press, 1932, 1936). Treating the Fourteenth and Fifteenth centuries, respectively; collaborative work useful principally for reference.

J. Huizinga, *The Waning of the Middle Ages* (*Anchor). Celebrated re-creation of the atmosphere of a whole era, with particular stress on France and the Low Countries.

M. Aston, *The Prospect of Europe: The Fifteenth Century* (Thames & Hudson, 1968). A bird's-eye view, emphasizing social and cultural history; abundantly illustrated.

NATIONAL MONARCHIES

A. J. Slavin, *The "New Monarchies" and Representative Assemblies: Medieval Constitutionalism or Modern Absolutism?* (*Heath). Illuminating exploration of the pros and cons about the degree of newness in the new monarchies.

G. Mattingly, *Renaissance Diplomacy* (*Penguin). Stimulating study of the origins of modern diplomatic techniques.

E. Perroy, *The Hundred Years' War* (*Capricorn). The standard work on the subject and the best introduction to French history in the fourteenth and fifteenth centuries.

H. Pirenne, *Early Democracies in the Low Countries: Urban Society and Political Conflict in the Middle Ages and Renaissance* (Harper, 1969). By a famous Belgian historian of the early twentieth century.

M. McKisack, *The Fourteenth Century*, and E. F. Jacob, *The Fifteenth Century* (Clarendon, 1959, 1961). Detailed, scholarly volumes in the Oxford History of England.

A. R. Myers, *England in the Late Middle Ages, 1307–1536* (*Penguin). Handy shorter account.

E. F. Jacob, *Henry V and the Invasion of France* (*Collier). Good popular treatment.

R. L. Storey, *The Reign of Henry VII* (Blandford, 1968). Revisionist study, questioning traditional estimates of Henry's personality and policies.

C. W. S. Williams, *Henry VII* (Barker, 1937). Standard older assessment.

B. Wilkinson, *The Constitutional History of Medieval England, 1216–1485* (Longmans, 1948–1964). Multivolumed detailed treatment.

S. B. Chrimes, *English Constitutional History*, 4th ed. (*Oxford Univ. Press). Reliable manual.

J. Lynch, *Spain under the Habsburgs,* Vol. I (Blackwell, 1964). Begins with a good brief evaluation of the work of Ferdinand and Isabella.

J. H. Elliott, *Imperial Spain, 1469–1716* (Edward Arnold, 1963). Another sound recent survey.

J. H. Mariéjol, *The Spain of Ferdinand and Isabella*, ed. B. Keen, (Rutgers Univ. Press, 1961). Celebrated older study by a French scholar, edited to bring it abreast of twentieth-century scholarship.

GERMANY AND ITALY

G. Barraclough, *The Origins of Modern Germany* (*Capricorn). The best general treatment of late medieval Germany in English.

F. L. Carsten, *Princes and Parliaments in Germany from the Fifteenth to the Eighteenth Century* (Clarendon, 1959). Scholarly study of Württemberg, Saxony, Bavaria, and a few other particular states.

J. Burckhardt, *The Civilization of the Renaissance in Italy,* 2 vols. (*Torchbooks). Very famous interpretation now more than a century old; its contention that the modern state originated in Renaissance Italy is no longer generally accepted.

J. A. Symonds, *The Age of the Despots* (*Capricorn). First volume of an extended nineteenth-century study of Renaissance Italy.

H. Baron, *The Crisis of the Early Italian Renaissance*, rev. ed. (*Princeton Univ. Press). Monograph incorporating recent scholarship, affording many insights into Renaissance politics.

F. Schevill, *Medieval and Renaissance Florence,* 2 vols., and *The Medici* (*Torchbooks). Clear, detailed studies, first written a generation ago.

M. B. Becker, *Florence in Transition,* 2 vols. (Johns Hopkins Univ. Press, 1967–1968). Up-to-date study of Florence in the fourteenth century.

C. M. Ady, *Lorenzo de' Medici and Renaissance Italy* (*Collier). Brief popular account.

E. Armstrong, *Lorenzo de' Medici* (Putnam's, 1941). Standard biography of *Il Magnifico*.

R. Sabatini, *The Life of Cesare Borgia* (Brentano's, 1912). By a capable picaresque novelist.

J. R. Hale, *Machiavelli and Renaissance Italy* (*Torchbooks). Good short biography.

G. Prezzolini, *Machiavelli* (Farrar, Straus, 1967). Detailed survey of his work, its origins, and its reception over the centuries.

H. Butterfield, *The Statecraft of Machiavelli* (*Collier). Useful statement of the traditional critical interpretation.

F. Chabod, *Machiavelli and the Renaissance* (*Torchbooks). Pithy, more sympathetic evaluation.

SOCIAL AND ECONOMIC DEVELOPMENTS

The Cambridge Economic History of Europe. Vol. II: *Trade and Industry in the Middle Ages;* Vol. III: *Economic Organization and Policies in the Middle Ages* (Cambridge, 1954, 1965). Advanced scholarly work and a mine of information.

F. C. Lane, *Venetian Ships and Shipping of the Renaissance* (Johns Hopkins Univ. Press, 1934). Unusually interesting monograph.

A. W. O. von Martin, *Sociology of the Renaissance* (*Torchbooks). Instructive study of Italian society in the fourteenth and fifteenth centuries.

M. Beard, *A History of Business,* 2 vols. (*Ann Arbor). With thumbnail sketches of Renaissance millionaires (formerly entitled *A History of the Businessman*).

R. de Roover, *Rise and Decline of the Medici Bank, 1397–1494* (*Norton). Case history of the profits and pitfalls of Renaissance finance.

R. Ehrenberg, *Capital and Finance in the Renaissance: A Study of the Fuggers and their Connections* (Harcourt, 1928). Another instructive case history.

SOURCES

J. Froissart, *Chronicles of England, France, and Spain* (*Dutton). A great narrative source of late medieval history.

S. Kinser and I. Cazeaux, *The Memoirs of Philippe de Commynes* (Univ. of South Carolina Press, 1969). Well-edited translation of the famous history by the contemporary of Louis XI and Charles the Bold.

Machiavelli, *The Prince* and *the Discourses*, ed. Max Lerner (*Modern Library).

FICTION

G. B. Shaw, *St. Joan* (*Penguin). Perhaps more successful as drama than as history; peppered with quirky Shavian observations.

W. Scott, *Quentin Durward* (*Signet). Celebrated romantic novel set in the France of Louis XI.

V. Hugo, *The Hunchback of Notre Dame* (*several editions). Even more celebrated romantic novel set in the same era.

C. Reade, *The Cloister and the Hearth* (*Washington Square). Famous nineteenth-century novel about fifteenth-century Europe; based on careful research.

T. B. Costain, *The Moneyman* (Doubleday, 1947). Jacques Coeur interpreted by a competent modern historical novelist.

J. Tey, *The Daughter of Time* (*Dell). A tour de force, in which a bedridden detective entertains himself rehabilitating the reputation of Richard III.

N. Balchin, *The Borgia Testament* (Houghton, 1949). Fictionalized autobiography as Cesare might have written it; by a veteran of intelligence services and accomplished writer of adventure tales.

Illustrations